THE UNITED STATES IN LITERATURE

America Reads

GOOD TIMES THROUGH LITERATURE

EXPLORING LIFE THROUGH LITERATURE

THE UNITED STATES IN LITERATURE

ENGLAND IN LITERATURE

ROBERT C. POOLEY, *General Editor*

THE United States IN Literature

BY

ROBERT C. POOLEY

WALTER BLAIR

THEODORE HORNBERGER

PAUL FARMER

SCOTT, FORESMAN AND COMPANY

Chicago   Atlanta   Dallas   Palo Alto   Fair Lawn, N.J.

For permission to reprint the poetry appearing on pages 13 through 20 the editors make grateful acknowledgment.

Lines by Stephen Vincent Benét (pages 14, 16, and 19). From *John Brown's Body,* published by Rinehart & Company, Inc. Copyright, 1927, 1928, by Stephen Vincent Benét.

Lines by Sarah Cleghorn (page 14). From "Vermont" in *Portraits and Protests* by Sarah Cleghorn, published by Henry Holt and Company.

Lines by William Vaughn Moody (page 15). From "Gloucester Moors" by William Vaughn Moody, published by Houghton Mifflin Company.

Lines by Robert Frost (page 15). From "The Onset" in *The Complete Poems of Robert Frost,* published by Henry Holt and Company.

Lines by Josephine Pinckney (page 16). From "Sea-Drinking Cities." Copyright, 1927, by Harper & Brothers.

Lines by Lola Ridge (page 16). From "New Orleans," by Lola Ridge, in *New Republic,* May 12, 1920. Reprinted through the courtesy of *New Republic.*

Lines by John Gould Fletcher (page 17). From "Down the Mississippi" in *Selected Poems* by John Gould Fletcher. Copyright 1938 by John Gould Fletcher, and reprinted by permission of Rinehart & Company, Inc., Publishers.

Lines by William Vaughn Moody (page 18). From "Ode in Time of Hesitation" by William Vaughn Moody, published by Houghton Mifflin Company.

Lines by Edwin Curran (page 19). From *Poems* by Edwin Curran, copyright 1919 by the Four Seas Co. Used by permission of Bruce Humphries, Inc.

Lines by Ruth Comfort Mitchell (page 19). From *Narratives in Verse* by Ruth Comfort Mitchell. Copyright, 1923, D. Appleton & Company. Reprinted by permission of the publishers, Appleton-Century-Crofts, Inc.

Lines by Ada Hastings Hedges (page 20). From "Desert Road" in *Desert Poems* by Ada Hastings Hedges, published by Binfords & Mort, Publishers.

Lines by Paul Engle (page 20). From "America Remembers" in *American Song* by Paul Engle, published by Doubleday & Company, Inc.

Lines by Robinson Jeffers (page 20). From "Ascent to the Sierras" in *Cawdor and Other Poems* by Robinson Jeffers. Reprinted by courtesy of Random House, Inc.

Preface

THE UNITED STATES IN LITERATURE, the third book in the *America Reads* series, is shaped by some years of thoughtful study of the chief problem in teaching American literature. This problem is: How can students be taught to enjoy good American writing, to grow in their appreciation of it, and to make the reading of it an enriching part of their lives?

Organization

The editors, like a growing number of teachers, feel that many American literature courses in the past have failed to answer that question satisfactorily because they have concentrated upon some single approach to the subject. In contrast, varied but interrelated approaches to the study of American literature are provided under the two major parts of *The United States in Literature*—"American Life Through Literature" and "The Pageant of American Literature":

In Part I, Division A, the student studies successively the great themes of America's growth as a nation: the settlement of the Eastern seaboard, the movement westward, the absorption into our expanding population of representatives of many Old World cultural strains, and the rise of science and industry. In Part I, Division B, provision is made for an analysis of those ideals that have come to represent the fundamental spirit of the American people.

In Part II, Division C ("Men and Books"), our literature is related to the life and times of the men and women who produced it. Chronologically presented, this survey differs in important ways from the traditional "history" of American literature. In this new and vital method, the story of six great periods of our literary history is brought into sharp focus through the study of one representative man of each period—Benjamin Franklin, Washington Irving, Henry David Thoreau, Walt Whitman, Mark Twain, and Stephen Vincent Benét. Reading the story of each representative author as an interesting personality; grasping his relationship to his contemporaries; and following his development as a writer through reading selections produced by him at successive periods of his career—in all these ways the student gains a clear and uncluttered understanding of changing trends in American literature. In Part II, Division D ("Changing Literary Patterns"), emphasis is placed on the significant contributions made by American writers, during successive periods of our literary history, to the development of the short story, lyric poetry, humor, biography, and drama.

Selections

The editors have carefully chosen each selection with relation to the needs, abilities, and interests of students. While the selections represent every period of American writing, the editors have remembered the attractiveness of modern selections for modern youth and have provided an abundance from among the best contemporary literature. Even in the units treating of early days, modern selections are mingled with the old. Thus Captain Smith's account of his rescue by Pocahontas is followed by Donald Culross Peattie's interpretation of Pocahontas' character. Authentic folk material is used generously to bring students the "feel" of a particular period. Care has been taken also to select the exactly *right* items to point up the unit themes. For example, in the unit treating of the

5

development of the American short story, not just any story by Hawthorne or Crane has been used but one which precisely exemplifies each man's contribution to the development of the short-story form.

Aids to Good Reading

The editorial features of *The United States in Literature* have been carefully planned to help the student grow in the effective use of the reading skills vital to sound interpretation:

Each division and each unit is prefaced by an introduction which sets the stage and arouses the student's interest in the material to be studied. Most selections, in turn, are prefaced by brief headnotes which supply pertinent information, raise a question, or provide a lead for purposeful reading.

The questions which follow most selections are designed to aid students in interpretation, to challenge personal reactions, and to promote critical evaluation.

Special editorial articles call attention to important points of literary craftsmanship. They offer every student stimulating challenges to put into practice the basic principle underlying the art of reading: to establish close, meaningful, enjoyable communication between author and reader. "Extending Interests" sections suggest interesting activities for exceptional students or the entire class.

A strong vocabulary program is provided for by the "Know Your Words" sections and by the extensive *dictionary-type* Glossary. Together these two features of the book form the basis for a coördinated program in promoting effective word perception.

"The Larger View" section at the end of each unit not only furnishes a review of the selections and the ideas covered in the unit but also suggests stimulating invitations to further exploration and learning.

The annotated bibliographies after each unit provide for the reading needs of students of various abilities.

Illustrations

The lavish illustrations, many of them in color, will not only delight the student's eye; they will aid him in catching the spirit of America. From the moment he looks at the handsome cover, with its vivid representation of typical Americana, he will be strongly influenced by the art work of the volume. In the eight pages of the Prelude, he will sense the American quality of varied regional scenes. In his study of the text selections, he will find the illustrations a powerful stimulus to comprehension and appreciation.

The illustrators, named at the bottom of this page, compose a distinguished group of American artists. Each one was selected because of a special gift for depicting sympathetically a specific aspect of the text matter. The result is that the illustrations for a particular unit, or even for a particular selection, are closely correlated with the reading matter they accompany. Such correlation is, we believe, of highest importance in stimulating creative reading of literature.

The Guidebook

While *The United States in Literature* is complete in itself, a *Guidebook* is provided as an aid to the all-too-busy teacher. Here may be found suggestions for developing interpretation of the various selections, for strengthening and extending vocabularies, for opening avenues to new interests, and for taking care of the needs of both the retarded and the exceptional student.

The illustrations for this book were done by the following artists:
Prelude, James Lewicki; Contents, Seymour Fleishman; Units I and II, Douglas Gorsline; Unit III, Seymour Fleishman; Unit IV, Harold Walter; Unit V, Brinton Turkle; Unit VI, Francis Stroebel; Units VII through XI, Rainey Bennett; Unit XII, Rainey Bennett and Fritz Kredel; Unit XIII, Raymond Breinin and Nathan Goldstein; Unit XIV, Richard Van Benthem; Unit XVI, Phoebe Moore; Unit XVII, Rainey Bennett and Salcia Bahnc.
The cover and the end sheets were designed by Arnold Ryan.

PART I:

American Life Through Literature

Contents

B. THE DEVELOPMENT OF AMERICAN IDEALS

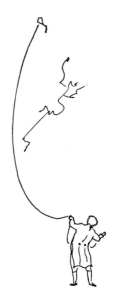

PART II

The Pageant of American Literature

C. MEN AND BOOKS 291

UNIT VII: BENJAMIN FRANKLIN
(*representing The Colonial Period*) 292

Introduction, 292; The Common-Sense Philosopher, 292; The Patriotic Penman, 302; The Scientist, 306; The Man of the World, 310

UNIT VIII: WASHINGTON IRVING
(*representing The Early National Period*) 322

Introduction, 322; Irving Contrasted with Franklin, 322; New York Amateur, 323; Irving and Europe, 329; Europe and America, 331; Irving's Romanticism, 343; Historian and Biographer, 351

UNIT IX: HENRY DAVID THOREAU
(representing America's "Golden Day")   360

Introduction, 360; Craftsman and Woodsman, 360; Humorous Philosopher, 366; The Walden Idea, 371; Rebel, 377

UNIT X: WALT WHITMAN
(representing The Period of Conflict)   386

Introduction, 386; The Early Whitman, 386; The New Whitman, 389; Poet in Wartime, 394; Postwar Themes, 401

UNIT XI: SAMUEL CLEMENS
(representing The Period of New Outlooks)   410

Introduction, 410; Journalist, 411; Yarnspinner, 419; Fiction Writer, 426

UNIT XII: STEPHEN VINCENT BENÉT
(representing The Twentieth Century)   444

Introduction, 444; Rebel of the 1920's, 444; Interpreter of America's Past, 448; Realist, 462; Patriot, 473

12

THE AMERICAN SCENE, *"from sea to shining sea,"*
as pictured by James Lewicki and various
American poets

...the chanting buildings rise,
Rivet and girder, motor and dynamo,
Pillar of smoke by day and fire by night
The steel-faced cities reaching to the skies.
Stephen Vincent Benét

Foliaged deep, the cool midsummer maples
Shade the porches of the long white street;
Trailing wide Olympian elms lean over
Tiny churches where the crossroads meet....
Sarah Cleghorn

A mile behind is Gloucester town
Where the fishing fleets put in,
A mile ahead the land dips down
And the woods and farms begin.
William Vaughn Moody

...the snow may heap
In long storms an undrifted four feet deep
As measured against maple, birch and oak.
Robert Frost

The South…the honeysuckle…the hot sun…
The taste of ripe persimmons and sugar cane…
The cloyed and waxy sweetness of magnolias…
White cotton, blowing like a fallen cloud,
And foxhounds belling the Virginia hills…

Stephen Vincent Benét

Sea-drunken sure are these—
Towns that doze—dream—and never wake at all,
While the soft supple wind slides through the trees,
And the sun sleeps against a yellow wall.

Josephine Pinckney

Honey-melon moon
Dripping thick sweet light
Where Canal Street saunters off by herself among
    quiet trees.
And the faint decayed patchouli—
Fragrance of New Orleans…

Lola Ridge

Loosely the river sways out, backward, forward,
Always fretting the outer side;
Shunning the invisible focus of each crescent,
Seeking to spread into shining loops over fields.

Like an enormous serpent, dilating, uncoiling,
Displaying a broad scaly back of earth-smeared gold;
Swaying out sinuously between the dull motionless forests,
As molten metal might glide down the lip of a vase of dark bronze.

John Gould Fletcher

...gigantic, wilful, young
Chicago sitteth at the northwest gates,
With restless violent hands and casual tongue
Moulding her mighty fates.

William Vaughn Moody

...the buffalo-ghost, the bronco-ghost
With dollar-silver in your saddle horn,
The cowboys riding in from Painted Post,
The Indian arrow in the Indian corn.
Stephen Vincent Benét

Desert and sagebrush; cactus, alkali,
Tiny, low-growing flowers brilliant, dry;
A vanishing coyote, lean and spare,
Lopes slowly homeward with a backward stare
To jigsaw hills cut sharp against the sky.
Ruth Comfort Mitchell

The rainbows all lie crumpled on these hills,
The red dawn scattered on their colored sills.
These hills have caught the lightning in its flight,
Caught colors from the skies of day and night
And shine with shattered stars and suns; they hold
Dyed yellow, red and purple, blue and gold.
Edwin Curran

And sometimes in the sunset mystery
　Of luminous dust along the golden span,
With phantom canvas gleaming, you may see
　In cloudy shapes a moving caravan.
Ada Hastings Hedges

...the land of the shining mountains, the cloud-high
West where the Indian god and the Indian ghost
Ride down the Montana wind...

Paul Engle

Beyond the great valley an odd instinctive rising
Begins to possess the ground, the flatness gathers to little
　humps and barrows, low and aimless ridges,
A sudden violence of rock crowns them. The crowded
　orchards end, they have come to a stone knife;
The farms are finished; the sudden foot of the sierra. Hill
　over hill, snow-ridge beyond mountain gather
The blue air of their height about them.

Robinson Jeffers

PART ONE

American Life Through Literature

The Growth of a Nation

WE WHO LIVE in the United States are truly heirs of good fortune. We are citizens of a democracy. Ours is a vast nation with many kinds of climate, many varied scenic beauties, many rich resources. We have good roads, schools, parks, stadiums, theaters, and museums. All of us enjoy comforts and services that could not have been purchased by even the wealthiest people only fifty years ago. Although we have burdens, we enjoy unlimited opportunity to make good in the world.

Such is the wealth of life in this nation to which we are born heirs. But heirs cannot claim credit for their inheritance, nor can they understand its nature without some effort. How did the life we know come to be? And how can we be worthy of our heritage? The purpose of "The Growth of a Nation" is to help you find the answers to these questions as they are given in our literature.

In the first division of this book you are to look at the story of the growth of our nation, not merely at the events but at the thoughts and feelings of the people who shaped its history. For only when you see what the events meant to those who took part in them do the happenings take on real meaning. For example, knowing that the *Mayflower* pilgrims landed at Plymouth Harbor in 1620 may leave you unmoved, whereas reading in Helen Grace Carlisle's "March 1621" of the day-by-day struggle of these earliest settlers against loneliness and fear, against a hostile land and its unknown inhabitants, can grip both mind and heart and make you know that you have come in touch with greatness. No historian who is satisfied to recount the dry facts of our western expansion can make real to you the deep longing that drove people across a continent in spite of mountains, deserts, rivers, and warlike Indians; to understand such matters, you must turn to such a story as John Steinbeck's "The Leader of the People." For many years statistics have been compiled to show the annual foreign immigration into the United States, but only a story such as Ruth Suckow's "Four Generations" can reveal the loneliness of an old immigrant in a new land.

The growth of ideas and ideals is a very precious part of every American's heritage. But like a fortune that is held in trust until an heir is able to spend it profitably, this inheritance is stored and waiting in our literature. You have inherited it, but you will never possess it until you have read about it, understood it, and made it a part of yourself.

UNIT I: SETTLING THE SEABOARD

THE EARLIEST colonial settlers in America were much too busy getting food, building homes, clearing land, and defending themselves against the wilderness to give much thought to literature as we think of it today. Yet a surprising amount of writing was done. Many descriptions of the new country were sent to friends back home, often in the hope of persuading these friends to join the settlers in "earth's only paradise." Since the New England colonists were numerous and since they were greatly interested in religion, religious writing at first made up a large and carefully finished part of our early literature. Because interest in government rivaled interest in religion, many wrote on political subjects. In time, as the Revolution drew nearer, publishers of pamphlets, books, and newspapers found a wide audience for political writings. The various other interests of colonial Americans also found expression in works such as histories, scientific observations, and occasional yarns.

But among these early works one must look to the autobiographical writings for material which immediately interests the general reader. Many of the colonists recorded personal experiences and reflections in letters, journals, and diaries. These personal writings, together with many modern stories, poems, and articles that make these old accounts come to life, are good reading. Moreover, they show how the early settlers of the seaboard became, not transplanted Englishmen, but Americans.

Captain Smith
Among the Indians

JOHN SMITH

In the spring of 1607, the first group of Englishmen to make a permanent settlement in the New World landed near the mouth of a river on the Virginia coast. In proper loyalty they named the river *James* and their settlement *Jamestown* in honor of their king, James I. Of the original 143 who had sailed from England, 105 had survived the voyage. Among them was Captain John Smith, a soldier of fortune distinguished by much of the daring that had marked English adventurers in the recent reign of Queen Elizabeth. As one of the council of seven appointed by the Virginia Company of London to govern the colony during the first year, Captain Smith was principally responsible for its success. He provided for the defense of the colony, procured food from the Indians, gave wise counsel, and led explorations into the surrounding country. On one of these expeditions he was captured by the Indians. The following account of this event and of his being saved by Pocahontas is no doubt his most famous story. It is famous partly because of the romantic quality of the adventure it recounts, partly because of the skill with which this man of action unfolded his narrative. Smith wrote of himself in the third person.

T HE WINTER [of 1607] approaching, the rivers became so covered with swans, geese, ducks, and cranes, that we daily feasted with good bread, Virginia peas, pumpkins, putchamins,[1] fish, fowl, and diverse sorts of wild beasts as fat as we could eat them, so that none of our tuftaffety humorists[2] desired to go for England.

But our comedies never endured long without a tragedy; some idle exceptions being muttered against Captain Smith for not discovering the head of Chickahamania River, and taxed by the Council to be too slow in so worthy an attempt. The next voyage he proceeded so far that with much labor by cutting of trees asunder he made his passage; but when his barge could pass no farther, he left her in a broad bay out of danger of shot, commanding none should go ashore till his return: himself with two English and two savages went up higher in a canoe, but he was not long absent but[3] his men went ashore, whose want of government gave both occasion and opportunity to the savages to surprise one George Cassen, whom they slew, and much failed not[4] to have cut off the boat and all the rest.

Smith, little dreaming of that accident, being got to the marshes at the river's head, twenty miles in the desert, had his two men slain (as is supposed) sleeping by the canoe, whilst himself by fowling sought them victual; who, finding he was beset with two hundred savages, two of them he slew, still defending himself with the aid of a savage his guide, whom he bound to his arm with his garters and used him as a buckler; yet he was shot in his thigh a little and had many arrows that stuck in his clothes but no great hurt, till at last they took him prisoner.

When this news came to Jamestown, much was their sorrow for his loss, few expecting what ensued.

Six or seven weeks those barbarians kept him prisoner, many strange triumphs and conjurations they made of him, yet he so demeaned himself amongst them, as he not only diverted them from surprising the fort, but procured his own liberty, and got himself and his company such estimation amongst them, that those savages admired him more than their own Quiyouckosucks.[5] The manner how they used and delivered him is as follows.[6]

The savages having drawn from George Cassen whither Captain Smith was gone, prosecuting that opportunity they followed him with three hundred bowmen, conducted by the King of Pamaunkee, who in divisions searching the turnings of the river, found Robinson and

---

[1]*putchamins* (put chä′minz), persimmons, yellow, plumlike fruits.
[2]*tuftaffety humorists,* critical, elegant gentlemen who prided themselves on following their whims (humors) and behaving in an unusual or eccentric fashion. Tuftaffeta was a fashionable silk fabric which had a pattern formed by tufts.

[3]*but,* until.
[4]*much failed not,* almost succeeded.
[5]*Quiyouckosucks* (kwē youk′ō suks), god before whose images the Indians of this region made offerings for rain.
[6]*as follows.* In the next paragraph Captain Smith retraces the circumstances that led to his being taken prisoner.

Emry[7] by the fire side; those they shot full of arrows and slew. Then finding the Captain, as is said, that used the savage that was his guide as his shield (three of them being slain and divers others so galled) all the rest would not come near him. Thinking thus to have returned to his boat, regarding them as he marched more than his way, slipped up to the middle in an oozy creek and his savage with him; yet durst they not come to him till being near dead with cold, he threw away his arms. Then according to their composition[8] they drew him forth and led him to the fire, where his men were slain. Diligently they chafed his benumbed limbs.

He demanding for their captain, they showed him Opechankanough, King of Pamaunkee, to whom he gave a round ivory double compass dial.[9] Much they marveled at the playing of the fly and needle, which they could see so plainly, and yet not touch it because of the glass that covered them. But when he demonstrated by that globelike jewel the roundness of the earth, the skies, the sphere of the sun, moon, and stars, and how the sun did chase the night round about the world continually; the greatness of the land and sea, the diversity of nations, variety of complexions, and how we were to them antipodes, and many other suchlike matters, they all stood as amazed with admiration.[10] Notwithstanding, within an hour after they tied him to a tree, and as many as could stand about him prepared to shoot him, but the King holding up the compass in his hand, they all laid down their bows and arrows, and in a triumphant manner led him to Orapaks, where he was after their manner kindly feasted and well used.

At last they brought him to Meronocomoco, where was Powhatan, their emperor. Here more than two hundred of these grim courtiers stood wondering at him, as he had been a monster; till Powhatan and his train had put themselves in their greatest braveries. Before a fire upon a seat like a bedstead, he[11] sat covered with a great robe, made of raccoon skins, and all the tails hanging by. On either hand did sit a young wench of sixteen or eighteen years, and along on each side the house, two rows of men, and behind them as many women, with all their heads and shoulders painted red; many of their heads bedecked with the white down of birds; but every one with something.

At his entrance before the King, all the people gave a great shout. The Queen of Appamatuck was appointed to bring him water to wash his hands, and another brought him a bunch of feathers, instead of a towel, to dry them. Having feasted him after their best barbarous manner they could, a long consultation was held; but the conclusion was, two great stones were brought before Powhatan: then as many as could laid hands on him, dragged him to them, and thereon laid his head, and being ready with their clubs to beat out his brains, Pocahontas, the King's dearest daughter, when

[11]*he*, Powhatan.

---

[7]*Robinson and Emry,* the two men mentioned as slain in a preceding paragraph. Smith was hunting near by.

[8]*composition,* agreement.

[9]*round ivory double compass dial.* This primitive type of compass was a ball containing liquid on which a magnetic needle floated.

[10]*admiration,* wonder, astonishment.

no entreaty could prevail, got his head in her arms, and laid her own upon his to save him from death: whereat the emperor was contented he should live to make him hatchets, and her bells, beads, and copper; for they thought him as well of all occupations as themselves. For the King himself will make his own robes, shoes, bows, arrows, pots; plant, hunt, or do anything so well as the rest.

Two days after, Powhatan having disguised himself in the most fearfullest manner he could, caused Captain Smith to be brought forth to a great house in the woods, and there upon a mat by the fire to be left alone. Not long after, from behind a mat that divided the house, was made the most dolefullest noise he ever heard; then Powhatan, more like a devil than a man, with some two hundred more as black as himself, came unto him and told him now they were friends and presently he should go to Jamestown to send him two great guns and a grindstone, for which he would give him the country of Capahowosick, and forever esteem him as his son Nantaquoud.

So to Jamestown with twelve guides Powhatan sent him. That night they quartered in the woods, he still expecting (as he had done all this long time of his imprisonment) every hour to be put to one death or other, for all their feasting. But almighty God, by His divine providence, had mollified the hearts of those stern barbarians with compassion. The next morning betimes they came to the fort, where Smith having used the savages with what kindness he could, he showed Rawhunt, Powhatan's trusty servant, two demi-culverins[12] and a millstone to carry Powhatan: they found them somewhat too heavy; but when they did see him discharge them, being loaded with stones, among the boughs of a great tree loaded with icicles, the ice and branches came so tumbling down that the poor savages ran away half dead with fear. But at last we regained some conference with them, and gave them such toys; and sent to Powhatan, his women, and children such presents, and gave them in general full content.

---

[12]*demi-culverins* (dem′i kul′vər inz), long cannons with about 4½-inch bore using balls of 9 to 13 pounds.

1. Imagine yourself at a meeting of the Council in Jamestown a few days before Captain Smith sets out on the expedition that he describes. What do the Council members say about the welfare and progress of the colony? What is their attitude toward Captain Smith?

2. Now picture a meeting of the Indian chieftains at the same time. How do you think the Indians have reacted to the presence of the colonists? Why would they be likely to have a special interest in Captain Smith?

3. What is the purpose of Captain Smith's exploration? How does the exploring party run into trouble?

4. What instances of bravery does Captain Smith reveal in his encounter with the Indians? How does he show his wisdom in dealing with his captors?

5. On what conditions does Powhatan release Captain Smith? Why are these conditions satisfactory to both sides?

6. Although born an Englishman, Captain Smith possessed some qualities that we associate with the typical American. What "American" qualities do you find him exhibiting in this selection?

7. Why do you think the story of Pocahontas and Captain Smith has always been a favorite episode in American legend?

In John Smith's words

Reread the first paragraph of the selection and choose the word or phrase that seems most unusual to you. Is it *putchamins,* or *tuftaffety humorists?* Certainly these are seldom heard today. Now look at the last four words in the paragraph, *to go for England.* Every word in the phrase is simple and familiar, yet the meaning of the expression may at first escape you. What *did* Captain Smith mean? How would you say what he put in such a quaint, old-fashioned way? What do the following expressions from the selection mean? Rereading them in their context will help you understand them. If necessary, consult a dictionary for the meaning of each italicized word.

1. some *idle exceptions* being muttered (page 25, column 1, paragraph 2)

2. *taxed* by the Council (page 25, column 1, paragraph 2)

3. whilst himself by *fowling* sought them *victual* (page 25, column 2, paragraph 1)

4. three of them being slain and *divers* others so *galled* (page 26, column 1, line 4)

5. had put themselves in their greatest *braveries* (page 26, column 1, paragraph 2)

6. thought him as well of all occupations as themselves (page 27, column 1, line 5)

America's First Great Lady

DONALD CULROSS PEATTIE

In recent years Pocahontas has become increasingly important in the thinking of those who study carefully the colonial beginnings of the United States. The following description of her heroic life was written in 1947. As you will see, it is a retelling, by a modern author, of some of the happenings recounted by Captain Smith in the selection which you have just read. The present selection points out the value of the Indian woman's friendship with the Jamestown colonists. As you read observe exactly how, according to Donald Culross Peattie, she "mothered the first colony in America."

HER REAL NAME was Matoaka. Her father, Wahunsonacock, chief of the Powhatans,[1] called her his little *Pocahontas,* "the playful one." And by that nickname she has come down to us, stepping light as a fawn out of the underbrush of legend into the bright clearing of history.

She was eleven when she first met Captain John Smith. The Captain was twenty-seven when he came to Virginia—in chains. His ship was one of three sailing into Chesapeake Bay, on an April night in 1607, to found the colony at Jamestown. So laden were they with fools and knaves that when John Smith had spoken his mind about the knavery, he was thrown into irons.[2]

But on the night after landing, weighing the advisability of swinging John Smith from a yardarm for "mutiny," the ship captains opened their sealed orders from the Virginia Company of London and found that Smith had been appointed one of the colony's seven councilors. So they had to strike off his shackles.

Of all the fine gentlemen in ruffs and laces who stepped ashore at Jamestown that spring morning, only John Smith was fit to meet the challenge of the American wilderness. Behind him lay a decade of adventuring and soldiering over half of Europe—fighting against the Turks, suffering capture and slavery, finally escaping to England. There he had presented himself before the honorable "gentlemen adventurers" of the Virginia Company of London. They adventured only their money. They had sent Smith forth to risk his skin for it.

None of the colonists wished to labor over crops or shelter, for few imagined they would stay longer in this savage place than the brief time it should take to grow immensely rich in the gold they expected to find. And none had any idea, that, within a year, more than half of them would be under the sod from malaria, starvation, Indian arrows, and hanging.

But Smith took the measure of this new land; he set forth to explore it and to find food. His first trip, up the James River, brought him the coöperation of the Indians and a fair store of corn. On his second trip he was captured. Even the savages recognized his stature and exhibited him all over the Tidewater country,[3] at last delivering him to the great Powhatan, Wahunsonacock himself. The "emperor," as Smith calls him, received his prisoner reclining on a high pile of blankets; around him Smith saw the glittering gaze of the painted braves, and the women in wampum. Did he observe, too, the girl-child with lovely and intent young face?

Having picked up much of the Indian language, Smith desperately began to talk for time. He showed the Powhatan his compass; he told of the North Pole and the rotation of the earth, eclipses of sun and moon. But at last he had to pause for breath, and Indian courtesy satis-

---

[1]*Wahunsonacock* (wä′hŭn sō nä′kok), *chief of the Powhatans.* Wahunsonacock was the real name of Pocahontas' father. Powhatan, as the colonists called him, was the name of one of the many tribes he governed.
[2]*thrown into irons,* imprisoned and bound by chains.

---

[3]*Tidewater country,* that part of Virginia near the seacoast. It is so called because it is drained by the great tidal rivers.

fied, Wahunsonacock gave the signal for the death ceremony.

The Captain's head was laid on a stone block. His executioners lifted high the rocks to crush his skull. There came a cry, a flash of slim bronze limbs, and childish arms were flung protectingly about the Captain's neck. Sharply the Powhatan motioned the executioners aside, for he had always gratified his daughter's whims. And it was a well-known custom among the red race that a woman might claim a prisoner's life.

So it was that John Smith got back to Jamestown, to find the colonists on the point of starvation. And then through the woods came Pocahontas, leading a string of grim warriors and curious women bearing great baskets of corn, slain deer, heaped-up wild turkeys with bronze feathers blowing. Every week or so she came again, with all wild America to lay at the Captain's feet.

Pocahontas would go through the fort finding the white children, and would vie with them in turning handsprings and somersaults. But somehow she always managed to land on her feet near the Captain, and in a breath she would tell him what was said at her father's council fires.

The Powhatan was temporizing until he could form a confederacy to sweep the palefaces into the sea. In the web of forest treachery Smith, now president of the Jamestown Council, had a guardian angel. Pocahontas would come miles through the night and forest to warn him that her father was having him ambushed. Grateful, he offered the child gifts. She refused, for they would betray her.

One day she tearfully bade her Captain farewell; he had been terribly burned in a gunpowder explosion, and must have medical care in England. His departure was hailed with rejoicing by the colonists, who did not care to mount sentry or raise crops; they would live lazily now, they thought, on the fat of the land. But Pocahontas did not come to the fort again; there was no more food from the Indians. Open warfare finally broke out, and during this period the colonists managed to capture Pocahontas and hold her as hostage. She was eighteen now, considered by all the most beautiful Indian woman they had ever seen.

And at last she heard of John Smith again, but bitter news. After a distinguished career exploring New England—it was he who gave it that name—he had been captured by a French pirate, the ship had been wrecked on the Brittany coast and had gone down with all hands.

The English treated Pocahontas as a captive princess. One young man, John Rolfe, could not keep his eyes from her as she came and went in her dignity and sweetness, learning the English language, the English ways, the Christian religion. Rolfe was making Virginia rich. By experiments with different tobacco strains and various ways of cultivating the crop he had produced a leaf that had suddenly outstripped all others in popularity with English smokers.

Now he began to examine his feelings about Pocahontas. He states that he fell "in love with one whose education hath been rude, her manners barbarous, her generation accursed, and so discrepant in all nurtriture[4] from myself." Nevertheless, in April 1614 were united John Rolfe and Rebecca, to give her her new baptismal name.

This international marriage insured an era of peace between red man and white, and the colony of Virginia took firm root. As the great plantation system was established, wealth came to the colony. A "wife ship" brought out marriageable women to provide mates and children for the men. It was Pocahontas who had made it safe for her white sisters in her native land.

But she was not there to welcome them. In 1616 with her infant son she accompanied her husband to England. There she learned that Captain John Smith still lived. On the very night the French pirate ship was wrecked he had escaped in a small boat and had been found by fishermen. When Smith and Mrs. Rolfe met in London, she now in the stays and choking ruff of a fine lady, she was overcome with emotion and fell fainting. Her first words came from her forest heart: "They did always tell me you were dead, and I never knew aught else until I came to Plymouth!"[5]

[4]discrepant in all nurtriture, different in training and education.
[5]Plymouth, a seaport in southwestern England.

Smith wrote the Queen a long letter, telling everything that "Lady Pocahontas" had done for him and for England. The story flew over the country, so that Pocahontas was already a heroine when she was presented at Court.

Captain Smith seldom came to see Pocahontas while her husband was in England; when John Rolfe's duties took him back to Virginia alone, the Captain scrupulously stayed away altogether. In her innocence Pocahontas could not understand this, and when they met socially by chance she would reproach him, as a child reproaches one for forgetting a promise.

But now Rolfe and his wife were to return to Virginia. She started with what mixed feelings only a woman could tell us and, waiting to take ship at Gravesend, was mortally stricken with smallpox. Pocahontas did not grieve when she learned that her loyal but divided heart must soon stop beating. Her only recorded words were: "I rejoice that my child liveth."

So, in her foreign clothes, on a foreign shore, among strangers, of a race hers only by the love she bore them and the good she had done them, died Pocahontas.

Captain Smith survived her by fourteen years, one of the first and best of those who are born by nature to be Americans. Wahunsonacock died a year after his daughter, and this was the signal for fresh Indian warfare. John Rolfe was one of its victims.

But his son, Thomas, the child in whom Pocahontas died rejoicing, lived to become the ancestor of many persons of distinction on both sides of the Atlantic; no Virginia family is prouder than the Randolphs, for instance, and they are proudest of all of that first patriot ancestor in a line of patriots, Matoaka Pocahontas Rebecca Rolfe.

For by the pure love she bore two men, faithful always to both, she mothered the first colony in America. Jamestown is gone, long since, though the place has become a national monument. There you will find only the empty shell of the church, and the gravestones, tilted by time. There is a great sense of loneliness in this brave and haunted place, and somewhere—if you could quite see it—at the heart of the dazzle of sunlight, there is a little figure turning handsprings on the quiet grass.

CONCERNING TWO EARLY AMERICANS

1. What facts in Peattie's article indicate that he got at least a part of his material from John Smith's journal? What additional facts about Captain Smith have you gained from reading this article?

2. Do you think Peattie is justified in entitling his article "America's First Great Lady"? In what ways do you consider Pocahontas a "great lady"?

3. Name the ways in which Pocahontas helped the Jamestown colonists. Which incidents show her fine dealings and broad sympathy?

4. What does the author mean by saying of Captain Smith that he was "one of the first and best of those who are born by nature to be Americans"?

With an eye toward style

1. Explain how Mr. Peattie's use of each of the following figurative passages helps arouse the sympathy of the reader for the character:

(*a*) And by that nickname she [Pocahontas] has come down to us, stepping light as a fawn out of the underbrush of legend into the bright clearing of history.

(*b*) ...only John Smith was fit to meet the challenge of the American wilderness.

(*c*) Every week or so she [Pocahontas] came again, with all wild America to lay at the Captain's feet.

(*d*) In the web of forest treachery Smith...had a guardian angel.

2. Contrast the style of Mr. Peattie with that of Captain Smith. Consider the following points: (*a*) the length of sentences and paragraphs; (*b*) sentence structure; (*c*) the use of "picture-making" words and phrases. Which author is primarily interested in narrating what happened? Which in making clear the importance of what happened?

Extending interests

1. Plan to read one of the following poems aloud to your classmates: "Pocahontas," from *A Book of Americans,* by Rosemary and Stephen Vincent Benét; "Pocahontas," by Vachel Lindsay, in *Poetry of Today,* edited by Rosa M. R. Mikels and Grace Shoup; "The Last Meeting of Pocahontas and the Great Captain," by Margaret Preston, and "Pocahontas," by George P. Morris, both in *Poems of American History,* edited by Burton Stevenson.

2. If you are interested in knowing more about Pocahontas, you will enjoy David Garnett's novel *Pocahontas,* which is a fascinating account of her life.

A Tobacco Deal

MARY JOHNSTON

Within twelve years after the settlement of Jamestown, the Virginia colonists were making money for themselves and for their English financiers, the London Company. John Rolfe's experiments with tobacco grown from seed imported from Trinidad and Venezuela had made this product the colony's staple crop. The great demand for Virginia tobacco in English markets practically made tobacco worth its weight in gold. Since little hard money was in circulation in the colony, tobacco became the accepted currency. Wages, salaries, and debts were paid in so many pounds of tobacco.

The effect of profitable tobacco raising upon the life of the colony was far-reaching. More and more men, many of them upper-class gentlemen, arrived from England to farm large plantations with slave labor. The fact that ships brought manufactured goods and small luxuries out to the gentlemen-planters and carried tobacco back to England gradually established closer ties between the homeland and the Virginia colony. The London Company sent out a shipload of young women, recommended as suitable wives for the lonely bachelors. Upon the acceptance of the marriage offer, each prospective husband had to pay 120 pounds of tobacco for his bride's passage to Virginia. The following selection is from the romantic novel *To Have and To Hold* (1900), whose heroine Jocelyn Leigh is one of these bartered brides. The hero, Captain Ralph Percy, who tells the story, is a young plantation owner from up the James River. He gets his first glimpse of Jocelyn at the church service just before the general matchmaking begins.

WHEN I FIRST saw her, she sat some ten feet from me, in the corner, and so in the shadow of a tall pew. Beyond her was a row of milkmaid beauties, red of cheek, free of eye, deep-bosomed, and beribboned like Maypoles. I looked again, and saw—and see—a rose amongst blowzed poppies and peonies, a pearl amidst glass beads, a Perdita[1] in a ring of rustics, a nonparella[2] of all grace and beauty! As I gazed with all my eyes, I found more than grace and beauty in that wonderful face—found pride, wit, fire, determination, finally shame and anger. For, feeling my eyes upon her, she looked up and met what she must have thought the impudent stare of an appraiser. Her face, which had been without color, pale and clear like the sky about the evening star, went crimson in a moment. She bit her lip and shot at me one withering glance, then dropped her eyelids and hid the lightning.

She stood up with the other maids. Her dress of dark woolen, severe and unadorned, her close ruff and prim white coif, would have cried "Puritan," had ever Puritan looked like this woman, upon whom the poor apparel had the seeming of purple and ermine.[3]

As for the maids, for a minute or more they made one cluster; then, shyly or with laughter, they drifted apart like the petals of a wind-blown rose, and silk doublet and hose[4] gave chase. Five minutes saw the goodly company of damsels errant and would-be bridegrooms scattered far and near over the smiling meadow. For the most part they went man and maid, but the fairer of the feminine cohort had rings of clamorous suitors from whom to choose. As for me, I walked alone; for if by chance I neared a maid, she looked (womanlike) at my apparel first, and never reached my face, but squarely turned her back. I saw a shepherdess fresh from Arcadia[5] wave back a dozen importunate gallants, then throw a knot of blue ribbon into their midst, laugh with glee at the scramble that ensued, and finally march off with the wearer of the favor. I saw a neighbor of mine, tall Jack

Pride, who lived twelve miles above me, blush and stammer, and bow again and again to a milliner's apprentice of a girl, not five feet high and all eyes, who dropped a curtsy at each bow. When I had passed them fifty yards or more, and looked back, they were still bobbing and bowing.

At the far end of the meadow, near to the fort, I met young Hamor, alone, flushed, and hurrying back to the more populous part of the field.

"Not yet mated?" I asked. "Where are the maids' eyes?"

"By—!" he answered, with an angry laugh. "If they're all like the sample I've just left, I'll buy me a squaw from the Paspaheghs!"

I smiled. "So your wooing has not prospered?"

His vanity took fire. "I have not wooed in earnest," he said carelessly, and hitched forward his cloak of sky-blue tuftaffeta with an air. "I sheered off quickly enough, I warrant you, when I found the nature of the commodity I had to deal with."

"Ah!" I said. "When I left the crowd they were going very fast. You had best hurry, if you wish to secure a bargain."

"I'm off," he answered; then, jerking his thumb over his shoulder, "if you keep on to the river and that clump of cedars, you will find Termagant in ruff and farthingale."[6]

When he was gone, I stood still for a while and watched the slow sweep of a buzzard high in the blue, after which I unsheathed my dagger, and with it tried to scrape the dried mud from my boots. Succeeding but indifferently, I put the blade up, stared again at the sky, drew a long breath, and marched upon the covert of cedars indicated by Hamor.

As I neared it, I heard at first only the wash of the river; but presently there came to my ears the sound of a man's voice, and then a woman's angry "Begone, sir!"

---

[1]*Perdita* (pèr′di tə), a character in Shakespeare's *The Winter's Tale.* She is a king's daughter who is brought up as a shepherdess.

[2]*nonparella* (non′pə rel′ə), one having no equal. Today we use the word *nonpareil* (non′pə rel′).

[3]*purple and ermine,* traditionally the garb of royalty.

[4]*silk doublet and hose.* This is a figurative way of speaking of the men, who were clad in close-fitting silk jackets (doublets) and tight pants (hose).

[5]*shepherdess fresh from Arcadia* (är kā′di ə). In literature Arcadia is the symbol of a peaceful, happy country place untouched by modern civilization. The girl looked like a shepherdess newly come from such an untroubled land.

[6]*Termagant* (tèr′mə gənt) *in ruff and farthingale.* Termagant was a violent, proud character in the religious plays of the Middle Ages. Hamor indicates that although the woman he has just had an encounter with was dressed in ruffled collar (ruff) and hoop skirt (farthingale) as any lady would be, she nevertheless had the disposition of Termagant.

"Kiss and be friends," said the man.

The sound that followed being something of the loudest for even the most hearty salutation, I was not surprised, on parting the bushes, to find the man nursing his cheek, and the maid her hand.

"You shall pay well for that, you sweet vixen!" he cried, and caught her by both wrists.

She struggled fiercely, bending her head this way and that, but his hot lips had touched her face before I could come between.

When I had knocked him down he lay where he fell, dazed by the blow, and blinking up at me with his small ferret eyes. I knew him to be one Edward Sharpless, and I knew no good of him. He had been a lawyer in England. He lay on the very brink of the stream, with one arm touching the water. Flesh and blood could not resist it, so assisted by the toe of my boot, he took a cold bath to cool his hot blood.

When he had clambered out and had gone away cursing, I turned to face her. She stood against the trunk of a great cedar, her head thrown back, a spot of angry crimson in each cheek, one small hand clenched at her throat. I had heard her laugh as Sharpless touched the water, but now there was only defiance in her face. As we gazed at each other, a burst of laughter came to us from the meadow behind. I looked over my shoulder and beheld young Hamor—probably disappointed of a wife—with Giles Allen and Wynne, returning to his abandoned quarry. She saw, too, for the crimson spread and deepened and her bosom heaved. Her dark eyes, glancing here and there like those of a hunted creature, met my own.

"Madam," I said, "will you marry me?"

She looked at me strangely. "Do you live here?" she asked at last, with a disdainful wave of her hand toward the town.

"No, madam," I answered. "I live up river, in Weyanoke Hundred,[7] some miles from here."

"Then, in God's name, let us be gone!" she cried, with sudden passion.

I bowed low, and advanced to kiss her hand.

The finger tips which she slowly and reluctantly resigned to me were icy, and the look with which she favored me was not such an one as poets feign for like occasions. I shrugged

---

[7]*Hundred.* In early Virginia, counties were divided into sections called *hundreds.*

the shoulders of my spirit, but said nothing. So, hand in hand, though at arms' length, we passed from the shade of the cedars into the open meadow, where we presently met Hamor and his party. They would have barred the way, laughing and making unsavory jests, but I drew her closer to me and laid my hand upon my sword. They stood aside, for I was the best swordsman in Virginia.

The meadow was now less thronged. The river, up and down, was white with sailboats, and across the neck of the peninsula went a line of horsemen, each with his purchase upon a pillion behind him. The Governor, the councilors, and the commanders had betaken themselves to the Governor's house, where a great dinner was to be given. But Master Piersey, the Cape Merchant, remained to see the Company reimbursed to the last leaf,[8] and the four ministers still found occupation, though one couple trod not upon the heels of another, as they had done an hour agone.

"I must first satisfy the treasurer," I said, coming to a halt within fifty feet of the now deserted high places.[9]

She drew her hand from mine, and looked me up and down.

"How much is it?" she asked at last. "I will pay it."

I stared at her.

"Can't you speak?" she cried, with a stamp of her foot. "At what am I valued? Ten pounds—fifty pounds—"[10]

"At one hundred and twenty pounds of tobacco, madam," I said dryly. "I will pay it myself. To what name upon the ship's list do you answer?"

"Patience Worth," she replied.

I left her standing there, and went upon my errand with a whirling brain. Her enrollment in that company proclaimed her meanly born, and she bore herself as of blood royal; of her own free will she had crossed an ocean to meet this day, and she held in passionate hatred this day and all that it contained; she was come to Virginia to better her condition, and the purse which she had drawn from her bosom was filled with gold pieces. To another I would have advised caution, delay, application to the Governor, inquiry; for myself I cared not to make inquiries.

The treasurer gave me my receipt, and I procured, from the crowd around him, Humfrey Kent, a good man and true, and old Belfield, the perfumer, for witnesses. With them at my heels I went back to her, and, giving her my hand, was making for the nearest minister, when a voice at a little distance hailed me, crying out, "This way, Captain Percy!"

I turned toward the voice, and beheld the great figure of Master Jeremy Sparrow sitting, cross-legged like the Grand Turk,[11] upon a grassy hillock, and beckoning to me from that elevation.

"Our acquaintance hath been of the shortest," he said genially, when the maid, the witnesses, and I had reached the foot of the hillock, "but I have taken a liking to you and would fain do you a service. Moreover, I lack employment. The maids take me for a hedge parson,[12] and sheer off to my brethren, who truly are of a more clerical appearance. Whereas if they could only look upon the inner man! You have been long in choosing, but have doubtless chosen —" He glanced from me to the woman beside me, and broke off with open mouth and staring

---

[11]*Grand Turk,* the Sultan of Turkey.
[12]*hedge parson,* an uneducated priest or minister.

---

[8]*Master Piersey...reimbursed to the last leaf.* It was the duty of Master Piersey, a representative of the company which had financed bringing the women to Virginia, to see that as the girls were married each husband paid in tobacco for her passage.

[9]*high places,* pulpits of turf where the ministers were stationed.

[10]*Ten pounds...fifty pounds.* The pound she refers to is a unit of English money. In money value of today it would be worth perhaps $50.

eyes. There was excuse, for her beauty was amazing. "A paragon," he ended, recovering himself.

"Marry us quickly, friend," I said. "Clouds are gathering, and we have far to go."

He came down from his mound, and we went and stood before him. I had around my neck the gold chain given me upon a certain occasion by Prince Maurice, and in lieu of other ring I now twisted off the smallest link and gave it to her.

"Your name?" asked Master Sparrow, opening his book.

"Ralph Percy, Gentleman."[13]

"And yours?" he demanded, staring at her with a somewhat too apparent delight in her beauty.

She flushed richly and bit her lip.

He repeated the question.

She stood a minute in silence, her eyes upon the darkening sky. Then she said in a low voice, "Jocelyn Leigh."

It was not the name I had watched the Cape Merchant strike off his list. I turned upon her and made her meet my eyes. "What is your name?" I demanded. "Tell me the truth!"

"I have told it," she answered proudly. "It is Jocelyn Leigh."

I faced the minister again. "Go on," I said briefly.

"The Company commands that no constraint be put upon its poor maids. Wherefore, do you marry this man of your own free will and choice?"

"Ay," she said, "of my own free will."

---

[13]*Gentleman*. In earlier times only men of a certain rank were permitted to use this title.

Well, we were married, and Master Jeremy Sparrow wished us joy, and Kent would have kissed the bride had I not frowned him off. He and Belfield strode away, and I left her there, and went to get her bundle from the house that had sheltered her overnight. Returning, I found her seated on the turf, her chin in her hand and her dark eyes watching the distant play of lightning.

I gave her my hand and led her to the shore; then loosed my boat and helped her aboard. A sudden puff of wind brought the sail around. The wind freshened, coming from the bay, and the boat was off like a startled deer.

Below Martin-Brandon we met a canoe full of Paspaheghs, bound upon a friendly visit to some one of the downriver tribes; for in the bottom of the boat reposed a fat buck, and at the feet of the young men lay trenchers of maize cakes and of late mulberries. I hailed them, and when we were alongside held up the brooch from my hat, then pointed to the purple fruit. The exchange was soon made; they sped away, and I placed the mulberries upon the thwart beside her.

"I am not hungry," she said coldly. "Take them away."

I bit my lip, and returned to my place at the tiller. This rose was set with thorns, and already I felt their sting. Presently she leaned back in the nest I had made for her. "I wish to sleep," she said haughtily, and turning her face from me, pillowed her head upon her arms.

I sat, bent forward, the tiller in my hand, and stared at my wife in some consternation. This was not the tame pigeon, the rosy, humble, domestic creature who was to make me a home and rear me children. A sea bird with broad

white wings swooped down upon the water, now dark and ridged, rested there a moment, then swept away into the heart of the gathering storm. She was liker such an one. Such birds were caught at times, but never tamed and never kept.

The lightning, which had played incessantly in pale flashes across the low clouds in the south, now leaped to higher peaks and became more vivid, and the muttering of the thunder changed to long, booming peals. Thirteen years before, the Virginia storms had struck us with terror. Compared with those of the Old World we had left, they were as cannon to the whistling of arrows, as breakers on an iron coast to the dull wash of level seas. Now they were nothing to me, but as the peals changed to great crashes as of falling cities, I marveled to see my wife sleeping so quietly. The rain began to fall, slowly, in large sullen drops, and I rose to cover her with my cloak. Then I saw that the sleep was feigned, for she was gazing at the storm with wide eyes, though with no fear in their dark depths. When I moved they closed, and when I reached her the lashes still swept her cheeks, and she breathed evenly through parted lips. But, against her will, she shrank from my touch as I put the cloak about her; and when I had returned to my seat, I bent to one side and

saw, as I had expected to see, that her eyes were wide open again. If she had been one whit less beautiful, I would have wished her back at Jamestown, back on the Atlantic, back at whatever outlandish place, where manners were unknown, that had owned her and cast her out. Pride and temper! I set my lips, and vowed that she should find her match.

The storm did not last. Ere we had reached Piersey's the rain had ceased and the clouds were breaking; above Chaplain's Choice hung a great rainbow; we passed Tants Weyanoke in the glory of the sunset, all shattered gold and crimson. Not a word had been spoken. I sat in a humor grim enough, and she lay there before me, wide awake, staring at the running water, and thinking that I thought she slept.

At last my own wharf rose before me through the gathering dusk, and beyond it shone out a light; for I had told Diccon to set my house in order, and to provide fire and torches, that my wife might see I wished to do her honor. I looked at that wife, and of a sudden the anger in my heart melted away. It was a wilderness vast and dreadful to which she had come. The mighty stream, the towering forests, the black skies and deafening thunder, the wild cries of bird and beast, the savages, uncouth and terrible—for a moment I saw my world as the woman

at my feet must see it, strange, wild, and menacing, an evil land, the other side of the moon. A thing that I had forgotten came to my mind: how that, after our landing at Jamestown, years before, a boy whom we had with us did each night fill with cries and lamentations the hut where he lay with my cousin Percy, Gosnold, and myself, nor would cease though we tried both crying shame and a rope's end.[14] It was not for homesickness, for he had no mother or kin or home; and at length Master Hunt brought him to confess that it was but pure panic terror of the land itself—not of the Indians or of our hardships, both of which he faced bravely enough, but of the strange trees and the high and long roofs of vine, of the black sliding earth and the white mist, of the fireflies and the whippoorwills—a sick fear of primeval Nature and her tragic mask.

This was a woman, young, alone, and friendless, unless I, who had sworn to cherish and protect her, should prove myself her friend. Wherefore, when, a few minutes later, I bent over her, it was with all gentleness that I touched and spoke to her.

"Our journey is over," I said. "This is home, my dear."

She let me help her to her feet, and up the wet and slippery steps to the level of the wharf. It was now quite dark, there being no moon, and thin clouds obscuring the stars. The touch of her hand, which I perforce held since I must guide her over the long, narrow, and unrailed trestle, chilled me, and her breathing was hurried, but she moved by my side through the gross darkness unfalteringly enough. Arrived at the gate of the palisade, I beat upon it with the hilt of my sword, and shouted to my men to open to us. A moment, and a dozen torches came flaring down the bank. Diccon shot back the bolts, and we entered. The men drew up and saluted; for I held my manor a camp, my servants soldiers, and myself their captain. At my own door I turned and spoke to the men, who had followed us up the ascent.

"This lady," I said, taking her hand as she stood beside me, "is my true and lawful wife,

your mistress, to be honored and obeyed as such. Who fails in reverence to her I hold as mutinous to myself, and will deal with him accordingly. She gives you tomorrow for holiday, with double rations, and to each a measure of rum. Now thank her properly."

They cheered lustily, of course, and Diccon, stepping forward, gave us thanks in the name of them all, and wished us joy. After which, with another cheer, they backed from out our presence, then turned and made for their quarters, while I led my wife within the house and closed the door.

Diccon was an ingenious scoundrel. I had told him to banish the dogs, to have the house cleaned and lit, and supper upon the table; but I had not ordered the floor to be strewn with rushes, the walls draped with flowering vines, a great jar filled with sunflowers, and an illumination of a dozen torches. Nevertheless, it looked well, and I highly approved the capon and maize cakes, the venison pasty and ale, with which the table was set. Through the open doors of the two other rooms were to be seen more rushes, more flowers, and more lights.

To the larger of these rooms I now led the way, deposited her bundle upon the settle, and saw that Diccon had provided fair water for her face and hands; which done, I told her that supper waited upon her convenience, and went back to the great room.[15]

She was long in coming, so long that I grew impatient and went to call her. The door was ajar, and so I saw her, kneeling in the middle of the floor, her head thrown back, her hands raised and clasped, on her face terror and anguish of spirit written so large that I started to see it. I stared in amazement, and had I followed my first impulse, would have gone to her, as I would have gone to any other creature in so dire distress. On second thoughts, I went noiselessly back to my station in the great room. She had not seen me, I was sure. Nor had I long to wait. Presently she appeared, and I could have doubted the testimony of my eyes, so changed were the agonized face and figure of a few moments before. Beautiful and disdain-

---

[14]*rope's end*, whipping.

[15]*great room*, the principal room of the house.

ful, she moved to the table, and took the great chair drawn before it with the air of an empress mounting a throne. I contented myself with the stool.

She ate nothing, and scarcely touched the canary I poured for her. I pressed upon her wine and viands—in vain; I strove to make conversation—equally in vain. Finally, tired of "yes" and "no" uttered as though she were reluctantly casting pearls before swine, I desisted, and applied myself to my supper in a silence as sullen as her own. At last we rose from table, and I went to look to the fastenings of door and windows, and returning found her standing in the center of the room, her head up and her hands clenched at her sides. I saw that we were to have it out then and there, and I was glad of it.

"You have something to say," I said. "I am quite at your command," and I went and leaned against the chimney piece.

The low fire upon the hearth burnt lower still before she broke the silence. When she did speak it was slowly, and with a voice which was evidently controlled only by a strong effort of a strong will. She said:

"When—yesterday, today, ten thousand years ago—you went from this horrible forest down to that wretched village yonder, to those huts that make your London, you went to buy you a wife?"

"Yes, madam," I answered. "I went with that intention."

"You had made your calculation? In your mind you had pitched upon such and such an article, with such and such qualities, as desirable? Doubtless you meant to get your money's worth?"

"Doubtless," I said dryly.

"Will you tell me what you were inclined to consider its equivalent?"

I stared at her, much inclined to laugh. The interview promised to be interesting.

"I went to Jamestown to get me a wife," I said at length, "because I had pledged my word that I would do so. I was not overanxious. I did not run all the way. But, as you say, I intended to do the best I could for myself; one hundred and twenty pounds of tobacco being a

considerable sum, and not to be lightly thrown away. I went to look for a mistress for my house, a companion for my idle hours, a rosy, humble, docile lass, with no aspirations beyond cleanliness and good temper, who was to order my household and make me a home. I was to be her head and her law, but also her sword and shield. That is what I went to look for."

"And you found—me!" she said, and broke into strange laughter.

I bowed.

"In God's name, why did you not go further?"

I suppose she saw in my face why I went no further, for into her own the color came flaming.

"I am not what I seem!" she cried out. "I was not in that company of choice!"

I bowed again. "You have no need to tell me that, madam," I said, "I have eyes. I desire to know why you were there at all, and why you married me."

She turned from me, until I could see nothing but the coiled wealth of her hair and the bit of white neck between it and the ruff. We stood so in silence, she with bent head and fingers clasping and unclasping, I leaning against the wall and staring at her, for what seemed a long time. At least I had time to grow impatient, when she faced me again, and all my irritation vanished in a gasp of admiration.

Oh, she was beautiful, and of a sweetness most alluring and fatal! Had Medea worn such a look, sure Jason had quite forgot the fleece,[16] and with those eyes Circe[17] had needed no other charm to make men what she would. Her voice, when she spoke, was no longer imperious; it was low pleading music. And she held out entreating hands.

"Have pity on me," she said. "Listen kindly, and have pity on me. You are a strong man and wear a sword. You can cut your way through trouble and peril. I am a woman, weak, friend-

---

[16]*Had Medea* (mi dē′ə) *worn such a look...forgot the fleece*. Jason (jā′sən) was a legendary Greek hero who underwent severe trials in his attempt to gain the Golden Fleece. He would have failed had it not been for the help of Medea, who had fallen in love with him. Ralph Percy feels that had Medea looked as Jocelyn did, Jason would have forgotten his quest for the fleece.

[17]*Circe* (sėr′sē), a sorceress in Greek mythology who could change men into animals.

less, helpless. I was in distress and peril, and I had no arm to save,[18] no knight to fight my battle. I do not love deceit. Ah, do not think that I have not hated myself for the lie I have been. But these forest creatures that you take—will they not bite against springe and snare? Are they scrupulous as to how they free themselves? I too was in the toils of the hunter, and I too was not scrupulous. There was a thing of which I stood in danger that would have been bitterer to me, a thousand times, than death. I had but one thought, to escape; how, I did not care—only to escape. I had a waiting woman named Patience Worth. One night she came to me, weeping. She had wearied of service, and had signed to go to Virginia as one of Sir Edwyn Sandys'[19] maids, and at the last moment her heart had failed her. There had been pressure brought to bear upon me that day—I had been angered to the very soul. I sent her away with a heavy bribe, and in her dress and under her name I fled from—I went aboard that ship. No one guessed that I was not the Patience Worth to whose name I answered. No one knows now —none but you, none but you."

"And why am I so far honored, madam?" I said bluntly.

She crimsoned, then went white again. She was trembling now through her whole frame. At last she broke out: "I am not of that crew that came to marry! To me you are the veriest stranger—you are but the hand at which I caught to draw myself from a pit that had been digged for me. It was my hope that this hour would never come. When I fled, mad for escape, willing to dare anything but that which I left behind, I thought, 'I may die before that ship with its shameless cargo sets sail.' When the ship set sail, and we met with stormy weather, and there was much sickness aboard, I thought, 'I may drown or I may die of the fever.' When, this afternoon, I lay there in the boat, coming up this dreadful river through the glare of the lightning, and you thought I slept, I was thinking, 'The bolts may strike me yet, and all will be well.' I prayed for that death, but the storm

passed. I am not without shame. I know that you must think all ill of me, that you must feel yourself gulled and cheated. I am sorry—that is all I can say—I am sorry. I am your wife—I was married to you today—but I know you not and love you not. I ask you to hold me as I hold myself, a guest in your house, nothing more. I am quite at your mercy. I am entirely friendless, entirely alone. I appeal to your generosity, to your honor——"

Before I could prevent her she was kneeling to me, and she would not rise, though I bade her do so.

I went to the door, unbarred it, and looked out into the night, for the air within the room stifled me. It was not much better outside. The clouds had gathered again, and were now hanging thick and low. From the distance came a rumble of thunder, and the whole night was dull, heavy, and breathless. Hot anger possessed me. In the servants' huts, a hundred yards away, lights were still burning, against rule, for the hour was late. Glad that there was something I could rail out against, I strode down upon the men, and caught them assembled in Diccon's cabin, dicing for tomorrow's rum. When I had struck out the light with my rapier, and had rated the rogues to their several quarters, I went back through the gathering storm to the brightly lit, flower-decked room, and to Mistress Percy.

She was still kneeling, her hands at her breast, and her eyes, wide and dark, fixed upon the blackness without the open door. I went up to her and took her by the hand.

"I am a gentleman, madam," I said. "You need have no fear of me. I pray you to rise."

She stood up at that, and her breath came hurriedly through her parted lips, but she did not speak.

"It grows late, and you must be weary," I continued. "Your room is yonder. I trust that you will sleep well. Good night."

I bowed low, and she curtsied to me. "Good night," she said.

On her way to the door, she brushed against the rack wherein hung my weapons. Among them was a small dagger. Her quick eye caught its gleam, and I saw her press closer to the wall,

[18]*no arm to save*, no one to keep me from harm.
[19]*Sir Edwin Sandys* (sandz), treasurer of the Virginia enterprise. Under his direction the colony flourished.

and with her right hand strive stealthily to detach the blade from its fastening. She did not understand the trick. Her hand dropped to her side, and she was passing on, when I crossed the room, loosened the dagger, and offered it to her, with a smile and a bow. She flushed scarlet and bit her lips, but she took it.

"There are bars to the door within," I said. "Again, good night."

"Good night," she answered, and, entering the room, she shut the door. A moment more, and I heard the heavy bars drop into place.

ENGLISH LADY AND VIRGINIA GENTLEMAN

1. Account for the differences between the appearance and behavior of Jocelyn Leigh and that of the other girls. How did her motives for coming to America differ from theirs?

2. The narrator gave his name to the minister as "Ralph Percy, Gentleman." Using *gentleman* in its modern sense, do you think Ralph Percy is entitled to be called by it? Which one do you think showed better breeding—the Virginia planter or the English girl? Why?

3. In what ways was the new land of Virginia and life in that land different from the England Jocelyn had left? How did these differences affect Jocelyn? In what respects was her view of Virginia different from Percy's?

Mary Johnston uses a narrator

Before writing *To Have and To Hold* Mary Johnston spent much time in careful study, consulting old journals, letters, records, and histories until she was familiar with every detail of life in earliest Virginia. She discovered that while life in the colony differed in many respects from life in England, the speech of educated men in both places was much the same. Therefore Ralph Percy, whom she presents as the narrator of her story, tells his tale in the manner that the fashionable romantic writers of England had made popular. His style is flowery and ornate; for example, he compares Jocelyn to "a rose amongst blowsed poppies and peonies, a pearl amidst glass beads." He uses many classical allusions, as when he compares Jocelyn's beauty to that of Perdita and Medea.

Select from the story several other examples of these characteristics of Ralph Percy's style. What effect does the style have on the mood and tone of the story?

March 1621

HELEN GRACE CARLISLE

When Captain John Smith was captured by French pirates in 1615, he was leading a band of colonists who planned to settle in the territory which he had explored the year before and had named New England. Five years later a group of Englishmen boarded the not-too-seaworthy *Mayflower* at Plymouth, England, and set sail for the same region. They were a mixed group, numbering 101, mainly Pilgrims fleeing from a king who had said, "I will make them conform, or I will harry them out of the land." Determined not to let the king force them into the Church of England, these refugees proposed to set up a religious state in America.

During the first bleak winter on the Massachusetts coast half of the Pilgrims died; over the remainder hung the dread of Indians. In the following account John Dexter, a Pilgrim father, tells of the first visit of the Indians to Plymouth.

WE FINISHED our house this month. I built it twenty feet by twenty feet, and made two rooms. The hearth we made of stone put together with clay. The sand here makes excellent mortar, mixed with the lime we brought with us. Our chimney we had to make of wood and mortar. For the time it must serve. We are too near the springtime to make a floor. But David and Sarah keep the earth floor strewn with fresh rushes. I have made two windows with oiled paper, and wood shutters which we can bar. Also trestles and boards for eating,[1] and some benches, Eleazar[2] helping. Our chests we have now from the hold of the ship, and our bedding.

The most are now living on the land, though we have only four houses finished besides the

---

[1]*trestles and boards for eating.* Tables were made by placing boards on trestles or sawhorses.

[2]*Eleazar* (el′i ā′zər), John's extremely religious brother. He was unmarried and lived with John and his family (his wife Anne, and their children David, Purity, and Sarah).

"March 1621," from *We Begin,* by Helen Grace Carlisle. Reprinted by permission of Random House, Inc. Copyright 1932 by Helen Grace Carlisle.

common house,[3] and several sheds for our stores. Captain Jones,[4] somewhat sobered by death, together with his men, has helped us hoist our six pieces of ordnance to our platform, our minion,[5] very heavy, weighing nearly half a ton. He brought us a fat goose in friendliness, and begged we not desert his men in their sickness. By his advice we have taken out the marks of our graves on the hill, and made the earth flat, so that the savages may not know our deaths. Thirteen died in March.

When I look back upon these several months, it is a miracle that we have put even two logs together. There have been days on end, when no man could put in even one nail, so terrible the sickness among us. There have been days when there were but half a dozen well to nurse all the rest. Anne, herself stricken, came ashore to minister to those who lay in the common house, their beds and pallets so close, there was no space to walk between.

But toward the end of the month, there came a day when I said to Anne, "Do you know, Anne, it is a week since any has died?" And the ice and snow began to melt away, and the frost to leave the ground.

---

[3]*common house,* the first building erected by the Pilgrims, to be used for storage and shelter while individual homes were being built.

[4]*Captain Jones,* captain of the *Mayflower.*

[5]*minion* (min'yən), a cannon of about 3-inch caliber.

Almost we were daring to breathe a little. Was the winter beginning to end? Was death beginning to be surfeited? Each man that had gone had taken with him some part of ourselves. With each loss, a wave of terror would sweep us clear, making our blood cease to run in our veins. And now it was a week since any had felt that dread emotion course from man to man like a destroying fire that for the moment almost swept away our courage.

And on that same day, David and Purity came running in.

"A robin! A robin! We've seen a robin!"

And I knew it was time.

I gathered together the men, and we went to our shed, and got from the shed our plows and our harrows. And we went to the fields, and harnessed ourselves with chains and leather to our plows, and we cut our first furrows. I could have wept for joy. All that day we turned the earth, still cold, and made her ready. And I knew that with our loving caress, she would soon grow warm and soft and yielding to our needs.

In the evening when I came home, there were Anne and David and Sarah, waiting to greet me. They were smiling. They had turned the piece of ground behind the house and a small strip before.

That night we sat by the fire and hope murmured gently in our hearts.

The next morning while I was in the fields, wondering whether it was time to set the corn, we heard the drum beat, the signal to return instantly to the village. Dropping my tools, I ran with the others. In the common house, Mr. Carver[6] informed us a band of savages had been seen approaching over the hill. So all that day we remained close to the town, and spent the time in training practice.

The next day I returned to the fields, but my tools were gone! When I reported this Captain Standish[7] called us together. Now we must think more deeply on our defense. He explained with warlike competence that bore traces of his Elizabethan commission[8] what our position was should attack come, from here or from there. But whilst we were in the midst of these affairs, we heard suddenly outside a great commotion, and opening the door of the common house, where we were meeting, we saw there in the afternoon sunlight a strange sight. For there walking straight to us was a tall savage, stark naked but for a leather around his middle, very fine of carriage, and altogether unafraid. His black hair was cut short before, and hung long behind. Over his shoulder he had his bow slung, and in a kind of leather case were his arrows. With him were two of our own men, on either side, guarding him with their muskets. And a swarm of women and children gaped. This was the first I had ever seen a savage, though we had been here all these months, for I had not been at First Encounter.[9]

As the Indian approached, he made with his right hand a round gesture, and then cried out,

to our utter amazement, in English: "Welcome! Welcome!"

We closed the door that he not see within, how few we were, and came outside. We were some few more than twenty men, and of our number eight were servants. This had death done to us.

When we had gathered round the savage, he once more saluted us, and cried "Welcome!" Our governor, Mr. Carver, stepped forward and answered him gravely, "Welcome!" And the savage said in English, "Me—Samoset! Sagamore! Chief!"

Mr. Carver asked him what he wished of us.

In English he replied, though we could scarcely understand at first until we grew accustomed to the sounds of his voice, for he could not mouth his *l*'s and *r*'s properly, the which we discovered in after times to be the like of all of them— he said he had much to disclose of us, and asked we receive him more properly. So we went all to Mr. Hopkins' house. We seated ourselves about the room, some standing guard without, not knowing what treachery might be in store, and some remained on the platform with our cannon.

The next word our savage uttered astonished us still the more. "Beer!" he cried. But we had none. We gave him instead a little aqua vitae, and some biscuit, and a little butter we still had left to us, though it smelled something strong, and a piece of cheese, also some cold cooked duck and pudding. As he ate, he made sounds of great enjoyment, and let us know it was not all strange fare to him.

When he had eaten a considerable quantity of food, we commenced to question him. Why were the savages fled from us? Why did we never see them? Why did we come upon their houses uninhabited? Did they fear us?

To all these things, he answered the savages had not fled from us, we never saw them because those from these parts were all dead.

---

[6]*Mr. Carver,* first governor of the colony.

[7]*Captain Standish,* the military leader of the colony. He was a professional soldier and not a member of the Pilgrim church.

[8]*his Elizabethan commission.* While Queen Elizabeth was ruling England, Miles Standish had been commissioned a lieutenant in the English army.

[9]*First Encounter.* Before the colonists landed at Plymouth, a party sent out from the *Mayflower* to explore the shores of Cape Cod Bay had been attacked by Indians.

"Dead," we asked, "how dead?"

This place, he said, was named Patuxet by the Indians. Two years before a great plague had swept here, he knew not what it was. The most had had sores, turned yellow, and all had died.

We asked him what of those we had met at First Encounter.

Those, he answered, were the Nausites. And then told us why they had set upon us.

Some five or six years before, Captain Smith had left behind one of his vessels in the hands of a Captain Hunt, to finish some trucking. Captain Hunt had been a rascal of first order, and had enticed upon his ship under guise of trade, some twenty Indians. Then he had hoisted sail and made away. He had called at Spain and there had sold them all for slaves for profit. Samoset said he would bring with him the next time he came, a friend, who could tell us more of this. Meanwhile the Nausites had not forgotten. Some few years before they had killed three English from one of Sir Gorges' ships[10] and would have eagerly killed us.

We asked what their number were. He answered about a hundred warriors.

Then we asked him whence he came. To which he replied he was from the tribe of Massassoit, a great sachem, farther north, who was our nearest neighbor. We asked him then what was his strength. Sixty braves, he answered.

What puzzled us most was where he had his English. At this he laughed, and said he was not like the other savages. He knew the English were strong, and some day they would come to the land for more than fish and trade, and so he had taken service from time to time with the fishing vessels near the Kennebec. From these vessels, he knew his English. Captain Jones asked him to name some of these vessels and their captains, to see if he told the truth, and this Samoset did willingly to the Captain's satisfaction.

In this wise, we used the afternoon. We took our leave of Samoset the next morning, having housed and guarded him with Mr. Hopkins for the night. We told him of our stolen tools, and he showed no surprise, but seemed to have had knowledge of this event. But he said that now he knew us not to be the kind of Englishmen like Captain Hunt, he would report our willingness for trade and friendship to his chief, Massassoit. Before he left us we gave him gifts for his chief, a knife, a bracelet, and a ring. He promised that he would soon return with Massassoit himself. And so with many expressions of friendship, he departed, and we returned to the common house to discuss this turn of our affairs.

"How mighty are the Lord's works!" cried Eleazar, "and how clear it is we are his chosen people. He sent the plague to the heathen, to clear the land for our coming. Praise the Lord in His wisdom."

"And for what mighty purpose has He sent the plague to us?" I asked somewhat dryly.

"That time will tell us; you may be sure it was for some reason."

But for the greater part we discussed what should be our face toward the savages. Men like Billington were all for a show of power. They were like children (just see how Samoset had fancied himself in the bracelet). Treat them as children therefore—and make them conform to us. But Will[11] was of another mind, and he had with him Mr. Carver, Mr. Brewster, and the wiser element. Since we were so few in numbers, we would keep ourselves always armed, always on guard, but at the same time we would deal fairly with them, and attempt to win their trust.

---

[10]*Sir Gorges' ships.* Sir Ferdinando Gorges (gôr′jəs) was one of the men instrumental in forming the Plymouth company. Before the Pilgrims left England, he had sent exploratory parties to America.

[11]*Will,* William Bradford, who became governor after the death of John Carver in April, 1621. Through his wise policies he did more than any other single person to make Plymouth a prosperous colony.

Therein lay Christian example and safety. The first we must do is discover to whom we owed for the corn we took.[12] And, indeed, we decided upon a friendly course, which we hoped would bring us their trade and keep us safe.

The next day was the Sabbath, and we were all at meeting for prayer, when once more we heard an interruption. Undoing the bar of the door, we saw indeed a brave and comely sight. Before us stood five tall most proper men, the foremost Samoset. Very straight they stood. All five wore clothes, every man wearing a deer's skin coat, but Samoset wore one of wild cat to show himself their leader. Also they wore long hose of leather, high up to their groins, and from their waist short leather trousers—so they looked for all the world like Irishmen. Their hair was cut in front and tied so that it spread like a fan, in which stood upright some feathers. Behind, the hair hung long. In addition, Samoset wore a fox's tail down his back, white tipped. The faces of all five were marked with paint, black and white and red in antic designs. They carried their bows and arrows; also some beaver

---

[12]*the corn we took*. Before Plymouth was settled, an exploring party had discovered some buried corn.

skins. My heart leaped when I saw in Samoset's hands my tools that had been taken.

Captain Standish went to them first and said they must lay down their arms at the edge of the town. This they did immediately with much soberness. Then they informed us they had come to truck with us. But we explained this was our Sabbath, our God's day, and we could conduct no business.

But we would gladly entertain them, so once more we repaired to Mr. Hopkins' house, carrying our muskets. We sent the women to fetch food from our stores, and it was astonishing what capacities our guests had. This we were to learn later was due to their long periods of lean, so they were accustomed to eat mightily when there was anything to eat at all. They had with them, however, a kind of food. It was like flour, made from the corn grains that had first been parched, then ground fine. Samoset explained that for traveling, this flour mixed with a little water was excellent, they could voyage for days on nothing else. It was called nokake.[13] We tasted of it. It was very good, somewhat like nuts.

---

[13]*nokake* (nō′kāk).

As Samoset would make known their minds to us, we could see they had great admiration for his knowledge, and in fact, he made every effort to make his impress on his fellows as upon us, sometimes speaking a great deal of gibberish very quickly that they might think he spoke the English tongue fluently.

We made plain with many signs our friendliness, and they also bore in their gestures much amity toward us, so that after a while, Samoset drew forth a small leather pouch of tobacco. Of this he drank[14] from a wood pipe, and then offered the pipe to us. We then informed them that if they would return with the beaver skins tomorrow, we would gladly trade with them, but today was our God's day, and we could do nothing.

At this Samoset held a few words with his friends, and then, all smiling, he informed us that as this was our God's day, he and his friends had an excellent dancing and singing for it. Before we could say a word, the five of them arose and commenced to run about in a circle, hopping and careening, uttering strange short weird cries, sometimes like a drum, sometimes like an animal. We were completely astonished. I for one did not know where to put my head for laughter, but I would not for very much have wished them to see me. But Eleazar came quickly forward and said we neither danced nor sang upon our God's day, and they were somewhat bewildered. And although they thought us as strange perhaps as we thought them, that we did not dance and sing on our God's day, they ceased their caperings and cavorting in great good nature.

With this we dismissed them, but after they had started up the town street, Samoset came running back, doubled himself in half and made the most dreadful grimaces, indicating that he was suffering. We could see well he was shamming, though what with having eaten butter a good six months old, of this we could not be too sure. But he asked if he could not have of Englishman's physic, and whether he could not remain with us the night. This we permitted him, housing him at Mr. Hopkins' dwelling, but

_____
[14]*drank,* smoked.

keeping good guard on him, especially as he made a most excellent meal, not at all like a sick man.

The next morning he departed.

THINKING OVER JOHN DEXTER'S STORY

1. What were some of the reasons that the Pilgrims rejoiced at the coming of the first spring? What had been the effect on them of the many deaths during the first winter? What passages best recapture for you the feelings of the survivors?

2. What was the main reason that the Pilgrims saw so little of the Indians during that first winter? How had this helped the Pilgrims?

3. How did it happen that Samoset was friendly to the Pilgrims? How did he explain the unfriendliness of the Indians met by the Pilgrims in the First Encounter?

4. What differing points of view regarding treatment of the Indians were voiced by Mr. Billington and Will Bradford? Whose advice did the Pilgrims follow? What reasons have you for believing that this was by far the wiser plan?

A BACKWARD GLANCE

1. Think over the four selections you have studied thus far. Which one was actually written in early colonial times? Which ones are written as if the narrator had lived in the seventeenth century? In which one is the author obviously writing as a twentieth-century narrator?

2. Which selection made you visualize most clearly the way the people lived? Which one do you think would be most valuable for a student who wished to increase his knowledge of life in the colonies? Which section of the country—the North or the South—is made more real by the selections?

Extending interests

John Dexter kept a day-by-day account of happenings in Plymouth. What might Captain John Smith have written about those days which he telescopes by saying, "Six or seven weeks those barbarians kept him prisoner, many strange triumphs and conjurations they made of him"? What do you think Pocahontas might have written about her impressions of England? What would Jocelyn Leigh have confided to her diary concerning those first strange days in America? Choose the character that interests you most and write several days' entries in a diary such as this person might have kept.

Housewifery

EDWARD TAYLOR

Seven years after the settlement of the Plymouth colony, the King of England gave a charter to the Massachusetts Bay Company. The leaders of this company were English Puritans, wealthy and well educated. Convinced that they could never reform the Church of England, they came to America because they hoped to found a "purified" church here. Other Puritans followed in great numbers. Among them was the most distinguished poet of colonial America, Edward Taylor, a young man who left England in 1668. Here he was graduated from Harvard College and became pastor of the frontier village of Westfield, Massachusetts. He quietly served the people of this village during the remainder of his life.

As a good churchman, Taylor was of course interested in the religious struggles of his time. A man of great piety, he was very strict in all religious observances. As a poet, he is distinguished for his sincerity of thought and feeling and for his use of homely metaphors drawn straight from personal experience. Watch for these qualities in the following poem, which describes his complete dedication to the service of God in terms of a process familiar in every colonial household, the weaving of cloth.

Single spindle wheel

MAKE ME, O Lord, Thy spinning wheel
    complete,
  Thy holy Word my distaff make for me;
Make mine affections Thy swift flyers neat,
    And make my soul Thy holy spool to be;
    My conversation make to be Thy reel,   5
    And reel the yarn thereon spun of Thy wheel.

Make me Thy loom then; knit therein this twine,
    And make Thy Holy Spirit, Lord, wind
      quills;
Then weave the web Thyself. The yarn is fine.
    Thine ordinances make my fulling mills.[1] 10

Then dye the same in heavenly colors choice,
All pinked[2] with varnished flowers of paradise.

Then clothe therewith mine understanding, will,
  Affections, judgment, conscience, memory;
My words and actions, that their shine may
    fill   15
  My ways with glory and Thee glorify.
  Then mine apparel shall display before Ye
  That I am clothed in holy robes for glory.

---

[1]*fulling mills,* places where cloth is cleaned and shrunk by moisture, pressure, and heat.

[2]*pinked,* adorned.

HOW WELL DID YOU UNDERSTAND?

1. Why would anyone living in Taylor's time have an easier time understanding this prayer than someone of modern times?

2. How does the author associate each of the various parts of a spinning wheel with his relationship with God?

3. In the second stanza what relationship with God does the poet find in the processes of weaving and of operating the fulling mill?

4. As Taylor expands his comparison, what parts of his personality does he ask God to improve?

5. For what reason does he order the stanzas as he does?

6. How does the poem illustrate the qualities of Taylor mentioned in the headnote?

Early Life in Manhattan

WASHINGTON IRVING

One would hardly suspect that the restless New York City of today was ever a place where "a sweet and holy calm reigned over the whole province." Yet the New Amsterdam which Washington Irving describes in the following selection from his *Knickerbocker's History of New York* (1809) was just such a place. Remember that the author was born about the time we won our independence from England. In this selection, however, he is writing about the Dutch settlement of New Amsterdam before it became an English-governed colony in 1664.

As you read, judge how well the author achieves his purpose: "to embody the traditions of our city in an amusing form; to illustrate its local humors, customs, and peculiarities; to clothe home scenes and places and familiar names with those imaginative and whimsical associations so seldom met with in our new country, but which live like charms and spells about the cities of the old world, binding the heart of the native inhabitant to his home."

IN THOSE good days of simplicity and sunshine, a passion for cleanliness was the leading principle in domestic economy, and the universal test of an able housewife—a character which formed the utmost ambition of our unenlightened grandmothers. The front door was never opened, except on marriages, funerals, New Year's days, the festival of St. Nicholas,[1] or some such great occasion. It was ornamented with a gorgeous brass knocker, curiously wrought, sometimes in the device of a dog, and sometimes of a lion's head, and was daily burnished with such religious zeal that it was ofttimes worn out by the very precautions taken for its preservation. The whole house was constantly in a state of inundation, under the discipline of mops and brooms and scrubbing brushes; and the good housewives of those days were a kind of amphibious animal, delighting exceedingly to be dabbling in water—insomuch that a historian of the day gravely tells us that many of his townswomen grew to have webbed fingers like unto a duck; and some of them, he had little doubt, could the matter be examined into, would be found to have the tails of mermaids—but this I look upon to be a mere sport of fancy, or, what is worse, a willful misrepresentation.

The grand parlor was the sanctum sanctorum,[2] where the passion for cleaning was indulged without control. In this sacred apartment no one was permitted to enter, excepting the mistress and her confidential maid, who visited it, once a week, for the purpose of giving it a thorough cleaning, and putting things to rights—always taking the precaution of leaving their shoes at the door, and entering devoutly on their stocking feet. After scrubbing the floor, sprinkling it with fine white sand, which was curiously stroked into angles and curves and rhomboids with a broom—after washing the windows, rubbing and polishing the furniture, and putting a new bunch of evergreens in the fireplace—the window shutters were again closed to keep out the flies, and the room carefully locked up until the revolution of time brought round the weekly cleaning day.

As to the family, they always entered in at the gate, and most generally lived in the kitchen. To have seen a numerous household assembled round the fire, one would have imagined that he was transported back to those happy days of primeval simplicity, which float before our imaginations like golden visions. The fireplaces were of a truly patriarchal magnitude, where the whole family, old and young, master and servant, black and white, nay, even the very cat and dog, enjoyed a community of privilege, and had each a right to a corner. Here the old burgher would sit in perfect silence, puffing his pipe, looking in the fire with half-shut eyes and thinking of nothing for hours together; the *goede vrouw*,[3] on the opposite side, would employ herself diligently in spinning yarn, or knitting stockings. The young folks would crowd

---

[1]*festival of St. Nicholas,* December 6. On this day the Dutch children of New Amsterdam received gifts from St. Nicholas, the forerunner of Santa Claus.

[2]*sanctum sanctorum* (sangk′təm sangk tō′rəm), holy of holies. Irving means that the parlor was considered too fine to be used.

[3]*the goede vrouw* (Hü′tə vrou), the good woman.

around the hearth, listening with breathless attention to some old crone of a Negro, who was the oracle of the family, and who, perched like a raven in a corner of the chimney, would croak forth for a long winter afternoon a string of incredible stories about New England witches—grisly ghosts, horses without heads—and hairbreadth escapes, and bloody encounters among the Indians.

In those happy days a well-regulated family always rose with the dawn, dined at eleven, and went to bed at sunset. Dinner was invariably a private meal, and the fat old burghers showed incontestable signs of disapprobation and uneasiness at being surprised by a visit from a neighbor on such occasions. But though our worthy ancestors were thus singularly averse to giving dinners, yet they kept up the social bands of intimacy by occasional banquetings, called tea parties.

These fashionable parties were generally confined to the higher classes, or noblesse,[4] that is to say, such as kept their own cows and drove their own wagons. The company commonly as-

sembled at three o'clock, and went away about six, unless it was in wintertime, when the fashionable hours were a little earlier, that the ladies might get home before dark. The tea table was crowned with a huge earthen dish, well stored with slices of fat pork, fried brown, cut up into morsels, and swimming in gravy. The company being seated around the genial board, and each furnished with a fork, evinced their dexterity in launching at the fattest pieces in this mighty dish—in much the same manner as sailors harpoon porpoises at sea, or our Indians spear salmon in the lakes. Sometimes the table was graced with immense apple pies, or saucers full of preserved peaches and pears; but it was always sure to boast an enormous dish of balls of sweetened dough, fried in hog's fat, and called doughnuts, or olykoeks[5]—a delicious kind of cake, at present scarce known in this city, except in genuine Dutch families.

The tea was served out of a majestic delft teapot, ornamented with paintings of fat little Dutch shepherds and shepherdesses tending pigs, with boats sailing in the air, and the houses built in the clouds, and sundry other ingenious Dutch fantasies. The beaux distinguished themselves by their adroitness in replenishing this pot from a huge copper teakettle, which would have made the pygmy macaronies[6] of these degenerate days sweat merely to look at it. To sweeten the beverage, a lump of sugar was laid beside each cup, and the company alternately nibbled and sipped with great decorum, until an improvement was introduced by a shrewd and economic old lady, which was to suspend a large lump directly over the tea table, by a string from the ceiling, so that it could be swung from mouth to mouth—an ingenious expedient, which is still kept up by some families in Albany, but which prevails without exception in Communipaw, Bergen, Flatbush, and all our uncontaminated Dutch villages.

At these primitive tea parties the utmost propriety and dignity of deportment prevailed. No flirting nor coquetting—no gambling of old ladies, nor hoyden chattering and romping of

[4]*noblesse* (nō bles′). This word originally meant persons of noble birth. Irving humorously applies it to the wealthier citizens.

[5]*olykoeks* (ol′i kukz′).
[6]*macaronies*, fashionable gentlemen; dandies.

young ones—no self-satisfied struttings of wealthy gentlemen, with their brains in their pockets, nor amusing conceits and monkey divertissements of smart young gentlemen, with no brains at all. On the contrary, the young ladies seated themselves demurely in their rush-bottom chairs, and knit their own woolen stockings; nor even opened their lips excepting to say *yah Mynheer*,[7] or *yah ya Vrouw*, to any question that was asked them; behaving in all things like decent, well-educated damsels. As to the gentlemen, each of them tranquilly smoked his pipe, and seemed lost in contemplation of the blue and white tiles with which the fireplaces were decorated; wherein sundry passages of Scripture were piously portrayed: Tobit and his dog[8] figured to great advantage; Haman swung conspicuously on his gibbet[9]; and Jonah appeared most manfully bouncing out of the whale,[10] like Harlequin[11] through a barrel of fire.

The parties broke up without noise and confusion. They were carried home by their own carriages, that is to say, by the vehicles nature had provided them, excepting such of the wealthy as could afford to keep a wagon. The gentlemen gallantly attended their fair ones to their respective abodes, and took leave of them with a hearty smack at the door: which, as it was an established piece of etiquette, done in perfect simplicity and honesty of heart, occasioned no scandal at that time, nor should it at the present—if our great-grandfathers approved of the custom, it would argue a great want of deference in their descendants to say a word against it.

In this dulcet period of my history, when the beauteous island of Manna-hata[12] presented a scene, the very counterpart of those glowing pictures drawn of the golden reign of Saturn,[13] there was, as I have before observed, a happy ignorance, an honest simplicity prevalent among its inhabitants, which, were I even able to depict, would be but little understood by the degenerate age for which I am doomed to write. Even the female sex, those arch innovators upon the tranquillity, the honesty, and graybeard customs of society, seemed for a while to conduct themselves with incredible sobriety and comeliness.

Their hair, untortured by the abominations of art, was scrupulously pomatumed back from their foreheads with a candle,[14] and covered with a little cap of quilted calico, which fitted exactly to their heads. Their petticoats of linsey-woolsey were striped with a variety of gorgeous dyes—though I must confess these gallant garments were rather short, scarce reaching below the

---

[13]*golden reign of Saturn.* Saturn, a character of ancient mythology, was banished from his throne by his son Jupiter. He fled to Italy, where he civilized the people and taught them agriculture. Because of his wise and mild rule his reign is called the Golden Age.

[14]*pomatumed* (pō mā′təmd)...*with a candle.* Using candle wax as a hair dressing (pomatum), the Dutch belles pulled their hair smoothly back from their foreheads.

---

[7]*yah Mynheer* (yä mĭn här′ *or* mĭn hēr′), yes, Sir. *Mynheer* is the Dutch word for *Sir* or *Mr.*

[8]*Tobit* (tō′bit) *and his dog. The Book of Tobit* is an ancient story relating the trials of an Old Testament Jew held captive in Nineveh. When his son Tobias (tō bī′əs) undertakes a journey for him, he is aided by the angel Raphael. A dog accompanies Tobias and the angel.

[9]*Haman* (hā′mən)...*on his gibbet.* Haman, an enemy of the Jews, was hanged on a gallows about seventy-five feet high. (Esther, Chapters 5-7.)

[10]*Jonah*...*bouncing out of the whale.* After spending three days in the whale's belly, Jonah was spit up onto dry land. (Jonah, Chapters 4 and 5.)

[11]*Harlequin* (här′lə kwin), a masked comic character dressed in a costume of varied colors.

[12]*Manna-hata* (ma′nə hat′ə), Manhattan.

knee, but then made up in the number, which generally equaled that of the gentleman's small-clothes; and what is still more praiseworthy, they were all of their own manufacture—of which circumstance, as may well be supposed, they were not a little vain.

I cannot say much in vindication of the shortness of the petticoats; it doubtless was introduced for the purpose of giving the stockings a chance to be seen, which were generally of blue worsted, with magnificent red clocks—or, perhaps, to display a well-turned ankle, and a neat, though serviceable foot, set off by a high-heeled leathern shoe, with a large and splendid silver buckle. Thus we find that the gentle sex in all ages have shown the same disposition to infringe a little upon the laws of decorum, in order to betray a lurking beauty, or gratify an innocent love of finery.

From the sketch here given, it will be seen that our good grandmothers differed considerably in their ideas of a fine figure from their scantily dressed descendants of the present day. A fine lady, in those times, waddled under more clothes, even on a fair summer's day, than would have clad the whole bevy of a modern ballroom. Nor were they the less admired by the gentlemen in consequence thereof. On the contrary, the greatness of a lover's passion seemed to increase in proportion to the magnitude of its object—and a voluminous damsel, arrayed in a dozen of petticoats, was declared by a Low-Dutch sonneteer[15] of the province to be radiant as a sunflower, and luxuriant as a full-blown cabbage. Certain it is, that in those days the heart of a lover could not contain more than one lady at a time; whereas the heart of a modern gallant has often room enough to accommodate half a dozen. The reason of which I conclude to be, that either hearts of the gentlemen have grown larger, or the persons of the ladies smaller: this, however, is a question for the physiologists to determine.

But there was a secret charm in these petticoats, which, no doubt, entered into the consideration of the prudent gallants. The wardrobe of a lady was in those days her only fortune; and she who had a good stock of petticoats and stockings was as absolutely an heiress as is a Kamchatka[16] damsel with a store of bearskins, or a Lapland[17] belle with a plenty of reindeer. The ladies, therefore, were very anxious to display these powerful attractions to the greatest advantage; and the best rooms in the house, instead of being adorned with caricatures of Dame Nature, in watercolors and needlework, were always hung round with abundance of homespun garments, the manufacture and the property of the females—a piece of laudable ostentation that still prevails among the heiresses of our Dutch villages.

The gentlemen, in fact, who figured in the circles of the gay world in these ancient times corresponded, in most particulars, with the beauteous damsels whose smiles they were ambitious to deserve. True it is, their merits would make but a very inconsiderable impression upon the heart of a modern fair: they neither drove their curricles, nor sported their tandems,[18] for as yet those gaudy vehicles were not even dreamt of; neither did they distinguish themselves by their brilliancy at the table, and their consequent rencounters with watchmen, for our forefathers were of too pacific a disposition to need those guardians of the night, every soul throughout the town being sound asleep before nine o'clock. Neither did they establish their claims to gentility at the expense of their tailors, for as yet those offenders against the pockets of society, and the tranquillity of all aspiring young gentlemen, were unknown in New Amsterdam; every good housewife made the clothes of her husband and family, and even the *goede vrouw* of Van Twiller[19] himself thought it no disparagement to cut out her husband's linsey-woolsey galligaskins.

Not but what there were some two or three

---

[15]*Low-Dutch sonneteer,* a poet, probably a poor poet, who wrote in the language of Holland.

[16]*Kamchatka* (kam chat′kə), peninsula of northeast Asia bordering Bering Sea.

[17]*Lapland,* region in northern Norway, Sweden, Finland, and northwest Russia.

[18]*curricles* (kėr′i kəlz)...*tandems,* horse-drawn carriages. A curricle was a two-wheeled vehicle; a tandem was a carriage drawn by two horses harnessed one behind the other.

[19]*Van Twiller* (van twil′ər), director general of New Amsterdam from 1633 to 1637.

youngsters who manifested the first dawning of what is called fire and spirit; who held all labor in contempt; skulked about docks and market places; loitered in the sunshine; squandered what little money they could procure at hustlecap and chuck farthing[20]; swore, boxed, fought cocks, and raced their neighbors' horses; in short, who promised to be the wonder, the talk, and abomination of the town, had not their stylish career been unfortunately cut short by an affair of honor with a whipping post.

Far other, however, was the truly fashionable gentleman of those days: his dress, which served for both morning and evening, street and drawing room, was a linsey-woolsey coat, made, perhaps, by the fair hands of the mistress of his affections, and gallantly bedecked with abundance of large brass buttons; half a score of breeches heightened the proportions of his figure; his shoes were decorated by enormous copper buckles; a low-crowned broad-rimmed hat overshadowed his burly visage; and his hair dangled down his back in a prodigious queue of eelskin.

Thus equipped, he would manfully sally forth, with pipe in mouth, to besiege some fair damsel's obdurate heart—not such a pipe, good reader, as that which Acis did sweetly tune in praise of his Galatea,[21] but one of true Delft manufacture, and furnished with a charge of fragrant tobacco. With this would he resolutely set himself down before the fortress, and rarely failed, in the process of time, to smoke the fair enemy into a surrender, upon honorable terms.

Such was the happy reign of Wouter Van Twiller, celebrated in many a long-forgotten song as the real golden age, the rest being nothing but counterfeit copper-washed coin. In that delightful period, a sweet and holy calm reigned over the whole province. The burgomaster smoked his pipe in peace; the substantial solace of his domestic cares, after her daily toils were done, sat soberly at the door, with her

arms crossed over her apron of snowy white, without being insulted with ribald strollers or vagabond boys—those unlucky urchins who do so infest our streets, displaying, under the roses of youth, the thorns and briers of iniquity. Then it was that the lover with ten breeches, and the damsel with petticoats of half a score, indulged in all the innocent endearments of virtuous love, without fear and without reproach; for what had that virtue to fear, which was defended by a shield of good linsey-woolseys, equal at least to the seven bull hides of the invincible Ajax[22]?

---

[22]*seven bull hides...Ajax* (ā′jaks). According to Greek mythology, Ajax, one of the greatest of the Greek heroes, had a shield made of seven layers of bull hide and an outside fold of brass.

CAN YOU ENTER IRVING'S MOOD?

1. Read again the author's statement of his purpose quoted in the headnote to this selection and discuss whether or not he has achieved his purpose. Go through the whole selection in finding evidence to support your answer.

2. When Irving's *Knickerbocker's History of New York* was first published, some old Dutch aristocratic families of the community were irritated by the author's treatment of their ancestors. Point out details in this selection that probably offended New Yorkers when they first read it. Why did New Yorkers of later times feel less distressed about these passages?

3. What great contrast does Irving note in the behavior of the early dwellers in Manhattan and in that of his own time (1809)? How does the author, despite his humor, let the reader know of his respect and genuine admiration for the early Dutch settlers?

4. Point out what seem to you the most amusing paragraphs. Cite good examples of Irving's choice of words and details to emphasize the humor.

Extending interests

You and some of your friends might enjoy preparing an illustrated report on old New Amsterdam—its history, size, appearance, the dress and customs of its inhabitants, their occupations and interests. Some of the group could do research reading and take notes on different aspects of the subject; others who like to draw might work with those doing the research, preparing illustrations to be posted on the bulletin board when the joint report is presented to the class.

---

[20]*hustlecap and chuck farthing,* ancient gambling games played with coins.
[21]*pipe...in praise of his Galatea* (gal′ə tē′ə). Acis (ā′sis), a Sicilian shepherd, loved the sea nymph Galatea. With his shepherd's pipe he played melodies to show his love.

Neighbors in Virginia

WILLIAM BYRD

The life of the Virginia colonists at the beginning of the eighteenth century was in sharp contrast to that of the early settlers. Prosperity continued to increase. The great landowners built large colonial manor houses, surrounded by fine gardens and furnished with the costliest of furniture, paintings, cut glass, and silver imported from England. Frequently they owned libraries containing hundreds of books and employed tutors for the education of the children. The young men of the families usually completed their education in England and on the Continent. In fact, everything befitting the life of gentlemen was to be found in the aristocracy of the Virginia colony. There hospitality and gentility became a tradition.

This way of life is best exemplified by Colonel William Byrd II, of Westover Plantation on the James River. Byrd had the finest library in all the colonies; he rolled into Williamsburg on business of state in his coach-and-six with liveried outriders; and he was thoroughly at home in English as well as Virginia drawing rooms. In addition to managing his vast plantations of almost 180,000 acres, he was for thirty years a member of the House of Burgesses, a frequent representative of the colony in England, a regular correspondent with members of the Royal Society (an English society devoted to the study of science), and in his later life a member of the King's Councilors.

Like many other colonists, Colonel Byrd kept journals in which he wrote of his affairs. The following selection from one of these journals, *A Progress to the Mines,* describes a trip made to inspect his frontier properties and to learn from a friend all that he could about the manufacture of iron. As you read, note his smoothness of manner, his witty and keen observations, and his charming way of combining graciousness with business.

I CAME INTO the main county road that leads from Fredericksburg to Germanna, which last place I reached in ten miles more. This famous town consists of Colonel Spotswood's enchanted castle on one side of the street, and a baker's dozen of ruinous tenements on the other, where so many German families had dwelt some years ago; but are now removed ten miles higher, in the fork of Rappahannock, to land of their own. There had also been a chapel about a bow-shot from the Colonel's house, at the end of an avenue of cherry trees, but some pious people had lately burnt it down, with intent to get another built nearer to their own homes. Here I arrived about three o'clock, and found only Mrs. Spotswood at home, who received her old acquaintance with many a gracious smile. I was carried into a room elegantly set off with pier glasses, the largest of which came soon after to an odd misfortune. Amongst other favorite animals that cheered this lady's solitude, a brace of tame deer ran familiarly about the house, and one of them came to stare at me as a stranger. But unluckily spying his own figure in the glass, he made a spring over the table that stood under it and shattered the glass to pieces, and falling back upon the tea table, made a terrible fracas among the china. This exploit was so sudden and accompanied with such a noise that it surprised me, and perfectly frightened Mrs. Spotswood. But 'twas worth all the damage to show the moderation and good humor with which she bore this disaster.

In the evening the noble Colonel came home from his mines, who saluted me very civilly, and Mrs. Spotswood's sister, Miss Theky, who had been to meet him *en cavalier,*[1] was so kind too as to bid me welcome. We talked over a legend[2] of old stories, supped about nine, and then prattled with the ladies till it was time for a traveler to retire. In the meantime I observed my old friend to be very uxorious, and exceedingly fond of his children. This was so opposite to the maxims he used to preach up before he was married that I could not forbear rubbing up the memory of them. But he gave a very good-natured turn to his change of sentiments, by alleging that whoever brings a poor gentlewoman into so solitary a place, from all her friends and acquaintance, would be ungrateful not to use her and all that belongs to her with all possible tenderness.

---

[1] *en cavalier* (än kä vä lyā′), on horseback.
[2] *legend,* legion, or great number.

We all kept snug in our several apartments till nine, except Miss Theky, who was the housewife of the family. At that hour we met over a pot of coffee, which was not quite strong enough to give us the palsy. After breakfast the Colonel and I left the ladies to their domestic affairs and took a turn in the garden, which has nothing beautiful but three terrace walks that fall in slopes one below another. I let him understand that besides the pleasure of paying him a visit I came to be instructed by so great a master in the mystery of making of iron, wherein he had led the way, and was the Tubal Cain of Virginia.[3] He corrected me a little there, by assuring me he was not only the first in this country,[4] but the first in North America, who had erected a regular furnace.[5] That they ran altogether upon bloomeries in New England and Pennsyl-

vania,[6] till his example had made them attempt greater works. But in this last colony, they have so few ships to carry their iron to Great Britain that they must be content to make it only for their own use, and must be obliged to manufacture it when they have done. That he hoped he had done the country very great service by setting so good an example. That the four furnaces now at work in Virginia circulated a great sum of money for provisions and all other necessaries in the adjacent counties. That they took off a great number of hands from planting tobacco and employed them in works that produced a large sum of money in England to the persons concerned, whereby the country is so much the richer.

Then I inquired after his own mines, and hoped, as he was the first that engaged in this great undertaking, that he had brought them to

---

[3] *the Tubal Cain* (tū′bəl kān) *of Virginia.* Tubal Cain is mentioned in the Bible (Genesis 4:22) as "an instructor of artificers in brass and iron." He is regarded as the inventor of the metal-working arts.

[4] *country,* colony.

[5] *a regular furnace,* a real plant for removing the iron from the ore and for reheating it for shaping into various forms.

[6] *they ran altogether upon bloomeries in New England and Pennsylvania.* A bloomery was the first forge in an ironworks where the metal, already separated from the ore, was made into lumps of iron. The manufacturers of New England and Pennsylvania had only bloomeries as contrasted with Colonel Spotswood's more modern furnace.

the most perfection. He told me he had iron in several parts of his great tract of land, consisting of 45,000 acres. But that the mine he was at work upon was thirteen miles below Germanna. That his ore (which was very rich) he raised a mile from his furnace, and was obliged to cart the iron, when it was made, fifteen miles to Massaponox, a plantation he had upon Rappahannock River; but that the road was exceeding good, gently declining all the way, and had no more than one hill to go up in the whole journey. For this reason his loaded carts went it in a day without difficulty. He said it was true his works were of the oldest standing, but that his long absence in England, and the wretched management of Mr. Greame, whom he had entrusted with his affairs, had put him back very much. That his furnace stood still a great part of the time, and all his plantations ran to ruin. That indeed he was rightly served for committing his affairs to the care of a mathematician, whose thoughts were always among the stars.

Our conversation on this subject continued till dinner, which was both elegant and plentiful. The afternoon was devoted to the ladies, who showed me one of their most beautiful walks. They conducted me through a shady lane to the landing, and by the way made me drink some very fine water that issued from a marble fountain, and ran incessantly. Just behind it was a covered bench, where Miss Theky often sat and bewailed her maiden state. Then we proceeded to the river, which is the south branch of Rappahannock, about fifty yards wide, and so rapid that the ferry boat is drawn over by a chain, and therefore called the Rapidan. At night we drank prosperity to all the Colonel's projects in a bowl of rack punch,[7] and then retired to our devotions.

Having employed about two hours in retirement, I sallied out at the first summons to breakfast, where our conversation with the ladies, like whip sillabub,[8] was very pretty, but had nothing in it. This it seems was Miss Theky's birthday, upon which I made her my compli-

ments, and wished she might live twice as long a married woman as she had lived a maid. I did not presume to pry into the secret of her age, nor was she forward to disclose it, for this humble reason, lest I should think her wisdom fell short of her years.

Then the Colonel and I took another turn in the garden, to discourse farther on the subject of iron. He was very frank in communicating all his dear-bought experience to me, and told me very civilly he would not only let me into the whole secret, but would make a journey to James River, and give me his faithful opinion of all my conveniences. For his part he wished there were many more iron works in the country, provided the parties concerned would preserve a constant harmony among themselves, and meet and consult frequently, what might be for their common advantage.

WHAT WERE THE CHARACTERISTICS OF COLONEL BYRD'S WORLD?

1. Contrast life in the Virginia colony at this time with the life of the earliest colonists. What evidences do you find of wealth, culture, and leisure?

2. Do you think that the author might be referred to as "William Byrd, Gentleman"? Would he be considered a gentleman today?

3. What information on the beginnings of industry in the colonies do you gain from this selection? How did Colonel Spotswood show himself to be proud of his standing in the iron industry? What was his attitude in giving the information asked for by the author?

4. Byrd's way of writing is described as witty, polished, and vivacious. Read illustrative passages and tell exactly why you would so describe each passage. How is Byrd's way of writing a natural development of his way of living?

Extending interests

A round-table discussion group might be formed to investigate the reasons for the growth of an aristocratic class in Virginia and the effect of this class on economic life, architecture, literature, education, and clothing in the colony. Before holding the discussion, a chairman should be appointed, the subject divided into its various aspects, and each member of the group made responsible for reading up on one phase of the problem.

---

[7]*rack punch*, a drink made with arrack, a liquor distilled from rum, and flavored with fruit.

[8]*whip sillabub*, a dessert made of eggs and sweetened cream whipped to a froth and flavored with wine.

An Escape from Alligators

WILLIAM BARTRAM

Among the early settlers were a few who had a great curiosity about the natural wonders of the new land; some of these kept records of their scientific explorations which were of great value to scientists both in Europe and in America. Perhaps the most interesting of these early scientific observations are those written by the naturalist William Bartram (1739-1823).

In April, 1773, William Bartram began an exploration of the southeastern part of the United States which he continued until January, 1778. Thirteen years later (1791) he published the account of this exploration in a book entitled *Travels Through North and South Carolina, Georgia, East and West Florida.* Episodes like the following explain the great appeal of the book to ordinary readers as well as to scientists. The events took place on the upper St. John's River in Florida.

THE EVENING was temperately cool and calm. The crocodiles[1] began to roar and appear in uncommon numbers along the shores and in the river. I fixed my camp in an open plain, near the utmost projection of the promontory, under the shelter of a large live oak, which stood on the highest part of the ground, and but a few yards from my boat. From this open, high situation, I had a free prospect of the river, which was a matter of no trivial consideration to me, having good reason to dread the subtle attacks of the alligators, who were crowding about my harbor. Having collected a good quantity of wood for the purpose of keeping up a light and smoke during the night, I began to think of preparing my supper, when, upon examining my stores, I found but a scanty provision. I thereupon determined, as the most expeditious way of supplying my necessities, to take my bob[2] and try for some trout. About one hundred yards above my harbor began a cove or bay of the river, out of which opened a large lagoon. The mouth or entrance from the river to it was narrow, but the waters soon after spread and formed a little lake, extending into the marshes; its entrance and shores within I observed to be verged with floating lawns of the pistia and nymphea[3] and other aquatic plants; these I knew were excellent haunts for trout.

The verges and islets of the lagoon were elegantly embellished with flowering plants and shrubs; the laughing coots with wings half spread were tripping over the little coves, and hiding themselves in the tufts of grass; young broods of the painted summer teal, skimming the still surface of the waters, and following the watchful parent unconscious of danger, were frequently surprised by the voracious trout; and he, in turn, as often by the subtle greedy alligator. Behold him rushing forth from the flags and reeds. His enormous body swells. His plaited tail, brandished high, floats upon the lake. The waters like a cataract descend from his opening jaws. Clouds of smoke issue from his dilated nostrils.[4] The earth trembles with his thunder. When immediately from the opposite coast of the lagoon, emerges from the deep his rival champion. They suddenly dart upon each

---

[1]*crocodiles.* Although the alligator differs in certain respects from the American crocodile, the author uses the terms interchangeably.

[2]*bob,* fishing rod.

---

[3]*pistia* (pis′ti ə) *and nymphea* (nim fē′ə). The former is a free-floating water plant found in tropical climates. The latter is the common water lily.

[4]*Clouds of smoke issue from his dilated nostrils.* When a bull alligator roars, a fine steamy vapor with a musky smell comes forth from the scent glands on the underside of his chin. The author apparently confused the source of this vapor.

other. The boiling surface of the lake marks their rapid course, and a terrific conflict commences. They now sink to the bottom folded together in horrid wreaths. The water becomes thick and discolored. Again they rise, their jaws clap together, reëchoing through the deep surrounding forests. Again they sink, when the contest ends at the muddy bottom of the lake, and the vanquished makes a hazardous escape, hiding himself in the muddy turbulent waters and sedge on a distant shore. The proud victor exulting returns to the place of action. The shores and forests resound his dreadful roar, together with the triumphing shouts of the plaited tribes around, witnesses of the horrid combat.

My apprehensions were highly alarmed after being a spectator of so dreadful a battle. It was obvious that every delay would but tend to increase my dangers and difficulties, as the sun was near setting, and the alligators gathered around my harbor from all quarters. From these considerations I concluded to be expeditious in my trip to the lagoon, in order to take some fish. Not thinking it prudent to take my fusee[5] with me, lest I might lose it overboard in case of a battle, which I had every reason to dread before my return, I therefore furnished myself with a club for my defense, went on board, and penetrating the first line of those which surrounded my harbor, they gave way; but being pursued by several very large ones, I kept strictly on the watch, and paddled with all my might toward the entrance of the lagoon, hoping to be sheltered there from the multitude of my assailants; but ere I had halfway reached the place, I was attacked on all sides, several endeavoring to overset the canoe.

My situation now became precarious to the last degree; two very large ones attacked me closely at the same instant, rushing up with their heads and part of their bodies above the water, roaring terribly and belching floods of water over me. They struck their jaws together so close to my ears as almost to stun me, and I expected every moment to be dragged out of the boat and instantly devoured. But I applied my weapons so effectually about me, though at random, that I was so successful as to beat them off a little; when, finding that they designed to renew the battle, I made for the shore, as the only means left me for my preservation; for by keeping close to it, I should have my enemies on one side of me only, whereas I was before surrounded by them; and there was a probability, if pushed to the last extremity, of saving myself by jumping out of the canoe on shore, as it is easy to outwalk them on land, although comparatively as swift as lightning in the water. I found this last expedient alone could fully answer my expectations, for as soon as I gained the shore, they drew off.

This was a happy relief as my confidence was, in some degree, recovered by it. On recollecting myself, I discovered that I had almost reached the entrance of the lagoon, and determined to venture in, if possible, to take a few fish, and then return to my harbor while daylight continued; for I could now, with caution and resolution, make my way with safety along shore; and indeed there was no other way to regain my camp without leaving my boat and making my retreat through the marshes and reeds, which, if I could even effect, would have been in a manner throwing myself away, for then there would have been no hopes of ever recovering my bark, and returning in safety to any settlements of men. I accordingly proceeded, and made good my entrance into the lagoon, though not without opposition from the alligators, who formed a line across the entrance but did not pursue me into it, nor was I molested by any there, though there were some very large ones in a cove at the upper end.

I soon caught more trout than I had present occasion[6] for, and the air was too hot and sultry to admit of their being kept for many hours, even though salted or barbecued. I now prepared for my return to camp, which I succeeded in with but little trouble, by keeping close to the shore; yet I was opposed upon reëntering the river out of the lagoon, and pursued near to my landing (though not closely attacked), particularly by an old daring one, about twelve feet in

---

[5]*fusee* (fū sē′), light musket.

[6]*occasion*, need.

length, who kept close after me; and when I stepped on shore and turned about, in order to draw up my canoe, he rushed up near my feet and lay there for some time, looking me in the face, his head and shoulders out of water. I resolved he should pay for his temerity, and having a heavy load in my fusee, I ran to my camp, and returning with my piece, found him with his foot upon the gunwale of the boat, in search of fish. On my coming up he withdrew sullenly and slowly into the water, but soon returned and placed himself in his former position, looking at me and seeming neither fearful nor any way disturbed. I soon dispatched him by lodging the contents of my gun in his head, and then proceeded to cleanse and prepare my fish for supper; and accordingly took them out of the boat, laid them down on the sand close to the water, and began to scale them; when, raising my head, I saw before me, through the clear water, the head and shoulders of a very large alligator moving slowly toward me.

I stepped back, when, with a sweep of his tail, he brushed off several of my fish. It was certainly most providential that I looked up at that instant, as the monster would probably, in less than a minute, have seized and dragged me into the river. This incredible boldness of the animal disturbed me greatly, supposing there could now be no reasonable safety for me during the night but by keeping continually on the watch; I therefore, as soon as I had prepared the fish, proceeded to secure myself and effects in the best manner I could. In the first place, I hauled my bark upon the shore, almost clear out of the water, to prevent their oversetting or sinking her; after this, every movable was taken out and carried to my camp, which was but a few yards off; then ranging some dry wood in such order as was the most convenient, I cleared the ground round about it, that there might be no impediment in my way in case of an attack in the night, either from the water or the land; for I discovered by this time that this small isthmus, from[7] its remote situation and fruitfulness, was resorted to by bears and wolves. Having prepared myself in the best manner I could, I charged my gun and proceeded to reconnoiter my camp and the adjacent grounds; when I discovered that the peninsula and grove, at the distance of about two hundred yards from my encampment, on the land side were invested

---

[7]*from*, because of.

by a cypress swamp covered with water, which below was joined to the shore of the little lake, and above to the marshes surrounding the lagoon; so that I was confined to an islet exceedingly circumscribed, and I found there was no other retreat for me, in case of an attack, but by either ascending one of the large oaks, or pushing off with my boat.

It was by this time dusk, and the alligators had nearly ceased their roar, when I was again alarmed by a tumultuous noise that seemed to be in my harbor, and therefore engaged my immediate attention. Returning to my camp, I found it undisturbed, and then continued on to the extreme point of the promontory, where I saw a scene, new and surprising, which at first threw my senses into such a tumult that it was some time before I could comprehend what was the matter; however, I soon accounted for the prodigious assemblage of crocodiles at this place, which exceeded everything of the kind I had ever heard of.

How shall I express myself so as to convey an adequate idea of it to the reader, and at the same time avoid raising suspicions of my veracity? Should I say that the river (in this place) from shore to shore, and perhaps near half a mile above and below me, appeared to be one solid bank of fish, of various kinds, pushing through this narrow pass of St. John's into the little lake, on their return down the river, and that the alligators were in such incredible numbers, and so close together from shore to shore, that it would have been easy to have walked across on their heads, had the animals been harmless? What expressions can sufficiently declare the shocking scene that for some minutes continued, whilst this mighty army of fish were forcing the pass? During this attempt, thousands, I may say hundreds of thousands, of them were caught and swallowed by the devouring alligators. I have seen an alligator take up out of the water several great fish at a time, and just squeeze them betwixt his jaws, while the tails of the great trout flapped about his eyes and lips, ere he had swallowed them. The horrid noise of their closing jaws, their plunging amidst the broken banks of fish, and rising with their prey some feet upright above the water,

the floods of water and blood rushing out of their mouths, and the clouds of vapor issuing from their wide nostrils, were truly frightful. This scene continued at intervals during the night, as the fish came to the pass. After this sight, shocking and tremendous as it was, I found myself somewhat easier and more reconciled to my situation; being convinced that their extraordinary assemblage here was owing to this annual feast of fish; and that they were so well employed in their own element, that I had little occasion to fear their paying me a visit.

CONCERNING WILLIAM BARTRAM

1. What incidents in this account make it read like an adventure story? If it were rewritten as a mere adventure story, how should the happenings be rearranged to mount to a climax?

2. What details let you know that the author is a scientist with a scientist's approach to a problem?

3. What qualities do you find in William Bartram similar to those exhibited by John Smith? Did he have any of the characteristics of William Byrd?

The way it's said

The eighteenth century was an age of graceful living and formal manners in England. There the prose of the century reflected this leisurely, cultured life. Along the Atlantic seaboard in America, the gentlemen of the colonies, with the hazards and privations of the earliest days well behind them, wrote as their English contemporaries did. William Byrd and William Bartram studded their language with words derived from Latin roots—many of them long and rather difficult words which gave a dignified, formal air to their writing. The italicized words in the phrases below from "An Escape from Alligators" are all of Latin derivation. How would you express the ideas they contain in informal English? What happens to Bartram's style when you change his words?

1. near the utmost *projection* of the *promontory*
2. the most *expeditious* way of *supplying* my *necessities*
3. I *concluded* to be *expeditious*
4. *multitude* of my *assailants*
5. my *situation* now became *precarious*
6. *confined* to an islet *exceedingly circumscribed*
7. the *prodigious assemblage* of crocodiles
8. raising *suspicions* of my *veracity*

The Larger View

I. Now that you have finished studying this unit, you will probably find it interesting to talk over the various ideas you have gained both from the text selections and the other reading you have done. One way to do this is to divide the class into round-table discussion groups. Each group selects a chairman to present the subject for discussion and to guide its development. You may wish to allow members of the class not in the round table to enter the discussion after those in the group have had their say. You may think of other items to add to those listed below as subjects for the round-table discussions.

1. The earliest settlers exhibited many qualities which we regard today as "typically American."
2. Colonial life offered more opportunities than does modern life for developing strong character.
3. The patterns of life developed in the various colonies have continued to shape life in certain sections of the country even into the present day.
4. The mental hazards faced by the first colonists were even greater than the physical dangers.
5. The colonists showed themselves shortsighted and cruel in their treatment of the Indians.
6. The early colonists showed an awareness of and interest in the natural resources and physical features of the country.
7. From its colonial period the United States has been the home of people of many nationalities.

II. Prepare to report to the class on one of the following topics.

1. The Lost Colony of Roanoke
2. How America Got Its Name
3. Colonial Ambitions in the Seventeenth Century as Compared to Colonial Ambitions in the Twentieth Century
4. Child Life in Colonial Times
5. Home Life in Colonial Times
6. A Day in a Colonial Household
7. Manners in Colonial Times
8. School Life in Colonial Times
9. Indian Sports and Games
10. Colonial Costumes (illustrated)
11. Growth of the Colonies (illustrated)

III. Plan with the other members of your class an art exhibit on "Colonial America in Pictures." Select a chairman who will be responsible for the organization of the exhibit. Perhaps you will need subchairmen for classifying the pictures, mounting them, and hanging them. Let each member of the class share in searching through magazines, newspapers, and other sources for appropriate pictures. Your library and art department will probably coöperate in the exhibit. If you are pleased with the result of your work, no doubt you will want to invite the faculty and student body as well as the school patrons to see it.

MORE GOOD READING

AUSTIN, JANE, *Standish of Standish*. (Houghton) Miles Standish and the Pilgrim fathers are the central characters in this account of love and adventure in earliest New England. Girls may find even more interest in the same author's *Betty Alden* (Houghton).

BARR, AMELIA E., *Bow of Orange Ribbon*. (Dodd) The setting is New York, the time is 1756, and the subject is a romance between a Dutch maiden and one of King George's officers.

BENÉT, STEPHEN VINCENT, *Western Star*. (Farrar) In his long narrative poem Benét brings back to vivid life the adventurers of Jamestown and the men and women of Plymouth. Reading it will increase your pride in being an American.

BENNETT, JOHN, *Barnaby Lee*. (Appleton) This is a tale of pirates and adventure at the period when the British captured New Amsterdam in 1664. Peter Stuyvesant and Governor Calvert of Maryland are among the characters.

DARINGER, HELEN FERN, *Pilgrim Kate*. (Harcourt) This is the story of how seventeen-year-old Kate Endicott, who lived in Scrooby, England, in the time of James I, became a Pilgrim.

FORBES, ESTHER, *Paradise*. (Harcourt) Jude Parre's poverty didn't keep him from marrying a wealthy London woman and setting out for Massachusetts Bay Colony. The action of this fine historical novel leads up to and includes King Philip's War.

FORESTER, C. S., *To the Indies*. (Little) A lawyer, sent by the Spanish rulers to investigate conditions in the New World, tells this story of Columbus' last expedition. C. S. Forester is an expert at writing sea stories and creating believable—and sometimes despicable—characters.

GALE, ELIZABETH, *Katrina van Ost and the Silver Rose*. (Putnam) Tiny New Amsterdam in the 1630's and '40's is the background for this story of a beautiful girl and the silver rose heirloom which plays a part in her romance.

HALL-QUEST, OLGA W., *Jamestown Adventure*. (Dutton) This fine account, which is based on original records and research, gives the reader the feeling of what life in Jamestown was like in its first perilous, exciting, and hard years.

HAWTHORNE, NATHANIEL, *The Scarlet Letter*. (Houghton) This is an American classic, one of the finest studies of the working of the Puritan conscience. If you are interested in action that takes place inside the minds and hearts of people, read this story of Hester Prynne.

JOHNSTON, MARY, *Croatan*. (Little) The story of the "lost colony," the little band of English settlers who disappeared from the island of Roanoke leaving only the word "Croatan" carved on a tree, has always been a favorite. Using Virginia Dare, the first white child born in America, as her central character, Mary Johnston has woven a fascinating story about the fate of the lost colonists.

KELLY, ERIC, *The Amazing Journey of David Ingram*. (Lippincott) This fascinating adventure story is based on David Ingram's account in Hakluyt's *Voyages* of his overland journey with two companions from the Bay of Mexico to the Kennebec River in 1568. Suspense and humor alternate in this tale of adventures with Indians in an unknown land.

KING, GRACE E., *La Dame de Sainte Hermine*. (Macmillan) Mystery attends the arrival of the beautiful prisoner, Marie Alorge, in early New Orleans. Girls will enjoy the mystery and romance of this novel.

LOVELACE, M. H., *Charming Sally, a Novel*. (Day) "Show business" has changed greatly since the first theatrical troop reached the American colonies. A romance enlivens the story.

MORROW, HONORÉ WILLSIE, *Yonder Sails the Mayflower*. (Morrow) The action of this story occurs while the *Mayflower* waits to depart for the New World. Most interesting is its picture of the Pilgrims as young and enthusiastic men and women.

PYLE, HOWARD, *Story of Jack Ballister's Fortunes*. (Appleton) Captain Edward Teach, commonly called Blackbeard, was a pirate who lives on in the history books. Fact and fiction are mingled in this tale of a young gentleman, who is kidnaped in 1719 and carried to Virginia, but who later falls in with Blackbeard.

ROBINSON, GERTRUDE, *Catch a Falling Star*. (Dutton) Whether to travel back to London with her father or to remain in the New World is the problem that Elspeth Converse faces. How she solves her problem makes an absorbing story.

SNEDEKER, CAROLINE DALE, *Uncharted Ways*. (Doubleday) The romance of Margaret Stevenson and Jonathan Coleman is set against a background of New England life in the days when the Quakers were being harried from the Puritan colonies. This is a fine and thoroughly American story.

SUBLETTE, CLIFFORD M., *Scarlet Cockerel*. (Little) Young Blaise de Breault, called "the Scarlet Cockerel," is a prominent member of the colony founded by the French Huguenots along the St. John's River in Florida. Heroes and villains emerge in startling contrast when French and Spaniards clash.

YOUNG, STANLEY, *Mayflower Boy*. (Rinehart) A real member of the Pilgrim band, Giles Hopkins, is the central character in this excellent account of the trials and dangers faced by the Pilgrims from the time they landed at Cape Cod until they celebrated their first Thanksgiving day.

UNIT II: MOVING WESTWARD

FOR THE land-hungry people who came to colonial America and for the millions who were to come later, the seaboard was not enough. The tall mountains and broad valleys lying westward gave new and wider visions to the pioneers. For one thing, the unclaimed land beyond the seaboard held a great promise to those who had been denied the security of land ownership in Europe. For another thing, the frontier offered an escape from the petty quarrels that had come to be a part of life in the young communities along the Eastern coast. So the western lands helped fulfill the dreams of those who continued to come to America.

Three aspects of the movement westward are particularly significant. First, it was rapid: In less than half the time required for the thirteen colonies to settle the seaboard and win their independence, the American people pushed the frontier to the Pacific and acquired all the land within the present boundaries of the United States. Second, the movement for a long time was one of native-born Americans: Until the end of the Civil War the people moving westward were largely of American birth. Third, Americans in the West were thrown upon their own resourcefulness as never before: Because life was crude, hard, and dangerous, it developed an amazing amount of self-reliance and independence. Out of Western life grew a respect for individualism that is basic in American democracy. Thus the frontier cultivated not only a new breed of men but also new ways of thinking.

The influence of the West in the development of America has been great. The importance of the West in literature is proportionately large. The lure of the plains and the mountains, the excitement and suspense of frontier adventuring and living, the exuberant humor of mighty men, and the vision and courage of the pioneers combine to make the West one of the most popular themes in American literature.

61

A Test of Fortitude

JAMES FENIMORE COOPER

The first American writer to capture the romance of the Westward Movement and of the conquest of a continent was James Fenimore Cooper (1789-1851). Partly because he was reared in a frontier community in central New York state, Cooper had the "feel" for pioneer character and life. In a series called "The Leatherstocking Tales," he wrote the first great novels about the white man's struggle with the American wilderness and with the Indians. The stories range in time from before the French and Indian War to well into the nineteenth century. They stretch in space from the Mohawk River in New York to west of the Platte River in Nebraska. The stories are interesting for their historical details, but they are even more famous as adventure stories, full of breathless suspense.

The events in the series of novels begin with *The Deerslayer* (1841), from which the following selection has been drawn. The time is between 1740 and 1745. The hero, Natty Bumppo, whose Indian name is Deerslayer, has been reared by the Delaware Indians. He therefore knows both forest lore and the ways of Indians. His closest friend is a young Delaware chief, Chingachgook, who is engaged to an Indian girl named Hist. This girl has been stolen by the Hurons and adopted into their tribe. In attempting to rescue her, Deerslayer himself has been captured by the Hurons.

I T WAS ONE of the common expedients of the savages, on such occasions, to put the nerves of their victims to the severest proofs. On the other hand, it was a matter of Indian pride to betray no yielding to terror or pain, but for the prisoner to provoke his enemies to such acts of violence as would soonest produce death. Many a warrior had been known to bring his own sufferings to a more speedy termination, by taunting reproaches and reviling language, when he found that his physical system was giving way under the agony of sufferings produced by a hellish ingenuity that might well eclipse all that has been said of the infernal devices of religious persecution. This happy expedient of taking refuge from the ferocity of his foes in their passions was denied Deerslayer, however, by his peculiar notions of the duty of a white man; and he had stoutly made up his mind to endure everything in preference to disgracing his color.

No sooner did the young men understand that they were at liberty to commence than some of the boldest and most forward among them sprang into the arena, tomahawk in hand. Here they prepared to throw that dangerous weapon, the object being to strike the tree as near as possible to the victim's head without absolutely hitting him. This was so hazardous an experiment that none but those who were known to be exceedingly expert with the weapon were allowed to enter the lists[1] at all, lest an early death might interfere with the expected entertainment. In the truest hands, it was seldom that the captive escaped injury in these trials; and it often happened that death followed even when the blow was not premeditated. In the particular case of our hero, Rivenoak[2] and the older warriors were apprehensive that the example of the Panther's fate[3] might prove a motive with some fiery spirit suddenly to sacrifice his conqueror, when the temptation of effecting it in precisely the same manner, and possibly with the identical weapon with which the warrior had fallen, offered. This circumstance, of itself, rendered the ordeal of the tomahawk doubly critical for the Deerslayer.

It would seem, however, that all who now entered what we shall call the lists were more disposed to exhibit their own dexterity than to resent the deaths of their comrades. Each prepared himself for the trial with the feelings of rivalry rather than with the desire for vengeance; and for the first few minutes the prisoner had little more connection with the result than grew out of the interest that necessarily attached itself to a living target. The young men were eager, instead of being fierce, and Rivenoak thought he still saw signs of being able to save the life of the captive when the vanity of

---

[1] *enter the lists,* join in the contest. The author is using a phrase borrowed from the tournaments of the Middle Ages.

[2] *Rivenoak* (riv′ən ōk′), a Huron chieftain who secretly wished Deerslayer to become a member of the Huron tribe.

[3] *the Panther's fate.* Deerslayer had recently killed the Panther, a Huron warrior, with his tomahawk.

the young men had been gratified, always admitting that it was not sacrificed to the delicate experiments that were about to be made.

The first youth who presented himself for the trial was called the Raven, having as yet had no opportunity of obtaining a more warlike sobriquet. He was remarkable for high pretension rather than for skill or exploits, and those who knew his character thought the captive in imminent danger when he took his stand and poised the tomahawk. Nevertheless, the young man was good-natured, and no thought was uppermost in his mind other than the desire to make a better cast than any of his fellows. Deerslayer got an inkling of this warrior's want of reputation by the injunctions that he had received from the seniors, who, indeed, would have objected to his appearing in the arena at all but for an influence derived from his father, an aged warrior of great merit, who was then in the lodges of the tribe.[4] Still, our hero maintained an appearance of self-possession. He had

made up his mind that his hour was come, and it would have been a mercy, instead of a calamity, to fall by the unsteadiness of the first hand that was raised against him.

After a suitable number of flourishes and gesticulations that promised much more than he could perform, the Raven let the tomahawk quit his hand. The weapon whirled through the air with the usual evolutions, cut a chip from the sapling to which the prisoner was bound, within a few inches of his cheek, and stuck in a large oak that grew several yards behind him. This was decidedly a bad effort, and a common sneer proclaimed as much, to the great mortification of the young man. On the other hand, there was a general but suppressed murmur of admiration at the steadiness with which the captive stood the trial. The head was the only part he could move, and this had been purposely left free, that the tormentors might have the amusement, and the tormented endure the shame, of dodging and otherwise attempting to avoid the blows. Deerslayer disappointed these hopes by a command of nerve that rendered his whole body as immovable as the tree to which he was bound. Nor did he even adopt the

[4] *in the lodges of the tribe*, at home with the main body of Hurons. The Indians who were torturing Deerslayer belonged to a group who had come within the English boundaries for hunting and fishing.

natural and usual expedient of shutting his eyes, the firmest and oldest warrior of the red men never having more disdainfully denied himself this advantage, under similar circumstances.

The Raven had no sooner made his unsuccessful and puerile effort than he was succeeded by Le Daim-Mose,[5] or the Moose, a middle-aged warrior, who was particularly skillful in the use of the tomahawk, and from whose attempt the spectators confidently looked for gratification. This man had none of the good nature of the Raven, but he would gladly have sacrificed the captive to his hatred of the pale-faces generally, were it not for the greater interest he felt in his own success as one particularly skillful in the use of this weapon. He took his stand quietly but with an air of confidence, poised his little ax but a single instant, advanced a foot with a quick motion, and threw. Deerslayer saw the keen instrument whirling toward him, and believed all was over; still he was not touched. The tomahawk had actually bound the head of the captive to the tree by carrying before it some of his hair, having buried itself deep beneath the soft bark. A general yell expressed the delight of the spectators, and the Moose felt his heart soften a little toward the prisoner, whose steadiness of nerve alone enabled him to give this evidence of his consummate skill.

Le Daim-Mose was succeeded by the Bounding Boy, or Le Garçon qui Bondi,[6] who came leaping into the circle like a hound or a goat at play. This was one of those elastic youths whose muscles seemed always in motion, and who either affected or who from habit was actually unable to move in any other manner than by showing the antics just mentioned. Nevertheless, he was both brave and skillful, and had gained the respect of his people by deeds in war as well as success in the hunts. A far nobler name would long since have fallen to his share had not a Frenchman of rank inadvertently given him this sobriquet, which he religiously preserved as coming from his great father who lived beyond the wide salt lake.[7] The Bounding Boy skipped about in front of the captive, menacing him with his tomahawk, now on one side and now on another and then again in front, in the vain hope of being able to extort some sign of fear by this parade of danger. At length Deerslayer's patience became exhausted by all this mummery, and he spoke for the first time since the trial had actually commenced.

"Throw away, Huron!" he cried, "or your tomahawk will forget its arr'nd.[8] Why do you keep loping about like a fa'an[9] that's showing its dam how well it can skip, when you're a warrior grown, yourself, and a warrior grown defies you and all your silly antics? Throw, or the Huron gals will laugh in your face."

Although not intended to produce such an effect, the last words aroused the "Bounding" warrior to fury. The same nervous excitability which rendered him so active in his person made it difficult to repress his feelings, and the words were scarcely past the lips of the speaker than the tomahawk left the hand of the Indian. Nor was it cast without good will, and a fierce determination to slay. Had the intention been less deadly, the danger might have been greater. The aim was uncertain, and the weapon glanced near the cheek of the captive, slightly cutting the shoulder in its evolutions. This was the first instance in which any other object than that of terrifying the prisoner and of displaying skill had been manifested; and the Bounding Boy was immediately led from the arena and was warmly rebuked for his intemperate haste, which had come so near defeating all the hopes of the band.

To this irritable person succeeded several other young warriors, who not only hurled the tomahawk but who cast the knife, a far more dangerous experiment, with reckless indifference; yet they always manifested a skill that prevented any injury to the captive. Several times Deerslayer was grazed, but in no instance did

---

[5]*Le Daim-Mose* (lə daɴ′mōz′), a French name meaning "the moose-deer." The Hurons made friends with the French, and many of them were called by names the French had given them.

[6]*Le Garçon qui Bondi* (lə gär sōɴ′ kē bōɴ di′), French for "the boy who bounds."

[7]*A far nobler name...salt lake.* Because the Indians regarded the French as more intelligent than they were, they usually prized the nicknames (sobriquets) the French gave them.

[8]*arr′nd,* errand.

[9]*fa'an,* fawn.

he receive what might be termed a wound. The unflinching firmness with which he faced his assailants, more especially in the sort of rally with which this trial terminated, excited a profound respect in the spectators; and when the chiefs announced that the prisoner had well withstood the trials of the knife and the tomahawk, there was not a single individual in the band who really felt any hostility toward him, with the exception of Sumach[10] and the Bounding Boy. These two discontented spirits got together, it is true, feeding each other's ire; but, as yet, their malignant feelings were confined very much to themselves, though there existed the danger that the others, ere long, could not fail to be excited by their own efforts into that demoniacal state which usually accompanied all similar scenes among the red men.

Rivenoak now told his people that the paleface had proved himself to be a man. He might live with the Delawares, but he had not been made woman with that tribe.[11] He wished to know whether it was the desire of the Hurons to proceed any further. Even the gentlest of the females, however, had received too much satisfaction in the late trials to forgo their expectations of a gratifying exhibition; and there was but one voice[12] in the request to proceed. The politic chief, who had some such desire to receive so celebrated a hunter into his tribe as a European minister has to devise a new and available means of taxation, sought every plausible means of arresting the trial in season; for he well knew if permitted to go far enough to arouse the more ferocious passions of the tormentors, it would be as easy to dam the waters of the great lakes of his own region as to attempt to arrest them in their bloody career. He therefore called four or five of the best marksmen to him and bid them put the captive to the proof of the rifle, while, at the same time, he cautioned them touching the necessity of their maintaining their own credit by the closest attention to the manner of exhibiting their skill.

When Deerslayer saw the chosen warriors step into the circle with their arms prepared for service, he felt some such relief as the miserable sufferer who had long endured the agonies of disease feels at the certain approach of death. Any trifling variance in the aim of this formidable weapon would prove fatal, since, the head being the target, or rather the point it was desired to graze without injury, an inch or two of difference in the line of projection must at once determine the question of life or death.

In the torture by the rifle there was none of the latitude permitted that appeared in the case of even Gessler's apple,[13] a hair's-breadth being, in fact, the utmost limits that an expert marksman would allow himself on an occasion like this. Victims were frequently shot through the head by too eager or unskillful hands; and it often occurred that, exasperated by the fortitude and taunts of the prisoner, death was dealt intentionally in a moment of ungovernable irritation. All this Deerslayer well knew, for it was in relating the traditions of such scenes, as well as of the battles and victories of their people, that the old men beguiled the long winter evenings in their cabins. He now fully expected the end of his career, and experienced a sort of melancholy pleasure in the idea that he was to fall by a weapon as much beloved as the rifle.

The warriors prepared to exhibit their skill, as there was a double object in view: that of putting the constancy of the captive to the proof, and that of showing how steady were the hands of the marksmen under circumstances of excitement. The distance was small, and, in one sense, safe. But in diminishing the distance taken by the tormentors, the trial to the nerves of the captive was essentially increased. The face of Deerslayer, indeed, was just removed sufficiently from the ends of the guns to escape the effects of the flash, and his steady eye was enabled to look directly into their muzzles, as it might be, in anticipation of the fatal messenger that was to issue from each. The cunning Hurons well knew this fact; and scarce one

---

[10]*Sumach* (sü′mak *or* shü′mak), sister of the Panther.
[11]*He might...that tribe*. Despite the fact that Deerslayer had lived with the Delawares, his manly courage had not lessened.
[12]*there was but one voice*, all spoke together in agreement.

[13]*Gessler's apple*. According to legend, Gessler was the Austrian tyrant who forced William Tell to shoot the apple from the head of his little son.

leveled his piece without first causing it to point as near as possible at the forehead of the prisoner, in the hope that his fortitude would fail him, and that the band would enjoy the triumph of seeing a victim quail under their ingenious cruelty. Nevertheless, each of the competitors was still careful not to injure, the disgrace of striking prematurely being second only to that of failing altogether in attaining the object.

Shot after shot was made, all the bullets coming in close proximity to the Deerslayer's head, without touching it. Still, no one could detect even the twitching of a muscle on the part of the captive, or the slightest winking of an eye. This indomitable resolution, which so much exceeded everything of its kind that any present had before witnessed, might be referred to three distinct causes. The first was resignation to his fate, blended with natural steadiness of deportment, for our hero had calmly made up his mind that he must die, and preferred this mode to any other; the second was his great familiarity with this particular weapon, which deprived it of all the terror that is usually connected with the mere form of the danger; and the third was this familiarity carried out in practice, to a degree so nice as to enable the intended victim to tell, within an inch, the precise spot where each bullet must strike, for he calculated its range by looking in at the bore of the piece. So exact was Deerslayer's estimation of the line of fire that his pride finally got the better of his resignation, and, when five or six had discharged their bullets into the trees, he could not refrain from expressing his contempt.

"You may call this shooting, Mingos,"[14] he exclaimed, "but we've squaws among the Delawares, and I have known Dutch gals on the Mohawk,[15] that could outdo your greatest indivors. Ondo these arms of mine; put a rifle into my hands; and I'll pin the thinnest war lock[16] in your party to any tree you can show

me, and this at a hundred yards—aye, or at two hundred, if the object can be seen—nineteen shots in twenty—or, for that matter, twenty in twenty, if the piece is creditable and trusty!"

A low, menacing murmur followed this cool taunt; the ire of the warriors kindled at listening to such a reproach from one who so far disdained their efforts as to refuse even to wink when a rifle was discharged as near his face as could be done without burning it. Rivenoak perceived that the moment was critical; and, still retaining his hope of adopting so noted a hunter into his tribe, the politic old chief interposed in time, probably, to prevent an immediate resort to that portion of the torture which must necessarily have produced death, through extreme bodily suffering if in no other manner. Moving into the center of the irritated group, he addressed them with his usual wily logic and plausible manner, at once suppressing the fierce movement that had commenced.

"I see how it is," he said. "We have been like the palefaces when they fasten their doors at night, out of fear of the red man. They use so many bars that the fire comes and burns them

---

[14]*Mingos* (ming′gōz), a name scornfully applied by the Delawares to their enemies.

[15]*Dutch gals on the Mohawk,* descendants of the Dutch settlers who lived in frontier settlements along the Mohawk River in central New York state.

[16]*war lock,* scalp lock, a long tuft of hair at the top of the head. Many warriors shaved their heads except for this lock.

before they can get out. We have bound the Deerslayer too tight; the thongs keep his limbs from shaking, and his eyes from shutting. Loosen him; let us see what his own body is really made of."

It is often the case when we are thwarted in a cherished scheme that any expedient, however unlikely to succeed, is gladly resorted to, in preference to a total abandonment of the project. So it was with the Hurons. The proposal of the chief found instant favor; and several hands were immediately at work cutting and tearing the ropes of bark from the body of our hero. In half a minute Deerslayer stood free from bonds. Some time was necessary that he should recover the use of his limbs, the circulation of the blood having been checked by the tightness of the ligatures; and this was accorded to him by the politic Rivenoak under the pretense that his body would be more likely to submit to apprehension if its true tone were restored, though really with a view to give time to the fierce passions which had been awakened in the bosoms of his young men to subside. This ruse succeeded; and Deerslayer, by rub-

bing his limbs, stamping his feet, and moving about, soon regained the circulation, recovering all his physical powers as effectually as if nothing had occurred to disturb them.

It is seldom men think of death in the pride of their health and strength. So it was with Deerslayer. Having been helplessly bound, and, as he had every reason to suppose, so lately on the very verge of the other world, to find himself so unexpectedly liberated, in possession of his strength, and with a full command of limb, acted on him like a sudden restoration to life, reanimating hopes that he had once absolutely abandoned. From that instant all his plans changed. In this he simply obeyed a law of nature; for while we have wished to represent our hero as being resigned to his fate, it has been far from our intention to represent him as anxious to die. From the instant that his buoyancy of feeling revived, his thoughts were keenly bent on the various projects that presented themselves as modes of evading the designs of his enemies; and he again became the quick-witted, ingenious, and determined woodsman, alive to all his own powers and resources. The change was so great that his mind resumed its elasticity; and, no longer thinking of submission, it dwelt only on the devices of the sort of warfare in which he was engaged.

As soon as Deerslayer was released, the band divided itself in a circle around him in order to hedge him in; and the desire to break down his spirit grew in them, precisely as they saw proofs of the difficulty there would be in subduing it. The honor of the band was now involved in the issue; and even the female sex lost all its sympathy with suffering, in the desire to save the reputation of the tribe. The voices of the girls, soft and melodious as nature had made them, were heard mingling with the menaces of the men; and the wrongs of Sumach suddenly assumed the character of injuries inflicted on every Huron female. Yielding to this rising tumult, the men drew back a little, signifying to the females that they left the captive, for a time, in their hands, it being a common practice on such occasions for the women to endeavor to throw the victim into a rage by their taunts and revilings, and then to turn him suddenly over to the men in a state of mind that was little favorable to resisting the agony of bodily suffering. Nor was this party without the proper instruments for effecting such a purpose. Sumach had a notoriety as a scold; and one or two crones had come out with the party, most probably as the conservators of its decency and moral discipline, such things occurring in savage as well as civilized life. It is unnecessary to repeat all that ferocity and ignorance could invent for such a purpose, the only difference between this outbreaking of feminine anger and a similar scene among ourselves consisting in the figures of speech and the epithets, the Huron women calling their prisoner by the names of the lower and least respected animals that were known to themselves.

But Deerslayer's mind was too much occupied to permit him to be disturbed by the abuse of excited hags; and their rage necessarily increasing with his indifference, as his indifference increased with their rage, the furies soon rendered themselves impotent by their own excesses.[17] Perceiving that the attempt was a complete failure, the warriors interfered to put a stop to this scene, and this so much the more because preparations were now seriously making for the commencement of the real tortures, or that which would put the fortitude of the sufferer to the test of severe bodily pain. Fragments of dried wood were rapidly collected near the sapling; the splinters which it was intended to thrust into the flesh of the victim, previously to lighting, were all collected; and the thongs were already produced that were again to bind him to the tree.

Suddenly a young Indian came bounding through the Huron ranks, leaping into the very center of the circle in a way to denote the utmost confidence or a temerity bordering on foolhardiness. Five or six sentinels were still watching the lake at different and distant points; and it was the first impression of Rivenoak that one of these had come in with tidings of

import. Still, the movements of the stranger were so rapid, and his war dress, which scarcely left him more drapery than an antique statue, had so little distinguishing about it, that, at the first moment, it was impossible to ascertain whether he were friend or foe. Three leaps carried this warrior to the side of Deerslayer. Not till this was effected did the stranger bestow a glance on any other object; then he turned and showed the astonished Hurons the noble brow, fine person, and eagle eye of a young warrior in the paint and panoply of a Delaware. He had a rifle in each hand, the butts of both resting on the earth, while from one dangled its proper pouch and horn.[18] This was Killdeer,[19] which even as he looked boldly and in defiance on the crowd around him, he suffered to fall back into the hands of the proper

---

[18]*pouch and horn.* Shot and patches (or wadding) for the rifle were carried in the pouch, powder in the horn. To load the gun the frontiersman poured in a measure of powder from the horn, rammed in a patch, inserted shot, and then put in another patch.

[19]*Killdeer,* Deerslayer's rifle.

---

[17]*the furies...excesses,* the Indian women became so angry that they were even more powerless than ever to affect Deerslayer. In Greek and Roman mythology the three Furies were the spirits of revenge. Because of their desire for vengeance Cooper calls the Indian women furies.

owner. The presence of two armed men, though it was in their midst, startled the Hurons. Their rifles were scattered about against the different trees and their only weapons were their knives and tomahawks. Still, they had too much self-possession to betray fear. It was little likely that so small a force would assail so strong a band; and each man expected some extraordinary proposition to succeed so decisive a step. The stranger did not seem disposed to disappoint them; he prepared to speak.

"Hurons," he said, "this earth is very big. The great lakes are big, too; there is room beyond them for the Iroquois; there is room for the Delawares on this side. I am Chingachgook, the son of Uncas, the kinsman of Tamenund. That paleface is my friend. My heart was heavy when I missed him. Come, let us say farewell, and go on our path."

"Hurons, this is your mortal enemy, the Great Serpent[20] of them you hate!" cried Briar-thorn.[21] "If he escape, blood will be in your moccasin prints from this spot to the Canadas.[22] *I am* all *Huron.*"[23]

As the last words were uttered, the traitor cast his knife at the naked breast of the Delaware. With a quick movement Chingachgook avoided the blow, the dangerous weapon burying its point in a pine. At the next instant a similar weapon glanced from the hand of the Serpent, and quivered in the recreant's heart. A minute had scarcely elapsed from the moment in which Chingachgook bounded into the circle, and that in which Briarthorn fell, like a dog, dead in his tracks. The rapidity of events prevented the Hurons from acting; but this catastrophe permitted no further delay. A common exclamation followed, and the whole party was in motion. At this instant a sound unusual to the woods was heard, and every Huron, male and female, paused to listen with ears erect and faces filled with expectation. The sound was regular and heavy, as if the earth were struck with beetles. Objects became visible among the trees of the background, and a body of troops was seen advancing with measured tread. They came upon the charge, the scarlet of the King's livery[24] shining among the bright green foliage of the forest.

The scene that followed is not easily described. It was one in which wild confusion, despair, and frenzied efforts were so blended as to destroy the unity and distinctness of the action. A general yell burst from the inclosed Hurons; it was succeeded by the hearty cheers of England.[25] Still, not a musket or rifle was fired, though that steady, measured tramp continued, and the bayonet was seen gleaming in advance of a line that counted nearly sixty men. The Hurons were taken at a fearful disadvantage. On three sides was the water, while their formidable and trained foes cut them off from flight on the fourth. Each warrior rushed for his arms, and then all on the point, man, woman, and child, eagerly sought cover. In this scene of confusion and dismay, however, nothing could surpass the discretion and coolness of Deerslayer. He threw himself on a flank of the retiring Hurons, who were inclining off toward the southern margin of the point, in the hope of escaping through the water. Deerslayer watched his opportunity, and finding two of his recent tormentors in range, his rifle first broke the silence of the terrific scene. The bullet brought down both at one discharge. This drew a general fire from the Hurons, and the rifle and war cry of the Serpent were heard in the clamor. Still the trained men returned no answering volley, if we except the short, prompt word of authority, and that heavy, measured, and menacing tread. Presently, however, the shrieks, groans, and denunciations that usually accompany the use of the bayonet followed. That terrible and deadly weapon was glutted in vengeance. The scene that succeeded was one of those of which so many have occurred in our own times, in which neither age nor sex forms an exemption to the lot of a savage warfare.

---

[20]*the Great Serpent*, Chingachgook. He was so called for his wisdom, cunning, and prudence.

[21]*Briarthorn*, a Delaware warrior, traitor to his tribe, who had joined the Hurons.

[22]*the Canadas*, Canada.

[23]*I am all Huron.* Briarthorn, the traitor, is asserting that he is more loyal than are the Hurons themselves.

[24]*the King's livery*, the uniforms of the army of George II of England.

[25]*cheers of England*, the shouts of the English soldiers.

1. What tests are made of Deerslayer's courage and endurance? How does the arrangement (that is, the order) of the tests build up suspense?

2. What happenings come as surprises? Why?

3. What is Deerslayer's attitude toward his captors and their attempts to break his nerve? How do the reactions of the Indians change as the trial progresses?

4. What typical Indian traits does the story bring out? Which of these traits does Deerslayer possess to a greater degree than most Indians?

5. In what ways does Deerslayer show himself to be "quick-witted, ingenious, and determined"?

6. Is the ending of the story pleasing to you? Why, or why not?

Evaluating Cooper's skill

Some critics have praised Cooper highly as a writer. Other critics have found nothing good to say about him. Judging from "A Test of Fortitude," decide whether each of the following statements is true or false.

1. Indians such as Cooper depicted never existed. They are either too good to be true, or they are complete villains.

2. Deerslayer is a true and accurate characterization of the frontiersman.

3. The events Cooper records, while exciting, are unbelievable.

4. Cooper has little distinction or beauty of style.

Know your words

Two thousand years ago the Romans used the word *fortis* meaning "strong." In the succeeding centuries French, Italian, and English words were derived from this Latin word. One English derivative is *fortitude,* which represents the theme of the selection you have just read. It is only one of many words in which *fort-* has the meaning "strong." Be prepared to point out how the italicized word in each of the following sentences carries this meaning.

1. The passages of the piano solo marked *forte* gave Janet's small fingers the most trouble.

2. The *fortress* commanded the southern approach to the lake.

3. He *fortified* himself for the coming ordeal by taking a long nap.

4. If you play the passage *fortissimo,* you will find it far more effective.

5. On the treeless plain the only *fortification* the emigrants could prepare was the close-drawn circle of their covered wagons.

Daniel Boone's Last Look Westward

CALE YOUNG RICE

One of the unforgettable names among the westward-moving pioneers is that of Daniel Boone (1734-1820). The story of Boone's crossing the Alleghenies, choosing the site for his settlement in Kentucky, and eventually leading a group of Carolinians to it was at one time a part of every American schoolboy's reading. After the Kentucky settlement was established, he moved on to the Missouri country. There he continued to hunt, fight Indians, and serve as scout for groups of settlers and explorers. As you read the following poem, imagine Daniel Boone, now a restless old man, sitting by the fire talking to his sons.

I'M ONLY four score year, my sons, and a few
To fill the measure up. And so I shouldn't
Be shut here like an old hound by the fire
To dream of deeds I still have wind to do.
Maybe I have performed enough for one man; 5
For there's Kentucky cut from the wilderness
And sewed fast to the States by law and order—
Which I'm not sayin' isn't good for them
Who like pullin' in harness with their neighbors.
But I keep seein' trails—runnin' to westward 10
And northwest—Indian-footed trails
That no white man has ever pierced an eye through;
And beyond them are prairie lands and forests
Which settlers comin' after me could scalp
And sell, if silver is the game they're seekin': 15
And the Almighty means my eyes to see them,
Else He'd have made my sight dim and rheumy
By now—and where's the deer or bear that gambols
Before my gun and goes away to say so?

It's kind of shiftless maybe, I'll allow, 20
To want to keep always *beyond* the settlements,
Not *in* them: ten near families is too many.
But the Lord never meant the plow to be
My instrument: I get to the end of a furrow

"Daniel Boone's Last Look Westward," reprinted from *Bitter Brew* by Cale Young Rice.

And there's the wilderness waitin', all crea-
tion,   25
And I just have to find a path across it—
As your ma, there, knows; though I never could
tell her
The reason, till they took Kentucky in.

And then I saw the cunnin' to be wise
With animals and savage was more   30
Than love of powder and shot; and that God
used
My ax to hew a realm out. And there's more
realms
Yet to be hewed—and God's grindin' the axes,
I'll tell you that. For, young Lewis and Clark,[1]
Sons of my two old friends, are comin' to-
morrow   35
With unblazed trails of the Northwest in their
eyes;
And who knows but that land's as big as
Kentucky
And Illinois too; and that they're comin'
For more than to look at an old hound by the
fire?
There's one run in me yet; and if I died   40
Somewhere upon a far new trail with them,
There's a coffin-board saved—and I'd sleep bet-
ter...

---

[1]*young Lewis and Clark.* Meriwether Lewis was not yet
thirty and William Clark barely thirty-three when they
began their famous expedition from St. Louis to the mouth
of the Columbia River.

Unless your ma, this time, wouldn't be willin'
To pack my kit and draw the latch of the door.[2]

She won't, eh? Then it's dodderin' here, I
reckon,   45
And dreamin'. Put a fresh log on, and let be.
Young Lewis and Clark will need a-many like
me, though,
Before they hew that Northwest into the world.

---

[2]*draw the latch of the door,* pull out the bar that fastens
the door.

DO YOU UNDERSTAND DANIEL BOONE?

*"Daniel Boone's Last Look Westward" is a dramatic
monologue, that is, a poem in which a single person
is represented as talking at a time when he is excited
about something and thereby revealing his true character more than he would in guarded conversation.
As you answer the following questions refer often to
the poem for lines that help you understand Daniel
Boone's mood and character.*

1. What coming event arouses Daniel Boone's complaint?
2. How does he explain his motive in refusing to
settle down anywhere? Do you think this motive or
the love of adventure was stronger in a pioneer like
Boone? Why?
3. Why is the kind of excitement that Boone shows
in this dramatic monologue particularly revealing of
his character? What are his traits? How does the poem
show them? Why is the simile "like an old hound by
the fire" unusually appropriate?

Crockett's Morning Hunt

A large part of American humor sprang from the frontier. People moving westward or living in the wilderness did not have much time for books, but always welcomed good storytellers around the camp or cabin fireside. Entertaining stories and hearty laughter helped them forget their hardships. Indeed the art of oral narration, particularly that of swapping tall tales and of composing and singing folk songs, flourished with the expanding frontier. In reading written versions of this oral literature, we come closest to getting the tang of the rugged land and the rigorous life of the people who explored and conquered the frontiers. Perhaps there too we come closest to finding our national heroes.

Among the most famous of these heroes is Davy Crockett, a typical example of a country boy who made good. As a great hunter and Indian fighter, a picturesque member of Congress, and a heroic defender of the Alamo, he naturally became the subject of fireside whoppers. Many tales about him, most of them written as if he himself were telling the story, appeared in almanacs, and in time made the great frontiersman more legend than fact. The following selection is such a tale.

O NE JANUARY morning it was so all-screwen-up cold that the forest trees war[1] so stiff they couldn't shake, and the very daybreak froze fast as it war tryin' to dawn. The tinderbox in my cabin would no more ketch fire than a sunk raft at the bottom o' the sea. Seein' that daylight war so far behind time, I thought creation war in a fair way for freezin' fast.

"So," thinks I, "I must strike a leetle fire from my fingers, light my pipe, travel out a few leagues, and see about it."

Then I brought my knuckles together like two thunderclouds, but the sparks froze up afore I could begin to collect 'em—so out I walked, and endeavored to keep myself unfriz by goin' at a hop, step, and jump gait, and whistlin' the tune of "Fire in the Mountains!" as I went along in three-double-quick time. Well, arter I had walked about twenty-five miles

up the peak o' Daybreak Hill, I soon discovered what war the matter. The airth had actually friz fast in her axis, and couldn't turn round; the sun had got jammed between two cakes o' ice under the wheels, an thar he had bin shinin' and workin' to get loose, till he friz fast in his cold sweat.

"C-r-e-a-t-i-o-n!" thought I, "this are the toughest sort o' suspension—somethin' must be done, or human creation is done for."

It war then so antediluvian and premature cold[2] that my upper and lower teeth an' tongue war all collapsed together as tight as a friz oyster. I took a fresh twenty-pound bear off o' my back that I'd picked up on the road, an' beat the animal agin the ice till the hot ile[3] began to walk out on him at all sides. I then took an' held him over the airth's axes,[4] an' squeezed him till I thaw'd 'em loose, poured about a ton on it over the sun's face, give the airth's cogwheel one kick backward till I got the sun loose, whistled "Push along, keep movin'!", an' in about fifteen seconds the airth gin a grunt and begun movin'—the sun walked up beautiful, salutin' me with sich a wind o' gratitude that it made me sneeze. I lit my pipe by the blaze o' his topknot, shouldered my bear, an' walked home, introducin' the people to fresh daylight with a piece of sunrise in my pocket, with which I cooked my bear steaks, an' enjoyed one o' the best breakfasts I had tasted for some time. If I didn't, jist wake some mornin' and go with me to the office o' sunrise!

---

[1]*war*, were.

[2]*antediluvian* (an′ti di lü′vi ən) *and premature cold.* The words describing the cold mean "before the Flood" and "before the proper time." They are used here to give comic emphasis to the fact that it was extremely cold.

[3]*ile*, oil.

[4]*axes* (ak′sēz), plural of axis.

The Saga of Pecos Bill

EDWARD O'REILLY

Pecos Bill, unlike Crockett, was not a real historical character; he sprang altogether from the minds of the cattlemen, humor-loving creators of "Texas windies." He has come down to us as a miracle man, a typical American comic demigod, who had an ordinary job to do but did it in a supercolossal way.

ACCORDING TO the most veracious historians, Bill was born about the time Sam Houston[1] discovered Texas. His mother was a sturdy pioneer woman who once killed forty-five Indians with a broom handle, and weaned him on moonshine liquor when he was three days old. He cut his teeth on a bowie knife, and his earliest playfellows were the bears and catamounts of East Texas.

When Bill was about a year old, another family moved into the country, and located about fifty miles down the river. His father decided the place was gettin' too crowded, and packed his family into a wagon and headed west.

One day after they crossed the Pecos River,[2] Bill fell out of the wagon. As there were sixteen or seventeen other children in the family, his parents didn't miss him for four or five weeks, and then it was too late to try to find him.

That's how Bill came to grow up with the coyotes along the Pecos. He soon learned the coyote language, and used to hunt with them and sit on the hills and howl at night. Being so young when he got lost, he always thought he was a coyote. That's where he learned to kill deer by runnin' them to death.

One day when he was about ten years old, a cowboy came along just when Bill had matched a fight with two grizzly bears. Bill hugged the bears to death, tore off a hind leg, and was just settin' down to breakfast when this cowboy loped up and asked him what he meant by runnin' around naked that way among the varmints.

"Why, because I am a varmint," Bill told him. "I'm a coyote."

The cowboy argued with him that he was a human, but Bill wouldn't believe him.

"Ain't I got fleas?" he insisted. "And don't I howl around all night, like a respectable coyote should do?"

"That don't prove nothin'," the cowboy answered. "All Texans have fleas, and most of them howl. Did you ever see a coyote that didn't have a tail? Well, you ain't got no tail; so that proves you ain't a varmint."

Bill looked, and, sure enough, he didn't have a tail.

"You sure got me out on a limb," says Bill. "I never noticed that before. It shows what higher education will do for a man. I believe you're right. Lead me to them humans, and I'll throw in with them."

Bill went to town with this cow-hand, and in due time he got to enjoyin' all the pleasant vices of mankind, and decided that he certainly was a human. He got to runnin' with the wild bunch, and sunk lower and lower, until finally he became a cowboy.

It wasn't long until he was famous as a bad man. He invented the six-shooter and train-robbin' and most of the crimes popular in the old days of the West. He didn't invent cow-stealin'. That was first discovered thousands of years ago by King David in the Bible,[3] but Bill improved on it.

There is no way of tellin' just how many men Bill did kill. Deep down he had a tender heart, however, and never killed women or children, or tourists out of season. He never scalped his

---

[1] *Sam Houston,* twice president of Texas before it joined the United States, and a favorite Texas hero. He first went to Texas in 1832 to negotiate treaties with the Indians.

[2] *Pecos River.* At one time this river in western Texas marked the end of law-abiding communities. On the high plateaus west of the Pecos the gun was the only law.

[3] *cow-stealin'...King David in the Bible.* There are frequent references in the Book of Samuel in the Old Testament to David's driving off herds of cattle as spoils after battles with the Philistines and other enemies.

"The Saga of Pecos Bill," by Edward O'Reilly, from *The Century Magazine,* October, 1923. Copyright, 1923, by The Century Co.

victims; he was too civilized for that. He used to skin them gently and tan their hides.

It wasn't long before Bill had killed all the bad men in West Texas, massacred all the Indians, and eat all the buffalo. So he decided to migrate to a new country where hard men still thrived and a man could pass the time away.

He saddled up his horse and hit for the West. One day he met an old trapper and told him what he was lookin' for.

"I want the hardest cow outfit in the world," he says. "Not one of these ordinary cow-stealin', Mexican-shootin' bunches of amateurs, but a real hard herd of hand-picked hellions that make murder a fine art and take some proper pride in their slaughter."

"Stranger, you're headed in the right direction," answers the trapper. "Keep right on down this draw for a couple of hundred miles, and you'll find that very outfit. They're so hard they can kick fire out of a flint rock with their bare toes."

Bill single-footed down that draw for about a hundred miles that afternoon; then he met with an accident. His horse stubbed his toe on a mountain and broke his leg, leavin' Bill afoot.

He slung his saddle over his shoulder and set off hikin' down that draw, cussin' and a-swearing. Profanity was a gift with Bill.

All at once a big ten-foot rattlesnake quiled[4] up in his path, set his tail to singin', and allowed he'd like to match a fight. Bill laid down his saddle, and just to be fair about it, he gave the snake the first three bites. Then he waded into that reptile and everlastingly frailed the pizen[5] out of him.

By and by that old rattler yelled for mercy, and admitted that when it came to fightin', Bill started where he let off. So Bill picked up his saddle and started on, carryin' the snake in his hand and spinnin' it in short loops at the Gila monsters.

About fifty miles further on, a big old mountain lion jumped off a cliff and lit all spraddled out on Bill's neck. This was no ordinary lion. It weighed more than three steers and a yearlin', and was the very same lion the State of Nuevo León[6] was named after down in old Mexico.

Kind of chucklin' to himself, Bill laid down his saddle and his snake and went into action. In a minute the fur was flyin' down the canyon until it darkened the sun. The way Bill knocked the animosity out of that lion was a shame. In about three minutes that lion hollered:

"I'll give up, Bill. Can't you take a joke?"

Bill let him up, and then he cinched the saddle on him and went down that canyon whoopin' and yellin', ridin' that lion a hundred feet at a jump, and quirtin' him down the flank with the rattlesnake.

It wasn't long before he saw a chuck wagon with a bunch of cowboys squattin' around it. He rode up to that wagon, splittin' the air with his war whoops, with that old lion a-screechin', and that snake singin' his rattles.

When he came to the fire he grabbed the old cougar by the ear, jerked him back on his haunches, stepped off him, hung his snake around his neck, and looked the outfit over. Them cowboys sat there sayin' less than nothin'.

Bill was hungry, and seein' a boilerful of beans cookin' on the fire, he scooped up a few handfuls and swallowed them, washin' them down with a few gallons of boilin' coffee out of the pot. Wipin' his mouth on a handful of prickly-pear cactus, Bill turned to the cowboys and asked:

"Who's boss around here?"

A big fellow about eight feet tall, with seven pistols and nine bowie knives in his belt, rose up and, takin' off his hat, said:

"Stranger, I was; but you be."

Bill had many adventures with this outfit. It was about this time he staked out New Mexico, and used Arizona for a calf pasture. It was here that he found his noted horse Widow-Maker. He raised him from a colt on nitroglycerin and dynamite, and Bill was the only man that could throw a leg over him....

Bill was a great roper. In fact, he invented

---

[4]*quiled*, coiled.
[5]*frailed the pizen*, beat the poison.

[6]*Nuevo León* (nwā′vō lā ōn′). Translated into English, these Spanish words mean "New Lion."

ropin'. Old-timers who admit they knew him say that his rope was as long as the equator, although the more conservative say that it was at least two feet shorter on one end. He used to rope a herd of cattle at one throw.

This skill once saved the life of a friend. The friend had tried to ride Widow-Maker one day, and was thrown so high he came down on top of Pike's Peak. He was in the middle of a bad fix, because he couldn't get down, and seemed doomed to a lingerin' death on high.

Bill came to the rescue, and usin' only a short calf-loop,[7] he roped his friend around the neck and jerked him down to safety in the valley, twenty thousand feet below. This man was always grateful, and became Bill's horse wrangler[8] at the time he staked out New Mexico....

The stories of Bill's love affairs are especially numerous. One of them may be told. It is the sad tale of the fate of his bride, a winsome little maiden called Slue-Foot Sue. She was a famous rider herself, and Bill lost his heart when he saw her riding a catfish down the Rio Grande with only a surcingle. You must remember that the catfish in the Rio Grande are bigger than whales and twice as active.

Sue made a sad mistake, however, when she insisted on ridin' Widow-Maker on her weddin' day. The old horse threw her so high she had to duck her head to let the moon go by. Unfortunately, she was wearin' her weddin' gown, and in those days the women wore those big steel-spring bustles.

Well, when Sue lit, she naturally bounced, and every time she came down she bounced again. It was an awful sad sight to see Bill implorin' her to quit her bouncin' and not be so nervous; but Sue kept right on, up and down, weepin', and throwin' kisses to her distracted lover, and carryin' on as a bride naturally would do under those circumstances.

She bounced for three days and four nights, and Bill finally had to shoot her to keep her from starvin' to death. It was mighty tragic. Bill never got over it. Of course he married lots of women after that. In fact, it was one of his

weaknesses; but none of them filled the place in his heart once held by Slue-Foot Sue, his bouncin' bride....

DAVY CROCKETT AND PECOS BILL

1. "Crockett's Morning Hunt" obviously belongs to the pioneer period. What conditions in frontier living probably led the yarnspinner to invent this particular adventure?

2. How does the narrative about Davy Crockett illustrate the fact that he is now largely legendary?

3. Point out some of the crude expressions that give the tale a "backwoods" atmosphere. Do they serve any other purpose? Why, for instance, is the language used more helpful to the humor of the highly imaginative tale than more elegant language would be? What picture does it give you of the yarnspinner?

4. How does the author of the selection about Pecos Bill suggest the atmosphere, the "tang," of the West? How do the language he uses and the way he tells his story add to the humor? How does his language differ from that in the Davy Crockett tale?

5. A recent writer on humor notes that many frontier stories satirize the Easterner's idea that Westerners are outrageously uncouth and tough. Do you see evidence of this in these tales? Where?

6. What qualities do these legends about Davy Crockett and Pecos Bill have in common? How do American legends like these differ from those you know from other countries?

7. One writer says, "A composite picture of the American hero would show him to be a plain, tough, practical fellow, equally good at a bargain or a fight, a star performer on the job and a hell-raiser off it, and something of a salesman and a showman, with a flair for prodigious stories, jokes, and stunts, and a general capacity for putting himself over." Test Davy Crockett and Pecos Bill for each of these qualities. Which man more nearly qualifies as the American hero?

Extending interests

Arrange to devote a period to spinning yarns about Davy Crockett, Pecos Bill, Paul Bunyan, and other American folk heroes, with a prize for the student who tells the tallest tale. In addition to the books about folk heroes listed in "More Good Reading" on pages 95-96, you might consult: *Pecos Bill*, by James C. Bowman; *Pecos Bill, Texas Cowpuncher*, by Harold Felton; *Paul Bunyan*, by Esther Shephard; *Paul Bunyan*, by James Stevens; *The Marvelous Adventures of Johnny Caesar Cicero Darling*, by M. A. Jagendorf; and *A Treasury of American Folklore*, edited by Benjamin Botkin.

---

[7]*calf-loop*, a cowboy's lasso.
[8]*horse wrangler*, man in charge of a herd of horses.

FOUR FOLK SONGS

We have just seen how the people moving westward laughed away many of their hardships and heartaches by spinning yarns, and how they jokingly revealed their pride in their great achievements by creating legendary heroes with the qualities of miracle men. The frontiersmen's thoughts and feelings also found expression in their songs. As others all over the world have done, the folk moving westward composed songs about people, situations, and happenings that appealed most strongly to their feelings and imaginations. They fitted the only kinds of words they knew to the only kind of music with which they were familiar. These songs they composed, sang, and learned by heart.

The folk songs that follow vary as widely as the interests and circumstances of those who sang them. "Sweet Betsy from Pike" belongs to Gold Rush days —to that time when great throngs of Overlanders from every section of the United States pushed westward over plains and mountains in a frenzied search for gold. "The Little Old Sod Shanty on the Claim" is the song of the Homesteaders who went westward after the Gold Rush, the men and women who built their sod homes on the wide plains of Kansas and Nebraska. "The Old Chisholm Trail" is a cowboy song, and "Billy the Kid" recounts the tale of a famous Western desperado. Like the folk songs of all nations, these American songs are part of a literature that is of, by, and for the people.

Sweet Betsy from Pike

D ID YOU EVER hear tell of Sweet Betsy from Pike,[1]
Who crossed the wide prairies with her lover Ike,
And two yoke of cattle, a large yaller dog,
A tall, shanghai rooster,[2] and one spotted hog.

CHORUS 1:
 Saying, "Good-by, Pike County, farewell for
  a while;   5
 We'll come back again when we've panned
  out[3] our pile."

One evening quite early they camped on the Platte,[4]
'Twas near by the road on a green shady flat;
Where Betsy, quite tired, lay down for repose,
While with wonder Ike gazed on his Pike County rose. 10
   (Chorus 1)

They soon reached the desert, where Betsy gave out,
And down on the sand she lay rolling about;
While Ike in great terror looked on in surprise,
Saying, "Betsy, get up, you'll get sand in your eyes."

CHORUS 2:
 Saying, "Good-by, Pike County, farewell for
  a while;   15
 I'd go back tonight, if it was but a mile."

Sweet Betsy got up in a great deal of pain,
And declared she'd go back to Pike County again;
Then Ike heaved a sigh and they fondly embraced,
And she traveled around with his arm round her waist. 20
   (Chorus 1)

---

[1]*Pike*, a county in Missouri. It was the birthplace of many of the first emigrants to set out across the western plains.
[2]*shanghai rooster*, a long-legged Asiatic domestic fowl.
[3]*panned out*, washed the gold from the gravel in a pan.
[4]*Platte* (plat), a river flowing through central Nebraska to the Missouri River. The most commonly traveled trail to the West paralleled this river for many miles.

The Injuns came down in a wild yelling horde,
And Betsy was skeered they would scalp her adored;
Behind the front wagon wheel Betsy did crawl,
And there she fought Injuns with musket and ball.
   (Chorus 1)

The alkali desert was burning and bare, 25
And Isaac's soul shrank from the death that lurked there:
"Dear old Pike County, I'll go back to you."
Says Betsy, "You'll go by yourself if you do."
   (Chorus 1)

The wagon tipped over with a terrible crash,
And out on the prairie rolled all sorts of trash; 30
A few baby clothes done up with great care
Looked rather suspicious; but 'twas all on the square.
   (Chorus 1)

The shanghai ran off and the cattle all died,
The last piece of bacon that morning was fried;
Poor Ike got discouraged, and Betsy got mad, 35
The dog wagged his tail and looked wonderfully sad.
   (Chorus 1)

They swam the wide rivers and crossed the tall peaks,
And camped on the prairie for weeks upon weeks.
Starvation and cholera and hard work and slaughter,
They reached California spite of hell and high water. 40
   (Chorus 1)

Long Ike and sweet Betsy got married of course,
But Ike getting jealous obtained a divorce;
And Betsy well satisfied, said with a shout:
"Good-by, you big lummox, I'm glad you backed out!"

CHORUS 3:
 Saying, "Good-by, dear Isaac, farewell for
  a while,   45
 But come back in time to replenish my pile."

The Little Old Sod Shanty on the Claim

I am look-ing rath-er seed-y now while hold-ing down my
Yet I rath-er like the nov-el-ty of liv-ing in this

claim, And my vict-uals are not al-ways of the best;___ And the
way, Though my bill of fare is al-ways rath-er tame,___ But I'm

mice play shy-ly round me as I nes-tle down to rest, In my
hap-py as a clam___ on the land of Un-cle Sam, In my

lit-tle old sod shant-y in the West.___
lit-tle old sod shant-y on my claim.___

CHORUS

The hing-es are of leath-er and the win-dows have no glass, While the

board roof lets the howl-ing bliz-zards in,___ And I hear the hun-gry ki-yote as he

slinks up through the grass, Round my lit-tle old sod shan-ty on my claim.___

"The Little Old Sod Shanty on the Claim," from *The American Songbag*, edited by **Carl** Sandburg, copyright, 1927, by Harcourt, Brace and Company, Inc.

I AM LOOKING rather seedy now while holding
  down my claim,[1]
And my victuals are not always of the best;
And the mice play shyly round me as I nestle
  down to rest,
In my little old sod shanty in the West.
Yet I rather like the novelty of living in this
  way,   5
Though my bill of fare is always rather tame,[2]
But I'm happy as a clam on the land of Uncle
  Sam,
In my little old sod shanty on my claim.

CHORUS:

  The hinges are of leather and the windows
    have no glass,
  While the board roof lets the howling bliz-
    zards in,   10
  And I hear the hungry kiyote as he slinks up
    through the grass,
  Round my little old sod shanty on my claim.

O when I left my Eastern home, a bachelor so
  gay,
To try and win my way to wealth and fame,
I little thought that I'd come down to burning
  twisted hay[3]   15

---

[1]*holding down my claim.* According to the Homestead
Act of 1862, a settler might claim up to 160 acres of public land by living on it for five years.
[2]*bill of fare is always rather tame.* The available food
lacked variety.
[3]*burning twisted hay.* Because of the scarcity of trees for
firewood, the early settlers on the plains twisted hay into
ropes and burned it.

In the little old sod shanty on my claim.
My clothes are plastered o'er with dough, I'm
  looking like a fright,
And everything is scattered round the room,
But I wouldn't give the freedom that I have out
  in the West
For the table of the Eastern man's old home. 20

Still I wish that some kind-hearted girl would
  pity on me take,
And relieve me from the mess that I am in;
The angel, how I'd bless her if this her home
  she'd make
In the little old sod shanty on my claim.
And we would make our fortunes on the prairies
  of the West,   25
Just as happy as two lovers we'd remain;
We'd forget the trials and troubles we endured
  at the first,
In the little old sod shanty on our claim.

And if kindly fate should bless us with now
  and then an heir,
To cheer our hearts with honest pride of
  fame,   30
O then we'd be contented for the toil that we
  had spent
In the little old sod shanty on our claim.
When time enough had lapsed and all of those
  little brats
To noble man- and womanhood had grown,
It wouldn't seem half so lonely as around us
  we should look,   35
And see the little old sod shanty on our claim.

The Old Chisholm Trail

COME ALONG, boys, and listen to my tale,
  I'll tell you of my troubles on the old
  Chisholm trail.[1]

CHORUS:

  Come ti yi youpy, youpy yea, youpy yea,
  Coma ti yi youpy, youpy yea.

---

[1]*Chisholm* (chiz′əm) *trail,* a famous cattle trail which
extended from the Red River in eastern Texas to southern
Kansas.

I started up the trail October twenty-third,   5
I started up the trail with the 2-U herd.

Oh, a ten-dollar hoss and a forty-dollar saddle,
And I'm goin' to punchin' Texas cattle.

I woke up one morning on the old Chisholm
  trail,
Rope in my hand and a cow by the tail.   10

I'm up in the mornin' afore daylight
And afore I sleep the moon shines bright.

My hoss throwed me off at the creek called Mud,
My hoss throwed me off round the 2-U herd.

Last time I saw him he was going 'cross the
    level   15
A-kicking up his heels and a-running like the
    devil.

Last night I was on guard and the leader broke
    the ranks,
I hit my horse down the shoulders and I spurred
    him in the flanks.

The wind commenced to blow, and the rain
    began to fall,
It looked, by grab, like we was goin' to lose
    'em all.   20

My slicker's in the wagon and I'm gittin' mighty
    cold,
And these longhorn sons-o'-guns are gittin' hard
    to hold.

Saddle up, boys, and saddle up strong
For I think these cattle have scattered along.

With my blanket and my gun and my rawhide
    rope,   25
I'm a-slidin' down the trail in a long, keen lope.

I don't give a hoot if they never do stop;
I'll ride as long as an eight-day clock.

We rounded 'em up and put 'em on the cars,
And that was the last of the old Two Bars.   30

Oh, it's bacon and beans most every day—
I'd as soon be a-eatin' prairie hay.

I went to the boss to draw my roll,
He had it figgered out I was nine dollars in the
    hole.

I'll sell my outfit just as soon as I can,   35
I won't punch cattle for no other man.

With my knees in the saddle and my seat in the
    sky,
I'll quit punching cows in the sweet by-and-
    by.

Fare you well, old trail-boss, I don't wish you
    any harm,
I'm quittin' this business to go on the farm.   40

Billy the Kid

I'LL SING you a true song of Billy the Kid,[1]
I'll sing of the desperate deeds that he did,
Way out in New Mexico long, long ago,
When a man's only chance was his own .44.

When Billy the Kid was a very young lad,   5
In old Silver City[2] he went to the bad;
Way out in the West with a gun in his hand
At the age of twelve years he first killed his man.

Fair Mexican maidens play guitars and sing
A song about Billy, their boy bandit king,   10
How ere his young manhood had reached its
    sad end
Had a notch on his pistol for twenty-one men.

'Twas on the same night when poor Billy
    died
He said to his friends: "I am not satisfied;
There are twenty-one men I have put bullets
    through,   15
And Sheriff Pat Garrett must make twenty-
two."

Now this is how Billy the Kid met his fate:
The bright moon was shining, the hour was
    late;
Shot down by Pat Garrett, who once was his
    friend,
The young outlaw's life had now come to its
    end.   20

There's many a man with a face fine and fair
Who starts out in life with a chance to be square,
But just like poor Billy he wanders astray
And loses his life in the very same way.

---

[1]*Billy the Kid.* This "bad man" of the Southwest, whose name was William Bonney, was twenty-two years old when he was killed in 1881 after years of wholesale cattle stealing.
[2]*Silver City,* an old silver-mining town in southwestern New Mexico.

"Billy the Kid," from *American Ballads and Folk Songs* by John A. and Alan Lomax by permission of the Estate of John A. Lomax. Copyright, 1934, by The Macmillan Company.

1. How do the four folk songs on pages 76-81 add to your knowledge of history?
2. Point out situations described in the ballads that show the ability of pioneers to laugh at themselves and to adapt themselves as well as possible to their predicaments. What does each of these songs reveal about the interests, sympathies, and ideals of the people who composed and sang them?
3. Give examples of localisms, idiomatic expressions, and slang found in the ballads. Why do these expressions add to the value of these songs?
4. Ballads are often praised because they say much in a few words and say it very well. Point out examples of this achievement.
5. Note that all of the ballads use a simple verse form and that three of them include a refrain. Of what value are these characteristics for group singing?

Extending interests

A song session will help you and your classmates catch the spirit of the old folk ballads. Select a number of songs that have become "folk" songs in the sense that "everyone" knows and sings them. You'll find the singing more fun if someone brings an accordion or banjo to class, or if arrangements are made to use a piano.

The Leader of the People

JOHN STEINBECK

When we look backward to the time that people were moving westward, we experience varying emotions. For one thing, the westward adventure seems so remote from our lives in the Machine Age that we have a hard time merely imagining the motives and the adventures of the pioneer. Again, while we admire his courage and strength, we are frequently amazed at his rashness and greediness. Our sense of gratitude for his effort and determination in making secure for later generations the wealth and opportunities of the West is mingled with regret for his disregard of the rights of Indians and his wastefulness of natural resources. Finally, we wonder what the disappearance of the old West and its impacts on our life mean and will mean to Americans.

John Steinbeck, a native Californian, has woven some of those conflicting feelings into the following short story. A restless old pioneer, living almost wholly with his memories, tries to put into words the meaning of the Westward Movement. But the words elude him; he cannot communicate his feeling to the people of today. As you read the story, decide whether or not he succeeds in making you understand his feelings.

O N SATURDAY afternoon Billy Buck, the ranch hand, raked together the last of the old year's haystack and pitched small forkfuls over the wire fence to a few mildly interested cattle. High in the air small clouds like puffs of cannon smoke were driven eastward by the March wind. The wind could be heard whishing in the brush on the ridge crests, but no breath of it penetrated down into the ranch-cup.[1]

The little boy, Jody, emerged from the house eating a thick piece of buttered bread. He saw Billy working on the last of the haystack. Jody tramped down scuffing his shoes in a way he had been told was destructive to good shoe leather. A flock of white pigeons flew out of the black cypress tree as Jody passed, and circled the tree and landed again. A half-grown tortoise-shell cat leaped from the bunkhouse porch, galloped on stiff legs across the road, whirled, and galloped back again. Jody picked up a stone to help the game along, but he was too late, for the cat was under the porch before the stone could be discharged. He threw the stone into the cypress tree and started the white pigeons on another whirling flight.

Arriving at the used-up haystack, the boy leaned against the barbed-wire fence. "Will that be all of it, do you think?" he asked.

The middle-aged ranch hand stopped his careful raking and stuck his fork into the ground. He took off his black hat and smoothed down his hair. "Nothing left of it that isn't soggy from ground moisture," he said. He replaced his hat and rubbed his dry leathery hands together.

"Ought to be plenty mice," Jody suggested.

"Lousy with them," said Billy. "Just crawling with mice."

"Well, maybe, when you get all through, I could call the dogs and hunt the mice."

"Sure, I guess you could," said Billy Buck. He lifted a forkful of the damp ground hay and threw it into the air. Instantly three mice leaped out and burrowed frantically under the hay again.

Jody sighed with satisfaction. Those plump, sleek, arrogant mice were doomed. For eight months they had lived and multiplied in the haystack. They had been immune from cats, from traps, from poison, and from Jody. They had grown smug in their security, overbearing and fat. Now the time of disaster had come; they would not survive another day.

Billy looked up at the top of the hills that surrounded the ranch. "Maybe you better ask your father before you do it," he suggested.

"Well, where is he? I'll ask him now."

---

[1] *ranch-cup,* the hollow between the hills where the ranch was located.

"He rode up to the ridge ranch after dinner. He'll be back pretty soon."

Jody slumped against the fence post. "I don't think he'd care."

As Billy went back to his work he said ominously, "You'd better ask him anyway. You know how he is."

Jody did know. His father, Carl Tiflin, insisted upon giving permission for anything that was done on the ranch, whether it was important or not. Jody sagged farther against the post until he was sitting on the ground. He looked up at the little puffs of wind-driven cloud. "Is it like to rain, Billy?"

"It might. The wind's good for it, but not strong enough."

"Well, I hope it don't rain until after I kill those damn mice." He looked over his shoulder to see whether Billy had noticed the mature profanity. Billy worked on without comment.

Jody turned back and looked at the sidehill where the road from the outside world came down. The hill was washed with lean March sunshine. Silver thistles, blue lupins, and a few poppies bloomed among the sage bushes. Halfway up the hill Jody could see Doubletree Mutt, the black dog, digging in a squirrel hole. He paddled for a while and then paused to kick bursts of dirt out between his hind legs, and he dug with an earnestness which belied the knowledge he must have had that no dog had ever caught a squirrel by digging in a hole.

Suddenly, while Jody watched, the black dog stiffened, and backed out of the hole and looked up the hill toward the cleft in the ridge where the road came through. Jody looked up too. For a moment Carl Tiflin on horseback stood out against the pale sky, and then he moved down the road toward the house. He carried something white in his hand.

The boy started to his feet. "He's got a letter," Jody cried. He trotted away toward the ranch house, for the letter would probably be read aloud and he wanted to be there. He reached the house before his father did, and ran in. He heard Carl dismount from his creaking saddle and slap the horse on the side to send it to the barn where Billy would unsaddle it and turn it out.

Jody ran into the kitchen. "We got a letter!" he cried.

His mother looked up from a pan of beans. "Who has?"

"Father has. I saw it in his hand."

Carl strode into the kitchen then, and Jody's mother asked, "Who's the letter from, Carl?"

He frowned quickly. "How did you know there was a letter?"

She nodded her head in the boy's direction. "Big-Britches Jody told me."

Jody was embarrassed.

His father looked down at him contemptuously. "He *is* getting to be a big-britches," Carl said. "He's minding everybody's busi-

ness but his own. Got his big nose into every-thing."

Mrs. Tiflin relented a little. "Well, he hasn't enough to keep him busy. Who's the letter from?"

Carl still frowned on Jody. "I'll keep him busy if he isn't careful." He held out a sealed letter. "I guess it's from your father."

Mrs. Tiflin took a hairpin from her head and slit open the flap. Her lips pursed judiciously. Jody saw her eyes snap back and forth over the lines. "He says," she translated, "he says he's going to drive out Saturday to stay for a little while. Why, this is Saturday. The letter must have been delayed." She looked at the post-mark. "This was mailed day before yesterday. It should have been here yesterday." She looked up questioningly at her husband, and then her face darkened angrily. "Now what have you got that look on you for? He doesn't come often."

Carl turned his eyes away from her anger. He could be stern with her most of the time, but when occasionally her temper rose, he could not combat it.

"What's the matter with you?" she demanded again.

In his explanation there was a tone of apology Jody himself might have used. "It's just that he talks," Carl said lamely. "Just talks."

"Well, what of it? You talk yourself."

"Sure I do. But your father only talks about one thing."

"Indians!" Jody broke in excitedly. "Indians and crossing the plains!"

Carl turned fiercely on him. "You get out, Mr. Big-Britches! Go on, now! Get out!"

Jody went miserably out the back door and closed the screen with elaborate quietness. Under the kitchen window his shamed, down-cast eyes fell upon a curiously shaped stone, a stone of such fascination that he squatted down and picked it up and turned it over in his hands.

The voices came clearly to him through the open kitchen window. "Jody's right," he heard his father say. "Just Indians and crossing the plains. I've heard that story about how the horses got driven off about a thousand times. He just goes on and on, and he never changes a word in the things he tells."

When Mrs. Tiflin answered, her tone was so changed that Jody, outside the window, looked up from his study of the stone. Her voice had become soft and explanatory. Jody knew how her face would have changed to match the tone. She said quietly, "Look at it this way, Carl. That was the big thing in my father's life. He led a wagon train[2] clear across the plains to the west coast, and when it was finished, his life was done. It was a big thing to do, but it didn't last long enough. Look!" she continued, "it's as though he was born to do that, and after he finished it, there wasn't anything more for him to do but think about it and talk about it. If there'd been any farther west to go, he'd have gone. He's told me so himself. But at last there was the ocean. He lives right by the ocean where he had to stop."

She had caught Carl, caught and entangled him in her soft tone.

"I've seen him," he agreed quietly. "He goes down and stares off west over the ocean." His voice sharpened a little. "And then he goes up to the Horseshoe Club in Pacific Grove, and he tells people how the Indians drove off the horses."

She tried to catch him again. "Well, it's everything to him. You might be patient with him and pretend to listen."

Carl turned impatiently away. "Well, if it gets too bad, I can always go down to the bunk-house and sit with Billy," he said irritably. He walked through the house and slammed the front door after him.

Jody ran to his chores. He dumped the grain to the chickens without chasing any of them. He gathered the eggs from the nests. He trotted into the house with the wood and interlaced it so carefully in the woodbox that two armloads seemed to fill it to overflowing.

His mother had finished the beans by now. She stirred up the fire and brushed off the stove top with a turkey wing. Jody peered cautiously at her to see whether any rancor toward him remained. "Is he coming today?" Jody asked.

"That's what his letter said."

[2] *wagon train,* group of emigrants moving westward in covered wagons.

"Maybe I better walk up the road to meet him."

Mrs. Tiflin clanged the stove lid shut. "That would be nice," she said. "He'd probably like to be met."

"I guess I'll just do it then."

Outside, Jody whistled shrilly to the dogs. "Come on up the hill," he commanded. The two dogs waved their tails and ran ahead. Along the roadside the sage had tender new tips. Jody tore off some pieces and rubbed them on his hands until the air was filled with the sharp wild smell. With a rush the dogs leaped from the road and yapped into the brush after a rabbit. That was the last Jody saw of them, for when they failed to catch the rabbit, they went back home.

Jody plodded on up the hill toward the ridge top. When he reached the little cleft where the road came through, the afternoon wind struck him and blew up his hair and ruffled his shirt. He looked down on the little hills and ridges below and then out at the huge green Salinas Valley.[3] He could see the white town of Salinas far out in the flat and the flash of its windows under the waning sun. Directly below him, in an oak tree, a crow congress had convened. The tree was black with crows all cawing at once.

Then Jody's eyes followed the wagon road down from the ridge where he stood, and lost it behind a hill, and picked it up again on the other side. On that distant stretch he saw a cart slowly pulled by a bay horse. It disappeared behind the hill. Jody sat down on the ground and watched the place where the cart would reappear again. The wind sang on the hilltops and the puff-ball clouds hurried eastward.

Then the cart came into sight and stopped. A man dressed in black dismounted from the seat and walked to the horse's head. Although it was so far away, Jody knew he had unhooked the checkrein, for the horse's head dropped forward. The horse moved on, and the man walked slowly up the hill beside it. Jody gave a glad

cry and ran down the road toward them. The squirrels bumped along off the road, and a road runner flirted its tail and raced over the edge of the hill and sailed out like a glider.

Jody tried to leap into the middle of his shadow at every step. A stone rolled under his foot and he went down. Around a little bend he raced, and there, a short distance ahead, were his grandfather and the cart. The boy dropped from his unseemly running and approached at a dignified walk.

The horse plodded stumble-footedly up the hill and the old man walked beside it. In the lowering sun their giant shadows flickered darkly behind them. The grandfather was dressed in a black broadcloth suit and he wore kid congress gaiters[4] and a black tie on a short, hard collar. He carried his black slouch hat in his hand. His white beard was cropped close and his white eyebrows overhung his eyes like mustaches. The blue eyes were sternly merry. About the whole face and figure there was a granite dignity, so that every motion seemed an impossible thing. Once at rest, it seemed the old man would be stone, would never move again. His steps were slow and certain. Once made, no step could ever be retraced; once headed in a direction, the path would never bend nor the pace increase nor slow.

[4]*congress gaiters,* high shoes with elastic sides.

[3]*Salinas* (sə lē′nəs) *Valley,* a valley in central California south of San Francisco and a few miles inland from Monterey Bay.

When Jody appeared around the bend, Grandfather waved his hat slowly in welcome, and he called, "Why, Jody! Come down to meet me, have you?"

Jody sidled near and turned and matched his step to the old man's step and stiffened his body and dragged his heels a little. "Yes, sir," he said. "We got your letter only today."

"Should have been here yesterday," said Grandfather. "It certainly should. How are all the folks?"

"They're fine, sir." He hesitated and then suggested shyly, "Would you like to come on a mouse hunt tomorrow, sir?"

"Mouse hunt, Jody?" Grandfather chuckled. "Have the people of this generation come down to hunting mice? They aren't very strong, the new people, but I hardly thought mice would be game for them."

"No, sir. It's just play. The haystack's gone. I'm going to drive out the mice to the dogs. And you can watch, or even beat the hay a little."

The stern, merry eyes turned down on him. "I see. You don't eat them, then. You haven't come to that yet."

Jody explained, "The dogs eat them, sir. It wouldn't be much like hunting Indians, I guess."

"No, not much—but then later, when the troops were hunting Indians and shooting children and burning tepees, it wasn't much different from your mouse hunt."

They topped the rise and started down into the ranch-cup, and they lost the sun from their shoulders. "You've grown," Grandfather said. "Nearly an inch, I should say."

"More," Jody boasted. "Where they mark me on the door, I'm up more than an inch since Thanksgiving even."

Grandfather's rich throaty voice said, "Maybe you're getting too much water and turning to pith and stalk. Wait until you head out,[5] and then we'll see."

Jody looked quickly into the old man's face

to see whether his feelings should be hurt, but there was no will to injure, no punishing nor putting-in-your-place light in the keen blue eyes. "We might kill a pig," Jody suggested.

"Oh, no! I couldn't let you do that. You're just humoring me. It isn't the time and you know it."

"You know Riley, the big boar, sir?"

"Yes. I remember Riley well."

"Well, Riley ate a hole into that same haystack, and it fell down on him and smothered him."

"Pigs do that when they can," said Grandfather.

"Riley was a nice pig, for a boar, sir. I rode him sometimes, and he didn't mind."

A door slammed at the house below them, and they saw Jody's mother standing on the porch waving her apron in welcome. And they saw Carl Tiflin walking up from the barn to be at the house for the arrival.

The sun had disappeared from the hills by now. The blue smoke from the house chimney hung in flat layers in the purpling ranch-cup. The puff-ball clouds, dropped by the falling wind, hung listlessly in the sky.

Billy Buck came out of the bunkhouse and flung a wash basin of soapy water on the ground. He had been shaving in midweek, for Billy held Grandfather in reverence, and Grandfather said that Billy was one of the few men of the new generation who had not gone soft. Although Billy was in middle age, Grandfather considered him a boy. Now Billy was hurrying toward the house too.

When Jody and Grandfather arrived, the three were waiting for them in front of the yard gate.

Carl said, "Hello, sir. We've been looking for you."

Mrs. Tiflin kissed Grandfather on the side of his beard, and stood still while his big hand patted her shoulder. Billy shook hands solemnly, grinning under his straw mustache. "I'll put up your horse," said Billy, and he led the rig away.

Grandfather watched him go, and then, turning back to the group, he said as he had said a hundred times before, "There's a good boy.

---

[5]*Maybe you're getting too much water...head out.* Grandfather compares Jody to a plant which may grow tall from too much water. As the plant's worth cannot be estimated until it gets ready to bloom, so Jody's growth cannot be judged until he matures.

I knew his father, old Mule-tail Buck. I never knew why they called him Mule-tail except he packed mules."[6]

Mrs. Tiflin turned and led the way into the house. "How long are you going to stay, Father? Your letter didn't say."

"Well, I don't know. I thought I'd stay about two weeks. But I never stay as long as I think I'm going to."

In a short while they were sitting at the white oilcloth table eating their supper. The lamp with the reflector hung over the table. Outside the dining-room windows the big moths battered softly against the glass.

Grandfather cut his steak into tiny pieces and chewed slowly. "I'm hungry," he said. "Driving out here got my appetite up. It's like when we were crossing. We all got so hungry every night we could hardly wait to let the meat get done. I could eat about five pounds of buffalo meat every night."

"It's moving around does it," said Billy. "My father was a government packer.[7] I helped him when I was a kid. Just the two of us could about clean up a deer's ham."

"I knew your father, Billy," said Grandfather. "A fine man he was. They called him Mule-tail Buck. I don't know why except he packed mules."

"That was it," Billy agreed. "He packed mules."

Grandfather put down his knife and fork and looked around the table, "I remember one time we ran out of meat—" His voice dropped to a curious low singsong, dropped into a tonal groove the story had worn for itself. "There was no buffalo, no antelope, not even rabbits. The hunters couldn't even shoot a coyote. That was the time for the leader to be on the watch. I was the leader, and I kept my eyes open. Know why? Well, just the minute the people began to get hungry they'd start slaughtering the team oxen. Do you believe that? I've heard of parties that just ate up their draft cattle. Started from the middle and worked toward the ends. Finally they'd eat the lead pair, and then the wheelers.[8] The leader of a party had to keep them from doing that."

In some manner a big moth got into the room and circled the hanging kerosene lamp. Billy got up and tried to clap it between his hands. Carl struck with a cupped palm and caught the moth and broke it. He walked to the window and dropped it out.

"As I was saying," Grandfather began again, but Carl interrupted him. "You'd better eat some more meat. All the rest of us are ready for our pudding."

Jody saw a flash of anger in his mother's eyes. Grandfather picked up his knife and fork. "I'm pretty hungry, all right," he said. "I'll tell you about that later."

When supper was over, when the family and Billy Buck sat in front of the fireplace in the other room, Jody anxiously watched Grandfather. He saw the signs he knew. The bearded head leaned forward; the eyes lost their sternness and looked wonderingly into the fire; the big lean fingers laced themselves on the black knees. "I wonder," he began, "I just wonder whether I ever told you how those thieving Piutes[9] drove off thirty-five of our horses."

"I think you did," Carl interrupted. "Wasn't it just before you went up into the Tahoe country[10]?"

Grandfather turned quickly toward his son-in-law. "That's right. I guess I must have told you that story."

"Lots of times," Carl said cruelly, and he avoided his wife's eyes. But he felt the angry eyes on him, and he said, " 'Course I'd like to hear it again."

Grandfather looked back at the fire. His fingers unlaced and laced again. Jody knew how he felt, how his insides were collapsed and empty. Hadn't Jody been called a big-britches

---

[6]*packed mules,* was in charge of a string of mules which carried goods or provisions.

[7]*government packer,* one who ran a string of pack mules owned by the government.

[8]*lead pair...wheelers.* The lead pair were the animals harnessed first in a team; the wheelers were placed immediately in front of the wheels of the wagon.

[9]*Piutes* (pī'ūtz), a term applied to various Shoshoni Indian tribes who were scattered from Arizona and Utah to Nevada, California, and Oregon.

[10]*Tahoe* (tä'hō *or* tā'hō) *country,* the high, forested land near Lake Tahoe, a lake at the base of the Sierra Nevada Mountains on the Nevada-California boundary.

that very afternoon? He arose to heroism and opened himself to the term big-britches again. "Tell about Indians," he said softly.

Grandfather's eyes grew stern again. "Boys always want to hear about Indians. It was a job for men, but boys want to hear about it. Well, let's see. Did I ever tell you how I wanted each wagon to carry a long iron plate?"

Everyone but Jody remained silent. Jody said, "No. You didn't."

"Well, when the Indians attacked, we always put the wagons in a circle and fought from between the wheels. I thought that if every wagon carried a long plate with rifle holes, the men could stand the plates on the outside of the wheels when the wagons were in the circle and they would be protected. It would save lives and that would make up for the extra weight of the iron. But of course the party wouldn't do it. No party had done it before, and they couldn't see why they should go to the expense. They lived to regret it, too."

Jody looked at his mother, and knew from her expression that she was not listening at all. Carl picked at a callus on his thumb and Billy Buck watched a spider crawling up the wall.

Grandfather's tone dropped into its narrative groove again. Jody knew in advance exactly what words would fall. The story droned on, speeded up for the attack, grew sad over the wounds, struck a dirge at the burials on the great plains. Jody sat quietly watching Grandfather. The stern blue eyes were detached. He looked as though he were not very interested in the story himself.

When it was finished, when the pause had been politely respected as the frontier of the story,[11] Billy Buck stood up and stretched and hitched his trousers. "I guess I'll turn in," he said. Then he faced Grandfather. "I've got an old powder horn[12] and a cap and ball pistol[13] down to the bunkhouse. Did I ever show them to you?"

Grandfather nodded slowly. "Yes, I think you did, Billy. Reminds me of a pistol I had when I was leading the people across." Billy stood politely until the little story was done, and then he said, "Good night," and went out of the house.

Carl Tiflin tried to turn the conversation then. "How's the country between here and Monterey[14]? I've heard it's pretty dry."

"It is dry," said Grandfather. "There's not a drop of water in the Laguna Seca.[15] But it's a long pull from '87.[16] The whole country was powder then, and in '61 I believe all the coyotes starved to death. We had fifteen inches of rain this year."

"Yes, but it all came too early. We could do with some now." Carl's eye fell on Jody. "Hadn't you better be getting to bed?"

Jody stood up obediently. "Can I kill the mice in the old haystack, sir?"

---

[11]*the frontier of the story.* The audience recognized that Grandfather had reached the limits, or end, of his story, and did not intend to go any further with it.

[12]*powder horn,* an animal's horn used as a flask for carrying gunpowder.

[13]*cap and ball pistol,* a single-shot pistol loaded with powder and ball (lead shot), fired by a hammer striking a percussion cap.

[14]*Monterey* (mon tə rā′), a seacoast city west of the Salinas Valley.

[15]*Laguna Seca* (lä gü′nä sä′kä), a shallow body of water whose name means "dry lagoon."

[16]*a long pull from '87,* not nearly so dry as it was in 1887.

"Mice? Oh! Sure, kill them all off. Billy said there isn't any good hay left."

Jody exchanged a secret and satisfying look with Grandfather. "I'll kill every one tomorrow," he promised.

Jody lay in his bed and thought of the impossible world of Indians and buffaloes, a world that had ceased to be forever. He wished he could have been living in the heroic time, but he knew he was not of heroic timber. No one living now, save possibly Billy Buck, was worthy to do the things that had been done. A race of giants had lived then, fearless men, men of a stanchness unknown in this day. Jody thought of the wide plains and of the wagons moving across like centipedes. He thought of Grandfather on a huge white horse, marshaling the people. Across his mind marched the great phantoms, and they marched off the earth and they were gone.

He came back to the ranch for a moment, then. He heard the dull rushing sound that space and silence make. He heard one of the dogs, out in the doghouse, scratching a flea and bumping his elbow against the floor with every stroke. Then the wind arose again, and the black cypress groaned, and Jody went to sleep.

He was up half an hour before the triangle sounded[17] for breakfast. His mother was rattling the stove to make the flames roar when Jody went through the kitchen. "You're up early," she said. "Where are you going?"

"Out to get a good stick. We're going to kill the mice today."

"Who is 'we'?"

"Why, Grandfather and I."

"So you've got him in it. You always like to have someone in with you in case there's blame to share."

"I'll be right back," said Jody. "I just want to have a good stick ready for after breakfast."

He closed the screen door after him and went out into the cool blue morning. The birds were noisy in the dawn and the ranch cats came down from the hill like blunt snakes. They had been hunting gophers in the dark, and although the four cats were full of gopher meat, they sat in a semicircle at the back door and mewed piteously for milk. Doubletree Mutt and Smasher moved sniffling along the edge of the brush, performing the duty with rigid ceremony, but when Jody whistled, their heads jerked up and their tails waved. They plunged down to him, wriggling their skins and yawning. Jody patted their heads seriously, and moved on to the weathered scrap pile. He selected an old broom handle and a short piece of inch-square scrap wood. From his pocket he took a shoelace and tied the ends of the sticks loosely together to make a flail. He whistled his new weapon through the air and struck the ground experimentally, while the dogs leaped aside and whined with apprehension.

Jody turned and started down past the house toward the old haystack ground to look over the field of slaughter, but Billy Buck, sitting patiently on the back steps, called to him, "You better come back. It's only a couple of minutes till breakfast."

Jody changed his course and moved toward the house. He leaned his flail against the steps.

---

[17] *the triangle sounded.* To call people to meals, Jody's mother struck a metal triangle with a metal rod.

"That's to drive the mice out," he said. "I'll bet they're fat. I'll bet they don't know what's going to happen to them today."

"No, nor you either," Billy remarked philosophically, "nor me, nor anyone."

Jody was staggered by this thought. He knew it was true. His imagination twitched away from the mouse hunt. Then his mother came out on the back porch and struck the triangle, and all thoughts fell in a heap.

Grandfather hadn't appeared at the table when they sat down. Billy nodded at his empty chair. "He's all right? He isn't sick?"

"He takes a long time to dress," said Mrs. Tiflin. "He combs his whiskers and rubs up his shoes and brushes his clothes."

Carl scattered sugar on his mush. "A man that's led a wagon train across the plains has got to be pretty careful how he dresses."

Mrs. Tiflin turned on him. "Don't do that, Carl! Please don't!" There was more of threat than of request in her tone. And the threat irritated Carl.

"Well, how many times do I have to listen to the story of the iron plates, and the thirty-five horses? That time's done. Why can't he forget it, now it's done?" He grew angrier while he talked, and his voice rose. "Why does he have to tell them over and over? He came across the plains. All right! Now it's finished. Nobody wants to hear about it over and over."

The door into the kitchen closed softly. The four at the table sat frozen. Carl laid his mush spoon on the table and touched his chin with his fingers.

Then the kitchen door opened and Grandfather walked in. His mouth smiled tightly and his eyes were squinted. "Good morning," he said, and he sat down and looked at his mush dish.

Carl could not leave it there. "Did—did you hear what I said?"

Grandfather jerked a little nod.

"I don't know what got into me, sir. I didn't mean it. I was just being funny."

Jody glanced in shame at his mother, and he saw that she was looking at Carl, and that she wasn't breathing. It was an awful thing that he was doing. He was tearing himself to pieces

to talk like that. It was a terrible thing to him to retract a word, but to retract it in shame was infinitely worse.

Grandfather looked sidewise. "I'm trying to get right side up," he said gently. "I'm not being mad. I don't mind what you said, but it might be true, and I would mind that."

"It isn't true," said Carl. "I'm not feeling well this morning. I'm sorry I said it."

"Don't be sorry, Carl. An old man doesn't see things sometimes. Maybe you're right. The crossing is finished. Maybe it should be forgotten, now it's done."

Carl got up from the table. "I've had enough to eat. I'm going to work. Take your time, Billy!" He walked quickly out of the dining room. Billy gulped the rest of his food and followed soon after. But Jody could not leave his chair.

"Won't you tell any more stories?" Jody asked.

"Why, sure I'll tell them, but only when—I'm sure people want to hear them."

"I like to hear them, sir."

"Oh! Of course you do, but you're a little boy. It was a job for men, but only little boys like to hear about it."

Jody got up from his place. "I'll wait outside for you, sir. I've got a good stick for those mice."

He waited by the gate until the old man came out on the porch. "Let's go down and kill the mice now," Jody called.

"I think I'll just sit in the sun, Jody. You go kill the mice."

"You can use my stick if you like."

"No, I'll just sit here a while."

Jody turned disconsolately away, and walked down toward the old haystack. He tried to whip up his enthusiasm with thoughts of the fat juicy mice. He beat the ground with his flail. The dogs coaxed and whined about him, but he could not go. Back at the house he could see Grandfather sitting on the porch, looking small and thin and black.

Jody gave up and went to sit on the steps at the old man's feet.

"Back already? Did you kill the mice?"

"No, sir. I'll kill them some other day."

The morning flies buzzed close to the ground and the ants dashed about in front of the steps. The heavy smell of sage slipped down the hill. The porch boards grew warm in the sunshine.

Jody hardly knew when Grandfather started to talk. "I shouldn't stay here, feeling the way I do." He examined his strong old hands. "I feel as though the crossing wasn't worth doing." His eyes moved up the sidehill and stopped on a motionless hawk perched on a dead limb. "I tell those old stories, but they're not what I want to tell. I only know how I want people to feel when I tell them.

"It wasn't Indians that were important, nor adventures, nor even getting out here. It was a whole bunch of people made into one big crawling beast. And I was the head. It was westering and westering. Every man wanted something for himself, but the big beast that was all of them wanted only westering. I was the leader, but if I hadn't been there, someone else would have been the head. The thing had to have a head.

"Under the little bushes the shadows were black at white noonday. When we saw the mountains at last, we cried—all of us. But it wasn't getting here that mattered, it was movement and westering.

"We carried life out here and set it down the way those ants carry eggs. And I was the leader. The westering was as big as God, and the slow steps that made the movement piled up and piled up until the continent was crossed.

"Then we came down to the sea, and it was done." He stopped and wiped his eyes until the rims were red. "That's what I should be telling instead of stories."

When Jody spoke, Grandfather started and looked down at him. "Maybe I could lead the people someday," Jody said.

The old man smiled. "There's no place to go. There's the ocean to stop you. There's a line of old men along the shore hating the ocean because it stopped them."

"In boats I might, sir."

"No place to go, Jody. Every place is taken. But that's not the worst—no, not the worst. Westering has died out of the people. Westering isn't a hunger any more. It's all done. Your father is right. It is finished." He laced his fingers on his knee and looked at them.

Jody felt very sad. "If you'd like a glass of lemonade, I could make it for you."

Grandfather was about to refuse, and then he saw Jody's face. "That would be nice," he said. "Yes, it would be nice to drink a lemonade."

Jody ran into the kitchen where his mother was wiping the last of the breakfast dishes. "Can I have a lemon to make a lemonade for Grandfather?"

His mother mimicked—"And another lemon to make a lemonade for you."

"No, ma'am. I don't want one."

"Jody! You're sick!" Then she stopped suddenly. "Take a lemon out of the cooler," she said softly. "Here, I'll reach the squeezer down to you."

UNDERSTANDING GRANDFATHER

1. Describe and account for the attitudes of Billy Buck, Carl Tiflin, and Mrs. Tiflin toward the grandfather. What is Jody's attitude?

2. What does the grandfather learn during the course of the story? Read the passage that best summarizes his feeling about the Westward Movement. What is his attitude toward the younger generation? Do you agree that "westering" has died out of the people? Explain your answer.

3. Discuss the various elements that make this story lifelike.

Getting to know Jody

John Steinbeck is a very skillful craftsman—so skillful that perhaps you did not realize as you read "The Leader of the People" that much of the time you were seeing through Jody's eyes. Jody looked on the California countryside, observed the small actions of various animals, got his knowledge of people from the tone of a voice or a fleeting expression. The author never slows the course of his story to tell you directly what kind of boy Jody is, but through letting you know what Jody saw and heard and felt he gives you a complete characterization of a very real boy.

1. Which of Jody's interests at the beginning of the story are typical "small boy"?

2. How do his reactions to the outdoor world and to animals show his powers of observation?

3. How do you know he thoroughly understood his father?

4. What happens to Jody in this story? In other words, how has he changed between the start and the conclusion? What is the reason for the change? How is what happens to the old man related to what happens to Jody?

Understanding the use of figurative language

Perhaps you are accustomed to think of figures of speech as mere ornaments, devices which an author uses to "decorate" his story or poem. But have you ever considered figures of speech as a necessary part of language, something without which a particular thought cannot be accurately expressed? John Steinbeck uses a simile to help the reader understand just how the great overland movement appeared in Jody's young imagination: "Jody thought of the wide plains and of *the wagons moving across like centipedes.*" Later, when the author wishes you to grasp the idea about crossing the country that Grandfather has failed to convey through his stories, he has the old man speak in metaphors: "It wasn't Indians that were important, nor adventures, nor even getting out here. It was a whole bunch of people made into one big crawling beast....Every man wanted something for himself, but *the big beast that was all of them* wanted only westering."

In addition to similes, metaphors, and other particular figures of speech, John Steinbeck often uses a single word or phrase figuratively to suggest a rich picture. When he introduces Grandfather, he writes: "About the whole face and figure there was a granite dignity." Can you grasp the idea that the figurative use of *granite* adds to the image of Grandfather? Is there any literal way of suggesting so briefly yet so clearly the simple strength, the integrity, and the unchanging quality of the old man?

What vivid impressions are added to your mind by the figurative language in each of the following sentences?

1. The hill was washed with lean March sunshine.
2. She had caught Carl, caught and entangled him in her soft tone.
3. His voice dropped into a curious low singsong, dropped into a tonal groove the story had worn for itself.
4. He wished he could have been living in the heroic time, but he knew he was not of heroic timber.
5. The birds were noisy in the dawn and the ranch cats came down from the hill like blunt snakes.
6. Then his mother came out on the back porch and struck the triangle, and all thoughts fell in a heap.

The Ideals of the Pioneer

FREDERICK J. TURNER

As all the stories, poems, and songs in this section have shown, the West has influenced life in the United States in many ways. Although it is impossible to separate entirely one of these elements of influence from another, writers have often tried to identify the elements and to describe the significance of each. Prominent among these writers is the historian Frederick J. Turner, who was born in Wisconsin in 1861. Until Turner's time, most American histories had been written by Easterners or Southerners who viewed the Atlantic seaboard as most important in shaping American character and ideals. But Turner, born and educated in the Midwest, saw the significance of the frontier in the making of America. In the following selection he gives a clear-cut statement of one important phase of this influence.

FROM THE beginning of the settlement of America, the frontier regions have exercised a steady influence toward democracy. In Virginia, to take an example, it can be traced as early as the period of Bacon's rebellion, a hundred years before our Declaration of Independence. The small landholders, seeing that their powers were steadily passing into the hands of the wealthy planters who controlled church and state and lands, rose in revolt. A generation later, in the governorship of Alexander Spotswood,[1] we find a contest between the frontier settlers and the property-holding classes of the coast. The democracy with which Spotswood had to struggle, and of which he so bitterly complained, was a democracy made up of small landholders, of the newer immigrants, and of indented servants,[2] who at the expiration of their time of servitude passed into the interior

---

[1] *Alexander Spotswood.* This is the same Colonel Spotswood with whom William Byrd talked about iron mines.

[2] *indented servants,* indentured servants. Many settlers were bound by contract to work as servants for a certain number of years before receiving their freedom.

"The Ideals of the Pioneer," condensed and adapted from the article "Contributions of the West to American Democracy," by Frederick J. Turner. Copyright, 1903, by *The Atlantic Monthly.* Reprinted by permission of *The Atlantic Monthly.*

to take up lands and engage in pioneer farming. Indeed, in the period before the outbreak of the American Revolution, one can trace a distinct belt of democratic territory extending from the back country of New England[3] down through western New York, Pennsylvania, and the South. In each colony this region was in conflict with the dominant classes of the coast. It constituted a quasi-revolutionary area[4] before the days of the Revolution, and it formed the basis on which the Democratic party was afterwards established. It was therefore in the West[5] that the struggle for democratic development first revealed itself, and in that area the essential ideas of American democracy had already appeared.

On the frontier of New England, along the western border of Pennsylvania, Virginia, and the Carolinas, and in the communities beyond the Allegheny Mountains, there arose a demand of the frontier settlers for independent statehood based on democratic provisions. There is a strain of fierceness in their energetic petitions demanding self-government under the theory that every people have the right to establish their own political institutions in an area which they have won from the wilderness. Those revolutionary principles based on natural rights, for which the seaboard colonies were contending, were taken up with frontier energy in an attempt to apply them to the lands of the West. No one can read their petitions denouncing the control exercised by the wealthy landholders of the coast, appealing to the record of their conquest of the wilderness, and demanding the possession of the lands for which they had fought the Indians, and which they had reduced by their ax to civilization, without recognizing in these frontier communities the cradle of a belligerent Western democracy. "A fool can sometimes put on his coat better than a wise man can do it for him"—such is the philosophy of its petitions.

Western democracy has been from the time of its birth idealistic. The very fact of the wilderness appealed to men as a fair, blank page on which to write a new chapter in the story of man's struggle for a higher type of society. The Western wilds, from the Alleghenies to the Pacific, constituted the richest free gift that was ever spread out before civilized man. To the peasant and artisan of the Old World, bound by the chains of social class,[6] as old as custom and as inevitable as fate, the West offered an exit into a free life and greater well-being among the bounties of nature, into the midst of resources that demanded manly exertion, and that gave in return the chance for indefinite ascent in the scale of social advance. "To each she offered gifts after his will." Never again can such an opportunity come to the sons of men. It was unique, and the thing is so near us, so much a part of our lives, that we do not even yet comprehend its vast significance. The existence of this land of opportunity has made America the goal of idealists from the days of the Pilgrim Fathers. With all the *materialism* of the pioneer movements, this idealistic conception of the vacant lands as an opportunity for a new order of things is unmistakably present. Kipling's "Song of the English" has given it expression:

We were dreamers, dreaming greatly, in the man-stifled town;
We yearned beyond the skyline where the strange roads go down.
Came the Whisper, came the Vision, came the Power with the Need,
Till the Soul that is not man's soul was lent us to lead.

American democracy is fundamentally the outcome of the experiences of the American people in dealing with the West. Western democracy through the whole of its earlier period tended to the production of a society of which the most distinctive fact was the freedom of the individual to rise under conditions of social mobility,[7] and whose ambition was the liberty and well-being of the masses. Let us see to it that the ideals of the pioneer in his log cabin

---

[3]*back country of New England,* the area stretching inland from the cities and towns along the Atlantic seaboard.

[4]*quasi-revolutionary area,* a section that was in a partial state of revolt.

[5]*the West,* that is, the western sections of New England, New York, Pennsylvania, and the present Southeast.

[6]*the chains of social class,* the rigid social system that made it impossible for people of one class to move upward through ability or hard work into a higher class.

[7]*social mobility,* the constantly changing conditions that allowed a person to move to a higher social class.

shall enlarge into the spiritual life of a democracy where civic power shall dominate and utilize individual achievement for the common good.

FOLLOWING THE AUTHOR'S ARGUMENT

1. How does the author support his statement that from the beginning of the settlement of America the frontier regions have steadily influenced democracy?
2. How was idealistic thinking naturally associated with the West?
3. How is American democracy fundamentally an outcome of the Westward Movement?
4. How does the author suggest that we keep alive the ideals of the pioneer? In what practical ways can we make use of this suggestion?

Know your words

Tractor is a word that stands for something you can see, hear, and touch. *Democracy* is a word that stands for something you cannot see, hear, or touch. If someone says to you, "My uncle likes his new *tractor* very much," there is not much danger you will misunderstand what the speaker means, since *tractor* probably suggests the same object to you that it does to him. However, if you write to a friend in a European country, "In recent years *democracy* has been broadened in the United States," your friend may not get exactly the meaning you intended from the word *democracy*. No one can see, hear, or touch *democracy* because *democracy* is an abstract term that stands for an idea —or for several ideas. Therefore what you mean by *democracy* may differ from your friend's understanding of the term. When you come upon words like *democracy, liberty,* and *freedom* in your reading, note carefully the context in which they are used and try to figure out what the writer means by them.

The phrases listed below are all taken from the first paragraph of "Ideals of the Pioneer." Explain as accurately as you can what the author meant by *democracy* or *democratic* in each of them.

1. ...a steady influence toward *democracy*.
2. ...a *democracy* made up of small landholders, of the newer immigrants, and of indented servants.
3. ...a distinct belt of *democratic* territory....
4. ...the struggle for *democratic* development....
5. ...the essential ideas of American *democracy*....

The Larger View

I. The Westward Movement is a vast subject. It covered millions of square miles of forest, mountain, and plain; it embraced over a hundred years in time; it gave a new life to thousands of people. The selections in this chapter can only serve to suggest to you the scope of this movement and its effect on American life and literature. It is only through wide and diversified reading that you can begin to appreciate and to understand it. Using the text selections and the outside reading you have already done as a basis, prepare to take part in discussing the following topics:

1. It was a natural outgrowth of frontier life to cast the Indian as villain in many stories.
2. The Indian has been unfairly treated in American literature.
3. One reason for the continuing popularity of Daniel Boone is that he exemplifies most of the qualities we like to think of as peculiarly American.
4. The size, strength, and good nature of Davy Crockett and Pecos Bill recur in most other great American folk heroes.
5. The qualities that the frontier yarnspinners gave to Pecos Bill are merely larger-than-life versions of characteristics most admired by pioneers.
6. Each light-hearted stanza of "Sweet Betsy from Pike" contains enough tragic truth to be the subject of a full-length novel.
7. The conditions described in "The Little Old Sod Shanty on the Claim" had their actual counterparts all across the central plains.
8. Stories about the cowboy often paint a glamorous picture of a life that was really hard.
9. The men who had endured the hardships of pioneering in their younger days often became discontented old men living in the past.

10. The frontier had a great effect on the development of certain American characteristics.

11. American literature was greatly affected in subject matter, mood, and style by the Westward Movement.

II. Interview some old resident of your community—perhaps your grandfather or grandmother—to learn at first hand something of earlier days. Prepare to report to the class interesting things you have discovered. If these reports show that your community is rich in stories of the past, it would be worth-while to write up these reminis-cences of old settlers, illustrating them if possible with photographs of the taletellers or of the locality. A committee might be appointed to compile the completed accounts into a community scrapbook.

III. Draw a large map of the United States, sketching in at the appropriate place figures recalling the various characters who appear in this unit and the preceding one. (You may want to add some character representing your own community.) Place a date under each character indicating approximately the age in which he lived.

MORE GOOD READING

ALDRICH, BESS STREETER, *A Lantern in Her Hand.* (Appleton) Just in case you've forgotten that there were women on the Western frontier, read this human and touching story of Abbie Dean, a pioneer Nebraska mother.

ALLEN, HERVEY, *The Forest and the Fort.* (Rinehart) This is the story of Salathiel Albine, who as a child was captured by Indians and grew up in an Indian village. Much of the action centers about the siege of Fort Pitt during the French and Indian War.

BAKELESS, JOHN, *Fighting Frontiersman: the Life of Daniel Boone.* (Morrow) The world of trackless wilderness, Indians, and the most famous of American frontiersmen are pictured in this fine biography.

BLAIR, WALTER, *Tall Tale America.* (Coward) The strength and the imagination of earlier America breathe through these humorous tales of Davy Crockett, Paul Bunyan, and other legendary heroes.

BOYD, JAMES, *The Long Hunt.* (Scribner) In Daniel Boone's day the way to the Mississippi lay through perilous Indian country. This is the exciting story of a "long hunter" who encountered hardship and danger alone in the wilderness.

CATHER, WILLA, *O Pioneers!* (Houghton) One of America's master craftsmen tells the courageous story of the Swedes, Bohemians, and French who fought the wild Nebraska land for a livelihood. Girls will particularly like the same author's *My Ántonia* (Houghton), the story of a strong and simple Bohemian immigrant girl on the Nebraska prairies.

DERLETH, AUGUST, *Wind over Wisconsin.* (Scribner) In the 1830's in Wisconsin fur traders were giving way to farmers, and the Indians, seeing themselves doomed by increasing numbers of white men, were making a last effort to hold their lands. Believable characters and tense situations make this an engrossing story.

EDMONDS, WALTER D., *Wilderness Clearing.* (Dodd) In the Mohawk Valley of New York in 1777, Indian attack loomed closer than British armies. Dick Mount became a man almost overnight, and proved to Maggie Gordon that together they could withstand any perils of the frontier.

GARLAND, HAMLIN, *Son of the Middle Border.* (Macmillan) This account of day-to-day living on an Iowa farm in pioneer days is one of the best of frontier autobiographies.

GUTHRIE, A. B. JR., *The Big Sky: an Edition for Younger Readers.* (William Sloan) Seventeen-year-old Boone Caudill ran away from his Kentucky home to become a mountain man. The beauty of the West and the dangers and rewards of life there have seldom been better described than in this exciting story.

HOUGH, EMERSON, *The Covered Wagon*. (Grosset) Two thousand men, women, and children bound overland to Oregon in 1848, the disruption of the wagon train on the news of gold in California, a love story—what more could you ask in a story of the Westward Movement?

JAMES, BESSIE, *Six Feet Six, the Heroic Story of Sam Houston*. (Bobbs) This fine biography, with its tales of border warfare, Indians, and frontiersmen, is as exciting as any fictional story. In addition it presents an understandable picture of a great American.

LANE, ROSE WILDER, *Let the Hurricane Roar*. (Longmans) Few stories of the frontier have been better loved than this brief, simple tale of a young pioneer wife and her brave husband in the early days in Dakota.

LOMAX, JOHN A. and ALAN (compilers), *Folk Song: U. S. A.* (Duell) This is an authentic collection of the words and music of 101 real American songs. The brief histories of the songs make fascinating reading, too.

MILLER, OLIVE K., *Heroes, Outlaws, and Funny Fellows of American Popular Tales*. (Doubleday) The outlaws are as fascinating as the folk heroes, and you'll find Captain Kidd and Pirate Jean LaFitte as well as John Henry and Paul Bunyan in this interesting collection of tales.

MORROW, HONORÉ WILLSIE, *On to Oregon*. (Morrow) You'll find this story of a thirteen-year-old boy who made the long journey across the Rockies in pioneer days even more fascinating when you realize that it is based on fact.

PARKMAN, FRANCIS, *The Oregon Trail*. (Rinehart) This is a first-hand account by a great American historian of his journey west in 1846. Here is an eyewitness record of encounters with Indians, buffalo hunts, and life on the prairie.

PEATTIE, DONALD C., *Forward the Nation*. (Putnam) The author has based his account of the Lewis and Clark expedition on original sources. This is a vivid, beautifully written retelling of an inspiring chapter in American history.

ROBERTS, KENNETH, *Northwest Passage*. (Doubleday) The old dream of a northwest passage through the continent to the Pacific Ocean inspired Major Robert Rogers, American ranger commander, as he journeyed west to the trading post at Mackinac. This is an excellent historical novel.

ROURKE, CONSTANCE, *Davy Crockett*. (Harcourt) From his Tennessee boyhood to his heroic death at the Alamo, Constance Rourke traces the life of Davy Crockett. The frontiersman's exciting life and the author's informal style of writing combine to provide a very readable biography.

SANDBURG, CARL (editor), *The American Songbag*. (Harcourt) From every corner of the country and from every period of American history Mr. Sandburg has collected these folk songs. The music is given too.

VESTAL, STANLEY, *Kit Carson: the Happy Warrior of the Old West*. (Houghton) The fact that the author knows intimately the country and the Indian tribes with which Kit Carson was associated adds to the interest of this colorful biography. You will also enjoy Mr. Vestal's *Jim Bridger, Mountain Man* (Morrow), a biography of one of the Old West's most famous hunters, trappers, and explorers.

WISTER, OWEN, *The Virginian*. (Macmillan) This is a classic story of the Western cowboy in the Wyoming cattle lands in early days. He wins, and fully deserves, the love of the pretty schoolteacher from Vermont.

UNIT III: FROM MANY DISTANT COUNTRIES

ONE OF the hardest things to explain to a native of another country is what we mean by the word *American*. We and many other people in the world have come to take for granted the fact that *American* refers to a citizen of the United States. So we are shocked when we discover a Brazilian or a Canadian or a Nicaraguan who thinks of himself as an American too. We would be ungracious to insist on our ownership of the name, because there is no place on the map labeled just *America* and because the complexion of various citizens of the United States may be black, white, yellow, red, or shades in between. Furthermore, just a glance at some of our family names shows that not one, but many nationalities, have been combined in making Americans. We so-called Americans, then, are without a common geographical, racial, or national background. Some of us boast of having ancestors who were here a little before others, but when the descendants of such ancestors brag, someone mentions the American Indian or the Norseman and invalidates the claim to priority. Most Americans, however, place more value upon the new than upon the old and refuse to be impressed by ancestors. "We care more about who and what you are," they say, "than about who your great-grandfather was." Thus the United States has gained a high degree of unity out of great diversity. In fact this blending of people from many distant countries is perhaps our most remarkable achievement.

Millions of people coming from every quarter of the globe have enriched not only our lives but also our literature beyond measure. A glance at the authors of the selections in this unit helps prove the point. Among them are immigrants from Austria, Poland, and Russia; and descendants of immigrants from England and Germany. Their differences in language, manners, and patterns of thinking have lent variety to their subject matter as well as the idiom and the form of their writing. The processes of many peoples' learning to live together have created situations that range from profound tragedy to delightful comedy—both the stuff of fine literature. The dreams and ideals that throughout the years have caused people to break away from their original homeland and to come to America for their fulfillment, and the adventures and experiences they had here, continue to be expressed in some of our most interesting literary works.

Immigrants

NANCY BYRD TURNER

"THESE FOREIGNERS with strange and avid
faces
Crowding our shores, marring our pleasant
places,
They must be curbed...." So mused King Powhatan,
Hundred per cent, red-blood American.

"Immigrants," reprinted by permission of Dodd, Mead & Company from *Star in a Well* by Nancy Byrd Turner. Copyright, 1935, by Dodd, Mead & Company, Inc.

The First Day

GEORGE and HELEN PAPASHVILY

In 1923, when George Papashvily, coauthor of the following selection, first came to the United States from Georgia in southern Russia, he thought of this country as a place where anything can happen. "And in twenty years," he says, "I never changed my mind." Here is an amusing—and heart-warming—description of his experiences during the first day in the United States.

AT FIVE in the morning the engines stopped, and after thirty-seven days the boat was quiet.

We were in America.

I got up and stepped over the other men and looked out the porthole. Water and fog. We

"The First Day" from *Anything Can Happen* by George and Helen Papashvily. Copyright, 1945, by George and Helen Waite Papashvily. Reprinted by permission of Harper & Brothers.

were anchoring off an island.[1] I dressed and went on deck.

Now began my troubles. What to do? This was a Greek boat and I was steerage, so of course by the time we were half way out I had spent all my landing money[2] for extra food.

Hassan, the Turk, one of the six who slept in the cabin with me, came up the ladder.

"I told you so," he said as soon as he saw me. "Now we are in America and you have no money to land. They send you home. No money, no going ashore. What a disgrace. In your position, frankly, I would kill myself."

Hassan had been satisfied to starve on black olives and salt cheese all the way from Gibraltar, and he begrudged every skewer of lamb I bribed away from the first-cabin steward.[3]

We went down the gangplank into the big room. Passengers with pictures in their hands was rushing around to match them to a relative. Before their tables the inspectors[4] was busy with long lines of people.

The visitors' door opened and fellow with big pile of caps, striped blue-and-white cotton caps with visors and a top button, came in. He went first to an old man with a karakul hat

[1] *an island*, Ellis Island in New York harbor, the chief inspection station of the United States Bureau of Immigration. Today most immigrants are examined aboard ship.

[2] *landing money*. Every immigrant to the United States must have either a certain sum of money to support himself until he gets a job or the promise of friends to support him.

[3] *first-cabin steward*, the man in charge of the food for the dining room of the passengers who had the most expensive accommodations.

[4] *inspectors*, United States government employees who checked immigrants' passports and other official papers and determined whether they were to be allowed to enter the country.

near the window, then to a Cossack[5] in the line. At last he came to me.

"Look," he said in Russian, "look at your hat. You want to be a greenhorn all your life? A karakul hat! Do you expect to see anybody in the U. S. A. still with a fur hat? The custom inspector, the doctor, the captain—are they wearing fur hats? Certainly not."

I didn't say anything.

"Look," he said. "I'm sorry for you. I was a greenhorn once myself. I wouldn't want to see anybody make my mistakes. Look, I have caps. See, from such rich striped material. Like wears railroad engineers, and house painters, and coal miners." He spun one around on his finger. "Don't be afraid. It's a cap in real American style. With this cap on your head, they couldn't tell you from a citizen. I'm positively guaranteeing. And I'm trading you this cap even for your old karakul hat. Trading even. You don't have to give me one penny."

Now it is true I bought my karakul coudie[6] new for the trip. It was a fine skin, a silver lamb, and in Georgia it would have lasted me a lifetime. Still—

"I'll tell you," the cap man said. "So you can remember all your life you made money the first hour you were in America, I give you a cap and a dollar besides. Done?"

I took off my coudie and put on his cap. It was small and sat well up on my head, but then in America one dresses like an American and it is a satisfaction always to be in the best style. So I got my first dollar.

Ysaacs, a Syrian, sat on the bench and smoked brown-paper cigarettes and watched all through the bargain. He was from our cabin, too, and he knew I was worried about the money to show the examiners. But now, as soon as the cap man went on to the next customer, Ysaacs explained a way to get me by the examiners—a good way.

Such a very good way, in fact, that when the inspector looked over my passport and entry permit I was ready.

"Do you have friends meeting you?" he asked me. "Do you have money to support yourself?"

I pulled out a round fat roll of green American money—tens, twenties—a nice thick pile with a rubber band around.

"O.K.," he said. "Go ahead." He stamped my papers.

I got my baggage and took the money roll back again to Ysaac's friend, Arapouleopolus, the moneylender, so he could rent it over again to another man. One dollar was all he charged to use it for each landing. Really a bargain.

On the outer platform I met Zurabeg, an Ossetian,[7] who had been down in steerage, too. But Zurabeg was no greenhorn coming for the first time. Zurabeg was an American citizen with papers to prove it, and a friend of Gospadin[8] Buffalo Bill besides. This Zurabeg came first to America twenty years before as a trick show rider, and later he was boss cook on the road with the Gospadin Buffalo Bill. Every few years, Zurabeg, whenever he saved enough money, went home to find a wife—but so far with no luck.

"Can't land?" he asked me.

"No, I can land," I said, "but I have no money to pay the little boat to carry me to shore." A small boat went chuffing back and forth taking off the discharged passengers.[9] "I try to make up my mind to swim, but if I swim how will I carry my baggage? It would need two trips at least."

"Listen, donkey-head," Zurabeg said. "This is America. The carrying boat is free. It belongs to my government. They take us for nothing. Come on."

So we got to the shore.

And there—the streets, the people, the noise! The faces flashing by—and by again. The screams and chatter and cries. But most of all the motion, back and forth, back and forth, pressing deeper and deeper on my eyeballs.

We walked a few blocks through this before I remembered my landing cards and passport and visas. I took them out and tore them into little pieces and threw them all in an ash can.

---

[5]Cossack (kos'ak), a man from southern Russia.
[6]coudie (kow'dye), hat.

[7]Ossetian (o set'i ən), a person from a region of Russia between the Black and Caspian seas.
[8]Gospadin (gus'pō dēn'), Mr.
[9]discharged passengers, those whose papers had been stamped by the inspectors to show permission to enter the United States.

"They can't prove I'm not a citizen, now," I said. "What we do next?"

"We get jobs," Zurabeg told me. "I show you."

We went to an employment agency. Conveniently, the man spoke Russian. He gave Zurabeg ticket right away to start in Russian restaurant as first cook.

"Now, your friend? What can you do?" he asked me.

"I," I said, "am a worker in decorative leathers, particularly specializing in the ornamenting of crop handles according to the traditional designs."

"My God!" the man said. "This is the U.S.A. No horses. Automobiles. What else can you do?"

Fortunately my father was a man of great foresight and I have two trades. His idea was that in the days when a man starves with one, by the other he may eat.

"I am also," I said, "a swordmaker. Short blades or long; daggers with or without chasing; hunting knives, plain or ornamented; tempering, fitting, pointing—" I took my certificate of successful completion of apprenticeship out of my *chemidon*.[10]

"My God! A crop maker—a sword pointer. You better take him along for a dishwasher," he said to Zurabeg. "They can always use another dishwasher."

We went down into the earth and flew through tunnels in a train. It was like the caves under the Kazbeck[11] where the giant bats sleep, and it smelled even worse.

The restaurant was on a side street and the lady owner, the *hasaika*,[12] spoke kindly. "I remember you from the tearoom," she said to Zurabeg. "I congratulate myself on getting you. You are excellent on the *piroshkis*,[13] isn't it?"

"On everything, madame," Zurabeg said grandly. "On everything. Buffalo Bill, an old friend of mine, has eaten thirty of my *piroshkis*

at a meal. My friend—" he waved toward me— "will be a dishwasher."

I made a bow.

The kitchen was small and hot and fat—like inside of a pig's stomach. Zurabeg unpacked his knives, put on his cap, and, at home at once, started to dice celery.

"You can wash these," the *hasaika* said to me. "At four we have party."

It was a trayful of glasses. And such glasses—thin bubbles that would hardly hold a sip—set on stems. The first one snapped in my hand, the second dissolved, the third to tenth I got washed, the eleventh was already cracked, the twelfth rang once on the pan edge and was silent.

Perhaps I might be there yet, but just as I carried the first trayful to the service slot,[14] the restaurant cat ran between my feet.

When I got all the glass swept up, I told Zurabeg, "Now, we have to eat. It's noon. I watch the customers eat. It makes me hungry. Prepare a *shashlik*[15] and some cucumbers, and

---

[10]*chemidon* (chŭ mə don′), suitcase.

[11]*Kazbeck* (käz bek′), a mountain that rises over 16,000 feet in the Caucasus Mountains in Russia.

[12]*hasaika* (hä sī′kə), a woman proprietor who acts as hostess.

[13]*piroshkis* (pēr rush′kēz), meat or cheese pies.

[14]*service slot*, opening in the wall between the kitchen and the dining rooms. From the dining-room side waiters could reach necessary glasses, china, etc.

[15]*shashlik* (shä′shlik), slices of mutton roasted on sticks.

we enjoy our first meal for good luck in the New World."

"This is a restaurant," Zurabeg said, "not a *duquani*[16] on the side of the Georgian road where the proprietor and the house[17] eat with the guests together at one table. This is a restaurant with very strict organization. We get to eat when the customers go, and you get what the customers leave. Try again with the glasses and remember my reputation. Please."

I found a quart of sour cream and went into the back alley and ate that and some bread and a jar of caviar which was very salty—packed for export, no doubt.

The *hasaika* found me. I stood up. "Please," she said, "please go on. Eat sour cream. But after, could you go away? Far away? With no hard feelings. The glasses—the caviar—it's expensive for me—and at the same time I don't want to make your friend mad. I need a good cook. If you could just go away? Quietly? Just disappear, so to speak? I give you five dollars."

"I didn't do anything," I said, "so you don't have to pay me. All in all, a restaurant probably isn't my fate. You can tell Zurabeg afterward."

She brought my cap and a paper bag. I went down through the alley and into the street. I walked. I walked until my feet took fire in my shoes and my neck ached from looking. I walked for hours. I couldn't even be sure it was the same day. I tried some English on a few men that passed. "What watch?" I said. But they pushed by me; so I knew I had it wrong. I tried another man. "How many clock?" He showed me on his wrist. Four-thirty.

A wonderful place. Rapidly, if one applies oneself, one speaks the English.

I came to a park and went in and found a place under a tree and took off my shoes and lay down. I looked in the bag the *hasaika* gave me. A sandwich from bologna and a nickel—to begin in America with.

What to do? While I decided, I slept.

A policeman was waking me up. He spoke. I shook my head I can't understand. Then with hands, with legs, rolling his eyes, turning his head, with motions, with gestures (really he was as good as marionettes I saw once in Tiflis[18]), he showed me to lie on the grass is forbidden. But one is welcome to the seats instead. All free seats in this park. No charge for anybody. What a country.

But I was puzzled. There were iron armrests every two feet along the benches. How could I distribute myself under them? I tried one leg. Then the other. But when I was under, how could I turn around? Then, whatever way I got in, my chin was always caught by the hoop. While I thought this over, I walked and bought peanuts for my nickel and fed the squirrels.

Lights began to come on in the towers around the park. It was almost dark. I found a sandy patch under a rock on little bluff above the drive. I cut a *shashlik* stick and built a fire of twigs and broiled my bologna over it and ate the bread. It lasted very short. Then I rolled up my coat for a pillow like the days during the war[19] and went to sleep.

I was tired from America and I slept some hours. It must have been almost midnight when the light flashed in my face. I sat up. It was from the head lamp of a touring car choking along on the road below me. While I watched, the engine coughed and died. A man got out. For more than an hour he knocked with tools and opened the hood and closed it again.

Then I slid down the bank. In the war there were airplanes, and of course cars are much the same except, naturally, for the wings. I showed him with my hands and feet and head, like the policeman: "Give me the tools and let me try." He handed them over and sat down on the bench.

I checked the spark plugs and the distributor, the timer, and the coils. I looked at the feed line, at the ignition, at the gas. In between, I cranked.[20] I cranked until I cranked my heart out onto the ground. Still the car wouldn't move.

---

[16]*duquani* (dü kwä'ni), inn frequented by peasants.
[17]*the house*, the employees.

[18]*Tiflis* (tif'lis, *Russian* tēf li ēs'), capital of Russian Georgia.
[19]*war*, the First World War, during which the author served in the Russian army.
[20]*cranked.* In those days automobiles had no automatic starters, but had to be cranked by hand.

I got mad. I cursed it. I cursed it for a son of a mountain *devi*. I cursed it for the carriage of the *diavels* in the cave. I cursed it by the black-horned goat,[21] and when I finished all I knew in Georgian I said it again in Russian to pick up the loose ends. Then I kicked the radiator as hard as I could. The car was old Model T, and it started with a snort that shook the chassis like an aspen.

The man came running up. He was laughing and he shook my hands and talked at me and asked questions. But the policeman's method didn't work. Signs weren't enough. I remembered my dictionary—English-Russian, Russian-English—it went both ways. I took it from my blouse pocket and showed the man. Holding it under the headlights, he thumbed through.

"Work?" he found in English.

I looked at the Russian word beside it and shook my head.

"Home?" he turned to that.

"No," again.

I took the dictionary. "Boat. Today."

"Come home—" he showed me the words—"with me—" he pointed to himself. "Eat. Sleep. Job." It took him quite a time between words. "Job. Tomorrow."

"Automobiles?" I said. We have the same word in Georgian.

"Automobiles!" He was pleased we found one word together.

We got in his car, and he took me through miles and miles of streets with houses on both sides of every one of them until we came to his own. We went in and we ate and we drank and ate and drank again. For that, fortunately, you need no words.

Then his wife showed me a room and I went to bed. As I fell asleep, I thought to myself: Well, now, I have lived one whole day in America and—just like they say—America is a country where anything, anything at all can happen.

And in twenty years—about this—I never changed my mind.

---

[21]*mountain devi...diavels in the cave...black-horned goat,* evil spirits believed in by superstitious people of Russian Georgia.

1. Which of the author's experiences caused him to think of America as a place where anything can happen? How does he show us that he was undismayed by experiences which others might have found crushing?

2. Specify some of the author's imaginative expressions such as "Listen, donkey-head" that add color and interest to his descriptions. How does he show by his style that he was not too familiar with our language?

3. This is a humorous piece. What's funny about it?

4. What reasons do you have for believing that George Papashvily will make a good American?

Know your words

The visa which George Papashvily so nonchalantly tore up and threw into an ash can had been one of the most important things he possessed twenty-four hours earlier. This visa was an endorsement on his passport signifying that it had been *seen* or examined and was in order. The idea of "see" or "seeing" appears in many words derived from the Latin root *vis-*. Rewrite each of the following sentences to bring out this idea without using the italicized word.

1. It was difficult for Papashvily to *envisage* a land so different from his native Georgia.

2. But he was no *visionary* who expected all things in the new land to be easy for him.

3. His *vision* of America was that of a practical, humorous, hard-working man.

4. He was *visibly* excited at the thought of the new experiences which awaited him.

Extending interests

1. Perhaps you know of other foreigners who have come to the United States and whose sense of humor and other personal traits and abilities have won respect and friendship. If you know such people, plan to tell the class about them.

2. After reading this story there are probably quite a few questions in your mind about immigration into the United States today. Are people of all races admitted? What qualifications must immigrants meet? How do they apply for admission? May all immigrants become citizens? What must an immigrant do to become a citizen? You and a group of your classmates might do some research on these and other questions about immigration. Then set yourself up as a panel of experts to answer the queries of the other students.

O'Meara, the Mayflower— and Mrs. MacLirr

DON MARQUIS

Racial pride, like family pride, is an admirable trait if it is not carried to excess. Perhaps the group most notable for holding loyalty in an even balance are the Americans of Irish descent. This fact is no doubt due to the keen sense of humor and vigorous imagination characteristic of the Irish. The following short story has both of these qualities. Mr. O'Meara's tale, as Don Marquis suggests, "sometimes reels and whirls and spins with an excess of imagination."

"IT'S A QUEER THING," said Terence O'Meara, with a wink at his brother Jack and a glance at the bald spot on the top of his father's head; "it's a queer thing that the Irish let the English and the French, the Spanish and the Dutch, all get ahead of them in exploring and settling America."

Mr. Timothy O'Meara, their father, had his face turned away from them, while he fumbled for a pipe-cleaner in the case of a great old clock that stood on the mantel. He grunted.

"I could never understand it myself," said Jack O'Meara, with an answering wink to his brother. "Why were none of the Irish great navigators?"

The senior O'Meara's bald spot suddenly flushed red, and the veins in it began to swell, and his sons, chuckling softly, knew just how his face would look when they saw it.

"Why were none of them discoverers?" continued Jack rhetorically. "Great sailors, or great whalers, or notable pioneers?"

Mr. Timothy O'Meara turned slowly and impressively toward them, where they sat at the table over their after-dinner pipes and coffee, and scorn made streaks and lines through the heat of his countenance. But when he spoke it was with a measure of dignity.

"Shame to you both," said he, "and sorrow to me that has such sons! The greatest navigator of thim all, not aven barrin' Noah and his ark, was an Irishman! And the greatest whale-catcher of all times, not aven exceptin' Jonah, who used to proffer himself for bait,[1] was an Irishman! Wan and the same Irishman they was, thim two, and his name was Timothy O'Meara, the same as me own, and my ancestor he was."

He suddenly tossed something hard upon the table, which he had taken out of the clock-case along with the pipe-cleaner, and the object rattled among the dishes.

"And what's that?" said Jack.

The young men were used to seeing their father take anything and everything out of that clock-case—valuable papers incidental to his contracting business, shirt studs and shoestrings, as well as bits of indeterminate junk of vast historical interest. Or, one might say, legendary interest, mythological interest, for the tales of Mr. O'Meara sometimes reeled and whirled and spun with an excess of imagination, as a muse might soar upon inebriate pinions. It was the delight of his sons to sting him to narration with insults; he usually retorted with an affectation of belief that his sons, who both had worthy records in the A. E. F.,[2] had really been dishonorably discharged from that organization.

"That," said Mr. O'Meara, "is a piece of Plymouth Rock. 'Twas chipped off by my ancestor, Timothy O'Meara, the day he landed the *Mayflower* outfit there, and quit his many wanderin's, and sittled down to colonize New England and America. And it has been kept in the family iver since, as a memento of the occasion."

He had a way of excluding his sons from the illustrious family in his stories as if they were unworthy to bear the name of O'Meara. Terence looked at the bit of stone, and it seemed to him that it bore a certain resemblance to a piece of rock that had once come out of the

---

[1] *Jonah* (jō′nə), *who used to proffer himself for bait.* Because Jonah was in the belly of the whale three nights and three days (Jonah 1:17), Mr. O'Meara says he caught a whale by offering himself as the bait.

[2] *A.E.F.,* American Expeditionary Force, the United States Army that served overseas during World War I.

clock-case as souvenir and evidence of the first gold discovery in California by a Timothy O'Meara. But he said nothing aloud. Internally he was asking himself:

"How the deuce is the old man going to get an Irish O'Meara aboard the *Mayflower?*"

There was a responsive wonder in Jack's countenance. Their father's visage was partially hidden again, as he bowed his head over his leisurely pipe-cleaning—if he was not wondering himself, he was at least arranging the details of his saga.

"Whales!" he murmured to himself "Whales! —not know whales? Of course he knew whales, did Tim O'Meara the navigator!"

Whales [said Mr. O'Meara, his pipe filled with plug-cut and drawing sweetly], whales are the most misunderstood of all God's craytures, by the common ginerality of mankind. The whale is the grandest and most intilligint and most ginerous of the bastes that roam the world, and it takes a large and noble nature to understand the whale—and a large and noble nature was that of Timothy O'Meara, my ancestor, that I'm going to tell you about. Whin the world was made, and the firmamint was set up as siperates the hivens from the earth, the whale was put into the seas and oceans, because there is so much more wather than there is land; and the nobility of the whale is fitted to a spacious elemint. He floats in grandeur and magnificence amidst the splendor of the icebergs at the pole, and he leaps through the glory and power of the hurricanes like a trout that is sportin' amongst the ripples of a brook. He's a large baste with large ideas, more intillictual than the iliphant, and with a heart as tinder as wan of these little red-footed pigeons on the roof.

For he isn't anny fish, the whale isn't, but he's warm-blooded like a man or a dog, with more gratitude than the wan and less suspicion than the other—and I don't know why I'm sayin' "he" all the time, for the faymale whales is equally mammalian and ginteel.[3]

'Twas this same Tim O'Meara I'm tellin' you of that understood whales as no man has iver understood thim before or afther, for the solitude and grandeur of the whale was in his own nature, and the melancholy of the whale was in his wild and tinder heart. And a roamer and a rover was this Tim O'Meara, and the rims of his eyelids was red with the salt of manny seas. 'Twas the woes of Ireland that drove him from her shores, and set him wanderin' here and there—the griefs of Ireland, and the impossibility of doin' anything about thim, on account of the Sassenach[4] that was mainly causin' thim. I have no prejudices of anny kind in me heart against anny man nor anny man's country—unless a giniral feelin' that 'twould be a good deal betther if there wasn't anny British Empire anny-wheres could be called a prejudice. Which it could not, for 'tis merely good sinse and sound logic. And this Tim O'Meara, me ancestor, was the same as me in his feelin's.

"If I could but spake to the King of England, Ireland, and Scotland personal," says he to him-silf oftentimes, "we might patch somethin' up betwixt us. But I will not bandy words with anny man less than the king himsilf! 'Twould not be fittin' for thim to do so that was kings in Ireland in the ould days. If I had me rights, wan of the thrones that he's sittin' on this day would be mine!"

And 'twas at sea he lived mostly, for the shores of inhabited countries would always put him in mind he didn't have anny happy country of his own; and 'twas fishin' and whalin' that he made his most notable success at. Greenland and Iceland was known to him, and the coasts of Labrador, and manny a wild rock that was islanded lonesome in the wild seas. 'Twas often he would sit in his boat amongst the sparklin' icebergs, singin' to his Irish harp, and watchin' thim Scandinavian fishers and whalers goin' back and forth 'twixt North America and Norway—for the bould men came and wint for long years before anny man bothered with the notion of makin' anny sittlements over here.

---

[3]*mammalian* (ma mā′li ən) *and ginteel.* The term *mammalian* merely refers to an animal that gives milk to its young, but Mr. O'Meara couples it with *genteel* to suggest that whales possess all the attributes of human beings.

---

[4]*Sassenach* (sas′ə nək), English. The name was first given to the Saxons of England by the original Gaelic (gāl′ik) inhabitants of Ireland and Great Britain.

And wan day whilst he was sittin' on wan of his lonely islands, singin' to the sea gulls and the seals, he heard some great crayture bellowin' and moanin' and sighin' and whooshin' in the vicinity, and he clambered to an eminence of rock and gazed about him.

'Twas a big faymale whale, and she was rollin' her bulk about, and bangin' around and sprawlin' hersilf against a reef near by, which the ebbin' tide had lift uncovered.

"What's the baste doin'?" says Tim to himsilf. And then he realized she was moanin' with pain as she batthered hersilf and twisted against the crooked stones.

"She's scratchin' her back on the reef," says Tim. And it puzzled him, for he'd never heard these bastes had fleas. He got into his dory, and rowed out as near as he dared to the turmoil she was makin'. And thin he saw that she was scratchin' her back indade.

Half a dozen broken harpoons was stickin' into it, and the intilligint animal was tryin' to get thim caught and hooked amongst the crooked rocks of the reef and pull and scrape hersilf rid of thim.

"Poor crayture!" says Tim. For though he had hunted manny a wan of thim to its death, gradual he had come to sympathize with thim and pity thim, for it was gettin' to his mind that they're really tinder-hearted bastes, full of kindness and gintleness there ain't anny feasible way for thim to expriss. "Poor crayture!" says Tim.

And just thin she cocked her eye in his direction, the poor sufferin' mammalian, and looked at him as speculative and considerin' and pitiful as a stray pup with a thorn in his foot. And she lay quiet and moaned.

"Do ye want me to pull thim out, ma'am?" says Tim, his heart bleedin' for her.

There was somethin' so respictable lookin' about her, like she might be the mother of ten childher, all bloated up with cares and nursin' and tay-drinkin' and housework, that he couldn't hilp callin' her ma'am.

She moaned again, and looked at him steady —a whale bein' the only wan of God's other craytures that can look a Christian steady in the eye and give him thought for thought. And that way they continued to gaze at aich other for some minutes, and the kindness that was in the heart of aich wan pinitrated to the bosom of the other—and there ain't anny matronly crayture annywheres that has an ampler bosom than a faymale whale.

"I'll do it, ma'am," says Timothy O'Meara, as she moaned again, and he stipped aboord of her and began pullin' out harpoons.

"Roll over a bit, till I get that ugly divil out of your side," says Tim. And, as if she understood, she rolled a bit, standin' the pain of all this extraction with the gallantry and fortitude of a woman. He blushed when he saw 'twas wan of his own old harpoons, with his initials in the shaft of it.

"And I'd axe your pardon, ma'am, if I thought ye remembered," says Tim; "I would that—Mrs. MacLirr!"

For it came to him with a rush and a shout what the name of the baste should be. The ould and ancient Irish deity of the boundless seas, before Saint Patrick came and made us Christians (praise God!), was Mananan MacLirr,[5] and this hugeous and intilligint baste, Timothy perceived, could be none other thin the wife of Mananan MacLirr, she hersilf. And 'twas always Mrs. MacLirr he called her iver afther that.

"Now, thin, Mrs. MacLirr," says Tim, "there's but wan more, and I'll be as aisy as I can!"

But 'twas nearly Tim's destruction, for whin Mrs. MacLirr felt the last barb lave her body she gave such a jump of joy and gratitude as took her twenty fathoms toward the smilin' sun, and down again she spanked her two thousand hundherd weight[6] into the wather, while the bould Tim wint whirlin' through a flock of screamin' gulls.

Back he swum to land, and from the beach he saw her out at sea, leapin' and cavortin' in her joy, and blowin' great fountains into the air.

---

[5]The old and ancient deity...Mananan MacLirr (man'a-nan mak lēr'). Mananan, son of Lir (Mac means "son of"), was lord of the sea and guide to the Islands of the Dead which lay beyond it. When St. Patrick christianized Ireland in the fifth century, the worship of the old Irish gods disappeared.

[6]two thousand hundherd weight, 200,000 pounds.

And thin she came as near as she could to the shore where she saw him standin'. And she poked first one eye out of the wather and thin the other, and she rolled and capered—tryin' to thank him, she was.

"Don't mintion it, Mrs. MacLirr!" says Tim, smilin' at the poor crayture, and at the same time feelin' the pathos of her, too. For 'tis wan of the most touchin' things about a whale that she has inside of her the sprightliness and coyness and good humor of a pup or a kitten, and wants to frolic and fawn and cuddle in her friends' laps; and, coupled with that, she has the bulk of an ocean liner.

If I hadn't heard it from me own grandfather and he from his grandad before him, and so by word of mouth down a line of O'Mearas, I would find it hard mesilf to belave all the details of the fri'ndship that grew up between Mrs. MacLirr and Timothy O'Meara. On all his voyages hither and yon she accompanied him and 'twas for her sake he give up huntin'

whales entirely. It was through her introduction and patronage that he became acquainted in a friendly way with manny another of thim splendid and poetic lords of the briny Atlantic.

Often he would sit in a cave on a rocky island playing the wild traditional music on his Irish harp, and singin' his Gaelic songs[7] across the waves, with the aurora borealis hangin' over him like a halo, and Mrs. MacLirr leapin' in the moonlight. And sometimes as manny as twinty or thirty of her friends would join her for a social avenin'—over whole leagues of tameless wather the harp of the O'Meara would be flingin' its strains of music and the sea would be spoutin' and boilin' with the magnificent dances of the whales, and misty moonbeams driftin' over all!

---

[7]*Gaelic* (gāl′ik) *songs*, old songs which had come down from the Gaels, the original inhabitants of Ireland and Great Britain.

He made a kind of a harness that fitted over Mrs. MacLirr's big head and fastened his boat to it with a rope, and he gave up sailin' entirely, for it was slow work and useless compared with the propulsion and the power that was now at his command. Or sometimes he would sit upon her back with the boat trailin' along behind and guide her by tappin' her on wan side of the head or the other, like wan of thim Orientals does with an iliphant. And a fine sight it must have been to see Mrs. MacLirr and me ancestor, Timothy O'Meara, ridin' a storm—with Timothy singin' and playin' his wild minstrelsy out of his wild heart, and the forked tongues of lightnin' showing the gleeful eyes of Mrs. MacLirr and the floatin' red beard and hair of Timothy O'Meara as they bulged across the boilin' seas.

Wan time ('twas in the winter of 1620 anno domino[8] is the word as it came down to me), Mrs. MacLirr and me bould ancestor were cruisin' quietly along about sunset, two or three hundherd miles due east of the prisint site of Boston, when what should they see limpin' up from the horizon like a draggled-wing duck but wan of thim small ships.

Timothy could tell aven at that distance that she was some sort of a family ship with but little nautical knowledge aboord of her annywheres, from the way she was bein' handled, and he steered Mrs. MacLirr nearer to her.

It was very near indade he got before aither of thim was noticed by the people on boord, for there was some kind of a row goin' on in the midst of this little windjammer that previnted anny of thim from takin' notice. Tim circled round her and came up behind and he noticed a signboard on the stern with the word *Mayflower* painted onto it with big letters. And just about the time he noticed that, Mrs. MacLirr, bein' full of fayminine curiosity, cocked her starboard eye over the rail of the vissil to take a look at what was transpirin' on the deck. And at the same time she opened her mouth to smile, bein' friendly by nature, and no longer frightened at the ways and works of humankind.

Anny wan that ain't used to havin' a whale ogle him in the eye and raise up and smile at him is apt to be narvous at the first expariance. And the people on boord the *Mayflower* are scarcely to be blamed for not realizin' the beneficince of Mrs. MacLirr's interest, for her lineamints was decaivin'.

There was wan gineral shout from the scores of people gathered on the deck and they scurried in all directions. But they couldn't run far, for the ship was small. And all the time they was cryin' out.

"A witch! A witch!" Timothy heard a dozen of thim callin' at the same time.

"She is a witch and she has called up a fiend out of the deep to save her!" says wan man.

" 'Tis the divil ridin' upon a dragon!" says another.

Tim, he leapt to the deck, and he walked right up to a solemn-lookin' man in black, who was standin' steady, with a hymnbook in wan hand and a soord in the other, apparently too proud to let himself be scairt, and he says to him very polite, says Tim:

"I'm the O'Meara, at your service, sir; and I am not plased with bein' mistook for the divil. I'll thank ye, sir, to ordher these people of yours to be more civil, or else there'll be trouble aboord the *Mayflower*. I take ye for the boss of this outfit, and I speak to ye as such."

"Mr. O'Meara," says this fella with the soord, "your appearance was the trifle unexpicted, as ye come red-bearded on that monster out of th' bloody wathers of the sunset. And I was shaken m'silf for a moment, albeit I have fought both man and fiend. And ye came on us dazzlin' like the flames of Tophet,"[9] says he, "at a time whin we were considerin' most serious matters of a ghostly nature."

"Be that as it may," says Tim, "go aisy with the divil stuff, or ye'll have to lave my part of the ocean. I'm a sinsitive man, and I will not

---

[8]*1620 anno domino.* The Latin phrase *anno Domini* (an'ō dom'ə nī) means "in the year of our Lord." Mr. O'Meara means that the event occurred 1620 years after the birth of Christ.

[9]*flames of Tophet* (tō'fet), fires of hell. Tophet was a place south of Jerusalem where the Jews offered human sacrifices to strange gods. (Jeremiah 19:4-6.) Later, when bonfires were kept burning there to consume rubbish, Tophet became symbolic of hell.

be miscalled out of me name. And what are these serious matters of yours?"

The man with the soord pointed to a lass that Tim now noticed for the first time.

Standin' by the mast she was, gold-haired and beautiful, with her chin in the air and a fire in her eyes. He seen manny of that ship's company was against her, and his heart wint out to her at wance, as was iver the case with Tim O'Meara whin he seen virtue and beauty in distress.

"She is on trial," says the man with the soord.

"She's innocint!" says Tim, prompt as a fist. "What's she charged with?"

"She whistled like a man," says he, "and that is an unseemly thing in a maiden. And she danced with her shadow as wan possessed by demons might. And when wan of the cocks crew, she crew again like a cock."

"What great matther is all this!" says Tim.

"Is this not the Sabbath day?" says he.

"Ye have the advantage of me there," says Tim. " 'Tis more than a year since I lost count. Come hither, colleen!"

The girl came forward, and she looked Tim straight between the eyes. And all the ship's company gathered as near as they dared, for their fright still clung to thim.

"Are ye guilty of these terrible crimes, as charged, my dear?" says Tim, smilin' at the darlin' thing.

"The sunshine seemed good," says she, smilin' back at him, "and I cut a bit of a caper on the deck."

There was a groan wint up from manny on that ship, but Tim and this swate crayture was lookin' so intintly at wan another they niver heeded it.

"They were plannin' to duck me over the side," said she, "and I cried out for help. And thin you came, and they said I was a witch and had called up a fiend from the sea!"

Tim, his forehead turned as red as his hair with exasperation. "Fine doin's this is!" says he, turnin' on thim all. "Where do you come from?"

They tould him they was fleein' from England.

" 'Tis more or less me own case," says Tim. "There's much in common between us—though I can't precisely put the name on it! At anny rate," says he, "we're both at outs with England —and that's somethin'! Drop this nonsinse about the colleen here, and I'll let ye sail the rest of the way acrost me ocean," he says. "But otherwise," says he, "Mrs. MacLirr and me will have siviral things to say to youse."

"Mrs. MacLirr?" says the man with the soord.

"Me pet whale there," says Tim.

They all turned toward her, where she was loomin' over the port side of the vissil, waitin' on Tim's word—and Tim noticed a curious thing: Mrs. MacLirr's eye was fastened in a stare upon the lass that Tim was befri'ndin', and there was a glint like 'twas jealousy in her look. And the girl looked back at Mrs. MacLirr with no friendliness in her gaze.

Whin they seen Mrs. MacLirr lookin' like that, and the girl lookin' back at her, the anxiety of thim Mayflowers was aroused again.

"Burn her!" says wan ould woman, with the shriek of a banshee in her voice. "Burn Mary Mullins—she's a witch!" And manny of the rist of thim began to murmur and repate it.

"Mrs. MacLirr," says Tim, "will you kindly open your mouth a few fathoms?"

And whin she done so he pointed at it loomin' forninst[10] the ship there, and he says:

---

[10] *forninst*, near. [*Irish*]

"If there is anny more talk about burnin' this young woman, or about witchcraft," says he, "into that mouth ye go, two at a time, as fast as I can throw ye from the deck here!"

And with Mrs. MacLirr dominatin' the situation in that way, Timothy had the trump hand[11] for the minute. But at the same time he was worried, for his words and actions only seemed to make thim the surer that there must be witchcraft somewheres about, and that Mary Mullins had called him up by the power of witchcraft to save her.

He called her to one side, and he bade the others to stand back while he conferred with her—and as he done so he realized that the circumstance looked bad in itsilf, in the eyes of the ship's company.

"Mary Mullins, my dear," says he, "I don't seem to be really helpin' you anny, with all the will in the world to do so. But there's wan thing certain, there's none shall burn ye, my child, while Timothy O'Meara is bossin' this part of the ocean!"

She laughed and she said: "Thank ye, Mr. O'Meara! And they wouldn't dare try to annyhow, on the ship here. They couldn't do it without burnin' the ship. It's a function they will have to postpone until we land somewheres."

"By the Lord," says Tim, "thin they'll niver land! I'll take ye aboord Mrs. MacLirr with me, and we'll batther the ould tub to pieces!"

"Ye'll not do that," says she, "for there's manny good people on boord here."

"That's what's the matther with thim evidently," says Tim, "they're too good!"

She laughed at that again, and thin she said: "No, Mr. O'Meara, I mane manny fine men and women, that would have nothin' to do whativer with this witchcraft idea if they were not scared to death. There's me sister Priscilla,[12]" she says, "as swate a girl as iver lived; and there's a couple of young men as is tryin' to shine up to her—dacent people, all of thim. And they'll have to be landed," says she, "or we'll niver get the United States of America started."

"Mary Mullins," says Tim, "how did ye come by that name? It sounds Irish to me."

"There must be Irish blood in us somewheres, Tim," says she, "or how could we have the name? And I think 'tis that Irish blood they're mistakin' for diviltry," says she. "They don't understand laughin' and dancin' and fancifulness."

And she smiled at me bould Tim, with the come-hither in her eyes—and there's no use postponin' the revelation anny longer; from that instant they was both madly in love with aich other.

"Moira,"[13] says Tim, just above a whisper, "by the hivens, I think 'tis a witch ye are, indade!"

"Tim," says she, in a low voice, laughin' and lookin' about her, "I belave ye have the rights of it! Sometimes I think I am!"

"'Tis somethin' to be carefully presarved, and not banished out of the world," says he.

He urged her wance more to come with him at wance. But she would not lave her sister behind her, nor anny other of the wans she liked.

"Tim," she says, "ye must be aisy with these people! For they'll niver get to land unless ye hilp thim. The rudder's gone from the ould tub now, and a bit of a gale would finish things."

"Come aboord Mrs. MacLirr with yer sister!" says Tim, "and have no care for the rist of thim!"

"No," says she; "and while we're on the subject, I don't like this Mrs. MacLirr of yours anny too well. And by the looks of her, she doesn't like me!"

And Mrs. MacLirr was peerin' at Tim and Moira in a way to confirm that, her eyes red and jealous.

There wasn't but wan way that Tim could see—to stay aboord the ship with the colleen until it landed, to protect her, and thin to marry her and take her away.

[11]*Timothy had the trump hand*, Timothy was in a position to make the others do as he wished. In card games a trump is any playing card of a suit that for the time ranks higher than the other suits. A hand of trumps only would be an unbeatable hand.

[12]*Priscilla*, famous in Longfellow's *Courtship of Miles Standish* as the girl who married John Alden. She is a real historical character.

[13]*Moira* (moi'rə), an Irish variant of the name Mary.

So he harnessed Mrs. MacLirr to the *Mayflower,* and he give her the signal full-speed-ahead, and whin the nixt mornin' came he drew up by the side of Plymouth Rock—the date he always remimbered, 'twas the siventeenth of March, Patrick's Day.[14] 'Tis written on that bit o' rock somewheres, if it hasn't been rubbed off.

And Timothy and Moira climbed aboord Mrs. MacLirr and sailed off and was married and sittled South Boston, which was the first permanent sittlement in New England, and predominates with their kinsmen to this day.[15] And if you don't belave that, go and look it up in the Boston tiliphone directory. And that's how the United States of America got its start, praise God!

And [said Jack] they lived happy in South Boston ever after!

I wish [said the old gentleman] as I could say the end was all happiness. But the truth is, it wasn't.

The most inordinate, unpleasant, and unreasonable jealousy sprung up betwixt Moira O'Meara and Mrs. MacLirr. For Tim, he went no more a-rovin', and Mrs. MacLirr used for to spout and caper in vain in the harbor below where the O'Mearas had built their house and was raisin' their childher. Tim, he paid but little attention to her; but Moira, she would call out to her now and thin, "Go away, you great ugly baste, you!" For well she knew that Mrs. MacLirr was trying to tempt her husband back to the wild, free life he'd lived before he married and sittled down, and that's a thing as no wife iver likes.

And wan spring Mrs. MacLirr disappeared, and ceased to haunt the harbor, and Moira be-

laved she was rid of her, and of the menace of her, foriver. And as for Tim, with the fickleness of all men he thought nothin' more about Mrs. MacLirr's tinder heart, wan way or the other, nor did he realize how bruised it was by his neglect. He should have known that the intilligint and sinsitive whale, bein' one of the most lovin' of all bastes, is therefore equally agitated whin 'tis insulted. For after Mrs. MacLirr had been gone six weeks, back she come wan afthernoon, and a hundherd whales was with her!

'Twas in the afthernoon of a breezy day whin Tim and Moira seen thim comin' into the harbor, and 'twas a sight majestic and splendid to see these noble monsters of the spacious deep movin' forward in naval formation, jettin' great fountains into the air, which the wind whipped to spray and the sunlight wove into flauntin' rainbows.

"Tim," says his wife, turnin' pale, for she had recognized Mrs. MacLirr in the lead of thim, "they mane diviltry!"

"They do not," says Tim; "they're all my ould friends! They've called on us for a bit of a frolic and some music!"

And he wint and got his harp, and sated himsilf upon a rock in front of his house, and out acrost the movin' wathers, he flung the wild music of his ancestors. And he sang the afthernoon away, and the rainbows ceased whin the sun laid low and level in the sky, and all thim scores of great mammalians danced in the red sunset; they danced a dance that was like the sport of naked thunders in the caves above the firmamint where the ragin' storms is made.

---

[14]*the date...'twas the siventeenth of March, Patrick's Day.* The Pilgrims landed at Plymouth on December 21, 1620, not, as Mr. O'Meara declared, on March 17, which the Irish celebrate as the feast of St. Patrick.

[15]*predominates with their kinsmen to this day.* South Boston is largely Irish.

"They intind no good," says Moira; "they're workin' themselves up to do some mischief!"

"They're wild with joy," says Tim; "they've found the O'Meara and his music again!"

And he harped the sunset out, and with the twilight the wather changed from burnin' brass to silver, and he harped the twilight out, and with the gatherin' dusk the wather turned to fire again; a phosphorescent fire it was that spouted whin they blew and rose and waved like plumes and fell again.

" 'Tis hatred and revenge they are afther!" cried Moira.

"They come in love and fri'ndship!" says Tim, exalted with his ringin' harp.

And which it was, no wan iver knew. As the dark thickened they all turned in the sea as wan whale, at a signal from Mrs. MacLirr, and came rushin' up the beach on the crest and reach of the risin' tide, as if they would fling themselves flamin' out of their fiery sea against the O'Meara house and the rocks on which it stood.

"The saints defend us!" screamed Moira, her knees turnin' wake and feeble.

Mrs. MacLirr was in the lead and comin' fast, but the wather receded from in under her far up the shore, and she hit her head against a point of rock, and groaned and died; and a dozen more was stranded and extinguished, perishin' like exploded rockets.

But Mrs. MacLirr, she give Tim just wan look before she died.

"I'm afraid," says Tim, lookin' melancholy at Mrs. MacLirr's remains, "that she's committed suicide out of a broken heart! Why couldn't ye have been nicer to her, Moira?"

"She tried to murther us all!" says Moira.

And nobody is quite sure to this day which the truth was. But it give Timothy and Moira somethin' to argue about for manny years—which is always a handy thing in ivery marriage. But don't ayther wan of you iver tell me again that the Irish niver projuced anny great navigators, nor great sailors, nor great whalers, nor great pioneer settlers; or I'll take wan of youse over aich knee and larrup ye, as I have done often in the past and as I am still well able to do, praise God!

1. How did Terence and Jack O'Meara prod their father into telling the tale of Timothy O'Meara and the whale? What attitude did Mr. O'Meara pretend to have toward his sons when he told the tale? How do you know that this was a pretended rather than a genuine attitude?

2. What was the origin of Mrs. MacLirr's name? What characteristics did she possess?

3. What historical facts and situations does Mr. O'Meara employ to make his story seem believable? What part of his story places the greatest strain upon the imagination? How does he develop this part so as to make it convincing?

4. What alleged characteristics of Irish temperament do you find in Mr. O'Meara? Do all Irishmen have such characteristics?

5. Why do you think the author wrote the story in Irish dialect? How does the dialect add to the appeal of the story?

The well-spun yarn

When Timothy O'Meara's sons goaded him into spinning a yarn, they knew in advance some of the qualities they might expect to find when, with his pipe drawing sweetly, Mr. O'Meara settled into his story. For Mr. O'Meara was a master of the Irish tale; he had the breadth of imagination necessary to conjure up a wide and sweeping story and to create characters whose heroic proportions would fit the adventures designed for them. But Mr. O'Meara knew that a wide-ranging yarn and larger-than-life characters were not enough. As a storyteller he realized that such a tale as his demanded words that would reflect the magnitude of the tale and catch something of the grandeur and beauty of the world in which his great characters adventured. So he matched his words to his theme, and gave his listeners a tale in which heroic imaginings were described in grand and exaggerated language. Prepare to read to the class the passage which you believe best represents this art. Why do you think this passage is outstanding?

Four Generations

RUTH SUCKOW

The process of becoming American and of replacing folkways brought from other lands with American ways of thinking and living has not always been easy. Children of immigrants have naturally forsaken the ways of their parents and have often felt an element of pride in losing the Old-World identity which marked them as different. Ruth Suckow skillfully portrays this situation in the following short story. Her own grandparents were born in Germany. She was reared in Iowa, where her observations of immigrant farmers and their descendants supplied her with first-class material for the ingenious realism for which she is famous.

1

"Move just a little closer together—the little girl more toward the center— that's good. Now I think we'll get it."

The photographer dived once more under the black cloth.

"Stand back, Ma," a husky voice said. "You'll be in the picture."

Aunt Em stepped hastily back with a panicky look. Mercy, she didn't want to show! She hadn't time to get her dress changed yet, had come right out of the kitchen, where she was baking pies, to see the photograph taken. She was in her old dark-blue kitchen dress and had her hair just wadded up until she could get time to comb it. It didn't give her much time for dressing up, having all this crowd to cook for.

The boys, and Uncle Chris, standing away back on the edges, grinned appreciatively. Fred whispered to Clarence, "Laugh if Ma'd got in it." The way she had jumped back, and her unconsciousness of the ends sticking up from her little wad of hair, delighted the boys. When they looked at each other, a little remembering glint came into their eyes.

There was quite a crowd of onlookers. Aunt Em, Uncle Chris in his good trousers, and his shirt sleeves, his sunburned face dark brown above the white collar that Aunt Em had made him put on because of Charlie's. Uncle Gus and Aunt Sophie Spfierschlage had come over to dinner, and stood back against the white house wall, Aunt Sophie mountainous in her checked gingham. The boys, of course, and Bernie Schuldt who was working for Chris, and another fellow who had come to look at some hogs and who was standing there, conscious of his old overalls and torn straw hat, mumbling, "Well, didn't know I was gona find anything like this goin' on."...Charlie's wife, Ella, had been given a chair where she could have a good view of the proceedings. She tried to smile and wave her handkerchief when little Phyllis looked around at her. Then she put the handkerchief to her eyes, lifting up her glasses with their narrow light shell rims, still smiling a little painfully. She had to think from how far Katherine had come....

Aunt Em and Aunt Sophie were whispering, "Ain't it a shame Edna couldn't get over! They coulda took one of Chris and her and Marine and Merle, with Grandpa, too....That little one looks awful cute, don't she?...Well, what takes him so long? Grandpa won't sit there

much longer. I should think they coulda had it taken by this time a'ready."

They all watched the group on the lawn. They had decided that the snow bushes[1] would "make a nice background." The blossoms were gone, but the leaves were dark green and thick. What a day for taking a picture! It would be so much better out here than in the house. Katherine had made them take it right after dinner, so that little Phyllis would not be late for her nap—nothing must ever interfere with that child's nap. It was the brightest, hottest time of day. The tall orange summer lilies seemed to open and shimmer in the heat. Things were so green —the country lawn with its thick grass, the heavy foliage of the maple trees against the blue summery sky of July. The thin varnished supports of the camera stand glittered yellow and sticky. The black cloth over the lens looked thick, dense, hot. The photographer's shirt was dazzling white in the sun, and when he drew his head out from under the cloth his round face shone pink. His coat made a black splotch tossed on the grass.

"The little girl more toward the center."

All three of the others tried anxiously to make little Phyllis more conspicuous. "Here, we've

—————
[1] *snow bushes,* snowball bushes, shrubs with white flowers in large ball-like clusters.

got to have you showing—my, my!—whether the rest of us do or not," Charlie said jovially. Grandpa's small aged frail hand moved a little as if he were going to draw the child in front of him, but, with a kind of delicacy, did not quite touch her arm.

They had to wait while a fleecy cloud crossed the sun, putting a brief cool shadow over the vivid lawn. In that moment the onlookers were aware of the waiting group. Four generations! Great-grandfather, grandfather, mother, daughter. It was all the more impressive when they thought of Katherine and Phyllis having come from so many miles away. The snowball bushes were densely green behind them—almost dusky in the heat. Grandpa's chair had been placed out there—a homemade chair of willow branches. To think that these four belonged together!

Grandpa, sitting in the chair, might have belonged to another world. Small, bent like a little old troll, foreign with his black cambric cap, his blue far-apart peasant eyes with their still gaze, his thin silvery beard. His hands, gnarled from years of farm work in a new country, clasped the homemade knotted stick that he held between his knees. His feet, in old felt slippers with little tufted wool flowers, were set flat on the ground. He wore the checked shirt of an old farmer....It hardly seemed that Char-

lie was his son. Plump and soft, dressed in the easy garments, of good quality and yet a trifle careless, of Middle Western small-town prosperity. His shaven face, paler now than it used to be and showing his age in the folds that had come about his chin; his glasses with shell rims and gold bows; the few strands of grayish hair brushed across his pale luminous skull. A small-town banker. Now he looked both impressed and shamefaced at having the photograph taken. ...And then Katherine, taking after no one knew whom. Slender, a little haggard and worn, still young, her pale delicate face and the cords of her long soft throat, her little collarbones, her dark intelligent weak eyes behind her thick-rimmed glasses. Katherine had always been like that. Refined, "finicky," studious, thoughtful. Her hand, slender and a trifle sallow, lay on Phyllis' shoulder.

Phyllis....Her little yellow frock made her vivid as a canary bird against the dark green foliage. Yellow—the relatives did not know whether they liked that bright yellow. Still, she did look sweet. They hadn't thought Katherine's girl would be so pretty. Of course the care that Katherine took of her—everything had to revolve around that child. There was something faintly exotic about her liquid brown eyes with their jet-black lashes, the shining straight gold-brown hair, the thick bangs, that lay, parted a little and damp with the heat, on the pure white of her forehead. Her little precise "Eastern accent".... Grandpa looked wonderingly at the bare arms, round and soft and tiny, white and moist in the heat. Fragile blue veins made a flowerlike tracery of indescribable purity on the white skin. Soft, tender, exquisite...*ach*,[2] what a little girl was here, like a princess!

The cloud passed. Katherine's white and Phyllis' yellow shone out again from the green. The others stood back watching, a heavy stolid country group against the white wall of the farmhouse that showed bright against the farther green of the grove. Beyond lay the orchard and the rank green spreading cornfields where little silvery clouds of gnats went shimmering over the moist richness of the leaves.

"Watch—he's taking it now!"

In the breathless silence they could hear the long whirr and rush of a car on the brown country road beyond the grove.

2

Well, the picture was taken. Everyone was glad to be released from the strain.

Grandpa's chair had been placed nearer the house, under some maple trees. Charlie stayed out there with him awhile. It was his duty, he felt, to talk to the old man awhile when he was here at the farm. He didn't get over very often —well, it was a hundred miles from Rock River, and the roads weren't very good up here in Sac township. His car stood out at the edge of the grove in the shade. The new closed car that he had lately bought, a "coach," opulent, shining, with its glass and upholstery and old-blue draperies, there against the background of the evergreen grove with its fallen branches and pieces of discarded farm machinery half visible in the deepest shade.

It wasn't really very hard to get away from Rock River and the bank. He and Ella took plenty of trips. He ought to come to see his father more than he did. But he seemed to have nothing to say to Grandpa. The old man had scarcely been off the place for years.

"Well, Pa, you keep pretty well, do you?"

"*Ja*,[3] pretty goot...*ja*, for so old as I am ——"

"Oh, now, you mustn't think of yourself as so old."

Charlie yawned, recrossed his legs. He lighted a cigar.

"Chris' corn doing pretty well this season?"

"*Ach,* dot I know nuttings about. Dey don't tell me nuttings."

"Well, you've had your day at farming, Pa."

"*Ja...ja, ja....*"

He fumbled in the pocket of his coat, drew out an ancient black pipe.

Charlie said cheerfully: "Have some tobacco?" He held out a can.

The old man peered into it, sniffed. "*Ach,* dot stuff? No, no, dot is shust like shavings. I smoke de real tobacco."

---

[2]*ach* (äн), a German exclamation like *oh*.

[3]*Ja* (yä), yes. [German]

"Like it strong, hey?"

They both puffed away.

Grandpa sat in the old willow chair. His blue eyes had a look half wistful, half resentful. Charlie was his oldest child. He would have liked to talk with Charlie. He was always wishing that Charlie would come, always planning how he would tell him things—about how the old ways were going and how the farmers did now, how none of them told him things—but when Charlie came, then that car was always standing there ready to take him right back home again, and there seemed nothing to be said. He always remembered Charlie as the young man, the little boy who used to work beside him in the field—and then when Charlie came, he was this stranger. Charlie was a town man now. He owned a bank! He had forgotten all about the country, and the old German ways. To think of Charlie, their son, being a rich banker, smoking cigars, riding around in a fine carriage with glass windows....

"Dot's a fine wagon you got dere."

Charlie laughed. "That's a coach, Pa."

"So? Coach, is dot what you call it? Like de old kings, like de emperors, de Kaisers,[4] rode around in. *Ja,* you can live in dot. Got windows and doors, curtains—is dere a table too, stove—no? *Ja,* dot's a little house on wheels."

He pursed out his lips comically. But *ach,* such a carriage! He could remember when he was glad enough to get to town in a lumber wagon. Grandma and the children used to sit in the back on the grain sacks. His old hands felt of the smooth knots of his stick. He went back, back, into reverie....He muttered just above his breath: "*Ach, ja, ja, ja*...dot was all so long ago...."

Charlie was silent too. He looked at the car, half drew out his watch, put it back....Katherine crossed the lawn. His eyes followed her. Bluish-gray, a little faded behind his modern glasses—there was resentment, bewilderment, wistfulness in them at the same time, and loneliness. He was thinking of how he used to bring Kittie out here to the farm when she was a little girl, when Chris used to drive to Germantown

and get them with a team and two-seated buggy. They had come oftener than now when they had the car...."Papa, *really* did you live out here—on this farm?" He had been both proud and a little jealous because she wasn't sunburned and wiry, like Chris' children. A little slim, long-legged, soft-skinned, dark-eyed girl. "Finicky" about what she ate and what she did—he guessed he and Ella had encouraged her in that. Well, he hadn't had much when he was a child, and he'd wanted his little girl to have the things he'd missed. He'd wanted her to have more than his brothers' and sisters' children. He was Charlie, the one who lived in town, the successful one. Music lessons, drawing lessons, college...and here she had grown away from her father and mother. Chris' children lived close around him, but it sometimes seemed to him that he and Ella had lost Kittie, living away off there in the East. And when she came home, although she was carefully kind and dutiful and affectionate, there was something aloof. He thought jealously, maybe it would have been better if they hadn't given her all those things, had kept her right at home with them....It hadn't been as much pleasure as he had anticipated having his little grandchild there. There was her "schedule" that Kittie was so pernickety about. He'd been proud to have people in Rock River see her beauty and perfection, but he hadn't been able to take her around and show her off as he'd hoped.

All day he had been seeing a slim fastidious girl in a white dress and white hair ribbons and black patent-leather slippers, clinging to his hand with little soft fingers when he took her out to see the cows and the pigs...."Well, Kittie, do you wish we lived out here instead of in town?" She shook her head, and her small underlip curled just a little....

He saw Chris and Gus off near the house. They could talk about how crops were coming, and he could tell them, with a banker's authority, about business conditions. He stirred uneasily, got up, yawned, stretched up his arms, said with a little touch of shame:

"Well, Pa, guess I'll go over and talk to Chris awhile. I'll see you again before we leave."

---

[4] *Kaisers* (kī′zərz), emperors of Germany.

"*Ja*—" The old man did not try to keep him. He watched Charlie's plump figure cross the grass. *Ja,* he had more to say to the young ones....

3

Aunt Em was through baking. She had gone into the bedroom to "get cleaned up." She had brought out chairs to the front porch. "Sit out here. Here's a chair, Ella—here, Katherine. *Ach,* Sophie, take a better chair than that." "Naw, this un'll do for me, Em."

"The womenfolks" — Katherine shuddered away from that phrase. She had always, ever since she was a little girl, despised sitting about this way with "the womenfolks." Planted squat in their chairs, rocking, yawning, telling over and over about births and deaths and funerals and sicknesses. There was a kind of feminine grossness about it that offended what had always been called her "finickiness."

Her mother enjoyed it. She was different from Aunt Em and Aunt Sophie, lived in a different way—a small plump elderly woman with waved grayish-silvery hair and a flowered voile dress with little fussy laces, feminine strapped slippers. But still there was something that she liked about sitting here in the drowsy heat and going over and over things with the other women. Sometimes, to Katherine's suffering disgust, she would add items about the birth of Katherine herself—"Well, I thought sure Kittie was going to be a boy. She kicked so hard——" "Oh, *Mother,* spare us!" Aunt Em would give a fat comfortable laugh—"Don't look so rambunctious now, does she? Kittie, ain't you ever gona get a little flesh on your bones? You oughta get out and ride the horses around like Edna does."

Aunt Sophie Spfierschlage—that was the way she sat rocking, her feet flat on the floor, her stomach comfortably billowing, beads of sweat on her heavy chin and lips and around the roots of her stiff dull hair. Well, thank goodness she was only Aunt Em's sister, she wasn't really related to the Kleins. Aunt Em was bad enough.

They used to laugh over her fastidious disgust, when she sat here, a delicate critical little girl who didn't want to get on one of the horses or jump from rafters into the hay. "Kittie thinks that's terrible. Well, Kittie, that's the way things happen." "*Ach,* she won't be so squeamish when she grows up and has three or four of her own." Now she sat beside them, delicate, still too thin to Aunt Em's amazement. "Ain't you got them ribs covered up yet? What's the matter? Don't that man of yours give you enough to eat?"—her soft skin pale and her eyes dark from the heat, dressed with a kind of fastidious precision, an ultrarefinement: a fragile bar pin holding the soft white silk of her blouse, her fine dark hair drooping about her face. "Well, you ain't changed much since you got married!" Aunt Em had said. They expected to admit her now to their freemasonry, to have *her* add interesting items about the birth of Phyllis.

Phyllis—her little darling! As if the exquisite miracle of Phyllis could have anything in common with these things! Katherine suffered just as she had always suffered from even small vulgarities. But she sat courteous and ladylike now, a slight dutiful smile on her lips.

"Where does she get them brown eyes? They ain't the color of yours, are they? Turn around and let's have a look at you—no, I thought yours was kinda darker."

Aunt Em had come out now, had squatted down into another chair. "I guess her papa's got the brown eyes."

"Yes, I think she looks a little like Willis."

Ella said almost resentfully, "Well, I don't know whether she takes after Willis' folks or not, but I can't see that she looks one bit like Kittie or any of us."

"Well," Aunt Em said, "but look at Kittie. She don't look like you or Charlie neither. But I guess she's yours just the same, ain't she, Ella?...Say, you remember that Will Fuchs? *Ja,* his girl's got one they say don't belong to who it ought to. Her and that young Bender from over south—"

Katherine did not listen. How long before they could leave? She had thought it right to bring Phyllis over here where her great-grandfather lived, as her father had wished. But it seemed worse to her than ever. She knew that Aunt Em wouldn't let them go without something more to eat, another of her great heavy meals with pie and cake and coffee. Her mother had always said, as if in extenuation of her visible enjoyment of the visit and the food, "Well, Aunt Em means well. Why don't you try and talk with her? She wants to talk with you." But Aunt Em and the Spfierschlages and the whole place seemed utterly alien and horrible to Katherine. For a moment, while they had been taking the photograph out on the lawn, she had felt touched with a sense of beauty. But she had never belonged here. She felt at home in Willis' quiet old frame house in New England, with his precise elderly New England parents—"refinement," "culture," Willis' father reading "the classics," taking the *Atlantic Monthly* ever since their marriage. She had always felt that those were the kind of people she ought to have had, the kind of home. Of course she loved Father and Mother and was loyal to them. They depended upon her as their only child.

This porch! It seemed to express the whole of her visits to the farm. It was old-fashioned now—a long, narrow porch with a fancy railing, the posts trimmed with red. Her ancestral home! It was utterly alien to her.

They were talking to her again.

"Where's the girl—in taking her nap yet?"

"Yes, she's sleeping."

"*Ach,* you hadn't ought to make her sleep all the time she's off visiting. I baked a little piece of pie crust for her. I thought I'd give it to her while it was nice and warm."

"Oh, better not try to give her pie crust," Ella said warningly.

"*Ach,* that ain't gona hurt her—nice home-made pie. Mine always et that."

"*Ja,* mine did too."

Katherine's lips closed firmly. She couldn't hurry and hurt Father and Mother—but oh, to get Phyllis home! Father—he was always trying to give the child something she shouldn't have, he wanted to spoil her as he had tried to spoil Katherine herself....She shut her lips tight to steel herself against the pitifulness of the sudden vision of Father—getting so much older these last few years—looking like a child bereft of his toy when she had firmly taken away the things with

which he had come trotting happily home for his grandchild. He had gradually drawn farther and farther away. Once he had hurt her by saying significantly, when Phyllis had wanted a pink blotter in the bank, "You'll have to ask your mother. Maybe there's something in it to hurt you. *Grandpa* don't know." He had wanted to take Phyllis to a little cheap circus that had come to town, to show her off and exhibit her. Mother was more sympathetic, even a little proud of retailing to the other "ladies" how careful Katherine was in bringing up the child, what a "nice family" Willis had. But even she was plaintive and didn't understand. Both she and Father thought that Katherine and Willis were "carrying it too far" when they decided to have Willis teach the child until they could find the proper school for her.

She heard a little sleepy startled voice from within the house—"Moth-uh!"

"Uh-huh! There's somebody!" Aunt Em exclaimed delightedly.

Katherine hurried into the darkened bedroom where Phyllis lay on Aunt Em's best bedspread. The shades were down, but there was the feeling of the hot sunlight back of them. Phyllis' bare arms and legs were white and dewy. Her damp golden-brown bangs were pushed aside. Katherine knelt adoring. She began to whisper.

"Is Mother's darling awake?...Shall we go home soon—see Father? Sleep in her own little room?"...Her throat tightened with a homesick vision of the little room with the white bed and the yellow curtains....

4

They had left Grandpa alone again. Charlie and the other men were standing out beside the car, bending down and examining it, feeling of the tires, trying the handles of the doors.

Grandpa had left his chair in the yard and gone to the old wooden rocker that stood just inside the door of his room. His room was part of the old house, the one that he and Grandma had had here on the farm. It opened out upon the back yard, with a little worn narrow plank out from the door. It looked out upon the mound of the old cyclone cellar, with its wooden door, where now Aunt Em kept her vegetables in sacks on the damp cool floor, with moist earthen jars of plum and apple butter on the shelf against the cobwebbed wall. The little triangular chicken houses were scattered about in the back yard, and beyond them was the orchard where now small apples were only a little lighter than the vivid summer green of the heavy foliage and where dark shiny bubbles of aromatic sap oozed out from the rough crusty bark.

The shadows in the orchard were drawing out long toward the east, and the aisles of sunlight too looked longer. The group of people moved about more. Everything had the freshened look of late afternoon.

Grandpa rocked a little. He puffed at his pipe, took it out and held it between his fingers. It left his lower lip moistened and shining above the fringe of silvery beard. His blue eyes kept looking toward the orchard, in a still, fathomless gaze. His lips moved at times.

"Ach, ja, ja, ja...." A kind of mild sighing groan. It had pleased him that they had wanted the photograph taken, with the little great-grandchild. But that was over now. They had left him alone. And again, with a movement of his head: *"Ja,* dot was all so long ago."

Beyond the orchard, beyond the dark-green cornfields that lay behind it, beyond the river and the town...beyond all the wide western country, and the ocean...what were his fixed blue eyes, intent and inward and sad, visioning now?

The rocker was framed in the doorway of his room. Even the odor of the room was foreign. His bed with a patchwork quilt, a little dresser, a chest of drawers. The ancient wallpaper had been torn off and the walls calcimined a sky blue. Against the inner one hung his big silver watch, slowly ticking....His eyes blue, and his hair under the little black cap, his beard, were silvery....A German text with gaudy flowers hung on a woolen cord above the bed. *"Der Herr ist mein Hirte."*[5]

He started. *"Nun[6]*— who is dot?"

He did not know that little Phyllis had been watching him. Standing outside the door, in her bright canary yellow, her beautiful liquid brown eyes solemnly studying him. She was half afraid. She had never seen anything so old as "Great-grandfather." The late afternoon sunlight shimmered in the fine texture of his thin silvery beard. It brought out little frostings and marks and netted lines on his old face in which the eyes were so blue. One hand lay upon his knee. She stared wonderingly at the knots that the knuckles made, the brownish spots, the thick veins, the queer look of the skin between the bones. She looked at his black pipe, his funny little cap, his slippers with the tufted flowers....

"Ach, so? You t'ink Grandpa is a funny old man den? You want to look at him? So?"

He spoke softly. A kind of pleased smiling look came upon his face. He stretched out his hand slowly and cautiously, as if it were a butterfly poised just outside his door. A sudden longing to get this small pretty thing nearer, an ingenuous delight, possessed him now that he was alone with her. He spoke as one speaks to a bird toward which one is carefully edging nearer, afraid that a sudden motion will startle its bright eyes and make it take wing.

"Is dis a little yellow bird? Can it sing a little song?"

A faint smile dawned on the serious parted lips. He nodded at her. She seemed to have

---

[5]*Der Herr ist mein Hirte,* The Lord is my Shepherd.
[6]*Nun* (nün), now. [German]

S. Fleischman

come a little closer. He too looked in wonderment, as he had done before, at the shining hair, the fragile blue veins on the white temples, the moist pearly white of the little neck, marveling at her as he would have marveled at some beautiful strange bird that might have alighted a moment on his doorstep....

"Can't sing a little song? No? Den Grandpa will have to sing one to you."

He had been thinking of songs as he sat here; they had been murmuring somewhere in his mind. Old, old songs that he had known long ago in the old country....His little visitor stood quite still as his faint quavering voice sounded with a kind of dim sweetness in the sunshine....

> *Du, du, liegst mir im Herzen,*
> *Du, du, liegst mir im Sinn,*
> *Du, du, machst mir viel Schmerzen,*
> *Weisst nicht wie gut ich dir bin—*
> *Ja, ja, ja, ja, weisst nicht wie gut ich dir bin.*[7]

The gaze of her brown shining eyes never wavered, and a soft glow of fascinated interest grew in them as the sad wailing simplicity of the old tune quavered on the summer air. For a

---

[7]*Du, du...ich dir bin:*
  Thou, thou liest in my heart,
  Thou, thou liest in my mind,
  Thou, thou makest me much pain,
  Thou knowest not how good I am to thee——
  Yes, yes, yes, yes, thou knowest not how good I am
  to thee.

moment she was quite near, they understood each other.

"You like dot? Like Grandpa's song?"

She nodded. A tiny pleased smile curved her fresh lips....Then suddenly, with a little delicate scared movement, as if after all she had discovered that the place was strange, she flitted away to her mother.

UNDERSTANDING VARIOUS POINTS OF VIEW

1. What is the significance of the title of this story? Read the passage that best describes and emphasizes the contrasts among the four generations.

2. What is pathetic about the attempt that Charlie makes to talk with his father? With which one do you sympathize most? Why? In what way is the relationship between Katherine and Charlie similar to that between Charlie and his father?

3. Describe the relationship between Katherine and the other women. Can you justify Katherine's attitude? Why, or why not?

4. Which two of the four generations come nearest to understanding one another? How is the fact that the grandfather twice almost touched Phyllis with his hand somewhat symbolic of their relationship?

Understanding a realistic story

When you read "A Test of Fortitude," you knew that the hero would be victorious in the end. Perhaps you knew this because in the stories you read in your growing-up years you learned to look for a happy ending—and you were seldom disappointed. Or perhaps you knew that the author of "A Test of Fortitude" wrote *romantic* novels, and in most romantic novels the villain gets his just deserts while the hero emerges victorious. Unfortunately, life does not always follow the pattern of the romantic storyteller. In life the hero may fail to attain his goal, and the wished-for happy ending may be replaced by disappointment, unhappiness, or tragedy. An author who pictures a world like that of our everyday life, who models his characters on ordinary men and women, and who believes that literature should mirror the happenings of life pretty accurately is called a *realist*. Ruth Suckow is such a writer, and "Four Generations" is a realistic story.

Glance over the story again. In what ways are the characters realistic? What realistic details does the author include in describing the setting? Do you think the story ends as a similar episode in real life might? Could a romantic storyteller have written this particular story?

Mr. K*a*p*l*a*n
Cuts a Gordian Knot

LEONARD Q. ROSS

In her autobiography, *The Promised Land,* Mary Antin, a Russian immigrant, says, "The public school has done its best for us foreigners, and for the country, when it has made us into good Americans." In the larger cities, night schools, opportunity schools, and vocational schools have helped the public schools generously and wisely in this process. Hyman Kaplan, the chief character in the following selection, attends an American night school. His behavior there as he gets into one tangle after another has been recounted in a very amusing book, *The Education of H*y*m*a*n K*a*p*l*a*n,*[1] by Leonard Q. Ross.

"Tonight," Mr. Parkhill said, "we shall devote the entire period to our—er—examination."

It was not really necessary for Mr. Parkhill to go through the formality of an examination. He knew, many weeks before the end of the year, which of the students in the beginners' grade deserved to be promoted to Miss Higby's Composition, Grammar, and Civics, and which students, by any measure of skill, would have to be held back. Miss Mitnick, for example, was unquestionably the best student in the class. There was no doubt about her right to promotion. Or that of Mr. Feigenbaum, who had submitted some of the best compositions. At the other extreme there were students like Mrs. Moskowitz. By no stretch of the pedagogical imagination could poor Mrs. Moskowitz be considered ready for Miss Higby. Nor could Mr. Hyman Kaplan.

Mr. Parkhill frowned as he thought of Mr. Kaplan. Mr. Kaplan was certainly his most energetic and ebullient pupil. He never missed a lesson; he never grew discouraged; the smile of undaunted hope and good will never left his cherubic face. But, unfortunately, Mr. Kaplan never seemed to *learn* anything. His spelling remained erratic, his grammar deplorable, his sentence structure fantastic. There was only one word for Mr. Kaplan's idioms—atrocious. As for Mr. Kaplan's speech, if anything it grew more astounding from day to day. Only last week Mr. Kaplan had announced that his wife suffered "fromm high blood pleasure." And in a drill on adjectives he had given the positive, comparative, and superlative forms of *cold* as "cold, colder, below zero." Mr. Parkhill often wondered whether there wasn't something sacrilegious in trying to impose the iron mold of English on so unfettered an intelligence.

Mr. Parkhill could go right through the class list that way, picking the promotion-worthy from the promotion-unworthy. He needed no examination to aid him in the task. But Mr. Parkhill realized that examinations lent a certain dignity and prestige to the American Night Preparatory School for Adults. They had a valuable *psychological* effect. And this was the night for which the examination had been announced.

"Please clear the arms of your chairs of everything except paper. Keep plenty of paper, please, and pens or pencils."

Smiles, frowns, and grins appeared on the faces of the students, according to their individual expectations.

"How's abot holdink bladders?" asked Mr. Kaplan.

"*Blotters,* Mr. Kaplan! Er—yes, you may keep blotters. Is everyone ready?"

Eyes alert, hearts pounding nervously, pens and pencils poised like falcons, the beginners' grade awaited the fateful event of examination. In the eyes of some students there were already visions of Composition, Grammar, and Civics, and Miss Higby.

"The first part of the examination will be a combined spelling-vocabulary test," said Mr. Parkhill. "Write a short sentence with each of the words I shall call off. Underline the word used. Is that clear to everyone?"

[1] *H*y*m*a*n K*a*p*l*a*n.* In class Mr. Kaplan always wrote his name in this way, with the asterisks in colored crayon.

From the agonized expression on Mrs. Moskowitz' face it was *too* clear.

"Very well, *knees*." Mr. Parkhill waited a moment and repeated, *"Knees!"* being careful to pronounce it as distinctly as possible: *"Neez."*

The class attacked *knees*. Mr. Kaplan promptly leaned his head back, closed his eyes, and held solemn communion with himself. This was done by whispering, in a semipublic tone, *"Neez....Neez....* A fonny void.... So be careful ....*Neez....* Aha! Has *two* minninks....Vun, a pot mine lag.... Also?...Aha! Mine brodder's daughter is mine nee—"

"Mr. Kaplan!" Mr. Parkhill was dismayed. "*Please.* You must not—er—disturb the class."

"I back you podden," murmured Mr. Kaplan with an injured air. Mr. Kaplan could think clearly *only* by whispering to himself, as if consulting a more rational self. Mr. Parkhill's edict, however much designed to preserve the peace of the classroom, was tantamount to an intellectual death sentence for Hyman Kaplan. It strangled cerebration at its very source. Mr. Kaplan shook his head sadly, marveling at the inhumanity of man to man.

"Heat," said Mr. Parkhill, not daring to meet Mr. Kaplan's melancholy gaze. *"Heat!"*

"*Heat,*" whispered Mr. Kaplan automatically, and with uncharacteristic feebleness. Then he caught himself, pressed his lips together resolutely, and wrote in silence. He looked pale. He seemed to grow paler and paler as he maintained the silence.

"*Pack....Excite....Throat.*"

Spelling-vocabulary continued on its even course. Mr. Parkhill announced the words slowly, allowing as much as three minutes for a word; he articulated each word with laudable precision. (*Excite* he repeated no less than four times.) So well did he time himself that he called the last of the twenty words on his list, *adorable,* just as the recess bell rang. The first part of the examination was over. A wave of relief swept through the class, like a sweet summer breeze. The students handed in their papers and swarmed into the corridors to relax from the grueling ordeal.

Mr. Parkhill began to sort the papers. He noticed that Miss Mitnick had, as usual, done excellently. Mrs. Friedman seemed to have struck disaster with *throat*. She had written several sentences, scratched them out, and left: "He throat the ball real fast." When Mr. Parkhill came to the paper headed "H*Y*M*A*N K*A*P*L*A*N," he sighed automatically. He read the sentences which Mr. Kaplan had contributed to knowledge.

1. My brother Maxs' little girl (I am Uncle) is my neece.
2. I heat him on the head, the big fool.
3. I am buyink a fine peck potatoes.
4. In a theater is the Insite, the Outsite, and the Exite. (for Fire).

Then Mr. Parkhill read no more.

At 8:40 the bell rang again, ending the recess, and the students returned to their purgatory. They looked serious, a trifle worried, and tense. Mr. Parkhill, the cadences of Mr. Kaplan's bizarre sentences still ringing in his ears, *felt* serious, a trifle worried, and tense.

Mrs. Moskowitz and Mr. Kaplan entered side by side. Mr. Kaplan beamed with some inner joy. He seemed to have forgiven and forgotten the heartless edict against his whispering. Mrs. Moskowitz was moaning, as if in pain.

"I'm shaking insite, Mr. Kaplan," she said.

Mr. Kaplan raised his head with a gallant flourish. "*Stop* shakink insite!" he cried. "Listen, Moskovitz. Kipp high de had! Kipp couratch! Dis pot haxemination vill be a tsinch, a *snep*. Dat's all, a *snep*."

Mrs. Moskowitz took a deep sigh, admiring Mr. Kaplan's morale. "I vish I had your noives, honist."

Mr. Kaplan accepted this tribute with a gracious nod. "I'll *halp* you mit de haxemination," he confided in a megaphonic whisper.[2] "An' ven you fillink blue, remamber de song dey sinking in U. S.: 'Heppy Dace Is Here Vunce More!'" Mr. Kaplan hummed a few bars of that classic ballad to lend weight to his counsel. "Vill give you strangt! 'Heppy Dace *Is* Here Vunce More!'"

Mr. Parkhill rapped his pencil on the desk at this point, interrupting an immortal conversation. Mr. Kaplan nodded encouragement to Mrs. Moskowitz again, sat down in his chair, and cried a last buoyant word across the room. "Don' give op de sheep, Moskovitz!" It was like a call to the colors.

Mr. Parkhill explained the second part of the examination. "A one-page composition," he said firmly. "On any subject."

Several fallen faces testified to the magnitude of this assignment.

"Please do *not* talk during this part of the examination. I shall not be able to answer any questions, so please do not ask them. And do not—er—try to get help from your neighbors." Mr. Parkhill sent a searching look in the general direction of Mr. Kaplan. Mr. Kaplan nodded loyally, and then shrugged his shoulders toward Mrs. Moskowitz. Mrs. Moskowitz looked as if the last psychic leg[3] had been cut from under her. "I suggest you begin at once. You will have the rest of the period for the composition."

Silence fell like a pall upon the beginners' grade. The wheels of creative imagination began to turn—rather slowly. Miss Caravello stared at the lithograph of George Washington on the wall, seeking inspiration, somehow, from that heroic visage. Mr. George Weinstein placed a hand over both eyes, signifying concentration. Mrs. Rodriguez yawned. Mr. Parkhill felt that "A Composition—Any Subject" would prove a decided success.

He waited a little while for the students to adjust themselves to their new problem, then sauntered down the aisle to see how the compositions were progressing. All the students were hard at work, grimacing through the opening paragraphs of their prose—all except Mrs. Moskowitz. She sat with a dumb, bewildered look. There was anguish in her eyes. Little beads of sweat on her upper lip proclaimed the effort of thought.

"Is anything wrong, Mrs. Moskowitz?" whispered Mr. Parkhill anxiously.

Mrs. Moskowitz raised a haggard face. "I ken't tink of a sobject!"

"Oh," murmured Mr. Parkhill. "Er—why not try 'My Ambition'?" "My Ambition" was a *very* popular topic.

Mrs. Moskowitz shook her head. Apparently Mrs. Moskowitz had no particular ambition.

"Er—how about 'My First Day in America'?"

"I'm sick of telling about dat," sighed Mrs. Moskowitz.

"I see," said Mr. Parkhill miserably. It was a desperate situation.

Suddenly a gentle whistle soared through the air. It was soft, but it had a haunting vibrance. Everyone looked up. The whistle caressed the lilting refrain of "Heppy Dace Is Here Vunce More."

"Mr. Kap—"

A disembodied whisper rose from the front row. "Sobjecks for composition...'Should Ladies Smoke?'...'Is Dere a God, Ectual?'...Tink abot a *qvastion*."

"Mr. Kaplan!" said Mr. Parkhill severely.

But the mysterious process of communication had been consummated. A light shone in Mrs. Moskowitz' eyes. "I'll write about a *quastion*," she said.

Mr. Parkhill moved on. He felt quite helpless. He wondered how Mr. Kaplan had heard the colloquy between him and Mrs. Moskowitz. He wondered whether Mr. Kaplan had some

---

[2]*megaphonic* (meg′ə fŏn′ik) *whisper*, a whisper as loud as one spoken through a megaphone would be.

[3]*psychic* (sī′kik) *leg*, imaginary leg or support.

sort of hyperaesthesia of the ears.[4] So entranced was he by this fancy that he did not notice that Mr. Kaplan had, for some strange reason, risen.

"Podden me, Mr. Pockheel—"

Mr. Parkhill shook his head at once. This was going too far. "I can*not* answer any questions, Mr. Kaplan."

Mr. Kaplan nodded humbly. "Is no qvastion," he said softly. "Is awful hot in de room, so maybe I should haupen op a vindow."

sf

Mr. Kaplan "haupened op" a window.

Five minutes after Mr. Kaplan had returned to his seat, Miss Rochelle Goldberg, on his left, began to whisper something to him.

Mr. Parkhill cleared his throat in patent reprimand.

Mr. Kaplan stood up again. "I must close *don* de vindow," he sighed. "Is on Goldboig's feet a tarrible graft."

He was "closing don" the window before Mr. Parkhill could say, "*D*raft, Mr. Kaplan, *d*raft."

It was with relief that Mr. Parkhill began to arrange the composition papers in a pile after the final bell had rung and the students were gone. The titles at the tops of the pages paraded before him. "My Friend's New House." "A Sad

---

[4]*hyperaesthesia* (hĭ′pər es thē′zhi ə) *of the ears,* a sense of hearing so acute that a person hears things not usually audible.

Night in Hospitel." "Should Be Dad Panelty for Murdering?" (That looked like an unmistakable Kaplan title; no, it was Mrs. Moskowitz' paper, but it showed Mr. Kaplan's advisory influence all too clearly.) "My 4 Children Make Me a Happy Life." "Liberty Stateu." "Thinking About."

Mr. Parkhill started. He read the title again. There it was, in bold letters: "Thinking About." Mr. Parkhill raised the sheet a little above the rest of the pile.

"Thinking About"
(Humans & Enimals)

Mr. Parkhill took a deep breath and raised the page a little higher yet.

by
H*Y*M*A*N K*A*P*L*A*N

Before he had weighed the full consequences of his folly, Mr. Parkhill was reading the composition graced by so provocative a title:

1.

Somtime I feel sad about how som people are living. Only sleeping eating working in shop. Not *thinking*. They are just like Enimals the same, which dont thinking also. Humans should not be like Enimals! They should *Thinking!* This is with me a deep idea.

Now we are having in school the axemination—a Comp. Mostly, will the students write a *story* for Comp. But I am asking, Why must allways be a story? Mr. P. must be sick and tierd from storys. Kaplan, be a man! No story! Tell better about *Thinking* somthing! Fine. Now I am thinking.

2.

In the recass was som students asking if is right to say Its Me or Its I—(because maybe we will have that question in axemination). Its Me or Its I—a planty hard question, no? Yes.

But it isn't so hard if we are *thinking about!* I figgure in this way:

If sombody is in hall besides my door, and makes knok, knok, knok; so I holler netcheral "Whose there"? Comes the anser "Its Me." A fine anser!! Who is that Me anyho? Can I tell? No! So is Its Me no good.

Again is knok, knok, knok. And again I holler "Whose there"? Now comes the anser "Its I." So who is now that I?? Still can I (Kaplan) tell?? Ha! Umpossible! So is Its I rotten also.

So it looks like is no anser. (Turn around paige)

As Mr. Parkhill turned the page "around"

(Mr. Kaplan had interpreted "a one-page composition" with characteristic generosity), he could see how, put that way, the problem of "Its Me" or "Its I" was a very Gordian knot.[5]

But must be *som kind anser.* So how we can find him out??? *By Thinking About.* (Now I show how Humans isnt Enimals)

3.

If *I* am in hall and make knok, knok, knok; and I hear insite (insite the room) sombody hollers "Whose there"?—I anser strong *"Its Kaplan!"!!*

Now is fine! Plain, clear like gold, no chance mixing up Me, I, Ect.

By *Thinking* is Humans making big edvences on Enimals. This we call Progriss.

T-H-E E-N-D

Only after he had read the composition twice did Mr. Parkhill notice that there was a postscript to this expedition into the realm of pure logic. It was like the signature to a masterpiece.

ps. I dont care if I dont pass, I *love* the class.

---

[5]*Gordian knot,* a problem impossible to solve. The expression comes from the legend of the mythical Gordius, King of Phrygia (frij′i ə), who tied a knot that could be undone only by the person who should rule Asia. Alexander the Great, unable to untie it, cut it with a sword.

"THINKING ABOUT"

1. How did Mr. Kaplan cut the Gordian knot? Do you approve of his solution of the problem? How did Mr. Parkhill feel about it? Do you think he should have promoted Mr. Kaplan? Why, or why not?

2. Why did the thought of Mr. Kaplan bring a frown to Mr. Parkhill's forehead? Describe the most amusing aspects of Mr. Kaplan's behavior. Why do you suppose the author described Mr. Kaplan's and Mrs. Moskowitz' conversation just before the second part of the examination as "immortal"?

3. What does Mr. Kaplan's postscript to his composition reveal about his character? What other qualities of his does the selection reveal?

4. Do you think Mr. Kaplan will be a good citizen? What Americans of similar racial origins have become great figures in our country?

5. Although "Mr. K*a*p*l*a*n Cuts a Gordian Knot" is a humorous story, it manages to give the reader a clear understanding of the author's point of view. What does Leonard Q. Ross think of Mr. Parkhill as a teacher? How much importance does he attach to certain rules of grammatical usage? What is his attitude toward Mr. Kaplan?

Awroopdedoop!

BENJAMIN APPEL

When people of varying backgrounds come together, conflict is likely to arise unless those people have understanding and sympathy. No one realizes this fact more keenly than Benjamin Appel. Of Polish descent, he was born in New York City and grew up in what is known as "Hell's Kitchen," a neighborhood of Irish, Italians, Greeks, Poles, French, and Germans. From such a background as this, he has seen people solve their differences and says, "I have faith in the ordinary folk of America." Observe how he illustrates this faith in the following short story.

ALL DAY LONG old Mrs. Elmer Knowles rocked on the porch of the big house and vowed she would have no tenants next summer. She had lived to see her guest houses used as bungalows by foreigners from the city who didn't know how to behave like decent Americans. Yes, terrible days had come to the country when the Knowleses of Knowlesville had been

---

"Awroopdedoop," by Benjamin Appel. Reprinted by permission of the author.

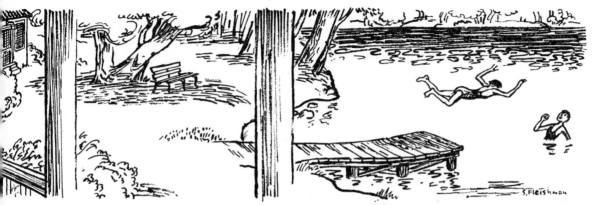

reduced to such a condition. The town and the lake were named after them, but what did that mean to the foreigners? She always thought of her tenants as the foreigners, the Jews, the Swedes, the Italians, instead of by their names.

Right now the two Swede girls were diving from their pier.

"Ooo, Elsie, watch me bellywhop," the younger child screamed.

"Awroopdedoop," Elsie cried. "This pier isn't so good for diving like Mrs. Knowles' pier. Awroopdedoop!" Elsie's vocabulary of fun was founded on the scream *awroopdedoop*.

Mrs. Knowles shuddered. Before the summer would be over, she would be driven mad by Elsie. She thought proudly of her two granddaughters, Phyllis and Elizabeth. Phyllis and Elizabeth were little ladies.

Sunlight ricocheted in yellow shafts from the arms of the Swede girls as they swam the crawl. They squirted water from between their teeth with raucous satisfaction.

The Swede boat rowed past the swimmers, the father at the oars, the son trolling for bass with a heavy sea line.

"Catch any fish, Paw?" Elsie yelled. She splashed water into the boat. "Awroopdedoop!"

The man at the oars heaved upright. He seemed baked and groggy from the sun. "Go away. We got a bass plug with nine hooks,[1] children. You want your skin ripped off, children?"

---

[1] *We got a bass plug with nine hooks,* we are using a bait with nine hooks on it especially designed for catching bass.

The boat rowed on, and Mrs. Knowles sniffed disgustedly. Before breakfast and after breakfast and going strong at twilight. These city people didn't know how to fish, and they refused her hired man's advice, as if they knew all about everything. They acted as if sky and water and woods had been especially built like a playground for their use over the summer. They should have realized that for years and years the lake was Knowles property, but they realized nothing. Only two days ago this imp Elsie had said, "Mrs. Knowles, can we use your big canoe? You never use it." These foreigners would only be content when they moved into her own house.

Now, out of the middle guest house where once the state senator had vacationed, the Italian father came rushing. He moved with the speed of a fat fast man; his white knickers were dazzling.

"Pa," his oldest son cried in agony. "Don't leave me." *Bang* went the screen door as the oldest son pursued his father.

"Don't leave me," the second son shouted. *Bang* went the screen door.

"Mama, they're leaving me," the third and smallest son bawled. "I don't want no cocoa. They're leaving me." *Bang* went the screen door.

At the end of the pier, the father set up a tin can. "Learn to shoot," he commanded with the zeal of a Daniel Boone.

His sons sprinted back to the bungalow. *Bang. Bang. Bang.* They returned with the air rifles and aimed carefully. *Plingk. Plingk. Plingk.*

Mrs. Knowles' tired gray eyes were hypnotized with attention like those of a small child at a three-ring circus. But finally she shifted her gaze to the third bungalow. The Jews' police dog, Julius, had begun to bark viciously at the faint bay of a hound miles distant. And she knew that soon she would hear Julius' master's voice. She loathed it as much as Elsie's *awroop-dedoop.*

"Come here, Julius." A husky boy of nineteen trotted out of his bungalow. He was Julius' master by right of endurance. He threw a branch into the lake, but instead of leaping to retrieve it, the police dog loped down from the end of the pier, dodged his master, and cannoned across Mrs. Knowles' lawn.

Disgraceful dog, Mrs. Knowles thought. And a disgraceful boy. He wears nothing but swimming trunks. Hasn't he any other clothes?

"Come here, Julius!" the boy shouted. "Wow, you mutt. Wait'll I catch you. Come here before I lose my temper."

Mrs. Knowles watched the muscles shape and unshape in the boy's legs as he sprinted, his blond face red from sun and fury. A wild boy. And if her only grandson, Reynold, wasn't disciplined....But Reynold was only eleven. There was some hope that Reynold would grow up to be a real Knowles and not a wild Indian.

"Come here. It's your last chance to be a good mutt," the boy bellowed, but the dog never seemed to have heard him. He changed his tactics and pleaded. "Nice mutt. Nice doggie."

Julius advanced across the lawn, wagging his tail doggishly but looking like a wolf. The boy retreated into the lake and yelled as if he were cowing a cage of lions. "Come on swimming, nice lil doggie."

"Tie Julius up," his mother ordered. As always, she was reading on the front porch of her bungalow. "And then get some sun." Her two daughters were rubbing olive oil on their arms.

Mrs. Knowles thought she had never seen such energy as the Jews and their dog had. It wasn't right. People she knew didn't have such energy.

And suddenly Mrs. Knowles stopped rocking. Why, the fishing and swimming Swedes, the

shooting Italians, the Jews and their dog owned Knowles Lake because they never got tired. She fought the notion out of consciousness because with it there was another idea she didn't like. The Knowleses, most of them, were tired. The Knowleses weren't like their grandfathers any more.

But on Friday night the real owners arrived, and Mrs. Knowles' big house seemed to be the big house of twenty years ago, when her husband had been alive. Her weak body became strong with the strength of seeing her daughter Mabel and Mabel's husband and children Phyllis and Elizabeth, and her son Alfred, his wife and his son Reynold. She kissed Phyllis and Elizabeth, but Reynold pulled back.

"I'm no girl," Reynold complained. He was a stocky boy and would be a heavier, stronger man than his father.

"I'm not a girl," his mother corrected.

"You are so," Reynold cried.

"Reynold," his father said sternly.

Yes, it was like the old days, the good days of youth and possession. It was heartening to see Alfred and Mabel and their families. She could almost forget they were all living on the last rag-ends of big properties and enterprises.[2] And when they sat down together in the dining room, Mrs. Knowles again felt they were back in the days of strength. The lights were bright, and they conversed in a glowing radiance of hearth and home and family.

"Let's all paddle out in the big canoe after dinner," Mrs. Knowles suggested. "We haven't done that in ever so long."

"Can I paddle, too, Grandma?" Reynold gripped his soup spoon as if it were a paddle and began to churn up the green lake of his pea soup.

"Stop that," his father commanded. Then he smiled in a lazy way at Mrs. Knowles. "But what for, Mother?"

And all the adults, Alfred and his wife, Mabel and her husband, seemed to be amused as if Mrs. Knowles' suggestion were the whim of a child. Even her two granddaughters, Phyllis

---

[2]*last rag-ends of big properties and enterprises,* the remnants of a once great fortune.

and Elizabeth, followed the lead of the grown-ups and smiled like prim, conservative people. Mrs. Knowles suddenly detested their almost lack of energy. It wasn't the old days, and she smiled with all her deepest love at Reynold. Reynold was the only Knowles who had the spirit of his ancestors.

After dinner, when the four adults sat down to bridge, Mrs. Knowles led her three grandchildren out on the porch. Almost immediately Elsie ran over.

"You want to play with us?" Elsie said. "We need more kids."

Elizabeth answered in a snobbish voice, a perfect imitation of her mother's. "No, thank you."

"Awroopdedoop." She stuck out her tongue. "Sissies. Sissies. Sissies. You're all sissies."

"Who's a sissy?" Reynold demanded. "Can I play, Grandma? It's no fun with Phyllis and Elizabeth."

"Yes, dear." Mrs. Knowles was amused and a little hurt at the surprise her granddaughters showed. They were so spotless, so languid, such pink small ladies. They weren't even a little bit like the Elizabeths and Phyllises after whom they had been named. The first Elizabeth Knowles had given birth to ten children. The first Phyllis had been lost one week in the forests, but when the searching party found her, she had been hale and hearty. She had built herself a lean-to and made snares for rabbits. She had built a fire and kept it going and greeted the frantic searchers calmly.

Mrs. Knowles' heart filled with a vast and surging remembering. The old days, the days of hearsay and legend and faded letters from another century. Once, the Knowleses had been strong. Her husband's grandfather had first come into the wilderness, and her husband's father had owned the forests, owned the sawmill, owned the factory that had made wood chemicals, but her husband had lived on his investments. And then had come the terrible arguments when her husband had sold the east shore of the lake and later the north shore, and invested the proceeds in more stocks and bonds. She didn't want to sell, but they had been great manorial days. Twenty and thirty guests used to stay with them in the big house for weeks on end. During the day they would fish and hunt. They would ride the horses along the sunlit trails. At night they would board the houseboat anchored in the lake and sing under the five-pointed wilderness of stars. But it was all gone into the grave. Oh, that her husband's grave could hold so much, forests and lands and fortunes. And yet her son and daughter still pretended that there had been no change.

As the twilight massed like snowdrift against the buildings Reynold shouted as loud as Elsie, and Mrs. Knowles grew a little more cheerful watching him lark about on the lawn. Thank heaven, one of her grandchildren had as much sap to him as the Knowleses of long ago. She glanced at Elizabeth and Phyllis seated like two miniature ladies next to her, and with an unwincing honesty she knew why Reynold was her favorite. Reynold had as much sap to him as the children of the foreigners.

"Watch out for the ninfantry," he kept shouting.

"Bing, bing, bing," Elsie's brother screamed.

And led by Elsie they all dashed over to the porch.

"G'wan, ask her," Elsie prompted.

"We want the big canoe," Reynold said. Then he capered toward the boathouse with Elsie's brothers careening after him, kicking their knees high like horses. Elsie smiled at Mrs. Knowles.

"Let's have it, Mrs. Knowles," she asked.

"You're too young, child, to be in a canoe."

"Giddyap," Elsie cried and galloped after her army.

It was black now, and the children were playing with glowworms in glasses. The green eerie light frolicked all over the lawn as the children ran about with their lanterns. Her heart expanded with the strength of this newest generation, with their brave voices, rich and furious with innocence. The children were ready to voyage out in the big canoe, her Reynold among them. Yes, they were willing. She began to think of the canoe as a rule to measure with. Oh, what a strange evening, and if it were not for her love for Reynold she would never have understood so many things. Reynold was the lens through which she was beginning to see the past and future.

One afternoon, after Reynold had returned to town, the Swede children took possession of the Knowleses' pier. Mrs. Knowles walked down to the smiling children, feeling futile before their positive ownership. "Don't you think you should swim from your own pier?"

"No," said Elsie. "This pier's better. You can dive off this pier, and you can't dive so good off our pier. We won't hurt your pier, and we won't hurt your old canoe." She dove in. Her two small brothers held their noses, galloped down the pier like ponies, and jumped in after her.

Mrs. Knowles sighed. Elsie was too fresh, but it was easier to forgive Elsie than her two granddaughters.

And having taken over the pier, the next weekend Elsie naturally led her partisans onto Mrs. Knowles' lawn and shouted for Reynold. It was night and time to play. Soon, she was ordering the small Italian boys and the Jewish girls to come over, until the dark swarmed with children like toadstools newly sprung up after a shower. They played tag, and their voices shrieked and gurgled and tinkled like bells.

Reynold's father hurried from the living room. "Reynold," he cried. "Stop that infernal rioting."

Mrs. Knowles laughed when Reynold, invisible but rebellious, bellowed, "Awroopdedoop!"

"Reynold." But now there was no reply, Reynold hiding in the night as if in a cave. His father patted the heads of Phyllis and Elizabeth. "Thank heaven, you children aren't like your cousin." He returned to his bridge game.

The next day, Mrs. Knowles had been watching the Italian father skin a woodchuck, and later he had come over with the pink meat in a bowl.

"How you eat woodchuck? How you prepare him?"

"Parboil it, Mr. Pagano. But I must first warn you the meat is very gamy. Years ago we used to break it down."[3] Mrs. Knowles glanced at the other Knowleses on the porch. How motionless, how refined they were. Her son and his wife. Her daughter and her husband. Her granddaughters. And none of them were even glancing at the Italian. Only Reynold stared with fascination.

---

[3]*break it down,* let it age until the flavor was less strong.

"When my wife prepare, it'll be fine," the Italian said simply. "What better to eat than God's little animals in the field."

"Did you shoot him yourself?" Reynold asked.

"Yes, sir." His eyes glittered with the hunter's lust for blood. He was as remorseless as any old-timer Knowles who had tracked down bear in the steep ridges, as remorseless as Reynold who was now aiming an imaginary rifle at the woodchuck meat. And now for the first time Mrs. Knowles understood her tenants. They were all like pioneers up here in the country. They had the strength, the get-up of the Knowleses who had settled the country a hundred years ago. They were crude, they were violent, they weren't as elegant as the present-day Knowleses. But they possessed the endurance, the solidity of Reynold's great-great-grandfathers. And above all Mrs. Knowles loved strength and courage in human beings.

"Missus Knowles," the hunter said hurriedly, as if he must retreat from the battery of condemning Knowleses. "I have company, and I wonder if you loan me the big canoe?"

"Of course, Mr. Pagano. We don't use it. We only play bridge nowadays."

The night was moonlit, the air scented with laurel and pine so that all the earth was fragrance. The Italians, man and wife, their two guests, their children, slipped out toward the middle of the lake where the houseboat had once been anchored, forgotten and unbelievable now as Noah's Ark. The canoe moved with a fatality, an ease that was like a happy fortune. The paddles dipped, many, many paddles; even the children had paddles, and the canoe became a mirage seen across the unbelievable stillness. The green peaks and the copper sky were twilight. The voices that had been dim sounding from the nostalgic distance, as if permeated with the dying light, gray, violet, now surged with the heartbreak of music heard on water, full-throated, harmony of male and female and the choir voices of the children...*Santa Lucia, Santa Lucia*.[4]...Mrs. Knowles, sitting on her

---

[4]*Santa Lucia* (sän′tə lü chē′ə). These words occur in the chorus of "Santa Lucia," a beautiful old boat song of Naples.

porch, dabbed her eyes with a tiny handkerchief.

These people were striking root in America as the Knowleses had struck root generations ago. For the first time she didn't think of the tenants as the Jews, the Swedes, the Italians, but as the Bergmans and Larsons and Paganos. New names. The world belonged to her grandson Reynold and to the strong of his generation. The canoe belonged to those who would use it.

The police dog barked. His master yelled with a ferocious energy. "Shut up, you mangy mutt." And Mrs. Knowles thought that the Knowleses of a hundred years ago were more like these foreigners than their own descendants.

"I wish I was out in that canoe," Reynold said.

"Go to bed, Reynold. You've played hard all day. Even Elsie is in bed."

"But why don't we go out in the canoe, Grandma?"

"You will some day, Reynold," Mrs. Knowles said. She smiled as Elsie responded in her own way to the singers.

"Awroopdedoop!" Elsie yodeled.

"Awroopdedoop!" Reynold yodeled back.

SEEING THROUGH
MRS. KNOWLES' EYES

1. What is Mrs. Knowles' attitude toward her tenants at the beginning of the story? What is her attitude toward them at the end? At what point in the story does the change take place? What causes the change? Read the lines that express each of these attitudes and the point of change respectively.

2. What specific quality distinguished Mrs. Knowles' tenants from her children? Why did she begin "to think of the canoe as a rule to measure with"? How was Reynold "the lens through which she was beginning to see the past and future"?

3. Did Mrs. Knowles admire everything about her tenants? Explain the reasons for the way in which you answer.

4. What event convinced Mrs. Knowles of the pioneer quality of her tenants? Did she find any qualities in them that you are accustomed to regard as typically American? What is her meaning when she says, "We only play bridge nowadays"?

"Scum o' the Earth"

ROBERT HAVEN SCHAUFFLER

Forgetting the fact—or never thinking of it—that their ancestors were once immigrants, citizens of this country too often look with scorn upon those who have come to our land more recently.

I

AT THE GATE of the West[1] I stand,
    On the island where nations throng.
We call them "scum o' the earth";

Stay, are we doing you wrong,
Young fellow from Socrates' land?[2]—   5
You, like a Hermes, lithe and strong,
Fresh from the master Praxiteles' hand?[3]
So you're of Spartan birth?[4]
Descended, perhaps, from one of the band—
Deathless in story and song—   10
Who combed their long hair at Thermopylae's
    pass?[5] . . .
Ah, I forget what straits (alas!),
More tragic than theirs, more compassion-
    worth,
Have doomed you to march in our "immigrant
    class"
Where you're nothing but "scum o' the earth."[15]

II

You Pole with the child on your knee,
What dower have you for the land of the free?
Hear her lips croon
The sad little tune
Chopin[6] once mined from the Polish air   20
And mounted in gold for us to wear.
Now a ragged young fiddler answers
In wild Czech[7] melody
That Dvořák[8] took whole from the dancers.
And the heavy faces bloom   25
In the wonderful Slavic way;
The dull little eyes, the foreheads' gloom,
Are suddenly fair and gay.
While, watching these folk and their mystery,
I forget that we,   30
In our scornful mirth,
Brand them as "polacks"[9]—and "scum o' the
    earth."

III

Genoese boy[10] of the level brow,
Lad of the lustrous, dreamy eyes
Agaze at Manhattan's pinnacles now   35
In the first, glad shock of a hushed surprise;
Within your far-rapt seer's eyes
I catch the glow of the wild surmise
That played on the *Santa Maria's* prow[11]
In that still gray dawn,   40
Four centuries gone,
When a world from the wave began to rise.
Oh, who shall foretell what high emprise
Is the goal that gleams
When Italy's dreams   45
Take wing and sweep into the skies?
Caesar dreamed him a world ruled well;

---

[1] *the gate of the West,* Ellis Island in New York Harbor, formerly the port of admission for immigrants to the United States. Today immigrants are examined aboard ship, and only those held for special inquiry are sent to Ellis Island.

[2] *Socrates'* (sok'rə tēz) *land,* Greece. Socrates was one of the greatest philosophers of ancient Greece.

[3] *like a Hermes* (hêr'mēz)...*Fresh from the master Praxiteles'* (praks it'ə lēz) *hand,* like a statue of the messenger-god Hermes newly modeled by the Greek sculptor Praxiteles. One of the greatest works of Praxiteles, who lived in the fourth century B.C., was a statue of Hermes noted for its strength and suppleness.

[4] *of Spartan birth,* from Sparta, a city in Greece, famous in ancient times for the hardiness of its people.

[5] *combed their long hair at Thermopylae's* (thər mop'ə-lēz) *pass.* In 480 B.C. three hundred Spartans defended the mountain pass at Thermopylae in Greece against an army of Persians until the last Spartan was killed. It was a custom of the Spartans to don fine garments and put garlands in their hair before going into battle.

[6] *Chopin* (shō pan'), a Polish composer, who wove many folk melodies into his compositions.

[7] *Czech* (chek), the most western branch of the Slavic peoples, including the Bohemians.

[8] *Dvořák* (dvôr'zhäk), Bohemian composer.

[9] "*polacks*" (pō'lakz), a scornful term for Polish people.

[10] *Genoese* (jen'ō ēz') *boy,* boy from Genoa, the seaport in northwest Italy which was the birthplace of Columbus.

[11] "*Santa Maria's*" *prow,* pointed front part of Columbus' flagship on his voyage of 1492.

"Scum o' the Earth," reprinted by permission of the author, from *New and Selected Poems* by Robert Haven Schauffler, New York, Dodd, Mead and Company, Inc., 1942.

S. Fleishman

Dante[12] dreamed Heaven out of Hell;
Angelo[13] brought us there to dwell;
And you, are you of a different birth?—   50
You're only a "dago,"[14]—and "scum o' the
    earth"!

IV

Stay, are we doing you wrong
Calling you "scum o' the earth,"
Man of the sorrow-bowed head,
Of the features tender yet strong—   55
Man of the eyes full of wisdom and mystery
Mingled with patience and dread?
Have I not known you in history,
Sorrow-bowed head?
Were you the poet-king, worth   60
Treasures of Ophir unpriced?[15]

Or were you the prophet[16] whose art
Foretold how the rabble would mock
That shepherd of spirits, erelong,
Who should gather the lambs to his heart   65
And tenderly feed his flock?
Man—lift that sorrow-bowed head....
Behold the face of the Christ!

The vision dies at its birth.
You're merely a butt for our mirth.   70
You're a "sheeny"[17]—and therefore despised
And rejected as "scum o' the earth."

V

Countrymen, bend and invoke
Mercy for us blasphemers,
For us who spat on these marvelous folk,   75
Nations of darers and dreamers,
Scions of singers and seers,
Our peers, and more than our peers.
"Rabble and refuse" we name them,

---

[12]*Dante* (dan′tē *or* dän′tā), Italian poet (1265-1321),
whose *Divine Comedy* is a vision of Hell, Purgatory, and
Paradise.
   [13]*Angelo*, Michelangelo (mĭ′kəl an′jə lō), great Italian
sculptor, painter, and architect of the Renaissance.
   [14]*"dago"* (dā′gō), a derogatory name for an Italian.
   [15]*the poet-king, worth treasures of Ophir* (ō′fər) *unpriced*. Solomon, king of Israel, received great treasures of
gold from the mines of Ophir. (I Kings 10:11-23.)

[16]*prophet*, Isaiah (ī zā′ə *or* ī zī′ə), greatest of the
Hebrew prophets, who foretold the birth, suffering, and
death of Christ. The next lines of the poem refer to Christ.
   [17]*"sheeny"* (shē′nē), vulgar, offensive name for a Jew.

And "scum o' the earth," to shame them.   80
Mercy for us of the few, young years,
Of the culture so callow and crude,
Of the hand so grasping and rude,
The lip so ready for sneers
At the sons of our ancient more-than-peers. 85
Mercy for us who dare despise
Men in whose loins our Homer lies;[18]
Mothers of men who shall bring to us
The glory of Titian,[19] the grandeur of Huss;[20]
Children in whose frail arms may rest   90
Prophets and singers and saints of the West.[21]

Newcomers all from the eastern seas,
Help us incarnate dreams like these.
Forgive and forget that we did you wrong.
Help us to father a nation strong   95
In the comradeship of an equal birth,
In the wealth of the richest bloods of earth.

---

[18]*Men in whose loins our Homer lies,* men from whom
will be descended our future great poets. Homer was the
greatest poet of ancient Greece.
  [19]*Titian* (tish'ən), an Italian Renaissance artist, famous
for the rich colors in his paintings.
  [20]*Huss* (hus), a Bohemian religious reformer.
  [21]*the West,* the Western hemisphere, particularly the
United States.

HOW WELL DO YOU UNDERSTAND?

1. Why is the expression "scum o' the earth" written in quotation marks? Why do you think the author chose this expression for the title of his poem?

2. What greatness of the past does the young Greek immigrant suggest to the author? Can you mention any other fields in which this lad's Greek forebears achieved fame?

3. What past greatness do the Polish mother crooning to her child and the ragged old fiddler suggest?

4. Of what past achievement does the boy from Genoa remind the poet? In what sense is this immigrant boy on a voyage of discovery? What fields of Italian genius are touched on in lines 47-49?

5. What past greatness does the "man of the sorrow-bowed head" suggest?

6. In Section V of the poem, the author suggests several reasons why native-born Americans should ask forgiveness for their scorn for the immigrant. State each of these reasons in your own words. In the last six lines, what does the author request of the immigrants? Why do you agree or disagree with the ideas expressed in this section of the poem?

A Nation of Nations

LOUIS ADAMIC

No American writer was better qualified to speak for the immigrant than Louis Adamic. Born in the part of Austria which is now Yugoslavia, he came to America when he was fourteen years old. Here he dug ditches, and worked in restaurants, textile mills, shoe factories, and at many other jobs. Later he became a reporter and finally won a Guggenheim Fellowship, which enabled him to visit his native land. Out of this experience came *The Native's Return* (1934). This was followed by many other books dealing with the same theme—the immigrant in America.

The following selection is from one of these books, *From Many Lands* (1940). By reading it we can get an idea of what America has meant to the immigrant, what the immigrant has meant to America, and what both can mean to us all.

EIGHTY-FIVE years ago, Walt Whitman[1] said of the United States: "This is not a nation but a teeming nation of nations." The United States has been that from the start. It was recognized as such by the Founding Fathers. John Adams, Benjamin Franklin, and Thomas Jefferson, who were a committee created for the purpose, recommended to Congress that the new national emblem of the country should contain, besides the emblems of the original thirteen states, also the national emblems of England, Scotland, Ireland, France, Germany, and Holland, as representing "the countries from which these States have been peopled.". . . This has always been a country of many strains.

There is no doubt, however, that once upon a time, early in its career, the United States was a much simpler place in its human make-up than it is today. Even, say, a hundred years ago the people of this country were largely derived

---

[1]*Walt Whitman,* a great nineteenth-century American poet, particularly noted for his strong faith in democracy.

from Britain: Anglo-Saxons, who—along with the other elements of the population at the time—were mostly Protestants. There were few Catholics and few Jews. There were, to be sure, great numbers of Negroes, but they were nearly all in the South, and slavery created the illusion that they were outside the processes of American culture. Upon a different basis, the same was true of the Indians.

As the dominant element, the Anglo-Saxon Americans in the East began to create a cultural pattern which was then stretched across the country as the people began to move West. The threads being woven into this pattern were the English heritage, the English language, the colonial experience, the Revolution and its ideas, the sense of the frontier, and, to no slight extent, particularly in the Northeast, the attitude to life called Puritanism. In connection with these cultural beginnings, there appeared a system of national hopes or aspirations that came to be called the American Dream—a matter mostly of faith in the human individual and the concepts of liberty, fraternity and equality, of general welfare and democracy, which were stated or embodied in the Declaration of Independence and the Constitution. This Dream was the flowering of the idealistic, socially creative urges of the early immigrants here and their descendants, whom I now like to call the old-stock Americans.

At the beginning of their story as a group in this New World were Jamestown and Plymouth Rock.

After the Revolution, which had occurred in part because England did not permit free immigration into the colonies, new people came over right along; but for a good while they were chiefly Anglo-Saxons with some Germans and Hollanders—Protestants nearly all of them.

We have no immigration figures prior to 1820. In that year about 8000 immigrants entered; in 1830 the number was 23,000; in 1840 approximately 84,000 came in. There were many Catholic Irish among the immigrants during these decades, but most of them still were Anglo-Saxons and Protestants of the German and Dutch strains.

Then the Machine roared its way onto the national scene, bringing on the Industrial Revolution and the passion to develop the country in a hurry and to get rich quick; and came, too, the Civil War or the War Between the States, which was a great drain on the man power; and there began the New Immigration.

In the last hundred years 38,000,000 immigrants came over; 24,000,000 in the last fifty years. And the majority of them were non-Anglo-Saxons and non-Protestants, and were not very closely attached to the attitude to life called Puritanism.

Some of these new people came in a spirit of adventure or with chiefly materialistic motives, or because they were lured over by American industrialists. Most of them, however, were escaping from oppression, terrorism, even massacres; from army service and militarism generally; from life in ghettos and from economic or personal frustration or fear of frustration. It was as if they came in response to the lines struck—in 1886—on the pedestal of the Statue of Liberty:

> Give me your tired, your poor,
> Your huddled masses yearning to breathe free,
> The wretched refuse of your teeming shore,
> Send these, the homeless, the tempest-tost, to me:
> I lift my lamp beside the golden door.[2]

To most of them, as it had been to most of the earliest immigrants, the Pilgrims, America was a refuge, a chance for a better life....They came and spilled themselves over America, 38,000,000 of them, in what was a mere moment in history; representing over fifty different national backgrounds, speaking as many languages and several hundred dialects, owing allegiance to over two score rulers and governments, and adhering to about a dozen different religions.

The majority of these new people went into the cities, to work in factories and mills, in small shops and stockyards, on the new bridges, roads, and skyscrapers; or into the small min-

---

[2]*"Give me your tired...golden door."* These lines are from "The New Colossus," by Emma Lazarus, a poem written in aid of the fund to raise money for the pedestal of the Statue of Liberty.

ing towns and camps. But many, too, went on the land as pioneers. Or they went into fishing along the various coasts of America and on the Great Lakes; or to the woods as timber workers. ...And everybody worked and built and dug and grubbed and carried burdens, and as America stands today, there is hardly a building here, hardly a bridge or mile of railway or highway, hardly a vehicle, hardly anything that is not, in part, a result of immigrant labor.

This is one of the greatest stories under the sun, the story of the coming and the meeting of all these peoples, in so brief a period, on this vast and beautiful continent. It is, as yet, a story little known and perhaps never to be written fully.

We have something over 300,000 Indians, who are mostly in reservations, a problem somewhat special and apart; and about 13,000,-000 Negroes, also a rather special and uniquely acute problem, possibly destined to be the ultimate and most severe test of our forming culture, of our pretensions to democracy—a test which the country will be able to meet, I feel, only if the white elements soon begin to solve the problems among themselves.

The whites number about 115,000,000. Slightly over half of them are Anglo-Saxons, or think they are, or pass as such, partly, largely, or wholly. They are Protestants or of Protestant background. There are about 20,000,000 other people here who are not Anglo-Saxons but are Protestants, or of Protestant background. About 10,000,000 are Irish Catholic, or of that background; between 15 and 20 millions of the German, about 5,000,000 of the Italian, about 4,000,000 of the Scandinavian, about 2,000,-000 of the French, and between 8 and 10 millions of the various Slavic backgrounds.[3] Half a million each will cover those of the Finnish, Lithuanian, and Greek backgrounds. Also, we have several hundred thousand Orientals,[4] and

there are not inconsiderable Mexican and Filipino elements. And we have 4,500,000 Jews, about 22,000,000 Catholics, and 5 or 6 million people of the Eastern Orthodox faiths[5] ....These are estimates, but I believe fairly close.

We have here now 12,000,000 immigrants and between 30 and 35 million American-born children of immigrants who are designated in the census as "native of foreign white stock." And we have, perhaps, 10 or 15 million grandchildren of immigrants who are not distinguished in the census. This constitutes about half of the white population. Most of this half is non-Anglo-Saxon and non-Protestant.

"This is not a nation but a teeming nation of nations," a country in process of becoming a nation; it always has been that, and, to my mind, it will be no tragedy should it remain that for some time to come, even forever. It always has been a heterogeneous country, a mixture of strains and religions, which has been, and is, the basis of much of its uniqueness in the world and the source of much of its power. It may be no accident that many of the most dynamic cities and regions in this country have been and are those which include the greatest variety of national and cultural backgrounds.

On its sound, positive side, America always has welcomed diversity, variety, differences. The Revolution, as I say, was fought, in part, because England did not permit free immigration into the colonies.

The Founding Fathers were mostly Anglo-Saxons, but eighteen of the signers of the Declaration of Independence were of non-English origin or descent. The springs of this country's central ideas and ideals have various sources. The Declaration of Independence, one of the greatest pieces ever written, *is* an Anglo-Saxon document, written by Jefferson in the English language; its contents, however, are not the exclusive patent of any one strain. In fact, there

---

[3]*Slavic* (släv′ik *or* slav′ik) *backgrounds,* eastern European groups including Poles, Czechs, Russians, Slovaks, Bulgarians, and Yugoslavs.

[4]*Orientals,* people from the East, as Turks, Arabs, Hindus, Chinese, and Japanese.

---

[5]*Eastern Orthodox faiths,* group of Christian churches in eastern Europe, western Asia, and Egypt that recognize the patriarch of Constantinople rather than the Pope as head of the church.

is good basis for believing that an early, if not the first, draft of the Declaration was written by an Italian, Mazzei,[6] who was a close friend and associate of Jefferson. No one strain has a monopoly on the ideas of liberty, equality, fraternity, democracy....Before the Revolution, the sermons of the anti-British preachers in New England were based on passages dealing with liberty in the Old Testament, a Jewish book.... Government based on the consent of the governed is an all-important concept. The Founding Fathers got it, as it has been shown by historians, from the thirteenth-century scholastic philosophers,[7] who were Spaniards, Italians, and Frenchmen.

At its best, Americanism is nobody's monopoly, but a happy concentrate of some of the highest aspirations and tendencies of humanity at its best nearly everywhere at one time or another. As it seems to me, it is the highest body of idealism in the world today. It is, among other things, a movement away from primitive racism, fear, and nationalism, and herd instincts and mentality; a movement toward freedom, creativeness, a universal or pan-human culture.[8]

Americanism welcomes differences, and if we can stand another motto, I suggest: Let's make America safe for differences. Let us work for unity within diversity. My guess is that if we try this, much of the diversity to which some of us possibly more or less object will cease to be important or objectionable. Let us begin to accept one another as we are. I don't mean, of course, that one should like everybody; I mean that one's decision to like or dislike or be indifferent to a man should be made on the basis of his essential qualities as a person, not on the basis of the fact that he was born an Albanian or Yankee, or that he came over in steerage or

that he can sport a Mayflower blossom on his family tree....

We need to be trained, or train ourselves, in the direction of becoming creatively, positively interested in a man partly *because* he is different; *because,* being different, he is apt to have something out of the ordinary to offer to us personally and contribute to the evolving culture and civilization. Emerson said, "It is the 'not-me' in my friend that charms me."

Inviting diversity, being interested in it, will tend to produce unity in a democratic country; will tend to make it dynamic; will operate against the concentration-camplike foreign sections and ghettos and restricted residential districts, and will encourage movement and dispersal, at the same time that it will work for harmony and fusion....Inviting diversity brings out the basic sameness of people, just as the opposite results only in more and sharper differences. It breaks down both the superiorities and inferiorities, which are equally bad—two ends of the same stick.

When this country was formed, there were people, Jefferson included, who believed that the hope of the world was here. They probably were right. But we must be careful. There is need of exerting our individual and collective intelligence. We have serious economic and social problems; as we proceed to try to solve them, we should watch out that prejudice and intolerance don't turn the American Dream into a nightmare.

The future, ours as the world's, is in unity within diversity. Our various backgrounds are important and valuable, but, in the long run, not in themselves, not as something perfect and final. They are important and valuable only as material for our future American culture. As I say, we have a chance to create a universal, a pan-human culture, more satisfying than anything humanity has as yet devised or experienced.

The American Dream is a lovely thing, but to keep it alive, to keep it from turning into a nightmare, every once in a while we've got to wake up.

---

[6]*Mazzei* (mät tsä′ə), a physician and merchant who acted as Colonial American agent in Europe from 1779 to 1784.

[7]*scholastic philosophers,* men who developed a system of philosophical and theological teaching based chiefly on the teachings of the Greek philosopher Aristotle and early Christian philosophers.

[8]*pan-human culture,* a civilization that embraces the people of all races.

WHAT IS AMERICA?

1. What is the significance of the title, "A Nation of Nations"? In what way is it a summary of Mr. Adamic's entire article?

2. What evidence does the author give to show that our Founding Fathers valued the mixture of races? What other evidence can you give to show this value?

3. What diversity of background is represented by the various people you have met in the selections studied in this unit? According to Mr. Adamic, what benefits shall we receive by welcoming differences among our citizens? Why do you agree or disagree with this point of view?

4. An immigrant himself, Mr. Adamic has examined the term *Americanism* and all that it represents far more carefully than have many native-born citizens. Explain each of the following statements to show how it contributes to his understanding of what constitutes America and Americans.

(*a*) [America is] a country in process of becoming a nation. (Page 134, column 2, paragraph 2.)

(*b*) On its sound, positive side, America always has welcomed diversity, variety, differences. (Page 134, column 2, paragraph 3.)

(*c*) At its best, Americanism is nobody's monopoly. (Page 135, column 1, paragraph 1.)

(*d*) It [Americanism] is, among other things, a movement away from primitive racism, fear, and nationalism, and herd instincts and mentality; a movement toward freedom, creativeness, a universal or pan-human culture. (Page 135, column 1, paragraph 1.)

(*e*) The American Dream is a lovely thing, but to keep it alive, to keep it from turning into a nightmare, every once in a while we've got to wake up. (Page 135, column 2, paragraph 5.)

5. How do Mr. Adamic's ideas of what constitutes America and Americans agree with or differ from your ideas?

Extending interests

Prepare a chart illustrating one of the following, and be ready to explain it to the class:

1. Number of immigrants to the United States for each decade since 1820.

2. Number of immigrants from various countries in the United States at present.

The Larger View

I. George Papashvily, Mr. O'Meara, and Hyman Kaplan probably gave you some good laughs, but if you really understood these gentlemen, they and the other immigrants you met in this unit gave you something else as well—a better understanding of the immigrant, his problems, and the part he has played in building America. The following questions may serve as a basis for an informal discussion:

1. How have your ideas about the people who make up America been enlarged or changed since you have studied the selections in Unit III?

2. Louis Adamic suggests as a motto: "Let's make America safe for differences. Let us work for unity within diversity." What ways can you think of for putting this motto to work?

3. What suggestions have you for helping the immigrant or newcomer adjust to life in your community?

II. Possibly your parents and your grandparents have a surprising fund of stories to tell you about the lands from which your ancestors came, the reasons for their decision to come to the United States, and the things that happened to them in earlier days in their new country. Select some colorful bit of history or anecdote about your ancestors. Write it up in as interesting a manner as you can and prepare to read it to the class. After all pupils have read their stories, you may wish to appoint a committee to make them into a booklet which class members might illustrate.

III. Appoint a committee to secure or make a large outline map of the world. Jot down on a slip of paper your name and the names of the country or countries from which your ancestors came. The members of the committee will type or print your name and attach it to the proper country or countries.

MORE GOOD READING

ADAMIC, LOUIS, *Native's Return*. (Harper) This account of Adamic's visit to Yugoslavia in 1932 after nineteen years in America gives a vivid picture of the country and its people as they appeared to a new American. *My America* (Harper) continues the autobiography by telling of Adamic's experiences in his adopted homeland.

ALDRICH, BESS STREETER, *Spring Came on Forever*. (Appleton) This novel of two German-American families who came to Nebraska in covered-wagon days bridges several generations. Here are the growth of a family, the development of a new country, and romance.

ANTIN, MARY, *The Promised Land*. (Houghton) To the little twelve-year-old girl from Russian Poland, America was "the promised land." Her autobiography is a vivid account of her new experiences, her school days, and above all her feelings of the freedom and opportunity her new land offered.

AUSLANDER, JOSEPH, and WURDEMANN, AUDREY, *My Uncle Jan; a Novel*. (Longmans) Forty years ago Uncle Jan arrived in Wisconsin from Czechoslovakia. This is his account of hilarious adventures in the New World.

BOJER, JOHAN, *The Emigrants*. (Appleton) Erik Foss' colony of Norwegians had high hopes as they began to farm sections of the Red River Valley in North Dakota. But drought, frost, and the terrible loneliness shattered their first plans. This is a vital, courageous novel.

BOK, EDWARD, *The Americanization of Edward Bok*. (Scribner) This is a true success story, the autobiography of a Dutch immigrant boy who became a magazine editor and a friend of the great of two continents.

CANNON, CORNELIA, *Red Rust*. (Little) Matts Swenson, a farmer of Swedish descent, struggled on the wheatlands of Minnesota to produce a grain that would be able to withstand red rust. Believable human relationships add to the values of this fine novel.

CARR, LORRAINE, *Mother of the Smiths*. (Macmillan) Sabe Smith's husband was a good-natured dreamer, but Sabe was determined to win an education for her six sons. You will find the adventures of the Smiths and their Mexican neighbors in Taos, New Mexico, make a vivid and humorous story.

CATHER, WILLA, *Song of the Lark*. (Houghton) Thea Kronborg, the daughter of a Swedish minister in Arizona, had one ambition. The account of Thea's development into a great singer is a fascinating story, beautifully written.

CHASE, MARY ELLEN, *Mary Christmas*. (Little) Mary Christmas was an Armenian peddler who came to play an important part in the life of a happy family in Maine. You'll find every page of this small book a delight.

DAHL, BORGHILD, *Karen*. (Random House) Karen came to the United States from Norway in 1870, imbued with courage, self-confidence, and optimism. On the Dakota prairies she struggled to establish a home. Karen emerges from this story as real as any historical character.

DANKOVSZKY, DORATHEA, *Sugar Bush*. (Nelson) For six years the Kolochecks, a Polish family, had saved to buy the farm at Meeting House Hill. This is the story of their life there and their learning to be a part of the community.

FERBER, EDNA, *American Beauty*. (Doubleday) Edna Ferber is a fine storyteller, and this story of the disintegration of the Oakes' estate and its rebirth under the hard-working hands of Polish immigrants moves with her usual skill and sureness.

FORBES, KATHRYN, *Mama's Bank Account*. (Harcourt) Few more heart-warming stories have been written than this account of a Norwegian carpenter's family in San Francisco.

HAVILL, EDWARD, *Big Ember; a Novel*. (Harper) Violent weather was not the only hazard faced by this group of Norwegian settlers in Minnesota; there was also the constant threat of marauding Indians. You'll find plenty happens to keep you turning the pages rapidly.

JORDAN, MILDRED A., *One Red Rose Forever*. (Knopf) The background of the story is mid-eighteenth century Pennsylvania; the hero is Baron Stiegel, a German immigrant who became famous as the maker of Stiegel glass.

NATHAN, ROBERT, *The Sea-Gull Cry*. (Knopf) Human kindness plays a large part in this story of a refugee girl and her small brother who set up housekeeping in a derelict barge on Cape Cod in the early days of World War II.

PUPIN, MICHAEL, *From Immigrant to Inventor*. (Scribner) From Serbian immigrant boy to professor at Columbia University and scientist is a long road to travel, yet Michael Pupin covered it all. His autobiography makes inspiring reading.

RIIS, JACOB, *The Making of an American*. (Macmillan) When Jacob Riis arrived in New York from Denmark in 1869 he was a penniless youth of twenty. After working at various trades he became a newspaper reporter and worked to better living conditions in the slums. You'll find Riis' rise from poverty to influence provides the material for an excellent autobiography.

RIZK, SALOM, *Syrian Yankee*. (Doubleday) At the age of twelve the Syrian boy found he could claim American citizenship through his mother; at seventeen he arrived in the United States. This is the simple and moving story of his life and the thrill he finds in being an American.

RÖLVAAG, OLE E., *Giants in the Earth*. (Harper) Per Hansa was a Norwegian immigrant who found the struggle with the Dakota prairie for a livelihood exhilarating, but his beloved wife Beret found only loneliness and terror. If you're a mature reader you'll enjoy this story of two fine people.

SAROYAN, WILLIAM, *My Name Is Aram.* (Harcourt) Each of the sketches in this book about an American-born boy of Armenian family in California is a story in itself; but each is so amusing or so unusual that you'll just have to go on and read the next.

SHIPPEN, KATHERINE B., *Passage to America; the Story of the Great Migrations*. (Harper) In a narrative that never fails to interest, the author covers the historical events that sent waves of immigrants to America, from the Dutch and Swedish groups of colonial days to refugees from concentration camps after World War II. Particularly valuable is the discussion of the contributions that each group of immigrants made to American culture.

WALKER, MILDRED, *Brewers' Big Horses*. (Harcourt) The brewer's son belonged to a German family; the girl was a member of a proud Michigan family. The opposition she encountered in her plans to live life in her own way makes the story.

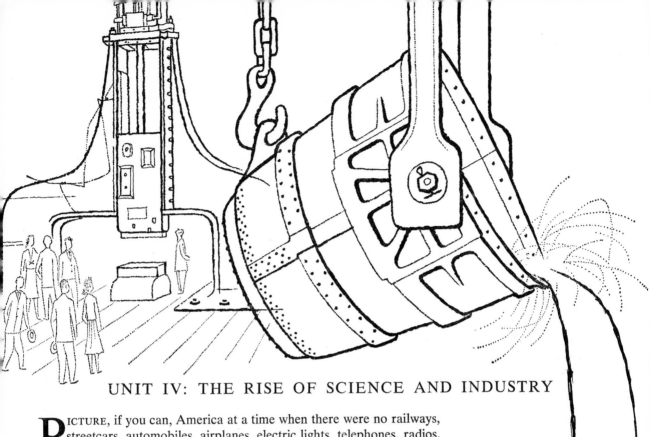

UNIT IV: THE RISE OF SCIENCE AND INDUSTRY

Picture, if you can, America at a time when there were no railways, streetcars, automobiles, airplanes, electric lights, telephones, radios, television sets, or moving-picture houses, and in which there were practically no factories and no scientific laboratories of the kind we know today. Consider next what must have happened to people's lives when, in a relatively short time, all these became common. If you have a lively imagination, you will see why the rise of science and industry revolutionized American living, and why we today are so often aware of existing in what is called "the machine age."

From colonial times many Americans were interested in natural phenomena and through their studies helped advance science. In the nineteenth century, as the people moved westward and began to discover the land's vast store of natural resources, forward-looking businessmen began to harness the recently invented steam engine to more and more machines. Physicists, chemists, and engineers worked diligently to supply useful aid to these industrialists. This coöperative effort served as a spur to both science and industry, and off they galloped without bothering to pay much attention to the effect upon human beings. In fact, this rapid movement forward of science and industry, although adding much to our material comfort, has created some of our gravest social problems. Among these are the waste of natural resources, the unwholesome living conditions in some factory towns and cities, the strained relationship between capital and labor and the consequent problem of governmental restraints of many sorts.

American authors show an increasing awareness of these problems, and many have tried to make us conscious of them. Others, merely interested in picturing life, have shown corners of industrial America with great faithfulness. Still others have told of the sorrow they feel because science has done so little to add to the freedom and happiness of mankind. A few have found beauty in the rhythms of the machine and grandeur in the energy and vastness of industrial America. Whatever the viewpoints of writers, the rise of science and industry has profoundly affected American life and is inescapably a part of our literature.

How to Make Lightning Rods

BENJAMIN FRANKLIN

The first selection in this unit serves to remind us that American authors were deeply interested in science even in colonial times. The passage is by the famed Benjamin Franklin, whose life nearly spanned the eighteenth century.

After Franklin had barely escaped shipwreck on one of his trips to England, he wrote to his wife: "Perhaps I should on this occasion vow to build a chapel to some saint; but...if I were to vow at all, it should be *to* build a lighthouse." This practical kind of thinking is characteristic of America's first great electrician and widely known scientist. His great desire to find out the *why* of things was matched by a desire to make his discoveries and inventions useful to mankind. This attitude is found throughout his writing. The following letter is typical.

To DAVID HUME[1]

London, January 24, 1762

Dear Sir,

In compliance with my Lord Marischal's request,[2] communicated to me by you, when I last had the pleasure of seeing you, I now send you what at present appears to me to be the shortest and simplest method of securing buildings, etc., from the mischiefs of lightning.

Prepare a steel rod five or six feet long, half an inch thick at its biggest end, and tapering

[1]*David Hume* (hūm), a Scottish historian and philosopher.

[2]*Lord Marischal's request.* Lord Marischal was the hereditary title of George Keith, a member of a noble Scottish family. Apparently he had asked Hume to inquire of Franklin about how to protect buildings against lightning.

to a sharp point; which point should be gilt to prevent its rusting. Let the big end of the rod have a strong eye or ring of half an inch diameter. Fix this rod upright to the chimney or highest part of the house, by means of staples, so as it may be kept steady. Let the pointed end be upward, and rise three or four feet above the chimney or building that the rod is fixed to. Drive into the ground an iron rod of about an inch diameter, and ten or twelve feet long, that has also an eye or ring in its upper end. It is best that the rod should be at some distance from the foundation of the building, not nearer than ten feet, if your ground will allow so much. Then take as much length of iron rod of about an inch diameter as will reach from the eye in the rod above to that in the rod below, and fasten it securely to those rods by passing its ends through the rings, and bending those ends till they likewise form rings.

This length of rod may either be in one or several pieces. If in several, let the ends of the pieces be also well hooked to the other. Then close and cover every joint with lead, which is easily done by making a strong bag of strong paper round the joint, tying it close below, and then pouring in the melted lead; it being of use in these junctures that there should be a considerable quantity of metalline contact between piece and piece. For, if they were only hooked together and so touched each other but in points, the lightning, in passing them, might melt and break them where they join. The lead will also prevent the weakening of the joints by rust. To prevent the shaking of this rod by the wind, you may secure it by a few staples to the building, till it comes down within ten feet of the ground, and thence carry it off to the ground rod, near to which should be planted a post, to support the iron conductor above the heads of the people walking under it.

If the building be large and long, as an hundred feet and upward, it may not be amiss to erect a pointed rod at each end, and form a communication by an iron rod between them. If there be a well near the house, so that you can by such a rod form a communication from your top rod to the water, it is rather better to do so than to use the ground rod above mentioned. It may also be proper to paint the iron, to render it more durable by preserving it from rust.

A building thus guarded will not be damaged by lightning, nor any person or thing therein killed, hurt, or set on fire. For, either the explosion will be prevented by the operation of the point; or, if not prevented, then the whole quantity of lightning exploded near the house, whether passing from the cloud to the earth or from the earth to the cloud, will be conveyed in the rods. And, though the iron be crooked around the corner of the building, or make ever so many turns between the upper and lower rod, the lightning will follow it and be guided by it, without affecting the building. I omit the philosophical reasons and experiments on which this practice is founded; for they are many, and would make a book. Besides they are already known to most of the learned throughout Europe. In the American British colonies, many houses have been, since the year 1752, guarded by these principles.

If I have not been explicit enough in my directions, I shall, on the least intimation, endeavor to supply the defect.

I am, &c.,

B. Franklin

WHAT ARE THE FACTS?

1. Are Franklin's directions for installing lightning rods clear? What qualities of his writing make the directions easy to follow? Be prepared to draw a diagram of Franklin's lightning rod on the blackboard.

2. What does Franklin admit, near the end of his letter, that he is omitting? What are his reasons for leaving these matters out? Do you think his reasons are sound?

3. How does this letter reflect Franklin's desire for the wide use of scientific improvements?

The Paper Mill in Devil's Dungeon

HERMAN MELVILLE

Toward the latter part of his long life, Benjamin Franklin wrote: "The rapid progress true science now makes occasions my regretting sometimes that I was born so soon. It is impossible to imagine the height to which may be carried, in a thousand years, the power of man over matter. O that *moral* science were in a fair way of improvement, that men would cease to be wolves to one another, and that human beings would at length learn what they now improperly call *humanity.*"

As Franklin foresaw, moral science has tended to lag behind pure science through the years. Herman Melville (1819-1891) noticed the fact in a prose sketch which he wrote about a New England paper mill in the early 1850's. Although the passage was written about a century ago and although we have since made progress in improving conditions, Melville makes a point which is still worth remembering. Wherever conditions similar to those described exist today, their greatest tragedy lies, as Melville says, in "the strange innocence of cruel-heartedness in usage-hardened" people.

AT FIRST I could not discover the paper mill.

Below me the whole hollow, called by the country people the Devil's Dungeon, gleamed with the white snow, except, here and there where a pinnacle of granite showed one wind-swept angle bare. The mountains stood pinned in shrouds—a pass of Alpine corpses.[1] Where stands the mill? Suddenly a whirling, humming sound broke upon my ear. I looked, and there, like an arrested avalanche, lay the large white-washed factory. It was subordinately surrounded by a cluster of other and smaller buildings, some of which, from their cheap, blank air, great length, gregarious windows, and comfortless expression, no doubt were boarding houses of the operatives. A snow-white hamlet amidst the snows.

[1] *The mountains...pass of Alpine corpses.* To the author the snow-covered trees on the mountainside looked like corpses in white shrouds.

Dismounting and warily picking my way down the dangerous declivity—horse and man both sliding now and then upon the icy ledges —at length I drove, or the blast drove me, into the largest square, before one side of the main edifice. Piercingly and shrilly the shotted blast[2] blew by the corner; and redly and demoniacally boiled Blood River at one side. A long wood-pile of many scores of cords, all glittering in mail of crusted ice, stood crosswise in the square. A row of horse posts, their north sides plastered with adhesive snow, flanked the factory wall. The bleak frost packed and paved the square as with some ringing metal.

Then, as I and my horse stood shivering in the wind-spray, a dark-complexioned, well-wrapped personage passed, making for the factory door.

"Is there no horse shed here, sir?"

"Yonder, the woodshed," he replied and disappeared inside the factory.

With much ado I managed to wedge in horse and pung[3] between the scattered piles of wood all sawn and split. Then, blanketing my horse and piling my buffalo[4] on the blanket's top, and tucking in its edges well around the breastband and breeching, I tied him fast and ran lamely for the factory door.

Immediately I found myself standing in a spacious place, intolerably lighted by long rows of windows, focusing inward the snowy scene without.

At rows of blank-looking counters sat rows of blank-looking girls, white folders in their blank hands, all blankly folding blank paper.

In one corner stood some huge frame of ponderous iron, with a vertical thing like a piston periodically rising and falling upon a heavy wooden block. Before it—its tame minister—stood a tall girl feeding the iron animal with half quires of rose-hued note paper, which, at every downward dab of the pistonlike machine, received in the corner the impress of a wreath of roses. I looked from the rosy paper to the pallid cheek, but said nothing.

[2]*shotted blast,* gust of wind with the force of a charge of shot.
[3]*pung,* sleigh with a boxlike body.
[4]*buffalo,* robe made of buffalo skin.

Seated before a long apparatus strung with long, slender strings like any harp, another girl was feeding it with foolscap sheets, which, so soon as they curiously traveled from her on the cords, were withdrawn at the opposite end of the machine by a second girl. They came to the first girl blank; they went to the second girl ruled.

I looked upon the first girl's brow, and saw it was young and fair; I looked upon the second girl's brow, and saw it was ruled and wrinkled. Then, as I still looked, the two—for some small variety to the monotony—changed places; and where had stood the young, fair brow, now stood the ruled and wrinkled one.

Perched high upon a narrow platform and still higher upon a high stool crowning it, sat another figure serving some other iron animal, while below the platform sat her mate in some sort of reciprocal attendance.

Not a syllable was breathed. Nothing was heard but the low, steady, overruling hum of the iron animals. The human voice was banished from the spot. Machinery—that vaunted slave of humanity—here stood menially served by human beings, who served mutely and cringingly as the slave serves the sultan. The girls did not so much seem accessory wheels to the general machinery as mere cogs to the wheels.

All this scene around me was instantaneously taken in at one sweeping glance—even before I had proceeded to unwind the heavy fur tippet from around my neck. I made known my business, concluded it satisfactorily, and then begged to be conducted throughout the place to view it.

"Cupid is the boy for that," said the dark-complexioned man. "Cupid!" and by this odd fancy name calling a dimpled, red-cheeked, spirited-looking, forward little fellow, the man bade him lead the stranger through the edifice.

"Come first and see the water wheel," said this lively lad, with the air of boyishly brisk importance.

Quitting the folding room, we crossed some damp, cold boards and stood beneath a great wet shed, incessantly showering with foam, like the green barnacled bow of some East India-

man[5] in a gale. Round and round here went the enormous revolutions of the dark colossal water wheel, grim with its one immutable purpose.

"This sets our whole machinery agoing, sir; in every part of all these buildings, where the girls work and all."

I looked, and saw that the turbid waters of Blood River had not changed their hue by coming under the use of man.

"You make only blank paper; no printing of any sort, I suppose? All blank paper, don't you?"

"Certainly; what else would a paper factory make?" The lad here looked at me as if suspicious of my common sense.

He took me up a wet and rickety stair to a great light room, furnished with no visible thing but rude, mangerlike receptacles running all round its sides; and up to these mangers, like so many mares haltered to the rack, stood rows of girls. Before each was vertically thrust up a long, glittering scythe, immovably fixed at bottom to the manger edge. The curve of the scythe, and its having no snath to it, made it look exactly like a sword. To and fro across the sharp edge the girls forever dragged long strips of rags, washed white, picked from baskets at one side, thus ripping asunder every seam and converting the tatters almost into lint. The air swam with the fine, poisonous particles, which from all sides darted, subtly, as motes in sunbeams, into the lungs.

"This is the rag room," coughed the boy.

---

[5]*barnacled bow of some East Indiaman*, front of a ship in the India trade crusted over with shell-covered animals.

"You find it rather stifling here," coughed I in answer, "but the girls don't cough."

"Oh, they are used to it."

"Where do you get such hosts of rags?" picking up a handful from a basket.

"Some from the country round about; some from far over sea—Leghorn and London."

"The edges of those swords, they are turned outward from the girls, if I see right; but their rags and fingers fly so, I cannot distinctly see."

"Turned outward."

Yes, murmured I to myself, I see it now; turned outward; and each erected sword is so borne, edge outward, before each girl. If my reading fails me not, just so, of old, condemned state prisoners went from the hall of judgment to their doom, an officer before bearing a sword, its edge turned outward in significance of their fatal sentence. So, through consumptive pallors of this blank, raggy life, go these white girls to death.

"Those scythes look very sharp," again turning toward the boy.

"Yes; they have to keep them so. Look!"

That moment two of the girls, dropping their rags, plied each a whetstone up and down the sword blade. My unaccustomed blood curdled at the sharp shriek of the tormented steel.

Their own executioners, themselves whetting the very swords that slay them, meditated I.

"What makes those girls so sheet-white, my lad?"

"Why"—with a roguish twinkle, pure ignorant drollery, not-knowing heartlessness—"I suppose the handling of such white bits of sheets all the time makes them so sheety."

"Let us leave the rag room now, my lad."

More tragical and more inscrutably mysterious than any mystic sight, human or machine, throughout the factory, was the strange innocence of cruel-heartedness in this usage-hardened boy.

"And now," said he cheerily, "I suppose you want to see our great machine, which cost us twelve thousand dollars only last autumn. That's the machine that makes the paper, too. This way, sir."

Following him, I crossed a large, bespattered place with two great round vats in it, full of a white, wet, woolly-looking stuff, not unlike the albuminous part of an egg, soft-boiled.

"There," said Cupid, tapping the vats carelessly, "these are the first beginnings of the paper, this white pulp you see. Look how it swims bubbling round and round, moved by the paddle here. From hence it pours from both vats into that one common channel yonder; and so goes, mixed up and leisurely, to the great machine. And now for that."

He led me into a room stifling with a strange, bloodlike, abdominal heat, as if here, true enough, were being finally developed the germinous particles[6] lately seen.

Before me, rolled out like some long Eastern manuscript, lay stretched one continuous length of iron framework, multitudinous and mystical, with all sorts of rollers, wheels, and cylinders in slowly measured and unceasing motion.

"Here first comes the pulp now," said Cupid. "See; first it pours out and spreads itself upon this wide, sloping board; and then—look—slides, thin and quivering, beneath the first roller there. Follow on now, and see it as it slides from under that to the next cylinder. There; see how it has become just a very little less pulpy now. One step more, and it grows still more to some slight consistence."

"Bless my soul!" said I, amazed at the elongation, interminable convolutions, and deliberate slowness of the machine; "it must take a long time for the pulp to pass from end to end, and come out paper."

"Oh, not so long," smiled the precocious lad, with a superior and patronizing air; "only nine minutes. But look; you may try it for yourself. Have you a bit of paper? Ah! here's a bit on the floor. Now mark that with any word you please, and let me dab it on here, and we'll see how long before it comes out at the other end."

"Well, let me see," said I, taking out my pencil. "Come, I'll mark it with your name."

Bidding me take out my watch, Cupid adroitly dropped the inscribed slip on an exposed part of the incipient mass.

---

[6]germinous particles. The author compares the making of paper to the growth of an animal or plant; he thinks of the pulp particles as the germ from which the organism develops.

Instantly my eye marked the second hand on my dial plate.[7]

Slowly I followed the slip, inch by inch, sometimes pausing for full half a minute as it disappeared beneath inscrutable groups of the lower cylinders, but only gradually to emerge again; and so on, and on, and on—inch by inch; now in open sight, sliding along like a freckle on the quivering sheet; and then again wholly vanished; and so on, and on, and on—inch by inch; all the time the main sheet growing more and more to final firmness—when, suddenly, I saw a sort of paper-fall, not wholly unlike a waterfall; a scissory sound smote my ear, as of some cord being snapped; and down dropped an unfolded sheet of perfect foolscap, with my "Cupid" half faded out, and still moist and warm.

My travels were at an end, for here was the end of the machine.

"Well, how long was it?" said Cupid.

"Nine minutes to a second," replied I.

"I told you so."

For a moment a curious emotion filled me, not wholly unlike that which one might experience at the fulfillment of some mysterious prophecy. But how absurd, thought I again; the thing is a mere machine, the essence of which is unvarying punctuality and precision.

Previously absorbed by the wheels and cylinders, my attention was now directed to a sad-looking woman standing by.

"That is rather an elderly person so silently tending the machine end here. She would not seem wholly used to it either."

"Oh," knowingly whispered Cupid through the din, "she only came last week. She was a nurse formerly. But the business is poor in these parts, and she's left it. But look at the paper she is piling there."

"Does that thin cobweb there," said I, pointing to the sheet in its more imperfect stage, "does that never tear or break? It is marvelous fragile, and yet this machine it passes through is so mighty."

"It never is known to tear a hair's point."

"Does it never stop—get clogged?"

"No, it *must* go. The machinery makes it go just *so*—just that very way, and at that very pace you there plainly *see* it go. The pulp can't help going."

Something of awe now stole over me, as I gazed upon this inflexible iron animal. Always, more or less, machinery of this ponderous, elaborate sort strikes, in some moods, strange dread into the human heart, as some living, panting behemoth might. But what made the thing I saw so specially terrible to me was the metallic necessity, the unbudging fatality which governed it. Though here and there I could not follow the thin, gauzy veil of pulp in the course of its more mysterious or entirely invisible advance, yet it was indubitable that at those points where it eluded me it still marched on in unvarying docility to the autocratic cunning of the machine. A fascination fastened on me. I stood spellbound and wandering in my soul. Before my eyes—there, passing in slow procession along the wheeling cylinders, I seemed to see, glued to the pallid incipience of the pulp, the yet more pallid faces of all the pallid girls I had eyed that heavy day. Slowly, mournfully, beseechingly, yet unresistingly, they gleamed along, their agony dimly outlined on the imperfect paper, like the print of the tormented face on the handkerchief of St. Veronica.[8]

"Hallo! the heat of the room is too much for you," cried Cupid, staring at me.

"No—I am rather chill, if anything."

"Come out, sir—out—out," and with the protecting air of a careful father the precocious lad hurried me outside.

In a few minutes, feeling revived a little, I went into the folding room—the first room I had entered—where the desk for transacting business stood, surrounded by the blank counters and blank girls engaged at them.

"Cupid here has led me a strange tour," said I to the dark-complexioned man before mentioned. "Yours is a most wonderful factory. Your great machine is a miracle of inscrutable intricacy."

---

[7] *dial plate,* face of a watch.

[8] *the print...handkerchief of St. Veronica.* According to legend a pious woman of Jerusalem named Veronica was moved with pity when she saw Christ carrying His cross to Calvary and gave Him her handkerchief to wipe His face. When Christ handed the handkerchief back to her, it miraculously bore a perfect imprint of His face.

"Yes, all our visitors think it so. But we don't have many. We are in a very out-of-the-way corner here. Few inhabitants, too. Most of our girls come from far-off villages."

"The girls," echoed I, glancing round at their silent forms. "Why is it, sir, that in most factories female operatives of whatever age are indiscriminately called girls, never women?"

"Oh! as to that—why, I suppose, the fact of their being generally unmarried—that's the reason, I should think. But it never struck me before. For our factory here, we will not have married women; they are apt to be off and on too much. We want none but steady workers: twelve hours to the day, day after day, through the three hundred and sixty-five days, excepting Sundays, Thanksgiving, and fast days. That's our rule. And so, having no married women, what females we have are rightly called girls."

"Then these are all maids," said I, while some pained homage to their pale virginity made me involuntarily bow.

"All maids."

Again the strange emotion filled me.

Remuffling myself and thrusting my hands into my huge sealskin mittens, I sallied out into the nipping air, and found poor Black, my horse, all cringing and doubled up with the cold.

Soon, wrapped in furs and meditations, I ascended from the Devil's Dungeon.

WHAT ARE THE AUTHOR'S IMPRESSIONS?

1. What details in the outdoor setting add to the bleakness and misery described later in the selection? In what way do the proper names used suggest unhappiness?

2. When the author entered the paper mill, what was his first impression? What details of his progress through the factory served to increase and strengthen this impression?

3. Why do you think the author refers to the machines several times as "iron animals"? What effect did the precision and perfection of these machines have on the author?

4. In what way were the author's questions, suggesting the inhuman working conditions, received by the lad? What fact did the author find "more tragical and more inscrutably mysterious than any mystic sight, human or machine"?

5. What conditions in the paper mill would not be permitted nowadays by health and labor laws? In what ways did the life and work of the girls differ from that of factory workers today?

6. What result might Melville have expected from widespread, immediate reading of his article? Would it have aroused you to any form of action?

Choosing words to create atmosphere

Herman Melville detested the paper mill; he felt that it robbed human beings of strength, joy, dignity, and, ultimately, of life itself. In writing of it, in order to convey to his readers the feeling of gloom and death with which it had affected him, he chose words that suggested its grim, inhuman atmosphere. To his sensitive mind even the surroundings partook of the general gloom. Death, the enemy of life, is suggested to him by the encircling mountains that "stood pinned in shrouds—a pass of Alpine corpses." The descent was down a "dangerous declivity" and over "icy ledges." In the square before the mill itself "piercingly and shrilly the shotted blast blew by the corner; and redly and demoniacally boiled Blood River at one side." There is the suggestion of steely hardness in Melville's description of the woodpile "all glittering in mail of crusted ice" and of the square "paved...as with some ringing metal."

The author finds the same cold, inhuman atmosphere within the paper mill. Glance through the selection again, finding passages in which you think Melville was particularly successful in using words to create a feeling of inhumanity.

Know your words

The prefixes *in-*, *im-*, and *un-* sometimes carry the meaning "not; the opposite of; the absence of." In his description of the mechanical devices which dominated the lives of the workers in the paper mill, Melville often uses words containing these prefixes. Explain each of the following phrases, in each case showing how the italicized word helps the author convey his feeling about the factory. What impression do you gain from considering all of the phrases together?

1. ...the enormous revolutions of the dark colossal water wheel, grim with its one *immutable* purpose....

2. ...a long glittering scythe, *immovably* fixed at bottom to the manger edge....

3. ...*interminable* convolutions and deliberate slowness of the machine....

4. ...this *inflexible* iron animal....

5. ...the metallic necessity, the *unbudging* fatality which governed it....

6. ...a miracle of *inscrutable* intricacy....

John Henry and the Machine in West Virginia

WALTER BLAIR

The United States is probably the only country in the world in which the idea of a contest between a man and a machine has been embodied in a folk tale. John Henry, like Davy Crockett, Mike Fink, Paul Bunyan, and others, is an American folk hero. The story of his show-down with the machine reflects the natural pride of men in their physical strength and achievement. John Henry's proud boast, "Before I let that steam drill beat me, I'll die with my hammer in my hand," is symbolic both of the tragic significance of the machine to a people that had earned its living largely by manual labor and of man's proud, unconquerable spirit. The following version of this folk tale is a chapter in a book written by one of the editors of this volume.

FROM HIS BIRTH, it was clear that John Henry's life would be out of the ordinary. The day before, there was a rainbow, and a coal-black preacher rode by the Henry cabin on a gray mule. The night was black, with a round red moon and no stars. Near by a cock crowed, a hound bayed, and somewhere in the forest panthers screamed. A great black cloud came from the southwest to cover the moon, and rain and forked lightning darted out of the cloud. And the thunder made a hammer of itself that pounded the earth till the trees quivered.

Then John Henry was born.

And the cloud went away, the moon shone white and bright, the stars came out, and the night birds started their singing. But in the moonlight, a coal-black preacher rode by the cabin again, and he was riding on a gray mule.

First thing John Henry knew, someone was saying, "He weigh thirty-three pound!" Next thing he knew, someone else was saying, "My, my, see them great big shoulders!"

"Course I weigh thirty-three pounds," says John Henry. "Course I got big shoulders! And I got me a voice that's deep and strong. And I got me a cravin' in my soul. What's more, I's hungry."

"My, my," John Henry's pappy said. "John Henry's talkin' already. What you aim to eat, son? Want a little old milk, son?"

"Milk's for babies," John Henry answered him back, "and already I's a natural boy, and soon I'll be a natural man. And I's hollow as an old dry well, sure as you born. So bring me seven hawg jowls and three kettle full of black-eyed peas. Bring me seven ham bones and three pot full of giant cabbage sloshed around in gravy. Bring me a bait of turnip greens[1] that's higher than my woolly head, and a like amount of ash cake[2] to soak in the potlicker."[3]

"Lawd, Lawd," says John Henry's mammy. "Sound like we got a bragful son on our weary hands. Pappy, maybe if we start right now and learn him his eyes is bigger than his stomach, it'll start him on a good life."

So, with the help of the neighbors, they got all those mountains of food together. And there wasn't room for all the food in the fireplace room, so they had to set it forth on seven tables in the yard.

When John Henry's pappy looked at all that food, he grinned from ear to ear. Then he went to that newborn son of his, and he said, "It's all there, son, set forth on seven tables. If you can eat it, it's steamin' in the moonlight."

John Henry walked to the tables, and he started to eat. The food began to fly, and everybody that watched him grinned to see the way he prized his food. Of course, they expected that he'd stop after the first or second table.

But soon every table was clean as a hound-dog's tooth and John Henry was untying his napkin from around his neck.

"My, my," his pappy said. "He done et up all that food."

---

[1] *a bait of turnip greens,* a meal of the boiled leaves of turnips.
[2] *ash cake,* corn bread cooked in hot ashes.
[3] *potlicker,* the liquid left in the kettle after boiling hog jowls and turnip greens.

"Course I did," says John Henry. "I told you I was hungry."

"We thought you was just a bragful son," his mammy said.

"No," John Henry told her, "I's not bragful and I's not humble. I's a natural boy, and what I says, I means. And now I's goin' to sleep for nine hours."

Nine hours after he went to sleep—nine hours on the dot—John Henry woke up. "I got me a cravin' in my soul, and I's hungry," he said. "Bring me thirteen possums with sweet taters piled treetop high around them. Bring me ninety-nine slices of fried razorback ham[4] and the red gravy. Bring me three gallons of hominy grits[5] to put the gravy onto. And bring me thirty-three buttermilk biscuits and tree-sweetnin'[6] for them, for to finish off with."

Knowing, by now, that the boy meant business, they brought what he asked, and served it forth on nine tables. He ate it, easy as could be, untied his napkin from around his neck, and went back to bed.

And it went like that for quite a few months, while John Henry grew and grew. By good luck, that was back in the slave days before the war, so Ole Massa[7] had to furnish all that food.

But John Henry grew fast, and his strength grew likewise.

He wasn't many weeks old when he got hold of a piece of steel and his pappy's five-pound hammer when the family was at meeting[8] one fine Sunday morning.

When the family was a good piece from the cabin—"Lawd, Lawd," says John Henry's mammy. "Hear that hammer ringin'. It sound like the meetin' house bells when they's tollin' for a buryin'."

When the family came to the house, they found John Henry had gone out with that piece of steel and that hammer. He'd found every big

stone he could find, and he'd used the steel and the five-pound hammer to break the big stones. He was working away on the biggest stone of the lot now, hammering the steel and singing in time:

If I die (*Wham!*)
A railroad man, (*Wham!*)
Go bury me (*Wham!*)
Under the sand, (*Wham!*)
With a pick and shovel (*Wham!*)
At my head and feet, (*Wham!*)
And a twenty-pound hammer (*Wham!*)
In my hand. (*Wham!*)

With the last wham, the rock broke in two, just as clean as if it'd been sawed, and John Henry stood up grinning, his white teeth shining in his dark face.

"Hello, folkses," says he. "Look like I's found what I want to do—swing a hammer and make the steel ring like a bell. Never been so happy in all my born days, and I's seven weeks old come Thursday. Seem like when I swings this old hammer, I don't have a cravin' in my soul—don't have a cravin' any more."

"My, my," his pappy said. "Look like our son was goin' to be a steel-drivin' man."

While he was saying this, though, there was the clump of hoofs on the red clay road that ran past the quarters. And the smile on John Henry's face faded, and he frowned a little. And the next thing John Henry said was:

"This hammer be the death of me." (He said it kind of puzzled-like, looking fair-to-middling dazed.)

"Lawd, Lawd," his mammy said. "Run out, one of you chillun, and see what that was ridin' by."

So one of the little children—all eight of them were smaller than John Henry by now—ran out and looked down the red clay road. When this little girl came back, she said, "It was nothin' but a coal-black preacher ridin' on an old gray mule."

"Lawd save us all," mammy said, "that's a bad, bad sign."

After that John Henry slept with his hammer every night, giving it a smacking big kiss before he went to sleep. And many of his childhood days he spent breaking big stones with his ham-

---

[4]*razorback ham*, ham from a razorback, a kind of thin, half-wild hog with a ridged back.

[5]*hominy grits*, a dish made of coarsely ground, hulled Indian corn.

[6]*tree-sweetnin'*, syrup, probably made from the sweet sap of maple trees.

[7]*Ole Massa*, Old Master, a common term for the owner of a plantation.

[8]*meeting*, church services.

mer and his steel. Not only would he break up stones; some of them he'd drive with his hammer. He could kill animals by driving the stones —a whirring partridge or a leaping rabbit, or even a whizzing deer. He didn't kill much game, though—just what he and the family needed for the pot. Because his heart was big in proportion to his size, and he was mighty big.

After a while, though, John Henry got so big and so strong that when he lifted the hammer with all his strength and whammed it down, he broke it. There wasn't any other hammer handy, and he wouldn't take that old hammer to his bed. But there'd be dark black nights when he'd wake up to find himself reaching for that old hammer and full of woe because he couldn't find it.

By the time he was fifteen, John Henry was bigger than any full-grown black man on the plantation. It was still slave days, then, so Old Massa had him go to the fields. The fields were snow-white with cotton, and it was cotton-picking time in the fields.

When the overseer looked at him, the overseer said, "You're big and strong beyond your years, John Henry, and maybe we can make a cotton-picker out of you, sure enough."

John Henry said, in his big deep voice: "Course I's big and strong beyond my years. But you don't need to *make* a cotton-picker out of me, 'cause I already *is* one. Bring me three sacks, big sacks—one for each shoulder and one for the middle of my back, and stand out of the way, 'cause I can pick more cotton—clean cotton, too, without any bolls and stalks in it—than any nine black men there is. Three bales a day is what I can pick, sure as you born."

"Oh! Oh!" says the overseer. "I see what you are, John Henry. You're bragful and you're uppity, high steppin' and proud. All right, folks, bring him the three sacks, big sacks, and stand out of the way. And be ready to laugh till your sides ache, 'cause John Henry's talked beyond his powers."

Every one of all those cotton pickers got to a place where he could see and where he had plenty of scope to laugh hearty. But they soon saw John Henry had a natural-born cotton-picker's ways. He bent his back and kept it

bent, in order that he might not tire. He passed his bent fingers over the bolls, cupped his hands to catch the cotton as it fell, and moved his hands all the time toward the sacks on his shoulders. What's more, the way a good cotton-picker does, he sang while he worked:

Ole Massa told the slaves,
Pick a bale of cotton,
Ole Massa told the slaves,
Pick a bale a day.

A-pick a bale, a-pick a bale, a-pick a bale of cotton,
A-pick a bale, a-pick a bale, a-pick a bale a day.

Ole Eli from Shilo
Can pick a bale of cotton,
Ole Eli from Shilo
Can pick a bale a day.

I believe to my soul
I pick three bales of cotton,
I believe to my soul
I pick three bales a day.

A-pick three bales, a-pick three bales, pick three bales of cotton,
A-pick three bales, a-pick three bales, pick three bales a day.

When John Henry first sang that about picking three bales, the workers laughed deep—

"Yugh, yugh, yugh," that way, slapped their knees, and said: "Sakes alive! Ain't he a bragful black man?" For nobody except Old Eli from Shilo had ever been known to pick as much as a bale a day, and that'd been his best day, too.

But when the copper sun was setting, and they weighed John Henry's cotton, there was forty-five hundred pounds—a good three bales—and it was clean cotton too, without any stalks or bolls in it. The workers' eyes got round as saucers, and the overseer said, "Well, John Henry, I thought you were bragful, and I thought you were uppity, and I thought you'd talked beyond and above your powers. But I see you picked what you promised."

"Course I did," says John Henry. "I's not bragful, I's not uppity, and I's not humble. I's a natural man and a natural-born cotton-picker, and what I says, I means."

For quite a time, John Henry was a cotton-picker on the plantation. Then, for quite a time, he was a tobacco-stripper. He was just as good with tobacco as with cotton, better than any other man on all the plantations. For he was a natural man and a natural-born tobacco-stripper.

In the fields, John Henry sang, he cracked jokes, and he worked hard. John Henry got religion, and he was baptized in Goodman Creek by Parson Day. John Henry married Polly Ann. She had shining black hair as wavy as the ocean, eyes that glowed like stars, teeth like pearls, a dimple on her cheek that came and went like a ripple on a bayou, slender little hands and dancing feet. He loved her more than tongue could tell, and she loved him likewise.

But instead of being as happy as a mocking-bird, John Henry had a craving in his soul. At night, he'd sit in front of the cabin, with Polly Ann's head on his weary shoulder, and he'd sing songs like this one:

I knows moonlight, I knows starlight,
  Lay this body down;
I walks in the moonlight, I walks in the starlight,
  To lay this body down.
I walks in the churchyard, I walks through the church-
    yard,
  To lay this body down;
I'll lie in the grass and stretch out my weary arms,
  Lay this body down.

Down the row of the cabins, John Henry's mammy could hear him sing. "Lawd, Lawd," she said to his pappy, "that boy's got a cravin' in his weary soul, and his home ain't here."

That was the way it was when the Civil War ended, and all the slaves were free. When John Henry heard he was free, he went to the overseer, and told the overseer this: "Now I's free, I thinks I's goin' to roam. I got me a cravin' in my weary soul, and my home's some place else. So, good-by, Mr. Overseer, good-by to you."

Polly Ann and John Henry started to roam and they roamed far and wide, sure enough. They'd be one place for a while, then they'd be another, but always, in the end, it'd be the same. John Henry would say what he could do, and then he would do it; for he was a natural man that meant what he said. At work, he'd joke and sing his songs—coonjine,[9] and he was a good worker. He was a roustabout for a while, a deckman on a steamboat for a while, a corn-picker for a while.

But always, sooner or later, he'd move along, because he had that craving that I mentioned awhile back in his soul.

John Henry and his loving Polly Ann were walking one day in West Virginia, looking for a place to call their home. It'd been a bad night the night before, with a great black cloud from the southwest covering up a copper moon, with forked lightning and rain coming out of the cloud, and with thunder making the ground shake as if a great big hammer had whammed it hard.

This day, though, was a fine day, with a rain-bow in the sky, the trees all a brand-new green, and the songbirds in the shiny leaves just sing-ing fit to kill. Polly Ann had a pretty red ribbon in her shining black hair, the dress she wore was blue, and she danced along in her little red shoes, happy as a singing lark. But John Henry, he was the one that was doing the singing. He sang a happy song that went like this:

I done walk till my feet's gone to rollin',
Just like a wheel, Lawd, just like a wheel;
But I got a feelin' my troubles is over.
That's how I feel, Lawd, that's how I feel.

---

[9]*coonjine*, songs made up and sung by Negro laborers.

Got me a rainbow shine in the heaven—
Ain't gonna rain, Lawd, ain't gonna rain.
So I got a feelin' my troubles is over;
I's found my home, Lawd, free from all pain.

"You sure sounds happy, John Henry," says Polly Ann. "I hope it's like you say it in the song—that we've found our home. For I's powerful tired of this life of roamin', John Henry, powerful tired."

"I got me a hunch that's more than a hunch," John Henry said. "I knows. We've had plenty of signs of this, too, Polly Ann. Look what year it is—1872. Add one and eight, and you gets nine. Add seven and two, and you gets nine, likewise. My lucky number is nine, Polly Ann. They's nine letters in my natural-born name. I weighed thirty-three pounds, on the dot, when I was born, and three times three is nine. This is bound to be my lucky year, sure as you born. Listen!"

What they heard when they listened was the ring of hammers on steel off in the distance, and the songs of black men working.

"That's the finest music I ever heard," John Henry told his Polly Ann. "I minds me of the time when I's a little bitty boy and I played with my pappy's hammer. I been huntin' a hammer all this livelong time, and now I knows it."

When they got to the place where the hammers were ringing, it was a mountain. And the men that were hammering and singing were at work building the Big Bend Tunnel for the C. & O. Railroad.[10]

This wasn't much of a railroad, so far as size went. But it was an important one, just the same. For one thing, it's just about the only railroad that will get into this history. For another thing, it stood for something mighty big that was happening in America along about this time: people were building a whole mess of railroads—the Union Pacific, the Santa Fé, the Southern Pacific, the Northern Pacific, and the Great Northern, to name just the biggest of them. Finally, it was going to be on this railroad

that a hero, namely, John Henry, would have it out with a machine.

Captain Tommy was the boss of the men that were working in the Big Bend Tunnel, down there in West Virginia. These men had the job of driving long rods of steel deep into the rock. When the holes were deep enough, and the men had gone far enough away, other men would put nitroglycerin or mica powder or dualin[11] into the holes and blow away the rock, huge hunks at a time.

"You look big and strong," says Captain Tommy, when John Henry braced him for a job, "and maybe we can make a steel-drivin' man out of you, sure enough."

John Henry answered him back, in his thunder voice, "Course I's big and strong—bigger and stronger than any black man a-workin' in the Big Bend Tunnel. But you don't need to *make* a steel-drivin' man out of me, 'cause I already *is* one. Bring me a twelve-pound hammer, and get me a shaker,[12] and stand out of my way, 'cause I can drive more steel than any nine men at work in this here tunnel."

"Oh! Oh!" says Captain Tommy. "Sounds to me as if this man that came to me and asked me for work might be just bragful and uppity. Here, you, Li'l Bill, come and shake for this big-mouthed man. And the rest of you stand back and be ready to laugh till you bust, because here's somebody that talks mighty big, and if his say-so is bigger than his do-so, we'll laugh him out of camp."

The shaker held the steel, and John Henry got himself organized to swing the hammer. Chiefly, to get organized, he got a feel of rhythm in his legs, in his stomach, in his chest, in his shoulders, in his arms, and in his head. Also, he started to sing, in time with the rhythm, and he brought down the hammer in time with the tune. He sang:

Oh, my hammer, *(Wham!)*
Hammer ring, *(Wham!)*
While I sing, Lawd, *(Wham!)*
Hear me sing! *(Wham!)*

[10]*Big Bend Tunnel...C. & O. Railroad.* The Chesapeake and Ohio Railroad (C. & O. Railroad) traverses some of the most mountainous territory in West Virginia. The Big Bend Tunnel, which was constructed by hand labor, is in the southern part of the state.

[11]*mica powder or dualin* (dū′əl in), different types of dynamite.
[12]*shaker,* a workman who holds the steel drill being hammered into the rock or coal.

(The whams came in on the rest of the song, the way they did on this verse, but I'll leave them out, because all those whams may be tiresome.)

Ain't no hammer,
Rings like mine,
Rings like gold, Lawd,
Ain't it fine?

Rings like silver,
Peal on peal,
Into the rock, Lawd,
Drive the steel.

If'n I dies, Lawd,
I command,
Bury the hammer
In my hand.

When John Henry first sang about his hammer ringing better than any other, the steel drivers laughed "Yugh, yugh, yugh," and hit their knees with the palms of their hands. "Ain't never heard such bragful singin' in all our born days!" they said. But when they watched the way John Henry's hot hammer swung in a rainbow arc around his shoulder, and when they saw the way Li'l Bill, the shaker, had to work to loosen and turn the steel after each ringing wham of the hammer, they stopped laughing and their eyes grew round as dinner plates.

Finally, Captain Tommy said, "Stop for a while, John Henry, while I see the work you've done." Then when Captain Tommy had looked, he said, "Well, well, John Henry, looks like your do-so is as good as your say-so, and you aren't just bragful and uppity, the way I thought you were. You drove steel as good as you promised—more than any nine men at work in the Big Bend Tunnel."

"Course he did," says Polly Ann, grinning with her pearl-white teeth. "He's not bragful and he's not uppity. He's a natural-born steel-drivin' man, and what he say, he mean. Praise the Lawd, we's done found our home."

"You work for me," Captain Tommy told John Henry, "and I'll give you four dollars a day and the rent of a company house[13] and enough vittles for you and Polly Ann. I like the way you make that hammer ring and the way the steel goes down."

"Thanks politely, Captain Tommy," John Henry answered him back. "I be proud to work for you, but I wants to ask one little favor. When you goes to town, I'd like to have you get me two twenty-pound hammers so I can make 'em ring and drive the steel."

"Anyone else asked for two twenty-pound hammers, I'd laugh right square in his face," Captain Tommy said. "But I've seen what you can do with a swinging hammer, so I'll get you what you want. Now pitch in and let me hear that steel ring, because you're working for me from now on."

So John Henry was working for Captain Tommy, and his loving Polly Ann was keeping house in one of the company houses.

It was hard work in the tunnel, of course. The smoke from the blackstrap lamps[14] and the dust from the hard red shale were so thick that a tall man working in the tunnel couldn't see his own feet without stooping almost double. The thick air was hot, and the men stripped to their waists before working.

But John Henry was the best steel-driving man in the world. He could sink a hole down or he could sink it sideways, in soft rock or hard—it made no difference. When he worked with two twenty-pound hammers, one in each hand, it sounded as if the Big Bend Tunnel was caving in, the ring of the steel was so loud.

And John Henry and his sweet Polly Ann were as happy as singing birds, for their roaming days were over, and they felt they'd found a home.

Everything was going fine until a man came along and tried to peddle his steam drill to Captain Tommy. This man had pictures of the steam drill in a book, and he had a wagging tongue in his head. "This steam drill of mine," he said, "will outdrill any twenty men. It doesn't have to rest or eat, either, so it'll save you lots of money."

"Hm, maybe," Captain Tommy said, *"may-*

---

[13]*the rent of a company house.* As part of his wages John Henry was given occupancy of a house owned by the railroad.

[14]*blackstrap lamps,* lamps such as miners wear attached to their caps.

be. But I've got one steel-driving man here that's the finest in the world, and I'm mighty fond of big John Henry. So I'll tell you what I think we might do. We might have a race between the steam drill and this man of mine. If the steam drill wins, I'll buy it. But if John Henry wins, you give me the steam drill and five hundred dollars."

"I heard about John Henry, all right, and I know he's good," the man said. "But I know a man is nothing but a man. So I'll have that race, the way you say."

"Fine," says Captain Tommy, "except for one thing: I've got to ask John Henry, but I know pretty well what he'll say." So he went to John Henry, and asked him if he'd race that drill for a favor and a hundred dollars to boot.

John Henry said, "Course I'll race it, and course I'll beat it. For I's a natural-born steel-drivin' man that can beat any nine men or any of the traps[15] that ever drove steel. I don't want any old machine to take my place at the happiest work I's ever found. So before I let that steam drill beat me, I'll die with my hammer in my hand."

The day of the race, country folks and all the steel-driving gangs in the whole section came to see whether John Henry meant what he said. The race was to be outside the mouth of the tunnel—out there by the blacksmith shops where the steels were sharpened and the hammers were fixed—a place where everybody could see. The steam drill, with a boiler about twenty feet long to make the steam, was on the right-hand corner, and the spot where John Henry was to drive was on the left. The crowd was sprinkled all around the edges of the quarry.

At the time the race was to start, the blacksmiths had sharpened piles of drills, the steam drill had its steam up, and the carriers were ready with pads on their shoulders to carry the sharpened steels from the shop and the dull ones back to be sharpened. When there was one minute to go, the steam drill whistled, and John Henry lifted one of his twenty-pound hammers.

Then Captain Tommy dropped his hat, and the race started.

Says John Henry to Li'l Bill, the shaker, "Boy, you'd better pray. 'Cause if I miss this piece of steel, tomorrow be your buryin' day, sure as you born."

[15]*traps*, contraptions, or machines.

Then the steam drill was chugging and John Henry was swinging and singing—singing "Oh, My Hammer," "Water Boy, Where Is You Hidin'," "If I Die a Railroad Man," and other hammer songs he could keep time to. The steel rang like silver, the carriers trotted to and from the blacksmith shops, and the crowd watched with all its might and main.

It wasn't long after the start that John Henry took the lead. The steam-drill salesman wasn't worried, though—or if he was, his talk didn't show it. "That man's a mighty man," he said. "But when he hits the hard rock, he'll weaken." Then when John Henry hit the hard rock, and kept driving fast as ever, the salesman said, "He can't keep it up."

John Henry did keep it up, though, swinging those two hammers and driving down the steel, stopping only once an hour, maybe, to take a drink of water from the dipper Polly Ann had carried in her slender little hands. Six hours—seven hours—eight hours of that nine-hour race, he made his hammer ring like gold. And though Li'l Bill got plumb played out and a new shaker had to take his place, all through the eighth hour John Henry was going strong as ever, with the rhythm in every muscle and joint helping him wham the steel.

It wasn't until the ninth hour that John Henry showed any signs of getting tired. Then, when Captain Tommy came up to ask him how things were going, he answered him back, "This rock is so hard and this steel is so tough, I feel my muscles givin' way. But," he went on to say, "before I let that machine beat me, I'll die with my hammer in my hand."

After that, the crowd that was watching could see signs that John Henry was a weary man—very, very tired and weary.

And John Henry wasn't singing any more. All you could hear was the ring of the hammer on the steel and the chug-chug of the steam drill.

When Captain Tommy, at the end of the ninth hour, looked at his watch and yelled, "The race is over," and when the drills stopped going down, everything was as still as a graveyard. Captain Tommy was looking at the holes. Then, when Captain Tommy said, "John Henry won—three holes ahead of the steam drill," every-

body cheered—everybody, that is, excepting the salesman and the steam-drill crew—and John Henry.

When the crowd looked at John Henry, they saw the great man was lying on the ground, and his loving Polly Ann was holding his head. John Henry was moaning, and he sort of mumbled, "Before I let that steam drill beat me, I'll die with my hammer in my hand." (Sure enough, he had *two* hammers in his big black hands.)

Then he said, "Give me a cool drink of water 'fore I die."

Polly Ann was crying when she gave him the water.

Then John Henry kissed his hammer and he kissed his loving Polly Ann. She had to stoop down so he could kiss her. Then he lay very still, and Polly Ann cried harder than ever—sounded mighty loud in that quiet quarry.

Just at that minute, there was the sound of hoofs, and a coal-black preacher came riding up on a gray mule. "You got troubles, sister?" he said to Polly Ann. "Can I help you?"

"Only way you can help," she answered him back, "is to read the buryin' service for my lovin' John Henry. 'Cause his home ain't here no more."

So the coal-black preacher read the burying services. They buried John Henry on a hillside

—with a hammer in each hand, a rod of steel across his breast, and a pick and shovel at his head and feet. And a great black cloud came out of the southwest to cover the copper sun.

THE QUALITIES OF A FOLK TALE

1. Soaring imagination is one of the characteristics of the folk tale. What are some of the most imaginative details concerning John Henry's infancy?

2. In what fields did John Henry achieve fame before he became a steel-driver? What historical event occurring in his early manhood made it possible for him to roam from one job to another?

3. When John Henry was a newborn infant, he indicated that he could eat a larger amount of food than babies ordinarily can eat. His father was doubtful. Then John Henry ate the food. Point out similar patterns of action throughout the story. What is the value of such patterns?

4. Folk heroes often are "fated" to be what they are. Point out foreshadowings of John Henry's becoming a great man with a hammer and of his tragic death. (Note particularly the first paragraph of the selection.)

5. What characteristics said to be typical of Negro life are important elements of this tale? Which of these characteristics are the most admirable?

6. Folk heroes are composite heroes; that is, in them are combined many of the traits and deeds of a people. In what ways does John Henry—a hero of the American people—measure up to this description of a folk hero?

7. Which of the following adjectives accurately describe the author's style: learned, simple, idiomatic, literal, figurative, unrhythmical, rhythmical? (If you don't know the meanings of these words, look them up in your dictionary.) Point out passages which justify your choice of each adjective. What additional points can you make about the language?

Extending interests

Folk heroes are associated with various aspects of the development of the United States. Tell the class the story of one of the following: Joe Magarac, steelman; Mike Fink, keelboatman; John Darling, canalman; Old Stormalong, deep-water sailor; Kemp Morgan, oil driller; Casey Jones, railroader. You'll find the following books good sources of information: *Heroes, Outlaws, and Funny Fellows of American Popular Tales,* by Olive K. Miller; *The Hurricane's Children,* by Carl Carmer; *Tall Tale America,* by Walter Blair; and *A Treasury of American Folklore,* edited by B. A. Botkin.

The Brute

WILLIAM VAUGHN MOODY

Melville's description of the paper mill and Blair's retelling of the John Henry legend reflect in very different ways the uneasiness of Americans in the machine age. The poet William Vaughn Moody also questioned whether scientific progress, the machine particularly, had brought happiness to man.

Moody, born shortly after the Civil War, lived through many of the changes which were brought by the machine age; as a teacher and a poet, he was interested in the way such changes were affecting the lives of men. In this poem, which sums up Moody's thought and feeling about our so-called "progressive" era, the "Brute" is the machine.

THROUGH his might men work their wills.
   They have boweled out the hills
For food to keep him toiling in the cages they
   have wrought;
And they fling him, hour by hour,
Limbs of men to give him power;   5
Brains of men to give him cunning; and for
   dainties to devour
Children's souls, the little worth; hearts of
   women, cheaply bought:
He takes them and he breaks them, but he gives
   them scanty thought.

For about the noisy land,
Roaring, quivering 'neath his hand,   10
His thoughts brood fierce and sullen or laugh
   in lust of pride
O'er the stubborn things that he
Breaks to dust and brings to be.
Some he mightily establishes, some flings down
   utterly.
There is thunder in his stride, nothing ancient
   can abide,   15
When he hales the hills together and bridles up
   the tide.

Quietude and loveliness,
Holy sights that heal and bless,
They are scattered and abolished where his iron
hoof is set;
When he splashes through the brae,   20
Silver streams are choked with clay;
When he snorts, the bright cliffs crumble and
the woods go down like hay;
He lairs in pleasant cities, and the haggard
people fret
Squalid 'mid their new-got riches, soot-begrimed
and desolate.

They who caught and bound him tight   25
Laughed exultant at his might,
Saying, "Now behold, the good time comes for
the weariest and the least!
We will use this lusty knave:
No more need for men to slave;
We may rise and look about us and have
knowledge ere the grave."   30
But the Brute said in his breast, "Till the mills
I grind have ceased,
The riches shall be dust of dust, dry ashes be
the feast!

"On the strong and cunning few
Cynic favors I will strew;
I will stuff their maw with overplus until their
spirit dies;   35
From the patient and the low
I will take the joys they know;
They shall hunger after vanities and still an-
hungered[1] go.
Madness shall be on the people, ghastly jeal-
ousies arise;
Brother's blood shall cry on brother up the
dead and empty skies.   40

"I will burn and dig and hack
Till the heavens suffer lack;
God shall feel a pleasure fail Him, crying to his
cherubim,
'Who hath flung yon mud-ball there
Where my world went green and fair?'   45
I shall laugh and hug me, hearing how his
sentinels declare,

[1]an-hungered, hungry.

' 'Tis the Brute they chained to labor! He has
made the bright earth dim.
Stores of wares and pelf a plenty, but they got
no good of him.' "

So he plotted in his rage:
So he deals it, age by age.   50
But even as he roared his curse a still small
Voice befell;
Lo, a still and pleasant voice bade them none
the less rejoice,
For the Brute must bring the good time on; he
has no other choice.
He may struggle, sweat, and yell, but he knows
exceeding well
He must work them out salvation ere they send
him back to hell.   55

All the desert that he made
He must treble bless with shade,
In primal wastes set precious seed of rapture
and of pain;
All the strongholds that he built
For the powers of greed and guilt—   60
He must strew their bastions down the sea and
choke their towers with silt;
He must make the temples clean for the gods to
come again,
And lift the lordly cities under skies without
a stain.

In a very cunning tether
He must lead the tyrant weather;   65
He must loose the curse of Adam[2] from the
worn neck of the race;
He must cast out hate and fear,
Dry away each fruitless tear,
And make the fruitful tears to gush from the
deep heart and clear.
He must give each man his portion, each his
pride and worthy place;   70
He must batter down the arrogant and lift the
weary face,
On each vile mouth set purity, on each low
forehead grace.

[2]the curse of Adam, work. When God drove Adam out
of the garden of Eden after he had sinned, He said to
him, "In the sweat of thy face shalt thou eat bread."
(Genesis 3:19.)

Then, perhaps, at the last day,
They will whistle him away,
Lay a hand upon his muzzle in the face of God,
and say,   75
"Honor, Lord, the Thing we tamed!"
Let him not be scourged or blamed,
Even through his wrath and fierceness was thy
fierce wroth world reclaimed!
Honor Thou thy servants' servant; let thy justice
now be shown."
Then the Lord will heed their saying, and the
Brute come to his own,   80
'Twixt the Lion and the Eagle, by the armpost
of the Throne.[3]

---

[3]*Lion and the Eagle...Throne.* In the book of Revelation (4:6-9) St. John speaks of a lion and an eagle among the four creatures which stand before the throne of God, eternally glorifying Him.

FOLLOWING THE POET'S THOUGHT

1. Describe the Brute as you picture him—his looks, actions, attitudes. Why would men wish to keep such a monster alive and to make him even more powerful?

2. In order to keep the Brute fed, what sacrifices do men make in regard to (*a*) their fellow human beings, (*b*) the beauty and natural resources of the land?

3. What line in the poem marks a turning point in Moody's point of view about the Brute? In what specific ways does he think "the Brute must bring the good time on"? Can you give any recent examples to show that Moody's optimism, expressed many years ago, has or has not been justified?

4. Cite parallels in the thoughts of William Vaughn Moody and Herman Melville about the machine. Do you find any differences? Which author—the poet or the prose writer—succeeded better in making you share his thoughts and feelings about the machine? In general, do you think poetry or prose is more effective in expressing such thoughts and feelings as are found in the two selections?

Extending interests

Read to the class a poem that has machinery as its subject. Be prepared to discuss briefly with your classmates how the idea in the poem you have read agrees or disagrees with that advanced in "The Brute." Among the poems that you might read are: "And Yet Fools Say," by George S. Holmes; "Pittsburgh," by James Oppenheim; and "The Steam Shovel," by Eunice Tietjens. All can be found in *Poems for Modern Youth,* edited by Gillis and Benét.

Tin Lizzie

JOHN DOS PASSOS

The following selection is from a novel called *The Big Money*. This novel is one of three which the author combined under the title *U. S. A.* His purpose in this trilogy seems to be to record a panoramic picture of American life, principally its social and economic aspects. So the author tells about not only imagined characters but also real men and women important in America at the time of the novel.

"Tin Lizzie" is a description of the mechanical and inventive mind of Henry Ford. As you read, notice the strange arrangement of the sentences and paragraphs and consider what is accomplished by the unusual way of writing.

"MR. FORD *the automobileer,*" the feature-writer wrote in 1900,

"*Mr. Ford the automobileer began by giving his steed three or four sharp jerks with the lever at the righthand side of the seat; that is, he pulled the lever up and down sharply in order, as he said, to mix air with gasoline and drive the charge into the exploding cylinder....Mr. Ford slipped a small electric switch handle and there followed a puff, puff, puff....The puffing of the machine assumed a higher key. She was flying along about eight miles an hour. The ruts in the road were deep, but the machine certainly went with a dreamlike smoothness. There was none of the bumping common even to a streetcar.... By this time the boulevard had been reached, and the automobileer, letting a lever fall a little, let her out. Whiz! She picked up speed with infinite rapidity. As she ran on there was a clattering behind, the new noise of the automobile.*

For twenty years or more,
ever since he'd left his father's farm when he was sixteen to get a job in a Detroit machine-shop, Henry Ford had been nuts about machinery. First it was watches, then he designed a steamtractor, then he built a horseless carriage with an engine adapted from the Otto gasen-

---

"Tin Lizzie," reprinted by permission of the author, from *U.S.A.,* copyright by John Dos Passos.

gine[1] he'd read about in *The World of Science,* then a mechanical buggy with a onecylinder fourcycle motor, that would run forward but not back;

at last, in ninetyeight, he felt he was far enough along to risk throwing up his job with the Detroit Edison Company, where he'd worked his way up from night fireman to chief engineer, to put all his time into working on a new gasoline engine,

(in the late eighties he'd met Edison[2] at a meeting of electriclight employees in Atlantic City. He'd gone up to Edison after Edison had delivered an address and asked him if he thought gasoline was practical as a motor fuel. Edison had said yes. If Edison said it, it was true. Edison was the great admiration of Henry Ford's life);

and in driving his mechanical buggy, sitting there at the lever jauntily dressed in a tight-buttoned jacket and a high collar and a derby hat, back and forth over the level illpaved streets of Detroit,

scaring the big brewery horses and the skinny trotting horses and the sleekrumped pacers with the motor's loud explosions,

looking for men scatterbrained enough to invest money in a factory for building automobiles.

He was the eldest son of an Irish immigrant who during the Civil War had married the daughter of a prosperous Pennsylvania Dutch farmer and settled down to farming near Dearborn[3] in Wayne County, Michigan;

like plenty of other Americans, young Henry grew up hating the endless sogging through the mud about the chores, the hauling and pitching manure, the kerosene lamps to clean, the irk and sweat and solitude of the farm.

He was a slender, active youngster, a good skater, clever with his hands; what he liked was to tend the machinery and let the others do the heavy work. His mother had told him not to drink, smoke, gamble, or go into debt, and he never did.

When he was in his early twenties his father tried to get him back from Detroit, where he was working as mechanic and repairman for the Drydock Engine Company that built the engines for steamboats, by giving him forty acres of land.

Young Henry built himself an uptodate square white dwellinghouse with a false mansard roof and married and settled down on the farm,

but he let the hired men do the farming;

he bought himself a buzzsaw and rented a stationary engine and cut the timber off the woodlots.

He was a thrifty young man who never drank or smoked or gambled..., but he couldn't stand living on the farm.

He moved to Detroit, and in the brick barn behind his house tinkered for years in his spare time with a mechanical buggy that would be light enough to run over the clayey wagonroads of Wayne County, Michigan.

By 1900 he had a practicable car to promote.

He was forty years old before the Ford Motor Company was started and production began to move.

Speed was the first thing the early automobile manufacturers went after. Races advertised the makes of cars.

Henry Ford himself hung up several records at the track at Grosse Pointe[4] and on the ice on Lake St. Clair.[5] In his 999[6] he did the mile in thirtynine and fourfifths seconds.

But it had always been his custom to hire others to do the heavy work. The speed he was busy with was speed in production, the records records in efficient output. He hired Barney Oldfield, a stunt bicyclerider from Salt Lake City, to do the racing for him.

---

[1]*Otto gasengine.* In 1876 a German technician named Nikolaus Otto produced a gas engine of the type that was later used in automobiles.

[2]*Edison,* Thomas Alva Edison (1847-1931), the electrical wizard, inventor of the phonograph, the incandescent lamp, and the moving-picture camera.

[3]*Dearborn,* a city near Detroit.

---

[4]*Grosse Pointe* (grōs point), a village east of Detroit.

[5]*Lake St. Clair,* a large lake east of Detroit which forms part of the waterway between Lake Huron and Lake Erie.

[6]*999,* a four-cylinder racing car built by Ford.

Henry Ford had ideas about other things than the designing of motors, carburetors, magnetos, jigs and fixtures, punches and dies; he had ideas about sales,

that the big money was in economical quantity production, quick turnover, cheap interchangeable easily-replaced standardized parts;

it wasn't until 1909, after years of arguing with his partners, that Ford put out the first Model T.

Henry Ford was right.

That season he sold more than ten thousand tin lizzies, ten years later he was selling almost a million a year.

In these years the Taylor Plan[7] was stirring up plantmanagers and manufacturers all over the country. Efficiency was the word. The same ingenuity that went into improving the perform-

ance of a machine could go into improving the performance of the workmen producing the machine.

In 1913 they established the assemblyline at Ford's. That season the profits were something like twentyfive million dollars, but they had trouble keeping the men on the job, machinists didn't seem to like it at Ford's.

Henry Ford had ideas about other things than production.

He was the largest automobile manufacturer in the world; he paid high wages; maybe if the steady workers thought they were getting a cut (a very small cut) in the profits, it would give trained men an inducement to stick to their jobs,

wellpaid workers might save enough money to buy a tin lizzie; the first day Ford's announced that cleancut...American workers who wanted jobs had a chance to make five bucks a day (of course it turned out that there were strings to it; always there were strings to it)

---

[7]*Taylor Plan,* a plan promoted by Frederick W. Taylor (1856-1915), whose purpose was to increase industrial efficiency.

such an enormous crowd waited outside the Highland Park plant[8]

all through the zero January night

that there was a riot when the gates were opened; cops broke heads, jobhunters threw bricks; property, Henry Ford's own property, was destroyed. The company dicks[9] had to turn on the firehose to beat back the crowd.

The American Plan[10]; automotive prosperity seeping down from above; it turned out there were strings to it.

But that five dollars a day

paid to good, clean American workmen

who didn't drink or smoke cigarettes or read or think...,

made America once more the Yukon of the sweated workers of the world[11];

made all the tin lizzies and the automotive age, and incidentally,

made Henry Ford the automobileer, the admirer of Edison, the birdlover,

the great American of his time.

---

[8]*Highland Park plant,* Ford's principal plant until the removal to Dearborn. Highland Park is a city entirely surrounded by Detroit.

[9]*dicks,* policemen.

[10]*American Plan,* Ford's profit-sharing, $5 minimum wage, eight-hour-day plan.

[11]*the Yukon of the sweated workers of the world.* As the gold in the Yukon had attracted adventurers from all the world, so the lure of money in industry attracted laborers from all nations.

CONCERNING THE GREAT AUTOMOBILEER

1. How did Henry Ford show his love of machinery before he produced a practicable automobile in 1900? How did Ford's inventive mind display itself after he had become a manufacturer?

2. What kind of person does Dos Passos show Ford to be; that is, what were his personal traits? How does Dos Passos show that he had these traits?

3. Do you think Dos Passos admires Ford unreservedly? What evidence can you cite for your opinion? Do you share Dos Passos' attitude?

4. Can you find any reasons whatever for the author's unusual spelling, capitalization, and paragraphing? Do you think Dos Passos used them merely to be "different"? Are they related in any way to his subject matter?

Reed of Virginia

CHARLES MORROW WILSON

The changes that the rise of science and industry brought into the lives of Americans are shown not only by the increasing dependence on machinery and the development of the assembly line but also by the great advances made in medical science. The story of Dr. Walter Reed, a pioneer bacteriologist, is a dramatic example of the way the tools of research were used to conquer one of mankind's greatest enemies—yellow fever.

IN ARLINGTON CEMETERY[1] there is a knoll that overlooks the Potomac River and the nation's capital. On that knoll stands a shaft of dark granite five feet high; the bronze tablet on it reads simply:

Walter Reed, M.D. of the University of Virginia
A.M. of Harvard University
LL.D. of the University of Michigan[2]
Professor of Bacteriology, Army Medical School

and

Columbian University, Washington, D. C.

"He gave to man control over that dreadful scourge, Yellow Fever."

A memorial as unpretentious as the man it commemorates, a doctor who was a pioneer among our ambassadors in white[3] and who proved himself one of the greatest of them. If the statement that Reed gave to man control over yellow fever is not quite so valid as it

---

[1]*Arlington Cemetery,* a military cemetery directly across the Potomac River from Washington, D. C. There are military dead from every conflict in which the nation has taken part buried here.

[2]*M.D...LL.D. of the University of Michigan.* The letters represent the degrees held by Walter Reed: Doctor of Medicine (M.D.), Master of Arts (A.M.), and Doctor of Laws (LL.D.).

[3]*ambassadors in white,* a term the author applies to doctors who bring the miracles of modern medical science to people outside the United States. These men are like ambassadors in that through their work they promote good will between their own country and others.

seemed when the monument was erected, the great Virginia doctor's achievement in pointing the way toward saving thousands of lives in every part of the world is not at all belittled by the fact that what he pointed out was the beginning and not the end of the way.

Walter Reed's first connection with the appalling medical problems left in the wake of the Spanish-American War[4] was as chairman of a committee appointed by the Army to study the typhoid ravaging the camps throughout the nation's eastern seaboard. In association with Dr. W. C. Vaughn, of the University of Michigan, and Dr. E. O. Shakespeare, of Philadelphia, Reed spent a busy year investigating training-camp typhoid and eventually published a report —*Report of the Origin and Spread of Typhoid Fever in the United States Military Camps during the Spanish-American War*—which, although not published until long after the death of its compilers, has become something of a medical classic. In this report Majors Reed and Shakespeare contended that infected water was not an important factor in the spread of typhoid; that flies unquestionably act as carriers of the disease; that the development of typhoid was characterized by series of epidemics in companies; that the infection was probably spread, to an additional measure, by blowing dust.

The study was painstaking, fearless, and little noticed. His typhoid report finished, Walter Reed returned to Washington and began to concentrate his thinking on yellow fever, which he preferred to call by its Spanish name—*el vomito negro*[5]—the black vomit.

Until the great Philadelphia epidemic of 1793, men had been inclined to regard the black vomit as a divine punishment. Then conflicting theories began to appear. Some contended that the malady was imported from the West Indies; others that it was a "spontaneous generation" from heat, filth, and moisture. One medical camp held that it was contagious, the other that it was not.

At the outbreak of the Spanish-American War, man's ignorance of this lethal disease was appalling. Except by Carlos Finlay in Havana, who believed that a certain type of mosquito transmitted the disease, nothing was learned of the yellow plague during the century that saw the actual birth of scientific medicine.

The ability of insects to carry disease was widely recognized, but the actual diseases they carried and their manner of passing them from host to victim was seldom clear. For centuries men of medicine had blamed flies and other winged creatures for the spreading of virtually every infectious or contagious disease known, including leprosy, tuberculosis, black plague, malaria, cholera, anthrax, and a hundred others.

Perhaps the first scientific proof of insect transmission of diseases was established about 1880 by Sir Patrick Manson,[6] who demonstrated beyond reasonable question that the mosquito acts as intermediary host and is thus directly instrumental in the production of elephantiasis scroti[7] and other maladies.

While the Spanish-American War was running its ambiguous course, Surgeon General Sternberg designated Dr. Walter Reed and Dr. James Carroll, a brilliant self-made Canadian bacteriologist, to study, confirm, or disprove the contention of the Italian Giuseppe Sanarelli, who claimed that he had discovered the specific cause of yellow fever in the form of a bacillus which he named *Bacillus icteroides*.[8]

Drs. Reed and Carroll promptly noted that Sanarelli's bacillus was no more than a rather common variety of the hog-cholera bacillus.

Early in 1900 yellow fever appeared among United States troops stationed at Havana. The surgeon general promptly appointed that Yellow Fever Board which was destined to be better known than his own name. Dr. Walter Reed was chairman and director; Dr. James Carroll directed its bacteriological investigations; Dr. Jesse W. Lazear led its mosquito research; Dr.

---

[4]*medical problems...Spanish-American War*. Since the land action in the Spanish-American War of 1898 was mainly in the tropics during the summer or wet season, many American soldiers sickened or died of malaria, yellow fever, and other diseases.

[5]*el vomito negro* (el vom′it ō nā′grō). [*Spanish*]

[6]*Sir Patrick Manson*, a British physician (1844-1922).

[7]*elephantiasis scroti* (el′ə fən tī′ ə sis skrō′ti), a disease caused by parasitic worms, that is characterized by swelling and broken and thickened skin in the affected part.

[8]*Bacillus icteroides* (bə sil′əs ik′tėr oi′dēz).

Aristides Agramonte had charge of autopsies and pathological research. Of the four, only Agramonte was immune to yellow fever. In childhood he had proved tough enough to survive an attack. Reed, Carroll, and Lazear, all nonimmunes, were quite evidently risking their lives.

Walter Reed was forty-nine. His skin was sun-browned and leathery. His blackish-brown hair, not yet showing a trace of gray, supported its customary frond trailing toward the left brow. Clean shaven during most of his life, he had begun work on a mustache.

James Carroll, second in command, was forty-six, black-haired and growing bald in front. He was married and the father of five children. In voting to risk his life in conquest of yellow jack it was plain that he had much to lose.

Jesse W. Lazear of Baltimore was the third member of the commission. In 1900 he was thirty-four and well established in medical research. Professionally, Lazear was the ideal man to undertake the experimental study of yellow fever. At Bellevue Hospital in New York he had begun investigation of malaria parasites. He had left Johns Hopkins[9] and his beginning family and proceeded to Cuba early in 1900. There he had been observing yellow fever, performing autopsies, and taking blood cultures.

The fourth and youngest member of the board was the handsome, thirty-two-year-old Cuban, Aristides Agramonte, son of the illustrious insurgent General Eduardo Agramonte,[10] who was killed in battle when Aristides was only four. The general's bereaved family found refuge in the United States. Aristides was raised in New York, attended the public schools of that city, and like Lazear, studied medicine at Columbia. Early in 1898, Agramonte joined the United States Army Medical Corps and was promptly sent to Cuba for duty. Late in the year he was ordered to Havana to study the bacteriology of yellow fever. During May, 1901, he

was made director of the Army Laboratory of the Division of Cuba.

Agramonte knew yellow fever and he knew Cuba. At the barracks in the town of Pinar del Rio, he diagnosed an epidemic of yellow jack in open contradiction to medical officers who had termed the contagion "pernicious malaria." Agramonte ridiculed their ignorance.

These were the four men who were about to make history. On the first day of summer Drs. Reed and Carroll sailed from New York en route to Havana. By early July the Yellow Fever Board was assembled and at work. On the last day of July, Walter Reed made his first yellow-fever autopsy in Cuba. During the same month yellow fever had appeared in an army guardhouse—a single cell occupied by nine prisoners. One contracted yellow fever and died in the post hospital twelve days later. The eight other prisoners in the one-room guardhouse did not take the disease. One slept in the bed vacated by the sick man. But he remained in good health.

Walter Reed pondered: As these nine prisoners had been kept under strict military guard, it was impossible that the individual attacked could have acquired his infection in Pinar del Rio, although Lazear had clearly shown that yellow fever existed there. The sick man simply could not have been there. He was, so far as could be ascertained, exposed to no source of infection to which his companions had not been equally exposed, and yet he alone acquired the disease. It was conjectured at the time that perhaps some insect...such as the mosquito, had entered through the cell window, bitten this particular prisoner, and then passed out again....

He had heard of the comments of a pair of English physicians, on the ideas which Carlos Finlay's work had given them. He wrote Finlay asking for more information. He was perhaps a little cold, afraid of showing too much interest in a suggestion that might turn out to be nonsense. His coldness was met by Finlay—with generous enthusiasm. The Cuban, more interested in results than in credit for them, offered the American commission his notes, his help, his materials, and the use of his laboratory. Reed may have been cold but he was far from mulish. It was not long before he realized that

---

[9]*Johns Hopkins,* a famous Baltimore hospital affiliated with the university of the same name. Lazear was bacteriologist here.

[10]*Eduardo Agramonte* (ā dwär′dō ä′grä mōn′tä), a Cuban who fought for independence from Spain, which at that time controlled Cuba.

the clue to the solution of the yellow-fever problem had for twenty years been in existence in Carlos Finlay's shrewd but unresolved work. Finlay, with that same imaginative inference which gave to the ancient Greeks scientific knowledge far in advance of their time, believed that the mosquito was the disseminating agent in yellow fever. In the homemade laboratory of Carlos Finlay, Walter Reed became acquainted at first hand with the suspected mosquito, *Stegomyia fasciata*[11] (now called *Aedes aegypti*[12]).

Reed observed the distinguishing characteristics of this particular genus: the silvery stripe on the lateral surface of the thorax and the white stripes at the base of the tarsal joints. He reflected on its special mode of existence—its preference for breeding places in clean, standing water, and realized that water of this kind was to be found principally in towns. The female, he found, laid her eggs at night—twenty-five to seventy to the "raft." The eggs were jet black and unusually tough. Freezing, even, did not easily destroy them. Stored in a dry box for three months they would still hatch.

---

[11]*Stegomyia fasciata* (stē′gō mǐ′ē ä fäs ē ā′tä).
[12]*Aedes aegypti* (ā ē′dēz ē jip′tǐ).

Reed, Carroll, Lazear, and Agramonte agreed that practical tests with human subjects was the next necessary step in proving Finlay's mosquito-transmission theory. That meant serious responsibility and serious risk. The four doctors agreed that members of the commission should not hestitate to take as much risk with their own lives as they asked of others. They resolved that each person subjected to the experiment should be a volunteer and fully informed of his risk.

Late in July, without forewarning and for no clearly convincing reason, Walter Reed was recalled to Washington. During his absence, Jesse Lazear was elected to begin experiments. He acquired a collection of yellow-fever-infected stegomyia mosquitoes hatched from eggs furnished by Carlos Finlay. He imprisoned them and allowed them to bite himself and several other subjects. At first there were no results. Then Dr. Lazear applied another infected mosquito to Dr. James Carroll's arm. The experiment was immediately successful. Within four days the meditative James Carroll was writhing with yellow fever.

By September 13, Carroll's recovery was comparatively certain. On that day Dr. Jesse

h. Walter

Lazear was at work in the yellow-fever ward of Las Animas Hospital in the suburbs of Havana. A mosquito settled on his hand. Lazear noticed the uninvited guest but believed it "a common brown mosquito." He allowed it to bite. Five days later, while James Carroll was leaving the hospital, Dr. Lazear was seized with a violent chill. Carroll examined his blood for malaria parasites; finding none, he termed the illness yellow fever.

The young man from Baltimore delivered his notes to Dr. Carroll and moved to the yellow-fever isolation ward of the hospital. For three days he held his own. Then the dread black vomit made its appearance. His diaphragm contracted spasmodically. His eyes showed tense alarm. On the sixth day he died.

In a sense, Lazear's death was accidental. But it was also gallant and valuable to the Americas and to medicine.

Walter Reed, still in Washington, considered the evidence invincible. But further proof was needed. The next step was the founding of Camp Lazear, in a sunny open pasture about one mile from the town of Los Quemados, Cuba, also a focus of yellow fever. Walter Reed took command. The original camp consisted of seven army tents and a flagstaff from which waved the Stars and Stripes. Reed, Carroll, and Agramonte moved to the location, taking with them Dr. Roger P. Ames, an immune, and Dr. Robert P. Cooke, a nonimmune, both of the Army Medical Corps; nine privates of the Hospital Corps, one of whom was immune, and an immune ambulance driver.

They established the camp in November of 1900 under strict quarantine—only the three immune men were allowed to leave or to re-enter. Temperature and pulse of all nonimmune residents were recorded three times daily so that any infected person entering the camp could be detected and removed.

Walter Reed and his associates proposed to try to produce the infection of nonimmunes in three ways—by the bites of mosquitoes which had previously bitten yellow-fever patients; by the injection of blood taken during the early stages from those suffering from the disease; by

exposure to fomites.[13] To supplement the seven tents which quartered the camp's personnel, Reed directed the construction of two frame buildings, each fourteen by twenty feet and alike except that one, the "Infected Mosquito Building," was divided near the middle by a permanent wire-screen partition and had good ventilation while the other, the "Infected Clothing Building," was purposely built to exclude ventilation. The houses were placed about eighty yards apart on opposite sides of a small valley, and both were provided with wire-screen windows and double-screen doors so that mosquitoes could be kept inside or outside as the experimenters desired.

The first need was for human subjects. Walter Reed called for volunteers among the troops. The first to answer were two boy privates from Ohio: John R. Kissinger, of the Hospital Corps, and John J. Moran, a headquarters clerk. Walter Reed explained to them the proposed experiment, pointing out the danger and suffering likely to be involved. When the youths expressed their willingness to go ahead, Walter Reed offered an official money reward. Both young men refused to accept the money. Private Kissinger explained that he had volunteered "solely in the interest of humanity and the cause of science."

Walter Reed knew a hero when he saw one. He drew himself up before Kissinger and Moran and saluted his subordinates. "Gentlemen, I salute you!" he said.

Private Kissinger was the first volunteer. On December 5 he permitted himself to be bitten by five *Aedes aegypti* mosquitoes which had bitten yellow-fever patients from fifteen to twenty-two days previously. Three days later Private Kissinger, who had been under strict quarantine for fifteen days, was seized with a chill which proved to be the beginning of yellow fever.

Walter Reed and his men, even Private Kissinger, were delighted. The commanding officer of Camp Lazear wrote to his wife:

Rejoice with me, sweetheart, as aside from the antitoxin of diphtheria and Koch's discovery of the

[13]*fomites* (fom′i tēz), bedding, clothing, or other material believed filled with germs because of use by infected persons.

tubercle bacillus,[14] this will be regarded as the most important piece of work scientifically during the 19th century....I do not exaggerate and I could shout for very joy....It was Finlay's theory and he deserves great credit for having suggested it, but as he did nothing to prove it, it was rejected by all, including General Sternberg. Now we have put it beyond cavil. ...Major Kean says that the discovery is worth more than the cost of the Spanish War, including lives lost and money expended....I suppose that old Dr. Finlay will be delighted beyond bounds, as he will see his theory at last fully vindicated. 9:30 P.M. Since writing the above our patient has been doing well....Everything points, so far as it can at this stage, to a favorable termination for which I feel so very happy.

At Camp Lazear, during the week that followed, four more cases of yellow fever were produced with the help of mosquitoes. Meanwhile the fomite experiment was in progress. Three soldiers—Private Levi E. Folk, of South Carolina; Private Warren G. Jernegan, of Florida; Dr. Robert P. Cooke, of Virginia and the Army Medical Corps—all Southerners and nonimmunes, moved into the "Fomite House," sleeping in the filthy bedding of yellow-fever patients, wearing castoff soiled clothes of yellow-fever patients, and adorning their cells with all manner of contaminated articles reckoned to spread the contagion by direct exposure.

For twenty days the three *norteamericanos*[15] followed through the repulsive experiment. After twelve days another box of contaminated clothing and linen from Las Animas Hospital was distributed about the room, while heat and humidity were kept high. On December 19 the three experimenters were placed in quarantine for five days, then given the liberty of the camp. All had remained in perfect health.

After fifteen days in the pesthouse, the three volunteers heard of the successes with mosquito infection....The observing Walter Reed noted:

With the occurrence of these cases of mosquito infection the countenances of these men, which had before borne the serious aspect of those who were bravely facing an unseen foe, suddenly took on the glad expression of school boys let out for a holiday,

and from this time their contempt for "fomites" could not find sufficient expression. Thus illustrating once more the old adage that familiarity, even with fomites, may breed contempt!

The fomite experiment was repeated three times. Volunteers slept in nightshirts that had been worn by yellow-fever patients. Still they did not contract the disease.

With the fomite theory blasted, the next challenge was to show just how a house becomes infected with yellow fever. Accordingly, on December 21, fifteen stegomyia mosquitoes, contaminated with yellow fever at intervals of five to twenty-four days previously, were released in one screened-in compartment of the Infected Mosquito Building. Five minutes after the mosquitoes were released, Field Clerk John J. Moran, who had been in quarantine for thirty-two days, freshly bathed and clad only in his nightshirt, entered the mosquito room and lay down on the bed. On the other side of the partition, where no mosquitoes were allowed to enter, three more volunteers took up residence.

On Christmas morning, four days later, Army Clerk Moran was stricken with yellow fever. Luckily the gallant Ohioan recovered. The nonimmunes on the other side of the screen partition remained in perfect health during fifteen days of confinement.

On New Year's night, 1900, Walter Reed wrote to his wife:

It has been permitted me and my assistants to lift the impenetrable veil that has surrounded the causation of this most wonderful, dreadful pest of humanity and put it on a rational and scientific basis....The prayer that has been mine for twenty years, that I might be permitted in some way or at some time to do something to alleviate human suffering, has been granted.

The work at Camp Lazear was ended. The last successful case of mosquito infection was made February 7, 1901. Its work done, the Yellow Fever Board disbanded. Agramonte remained at Havana, a full-fledged member of the faculty of medicine. James Carroll returned to New York and Washington in company with Walter Reed. Yellow fever was being beaten from Cuba. Lives were being saved. For the American tropics a new era was dawning.

---

[14]*Koch's discovery of the tubercle bacillus.* Robert Koch (kôH), a German doctor and bacteriologist, discovered the germ that causes tuberculosis.

[15]*norteamericanos* (nôr′tä ə mer′i kä′nōs), used here to mean "people from the United States."

HOW DID WALTER REED ATTACK HIS PROBLEM?

1. What various theories about yellow fever were current when Walter Reed began to study it during the Spanish-American War?

2. What previous experience had Reed had that would make Surgeon General Sternberg feel he was capable of heading the Yellow Fever Board? What were the qualifications for this work of each of the other three men?

3. Why was Reed able to convince the medical world that a certain type of mosquito transmitted yellow fever while Finlay, who had preached this theory for twenty years, was scorned?

4. Trace the steps, from the formation of the Yellow Fever Board to the closing of Camp Lazear, by which Reed and his associates (*a*) proved how yellow fever is transmitted and (*b*) showed how it can be controlled.

5. In what ways does this article illustrate how the rise of science has aided progress in medicine? What other developments in medicine can you mention that science has made possible?

Know your words

On a sheet of paper answer the following questions. Be ready to explain why you decided as you did. Use the Glossary if necessary.

1. If a medical problem is *appalling,* is it practically solved, dismaying, or primarily a result of war?

2. If a doctor tells you a certain disease is *lethal,* do you understand it to be deadly, mild, or of long duration?

3. If this disease is being rapidly *disseminated,* is it under complete control, spreading, or practically wiped out?

4. If a doctor performs an *autopsy,* is he investigating the cause of death, demonstrating a new operating technique, or examining a patient?

Extending interests

Research on any one of the following subjects might be the basis for an interesting report:
1. Reed's life before his rise to fame
2. Yellow fever today
3. The wonder drugs
4. Atomic energy in medicine
5. Recent discoveries in medicine (This might be the basis for several reports dealing with special fields of medicine.)
6. The accomplishments of some other ambassador in white.

Wheels in His Head

M. M. MUSSELMAN

Inventors, who are largely responsible for advances in industry, must be at the same time original and practical, unconventional and responsive to popular demands. Every year patents are taken out on about 25,000 devices at the United States Patent Office. Many of these, of course, never reach a factory. Either the ideas are not practical or the demand is insufficient.

The following article shows an inventor at work, and indicates how he took advantage of the kind of opportunity available to ingenious men in the United States.

EVERYBODY, including Grandma, said A. J.[1] would never amount to anything because he just wouldn't stick to a good job when he had one. In more or less chronological order he was a bicycle racer, hardware buyer, sporting-goods dealer, bicycle salesman, assistant manager of a mail-order house, tire salesman, manufacturer of golf clubs, real-estate subdivider, country-club promoter, research engineer, and gentleman farmer. And always he was an inventor. Inventors sometimes become very wealthy, but more often they go bankrupt. For many years A. J. danced a jig between the two, but in the end, to everyone's amazement, he did all right.

The first invention on which he was granted a patent was a game called "Parlor Golf," which he sold to Parker Brothers[2] for one hundred dollars, spot cash. The most remarkable thing about this was that, when he invented it, A. J. had never seen a game of golf. But apparently neither had Parker Brothers, for the game resembled golf about as much as Paris, Illinois, resembles that other and more famous Paris.

The idea of the game was to flick a marble, with thumb and forefinger, up a series of nine grooved and undulated inclines, into nine little

---

[1] *A. J.,* Alvin J. Musselman, father of the author of this selection.

[2] *Parker Brothers,* a firm which manufactures games.

holes. In all Wichita, where A. J. by this time owned a bicycle repair shop, he was the only person who had the patience or skill to accomplish this feat in less than par. Everyone else grew infuriated at the thing and gave up, leaving A. J. the first undisputed Western Open Golf Champion (Parlor Division).

A. J. claims that inventing Parlor Golf was not in itself a deterrent factor in his normal development as a bicycle merchant. It was selling the monstrosity that did the harm. The acquisition of one hundred dollars in a lump sum was A. J.'s first taste of wealth. It excited his imagination. He reasoned that all he had to do was think up one invention a week and he'd be about the richest man in Wichita. When he discovered that inventors could get royalties for their creations, he went hog-wild figuring how rich he'd be in a year or two.

There followed a number of remarkable inventions, all of which, for one reason or another, failed to produce quick riches.

The Tearless Onion Peeler was a gadget that should have been a welcome addition to every kitchen. It was an affair of wheels and knives with a crank to operate it. For large consumers of onions, such as hotels and restaurants, A. J. devised a model which had a foot treadle for motive power. With this super-job one man (or woman) could peel, A. J. estimated roughly, seven bushels of onions per hour without shedding a single tear. And by a simple adjustment, the machine could be converted to a potato, apple, peach, turnip, or rutabaga peeler. In those days, however, labor was plentiful and cheap; consequently, manufacturers of kitchen implements were of the unanimous opinion that A. J.'s Tearless Onion Peeler was no substitute for a ten-cent paring knife.

"It was a good invention," A. J. once told me, "but nobody wanted to buy it. That's always been the trouble with the world. People are suspicious of new ideas. If you spend a year inventing something new, you have to spend two years cramming it down people's throats. There are lots of easier ways to get rich."

After the Tearless Onion Peeler, A. J. invented his Wind-Proof Umbrella. "It Can't Blow Inside Out," read the prospectus.

A. J. was sure he had a winner. Every household needed an umbrella, more especially one that would not collapse at the first gust of wind. And certainly rain was usually accompanied by wind; at least it was in Kansas. He figured that if he could collect a royalty of five cents per umbrella, he ought to make a million dollars in five years.

At the time he perfected the new umbrella, he was enamored of a girl in Wichita, whose name, according to Aunt Ora, was Bertha. A. J. usually maintains a discreet silence regarding Bertha and sometimes vehemently denies that this was her name; but there definitely was a girl who, despite A. J., has become known in family legends as Bertha.

She was the clinging-vine type, just a slip of a thing, too frail for this world's sorrows. That was a day when it was fashionable for women to be weak and helpless. Men adored Bertha; women hated her.

"It was an act," Aunt Ora used to say. "She was frail like an amazon and about as helpless as Cleopatra."[3]

A. J. told Bertha about his newest invention. She listened with round-eyed admiration and assured him, breathlessly, that he must be the cleverest man in Wichita. And would he, pretty please, give her one of his patent umbrellas when he became a famous millionaire?

A. J. didn't wait to become a millionaire. He rushed right down to Innes' Department Store and bought a lady's silk umbrella, priced at three dollars. Then he took it to his shop and rebuilt it, with the cross-bracing, truss arrangement which was the feature of his Wind-Proof Umbrella.

On Bertha's birthday he presented it to her. She protested that it was far too expensive a gift but rewarded A. J. by calling him a "wonderful, darling man."

For a week or so, Bertha displayed her umbrella as proudly as a queen with a new scepter; and A. J. was elevated to the position of chief swain in her retinue of admirers. His head was

---

[3]*Cleopatra* (klē′ə pat′rə *or* klē′ə pā′trə), queen of Egypt 69?-30 B.C., whose beauty, charm, and influence over men were legendary. She gained the love of both Julius Caesar and Mark Antony.

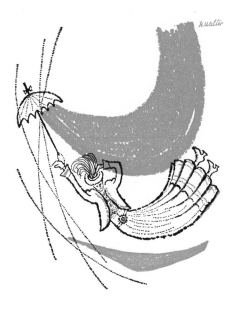

Cissie's house, the wind filled her umbrella and tried to tear it from her grasp. But the loop about her wrist prevented this. Instead, she and the umbrella were swept along like two chips on a raging torrent.

Bertha screamed for help, but gallant male pedestrians dashing for shelter could only make futile grabs at her as she bounded past with arms, legs, and petticoats flying. Then the wind dragged her out into the street, where she tripped and fell. As she skidded and rolled through the mud, she prayed for the total collapse of A. J.'s indestructible umbrella—but in vain. By the time she piled up against the Onderdonks' picket fence, bruised, battered, and humiliated, the romance between Bertha and the inventor of the Patented Wind-Proof Umbrella was definitely ended.

in the clouds, the perfume of orange blossoms was in the air, and the tinkle of wedding bells in the offing. And then—the rains came.

It happened while Bertha was on her way downtown, clad in a new spring outfit. The sky was slightly overcast, so she was carrying her Patented Wind-Proof Umbrella. But aside from the threatening clouds there was no portent of the coming tragedy. When the first drops fell, Bertha struggled for a minute or two with the mechanism of the Wind-Proof Umbrella and finally opened it. Then, with an efficient gesture, she slipped her hand through the umbrella's stout wrist-loop, grasped the handle, and quickened her pace along Douglas Avenue toward the center of town.

The raindrops were growing fatter and falling faster. Bertha could have turned in at her Aunt Cissie's house until the summer storm passed over, but she continued on with complacent assurance, feeling completely secure beneath her handsome, ample Wind-Proof Umbrella.

Then suddenly the rain began to slant; overhead, tree branches bent and groaned as a rush of wind struck them; and the sky turned a threatening yellowish gray. Bertha grasped her umbrella with both hands and stopped in her tracks. She had lived in Kansas all her life and she knew what was coming: a Kansas tornado. As she turned to dash back toward her Aunt

Even as a boy back on the farm A. J. had an unnatural passion for things that went round and round. Wheels! Anything with wheels attached to it started him off on a mental tangent. An unattached wheel would leave him in a state of suspended animation, while he gawked at it with a dreamy, speculative expression.

The invention of which he is proudest is his method for making the tires now used on airplanes, farm tractors, and other vehicles. This invention created a new principle in tire construction, by means of which the cross section of a tire could be nearly as great as one half the diameter, resulting in very low air pressures. These tires made it possible for planes to land or take off on rough or muddy fields; they also reduced ground looping[4] and eliminated crackups due to wheel failure. Unfortunately, he sold his patent before anyone could foresee the enormous production of planes that World War II would bring. So the invention which has brought him the greatest financial return is his bicycle coaster brake.

Over a period of some fifty years, A. J. has conceived more than a hundred other inventions, among which are such widely divergent devices as the low-pressure, single-tube tire, as

[4]*ground looping,* an uncontrollable sharp turn made by an airplane while running along the ground during landing or taking-off.

used on wheelbarrows and toy vehicles, a mechanics' soap, a pneumatic auto bumper, a radio aerial, a bicycle pedal, the zipper golf bag, a two-speed coaster brake, and an airplane brake.

"I got the idea for my bicycle coaster brake back in 1894," A. J. always begins one of his best stories. "It was while I was traveling about ninety miles an hour down the slopes of the Rockies on a bicycle. Lucky thing I didn't kill myself or I never could have invented it."

Grandma used to smile indulgently whenever A. J. would start this yarn. She took that business about the Rocky Mountains with a grain of salt.

But anyway, as A. J. tells the story, he unlocked his bike shop one July morning and discovered that the window on the alley was standing wide open. Then he noticed that his pride and joy, a red and white Peerless bicycle, the latest thing in cycledom,[5] was missing. It was the most expensive one in the store—priced at $125. The plush-lined traveling case, for shipping via railroad, was undisturbed, so A. J. knew that the thief had ridden his loot away.

He hurried over to the police station, where inquiry revealed that a stranger, who had skipped out of the local hotel without paying his bill, had been seen the night before, by Patrolman Murphy, hightailing toward Hutchinson on the Peerless.

A. J. was fit to be tied. "Why didn't Murphy pinch that fellow?" he demanded. "That was the only red and white Peerless bike in Wichita and everybody knew it belonged to me."

The Chief of Police shrugged. "Maybe Murphy thought the guy had bought it."

A. J. was mad enough to have chewed a sprocket. He hurried over to the bank and drew out twenty dollars for expense money, then dashed back to his store, shouted to Aunt Ora that he was on the trail of a bicycle thief, and climbed on his Ariel roadracer, and started for Hutchinson.

As A. J. likes to point out, he was pretty sharp on a bicycle in those days—an amateur circuit racer[6] and one of the best riders west of the Mississippi. He thought he could overtake the bike-rustler before nightfall, because the red and white Peerless was bound to attract as much attention as though the thief had been riding a zebra.

But he soon discovered that his quarry was a fast rider himself. For when he arrived at Great Bend, about nine o'clock that night, the Peerless had been there and gone. A. J. started out next morning at daybreak, hoping to overtake the bike-snatcher before he lost the trail. He was at a disadvantage, of course, because he had to stop at every crossroad and make inquiries; but the trail stayed hot—as A. J. says, "hotter'n an iron pump handle in August."

The second afternoon, under a scorching sun, he came to an interminable stretch of lonely Kansas prairie without a farmhouse or a tree in sight for miles. His tongue became parched and swollen, until it seemed too large for his mouth. He had almost given up hope of ever reaching water, when he finally sighted a water tank along the Missouri Pacific Railroad. For the next half hour he sat in the shade and sipped water until he had slaked his thirst and re-

[6]*circuit racer*, one who entered bicycle races held at scheduled intervals in connection with county fairs and other gatherings. The circuit racer went from one contest to another.

[5]*cycledom*, in the world of bicycles.

gained his strength. Then, with a bottle of water slung over his shoulder, he started out again. Never before had an amateur rider given him such a run for his money; he was determined to catch him.

Finally he arrived at a desolate group of shanties beside the railroad. One of these was a fly-infested lunchroom, where he ordered a sandwich and inquired about the man on the Peerless.

"Yeah," answered the proprietor. "There was a fellow come through here on a bike like that."

"How long ago?"

"Couple hours. Told me he was headin' for Colorado Springs.[7] Purty long ride, if you ask me."

A. J. didn't wait to finish his sandwich. He hit the road and settled down to ride his fox to earth. He claims this was the best race he ever pedaled in his life, but somehow the thief evaded him. He thinks the man may have bribed a brakeman on a freight train to give him and the Peerless a lift in an empty boxcar.

A. J. reached Colorado Springs early one morning. As soon as the stores were open he canvassed every bike shop in town, but nobody had seen the Peerless. As a last resort he went to the police station.

"Saw a fellow ridin' a bike toward Cripple Creek[8] this morning," one of the cops told him.

"Was it a red and white Peerless?"

"Didn't notice."

A. J. took a chance and headed for Cripple Creek. He had never seen mountains before and hadn't the vaguest idea what he was in for. The last ten miles into the little mining town were so steep he had to get off his bike and push. As he plugged up those weary miles, he had an uncomfortable feeling that he had been sent on a wild-goose chase. Sure enough, nobody in Cripple Creek had seen the Peerless.

A. J. was a very unhappy man—tired, defeated, six hundred miles from home, and with only about six dollars left in his jeans. His one consoling thought was that he would be able to coast all the way back to Colorado Springs and a bed.

So he climbed on his bike and started, with never a thought of more trouble ahead. But before he was half a mile out of town, he suddenly realized that he was traveling too fast. For although the Cripple Creek road didn't look so steep, it was something like the first dip on a roller coaster. He tried to slow down by throwing his weight against the pedals, but that was no help. He just kept gaining speed and before he knew it was heading down that road faster than a hound dog with a hive of bees on his tail.

In those days a cyclist used to brake his bike by slipping one toe under the frame and pressing on the front tire with the sole of his shoe. A. J. tried that. For a moment it worked; then suddenly friction made the sole of his shoe fiery hot. He let out a startled yell and jerked his foot from beneath the frame.

Then gravity took charge once more and away he went. It quickly flashed into his mind that it was time to think of something ingenious. But the only bright idea his inventive brain could contrive was to fall off, which he did. He hit the dirt with a thud that knocked the wind completely out of him; then in one bounce he was off the road and rolling down the mountainside. He finished upside down against a scrub pine fifty feet from the road.

For a minute or two he just lay there regaining his wind and wondering if he was all in one piece. Finally he rose groggily and shook his head until the world came back into focus. Setting his jaw determinedly, he scrambled up to the road and looked about for the bicycle. It was nowhere in sight. After a twenty-minute search, he found it caught in a thicket of sagebrush some distance from the point at which he had abandoned it.

Grimly he hauled the bike back to the road, straightened the handle bars, and climbed aboard. But this time he was prepared for that deceptive grade and intended to master it. So he tried tacking from one side of the road to the other to slow up his descent; he dragged one foot until his toes were numb; he tried every

---

[7]*Colorado Springs,* a city in Colorado lying at the foot of the Rocky Mountains.

[8]*Cripple Creek,* a gold-mining town lying in the mountains more than half a mile higher than Colorado Springs and almost forty miles away.

trick he could think of. And the end result? As A. J. so graphically puts it, "I'll be jumped-up-and-knocked-down if the same thing didn't happen all over again."

When he picked himself up the second time, he had a new respect for the law of gravity. And after another extensive search, he found his bike with eight spokes broken and the frame bent; but he finally fixed the machine so that it would run. Then he sat down by the roadside to evolve a method by which he could ride back to Colorado Springs without the risk of killing himself.

His pondering resulted in the invention of his first "coaster brake." He manufactured it on the spot by cutting several pine branches and tying them into a bundle with a piece of rope from his tool kit. The end of the rope was then attached to his saddle post so that the pine branches dragged behind on the road.

It worked like a charm. The bundle of branches was just enough brake to keep things under control. He went steaming down the mountain road, throwing up a dust cloud big enough for thirty head of cattle.

For about six miles A. J. was mighty proud of his invention; then to his dismay, he discovered that it was an infringement. He was informed of this fact by a deputy sheriff who halted him with a .44 and a vocabulary of four-letter words that would have shriveled an alligator's hide.

Using a drag for a brake was old stuff in those parts. Wagon freighters had invented the device years before. The trouble was that it ruined good roads, so the state had passed a law against that invention. A. J. had to wire back to Wichita for money to pay his fine.

"And that's one reason," A. J. has often told me, "that I conceived the idea of putting a coaster brake on a bicycle."

The idea was a long time hatching, for it was not until about 1907 that he applied for a patent. But since 1908 five million bicycles have been equipped with A. J.'s coaster brake, and even Grandma had to admit, before she died, that somehow "one of Alvey's fool inventions turned out purty good."

DO YOU AGREE THAT A. J. "DID ALL RIGHT"?

1. Why do you think the author chose "Wheels in His Head" as a title for his account of an inventor's life?

2. How do you account for A. J.'s success as an inventor? What qualities did he possess to a marked degree? Which was most important to his success?

3. In what ways does the author make A. J. seem a likable and interesting person?

4. Which of A. J.'s inventions was of most importance to industry? How have A. J. and other inventors aided in the development of the industrial age in America?

Machines
With and Without Freedom

DAVID E. LILIENTHAL

Perhaps few men realize more fully the impact of the progress of science on American life than David Lilienthal. When the Tennessee Valley Authority was authorized by Congress in 1933 to harness the Tennessee River by a series of twenty-one dams, thereby developing hydro-electric power, aiding flood control, and promoting navigation, he became one of three directors. From 1941 to 1946 he served as chairman of the Authority. When the U. S. Atomic Energy Commission was set up following the development of atomic power during World War II, Lilienthal was appointed chairman. He resigned from this position at the end of 1949. In the following article he presents his views as to how men can remain free in the machine age.

To SOME PEOPLE modern technology is plainly evil. To them, the more gadgets the more unpalatable is life. The more things we produce, the faster we can travel, the more complex the machines we invent, the nearer—they assert—we move to the edge of a bottomless pit. They ask: "Is not scientific warfare the inevitable fruit of technology? Are not ever more devastating atomic bombs the ultimate proof that modern applied science is a curse, an unmitigated blight?" Even great figures are heard to say: "Let us cease learning more of the world, let scientists declare a moratorium in their ceaseless prying into Nature's secrets." They are homesick for that simpler life, before the days when man produced so much and knew so much. They want to flee. But where and how? They cannot say. They cry out against science and the machine and call them evil; but their voices are the voices of despair and defeat.

There are others of our contemporaries who have an almost opposite view of the machine. You will find them all over the world. What they say is exuberant and uncritical. "Of course technology is good," they say, "for it produces more and more things; and isn't production the answer to everything?" They are usually skeptical of God, but they openly worship the machine.

"Of course the machine is good," they say. "When assembly lines cut costs, when production curves are upward[1] or when Five-Year Plans[2] are fulfilled—those are the important things; let's not agonize over the effect of the machine on the freedom of men."

Technology, they seem to say, is good as an end in itself. If the spirit of man balks, if the yearning to be human increases cost of production or requires coercion—well, man must be redesigned to fit the assembly line, not the assembly line revised for man. The supertechnologists of the world are quite prepared to re-create man in the image of the machine.

I venture to say that neither of these views—of the defeatist or the technolator[3]—will appeal to most Americans.

The machine and technology are neither good nor evil in themselves. They are good only when man uses them for good. They are evil only if he puts them to evil purposes.

The machine can, of course, be so used as to degrade and enslave man. It can be used to exhaust the land and with it the human dignity of those who live on the land; it can poison the air, foul the streams, devastate the forests, and thereby doom men and women and children to the spiritual degradation of great poverty. But it can also open wider—and it has so opened—the doors of human opportunity; it can nourish the spirit of men. Technology can be used to eliminate filth and congestion and disease; to

---

[1]*production curves are upward.* On a chart showing the manufacture of one or more articles, an upward curve indicates increased production.

[2]*Five-Year Plans,* plans designed to stimulate production by laying down a certain quota to be reached each year. Such plans have been used as a spur to industrialization, particularly in totalitarian countries.

[3]*technolator,* a coined word meaning one who worships technology or who believes it can accomplish all things.

strengthen the soil; to conserve the forests; to humanize man's environment.

The machine can be so used as to make men free as they have never been free before.

We have a choice—that, it seems to me, is the shining and hopeful fact. If we are wise enough, if we follow our democratic precepts, we can control and direct technology and the machine and make them serve for good.

I believe in the great potentialities for well-being of the machine and technology; and though they do hold a real threat of enslavement and frustration for the human spirit, I believe those dangers can be averted. I believe that through the methods of democracy the world of technology holds out the greatest opportunity in all history for the development of the individual, according to his own talents, aspirations, and willingness to shoulder the responsibilities of a free man. I believe men can make themselves free. Men can direct technology so that it can carry mankind toward the fulfillment of the greatest promise for human life and the human spirit in all history.

But this result is by no means inevitable. It is equally possible that technology may yield a harvest of bitter fruit.

More huge cyclotrons and nuclear research reactors[4] are not enough. More fine laboratories, more extensive projects in physical and social research are not enough. More *use* of technology, more factories, more gadgets, whether in

[4]*cyclotrons and nuclear research reactors,* machines used in releasing atomic energy.

this country or in the undeveloped reaches of Africa and Asia and South America is not enough. Those who encourage a contrary belief are playing a dangerous game or are quite blind to the realities.

Unless the applications of research and technology are consciously related to a central purpose of human welfare, unless technology is defined and directed by those who believe in people and in democratic and ethical ends and means, it could be that the more research money we spend the further we miss the mark. It is like driving in an automobile that is going in the wrong direction; the faster and faster you drive the farther away from your destination you will be.

The guiding of technical activity is safe, in terms of the human spirit, only when it is in the hands of those, in private business and in public agencies, who have faith in the individual human being. It is only safe when it is carried on by methods that are in furtherance of that faith, and methods that insure accountability to the people for the results.

This is not always the case with modern technology. There are times when these matters are controlled by men who lack a faith in people. People, to them, are only a "market." They are a market to whom to sell new gadgets; a labor market with which to make the gadgets; a political market to be cajoled and organized and voted and coerced. Technical development under such direction will not further freedom or will do so only by accident, by sheer coincidence.

We know what amazing things applied research can do to increase the destructive powers of armies and navies and air forces—our own, or a potential enemy's. But we still must ask: What can technology do to nourish and strengthen the human spirit? What can technology do to safeguard and strengthen men's freedom?

That modern man can completely change his environment is a matter of common observation. Perhaps as widely known an illustration in other parts of the world is afforded by the development in the Tennessee Valley.

In a single decade the face of a region larger than England was substantially altered, a region comprising parts of seven Southern states. The great Tennessee River has been changed: more than a score of huge dams make it do what men tell it to do. The farming land is changed—millions of acres—and the forests and woodlands. New factories, large and small, barges on the new river channel, and yards building ships; fields once dead and hideous with gullies now fruitful and green to the sun, secure with pastures and meadows; electric pumps in farmyards; new local and regional libraries; state parks and county health facilities—these and many other changes make it a new valley today. The job of development is not done, of course—such a task never is—but it is well on the way. It is one more demonstration that modern technical tools and managerial skills can control nature and change the physical setting of our life in almost any way we choose—there is the point—in whatever way we as a people choose.

These changes in that valley—these physical changes—strike the eye. They are unmistakable evidence of what can be done. Equally impressive are the evidences of increased production of farm and factory, of rising individual income among people who have suffered under shockingly sparse incomes. But most important of all the changes is the change in the spirit of the valley's people. One of Alabama's younger leaders described it in these words:

We can write of great dams...of the building of home-grown industry and of electricity at last coming to the farms of thousands of farm people in the valley. Yet the significant advances have been made in the thinking of a people. They are no longer afraid. They have caught the vision of their own powers. They can stand now and talk out in meeting....

And they do!

The real significance to many observers of what has taken place in the valley of the Tennessee is this: This American experiment has fortified confidence that men need not be chained to the wheel of technology. If their purpose is firm and clear, and if they insist upon ways and means to make that purpose effective, man can use the machine in the interest of human welfare and the human spirit.

A great many men and women from foreign countries have come to study the TVA.[5] They have come from more than fifty countries, and in particular from the technically undeveloped regions of the world, and from areas in which unsparing and unwise exploitation threatens their natural resources with utter exhaustion. These visitors have not only seen new life come to a dying soil; they have also seen how a new hope and faith return to people living on that soil, have seen men's pride and their human dignity strengthened as their soil was strengthened. They have not only seen the once wasted energies of a great river turned into electricity but they have also seen the way that electricity has put an end to degrading drudgery in tens of thousands of homes. They have seen businessmen, farmers, laborers—all kinds of men and women—joining together to apply the lessons of science and technology to the building of their region, and in the very act of joining together for that common purpose have seen many of them become better neighbors, kinder and more generous and more coöperative human beings.

These hundreds of foreign visitors see with particular clarity that the new Tennessee Valley speaks in a tongue that is universal among men, a language of things close to the everyday lives of people: soil, forests, factories, minerals, rivers. No English interpreter is needed when a Chinese or a Hindu or a Peruvian sees these products of a working technology, sees a series of working dams, or a hillside pasture brought back to life by phosphate and lime and an un-

[5]*TVA*, Tennessee Valley Authority.

derstanding of soils. For it is not really Fontana Dam on a North Carolina stream or a farm in Kentucky that he sees, but a river, a valley, a farm in China or India or Peru.

Because it is an illustration with which I am familiar, I have pointed to the Tennessee Valley as one bit of American evidence that *it can be done,* that men can use science and technology in the interest of the human spirit. It does not make the demonstration less relevant that only a beginning has been made in that valley, that the people of the valley realize what a long, long way there is yet to travel. And it should surely not be necessary to utter the warning that no one should regard the TVA, or any other one effort in this direction, as a single way out. The paths are many, and TVA is but one of the many moving toward the same goal.

We have a choice. We can choose deliberately and consciously whether the machine or man comes first. But that choice will not be exercised on a single occasion, surrounded by spectacle and drama. We will move from decision to decision, from issue to issue, and we will be in the midst of this struggle for the rest of our days.

We cannot master the machine in the interest of the human spirit unless we have a faith in people. This is the foundation of everything. The rock upon which all these efforts rest must be a deep and abiding faith in human beings, which is a faith in the supreme worth of life. The machine can only add to the dignity and integrity of human existence if it is deliberately used in furtherance of such faith in people. It is the purpose for which the machine is used, and particularly the methods pursued in carrying out that purpose, that determine whether technology is likely to further human well-being or to threaten it.

CAN MAN RULE THE MACHINE?

1. According to Lilienthal, what is the view of the defeatist toward modern technology? What is the view of the supertechnologist? What is the author's viewpoint? Select statements from the article which explain each of these viewpoints.

2. What sort of man does Lilienthal believe should control technical activity? What is his criticism of men to whom people are only a "market"?

3. What physical differences has TVA made in the Southern states which the Tennessee River and its tributaries drain? What differences, according to Lilienthal, has it made in the lives of the people? In their spirit? Which does he believe are the most important changes?

4. Why do you think Lilienthal discussed the Tennessee Valley in an article entitled "Machines With and Without Freedom"?

5. Compare Lilienthal's view of the machine with that of Melville and Moody. How do you think that Melville would answer Lilienthal's argument that "the machine can be so used as to make men free as they have never been free before"? What is your own view?

A scientist uses figurative language

You have known for years that poets use figurative language. Perhaps since studying "The Leader of the People" you have come to realize that the novelist and the short-story writer also need figurative language to help them convey particular ideas; but have you considered that the scientist also may find figurative expressions helpful in explaining his thoughts? In "Machines With and Without Freedom" David Lilienthal explains his belief as to how the machine can be made a friend rather than an enemy of man; in doing so he frequently uses figurative language to make his ideas understandable.

Pick out the figurative expressions in the following sentences. Then try to restate the sentences literally. How often does literal language require more words to express an idea? Why, as a rule, does it fail to express it as satisfactorily?

1. But it [the machine] can also open wider—and it has so opened—the doors of human opportunity; it can nourish the spirit of men.

2. It is equally possible that technology may yield a harvest of bitter fruit.

3. Those who encourage a contrary belief are playing a dangerous game or are quite blind to the realities.

4. This American experiment [TVA] has fortified confidence that men need not be chained to the wheel of technology.

5. These hundreds of foreign visitors see with particular clarity that the new Tennessee Valley speaks in a tongue that is universal among men, a language of things close to the everyday lives of people.

6. The paths are many, and TVA is but one of the many moving toward the same goal.

7. The rock upon which all these efforts rest must be a deep and abiding faith in human beings, which is a faith in the supreme worth of life.

The Larger View

I. Each of the numbered items in Group A describes a man whom you have met in this unit. Each of the lettered statements in Group B is a quotation from one of the unit selections. On a sheet of paper write the numbers 1 through 8. After each number write the name of the man whom the item in Group A characterizes; then write the letter indicating the quotation in Group B which presents the man's ideas.

Group A

1. A manual laborer who refused to give way to the machine.
2. A public servant who believes in the worth and wisdom of free men.
3. An industrialist who pinned his faith on the assembly line.
4. A poet who believed that the machine would ultimately work for man's good.
5. A scientist who was more interested in practical results than in theory.
6. An inventor who loved gadgets.
7. An observer who saw man debased by machinery.
8. A man who used science to conquer disease.

Group B

a. He must loose the curse of Adam from the worn neck of the race.

b. ...it had always been his custom to hire others to do the heavy work. The speed he was busy with was speed in production, the records records in efficient output.

c. I don't want any old machine to take my place at the happiest work I's ever found. So before I let that steam drill beat me, I'll die with my hammer in my hand.

d. It has been permitted me and my assistants to lift the inpenetrable veil that has surrounded the causation of this most wonderful, dreadful pest of humanity and put it on a rational and scientific basis.

e. Anything with wheels attached to it started him off on a mental tangent. An unattached wheel would leave him in a state of suspended animation.

f. We cannot master the machine in the interest of the human spirit unless we have a faith in people.

g. Machinery—that vaunted slave of humanity—here stood menially served by human beings, who served mutely and cringingly as the slave serves the sultan.

h. I now send you what at present appears to me to be the shortest and simplest method of securing buildings, etc., from the mischiefs of lightning.

II. Prepare to talk over the following questions, wherever possible using books, magazines, and newspapers you have read, movies or television programs you have seen, or radio programs you have heard to enlarge the discussion or to give concrete examples.

1. What do you think Benjamin Franklin's reaction to TVA would be? Do you think today's advances in the living and working conditions of the laboring man would convince Herman Melville that machines can be used for man's good?

2. Which selections in this unit would you say present only the bright side of scientific or industrial improvement? Which ones concentrate on the social abuses that have accompanied change? In which selections can you find both good and bad aspects of increased industrialization?

3. Which selection succeeds best in your opinion in developing the phase of our industrial and scientific progress of which it treats? Have you read any book or article that develops this same phase? Would you say it was more or less successful than the text selection? What discussions have you read of phases of our scientific and industrial growth not represented in these selections?

4. Comment on the following statement, giving your reasons for agreeing or disagreeing with it: On the whole the rise of science and industry has improved and will continue to improve the lot of the ordinary man.

5. In what ways have the selections in this unit enlarged your understanding of the problems facing modern man?

MORE GOOD READING

BURLINGAME, ROGER, *Whittling Boy; The Story of Eli Whitney*. (Harcourt) The man who invented the cotton gin was a genius in mechanics. Born before the world was ready for his ideas, he spent his life dreaming of and working for a mechanical world. Roger Burlingame makes Whitney's life an absorbing story.

CONKLIN, GROFF (editor), *Best of Science Fiction*. (Crown) The best science fiction of the past hundred years, from Edgar Allan Poe and A. Conan Doyle to the atom bomb, is assembled in this volume.

DE KRUIF, PAUL, *Hunger Fighters*. (Harcourt) Here are the stories of men who worked from a fact to its implications and so taught the world to overcome various plant and animal diseases. Equally interesting is De Kruif's *Microbe Hunters* (Harcourt).

DITMARS, RAYMOND L., *Confessions of a Scientist*. (Macmillan) If you're interested in reading an informal account of a naturalist's day-to-day work in field and laboratory with its full quota of excitement, danger, and unexpected happenings, this is the book for you.

EVERSON, GEORGE, *Story of Television; the Life of Philo T. Farnsworth*. (Norton) Young Farnsworth was fifteen when he told his high-school teacher his dream of sending pictures through the air, but it was twenty-two years before he saw his dream come true. Whether or not you're interested in science, you'll enjoy this biography.

FIELD, RACHEL, *And Now Tomorrow*. (Macmillan) Rachel Field's skill as a fine novelist is apparent in the realness of the characters who fight hard times in a New England mill town.

GARBEDIAN, HAIG G., *George Westinghouse: Fabulous Inventor*. (Dodd) Few men played so important a part in the industrial age which followed the Civil War as George Westinghouse, a country boy who became a world-renowned inventor.

HAMMOND, J. W., *Magician of Science; The Boy's Life of Steinmetz*. (Appleton) The story of Steinmetz, a poor crippled Jewish immigrant who became a scientific and mathematical genius honored by all America, is one of the most inspiring ever told. You'll find this version of it interesting and easy to understand.

HOLT, RACKHAM, *George Washington Carver; an American Biography*. (Doubleday) The wizened little Negro, born a slave, unlocked the secrets hidden in various plants as no one before him had ever done. This is one of the best of recent biographies.

HORAN, KENNETH, *Bashful Woman*. (Doubleday) Girls, particularly, will be interested in this novel about Sally Benson, who persuaded her first husband to study the outlandish contraption called the horseless carriage. The picture of the development of the automobile business in Michigan will appeal to all.

LAWRENCE, JOSEPHINE, *If I Have Four Apples*. (Stokes) If you insist on believing that four apples plus two apples equals eight apples, you'll face the same sort of troubles that befell the Hoe family. This is a likable, readable novel.

LEVINGER, ELMA, *Albert Einstein*. (Messner) From the boy who hated school because he could not ask "why" to the man acknowledged the greatest living scientist—this is the wide territory covered in a biography of particular interest to young scientists.

LEWIS, SINCLAIR, *Arrowsmith*. (Harcourt) Few American novels ever enjoyed wider popularity over a period of time than Sinclair Lewis' Pulitzer-prize winning story of Martin Arrowsmith, a young physician and bacteriologist who struggled with problems in medicine as well as in his personal life.

MEADOWCROFT, WILLIAM H., *Boy's Life of Edison*. (Harper) Among the greatest charms of this biography, written by a member of Edison's staff, are the amusing anecdotes in the inventor's own words which enliven the story.

STEVENSON, O. J., *Talking Wire; the Story of Alexander Graham Bell*. (Messner) This history of the development of the telephone is fact that reads like fiction. There is fascination in the details of Bell's experiments and in the account of his early struggles.

The Development of American Ideals

AMERICAN LITERATURE, as we have seen, is the record of the growth of the nation from small beginnings in a strange and newly discovered continent to the immensely complicated factory and machine world of today. It tells us the story of men and women in America from the time John Smith met Pocahontas in the wilds of Virginia to the age of airliners and television. American literature, however, is more than a story of the vast changes in man's life in this land. In the United States, more perhaps than in most countries, written words are the slender but strong bonds which hold together thousands of persons who as individuals differ in almost every way one can think of—in their family backgrounds and training, in their religion, in their wealth, in their opinions, in their tastes, and in their places and ways of living.

Some years ago, when the Freedom Train toured the country, hundreds of thousands of Americans, young and old, stood in line for hours, waiting for a chance to look briefly at some words written on pieces of paper. They looked reverently at the Mayflower Compact, the Declaration of Independence, and the Constitution. All who visited the train realized the amazing power of the written word. These fragments of paper, covered with faded ink, represent the oneness, the unity, of the American people. Like the flag, they symbolize the nation.

Not all literature, of course, has the almost sacred associations of the documents which were displayed on the Freedom Train. Yet much American literature is a similar expression of American ideals. It tells us the things for which Americans have been willing to sacrifice their comfort and their money, the beliefs which they have held in common, the steps they have taken toward building a world where all groups can dwell together in unity.

The literature of American idealism gives us courage and strength. It is good to know the dreams and to understand the achievements of our predecessors, because, in a free society, each of us must make up his mind about many disputes whose outcome affects the success of that society. This is not to say that American literature is the final word about democracy. On the contrary, it tends to suggest that there will always be new problems, that every generation will have to find its own solutions. That the living generation may find wise solutions is the main reason for exploring the literature of ideals.

UNIT V: THE PRICE OF LIBERTY

WE AMERICANS sing that our country is "the land of the free," "sweet land of liberty." We boast that the rights which the individual cannot give up or have taken from him are "life, liberty, and the pursuit of happiness." We do not always remember that liberty has been hard to get and that it is even harder to keep.

Liberty has meant different things at different times. To one generation of Americans it meant self-government, "no taxation without representation." To another it meant fighting to free the Negro slaves or to preserve states' rights. To still another it has meant global war to eliminate the threat of secret police and concentration camps. In the Bill of Rights, the first ten amendments to the Constitution, liberty meant freedom of religion, freedom of speech, freedom of the press, freedom of assembly, safety of person and property from seizure by other than due and public legal processes, trial by jury, and similar securities.

One might think that these liberties, so central to American democracy, can be taken for granted, that we need not worry about them after all these years. But experience has shown that they are not easily kept. The preservation of civil liberties is an endless struggle against ignorance and prejudice, a struggle to which a good citizen cannot honorably be indifferent. The price of liberty is constant watchfulness. We must constantly endeavor to treat fairly all those who are in one way or another unlike our own group of intimate associates, and we must untiringly seek for accurate information before taking a stand on questions of public concern.

No thoughtful American scrawls dirty names on the walls of a church whose faith is unlike his own, hoots down opinions with which he disagrees, or tries to drive out of his community persons whom he does not care to meet socially. Yet these things happen every day—despite constitutional and legal ideals to which most Americans subscribe; and they will continue to happen until everyone learns that in a free society there can be no second-class citizens, no cruel attacks upon the dignity and self-respect of one's fellows.

Today, moreover, as never before, the price of liberty includes awareness of the problems and aspirations of other peoples, in other continents than our own. The airplane and the other developments of applied science have made the world so small, and the parts of it so dependent one upon another, that freedom is much more complicated than it seemed to the founders of our nation. Intelligent understanding of the needs and hopes of distant lands is an urgent necessity for Americans if they are to survive, let alone be free. No people, perhaps, has ever faced so great a responsibility for world peace and human progress. We have learned to live together in the United States, not perfectly but reasonably well; now we must learn to live together in the world, with folk who do not always speak our language or understand our ideals. As Vannevar Bush says, in the last selection in this unit of our book, if we lose our liberties "it will be because we abandon them." What our literature tells us is what we would be abandoning.

Sweet Land of Liberty

Freedom Is a Habit

CARL SANDBURG

Thoughtful Americans have always known that the reality of liberty, the feeling which lies underneath and behind the word *freedom,* is not to be had cheaply. It has taken two world wars, however, to bring to twentieth-century Americans the realization of what a mysterious, priceless thing freedom really is. This new awareness is the theme of Carl Sandburg's wartime poem.

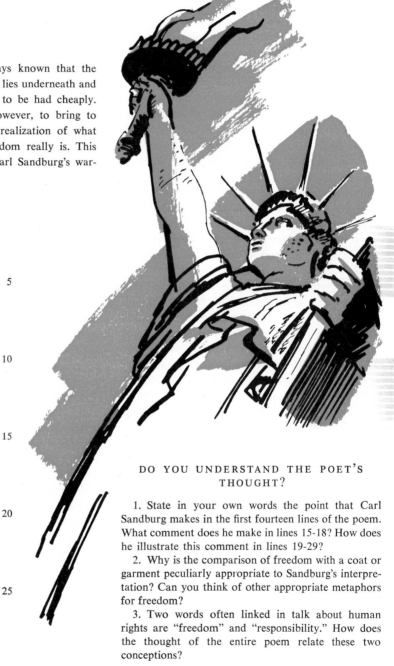

FREEDOM is a habit
and a coat worn
some born to wear it
some never to know it.
Freedom is cheap   5
or again as a garment
is so costly
men pay their lives
rather than not have it.
Freedom is baffling: 10
men having it often
know not they have it
till it is gone and
they no longer have it.
What does this mean?   15
Is it a riddle?
Yes, it is first of all
in the primers of riddles.
To be free is so-so:
you can and you can't: 20
walkers can have freedom
only by never walking
away their freedom:
runners too have freedom
unless they overrun: 25
eaters have often outeaten
their freedom to eat
and drinkers overdrank
their fine drinking freedom.

DO YOU UNDERSTAND THE POET'S THOUGHT?

1. State in your own words the point that Carl Sandburg makes in the first fourteen lines of the poem. What comment does he make in lines 15-18? How does he illustrate this comment in lines 19-29?

2. Why is the comparison of freedom with a coat or garment peculiarly appropriate to Sandburg's interpretation? Can you think of other appropriate metaphors for freedom?

3. Two words often linked in talk about human rights are "freedom" and "responsibility." How does the thought of the entire poem relate these two conceptions?

The Gray Champion

NATHANIEL HAWTHORNE

One of the most persistent themes of folklore is that of a great popular leader who appears whenever he is desperately needed. Nathaniel Hawthorne combined this theme with his thorough knowledge of New England history in a story which is one of the best literary expressions of the concept of liberty.

Important to the understanding of the story are some facts about the history of England and her colonies. For the better part of a hundred years the Stuarts—proud, haughty, self-willed men—had ruled England. They had constantly proclaimed the Divine Right of Kings—the theory that a king receives his power to rule from God and need respect no other authority—and had overridden the will of Parliament and people. They had suppressed the Puritans, many of whom had fled their homes to settle the New England colonies. Now fear and hatred of the king and his representatives united the people of colonial New England.

The events related by Hawthorne take place in 1689, shortly after James II, the last of the Stuart kings, had been obliged to flee from England. The king's daughter Mary and her husband, William of Orange, had been declared joint rulers of England. But no sailing ship had yet brought this momentous news to the colonies. New England still chafed under the rule of Sir Edmund Andros, the royal governor appointed by James II.

The Gray Champion is, as Hawthorne says, "the type [that is, the symbol] of New England's hereditary spirit"; he may also be said to be the symbol of the American determination to be free of autocratic rule.

T HERE WAS ONCE a time when New England groaned under the actual pressure of heavier wrongs than those threatened ones which brought on the Revolution. James II, the bigoted successor of Charles the Voluptuous,[1] had annulled the charters of all the colonies, and sent a harsh and unprincipled soldier to take away our liberties and endanger our religion. The administration of Sir Edmund Andros lacked scarcely a single characteristic of tyranny: a Governor and Council, holding office from the King, and wholly independent of the country; laws made and taxes levied without concurrence of the people immediate or by their representatives; the rights of private citizens violated, and the titles of all landed property declared void; the voice of complaint stifled by restrictions on the press; and, finally, disaffection overawed by the first band of mercenary troops that ever marched on our free soil. For two years our ancestors were kept in sullen submission by that filial love which had invariably secured their allegiance to the mother country, whether its head chanced to be a Parliament, Protector, or Monarch.[2] Till these evil times, however, such allegiance had been merely nominal, and the colonists had ruled themselves, enjoying far more freedom than is even yet the privilege of the native subjects of Great Britain.

At length a rumor reached our shores that the Prince of Orange had ventured on an enterprise,[3] the success of which would be the triumph of civil and religious rights and the salvation of New England. It was but a doubtful whisper; it might be false, or the attempt might fail; and, in either case, the man that stirred against King James would lose his head. Still the intelligence produced a marked effect. The people smiled mysteriously in the streets, and threw bold glances at their oppressors; while far and wide there was a subdued and silent agitation, as if the slightest signal would rouse the whole land from its sluggish despondency. Aware of their danger, the rulers resolved to avert it by an imposing display of strength, and perhaps to confirm their despotism by yet harsher measures. One afternoon in April, 1689, Sir Edmund Andros and his favorite councilors, being warm with wine, assembled the redcoats of the Governor's Guard, and made their appearance in the streets of Boston. The sun was near setting when the march commenced.

---

[1] *Charles the Voluptuous,* Charles II, ruler of England from 1660 to 1685. He was a brother of James II.

[2] *whether its head chanced to be...Monarch.* Although England has usually been governed by a monarch, Parliament ruled the country after Charles I was beheaded in 1649 at the close of the English civil wars. In 1653 Oliver Cromwell, who had led the Puritan armies during the wars, dissolved Parliament and made himself Lord Protector.

[3] *a rumor...enterprise.* The rumor was that Prince William of Orange, with the sympathy and assistance of the majority of the English people, was moving with an army against James II.

The roll of the drum at that unquiet crisis seemed to go through the streets, less as the martial music of the soldiers than as a muster call[4] to the inhabitants themselves. A multitude, by various avenues, assembled in King Street, which was destined to be the scene, nearly a century afterwards, of another encounter between the troops of Britain and a people struggling against her tyranny.[5] Though more than sixty years had elapsed since the Pilgrims came, this crowd of their descendants still showed the strong and somber features of their character—perhaps more strikingly in such a stern emergency than on happier occasions. There were the sober garb, the general severity of mien, the gloomy but undismayed expression, the scriptural forms of speech, and the confidence in Heaven's blessing on a righteous cause which would have marked a band of the original Puritans when threatened by some peril of the wilderness. Indeed, it was not yet time for the old spirit to be extinct; since there were men in the street that day who had worshiped there beneath the trees, before a house was reared to the God for whom they had become exiles. Old soldiers of the Parliament[6] were here, too, smiling grimly at the thought that their aged arms might strike another blow against the house of Stuart. Here, also, were the veterans of King Philip's War,[7] who had burned villages and slaughtered young and old, with pious fierceness, while the godly souls throughout the land were helping them with prayer. Several ministers were scattered among the crowd, which, unlike all other mobs, regarded them with such reverence, as if there were sanctity in their very garments. These holy men exerted their influence to quiet the people, but not to disperse them. Meantime, the purpose of the Governor, in disturbing the peace of the town at a period when the slightest commotion might throw the country into a ferment, was almost the universal subject of inquiry, and variously explained.

"Satan will strike his master stroke presently," cried some, "because he knoweth that his time is short. All our godly pastors are to be dragged to prison! We shall see them at a Smithfield fire[8] in King Street!"

Hereupon the people of each parish gathered closer round their minister, who looked calmly upwards and assumed a more apostolic dignity, as well befitted a candidate for the highest honor of his profession, the crown of martyrdom. It was actually fancied, at that period, that New England might have a John Rogers of her own to take the place of that worthy in the Primer.[9]

"We are to be massacred, man and male child!" cried others.

Neither was this rumor wholly discredited, although the wiser class believed the Governor's object somewhat less atrocious. His predecessor under the old charter, Bradstreet,[10] a venerable companion of the first settlers, was known to be in town. There were grounds for conjecturing that Sir Edmund Andros intended at once to strike terror by a parade of military force, and to confound the opposite faction by possessing himself of their chief.

"Stand firm for the 'old charter' Governor!" shouted the crowd, seizing upon the idea. "The good old Governor Bradstreet!"

While this cry was at the loudest, the people were surprised by the well-known figure of Governor Bradstreet himself, a patriarch of nearly ninety, who appeared on the elevated steps of a door, and, with characteristic mildness, besought them to submit to the authorities.

---

[4]*a muster call,* a call to come together or assemble.

[5]*another encounter...tyranny,* the Boston Massacre of March 5, 1770. King Street later became State Street.

[6]*Old soldiers of the Parliament,* men of Oliver Cromwell's army, which had driven Charles I from his throne.

[7]*King Philip's War,* 1675-1676, a conflict between the English settlers and various Indian tribes of New England united under Philip, or Metacomet (mā′tä kō′met). Philip, chief of the Wampanoag (wäm′pä nō′äg) tribe, was a son of Massasoit.

[8]*a Smithfield fire.* In the sixteenth century religious heretics were burned at Smithfield, an open space outside the northwest walls of London.

[9]*that New England...Primer.* John Rogers, a noted Protestant clergyman, was executed by order of Queen Mary I of England at Smithfield in 1555. The first of nearly three hundred Protestants executed during Mary's reign, he was known to New Englanders both through the *New England Primer* (first published about 1690) and through John Foxe's *Book of Martyrs* (1563).

[10]*His predecessor...Bradstreet.* Simon Bradstreet (1603-1697) had governed Massachusetts from 1679 to 1686. Thus he was governor at the time the charter was revoked and Massachusetts made a royal colony.

"My children," concluded this venerable person, "do nothing rashly. Cry not aloud, but pray for the welfare of New England, and expect patiently what the Lord will do in this matter!"

The event was soon to be decided. All this time, the roll of the drum had been approaching through Cornhill,[11] louder and deeper, till with reverberations from house to house, and the regular tramp of martial footsteps, it burst into the street. A double rank of soldiers made their appearance, occupying the whole breadth of the passage, with shouldered matchlocks, and matches burning,[12] so as to present a row of fires in the dusk. Their steady march was like the progress of a machine, that would roll irresistibly over everything in its way. Next, moving slowly, with a confused clatter of hoofs on the pavement, rode a party of mounted gentlemen, the central figure being Sir Edmund Andros, elderly, but erect and soldierlike. Those around him were his favorite councilors, and the bitterest foes of New England. At his right hand rode Edward Randolph,[13] our archenemy, that "blasted wretch," as Cotton Mather[14] calls him, who achieved the downfall of our ancient government, and was followed with a sensible curse, through life and to his grave. On the other side was Bullivant,[15] scattering jests and mockery as he rode along. Dudley[16] came behind, with a downcast look, dreading, as well he might, to meet the indignant gaze of the

---

[11]*Cornhill,* a street near King Street where the crowds were assembling.

[12]*shouldered matchlocks, and matches burning.* A matchlock was a gun fired by lighting the powder with a wick or cord called a match. The soldiers were carrying their guns almost upright with the barrel resting in the hollow of the shoulder and the butt in the hand. The burning cord (match) to light the powder was carried in the other hand.

[13]*Edward Randolph,* an officer in the royal government of New England. After visiting in Massachusetts in 1676 as an agent of Charles II, he had made reports as a result of which the charter of Massachusetts was withdrawn.

[14]*Cotton Mather,* a famous Boston clergyman active in the opposition to Andros. He wrote *Magnalia Christi Americana* (1702), a part of which tells the story of the revolt against Andros.

[15]*Bullivant.* Benjamin Bullivant was a minor figure in Andros' government.

[16]*Dudley.* Joseph Dudley, American-born son of a governor of Massachusetts, was himself governor for a few months in 1686 immediately before Andros took office. At the time of which Hawthorne writes he was chief justice of the superior court of Massachusetts and the most influential member of Andros' council.

people, who beheld him, their only country-man by birth, among the oppressors of his native land. The captain of a frigate in the harbor, and two or three civil officers under the Crown, were also there. But the figure which most attracted the public eye, and stirred up the deepest feeling, was the Episcopal clergyman of King's Chapel,[17] riding haughtily among the magistrates in his priestly vestments, the fitting representative of prelacy and persecution, the union of church and state, and all those abominations which had driven the Puritans to the wilderness. Another guard of soldiers, in double rank, brought up the rear.

The whole scene was a picture of the condition of New England, and its moral, the deformity of any government that does not grow out of the nature of things and the character of the people. On one side the religious multitude, with their sad visages and dark attire, and on the other, the group of despotic rulers, with the high churchman in the midst, all magnificently clad, flushed with wine, proud of unjust authority, and scoffing at the universal groan. And the mercenary soldiers, waiting but the word to deluge the street with blood, showed the only means by which obedience could be secured.

"O Lord of Hosts," cried a voice among the crowd, "provide a Champion for Thy people!"

This ejaculation was loudly uttered, and served as a herald's cry to introduce a remarkable personage. The crowd had rolled back, and were now huddled together nearly at the extremity of the street, while the soldiers had advanced no more than a third of its length. The intervening space was empty—a paved solitude, between lofty edifices, which threw almost a twilight shadow over it. Suddenly, there was seen the figure of an ancient man, who seemed to have emerged from among the people, and was walking by himself along the center of the street, to confront the armed band. He wore the old Puritan dress, a dark cloak and a steeple-crowned hat, in the fashion of at least fifty years before, with a heavy sword upon his thigh, but a staff in his hand to assist the tremulous gait of age.

---

[17]*the Episcopal clergyman of King's Chapel,* Robert Ratcliffe, the first minister of an Anglican parish in Massachusetts. King's Chapel, the first Episcopalian church in the colony, was formed in 1688.

When at some distance from the multitude, the old man turned slowly round, displaying a face of antique majesty, rendered doubly venerable by the hoary beard that descended on his breast. He made a gesture at once of encouragement and warning, then turned again, and resumed his way.

"Who is this gray patriarch?" asked the young men of their sires.

"Who is this venerable brother?" asked the old men among themselves.

But none could make reply. The fathers of the people, those of fourscore years and upwards, were disturbed, deeming it strange that they should forget one of such evident authority, whom they must have known in their early days, the associate of Winthrop[18] and all the old councilors, giving laws, and making prayers, and leading them against the savage. The elderly men ought to have remembered him, too, with locks as gray in their youth as their own were now. And the young! How could he have passed so utterly from their memories—that hoary sire, the relic of long-departed times, whose awful benediction had surely been bestowed on their uncovered heads in childhood?

"Whence did he come? What is his purpose? Who can this old man be?" whispered the wondering crowd.

Meanwhile, the venerable stranger, staff in hand, was pursuing his solitary walk along the center of the street. As he drew near the advancing soldiers, and as the roll of their drum came full upon his ear, the old man raised himself to a loftier mien, while the decrepitude of age seemed to fall from his shoulders, leaving him in gray but unbroken dignity. Now, he marched onward with a warrior's step, keeping time to the military music. Thus the aged form advanced on one side, and the whole parade of soldiers and magistrates on the other, till, when scarcely twenty yards remained between, the old man grasped his staff by the middle, and held it before him like a leader's truncheon.

"Stand!" cried he.

The eye, the face, and attitude of command; the solemn, yet warlike peal of that voice, fit either to rule a host in the battlefield or be raised to God in prayer, were irresistible. At the old man's word and outstretched arm, the roll of the drum was hushed at once, and the advancing line stood still. A tremulous enthusiasm seized upon the multitude. That stately form, combining the leader and the saint, so gray, so dimly seen, in such an ancient garb, could only belong to some old champion of the righteous cause, whom the oppressor's drum had summoned from his grave. They raised a shout of awe and exultation, and looked for the deliverance of New England.

The Governor, and the gentlemen of his party, perceiving themselves brought to an unexpected stand, rode hastily forward, as if they would have pressed their snorting and affrighted horses right against the hoary apparition. He, however, blenched not a step, but glancing his severe eye round the group, which half encompassed him, at last he bent it sternly on Sir Edmund Andros. One would have thought that the dark old man was chief ruler there, and that the Governor and Council, with soldiers at their back, representing the whole power and authority of the Crown, had no alternative but obedience.

"What does this old fellow here?" cried Edward Randolph fiercely. "On, Sir Edmund! Bid the soldiers forward, and give the dotard the same choice that you give all his countrymen—to stand aside or be trampled on!"

"Nay, nay, let us show respect to the good grandsire," said Bullivant, laughing. "See you not, he is some old round-headed dignitary,[19] who hath lain asleep these thirty years, and knows nothing of the change of times? Doubtless, he thinks to put us down with a proclamation in Old Noll's name!"[20]

"Are you mad, old man?" demanded Sir Edmund Andros in loud and harsh tones.

_____

[18]*Winthrop.* John Winthrop (1588-1649) was the first governor of the Massachusetts Bay Colony and until his death its chief political leader.

_____

[19]*round-headed dignitary,* Puritan. During the civil wars, Puritans were called Roundheads because they wore their hair cut short in contrast to the long curls of their opponents, the Cavaliers or Royalists.

[20]*Old Noll's name.* "Old Noll" was a nickname for Oliver Cromwell, leader of the Puritans in the civil wars and Lord Protector of England.

"How dare you stay the march of King James' Governor?"

"I have stayed the march of a King himself, ere now," replied the gray figure, with stern composure. "I am here, Sir Governor, because the cry of an oppressed people hath disturbed me in my secret place; and beseeching this favor earnestly of the Lord, it was vouchsafed me to appear once again on earth, in the good old cause of his saints. And what speak ye of James? There is no longer a tyrant on the throne of England, and by tomorrow noon his name shall be a byword in this very street, where ye would make it a word of terror. Back, thou that wast a Governor, back! With this night thy power is ended—tomorrow, the prison!—back, lest I foretell the scaffold!"

The people had been drawing nearer and nearer, and drinking in the words of their champion, who spoke in accents long disused, like one unaccustomed to converse except with the dead of many years ago. But his voice stirred their souls. They confronted the soldiers, not wholly without arms, and ready to convert the very stones of the street into deadly weapons. Sir Edmund Andros looked at the old man; then he cast his hard and cruel eye over the multitude, and beheld them burning with that lurid wrath, so difficult to kindle or to quench; and again he fixed his gaze on the aged form, which stood obscurely in an open space, where neither friend nor foe had thrust him-

self. What were his thoughts, he uttered no word which might discover. But whether the oppressor were overawed by the Gray Champion's look, or perceived his peril in the threatening attitude of the people, it is certain that he gave back, and ordered his soldiers to commence a guarded retreat. Before another sunset, the Governor, and all that rode so proudly with him, were prisoners, and long ere it was known that James had abdicated, King William was proclaimed throughout New England.

But where was the Gray Champion? Some reported that, when the troops had gone from King Street, and the people were thronging tumultuously in their rear, Bradstreet, the aged governor, was seen to embrace a form more aged than his own. Others soberly affirmed that while they marveled at the venerable grandeur of his aspect, the old man had faded from their eyes, melting slowly into the hues of twilight, till, where he stood, there was an empty space. But all agreed that the hoary shape was gone. The men of that generation watched for his reappearance, in sunshine and in twilight, but never saw him more, nor knew when his funeral passed, nor where his gravestone was.

And who was the Gray Champion? Perhaps his name might be found in the records of that stern Court of Justice[21] which passed a sentence, too mighty for the age, but glorious in all after-times, for its humbling lesson to the monarch and its high example to the subject. I have heard, that whenever the descendants of the Puritans are to show the spirit of their sires, the old man appears again. When eighty years had passed, he walked once more in King Street.[22] Five years later, in the twilight of an April morning, he stood on the green, beside the meeting house at Lexington, where now the obelisk of granite, with a slab of slate inlaid, commemorates the first fallen of the Revolution. And when our fathers were toiling at the breastwork on Bunker's Hill, all through that night the old warrior walked his rounds. Long, long may it be, ere he comes again! His hour is one of darkness, and adversity, and peril. But should domestic tyranny oppress us, or the invader's step pollute our soil, still may the Gray Champion come, for he is the type of New England's hereditary spirit; and his shadowy march, on the eve of danger, must ever be the pledge that New England's sons will vindicate their ancestry.

WHO IS THE GRAY CHAMPION?

1. Why did the people of New England need a champion at this particular time?
2. What devices did Hawthorne use to make this tale of the "gray patriarch" seem like something that might really have occurred? What details had the greatest effect in giving the story reality in your eyes?
3. What does the Gray Champion represent? How does Hawthorne make this clear in his picture of the figure? How does the story emphasize the point that freedom must be won anew in every generation?

Using a character to emphasize an idea

To readers of the Arthurian legends or of romances of the days of chivalry, the word *champion* suggests a man clad in flashing armor, a peerless knight mounted on a charging steed. Nathaniel Hawthorne's champion is a very different sort of man—a "gray champion." From the time he first makes his appearance in the darkening street, the author describes him in words that blend with the twilight in which he has appeared. Find phrases which emphasize his grayness and his age. What effect does the author gain by using some of the same descriptive terms several times? How do the appearance, the actions, and the history of the champion develop the idea of the tale? Why is such a champion as Hawthorne describes better suited to the theme of this particular story than a dashing warrior would be?

Extending interests

"The Gray Champion" is based upon the story of William Goffe, a Puritan who fled England under unusual circumstances. If you would like to make a report to the class about this mysterious individual, among books you might consult for information are *Encyclopedia Americana, Columbia Encyclopedia,* and *The Oxford Companion to American Literature.*

---

[21]*Court of Justice,* the court which condemned Charles I to death. There is a tradition that some of the members of this court, the so-called "regicides," fled to New England at the Restoration and lived out their lives in hiding.

[22]*When eighty years...King Street.* According to legend, the Gray Champion appeared again in King Street at the time of the Boston Massacre in 1770.

Light and Truth

FROM *A Scheme for Education in a New Republic*

THOMAS JEFFERSON

Americans have given much thought to the best means of preserving their liberties. High on the list of means has always been education, because a well-informed and enlightened citizenry is one of the best protections of a true democracy. While ignorant people can be fooled by selfish and unprincipled leaders, people who are trained to read and listen and speak intelligently can take an active part in the difficult business of self-government. Thomas Jefferson, although not the only one of the Founding Fathers to preach the necessity of education, is often regarded as largely responsible for the idea of education for citizenship, the idea which has produced the great public-school system of the United States. The following passage from his *Notes on the State of Virginia* (1784) offers a typical plea for public support of schools and shows the temper of the representative legislatures of Jefferson's day.

MANY OF THE LAWS which were in force during the monarchy being relative merely to that form of government, or inculcating principles inconsistent with republicanism, the first assembly which met after the establishment of the commonwealth appointed a committee to revise the whole code.[1]

One object of the revisal is to diffuse knowledge more generally through the mass of the people. This bill proposes to lay off every county into small districts of five or six miles square, called hundreds,[2] and in each of them to establish a school for teaching reading, writing, and arithmetic. The tutor to be supported by the hundred, and every person in it entitled to send their children three years gratis, and as much longer as they please, paying for it. These schools to be under a visitor[3] who is annually to choose the boy of the best genius in the school, of those whose parents are too poor to give them further education, and to send him forward to one of the grammar schools,[4] of which twenty are proposed to be erected in different parts of the country,[5] for teaching Greek, Latin, geography, and the higher branches of numerical arithmetic. Of the boys thus sent in one year, trial is to be made at the grammar schools one or two years, and the best genius of the whole school selected, and continued six years, and the residue dismissed. By this means twenty of the best geniuses will be raked from the rubbish annually, and be instructed, at the public expense, so far as the grammar schools go. At the end of six years' instruction, one half are to be discontinued (from among whom the grammar schools will probably be supplied with future masters); and the other half, who are to be chosen for the superiority of their parts and disposition,[6] are to be sent and continued three years in the study of such sciences as they shall choose, at William and Mary College,[7] the plan of which is proposed to be enlarged and extended to all the useful sciences.

The ultimate result of the whole scheme of education would be the teaching all of the state reading, writing, and common arithmetic; turning out ten annually, of superior genius, well

---

[1] *Many of the laws...code.* After the United States had declared its independence from England in 1776, Virginia adopted its first constitution as a state (commonwealth). The general assembly appointed a committee composed of Thomas Jefferson, George Wythe, and Edmund Pendleton to change the laws of the state to agree with democratic principles rather than with the laws of the English monarchy which had previously been in force.

[2] *hundreds,* old English divisions of a county. Observe that the six-mile squares here suggested later became, as townships, the basis of land division in the American West. For this Jefferson was chiefly responsible.

[3] *visitor,* inspector or examiner.

[4] *grammar schools.* Jefferson used the term as present-day Englishmen do, to mean a secondary or high school emphasizing Latin and Greek.

[5] *country,* state.

[6] *their parts and disposition,* their abilities or talents and their character.

[7] *William and Mary College,* the second oldest college in the United States, one of the two colleges at this time in Virginia. Since its founding in 1693, it had been partially supported by the colony.

taught in Greek, Latin, geography, and the higher branches of mathematics; turning out ten others annually, of still superior parts, who, to those branches of learning, shall have added such of the sciences as their genius shall have led them to; the furnishing to the wealthier part of the people convenient schools at which their children may be educated at their own expense. The general objects of this law are to provide an education adapted to the years, to the capacity, and the condition of everyone, and directed to their freedom and happiness.

By that part of our plan which prescribes the selection of the youths of genius from among the classes of the poor, we hope to avail the state of those talents which nature has sown as liberally among the poor as the rich, but which perish without use, if not sought for and cultivated. But of the views of this law none is more important, none more legitimate, than that of rendering the people the safe, as they are the ultimate, guardians of their own liberty. For this purpose the reading in the first stage, where they will receive their whole education,[8] is proposed to be chiefly historical. History, by apprising them of the past, will enable them to judge of the future; it will avail them of the experience of other times and other nations; it will qualify them as judges of the actions and designs of men; it will enable them to know ambition[9] under every disguise it may assume; and knowing it, to defeat its views. In every government on earth is some trace of human weakness, some germ of corruption and degeneracy, which cunning will discover, and wickedness insensibly open, cultivate, and improve. Every government degenerates when trusted to the rulers of the people alone. The people themselves therefore are its only safe depositories. And to render even them safe, their minds must be improved to a certain degree. This indeed is not all that is necessary, though it be essentially necessary. An amendment of our constitution must here come in aid of the public education. The influence over government must be shared among all the people. If every individual which composes their mass participates of the ultimate authority, the government will be safe; because the corrupting the whole mass will exceed any private resources of wealth; and public ones cannot be provided but by levies on the people. In this case every man would have to pay his own price. The government of Great Britain has been corrupted, because but one man in ten has a right to vote for members of Parliament. The sellers of that government, therefore, get nine-tenths of their price clear. It has been thought that corruption is restrained by confining the right of suffrage to a few of the wealthier of the people; but it would be more effectually restrained by an extension of that right to such number as would bid defiance to the means of corruption.

WHAT WERE JEFFERSON'S IDEAS ON EDUCATION?

1. Outline briefly Jefferson's plan to assure some schooling to all the children of the state. Under his plan who would receive a secondary-school education? A college education?

2. Why did Jefferson believe it necessary for all citizens to have a certain degree of education? What were his reasons for stressing the study of history, particularly in the elementary schools?

3. To what extent does education in the United States today follow the plan proposed by Jefferson? Name some ways in which the modern educational system goes beyond his ideas.

4. What common theme is developed by Sandburg's "Freedom Is a Habit," Hawthorne's "The Gray Champion," and this selection? What point does Jefferson stress that is not made by either of the other authors?

Extending interests

To give your class some idea of the extent of public education today, prepare a chart giving as many of the following statistics as possible for your state: (a) number of elementary schools, high schools, colleges; (b) number of pupils attending elementary school, high school, college; (c) average yearly expenditure per pupil. You might also compare the figures for your state with those for the United States as a whole. Almanacs are a good source of information.

---

[8]*the first stage...whole education.* By *they* Jefferson means the great majority of the people, who will receive no education beyond that offered by the elementary schools.

[9]*ambition,* used here to mean the pursuing of selfish aims which will harm the people as a whole.

Henry Cogdal

EDGAR LEE MASTERS

Education as a safeguard of political liberty does not depend entirely, of course, upon the schools. Newspapers, magazines, and books are also powerful instruments in the shaping of public opinion. One argument for a free press, as a chief means of acquainting people with differing points of view, is stated by the speaker in the following poem. "Henry Cogdal" is taken from *The New Spoon River*, by Edgar Lee Masters. This book, like Masters' earlier *Spoon River Anthology*, consists of a series of epitaphs in which the people buried in a Midwestern cemetery reveal their true selves.

BRING FROM the Big Creek a huge boulder,
   Put it at the head of me,
And bolt upon it a tablet of bronze
With these words:
Here was buried the body of Henry Cogdal,   5
A private who fell in the war for Wisdom,
And Beauty and Truth.
He strove to be a guide to the creative spirit,
And to uphold the singers and tellers of stories,
Who keep the vision of a nation   10
Upon the clear realities of life.
At the height of his power and work
He lost his place and means of support
Through a rich manufacturer who bought the
   newspaper,
And began to popularize it,   15
And to lower its criticisms
To the level of advertisers and optimists:—
There will come a time when crimes against
   culture
Will be punished the same as murder!

WHAT DOES HENRY COGDAL STAND FOR?

1. What satisfactions did Henry Cogdal find in being the editor of a newspaper? Why did he regard his work as important? Why does he characterize himself as "a private who fell in the war for Wisdom"?

2. In which of these facts does the evil that Henry Cogdal complains about lie: (*a*) the newspaper was bought by a wealthy man; (*b*) the editor was no longer able to tell the truth as he saw it? Explain your answer.

3. In what way would domination of the press by any group be a crime against culture? Do you agree or disagree with Cogdal's closing prediction?

Extending interests

One of the first heroes of the struggle for freedom of the press in America was the New York publisher, John Peter Zenger. Among the interesting accounts written about him are the articles "Freedom on Trial —the Zenger Case," by Donald Culross Peattie in the *Reader's Digest* for July, 1947, and "He Dared to Talk Back" in *Scholastic* for October 27, 1947. You will also find a good treatment of Zenger in each of the following books: *Fighting Editors*, edited by W. C. Howey; *North of Manhattan*, by Harry Hansen; and *For the Rights of Man*, by Carl Carmer. Any one of these would furnish material for an interesting report.

Rights and Duties

FROM *First Inaugural Address, March 4, 1801*

THOMAS JEFFERSON

One of the best statements of the political faith of Americans, next to the Declaration of Independence and the Bill of Rights, is the First Inaugural of Thomas Jefferson. Behind it lay one of the bitterest election contests in our history, settled by the narrowest of margins in the House of Representatives. The things Jefferson had to say about yielding to the will of the majority, about the rights of the minority, and about the essential principles of government apply as well today as they did a century and a half ago.

F RIENDS AND FELLOW CITIZENS:
   Called upon to undertake the duties of the first executive office of our country, I avail myself of the presence of that portion of my fellow citizens which is here assembled to express my grateful thanks for the favor with which they have been pleased to look toward me. During the contest of opinion[1] through which we have passed, the animation of discussions and of exertions has sometimes worn an aspect which might impose on strangers unused to think freely, and to speak and to write

what they think. But this[2] being now decided by the voice of the nation, announced according to the rules of the Constitution, all will of course arrange themselves under the will of the law and unite in common efforts for the common good. All too will bear in mind this sacred principle, that though the will of the majority is in all cases to prevail, that will, to be rightful, must be reasonable; that the minority possess their equal rights, which equal laws must protect, and to violate would be oppression.

Let us then, fellow citizens, unite with one heart and one mind—let us restore to social intercourse that harmony and affection without which liberty, and even life itself, are but dreary things. We are all Republicans; we are all Federalists.[3]

If there be any among us who would wish to dissolve this union or to change its republican form, let them stand undisturbed as monuments of the safety with which error of opinion may be tolerated where reason is left free to combat it. I know indeed that some honest men feel that a republican government cannot be strong; that this government is not strong enough. But would the honest patriot, in the full tide of successful experiment, abandon a government

---

[1] *contest of opinion,* the election of 1800.

[2] *this,* the election.
[3] *Republicans...Federalists,* the names of the political parties in Jefferson's day. Jefferson was a Republican.

which has so far kept us free and firm on the theoretic and visionary fear that this government, the world's best hope, may, by possibility, want energy to preserve itself? I trust not. I believe this, on the contrary, the strongest government on earth. I believe it the only one where every man, at the call of the law, would fly to the standard of the law and would meet invasions of the public order as his own personal concern.

Sometimes it is said that man cannot be trusted with the government of himself. Can he then be trusted with the government of others? Or have we found angels in the form of kings to govern him? Let history answer this question.

Let us then with courage and confidence pursue our own federal and republican principles, our attachment to our Union and representative government. Kindly separated by nature and a wide ocean from the exterminating havoc of one quarter of the globe[4]; too high-minded to endure the degradations of the others; possessing a chosen country, with room enough for our descendants to the thousandth and thousandth generation; entertaining a due sense of our equal right to the use of our own faculties, to the acquisitions of our own industry, to honor and confidence from our fellow citizens resulting not from birth but from our actions and their sense of them; enlightened by a benign religion, professed indeed and practiced in various forms, yet all of them inculcating honesty, truth, temperance, gratitude, and the love of man; acknowledging and adoring an overruling Providence, which by all its dispensations proves that it delights in the happiness of man here and his greater happiness hereafter—with all these blessings, what more is necessary to make us a happy and a prosperous people? Still one thing more, fellow citizens, a wise and frugal government, which shall restrain men from injuring one another, shall leave them otherwise free to regulate their own pursuits of industry and improvement, and shall not take from the mouth of labor the bread it has earned. This is the sum of good government, and this is necessary to close the circle of our felicities.

About to enter, fellow citizens, on the exercise of duties which comprehend everything dear and valuable to you, it is proper you should understand what I deem the essential principles of our government and consequently those which ought to shape its administration. I will compress them in the narrowest compass they will bear, stating the general principle but not all its limitations:

Equal and exact justice to all men, of whatever state or persuasion, religious or political;

Peace, commerce, and honest friendship with all nations; entangling alliances with none;

The support of the state governments in all their rights, as the most competent administrations for our domestic concerns, and the surest bulwarks against antirepublican tendencies;

The preservation of the general government in its whole constitutional vigor, as the sheet anchor[5] of our peace at home and safety abroad;

A jealous care of the right of election by the people, a mild and safe corrective of abuses, which are lopped by the sword of revolution where peaceable remedies are unprovided;

Absolute acquiescence in the decisions of the majority, the vital principle of republics, from which is no appeal but to force, the vital principle and immediate parent of despotism;

A well-disciplined militia, our best reliance in peace, and for the first moments of war, till regulars may relieve them;

The supremacy of the civil over the military authority;

Economy in the public expense, that labor may be lightly burdened;

The honest payment of our debts, and sacred preservation of the public faith;

Encouragement of agriculture and of commerce as its handmaid[6];

The diffusion of information, and arraignment of all abuses at the bar of public reason;

---

[4]*exterminating havoc of one quarter of the globe.* At the time Jefferson spoke, the Napoleonic Wars, beginning in 1799, had brought great destruction as they spread over most of Europe.

[5]*sheet anchor,* chief reliance. A sheet anchor is a large anchor used only in emergencies.

[6]*commerce as its handmaid.* In the agricultural society of his day, Jefferson saw the relation between agriculture and commerce like that between mistress and maid. Commerce was to aid agriculture.

Freedom of religion, freedom of the press, and freedom of person under the protection of the habeas corpus;

Trial by juries, impartially selected.

These principles form the bright constellation which has gone before us and guided our steps through an age of revolution and reformation. The wisdom of our sages and the blood of our heroes have been devoted to their attainment; they should be the creed of our political faith, the text of civic instruction, the touchstone by which to try the services of those we trust; and should we wander from them in moments of error or of alarm, let us hasten to retrace our steps and to regain the road which alone leads to peace, liberty, and safety.

WHAT WERE JEFFERSON'S IDEAS ON GOVERNMENT?

1. In what did Jefferson believe the chief strength of this government lay? Why did he regard it as "the world's best hope"?

2. What was Jefferson's conception of the purpose of government? What principles did he regard as essential to the preservation of the government of the United States?

3. Some of the ideas which Louis Adamic advances in his article, "A Nation of Nations" (pages 132-136), were originally stated by Jefferson. Do you think Jefferson would have agreed with the motto Adamic suggests: "Let's make America safe for differences. Let us work for unity within diversity"? Cite evidence from Jefferson's First Inaugural to support your answer.

4. If Jefferson were living today, do you think he would subscribe to all the principles he listed as essential in 1801? If so, why? If not, why not? Would he advocate any additional principles?

Extending interests

1. Prepare a report to the class on the circumstances of the election of 1800 and the issues on which the Republicans and the Federalists differed.

2. Organize a discussion group of three or four students to compare Jefferson's list of "essential principles" with the Bill of Rights, noting particularly which of Jefferson's "essential principles" are not covered by that portion of the Constitution.

Practical Politics

FIORELLO H. LA GUARDIA

We all know well enough that in a successful democracy there must be active participation in party politics. Yet many Americans are still inclined to think of precinct caucuses and the rest of the machinery of choosing representatives and public officials as a dirty business, too corrupt or too time-consuming to get mixed up in. Fiorello La Guardia, the young lawyer who later served as mayor of New York City for more than ten years, believed that politics was every honest man's business. He studied political and economic conditions in his city, became an active member of the local Republican organization, followed all the proceedings of Congress in the *Congressional Record,* and hoped some day to become a member of the House of Representatives. The following selection from his autobiography, *The Making of an Insurgent* (1948), tells how he finally realized this ambition.

ONE NIGHT I happened to be in the club rooms of the 25th Assembly District,[1] my own district, where I was an election district captain for a time, when the boys were filling in petitions for the nomination for Congress. It was in the late summer of 1914. The petitions were printed, and the names of state and county candidates appeared on them. There were blanks left for the local candidates for the state senate and assembly and for representatives in Congress.

Someone hollered out, "Who is the candidate for Congress?"

The leader of the district—I think it was Clarence Fay—came from his backroom office. He shouted out, "Who wants to run for Congress?"

That was my chance. "I do," I said.

"O.K., put La Guardia down," Clarence said.

---

[1] *25th Assembly District,* a political division of New York State located in the southern part of Manhattan Island in New York City.

That was all there was to it. But I darn near missed out even so. One of the men asked, "Hey, La Guardia, what's your first name?"

I said, "Fiorello."

"Oh, no!" he said; "let's get someone whose name we can spell."

I spelled the name carefully and slowly and had to argue hard to get it on the petitions.

I took my nomination seriously. I soon learned that I was not supposed to take it seriously. When September came along, I attended my first political meeting. It was in one of the district clubhouses. Pamphlets were distributed throughout the district announcing the meeting, and stating that all the prominent candidates would talk. I was there bright and early. The meeting started. Candidate after candidate spoke. The state candidates came in, and they had the right of way. I waited and waited for my turn. Two or three times in the course of the evening I was sure that I was next when the chairman would say, "And now we will hear from a young and promising candidate." I would get up each time, only to see that someone else was being introduced.

The meeting ended around 11:30 that night. I had not been called on. I protested to the chairman, who was talking to the district leader. "How come?" I asked.

Everyone had a good laugh. "Why, Fiorello, you haven't a chance of winning," they told me. "We've never elected a Republican to Congress from this district. Now, what you should do is go out and campaign for the state senator and assemblyman, help elect the ticket. That is all you can do."

"Could I try?" I pleaded.

"Oh, no, don't be foolish. You just go out now and help the others, and some day you may get a nomination for an office you can win."

I didn't think that was quite on the level. A few of the boys in the district agreed with me, among them Harry Andrews, who was district secretary, Louis Espresso, and old Mike Kehoe. Kehoe, who was in his late seventies, was a master mind and a good political strategist. He was very much amused at my predicament. "Kid, don't be discouraged," he said, "but go out and try."

I discovered that the procedure at that first meeting was repeated at all the regular party meetings. I was not to get a chance to speak at any of them. I went out and bought a second-hand Ford. Harry Andrews and I plastered it with signs, and I started out on my own private, individual campaign. We went from corner to corner every night in that district, and we never missed a wedding, a funeral, a christening, or any other kind of a gathering we could get into.

The 14th Congressional District ran from the Hudson River clear across Manhattan to the East River. It included some of the tenement sections of the lower East Side, teeming with Italian and Jewish immigrants. My knowledge of Italian and Yiddish[2] came in handy. I rang doorbells and talked to the immigrant families. At outdoor meetings I would wait until the regular political rally had ended, pull up in my Ford as the people were leaving, gather a crowd and do my talking.

---

[2]*My knowledge of Italian and Yiddish.* Yiddish is a German dialect containing many Hebrew words. Because of his Italian and Jewish ancestry, La Guardia knew both languages.

My opponent was Congressman Michael Farley—a saloonkeeper and president of the National Liquor Dealers' Association. He had been the regular Tammany[3] representative in Congress from that district for some time. I was called down once or twice for being "too rough" on him. Distinguished and serious gentlemen in the community pointed out to me that the retail liquor business was a lawful occupation and urged me not to disparage the congressman who was in that business. I did not disparage him. I merely pointed out that he was not a good congressman and wasn't even a good bartender.

When the votes were counted that November 1914, Congressman Farley was reëlected by the small margin of 1700 votes. Never before had the Democratic majority in that district been less than 16,000 votes. Both my Republican colleagues and my Democratic opponents began to take notice of me. The Republicans began to think that maybe I had a future in politics because I could put on a campaign that got the public interested and therefore it would be wise to keep me in the political family. The showing I made attracted enough attention among the politicians to make them think it worth while to give me the appointment of Deputy Attorney General of the State of New York.

I kept pretty busy in 1915 and 1916, what with my work in the Attorney General's office, learning to fly, and building my fences for the 1916 Congressional campaign.[4] I had my heart still set on going to Congress, and my first defeat did not discourage me. Once when I was in Washington, a member of Congress gave me a card to the "family" gallery. I would not go. I did not want to enter the House of Representatives until I could go on the floor as a member. But I read the *Congressional Record* religiously. That was the easiest part of my preliminary training. The big job was making friends, so that I could win the election.

I knew that I could not depend much on the Republican organization, because of my first experience with it in 1914. It was pretty clear to me that the seat in Congress from my district appeared to belong to the National Liquor Dealers' Association in the name of Michael Farley, the Democratic incumbent, by tacit agreement with the Republicans.[5] But I kept building up my contacts. My law office was a regular Legal Aid Society, and after office hours at the Attorney General's office I made many friends useful to me in politics by going to clambakes,[6] balls, weddings, and funerals—functions inseparable from the life of a man in politics. I got to know a great many people in my district.

---

[5]*the seat in Congress...Republicans.* Though apparently the Republicans were trying to win the election in New York's 14th Congressional District, actually both Republicans and Democrats regarded the seat as belonging to the National Liquor Dealers' Association, whose interests were represented by Michael Farley.

[6]*clambakes.* La Guardia uses the term to suggest various types of gatherings, from picnics to large family parties.

---

[3]*Tammany,* Democratic. *Tammany* is the name commonly applied to the political organization of the Democratic Party in New York City. The name comes from Tammany Hall, the home of a political society founded in 1789 and today the headquarters of the New York City Democratic organization.

[4]*building my fences...campaign,* attending gatherings, making friends, and in general doing the things that would aid in winning an election.

When the time came for the Congressional nomination in 1916, I was surprised, shocked, and hurt to learn that I was not slated for the place on the Republican ticket. I felt I was entitled to it because of the run I had made in the previous election two years before. But that run had attracted a great deal of interest in the nomination. Everybody was nice, giving me good advice about not taking another licking. I was destined, they said, to be a judge or something big like that. "Just be a good boy, go along with the organization, help wherever you can," they told me. That didn't register very well with me.

I got my petitions printed. I was told that was not in the books,[7] that recognition had been given me by my appointment as Deputy Attorney General; I must not hurt my own interest, but just go along and be a good soldier. I insisted that I would contest any nomination made by the party and run in the primaries against another Republican organization choice.

Finally, I made an appointment to see Fred Tanner, who was then Republican State Chairman. He had been leader of my home district. Fred Tanner was a prominent lawyer, scholarly and gentlemanly, who was interested in politics. I had an interesting talk with him. He repeated the old gaff[8] about my future in politics, and he tried to convince me that it was to my interest to stay put that year. I was not a bit impressed. He was frank enough to tell me that a young outsider wanted the Congressional nomination badly that year. And this young man's friends had promised to make a substantial contribution to the Republican Party, if he got the nomination.

Fred Tanner made one blunder in his effort to talk me out of running that year. He said that if I had gone to any expense, such as printing my petitions, or anything else, he would see that I was reimbursed. Well, I just hit the ceiling. I don't think Fred meant it the way I took it. But I blew up, and that just about ended our talk. As I started out of his office, Fred shouted to me, "Fiorello, hold your horses. If you want to run, go ahead and do it. Don't blame me if you're licked again."

Harry Andrews was a very useful man around our district. He was young, a good stenographer, did most of the clerical work, and acted as secretary to the district leader. He had a job as a secretary to a judge. I learned a great deal about politics from Harry, and he, I believe, learned some things about government from me.

We got my petitions signed and filed. Though I never got a nod or a word from the Republican Party officials, no opposition developed, much to my surprise, and I entered the primaries unopposed. I did have opposition for the Progressive Party nomination.[9] My friend Ben Marsh, a real liberal who has been on the right side of many losing causes, was my opponent. I won the Progressive nomination, too, and always had a feeling that Ben voted for me.

The campaign was hot. I got a tremendous start on my opponent, the sitting congressman. His office-holding had gone to his head, and he was terribly inflated. He seldom showed up at his saloon, and when he did, forgot to treat the boys. He had become a "big shot," and was seldom seen in the district. That would not have been so bad if he had ever done anything in Washington. So I had plenty of material to work on.

This time I did not wait for the party leaders to get me started. I was 'way ahead of them. The campaign was difficult because my district had such varied interests. The East Side section was interested in economics and the future of Europe; Washington Square, before Greenwich Village had become The Village,[10] was most conservative—for higher tariffs, lower taxes, big-business stuff; and the West Side Irish were anti-British and completely Tammanyized.[11]

---

[7]*not in the books,* not what the political party wished.
[8]*gaff,* a line of talk.

[9]*I did have opposition...nomination.* La Guardia wished to run as the candidate of both the Republican and the Progressive parties.
[10]*Washington Square...The Village.* Washington Square is an area adjoining the part of southern Manhattan known as Greenwich (gren'ich) Village. As the fine old homes and apartments gradually became boarding houses and small flats attracting artists, authors, and students, the character of the neighborhood changed and it was often called The Village.
[11]*Tammanyized,* strong in their support of Tammany or Tammany Hall, the Democratic organization of New York City.

While I had many friends in the Socialist Party, they waged their fight against me on the East Side. It was their tactics to accept an ultra-conservative rather than a progressive. Tammany was counting on a heavy vote in the West Side section of the district and the solid Little Tim Sullivan Third District on the East Side.

This time my candidacy was not taken by Tammany Hall as the joke it had been to its henchmen two years before. They were in a dilemma. They didn't dare put Mike Farley, their candidate, on the stump.[12] So all sorts of stump speakers were imported into the district. We had a great time with them. I covered every corner in that district, I think. We would start early in the evening, on the West Side, keep going east, and it was not unusual for the last street meeting to end 'way past one o'clock in the morning. Then, to Stuyvesant Hall or some coffee house on the East Side for another hour or two of campaigning.

Tammany was not really worried. They depended on two things: on the Democratic majority usual in that Congressional district, which they considered overwhelming, and on the count.[13] Republican leaders in the West Side districts and in some of the East Side districts were not only weak but untrustworthy and venal. The Republican leader in Little Tim Sullivan's East Side district was an Italian who had made a fortune as a padrone for the Erie Railroad. He worked very closely with Tammany Hall and would do nothing to incur its displeasure. He always got advice, protection, and help from the national Republican administration. He was illiterate, ignorant, and arrogant. He didn't even treat his family well. The Tammany leader in the same district was one of the Sullivan clan. Little Tim Sullivan was personally a nice fellow, but as tough a Tammany leader as they came. We prepared for fraud by organizing a corps of volunteer watchers for the count, a precaution I have always taken in my subsequent campaigns.

[12]*put Mike Farley...stump,* allow him to make political speeches at various places in the district.
[13]*the count,* the counting of votes in a precinct. Tammany expected chances to alter the returns in their favor.

We were all pretty tired that last Monday night before election day. We stuck it out at meetings until two o'clock in the morning. We had to get up very early on election day, for we had a job to do. After about three hours' sleep, we covered the two or three lodging houses in the district—flop houses. At five o'clock we visited these, for we knew that Tammany planned to vote the inhabitants in a pack between eight and nine that morning. Our boys were ready with coffee and rolls and doughnuts, so that by the time the Tammany men came around, the flop-house inhabitants had already voted. It was the first time in years, some of the old timers remarked, that the guests of these flop houses had voted sober.

We had a little trouble early in the morning when word was spread, allegedly by one of the Republican leaders, "La Guardia hasn't got a chance, so trade votes for Congress for a Republican assemblyman." We got hold of that leader quickly, took him in the car with us, and went from polling place to polling place straightening out that one.

Our real trouble started when the polls closed and the count began. In those days we still had paper ballots. The count was long and tedious. There was ample time and opportunity for marking ballots so that they would be disqualified, for substituting ballots, and every other kind of dirty, dishonest political trick.

I took the toughest district on the water front to watch. This attracted a lot of attention, and finally Charles Culkin, one of the top men in Tammany Hall, who held high office from time to time and was the Tammany leader of that district, came to the polling place. He gently told me, "Why, La Guardia, what are you doing here? You shouldn't be here. Everything is all right."

"Everything is not all right," I said, "and what is more, Charlie, you sit here and help me watch this count. There is going to be an honest count, and, if not, someone is going to go to jail, and I mean you, Charlie. You stay here and protect your own district."

He did.

I had all sorts of people watching that district of Charlie Culkin's as well as the other

I got quite a reception on the East Side. Sam Koenig, who was the Republican county chairman, was genuinely elated at my victory. There is one thing I could always say about Sam Koenig then and during the many years following: if he gave you his word about something, he kept it. I anticipated an enthusiastic reception in other parts of the 14th Congressional District. After all, it was the first time a Republican had been elected to Congress below 14th Street since the foundation of the Republican Party. I particularly thought I would get a riotous reception in my own home district. I never saw such gloom anywhere. The hangers-on at the club hardly nodded to me. Someone was on the telephone in the rear office, assuring the Democratic leader of the district, who was supposed to be his rival, "No, Joe, we didn't double-cross you; we didn't do anything for this fellow. You just can't control him." An apology for my victory is what I heard instead of congratulations! Those are just some of the little things that have made me an incurable insurgent.

districts. There were school teachers, doctors, businessmen, longshoremen, and some tough guys on our side. In the final count in the district where I was helping to watch, I defeated my Tammany opponent by a very small margin. The Democratic vote in that district was usually five to one against the Republican. Charlie Culkin's jaw dropped. He shook his head and asked me if I was satisfied with the count. "Yes," I said, "as soon as the certificate is signed and turned over to the police." It was.

All through the Democratic districts on the West Side river front I was running 'way ahead of the ticket. We knew then that if we could keep up that lead, we would overcome the normal majority for the Democrats. We were going well on the East Side. It, too, was well organized. All of our watchers were instructed to remain on duty until the count was entirely completed, the returns officially signed, and the ballot boxes sealed.

It was about four in the morning before we could get a final count. I had won the election. But it was a good thing we had watched that count carefully, for I won by 357 votes—7272 for me, 6915 for Farley.

WHAT DID LA GUARDIA LEARN?

1. Judging from La Guardia's experience, what are the chief difficulties in the way of an ordinary American with political ambitions? How did La Guardia overcome those difficulties?
2. What qualities did La Guardia show in his fight to become a Congressman that, in your opinion, aided him later to be elected mayor of New York City? What characteristics do you think were important in making him an outstanding success in this position?

Know your words

On a sheet of paper complete each statement below in such a way as to bring out the meaning of the italicized word. Consult the Glossary or a dictionary if necessary.

1. La Guardia called himself an *insurgent* because....
2. He believed there was a *tacit* understanding between Democrats and Republicans because....
3. When La Guardia ran against the Democratic incumbent for the second time, Tammany was in a *dilemma* because....
4. He opposed *venal* politicians because....
5. He might be called a good political *strategist* because....

The Poor Voter on Election Day

JOHN GREENLEAF WHITTIER

"Good government is everybody's business"—so read
the signs in city streetcars and village halls. As Whittier's
poem (published in 1884) suggests, this is no new
idea. The privilege of voting was once restricted to
those with property or to the members of particular
churches. But to believe in democracy is to believe in
the collective wisdom of all.

THE PROUDEST now is but my peer,
    The highest not more high;
Today, of all the weary year,
    A king of men am I.
Today, alike are great and small,   5
    The nameless and the known;
My palace is the people's hall,
    The ballot box my throne!

Who serves today upon the list
    Beside the served shall stand;   10
Alike the brown and wrinkled fist,
    The gloved and dainty hand!
The rich is level with the poor,
    The weak is strong today;
And sleekest broadcloth counts no more   15
    Than homespun frock of gray.

Today let pomp and vain pretense
    My stubborn right abide;
I set a plain man's common sense
    Against the pedant's pride.   20
Today shall simple manhood try
    The strength of gold and land;
The wide world has not wealth to buy
    The power in my right hand!

While there's a grief to seek redress,   25
    Or balance to adjust,
Where weighs our living manhood less
    Than Mammon's vilest dust[1]—
While there's a right to need my vote,
    A wrong to sweep away,   30
Up! clouted[2] knee and ragged coat!
    A man's a man today!

---

[1]*Mammon's vilest dust,* money. *Mammon* personifies
greed for wealth. See Matthew 6:24 and Luke 16:9.
    [2]*clouted,* patched.

HOW IMPORTANT IS VOTING?

1. What is the significance of election day to the
"poor voter"? Read aloud the lines that you feel best
express its importance. What lines show that Whittier
regards voting as more than a privilege or right?

2. What indications do you find in the last two
stanzas that Whittier thought of politics as a class
conflict? What groups does he indicate are ranged
against one another? Do you believe that there is
more, or less, conflict between these various groups
in the United States today?

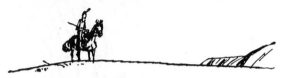

Lone Wolf's Old Guard

HAMLIN GARLAND

One of the great problems of democracy, clearly recognized by Jefferson, is that the will of the majority
may sometimes prove unjust to minorities. Hamlin
Garland's story of the distinction made by Lone Wolf
between greedy white men and the government at
Washington shows an age-old conflict between economic and social forces on the one hand and justice
to minorities on the other. That conflict is still with
us, in many forms and in many places, some of them
as dramatic as was the situation in Oklahoma Territory after the War Between the States.

NOW IT HAPPENED that Lone Wolf's camp
was on the line between the land of the
Cheyennes and the home of his own people,
the Kiowas,[1] but he did not know this. He had
lived there long, and the white man's maps
were as unimportant to him as they had been
to the Cheyennes. When he moved there he
considered it to be his—a gift direct from the
Creator—with no prior rights to be overstepped.

---

[1]*the land of the Cheyennes* (shī enz′)...*Kiowas* (kī′ō-
wāz or kī′ō wəz). These tribes of Indians, both of which
had originally hunted buffalo on the Great Plains, had
been settled on adjoining reservations in western Oklahoma
Territory.

"Lone Wolf's Old Guard," from *The Book of the American
Indian,* copyright, 1923, by Hamlin Garland. Published
  by Harper and Brothers. Reprinted by permission of
  Constance Garland Doyle and Isabel Garland Lord.

But the Consolidated Cattle Company, having secured the right to enclose a vast pasture, cared nothing for any red man's claim, provided they stood in with the government. A surveying party was sent out to run lines for fences.

Lone Wolf heard of these invaders while they were at work north of him, and learned in some mysterious way that they were to come down the Elk[2] and cut through his camp. To his friend, John, the interpreter,[3] he sent these words:

"The white man must not try to build a fence across my land. I will fight if he does. Washington[4] is not behind this thing. He would not build a fence through my lines without talking with me. I have sent to the agent of the Kiowas[5]; he knows nothing about it—it is all a plan of the cattlemen to steal my lands. Tell them that we have smoked over this news—we have decided. This fence will not be built."

When "Johnny Smoker" brought this stern message to the camp of the surveyors, some of them promptly threw up their hands. Jim Bellows, scout and interpreter, was among these, and his opinion had weight, for he wore his hair long and posed as an Indian fighter of large experience.

"Boys," he began, impressively, "we got to get out o' here as soon as darkness covers us. We're sixty miles from the fort, and only fifteen all told, and not half armed. Old Lone Wolf holds over us, and we might as well quit and get help."

This verdict carried the camp, and the party precipitately returned to Darlington[6] to confer with the managers of the company.

Pierce, the chief man, had reasons for not calling on the military authorities. His lease was as yet merely a semiprivate arrangement between the Secretary of the Interior[7] and himself, and he feared the consequences of a fight with Lone Wolf—publicity, friction—might cause the withdrawal of his lease; therefore he called in John Seger and said, "Jack, can you put that line through?"

"I could, but I don't want to. Lone Wolf is a good friend of mine, and I don't want to be mixed up in a mean job."

"Oh, come now—you mustn't show the white flag.[8] I need you. I want you to pick out five or six men of grit and go along and see that this line is run. I can't be fooling around here all summer. Here's my lease, signed by the Secretary, as you see. It's all straight, and this old fool of an Indian must move."

Jack reluctantly consented, and set to work to hire a half-dozen men of whose courage he had personal knowledge. Among these was a man by the name of Tom Speed, a borderman of great hardihood and experience. To him he said, "Tom, I don't like to go into this thing; but I'm hard up, and Pierce has given me the contract to build this fence if we run the line, and it looks like we got to do it. Now I wish you'd saddle up and help me stave off trouble. How does it strike you?"

"It's nasty business, Jack; but I reckon we might better do it than let some tenderfoot go in and start a killin'. I'm busted flat, and if the pay is good, I jest about feel obliged to take it."

So it happened that two avowed friends of the red man led this second expedition against Lone Wolf's camp. Pierce sent his brother as boss, and with him went the son of one of the principal owners, a Boston man by the name of Ross. Speed always called him "the Dude," though he dressed quite simply, as dress goes in Roxbury.[9] He wore a light suit of gray wool, "low-quartered shoes," and a "grape box hat." He was armed with a pistol, which wouldn't kill a turtledove at fifteen feet. Henry Pierce, on the contrary, was a reckless and determined man.

---

[2]*the Elk,* a creek in western Oklahoma.

[3]*John, the interpreter,* John Seger, often called "Johnny Smoker" by the Indians.

[4]*Washington,* the white man's government at Washington.

[5]*the agent of the Kiowas,* the white man appointed as Indian agent by the Secretary of the Interior to protect the interests of this particular tribe.

[6]*Darlington,* a small village. White men having business with the Indians made it their headquarters. The Indian Agency, licensed shops, and a school for Indians were located here.

---

[7]*Secretary of the Interior,* the member of the Cabinet in charge of Indian affairs.

[8]*show the white flag,* back down. The white flag is used as a sign of truce or surrender.

[9]*Roxbury,* a section of Boston, once a separate town.

Moving swiftly across the Divide,[10] they took up the line on Elk Creek, and started directly toward Lone Wolf's camp. As they were nearing the bend in the river where Lone Wolf was camped, a couple of young warriors came riding leisurely up from the south. They were very cordial in their greeting, and after shaking hands all around pleasantly inquired, "What are you doing here?"

"Running a line to mark out the land which the cattlemen have leased of the Cheyennes."

"We will go along and see where you are going," they replied.

A couple of hours later, while they were still with the camp, two others came riding quietly in from the east. They said, "We are looking for horses," and after shaking hands and asking Seger what the white men were doing, rode forward to join their companions, who seemed deeply interested in the surveyors and their instruments.

Turning to Pierce, Jack said, "You noticed that these four men were armed, I reckon?"

"Oh, yes, but they are all right. Didn't you see how they shook hands all round? They're just out hunting up ponies."

"Yes, I saw that; but I noticed they had plenty of ammunition and that their guns were bright. Indians don't hunt horses in squads, Mr. Pierce."

Pierce smiled, giving Seger a sidewise glance. "Are you getting nervous? If you are, you can drop to the rear."

Now Seger had lived for the larger part of his life among the red people, and knew their ways. He answered quietly, "There are only four of them now; you'll see more of them soon," and he pointed away to the north, where the heads of three mounted men were rising into sight over a ridge. These also proved to be young Kiowas, thoroughly armed, who asked the same question of the manager, and in conclusion pleasantly said:

"We'll just go along and see how you do it."

As they rode forward Seger uttered a more pointed warning. "Mr. Pierce, I reckon you'd

better make some better disposition of your men. They are all strung out here with their guns on their backs, in no kind of shape to make a defense."

Pierce was a little impressed by the scout's earnestness, and took trouble to point out the discrepancy between "a bunch of seven cowardly Indians" and his own band of twenty brave and experienced men.

"That's all right," replied Seger; "but these seven men are only spies, sent out to see what we are going to do. We'll have to buckle up with Lone Wolf's whole band very soon."

A few minutes later the seven young men rode quietly by and took a stand on a ridge a little in front of the surveyors. As he approached them, Seger perceived a very great change in their demeanor. They no longer smiled; they seemed grim, resolute, and much older. From a careless, laughing group of young men they had become soldiers—determined, disciplined, and dignified. Their leader, riding forth, held up his hand, and said, "Stop; you must wait here till Lone Wolf comes."

Meanwhile, in the little city of tents, a brave drama was being enacted. Lone Wolf, a powerful man of middle age, was sitting in council with his people. The long-expected had happened—the cattlemen had begun to mark off the red man's land as their own, and the time had come either to submit or to repel the invaders. To submit was hard, to fight was hopeless. Their world was still narrow, but they had a benumbing conception of the power and the remorseless greed of the white man.

"We can kill those who come," said Lone Wolf. "They are few, but behind them are the soldiers and men who plough."

At last old White Buffalo rose—he had been a great leader in his day, and was still much respected, though he had laid aside his chieftainship. He was bent and gray and wrinkled, but his voice was still strong and his eyes keen.

"My friends, listen to me! During seventy years of my life I lived without touching the hand of a white man. I have always opposed warfare, except when it was necessary; but now the time has come to fight. Let me tell you what to do. I see here some thirty old men, who, like

[10]*the Divide,* the land that separated Darlington from Elk Creek.

202   THE PRICE OF LIBERTY

me, are nearing the grave. This thing we will do—we old men—we will go out to war against these cattlemen. We will go forth and die in defense of our lands. Big Wolf, come—and you, my brother, Standing Bear."

As he called the roll of the gray old defenders, the old women broke into heart-piercing wailing, intermingled with exultant cries as some brave wife or sister caught the force of the heroic responses, which leaped from the

lips of their fathers and husbands. A feeling of awe fell over the young men as they watched the fires flame once more in the dim eyes of their grandsires, and when all had spoken, Lone Wolf rose and stepped forth, and said, "Very well; then I will lead you."

"Whosoever leads us goes to certain death," said White Buffalo. "It is the custom of the white men to kill the leader. You will fall at the first fire. I will lead."

Lone Wolf's face grew stern. "Am I not your war chief? Whose place is it to lead? If I die, I fall in combat for my land, and you, my children, will preserve my name in song. We do not know how this will end, but it is better to end in battle than to have our lands cut in half beneath our feet."

The bustle and preparation began at once. When all was ready the thirty gray and withered old men, beginning a low humming song, swept through the camp and started on their desperate charge, Lone Wolf leading them. "Some of those who go will return, but if the white men fight, I will not return," he sang, as they began to climb the hill on whose top the white men could be seen awaiting their coming.

Halfway up the hill they met some of the young warriors. "Go bring all the white men to the council," said Lone Wolf.

As the white men watched the band leaving the village and beginning to ascend the hill, Speed turned and said: "Well, Jack, what do you think of it? Here comes a war party—Here comes a war party—painted and armed."

"I think it's about an even chance whether we ever cross the Washita[11] again or not. Now, you are a married man with children, and I wouldn't blame you if you pulled out right this minute."

"I feel meaner about this than anything I ever did," replied Speed, "but I am going to stay with the expedition."

As Lone Wolf and his heroic old guard drew near, Seger thrilled with the significance of this strange and solemn company of old men in full war paint, armed with all kinds of old-fashioned guns, and bows and arrows. As he looked into their wrinkled faces, the scout perceived that these grandsires had come resolved to die. He divined what had taken place in camp. Their exalted heroism was written in the somber droop of their lips. "We can die, but we will not retreat!" In such wise our grandsires fought.

---

[11] the Washita (wosh′i tô), a river to the east of Elk Creek.

Lone Wolf led his Spartan host[12] steadily on till near enough to be heard without effort. He then halted, took off his war bonnet and hung it on the pommel of his saddle. Lifting both palms to the sky, he spoke, and his voice had a solemn boom in it: "The Great Father is looking down on us. He sees us. He knows I speak the truth. He gave us this land. We are the first to inhabit it. No one else has any claim to it. It is ours, and I will go under the sod before any cattlemen shall divide it and take it away from us. I have said it."

When this was interpreted to him, Pierce with a look of inquiry turned to Speed. "Tell the old fool this line is going to be run, and no old scarecrows like these can stop us."

Seger, lifting his hand, signed: "Lone Wolf, you know me. I am your friend. I do not come to do you harm. I come to tell you you are wrong. All the land on my left hand the Great White Father[13] says is Cheyenne land. All on my right is Kiowa land. The Cheyennes have sold the right to their land to the white man, and we are here to mark out the line. We take only Cheyenne land."

"I do not believe it," replied the chief. "My agent knows nothing of it. Washington has not written anything to me about it. This is the work of robbers. Cattlemen will do anything for money. They are wolves. They shall not go on."

"What does he say?" asked Pierce.

"He says we must not go on."

"You tell him that he can't run any such bluff on me with his old scarecrow warriors. This line goes through."

Lone Wolf, tense and eager, asked, "What says the white chief?"

"He says we must run the line."

Lone Wolf turned to his guard. "You may as well get ready," he said, quietly.

The old men drew closer together with a mutter of low words, and each pair of dim eyes selected their man. The clicking of their guns was ominous, and Pierce turned white.

Speed drew his revolver holster round to the front. "They're going to fight," he said. "Every man get ready!"

But Seger, eager to avoid the appalling contest, cried out to Pierce, "Don't do that! It's suicide to go on. These old men have come out to fight till death." To Lone Wolf he signed: "Don't shoot, my friend!—let us consider this matter. Put up your guns."

Into the hot mist of Pierce's wrath came a

[12]*Spartan host,* a group of men who would die rather than surrender. In 480 B.C., during the war between Greece and Persia, three hundred Spartans died to the last man while defending the mountain pass at Thermopylae (thər-mop′ə lē) against the Persian army.

[13]*Great White Father,* the President of the United States.

realization that these old men were in mighty earnest. He hesitated.

Lone Wolf saw his hesitation, and said: "If you are here by right, why do you not get the soldier chief to come and tell me? If the Great White Father has ordered this—then I am like a man with his hands tied. The soldiers do not lie. Bring them!"

Seger grasped eagerly at this declaration. "There is your chance, Pierce. The chief says he will submit if the soldiers come to make the survey. Let me tell him that you will bring an officer from the fort to prove that the government is behind you."

Pierce, now fully aware of the desperate bravery of the old men, was looking for a knot-hole of escape. "All right, fix it up with him," he said.

Seger turned to Lone Wolf. "The chief of the surveyors says, 'Let us be friends. I will not run the line.' "

"Ho, ho!" cried the old warriors, and their faces, grim and wrinkled, broke up into smiles. They laughed, they shook hands, while tears of joy filled their eyes. They were like men delivered from sentence of death. The desperate courage of their approach was now revealed even to Pierce. They were as joyous as children over their sudden release from slaughter.

Lone Wolf, approaching Seger, dismounted, and laid his arm over his friend's shoulder. "My friend," he said, with grave tenderness, "I wondered why you were with these men, and my heart was heavy; but now I see that you were here to turn aside the guns of the cattlemen. My heart is big with friendship for you. Once more you have proved my good counselor." And tears dimmed the fierceness of his eyes.

A week later, a slim, smooth-cheeked second lieutenant, by virtue of his cap and the crossed arms which decorated his collar, ran the line, and Lone Wolf made no resistance. "I have no fight with the soldiers of the Great White Father," he said; "they do not come to gain my land. I now see that Washington has decreed that this fence shall be built." Nevertheless, his heart was heavy, and in his camp his heroic old guard sat waiting, waiting!

UNDERSTANDING CONFLICTING ATTITUDES

1. What is Lone Wolf's attitude toward the government at Washington? Toward the cattlemen? Why does he allow the young lieutenant to run the lines for fences?

2. What is White Buffalo's reason for suggesting that the thirty old men of the tribe go to war?

3. Contrast the attitude of Pierce toward the Indians with that of Seger. How do you explain the difference?

4. How would you describe the author's attitude toward the taking of Indian lands by the white cattlemen?

5. What differences do you find between James Fenimore Cooper's and Hamlin Garland's attitudes toward the Indian?

Know your words

Many words have several different meanings. Only by seeing or hearing such words in their context is it possible to determine which meaning is intended. Note the italicized words in the sentences below. First decide the meaning of the word as Hamlin Garland uses it in "Lone Wolf's Old Guard." Then write at least one sentence using the word in another sense.

1. "...I reckon you'd better make some better *disposition* of your men."

2. "They are all strung out here...in no kind of *shape* to make a defense."

3. He *divined* what had taken place in camp.

4. They were like men delivered from *sentence* of death.

Extending interests

Consult encyclopedias, almanacs, or other reference works for answers to one of the following groups of questions. Your answers will form the basis of an interesting report to the class. If you are very ambitious, you may extend your report to cover all three groups of questions.

1. What is the status of the Indian today? Is he a citizen? Does he have the right to vote? What part has the Indian played in the armed forces?

2. What is the total amount of land in Indian reservations today? In what states are the largest reservations located? What is the total Indian population? In what states do Indians live?

3. What provisions are made for educating Indian children? How do schools on the reservations differ from most other public schools?

What Americans Have Fought For

A Tooth for Paul Revere

STEPHEN VINCENT BENÉT

Sometimes nations of peace-loving people have to go to war, to fight for their freedoms and their way of life. They always do so reluctantly. Wearing the uniforms, marching behind the military bands, winning the ribbons and the medals and—too often—the white wooden crosses in long lines in the military cemeteries, are boys and men who for the most part would rather be home. The theme of Benét's "A Tooth for Paul Revere" is that history belongs to the common man as much as to his leaders. This story incidentally tells us much about what Americans fought for in the Revolutionary War.

I

SOME SAY it all happened because of Hancock and Adams[1] (said the old man, pulling at his pipe), and some put it back to the Stamp Act[2] and before. Then there's some hold out for Paul Revere[3] and his little silver box. But the way I heard it, it broke loose because of Lige Butterwick and his tooth.

What's that? Why, the American Revolution, of course. What else would I be talking about? Well, your story about the land down South that they had to plow with alligators reminded me.

No, this is a true story—or at least that's how I heard it told. My great-aunt was a Butterwick and I heard it from her. And, every now and then, she'd write it out and want to get it put in the history books. But they'd always put her off with some trifling sort of excuse. Till, finally, she got her dander up and wrote direct to the President of the United States. Well, no, he didn't answer himself exactly—the President's apt to be a pretty busy man. But the letter said he'd received her interesting communication and thanked her for it, so that shows you. We've got it framed, in the trailer—the ink's a little faded, but you can make out the man's name who signed it. It's either Bowers or Thorpe and he wrote a very nice hand.

You see, my great-aunt, she wasn't very respectful to the kind of history that does get into the books. What she liked was the queer corners of it and the tales that get handed down in families. Take Paul Revere, for instance—all most folks think about, with him, is his riding a horse. But when she talked about Paul Revere—why, you could just see him in his shop, brewing the American Revolution in a silver teapot and waiting for it to settle. Oh yes, he was a silversmith by trade—but she claimed he was something more. She claimed there was a kind of magic in that quick, skillful hand of his—and that he was one of the kind of folks that can see just a little bit farther into a millstone than most. But it was when she got to Lige Butterwick that she really turned herself loose.

For she claimed that it took all sorts to make a country—and that meant the dumb ones, too. I don't mean ijits[4] or nincompoops—just the ordinary folks that live along from day to day. And that day may be a notable day in history—but it's just Tuesday to them, till they read all about it in the papers. Oh, the heroes and the great men—they can plan and contrive and see ahead. But it isn't till the Lige Butterwicks get

---

[1]*Hancock and Adams*, John Hancock and Sam Adams, leaders of the American Revolution in the Boston area.

[2]*Stamp Act*, a measure passed by the British Parliament in 1765, but repealed the next year after vigorous protests by the Americans. It was a scheme for gaining revenue by internal taxes, whose payment was to be indicated by placing stamps on legal documents, newspapers, etc.

[3]*Paul Revere*. Although Paul Revere is best known today for his ride to Lexington in April 1775 to warn of the approach of British troops, he won fame in his own time as one of the finest silversmiths and goldsmiths in the colonies, a skilled engraver, and a dentist specializing in artificial teeth.

[4]*ijits*, idiots.

stirred up that things really start to happen. Or so she claimed. And the way that they do get stirred up is often curious, as she'd tell this story to prove.

For, now you take Lige Butterwick—and, before his tooth started aching, he was just like you and me. He lived on a farm about eight miles from Lexington, Massachusetts, and he was a peaceable man. It was troubled times in the American colonies, what with British warships in Boston Harbor and British soldiers in Boston and Sons of Liberty[5] hooting the British soldiers—not to speak of Boston tea parties and such. But Lige Butterwick, he worked his farm and didn't pay much attention. There's lots of people like that, even in troubled times.

When he went into town, to be sure, there was high talk at the tavern. But he bought his goods and came home again—he had ideas about politics, but he didn't talk about them much. He had a good farm and it kept him busy—he had a wife and five children and they kept him humping. The young folks could argue about King George[6] and Sam Adams— he wondered how the corn was going to stand that year. Now and then, if somebody said that this and that was a burning shame, he'd allow as how it might be, just to be neighborly. But, inside, he was wondering whether next year he mightn't make an experiment and plant the west field in rye.

Well, everything went along for him the way that it does for most folks with good years and bad years, till one April morning, in 1775, he woke up with a toothache. Being the kind of man he was, he didn't pay much attention to it at first. But he mentioned it that evening, at supper, and his wife got a bag of hot salt for him. He held it to his face and it seemed to ease him, but he couldn't hold it there all night, and, next morning, the tooth hurt worse than ever.

Well, he stood it the next day and the next,

but it didn't improve any. He tried tansy tea[7] and other remedies—he tried tying a string to it and having his wife slam the door. But, when it came to the pinch, he couldn't quite do it. So, finally, he took the horse and rode into Lexington town to have it seen to. Mrs. Butterwick made him—she said it might be an expense, but anything was better than having him act as if he wanted to kick the cat across the room every time she put her feet down hard.

When he got into Lexington, he noticed that folks there seemed kind of excited. There was a lot of talk about muskets and powder and a couple of men called Hancock and Adams who were staying at Parson Clarke's. But Lige Butterwick had his own business to attend to— and, besides, his tooth was jumping so he wasn't in any mood for conversation. He set off for the local barber's, as being the likeliest man he knew to pull a tooth.

The barber took one look at it and shook his head.

"I can pull her, Lige," he said. "Oh, I can pull her, all right. But she's got long roots and strong roots and she's going to leave an awful gap when she's gone. Now, what you really need," he said, kind of excited, for he was one of those perky little men who's always interested in the latest notion, "what you really need—though it's taking away my business—is one of these-here artificial teeth to go in the hole."

"Artificial teeth!" said Lige. "It's flying in the face of Nature!"

The barber shook his head. "No, Lige," he said, "that's where you're wrong. Artificial teeth is all the go these days, and Lexington ought to keep up with the times. It would do me good to see you with an artificial tooth—it would so."

"Well, it might do *you* good," said Lige, rather crossly, for his tooth was jumping, "but, supposing I did want one—how in tunket will I get one in Lexington?"

"Now you just leave that to me," said the barber, all excited, and he started to rummage around. "You'll have to go to Boston for it, but

[5]*Sons of Liberty,* a patriotic secret society organized at the time of the Stamp Act. The society was active in organizing resistance to paying the British taxes.

[6]*King George,* George III, king of England from 1760 to 1820.

[7]*tansy tea,* a drink made from an aromatic plant of the aster family.

I know just the man." He was one of those men who can always tell you where to go and it's usually wrong. "See here," he went on. "There's a fellow called Revere in Boston that fixes them and they say he's a boss workman. Just take a look at this prospectus"—and he started to read from a paper: " 'Whereas many persons are so unfortunate as to lose their foreteeth'—that's you, Lige—'to their great detriment, not only in looks but in speaking, both in public and private, this is to inform all such that they may have them replaced by artificial ones'—see?— 'that look as well as the natural and answer the end of speaking to all intents'—and then he's got his name—'Paul Revere, goldsmith, near the head of Dr. Clarke's wharf, Boston.' "

"Sounds well enough," said Lige, "but what's it going to cost?"

"Oh, I know Revere," said the barber, swelling up like a robin. "Comes through here pretty often, as a matter of fact. And he's a decent fellow, if he is a pretty big bug in the Sons of Liberty. You just mention my name."

"Well, it's something I hadn't thought of," said Lige, as his tooth gave another red-hot jounce, "but in for a penny, in for a pound. I've missed a day's work already and that tooth's got to come out before I go stark, staring mad. But what sort of a man is this Revere, anyway?"

"Oh, he's a regular wizard!" said the barber. "A regular wizard with his tools."

"Wizard!" said Lige. "Well, I don't know about wizards. But if he can fix my tooth I'll call him one."

"You'll never regret it," said the barber— and that's the way folks always talk when they're sending someone else to the dentist. So Lige Butterwick got on his horse again and started out for Boston. A couple of people shouted at him as he rode down the street, but he didn't pay any attention. And, going by Parson Clarke's, he caught a glimpse of two men talking in the parson's front room. One was a tallish, handsomish man in pretty fine clothes and the other was shorter and untidy, with a kind of bulldog face. But they were strangers to him and he didn't really notice them—just rode ahead.

II

But as soon as he got into Boston he started to feel queer—and it wasn't only his tooth. He hadn't been there in four years and he'd expected to find it changed, but it wasn't that. It was a clear enough day and yet he kept feeling there was thunder in the air. There'd be knots of people, talking and arguing, on street corners, and then, when you got closer to them, they'd kind of melt away. Or, if they stayed, they'd look at you, out of the corners of their eyes. And there, in the Port of Boston, were the British warships, black and grim. He'd known they'd be there, of course, but it was different, seeing them. It made him feel queer to see their guns pointed at the town. He'd known there was trouble and dispute, in Boston, but the knowledge had passed over him like rain and hail. But now here he was in the middle of it—and it smelt like earthquake weather. He couldn't make head or tail of it, but he wanted to be home.

All the same, he'd come to get his tooth fixed, and, being New England, he was bound to do it. But first he stopped at a tavern for a bite and a sup, for it was long past his dinnertime. And there, it seemed to him, things got even more curious.

"Nice weather we're having, these days," he said, in a friendly way, to the barkeep.

"It's bitter weather for Boston," said the

barkeep, in an unfriendly voice, and a sort of low growl went up from the boys at the back of the room and every eye fixed on Lige.

Well, that didn't help the toothache any, but, being a sociable person, Lige kept on.

"May be, for Boston," he said, "but out in the country we'd call it good planting weather."

The barkeep stared at him hard.

"I guess I was mistaken in you," he said. "It *is* good planting weather—for some kinds of trees."

"And what kind of trees were you thinking of?" said a sharp-faced man at Lige's left, and squeezed his shoulder.

"There's trees and trees, you know," said a red-faced man at Lige's right, and gave him a dig in the ribs.

"Well, now that you ask me——" said Lige, but he couldn't even finish before the red-faced man dug him hard in the ribs again.

"The liberty tree!"[8] said the red-faced man. "And may it soon be watered in the blood of tyrants!"

"The royal oak of England!" said the sharp-faced man. "And God save King George and loyalty!"

Well, with that it seemed to Lige Butterwick as if the whole tavern kind of riz up at him. He was kicked and pummeled and mauled and thrown into a corner and yanked out of it again, with the red-faced man and the sharp-faced man and all the rest of them dancing quadrilles over his prostrate form. Till, finally, he found himself out in the street with half his coat gone galley-west.

"Well," said Lige to himself, "I always heard city folks were crazy. But politics must be getting serious in these American colonies when they start fighting about trees!"

Then he saw the sharp-faced man was beside him, trying to shake his hand. He noticed with some pleasure that the sharp-faced man had the beginnings of a beautiful black eye.

"Nobly done, friend," said the sharp-faced man, "and I'm glad to find another true-hearted Loyalist in this pestilent, rebellious city."

---

[8]*liberty tree,* a Boston elm from which royal officials were hung in effigy.

"Well, I don't know as I quite agree with you about that," said Lige. "But I came here to get my tooth fixed, not to talk politics. And as long as you've spoken so pleasant, I wonder if you could help me out. You see, I'm from Lexington way—and I'm looking for a fellow named Paul Revere——"

"Paul Revere!" said the sharp-faced man, as if the name hit him like a bullet. Then he began to smile again—not a pleasant smile.

"Oh, it's Paul Revere you want, my worthy and ingenuous friend from the country," he said. "Well, I'll tell you how to find him. You go up to the first British soldier you see and ask the way. But you better give the password first."

"Password?" said Lige Butterwick, scratching his ear.

"Yes," said the sharp-faced man, and his smile got wider. "You say to that British soldier, 'Any lobsters for sale today?' Then you ask about Revere."

"But why do I talk about lobsters first?" said Lige Butterwick, kind of stubborn.

"Well, you see," said the sharp-faced man, "the British soldiers wear red coats. So they like being asked about lobsters. Try it and see." And he went away, with his shoulders shaking.

Well, that seemed queer to Lige Butterwick, but no queerer than the other things that had happened that day. All the same, he didn't quite trust the sharp-faced man, so he took care not to come too close to the British patrol when he asked them about the lobsters. And it was lucky he did, for no sooner were the words out of his mouth than the British soldiers took after him and chased him clear down to the wharves before he could get away. At that, he only managed it by hiding in an empty tar barrel, and when he got out he was certainly a sight for sore eyes.

"Well, I guess that couldn't have been the right password," he said to himself, kind of grimly, as he tried to rub off some of the tar. "All the same, I don't think soldiers ought to act like that when you ask them a civil question. But, city folks or soldiers, they can't make a fool out of me. I came here to get my tooth fixed and get it fixed I will, if I have to surprise the whole British Empire to do it."

And just then he saw a sign on a shop at the end of the wharf. And, according to my great-aunt, this was what was on the sign. It said "PAUL REVERE, SILVERSMITH" at the top, and then, under it, in smaller letters, "Large and small bells cast to order, engravings and printing done in job lots, artificial teeth sculptured and copper boilers mended, all branches of goldsmith and silversmith work and revolutions put up to take out. Express Service, Tuesdays and Fridays, to Lexington, Concord and Points West."

"Well," said Lige Butterwick, "kind of a jack-of-all-trades. Now maybe I can get my tooth fixed." And he marched up to the door.

III

Paul Revere was behind the counter when Lige came in, turning a silver bowl over and over in his hands. A man of forty-odd he was, with a quick, keen face and snapping eyes. He was wearing Boston clothes, but there was a French look about him—for his father was Apollos Rivoire from the island of Guernsey,[9] and good French Huguenot[10] stock. They'd changed the name to Revere when they crossed the water.

It wasn't such a big shop, but it had silver pieces in it that people have paid thousands for, since. And the silver pieces weren't all. There were prints and engravings of the Port of Boston and caricatures of the British and all sorts of goldsmith work, more than you could put a name to. It was a crowded place, but shipshape. And Paul Revere moved about it, quick and keen, with his eyes full of life and hot temper—the kind of man who knows what he wants to do and does it the next minute.

There were quite a few customers there when Lige Butterwick first came in—so he sort of scrooged back in a corner and waited his chance. For one thing, after the queer sign and the barber's calling him a wizard, he wanted to be sure about this fellow, Revere, and see what kind of customers came to his shop.

[9]*Guernsey* (gẽrn′zi), an island in the English Channel. Although it is ruled by England, the population is largely of French descent.
[10]*French Huguenot* (hū′gə not), French Protestant.

Well, there was a woman who wanted a christening mug for a baby and a man who wanted a print of the Boston Massacre. And then there was a fellow who passed Revere some sort of message, under cover—Lige caught the whisper, "powder" and "Sons of Liberty," though he couldn't make out the rest. And, finally, there was a very fine silk-dressed lady who seemed to be giving Revere considerable trouble. Lige peeked at her round the corner of his chair, and, somehow or other, she reminded him of a turkey-gobbler, especially the strut.

She was complaining about some silver that Paul Revere had made for her—expensive silver it must have been. And "Oh, Master Revere, I'm so disappointed!" she was saying. "When I took the things from the box, I could just have cried!"

Revere drew himself up a little at that, Lige noticed, but his voice was pleasant.

"It is I who am disappointed, madam," he said, with a little bow. "But what was the trouble? It must have been carelessly packed. Was it badly dented? I'll speak to my boy."

"Oh, no, it wasn't dented," said the turkey-gobbler lady. "But I wanted a really impressive silver service—something I can use when the Governor comes to dinner with us. I certainly *paid* for the best. And what have you given me?"

Lige waited to hear what Paul Revere would say. When he spoke, his voice was stiff.

"I have given you the best work of which I am capable, madam," he said. "It was in my hands for six months—and I think they are skillful hands."

"Oh," said the woman, and rustled her skirts. "I know you're a competent artisan, Master Revere—"

"Silversmith, if you please—" said Paul Revere, and the woman rustled again.

"Well, I don't care what you call it," she said, and then you could see her fine accent was put on like her fine clothes. "But I know I wanted a real service—something I could show my friends. And what have you given me? Oh, it's silver, if you choose. But it's just as plain and simple as a picket fence!"

Revere looked at her for a moment and Lige Butterwick thought he'd explode.

"Simple?" he said. "And plain? You pay me high compliments, madam!"

"Compliments indeed!" said the woman, and now she was getting furious. "I'm sending it back tomorrow! Why, there isn't as much as a lion or a unicorn on the cream jug. And I told you I wanted the sugar bowl covered with silver grapes! But you've given me something as bare as the hills of New England! And I won't stand it, I tell you! I'll send to England instead."

Revere puffed his cheeks and blew, but his eyes were dangerous.

"Send away, madam," he said. "We're making new things in this country—new men—new silver—perhaps, who knows, a new nation. Plain, simple, bare as the hills and rocks of New England—graceful as the boughs of her elm trees—if my silver were only like that indeed! But that is what I wish to make it. And, as for you, madam"—he stepped toward her like a cat —"with your lions and unicorns and grape leaves and your nonsense of bad ornament done by bad silversmiths—your imported bad taste and your imported British manners—puff!" And he blew at her, just the way you blow at a turkey-gobbler, till she fairly picked up her fine silk skirts and ran. Revere watched her out of the door and turned back, shaking his head.

"William!" he called to the boy who helped him in the shop. "Put up the shutters—we're closing for the day. And William—no word yet from Dr. Warren[11]?"

"Not yet, sir," said the boy, and started to put up the shutters. Then Lige Butterwick thought it was about time to make his presence known.

So he coughed, and Paul Revere whirled and Lige Butterwick felt those quick, keen eyes boring into his. He wasn't exactly afraid of them, for he was stubborn himself, but he knew this was an unexpected kind of man.

"Well, my friend," said Revere, impatiently, "and who in the world are you?"

"Well, Mr. Revere," said Lige Butterwick. "It is Mr. Revere, isn't it? It's kind of a long story. But, closing or not, you've got to listen to me. The barber told me so."

[11]*Dr. Warren.* Joseph Warren (1741-1775) was active on Boston patriotic committees from the time of the Stamp Act. It was he who sent Revere and William Dawes (Revere's less remembered companion) to Lexington to warn Hancock and Adams of the impending raid. He was killed in the Battle of Bunker Hill.

"The barber!" said Revere, kind of dumfounded.

"Uh-huh," said Lige, and opened his mouth. "You see, it's my tooth."

"Tooth!" said Revere, and stared at him as if they were both crazy. "You'd better begin at the beginning. But wait a minute. You don't talk like a Boston man. Where do you come from?"

"Oh, around Lexington way," said Lige. "And, you see—"

But the mention of Lexington seemed to throw Revere into a regular excitement. He fairly shook Lige by the shoulders.

"Lexington!" he said. "Were you there this morning?"

"Of course I was," said Lige. "That's where the barber I told you about—"

"Never mind the barber!" said Revere. "Were Mr. Hancock and Mr. Adams still at Parson Clarke's?"

"Well, they might have been, for all I know," said Lige. "But I couldn't say."

"Great heaven!" said Revere. "Is there a man in the American colonies who doesn't know Mr. Hancock and Mr. Adams?"

"There seems to be me," said Lige. "But, speaking of strangers—there *was* two of them staying at the parsonage, when I rode past. One was a handsomish man and the other looked more like a bulldog—"

"Hancock and Adams!" said Revere. "So they are still there." He took a turn or two up and down the room. "And the British ready to march!" he muttered to himself. "Did you see many soldiers as you came to my shop, Mr. Butterwick?"

"See them?" said Lige. "They chased me into a tar barrel. And there was a whole passel[12] of them up the Common[13] with guns and flags. Looked as if they meant business."

Revere took his hand and pumped it up and down.

"Thank you, Mr. Butterwick," he said.

---

[12]*passel*, crowd.

[13]*Common*, Boston Common, an open space in the heart of Boston, originally set aside for training militia and pasturing cattle. It exists as a park today.

"You're a shrewd observer. And you have done me—and the colonies—an invaluable service."

"Well, that's nice to know," said Lige. "But, speaking about this tooth of mine—"

Revere looked at him and laughed, while his eyes crinkled.

"You're a stubborn man, Mr. Butterwick," he said. "All the better. I like stubborn men. I wish we had more of them. Well, one good turn deserves another—you've helped me and I'll do my best to help you. I've made artificial teeth—but drawing them is hardly my trade. All the same, I'll do what I can for you."

So Lige sat down in a chair and opened his mouth.

"Whew!" said Revere, with his eyes dancing. His voice grew solemn. "Mr. Butterwick," he said, "it seems to be a compound, agglutinated infraction of the upper molar. I'm afraid I can't do anything about it tonight."

"But—" said Lige.

"But here's a draft—that will ease the pain for a while," said Revere, and poured some medicine into a cup. "Drink!" he said, and Lige drank. The draft was red and spicy, with a queer, sleepy taste, but pungent. It wasn't like anything Lige had ever tasted before, but he noticed it eased the pain.

"There," said Revere. "And now you go to a tavern and get a good night's rest. Come back to see me in the morning—I'll find a tooth-drawer for you, if I'm here. And—oh yes—you'd better have some liniment."

He started to rummage in a big cupboard at the back of the shop. It was dark now, with the end of day and the shutters up, and whether it was the tooth, or the tiredness, or the draft Paul Revere had given him, Lige began to feel a little queer. There was a humming in his head and a lightness in his feet. He got up and stood looking over Paul Revere's shoulder, and it seemed to him that things moved and scampered in that cupboard in a curious way, as Revere's quick fingers took down this box and that. And the shop was full of shadows and murmurings.

"It's a queer kind of a shop you've got here, Mr. Revere," he said, glad to hear the sound of his own voice.

"Well, some people think so," said Revere—and that time Lige was almost sure he saw something move in the cupboard. He coughed. "Say—what's in that little bottle?" he said, to keep his mind steady.

"That?" said Paul Revere, with a smile, and held the bottle up. "Oh, that's a little chemical experiment of mine. I call it Essence of Boston. But there's a good deal of East Wind in it."

"Essence of Boston," said Lige, with his eyes bulging. "Well, they did say you was a wizard. It's gen-u-wine magic, I suppose?"

"Genuine magic, of course," said Revere, with a chuckle. "And here's the box with your liniment. And here—"

He took down two little boxes—a silver and a pewter one—and placed them on the counter. But Lige's eyes went to the silver one—they were drawn to it, though he couldn't have told you why.

"Pick it up," said Paul Revere, and Lige did so and turned it in his hands. It was a handsome box. He could make out a growing tree and an eagle fighting a lion.[14] "It's mighty pretty work," he said.

"It's my own design," said Paul Revere. "See the stars around the edge—thirteen of them? You could make a very pretty design with stars —for a new country, say—if you wanted to—I've sometimes thought of it."

"But what's in it?" said Lige.

"What's in it?" said Paul Revere, and his voice was light but steely. "Why, what's in the air around us? Gunpowder and war and the making of a new nation. But the time isn't quite ripe yet—not quite ripe."

"You mean," said Lige, and he looked at the box very respectful, "that this-here revolution folks keep talking about—"

"Yes," said Paul Revere, and he was about to go on. But just then his boy ran in, with a letter in his hand.

"Master!" he said. "A message from Dr. Warren!"

---

[14]*eagle...lion.* The eagle symbolized the colonies; the lion, England. Revere is believed to have been the first man to use the eagle to represent America.

IV

Well, with that Revere started moving, and, when he started to move, he moved fast. He was calling for his riding boots in one breath and telling Lige Butterwick to come back tomorrow in another—and, what with all the bustle and confusion, Lige Butterwick nearly went off without his liniment after all. But he grabbed up a box from the counter, just as Revere was practically shoving him out of the door—and it wasn't till he'd got to his tavern and gone to bed for the night that he found out he'd taken the wrong box.

He found it out then because, when he went to bed, he couldn't get to sleep. It wasn't his tooth that bothered him—that had settled to a kind of dull ache and he could have slept through that. But his mind kept going over all the events of the day—the two folks he'd seen at Parson Clarke's and being chased by the British and what Revere had said to the turkey-gobbler woman—till he couldn't get any peace. He could feel something stirring in him, though he didn't know what it was.

" 'Tain't right to have soldiers chase a fellow down the street," he said to himself. "And 'tain't right to have people like that woman run down New England. No, it ain't. Oh me—I better look for that liniment of Mr. Revere's."

So he got up from his bed and went over and found his coat. Then he reached his hand in the pocket and pulled out the silver box.

Well, at first he was so flustrated that he didn't know rightly what to do. For here, as well as he could remember it, was gunpowder and war and the makings of a new nation—the revolution itself, shut up in a silver box by Paul Revere. He mightn't have believed there could be such things before he came to Boston. But now he did.

The draft was still humming in his head, and his legs felt a mite wobbly. But, being human, he was curious. "Now, I wonder what *is* inside that box," he said.

He shook the box and handled it, but that seemed to make it warmer, as if there was something alive inside it, so he stopped that right quick. Then he looked all over it for a keyhole, but there wasn't any keyhole, and, if there had been, he didn't have a key.

Then he put his ear to the box and listened hard. And it seemed to him that he heard, very tiny and far away, inside the box, the rolling fire of thousands of tiny muskets and the tiny, faraway cheers of many men. "Hold your fire!" he heard a voice say. "Don't fire till you're fired on—but, if they want a war, let it begin here!"[15] And then there was a rolling of drums and a squeal of fifes. It was small, still, and far away, but it made him shake all over, for he knew he was listening to something in the future—and something that he didn't have a right to hear. He sat down on the edge of his bed, with the box in his hands.

"Now, what am I going to do with this?" he said. "It's too big a job for one man."

Well, he thought, kind of scared, of going down to the river and throwing the box in, but, when he thought of doing it, he knew he couldn't. Then he thought of his farm near Lexington and the peaceful days. Once the revolution was out of the box, there'd be an end to that. But then he remembered what Revere had said when he was talking with the woman about the silver—the thing about building a new country and building it clean and plain. "Why, I'm not a Britisher," he thought. "I'm a New Englander. And maybe there's something beyond that—something people like Hancock and Adams know about. And, if it has to come with a revolution—well, I guess it has to come. We can't stay Britishers forever, here in this country."

He listened to the box again, and now there wasn't any shooting in it—just a queer tune[16] played on a fife. He didn't know the name of the tune, but it lifted his heart.

He got up, sort of slow and heavy. "I guess I'll have to take this back to Paul Revere," he said.

Well, the first place he went was Dr. Warren's, having heard Revere mention it, but he didn't get much satisfaction there. It took quite a while to convince them that he wasn't a spy, and, when he did, all they'd tell him was that Revere had gone over the river to Charlestown.[17] So he went down to the water front to look for a boat. And the first person he met was a very angry woman.

"No," she said, "you don't get any boats from me. There was a crazy man along here an hour ago and he wanted a boat, too, and my husband was crazy enough to take him. And then, do you know what he did?"

"No, mam," said Lige Butterwick.

"He made my husband take my best petticoat to muffle the oars so they wouldn't make a splash when they went past that Britisher ship," she said, pointing out where the man-of-war *Somerset* lay at anchor. "My best petticoat, I tell you! And when my husband comes back he'll get a piece of my mind!"

"Was his name Revere?" said Lige Butterwick. "Was he a man of forty-odd, keen-looking and kind of Frenchy?"

"I don't know what his right name is," said the woman, "but his name's mud with me. My best petticoat tore into strips and swimming in that nasty river!" And that was all he could get out of her.

All the same, he managed to get a boat at last—the story doesn't say how—and row across the river. The tide was at young flood and the moonlight bright on the water, and he passed under the shadow of the *Somerset,* right where Revere had passed. When he got to the Charlestown side, he could see the lanterns in North Church,[18] though he didn't know what they signified. Then he told the folks at Charlestown he had news for Revere and they got him a horse and so he started to ride. And, all the while, the silver box was burning his pocket.

Well, he lost his way more or less, as you well might in the darkness, and it was dawn when he came to Lexington by a side road. The dawn in that country's pretty, with the dew still on the grass. But he wasn't looking at the dawn.

---

[15]*"Hold your fire!...begin here."* This is one version of the speech of Captain John Parker, commander of the Minute Men at Lexington.

[16]*a queer tune,* probably "Yankee Doodle."

[17]*Charlestown,* a town across the Charles River from Boston. From here Revere started on his famous ride.

[18]*lanterns in North Church.* Lanterns had been hung in the spire as a signal that the British had left Boston for Concord.

He was feeling the box burn his pocket and thinking hard.

Then, all of a sudden, he reined up his tired horse. For there, on the side road, were two men carrying a trunk—and one of them was Paul Revere.

They looked at each other and Lige began to grin. For Revere was just as dirty and mud-splashed as he was—he'd warned Hancock and Adams all right, but then, on his way to Concord, he'd got caught by the British and turned loose again. So he'd gone back to Lexington to see how things were there—and now he and the other fellow were saving a trunk of papers that Hancock had left behind, so they wouldn't fall into the hands of the British.

Lige swung off his horse. "Well, Mr. Revere," he said, "you see, I'm on time for that little appointment about my tooth. And, by the way, I've got something for you." He took the box from his pocket. And then he looked over toward Lexington Green and caught his breath. For, on the Green, there was a little line of Minute Men—neighbors of his, as he knew—and, in front of them, the British regulars. And,

even as he looked, there was the sound of a gunshot, and, suddenly, smoke wrapped the front of the British line and he heard them shout as they ran forward.

Lige Butterwick took the silver box and stamped on it with his heel. And with that the box broke open—and there was a dazzle in his eyes for a moment and a noise of men shouting —and then it was gone.

"Do you know what you've done?" said Revere. "You've let out the American Revolution!"

"Well," said Lige Butterwick, "I guess it was about time. And I guess I'd better be going home, now. I've got a gun on the wall there. And I'll need it."

"But what about your tooth?" said Paul Revere.

"Oh, a tooth's a tooth," said Lige Butterwick. "But a country's a country. And anyhow, it's stopped aching."

All the same, they say Paul Revere made a silver tooth for him, after the war. But my great-aunt wasn't quite sure of it, so I won't vouch for that.

1. What kind of person is Lige Butterwick as he sets out for Boston to have a tooth pulled? What are his interests?

2. What is the effect upon Lige of (*a*) the conversation in the tavern, (*b*) his encounter with the redcoats, (*c*) the conversation between Paul Revere and the "turkey-gobbler" woman?

3. What is symbolized by the silver box? Would its meaning have been at all apparent to Lige on the morning of his eventful day? Why does he stamp on it? What does this action reveal about the change that has come over him in less than twenty-four hours?

4. What idea of Paul Revere do you draw from this story? Does it differ in any way from the accounts of him you have read in history? If so, how? Explain why you like or dislike Benét's characterization of Revere.

5. What kind of person narrates this story? Why is the character of the narrator well suited to the unfolding of such a story?

6. What "tall tale" elements appear in the story? Considering the story as a whole, would you describe it as a typical tall tale? Why, or why not?

Understanding from a historical perspective

One of the joys of reading for most people is being aware of the significance of events that are completely hidden from the characters in the tale. This is particularly true of stories set in the past, in which famous names and noteworthy times and places jog the reader's memory and make him anticipate what is to come. Much of the pleasure of reading "A Tooth for Paul Revere" lies in this historical understanding of things of which Lige Butterwick is ignorant. For example, when Lige rides into Lexington to have his tooth pulled at the barber's, he hears about "a couple of men called Hancock and Adams who were staying at Parson Clarke's." The reader realizes who these men are and senses that Lige is about to be drawn into historic events, but Lige thinks only about his aching tooth.

Run through the story again, making a list of names and phrases that have more significance for modern readers than they had for Lige.

Extending interests

You may enjoy reading to the class a poem based on the same historical events that served as a background for "A Tooth for Paul Revere." Among poems that might be chosen are: "Paul Revere's Ride," by Henry Wadsworth Longfellow; "Concord Hymn," by Ralph Waldo Emerson; and "New England's Chevy Chase," by Edward Everett Hale, in *A Home Book of Verse for Young Folks,* edited by Burton Stevenson.

The Declaration of Independence

First among the state papers of the United States is the Declaration announcing to the world the separation from Great Britain. It is, in outline, the colonists' story of ten years of conflict, as well as a statement of the political principles which Americans had come to believe in. It is also a presentation of a case to the world, skillfully directed chiefly against George III rather than against Parliament or the English people. The chief author was Thomas Jefferson, but John Adams and Benjamin Franklin were also on the committee which composed it, and numerous changes were made by the Continental Congress before final adoption. It was agreed to and "authenticated" by the signatures of the president and secretary of the Congress on July 4, 1776. The formal signing by the members of the Congress took place on August 2. Today, the most important passage of the Declaration is the second paragraph, upon which rests the faith of Americans in self-government.

W HEN, in the course of human events, it becomes necessary for one people to dissolve the political bands which have connected them with another, and to assume, among the Powers of the earth, the separate and equal station to which the Laws of Nature and of Nature's God entitle them, a decent respect to the opinions of mankind requires that they should declare the causes which impel them to the separation.

We hold these truths to be self-evident: that all men are created equal; that they are endowed by their Creator with certain inalienable Rights; that among these are Life, Liberty, and the pursuit of Happiness. That, to secure these

Rights, Governments are instituted among Men, deriving their just powers from the consent of the governed—That, whenever any Form of Government becomes destructive of these ends, it is the Right of the People to alter or abolish it, and to institute new Government, laying its foundation on such Principles, and organizing its Powers in such form, as to them shall seem most likely to effect their Safety and Happiness. Prudence, indeed, will dictate that Governments long established should not be changed for light and transient causes; and, accordingly, all experience hath shown that mankind are more disposed to suffer, while evils are sufferable, than to right themselves by abolishing the forms to which they are accustomed. But, when a long train of abuses and usurpations, pursuing invariably the same Object, evinces a design to reduce them under absolute Despotism, it is their right, it is their duty, to throw off such Government, and to provide new Guards for their future security. Such has been the patient sufferance of these Colonies, and such is now the necessity which constrains them to alter their former Systems of Government. The history of the present King of Great Britain is a history of repeated injuries and usurpations, all having in direct object the establishment of an absolute Tyranny over these States. To prove this, let Facts be submitted to a candid world:

He has refused his Assent to Laws the most wholesome and necessary for the public good.

He has forbidden his Governors to pass Laws of immediate and pressing importance, unless suspended in their operation till his Assent should be obtained; and, when so suspended, he has utterly neglected to attend to them.

He has refused to pass other Laws for the accommodation of large districts of people, unless those people would relinquish the rights of Representation in the Legislature; a right inestimable to them, and formidable to tyrants only.

He has called together legislative bodies at places unusual, uncomfortable, and distant from the depository of their Public Records, for the sole purpose of fatiguing them into compliance with his measures.

He has dissolved Representative Houses repeatedly for opposing, with manly firmness, his invasions on the rights of the people.

He has refused for a long time after such dissolutions to cause others to be elected; whereby the Legislative Powers, incapable of Annihilation, have returned to the People at large for their exercise; the State remaining, in the meantime, exposed to all the dangers of invasions from without, and convulsions within.

He has endeavored to prevent the Population of these States; for that purpose obstructing the Laws for Naturalization of Foreigners; refusing to pass others to encourage their migrations hither, and raising the conditions of new Appropriations of Lands.

He has obstructed the Administration of Justice by refusing his Assent to Laws for establishing Judiciary Powers.

He has made Judges dependent on his Will alone for the tenure of their offices, and the amount and Payment of their salaries.

He has erected a multitude of New Offices, and sent hither swarms of Officers to harass our People and eat out their substance.

He has kept among us, in times of Peace, Standing Armies, without the Consent of our legislatures.

He has affected to render the Military independent of and superior to the Civil Power.

He has combined with others to subject us to a jurisdiction foreign to our constitution, and unacknowledged by our laws: giving his Assent to their Acts of pretended Legislation:

For quartering large bodies of armed troops among us;

For protecting them, by a mock Trial, from Punishment for any Murders which they should commit on the Inhabitants of these States;

For cutting off our Trade with all parts of the world;

For imposing Taxes on us without our Consent;

For depriving us, in many cases, of the benefits of Trial by Jury;

For transporting us beyond Seas to be tried for pretended offences;

For abolishing the free System of English Laws in a neighboring Province,[1] establishing therein an Arbitrary government, and enlarging its Boundaries, so as to render it at once an example and fit instrument for introducing the same absolute rule into these Colonies;

For taking away our Charters, abolishing our most valuable Laws, and altering, fundamentally, the Forms of our Governments;

For suspending our own Legislatures, and declaring themselves invested with Power to legislate for us in all cases whatsoever.

He has abdicated Government here by declaring us out of his Protection, and waging War against us.

He has plundered our seas, ravaged our Coasts, burnt our towns, and destroyed the Lives of our People.

He is, at this time, transporting large Armies of foreign Mercenaries to complete the works of death, desolation, and tyranny, already begun with circumstances of Cruelty and Perfidy scarcely paralleled in the most barbarous ages,

---

[1] *a neighboring Province,* Quebec, which England had acquired as a result of the French and Indian Wars. According to the Quebec Act of 1774, French Civil Law was established, a royal governor and council were appointed, and the boundaries were enlarged to include much of the country between the Ohio and the Mississippi rivers.

and totally unworthy the Head of a civilized nation.

He has constrained our fellow Citizens, taken Captive on the high Seas, to bear Arms against their Country, to become the executioners of their friends and Brethren, or to fall themselves by their Hands.

He has excited domestic insurrections amongst us, and has endeavored to bring on the inhabitants of our frontiers the merciless Indian Savages, whose known rule of warfare is an undistinguished destruction of all ages, sexes, and conditions.

In every stage of these Oppressions, We have Petitioned for Redress, in the most humble terms: Our repeated Petitions have been answered only by repeated injury. A Prince, whose character is thus marked by every act which may define a Tyrant, is unfit to be the ruler of a free People.

Nor have We been wanting in attentions to our British brethren. We have warned them, from time to time, of attempts by their legislature to extend an unwarrantable jurisdiction over us. We have reminded them of the circumstances of our emigration and settlement here. We have appealed to their native justice and magnanimity, and we have conjured them, by the ties of our common kindred, to disavow these usurpations, which would inevitably interrupt our connections and correspondence. They, too, have been deaf to the voice of justice and of consanguinity. We must, therefore, acquiesce in the necessity which denounces our Separation, and hold them, as we hold the rest of mankind—Enemies in War—in Peace, Friends.

WE, THEREFORE, the REPRESENTATIVES of the UNITED STATES OF AMERICA, in GENERAL CONGRESS Assembled, appealing to the Supreme Judge of the world for the rectitude of our intentions, Do, in the Name and by the Authority of the good People of these Colonies, solemnly PUBLISH and DECLARE, That these United Colonies are, and of Right ought to be, FREE AND INDEPENDENT STATES; that they are Absolved from all Allegiance to the British Crown, and that all political connection between them and the State of Great Britain is, and ought to be, totally dissolved; and that, as

FREE and INDEPENDENT STATES, they have full Power to levy War, conclude Peace, contract Alliances, establish Commerce, and to do all other Acts and Things which INDEPENDENT STATES may of right do. And, for the support of this Declaration, with a firm reliance on the Protection of Divine Providence, we mutually pledge to each other our Lives, our Fortunes, and our Sacred Honor.

CAN YOU UNDERSTAND THE DOCUMENT?

1. Under what conditions did the signers of the Declaration of Independence believe men are justified in setting up a new government? What did they give as a reason for making this document public?

2. Why is the second paragraph of the Declaration considered the most important passage? To what rights does it say all men are entitled? What is the significance of the phrase, "pursuit of happiness"?

3. Why was it shrewd to lay most of the blame for the conflict with England on George III? Name some of the abuses of which the makers of the Declaration declared him guilty.

4. What are the most emotional passages of the document?

Thomas Jefferson's ideas

Thomas Jefferson himself chose his epitaph. It reads: "Here was buried Thomas Jefferson, author of the Declaration of American Independence, of the statute of Virginia for religious freedom, and father of the University of Virginia." No mention of his years as Minister to France, as Secretary of State in Washington's Cabinet, or as President of the United States! The three things by which he chose to be remembered highlight his belief in political democracy, in religious freedom, and in education.

Thomas Jefferson's ideas had a greater effect upon shaping the institutions of his new country than did those of any other man. And more than any other of the Founding Fathers he possessed the ability to put his ideas about democracy and all that a true democracy includes into clear, precise, and inspiring language. Glance again through the three selections by Jefferson included in this unit. Which passage do you believe best expresses each of these things: (a) his trust in the people; (b) the rights to which those people are entitled; (c) the position of minorities; (d) the importance of education for all? What idea do the three selections taken together give you of Jefferson's interests and sympathies?

Second Inaugural Address, March 4, 1865

ABRAHAM LINCOLN

The War Between the States was undoubtedly the most tragic conflict in which our nation has engaged. Lincoln recognized that both North and South believed themselves in the right, that neither was wholly so, and that vindictiveness has no place in a democratic society however bitter its divisions. His forgiving spirit and his vision of a nation once more united shine through the simple words of his Second Inaugural Address.

FELLOW COUNTRYMEN: At this second appearing to take the oath of the presidential office, there is less occasion for an extended address than there was at the first. Then a statement, somewhat in detail, of a course to be pursued, seemed fitting and proper. Now, at the expiration of four years, during which public declarations have been constantly called forth on every point and phase of the great contest which still absorbs the attention and engrosses the energies of the nation, little that is new could be presented. The progress of our arms, upon which all else chiefly depends, is as well known to the public as to myself; and it is, I trust, reasonably satisfactory and encouraging to all. With high hope for the future, no prediction in regard to it is ventured.

On the occasion corresponding to this four years ago, all thoughts were anxiously directed to an impending civil war. All dreaded it—all sought to avert it. While the inaugural address was being delivered from this place, devoted altogether to saving the Union without war, insurgent agents were in the city seeking to destroy it without war—seeking to dissolve the Union, and divide effects, by negotiation. Both parties deprecated war; but one of them would make war rather than let the nation survive; and the other would accept war rather than let it perish. And the war came.

One eighth of the whole population were colored slaves, not distributed generally over the Union, but localized in the southern part of it. These slaves constituted a peculiar and powerful interest. All knew that this interest was, somehow, the cause of the war. To strengthen, perpetuate, and extend this interest was the object for which the insurgents would rend the Union, even by war; while the government claimed no right to do more than to restrict the territorial enlargement of it.

Neither party expected for the war the magnitude or the duration which it has already attained. Neither anticipated that the cause of the conflict might cease with, or even before, the conflict itself should cease. Each looked for an easier triumph and a result less fundamental and astounding. Both read the same Bible, and pray to the same God; and each invokes His aid against the other. It may seem strange that any man should dare to ask a just God's assistance in wringing their bread from the sweat of other men's faces; but let us judge not, that we be not judged.[1] The prayers of both could not be answered—that of neither has been answered fully.

The Almighty has His own purposes. "Woe unto the world because of offenses! for it must needs be that offenses come; but woe to that man by whom the offense cometh."[2] If we shall suppose that American slavery is one of those offenses which in the providence of God, must needs come, but which, having continued

[1]*judge not...judged.* Matthew 7:1.
[2]*"Woe unto the world...the offense cometh."* Matthew 18:5.

through His appointed time, He now wills to remove, and that He gives to both North and South this terrible war, as the woe due to those by whom the offense came, shall we discern therein any departure from those divine attributes which the believers in a living God always ascribe to Him? Fondly do we hope—fervently do we pray—that this mighty scourge of war may speedily pass away. Yet, if God wills that it continue until all the wealth piled by the bondman's two hundred and fifty years of unrequited toil shall be sunk, and until every drop of blood drawn with the lash shall be paid by another drawn with the sword, as was said three thousand years ago, so still it must be said, "The judgments of the Lord are true and righteous altogether."[3]

With malice toward none; with charity for all; with firmness in the right, as God gives us to see the right, let us strive on to finish the work we are in; to bind up the nation's wounds; to care for him who shall have borne the battle, and for his widow and his orphan—to do all which may achieve and cherish a just and lasting peace among ourselves, and with all nations.

---

[3]"The judgments...righteous altogether." Psalms 19:9.

WHAT WERE LINCOLN'S VIEWS?

1. What does Lincoln say was the purpose of the North in the war?
2. What, judging by this address, was his own attitude toward slavery?
3. How did Lincoln feel about the preservation of the Union?
4. How are the quotations from the Bible useful in the development of the point being made in the final paragraphs?
5. Why is this speech regarded as a great piece of literature? Consider such points as: (a) word choice, (b) word order, (c) variation in sentence structure, (d) figures of speech, (e) mood, or tone.

Extending interests

Read Lincoln's Gettysburg Address aloud several times in preparation for reading it to the class. Your reading of the speech will be more interesting to your classmates if you preface it with a brief account of the circumstances under which it was given.

Message Asking for Declaration of War, December 8, 1941

FRANKLIN DELANO ROOSEVELT

When Abraham Lincoln gave his Second Inaugural Address in Washington, it was weeks before people in the far corners of the nation heard what their President had said. But when, seventy-six years later, Franklin Delano Roosevelt addressed Congress to ask for a declaration of war against Japan, his message was heard from coast to coast. Once again a united people sprang forward to fight for the liberties they had cherished since the founding of the nation.

MR. VICE PRESIDENT, Mr. Speaker, Members of the Senate and the House of Representatives:

Yesterday, December 7th, 1941—a date which will live in infamy—the United States of America was suddenly and deliberately attacked by naval and air forces of the Empire of Japan.

The United States was at peace with that nation, and, at the solicitation of Japan, was still in conversation[1] with its government and its Emperor looking toward the maintenance of peace in the Pacific. Indeed, one hour after Japanese air squadrons had commenced bombing in the American island of Oahu,[2] the Japanese ambassador to the United States and his colleague delivered to our Secretary of State a formal reply to a recent American message. While this reply stated that it seemed useless to continue the existing diplomatic negotiations, it contained no threat or hint of war or of armed attack.

It will be recorded that the distance of Hawaii from Japan makes it obvious that the attack was deliberately planned many days or even weeks ago. During the intervening time the Japanese government has deliberately sought

---

[1]still in conversation. Kichisaburo Nomura (kē′chē′-sä′bů rō nô mü′rä′) became ambassador to the United States in November, 1940; a year later a special envoy, Saburo Kurusu (sä′bů′rō′ kü′rü′sü′) arrived in Washington to negotiate with the Department of State.
[2]Oahu (ō ä′hü), third largest of the Hawaiian Islands. Pearl Harbor, the American naval base, is located there.

to deceive the United States by false statements and expressions of hope for continued peace.

The attack yesterday on the Hawaiian Islands has caused severe damage[3] to American naval and military forces. I regret to tell you that very many American lives have been lost. In addition, American ships have been reported torpedoed on the high seas between San Francisco and Honolulu.

Yesterday the Japanese government also launched an attack against Malaya. Last night Japanese forces attacked Hong Kong. Last night Japanese forces attacked Guam. Last night Japanese forces attacked the Philippine Islands. Last night the Japanese attacked Wake Island. And this morning the Japanese attacked Midway Island.

Japan has, therefore, undertaken a surprise offensive extending throughout the Pacific area. The facts of yesterday and today speak for themselves. The people of the United States have already formed their opinions and well understand the implications to the very life and safety of our nation.

As Commander in Chief of the Army and Navy I have directed that all measures be taken for our defense, but always will our whole nation remember the character of the onslaught against us. No matter how long it may take us to overcome this premeditated invasion, the American people in their righteous might will win through to absolute victory. I believe that I interpret the will of the Congress and of the people when I assert that we will not only defend ourselves to the uttermost but will make it very certain that this form of treachery shall never again endanger us.

Hostilities exist. There is no blinking at the fact that our people, our territory, and our interests are in grave danger. With confidence in our armed forces, with the unbounded determination of our people, we will gain the inevitable triumph, so help us God.

---

[3]*severe damage.* The extent of damage was withheld until December 5, 1942. Ten ships, including five battleships, were sunk or put out of commission; eight ships were damaged; eighty aircraft were destroyed and seventy disabled; over 2300 enlisted men and officers were killed and over 1200 wounded.

I ask that the Congress declare that since the unprovoked and dastardly attack by Japan on Sunday, December 7th, 1941, a state of war has existed between the United States and the Japanese Empire.

HOW DID ROOSEVELT SAY IT?

1. What circumstances attending the Japanese attack led Roosevelt to characterize December 7, 1941, as "a date which will live in infamy"?

2. How, in this short address, did Roosevelt manage to impress on the American people the gravity and the magnitude of the attack?

3. Why do you suppose Roosevelt made this address so simple, with so few flourishes of rhetoric? What effective phrases and emotion-laden words did he use?

The Future for Democracy

VANNEVAR BUSH

Between 1942 and 1946 Vannevar Bush was chairman of the Joint Committee on New Weapons and Equipment of the Joint United States Chiefs of Staffs; in 1950 he became chairman of the National Science Foundation. No person, in other words, is better informed about the much-discussed problem of modern science and its enormous power for evil and for good in a world harassed by war and threats of war.

IF WE LOSE our liberties it will be because we abandon them.

It is a hazardous world; it has always been a hazardous world, beset by the perils of harsh nature and the greater perils of harsh men. Ambition and cunning and the ignorance of multitudes have created rigid systems that have suppressed all liberties, and from these men have broken away into freedom at times, have

---

"The Future for Democracy," adapted from *Modern Arms and Free Men.* Copyright, 1949, by The Trustees of Vannevar Bush Trust. Reprinted by permission of Simon and Schuster, Publishers.

become confused in their councils, and have again succumbed. This time there is hope, for free men have at last created a democracy more effective, as long as it retains its hallmark,[1] than any dictatorship can ever be in dealing with the intricacies of civilization.

There have been recurrent wars, and these have harassed men in their progress toward health, the control of the forces of nature, and the blessings of saved wealth, harassed but not halted advance toward better material things. They have burdened the spirit of man and kept his eyes on the mud about him when he might perhaps have lifted them to the heights.

Now comes the application of science, and it renders war more swift and more rapidly destructive of life and goods. It calls, as never before, for intelligence and common action among whole peoples for its prosecution.

There need be no more great wars; yet there may be. If democracy enhances its latent strength, and free men join in a common purpose, resisting the temptations of avarice and the diversions of petty causes, they can prevent great wars. They can finally mold the whole earth in their pattern of freedom and create one world under law. If democracy loses its touch, then no great war will be needed in order to overwhelm it. If it keeps and enhances its strength, no great war need come again. Yet there is chance and change, a great war may come in ways we do not see, and free men must be ready.

Still, the specter of war should not paralyze as does the glare of the cobra. To intrigue and deception there is now added the weapon of terror in the armament of those who would dominate. All these weapons must be resisted in the uneasy days of peace. Strength cannot be built in unreasoning fear, and strength is essential to prevent a holocaust. Fear cannot be banished, but it can be calm and without panic, and it can be mitigated by reason and evaluation. A new great war would not end the progress of civilization, even in the days of the riven atom, even with the threat of disease marshaled for conquest.[2] It is even possible that defenses may become tightened, not made absolute, but competent to halt the full flood of death from the air. As science goes forward it distributes its uses both to those who destroy and to those who preserve. A great war would be terrible; it would not utterly destroy. It need not destroy democracy, for the organization of free men tends to become refined under stress, whether the stress be hot or cold, and meets its greatest hazards when the times are soft. This has always been true since men have begun to learn their strength in freedom.

The course of history is determined by the faith that men are guided by. If they misread the lessons of expanding knowledge and in their brazen egotism believe that all things are known or knowable, then they will see nothing but an endlessly repeating pattern of sordid strife, the ascendancy of ruthlessness and cunning, man damned to exist a little time on an earth where there is nothing higher than to seize and kill and dominate. If they see beyond this they will see by faith, and not by reading instruments or combining numbers. They may look beyond by religious faith, or they may look merely because they feel validity in the heart's desire and conviction that good will is not a delusion. If they have faith they will build, and they will grow strong that their buildings may endure.

Their greatest buildings will be those of relations between man and man, systems and organizations and law. If they build well the structure will preserve the resourcefulness and initiative of freedom, and further the urge to create, with no stifling regimentation or deadening mediocrity. They will build so that the ambition of youth may have an outlet without artificial barriers, so that genius may rise and innovate for the benefit of all. They will build their structure so as to marshal their full strength in powerful array, designed to deal with assault of any form, whether it come in the full light or skulk in the dark.

If they build thus, and keep the faith, no power on earth can destroy what they create.

---

[1]*hallmark,* originally a mark used by goldsmiths to guarantee the purity of their product; here used to mean *authenticity.*

[2]*disease marshaled for conquest,* an allusion to "germ warfare."

1. What arguments does Vannevar Bush advance to prove the statement with which he begins his essay?

2. What does he regard as the main steps to be taken to avoid war?

3. What view of science does the essay present? How does this view compare with that outlined by David Lilienthal in "Machines With and Without Freedom" (pages 172-175)?

4. Does Vannevar Bush's essay give you more confidence about the future? Why, or why not?

Understanding the effect of figurative language

1. In his discussion of war and its effect upon men, Vannevar Bush makes frequent use of figurative language. Explain the figurative expressions in the sentences below and analyze what effect is gained by their use.

(a) They [wars] have burdened the spirit of man and kept his eyes on the mud about him when he might perhaps have lifted them to the heights.

(b) Still, the specter of war should not paralyze as does the glare of the cobra.

(c) It is even possible that defenses may become ...competent to halt the full flood of death from the air.

(d) It [a great war] need not destroy democracy, for the organization of free men tends to become refined under stress, whether the stress be hot or cold, and meets its greatest hazards when the times are soft.

2. In speaking of the future of men in a democracy, Vannevar Bush writes: "If they have faith they will build, and they will grow strong that their buildings may endure." How does he develop this "building" metaphor? Why is this metaphor especially appropriate to the essay?

Know your words

The words listed below will be valuable additions to your vocabulary. Study each word, checking its pronunciation and meaning in your Glossary if necessary. Then read the sentences below and decide which one of the listed words belongs in each sentence. On a sheet of paper write the appropriate word after the sentence number. Three of the words will not be used.

latent	holocaust
recurrent	succumb
egotism	validity
innovate	intricacy

1. Much of man's trouble can be traced to his _____.

2. He makes little effort to check the _____ of his conclusions.

3. Unthinkingly he is apt to _____ to the counsels of any new voice.

4. Thus, much of the _____ power of democracy remains undiscovered.

5. Man continues to face _____ crises.

The Larger View

I. Over one hundred and fifty years of life in the United States have only served to prove the truth of Thomas Jefferson's ideas as to what the principles of democratic government should be. The following statements are taken from writings of Jefferson that you have studied in this unit. Read each statement carefully, identifying the selection from which it is taken and talking over with your classmates its essential meaning. Then consider each statement in relation to the other selections from this unit or the outside reading you have done. What examples can you cite in which adherence to one of Jefferson's ideas is shown? Can you point out instances where disregard of Jefferson's ideas has led to unhappiness, injustice, or war?

1. We hold these truths to be self-evident: that all men are created equal; that they are endowed by their Creator with certain inalienable Rights; that among these are Life, Liberty, and the pursuit of Happiness.

2. Every government degenerates when trusted to the rulers of the people alone. The people themselves therefore are its only safe depositories. And

to render even them safe, their minds must be improved to a certain degree.

3. A jealous care of the right of election by the people, a mild and safe corrective of abuses, which are lopped by the sword of revolution where peaceable remedies are unprovided.

4. All too will bear in mind this sacred principle, that though the will of the majority is in all cases to prevail, that will, to be rightful, must be reasonable; that the minority possess their equal rights, which equal laws must protect, and to violate would be oppression.

5. I know indeed that some honest men feel that a republican government cannot be strong; that this government is not strong enough. But would the honest patriot, in the full tide of successful experiment, abandon a government which has so far kept us free and firm on the theoretic and visionary fear that this government, the world's best hope, may, by possibility, want energy to preserve itself? I trust not. I believe this, on the contrary, the strongest government on earth.

II. Some of the following individuals appear in "The Price of Liberty"; some do not. Explain how each one represents some phase of the continuing struggle of Americans to achieve the privileges of a free society for all.

1. The Gray Champion
2. Henry Cogdal
3. A poor man casting his vote for president
4. Thomas Jefferson
5. An Italian immigrant learning English in an adult education class
6. Fiorello La Guardia
7. Paul Revere
8. A girl studying history in a free public high school
9. A refugee from Europe attending church services
10. Abraham Lincoln
11. A naturalized American casting his first vote
12. Lone Wolf
13. Lige Butterwick

MORE GOOD READING

BELL, MARGARET ELIZABETH, *The Totem Casts a Shadow*. (Morrow) In this love story of Alaska in the 1880's, the prejudice of white settlers against Indians threatens the happiness of Gregory Monroe. How he defies his father and marries his Indian sweetheart and how the other members of the family react form a thoughtful, interesting story.

BENÉT, ROSEMARY and STEPHEN VINCENT, *A Book of Americans*. (Rinehart) In this collection of light, rollicking verses the Benéts call the roll of famous Americans from Pocahontas and Johnny Appleseed to Abraham Lincoln and Woodrow Wilson.

BOWEN, CATHERINE DRINKER, *Yankee from Olympus; Justice Holmes and His Family*. (Little) Through this always human, always engrossing biography of a great justice of the Supreme Court, the reader learns how the courts protect the liberties of the American citizen.

CARSON, JULIA M., *Son of Thunder; Patrick Henry*. (Longmans) You'll find it interesting to trace Patrick Henry's life from the days when he was an average boy who hated school until he became a fiery protector of the rights of American citizens.

COOPER, JAMES FENIMORE, *The Spy*. (Scribner) Harvey Birch posed as a peddler, but in reality he was a secret agent employed by Washington. There's plenty of suspense and action in this spy story of the Revolution.

COOPER, KENT, *Anna Zenger, Mother of Freedom*. (Farrar) This is the story of Anna Zenger, of her husband Peter, imprisoned for publishing the truth, and of their battle to establish freedom of the press in America.

DAUGHERTY, JAMES, *Abraham Lincoln*. (Viking) The heroic character of one of the best loved of all Americans emerges clearly in this fine biography especially written for students.

EATON, JEANETTE, *Leader By Destiny; George Washington, Man and Patriot.* (Harcourt) Miss Eaton's well-written biography portrays the gradual growth of a Virginia gentleman into a great leader who, both as general and as president, fought for the liberties of Americans.

ERDMAN, LOULA GRACE, *Fair Is the Morning.* (Longmans) Connie Thurman believed that rural schools needed experienced teachers. What happens when she turns down a position in a fine new school to teach in the poorest school in the county makes an interesting story.

FISHER, DOROTHY CANFIELD, *Seasoned Timber.* (Harcourt) When the issue of race prejudice becomes involved in the township election in Windward County, Vermont, Timothy Hulme, principal of the academy, and his students get into the fight. You'll find this novel full of life-like people and believable situations.

FORBES, ESTHER, *Paul Revere and the World He Lived In.* (Houghton) All the aspects of the many-sided life of Paul Revere are developed in this fascinating picture of a man and his times. If you prefer fiction to biography, try the same author's *Johnny Tremain* (Houghton), the story of a Boston apprentice who grows to manhood in the stirring days of the Revolution.

FORD, PAUL LEICESTER, *Janice Meredith.* (Dodd) The central figure in this exciting historical novel is a beautiful girl who becomes involved in several perilous episodes during the Revolutionary War. You'll be particularly interested in the part Washington plays.

GARST, DORIS SHANNON, *Crazy Horse.* (Houghton) This fictionized biography follows the great Sioux leader from his boyhood to his defeat of Custer and his pathetic death. Here in an account full of action and suspense the reader learns of the last days of Sioux freedom from the point of view of the Indian.

HUNGERFORD, EDWARD BUELL, *Escape to Danger.* (Wilcox) Nat Huntley, the hero of this story based on actual events, is a young Yankee seaman who is captured by the British during the Revolution and thrown into Mill Prison. His escape from prison, his flight to France to join John Paul Jones, and his part in battles on the *Bonne Homme Richard* provide plenty of excitement.

LISITZKY, GENEVIEVE, *Thomas Jefferson.* (Viking) This biography paints a vivid picture of Jefferson and the great part he played in the development of democracy in the United States.

MEANS, FLORENCE CRANNELL, *The Moved Outers.* (Houghton) Sue Ohara, a California high-school girl of Japanese-American descent, moves with her family to a relocation camp after the Japanese attack on Pearl Harbor. The way in which this change in her life affects Sue will interest all girls.

MORROW, HONORÉ WILLSIE, *Great Captain; the Lincoln Trilogy.* (Morrow) Three novels— *Forever Free, With Malice Toward None,* and *The Last Full Measure*—make up this fine trilogy dealing with Lincoln's years as president.

PAGE, ELIZABETH, *Tree of Liberty.* (Rinehart) This long, interest-packed novel covers the years from 1754 to 1806 and shows the part three generations of an American family played in the half century when the nation was taking form.

PATTERSON, EMMA L., *Midnight Patriot.* (Longmans) Philip Van Dorn had no desire to serve as a secret agent for the patriots; he knew that doing so might cost him his reputation and the love of his wife. But he did become a spy—and therein lies the plot of a very exciting story.

ROOSEVELT, ELEANOR, and FERRIS, HELEN, *Partners: United Nations and Youth.* (Doubleday) This book for and about young people will help you to see your contemporaries in other lands with sympathetic interest and understanding.

RUSH, WILLIAM, *Red Fox of the Kinapoo.* (Longmans) This tale of the Nez Percé Indians between 1872 and 1877 gives an honest picture of Indian pride and courage. The principal character is John Child, who was educated in the white man's school but who returns to help Chief Joseph make his last stand against the land-hungry settlers.

SHERWOOD, ROBERT, *Roosevelt and Hopkins.* (Harper) The mature reader will appreciate this intimate account of important people and great events during World War II.

WASHINGTON, BOOKER T., *Up from Slavery.* (Doubleday) No student can fail to understand this simply written autobiography of a Negro slave who became a famous educator yet never lost touch with the needs of his people.

UNIT VI: THE PURSUIT OF HAPPINESS

LIFE, liberty—and the pursuit of happiness: these, wrote Jefferson, are among the inalienable rights of men; that is, we cannot take them from another even if we wish to. American writers, as the pages which follow will show, have had much to say about the pursuit of happiness—its obstacles, its innumerable bypaths, its lasting satisfactions. As the plains and mountains and rivers have unfolded like a great panorama to successive waves of men and women from many nations and of many races, America has echoed with laughter and with tears, with music and with the sounds of work and machinery, with song and with story. The farms, the small towns, and the great cities have been created by men and women, with the help of their dreams. And Americans have found it all good, for the most part, although not always as good as it might be. It is a spacious land, this one of ours, and all the powerful forces of modern technology, which tend usually toward standardizing all things, have not been able to destroy its diversity. Nowhere, perhaps, has the pursuit of happiness led people into more different paths.

Our literature tells us not only that what is happiness for one person may be boredom for another, but also that here in America there is room for more than one version of the good life. To have a sympathetic insight of the other fellow's way is the first and greatest step toward living with him happily.

We turn, then, to writing which is a revelation of history and of ideals through personal, first-hand records of the ways in which men and women in America have looked at their work and play, their companionship with others, and their own personal faith.

227

Farm and City

I Hear America Singing

WALT WHITMAN

Of all our American poets, none appreciated more fully than Walt Whitman the satisfactions of living and working in a democracy or spoke more vigorously of them. In this brief poem, first published in 1860, he interprets for us what to him was the essence of America—a nation of people who chose their own varied methods of living and labored with a song on their lips.

I HEAR America singing, the varied carols I
    hear,
Those of mechanics, each one singing his as it
    should be blithe and strong,
The carpenter singing his as he measures his
    plank or beam,
The mason singing his as he makes ready for
    work, or leaves off work,
The boatman singing what belongs to him in
    his boat, the deck hand singing on the steam-
    boat deck,   5
The shoemaker singing as he sits on his bench,
    the hatter singing as he stands,
The woodcutter's song, the plowboy's on his
    way in the morning, or at noon intermission
    or at sundown,
The delicious singing of the mother, or of the
    young wife at work, or of the girl sewing or
    washing,
Each singing what belongs to him or her and
    to none else,
The day what belongs to the day—at night the
    party of young fellows, robust, friendly,   10
Singing with open mouths their strong melodi-
    ous songs.

WHAT SONGS DOES AMERICA SING?

1. What, judging from this poem, did Walt Whitman think was the most important element in happiness?

2. What does Whitman imply in line 9, "Each singing what belongs to him or her and to none else"?

3. What does this poem tell you about the kind of life which was common in the United States about a hundred years ago? If Whitman were writing this poem today, what kinds of workers do you think he might substitute for some of those he has named?

Life on the Farm

SAMUEL CLEMENS

For many generations, Americans were a rural people and looked for happiness in life on the farm. In
his autobiography Samuel Clemens (1835-1910), who
is perhaps better known by his pseudonym, Mark
Twain, recalled lovingly what a wonderful place a
Missouri farm was for a boy more than a hundred
years ago. He gives us a rosy view of the type of life
which was probably most desired by our forefathers,
a life, moreover, which millions of them achieved for
themselves and for their families. Its rewards were
self-sufficiency and freedom; its philosophy was that
rugged individualism which has become more and
more difficult to preserve in an interdependent world.

MY UNCLE, John A. Quarles, was a farmer,
and his place was in the country four
miles from Florida.[1]...I have not come across a
better man than he was. I was his guest for two or
three months every year, from the fourth year
after we removed to Hannibal till I was eleven
or twelve years old. I have never consciously
used him or his wife in a book, but his farm
has come very handy to me in literature once
or twice. In *Huck Finn* and in *Tom Sawyer, Detective* I moved it down to Arkansas. It was all
of six hundred miles, but it was no trouble; it
was not a very large farm—five hundred acres,
perhaps—but I could have done it if it had been
twice as large. And as for the morality of it, I
cared nothing for that; I would move a state if
the exigencies of literature required it.

It was a heavenly place for a boy, that farm
of my Uncle John's. The house was a double
log one, with a spacious floor (roofed in) connecting it with the kitchen. In the summer the
table was set in the middle of that shady and
breezy floor, and the sumptuous meals—well, it
makes me cry to think of them. Fried chicken,
roast pig; wild and tame turkeys, ducks, and
geese; venison just killed; squirrels, rabbits,
pheasants, partridges, prairie chickens; biscuits,
hot batter cakes, hot buckwheat cakes, hot
wheat bread, hot rolls, hot corn pone; fresh corn
boiled on the ear, succotash, butter beans, string
beans, tomatoes, peas, Irish potatoes, sweet
potatoes; buttermilk, sweet milk, clabber; water-
melons, muskmelons, cantaloupes—all fresh
from the garden; apple pie, peach pie, pumpkin
pie, apple dumplings, peach cobbler—I can't
remember the rest.

The way that the things were cooked was
perhaps the main splendor—particularly a certain few of the dishes. For instance, the corn
bread, the hot biscuits and wheat bread, and
the fried chicken. These things have never been
properly cooked in the North—in fact, no one
there is able to learn the art, so far as my experience goes. The North thinks it knows how to
make corn bread, but this is a mere superstition.
Perhaps no bread in the world is quite so good
as Southern corn bread, and perhaps no bread
in the world is quite so bad as the Northern
imitation of it. The North seldom tries to fry
chicken, and this is well; the art cannot be
learned north of the line of Mason and Dixon,[2]
nor anywhere in Europe. This is not hearsay;
it is experience that is speaking....

The farmhouse stood in the middle of a very
large yard, and the yard was fenced on three
sides with rails and on the rear side with high
palings; against these stood the smokehouse;
beyond the palings was the orchard; beyond
the orchard were the tobacco fields. The front
yard was entered over a stile made of sawed-off
logs of graduated heights; I do not remember
any gate. In a corner of the front yard were a
dozen lofty hickory trees and a dozen black
walnuts, and in the nutting season riches were
to be gathered there.

Down a piece, abreast the house, stood a
little log cabin against the rail fence; and there
the woody hill fell sharply away, past the barns,
the corncrib, the stables, and the tobacco-cur-

---

[1]*Florida,* a small town in northeastern Missouri. Mark
Twain lived here until he was four years old, at which
time the family moved to Hannibal, a Missouri town on
the Mississippi River.

[2]*the line of Mason and Dixon,* the boundary between
Pennsylvania and Maryland. It is often thought of as
separating the North from the South.

ing house,[3] to a limpid brook which sang along over its gravelly bed and curved and frisked in and out and here and there and yonder in the deep shade of overhanging foliage and vines—a divine place for wading, and it had swimming pools, too, which were forbidden to us and therefore much frequented by us. For we were little Christian children and had early been taught the value of forbidden fruit....

I can see the farm yet, with perfect clearness. I can see all its belongings, all its details: the family room of the house, with a trundle bed in one corner and a spinning wheel in another—a wheel whose rising and falling wail, heard from a distance, was the mournfulest of all sounds to me, and made me homesick and low-spirited, and filled my atmosphere with the wandering spirits of the dead; the vast fireplace, piled high, on winter nights, with flaming hickory logs from whose ends a sugary sap bubbled out, but did not go to waste, for we scraped it off and ate it; the lazy cat spread out on the rough hearthstones; the drowsy dogs braced against the jambs and blinking; my aunt in one chimney corner, knitting; my uncle in the other, smoking his corncob pipe; the slick and carpet-less oak floor faintly mirroring the dancing

flame tongues and freckled with black indentations where fire coals had popped out and died a leisurely death; half a dozen children romping in the background twilight; split-bottomed chairs[4] here and there, some with rockers; a cradle—out of service, but waiting, with confidence; in the early cold mornings a snuggle of children in shirts and chemises, occupying the hearthstone and procrastinating—they could not bear to leave that comfortable place and go out on the wind-swept floor space between the house and kitchen where the general tin basin stood, and wash.

Along outside of the front fence ran the country road, dusty in the summertime, and a good place for snakes—they liked to lie in it and sun themselves; when they were rattle-snakes or puff adders, we killed them; when they were blacksnakes, or racers, or belonged to the fabled hoop breed,[5] we fled, without shame; when they were house snakes,[6] or garters, we carried them home and put them in Aunt Patsy's workbasket for a surprise; for she was prejudiced against snakes, and always when

---

[3]*the tobacco-curing house,* a shed in which tobacco leaves were hung to dry (cure).

[4]*split-bottomed chairs,* chairs with seats made of strips (splits) of hickory or oak.

[5]*the fabled hoop breed,* a large, harmless snake which was called a "hoop" snake because people mistakenly believed it moved by putting its tail in its mouth and rolling like a hoop.

[6]*house snakes,* harmless milk snakes.

she took the basket in her lap and they began to climb out of it, it disordered her mind. She never could seem to get used to them; her opportunities went for nothing. And she was always cold toward bats, too, and could not bear them; and yet I think a bat is as friendly a bird as there is. My mother was Aunt Patsy's sister and had the same wild superstitions. A bat is beautifully soft and silky; I do not know any creature that is pleasanter to the touch or is more grateful for caressings, if offered in the right spirit. I know all about these Coleoptera,[7] because our great cave, three miles below Hannibal, was multitudinously stocked with them, and often I brought them home to amuse my mother with. It was easy to manage if it was a school day, because then I had ostensibly been to school and hadn't any bats. She was not a suspicious person, but full of trust and confidence; and when I said, "There's something in my pocket for you," she would put her hand in. But she always took it out again, herself; I didn't have to tell her. It was remarkable, the way she couldn't learn to like private bats. The more experience she had, the more she could not change her views....

Beyond the road where the snakes sunned themselves was a dense young thicket, and through it a dim-lighted path led a quarter of a mile; then out of the dimness one emerged abruptly upon a level great prairie which was covered with wild strawberry plants, vividly starred with prairie pinks, and walled in on all sides by forests. The strawberries were fragrant and fine, and in the season we were generally there in the crisp freshness of the early morning, while the dew beads still sparkled upon the grass and the woods were ringing with the first songs of the birds....

The country schoolhouse was three miles from my uncle's farm. It stood in a clearing in the woods and would hold about twenty-five boys and girls. We attended the school with more or less regularity once or twice a week, in summer, walking to it in the cool of the morning by the forest paths, and back in the gloaming at the end of the day. All the pupils brought their dinner in baskets—corn dodger,[8] buttermilk, and other good things—and sat in the shade of the trees at noon and ate them. It is the part of my education which I look back upon with the most satisfaction. My first visit to the school was when I was seven. A strapping girl of fifteen, in the customary sunbonnet and calico dress, asked me if I "used tobacco"—meaning did I chew it. I said no. It roused her scorn. She reported me to all the crowd, and said:

"Here is a boy seven years old who can't chew tobacco."

By the looks and comments which this produced I realized that I was a degraded object, and was cruelly ashamed of myself. I determined to reform. But I only made myself sick; I was not able to learn to chew tobacco. I learned to smoke fairly well, but that did not conciliate anybody and I remained a poor thing, and characterless. I longed to be respected, but I never was able to rise. Children have but little charity for one another's defects.

As I have said, I spent some part of every year at the farm until I was twelve or thirteen years old. The life which I led there with my cousins was full of charm, and so is the memory of it yet. I can call back the solemn twilight and mystery of the deep woods, the earthy smells, the faint odors of the wild flowers, the sheen of rain-washed foliage, the rattling clatter of drops when the wind shook the trees, the far-off hammering of woodpeckers and the muffled drumming of wood pheasants in the remoteness of the forest, the snapshot glimpses of disturbed wild creatures scurrying through the grass—I can call it all back and make it as real as it ever was, and as blessed.

I can call back the prairie, and its loneliness and peace, and a vast hawk hanging motionless in the sky, with his wings spread wide and the blue of the vault showing through the fringe of their end feathers. I can see the woods in their autumn dress, the oaks purple, the hickories washed with gold, the maples and the sumacs

---

[7]*Coleoptera* (kō′li op′tər ə *or* kol′i op′tər ə), an order of insects which includes the beetles. Bats are not Coleoptera. Mark Twain uses this incorrect scientific name humorously.

[8]*corn dodger*, a kind of corn bread baked hard under embers.

luminous with crimson fires, and I can hear the rustle made by the fallen leaves as we plowed through them. I can see the blue clusters of

wild grapes hanging among the foliage of the saplings, and I remember the taste of them and the smell. I know how the wild blackberries looked, and how they tasted, and the same with the papaws, the hazelnuts, and the persimmons; and I can feel the thumping rain,  upon my head, of hickory nuts and walnuts when we were out in the frosty dawn to scramble for them with the pigs, and the gusts of wind loosed them and sent them down.

I know the stain of blackberries, and how pretty it is, and I know the stain of walnut hulls, and how little it minds soap and water; also what grudged experience it had of either of them. I know the taste of maple sap, and when to gather it, and how to arrange the troughs and the delivery tubes, and how to boil down the juice, and how to hook the sugar after it is made, also how much better hooked sugar tastes than any that is honestly come by, let bigots say what they will.

I know how a prize watermelon looks when it is sunning its fat rotundity among pumpkin vines and "simblins"[9]; I know how to tell when it is ripe without plugging it; I know how inviting it looks when it is cooling itself in a tub of water under the bed, waiting; I know how it looks when it lies on the table in the sheltered great floor space between house and kitchen, and the children gathered for the sacrifice and their mouths watering; I know the crackling sound it makes when the carving knife enters its end, and I can see the split fly along in front of the blade as the knife cleaves its way to the other end; I can see its halves fall apart and display the rich red meat and the black seeds, and the heart standing up, a luxury fit for the

[9]"*simblins*" (sim'linz), a variety of squash.

elect; I know how a boy looks behind a yard-long slice of that melon, and I know how he feels; for I have been there. I know the taste of the watermelon which has been honestly come by, and I know the taste of the watermelon which has been acquired by art. Both taste good, but the experienced know which tastes best.

I know the look of green apples and peaches and pears on the trees, and I know how entertaining they are when they are inside of a person. I know how ripe ones look when they are piled in pyramids under the trees, and how pretty they are, and how vivid their colors. I know how a frozen apple looks in a barrel down cellar in the wintertime, and how hard it is to bite, and how the frost makes the teeth ache, and yet how good it is, notwithstanding. I know the disposition of elderly people to select the specked apples for the children, and I once knew ways to beat the game. I know the look of an apple that is roasting and sizzling on a hearth on a winter's evening, and I know the comfort that comes of eating it hot, along with some sugar and a drench of cream. I know the delicate art and mystery of so cracking hickory nuts and walnuts on a flatiron with a hammer that the kernels will be delivered whole, and I know how the nuts, taken in conjunction with winter apples, cider, and doughnuts, make old people's old tales and old jokes sound fresh and crisp  and enchanting, and juggle an evening away before you know what went with the time.

I know the look of Uncle Dan'l's kitchen as it was on the privileged nights when I was a child, and I can see the white and black children grouped on the hearth, with the firelight playing on their faces and the shadows flickering upon the walls, clear back toward the cavernous gloom of the rear, and I can hear Uncle Dan'l telling the immortal tales which Uncle Remus

Harris[10] was to gather into his book and charm the world with, by and by; and I can feel again the creepy joy which quivered through me when the time for the ghost story was reached —and the sense of regret, too, which came over me, for it was always the last story of the evening and there was nothing between it and the unwelcome bed.

I can remember the bare wooden stairway in my uncle's house, and the turn to the left above the landing, and the rafters and the slanting roof over my bed, and the squares of moonlight on the floor, and the white cold world of snow outside, seen through the curtainless window. I can remember the howling of the wind and the quaking of the house on stormy nights, and how snug and cozy one felt, under the blankets, listening; and how the powdery snow used to sift in, around the sashes, and lie in little ridges on the floor and make the place look chilly in the morning and curb the wild desire to get up—in case there was any. I can remember how very dark that room was, in the dark of the moon, and how packed it was with ghostly stillness when one woke up by accident away in the night, and forgotten sins came flocking out of the secret chambers of the memory and wanted a hearing; and how ill-chosen the time seemed for this kind of business; and how dismal was the hoo-hooing of the owl and the wailing of the wolf, sent mourning by on the night wind.

I remember the raging of the rain on that roof, summer nights, and how pleasant it was to lie and listen to it, and enjoy the white splendor of the lightning and the majestic booming and crashing of the thunder. It was a very satisfactory room, and there was a lightning rod which was reachable from the window, an adorable and skittish thing to climb up and down, summer nights, when there were duties on hand of a sort to make privacy desirable.

I remember the 'coon and 'possum hunts, nights, with the Negroes, and the long marches through the black gloom of the woods, and the excitement which fired everybody when the distant bay of an experienced dog announced that the game was treed; then the wild scramblings and stumblings through briers and bushes and over roots to get to the spot; then the lighting of a fire and the felling of the tree, the joyful frenzy of the dogs and the Negroes, and the weird picture it all made in the red glare—I remember it all well, and the delight that everyone got out of it, except the 'coon.

I remember the pigeon seasons, when the birds would come in millions and cover the trees and by their weight break down the branches. They were clubbed to death with sticks; guns were not necessary and were not used. I remember the squirrel hunts, and prairie-chicken hunts, and wild-turkey hunts, and all that; and how we turned out, mornings while it was still dark, to go on these expeditions, and how chilly and dismal it was, and how often I regretted that I was well enough to go. A toot on a tin horn brought twice as many dogs as were needed, and in their happiness they raced and scampered about, and knocked small people down, and made no end of unnecessary noise. At the word, they vanished away toward the woods, and we drifted silently after them in the melancholy gloom. But presently the gray dawn stole over the world, the birds piped up, then the sun rose and poured light and comfort all around, everything was fresh and dewy and fragrant, and life was a boon again. After three hours of tramping we arrived back wholesomely tired, overladen with game, very hungry, and just in time for breakfast....

REMEMBERING A HAPPY CHILDHOOD

1. How many of the experiences which Mark Twain enjoyed would he be likely to find on a farm today? How do you account for the loss of those now rarely met with?

2. What impressions does this selection give you of Twain as a boy? Cite passages for each impression.

3. What, judging from this selection, did Mark Twain believe to be the most durable satisfactions of life? Do you agree with him?

4. In this selection Mark Twain tries to describe for his readers the sights, smells, sounds, tastes, and feelings of life on the farm. Find passages which are particularly strong in their appeal to each of the five senses. To which of your senses is the selection as a whole most vivid?

[10]*Uncle Remus Harris,* Joel Chandler Harris (1848-1908). He is famous for a series of stories supposedly told by Uncle Remus, an old Negro storyteller.

A Holiday with Father

CLARENCE DAY

As the United States became an industrial nation and cities and towns multiplied, for many Americans the patterns of life which Mark Twain knew in his boyhood were gradually replaced by more urban patterns. To the city-bred man or woman, however, the sights and sounds and smells of a great metropolis are as fascinating and pleasant as those of the country; and with an ever greater part of the population growing up in towns and cities, urban life has come to have a more and more conspicuous place in our literature.

Life with Father, originally a series of sketches and later successful both as a play and as a motion picture, is the story of an extraordinary family and a picture of life in New York City at the time when telephones and typewriters were new inventions. Clarence Day's father, the real hero of the following piece, was a wealthy stockbroker and a governor of the New York Stock Exchange. He knew what kind of life he wanted, what "civilized" folk did. Like Mark Twain's, his pattern of life has been one which great numbers of Americans have found desirable.

ONCE IN A LONG WHILE, as a great treat, Father took me down to his office. This could happen only on a Saturday morning, when there was no school. I felt very important and grown-up on the days I went to "The Office"—not after I got there, to be sure, but as I was leaving the house, with Mother and my three little brothers respectfully seeing me off.

If it was a rainy day, Father would prepare for rough weather by wearing a derby hat and a black rubber mackintosh over his usual tailed coat.[1] (He seldom was informal enough to wear a sack suit in town except on warm days, or when he left New York to go to the country, in summer.) If the sun was out, he wore a silk hat and carried a cane, like his friends. When he and they passed each other on the street,

they raised their canes and touched the brims of their hats with them, in formal salute.

I admired this rich and splendid gesture, and wished I could imitate it, but I was too young for a cane. I was soberly dressed in a pepper-and-salt sack suit with short pants and the usual broad flat white Eton collar that boys wore in the eighties—a collar that started out very stiff and immaculate every morning and was done for by dinner time. Black laced or buttoned shoes and black stockings. We only wore brown in the country in summer.

On one of these Saturdays, although it was sunny, Father put on his derby. I didn't know why until later. I hopped along by his side as he walked through the long rows of comfortable-looking brownstone houses from Madison Avenue over to Sixth,[2] climbed the stairs of the

---

[1] *tailed coat.* In Clarence Day's time the prosperous businessman wore a black suit with a coat with long tails, much like the suits customary for formal wear today. Ordinary suits (sack suits) were thought to lack dignity.

[2] *Sixth,* Sixth Avenue, a north-south thoroughfare in Manhattan, now called The Avenue of the Americas. In Clarence Day's time an elevated railroad ran above this street.

Elevated, and stood on the platform, chatting with one of his friends, while we waited for the next train.

Soon a stubby little steam engine, with its open coal car piled full of anthracite, and its three or four passenger cars swinging along behind, appeared round the curve. White smoke poured from the smokestack. The engineer leaned out from his window. "Too-oot, too-too-toot!" whistled the engine as it came puffing in. We got on board and walked leisurely through the cars till Father found a seat that he liked.

During the journey downtown, except when the smoke from the engine was too thick for me to see out, I stared fascinatedly into the windows of cheap red brick tenements, or at the even more interesting interiors of lodging houses for tramps. The second-floor rooms of the lodging houses were crowded, but I envied the tramps in them. They looked so easy-going. Not a thing to do; just tilt their chairs back against the wall, in comfortable old clothes, and smoke. If I were a tramp, I wouldn't have to scrub every last bit of grime out of my knuckles each Friday, and put on tight white kid gloves, and pull some unwieldy little girl around a waxed floor at dancing school. It wouldn't cost so very much either. The lodging-house sign said in big letters, "Ten Cents a Night."

I never had a chance to see such sights except when I went downtown with Father, for Mother kept away from the Elevated. It was comparatively new, and she felt that the horsecars[3] were better. Besides, Sixth Avenue was so cindery and sooty that ladies disliked it. They did go that far west sometimes, to shop, and they went as far east as Lexington, but in general they lived and walked in the long narrow strip between those two boundaries.

When Father and I left the train at the end of our journey, I found myself in a tangle of little streets full of men and boys but no women. If some lonely bonnet chanced to be bobbing along in the crowd, we all stared at it. Most of the business buildings were old and many of them were dirty, with steep, well-worn wooden stairways, and dark, busy basements.

[3]*horsecars*, streetcars pulled by horses.

Exchange Place and Broad Street were full of these warrens, and there were some even on Wall Street. The southern corner of Wall Street and Broadway was one of the dingiest. Father raised his cane and said as we passed, "That's where Great-Aunt Lavinia was born."

A few doors beyond the Assay Office[4] we came to a neat but narrow five-story building and walked up the front stoop. This was No. 38 Wall Street. Father's office occupied the ground floor, at the top of the stoop, and on the back part of the second floor he had a small store-room.

The office was busy in what seemed to me a mysterious way. The cashier, who never would let me go inside his cage, sat in there on a stool, with a cash drawer, a safe full of books, another safe for securities, and a tin box full of postage stamps, which he doled out as needed. One or two bookkeepers were making beautifully written entries in enormous leather-bound ledgers. They had taken the stiff white detachable cuffs off their shirt sleeves and stacked them in a corner, and they had exchanged their regular jackets for black alpaca coats. Future

[4]*Assay Office*, United States government office where gold and silver in any form—jewelry, coins, etc.—were analyzed (assayed) for the amount of pure metal contained.

bookkeepers or brokers who now were little office boys ran in and out. Western Union messengers rushed in with telegrams. In the front room there was a long table full of the printed reports issued by railroads about their earnings and traffic. Only twenty or thirty industrial stocks were traded in on the Exchange[5] in those days, and Father's office ignored them. On or around the table were the *Commercial & Financial Chronicle,* the *Journal of Commerce,* a blackboard, a ticker,[6] and four or five whiskery men. Two were arguing heatedly about Henry Ward Beecher,[7] and the others were shaking their heads over some crazy proposal by the Knights of Labor[8] to have an eight-hour day.

Father went into his private office, where a little coal fire was burning, hung his hat on a rack, and unlocked and sat down at his desk. While he opened his mail, I proudly brought in two stone jugs of ink, one of greenish black made in England, and one to use when he wrote letters of which he wished to keep copies, because with this ink impressions could be taken to put in his files. I cleaned and filled all Father's inkwells, and put fresh steel pens in his penholders. He had quill pens at home, but he used only steel pens at the office, and as he had no stenographer he wrote a good share of the firm's letters in longhand, himself.

There were lots of things to do in the office besides filling inkwells. It was fun to scamper around the streets carrying all the messages (which are telephoned nowadays), or to roll colored pencils down the clerks' slanting desks, or try to ring the bell on the typewriter. The latter was a new contraption which seldom was used except on important occasions, when the bookkeeper or one of the office boys had to stop work and pick at it.

All of a sudden it was noon. The customers left. The ticker came to a stop. At half-past twelve Father called to me and we went out for lunch.

"Will you be back, Mr. Day?" the cashier asked respectfully, but eagerly too. On days when Father said yes, all the clerks looked disappointed. They bent over their desks, saying nothing, till Father went out of the door, but if I lingered behind for a moment I heard them slamming their ledgers about. Not only did they and the office boys all have to stay, but the rule was that they couldn't even smoke until Father had gone home for the day.

Today he said no, however. I saw them getting out their sulphur matches as he was crossing the threshold, and the instant he stepped into the hall they struck them on the seats of their pants.

I trotted at Father's side down to Beaver Street, where there stood a mellow old building. It had the look of a friendly, hospitable country hotel. There were green blinds and little outside balconies on its upper floors, and windows with looped lacy curtains; and white pillars stood at the entrance, at the top of a low flight of steps.

This was Delmonico's,[9] and the food was so good there that even I had heard it talked of, uptown.[10] It was one of the places that just suited people like Father.

Delmonico's stood upon a triangular-shaped plot of ground, with the front doors at the apex, and when we arrived we met a bottle-necked jam at the entrance. Silk-hatted men, who had been lunching in a lingering way, had suddenly remembered apparently that they were due back in Wall Street, and they were shoving each other, politely but urgently, to force their way out.

As Father and I went in the long crowded room, the head waiter led us with a flourish to

---

[5] *the Exchange,* the New York Stock Exchange, where stocks are bought, sold, and traded.

[6] *a ticker,* a telegraphic instrument that printed up-to-the-minute market reports on a paper tape.

[7] *Henry Ward Beecher,* clergyman and reformer. His ideas were supported by many and opposed by many others.

[8] *Knights of Labor,* an organization designed to bring together all workingmen without division by trades or occupations. Founded in 1869, it was strongest between 1881 and 1886. At the time Clarence Day is writing about, the average working day was ten or more hours long.

[9] *Delmonico's* (del mon′i kōz), a restaurant which made New York famous for good food, under the direction of Lorenzo Delmonico, a Swiss immigrant in 1832. Of the several locations, the one at the corner of Beaver and William streets was among the oldest, dating from 1835.

[10] *uptown,* the residential area north of the financial and manufacturing district at the southern end of Manhattan Island.

a table for two. The air was fragrant with cigar smoke and the appetizing smell of rich, greasy cooking. A stately-looking foreigner who was standing at the side of the room caught Father's eye and bowed to him in a dignified way.

"Lorenzo," Father said to him as he approached us, "this is my son."

I bobbed my head at him rather embarrassed, and Mr. Lorenzo Crist Delmonico bowed and said he was happy to meet me.

As he left us, old François, Father's regular waiter, hurried up to our table, and he and Father had a talk, in French, about the best dish to order. They spoke so rapidly that I couldn't understand a word of it, except that François kept assuring Father that we could rely on the sauce. *"Parfaitement."*[11] It seems that the last time Father had relied on this sauce, an admittedly difficult kind, he had had a severe disappointment.

When anything of this sort occurred, I had noted, François had a healing way of dealing with such a catastrophe. He seemed even more shocked and perturbed at a failure than Father, and he would snatch the offending dish away and come racing back with a substitute. Usually he was accompanied at such moments by

one of the Delmonico family—Lorenzo or Charles—who bent over the table to examine the new dish as it was placed before Father, murmuring most sympathetically about the unhappy misfortune.

Today the sauce and everything else was not only successful but perfect, and Father and François smiled and nodded in a congratulatory way to each other. I used to wonder why Father never got into rages at Delmonico's as he did at home,[12] but I see now that he may have felt lonely at home, where there were no brother experts.

Father was fond of French cooking and of being served by French waiters. At home he had to put up with an Irish waitress who was changed every few months, and with cooking which, though excellent of its kind, after all wasn't French. He ate it with relish and gusto, when it came up to his standards, but he did so like a city man in the country, enjoying good, simple fare.

I didn't always appreciate French cooking myself. It tasted all right, but it was dainty and there wasn't much of it. It seemed to me that

---

[11]*Parfaitement* (pär fet mäN′), perfectly. [*French*]

[12]*Father never got into rages…did at home.* When Father was disappointed in a particular dish served at home, he would thump three times on the floor to summon the cook to take the offending food away.

Father got along with a very light lunch. When he was having his demitasse, however, and saw a hungry look on my face, he smiled understandingly and beckoned to François, who smiled too and presently came running back with a large chocolate éclair. The richness of its soft, thick yellow interior and the meltingness of its chocolate outside were so delicious that time stood still as I happily ate it, and I almost forgot where I was.

After lunch, instead of taking me back uptown, Father walked down to the Battery,[13] and to my surprise we got on the boat at South Ferry. We had never done this before. I now saw why he was wearing his derby. We were going out to the country. Off we steamed across the sweet-smelling bay filled with sailboats and four-masted schooners and tugboats and barges, and when we landed on Staten Island[14] Father told me that we were going to see Buffalo Bill.[15]

We got seats in a flimsy wooden stand full of splintery benches, and there was the Wild West spread out before us—dust, horses, and all. The wonderful marksmanship of riders who hit glass balls with their rifles—balls tossed into the air and shot at with careless ease as the horsemen dashed by; the herds of cattle, the lariats, the brass band, the old Deadwood Stage Coach, the thrilling attack on it by Indians, the last-minute rescue. Father dragged me out just before the rescue so that we could get seats on the ferry-boat, but I caught a glimpse of it anyway as I was being hauled through the exit.

I wanted to be a cowboy. I told Father on the way home. He chuckled and said no I didn't. He said I might as well be a tramp.

I wondered if I'd better tell him that this idea, too, had occurred to me, no further back than that very morning. I decided that upon the whole it mightn't be a good day to mention it, just after Father had taken me to lunch at Delmonico's. I did venture to ask him, however, what was the matter with cowboys.

Father briefly explained that their lives, their food, and their sleeping accommodations were outlandish and "slummy." They lived in the wilds, he informed me, and they had practically gone wild themselves. "Put your cap on straight," he added. "I am trying to bring you up to be a civilized man."

I adjusted my cap and walked on, thinking over this future. The more I thought about it, the less I wanted to be a civilized man. After all, I had had a very light lunch, and I was tired and hungry. What with fingernails and improving books and dancing school, and sermons on Sundays, the few chocolate éclairs that a civilized man got to eat were not worth it.

WHAT DOES THE CITY OFFER?

1. What are the "advantages" of city life as Father saw them? What were some of the disadvantages, from the point of view of his son? How do you think Mark Twain would have regarded the things which Father considered "civilized"?

2. What differences do you find between the way work was done in Father's office and the methods used in offices today? What changes are apparent in the kind of employee hired and in working conditions?

3. What attitude does the author have toward Father? How does the sketch convey this attitude to you?

Know your words

In rainy weather Father wore a mackintosh and a derby to his office. Like many other words in the English language, *mackintosh* and *derby* came from proper names. The mackintosh is named after its inventor, Charles Mackintosh, who in 1823 patented capes and cloaks for rainy-weather wear. The derby takes its name from the kind of hat worn by men at the most famous English horse race, the Derby, which was instituted by the twelfth Earl of Derby in 1780.

Other articles of clothing also derived their names from proper names. You may be interested in tracing the history of the following words: *cardigan, chesterfield, fedora, panama, jeans, jodhpurs, ulster,* and *tuxedo.* Consult an unabridged dictionary or any of various books on word derivation for information. Eric Partridge's *Name into Word* gives detailed accounts.

---

[13]*the Battery,* a small park at the southern extremity of Manhattan. It takes its name from the fort which occupied the area in early colonial days.

[14]*Staten* (stat′ən) *Island,* an island in New York Bay south of Manhattan Island. It is now a part of New York City.

[15]*Buffalo Bill,* William Frederick Cody (1846–1917), who had started his "Wild West" show in 1883 after a colorful career as a scout and actor.

The Work We Do

Mowing

ROBERT FROST

Whatever the overall pattern of our lives—rural, urban, or small town—the pursuit of happiness is perhaps most closely related to the work we do. One of the biggest satisfactions in life is to do something well, something whose meaning and usefulness are immediately apparent. Failure in our work and a sense of its insignificance are among the greatest causes of discontent. How American writers have felt about work is the theme of the next few selections, appropriately introduced by Robert Frost's "Mowing."

THERE WAS never a sound beside the wood but one,
And that was my long scythe whispering to the ground.
What was it it whispered? I knew not well myself;
Perhaps it was something about the heat of the sun,
Something, perhaps, about the lack of sound— 5
And that was why it whispered and did not speak.
It was no dream of the gift of idle hours,
Or easy gold at the hand of fay or elf:
Anything more than the truth would have seemed too weak
To the earnest love that laid the swale in rows, 10
Not without feeble-pointed spikes of flowers
(Pale orchises), and scared a bright green snake.
The fact is the sweetest dream that labor knows.
My long scythe whispered and left the hay to make.

UNDERSTANDING THE POET'S IDEA

1. The good workman loves the tools he uses and identifies himself with them. How is this idea suggested in the poem?

2. The good workman *enjoys* his labor, and does not work merely for material gains. What lines best express this idea?

3. Which line do you think carries the main point of the poem? Explain what this line means to you.

The Year of the Hot Winter

JAMES STEVENS

Humorous glorification of the great achievement of workers probably reaches its height in the folk tales about Paul Bunyan, the fantastically powerful hero of the lumbermen. Paul and Babe, his blue ox, have been talked about by yarnspinners in the camps from Maine to Washington, and there is no sign that Americans are weary of tall tales about their strength. Paul's greatest happiness, like that of outdoor men everywhere, was in devising ingenious means to defy the handicaps which nature imposes on man in accomplishing his work.

NO REGION of Real America,[1] save Kansas, boasted of its weather in Paul Bunyan's time. In the heyday of the mighty logger the climates and seasons were not systematized; they came and went and behaved without rule or reason. There were many years with two winters, and sometimes all four seasons would come and go in one month. The wind would frequently blow straight up and then straight down. Sometimes it would simply stand still and blow in one place. In its most prankish moods it would blow all ways at once. The weather was indeed powerful strange in those days and it got itself talked about. And nowhere were its ways more evil than in Utah.

When Paul Bunyan moved his camp to the state of Utah for the purpose of logging off its forests of stonewood trees, he was not careless of the climate; he merely failed to suspect its treachery. Besides, other troubles beset him. The gritty texture of the stonewood timber dulled the edge of an ax bit in two strokes. At the end of their twelve-hour day in the woods the loggers had to sharpen axes for seven hours. They were always fagged out. Then there was only one small river near the forests, and Babe, the blue ox, who had got hayfever again since coming West, drank it dry every fifteen minutes. The loggers thirsted, and they were bedeviled by sand in their blankets and in the beans, for every time Babe sneezed he raised a dust storm that rolled its clouds through the cookhouse and the bunkhouses and covered the great plain and the hills around the camp. A spirit of dark and evil melancholy settled on the loggers.

Paul Bunyan hoped for an adequate water supply from the December snows. And he brought all his inventive powers to the problem of felling the stonewood trees. In eleven days and nights he devised eight hundred and five systems, machines, and implements, and from this galaxy he selected a noble tool.

Paul's new invention was the double-bitted ax, which is used everywhere in the woods today. Paul Bunyan devised it so that a feller could chop with one blade, then twist the handle, and whet the other blade on the gritty stonewood with the backward swing.

But even with the new axes the logging went on slowly. The camp supply of elbow grease gave out, and the loggers suffered stiffened joints. The December snows were light, and the thirsty blue ox continued to drink the entire water supply. The bunkhouses came to be dens of ominous brooding and quiet instead of gay and noisy habitations. Finally the shipment of web-footed turkeys from the Great Lakes arrived too late for Christmas dinner. The loggers became dour, gaunt, embittered men.

Then came New Year's Day and outrageous fortune. When the loggers went to work at the first thinning of darkness, they attributed the peculiar oppressive warmth of the morning to an unusual Chinook wind.[2] There was, however, no wind at all. Then the rising sun shot blazing rays into a cloudless sky. Even then the loggers did not realize that they were witnessing an Event. This was the beginning of a notable year, the Year of the Hot Winter. As the sun climbed higher, the heat grew more intense.

---

[1]*Real America.* This was the name by which Paul Bunyan, who was Canadian-born, called the United States.

[2]*Chinook* (chi nŭk' *or* chi nŭk') *wind,* a southwest wind of the Northwest, usually warm and moist.

"The Year of the Hot Winter." Reprinted from *Legends of Paul Bunyan* by Harold Felton as adapted by him from *Paul Bunyan* by James Stevens, by permission of Alfred A. Knopf, Inc., copyright 1947 by Alfred A. Knopf, Inc.

The Christmas snow had vanished at the first burning touch of day. The ground baked and cracked. The stonewood trees glittered in a fierce light. Each logger threw off his mackinaw, muffler, sweater, stagged shirt, woolen overshirt and undershirt; his paraffin pants, mackinaw pants, and overalls; and his Arctic socks, heavy wool socks, light wool socks, and cotton socks. All heavy clothing was speedily thrown aside, and everywhere in the plain, in the valleys, and on the hillsides were piles of garments, and by each pile a logger toiled, clad only in drawers and calked boots. But still sweat dripped and trickled from their bodies; they labored more and more languorously. Each quarter of an hour the blue ox, with lolling tongue, dashed madly for the river and drank it dry.

Paul Bunyan was distressed by this change in his affairs, but he was not daunted. Confident that his loggers would do their best in the meanwhile, he again retired to solitude, hoping to devise something that would conquer the hostile and unnatural season. He returned with the great timber scythe, with which he could fell a full section of timber[3] with one swing of his mighty arms. Carrying the timber scythe over his shoulder, Paul Bunyan strode toward his camp. His tread was vigorous despite the deadening heat. Benevolent ideas stirred his heart. He himself would do the arduous labor of felling the stonewood trees; the loggers would be asked only to do the lighter work of trimming and bucking[4] the trees into logs. They were a fine bunch of savages; ordinarily they would not allow even Paul Bunyan to do their natural work. Perhaps they would resist such intrusion now. But the great logger was sure of his persuasive powers.

As he neared the camp, busy as he was with philanthropic thoughts, he failed to note an unusual silence in the woods and about the bunkhouses. Not until he saw Babe and the Big Swede[5] sleeping in the stable was he made aware of the extraordinary. Paul Bunyan went next to the camp office. Johnny Inkslinger,[6] that tower of energy, was sleeping at his desk! His fountain pen had dropped from his hand, and as it was fed by hose lines from twenty-five barrels of ink, a black stream gushed from its point and flooded the floor. A chorus of faint snores came from each bunkhouse. The cookhouse looked gloomy and deserted. In the woods the axes and saws lay where the loggers had left them. For one hundred and seventy-nine minutes Paul Bunyan stood silently in the midst of his camp, tormented by wrath, regret, and sorrow. His outfit had failed him. After all these years of comradeship in labor they had allowed a mere hot winter to provoke them into faithlessness. He had left them without an idea that they would be untrue to the job while he was scheming to make it a success. But they had weakened. Very well, he thought, after his brief period of emotion, he would perform their labor for them while they snored. They should awaken to shame.

One stride brought him into the first clearing made among the stonewood trees. Without losing a second, he threw the timber scythe from his shoulder, he grasped its handles, then took a long swing, and the first section of trees thundered to the ground. On he went, making a circular swath. As he stepped with his right foot the sharp scythe blade crashed through the trees on the cutting stroke, and as he stepped with his left he brought the scythe behind him with a vigorous swing. On and on he labored, his steps coming faster as the circle widened. Every seven hours he paused to whet the blade of the timber scythe on a bundle of the stonewood trees which he carried in his hip pocket. The hot winter drove its fires upon him, but his passion of toil repelled them with a stronger flame. The great logger's walk became a run; the dazzling blade of the timber scythe flashed in strokes of inconceivable rapidity; the sections of stonewood trees fell in a steady roar.

Then Paul Bunyan began to sweat. He had labored before this, but never so savagely, nor in such penetrating heat. Only the man who raises a good sweat for the first time can realize

---

[3]*section of timber*, an area of forest one mile square.
[4]*bucking*, cutting.
[5]*the Big Swede*, Hels Helson, Paul Bunyan's foreman.

[6]*Johnny Inkslinger*, camp timekeeper and bookkeeper.

what an astounding store of perspiration the human body can hold. On occasion it gushes from innumerable springs, seeming inexhaustible. It streams down the crevices and valleys of the body and floods the flat spaces; it soaks the clothing and drips to the ground. Imagine then what happened when Paul Bunyan's stored perspiration was unloosed. As he toiled on, ever more fiercely, his sweat flooded his boots, it surged over their tops and foamed toward the ground like two Niagaras. His swinging body and flying arms flung out clouds of spray. These strange waters coursed over the plains in torrents and gathered in heaving pools. The little river was submerged, drowned, exterminated. The waters crept toward the camp. Paul Bunyan, more and more engrossed with his labor as time went on, did not note the rising flood. His circle grew wider and wider. It left the plain and swung around the bordering slopes. Section after section of the trees was felled, only to be covered by water, for the stonewood timber was too heavy to float. But Paul Bunyan labored around and around the circle, quite unaware of the tragical consequence of his efforts.

For five days and nights the loggers lay in their bunks, too lazy to get up to eat, too lazy to do aught but drowse and dream. But at twelve o'clock on the fifth night the waters had reached the bunkhouses, and they learned of their peril. Yells of fear arose from every quarter, and in a few moments the whole camp, with the exception of Babe, the Big Swede, and Johnny Inkslinger, was aroused. Fright made the loggers forget the hot winter, and gave them energy. When they looked out on a vast lake glittering in the moonlight, and saw in the dim distance the twin rivers roaring from Paul Bunyan's boots, they knew that speedy and efficient action was necessary to save their lives. The best swimmers swam out to the tool house and brought back hammers, saws, and nails. Each logger then began to build a boat from his bunk, and for three hours they worked feverishly and silently constructing the vessels. When the last one was finished the word was passed along, and in a few moments the boats, each one carrying a logger and his blankets, swarmed from the bunkhouses. Before the armada had gone twenty feet the boats all filled with water and sank, while the loggers uttered lamentable cries. These changed to sounds of rejoicing, however, when it was discovered that the water was only waist deep. The loggers rescued their bundles from the boats and scampered to the shore like a holiday host at a beach.

But their joy did not last; it quickly gave way to dread. Paul Bunyan, toiling more desperately every moment, was rapidly moving around the circle. In a short time he would be upon them, and at any instant he might discover the fate of his trees, the flooding of his camp, his complete disaster. The loggers all understood the reason for the mighty man's wrathful labor. Their sense of blame confused them and smothered their native courage. The host began to move over the hills, haltingly at first, and with heads bowed like penitents. Then, as the volleying thunder of Paul Bunyan's timber scythe sounded nearer and nearer, they lifted their heads and struck a faster pace. Then guilty fears possessed them and every logger of the lot began to gallop madly. Someone yelled, "Ol' Paul's a-comin'!" and the warning cry was echoed from thousands of throats all over the hills. The loggers were taken by panic; the runaway became a stampede. By dawn they were making such running leaps that each logger would hit his chin with his front knee and his head with his back heel at every stride. They were so scared that they never stopped until they got to Kansas.

For many days and nights after the stampede of his loggers Paul Bunyan had toiled on, swinging his timber scythe with undiminished rapidity. He had not observed the desertion of his men, or the flooding of his camp, or the fate of the stonewood trees. But at last his energy and strength began to fail, his pace slackened, he swung the scythe with slower strokes, and the intervals between the rolling thunders of falling trees became longer and longer. Then the timber scythe dropped from his hands, and he sank to the ground. Now he saw for the first time the shimmering distances of salt water which covered the stonewood trees and all but the tallest buildings of his camp. For seven hours he gazed on the lamentable scene, then his head dropped to the ground. He was not disheartened; he was only tired. He slept.

Days and nights went by with little change in the unnatural season. The days of springtime came, but here there was no spring. Summer days began, the sultriness of the nights got increasingly heavy and thick, and in the daytime the overpowering blaze of the sun seemed to make the very hills shrink, while the surface of the lake was veiled in steaming mists. The slumbers of Paul Bunyan, Johnny Inkslinger, the Big Swede, and the blue ox became so deep that the active careers of all of them might have ended there ingloriously, had it not been for Babe's appetite, which always tormented him, sleeping or waking. The Big Swede was couched on the high-piled hay in the manger, and Babe's chin rested on his body. Stirred by a hunger that would not be denied, his jaws began to work mechanically; they closed over the fifty-pound plug of chewing tobacco that the Big Swede always carried in his hip pocket, and it was swallowed like a blade of grass. Babe gasped, groaned, and shuddered; then he lunged to his feet, snorting and bellowing, for chewing tobacco was as poisonous to him as to a circus elephant. He gouged the Big Swede viciously with his horns until he awoke with yells of agony and astonishment. And not until he saw, through the stable door, Paul Bunyan asleep on the far side of the lake did Babe heed the fore-man's powerful remonstrances. With a last angry toss of his horns, which threw the Big Swede through the stable window, Babe turned and plunged into the water. So fast did he run that he threw foaming waves to the furthest reaches of the lake. When he reached Paul Bun-yan he emitted a joyous bellow and eagerly began licking the great logger's neck. For one hour and twenty-seven minutes Babe assidu-ously tickled him, and then Paul Bunyan sprang to his feet with a great roar of laughter. He felt strong and fresh; he smiled cheerfully at the blue ox, who capered around him. He strad-dled Babe and rode him across the lake to the flooded camp.

LYING FOR THE FUN OF IT

1. At what point in the story do you first realize that it is a tall tale? What pleasure do you find in exaggeration of this kind?

2. What details seemed to you the best examples of the type of exaggeration typical of a tall tale?

3. What was the normal attitude of the loggers toward their work? What had caused their unusual be-havior on this occasion?

4. What was Paul Bunyan's purpose in felling the stonewood trees himself? To what near-tragedy did his energy lead?

5. Can you identify a great natural wonder in the state of Utah that might have resulted from Paul's labor?

6. Compare Paul Bunyan with Pecos Bill and John Henry, taking into account the characteristics of each and the work each did. Select the one who you be-lieve most nearly fulfills the idea of the American folk hero and give reasons for your choice.

The Riverman

STEWART EDWARD WHITE

Stewart Edward White's stories of men who work in the outdoors are full of action and everyday heroism. They are often concerned with how men work at jobs which require ingenuity and physical fitness. As in "The Riverman," the qualities of ordinary workers some-times approach the fabulous powers of Paul Bunyan.

I FIRST MET HIM one Fourth of July after-noon in the middle eighties. The sawdust streets and high board sidewalks of the lumber town were filled to the brim with people. The permanent population, dressed in the stiffness of its Sunday best, escorted gingham wives or sweethearts; a dozen outsiders like myself tried not to be too conspicuous in a city smartness; but the great multitude was composed of the men of the woods. I sat, chair-tilted by the hotel, watching them pass. Their heavy woolen shirts crossed by the broad suspenders, the red of their sashes or leather shine of their belts, their short kersey trousers "stagged" off[1] to leave a gap between the knee and the heavily spiked "cork boots"—all these were distinctive enough of their class, but most interesting to me were the eyes that peered from beneath their little round hats tilted rakishly askew. They were all subtly alike, those eyes. Some were black, some were brown, or gray, or blue, but all were steady and unabashed, all looked straight at you with a strange humorous blend-ing of aggression and respect for your own busi-ness, and all without exception wrinkled at the corners with a suggestion of dry humor. In my half-conscious scrutiny I probably stared harder than I knew, for all at once a laughing pair of the blue eyes suddenly met mine full, and an ironical voice drawled, "Say, bub, you look as interested as a man killing snakes. Am I your long-lost friend?"

---

[1] *"stagged" off,* cut off.

"The Riverman," from *Blazed Trail Stories* by Stewart Edward White. Copyright 1904 by Stewart Edward White, reprinted by permission of Doubleday & Company, Inc.

The tone of the voice matched accurately the attitude of the man, and that was quite non-committal. He stood cheerfully ready to meet the emergency. If I sought trouble, it was here to my hand; or if I needed help, he was willing to offer it.

"I guess you are," I replied, "if you can tell me what all this outfit's headed for."

He thrust back his hat and ran his hand through a mop of closely cropped light curls.

"Birling match,"[2] he explained briefly. "Come on."

I joined him, and together we followed the crowd to the river, where we roosted like cormorants on adjacent piles overlooking a patch of clear water among the filled booms.[3]

"Drive's just over," my new friend informed me. "Rear come down last night. Fourther July celebration...."

A half-dozen men with peaveys rolled a white-pine log of about a foot and a half diameter into the clear water, where it lay rocking back and forth, three or four feet from the boom piles. Suddenly a man ran the length of the boom, leaped easily into the air, and landed with both feet square on one end of the floating log. That end disappeared in an ankle-deep swirl of white foam, the other rose suddenly, the whole timber, projected forward by the shock, drove headlong to the middle of the little pond. And the man, his arms folded, his knees just bent in the graceful nervous attitude of the circus rider, stood upright like a statue of bronze.

A roar approved this feat.

"That's Dickey Darrell," said my informant, "Roaring Dick....Watch him."

The man on the log was small, with clean beautiful haunches and shoulders, but with hanging baboon arms. Perhaps his most striking feature was a mop of reddish-brown hair that overshadowed a little triangular white face accented by two reddish-brown quadrilaterals

that served as eyebrows and a pair of inscrutable chipmunk eyes.

For a moment he poised erect in the great calm of the public performer. Then slowly he began to revolve the log under his feet. The lofty gaze, the folded arms, the straight supple waist budged not by a hair's-breadth; only the feet stepped forward, at first deliberately, then faster and faster, until the rolling log threw a blue spray a foot into the air. Then suddenly *slap! slap!* the heavy calks stamped a reversal. The log came instantaneously to rest, quivering exactly like some animal that had been spurred through its paces.

"Magnificent!" I cried.

"That's nothing!" my companion repressed me, "anybody can birl a log. Watch this."

Roaring Dick for the first time unfolded his arms. With some appearance of caution he balanced his unstable footing into absolute immobility. Then he turned a somersault.

This was the real thing. My friend uttered a wild yell of applause which was lost in a general roar.

A long pike-pole shot out, bit the end of the timber, and towed it to the boom pile. Another man stepped on the log with Darrell. They stood facing each other, bent-kneed, alert. Suddenly with one accord they commenced to birl the log from left to right. The pace grew hot. Like squirrels treading a cage their feet twinkled. Then it became apparent that Darrell's opponent was gradually being forced from the top of the log. He could not keep up. Little by little, still moving desperately, he dropped back to the slant, then at last to the edge, and so off into the river with a mighty splash.

"Clean birled!" commented my friend.

One after another a half-dozen rivermen tackled the imperturbable Dick, but none of them possessed the agility to stay on top in the pace he set them. One boy of eighteen seemed for a moment to hold his own, and managed at least to keep out of the water even when Darrell had apparently reached his maximum speed. But that expert merely threw his entire weight into two reversing stamps of his feet, and the young fellow dove forward as abruptly as though he had been shied over a horse's head.

---

[2]*Birling match,* a traditional logger's contest in which two men stand at opposite ends of a floating log and spin (birl) it by movements of their feet. The object of the contest is to dislodge the other man.

[3]*filled booms.* A boom is a line of connecting logs stretched across a river. The area upriver from the booms had been filled with logs floating downstream.

The crowd was by now getting uproarious and impatient of volunteer effort to humble Darrell's challenge. It wanted the best, and at once. It began, with increasing insistence, to shout a name.

"Jimmy Powers!" it vociferated, "Jimmy Powers."

And then by shamefaced bashfulness, by profane protest, by muttered and comprehensive curses I knew that my companion on the other pile was indicated.

A dozen men near at hand began to shout. "Here he is!" they cried. "Come on, Jimmy." "Don't be a high banker."[4] "Hang his hide on the fence."

Jimmy, still red and swearing, suffered himself to be pulled from his elevation and disappeared in the throng. A moment later I caught his head and shoulders pushing toward the boom piles, and so in a moment he stepped warily aboard to face his antagonist.

---

[4]*high banker,* a riverman's term for a greenhorn.

This was evidently no question to be determined by the simplicity of force or the simplicity of a child's trick. The two men stood half-crouched, face to face, watching each other narrowly, but making no move. To me they seemed like two wrestlers sparring for an opening. Slowly the log revolved one way; then slowly the other. It was a mere courtesy of salute. All at once Dick birled three rapid strokes from left to right as though about to roll the log, leaped into the air and landed square with both feet on the other slant of the timber. Jimmy Powers felt the jar, and acknowledged it by the spasmodic jerk with which he counterbalanced Darrell's weight. But he was not thrown.

As though this daring and hazardous maneuver had opened the combat, both men sprang to life. Sometimes the log rolled one way, sometimes the other, sometimes it jerked from side to side like a crazy thing, but always with the rapidity of light, always in a smother of spray and foam. The decided *spat, spat, spat* of the reversing blows from the calked boots sounded

like picket firing. I could not make out the different leads, feints, parries, and counters of this strange method of boxing, nor could I distinguish to whose initiative the various evolutions of that log could be described. But I retain still a vivid mental picture of two men nearly motionless above the waist, nearly vibrant below it, dominating the insane gyrations of a stick of pine.

The crowd was appreciative and partisan—for Jimmy Powers. It howled wildly, and rose thereby to ever higher excitement. Then it forgot its manners utterly and groaned when it made out that a sudden splash represented its favorite, while the indomitable Darrell still trod the quarterdeck[5] as champion birler for the year.

I must confess I was as sorry as anybody. I climbed down from my cormorant roost, and picked my way between the alleys of aromatic piled lumber in order to avoid the press....In this manner I happened on Jimmy Powers himself seated dripping on a board and examining his bared foot.

"I'm sorry," said I behind him. "How did he do it?"

He whirled, and I could see that his laughing boyish face had become suddenly grim and stern, and that his eyes were shot with blood.

"Oh, it's you, is it?" he growled disparagingly. "Well, that's how he did it."

He held out his foot. Across the instep and at the base of the toes ran two rows of tiny round punctures from which the blood was oozing. I looked very inquiring.

"He corked me!" Jimmy Powers explained. "Jammed his spikes into me! Stepped on my foot and tripped me...." Jimmy Powers certainly could swear.

"Why didn't you make a kick?" I cried.

"That ain't how I do it," he muttered, pulling on his heavy woolen sock.

"But no," I insisted, my indignation mounting. "It's an outrage! That crowd was with you. All you had to do was to say something—"

He cut me short. "And give myself away as a fool—sure Mike. I ought to know Dickey Dar-

rell by this time, and I ought to be big enough to take care of myself." He stamped his foot into his driver's shoe and took me by the arm, his good humor apparently restored. "No, don't you lose any hair, bub; I'll get even with Roaring Dick"....

The following year, but earlier in the season, I again visited my little lumber town. In striking contrast to the life of that other midsummer day were the deserted streets. The landlord knew me, and after I had washed and eaten, approached me with a suggestion.

"You got all day in front of you," said he; "why don't you take a horse and buggy and make a visit to the big jam? Everybody's up there more or less."

In response to my inquiry, he replied:

"They've jammed at the upper bend, jammed bad. The crew's been picking at her for near a week now, and last night Darrell was down to see about some more dynamite. It's worth seein'. The breast of her is near thirty foot high, and lots of water in the river."

"Darrell?" said I, catching at the name.

"Yes. He's rear boss this year. Do you think you'd like to take a look at her?"

"I think I should," I assented.

The horse and I jogged slowly along a deep sand road, through wastes of pine stumps and belts of hardwood beautiful with the early spring, until finally we arrived at a clearing in which stood two huge tents, a mammoth kettle slung over a fire of logs, and drying racks about the timbers of another fire. A fat cook in the inevitable battered derby hat, two bare-armed cookees,[6] and a chore "boy" of seventy-odd summers were the only human beings in sight. One of the cookees agreed to keep an eye on my horse. I picked my way down a well-worn trail toward the regular *clank, clank, click* of the peaveys.

I emerged finally to a plateau elevated some fifty or sixty feet above the river. A half-dozen spectators were already gathered. Among them I could not but notice a tall, spare, broad-shouldered young fellow dressed in a quiet busi-

---

[5]*trod the quarterdeck.* The author is using ship terminology to suggest that Dick Darrell, like the captain of a ship, was entitled to walk the quarterdeck.

[6]*cookees,* cooks' helpers.

ness suit, somewhat wrinkled, whose square, strong, clean-cut face and muscular hands were tanned by the weather to dark umber-brown. In another moment I looked down on the jam.

The breast, as my landlord had told me, rose sheer from the water to the height of at least twenty-five feet, bristling and formidable. Back of it pressed the volume of logs packed closely in an apparently inextricable tangle as far as the eye could reach. A man near informed me that the tail was a good three miles up stream. From beneath this wonderful *chevaux de frise*[7] foamed the current of the river, irresistible to any force less mighty than the statics of such a mass.

A crew of forty or fifty men were at work. They clamped their peaveys to the reluctant timbers, heaved, pushed, slid, and rolled them one by one into the current, where they were caught and borne away. They had been doing this for a week. As yet their efforts had made but slight impression on the bulk of the jam, but some time, with patience, they would reach the key logs. Then the tangle would melt like sugar in the freshet, and these imperturbable workers would have to escape suddenly over the plunging logs to shore.

My eye ranged over the men, and finally rested on Dickey Darrell. He was standing on the slanting end of an upheaved log dominating the scene. His triangular face with the accents of the quadrilateral eyebrows was pale with the blaze of his energy, and his chipmunk eyes seemed to flame with a dynamic vehemence that caused those on whom their glance fell to jump as though they had been touched with a hot poker. I had heard more of Dickey Darrell since my last visit, and was glad of the chance to observe Morrison and Daly's[8] best "driver" at work.

The jam seemed on the very edge of breaking. After half an hour's strained expectation

it seemed still on the very edge of breaking. So I sat down on a stump. Then for the first time I noticed another acquaintance, handling his peavey near the very person of the rear boss.

"Hullo," said I to myself, "that's funny. I wonder if Jimmy Powers got even; and if so, why he is working so amicably and so near Roaring Dick."

At noon the men came ashore for dinner. I paid a quarter into the cook's private exchequer and so was fed. After the meal I approached my acquaintance of the year before.

"Hello, Powers," I greeted him, "I suppose you don't remember me?"

"Sure," he responded heartily. "Ain't you a little early this year?"

"No," I disclaimed, "this is a better sight than a birling match."

I offered him a cigar, which he immediately substituted for his corncob pipe. We sat at the root of a tree.

"It'll be a great sight when that jam pulls," said I.

"You bet," he replied, "but she's a teaser. Even old Tim Shearer would have a picnic to make out just where the key logs are. We've started her three times, but she's plugged tight every trip. Likely to pull almost any time."

We discussed various topics. Finally I ventured: "I see your old friend Darrell is rear boss."

"Yes," said Jimmy Powers, dryly.

"By the way, did you fellows ever square up on that birling match?"

"No," said Jimmy Powers; then after an instant, "not yet."

I glanced at him to recognize the square set to the jaw that had impressed me so formidably the year before. And again his face relaxed almost quizzically as he caught sight of mine.

"Bub," said he, getting to his feet, "those little marks are on my foot yet. And just you tie into one idea: Dickey Darrell's got it coming." His face darkened with a swift anger.... I glimpsed the flare of an undying hate.

About three o'clock that afternoon Jimmy's prediction was fulfilled. Without the slightest warning the jam "pulled." Usually certain premonitory *cracks,* certain sinkings down, groan-

---

[7]*chevaux de frise* (shə vō′ də frēz), Friesland "horses," so-called from the Dutch province where they were invented. They were ten-to-twelve-foot pieces of wood with spikes sticking out of them, once used to hinder the advance of enemy cavalry. To the writer the tangled jumble of logs suggested these ancient military devices.

[8]*Morrison and Daly,* the name of the company for which Darrell worked.

ings forward, grumblings, shruggings, and sullen, reluctant shiftings of the logs give opportunity for the men to assure their safety. This jam, after inexplicably hanging fire for a week, as inexplicably started like a sprinter almost into its full gait. The first few tiers toppled smash into the current, raising a waterspout like that made by a dynamite explosion; the mass behind plunged forward blindly, rising and falling as the integral logs were upended, turned over, thrust one side, or forced bodily into the air by the mighty power playing jackstraws with them.

The rivermen, though caught unaware, reached either bank. They held their peaveys across their bodies as balancing poles, and zig-zagged ashore with a calmness and lack of haste that were in reality only an indication of the keenness with which they fore-estimated each chance. Long experience with the ways of the saw logs brought them out. They knew the correlation of these many forces just as the expert billiard player knows instinctively the various angles of incident and reflection between his cue ball and its mark. Consequently they avoided the centers of eruption, paused on the spots steadied for the moment, dodged moving logs, trod those not yet under way, and so arrived on solid ground. The jam itself started with every indication of meaning business, gained momentum for a hundred feet, and then plugged to a standstill. The break was abortive.

Now we all had leisure to notice two things. First, the movement had not been of the whole jam, as we had at first supposed, but only of a block or section of it twenty rods or so in extent. Thus between the part that had moved and the greater bulk that had not stirred lay

a hundred feet of open water in which floated a number of loose logs. The second fact was, that Dickey Darrell had fallen into that open stretch of water and was in the act of swimming toward one of the floating logs. That much we were given just time to appreciate thoroughly. Then the other section of the jam rumbled and began to break. Roaring Dick was caught between two gigantic millstones moving to crush him out of sight.

An active figure darted down the tail of the first section, out over the floating logs, seized Darrell by the coat collar, and so burdened began desperately to scale the very face of the breaking jam.

Never was a more magnificent rescue. The logs were rolling, falling, diving against the laden man. He climbed as over a treadmill, a treadmill whose speed was constantly increasing. And when he finally gained the top, it was as the gap closed splintering beneath him and the man he had saved.

It is not in the woodsman to be demonstrative at any time, but here was work demanding attention. Without a pause for breath or congratulation they turned to the necessity of the moment. The jam, the whole jam, was moving at last. Jimmy Powers ran ashore for his peavey. Roaring Dick, like a demon incarnate, threw himself into the work.

Forty men attacked the jam at a dozen places, encouraging the movement, twisting aside the timbers that threatened to lock anew, directing pygmylike the titanic forces into the channel of their efficiency. Roaring like wild cattle the logs swept by, at first slowly, then with the railroad rush of the curbed freshet. Men were everywhere, taking chances, like cowboys before the stampeded herd. And so, out of sight around the lower bend swept the front of the jam in a swirl of glory, the rivermen riding the great boom back of the creature they subdued, until at last, with the slackening current, the logs floated by free, cannoning with hollow sound one against the other. A half-dozen watchers, leaning statuesquely on the shafts of their peaveys, watched the ordered ranks pass by.

One by one the spectators departed. At last only myself and the brown-faced young man remained. He sat on a stump, staring with sightless eyes into vacancy. I did not disturb his thoughts.

The sun dipped. A cool breeze of evening sucked up the river. Over near the cook-camp a big fire commenced to crackle by the drying frames. At dusk the rivermen straggled in from the downriver trail.

The brown-faced young man arose and went to meet them. I saw him return in close conversation with Jimmy Powers. Before they reached us he had turned away with a gesture of farewell.

Jimmy Powers stood looking after him long after his form had disappeared, and indeed even after the sound of his wheels had died toward town. As I approached, the riverman turned to me a face from which the reckless, contained self-reliance of the woods-worker had faded. It was wide-eyed with an almost awe-stricken wonder and adoration.

"Do you know who that is?" he asked me in a hushed voice. "That's Thorpe, Harry Thorpe. And do you know what he said to me just now, *me?* He told me he wanted me to work in Camp One next winter, Thorpe's One. And he told me I was the first man he ever hired straight into One."

His breath caught with something like a sob.

I had heard of the man and of his methods. I knew he had made it a practice of recruiting for his prize camp only from the employees of his other camps, that, as Jimmy said, he never "hired straight into One." I had heard, too, of his reputation among his own and other woodsmen. But this was the first time I had ever come into personal contact with his influence. It impressed me the more in that I had come to know Jimmy Powers and his kind.

"You deserve it, every bit," said I. "I'm not going to call you a hero, because that would make you tired. What you did this afternoon showed nerve. It was a brave act. But it was a better act because you rescued your enemy, because you forgot everything but your common humanity when danger——"

I broke off. Jimmy was again looking at me with his ironically quizzical grin.

"Bub," said he, "if you're going to hang any stars of Bethlehem on my Christmas tree, just call a halt right here. I didn't rescue that scalawag because I had any Christian sentiments, nary bit. I was just naturally savin' him for the birling match next Fourther July."

CONSIDERING AN ACTION-FILLED STORY

1. Who tells the story? Why do you think Stewart Edward White chose such a narrator?

2. What is there in the description of the "men of the woods" which suggests their pride in their work? What passages indicate most clearly the skill these men have developed?

3. In describing Jimmy Powers and Roaring Dick what details does the author use to present a vivid portrait of each?

4. How do the comparisons with wrestling and boxing make the descriptions of the birling matches more vivid?

5. What purpose does Harry Thorpe serve in the story?

America Was Schoolmasters

ROBERT P. TRISTRAM COFFIN

A modern New England poet here pays tribute to the teachers of past generations. Usually the teacher was a man, and he held classes in the "little red schoolhouse on the hill." His pay was small, his duties many. He asked no greater reward than that of seeing his pupils developing into clear-thinking, soundhearted Americans.

AMERICA was forests,
America was grain,
Wheat from dawn to sunset,
And rainbows trailing rain.

America was beavers, 5
Buffalo in seas,
Cornsilk and the johnnycake,
Song of scythes and bees.

America was brown men
With eyes full of the sun, 10
But America was schoolmasters,
Tall one by lonely one.

They hewed oak, carried water,
Their hands were knuckle-boned,
They piled on loads of syntax 15
Till the small boys groaned.

They taught the girls such manners
As stiffened them for life,
But made many a fine speller,
Good mother and good wife. 20

They took small wiry children,
Wild as panther-cats,
And turned them into reasoning
Sunny democrats.

They caught a nation eager, 25
They caught a nation young,
They taught the nation fairness,
Thrift, and the golden tongue.

They started at the bottom
And built up strong and sweet, 30
They shaped our minds and morals
With switches on the seat!

INTERPRETING THE POEM

1. What does the poet mean by saying "America was schoolmasters"?

2. Do you think the old-time schoolmasters succeeded in developing "clear-thinking, sound-hearted Americans"? Explain your reasons.

3. In your opinion were the old-time teachers *liked and respected* or *disliked and feared* by their pupils? Cite evidence for your answer.

4. Explain the meaning of lines 21-24. (Be sure to notice that the last word of line 24 begins with a small *d*, not a capital *D*. What difference does this make in the meaning of the word?)

Chicago

CARL SANDBURG

When Carl Sandburg's first volume, *Chicago Poems*, appeared in 1916, it startled its readers by its use of slangy diction, irregular rhythms, and realistic pictures of the commonplace (and often crude) life that the poet had known from first-hand experience. In "Chicago," the title poem of the volume, Sandburg expresses his admiration for the power that gets work done, even when it is rough and possibly ugly work.

Hog butcher for the World,
  Tool Maker, Stacker of Wheat,
Player with Railroads and the Nation's
  Freight Handler;
Stormy, husky, brawling,
City of the Big Shoulders: 5

They tell me you are wicked and I believe them,
  for I have seen your painted women under
  the gas lamps luring the farm boys.
And they tell me you are crooked and I answer:
  Yes, it is true I have seen the gunman kill
  and go free to kill again.
And they tell me you are brutal and my reply
  is: On the faces of women and children I
  have seen the marks of wanton hunger.
And having answered so I turn once more to
  those who sneer at this my city, and I give
  them back the sneer and say to them:
Come and show me another city with lifted
  head singing so proud to be alive and
  coarse and strong and cunning.   10
Flinging magnetic curses amid the toil of piling
  job on job, here is a tall bold slugger set
  vivid against the little soft cities;
Fierce as a dog with tongue lapping for action,
  cunning as a savage pitted against the
  wilderness,
    Bareheaded,
    Shoveling,
    Wrecking,   15
    Planning,
    Building, breaking, rebuilding,

Under the smoke, dust all over his mouth,
  laughing with white teeth,
Under the terrible burden of destiny laughing
  as a young man laughs,
Laughing even as an ignorant fighter laughs who
  has never lost a battle,   20
Bragging and laughing that under his wrist is
  the pulse, and under his ribs the heart of
  the people,
    Laughing!
Laughing the stormy, husky, brawling laughter
  of Youth, half-naked, sweating, proud to
  be Hog Butcher, Tool Maker, Stacker of
  Wheat, Player with Railroads and Freight
  Handler to the Nation.

HOW DOES SANDBURG DEFEND INDUSTRIALISM?

1. What is Sandburg's defense of Chicago?
2. To what does Sandburg compare Chicago? Read aloud the lines that develop this comparison. Describe in your own words the mental picture these lines give you.
3. What does Sandburg mean by "the terrible burden of destiny" (line 19)?
4. How does this poem illustrate the satisfactions to be gained even from hard, unpleasant work?
5. Compare "Chicago" with Whitman's "I Hear America Singing" (page 228). What do the two poems have in common? Explain the differences that you find.

Extending interests

1. You may find it interesting to compare other poems about cities with Sandburg's "Chicago." Among those that you might read are: "Skyscraper," by Carl Sandburg, in Sandburg's *Chicago Poems;* "Proud New York," by John Reed, and "Dusk" (Charleston, South Carolina), by Du Bose Heyward, in *The Home Book of Modern Verse,* edited by Burton Stevenson; and "Mannahatta," by Walt Whitman. This last poem, which pictures New York in an earlier day, may be found in *The Home Book of Verse,* edited by Burton Stevenson.
2. If you like to make posters, you may find that Sandburg's "tall bold slugger" offers an interesting idea for a poster of the type that the city of Chicago might use to illustrate its industrial progress.

Good Times

Circus at Dawn

THOMAS WOLFE

Although work has been one of the main routes to happiness for Americans, entertainment and play have been its rival. Americans spend their leisure time in innumerable ways. On a summer's day, however, few can resist a circus if there is one in town. For many generations the circus has been one of the windows of the American imagination, opening to a romantic, unfamiliar world of strange smells and sounds and sights. Thomas Wolfe, whose love of sense experience is comparable to that of Walt Whitman and Mark Twain, tells us how meeting the circus train in early morning impressed him when he was a newspaper carrier in Asheville, North Carolina, nearly a half century ago.

THERE WERE TIMES in early autumn—in September—when the greater circuses would come to town—the Ringling Brothers, Robinson's, and Barnum and Bailey shows,[1] and when I was a route-boy on the morning paper, on those mornings when the circus would be coming in I would rush madly through my route in the cool and thrilling darkness that comes just before break of day, and then I would go back home and get my brother out of bed.

Talking in low excited voices we would walk rapidly back toward town under the rustle of September leaves, in cool streets just grayed now with that still, that unearthly and magical first light of day which seems suddenly to rediscover the great earth out of darkness, so that the earth emerges with an awful, a glorious sculptural stillness, and one looks out with a feeling of joy and disbelief, as the first men on this earth must have done, for to see this happen is one of the things that men will remember out of life forever and think of as they die.

At the sculptural still square where at one corner, just emerging into light, my father's shabby little marble shop[2] stood with a ghostly strangeness and familiarity, my brother and I would "catch" the first streetcar of the day bound for the "depot" where the circus was—or sometimes we would meet someone we knew, who would give us a lift in his automobile.

Then, having reached the dingy, grimy, and rickety depot section, we would get out, and walk rapidly across the tracks of the station yard, where we could see great flares and steamings from the engines, and hear the crash and bump of shifting freight cars, the swift sporadic thunders of a shifting engine, the tolling of bells, the sounds of great trains on the rails.

And to all these familiar sounds, filled with their exultant prophecies of flight, the voyage, morning, and the shining cities—to all the sharp and thrilling odors of the trains—the smell of cinders, acrid smoke, of musty, rusty freight cars, the clean pine-board of crated produce, and the smells of fresh stored food—oranges, coffee, tangerines and bacon, ham and flour and beef—there would be added now, with an unforgettable magic and familiarity, all the strange sounds and smells of the coming circus.

The gay yellow sumptuous-looking cars in which the star performers lived and slept, still dark and silent, heavily and powerfully still,

[1] *the Ringling Brothers, Robinson's, and Barnum and Bailey shows,* all famous circuses of the latter part of the nineteenth century and of the twentieth century. Barnum and Bailey's was started in 1871 by P. T. Barnum, most famous of American showmen, and ten years later combined with its chief rival, the show of James Anthony Bailey. Ringling Brothers was organized in 1884 by five brothers, the guiding spirit being Charles Ringling. It later absorbed the circus of "Yankee" Robinson. All three are now a single circus, the biggest in the world.

[2] *my father's shabby little marble shop.* The author's father was a stonecutter, a maker of tombstones.

would be drawn up in long strings upon the tracks. And all around them the sounds of the unloading circus would go on furiously in the darkness. The receding gulf of lilac and departing night would be filled with the savage roar of the lions, the murderously sudden snarling of the great jungle cats, the trumpeting of the elephants, the stamp of the horses, and with the musty, pungent, unfamiliar odor of the jungle animals: the tawny camel smells, and the smells of panthers, zebras, tigers, elephants, and bears.

Then, along the tracks, beside the circus trains, there would be the sharp cries and oaths of the circus men, the magical swinging dance of lanterns in the darkness, the sudden heavy rumble of the loaded vans and wagons as they were pulled along the flats and gondolas, and down the runways to the ground. And everywhere, in the thrilling mystery of darkness and awakening light, there would be the tremendous conflict of a confused, hurried, and yet orderly movement.

The great iron-gray horses, four and six to a team, would be plodding along the road of thick white dust to a rattling of chains and traces and the harsh cries of their drivers. The men would drive the animals to the river which flowed by beyond the tracks, and water them; and as first light came one could see the elephants wallowing in the familiar river and the big horses going slowly and carefully down to drink.

Then, on the circus grounds, the tents were going up already with the magic speed of dreams. All over the place (which was near the tracks and the only space of flat land in the town that was big enough to hold a circus) there would be this fierce, savagely hurried, and yet orderly confusion. Great flares of gaseous circus light would blaze down on the seared and battered faces of the circus toughs as, with the rhythmic precision of a single animal—a human riveting machine—they swung their sledges at the stakes, driving a stake into the earth with the incredible instancy of accelerated figures in a motion picture. And everywhere, as light came, and the sun appeared, there would be a scene of magic, order, and of violence. The drivers would curse and talk their special language to their teams, there would be the loud, gasping and uneven labor of a gasoline engine, the shouts and curses of the bosses, the wooden riveting of driven stakes, and the rattle of heavy chains.

Already in an immense cleared space of dusty beaten earth, the stakes were being driven for the main exhibition tent. And an elephant would lurch ponderously to the field, slowly lower his great swinging head at the command of a man who sat perched upon his skull, flourish his gray wrinkled snout a time or two, and then solemnly wrap it around a tent pole big as the mast of a racing schooner. Then the elephant would back slowly away, dragging the great pole with him as if it were a stick of matchwood.

And when this happened, my brother would break into his great "whah-whah" of exuberant

laughter, and prod me in the ribs with his clumsy fingers....

Meanwhile, the circus food-tent—a huge canvas top without concealing sides—had already been put up, and now we could see the performers seated at long trestled tables underneath the tent, as they ate breakfast. And the savor of the food they ate—mixed as it was with our strong excitement, with the powerful but wholesome smells of the animals, and with all the joy, sweetness, mystery, jubilant magic and glory of the morning and the coming of the circus—seemed to us to be of the most maddening and appetizing succulence of any food that we had ever known or eaten.

We could see the circus performers eating tremendous breakfasts, with all the savage relish of their power and strength: they ate big fried steaks, pork chops, rashers of bacon, a half-dozen eggs, great slabs of fried ham and great stacks of wheat cakes which a cook kept flipping in the air with the skill of a juggler, and which a husky-looking waitress kept rushing to their tables on loaded trays held high and balanced marvelously on the fingers of a brawny hand. And above all the maddening odors of the wholesome and succulent food, there brooded forever the sultry and delicious fragrance—that somehow seemed to add a zest and sharpness to all the powerful and thrilling life of morning —of strong boiling coffee, which we could see sending off clouds of steam from an enormous polished urn, and which the circus performers gulped down, cup after cup.

And the circus men and women themselves —these star performers—were such fine-looking people, strong and handsome, yet speaking and moving with an almost stern dignity and decorum, that their lives seemed to us to be as splendid and wonderful as any lives on earth could be. There was never anything loose, rowdy, or tough in their comportment....

Rather, these people in an astonishing way seemed to have created an established community which lived an ordered existence on wheels, and to observe with a stern fidelity unknown in towns and cities the decencies of family life. There would be a powerful young man, a handsome and magnificent young woman with blonde hair and the figure of an Amazon,[3] and a powerfully built, thick-set man of middle age, who had a stern, lined, responsible-looking face and a bald head. They were probably the members of a trapeze team—the young man and woman would leap through space like projectiles, meeting the grip of the older man and hurling back again upon their narrow perches, catching the swing of their trapeze in mid-air, and whirling thrice before they caught it, in a perilous and beautiful exhibition of human balance and precision.

But when they came into the breakfast tent, they would speak gravely yet courteously to other performers, and seat themselves in a family group at one of the long tables, eating their

---

[3] *Amazon,* one of a legendary race of women soldiers, notable for size and strength. According to mythology, the Amazons lived near the Black Sea.

tremendous breakfasts with an earnest concentration, seldom speaking to one another, and then gravely, seriously, and briefly.

And my brother and I would look at them with fascinated eyes: my brother would watch the man with the bald head for a while and then turn toward me, whispering:

"D-d-do[4] you see that f-f-fellow there with the bald head? W-w-well he's the heavy man," he whispered knowingly. "He's the one that c-c-c-catches them! That f-f-fellow's got to know his business! You know what happens if he m-m-misses, don't you?" said my brother.

"What?" I would say in a fascinated tone.

My brother snapped his fingers in the air.

"Over!" he said. "D-d-done for! W-w-why, they'd be d-d-d-dead before they knew what happened. Sure!" he said, nodding vigorously. "It's a f-f-f-fact! If he ever m-m-m-misses it's all over! That boy has g-g-g-got to know his s-s-s-stuff!" my brother said. "W-w-w-why," he went on in a low tone of solemn conviction, "it w-w-w-wouldn't surprise me at all if they p-p-p-pay him s-s-seventy-five or a hundred dollars a week! It's a fact!" my brother cried vigorously.

And we would turn our fascinated stares again upon these splendid and romantic creatures, whose lives were so different from our own, and whom we seemed to know with such familiar and affectionate intimacy. And at length, reluctantly, with full light come and the sun up, we would leave the circus grounds and start for home.

And somehow the memory of all we had seen and heard that glorious morning, and the memory of the food-tent with its wonderful smells, would waken in us the pangs of such a ravenous hunger that we could not wait until we got home to eat. We would stop off in town at lunchrooms and seated on tall stools before the counter, we would devour ham-and-egg sandwiches, hot hamburgers red and pungent at their cores with coarse spicy sanguinary beef, coffee, glasses of foaming milk and doughnuts, and then go home to eat up everything in sight upon the breakfast table.

_____
[4] *D-d-do.* Thomas Wolfe's brother Fred stuttered.

THOMAS WOLFE AND THE CIRCUS

1. How do you learn that Thomas Wolfe and his brother looked on the coming of the circus as a very important event? What passages do you think best show the intensity of feeling which this event caused?

2. What are some of the highlights in Thomas Wolfe's description of the circus? Which part of his experience is most vivid to you?

Appreciating sensory imagery

In one of his books Thomas Wolfe tells of his almost maddening desire to recapture the exact, detailed impressions of past experiences. And through his brilliant use of sensory imagery he does succeed in re-creating the sights, sounds, smells, tastes, and feelings of that day, long ago, when the circus train arrived at a spot near Asheville. The reader feels the urgency of the paper-boy hurrying through his route "in the cool and thrilling darkness that comes just before break of day," shares with him the mystery of the earth emerging from darkness "with an awful, a glorious sculptural stillness," and knows the stretching of imagination the boy feels at hearing the various noises of the trains "filled with their exultant prophecies of flight, the voyage, morning, and the shining cities." Then there is the circus itself—an almost overwhelming profusion of sense impressions.

Select passages that are particularly strong in sensory imagery, noting which words are most important in creating a vivid impression. Select also examples of Wolfe's habit of repeating certain sensory words and phrases, and explain why this device is probably used.

Remember that the trick isn't for the author to employ as many sensory details as possible but to *select* those which will give exactly the impression desired. What rules for the choice of sensory details can you formulate and illustrate?

Compare this selection with Mark Twain's "Life on the Farm," which is also very rich in sensory imagery. Consider the things that delight the authors, their skill in making you visualize the things they describe, and the ability of each to choose the right details.

Extending interests

Walter Edmond's *Chad Hanna* tells an interesting story of a nineteenth-century circus in New York State. Chapter XXII, "Why the Lynching Bee Failed," in *The Adventures of Huckleberry Finn*, by Samuel Clemens, contains Huck's own account of the glories of a circus. You may also enjoy Harvey Woods Root's *Boys' Life of Barnum* or Barnum's own *Here Comes Barnum*, arranged by Helen Ferris.

Fiddler Jones

EDGAR LEE MASTERS

Folk dancing has recently become one of the most fashionable of American recreations, a fact which is new evidence of the deeply ingrained love of play and music in our people. In "Fiddler Jones," one of the few poems in *Spoon River Anthology*[1] which suggests that men and women can find some happiness, Edgar Lee Masters catches part of the spirit of music in a people. His poem is in its way a stout defense of a life devoted to delighting others in one of the most universal ways man has found.

T HE EARTH keeps some vibration going
There in your heart, and that is you.
And if the people find you can fiddle,
Why, fiddle you must, for all your life.
What do you see, a harvest of clover?   5
Or a meadow to walk through to the river?
The wind's in the corn; you rub your hands
For beeves hereafter ready for market;
Or else you hear the rustle of skirts
Like the girls when dancing at Little Grove.   10
To Cooney Potter a pillar of dust
Or whirling leaves meant ruinous drouth;
They looked to me like Red-Head Sammy
Stepping it off, to "Toor-a-Loor."[2]
How could I till my forty acres   15
Not to speak of getting more,
With a medley of horns, bassoons, and piccolos
Stirred in my brain by crows and robins
And the creak of a windmill—only these?
And I never started to plow in my life   20
That some one did not stop in the road
And take me away to a dance or picnic.
I ended up with forty acres;
I ended up with a broken fiddle—
And a broken laugh, and a thousand memories,
And not a single regret.   26

---

[1]See the headnote for "Henry Cogdal" (page 191) for an explanation of the organization of *Spoon River Anthology*.

[2]*Toor-a-Loor,* a folk tune.

1. What was the secret of Fiddler Jones' happiness? How do you imagine his more prosperous neighbors looked upon his way of living? Can you defend him?

2. What is the meaning of the first two lines of the poem? Why are these lines particularly appropriate to introduce a fiddler's account of his life?

3. What did each of the following suggest to Fiddler Jones: a field of clover, the wind in the corn, a pillar of dust, a robin's song, the creak of a windmill?

At the Symphony (César Franck,[1] D Minor)

ROBERT NATHAN

At the opposite end of the scale from the folk song in the world of music is the highly sophisticated art music of the concert halls. In recent years Americans have learned from the radio and television and through the wide development of music in the schools that "highbrow" music brings some of the most genuine satisfactions of life. Robert Nathan in this brief poem tells us how great music can transport us from our prosy everyday life into a new and thrilling world.

T HE 'CELLOS, setting forth apart,
Grumbled and sang, and so the day
From the low beaches of my heart
Turned in tranquillity away.

And over weariness and doubt   5
Rose up the horns like bellied sails,
Like canvas of the soul flung out
To rising and orchestral gales;

Passed on and left irresolute
The ebony, the silver throat;   10

Low over clarinet and flute
Hung heaven upon a single note.

---

[1]*César Franck* (sā′ zär′ frängk), a nineteenth-century French composer and organist.

1. This poem depends heavily upon figurative language for its effect. Analyze the various similes and metaphors that the poet uses in explaining the thoughts aroused in him by the following musical instruments: the 'cellos, the horns, the clarinet, and the flute. Why does he arrange the instruments in this order?

2. What relation to his own life does the poet find in the music of the various instruments? What is the effect of the symphony upon him?

Extending interests

Suggest to your teacher that arrangements be made to have a recording of César Franck's *Symphony in D Minor* played for the class. As a preparation for listening to the music, one member of the class might give a brief report on Franck's work, with emphasis on the *Symphony in D Minor*. After the music has been played, read the poem again. What added insight into the poet's meaning do you gain from hearing the music?

Life and Love

Sixteen

MAUREEN DALY
(*adapted as a radio play by*
BETTY KEPPLER)

Happiness may be found in work or in play, but it is also found, and perhaps more universally, in the affection and love with which we all like to be surrounded. The well-worn statement that it is love which makes the world go round still has truth in it, for we all know that the love of parents for their children, of boy for girl, of husband for wife constitutes one of the strongest forces in our lives.

Just when the boy-meets-girl type of love first strikes varies greatly, but the traditional age for girls is sixteen, for boys perhaps a little later. Maureen Daly's short story, "Sixteen," here given in an adaptation for radio presentation, tells a lot about it, but not perhaps the very special things that one must learn, and cherish, for oneself.

CHARACTERS

VOICE	MOTHER
MAUREEN	BOB
BOY	

[*Music: "Near You"—Strings.*]

VOICE. Now don't get me wrong. I mean, I want you to understand from the beginning that I'm not really so dumb. I know what a girl should do, and what she shouldn't. I get around. I read. I listen to the radio. And I have two older sisters. So you see, I know what the score is. I read Winchell's column[1]—you get to know what New York boy is that way about what pineapple princess on the West Coast and what Broadway pretty is currently the prettiest. But I'm sort of drifting. This isn't what I wanted to tell you. I just wanted to give you the general idea of how I'm not so dumb. It's important that you understand that. You see...it was funny how I met him. It was a winter night like any other night....

MAUREEN (*half singing, half humming "Near You"*). "There's just one...hmmmm hmmm me, near you. It's like heaven...hmmm... hmmm...hm hm"...Latin...Phooey! Fuisti... fuerit...fueramus...fueratis...fuerant.[2]

---

[1] *Winchell's column,* a miscellany of New York gossip and doubtful prophecies which appears in many newspapers.
[2] *Fuisti...fuerant.* Maureen is memorizing the Latin forms of the verb "to be."

[*Sound of book being slammed shut.*]

MAUREEN. Gosh, but it looks like a wonderful night out! *(Calling.)* Mother...hey, Moms. ...You downstairs?...Can I go out for a while?

MOTHER. *May* I, Maureen. Where do you want to go?

MAUREEN. I think I'd like to go skating.

MOTHER. It's getting on toward eight-thirty, you know, dear. Have you all your homework finished?

MAUREEN. We-ee-ll, all except my Latin... that's started, Moms. I wouldn't stay long... just long enough to get some fresh air in my lungs and to keep my skates in practice.

MOTHER. All right. If you promise to come in early. Why don't you call Mary Jane and ask her to go along? I think that would be nice.

[*Sound of boxes and shoes pushed around.*]

MAUREEN. Oh, no, Moms. I'm not in the mood for Mary Jane tonight...hey, do you know where my yellow skating socks are? My red ones have a hole in the toe of one of 'em....

MOTHER. Ellen's got them on, Maureen. I didn't know you were planning to go out, so I told her she could borrow them. Is the hole in your red ones a big one, dear? Couldn't you darn it?

MAUREEN *(to herself).* Well, if I must, I must ...I guess. *(Pause.)* Hey, Moms, do you know where the darning egg is?

MOTHER. Isn't it in its usual place...the left side of my sewing table?

[*Sound of drawer opened.*]

MAUREEN. Oh, yes, I have it now; I was looking in the wrong place....*(Drawer shut....To herself.)* Why does everything have to happen to me? Ellen's socks don't keep wearing out on her. *(Hums "Near You" to herself a moment.)* There. Hole closed. On you go! *(Humming.... To Mother.)* Where are my skates, Mom?

MOTHER. I suppose they're hanging by the back door; that's where they were the last time I saw them. *(Pause.)* Maureen, whatever are you doing now? Soon it'll be nine o'clock and too late for you to go out.

MAUREEN. Be right down...just brushing my hair....*(To herself.)* Gloves, scarf...there! *(To Mother.)* O. K., Moms, here I come....

[*Sound of rapid footsteps going downstairs.*]

MAUREEN. And here I go....Bye! Be seeing you. *(Door slams.)*

[*Music: soft, clear, low strings. Up, under, out slow.[3]*]

VOICE. My skates were all nice and shiny because I'd only worn them once since I got them for Christmas and they smelled so funny ...just like fresh smoked ham. My dog walked with me as far as the corner....My skates thumped me good-naturedly on the back as I walked...and the night was breathlessly quiet ...and the stars winked down like a million flirting eyes. It was very lovely. *(Pause.)* I ran

most of the way...so it was lucky that the sidewalks had ashes on them or I'd have slipped surely. The ashes made funny crunchy noises as I stepped on them, and I could feel their cindery shapes through my shoes. I was out of breath when I got to the warming shanty...out of breath from running and from the loveliness of the night. *(Pause.)* Shanties are always such friendly places...the floor all hacked into wet splinters from the skate runners and the walls scribbled up with paired initials....

---

[3]*Up, under, out slow.* These are directions telling how the music should be played: first loud *(up)*, then softer *(under)* and gradually fading out *(out slow).*

[*Door opens. Laughing conversations. A crackling fire. Skate runners thudding on wood floor. Fade into:*]

BOB. Hi, Maureen. Hey, fellows, Maureen's here....

MAUREEN. Hello, Bob....Hello, everybody.

[*Door closes.*]

BOB. Hey, Maureen, where are you going? C'mon over here and I'll put your skates on for you....

MAUREEN. Thanks, but I can....

BOB (*close*). You can, but you're not going to....You're coming over here and I'm putting them on for you....See?

MAUREEN. All right, Bob, if you want to.

BOB. If I want to....Say, what's the matter with you tonight, anyway? You're in a daze.

MAUREEN. Not in a daze, I'm just not in a talkative mood.

BOB. Well, I guess that tells me where I stand....Say, maybe you don't want to go skating at all...maybe you'd rather go down to the Dive and have a soda and listen to the new bunch of records that just came in....How does that strike you, huh?

MAUREEN. Go down to the Dive and sit inside on a night like this? Oh, Bob, how could you? Haven't you seen the night out tonight? It's too wonderful for words...and you talk about going down to the Dive...gosh!

BOB. I can't see anything so extra special about this night. Say, what is wrong with you?

MAUREEN. Nothing's wrong with me....I'm just not in your kind of mood, that's all.... Well, thanks for putting my skates on for me.

VOICE. I stuck my shoes under the bench ...far back where they'd be easy to find and wouldn't get kicked around. Then I walked out on my toes and the shiny runners of my new skates dug deep into the sodden floor.

[*Door closes. Background cuts.[4]*]

VOICE. It was snowing a little outside, quick little flakes, that melted as soon as they touched your hand. I don't know where the snow came from, 'cause there were stars out...or maybe there weren't and I just thought so, I don't know....That was the kind of a night it was... I waited a moment. You know, starting to skate at a crowded rink is like jumping on a moving merry-go-round. The skaters go skimming around in a colored blur like the painted horses, and the shrill musical clatter echoes into the night like the merry-go-round's organ. Once in, I went all right. At least, I went all right after I found exactly where the rough spot was, it was round, round, round, jump the rut, round, round, round, jump the rut, round, round.

[*Music: "Skater's Waltz."*]

VOICE. And then *he* came! All of a sudden his arm was around my waist so warm and so tight and he said very casually—

HE. Mind if I skate with you?

VOICE. And then he took my other hand. That's all there was to it....Just that. And then we were skating. It wasn't that I'd never skated with a boy before. Don't be silly. I told you before that I get around. But this was different. *He* was smooth. He was a big shot up at school and he went to all the big dances and he was the very best dancer in town. All the girls know that! Don't you see?...This was different.

[*Music: waltz up and end.*]

[*Sound of skates cutting into ice. Low tinkle of bells.*]

HE. Didn't your mother ever tell you that you shouldn't go out alone at night?

MAUREEN. Why...sure...but this—this is just skating....It's not going out alone at night.

HE. Well, take my word for it, when a girl's as special as you are, it's very dangerous.

MAUREEN. Really? (*Laughs.*) Ooops, excuse me...that rough spot again....Hi, Mary!... Hello, Jean....

GIRLS. *Adlibbed Hellos.[5]*

HE. Hi, girls. (*Pause.*) Here's that bump again. (*Laughs.*)

MAUREEN. I guess they just didn't know we were coming or they'd have had that fixed.

HE. Remind me to speak to the mayor about it in the morning. Say, what are those bells? Are they on you somewhere?

MAUREEN. Uh-huh, they're on my bracelet ...see? (*Bells.*) Oh! Look out! (*Thud of bodies*

---

[4]*Background cuts.* With the closing of the door all background noises—conversations, skates thudding on floor, etc. —should stop.

[5]*Adlibbed Hellos.* Girls make up (adlib) a brief phrase of greeting or merely say "hello."

on ice, scraping of skates.) Well, anyway, now that we're sitting down, you can see it better. *(They laugh.)*

HE. It's cute...and like you....Well, give me your hand...up you go. Thank you. Would you like to sit this skate out, Mademoiselle? In a cozier place, I mean.

MAUREEN. What did you have in mind?

HE. I know of a very special snowbank.

MAUREEN. It sounds wonderful.

HE. Oh, it is....Here you go.

MAUREEN. B-R-R, it's cold!

HE. Maybe this'll warm you up....It's called the snow treatment....The idea behind it is to....*(Scuffling.)*

MAUREEN. Oh, don't, oh...help....

HE. Shhh, or I'll be lynched for attempting to murder this town's most beautiful girl.... You wouldn't want me lynched, would you?

MAUREEN. We-e-ll.

HE. Beautiful but hard-hearted....But seriously though, aren't you warmer now? Here, let me brush you off.

VOICE. He leaned over to brush me off. I held my breath. The night stood still. *(Pause.)*

HE. Well, it looks like the town's turning in. There go the lights in the Rogers' house. We'd better start for home.

VOICE. Not "shall I take you home" or "do you live far" but "we'd better start for home." See? That's how I knew he really wanted to take me home. He went to the shanty to get my shoes....

MAUREEN. Black ones...same size as Garbo's....They're under the bench by the old stove....Think you can find them?

HE. I can do anything...especially tonight. You're an inspiration. Be right back...*with* the shoes....Miss me while I'm gone, will you?

MAUREEN. Uh-huh....

VOICE. He was laughing when he left me and ran toward the shanty...he had a wonderful laugh...everything about him was wonderful ...and the night...it was beautiful....He was still smiling when he came back. He took off my skates and tied the wet strings in a soggy knot and put them over his shoulder. Then he held out his hands and I slid off the snow bank.

HE. All ready?

MAUREEN. All ready, sir.

HE. O. K. Let's go.

VOICE. It was snowing harder now. Big, quiet flakes that stuck to the twiggy branches and drifted against the tree trunks. The night was black and white. It was all so lovely that I was sorry I lived only a few blocks away. We talked quietly as we walked....

[*Sound of crunching footsteps in snow.*]

HE. Have you heard Stan Kenton[6] lately? He changed his style, sort of....I never used to like him, but now I think he's just about tops.

MAUREEN. I think he's wonderful. I just love to dance to his records down at the Dive...and I danced to him in person, once, too. It was when he was here playing that Legion benefit.

HE. Were you at that benefit? Funny I didn't see you there. I could have used a good dancing partner, too....I'll bet you're a good dancer, aren't you?

MAUREEN. Well now, I've never danced with me...I wouldn't know.

HE. Well, then, I'll have to find out for myself....I suppose you'll be going away to college next fall?

MAUREEN. Well, I don't know yet...maybe I'm not going to college at all...sometimes I think it's a waste of time for a girl to go to college.

HE. What is it? Out with it....You can tell your old uncle here, marriage or a career?

MAUREEN. Oh, neither, really. I don't have anything special in my mind....I just don't know if I want to go away....Mother and Dad want me to go East to school like Ellen and Ruthie, you see....

HE. I think that would be wonderful....I'm going...to Princeton, I think.

MAUREEN. Oh, really? I didn't think you would be going East. Then it might be fun if I went to Vassar!

HE. I think it could be. *(Pause.)* How lovely you look with that snow in your hair....

MAUREEN. That's just the night...everything looks sort of special and nice tonight....

HE. There *is* something about tonight, you're right....Have you ever seen the moon so close?

---

[6]*Stan Kenton*, a dance-band leader.

MAUREEN. Nope, it's never seemed quite as big or as near to me before...it must be magic....

VOICE. The moon was following us as we walked and ducking playfully behind a chimney every time we turned to look at it. Then we were home. The porch light was on....Mother always puts the porch light on when I'm out at night. We stood there a moment by the front steps....

HE. Well, I guess it's time for me to be getting home. My mother hasn't seen me since breakfast....

MAUREEN. Why, how terrible! I'm glad you went skating, though....

HE. I'm glad you're glad....I'm glad too....

MAUREEN. I suppose I could go on and say that I'm glad that you're glad that I'm glad, but I won't....*(Laugh.)* I am, though....

VOICE. As we stood there, the snow turned pinkish in the glow of the colored light and a few feathery flakes settled in his hair. Then he took my skates and put them over my shoulder and said....

HE. Good night now. I'll call you.

VOICE. Just that, nothing more. I'll call you. I'll call you, he said. I went inside then, and in a moment he was gone. I watched him from the window as he went down the street. He was whistling when he left me, and I waited till the sound faded away so that I couldn't tell if it was he or my heart whistling...out there in the night. And then he was gone...really gone....I shivered....

[*Door closes softly.*]

MOTHER (*off[7]*). Maureen, is that you? Isn't it very late? Where were you so long? Did you meet Mary Jane?

MAUREEN. Yes, Mother...I mean "yes" it's me, and "yes," it is late, but "no" I didn't meet Mary Jane...I was just skating...that's all...and the time sort of passed quicker than I realized it was. It was just wonderful out tonight, Moms, so clear and cold and nice....

MOTHER. I think you'd better go to bed now and get up to do your Latin in the morning. Good night...pleasant dreams....

[*Sound of feet ascending stairs.*]

VOICE. I went into my room and right over to the window. Somehow—outside it seemed changed. The stars were like little chips of hard light way up in the sky...the wonderful moon of a few minutes ago now was throwing down a sullen yellow glare. The air was tense with bitter cold and a big gust of wind had already blown his footprints away. Everything was quiet. I'll call you, he'd said...I'll call you.

[*Music, mysterious, light.*]

VOICE. And that was Thursday. Tonight is Tuesday...and my homework's—*(Aloud.)* Was that the phone? I'll get it.

[*Sound of running footsteps, lifted receiver.*]

MAUREEN. Hello?...oh...just a minute, please, and I'll call her....Mother, Mother, Mrs. Garrison's on the phone....She wants to speak to you about the cake sale or something.... Hello? Mother will be right with you...you're quite welcome....

[*Sound of receiver being put down. Mother enters.*]

MOTHER. Hello...oh, hello, Mattie...just fine, thank you. Yes, he's fine too....How's Thad?...Good...you do?...Well, I've...my goodness, but this is a bad connection...it's buzzing like a beehive.

MAUREEN (*excitedly*). Maybe someone's trying to get us, Mother, why don't you hang up and see....

---

[7]*off*, at a distance from the microphone.

MOTHER. Shhh, Maureen, I can't hear Mrs. Garrison as it is....Well, all right, if you're in a jam I'll tackle a chocolate cake, too. Sure, Mattie. That's all right....Good-by. *(Hangs up.)* My goodness, Maureen, I could hardly hear as it was, without having to try to listen to two people....

[*Phone rings.*]

BOTH. I'll get it....

[*Phone up.*]

MOTHER. Hello?...Maureen?...

MAUREEN. For me?...Boy or girl?

MOTHER. Yes, she's right here, Mary Jane....

MAUREEN. Mary Jane, ohhhh....Hello, Mary Jane...m-m-m-mine's all done. I didn't think it was hard....No, I couldn't go skating to-night....I have work to do....Well, Latin isn't the only thing I take....I know I haven't been over all week, but....Well, I've been awfully busy, Mary Jane. Well, I'm sorry....Bye....

[*Hang up phone.*]

MOTHER. Why did you say you couldn't go out, dear? I'm sure your Father and I wouldn't have minded, and you don't seem to be doing any of the work that you told her about any-way....Why don't you run over?

MAUREEN. Uh-uh. I just don't feel like go-ing over to Mary Jane's tonight...anyway, she wanted to go skating....

MOTHER. Well, what's wrong with skating all of a sudden? This is the first time in my life I've ever heard you turn down an invitation to go skating....You haven't felt like doing anything all week. What's the trouble, dear, tell me....

MAUREEN. Nothing...leave me alone!...I'm sorry, Moms...I'm not feeling so good tonight. How's about a little music?...

VOICE. Tonight is Tuesday and my home-work's done, and I darned some stockings that didn't really need it, and I worked a crossword puzzle, and I listened to the radio and now I'm just sitting. I'm just sitting because I can't think of anything else to do. I can't think of anything, anything but snowflakes and ice skates and yel-low moons and Thursday night. My heart still prays and my mind just laughs. Outside the night is still, so still I think I'll go crazy, and the white snow's all dirtied and smoked into grayness and the wind is blowing the arc light

so it throws weird, waving shadows from the trees onto the lawn—like thin, starved arms begging for I don't know what. And so I'm just sitting here and I'm not feeling anything. I'm not even sad because all of a sudden I know. All of a sudden I know. I can sit here now forever and laugh and laugh and laugh while the tears run salty in the corners of my mouth. For all of a sudden I know, I know what the stars knew all the time—he'll never call—never.

GETTING TO KNOW MAUREEN AND THE BOY

1. Maureen begins her account by saying: "Now don't get me wrong. I mean, I want you to understand from the beginning that I'm not really so dumb." What leads her to fear that the reader will think that she is "dumb"?

2. What circumstances cast a special glow over the evening Maureen describes? When do you think she first realized the boy would not call her? Why in your opinion was it almost a week before she faced the facts squarely?

3. What is your opinion of the boy? Can you justify his actions?

4. Does Maureen seem like a real girl to you? Why, or why not?

Using an old device

The soliloquy was a favorite device in Shakespeare's plays. Often, when the great dramatist wished the audience to know what a character was thinking or feeling, he had that character think aloud. Thus the character spoke directly to the audience, supposedly unheard by the other players on the stage.

Modern playwrights, for the most part, avoid the soliloquy. To today's audience there is something false in having one player speak lines apparently not heard by the rest of the cast. But because in a radio play the characters are not seen by the audience, one of the newest of dramatic forms is able to make effective use of a variation on this old device. In the radio play you have just read, the principal character appears both as Maureen and as the Voice. The part of the Voice forms a kind of running soliloquy throughout the play.

What information does the Voice give you? What is the difference in mood between the lines spoken by the Voice and those spoken by Maureen? Which lines—those spoken by Maureen or those spoken by the Voice—give you a better idea of the girl's personality? Why does the Voice both begin and end the play?

I Can't Breathe

RING LARDNER

Courtship almost always has its ups and downs, especially if it is based more upon being in love with love than upon genuine and mutual affection. The unnamed heroine of Ring Lardner's story in diary form faced the troubles of being eighteen and in love in the 1920's; although the popular songs she sang seem old-fashioned now, you will probably admit, ruefully, that human nature hasn't changed at all.

July 12

I AM STAYING here at the Inn for two weeks with my Uncle Nat and Aunt Jule and I think I will keep a kind of a diary while I am here to help pass the time and so I can have a record of things that happen though goodness knows there isn't lightly to anything happen, that is anything exciting with Uncle Nat and Aunt Jule making the plans as they are both at least 35 years old and maybe older.

Dad and mother are abroad to be gone a month and me coming here is supposed to be a recompence for them not taking me with them. A fine recompence to be left with old people that come to a place like this to rest. Still it would be a heavenly place under different conditions, for instance if Walter were here, too. It would be heavenly if he were here, the very thought of it makes my heart stop.

I can't stand it. I won't think about it.

This is our first seperation since we have been engaged, nearly 17 days. It will be 17 days tomorrow. And the hotel orchestra at dinner this evening played that old thing "Oh how I miss you tonight"[1] and it seemed as if they must be playing it for my benefit though of course the person in that song is talking about how they miss their mother though of course I miss mother too, but a person gets used to missing their mother and it isn't like Walter or the person you are engaged to.

But there won't be any more seperations much longer, we are going to be married in December even if mother does laugh when I talk to her about it because she says I am crazy to even think of getting married at 18.

She got married herself when she was 18, but of course that was "different," she wasn't crazy like I am, she knew whom she was marrying. As if Walter were a policeman or a foreigner or something. And she says she was only engaged once while I have been engaged at least five times a year since I was 14, of course it really isn't as bad as that and I have only been really what I call engaged six times altogether, but is getting engaged my fault when they keep insisting and hammering at you and if you didn't say yes they would never go home.

But it is different with Walter. I honestly believe if he had not asked me I would have asked him. Of course I wouldn't have, but I would have died. And this is the first time I have ever been engaged to be really married. The other times when they talked about when should we get married I just laughed at them, but I hadn't been engaged to Walter ten minutes when he brought up the subject of marriage and I didn't laugh. I wouldn't be engaged to him unless it was to be married. I couldn't stand it.

Anyway mother may as well get used to the idea because it is "No Foolin' "[2] this time and we have got our plans all made and I am going to be married at home and go out to California and Hollywood on our honeymoon. December, five months away. I can't stand it. I can't wait.

There were a couple of awfully nice looking boys sitting together alone in the dining room tonight. One of them wasn't so much, but the other was cute. And he—

There's the dance orchestra playing "Always,"[3] what they played at the Biltmore the day I met Walter. "Not for just an hour not for just a day." I can't live. I can't breathe.

---

[1] *"Oh how I miss you tonight,"* a song by Benny Davis, Joe Burke, and Mark Fisher (1924).

[2] *"No Foolin',"* a song by Gene Buck and James F. Hanley.

[3] *"Always,"* a song by Irving Berlin (1925). The words the girl quotes in the next line are from this song.

This has been a much more exciting day than I expected under the circumstances. In the first place I got two long night letters, one from Walter and one from Gordon Flint. I don't see how Walter ever had the nerve to send his, there was everything in it and it must have been horribly embarrassing for him while the telegraph operator was reading it over and counting the words to say nothing of embarrassing for the operator.

But the one from Gordon was a kind of a shock. He just got back from a trip around the world, left last December to go on it and got back yesterday and called up our house and Helga gave him my address, and his telegram, well it was nearly as bad as Walter's. The trouble is that Gordon and I were engaged when he went away, or at least he thought so and he wrote to me right along all the time he was away and sent cables and things and for a while I answered his letters, but then I lost track of his itinery[4] and couldn't write to him any more and when I got really engaged to Walter I couldn't let Gordon know because I had no idea where he was besides not wanting to spoil his trip.

And now he still thinks we are engaged and he is going to call me up tomorrow from Chicago and how in the world can I explain things and get him to understand because he is really serious and I like him ever and ever so much and in lots of ways he is nicer than Walter, not really nicer but better looking and there is no comparison between their dancing. Walter simply can't learn to dance, that is really dance. He says it is because he is flat-footed, he says that as a joke, but it is true and I wish to heavens it wasn't.

All forenoon I thought and thought and thought about what to say to Gordon when he calls up and finally I couldn't stand thinking about it any more and just made up my mind I wouldn't think about it any more. But I will tell the truth though it will kill me to hurt him.

I went down to lunch with Uncle Nat and Aunt Jule and they were going out to play golf this afternoon and were insisting that I go with them, but I told them I had a headache and then I had a terrible time getting them to go without me. I didn't have a headache at all and just wanted to be alone to think about Walter and besides when you play with Uncle Nat he is always correcting your stance or your swing or something and always puts his hands on my arms or shoulders to show me the right way and I can't stand it to have old men touch me, even if they are your uncle.

I finally got rid of them and I was sitting watching the tennis when that boy I saw last night, the cute one, came and sat right next to me and of course I didn't look at him and I was going to smoke a cigarette and found I had left my lighter upstairs and I started to get up and go after it when all of a sudden he was offering me his lighter and I couldn't very well refuse it without being rude. So we got to talking and he is even cuter than he looks, the most original and wittiest person I believe I ever met and I haven't laughed so much in I don't know how long.

For one thing he asked me if I had heard Rockefeller's song and I said no and he began singing "Oil alone."[5] Then he asked me if I knew the orange juice song and I told him no again and he said it was "Orange juice sorry you made me cry."[6] I was in hysterics before we had been together ten minutes.

His name is Frank Caswell and he has been out of Darthmouth a year and is 24 years old. That isn't so terrible old, only two years older than Walter and three years older than Gordon. I hate the name Frank, but Caswell is all right and he is so cute.

He was out in California last winter and visited Hollywood and met everybody in the world and it is fascinating to listen to him. He met Norma Shearer[7] and he said he thought she was the prettiest thing he had ever seen. What he

---

[4]*itinery*, itinerary, or route of travel.

[5]"*Oil alone*," a pun on the title of Irving Berlin's song "All Alone" (1924). Rockefeller made his fortune from oil.

[6]"*Orange juice sorry...cry*," another pun, this time a variation on the popular song "I'm Sorry I Made You Cry," by N. J. Clesi (1918).

[7]*Norma Shearer*, a movie actress who was very popular in the 1920's and 1930's.

said was "I did think she was the prettiest girl in the world, till today." I was going to pretend I didn't get it, but I finally told him to be sensible or I would never be able to believe anything he said.

Well, he wanted me to dance with him tonight after dinner and next question was how to explain how we had met each other to Uncle Nat and Aunt Jule. Frank said he would fix that all right and sure enough he got himself introduced to Uncle Nat when Uncle Nat came in from golf and after dinner Uncle Nat introduced him to me and Aunt Jule too and we danced together all evening, that is not Aunt Jule. They went to bed, thank heavens.

He is a heavenly dancer, as good as Gordon. One dance we were dancing and for one of the encores the orchestra played "In a cottage small by a waterfall"[8] and I simply couldn't dance to it. I just stopped still and said "Listen, I can't bear it, I can't breathe" and poor Frank thought I was sick or something and I had to explain that that was the tune the orchestra played the night I sat at the next table to Jack Barrymore[9] at Barney Gallant's.

I made him sit out that encore and wouldn't let him talk till they got through playing it. Then they played something else and I was all right again and Frank told me about meeting Jack Barrymore. Imagine meeting him. I couldn't live.

I promised Aunt Jule I would go to bed at eleven and it is way past that now, but I am all ready for bed and have just been writing this. Tomorrow Gordon is going to call up and what will I say to him? I just won't think about it.

July 14

Gordon called up this morning from Chicago and it was wonderful to hear his voice again though the connection was terrible. He asked me if I still loved him and I tried to tell him no, but I knew that would mean an explanation and the connection was so bad that I never could make him understand so I said yes, but I almost whispered it purposely, thinking he wouldn't hear me, but he heard me all right and he said that made everything all right with the world. He said he thought I had stopped loving him because I had stopped writing.

I wish the connection had been decent and I could have told him how things were, but now it is terrible because he is planning to get to New York the day I get there and heaven knows what I will do because Walter will be there, too. I just won't think about it.

Aunt Jule came in my room just after I was through talking to Gordon, thank heavens. The room was full of flowers. Walter had sent me some and so had Frank. I got another long night letter from Walter, just as silly as the first one. I wish he would say those things in letters instead of night letters so everybody in the world wouldn't see them. Aunt Jule wanted me to read it aloud to her. I would have died.

While she was still in the room, Frank called up and asked me to play golf with him and I said all right and Aunt Jule said she was glad my headache was gone. She was trying to be funny.

[8]*In a cottage small by a waterfall,* "Just a Cottage Small (by a Waterfall)," a song by Bud De Sylva and James F. Hanley (1925).

[9]*Jack Barrymore,* John Barrymore (1882-1942), probably the most popular hero of stage and screen in his generation.

I played golf with Frank this afternoon. He is a beautiful golfer and it is thrilling to watch him drive, his swing is so much more graceful than Walter's. I asked him to watch me swing and tell me what was the matter with me, but he said he couldn't look at anything but my face and there wasn't anything the matter with that.

He told me the boy who was here with him had been called home and he was glad of it because I might have liked him, the other boy, better than himself. I told him that couldn't be possible and he asked me if I really meant that and I said of course, but I smiled when I said it so he wouldn't take it too seriously.

We danced again tonight and Uncle Nat and Aunt Jule sat with us awhile and danced a couple of dances themselves, but they were really there to get better acquainted with Frank and see if he was all right for me to be with. I know they certainly couldn't have enjoyed their own dancing, no old people really can enjoy it because they can't really *do* anything.

They were favorably impressed with Frank I think, at least Aunt Jule didn't say I must be in bed at eleven, but just not to stay up too late. I guess it is a big surprise to a girl's parents and aunts and uncles to find out that the boys you go around with are all right, they always seem to think that if I like somebody and the person pays a little attention to me, why he must be a convict or a policeman or a drunkard or something queer.

Frank had some more songs for me tonight. He asked me if I knew the asthma song and I said I didn't and he said "Oh, you must know that. It goes yes, sir, asthma baby."[10] Then he told me about the underwear song, "I underwear my baby is tonight."[11] He keeps you in hysterics and yet he has his serious side, in fact he was awfully serious when he said good night to me and his eyes simply shown. I wish Walter were more like him in some ways, but I mustn't think about that.

[10]"*yes, sir, asthma baby*," a pun on the title of "Yes, Sir, That's My Baby," by Gus Kahn and Walter Donaldson (1925).

[11]"*I underwear my baby is tonight*," more punning of the same type on the title of "I Wonder Where My Baby Is Tonight," by Gus Kahn and Walter Donaldson (1925).

July 15

I simply can't live and I know I'll never sleep tonight. I am in a terrible predicament or rather I won't know whether I really am or not till tomorrow and that is what makes it so terrible.

After we had danced two or three dances, Frank asked me to go for a ride with him and we went for a ride in his car and he had had some cocktails, and during the ride he had some drinks out of a flask and finally he told me he loved me and I said not to be silly, but he said he was perfectly serious and he certainly acted that way. He asked me if I loved anybody else and I said yes and he asked if I didn't love him more than anybody else and I said yes, but only because I thought he had probably had too much to drink and wouldn't remember it anyway and the best thing to do was humor him under the circumstances.

Then all of a sudden he asked me when I could marry him and I said, just as a joke, that I couldn't possibly marry him before December. He said that was a long time to wait, but I was certainly worth waiting for and he said a lot of other things and maybe I humored him a little too much, but that is just the trouble, I don't know.

I was absolutely sure he was tight and would forget the whole thing, but that was early in the evening, and when we said good night he was a whole lot more sober than he had been and now I am not sure how it stands. If he doesn't remember anything about it, of course I am all right. But if he does remember and if he took me seriously, I will simply have to tell him about Walter and maybe about Gordon too. And it isn't going to be easy. The suspense is what is maddening and I know I'll never live through this night.

July 16

I can't stand it, I can't breathe, life is impossible. Frank remembered everything about last night and firmly believes we are engaged and going to be married in December. His people live in New York and he says he is going back when I do and have them meet me.

Of course it can't go on and tomorrow I will tell him about Walter or Gordon or both of them. I know it is going to hurt him terribly, perhaps spoil his life and I would give anything in the world not to have had it happen. I hate so to hurt him because he is so nice besides being so cute and attractive.

He sent me the loveliest flowers this morning and called up at ten and wanted to know how soon he could see me and I hope the girl wasn't listening in because the things he said were, well, like Walter's night letters.

And that is another terrible thing, today I didn't get a night letter from Walter, but there was a regular letter instead and I carried it around in my purse all this afternoon and evening and never remembered to read it till ten minutes ago when I came up in the room. Walter is worried because I have only sent him two telegrams and written him one letter since I have been here, he would be a lot more worried if he knew what has happened now, though of course it can't make any difference because he is the one I am really engaged to be married to and the one I told mother I was going to marry in December and I wouldn't dare tell her it was somebody else.

I met Frank for lunch and we went for a ride this afternoon and he was so much in love and so lovely to me that I simply did not have the heart to tell him the truth, I am surely going to tell him tomorrow and telling him today would have just meant one more day of unhappiness for both of us.

He said his people had plenty of money and his father had offered to take him into partnership and he might accept, but he thinks his true vocation is journalism with a view to eventually writing novels and if I was willing to undergo a few hardships just at first we would probably both be happier later on if he was doing something he really liked. I didn't know what to say, but finally I said I wanted him to suit himself and money wasn't everything.

He asked me where I would like to go on my honeymoon and I suppose I ought to have told him my honeymoon was all planned, that I was going to California, with Walter, but all I said was that I had always wanted to go to California and he was enthusiastic and said that is where we would surely go and he would take me to Hollywood and introduce me to all those wonderful people he met there last winter. It nearly takes my breath away to think of it, going there with someone who really knows people and has the entrée.

We danced again tonight, just two or three dances, and then went out and sat in the tennis court, but I came upstairs early because Aunt Jule had acted kind of funny at dinner. And I wanted to be alone, too, and think, but the more I think the worse it gets.

Sometimes I wish I were dead, maybe that is the only solution and it would be best for everyone concerned. I *will* die if things keep on the way they have been. But of course tomorrow it will be all over, with Frank I mean, for I must tell him the truth no matter how much it hurts us both. Though I don't care how much it hurts me. The thought of hurting him is what is driving me mad. I can't bear it.

July 18

I have skipped a day. I was busy every minute of yesterday and so exhausted when I came upstairs that I was tempted to fall into bed with all my clothes on. First Gordon called me up from Chicago to remind me that he would be in New York the day I got there and that when he comes he wants me all to himself all the time and we can make plans for our wedding. The connection was bad again and I just couldn't explain to him about Walter.

I had an engagement with Frank for lunch and just as we were going in another long distance call came, from Walter this time. He wanted to know why I haven't written more letters and sent him more telegrams and asked me if I still loved him and of course I told him yes because I really do. Then he asked if I had met any men here and I told him I had met one, a friend of Uncle Nat's. After all it was Uncle Nat who introduced me to Frank. He reminded me that he would be in New York on the 25th which is the day I expect to get home, and said he would have theater tickets for that night and we would go somewhere afterwards and dance.

Frank insisted on knowing who had kept me talking so long and I told him it was a boy I had known a long while, a very dear friend of mine and a friend of my family's. Frank was jealous and kept asking questions till I thought I would go mad. He was so serious and kind of cross and gruff that I gave up the plan of telling him the truth till some time when he is in better spirits.

I played golf with Frank in the afternoon and we took a ride last night and I wanted to get in early because I had promised both Walter and Gordon that I would write them long letters, but Frank wouldn't bring me back to the Inn till I had named a definite date in December. I finally told him the 10th and he said all right if I was sure that wasn't a Sunday. I said I would have to look it up, but as a matter of fact I know the 10th falls on a Friday because the date Walter and I have agreed on for our wedding is Saturday the 11th.

Today has just been the same thing over again, two more night letters, a long distance call from Chicago, golf and a ride with Frank, and the room full of flowers. But tomorrow I am going to tell Frank and I am going to write Gordon a long letter and tell him, too, because this simply can't go on any longer. I can't breathe. I can't live.

July 21

I wrote to Gordon yesterday, but I didn't say anything about Walter because I don't think it is a thing a person ought to do by letter. I can tell him when he gets to New York and then I will be sure that he doesn't take it too hard and I can promise him that I will be friends with him always and make him promise not to do anything silly, while if I told it to him in a letter there is no telling what he would do, there all alone.

And I haven't told Frank because he hasn't been feeling well, he is terribly sunburned and it hurts him terribly so he can hardly play golf or dance, and I want him to be feeling his best when I do tell him, but whether he is all right or not I simply must tell him tomorrow because he is actually planning to leave here on the same train with us Saturday night and I can't let him do that.

Life is so hopeless and it could be so wonder-ful. For instance how heavenly it would be if I could marry Frank first and stay married to him five years and he would be the one who would take me to Hollywood and maybe we could go on parties with Norman Kerry and Jack Barrymore and Buster Collier and Marion Davies and Lois Moran.[12]

And at the end of five years Frank could go into journalism and write novels and I would only be 23 and I could marry Gordon and he would be ready for another trip around the world and he could show me things better than someone who had never seen them before.

Gordon and I would separate at the end of five years and I would be 28 and I know of lots of women that never even got married the first time till they were 28 though I don't suppose that was their fault, but I would marry Walter then, for after all he is the one I really love and want to spend most of my life with and I wouldn't care whether he could dance or not when I was that old. Before long we would be as old as Uncle Nat and Aunt Jule and I certainly wouldn't want to dance at their age when all you can do is just hobble around the floor. But Wal-ter is so wonderful as a companion and we would enjoy the same things and be pals and maybe we would begin to have children.

But that is all impossible though it wouldn't be if older people just had sense and would look at things the right way.

It is only half-past ten, the earliest I have gone to bed in weeks, but I am worn out and Frank went to bed early so he could put cold cream on his sunburn.

Listen, diary, the orchestra is playing "Lime-house Blues."[13] The first tune I danced to with Merle Oliver, two years ago. I can't stand it. And how funny that they should play that old tune tonight of all nights, when I have been thinking of Merle off and on all day, and I hadn't thought of him before in weeks and weeks. I wonder where he is, I wonder if it is

---

[12]*Norman Kerry...Buster Collier and Marion Davies and Lois Moran.* All movie actors and actresses who were popular stars of the silent screen at the time of the story.
[13]*"Limehouse Blues,"* a song by Douglas Furber and Philip Braham (1924).

just an accident or if it means I am going to see him again. I simply mustn't think about it or I'll die.

July 22

I knew it wasn't an accident. I knew it must mean something, and it did.

Merle is coming here today, here to this Inn, and just to see me. And there can only be one reason. And only one answer. I knew that when I heard his voice calling from Boston. How could I ever have thought I loved anyone else? How could he ever have thought I meant it when I told him I was engaged to George Morse?

A whole year and he still cares and I still care. That shows we were always intended for each other and for no one else. I won't make *him* wait till December. I doubt if we even wait till dad and mother get home. And as for a honeymoon I will go with him to Long Beach or the Bronx Zoo,[14] wherever he wants to take me.

After all this is the best way out of it, the only way. I won't have to say anything to Frank, he will guess when he sees me with Merle. And when I get home Sunday and Walter and Gordon call me up, I will invite them both to dinner and Merle can tell them himself, with two of them there it will only hurt each one half as much as if they were alone.

The train is due at 2:40, almost three hours from now. I can't wait. And what if it should be late? I can't stand it.

---

[14]*Long Beach or the Bronx Zoo,* recreation areas in or near New York City. Long Beach is a bathing resort on the southern shore of Long Island, and Bronx Zoo is in a borough of the city on the mainland north of Manhattan.

WHAT DO YOU LEARN FROM THE DIARY?

1. Do you think Ring Lardner chose wisely when he decided on the diary form for this story? Explain.

2. What do you learn about the writer from the writing itself? What does the title of the story tell you about the girl?

3. As the story progresses the writer gets more and more involved in difficulties. How does each of the following excerpts from her diary show that she herself causes most of her troubles?

(*a*) I won't think about it.

(*b*)…when I got really engaged to Walter I couldn't let Gordon know because I had no idea where he was besides not wanting to spoil his trip.

(*c*)…I am surely going to tell him [Frank] tomorrow and telling him today would have just meant one more day of unhappiness for both of us.

(*d*)…I will invite them both [Walter and Gordon] to dinner and Merle can tell them himself, with two of them there it will only hurt each one half as much….

4. Do you think the writer is ready to get married? Why, or why not?

5. (*For girls only.*) To what do you attribute the girl's apparently irresistible charm?

6. Which of the following statements do you think explain the author's reasons for writing "I Can't Breathe": (*a*) to entertain, (*b*) to present a realistic picture of a girl in love, (*c*) to satirize a certain type of young girl, (*d*) to prove that no one should marry at eighteen?

Annabel Lee

EDGAR ALLAN POE

The poets, of course, have made love their special province. Their thoughts on the subject range from ecstatic approval of the idea itself to disillusion and cynicism. Poe's famous "Annabel Lee" sings of the immortal power of love over all difficulties, even over death itself. The poem is an idealized account of Poe's child-wife, Virginia Clemm, who died in 1847, two years before Poe died.

IT WAS many and many a year ago,
  In a kingdom by the sea,
That a maiden there lived whom you may know
  By the name of Annabel Lee;
And this maiden she lived with no other thought
  Than to love and be loved by me.   6

I was a child and *she* was a child,
  In this kingdom by the sea,
But we loved with a love that was more than love—

I and my Annabel Lee;   10
With a love that the wingèd seraphs of heaven
  Coveted her and me.

And this was the reason that, long ago,
  In this kingdom by the sea,
A wind blew out of a cloud, chilling   15
  My beautiful Annabel Lee;
So that her highborn kinsmen came
  And bore her away from me,
To shut her up in a sepulcher
  In this kingdom by the sea.   20

The angels, not half so happy in heaven,
  Went envying her and me—
Yes! that was the reason (as all men know,
  In this kingdom by the sea)
That the wind came out of the cloud by night,
  Chilling and killing my Annabel Lee.   26

But our love it was stronger by far than the love
  Of those who were older than we,
  Of many far wiser than we;
And neither the angels in heaven above,   30
  Nor the demons down under the sea,
Can ever dissever my soul from the soul
  Of the beautiful Annabel Lee;

For the moon never beams, without bringing me
    dreams
  Of the beautiful Annabel Lee;   35
And the stars never rise, but I feel the bright
    eyes
  Of the beautiful Annabel Lee;
And so, all the night-tide, I lie down by the side
Of my darling—my darling—my life and my
    bride,
  In the sepulcher there by the sea,   40
  In her tomb by the sounding sea.

HOW DOES POE LOOK AT LOVE?

1. How does this poem illustrate the power of love
over death? How do you interpret the last four lines?
2. Why is this poem considered a ballad?
3. Point out words and phrases that the poet uses
to give the poem the unreal atmosphere of a fairy
tale. How does this device add to the idea of the time-
lessness of love?

Give All to Love

RALPH WALDO EMERSON

The poem "Give All to Love" is by a man more
famous as philosopher than as poet. Descended from
nine generations of ministers, Ralph Waldo Emerson
himself became a clergyman, but gave up his ministry
to devote his life to lecturing and writing. However,
in his insistence, both as a lecturer and as a writer,
that man seek his own soul and develop the best that
is in him, he remained always a preacher.

To some people Emerson has seemed austere and
cold, yet he understood better than many another poet
the power and exhilaration of love, its mysterious and
lightning-like appearance and its swift departure.
"Give All to Love" is one of the great literary glori-
fications of the driving force of love.

GIVE ALL to love;
  Obey thy heart;
Friends, kindred, days,
Estate, good fame,
Plans, credit and the Muse[1]—   5
Nothing refuse.

'Tis a brave master;
Let it have scope:
Follow it utterly,
Hope beyond hope: 10
High and more high
It dives into noon,
With wing unspent,
Untold intent;
But it is a god,   15
Knows its own path
And the outlets of the sky.

It was never for the mean;
It requireth courage stout.
Souls above doubt,   20
Valor unbending,
It will reward—
They shall return
More than they were,
And ever ascending.   25

---

[1] the Muse, one of the nine Greek goddesses of the arts
and sciences, here probably the goddess of poetry.

Leave all for love;
Yet, hear me, yet,
One word more thy heart behooved,
One pulse more of firm endeavor—
Keep thee today,   30
Tomorrow, forever,
Free as an Arab[2]
Of thy beloved.

Cling with life to the maid;
But when the surprise,   35
First vague shadow of surmise
Flits across her bosom young,
Of a joy apart from thee,
Free be she, fancy-free;
Nor thou detain her vesture's hem,   40
Nor the palest rose she flung
From her summer diadem.

Though thou loved her as thyself,
As a self of purer clay,
Though her parting dims the day,   45
Stealing grace from all alive;
Heartily know,
When half-gods go,
The gods arrive.

---

[2]*Free as an Arab.* Among the Mohammedan Arabs divorce was allowed the husband at his will.

WHAT IS EMERSON'S VIEW ON LOVE?

1. Like many of Emerson's poems, this one is rather difficult to understand because the poet states his ideas in so few words and omits many words needed to complete the meaning. Work out the poet's argument for each stanza in your own words, supplying any words necessary to make the meaning clear.

2. What is the poet's advice in lines 1-25? How do you explain the paradox of lines 26-33? What is the meaning of lines 34-42?

3. At the end of his essay on "Friendship" Emerson wrote: "It is thought a disgrace to love unrequited. But the great will see that true love cannot be unrequited. True love transcends instantly the unworthy object, and dwells and broods on the eternal, and when the poor, interposed mask crumbles, it is not sad, but feels rid of so much earth, and feels its independency the sooner." Does this idea help explain any part of this poem? How?

I Shall Not Care

SARA TEASDALE

Love unreturned is always painful. In this brief poem Sara Teasdale expresses the feelings of many who have suffered the pangs of unrequited love.

WHEN I AM DEAD and over me bright April
    Shakes out her rain-drenched hair,
Though you should lean above me broken-
    hearted,
    I shall not care.

I shall have peace, as leafy trees are peaceful
    When rain bends down the bough;
And I shall be more silent and cold-hearted
    Than you are now.

WHAT IS THE POET'S MOOD?

1. In what way do the figures of speech used in this poem reflect the mood of the poem? What is peculiarly feminine about the imagery in the first stanza?

2. Read aloud the lines which you think are most effective. How do you explain their effectiveness?

Personal Faith

The Creation

JAMES WELDON JOHNSON

Work and play and love may make everyday living good, but the fullest satisfactions of life depend also upon deep convictions of its meaning. In some form or other, religion has given such convictions to most Americans. In the great personal crises of serious illness and death, worship is a consolation. In the days of well-being and thanksgiving, religion is joy and exhilaration. *God's Trombones,* from which comes the following Negro sermon in verse, was suggested to James Weldon Johnson by the primitive poetry of an old-time preacher who was thoroughly familiar with the sublime phrases of the Hebrew prophets.

AND GOD stepped out on space,
    And he looked around and said:
I'm lonely—
I'll make me a world.

And as far as the eye of God could see   5
Darkness covered everything,
Blacker than a hundred midnights
Down in a cypress swamp.

Then God smiled,
And the light broke,   10
And the darkness rolled up on one side,
And the light stood shining on the other,
And God said: That's good!

Then God reached out and took the light in his
    hands,
And God rolled the light around in his hands 15
Until he made the sun;
And he set that sun a-blazing in the heavens.
And the light that was left from making the sun
God gathered it up in a shining ball
And flung it against the darkness,   20
Spangling the night with the moon and stars.
Then down between

The darkness and the light
He hurled the world;
And God said: That's good!   25

Then God himself stepped down—
And the sun was on his right hand,
And the moon was on his left;
The stars were clustered about his head,
And the earth was under his feet.   30
And God walked, and where he trod
His footsteps hollowed the valleys out
And bulged the mountains up.

Then he stopped and looked and saw
That the earth was hot and barren.   35
So God stepped over to the edge of the world
And he spat out the seven seas—
He batted his eyes, and the lightnings flashed—
He clapped his hands, and the thunders rolled—
And the waters above the earth came down, 40
The cooling waters came down.

Then the green grass sprouted,
And the little red flowers blossomed,
The pine tree pointed his finger to the sky,
And the oak spread out his arms,   45
The lakes cuddled down in the hollows of the
    ground,
And the rivers ran down to the sea;
And God smiled again,
And the rainbow appeared,
And curled itself around his shoulder.   50

Then God raised his arm and he waved his hand
Over the sea and over the land,
And he said: Bring forth! Bring forth!
And quicker than God could drop his hand,
Fishes and fowls   55
And beasts and birds
Swam the rivers and the seas,
Roamed the forests and the woods,
And split the air with their wings.
And God said: That's good!   60

Then God walked around,
And God looked around
On all that he had made.
He looked at his sun,
And he looked at his moon,   65
And he looked at his little stars;
He looked on his world
With all its living things,
And God said: I'm lonely still.

Then God sat down—   70
On the side of a hill where he could think;
By a deep, wide river he sat down;
With his head in his hands,
God thought and thought,
Till he thought: I'll make me a man!   75

Up from the bed of the river
God scooped the clay;
And by the bank of the river
He kneeled him down;
And there the great God Almighty   80
Who lit the sun and fixed it in the sky,
Who flung the stars to the most far corner of
   the night,
Who rounded the earth in the middle of his
   hand;
This Great God

Like a mammy bending over her baby,   85
Kneeled down in the dust
Toiling over a lump of clay
Till he shaped it in his own image;

Then into it he blew the breath of life,
And man became a living soul.   90
Amen. Amen.

INTERPRETING THE POET'S IDEA

1. Point out the imagery that the preacher uses to bring God close to the everyday experience of his congregation.

2. "God made man in His own image, but man also makes God in his own image." By referring to the poem explain what this statement means.

3. How would you describe the tone of the poem?

4. Which lines in their rhythm and phraseology are most like Biblical language?

Extending interests

Read M. C. Connelly's fine play, *Green Pastures,* a Negro interpretation of the Bible. You may also enjoy reading some of the other Negro sermons in verse from *God's Trombones,* by James Weldon Johnson. Which author better (*a*) portrays the faith of the simple and devout Negro, (*b*) conveys his love of the people of whom he writes?

THREE SPIRITUALS

Much of the delight which we all find in the spirituals or religious songs of the American Negroes lies in the haunting melodies, at once supremely sad and mysteriously lovely. But the spirituals have fine poetic qualities, too. They are simple and compact. They have vivid imagery, often drawn from a fresh, direct view of commonplace experience, as in "This Train." They have subtle rhythmic patterns, the result of various kinds of repetition and refrain. The three which follow are a sample of many—the poetry of humble people, much put upon in this life, but finding solace and beauty in the Christian promise of a better world to come.

Oh, Lawd, How Long?

BEFORE THIS TIME another year I may be
   gone,
And in some lonesome graveyard—oh, Lawd,
   how long?

Jes' so de tree fall, jes' so it lie,
Jes' so de sinner live, jes' so he die.

My mother's broke the ice and gone—oh, Lawd,
   how long?   5
An' soon she'll sing dat heavenly song—oh,
   Lawd, how long?

Joshua Fit de Battle ob Jericho[1]

Joshua fit de battle ob Jericho—Jericho—
Jericho—
Joshua fit de battle ob Jericho,
And de walls came a-tumblin' down.

You may talk about yo' King ob Gideon,[2]
You may talk about yo' man of Saul,[3]   5
Dere's none like good ole Joshua,
At de battle ob Jericho.

Up to de walls ob Jericho
He marched wid spear in han',
"Go blow dem ram horns," Joshua cried,   10
"Kase de battle am in my han'."

Den de lam' ram sheep-horns begin to blow,
Trumpets begin to soun',
Joshua commanded de chillun to shout,
An' de walls came a-tumblin' down.   15

Dat mornin'—
Joshua fit de battle ob Jericho—Jericho—Jericho,
Joshua fit de battle ob Jericho,
An' de walls came a-tumblin' down.

---

[1]*Joshua...Jericho.* According to Chapter 6 of the Book of Joshua, the Lord commanded Joshua to have his people march for seven days around Jericho, a city in Canaan, the land the Lord had promised to the Israelites. On the seventh day as the priests blew on the rams' horn trumpets, the walls fell and the city was taken.

[2]*King ob Gideon,* a Hebrew hero who delivered the Israelites from the Midianites and other desert raiders. (Judges, Chapters 6-8.)

[3]*Saul,* first king of Israel.

This Train

This train is bound for glory, this train,
This train is bound for glory, this train,
This train is bound for glory,
If you ride it, you must be holy, this train.

This train don' pull no extras, this train,   5
Don' pull nothin' but de Midnight Special.

This train don' pull no sleepers, this train,
Don' pull nothin' but the righteous people, this train.

This train don' pull no jokers, this train,
Neither don' pull no cigar smokers, this train. 10

This train is boun' for glory, this train,
If you ride it, you mus' be bold, this train.

Wha—a-hoo—wha-awha-a-hoo—

WHAT IDEAS DO YOU GET FROM THE SPIRITUALS?

1. How could "Oh, Lawd, How Long?" be expanded in singing? (A clue may be found in the last two lines.) What other spirituals of this type do you know?
2. How would you state the theme or underlying meaning of "Oh, Lawd, How Long?"
3. Why do you think the story of Joshua had particular appeal to a people in slavery?
4. What indications do you find that "This Train" was probably composed later than the other two spirituals?
5. Which spiritual do you like best? Why?

Extending interests

With your teacher's permission, devote a class period to playing recordings of Negro spirituals. Among selections that might be included are: "Joshua Fit de Battle ob Jericho," sung by both the Golden Gate Quartet (in Columbia album C-145) and the Hall Johnson Choir (Victor 4460); "Dry Bones" and "Ole Moses Put Pharaoh in His Place" (Decca 23948), sung by Fred Waring's Pennsylvanians; "City Called Heaven" (Victor 8958) and "Deep River" (Victor 2032), sung by Marian Anderson; or spirituals from the albums *Negro Spirituals Sung by Dorothy Maynor* (Victor M-879) and *Golden Gate Spirituals* (Columbia C-145). Your classmates may suggest other good recordings of spirituals to be included in the program.

Evening and Morning Prayer

JOHN MAYO GOSS

That it often takes bitter experience to know what some of the basic values of religion are is the theme of John Mayo Goss' story of a boy and his grandfather. Its wealth of descriptive detail, its vivid action, its quiet revelation of the wide gap between rebellion against the blows of circumstance and acceptance of the inscrutable—these make it a memorable picture of an almost universal part of growing up.

THE CLOCK on the mantel had not struck—its minute hand had yet a sliver of space to travel before the hour of nine would sound—but Tuck's grandfather always seemed to know the time without benefit of clocks. With a neat thump, he closed the red-bound copy of the Waverley novel[1] he had been reading since supper and took off his spectacles. The boy's aunt and uncle disposed of their reading matter, one a book, one a magazine. Tuck pushed the stereoscope and its cards, with which he had been engaged, toward the middle of the table and sat up straight on the piano stool. This was not easy, because it had been raised as high as it would go, and wobbled.

The moment was significant. It was the first time Tuck had been permitted, on a visit to the farm, to stay up for evening prayers. It was the high point of a significant day. That morning, his mother had put him on the bus in the town where they lived, and he had traveled alone the thirty miles to the crossroad nearest the farm. There his grandfather had met him with the potato surrey and the light team, and as they had driven along the country road, Tuck had stood between his grandfather's knees and held the lines, for he was seven and a man. It was at seven, in his estimation, that men were made, and it was with overpowering pride that

he now saw his aunt reach for the Bible, open it at the place marked by a green ribbon, pinch her glasses a little higher on her nose, and settle back in her rocker to read aloud.

Her voice was low but precise, and went on and on until it became part of the room, part of the shadows in the corners, part of the light from the lamp. The shade was a beautiful dark green, and around the copper stomach of the lamp a copper lizard followed a copper fly in everlasting pursuit. The night was sultry and the heat from the lamp oppressive. That afternoon, Tuck's grandfather had said there was rain in the air (though there had not been a cloud in the sky), and he and Uncle Charles had worked late getting in the last of a field of timothy hay. They had come in wet with sweat; Tuck could smell it still through the straw smell of the matting on the parlor floor and the dust smell of old rugs, old hangings, and old furniture upholstery. He shaded his eyes with a hand, as his uncle was doing. Perhaps men understood more easily with the eyes shaded, he thought.

A change in his aunt's voice aroused him. It took on the emphasis of finality and then stopped. Tuck dropped his hand to see his

---

[1]*Waverley novel,* one of a series by Sir Walter Scott (1771-1832), author of *Waverley* (1814) and many other enormously popular novels, including *Ivanhoe* (1819).

grandfather standing erect. No one else looked like his grandfather. No one else had such a fine, full, sturdy white beard. No one else had such thick, flowing white hair. When friends of Tuck's aunt, ladies from town, drove out to the farm of a Sunday, they would exclaim to her at sight of him, "What a splendid old gentleman!" and "What a noble head!" Mrs. Crashaw, who painted in water colors, would breathe, "Ah, that I were Michelangelo,[2] that I might do him justice!" Tuck went so far in agreeing with these ladies as to wonder what God could look like if not like his grandfather.

The old man stood for a moment in benign authority before he said, "Let us pray." When they had all knelt and the only sound in the room was the clock's tick, he spoke the Lord's Prayer. Tuck was disappointed, for he had hoped for something more dramatic than those familiar words, but he joined in dutifully.

Then his grandfather went on alone, and that was more like it. He besought protection from the dangers and perils of the night in a voice that sounded as if he fully expected a cyclone to whirl the family away or an earthquake to bury it, and as if only by calling the

Lord's particular attention to their plight could any of them be saved.

It was impressive. Tuck felt that they had been placed so firmly in the hollow of the Lord's hand that they would all be wafted, wordless, to bed, and when prayers had ended and they were on their feet again, he was surprised to hear his uncle say, in his ordinary tone, "Whew! It's close as a grain bin tonight. I'd better turn the cows out."

His grandfather nodded and said, "Yes, we're going to get that rain. I'm glad we got the hay in." His tone, too, was no more fervent than if he had been asking for a second baked apple at the supper table.

"And now you'd better go to bed, Tuck," said his aunt. "Sure you don't want me to go up with you?" She smiled at the shake of his head and lighted one of the candles standing in their small holders on the hall table and gave it to him.

Always before when Tuck had been at the farm without his mother, he had slept on a cot in the dressing room off his aunt's bedroom, and she had always gone upstairs with him soon after supper to see him safe in bed. On this memorable day, she had told him when he arrived to take his suitcase up to the south room, and on this memorable evening he climbed the stairs alone and marched past all the other bedrooms along the narrow upstairs hallway to his own room with a proud consciousness of his maturity. He undressed, got into his pajamas, blew out the candle, opened the window, and hoisted himself into the big bed in an exalted frame of mind.

It was dark, but Tuck was not afraid. In years long gone—last year and the year before—he would have glanced up at the ceiling before blowing out the candle, to see if the opening into the attic was properly closed. There were no attic stairs at the farm—no one, as far as Tuck knew, had ever been up there—but when the house was built, an oblong hole big enough for a man to squeeze through had been cut in the ceiling of each bedroom. These apertures had sliding covers, which sometimes (by what supernatural means Tuck could not guess) would be standing open two or three inches. With the

[2]*Michelangelo* (mī′kəl an′jə lō), Italian sculptor, painter, and architect who lived from 1475 to 1564.

cover in this position, the holes in the ceiling had always seemed to Tuck to make an ideal crevice through which hands or paws, feet or claws, or even narrow, elongated heads might emerge. On this night, though, he gave no thought to such childish fancies. Never had he felt so safe, so confident. The dangers and perils of the night? There were none.

What would he do the next day? Things he had never done: He would climb to the highest beam in the loft of the barn and do a flip-flop to the hay below, as he had seen a twelve-year-old cousin do; he would do a *double* flip-flop; he would go into Grandfather's workshop and make a boat, and Grandfather would let him use the saw and the drawknife, now that he was a man; he would ride Vixen bareback—no, he would ride Vixen's colt Foxcub, whom no one but his uncle had ever been able to ride. He would ride him down into the woods, clear down to the creek, all by himself; he would—he would....

Tuck woke to deathly darkness, deathly stillness. His head turned instinctively to the open window. It had no outline. Without and within, the darkness pressed. There was no house in that darkness, no room, no bed, only the darkness to hold him up and press him down. "I have you now," said the darkness. "Oh, Lord, we beseech thee...." thumped his heart.

He was wide awake, lying in rigid premonition, when the shock came and the universe was split with a knife of flame. There was no thunder, no echo, no reverberation. The world leapt into instantaneous white light and was gone again into nothingness.

Then his aunt was standing in his doorway, smiling at him over her lighted candle. "Goodness," she said, "that was a near one, wasn't it? Did it scare you, Tuck?" She looked tall in her dressing gown as she moved across the room. "I'd better close your window. It'll be raining cats and dogs in a minute."

But she did not close the window. She stood for a moment before it, the fingers of her right hand hooked over the sash, her left hand holding the candle away from the curtains. Then, as she bent forward to look out, the candle jumped in her hand, and she turned and hurried for the door. The candle flame was a shred of light clinging to the wick as she ran.

"Charles!" she cried in the hall. "Charles! The barn! The barn's been hit! It's on fire!"

The house came alive with movement, with quick questions and answers. Tuck's spine straightened at another lightning flash, but it was not so close. This time, there was thunder, and he was out of bed and at the window before it had done growling.

He looked to the left, where the barn would be if there were light enough to see. Nothing. Blackness. Then, there it was—a match flame in the night, high up under the barn's eaves, at the opening where, that afternoon, the big, two-tined unloading fork had swung through from the hayrack outside to drop its loads onto the mow within. It was a small flame, but it gave a lurch as Tuck looked, filled the opening, and spread, fast as an outflung hand, higher than the peak of the barn.

Tuck ran downstairs, and in the kitchen his aunt was twirling the handle of the box telephone on the wall, but the handle was dead, and it gave no more tinkle than the handle of a meat grinder. She dropped both hands helplessly, and the receiver she had held banged against the wall. Tuck raced by her and out the door, and by the time he pulled up inside the barnyard gate, the first thin steeple of flame had reached along the roof and the whole end of the building was on fire. Barefooted and still in his pajamas, he gaped while jets from the blazing hay beneath pierced the dry, age-curled shingles here and there, rose, fell, and rose higher and higher.

The rain held off; there was no wind; the sparks flicked up and died in the dark or were absorbed in the intermittent lightning. The great old bell on top of the house commenced to ring, but not in the measured tones it announced noonday in the fields; now its clapper stuttered in a hysterical call for help. His aunt again, Tuck knew. He heard his uncle's voice, tight with urgency, from within the barn, "Pull up now, Curly. Get around there, Doll." All the stock except the two work teams had been turned in to the pasture, and the four horses

appeared, singly, at the door from the stalls. They each hung back, breathed gustily, and then stumbled out at a slap on their rumps and ran down the pasture lane in their clumsy, work-horse canter.

The barnyard was as bright as day. The shadows of the crib and sheds and trees shifted and swung. Now and then, a lightning flash wiped them out, but they reappeared in their places again. The bell beat through the thunder. Smoke bulged from the barn door.

Tuck's grandfather pushed out through the smoke, bowed down under the horses' harness. Then his uncle appeared, and he, too, was all hung about with collars and pads and hames and breeching and traces. Both men wore their nightshirts thrust into their trousers, and both, like Tuck, were barefoot. Uncle Charles dropped his load just outside the door, pulled his white-sleeved arm hard down over his eyes and face, and ran back through the doorway. Grandfather dragged the gear farther from the barn, and Uncle Charles staggered out with another load. In and out he went, bringing more harness, then saddles and blankets, bushel baskets, piles of gunny sacks and tarpaulins, and the heavy logging tools—axes and chains, the maul, the wedges, and the two-man saw.

Now the roof was one great flame. The lightning fell into it and was gone; the thunder was part of its eager, omnivorous roar. The boy was held motionless in its glare, though his face burned with it. Then his aunt stood beside him, and he realized that the bell had stopped ringing. She was carrying two buckets of water, but she went no farther. With her eyes on the fire, she lowered the pails to the ground and stood erect between them, twisting one wrist forward and back in the fingers of her other hand, as if she were trying to break her own clasp.

Tuck watched his uncle materialize, empty-handed, in the smoke of the doorway and felt his aunt start forward as his uncle swayed and held himself upright against the doorjamb. But in an instant Tuck's grandfather was at his side and he put an arm around his back and helped him across the barnyard. Tuck's aunt turned and ran for the house.

As the two men passed Tuck, his grandfather swept him up with his free arm and set him down again just outside the barnyard gate. There they turned, the three of them, to face the fire once more. Tuck's uncle crossed his arms on top of the gate and laid his forehead on them as his shoulders rose and fell with tearing breaths. He did not raise his head when one section of the roof went in, though it made a whoof like a man hit in the stomach, and the sparks filled the sky.

The maple tree beside them stirred, and they could feel a wind at their backs. The crest of the great flame bowed away, straightened, and bent again more deeply as the wind came in a gust. On the gust was rain—big, smacking drops. Tuck looked up at his grandfather, who shook his head, turned about, and lifted his face while the drops beat upon him, faster and faster. The rain gathered into a downpour, and they started for the house.

When they reached the kitchen, they were as wet as they could be. Tuck's aunt was feeding a double handful of cobs into the range as they entered, and did not look up. His uncle crossed to the east window, through which the fire, glowing red in the rain, made a stronger light than the lamp on the wall, and pulled down the shade. He sat down slowly in a straight chair. His eyes were red-rimmed and bloodshot; his face and nightshirt were streaked; one sleeve was ripped to the shoulder. He filled and emptied his chest again and again with clean air, then his head fell loosely forward and his hands fell limply between his legs. At the gesture, nervous tears forced themselves into Tuck's eyes.

A car racketed up beside the house. A man yelled "Wow!" and a woman cried, "Ain't that awful, Gus, ain't that awful!"

"That will be the Crumpaughs," said Tuck's grandfather quite steadily, "the first of our neighbors."

The boy was crying now and, ashamed of his tears, he fled from the kitchen to his room.

When Tuck woke the next morning, he lay for a moment in the continued contemplation of the hero-sized deeds he had been planning when first he had gone to sleep the night before —somersaults to be turned from great heights, clipper ships to be built and rigged, fiery steeds to be ridden far distances. Then the lightning flash and the burning of the barn came back to him, and he swung from the bed to the window.

He knew that it had not been a dream. He knew that he would not see the barn as it had always been, looming protectively over the smaller buildings about it, over the corncrib and the workshop, the pig house and the chicken house, the machine shed and the wagon shed, yet he was not prepared for the reality. It did not seem that the fire's magnificence in the night could leave anything so stark for the daylight.

He stood naked before the window, for when he had gone back to bed, he had wriggled out of his rain-soaked pajamas, and now he shivered in the morning air as he looked out upon the ugly, jagged black oblong, as low as a fence, that was all that was left of the barn. From within the enclosure, a few charred timbers projected, misshapen, as if in pain, and a vague column of whitish, steamy smoke ascended thinly. The smell of the smoke and wet wood ash and wet hay ash—the smell came through the window, the smell of disaster.

Tuck dressed (with no pride in his new overalls and knee-high rubber boots), went downstairs, and slipped out the side door, for he could hear his aunt in the kitchen and he had no wish to talk to her. He still did not feel too sure of himself. He might suddenly begin to cry again. But at the barnyard gate he stopped, half ready to return to the house and to any companionship he might find.

The barnyard was deserted, and there were none of the usual sounds of the farm getting up. The lesser buildings looked abandoned and dilapidated, as if they were already falling hopelessly apart now that their chief member had been taken from them. Tuck saw no sign of his grandfather, who should have been milking somewhere or in the corncrib getting nubbins for the cows. And he missed hearing his uncle talking to the horses as he curried and harnessed them, shouting, "What're you doing there?" and "Back up now," as if he were out of all patience with them, though he loved the horses and his care of them was a joke throughout the countryside. Even the pigs were quiet in their pen, and the chickens, which usually crowded the door of the barn, moved warily about their own quarters.

Then Tuck saw his uncle coming up the lane, dangling an empty bushel basket by one handle, and knew he had been down in the pasture with corn. He must be very tired, Tuck thought, for as he walked, he sagged as wearily as he had the evening before, after getting in the last load of hay. He tossed the basket toward the door of the crib and, without looking to right or left, went directly to the pile of equipment that had been salvaged from the fire. He regarded the tangled, muddy mess before him with bent head and hanging arms. Then he raised a saddle with the toe of his boot from the puddle in which it lay, and let it drop with a splash. And again Tuck saw his grandfather lift his closed eyes to a rain that had come too late.

When Tuck's uncle turned and noticed the intentness with which he was being watched, he straightened, walked over to him, and said, "Come along, young fella. We'll be late for morning prayers," and he laughed as if he had made a joke. Tuck had taken two quick steps at his side before he realized what had been said. He would have stopped in his tracks if it hadn't been for the urging hand of his uncle on his shoulder, for he recalled the prayers of the night before, when his grandfather had so trustingly given the farm and all that was in it into the safekeeping of the Almighty.

On the back porch, Tuck pulled off his prized new boots and slammed them down so hard that the cat by the kitchen door was stung by the spattered mud and took refuge behind a basket of cobs. Once again, he looked at the desolation across the barnyard fence as he turned to follow his uncle into the house. Prayers again. For what? But there was no escaping the ritual. As he walked behind his uncle, both of them padding across the kitchen in their stocking feet—two men together—his aunt abandoned her stove and fell in behind him, making a little procession, with him in the middle. His grandfather was in the parlor before them, standing by the center table, turning the deer-foot-handled paper knife over and over. His hair and beard were beautifully brushed and he wore a clean white shirt, though it was only Thursday. He looked at them, one after the other, and then his eyes rested on the face of Tuck's uncle. After a

long moment, he said, "Charles, remember that yesterday there was no house here and no trees but the little butternut by the hedge. There was only empty prairie." Slowly, he took them all in again with his eyes; then he said, "Let us pray."

Tuck knelt with the rest, but only after he had stomped independently across the room to the curved seat by the bow window, and he did not put his hands before his face or close his eyes, nor did he join in the Lord's Prayer when his grandfather commenced. Grief and anger kept his lips tight shut and his eyes smarting. Resolutely, he paid no attention as his grandfather prayed. He looked out the window at the slope of the front yard dropping away to the white board fence along the road, winking to clear the tears from his eyes.

There were trees in the front yard—sweeping soft maples, shading the house and the lawn, stately trees, well cared for and lusty in their prime—and his head went slowly around until he could see, out of the corners of his eyes, the butternut tree, off by itself beside the hedge. It was lopsided, for one of its limbs had been ripped off in a wind, and some of its upper branches were dead; it was bent and it was old. "Empty prairie," he thought.

"Grant us patience under our afflictions." Tuck's grandfather's voice had not been raised, but it had taken on such resonance that the boy could no longer help distinguishing the words. "Give us grace to be just and upright in all our dealings; quiet and peaceable; full of compassion; and ready to do good to all men, according to our abilities and opportunities...."

Colin, the collie dog, who always absented himself under the back porch when it stormed, came swinging loosely around the corner of the house, stopped squarely under the bow window, looked up at Tuck, and wagged his tail, inviting him out. And suddenly Tuck became aware of odors that he had not even noticed as he had crossed the kitchen. He smelled coffee and bacon and pancakes.

"...These things, and whatever else thou shalt see to be necessary and convenient to us, we humbly beg...."

Across the road, the south cornfield was a rich blue green in the early sunlight, and beyond it the woods were a soft gray green. The sky was bluer than Tuck had ever seen it.

"Amen," he heard his grandfather and his aunt and his uncle all say together, and his uncle's voice was as strong and clear as the others. He heard them getting to their feet. His eyes flicked round again to the butternut tree, and, quickly, he whispered his own "Amen."

REBELLION AND RESIGNATION

1. What are the characteristics of Tuck's aunt, his uncle, and his grandfather? Which of these is the dominant personality?

2. What are Tuck's feelings at evening prayers? What is his reaction when he is called for prayer in the morning? How does he show his feelings?

3. What makes the description of the fire particularly effective?

4. What adult reacts to the fire in much the same way Tuck does? How do you know?

5. What does the butternut tree symbolize?

6. What are the several steps leading to Tuck's acceptance as a man by his elders?

7. In what instances does the author allude to sounds or odors to add vividness to his story?

Know your words

From the list below choose the word that might be used to replace the italicized word or words in each sentence without changing the meaning. You may use the Glossary or a dictionary for help.

reverberation	resonance	intermittent
instantaneous	elongated	oppressive
omnivorous	premonition	misshapen
salvaged	aperture	charred

1. Tuck stood watching the *all-devouring* flames lick at the barn.
2. Their *long, narrow* tongues reached for the sky.
3. *Occasional* flashes of lightning illumined the yard.
4. The blinding light was followed by the *echo* of thunder.
5. The men *saved* what they could from the flames.
6. By morning only a heap of *burned* timbers remained of the barn.

Jim Bludso, of the Prairie Belle

JOHN HAY

For the good life, men need not only religious faith but other kinds of faith also. "Jim Bludso of the *Prairie Belle*" was written by a man who lived in an age when the steamboat officer was an American hero. It is a tale of heroism and human greatness based upon a deep faith in duty. Jim's standards, like those of many a steamboat man in the heyday of Mississippi River transportation, were peculiar but humane. He had something to live by.

WAL, NO! I can't tell whar he lives,
    Because he don't live, you see;
Leastways, he's got out of the habit
    Of livin' like you and me.
Whar have you been for the last three year   5
    That you haven't heard folks tell
How Jimmy Bludso passed in his checks
    The night of the *Prairie Belle?*

He weren't no saint—them engineers
    Is all pretty much alike—   10
One wife in Natchez-under-the-Hill[1]
    And another one here, in Pike[2];
A keerless man in his talk was Jim,
    And an awkward hand in a row,
But he never flunked, and he never lied—   15
    I reckon he never knowed how.

And this was all the religion he had—
    To treat his engine well;
Never be passed on the river;
    To mind the pilot's bell;   20
And if ever the *Prairie Belle* took fire—
    A thousand times he swore,
He'd hold her nozzle agin the bank
    Till the last soul got ashore.

All boats has their day on the Mississip,   25
    And her day come at last—
The *Movastar* was a better boat,

---

[1]*Natchez-under-the-Hill,* the tough river-front section of Natchez, Mississippi.

[2]*Pike,* a county in Missouri, up the river from St. Louis. Hay, however, used "Pike" in *Pike County Ballads* (1871), from which this poem comes, as a term meaning rural Missourian.

But the *Belle* she *wouldn't* be passed.
  And so she come tearin' along that night—
    The oldest craft on the line—   30
With a feller squat on her safety valve,
  And her furnace crammed, rosin and pine.

The fire bust out as she clared the bar,
  And burnt a hole in the night,
And quick as a flash she turned, and made 35
  For that willer-bank on the right.
There was runnin' and cursin', but Jim yelled
    out
    Over all the infernal roar,
"I'll hold her nozzle agin the bank
  Till the last galoot's ashore."   40

Through the hot, black breath of the burnin'
    boat
  Jim Bludso's voice was heard,
And they all had trust in his cussedness,
  And knowed he would keep his word.
And, sure's you're born, they all got off   45
  Afore the smokestacks fell—
And Bludso's ghost went up alone
  In the smoke of the *Prairie Belle.*

He weren't no saint—but at jedgment
  I'd run my chance with Jim,   50
'Longside of some pious gentlemen
  That wouldn't shook hands with him.
He seen his duty, a dead-sure thing—
  And went for it thar and then;
And Christ ain't a-going to be too hard   55
  On a man that died for men.

WHAT DOES JIM BLUDSO STAND FOR?

1. Analyze Jim's "religion" as stated in the third stanza. How well did he live up to it?
2. What do the last two lines tell you about the narrator's idea of Jim's "religion"?
3. Why do you think the poet has an uneducated narrator tell the story of Jim Bludso?

FROM *Self-Reliance*

RALPH WALDO EMERSON

Ralph Waldo Emerson stands in the front rank of American essayists. He himself wrote that in his essays as in his lectures he taught only one doctrine, "the infinitude of the private man," or the unlimited possibilities of the individual. His essay "Self-Reliance" is the best-known statement of the doctrine of individualism, which has long been one of the cherished faiths of Americans. In this excerpt one can see the religious and philosophical basis from which Emerson's confidence stems—a belief that to live wisely man must listen to the voice within himself, intuition.

TO BELIEVE your own thought, to believe that what is true for you in your private heart, is true for all men—that is genius. A man should learn to detect and watch that gleam of light which flashes across his mind from within, more than the luster of the firmament of bards and sages.[1] Yet he dismisses without notice his thought, because it is his. In every work of genius we recognize our own rejected thoughts; they come back to us with a certain alienated majesty. Great works of art have no more affecting lesson for us than this. They teach us to abide by our spontaneous impression with good-humored inflexibility. Else, tomorrow a stranger will say with masterly good sense precisely what we have thought and felt all the time, and we shall be forced to take with shame our own opinion from another.

There is a time in every man's education when he arrives at the conviction that envy is ignorance; that imitation is suicide; that he must take himself for better, for worse, as his portion; that though the wide universe is full of good, no kernel of nourishing corn can come to him but through his toil bestowed on that plot of ground which is given to him to till. The power which resides in him is new in nature, and none but he knows what that is which he can do, nor does he know until he has tried.

Trust thyself: every heart vibrates to that iron string. Accept the place the Divine Providence has found for you; the society of your contemporaries, the connection of events. Great men have always done so and confided themselves childlike to the genius of their age, betraying their perception that the Eternal was stirring at their heart, working through their hands, predominating in all their being.

Society everywhere is in conspiracy against the manhood of every one of its members. The virtue in most request is conformity. Self-reliance is its aversion. It loves not realities and creators, but names and customs.

Whoso would be a man, must be a nonconformist. He who would gather immortal palms must not be hindered by the name of goodness, but must explore if it be goodness. Nothing is at last sacred but the integrity of your own mind.

The other terror[2] that scares us from self-trust is our consistency; a reverence for our past act or word because the eyes of others have no other data for computing our orbit than our past acts, and we are loath to disappoint them.

But why should you keep your head over your shoulder? Why drag about this corpse of your memory, lest you contradict somewhat[3] you have stated in this or that public place? Suppose you should contradict yourself; what then? It seems to be a rule of wisdom never to rely on your memory alone, scarcely even in acts of pure memory, but to bring the past for judgment into the thousand-eyed present, and live ever in a new day.

A foolish consistency is the hobgoblin of little minds, adored by little statesmen and philosophers and divines. With consistency a great soul has simply nothing to do. He may as well concern himself with his shadow on the wall. Speak what you think now in hard words and tomorrow speak what tomorrow thinks in hard words again, though it contradict everything you said today.—"Ah, so you shall be sure to be misunderstood."—Is it so bad then to be misunderstood? Pythagoras was misunderstood, and Socrates, and Jesus, and Luther, and Copernicus, and Galileo, and Newton,[4] and every pure and wise spirit that ever took flesh. To be great is to be misunderstood.

The magnetism which all original action exerts is explained when we inquire the reason of self-trust. Who is the Trustee? What is the aboriginal Self, on which a universal reliance may be grounded? The inquiry leads us to that source, at once the essence of genius, of virtue, and of life, which we call Spontaneity or Instinct. We denote this primary wisdom as Intuition. In that deep force, the last fact behind which analysis cannot go, all things find their common origin. Here is the fountain of action and of thought. Here are the lungs of that inspiration which giveth man wisdom and which cannot be denied without impiety and atheism.

[1]*the luster...bards and sages,* the brilliance of the multitudes of poets and wise men.
[2]*other terror.* Emerson sees fear of not conforming as the first terror.

[3]*somewhat,* something.
[4]*Pythagoras* (pi thag′ə rəs) ... *Newton,* philosophers, scientists, and teachers of morality.

Man is timid and apologetic; he is no longer upright; he dares not say "I think," "I am," but quotes some saint or sage. He is ashamed before the blade of grass or the blowing rose. These roses under my window make no reference to former roses or to better ones; they are for what they are; they exist with God today. There is no time to them. There is simply the rose; it is perfect in every moment of its existence. Before a leaf-bud has burst, its whole life acts; in the full-blown flower there is no more; in the leafless root there is no less. Its nature is satisfied and it satisfies nature in all moments alike. But man postpones or remembers; he does not live in the present, but with reverted eye laments the past, or, heedless of the riches that surround him, stands on tiptoe to foresee the future. He cannot be happy and strong until he too lives with nature in the present, above time.

This should be plain enough. Yet see what strong intellects dare not hear God himself unless he speak the phraseology of I know not what David, or Jeremiah, or Paul.[5] We shall not always set so great a price on a few texts, on a few lives. If we live truly, we shall see truly. It is as easy for the strong man to be strong, as it is for the weak to be weak. When we have new perception, we shall gladly disburden the memory of its hoarded treasures as old rubbish. When a man lives with God, his voice shall be as sweet as the murmur of the brook and the rustle of the corn.

---

[5]*David, or Jeremiah* (jer'ə mī'ə), *or Paul.* David, second king of Israel, was noted as a singer and poet; Jeremiah was a Hebrew prophet who in powerful language denounced the evils of his time; Paul was the apostle who wrote most of the epistles in the New Testament.

UNDERSTANDING EMERSON'S IDEAS

1. What does Emerson advance as the basis for his belief that a man should trust his own ideas?
2. Is Emerson's "intuition" the same thing as "conscience"? If not, how does it differ?
3. What, according to Emerson, are the two most common enemies of self-reliance? What arguments does he advance against yielding to these enemies?

4. What, in general, seems to be Emerson's attitude toward the past?
5. What does Emerson seem to think the relation between God and man should be? Is it what you regard as an orthodox religious view?

Emerson as thinker

Ralph Waldo Emerson was one of America's great thinkers. He wrote and lectured, not to entertain but to instruct. On countless lecture platforms he urged his belief that each man must rely upon himself, that by heeding the voice of intuition man can become an independent, self-sustaining individual. In his essays, which he prepared from his journals and from the manuscripts of his speeches, he expounded the same basic ideas. Because in these essays he condensed the material he had used in his lectures, a paragraph is often so packed with thought that the reader has difficulty grasping the philosopher's whole idea. Yet the ideas in Emerson's essays are worth struggling for, and Emerson's ability to state his thoughts with brevity and grace has made him one of the most quoted American writers.

Read carefully each of the sentences below, which are taken from "Self-Reliance" and other essays. Then explain in your own words what Emerson means.

1. In every work of genius we recognize our own rejected thoughts; they come back to us with a certain alienated majesty.
2....though the wide universe is full of good, no kernel of nourishing corn can come to [man] but through his toil bestowed on that plot of ground which is given him to till.
3. Trust thyself: every heart vibrates to that iron string.
4. Self-trust is the essence of heroism.
5. The reward of a thing well done is to have done it.
6. The only gift is a portion of thyself.
7. A foolish consistency is the hobgoblin of little minds.
8. Hitch your wagon to a star.

Extending interests

"To be great is to be misunderstood," Emerson says in his essay on "Self-Reliance," and lists the following as examples of great men misunderstood by their contemporaries: Pythagoras, Socrates, Jesus, Luther, Copernicus, Galileo, and Newton. Report on one of these to the class, emphasizing particularly the ways in which the teachings or ideas of the person you have chosen differed from those of his age. You might prefer to make your report on some other great figure who was also scorned in his own time.

Credo

EDWIN ARLINGTON ROBINSON

In the generations after Emerson many men questioned his optimistic faith. Edwin Arlington Robinson, a leading poet of the early twentieth century, reflected the doubts of his contemporaries; yet in "Credo" he, too, even in the silent blackness of isolation and the remoteness of faith, ends on a note of hope.

I CANNOT find my way: there is no star
  In all the shrouded heavens anywhere;
And there is not a whisper in the air
Of any living voice but one so far
That I can hear it only as a bar   5
Of lost, imperial music, played when fair
And angel fingers wove, and unaware,
Dead leaves to garlands where no roses are.

No, there is not a glimmer, nor a call,
For one that welcomes, welcomes when he
  fears,   10
The black and awful chaos of the night;
For through it all—above, beyond it all—
I know the far-sent message of the years,
I feel the coming glory of the Light!

"Credo," from *Children of the Night,* published by Charles Scribner's Sons.

°INTERPRETING THE POET'S THOUGHT

1. What does the title mean? Do you think the poet would have used this title if his poem had ended on a note of disbelief or despair?

2. At what point does one realize that Robinson is describing no actual experience but his belief? What is that belief?

Understanding a sonnet

For centuries poets have lavished their skill upon the sonnet. Shakespeare wrote great sonnets, and Milton and Wordsworth, as well as many lesser poets. "Credo" is a sonnet. You will understand the poem better and appreciate it more if you know something of its form.

The sonnet is a fourteen-line poem which originated in Italy and was introduced into England in the sixteenth century. The meter is iambic pentameter; that is, there are five measures in each line, each measure consisting of a short and a long syllable, the first one being unaccented and the second accented. There are two main types of sonnet, the *Italian* and the *English.* These differ in their rhyme schemes and in the fact that the English sonnet has no break in its structure, while the Italian sonnet is divided into two parts, an eight-line *octave* and a six-line *sestet.* The octave develops one side of a thought, while the sestet develops an answering side.

"Credo" is a regular Italian sonnet. Using *a* to represent the rhyme-sound (*star*) at the end of the first line, and *b* to indicate the next rhyme-sound (*-where*), chart the rhyme scheme of "Credo." When you have finished, you will have the usual rhyme scheme for the octave of an Italian sonnet and one of the patterns most used for the sestet. The rhyme scheme of the English sonnet is *abab, cdcd, efef, gg.*

Scan several lines of "Credo," either by beating a finger on your desk to mark each accented syllable and noting the number of accents in each line, or by writing several lines on the blackboard and indicating unaccented and accented syllables in this manner:

Ĭ cán | nŏt fínd | mў wáy; | thĕre ís | nŏ stár |

Read the sonnet again, noting the break between octave and sestet. What is the mood of the octave? What happens in the sestet?

Reread Robert Frost's "Mowing" (page 239), noting the ways in which it resembles a sonnet and the points in which it differs from a sonnet.

The Larger View

I. The theme of the unit you have just studied is "the pursuit of happiness." You realize that each person's happiness is made up of many strains. The quotations below suggest ways in which the various writers whose selections you have read believe some aspect of happiness may be found. Explain how the idea contained in each quotation fits into the total concept of happiness. Identifying each quotation as to author and selection may help you to interpret the thought.

1. They caught a nation eager,
They caught a nation young,
They taught a nation fairness,
Thrift, and the golden tongue.
2. Give all to love;
Obey thy heart....
3. He seen his duty, a dead-sure thing—
And went for it thar and then....
4. Each singing what belongs to him or her
and to none else.
5. Accept the place the Divine Providence has found for you....

6. And over weariness and doubt
Rose up the horns like bellied sails,
Like canvas of the soul flung out
To rising and orchestral gales....
7. Trust thyself: every heart vibrates to that iron string.
8. I know the far-sent message of the years,
I feel the coming glory of the Light!
9. And if the people find you can fiddle,
Why, fiddle you must, for all your life.

II. To the people of the eighteenth century the most startling and original idea stated in the Declaration of Independence was probably the conception of "the pursuit of happiness" as a right that should be guaranteed to all men. "Life, liberty, and property"—these were the usual rights. The American declaration that men were entitled to something more was a new idea. Think over your own life as a citizen of the United States. Then write a brief essay explaining what benefits this right to "the pursuit of happiness" has already gained for you and will secure for you in the years to come.

MORE GOOD READING

ANNIXTER, PAUL, *Swiftwater*. (Wyn) For years Bucky and his father had dreamed of establishing a sanctuary for wild geese in the woods of northern Maine. The beauty and dangers of wilderness life surround this story of their struggle toward their goal.

BRO, MARGUERITE, *Sarah*. (Doubleday) From girlhood the heroine of this story had concentrated on becoming a great pianist. The sorrows and joys she encounters as she matures make this an engrossing, sympathetic novel.

BROMFIELD, LOUIS, *The Farm*. (Harper) The rhythm of the seasons and the fruitfulness of work in the outdoors run through this account of four generations on an Ohio farm.

CARROLL, GLADYS, *West of the Hill*. (Macmillan) This charming love story of Maine in the 1880's concerns Molly, who married to escape from a home where she was misunderstood, and the good life that resulted from her marriage.

CATHER, WILLA, *Death Comes for the Archbishop*. (Knopf) Faith and charity illumine this beautifully written story of young Father Latour and his friend who went to New Mexico in the middle years of the nineteenth century.

CHASE, MARY ELLEN, *A Goodly Fellowship*. (Macmillan) From Maine to Montana as student and teacher Mary Ellen Chase examined the life of America. This book is a delightful commentary on what she saw and thought and felt.

DALY, MAUREEN, *Seventeenth Summer*. (Dodd) The boy was eighteen and the girl was seventeen and their love affair covered three summer months. There is a rare feeling of reality and truth in this simple, appealing story.

DOUGLAS, WILLIAM O., *Of Men and Mountains*. (Harper) An Associate Justice of the Supreme Court who is an amateur naturalist, mountain climber, and fisherman writes of the rewarding experiences and the enlarged view of life that his hobbies have brought him.

EMERY, ANNE, *Going Steady*. (Westminster) By the end of their senior year in high school Scotty and Sally were "going steady," and during summer vacation they decided to get married instead of going on to college. The experiences that led them to change their plans form the plot of the story.

FERBER, EDNA, *So Big*. (Doubleday) Widowed Selina had a truck farm to run and a son to raise, but through all her troubles she never lost sight of the beauty of work and the sense of accomplishment it brought her.

FISHER, DOROTHY CANFIELD, *The Bent Twig*. (Holt) The "twig" was the daughter of a Midwestern university professor who longed for a more glamorous life than the simple, unpretentious one of her parents. She found, however, that their ideals upheld her in times of indecision.

GOLLOMB, JOSEPH, *Albert Schweitzer: Genius in the Jungle*. (Vanguard) This biography traces the life of a man who has lived for others from his sickly boyhood to his manhood experiences as a doctor in the African jungle.

LOMAX, JOHN A., *Adventures of a Ballad Hunter*. (Macmillan) John Lomax followed the trail of folk songs all over America, did a fine job, and had a wonderful time doing it. His enthusiasm shines through his account of his adventures.

McGRAW, ELOISE JARVIS, *Sawdust in His Shoes*. (Coward) Joe Lang was born in a circus tent and grew up in the circus, but after his father's death he was shipped off to an industrial school.

Joe's adventures and the allurement of circus life combine to form an unusual, exciting story.

MORLEY, CHRISTOPHER, *Parnassus on Wheels*. (Lippincott) This is the delightful story of the spinster who bought a wagon van of books, of the shy professor who coached her, and of her adventures with her book van on country roads.

SKINNER, CORNELIA OTIS, *Family Circle*. (Houghton) In these amusing reminiscences one of the great figures in the theater today tells of her own childhood and of her father's rise to become one of the theater idols of his generation.

TARKINGTON, BOOTH, *Seventeen*. (Harper) Love illuminated the life of Willie Baxter for the first time when he met Lola Pratt, his baby-talk lady. You'll laugh at Willie's difficulties with circumstances and with his family, but you'll also have a feeling of kinship with him.

TUNIS, JOHN R., *Highpockets*. (Morrow) This is the story of a Dodger ballplayer who thought his own batting average more important than the team. How he straightens out his sense of values makes the story.

TURNBULL, AGNES S., *The Rolling Years*. (Macmillan) This fine novel traces the lives of three generations of women in a hard-working Scotch family in Pennsylvania and shows how in each generation religious beliefs affect their attitudes toward life.

WHITE, STEWART EDWARD, *The Blazed Trail*. (Doubleday) Once you start this exciting adventure story of a young lumberman's struggle in the Michigan lumber camps with an unscrupulous firm, you won't be able to stop until you've reached the end.

WILDER, THORNTON, *The Bridge of San Luis Rey*. (Grosset) Two centuries ago an osier bridge across an abyss in Peru collapsed, hurling five people to their death. Franciscan Brother Juniper traces the life of each victim to show that his presence on the bridge at that moment was all a part of God's plan. This is a brief, beautifully written novel for the thoughtful reader.

PART TWO

The Pageant of American Literature

Men and Books

THE FIRST two divisions of this book—"The Growth of a Nation" and "The Development of American Ideals"—have shown you that American literary works are interesting as records of the history of our countrymen: their problems, their struggles, their thoughts, their aspirations. Those divisions have indicated to you what life in America has signified to succeeding generations. The purpose of the last two divisions of this book—"Men and Books" and "Changing Literary Patterns"—is to show you that literary works are interesting in other ways: (1) as the expressions of varied personalities and differing periods, and (2) as examples of evolving literary forms, such as the short story, biography, and drama.

"Men and Books" will illustrate how, throughout our history, the lives and times of authors shaped their writings, and, also, how their writings helped shape the times in which they lived. There are six units in this division; each of them develops the story of one outstanding writer, sketches in the literary and historical background of his era, shows his relationship to his contemporaries, and provides for the study of selections that are representative of the various periods of his work. First of the six authors studied is Benjamin Franklin, whose diversified interests and writings in various fields typify the Colonial Period. A unit on Washington Irving represents the Early National Period. The ascendancy of the New England writers in America's "Golden Day" is developed through the study of Henry David Thoreau. Walt Whitman, the strange and misunderstood figure whose poems sounded a new note in American literature, represents the Period of Conflict, where differences between the South and the North led to war. The vigor of the postwar period and the increasing influence of the West in literature are developed through a study of Mark Twain, representing the Period of New Outlooks. Stephen Vincent Benét is the subject of the last of these six units; through studying the diversity and variety of this man's work, you will become more aware of the many interesting facets of literature in the Twentieth Century.

As you read "Men and Books" you will find unexpected pleasures in relating an author to his work. You will discover that the man who produces an interesting piece of literature in most cases is himself an interesting person. And you will come to realize that life and culture in the United States have been immeasurably enriched by the work of literary men.

UNIT VII: BENJAMIN FRANKLIN
(*representing* THE COLONIAL PERIOD)

ALTHOUGH HE has been dead for a century and a half, Benjamin Franklin is still a very popular American. We see his familiar round face almost daily—on the contents page of the *Saturday Evening Post* (successor to a magazine he founded), in advertisements, and (with luck) on new fifty-cent pieces. Many of his wise sayings are constantly quoted. Some of his inventions (such as bifocal lenses, lightning rods, and stoves) still play important parts in our lives. And anyone who reads our country's history is likely to feel that Benjamin Franklin may have equal claims with George Washington to the title "The Father of Our Country."

Naturally a man of such enduring fame has tended to become a legend, or indeed, several legends. In the popular mind today, there are several different Franklins. There is Franklin the Patriot, making eloquent speeches and signing declarations and treaties. There is Franklin the Workman, running his printing presses or wheeling his barrow down the street. There is Franklin the Philosopher, spouting profound maxims about the virtues of thrift, temperance, and self-discipline. There is Franklin the Scientist, catching lightning or carrying out ingenious experiments in his laboratory.

All these pictures of Franklin have elements of truth in them, yet none portrays the true Franklin. He was indeed a great patriot, a hard-working laborer and businessman, a coiner of wise maxims, and a great scientist. But he was not a stuffy paragon. Any true picture of Franklin would show a warmly human being, witty and clever in small as in great matters, a man who fell short of his wise maxims through pride, impatience, laziness, and a general love of good food, good drink, and good times. He was less perfect and more given to ordinary faults and failings than popular concepts show him to be.

Here you will be concerned with Franklin as a writer. But because his writings cover the range of his interests and occupations, you will see that much of Franklin the man emerges in his literary works. You will find him a person who is likable, who would be called great in any age, yet who was peculiarly a man of his own period.

❧ I THE COMMON-SENSE PHILOSOPHER

Born in 1706, the tenth son of a candlemaker, Benjamin Franklin—like practically all poor children in those days—had little chance to go to school. Yet he learned much from living with the other members of a large family, and he had experiences which taught him important lessons. Years after the event, he wrote of an early incident:

When I was a child of seven years old, my friends, on a holiday, filled my pockets with coppers. I went directly to a shop where they sold toys; and being charmed with the sound of a *whistle,* that I met by the way in the hands of another boy, I voluntarily offered and gave all my money for one. I then came home, and went whistling all over the house, much pleased with my *whistle,* but disturbing all the family. My brothers, and sisters, and cousins, understanding the bargain I had made, told me I had given four times as much for it as it was worth; put me in mind what good things I might have bought with the rest of the money; and laughed at me so much for my folly that I cried with vexation; and the reflection gave me more chagrin than the *whistle* gave me pleasure.

This, however, was afterward of use to me, the impression continuing on my mind; so that often, when I was tempted to buy some unnecessary thing, I said to myself, *Don't give too much for the whistle;* and I saved my money.

Franklin attended school for only two years before he started to earn a living. He worked for his father for a time before, at twelve, he was apprenticed to his brother James in his native city, Boston, to learn the printer's trade. In the printshop, the beginner did all the chores a beginner was assigned—sorted type, cut paper, ran the hand press, delivered and sold papers, and made himself generally useful. Before long, he began to set type, and this naturally resulted in his reading practically everything which went through the press.

Boston and the vicinity in those years was influenced by a controversy which affected Franklin's earliest and even his later writings. The rising laborers and farmers were beginning to feel that the aristocrats and the rich merchants had more privileges and more power than was fair. There was a hot contest, for instance, between the Council (made up of aristocrats and wealthy businessmen) and the House of Representatives (made up largely of tradesmen, farmers, mechanics, and laborers). In 1722 a Boston mason noticed: "There is great disputing about prerogative and property. The rich oppress. The poor complain."

James Franklin's printing shop issued the *Courant,* and there was no question about the sympathies of its printer-editor, Benjamin's brother. The newspaper was intended to appeal particularly to the workingmen and the farmers in and around Boston, and to champion their cause. Its bold and direct attacks on some well-to-do and influential Bostonians more than once landed James in jail. The writers for the *Courant* worded their pieces, as one of them said, "in a very easy and familiar manner, as that the meanest plowman may understand." They voiced the attitudes of common folk and signed their articles with names such as Timothy Turnstone, Ichabod Henroost, Homespun Jack, and Betty Frugal.

One day, Benjamin secretly wrote an article in a disguised hand. That night he sneaked it under the printing-house door.[1] The next morning, as he stood at his printing case, he had the pleasure of hearing James and the other *Courant* men speak with admiration of his first effort.

It is not surprising that the piece was admired and that it, and later pieces in the same style, were subsequently printed. The boy followed the *Courant* method of writing. He used a style of homely, direct language which would catch the attention of the humble citizens of Boston and

[1]This paper is printed on pages 295-296 under the title "Dogood Papers, No. 1."

speak to them in their own tongue, and he signed the piece with the name of a character who might well write in such a style—Mistress Silence Dogood. Thus he created his first character, a widow residing near Boston on a farm, associating with and friendly to the workers, farmers, and poor people. Uneducated but wise by experience, Mistress Dogood was a figure likely to appeal to uneducated readers who preferred wisdom based upon experience to wisdom drawn from books.

In fact, she was the sort of character likely to appeal to Americans of many places and in many periods. For dear to the American heart is the bluff and uneducated but keen-minded person who has emerged from the school of hard knocks with a highly practical philosophy. Such a character is one who finds popular, common-sense answers to problems of all sorts. The Widow Dogood was an ancestor of a whole line of very popular "horse-sense philosophers" such as Mark Twain and Will Rogers.

Thus Franklin's laboring-class background and the literary style of his brother's newspaper helped him hit upon a character and a way of writing certain to appeal to Americans. It was a lesson which he was to remember throughout his long life.

A little over a year later Franklin left his brother's shop and home to start life on his own in Philadelphia. Here he became a printer in his own shop. He printed business forms, legal papers, official notices, books of all kinds, and a succession of journals. His most successful publication, however, was one which utilized a second horse-sense character.

Various American printers, like British printers before them, had found that the annual publication of almanacs brought good returns. Because an almanac gave tables of the moon and the tides, predicted the weather (perhaps!), and included useful recipes and household hints, it was likely to sell in rural homes where the only other book might be a Bible. Always a good businessman, Franklin decided to enter the field. His almanac purported to be the publication of a certain Richard Saunders, who came to be known as Poor Richard. To fill spaces and liven the dull matter of tides and weather, Franklin inserted maxims and proverbs which were supposedly the sayings of Poor Richard. Bit by bit something of the character of Poor Richard emerged. He was a poor man, living quietly and virtuously in the country with his pious and worthy, but rather uninteresting, wife. He was short on education but long on experience and wit—in short, another horse-sense character like Widow Dogood.

The sayings of Poor Richard struck the popular fancy and were much quoted. Richard spoke in the language of the people, reducing the difficulties of life to homely expressions easily remembered. Many maxims urged the dull virtues which all men acknowledged were admirable though most people might fall short in practicing them. Typical of such sayings are these: Eat to live, and not live to eat. He that drinks fast pays slow. Experience keeps a dear school, yet fools will learn in no other.

Less well known, less frequently quoted, but equally typical are a group of earthy sayings scattered throughout the almanacs, such as: Fish and visitors smell in three days. Let thy maidservant be faithful, strong, and homely. There's more old drunkards than old doctors. A country man between two lawyers is like a fish between two cats.

The almanacs, started in 1732 and published over a span of twenty-five years, provided ample opportunity for Poor Richard to air his homely wisdom. Franklin drew on all his background for these sayings—from his reading, from the folk-wisdom of the people about him, and from his own inventive mind. Much later, in 1757, he made a collection of the sayings of Poor Richard which formed a running text. This text was supposed to be the speech of "Father Abraham," a simple country man talking about thrift and how to get along in the world. Published under the title of *The Way to Wealth*, it became Franklin's—and Poor Richard's—most popular work.

This single work has done much to create the myth of Franklin's being merely a frugal, prudent, hard-working, and virtuously dull businessman. The picture is misleading, for Franklin confesses himself to have been lazy, a lover of good food and drink, a seeker after luxuries, and in general, one who frequently fell below the standards of conduct which he set for himself. Nevertheless, there is some truth in the picture also, for Franklin did set goals for himself in terms of virtuous maxims, some of which he followed sincerely and others of which he was not above following for appearance' sake.

His famous *Autobiography*, written in 1771, 1784, and 1790, shows him both as a practical man, learning by experience, striving for virtue; and as an all-too-human being, who (as he ruefully admitted) often fell short of his aims. Here he confessed that despite his belief in thrift, frugality was "a virtue I never could acquire myself." Here he told how his vow to become a vegetarian was shattered when he became hungry on a sea voyage and could get only fish to eat. And here he told how he learned that "honesty was the best policy" by experimenting with the opposite. Here, too, for the benefit of his son (for whose guidance the book was written) he set down practical experiments he had conducted in living. In this book as in others, therefore, Franklin showed himself to be the great common-sense philosopher.

Dogood Papers, No. 1

FROM MONDAY, March 26, to Monday, April 2, 1722

To the Author of *The New-England Courant*

Sir,

It may not be improper in the first place to inform your readers that I intend once a fortnight to present them, by the help of this paper, with a short epistle, which I presume will add somewhat to their entertainment.

And since it is observed that the generality of people, nowadays, are unwilling either to commend or dispraise what they read, until they are in some measure informed who or what the author of it is, whether he be *poor* or *rich, old* or *young*, a *scholar* or a *leather-apron man*, etc., and give their opinion of the performance, according to the knowledge which they have of the author's circumstances, it may not be amiss to begin with a short account of my past life and present condition, that the reader may not be at a loss to judge whether or no my lucubrations are worth his reading.

"Dogood Papers, No. 1," from *The Writings of Benjamin Franklin*, edited by Albert H. Smyth. Copyright 1905 by The Macmillan Company.

At the time of my birth, my parents were on shipboard in their way from *London* to *N. England*. My entrance into this troublesome world was attended with the death of my father, a misfortune, which though I was not then capable of knowing, I shall never be able to forget; for as he, poor man, stood upon the deck rejoicing at my birth, a merciless wave entered the ship, and in one moment carried him beyond reprieve. Thus was the *first* day which I saw, the *last* that was seen by my father; and thus was my disconsolate mother at once made both a *parent* and a *widow*.

When we arrived at Boston (which was not long after) I was put to nurse in a country place, at a small distance from the town, where I went to school, and passed my infancy and childhood in vanity and idleness, until I was bound out apprentice, that I might no longer be a charge to my indigent mother, who was put to hard shifts for a living.

My master was a country minister, a pious good-natured young man, and a bachelor. He labored with all his might to instill virtuous and godly principles into my tender soul, well knowing that it was the most suitable time to make deep and lasting impressions on the mind, while it was yet untainted with vice, free and unbiased. He endeavored that I might be instructed in all that knowledge and learning which is necessary for our sex, and denied me no accomplishment that could possibly be attained in a country place, such as all sorts of needlework, writing, arithmetic, etc., and observing that I took a more than ordinary delight in reading ingenious books, he gave me the free use of his library, which though it was but small, yet it was well chosen to inform the understanding rightly and enable the mind to frame great and noble ideas.

Before I had lived quite two years with this reverend gentleman, my indulgent mother departed this life, leaving me as it were by myself, having no relation on earth in my knowledge.

I will not abuse your patience with a tedious recital of all the frivolous accidents of my life, that happened from this time until I arrived to years of discretion, only inform you that I lived a cheerful country life, spending my leisure time either in some innocent diversion with the neighboring females, or in some shady retirement, with the best of company, *books*. Thus I passed away the time with a mixture of profit and pleasure, having no affliction but what was imaginary and created in my own fancy; as nothing is more common with us women than to be grieving for nothing, when we have nothing else to grieve for.

As I would not engross too much of your paper at once, I will defer the remainder of my story until my next letter; in the meantime desiring your readers to exercise their patience, and bear with my humors now and then, because I shall trouble them but seldom. I am not insensible of the impossibility of pleasing all, but I would not willingly displease any; and for those who will take offense where none is intended, they are beneath the notice of

Your humble servant,

Silence Dogood

As the favor of Mrs. Dogood's correspondence is acknowledged by the publisher of this paper, lest any of her letters should miscarry, he desires they may for the future be delivered at his printing-house, or at the Blue Ball in Union Street, and no questions shall be asked of the bearer.

Project of Arriving at Moral Perfection, FROM *the Autobiography*

IT WAS about this time I conceived the bold and arduous project of arriving at moral perfection. I wished to live without committing any fault at any time; I would conquer all that either natural inclination, custom, or company might lead me into. As I knew, or thought I knew, what was right and wrong, I did not see why I might not always do the one and avoid the other. But I soon found I had undertaken a task of more difficulty than I had imagined. While my care was employed in guarding against one fault, I was often surprised by another; habit took the advantage of inattention; inclination was sometimes too strong for reason. I concluded, at length, that the mere speculative conviction that it was our interest to be completely virtuous was not sufficient to prevent our slipping; and that the contrary habits must be broken, and good ones acquired and established, before we can have any dependence on a steady, uniform rectitude of conduct. For this purpose I therefore contrived the following method.

In the various enumerations of the moral virtues I had met with in my reading, I found the catalogue more or less numerous, as different writers included more or fewer ideas under the same name. Temperance, for example, was by some confined to eating and drinking, while by others it was extended to mean the moderating every other pleasure, appetite, inclination, or passion, bodily or mental, even to our avarice and ambition. I proposed to myself, for the sake of clearness, to use rather more names, with fewer ideas annexed to each, than a few names with more ideas; and I included under thirteen names of virtues all that at that time occurred to me as necessary or desirable, and annexed to each a short precept, which fully expressed the extent I gave to its meaning.

These names of virtues, with their precepts were:

1. TEMPERANCE
Eat not to dullness; drink not to elevation.

2. SILENCE
Speak not but what may benefit others or yourself; avoid trifling conversation.

3. ORDER
Let all your things have their places; let each part of your business have its time.

4. RESOLUTION
Resolve to perform what you ought; perform without fail what you resolve.

5. FRUGALITY
Make no expense but to do good to others or yourself; i.e., waste nothing.

6. INDUSTRY
Lose no time; be always employed in something useful; cut off all unnecessary actions.

7. SINCERITY
Use no hurtful deceit; think innocently and justly and, if you speak, speak accordingly.

8. JUSTICE
Wrong none by doing injuries, or omitting the benefits that are your duty.

9. MODERATION
Avoid extremes; forbear resenting injuries so much as you think they deserve.

10. CLEANLINESS
Tolerate no uncleanliness in body, clothes, or habitation.

11. TRANQUILLITY
Be not disturbed at trifles, or at accidents common or unavoidable.

12. CHASTITY

13. HUMILITY
Imitate Jesus and Socrates.

My intention being to acquire the *habitude* of all these virtues, I judged it would be well not to distract my attention by attempting the whole at once, but to fix it on one of them at a time; and, when I should be master of that, then to proceed to another, and so on, till I should have gone through the thirteen; and as the previous acquisition of some might facilitate the acquisition of certain others, I arranged them with that view, as they stand above. *Temperance* first, as it tends to procure that coolness and clearness of head which is so necessary where constant vigilance was to be kept up, and guard maintained against the unremitting attraction of ancient habits and the force of perpetual temptations. This being acquired and established, *Silence* would be more easy; and my desire being to gain knowledge at the same time that I improved in virtue, and considering that in conversation it was obtained rather by the use of the ears than of the tongue, and therefore wishing to break a habit I was getting into of prattling, punning, and joking, which only made me acceptable to trifling company, I gave *Silence* the second place. This and the next, *Order,* I expected would allow me more time for attending to my project and my studies. *Resolution,* once become habitual, would keep me firm in my endeavors to obtain all the subsequent virtues; *Frugality* and *Industry* freeing me from my remaining debt, and producing affluence and independence, would make more easy the practice of *Sincerity* and *Justice,* etc., etc. Conceiving then, that, agreeably to the advice of

Pythagoras in his Golden Verses,[1] daily examination would be necessary, I contrived the following method for conducting that examination.

I made a little book, in which I allotted a page for each of the virtues. I ruled each page with red ink, so as to have seven columns, one for each day of the week, marking each column with a letter for the day. I crossed these columns with thirteen red lines, marking the beginning of each line with the first letter of one of the virtues, on which line, and in its proper column, I might mark, by a little black spot, every fault I found upon examination to have been committed respecting that virtue upon that day.

Form of the pages

TEMPERANCE							
EAT NOT TO DULLNESS; DRINK NOT TO ELEVATION.							
	S.	M.	T.	W.	T.	F.	S.
T.							
S.	*	*		*		*	
O.	* *	*	*		*	*	*
R.			*			*	
F.		*			*		
I.			*				
S.							
J.							
M.							
C.							
T.							
C.							
H.							

I determined to give a week's strict attention to each of the virtues successively. Thus, in the first week, my great guard was to avoid even the least offense against *Temperance,* leaving the other virtues to their ordinary chance, only marking every evening the faults of the day. Thus, if in the first week I could keep my first line, marked T, clear of spots, I supposed the habit of that virtue so much strengthened, and its opposite weakened, that I might venture extending my attention to include the next, and for the following week keep both lines clear of spots. Proceeding thus to the last, I could go through a course complete in thirteen weeks, and four courses in a year. And like him who, having a garden to weed, does not attempt to eradicate all the bad herbs at once, which would exceed his reach and his strength, but works on one of the beds at a time, and, having accomplished the first, proceeds to a second, so I should have, I hoped, the encouraging pleasure of seeing on my pages the progress I made in virtue, by clearing successively my lines of their spots, till in the end, by a number of courses, I should be happy in viewing a clean book, after a thirteen weeks' daily examination....

The precept of *Order* requiring that *every part of my business should have its allotted time,* one page in my little book contained the following scheme of employment.[2]

I entered upon the execution of this plan for self-examination, and continued it with occasional intermissions for some time. I was surprised to find myself so much fuller of faults than I had imagined; but I had the satisfaction of seeing them diminish. To avoid the trouble of renewing now and then my little book, which, by scraping out the marks on the paper of old faults to make room for new ones in a new course, became full of holes, I transferred my tables and precepts to the ivory leaves of a memorandum book, on which the lines were drawn with red ink, that made a durable stain, and on those lines I marked my faults with a black lead pencil, which marks I could easily wipe out with a wet sponge. After a while I went through one course only in a year, and after-

---

[1]*Pythagoras* (pi thag′ə rəs) *in his Golden Verses.* The Golden Verses of Pythagoras, an ancient Greek philosopher, suggest a system for attaining spiritual perfection much like that adopted by Franklin.

[2]*scheme of employment.* See page 299.

THE MORNING.	5	Rise, wash, and address *Powerful Goodness!*[3] Contrive day's business, and take the resolution of the day; prosecute the present study, and breakfast.
Question. What good shall I do this day?	6	
	7	
	8	Work.
	9	
	10	
	11	
NOON.	12	Read, or overlook my accounts, and dine.
	1	
	2	Work.
	3	
	4	
	5	
EVENING.	6	Put things in their places. Supper. Music or diversion, or conversation. Examination of the day.
	7	
Question. What good have I done today?	8	
	9	
	10	Sleep.
	11	
	12	
NIGHT.	1	
	2	
	3	
	4	

ward only one in several years, till at length I omitted them entirely, being employed in voyages and business abroad, with a multiplicity of affairs that interfered; but I always carried my little book with me.

My scheme of *Order* gave me the most trouble; and I found that, though it might be practicable where a man's business was such as to leave him the disposition of his time, that of a journeyman printer,[4] for instance, it was not possible to be exactly observed by a master, who must mix with the world and often receive people of business at their own hours. *Order,* too, with regard to places for things, papers, etc., I found extremely difficult to acquire. I had not been early accustomed to it, and, having an exceeding good memory, I was not so sensible of the inconvenience attending want of method.

[3]*Powerful Goodness,* God.

[4]*journeyman printer,* a workman who had completed his apprenticeship but had not become an employer, or master printer.

This article, therefore, cost me so much painful attention, and my faults in it vexed me so much, and I made so little progress in amendment, and had such frequent relapses, that I was almost ready to give up the attempt and content myself with a faulty character in that respect, like the man who, in buying an ax of a smith, my neighbor, desired to have the whole of its surface as bright as the edge. The smith consented to grind it bright for him if he would turn the wheel; he turned, while the smith pressed the broad face of the ax hard and heavily on the stone, which made the turning of it very fatiguing. The man came every now and then from the wheel to see how the work went on, and at length would take his ax as it was, without further grinding. "No," said the smith, "turn on, turn on; we shall have it bright by and by; as yet, it is only speckled." "Yes," says the man, *"but I think I like a speckled ax best."* And I believe this may have been the case with many, who, having, for want of some such means as I employed, found the difficulty of obtaining good and breaking bad habits in other points of vice and virtue, have given up the struggle and concluded that *"a speckled ax was best";* for something, that pretended to be reason, was every now and then suggesting to me that such extreme nicety as I exacted of myself might be a kind of foppery in morals, which, if it were known, would make me ridiculous; that a perfect character might be attended with the inconvenience of being envied and hated; and that a benevolent man should allow a few faults in himself, to keep his friends in countenance.

In truth, I found myself incorrigible with respect to *Order;* and now I am grown old, and my memory bad, I feel very sensibly the want of it. But, on the whole, though I never arrived at the perfection I had been so ambitious of obtaining, but fell far short of it, yet I was, by the endeavor, a better and a happier man than I otherwise should have been if I had not attempted it; as those who aim at perfect writing by imitating the engraved copies, though they never reach the wished-for excellence of those copies, their hand is mended by the endeavor, and is tolerable while it continues fair and legible.

It may be well my posterity should be informed that to this little artifice, with the blessing of God, their ancestor owed the constant felicity of his life, down to his 79th year, in which this is written. What reverses may attend the remainder is in the hand of Providence; but, if they arrive, the reflection on past happiness enjoyed ought to help his bearing them with more resignation. To *Temperance* he ascribes his long-continued health, and what is still left to him of a good constitution; to *Industry* and *Frugality,* the early easiness of his circumstances and acquisition of his fortune, with all that knowledge that enabled him to be a useful citizen and obtained for him some degree of reputation among the learned; to *Sincerity* and *Justice,* the confidence of his country and the honorable employs it conferred upon him; and to the joint influence of the whole mass of the virtues, even in the imperfect state he was able to acquire them, all that evenness of temper, and

that cheerfulness in conversation, which makes his company still sought for and agreeable even to his younger acquaintance. I hope, therefore, that some of my descendants may follow the example and reap the benefit....

My list of virtues contained at first but twelve; but a Quaker friend having kindly informed me that I was generally thought proud, that my pride showed itself frequently in conversation, that I was not content with being in the right when discussing any point, but was overbearing and rather insolent (of which he convinced me by mentioning several instances), I determined endeavoring to cure myself, if I could, of this vice or folly among the rest, and I added *Humility* to my list, giving an extensive meaning to the word.

I cannot boast of much success in acquiring the *reality* of this virtue, but I had a good deal with regard to the *appearance* of it. I made it a rule to forbear all direct contradiction to the sentiments of others, and all positive assertion of my own. I even forbid myself, agreeably to the old laws of our Junto,[5] the use of every word or expression in the language that imported a fixed opinion, such as *certainly, undoubtedly,* etc., and I adopted, instead of them *I conceive, I apprehend,* or *I imagine* a thing to be so or so; or *it so appears to me at present.* When another asserted something that I thought an error, I denied myself the pleasure of contradicting him abruptly and of showing immediately some absurdity in his proposition; and in answering I began by observing that in certain cases or circumstances his opinion would be right, but in the present case there *appeared* or *seemed* to me some difference, etc. I soon found the advantage of this change in my manner; the conversations I engaged in went on more pleasantly. The modest way in which I proposed my opinions procured them a readier reception and less contradiction; I had less mortification when I was found to be in the wrong, and I more easily prevailed with others to give up their mistakes and join with me when I happened to be in the right.

---

[5] *our Junto* (jun′tō), a literary and debating club founded by Franklin in 1727.

And this mode, which I at first put on with some violence to natural inclination, became at length so easy, and so habitual to me, that perhaps for these fifty years past no one has ever heard a dogmatical expression escape me. And to this habit (after my character of integrity) I think it principally owing that I had early so much weight with my fellow citizens when I proposed new institutions or alterations in the old, and so much influence in public councils when I became a member; for I was but a bad speaker, never eloquent, subject to much hesitation in my choice of words, hardly correct in language, and yet I generally carried my points.

In reality, there is, perhaps, no one of our natural passions so hard to subdue as *pride*. Disguise it, struggle with it, beat it down, stifle it, mortify it as much as one pleases, it is still alive, and will every now and then peep out and show itself; you will see it, perhaps, often in this history; for, even if I could conceive that I had completely overcome it, I should probably be proud of my humility.

CONCERNING BENJAMIN FRANKLIN

1. To what class of society did Franklin belong? What effect did being a member of this class have on his education and sympathies?

2. How did working on his brother's paper, the *Courant*, lead to Benjamin Franklin's first venture into journalism? How did this experience affect his viewpoint in much of his later writing?

3. What circumstances led to the creation of Poor Richard? In what ways are Poor Richard, Father Abraham, and the Widow Dogood alike?

4. What idea of Franklin as a man did later generations adopt as a result of the popularity of *The Way to Wealth*? How does this idea agree with the picture of the man presented in the *Autobiography*?

CONCERNING "DOGOOD PAPERS, NO. 1" AND "PROJECT OF ARRIVING AT MORAL PERFECTION"

1. Do you agree with the Widow Dogood's statement that people "are unwilling either to commend or dispraise what they read" until they know something about the author? Give reasons for your answer.

2. Why do you think readers of the *Courant* were interested in what the Widow Dogood had to say?

3. What details in the way Franklin set up and carried out his project for acquiring the moral virtues show him to have been a very practical man?

4. What did Franklin mean by saying he concluded at times that "a speckled ax was best"?

5. What benefits did Franklin himself believe he had gained from his attempts to arrive at moral perfection?

Know your words

Synonymous words cannot always be used interchangeably. For example, *soften* and *mitigate* are sometimes synonyms, and either could be used in the sentence "A kindly manner will often _____ the sting of criticism." But only one of these words would be correct in the sentence "Hot weather will _____ the butter."

Above each pair of sentences below are two words which are synonymous in one sense but not in others. In each case decide in which sentence the words might be used interchangeably and in which only one word is correct. Then on a sheet of paper copy the numbers 1 through 10 and after each number write the word or words that could be correctly used in the corresponding sentence.

poor; indigent

1. Care and tact must be exercised in caring for _____ families.

2. These are very _____ examples of this type of weaving.

assist; facilitate

3. The ushers will _____ people to their places.

4. My work in preparing the report was greatly _____ by the use of a good dictionary.

sensible; aware

5. The students seemed fully _____ of the honor they were about to receive.

6. Doing his homework before going out to play ball seemed _____ to John.

import; signify

7. We _____ much raw rubber from Sumatra.

8. What do you think Mr. Atkinson's recent actions _____?

habitual; regular

9. His _____ morning walk takes him through the park.

10. Along the street elm trees are planted at _____ intervals.

Franklin was successful in his own business, respected by his neighbors and associates. Always he was among the first to donate to worthy causes. Often he was the author of practical schemes for the improvement of his city and its citizens: to him, Philadelphia credits her public library, her fire department, her street-lighting system, and her university.

Such a man was quickly sought out for public office. Thus at the age of thirty, when many men are barely starting in life, Franklin was chosen clerk of the General Assembly of Pennsylvania. In this office he began a career of service to the public which extended throughout his life. At one time or another he served as deputy postmaster of Philadelphia, member of the Philadelphia Council, deputy postmaster-general of the American colonies, agent of the Pennsylvania colony in England, and later agent of several colonies, the first American postmaster-general of North America, president of the convention to frame a constitution for Pennsylvania, American diplomat in France, and delegate to the convention which framed the Constitution of the United States. This list names only the chief among the public offices held by Franklin.

There were two principal reasons for Franklin's many public services. One was his character, which combined a genuine and continuing zeal for the public good with sound sense and practical methods for getting things done. The second reason was Franklin's ability as a writer, which extended his ideas and influence far beyond his home community. Franklin was from the earliest days of his connection with printing what we now call a "propagandist"—a man who expresses and circulates arguments for or against current issues—and in this rôle his public services won him wide acclaim.

The newspapers which Franklin published or contributed to over many years provided a continuous outlet for his ideas on public matters. In addition, he frequently published pamphlets on a single subject, the kind that a man could take home, read, and discuss with his neighbors by the fireside or at a tavern.

In an age of no radio, moving pictures, telegraph or telephone, newspapers and such pamphlets were the principal means of spreading ideas and influencing people. It was a period when writers were particularly important in politics. Such contemporaries of Franklin as Samuel Adams, Thomas Paine, Alexander Hamilton, James Madison, and Thomas Jefferson all were among the great writers of the period—and all used their pens to argue about political questions. Not surprisingly, Franklin, as skilled

as any of these writers, extended the influence of his pen throughout the colonies and beyond them.

Beginning with matters close at home, Franklin wrote letters and articles proposing improvements for Philadelphia, such as the development of a police force, the creation of a hospital, and the foundation of an academy. It was not long before his efforts extended to wider interests: the public attitude toward smuggling, the need for paper currency in the colonies, and the desirability of improvement of the mails.

Late in 1763 Franklin was influential in stopping a growing riot which might have torn the Pennsylvania colony apart. Some settlers in western Pennsylvania killed a group of innocent Indians without cause, and then marched toward Philadelphia demanding more scalps. The Indian survivors fled before them in terror into the city. In a pamphlet called "A Narrative of the Late Massacres in Lancaster County," Franklin pleaded with the rioters to return home and to treat the Indians justly. In glowing language he appealed to the best natures of men to see that the wrongdoers were punished and the innocent protected for the sake of the peace and prosperity of all.

As the years passed Franklin continued to serve his country by proposing plans for greater unity of the American colonies. He was prominent in defending the rights and privileges of the colonists while they remained under British rule and British officials. And until the exchange of shots at Lexington, he worked ceaselessly to secure justice for the American colonies from the mother country. During the Revolution he spoke for the Colonial cause. After the war, he was helpful in shaping the new government.

It may well be asked, why was this Pennsylvania printer and businessman so successful as a political writer? He was, in the first place, convinced of the rightness of the causes for which he wrote, and he carried conviction to his readers. He had good sense, practical ideas, and appealing schemes for carrying out his ideas. Furthermore, he wrote clearly and logically, developing his points step by step, patiently leading his readers to the inevitable conclusion. Above all, he was a man whose personality colored everything he wrote. His readers delighted in his personal touches, his little laughs at his own mistakes and weaknesses, his ready wit, and his clever satire. Despite the fact that he wrote of serious and sometimes crucial matters, he was fair in his judgments, humane in his treatment of others, seldom dull and frequently amusing. The following extracts from his writings will illustrate his success as a writer for the public good.

Protection of Towns from Fire

On February 4, 1735, Franklin published in his own newspaper, *The Pennsylvania Gazette,* a letter supposedly from an old citizen, which described efficient ways to fight fire. Part of this letter is printed below.

A S TO OUR CONDUCT in the affair of extinguishing fires, though we do not want hands or good will, yet we seem to want order and method, and therefore I believe I cannot do better than to offer for our imitation the example of a city in a neighboring province.[1] There is, as I am well informed, a club or society of active men belonging to each fire engine, whose business is to attend all fires with it whenever they happen, and to work it once a quarter[2] and see it kept in order; some of these are to handle the fire hooks,[3] and others the axes, which are always kept with the engine; and for this service they are considered in an abatement or exemption in the taxes. In time of fire, they are commanded by officers appointed by law, called *fire wards,* who are distinguished by a red staff of five feet long, headed with a brass flame of six inches; and being men of prudence and authority, they direct the opening and stripping of roofs by the axmen, the pulling down burning timbers by the hookmen, and the playing of the engines, and command the making of lanes,[4] etc., and they are empowered to require assistance for the removing of goods out of houses on fire or in danger of fire, and to appoint guards for securing such goods; and disobedience to these officers in any way, at such times, is punished by a fine of 40*s.*[5] or ten days imprisonment.

---

[1]*a city in a neighboring province,* Boston. Franklin had returned from a visit there shortly before writing this letter.

[2]*quarter,* period of three months.

[3]*fire hooks,* strong hooks for tearing down beams, walls, etc., attacked by fire.

[4]*lanes,* fire lanes, or areas from which inflammable material is cleared to prevent the spread of fire.

[5]*40s,* forty shillings. In colonial America the value of the shilling varied from one colony to another. It was originally based on the English shilling, which equaled twelve pence or about 25 cents in U. S. money today.

"Protection of Towns from Fire," adapted from *The Writings of Benjamin Franklin,* edited by Albert H. Smyth. Copyright 1905 by The Macmillan Company.

These officers, with the men belonging to the engine, at their quarterly meetings, discourse of fires, of the faults committed at some, the good management in some cases at others, and thus communicating their thoughts and experience they grow wise in the things, and know how to command and to execute in the best manner upon every emergency. Since the establishment of this regulation, it seems there has been no extraordinary fire in that place; and I wish there never may be any here. But they suffered before they made such a regulation, and so must we; for Englishmen[6] feel but cannot see, as the Italian says of us. And it has pleased God that in the fires we have hitherto had all the bad circumstances have never happened together, such as dry season, high wind, narrow street, and little water: which perhaps tends to make us secure in our own minds; but if a fire with those circumstances, which God forbid, should happen, we should afterwards be careful enough.

---

[6]*Englishmen.* At this time (1735) the colonists were English subjects and thought of themselves as Englishmen.

Let Us Now Forgive and Forget

Jonathan Shipley, an English bishop, was Franklin's friend for many years. It was at Shipley's country home at Twyford near Winchester that Franklin wrote the first section of his *Autobiography.* Later, when Franklin was in France acting as one of the commissioners appointed by Congress to negotiate peace with England, he wrote the following letter to his old friend. Although the treaty was not signed until September 3, 1783, at the time Franklin wrote, the main points had been agreed upon and made public.

T O JONATHAN SHIPLEY

Passy,[1] March 17, 1783

I received with great pleasure my dear and respected friend's letter of the 5th instant,[2] as it informed me of the welfare of a family I so much esteem and love.

---

[1]*Passy* (pä sē′), a village near Paris where Franklin lived.

[2]*the 5th instant,* the fifth day of the present month.

The clamor against the peace in your Parliament would alarm me for its duration, if I were not of opinion with you that the attack is rather against the minister.[3] I am confident none of the opposition would have made a better peace for England, if they had been in his place; at least, I am sure that Lord Stormont, who seems loudest in railing at it, is not the man that could have mended it. My reasons I will give you, when I have, what I hope to have, the great happiness of seeing you once more and conversing with you.

They talk much of there being no *reciprocity* in our treaty. They think nothing, then, of our passing over in silence the atrocities committed by their troops, and demanding no satisfaction for their wanton burnings and devastations of our fair towns and countries. They have heretofore confessed the war to be unjust, and nothing is plainer in reasoning than that the mischiefs done in an unjust war should be repaired. Can Englishmen be so partial to themselves as to imagine they have a right to plunder and destroy as much as they please, and then, without satisfying for the injuries they have done, to have peace on equal terms? We were favorable, and did not demand what justice entitled us to. We shall probably be blamed for it by our constituents; and I still think it would be the interest of England voluntarily to offer reparation of those injuries, and effect it as much as may be in her power. But this is an interest she will never see.

Let us now forgive and forget. Let each country seek its advancement in its own internal advantages of arts and agriculture, not in retarding or preventing the prosperity of the other. America will, with God's blessing, become a great and happy country; and England, if she has at length gained wisdom, will have gained something more valuable, and more essential to her prosperity, than all she has lost; and will still be a great and respectable nation. Her great

disease at present is the number and enormous salaries and emoluments of office. Avarice and ambition are strong passions, and, separately, act with great force on the human mind; but, when both are united, and may be gratified in the same object, their violence is almost irresistible, and they hurry men headlong into factions and contentions, destructive of all good government. As long, therefore, as these great emoluments subsist, your Parliament will be a stormy sea, and your public councils confounded by private interests. But it requires much public spirit and virtue to abolish them; more perhaps than can now be found in a nation so long corrupted.

I am, &c.,

B. Franklin

CONSIDERING BENJAMIN FRANKLIN

1. Name some of the important offices held by Franklin. What qualities did he possess which made him an excellent public servant?

2. Why were newspapers and pamphlets very important in forming opinions in the American colonies? Besides Franklin, what great Americans of his day might you consider propagandists? Do you think that the written word exerted more influence then than now? Why, or why not?

3. In what ways did Franklin's writings further his influence and lead to his holding public office?

CONSIDERING "PROTECTION OF TOWNS FROM FIRE" AND "LET US NOW FORGIVE AND FORGET"

1. What points made by Franklin in "Protection of Towns from Fire" do you consider most effective in persuading the citizens of Philadelphia to accept his proposal?

2. In writing to Bishop Shipley, what arguments did Franklin advance to counter Parliament's claims that there was no reciprocity in the treaty: that is, that the Tories were not being reimbursed for lost properties? Why was his argument a very clever one?

3. Read again paragraph 4, page 303, which explains Franklin's success as a political writer. Then point out in the selections you have just studied passages which illustrate as many as possible of the points made there.

---

[3] *the minister,* Lord Shelburne, the prime minister. He was forced to resign because of strong opposition to certain provisions of the peace treaty with the United States. Most violently opposed was the article that Loyalists (Americans who had sided with the British) were not to be compensated for lost or destroyed property.

Modern science, historians say, had its start in the seventeenth and eighteenth centuries. Modern methods of learning scientific facts were initiated by Francis Bacon (1561-1626). In the seventeenth century the discoveries of the chemist Robert Boyle, who was born the year after Bacon's death, advanced scientific knowledge. Isaac Newton, the great mathematician and physicist, made most of his discoveries in the last half of the same century. The work of the French astronomer and mathematician, Pierre Simon Laplace, bridges the time from the late eighteenth to the early nineteenth century. These were only a few of many men who opened new vistas to science.

In Franklin's period and in the preceding century, many intellectual Americans who were not professional scientists followed developments with interest and at times made contributions to growing knowledge. William Byrd (1674-1744), the Virginia planter, for example, filled his journals with botanical and zoölogical observations. He was a member of the great British scientific organization, the Royal Society. Jonathan Edwards (1703-1758), a leading New England clergyman, wrote numerous scientific papers. And the great Thomas Jefferson (1743-1826) carried on experiments in agriculture and was chided by his enemies for his interest in scientific "gadgets."

Franklin shared the general interest of thinking men in science, partly because this new study was attracting such wide attention, partly because his character impelled him toward science. The curiosity which was a leading trait of his made him try to pry into nature's secrets. His common-sense approach helped him sound out ingenious ways of working. Once his interest was aroused in any question, he carefully stated the problem to be solved, conducted novel experiments with apparatus of his own invention, made observations which he recorded for later study, and, after checking his facts, drew conclusions which for the most part are still considered sound. In addition to his curiosity, two other characteristics extended the usefulness of his discoveries. In the first place, because he was practical and interested in human welfare, he was not content to let his conclusions rest as laboratory results; he tried immediately to find useful applications which would serve his fellow men. (One of his inventions, for instance, was a superior type of stove, still in use.) In the second place, because he was a skilled writer, he wrote so clearly and engagingly about his discoveries that hundreds of readers on both sides of the Atlantic were fascinated and instructed.

In 1744 Franklin founded the American Philosophical Society of Philadelphia, an organization to promote the study of the sciences, and to distribute among the members by means of published papers the discoveries made by each. This society helped advance science.

In 1746 Franklin embarked upon experiments in electricity, throwing himself with all his time and energy into learning all that was then known on this subject and conducting experiments of his own to advance this knowledge. Before long he was leading the world in experimental electricity, not only in conducting thorough and carefully reported experiments, but in the development of a theory of electricity as a fluid, with positive and negative characteristics. Everyone knows of Franklin's brilliant discovery and demonstration that lightning is electricity.

Always a practical man, Franklin made almost immediate use of his discovery in the development of the lightning rod to protect buildings from the effects of electrical storms.[1] The following paragraph from a letter addressed to his English friend and correspondent in the Royal Society, Peter Collinson, dated September, 1753, will show Franklin's keen observation, his careful analysis, and his sound conclusions on the subject of lightning.

In every stroke of lightning, I am of opinion that the stream of electric fluid, moving to restore the equilibrium between the cloud and the earth, does always previously find its passage, and mark out, as I may say, its own course, taking in its way all the conductors it can find, such as metals, damp walls, moist wood, etc. and will go considerably out of a direct course, for the sake of the assistance of good conductors; and that, in this course, it is actually moving, though silently and imperceptibly, before the explosion, in and among the conductors; which explosion happens only when the conductors cannot discharge it as fast as they receive it, by reason of their being incomplete, disunited, too small, or not of the best materials for conducting. Metalline rods, therefore, of sufficient thickness, and extending from the highest part of an edifice to the ground, being of the best materials and complete conductors, will, I think, secure the building from damage, either by restoring the equilibrium so fast as to prevent a stroke, or by conducting it in the substance of the rod as far as the rod goes, so that there shall be no explosion but what is above its point, between that and the clouds.

Almost two hundred years of scientific advance have done little to change the fundamental assumptions Franklin makes in this summary. Note, too, his use of terms like *stream of electric fluid, equilibrium, conductors*. These and many other of the commonest terms of electrical science were first used by Franklin (for example: *positive, negative, charge,* and *battery*).

Despite Franklin's serious interest in science, he was not above having a little fun with it. A number of the experiments reported in his letters were of a humorous character, and he entertained himself and his friends for years with a device in his home which caused bells to ring whenever an electrified cloud passed over the house.

While Franklin did his most important scientific work in electricity, his interests were much wider. He was the first to explain the progress of cyclonic storms across the eastern United States; he developed an important theory regarding the Gulf Stream; he discovered and reported the effect of the depth of canals on the movements of boats in them; he invented a musical instrument in which whirling glasses gave off sweet tunes; and he developed a theory concerning the common cold which is still substantially sound. In his work on every problem which his curious mind led him to examine, his careful observation and brilliant deductions led to conclusions of scientific importance. It is no wonder that he was regarded as the leading scientist of the Western Hemisphere, and was honored by election to the exclusive Royal Society of England. The following selections show Franklin in the rôle of a writer on science.

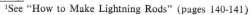
[1]See "How to Make Lightning Rods" (pages 140-141)

The Electrical Kite

To PETER COLLINSON

Philadelphia, October 1, 1752

Sir,

As frequent mention is made in public papers from Europe of the success of the Philadelphia experiment for drawing the electric fire from clouds by means of pointed rods of iron erected on high buildings, etc., it may be agreeable to the curious to be informed that the same experiment has succeeded in Philadelphia, though made in a different and more easy manner, which is as follows:

Make a small cross of two light strips of cedar, the arms so long as to reach to the four corners of a large thin silk handkerchief when extended; tie the corners of the handkerchief to the extremities of the cross, so you have the body of a kite, which, being properly accommodated with a tail, loop, and string, will rise in the air, like those made of paper; but this being of silk, is fitter to bear the wet and wind of a thundergust[1] without tearing. To the top of the upright stick of the cross is to be fixed a very sharp-pointed wire, rising a foot or more above the wood. To the end of the twine, next the hand, is to be tied a silk ribbon, and where the silk and twine join, a key may be fastened. This kite is to be raised when a thundergust appears to be coming on, and the person who holds the string must stand within a door or window or under some cover, so that the silk ribbon may not be wet; and care must be taken that the twine does not touch the frame of the door or window. As soon as any of the thunderclouds come over the kite, the pointed wire will draw the electric fire from them, and the kite, with all the twine, will be electrified, and the loose filaments of the twine will stand out every way, and be attracted by an approaching finger. And when the rain has wet the kite and twine, so that it can conduct the electric fire freely, you will find it stream out plentifully from the key on the approach of your knuckle. At this key the phial[2] may be charged; and from electric fire thus obtained, spirits may be kindled,[3] and all the other electric experiments be performed, which are usually done by the help of a rubbed glass globe or tube,[4] and thereby the sameness of the electric matter with that of lightning completely demonstrated.

B. Franklin

[1] *thundergust,* thunderstorm.

[2] *the phial,* a Leyden jar. This is a glass jar, lined inside and out with tin foil for most of its height, which may be used to accumulate frictional electricity.

[3] *spirits may be kindled,* alcohol may be lighted. This was a common electrical experiment.

[4] *all the other electric experiments...rubbed glass globe or tube.* In earlier experiments electric charges had been produced by rubbing glass on silk.

First Aerial Voyage by Man

In 1783, the year in which the treaty of peace between England and the new United States was signed, the people of France were greatly excited by balloon ascensions. The first practical balloon, a linen globe inflated over a fire fed by bundles of straw, had been tried out near Lyons by the Montgolfier brothers in June, 1783. Other experiments had followed this first one, including several in which a man, protected by guide ropes, went up in a balloon.

Franklin, who was living at Passy, near Paris, followed the accounts of these experiments with interest and sent reports on them to his friend Sir Joseph Banks, a member of the Royal Society. In the following extract from one of these letters, Franklin first refers to his earlier correspondence and then gives an eyewitness account of the first ascent of men in a free balloon.

To SIR JOSEPH BANKS

Passy, Nov. 21, 1783

Dear Sir,

I received your friendly letter of the 7th instant. I am glad my letters respecting the aerostatic experiment were not unacceptable. But as more perfect accounts of the construction and management of that machine have been and will be published before your transactions,[1] and from which extracts may be made that will be more particular and therefore more satisfactory, I think it best not to print those letters. I say this in answer to your question, for I did not indeed write them with a view of their being inserted. M. Faujas de St. Fond[2] acquainted me yesterday that a book on the subject, which has been long expected, will be published in a few days, and I shall send you one of them. Enclosed is a copy of the *proces verbal*[3] taken of the experiment made yesterday in the garden of the queen's palace, la Muette, where the Dauphin[4] now resides, which being near my house I was present. This paper was drawn up hastily, and may in some places appear to you obscure; therefore I shall add a few explanatory observations.

This balloon was larger than that which went up from Versailles and carried the sheep, etc.[5] Its bottom was open, and in the middle of the opening was fixed a kind of basket grate in which fagots and sheaves of straw were burnt. The air, rarefied in passing through this flame, rose in the balloon, swelled out its sides, and filled it.

The persons, who were placed in the gallery made of wicker and attached to the outside near the bottom, had each of them a port through which they could pass sheaves of straw into the grate to keep up the flame, and thereby keep the balloon full. When it went over our heads, we could see the fire, which was very considerable. As the flame slackens, the rarefied air

cools and condenses, the bulk of the balloon diminishes and it begins to descend. If these in the gallery see it likely to descend in an improper place, they can, by throwing on more straw and renewing the flame, make it rise again, and the wind carries it farther.

La Machine poussée par le Vent s'est dirigée sur une des Allées du Jardin.[6] That is, against the trees of one of the walks. The gallery hitched among the top boughs of those trees which had been cut and were stiff, while the body of the balloon leaned beyond and seemed likely to overset. I was then in great pain for the men, thinking them in danger of being thrown out or burnt, for I expected that the balloon being no longer upright, the flame would have laid hold of the inside that leaned over it. But by means of some cords that were still attached to it, it was soon brought upright again, made to descend, and carried back to its place. It was, however, much damaged.

Planant sur l'Horizon.[7] When they were as high as they chose to be, they made less flame and suffered the machine to drive horizontally with the wind, of which, however, they felt very little, as they went with it, and as fast. They say they had a charming view of Paris and its environs, the course of the river, etc., but that they were once lost, not knowing what part they were over, till they saw the Dome of the Invalids,[8] which rectified their ideas. Probably while they were employed in keeping up the fire, the machine might turn, and by that means they were *désorienté,*[9] as the French call it.

There was a vast concourse of gentry in the garden, who had great pleasure in seeing the adventures go off so cheerfully, and applauded them by clapping, etc., but there was at the same time a good deal of anxiety for their safety. Multitudes in Paris saw the balloon passing, but did not know there were men with it, it being then so high that they could not see them.

---

[1] *your transactions.* In its yearly publication called *Transactions* the Royal Society carried accounts of new scientific developments. Certain of Franklin's letters, such as his letter to Peter Collinson containing the account of the electric kite, had been published in *Transactions.* Banks had suggested to Franklin that his previous letters on aerial voyages might be inserted in the forthcoming volume.

[2] *Monsieur Faujas de St. Fond* (mə syœ′ fō zhäs′ də saṉ fôn′), a French geologist who had set on foot the subscription to finance the ascent of the first hydrogen-filled balloon.

[3] *proces verbal* (prô sä′ vėr bäl′), written report.

[4] *the Dauphin* (dô′fən), the eldest son of the king of France by traditional title. The Dauphin at this time was a two-year-old boy.

[5] *that which went up from Versailles* (vär sī′)...*sheep, etc.* On September 19 Joseph Montgolfier sent up a balloon carrying a sheep, a cock, and a duck—the first aerial travelers.

[6] *La Machine...Allées du Jardin.* The machine, driven by the wind, blew against one of the walks of the garden.

[7] *Planant sur l'Horizon,* hovering on the horizon.

[8] *the Dome of the Invalids,* the dome of the Hotel des Invalides (ō tel′ dä zäṉ vä lēd′), a hospital for old or sick soldiers in Paris.

[9] *they were "désorienté"* (dā zô′rē än tā′), they had lost their sense of direction.

Developant du Gaz.[10] That is, in plain English, *burning more straw;* for though there is a little mystery made concerning the kind of air with which the balloon is filled, I conceive it to be nothing more than hot smoke or common air rarefied—though in this I may be mistaken;...

Ayant encore dans leur Galerie le deux tiers de leur approvisionment.[11] That is, their provision of straw, of which they carried up a great quantity. It was well that, in the hurry of so hazardous an experiment, the flame did not happen by any accidental mismanagement to lay hold of this straw; though each had a bucket of water by him by way of precaution.

One of these courageous philosophers, the Marquis d'Arlandes, did me the honor to call upon me in the evening after the experiment, with Mr. Mongolfier, the very ingenious inventor. I was happy to see him safe. He informed me they lit gently without the least shock, and the balloon was very little damaged....

With great and sincere esteem, I am, dear sir, your most obedient and humble servant,

B. Franklin

---

[10]*Developant du Gaz,* developing gas.

[11]*Ayant encore...approvisionment,* still having in their gallery two-thirds of their provisions.

CONCERNING BENJAMIN FRANKLIN

1. Which of Franklin's characteristics were of most value to him as a scientist?

2. How did Franklin's activities as a scientist confirm what you have already learned of him as a man greatly interested in the public good?

3. In what way did Franklin's career as a newspaperman increase his value as a scientist?

CONCERNING "THE ELECTRICAL KITE" AND "FIRST AERIAL VOYAGE BY MAN"

1. What similarities do you find between "How to Make Lightning Rods" (pages 140-141) and "The Electrical Kite"? Using these two letters as a basis for your argument, explain why you think Franklin's experiments aroused such wide general interest.

2. Which details in "First Aerial Voyage by Man" show Franklin's interest in the balloon ascension as a scientific experiment? Which details would have no place in a purely scientific paper? Why do you think Franklin included in his letter details which had no bearing on the scientific aspects of the experiment?

Extending interests

If newspapers of the modern type had existed in 1783, the balloon ascension Franklin described would have rated a banner head on page 1. Like the good reporter he was, Franklin gave all the facts that would be needed for a newspaper article. Try your hand at turning them into a front-page story.

❧ IV THE MAN OF THE WORLD

Occupied though he was with business, science, and politics, Franklin somehow found time to enjoy to the full the crowded social life of his time. In the colonies where he spent the first half of his long life, in England, and later in France, he entered wholeheartedly into the favorite diversion of the eighteenth century—carrying on lively, intelligent conversation.

Franklin early discovered the fascination of good talk. While he was still a printer's apprentice he read with delight *The Spectator Papers,* a series of essays by Joseph Addison and Richard Steele which recounted, among other things, the interesting conversations of a group of English gentlemen called the Spectator Club. To provide for lively discussions in his own circle, in 1727 Franklin founded the Junto Club in Philadelphia. This group of twelve men met weekly for many years.

When Franklin went to London as agent for the American colonies, he found the new coffee houses the center of amusing talk. Here gentle-

men foregathered regularly for social evenings. Here the clubs met, among them Dr. Samuel Johnson's famous group. Dr. Johnson, brilliant conversationalist, author, and dictionary-maker, was the acknowledged literary leader of London. His group included, among others, Goldsmith the poet, Burke the orator, and Garrick the actor. Franklin thoroughly enjoyed the easy sociability and stimulating conversation in the coffee houses. Years later, as an old man of seventy-six, he wrote to his friend Dr. Priestley, the English clergyman and chemist: "I long to see you and the honest souls who meet in the coffee houses once more, that I may be happy in your sweet society."

Between 1776 and 1785, when Franklin was in France serving as agent for the new United States, his business brought him into daily contact with the brilliant society surrounding the court of the French king. In this assemblage of clever men and women Dr. Franklin, as he was then called, occupied a unique place as a scientist of international fame, the American minister to France, a philosopher out of the new world, and a brilliant conversationalist famous for his quickness in witty exchanges. A widely circulated story is illustrative: At a Paris banquet, the diplomats present were asked to toast their respective countries. The British ambassador said, "To England!—the Sun, whose warm beneficent rays encourage the growth of industry and assist in the expansion of labor in every form throughout the world!" The French minister said, "To France!—the Moon, whose soft glow encourages the flowering of literature and the mellowing of the arts!" When Franklin stood, the audience tittered, for it appeared that he was left with nothing important to claim. But unhesitatingly he said, "To the United States!—the Joshua at whose command the sun and the moon stand still!"

Not only in society but in books as well, Franklin found stimulating companionship. Although he often pictured characters who gloried in their lack of book learning, he himself read widely and with great pleasure. His favorite authors ranged from the ancient Greeks and Romans to his own contemporaries in England and France. Among the Greek writings he particularly enjoyed were the fables of Aesop, the philosophical writings of Plato, and the histories of Herodotus. He found pleasure in the Roman writers: Virgil, the epic poet; Horace, poet and satirist; and Cicero, orator and statesman. His favorites among English writers of previous centuries included the essayist Bacon and the poets Milton and Dryden; and the wideness of his reading interests is shown by his liking for two French authors, the great Renaissance satirist Rabelais and the philosophical churchman Fénelon. Addison and Steele remained among his favorite English writers of recent times; he read much, too, in the urbane and witty pages of his contemporaries: Alexander Pope, English poet; Jonathan Swift, Irish-born satirist; and Voltaire, French satirical poet and dramatist.

Not surprisingly, the author who could assume the rôle of an unlearned Widow Dogood or Poor Richard was equally at home when he wrote as a sophisticated man of the world. In Philadelphia, at one time for instance, Franklin wrote a series of articles for the *American Weekly Mercury* over the signature of "Busy-Body." In the first article he announces to the editor that he has taken upon himself the rôle of author, not from vanity, but for the public good. He observes that since the *Mercury* is from time to time somewhat dull, and since, moreover, the growing vices and follies of his fellow citizens call for restraining comment, he will provide a series of articles to enliven the pages of the *Mercury* and at the same time reform society. After outlining his plan of procedure, he concludes the first article in this way:

> It is very common with authors, in their first performances, to talk to their readers thus: "If this meets with a suitable reception; or, If this should meet with due encouragement, I shall hereafter publish, etc." This only manifests the value they put on their own writings, since they think to frighten the public into their applause, by threatening, that unless you approve what they have already written, they intend never to write again; when perhaps it mayn't be a pin matter whether they ever do or no. As I have not observed the critics to be more favorable on this account, I shall always avoid saying anything of the kind; and conclude with telling you that, if you send me a bottle of ink and a quire of paper by the bearer, you may depend on hearing further from, Sir, your most humble servant,—The Busy-Body.

Franklin contributed short articles over the years to many journals, sometimes signing his own name, but frequently creating a fictitious character as the supposed author. Such a character was Alice Addertongue, who commented on gossip and scandal in *The Pennsylvania Gazette*.

During his years in France as agent for the United States, Franklin entertained his friends at his home in Passy. Here he wrote little essays known as "bagatelles" for their amusement. He set up a press to amuse himself and his friends by printing them. Among these pieces is the famous "Ephemera," which was addressed as a letter to Franklin's friend, Madame Brillon. This shows very well what Franklin could do when he wrote as a man of the world.

Other humorous bits from the same collection show the range of Franklin's skill in the light and charming essay, from gently ironical commentaries on human life to broad and indelicate satire on the pretensions of scholars. In one of the best of these pieces Franklin takes himself to task for eating and drinking too much and exercising too little. He called it "Dialogue Between Franklin and the Gout."

The illustrations of Franklin's humor come chiefly from his later life, partly because greater leisure and the applause of an admiring circle of friends encouraged his putting his wit and humor into little essays. Throughout his life, however, the same quickness of wit, the same appreciation of the ridiculous, and the same skill at satire characterized his conversation and sometimes crept into his writing. No better example can be offered than that at the age of twenty-two (sixty-two years before his death in 1790) Franklin wrote his own epitaph in the following terms:

Epitaph Written 1728
The Body of
B Franklin Printer,
(Like the Cover of an old Book
Its Contents torn out
And stript of its Lettering & Gilding)
Lies here, Food for Worms.
But the Work shall not be lost;
For it will, (as he believ'd) appear once more,
In a new and more elegant Edition
Revised and corrected,
By the Author.

The following selections show Franklin writing in the rôle of a man of the world.

The Ephemera

AN EMBLEM OF HUMAN LIFE

YOU MAY REMEMBER, my dear friend, that when we lately spent that happy day in the delightful garden and sweet society of the Moulin Joly,[1] I stopped a little in one of our walks and stayed some time behind the company. We had been shown numberless skeletons of a kind of little fly, called an ephemera, whose successive generations, we were told, were bred and expired within the day. I happened to see a living company of them on a leaf, who appeared to be engaged in conversation. You know I understand all the inferior animal tongues. My too great application to the study of them is the best excuse I can give for the little progress I have made in your charming language.[2] I listened through curiosity to the discourse of these little creatures; but as they, in their national vivacity, spoke three or four together, I could make but little of their conversation. I found, however, by some broken expressions that I heard now and then, they were disputing warmly on the merit of two foreign musicians, one a *cousin,* the other a *moscheto*[3]; in which dispute they spent their time, seemingly as regardless of the shortness of life as if they had been sure of living a month. Happy people! thought I, you are certainly under a wise, just, and mild government, since you have no public grievances to complain of, nor any subject of contention but the perfections and imperfections of foreign music! I turned my head from them to an old

---

[1]*Moulin Joly* (mü laN′ zhô lē′), the name of the home of a friend of Franklin's on an island in the Seine (sān). Here in the summer of 1778 Franklin spent a day with Madame Brillon and other friends. Later in the selection Franklin uses *Moulin Joly,* which means "the pretty mill," to represent the whole world.

[2]*your charming language,* French.
[3]*two foreign musicians...cousin* (kü zaN′) *...moscheto* (mō skāt′tō). At the time Franklin wrote "The Ephemera," Parisians were disputing about the relative merits of a German and an Italian musician. Franklin satirizes this argument by having the insects discuss the music of the *cousin* (the French word for a gnat) and the *moscheto* (the Italian word for a mosquito).

gray-headed one, who was single on another leaf, and talking to himself. Being amused with his soliloquy, I put it down in writing, in hopes it will likewise amuse her[4] to whom I am so much indebted for the most pleasing of all amusements, her delicious company and heavenly harmony.

"It was," said he,[5] "the opinion of learned philosophers of our race, who lived and flourished long before my time, that this vast world, the Moulin Joly, could not itself subsist more than eighteen hours; and I think there was some foundation for that opinion, since, by the apparent motion of the great luminary[6] that gives life to all nature, and which in my time has evidently declined considerably toward the ocean at the end of our earth, it must then finish its course, be extinguished in the waters that surround us, and leave the world in cold and darkness, necessarily producing universal death and destruction. I have lived seven of those hours, a great age, being no less than four hundred and twenty minutes of time. How very few of us continue so long! I have seen generations born, flourish, and expire. My present friends are the children and grandchildren of the friends of my youth, who are now, alas, no more! And I must soon follow them; for, by the course of nature, though still in health, I cannot expect to live above seven or eight minutes longer. What now avails all my toil and labor in amassing honeydew on this leaf, which I cannot live to enjoy! What the political struggles I have been engaged in for the good of my compatriot inhabitants of this bush, or my philosophical studies for the benefit of our race in general! for in politics, what can laws do without morals? Our present race of ephemerae will in a course of minutes become corrupt, like those of other and older bushes, and consequently as wretched. And in philosophy how small our progress! Alas! art is long, and life is short! My friends would comfort me with the idea of a name they say I shall leave behind me; and they tell me I have lived long enough to nature and to glory. But what will fame be to an ephemera who no

longer exists? And what will become of all history in the eighteenth hour, when the world itself, even the whole Moulin Joly, shall come to its end, and be buried in universal ruin?"

To me, after all my eager pursuits, no solid pleasures now remain but the reflection of a long life spent in meaning well, the sensible conversation of a few good lady ephemerae, and now and then a kind smile and a tune from the ever amiable *Brillante*.[7]

B. Franklin

---

[7]*Brillante* (bri yaNt′), shining one. Franklin is punning on Madame Brillon's name, the pronunciation of which is similar to that of *Brillante*.

Dialogue Between Franklin and the Gout

Midnight, October 22, 1780

FRANKLIN. Eh! oh! eh! What have I done to merit these cruel sufferings?

GOUT. Many things; you have ate and drank too freely, and too much indulged those legs of yours in their indolence.

FRANKLIN. Who is it that accuses me?

GOUT. It is I, even I, the Gout.

FRANKLIN. What! my enemy in person?

GOUT. No, not your enemy.

FRANKLIN. I repeat it: my enemy; for you would not only torment my body to death, but ruin my good name; you reproach me as a glutton and a tippler; now all the world, that knows me, will allow that I am neither the one nor the other.

GOUT. The world may think as it pleases; it is always very complaisant to itself, and sometimes to its friends; but I very well know that the quantity of meat and drink proper for a man who takes a reasonable degree of exercise would be too much for another who never takes any.

FRANKLIN. I take—eh! oh!—as much exercise —eh!—as I can, Madam Gout. You know my

---

[4]*her*, Madame Brillon, the one to whom he is writing.
[5]*he*, the old ephemera who is giving the soliloquy.
[6]*the great luminary*, the sun.

sedentary state, and on that account, it would seem, Madam Gout, as if you might spare me a little, seeing it is not altogether my own fault.

Gout. Not a jot; your rhetoric and your politeness are thrown away; your apology avails nothing. If your situation in life is a sedentary one, your amusements, your recreations, at least, should be active. You ought to walk or ride; or, if the weather prevents that, play at billiards. But let us examine your course of life. While the mornings are long, and you have leisure to go abroad, what do you do? Why, instead of gaining an appetite for breakfast, by salutary exercise, you amuse yourself with books, pamphlets, or newspapers, which commonly are not worth the reading. Yet you eat an inordinate breakfast, four dishes of tea, with cream, and one or two buttered toasts, with slices of hung beef,[1] which I fancy are not things the most easily digested. Immediately afterward you sit down to write at your desk, or converse with persons who apply to you on business. Thus the time passes till one, without any kind of bodily exercise. But all this I could pardon, in regard, as you say, to your sedentary condition. But what is your practice after dinner? Walking in the beautiful gardens of those friends with whom you have dined would be the choice of men of sense; yours is to be fixed down to chess, where you are found engaged for two or three hours! This is your perpetual recreation, which is the least eligible of any for a sedentary man, because, instead of accelerating the motion of the fluids,[2] the rigid attention it requires helps to retard the circulation and obstruct internal secretions. Wrapt in the speculations of this wretched game, you destroy your constitution. What can be expected from such a course of living, but a body replete with stagnant humors,[3] ready to fall a prey to all kinds of dangerous maladies, if I, the Gout, did not occasionally bring you relief by agitating those humors, and so purifying or dissipating them? If it was in some nook or alley in Paris, deprived of walks, that you played awhile at chess after dinner, this might be excusable; but the same taste prevails with you in Passy, Auteuil, Montmartre, or Sanoy,[4] places where there are the finest gardens and walks, a pure air, beautiful women, and most agreeable and instructive conversation; all which you might enjoy by frequenting the walks. But these are rejected for this abominable game of chess. Fie, then, Mr. Franklin! But amidst my instructions, I had almost forgot to administer my wholesome corrections; so take that twinge—and that.

Franklin. Oh! eh! oh! ohhh! As much instruction as you please, Madam Gout, and as many reproaches; but pray, Madam, a truce with your corrections!

Gout. No, Sir, no—I will not abate a particle of what is so much for your good—therefore—

Franklin. Oh! ehhh!—It is not fair to say I take no exercise, when I do very often, going out to dine and returning in my carriage.

Gout. That, of all imaginable exercises, is the most slight and insignificant, if you allude to the motion of a carriage suspended on springs. By observing the degree of heat obtained by different kinds of motion, we may form an estimate of the quantity of exercise given by each. Thus, for example, if you turn out to walk in winter with cold feet, in an hour's time you will be in a glow all over; ride on horseback, the same effect will scarcely be perceived by four hours' round trotting; but if you loll in a carriage, such as you have mentioned, you may travel all day and gladly enter the last inn to warm your feet by a fire. Flatter yourself then no longer that half an hour's airing in your carriage deserves the name of exercise. Providence has appointed few to roll in carriages, while he has given to all a pair of legs, which are machines infinitely more commodious and serviceable. Be grateful, then, and make a proper use of yours. Would you know how they forward the circulation of your fluids, in the very action of transporting you from place to place,

---

[1] *hung beef*, beef which is salted and hung up to dry.

[2] *fluids*, substances within the body other than solids.

[3] *stagnant humors*. In Franklin's time men believed that the various body fluids (humors) determined a person's health and disposition. The Gout says Franklin's humors are stagnant or sluggish because of his inactive life.

[4] *Passy, Auteuil* (ō tė′yə), *Montmartre* (mōɴ′mär′trə), *or Sanoy* (sä nwä′). The first three places were villages in Franklin's day but are now within the city of Paris. Sanoy (Sannois) is a town a few miles north of the city.

observe when you walk that all your weight is alternately thrown from one leg to the other; this occasions a great pressure on the vessels of the foot, and repels their contents; when relieved, by the weight being thrown on the other foot, the vessels of the first are allowed to replenish, and, by a return of this weight, this repulsion again succeeds, thus accelerating the circulation of the blood. The heat produced in any given time depends on the degree of this acceleration; the fluids are shaken, the humors attenuated, the secretions facilitated, and all goes well; the cheeks are ruddy, and health is established. Behold your fair friend[5] at Auteuil, a lady who received from bounteous nature more really useful science than half a dozen such pretenders to philosophy as you have been able to extract from all your books. When she honors you with a visit, it is on foot. She walks all hours of the day, and leaves indolence, and its concomitant maladies, to be endured by her horses. In this, see at once the preservative of her health and personal charms. But when you go to Auteuil, you must have your carriage, though it is no further from Passy to Auteuil than from Auteuil to Passy.

FRANKLIN. Your reasonings grow very tiresome.

GOUT. I stand corrected. I will be silent and continue my office; take that, and that.

FRANKLIN. Oh! ohh! Talk on, I pray you!

GOUT. No, no; I have a good number of twinges for you tonight, and you may be sure of some more tomorrow.

FRANKLIN. What, with such a fever! I shall go distracted. Oh! eh! Can no one bear it for me?

GOUT. Ask that of your horses; they have served you faithfully.

FRANKLIN. How can you so cruelly sport with my torments?

GOUT. Sport! I am very serious. I have here a list of offenses against your own health distinctly written, and can justify every stroke inflicted on you.

FRANKLIN. Read it then.

GOUT. It is too long a detail; but I will briefly mention some particulars.

FRANKLIN. Proceed, I am all attention.

GOUT. Do you remember how often you have promised yourself, the following morning, a walk in the grove of Boulogne,[6] in the garden de la Muette,[7] or in your own garden, and have violated your promise, alleging, at one time, it was too cold, at another too warm, too windy, too moist, or what else you pleased; when in truth it was too nothing but your insuperable love of ease?

FRANKLIN. That I confess may have happened occasionally, probably ten times in a year.

GOUT. Your confession is very far short of the truth; the gross amount is one hundred and ninety-nine times.

FRANKLIN. Is it possible?

GOUT. So possible that it is fact; you may rely on the accuracy of my statement. You know M. Brillon's gardens,[8] and what fine walks they contain; you know the handsome flight of an hundred steps, which lead from the terrace above to the lawn below. You have been in the practice of visiting this amiable family twice a week, after dinner, and it is a maxim of your own that "a man may take as much exercise in walking a mile, up and down stairs, as in ten on level ground." What an opportunity was here for you to have had exercise in both these ways! Did you embrace it, and how often?

FRANKLIN. I cannot immediately answer that question.

GOUT. I will do it for you; not once.

FRANKLIN. Not once?

GOUT. Even so. During the summer you went there at six o'clock. You found the charming lady, with her lovely children and friends, eager to walk with you, and entertain you with their agreeable conversation; and what has been your choice? Why, to sit on the terrace, satisfying

---

[5]*your fair friend,* Madame Helvétius (mä däm′ el vā-syǝs′), the widow of a French philosopher. Franklin once addressed a half-serious proposal of marriage to her.

[6]*the grove of Boulogne,* the Bois de Boulogne (bwä′ dǝ bü lōn′). This wooded area just west of Passy is now a large public park in Paris.

[7]*the garden de la Muette* (dǝ lä myǝt′), the garden of the queen's palace. It was here that Franklin watched the balloon ascension.

[8]*M. Brillon's gardens.* The Brillons lived not far from Franklin at Passy.

yourself with the fine prospect and passing your eye over the beauties of the garden below, without taking one step to descend and walk about in them. On the contrary, you call for tea and the chessboard; and lo! you are occupied in your seat till nine o'clock, and that besides two hours' play after dinner; and then, instead of walking home, which would have bestirred you a little, you step into your carriage. How absurd to suppose that all this carelessness can be reconcilable with health, without my interposition!

FRANKLIN. I am convinced now of the justness of Poor Richard's remark that "Our debts and our sins are always greater than we think for."

GOUT. So it is. You philosophers are sages in your maxims and fools in your conduct.

FRANKLIN. But do you charge among my crimes that I return in a carriage from Mr. Brillon's?

GOUT. Certainly; for, having been seated all the while, you cannot object the fatigue of the day, and cannot want therefore the relief of a carriage.

FRANKLIN. What then would you have me do with my carriage?

GOUT. Burn it if you choose; you would at least get heat out of it once in this way; or, if you dislike that proposal, here's another for you. Observe the poor peasants, who work in the vineyards and grounds about the villages of Passy, Auteuil, Chaillot,[9] etc.; you may find everyday, among these deserving creatures, four or five old men and women, bent and perhaps crippled by weight of years, and too long and too great labor. After a most fatiguing day, these people have to trudge a mile or two to their smoky huts. Order your coachman to set them down. This is an act that will be good for your soul; and, at the same time, after your visit to the Brillons, if you return on foot, that will be good for your body.

FRANKLIN. Ah! how tiresome you are!

GOUT. Well, then, to my office; it should not be forgotten that I am your physician. There.

FRANKLIN. Ohhh! what a devil of a physician!

GOUT. How ungrateful you are to say so! Is it not I who, in the character of your physician, have saved you from the palsy, dropsy, and apoplexy? One or other of which would have done for you long ago but for me.

FRANKLIN. I submit, and thank you for the past, but entreat the discontinuance of your visits for the future; for, in my mind, one had better die than be cured so dolefully. Permit me just to hint that I have also not been unfriendly to *you*. I never feed physician or quack of any kind, to enter the list against you[10]; if then you do not leave me to my repose, it may be said you are ungrateful too.

GOUT. I can scarcely acknowledge that as any objection. As to quacks, I despise them; they may kill you indeed, but cannot injure me. And, as to regular physicians, they are at last convinced that the gout, in such a subject as you are, is no disease, but a remedy; and wherefore cure a remedy?—but to our business—there.

FRANKLIN. Oh! oh!—for Heaven's sake leave me! and I promise never more to play at chess, but to take exercise daily, and live temperately.

GOUT. I know you too well. You promise fair; but, after a few months of good health, you will return to your old habits; your fine promises will be forgotten like the forms of last year's clouds. Let us then finish the account, and I will go. But I leave you with an assurance of visiting you again at a proper time and place; for my object is your good, and you are sensible now that I am your *real friend*.

_____

[10]*I never feed physician...against you,* I never engage a physician or anyone who pretends to be a doctor to attempt to cure my gout.

CONCERNING BENJAMIN FRANKLIN

1. What were some of the characteristics of life in the eighteenth century? In what ways do Franklin's interests reflect the life of this age?

2. Franklin was seventy years old when he went to France, yet he soon became the center of a brilliant circle. What qualities of his do you think won the regard of courtiers, diplomats, and intellectuals?

3. Franklin's writings had aided his influence both as public servant and as scientist. Show how his pen was of value to him also as man of the world.

_____

[9]*Chaillot* (shä yō′), a village a short distance from Passy, today a part of Paris.

CONCERNING "THE EPHEMERA" AND
"DIALOGUE BETWEEN FRANKLIN
AND THE GOUT"

1. What is the basic idea of "The Ephemera"? In stating this idea use an adjective that is derived from the word *ephemera*.

2. Why did Franklin choose "an old gray-headed" ephemera to deliver the soliloquy? What points of comparison with the world in general and with Franklin's own life can you find in the soliloquy?

3. What idea of Franklin do you gain from reading "Dialogue Between Franklin and the Gout"? How does this compare with the idea of the man you received from reading "Project of Arriving at Moral Perfection"?

Franklin as a satirist

In England the eighteenth century was the age of satire. The poets Dryden and Pope, the essayists Addison, Steele, and Swift, the novelist Fielding were all satirists. With the sharp shafts of satire they mocked the pretensions of society, probed the inequalities of social justice, and sought to show men the frailties of human institutions. Together they made satire a dominant note in the literature of the first half of the eighteenth century; and even after the last of this famous group had died their influence continued to affect the writing and conversation of their successors.

Franklin, the American, shared to some extent the satirical view of life popular in England—in fact, his early literary tastes had been partially formed by reading the essays of Addison and Steele. The vein of satire crops out occasionally in the writing he did throughout his life but is particularly noticeable in the work of his later years.

Consider "The Ephemera." How does the very idea of the piece show Franklin's satirical bent? What particular habits and ideas of man does he satirize? Is the satire biting or relatively mild?

What evidences of satire do you find in "Dialogue Between Franklin and the Gout"? How does the satire here differ from that in "The Ephemera"?

The Larger View

I. Each of the paragraphs below has reference to some phase of Franklin's life. Read them carefully, and look up any unfamiliar references. Then discuss with your classmates which characteristics of the man and which aspects of his life are illustrated by each of the paragraphs.

1. As the story goes, on the momentous occasion when the Declaration of Independence was to be signed, John Hancock, President of the Second Continental Congress, stepped up first to affix his name to the document. He said, "We must be unanimous; there must be no pulling different ways; we must all hang together." "Yes," said Franklin; "we must indeed all hang together, or most assuredly we shall all hang separately."

2. Voltaire, the famous French philosopher and writer, and Franklin were both old men when a meeting was arranged between them at the Academy of Sciences in Paris. At the insistence of the crowd they embraced and kissed each other's cheek. Then from the crowd arose the cry: "How charming it is to see Solon and Sophocles embrace!"

3. When Franklin was a young apprentice of his brother James, James paid his board, as was customary. Benjamin asked to be given half of what his brother paid for his board, and agreed to board himself. He found he was able to save half of his money, and with it he bought books.

4. Franklin was considering publishing a book by a scholar on which he might lose money. He said, "If I can be the means of communicating anything valuable to the world, I do not always think of gaining, or even of saving, by my business."

5. Immanuel Kant, the famous German philosopher, on one occasion characterized Franklin as a new Prometheus who had stolen fire from heaven.

6. When Franklin's son Francis died of smallpox in 1736, the rumor spread over Philadelphia that the child had died as a result of being inoculated for the disease. Franklin published a notice in *The Pennsylvania Gazette* declaring that, because of a previous illness, the child had not been inoculated, but that he had intended to have him inoculated as soon as his health permitted.

II. Talk over the following questions with your classmates, wherever possible bringing into the discussion ideas you have gained as a result of your outside reading.

1. Which of the selections by Franklin that you have read did you enjoy most? Give reasons for your answer.

2. You have studied Franklin in a course in literature. In what other studies would he also be included? In your opinion in what field did he make his greatest contributions?

3. The introduction to Unit VI in this book speaks of writing "which is a revelation of history and of ideals through personal, first-hand records of the ways in which men and women in America have looked at their work and play, their companionship with others, and their own personal faith." Do any of the selections by Franklin fall into these classes? Explain your answer.

4. How would you characterize Franklin's style?

5. Why do you think Franklin's works continue to be read?

MORE GOOD READING

BURT, MAXWELL STRUTHERS, *Philadelphia, Holy Experiment.* (Doubleday) The chapters in this book which treat of pre-Revolutionary War Philadelphia will give you an engrossing picture of the city in which Franklin lived.

DAUGHERTY, JAMES, *Poor Richard.* (Viking) This biography of Franklin, which emphasizes his contributions to Americanism rather than his inventions, is a good account of a great patriot.

FRANKLIN, BENJAMIN, *Autobiography.* (Houghton) This account of his life which Franklin wrote for his son is perhaps the most famous of American autobiographies. You will find the first part, in which Franklin describes his early struggles, particularly interesting.

FRANKLIN, BENJAMIN, *The Benjamin Franklin Reader,* edited by Nathan Goodman. (Crowell) This is a fine book for browsing. You can glance through the pages, reading the letters and articles which treat of subjects that interest you.

FRANKLIN, BENJAMIN, *Poor Richard's Almanac.* (McKay) The pithy sayings and wise maxims which enlivened Franklin's almanac for many years are collected in this book.

HAWTHORNE, HILDEGARDE, *His Country Was the World; a Life of Thomas Paine.* (Longmans) Tom Paine, one of the great spokesmen of the rights of Americans, was born in poverty in England. It was Franklin who helped him come to America. This is a fine biography.

LAWSON, ROBERT, *Ben and Me.* (Little) Adults and children alike will enjoy this humorous life of Franklin told by the mouse who lived in the great man's famous fur cap. The line drawings are as sophisticated and clever as the text.

MEADOWCROFT, ENID, *Benjamin Franklin.* (Crowell) This readable biography emphasizes Franklin's boyhood and youth but also provides for an understanding of his later life.

MEIGS, CORNELIA L., *Mounted Messenger.* (Macmillan) The United States postal service owes its beginnings to Franklin. This is the story of young Tom Wetherall, who rides with mail for Franklin, and of his adventures in working for the unity of the American colonies.

MELVILLE, HERMAN, *Israel Potter.* (Page) This fictionized biography by a great American writer tells the story of a contemporary of Franklin and introduces such figures as King George III and John Paul Jones. And Melville's picture of Franklin himself is malicious but amusing.

RICHTER, CONRAD, *Free Man.* (Knopf) Pennsylvania in Franklin's day is the background for this novel of a German immigrant boy who is sold as an indentured servant in Philadelphia. How he escapes, flees from the city, and takes up arms against the British in his pursuit of a free life makes an inspiring story.

VAN DOREN, CARL, *Benjamin Franklin.* (Viking) Franklin's *Autobiography* covers only part of his life, but this full, scholarly, and interesting biography treats in detail of all the years of his long and varied life. The mature student will find it rewarding reading.

LITERATURE	HISTORICAL EVENTS
1721 Cotton Mather, *The Christian Philosopher*	
1722 Benjamin Franklin, *Dogood Papers*	
	William Byrd helped run boundary line between 1728 Virginia and North Carolina
1729 Edward Taylor died, leaving his *Poems* in manuscript	
1732 William Byrd, *Progress to the Mines*	George Washington born 1732
1733 Benjamin Franklin, *Poor Richard's Almanac* (first issue)	Oglethorpe established first settlement in Georgia 1733
1751 Benjamin Franklin, *Experiments and Observations on Electricity* (first edition)	First regular theatrical company visited colonies 1752
	Washington accompanied Braddock on his campaign 1755
1757 Benjamin Franklin, *The Way to Wealth*	
	Treaty of Paris ending the French and Indian 1763 War signed
	Great Britain passed the Stamp Act 1765
	Boston Massacre heightened ill feeling against 1770 England
1771 Benjamin Franklin wrote first part of *Autobiography*	
1774 Thomas Jefferson, *Summary of the Rights of British America*	
1775 Patrick Henry, "Liberty or Death"	Battles of Lexington and Concord fought 1775
Thomas Paine, *Common Sense*	
1776 "Declaration of Independence"	Independence from Great Britain declared 1776
Thomas Paine, *The American Crisis*	
1778 Francis Hopkinson, "Battle of the Kegs"	
1781 Philip Freneau, *The British Prison-Ship*	Cornwallis surrendered at Yorktown 1781
	Treaty of Paris concluding Revolution signed 1783
1784 Thomas Jefferson, *Notes on the State of Virginia*	
1786 Philip Freneau, *The Poems of Philip Freneau*	
	Northwest Ordinance passed 1787
1788 Alexander Hamilton, *The Federalist*	Constitution of the United States ratified 1788
1789 George Washington, "First Inaugural"	Washington became first President 1789
1791 William Bartram, *Travels*	

Benjamin Franklin 1706-1790

SOME PROMINENT WRITERS OF THE COLONIAL AND REVOLUTIONARY PERIOD

WILLIAM BARTRAM, 1739-1823

William Bartram was the son of one of Franklin's friends, the botanist John Bartram, a member of the American Philosophical Society founded by Franklin. With his father, William wandered into the back country around Philadelphia to collect seeds and plants. His careful observations might have made him a famous scientist, but this shy and humble man was content to share his knowledge with his friends. In 1773 he ventured into the unexplored wildernesses of the Southeastern states. *Travels Through North and South Carolina, Georgia, East and West Florida*, published in 1791, gives poetic descriptions of his travels and philosophical passages as well as notes on the plants, animals, and Indian inhabitants of these regions. (See "An Escape from Alligators" on pages 55-58.) This was the first American book to have a wide audience abroad, for within a few years translations appeared in German, Dutch, and French.

WILLIAM BYRD, 1674-1744

Virginia-born William Byrd was educated in England and on the Continent according to the custom of the colonial Southern aristocracy. When he returned to America, he not only managed his large plantation and served in the Virginia House of Burgesses, but also found time to practice lavish hospitality and devote himself to studying the classics from his own well-stocked library of 3500 volumes. A man of wide interests, Byrd furnished his mansion with the costliest objects of art, planned the city of Richmond on his own lands, and was a fellow of the Royal Society. Byrd's journals, not published until almost a century after his death, reveal the witty, sophisticated manner he admired in his British contemporaries, Swift and Pope. *The History of the Dividing Line* tells of a surveying trip to determine the Virginia-North Carolina boundary. *A Progress to the Mines* (see "Neighbors in Virginia" on pages 52-54) and *A Journey to the Land of Eden* are accounts of travels to his frontier properties.

ALEXANDER HAMILTON, 1757-1804

Alexander Hamilton, who was born in the West Indies, was sent to the mainland to finish his education. While a student at King's College (now Columbia University) he became interested in the patriot cause and wrote several pamphlets eloquently protesting England's treatment of her American colonies. During the Revolutionary War he served brilliantly on Washington's staff, but it was in the years after the war that he paid his greatest services to his adopted country. It was he who made the first proposal for a constitutional convention and by his pen excited interest in the project. And it was the series of newspaper articles written in the main by Hamilton and later gathered under the title *The Federalist* which more than any other factor won the acceptance of the Constitution.

THOMAS JEFFERSON, 1743-1826

Jefferson, like Byrd, was born into the Virginia planter aristocracy. Through his mother he claimed kinship with the famous Randolph family, which traced its descent back to Pocahontas. At fourteen young Tom inherited nearly three thousand acres of land. He attended William and Mary College, where he gained recognition not only as a student but also as a social leader and a friend of the colonial governor and other Virginia notables. His marriage to a wealthy young widow, his beloved Martha, soon brought him forty thousand acres of land. Such a background does not often breed revolutionists, yet Jefferson's entire adult life was a battle against the old order of things and a struggle for a better life for the average man. In 1774 he presented his arguments for self-government for the colonies in *Summary of the Rights of British America*. In 1776 he roused the spirit of freedom with the ringing words of the Declaration of Independence (see pages 216-219). In his public offices—as minister to France, as Washington's Secretary of State, as President—he fought with his powerful pen, his voice, and his actions for his ideal of American democracy.

THOMAS PAINE, 1737-1809

Thomas Paine had thirty-seven years of failure and disappointment behind him when Benjamin Franklin met him in England in 1774. But Franklin saw promise in this Englishman who was, like himself, a man of many ideas, and encouraged him to try America. Within a year he had justified Franklin's confidence. In *Common Sense* he tried to convince his adopted countrymen that "nothing can settle our affairs so expeditiously as an open and determined *Declaration for Independence*." In 1776 Paine joined the Revolutionary army. In the dark days of the retreat across New Jersey he wrote the first of the pamphlets now known as *The American Crisis,* a series of sixteen papers which helped greatly in upholding the courage and spurring on the efforts of the patriots during the critical days of war. The last years of Paine's life were full of controversy, but he holds a secure place in literary history because of his inspiring writings during the American Revolution.

UNIT VIII: WASHINGTON IRVING
(*representing* THE EARLY NATIONAL PERIOD)

WASHINGTON IRVING'S mother suggested his name. "George Washington's work is ended," she is reported to have said, "and the child shall be named for him."

Mrs. Irving's words underline the fact that her son's birth came at an important moment in our history. It occurred in New York, April 3, 1783, five months before peace was proclaimed between Great Britain and the colonies. Washington Irving was to live all but the first few months of his long life (he died in 1859) not as a British colonist but as a citizen of a young republic. His best writings appeared in what students call "the Early National Period" of our literary development.

❧ I IRVING CONTRASTED WITH FRANKLIN

Irving's career differed greatly from that of Benjamin Franklin. Much of Franklin's energy, as we have seen, was spent in the colonial fight for independence. Several of his most important works furthered the rift between Great Britain and America, setting off the New World from the Old. Irving, by contrast, was to win the name of "Ambassador of the New World to the Old." He was destined not only to help England and Europe understand the United States better but also to help this country understand England and Europe better.

Irving's career differed from Franklin's in a second important way. Colonist Franklin, even though he fought against the political ways of the Old World, did not rebel against the Old World literary fashions of an earlier period. To the day of his death, Franklin wrote pretty much in the manner of British authors who flourished before he was born or during his boyhood. Irving, to be sure, started as an imitator of some of Franklin's models, and to some extent his writings always echoed these early teachers. In time, however, he caught up with the contemporary parade, and indeed became a leader in a world-wide literary movement of the day.

A final contrast between Irving's career and Franklin's becomes clear when we compare their writing aims. Franklin's chief purpose, in almost everything he wrote, was to give information to his readers or to persuade them to act in certain ways. His writings, ordinarily, were factual. As a rule, Irving's chief aim, on the other hand, was to entertain his readers. His best writings were imaginative. Even when he wrote biography and history, he pictured scenes, characters, and events in the interesting fashion of a novelist.

These contrasts between Franklin and Irving typify those which may be drawn between other authors of the Colonial Period and the Early

National Period. Such contrasts represent changes in writing which naturally took place when a group of colonies became a nation. A friendlier feeling toward the Old World, up-to-dateness in writing methods, a shift from utilitarian writing to imaginative writing are evident not only in Irving's work but also in the work of William Cullen Bryant (1794-1878), James Fenimore Cooper (1789-1851), Edgar Allan Poe (1809-1849), and many of Irving's less famous contemporaries.

❧ II NEW YORK AMATEUR

As we study Irving, it is valuable to see him as representative of his age. It is also valuable to see him as an interesting personality whose distinctive qualities are reflected in his works.

Irving's life falls into three stages. Up to 1815, he was a playful amateur in letters who wrote chiefly of his native city, New York. Between 1815 and 1826, he became a professional writer who was internationally famous, and, since he spent these years in Europe, the Old World loomed large in his books. Between 1826 and 1859, his best work done, he turned to the composition of histories and biographies. Our first concern is with the young Irving, amateur in arts.

During Irving's lifetime, the general trend in our country was away from the stern religiousness of colonial days to less stern religious views. In New England, for instance, many turned from the grim beliefs brought to these shores by the Puritans to the more genial beliefs of the Unitarians. In their thinking and in their living, the people of New England and other sections as well were beginning to emphasize joy in the afterworld less, enjoyment in this world more.

Irving himself made the shift many others were making when he was still a youngster. His father was a zealous Scotch Presbyterian from the Orkney Islands,[1] and a deacon in his church. He held that everything enjoyable was wicked. For family reading Deacon Irving prescribed the Bible, the catechism, and that Puritan masterpiece by John Bunyan— *Pilgrim's Progress.* He made a great effort to pass along his harsh beliefs, his strict rules for living, to his son.

But Irving's mother, an Englishwoman, was tender and kind, and four brothers and three sisters—all older than Washington—already had rebelled against their father's dour faith. Moreover, the boy's environment seemed to encourage play rather than piety. The town of New York, so travelers said, was the gayest in all the country. There the fashionably dressed belles and beaux enjoyed the society of the drawing room and the ballroom and knew the excitement of the arts—music, literature, and the drama. And a New York boy in the upper-middle class was bound to feel the influence of his surroundings.

Young Washington, from the start, was spoiled by his mother, his brothers, and his sisters. One reason was that he tended to be sickly—a sister called him "a little rack of bones." A more important reason was that, from infanthood, he was a lovable little rascal—light-hearted and friendly, though with a sometimes troublesome talent for mischief. "Oh,

---

[1]*Orkney* (ôrk′ni) *Islands,* a group of islands northeast of, and belonging to, Scotland.

Washington!" his mother would often say, after some prank, "if you were only good!"

It did not take the boy long to decide that he did not care for his father's beliefs. "When I was a child," he wrote later, "religion was forced upon me...in its most ungracious forms. I was tasked with it; thwarted with it; wearied with it in a thousand harsh and disagreeable ways, until I was disgusted with...its forms and observances." So he decided that he would pay as little attention to religion as possible, and that he would have all the fun he could.

In the series of schools he attended before leaving classrooms, for good, at sixteen, he learned as little as his teachers allowed. He wandered around New York and its fringes, sailing boats in the straits of Hellgate,[2] standing by the harbor and watching ships move seaward, exploring nearby farms, or hunting squirrels in the woods along the Hudson. He took drawing lessons and learned to play the flute. In time, he discovered the fascination of the playhouse. Whenever he could afford it, he went in the evening to a nearby theater. There he watched the actors until nine, when he hurried home for family prayers. After prayers, he quickly climbed to his room, slipped through his window, clambered down the roof, and ran to the theater so that he might enjoy the last part of the show. And his favorite books were not religious tomes but accounts of travel to far countries and adventure stories such as *Robinson Crusoe* and *Sinbad the Sailor*.

When the time came for Washington to prepare to earn a living, naturally he had to disappoint his father's hopes that he would study for the ministry. He had no urge, then or later, to preach. After some family counsels, he followed the example of his brother John and entered a law office to study law. There, it was soon clear that his easy-going life had not prepared him for rigorous study. As he said, he found "the dull routine of a lawyer's office" unattractive. His legal training, interrupted by a trip to Europe for his health between 1804 and 1806, did not culminate until late in 1806, when he passed his bar examinations. And even after he became a lawyer, he never did much with his legal training.

Instead of buckling down to work while studying or practicing law, he drifted, and his indulgent family tried to satisfy his every whim. Fortunately, though neither he nor his family knew it, he was drifting toward a literary career. He embarked on a gay life which happened to furnish the first impetus toward literature.

Curly-haired, handsome, pleasant in manner and with a fine spontaneous smile, young Irving had a talent for good fellowship. He became a consistent theater-goer. He became a boon companion of the gallants of the town. Like them, he dressed in the height of style, and danced and flirted a great deal. A group of them which he joined had gay times when their informal club got together. It called itself "The Nine Worthies" or "The Lads of Kilkenny." It dined in the most fashionable or the most picturesque public houses, then chatted and sang for hours on end. Week-

---

[2]*straits of Hellgate,* a narrow passage in the East River between Manhattan and the western tip of Long Island.

ends, Irving and some of his friends drove by stagecoach to Cockloft Hall, in the highlands near Newark, where they were entertained by the Kembles.[3] During the day, they played leapfrog on the lawn; far into the night, they gossiped about New York society or talked of their chief diversions—the drama, art, and literature.

Irving's interests and those of his friends led him to try his hand at writing. His first published pieces, which he wrote when nineteen and twenty, were jocose newspaper essays about fashions, marriage customs, dueling, and the theater. In 1807 and 1808, Irving, his brother William, and his friend James K. Paulding wrote and published a series of papers in which the talk of the Worthies and gossip at the Kemble mansion figured largely. The periodical was called *Salmagundi,* after a spicy appetizer, and it was put out at intervals—whenever its easy-going editors managed to write out enough material to fill an issue. In these papers, the writers took the rôles of members of an eccentric club—Anthony Evergreen, Lancelot Langstaff, and William Wizard. "We intend," they said in their first number, "to present a striking picture of the town; and as everybody is anxious to see his own phiz on canvas, however stupid or ugly it may be, we have no doubt but the whole town will flock to our exhibition." They would moralize infrequently, they promised, and they were more eager to make their readers laugh than cry. "We are," they said, "laughing philosophers, and clearly of opinion that...true wisdom is a plump, jolly dame, who sits in her armchair, laughs right merrily at the farce of life, and takes the world as it goes."

In the *Salmagundi* papers which followed, the authors were impudent and amusing as they pictured the life and the personalities of New York. Comically, they described social and political activities. They offered satirical sketches of social climbers, politicians, military men, critics, and, of course, the belles whose company they so enjoyed. The society folk of New York read the magazine with delight and amusement.

Irving's next book pushed the satire of his native city into the past. He and his brother Peter started to write *A History of New York* as a parody of a pompous and dull book by S. L. Mitchell, *The Picture of New York,* published in 1807. When Irving's brother withdrew from the collaboration, Irving, as he put it, "altered the plan of the work." "Discarding all idea of a parody," he said, "I determined that what had been originally intended as an introductory sketch should comprise the whole work, and afford a comic history of the city." The result, published in 1809, was a playful account of New York (as the title page modestly proclaimed) "from the Beginning of the World to the End of the Dutch Dynasty... being the only Authentic History of the Times that has ever been, or ever will be Published." Supposedly written by an antiquarian named Diedrich Knickerbocker, it told hilarious stories about the old-time Dutch governors and playfully spoofed some of the leading Dutch families. Descendants of those families at first did not appreciate the humor very well. An old lady in Albany, for instance, misplaced her elegant manners long

---

[3]*Cockloft Hall...the Kembles.* Gouverneur (guv ər nir′) Kemble's large mansion stood on the Passaic River near Newark, New Jersey. It is famous in literature as Cockloft Hall, a name Irving gave it.

enough to say, with fervor, that she wished she could horsewhip the author. "It was a confounded impudent thing," Irving said years later, "in such a youngster as I was to be meddling in this way with old family names." But New Yorkers who were not so touchy and folk outside of New York, some of them in Great Britain, thought the book very funny. The great contemporary novelist Walter Scott said that he laughed at it until his sides ached, and, years later, Charles Dickens read and reread his copy until he wore it to pieces.

The following is a selection from *Knickerbocker's History of New York* from which "Early Life in Manhattan" (pages 47-51) is also taken.

Father Knickerbocker redrawn from an old print from The Bettmann Archive

The Golden Reign of Wouter Van Twiller

IN TREATING of the early governors of the province, I must caution my readers against confounding them, in point of dignity and power, with those worthy gentlemen who are whimsically denominated governors in this enlightened republic—a set of unhappy victims of popularity, who are, in fact, the most dependent, henpecked beings in the community; set up, like geese at Christmas holidays, to be pelted and shot at by every whipster[1] and vagabond in the land. On the contrary, the Dutch governors enjoyed that uncontrolled authority vested in all commanders of distant colonies or territories. They were, in a manner, absolute despots in

their little domains, lording it, if so disposed, over both law and gospel,[2] and accountable to none but the mother country. This hint will be of importance, to prevent my readers from being seized with doubt and incredulity, whenever, in the course of this authentic history, they encounter the uncommon circumstance of a governor acting with independence, and in opposition to the opinions of the multitude.

To assist the doubtful Wouter[3] in the arduous business of legislation, a board of magistrates was appointed. This potent body consisted of a *schout*,[4] or bailiff, with powers between those of the present mayor and sheriff; five *burgermeesters*,[5] who were equivalent to aldermen; and five *schepens*,[6] who officiated as scrubs, subdevils, or bottleholders to the *burgermeesters*, in the same manner as do assistant aldermen to their principals at the present day. It was their duty to fill the pipes of the lordly *burgermeesters*, hunt the markets for delicacies for corporation dinners, and to discharge such other little offices of kindness as were occasionally required. It was, moreover, tacitly understood that they should consider themselves as butts for the blunt wits of the *burgermeesters*, and should laugh most heartily at all their jokes. But this

---

[1]*whipster*, whippersnapper, an insignificant person who thinks he is smart or important.

[2]*lording it...over both law and gospel*, ruling, if so inclined, both civil affairs (law) and the church (gospel).

[3]*Wouter*, Wouter Van Twiller (vou′tər van twil′ər), governor, or director general, of New Amsterdam (later renamed New York) from 1633 to 1637.

[4]*schout* (skout).

[5]*burgermeesters* (bür′gər mās′tərz), burgomasters, or chief magistrates of Dutch towns.

[6]*schepens* (skā′pənz).

last was a duty as rarely called in action in those days as it is at present, and was shortly remitted, in consequence of the tragical death of a fat little *schepen,* who actually died of suffocation in an unsuccessful effort to force a laugh at one of *Burgermeester* Van Zandt's best jokes.

In return for these humble services, they were permitted to say *yes* and *no* at the councilboard, and to have that enviable privilege, the run of the public kitchen—being graciously permitted to eat, and drink, and smoke at all those public gormandizings for which the ancient magistrates were equally famous with their modern successors. The post of *schepen,* therefore, like that of assistant alderman, was eagerly coveted by all your burghers of a certain description, who have a huge relish for good feeding and an humble ambition to be great men in a small way—who thirst after a little brief authority, that shall render them the terror of the almshouse and the bridewell, that shall enable them to lord it over obsequious poverty, vagrant vice, and hunger-driven dishonesty.

The ancient magistrates of this city correspond with those of the present time no less in form, magnitude, and intellect than in prerogative and privilege. The burgomasters, like our aldermen, were generally chosen by weight—and not only the weight of the body, but likewise the weight of the head. It is a maxim practically observed in all honest, plain-thinking, regular cities that an alderman should be fat—and the wisdom of this can be proved to a certainty. That the body is in some measure an image of the mind, or rather that the mind is molded to the body, has been insisted on by many philosophers who have made human nature their peculiar study. Thus we see that a lean, spare, diminutive body is generally accompanied by a petulant, restless, meddling mind: either the mind wears down the body, by its continual motion, or else the body, not affording the mind sufficient houseroom, keeps it continually in a state of fretfulness, tossing and worrying about from the uneasiness of its situation. Whereas your round, sleek, fat, unwieldy periphery is ever attended by a mind like itself, tranquil, torpid, and at ease; and we may always observe that your well-fed, robustious burghers are in general very tenacious of their ease and comfort, being great enemies to noise, discord, and disturbance—and surely none are more likely to study the public tranquillity than those who are so careful of their own. Who ever hears of fat men heading a riot, or herding together in turbulent mobs? No—no. It is your lean, hungry men who are continually worrying society, and setting the whole community by the ears.

As a board of magistrates, formed on this principle, think but very little, they are the less likely to differ and wrangle about favorite opinions; and as they generally transact business upon a hearty dinner, they are naturally disposed to be lenient and indulgent in the administration of their duties. Charlemagne[7] was conscious of this, and therefore ordered that no judge should hold a court of justice except in the morning, on an empty stomach—a pitiful rule, which I can never forgive, and which I warrant bore hard upon all the poor culprits in the kingdom. The more enlightened and humane generation of the present day have taken an opposite course, and have so managed that the aldermen are the best-fed men in the community; feasting lustily on the fat things of the land, and gorging so heartily on oysters and turtles that in process of time they acquire the activity of the one, and the form, the waddle, and the green fat of the other. The consequence is, as I have just said, these luxurious feastings do produce such a dulcet equanimity and repose of the soul that their transactions are proverbial for unvarying monotony; and the profound laws which they enact in their dozing moments are quietly suffered to remain as dead letters, and never enforced, when awake.

Nothing could equal the profound deliberations that took place between the renowned Wouter and these his worthy compeers, unless it be the sage divans of some of our modern corporations.[8] They would sit for hours, smoking and dozing over public affairs, without

---

[7]*Charlemagne* (shär′lə mān), Charles the Great, king of the Franks. Crowned head of the Holy Roman Empire in 800 A.D., he ruled most of Christian Europe and reformed government and education in France.

[8]*divans* (di vanz′)...*corporations,* rulers of present-day city governments.

speaking a word to interrupt that perfect stillness so necessary to deep reflection. Under the sober sway of Wouter Van Twiller and these his worthy coadjutors, the infant settlement waxed vigorous apace, gradually emerging from the swamps and forests, and exhibiting that mingled appearance of town and country customary in new cities.

It was a pleasing sight, in those times, to behold the honest burgher, like a patriarch of yore, seated on the bench at the door of his whitewashed house, under the shade of some gigantic sycamore or overhanging willow. Here would he smoke his pipe of a sultry afternoon, enjoying the soft southern breeze, and listening with silent gratulation to the clucking of his hens, the cackling of his geese, and the sonorous grunting of his swine.

The modern spectator who wanders through the streets of this populous city can scarcely form an idea of the different appearance they presented in the primitive days of the Doubter.[9] The busy hum of multitudes, the shouts of revelry, the rumbling equipages of fashion, the rattling of accursed carts, and all the spirit-grieving sounds of brawling commerce were unknown in the settlement of New Amsterdam. The grass grew quietly in the highways; the bleating sheep and frolicsome calves sported about the verdant ridge where now the Broadway loungers take their morning stroll[10]; the cunning fox or ravenous wolf skulked in the woods where now are to be seen the dens of money brokers[11]; and flocks of vociferous geese cackled about the fields where now the great Tammany wigwam and the patriotic tavern of Martling[12] echo with the wranglings of the mob.

Thrice happy and ever to be envied little burgh, existing in all the security of harmless insignificance—unnoticed and unenvied by the world, without ambition, without vainglory, without riches, without learning, and all their train of carking cares! Such are the comfortable and thriving effects of a fat government. The province of the New Netherlands,[13] destitute of wealth, possessed a sweet tranquillity that wealth could never purchase. There were neither public commotions nor private quarrels; neither parties nor sects nor schisms; neither persecutions nor trials nor punishments; nor were there counselors, attorneys, catchpoles,[14] nor hangmen. Every man attended to what little business he was lucky enough to have, or neglected it if he pleased, without asking the opinion of his neighbor. In those days nobody meddled with concerns above his comprehension; nor thrust his nose into other people's affairs; nor neglected to correct his own conduct, and reform his own character, in his zeal to pull to pieces the characters of others; but, in a word, every respectable citizen ate when he was not hungry, drank when he was not thirsty, and went regularly to bed when the sun set and the fowls went to roost, whether he was sleepy or not. Everything, therefore, went on exactly as it should do, and in the usual words employed by historians to express the welfare of a country, "the profoundest *tranquillity* and *repose* reigned throughout the province."

---

[13]*the province of the New Netherlands,* the Dutch colony which included the land that became New York and New Jersey.

[14]*catchpoles,* tax collectors.

---

[9]*the Doubter,* Van Twiller, so called because, according to Irving, "he had his doubts about the matter" and could never make up his mind on any subject.

[10]*the verdant ridge...morning stroll.* Broadway, a busy street running the length of Manhattan Island, was at the time Irving wrote a short avenue lined with poplars.

[11]*where now...dens of money brokers,* Wall Street, which, in Irving's day, was already becoming the financial center of the United States.

[12]*the great Tammany wigwam...tavern of Martling.* Tammany, now the New York City Democratic organization, was originally a social club whose officers were given Indian titles. For a period beginning in 1805, Tammany met in the long room of Martling's Tavern near the tip of Manhattan.

CONCERNING WASHINGTON IRVING

1. How were Irving's attitudes influenced by (*a*) his family and (*b*) his environment?

2. Contrast Irving's purposes in his writings with Franklin's. How do these purposes reflect the differences in the times of the two men?

3. Name some of Irving's famous literary contemporaries. What selections by these men have you read? How are these men related to Irving in the purpose for which they wrote?

4. Illustrate the statement that Irving was "a playful amateur" in his first period as a writer.

CONCERNING "THE GOLDEN REIGN
OF WOUTER VAN TWILLER"

1. What contrast does Irving draw in the first paragraph of the selection? What does he satirize by means of the contrast?

2. Explain the organization of the board of magistrates in Wouter's time, as outlined in the second paragraph of the selection. What human foibles does Irving joke about in his account of the *schepens* in this and the following paragraph? Where may such foibles best be observed today?

3. Trace the development in the fourth and fifth paragraphs of the selection of the ideas summarized in the first sentence of the fourth paragraph. How do these paragraphs prepare for the picture of the "deliberations" given in the sixth paragraph?

4. What contrasts are drawn in the last two paragraphs of the selection? Are the contrasts to the discredit of old New York, Irving's New York, or both? Explain.

5. In what ways are "The Golden Reign of Wouter Van Twiller" and "Early Life in Manhattan" (pages 47-51) representative of the sort of person Irving was when he wrote *Knickerbocker's History?*

Understanding Washington Irving's
type of humor

The distinctive quality of Washington Irving's humor lies not so much in what he says as in his manner of saying it. He takes the eighteenth-century habit of using long sentences and many words of Latin derivation, exaggerates it grandly, and produces a species of humor which holds its charm even for the present-day reader. For example, there is nothing amusing in the statement, "Under the rule of Wouter Van Twiller and his council the settlement grew rapidly." But when Irving rolls out, "Under the sober sway of Wouter Van Twiller and these his worthy coadjutors, the infant settlement waxed vigorous apace," the abundance of dignified words produces a half-mocking, tongue-in-cheek effect.

Select four or five sentences from either "The Golden Reign of Wouter Van Twiller" or "Early Life in Manhattan" (pages 47-51) which are representative of this type of humor. In each case pick out words and phrases which help create the effect. Then consider what additional ideas about Irving as a person you have gained from studying this aspect of his style of writing.

❧ III IRVING AND EUROPE

A History of New York won wide recognition for its author. It succeeded financially, too, earning Irving about three thousand dollars. It hardly would have been surprising if its reception had caused its author to decide, once and for all, to earn his living by writing. But nothing of the sort happened. For one thing, the family was enjoying good times financially, and Irving's brothers were happy to share the large returns from their importing business with their favorite. There was no financial need to drive him on. For another thing, Irving was still lamenting—as indeed he had been while writing his history—the recent death of a young woman, Matilda Hoffman, to whom he had been engaged. The tragic end of a romance which he was to remember to his dying day (he was never to marry) had weakened his initiative.

So there were still more years of indecision and inaction. Then the beginning of a new stage in his career was marked by his going to Europe for a stay which, unexpectedly, lasted for seventeen years.

When Irving had gone to Europe before, between 1804 and 1806, for his health, the journey had been a tonic. At the time he had been helped aboard ship, the captain had glumly remarked, "There's a chap who will go overboard before we get across." But Irving had completed the ocean journey and then had spent twenty-three months traveling through southern Europe, to Paris, and to London. He had taken difficulties—many great difficulties—in his stride, and had made a miraculous recovery.

As he had undergone trips through mountains swarming with bandits, capture by Mediterranean pirates, uncomfortable journeys, and stopovers in dirty and disagreeable inns, his health had thrived. "When I cannot get a dinner to suit my taste," he had written, "I endeavor to get a taste to suit my dinner."

Irving's pleasant memories of this tour abroad naturally made him think, in time, of another such trip. And in 1815, as he was making plans, it happened that a real need arose for him to go to England. The War of 1812 had been followed by many financial upsets, and the Irving family's importing business was in a bad tangle. Although Irving had been a rather inactive partner, there seemed to be a chance that he might be of assistance in straightening out the firm's affairs.

So he went to Liverpool immediately—fortunately, it developed, since soon after his arrival, his brother Peter, Liverpool agent for the firm, became too ill to do any work. Irving had to learn what he could of the business and to take charge at once. Even such a greenhorn as Irving could soon see that the firm was headed for disaster; but he did everything in his power to postpone the crash. He wrote:

The struggle was certainly vain, yet the disgrace must be kept off as long as possible. There it was, day after day; work hard all day and then to bed late, a troubled sleep, for three hours perhaps, and then wake up; thump, thump, thump, at the heart comes the care. No more sleep for that night; then up and off....Payments must be made, and nowhere for remittances to come from....And the same thing over, day after day, week after week.

The task was hopeless as well as harrowing. In 1818, the Irving firm was forced into bankruptcy.

It was only at this time that Irving made up his mind that, if possible, he would use his pen to earn a living. Offers of a magazine editorship and a political appointment came along, but he rejected them. He intended to see, once and for all, whether he could support himself and help his family by writing. He wrote a brother at home:

I consider myself...as making a literary experiment in the course of which I only care to be kept in bread and cheese. Should it not succeed—should my writings not acquire critical applause, I am content to throw up my pen and take to any commonplace employment.

The die was cast. Either his writings succeeded or he would go into magazine editing, politics, business, or something equally horrible to him.

This was the background of the publication of *The Sketch Book,* issued in installments in 1819 and 1820. Most of this series of papers consisted of charming essays on English life and manners, but it is chiefly remembered today for two short stories, "Rip Van Winkle" and "The Legend of Sleepy Hollow."

The Sketch Book appeared in America first, and Irving waited impatiently in England for news of its reception to make its slow way across the ocean. He had sent off the first number in March, 1819. At the end of July he was still waiting—"a little nervous," he said. He received no word until September 9, a few days before the third number appeared in the United States.

The news, when it finally came, was wonderful. Irving said that he was so "overwhelmed" by the praise that he feared "it could not be real." The later numbers as well as the first were hailed by American critics and readers alike as masterpieces. English publishers, who had been cool when Irving first offered them the pieces in the collection, now were willing to print the entire volume. The English public joined the American public in making it a success.

This was the turning point in Irving's career. Other books written during this period—*Bracebridge Hall* (1822) and *Tales of a Traveller* (1824)—were also successful. Irving had established himself as an author. He had, moreover, improved relationships between England and the United States, and he had made important contributions to literature.

❧ IV EUROPE AND AMERICA

Surprising as it may seem to us in these days when Great Britain and the United States are great friends and allies, the two countries were not on very good terms between 1783, when Irving was born, and 1819, when he began to publish *The Sketch Book*. The reasons, if we think about them, are not hard to find: The people of America had rebelled against British rule and had set up a new nation. They had fought against Great Britain again in the War of 1812. Furthermore, the cocky young nation was constantly showing its youth by boasting that it was the greatest country in the world. No wonder old England was somewhat resentful. And no wonder the writers of old England tended to look for faults in the United States, and tended to overemphasize the flaws when they found them.

Travelers who visited America and who published accounts of what they saw devoted many pages to the bad manners of the crude Americans. They told of the disgusting habit Americans had of chewing tobacco; they claimed that Americans drank too much. They held that neither men nor women knew how to behave in society. They admitted that the United States was doing what it could to promote education, but they were sure that it had, as yet, made little progress.

Not only travelers but also critics agreed that the United States lagged woefully behind the world in art and literature. In February, 1819, the *British Critic* said:

The Americans have no national literature, and no learned men....The talents of our transatlantic brethren show themselves chiefly in political pamphlets. The Americans are too young to rival in literature the old nations of Europe. They have neither history, nor romance, nor poetry, nor legends on which to exercise their genius and kindle their imagination. The inhabitants of the United States will never have to boast of a native poetry, or a native music....

Shortly after this, Sydney Smith, English wit and critic, was asking in *The Edinburgh Review:* "In the four quarters of the globe, who reads an American book? or goes to an American play? or looks at an American picture?" Some writers went so far as to suggest that life in the wilds of the North American continent had brutalized the inhabitants and had finally produced a degenerate race of men.

Irving met such criticisms in two ways—by making fun of them and by

proving that, so far as his achievement as a writer was concerned, they were unjustified. Several times in *The Sketch Book,* he humorously referred to the European belief in our inferiority. In "The Author's Account of Himself" at the start of the book, for instance, he wrote:

I was anxious to see the great men of Europe; for I had read in the works of various philosophers that all animals had degenerated in America, and man among the number. A great man of Europe, thought I, must therefore be as superior to a great man of America as a peak of the Alps is to a highland of the Hudson; and in this I was confirmed by observing the comparative importance and swelling magnitude of many English travelers among us, who, I was assured, were very little people in their own country. I will visit this land of wonders, thought I, and see the gigantic race from which I am degenerated.

In addition, he included one paper in *The Sketch Book,* "English Writers on America," which offered temperate and sensible arguments against the ill nature and the harsh criticism of America by the British writers, and against the hot-headed answers which Americans were likely to make. Both countries, he pointed out, had too little to gain and too much to lose to risk such bickering.

Perhaps even more important, in papers such as "John Bull," a sketch of British character, and such as "Rural Life in England," "The Christmas Dinner," and "The Boar's Head Tavern," which sketched British life, he showed a sympathetic understanding of the folk of Great Britain. *Bracebridge Hall* continued to picture England in a way which showed that Irving, despite his japes, loved her history and her people.

British readers were very pleased with the pictures. Here, they said, was an American who appreciated them—one who at times portrayed English life as well as their own best authors had. The *British Critic,* which had been so harsh in February, 1819, said in November, 1820:

We would gladly believe, and will take our author's word for the fact, that a country in which the author of these Sketches received his education and formed his opinions, cannot be deserving of all the bitter sarcasm and reproach which writers in this island have heaped upon it. For our own parts, we hope to see the day when all animosities and mean jealousies between this country and that of our author will be sunk in oblivion. A few such writers as this before us, on both sides of the Atlantic, would do more to promote this happy consummation than could be effected, possibly, by events of apparently much greater moment.

Irving's genial writing also improved the feelings of Americans toward the British. He showed his countrymen the charm of British life, and he helped them appreciate the real virtues of the English. Professor Henry Seidel Canby, a twentieth-century American critic, pictures Irving as "an American Marco Polo, bringing home the romance of other countries, bearing their gifts of suavity, detachment, ease, and beauty to a raw country dependent upon its vulgar strength, stronger in brains than in manners, yet not devoid in a craving for civility." Such a service was an important achievement of other authors as well as Irving in the first half of the nineteenth century. Ralph Waldo Emerson, Oliver Wendell Holmes, James Russell Lowell, Henry Wadsworth Longfellow, and others brought Europe to America by portraying distant lands or by introducing their countrymen to foreign literary masterpieces.

Irving acquainted his countrymen not only with England but also with other lands. In *Tales of a Traveller,* for instance, German and Italian, as well as British, scenes and stories were presented. And in the historical works of his final period, as we shall see, he transported his readers to still other scenes.

The selection which follows is composed of excerpts from five of the essays Irving included in *The Sketch Book.* All of them treat of various aspects of Christmas time and show Irving as a sympathetic interpreter of English life.

Christmas

1

NOTHING IN ENGLAND exercises a more delightful spell over my imagination than the lingerings of the holiday customs and rural games of former times. Of all the old festivals, that of Christmas awakens the strongest and most heartfelt associations. There is a tone of solemn and sacred feeling that blends with our conviviality, and lifts the spirit to a state of hallowed and elevated enjoyment.

In the course of a December tour in Yorkshire,[1] I rode for a long distance in one of the public coaches, on the day preceding Christmas. The coach was crowded, both inside and out, with passengers, who, by their talk, seemed principally bound to the mansions of relations or friends, to eat the Christmas dinner. It was loaded also with hampers of game and baskets and boxes of delicacies; and hares hung dangling their long ears about the coachman's box, presents from distant friends for the impending feast. I had three fine rosy-cheeked schoolboys for my fellow passengers inside, full of the buxom health and manly spirit which I have observed in the children of this country. They were returning home for the holidays in high glee, and promising themselves a world of enjoyment. It was delightful to hear the gigantic plans of the little rogues, and the impracticable feats they were to perform during their six weeks' emancipation from the abhorred thralldom of book, birch, and pedagogue.

They were under the particular guardianship of the coachman, to whom, whenever an opportunity presented, they addressed a host of questions, and pronounced him one of the best fellows in the world. Indeed, I could not but notice the more than ordinary air of bustle and importance of the coachman, who wore his hat a little on one side, and had a large bunch of Christmas greens stuck in the buttonhole of his coat.

In the evening we reached a village where I had determined to pass the night. I had not been long at the inn when a post chaise drove up to the door. A young gentleman stepped out, and by the light of the lamps, I caught a glimpse of a countenance which I thought I knew. I moved forward to get a nearer view, when his eye caught mine. I was not mistaken; it was Frank Bracebridge, a sprightly good-humored young fellow, with whom I had once traveled on the continent.[2] Our meeting was extremely cordial, for the countenance of an old fellow traveler always brings up the recollection of a thousand pleasant scenes, odd adventures, and excellent jokes. To discuss all these in a transient interview at an inn was impossible; and finding that I was not pressed for time, and was merely making a tour of observation, he insisted that I should give him a day or two at his father's countryseat, to which he was going to pass the holidays, and which lay at a few miles' distance. "It is better than eating a solitary Christmas dinner at an inn," said he, "and I can assure you of a hearty welcome in something of the old-fashioned style." His reasoning was cogent, and I must confess the preparation I had

---

[1] *Yorkshire* (yôrk′shir), a shire, or county, in northern England.

[2] *the continent,* Europe.

seen for universal festivity and social enjoyment had made me feel a little impatient of my loneliness. I closed, therefore, at once, with his invitation; the chaise drove up to the door, and in a few moments I was on my way to the family mansion of the Bracebridges.

It was a brilliant moonlight night, but extremely cold; our chaise whirled rapidly over the frozen ground; the postboy smacked his whip incessantly, and a part of the time his horses were on a gallop. "He knows where he is going," said my companion, laughing, "and is eager to arrive in time for some of the merriment and good cheer of the servants' hall. My father, you must know, is a bigoted devotee of the old school, and prides himself upon keeping up something of old English hospitality. From early years, he determined, in his own mind, that there was no condition more truly honorable and enviable than that of a country gentleman on his paternal lands, and therefore passes the whole of his time on his estate. He is a strenuous advocate for the revival of the old rural games and holiday observances, and is deeply read in the writers, ancient and modern, who have treated on the subject. Being representative of the oldest family in the neighborhood, and a great part of the peasantry being his tenants, he is much looked up to, and, in general, is known simply by the appellation of 'The Squire,' a title which has been accorded to the head of the family since time immemorial."

We had passed for some time along the wall of a park, and at length the chaise stopped at the gate. It was in a heavy magnificent old style, of iron bars, fancifully wrought at top into flourishes and flowers.

The postboy rang a large porter's bell,[3] which resounded through the still frosty air, and was answered by the distant barking of dogs, with which the mansion house seemed garrisoned. An old woman immediately appeared at the gate. As the moonlight fell strongly upon her, I had a full view of a little primitive dame, dressed very much in the antique taste, with a neat kerchief and stomacher, and her silver hair peeping from under a cap of snowy whiteness. She came curtsying forth, with many expressions of simple joy at seeing her young master. Her husband, it seemed, was up at the house keeping Christmas Eve in the servants' hall; they could not do without him, as he was the best hand at a song and story in the household.

My friend proposed that we should alight and walk through the park to the hall,[4] which was at no great distance, while the chaise should follow on. Our road wound through a noble avenue of trees, among the naked branches of which the moon glittered as she rolled through the deep vault of a cloudless sky. The lawn beyond was sheeted with a slight cover of snow.

My companion looked around him with transport. "How often," said he, "have I scampered up this avenue, on returning home on school vacations! My father was always scrupulous in exacting our holidays, and having us around him on family festivals. He was very particular that we should play the old English games according to their original form; and consulted old books for precedent and authority for every 'merrie disport.' It was the policy of the good old gentleman to make his children feel that home was the happiest place in the world; and I value this delicious home feeling as one of the choicest gifts a parent could bestow."

We were interrupted by the clamor of a troop of dogs of all sorts and sizes, "mongrel, puppy, whelp and hound, and curs of low degree,"[5] that, disturbed by the ring of the porter's bell, and the rattling of the chaise, came bounding, open-mouthed, across the lawn.

"—The little dogs and all,
Tray, Blanch, and Sweetheart—see, they bark at me!"[6]

cried Bracebridge, laughing. At the sound of his voice, the bark was changed into a yelp of delight, and in a moment he was surrounded and almost overpowered by the caresses of the faithful animals.

---

[3]*porter's bell*, bell which signals a gatekeeper to open the gate giving entrance to the mansion grounds.

[4]*the hall*, the mansion house.
[5]*"mongrel...curs of low degree."* Irving is quoting from "Elegy on the Death of a Mad Dog," by Oliver Goldsmith, one of his favorite British authors.
[6]*"The little dogs...bark at me,"* lines from **Shakespeare's** play *King Lear*.

2

We had now come in full view of the old family mansion. It was an irregular building, of some magnitude, and seemed to be of the architecture of different periods.

As we approached the house, we heard the sound of music, and now and then a burst of laughter. This, Bracebridge said, must proceed from the servants' hall, where a great deal of revelry was permitted, and even encouraged, by the squire, throughout the twelve days of Christmas,[7] provided everything was done conformably to ancient usage.

So intent were the servants upon their sports that we had to ring repeatedly before we could make ourselves heard. On our arrival being announced, the squire came out to receive us, accompanied by his two other sons; one a young officer in the army, home on leave of absence; the other an Oxonian,[8] just from the university. The squire was a fine healthy-looking old gentleman, with silver hair curling lightly round an open florid countenance.

The family meeting was warm and affectionate. As the evening was far advanced, the squire would not permit us to change our traveling dresses, but ushered us at once to the company, which was assembled in a large old-fashioned hall. It was composed of different branches of a numerous family connection, where there were the usual proportion of old uncles and aunts, comfortable married dames, superannuated spinsters, blooming country cousins, half-fledged striplings, and bright-eyed boarding-school hoydens. They were variously occupied; some at a round game of cards[9]; others conversing around the fireplace; at one end of the hall was a group of the young folks, some nearly grown up, others of a more tender and budding age, fully engrossed by a merry game.

---

[9] *a round game of cards*, a card game in which the players have no partners.

The Bettmann Archive

---

[7] *twelve days of Christmas.* Traditionally in England the Christmas celebrations lasted until Twelfth Night, or the Feast of the Epiphany (i pif′ə ni). This feast, which is observed on January 6, commemorates the visit of the Wise Men.

[8] *an Oxonian* (oks ō′ni ən), a student at Oxford University.

While the mutual greetings were going on between young Bracebridge and his relatives, I had time to scan the apartment. I have called it a hall, for so it had certainly been in old times, and the squire had evidently endeavored to restore it to something of its primitive state. Over the heavy projecting fireplace was suspended a picture of a warrior in armor, standing by a white horse, and on the opposite wall hung a helmet, buckler and lance. At one end an enormous pair of antlers were inserted in the wall, the branches serving as hooks on which to suspend hats, whips, and spurs; and in the corners of the apartment were fowling pieces, fishing rods, and other sporting implements. The furniture was of the cumbrous workmanship of former days.

The grate had been removed from the wide, overwhelming fireplace to make way for a fire of wood, in the midst of which was an enormous log glowing and blazing, and sending forth a vast volume of light and heat; this I understood was the Yule log, which the squire was particular in having brought in and illumined on a Christmas Eve, according to ancient custom.

It was really delightful to see the old squire seated in his hereditary elbowchair, by the hospitable fireplace of his ancestors, and looking around him like the sun of a system, beaming warmth and gladness to every heart. I had not been seated many minutes by the comfortable hearth of the worthy old cavalier before I found myself as much at home as if I had been one of the family.

Supper was announced shortly after our arrival. It was served up in a spacious oaken chamber, the panels of which shone with wax, and around which were several family portraits decorated with holly and ivy. Besides the accustomed lights, two great wax tapers, called Christmas candles, wreathed with greens, were placed on a highly polished buffet among the family plate. The table was abundantly spread with substantial fare; but the squire made his supper of frumenty, a dish made of wheat cakes boiled in milk, with rich spices, being a standing dish in old times for Christmas Eve.

The mirth of the company was greatly promoted by the humors of an eccentric personage whom Mr. Bracebridge always addressed with the quaint appellation of Master Simon. He was a tight brisk little man, with the air of an arrant old bachelor. His nose was shaped like the bill of a parrot; his face slightly pitted with the smallpox, with a dry perpetual bloom on it like a frostbitten leaf in autumn. He had an eye of great quickness and vivacity, with a drollery and lurking waggery of expression that was irresistible.

He was evidently the wit of the family, dealing very much in sly jokes and innuendoes with the ladies, and making infinite merriment by harpings upon old themes; which, unfortunately, my ignorance of the family chronicles did not permit me to enjoy. Indeed, he was the idol of the younger part of the company, who laughed at everything he said or did, and at every turn of his countenance. I could not wonder at it; for he must have been a miracle of accomplishments in their eyes. He could imitate Punch and Judy[10]; make an old woman of his hand with the assistance of a burnt cork and pocket handkerchief; and cut an orange into such a ludicrous caricature that the young folks were ready to die with laughing.

No sooner was supper removed, and spiced wines and other beverages peculiar to the season introduced, than Master Simon was called on for a good old Christmas song. He bethought himself for a moment, and then, with a sparkle of the eye and a voice that was by no means bad, excepting that it ran occasionally into a falsetto, like the notes of a split reed, he quavered forth a quaint old ditty.

> Now Christmas is come,
> Let us beat up the drum,
> And call all our neighbors together,
> And when they appear,
> Let us make them such cheer,
> As will keep out the wind and the
> weather, etc.

The supper had disposed everyone to gaiety, and an old harper was summoned from the servants' hall, where he had been strumming all

[10]*Punch and Judy,* characters in a puppet show. Punch, the humpbacked, hook-nosed husband, quarrels ludicrously with his wife Judy.

the evening, and to all appearance comforting himself with some of the squire's home-brewed.

The dance, like most dances after supper, was a merry one; some of the older folks joined in it, and the squire himself figured down several couple with a partner with whom he affirmed he had danced at every Christmas for nearly half a century. Master Simon, who seemed to be a kind of connecting link between the old times and the new, and to be withal a little antiquated in the taste of his accomplishments, evidently piqued himself on his dancing, and was endeavoring to gain credit by the heel and toe, riga-doon,[11] and other graces of the ancient school; but he had unluckily assorted himself with a little romping girl from boarding school, who, by her wild vivacity, kept him continually on the stretch and defeated all his sober attempts at elegance.

The party now broke up for the night with the kind-hearted old custom of shaking hands. As I passed through the hall, on my way to my chamber, the dying embers of the Yule log still sent forth a dusky glow, and had it not been the season when "no spirit dares stir abroad,"[12] I should have been half tempted to steal from my room at midnight and peep whether the fairies might not be at their revels about the hearth.

3

When I woke the next morning, I heard the sound of little feet pattering outside of the door, and a whispering consultation. Presently a choir of small voices chanted forth an old Christmas carol, the burden of which was

> Rejoice, our Savior He was born
> On Christmas day in the morning.

I rose softly, slipped on my clothes, opened the door suddenly, and beheld one of the most beautiful little fairy groups that a painter could imagine. It consisted of a boy and two girls, the eldest not more than six, and lovely as seraphs. They were going the rounds of the house, and singing at every chamber door; but my sudden appearance frightened them into mute bashful-ness. They remained for a moment playing on their lips with their fingers, and now and then stealing a shy glance from under their eyebrows, until, as if by one impulse, they scampered away, and as they turned an angle of the gallery, I heard them laughing in triumph at their escape.

Everything conspired to produce kind and happy feelings in this stronghold of old-fashioned hospitality. I had scarcely dressed myself, when a servant appeared to invite me to family prayers. He showed me the way to a small chapel in the old wing of the house, where I found the principal part of the family already assembled in a kind of gallery, furnished with cushions, hassocks, and large prayer books; the servants were seated on benches below. The old gentleman read prayers from a desk in front of the gallery, and Master Simon acted as clerk, and made the responses; and I must do him the justice to say that he acquitted himself with great gravity and decorum.

Our breakfast consisted of what the squire denominated true old English fare—a brave display of cold meats, wine, and ale on the sideboard.

After breakfast, I walked about the grounds with Frank Bracebridge and Master Simon, or Mr. Simon, as he was called by everybody but the squire. We were escorted by a number of gentlemanlike dogs, that seemed loungers about the establishment, from the frisking spaniel to the steady old staghound, the last of which was of a race that had been in the family time out of mind.

While we were talking, we heard the distant toll of the village bell, and I was told that the squire was a little particular in having his household at church on a Christmas morning, considering it a day of pouring out of thanks and rejoicing. As the morning, though frosty, was remarkably fine and clear, the most of the family walked to the church, which was a very old building of gray stone, and stood near a village, about half a mile from the park gate. Adjoining it was a snug parsonage, which seemed coeval with the church. As we passed this sheltered nest, the parson issued forth and preceded us.

---

[11]*heel and toe, rigadoon* (rig′ə dün′), old-fashioned dances.

[12]*"no spirit dares stir abroad."* Irving is quoting from *Hamlet,* by Shakespeare.

The interior of the church was venerable but simple; on the walls were several mural monuments of the Bracebridges, and just beside the altar was a tomb of ancient workmanship, on which lay the effigy of a warrior in armor, with his legs crossed, a sign of his having been a crusader.

During service, Master Simon stood up in the pew and repeated the responses very audibly, evincing that kind of ceremonious devotion punctually observed by a gentleman of the old school and a man of old family connections. But he was evidently most solicitous about the musical part of the service, keeping his eye fixed intently on the choir and beating time with much gesticulation and emphasis.

The orchestra was in a small gallery, and presented a most whimsical grouping of heads, piled one above the other, among which I particularly noticed that of the village tailor, a pale fellow with a retreating forehead and chin, who played on the clarinet, and seemed to have blown his face to a point; and there was another, a short pursy man, stooping and laboring at a bass viol, so as to show nothing but the top of a round bald head, like the egg of an ostrich. There were two or three pretty faces among the female singers, to which the keen air of a frosty morning had given a bright rosy tint; but the gentlemen choristers had evidently been chosen, like old Cremona fiddles,[13] more for tone than looks; and as several had to sing from the same book, there were clusterings of

I had expected to see a sleek well-conditioned pastor, such as is often found in a snug living in the vicinity of a rich patron's table, but I was disappointed. The parson was a little, meager, black-looking man, with a grizzled wig that was too wide, and stood off from each ear, so that his head seemed to have shrunk away within it, like a dried filbert in its shell. He wore a rusty coat, with great skirts, and pockets that would have held the church Bible and prayer book; and his small legs seemed still smaller, from being planted in large shoes, decorated with enormous buckles.

[13]*old Cremona* (kri mō′nə) *fiddles,* the world's finest violins, which were made in Cremona in northern Italy by Stradivarius (strad′i vär′i əs) and Amati (ä mä′ti) in the seventeenth and eighteenth centuries.

odd physiognomies, not unlike those groups of cherubs we see on country tombstones.

The usual services of the choir were managed tolerably well, the vocal parts generally lagging a little behind the instrumental, and some loitering fiddler now and then making up for lost time by traveling over a passage with prodigious celerity, and clearing more bars than the keenest fox hunter to be in at the death.[14] But the great trial was an anthem that had been prepared and arranged by Master Simon, and on which he had founded great expectation. Unluckily there was a blunder at the very onset; the musicians became flurried; Master Simon was in a fever, everything went on lamely and irregularly until they came to a chorus beginning "Now let us sing with one accord," which seemed to be a signal for parting company: all became discord and confusion; each shifted for himself, and got to the end as well, or rather, as soon as he could, excepting one old chorister in a pair of horn spectacles bestriding and pinching a long sonorous nose, who happened to stand a little apart, and, being wrapped up in his own melody, kept on a quavering course, wriggling his head, ogling his book, and winding all up by a nasal solo of at least three bars' duration.

The parson gave us a most erudite sermon on the rites and ceremonies of Christmas, and the propriety of observing it not merely as a day of thanksgiving, but of rejoicing; and concluded by urging his hearers, in the most solemn and affecting manner, to stand to the traditional customs of their fathers, and feast and make merry on this joyful anniversary of the church.

I have seldom known a sermon attended apparently with more immediate effects; for on leaving the church the congregation seemed one and all possessed with the gaiety of spirit so earnestly enjoined by their pastor. The elder folks gathered in knots in the churchyard, greeting and shaking hands; and the children ran about crying "Ule! Ule!" and repeating some uncouth rhymes which the parson, who had joined us, informed me had been handed down from days of yore. The villagers doffed their hats to the squire as he passed, giving him the good wishes of the season with every appearance of heartfelt sincerity, and were invited by him to the hall, to take something to keep out the cold of the weather; and I heard blessings uttered by several of the poor, which convinced me that, in the midst of his enjoyments, the worthy old cavalier had not forgotten the true Christmas virtue of charity.

We had not been long home when the sound of music was heard from a distance. A band of country lads, without coats, their shirt sleeves fancifully tied with ribands, their hats decorated with greens, and clubs in their hands, were seen advancing up the avenue, followed by a large number of villagers and peasantry. They stopped before the hall door, where the music struck up a peculiar air, and the lads performed a curious and intricate dance, advancing, retreating, and striking their clubs together, keeping exact time to the music; while one, whimsically crowned with a fox's skin, the tail of which flaunted down his back, kept capering round the skirts of the dance, and rattling a Christmas box, with many antic gesticulations.

The squire eyed this fanciful exhibition with great interest and delight, and gave me a full account of its origin, which he traced to the times when the Romans held possession of the island,[15] plainly proving that this was a lineal descendant of the sword dance of the ancients.

After the dance was concluded, the whole party was entertained with brawn and beef, and stout home-brewed. The whole house seemed abandoned to merriment; as I passed to my room to dress for dinner, I heard the sound of music in a small court, and looking through a window that commanded it, I perceived a band of wandering musicians, with Pandean pipes[16] and tambourine; a pretty, coquettish housemaid was dancing a jig with a smart country lad, while several of the other servants looked on.

---

[14]*clearing more bars...in at the death.* Just as the fox hunter on horseback tries to clear all obstacles (bars) in order to catch up with the hounds by the time the fox is run down and killed, the fiddlers hurried over the bars of music to catch up with the other players before the piece ended.

[15]*the Romans held possession of the island.* From 43 B.C. until the beginning of the fifth century A.D. England was ruled by Rome.

[16]*Pandean* (pan dē′ən) *pipes,* ancient wind instruments made of hollow reeds of various lengths. They were said by the Greeks to have been invented by the god Pan.

4

I had finished my toilet, and was loitering with Frank Bracebridge in the library, when we heard a distinct thwacking sound, which he informed me was a signal for the serving up of the dinner. The squire kept up old customs in kitchen as well as hall; and the rolling pin, struck upon the dresser by the cook, summoned the servants to carry in the meats.

The dinner was served up in the great hall, where the squire always held his Christmas banquet. A blazing crackling fire of logs had been heaped on to warm the spacious apartment, and the flame went sparkling and wreathing up the wide-mouthed chimney. The great picture of the crusader and his white horse had been profusely decorated with greens for the occasion; and holly and ivy had likewise been wreathed round the helmet and weapons on the opposite wall, which I understood were the arms of the same warrior. A sideboard was set out just under this chivalric trophy, on which was a display of plate that might have vied (at least in variety) with Belshazzar's parade of the vessels of the temple[17]; "flagons, cans, cups, beakers, goblets, basins, and ewers"; the gorgeous utensils of good companionship that had gradually accumulated through many generations of jovial housekeepers. Before these stood the two Yule candles, beaming like two stars of the first magnitude; other lights were distributed in branches, and the whole array glittered like a firmament of silver.

We were ushered into this banqueting scene with the sound of minstrelsy, the old harper being seated on a stool beside the fireplace, and twanging his instrument with a vast deal more power than melody. Never did Christmas board display a more goodly and gracious assemblage of countenances; those who were not handsome were, at least, happy; and happiness is a rare improver of your hard-favored visage.

The parson said grace, which was not a short familiar one, such as is commonly addressed to the Deity in these unceremonious days, but a long, courtly, well-worded one of the ancient school. There was now a pause, as if something was expected, when suddenly the butler entered the hall with some degree of bustle. He was attended by a servant on each side with a large wax light, and bore a silver dish, on which was an enormous pig's head, decorated with rosemary, with a lemon in its mouth, which was placed with great formality at the head of the table. The moment this pageant made its appearance, the harper struck up a flourish; at the conclusion of which the young Oxonian, on receiving a hint from the squire, gave, with an air of the most comic gravity, an old carol.

The parade with which so odd a dish was introduced somewhat perplexed me, until I gathered from the conversation of the squire and the parson that it was meant to represent the bringing in of the boar's head, a dish formerly served up with much ceremony and the sound of minstrelsy and song, at great tables, on Christmas day.

The table was literally loaded with good cheer, and presented an epitome of country abundance, in this season of overflowing larders. A distinguished post was allotted to "ancient sirloin," as mine host termed it; being, as he added, "the standard of old English hospitality, and a joint of goodly presence, and full of expectation." There were several dishes quaintly decorated, and which had evidently something traditional in their embellishments; but about which, as I did not like to appear overcurious, I asked no questions.

When the cloth was removed,[18] the butler brought in a huge silver vessel of rare and curious workmanship, which he placed before the squire. Its appearance was hailed with acclamation, being the Wassail Bowl, so renowned in Christmas festivity. The contents had been prepared by the squire himself; for it was a beverage in the skillful mixture of which he particularly prided himself. It was a potation, indeed, that might well make the heart of a toper leap within him; being composed of the richest and

---

[17]*Belshazzar's* (bel shaz′ərz) *parade of the vessels of the temple.* Belshazzar, king of Babylon, used the golden vessels his father had taken from the temple at Jerusalem for a great feast. As a result of his sacrilege his kingdom was destroyed. (Daniel, Chapter 5.)

[18]*When the cloth was removed,* when the meal was over.

raciest wines, highly spiced and sweetened, with roasted apples bobbing about the surface.

The old gentleman's whole countenance beamed with a serene look of indwelling delight, as he stirred this mighty bowl. Having raised it to his lips, with a hearty wish of merry Christmas to all present, he sent it brimming round the board, for everyone to follow his example, according to the primitive style.

After the dinner table was removed, the hall was given up to the younger members of the family, who, prompted to all kind of noisy mirth by the Oxonian and Master Simon, made its old walls ring with their merriment, as they played at romping games. I could not help stealing out of the drawing room on hearing one of their peals of laughter. I found them at the game of blindman's buff. Master Simon, who was the leader of their revels, was blinded in the midst of the hall. The little beings were as busy about him as the mock fairies about Falstaff[19]; pinching him, plucking at the skirts of his coat, and tickling him with straws. One fine blue-eyed girl of about thirteen, with her flaxen hair all in beautiful confusion, her frolic face in a glow, her frock half torn off her shoulders, a complete picture of a romp, was the chief tormentor; and, from the slyness with which Master Simon avoided the smaller game, and hemmed this wild little nymph in corners, and obliged her to jump shrieking over chairs, I suspected the rogue of being not a whit more blinded than was convenient.

When I returned to the drawing room, I found the company seated round the fire listening to the parson, who was deeply ensconced in a high-backed oaken chair, the work of some cunning artificer of yore, which had been brought from the library for his particular accommodation. From this venerable piece of furniture, with which his shadowy figure and dark weazen[20] face so admirably accorded, he was dealing out strange accounts of the popular superstitions and legends of the surrounding country.

Whilst we were all attention to the parson's stories, our ears were suddenly assailed by a burst of heterogeneous sounds from the hall, in which were mingled something like the clang of rude minstrelsy, with the uproar of many small voices and girlish laughter. The door suddenly flew open, and a train came trooping into the room.

That indefatigable spirit, Master Simon, had conceived the idea of a Christmas mummery or masking; and having called in to his assistance the Oxonian and the young officer, who were equally ripe for anything that should occasion romping and merriment, they had carried it into instant effect. The old housekeeper had been consulted; the antique clothes presses and wardrobes rummaged and made to yield up the relics of finery that had not seen the light for several generations; the younger part of the company had been privately convened from the parlor and hall, and the whole had been bedizened out into a burlesque imitation of an antique masque.

Master Simon led the van as Ancient Christmas, quaintly appareled in a ruff, a short cloak, which had very much the aspect of one of the old housekeeper's petticoats, and a hat that might have served for a village steeple, and must indubitably have figured in the days of the Covenanters.[21] From under this his nose curved boldly forth, flushed with a frostbitten bloom, that seemed the very trophy of a December blast. He was accompanied by the blue-eyed romp, dished up as Dame Mince Pie, in the venerable magnificence of a faded brocade, long stomacher, peaked hat, and high-heeled shoes.

The rest of the train had been metamorphosed in various ways; the girls trussed up in the finery of the ancient belles of the Bracebridge line, and the striplings bewhiskered with burnt cork, and gravely clad in broad skirts, hanging sleeves, and full-bottomed wigs, to represent the character of Roast Beef, Plum Pud-

---

[19]*The little beings...mock fairies about Falstaff.* In Shakespeare's play *The Merry Wives of Windsor,* Falstaff is tricked into a forest meeting. Children dressed as fairies dance about him, pinch him, and burn him.

[20]*weazen* (wē′zən), a variant of *wizened* (wiz′ənd), which means "thin" or "shrunken."

[21]*Covenanters* (kuv′ə nən tərz *or* kuv′ə nan′tərz), supporters of the Scotch Presbyterian Church when it was under attack by the kings of England during the seventeenth century.

ding, and other worthies celebrated in ancient maskings.

The irruption of this motley crew, with beat of drum, according to ancient custom, was the consummation of uproar and merriment. Master Simon covered himself with glory by the stateliness with which, as Ancient Christmas, he walked a minuet with the peerless, though giggling, Dame Mince Pie. It was followed by a dance of all the characters, which, from its medley of costumes, seemed as though the old family portraits had skipped down from their frames to join in the sport.

The worthy squire contemplated these fantastic sports, and this resurrection of his old wardrobe, with the simple relish of childish delight. He stood chuckling and rubbing his hands, and scarcely hearing a word the parson said. For my part I was in a continual excitement, from the varied scenes of whim and innocent gaiety passing before me. It was inspiring to me to see wild-eyed frolic and warm-hearted hospitality breaking out from among the chills and glooms of winter, and old age throwing off his apathy and catching once more the freshness of youthful enjoyment. I felt also an interest in the scene, from the consideration that these fleeting customs were posting fast into oblivion, and that this was, perhaps, the only family in England in which the whole of them were still punctiliously observed. There was a quaintness, too, mingled with all this revelry, that gave it a peculiar zest: it was suited to the time and place; and as the old manor house almost reeled with mirth and wassail, it seemed echoing back the joviality of long-departed years.

CONCERNING WASHINGTON IRVING

1. List all the reasons why Irving did not decide to become a professional writer after his first literary success. When and why did he decide to write professionally?

2. Give an account of the publication and reception of *The Sketch Book.*

3. What attitude did England have toward America before 1819? Why? In what two ways did Irving help change this attitude?

4. How did Irving help change America's attitude toward Europe?

CONCERNING "CHRISTMAS"

1. How do the opening three paragraphs relate to the author's decision to spend Christmas with his friend?

2. What was the keynote of the Christmas celebration at the Bracebridge mansion?

3. How does the celebration described resemble a present-day American celebration? In what important ways does it differ?

4. In paragraph 1, Irving speaks of "a tone of solemn and sacred feeling that blends with our conviviality." To what extent, and in what ways, does Irving convey the "tone" here mentioned? Contrast that tone with the tone of "The Golden Reign of Wouter Van Twiller."

5. What qualities of the British are indicated? How are they indicated? What effect would the portrayal of such qualities have upon Irving's contemporaries in America? What would the effect upon his English contemporaries be?

Know your words

Often the meaning of an unfamiliar word is made clear by its context. If you do not know the meanings of the italicized words in the sentences below, you can probably figure them out by studying the way Irving uses them. Write the numbers 1 through 7 on a sheet of paper. After each number rewrite the corresponding sentence, substituting another word or group of words for each word in italics. When you have finished, use the Glossary as a check on the correctness of your work.

1. [He] is known simply by the *appellation* of "The Squire," a title which had been *accorded* to the head of the family since time *immemorial.*

2. ...everything was done *conformably* to ancient usage.

3. [Master Simon] cut an orange into such a *ludicrous caricature* that the young folks were ready to die with laughing.

4. Our breakfast consisted of what the squire *denominated* true old English fare....

5. ...those who were not handsome were, at least, happy; and happiness is a *rare* improver of your *hard-favored visage.*

6. [The parson] was deeply *ensconced* in a high-backed oaken chair, the work of some cunning *artificer of yore.*

7. I felt also an interest in the scene, from the consideration that these fleeting customs were *posting* fast into *oblivion,* and that this was, perhaps, the only family in England in which the whole of them were still *punctiliously* observed.

One very important thing which Irving did in his books after 1809 helped account for his fame: he embodied in them the spirit of the new Romantic Movement. He had started as a child of the eighteenth century —a writer not very different in his style from Benjamin Franklin. His first papers had been signed with the pseudonym Jonathan Oldstyle; and he was an old-style writer—one who echoed the voices of British authors such as Addison, Steele, and Goldsmith, all of whom had died before Irving was born. *Salmagundi* and *A History of New York* both were in the outmoded tradition.

But in 1810, Sir Walter Scott's thrilling narrative poem about old-time Scotland, *The Lady of the Lake,* came into Irving's hands, and he read it with great pleasure. This was followed by Byron's poetic romances, *Childe Harold, The Corsair,* and others, which also pleased him. These were the products of a great literary movement which was under way in several parts of the Old World—the Romantic Movement. Many trends made up this movement, but we may note three in particular: (1) An emphasis upon emotion in literature—emotion ranging from sentimentality to deep feeling. (2) A great interest in the picturesque elements of the past. (3) An enthusiasm about portraying national life and character— such an enthusiasm as is evident, for example, in Scott's narrative poems and in his historical novels.

During the months before *The Sketch Book* was written, Irving met many British authors, and talked with them about their new enthusiasms. More important, during a holiday late in the August of 1817, he paid a visit to Walter Scott. He rode up to Scott's home, Abbotsford, in a post chaise, and sent in a letter of introduction. Soon, Scott's hunting dogs came barking out to the road, and then the famous author himself, wearing "an old green shooting coat, with a dog-whistle at the button hole," came out and hospitably greeted him. Scott had admired *A History of New York,* and he found Irving attractive personally. Therefore he welcomed his visitor warmly, put him up for four days, rambled around the countryside with him, and just about talked Irving's arm off.

Irving discovered that his host was the very embodiment of what he admired—an author who, in a light-hearted spirit, wrote of the lore of his own countryside. "I never met with an antiquarian so delightful, either in his writings or his conversation," said Irving, "and the quiet subacid humor that was prone to mingle with his disquisitions gave them, to me, a peculiar and exquisite flavor." What is more, Scott probably told Irving that treasures of the kind he sought might be found in German literature; for soon the American author plunged into the study of German. In May, 1818, he wrote a friend, "I have been for some time past engaged in the study of the German language, and have got so far as to be able to read and splutter a little. It is a severe task, and has required hard study; but the rich mine of German literature holds forth abundant reward."

Romantic influences shaped Irving's writings from that time on. As he wrote of England or of other countries, Irving showed that he loved, as he said, "to loiter about the ruined castle, to meditate on the falling tower, to escape, in short, from the commonplace realities of the present, and lose myself among the shadowy grandeurs of the past." In his most successful short stories—"Rip Van Winkle" and "A Legend of Sleepy Hollow" in *The Sketch Book* and "The Devil and Tom Walker" in *Tales of a Traveller*—he did these things: (1) Like Scott, he told legendary and historical narratives about his own native countryside. (2) Like Scott, he treated his legendary lore lightly or semi-humorously. (3) He drew upon German literature for the suggestion of legends, which he adapted to the American scene. (4) Like most romantic writers, he so wrote as to express emotion and to create an emotional effect. Thus this famous author allied himself with the leaders of the world-wide Romantic Movement, and, by his example, helped American writers fall into step with the writers of their day.

The Devil and Tom Walker

A FEW MILES from Boston in Massachusetts, there is a deep inlet, winding several miles into the interior of the country from Charles Bay, and terminating in a thickly wooded swamp or morass. On one side of this inlet is a beautiful dark grove; on the opposite side the land rises abruptly from the water's edge into a high ridge, on which grow a few scattered oaks of great age and immense size.

Under one of these gigantic trees, according to old stories, there was a great amount of treasure buried by Kidd the pirate. The inlet allowed a facility to bring the money in a boat secretly and at night to the very foot of the hill; the elevation of the place permitted a good lookout to be kept that no one was at hand; while the remarkable trees formed good landmarks by which the place might easily be found again. The old stories add, moreover, that the devil presided at the hiding of the money, and took it under his guardianship; but this, it is well known, he always does with buried treasure, particularly when it has been ill-gotten. Be that as it may, Kidd never returned to recover his wealth, being shortly after seized at Boston, sent out to England, and there hanged for a pirate.

About the year 1727, just at the time that earthquakes were prevalent in New England, and shook many tall sinners down upon their knees, there lived near this place a meager, miserly fellow, of the name of Tom Walker. He had a wife as miserly as himself; they were so miserly that they even conspired to cheat each other. Whatever the woman could lay hands on, she hid away; a hen could not cackle but she was on the alert to secure the new-laid egg. Her husband was continually prying about to detect her secret hoards, and many and fierce were the conflicts that took place about what ought to have been common property.

They lived in a forlorn-looking house that stood alone, and had an air of starvation. A few straggling savin trees, emblems of sterility, grew near it; no smoke ever curled from its chimney; no traveler stopped at its door. A miserable horse, whose ribs were as articulate as the bars of a gridiron, stalked about a field, where a thin carpet of moss, scarcely covering the ragged beds of pudding stone, tantalized and balked his hunger; and sometimes he would lean his head over the fence, look piteously at the passerby, and seem to petition deliverance from this land of famine.

The house and its inmates had altogether a bad name. Tom's wife was a tall termagant, fierce of temper, loud of tongue, and strong of arm. Her voice was often heard in wordy warfare with her husband; and his face sometimes showed signs that their conflicts were not confined to words. No one ventured, however, to interfere between them. The lonely wayfarer shrunk within himself at the horrid clamor and clapper-clawing,[1] eyed the den of discord askance; and hurried on his way, rejoicing, if a bachelor, in his celibacy.

One day that Tom Walker had been to a distant part of the neighborhood, he took what he considered a short cut homeward, through the swamp. Like most short cuts, it was an ill-chosen route. The swamp was thickly grown with great gloomy pines and hemlocks, some of them ninety feet high, which made it dark at noonday and a retreat for all the owls of the neighborhood. It was full of pits and quagmires, partly covered with weeds and mosses, where the green surface often betrayed the traveler into a gulf of black, smothering mud; there were also dark and stagnant pools, the abodes of the tadpole, the bullfrog, and the water snake,

where the trunks of pines and hemlocks lay half-drowned, half-rotting, looking like alligators sleeping in the mire.

Tom had long been picking his way cautiously through this treacherous forest, stepping from tuft to tuft of rushes and roots, which afforded precarious footholds among deep sloughs; or pacing carefully, like a cat, along the prostrate trunks of trees, startled now and then by the sudden screaming of the bittern, or the quacking of wild duck rising on the wing from some solitary pool. At length he arrived at a firm piece of ground, which ran out like a peninsula into the deep bosom of the swamp. It had been one of the strongholds of the Indians during their wars with the first colonists. Here they had thrown up a kind of fort, which they had looked upon as almost impregnable, and had used as a place of refuge for their squaws and children. Nothing remained of the old Indian fort but a few embankments, gradually sinking to the level of the surrounding earth and already overgrown in part by oaks and other forest trees, the foliage of which formed a contrast to the dark pines and hemlocks of the swamp.

It was late in the dusk of evening when Tom Walker reached the old fort, and he paused there awhile to rest himself. Anyone but he would have felt unwilling to linger in this lonely, melancholy place, for the common people had a bad opinion of it, from the stories handed down from the time of the Indian wars, when it was asserted that the savages held incantations here and made sacrifices to the evil spirit.

Tom Walker, however, was not a man to be troubled with any fears of the kind. He reposed himself for some time on the trunk of a fallen hemlock, listening to the boding cry of the tree toad, and delving with his walking staff into a mound of black mold at his feet. As he turned up the soil unconsciously, his staff struck against something hard. He raked it out of the vegetable mold, and lo! a cloven skull, with an Indian tomahawk buried deep in it, lay before him. The rust on the weapon showed the time that had elapsed since this deathblow had been given. It was a dreary memento of the fierce struggle that

---
[1]*clapper-clawing,* an argument accompanied by scratching and slapping.

had taken place in this last foothold of the Indian warriors. "Humph!" said Tom Walker as he gave it a kick to shake the dirt from it.

"Let that skull alone!" said a gruff voice. Tom lifted up his eyes and beheld a great black man seated directly opposite him, on the stump of a tree. He was exceedingly surprised, having neither heard nor seen anyone approach; and he was still more perplexed on observing, as well as the gathering gloom would permit, that the stranger was neither Negro nor Indian. It is true he was dressed in a rude half-Indian garb, and had a red belt or sash swathed round his body; but his face was neither black nor copper color, but swarthy and dingy, and begrimed with soot, as if he had been accustomed to toil among fires and forges. He had a shock of coarse black hair that stood out from his head in all directions, and bore an ax on his shoulder.

He scowled for a moment at Tom with a pair of great red eyes.

"What are you doing on my grounds?" said the black man, with a hoarse, growling voice.

"Your grounds!" said Tom, with a sneer, "no more your grounds than mine; they belong to Deacon Peabody."

"Deacon Peabody be damned," said the stranger, "as I flatter myself he will be, if he does not look more to his own sins and less to those of his neighbors. Look yonder, and see how Deacon Peabody is faring."

Tom looked in the direction that the stranger pointed and beheld one of the great trees, fair and flourishing without, but rotten at the core, and saw that it had been nearly hewn through, so that the first high wind was likely to blow it down. On the bark of the tree was scored the name of Deacon Peabody, an eminent man who had waxed wealthy by driving shrewd bargains with the Indians. He now looked around, and found most of the tall trees marked with the name of some great man of the colony, and all more or less scored by the ax. The one on which he had been seated, and which had evidently just been hewn down, bore the name of Crowninshield; and he recollected a mighty rich man of that name, who made a vulgar display of wealth, which it was whispered he had acquired by buccaneering.

"He's just ready for burning!" said the black man, with a growl of triumph. "You see I am likely to have a good stock of firewood for winter."

"But what right have you," said Tom, "to cut down Deacon Peabody's timber?"

"The right of a prior claim," said the other. "This woodland belonged to me long before one of your white-faced race put foot upon the soil."

"And pray, who are you, if I may be so bold?" said Tom.

"Oh, I go by various names. I am the wild huntsman in some countries; the black miner in others. In this neighborhood I am known by the name of the black woodsman. I am he to whom the red men consecrated this spot, and in honor of whom they now and then roasted a white man, by way of sweet-smelling sacrifice. Since the red men have been exterminated by you white savages, I amuse myself by presiding at the persecutions of Quakers and Anabaptists[2]; I am the great patron and prompter of slave dealers, and the grand master of the Salem witches."[3]

"The upshot of all which is, that, if I mistake not," said Tom, sturdily, "you are he commonly called Old Scratch."

"The same, at your service!" replied the black man, with a half-civil nod.

Such was the opening of this interview, according to the old story; though it has almost too familiar an air to be credited. One would think that to meet with such a singular personage, in this wild, lonely place, would have shaken any man's nerves; but Tom was a hard-minded fellow, not easily daunted, and he had lived so long with a termagant wife that he did not even fear the devil.

It is said that after this commencement they had a long and earnest conversation together, as Tom returned homeward. The black man told him of great sums of money buried by Kidd the pirate, under the oak trees on the high ridge, not far from the morass. All these were under his

[2]*Anabaptists* (an′ə bap′tists), members of a Protestant sect which originated in Switzerland in the sixteenth century. Quakers and Anabaptists were persecuted in the Massachusetts colony.

[3]*the Salem witches*, old women accused of witchcraft in the Salem witch trials of 1692.

command, and protected by his power, so that none could find them but such as propitiated his favor. These he offered to place within Tom Walker's reach, having conceived an especial kindness for him; but they were to be had only on certain conditions. What these conditions were may be easily surmised, though Tom never disclosed them publicly. They must have been very hard, for he required time to think of them, and he was not a man to stick at trifles when money was in view.

When they had reached the edge of the swamp, the stranger paused. "What proof have I that all you have been telling me is true?" said Tom. "There's my signature," said the black man, pressing his finger on Tom's forehead. So saying, he turned off among the thickest of the swamp, and seemed, as Tom said, to go down, down, down, into the earth, until he totally disappeared.

When Tom reached home, he found the black print of a finger burned, as it were, into his forehead, which nothing could obliterate.

The first news his wife had to tell him was the sudden death of Absalom Crowninshield, the rich buccaneer. It was announced in the papers with the usual flourish that "A great man had fallen in Israel."[4]

Tom recollected the tree which his black friend had just hewn down and which was ready for burning. "Let the freebooter roast," said Tom; "who cares!" He now felt convinced that all he had heard and seen was no illusion.

He was not prone to let his wife into his confidence; but as this was an uneasy secret, he willingly shared it with her. All her avarice was awakened at the mention of hidden gold, and she urged her husband to comply with the black man's terms, and secure what would make them wealthy for life. However Tom might have felt disposed to sell himself to the devil, he was determined not to do so to oblige his wife; so he flatly refused, out of the mere spirit of contradiction. Many were the quarrels they had on the subject; but the more she talked, the more resolute was Tom not to be damned to please her.

<hr>

[4]*Israel*, Massachusetts. The Puritans of Massachusetts regarded their colony as the Promised Land (Israel).

At length she determined to drive the bargain on her own account, and if she succeeded, to keep all the gain to herself. Being of the same fearless temper as her husband, she set off for the old Indian fort toward the close of a summer's day. She was many hours absent. When she came back, she was reserved and sullen in her replies. She spoke something of a black man, whom she met about twilight hewing at the root of a tall tree. He was sulky, however, and would not come to terms; she was to go again with a propitiatory offering, but what it was she forbore to say.

The next evening she set off again for the swamp, with her apron heavily laden. Tom waited and waited for her, but in vain; midnight came, but she did not make her appearance; morning, noon, night returned, but still she did not come. Tom now grew uneasy for her safety, especially as he found she had carried off in her apron the silver teapot and spoons, and every portable article of value. Another night elapsed, another morning came; but no wife. In a word, she was never heard of more.

What was her real fate nobody knows, in consequence of so many pretending to know. It is one of those facts which have become confounded by a variety of historians. Some asserted that she lost her way among the tangled mazes of the swamp, and sank into some pit or slough; others, more uncharitable, hinted that she had eloped with the household booty, and made off to some other province; while others surmised that the tempter had decoyed her into a dismal quagmire, on the top of which her hat was found lying. In confirmation of this, it was said a great black man, with an ax on his shoulder, was seen late that very evening coming out of the swamp, carrying a bundle tied in a check apron, with an air of surly triumph.

The most current and probable story, however, observes that Tom Walker grew so anxious about the fate of his wife and his property that he set out at length to seek them both at the Indian fort. During a long summer's afternoon he searched about the gloomy place, but no wife was to be seen. He called her name repeatedly, but she was nowhere to be heard. The bittern alone responded to his voice, as he flew screaming by; or the bullfrog croaked dolefully from a neighboring pool. At length, it is said, just in the brown hour of twilight, when the owls began to hoot, and the bats to flit about, his attention was attracted by the clamor of carrion crows hovering about a cypress tree. He looked up and beheld a bundle tied in a check apron and hanging in the branches of the tree, with a great vulture perched hard by, as if keeping watch upon it. He leaped with joy; for he recognized his wife's apron and supposed it to contain the household valuables.

"Let us get hold of the property," said he consolingly to himself, "and we will endeavor to do without the woman."

As he scrambled up the tree, the vulture spread its wide wings and sailed off screaming into the deep shadows of the forest. Tom seized the checked apron, but, woeful sight! found nothing but a heart and liver tied up in it!

Such, according to this most authentic old story, was all that was to be found of Tom's wife. She had probably attempted to deal with the black man as she had been accustomed to deal with her husband; but though a female scold is generally considered a match for the devil, yet in this instance she appears to have had the worst of it. She must have died game, however; for it is said Tom noticed many prints of cloven feet deeply stamped upon the tree, and found handfuls of hair that looked as if they had been plucked from the coarse black shock of the woodsman. Tom knew his wife's prowess by experience. He shrugged his shoulders as he looked at the signs of a fierce clapper-clawing. "Egad," said he to himself, "Old Scratch must have had a tough time of it!"

Tom consoled himself for the loss of his property with the loss of his wife, for he was a man of fortitude. He even felt something like gratitude toward the black woodsman, who, he considered, had done him a kindness. He sought, therefore, to cultivate a further acquaintance with him, but for some time without success; the old black-legs played shy, for whatever people may think, he is not always to be had for calling for; he knows how to play his cards when pretty sure of his game.

At length, it is said, when delay had whetted Tom's eagerness to the quick, and prepared him to agree to anything rather than not gain the promised treasure, he met the black man one evening in his usual woodsman's dress, with his ax on his shoulder, sauntering along the swamp and humming a tune. He affected to receive Tom's advances with great indifference, made brief replies, and went on humming his tune.

By degrees, however, Tom brought him to business, and they began to haggle about the terms on which the former was to have the pirate's treasure. There was one condition which need not be mentioned, being generally understood in all cases where the devil grants favors; but there were others about which, though of less importance, he was inflexibly obstinate. He insisted that the money found through his means should be employed in his service. He proposed, therefore, that Tom should employ it in the black traffic; that is to say, that he should fit out a slave ship. This, however, Tom resolutely refused; he was bad enough in all conscience, but the devil himself could not tempt him to turn slave trader.

Finding Tom so squeamish on this point, he did not insist upon it, but proposed, instead, that he should turn usurer, the devil being extremely anxious for the increase of usurers, looking upon them as his peculiar people.

To this no objections were made, for it was just to Tom's taste.

"You shall open a broker's shop in Boston next month," said the black man.

"I'll do it tomorrow, if you wish," said Tom Walker.

"You shall lend money at two per cent a month."

"Egad, I'll charge four!" replied Tom Walker.

"You shall extort bonds, foreclose mortgages, drive the merchants to bankruptcy——"

"I'll drive them to the devil," cried Tom Walker.

"You are the usurer for my money!" said black-legs with delight. "When will you want the rhino[5]?"

"This very night."

"Done!" said the devil.

---

[5]*rhino* (rī′nō), money. [*Slang*]

"Done!" said Tom Walker. So they shook hands and struck a bargain.

A few days' time saw Tom Walker seated behind his desk in a counting house in Boston.

His reputation for a ready-moneyed man, who would lend money out for a good consideration, soon spread abroad. Everybody remembers the time of Governor Belcher,[6] when money was particularly scarce. It was a time of paper credit.[7] The country had been deluged with government bills, the famous Land Bank[8] had been established; there had been a rage for speculating; the people had run mad with schemes for new settlements, for building cities in the wilderness; land jobbers[9] went about with maps of grants, and townships, and El Dorados,[10] lying nobody knew where, but which everybody was ready to purchase. In a word, the great speculating fever which breaks out every now and then in the country had raged to an alarming degree, and everybody was dreaming of making sudden fortunes from nothing. As usual the fever had subsided; the dream had gone off, and the imaginary fortunes with it; the patients were left in doleful plight, and the whole country resounded with the consequent cry of "hard times."

At this propitious time of public distress did Tom Walker set up as usurer in Boston. His door was soon thronged by customers. The needy and adventurous, the gambling speculator, the dreaming land jobber, the thriftless tradesman, the merchant with cracked credit—in short, everyone driven to raise money by desperate means and desperate sacrifices hurried to Tom Walker.

Thus Tom was the universal friend of the needy, and acted like a "friend in need"; that is to say, he always exacted good pay and good security. In proportion to the distress of the applicant was the hardness of his terms. He accumulated bonds and mortgages; gradually squeezed his customers closer and closer; and sent them at length, dry as a sponge, from his door.

In this way he made money hand over hand; became a rich and mighty man, and exalted his cocked hat[11] upon 'Change.[12] He built himself, as usual, a vast house, out of ostentation; but left the greater part of it unfinished and unfurnished, out of parsimony. He even set up a carriage in the fullness of his vainglory, though he nearly starved the horses which drew it; and as the ungreased wheels groaned and screeched on the axletrees, you would have thought you heard the souls of the poor debtors he was squeezing.

As Tom waxed old, however, he grew thoughtful. Having secured the good things of this world, he began to feel anxious about those of the next. He thought with regret on the bargain he had made with his black friend, and set his wits to work to cheat him out of the conditions. He became, therefore, all of a sudden, a violent churchgoer. He prayed loudly and strenuously, as if heaven were to be taken by force of lungs. Indeed, one might always tell when he had sinned most during the week by the clamor of his Sunday devotion. The quiet Christians who had been modestly and steadfastly traveling Zionward,[13] were struck with self-reproach at seeing themselves so suddenly outstripped in their career by this new-made convert. Tom was as rigid in religious as in money matters; he was a stern supervisor and censurer of his neighbors, and seemed to think every sin entered up to their account became a credit on his own side of the page. He even talked of the expediency of reviving the persecution of Quakers and Anabaptists. In a word, Tom's zeal became as notorious as his riches.

Still, in spite of all this strenuous attention to forms, Tom had a lurking dread that the devil,

---

[6]*Governor Belcher*, Jonathan Belcher, who governed Massachusetts from 1730 to 1741.

[7]*paper credit*, assets that existed on paper but were actually of no value.

[8]*Land Bank*, a scheme to relieve the shortage of gold in Massachusetts by establishing a bank whose resources rested on real-estate mortgages.

[9]*land jobbers*, men who bought tracts of undeveloped land as a speculation and sold them to others.

[10]*El Dorados* (el də rä′dōz), fabulously wealthy places. The term comes from the name given to a legendary city of great wealth, sought by the early Spanish explorers in South America.

[11]*cocked hat*, a three-cornered hat with a turned-up brim.

[12]*'Change*, the Exchange, or the financial center of Boston, where merchants, traders, and brokers do business.

[13]*Zionward*, toward heaven. Zion, originally the hill in Jerusalem on which the temple stood, is often used to typify heaven.

after all, would have his due. That he might not be taken unawares, therefore, it is said he always carried a small Bible in his coat pocket. He had also a great folio Bible on his counting-house desk, and would frequently be found reading it when people called on business; on such occasions he would lay his green spectacles in the book, to mark the place, while he turned round to drive some usurious bargain.

Some say that Tom grew a little crack-brained in his old days, and that, fancying his end approaching, he had his horse new shod, saddled and bridled, and buried with his feet uppermost; because he supposed that at the last day the world would be turned upside down in which case he should find his horse standing ready for mounting, and he was determined at the worst to give his old friend a run for it. This, however, is probably a mere old wives' fable. If he really did take such a precaution, it was totally superfluous; at least so says the authentic old legend, which closes his story in the following manner.

One hot summer afternoon in the dog days, just as a terrible black thundergust was coming up, Tom sat in his counting house in his white cap and India-silk morning gown. He was on the point of foreclosing a mortgage, by which he would complete the ruin of an unlucky land speculator for whom he had professed the greatest friendship. The poor land jobber begged him to grant a few months' indulgence. Tom had grown testy and irritated, and refused another day.

"My family will be ruined and brought upon the parish,"[14] said the land jobber.

"Charity begins at home," replied Tom; "I must take care of myself in these hard times."

"You have made so much money out of me," said the speculator.

Tom lost his patience and his piety. "The devil take me," said he, "if I have made a farthing!"[15]

Just then there were three loud knocks at the street door. He stepped out to see who was there. A black man was holding a black horse, which neighed and stamped with impatience.

"Tom, you're come for," said the black fellow, gruffly. Tom shrank back, but too late. He had left his little Bible at the bottom of his coat pocket, and his big Bible on the desk buried under the mortgage he was about to foreclose; never was sinner taken more unawares. The black man whisked him like a child into the saddle, gave the horse the lash, and away he galloped, with Tom on his back, in the midst of the thunderstorm. The clerks stuck their pens behind their ears, and stared after him from the windows. Away went Tom Walker, dashing down the streets, his white cap bobbing up and down, his morning gown fluttering in the wind, and his steed striking fire out of the pavement at every bound. When the clerks turned to look for the black man, he had disappeared.

Tom Walker never returned to foreclose the mortgage. A countryman, who lived on the border of the swamp, reported that in the height of the thundergust he had heard a great clattering of hoofs and a howling along the road, and running to the window caught sight of a figure, such as I have described, on a horse that galloped like mad across the fields, over the hills, and down into the black hemlock swamp toward the old Indian fort; and that shortly after, a thunderbolt falling in that direction seemed to set the whole forest in a blaze.

The good people of Boston shook their heads and shrugged their shoulders, but had been so much accustomed to witches and goblins and tricks of the devil in all kinds of shapes, from the first settlement of the colony, that they were not so much horror-struck as might have been expected. Trustees were appointed to take charge of Tom's effects. There was nothing, however, to administer upon. On searching his coffers, all his bonds and mortgages were found reduced to cinders. In place of gold and silver, his iron chest was filled with chips and shavings; two skeletons lay in his stable instead of his half-starved horses, and the very next day his great house took fire and burned to the ground.

Such was the end of Tom Walker and his ill-gotten wealth. Let all griping money brokers lay

---

[14]*brought upon the parish*, forced to depend upon public charity for support.

[15]*farthing*, a British coin worth about half a cent in United States money. At the time of the story the colonists used the British money system.

this story to heart. The truth of it is not to be doubted. The very hole under the oak trees whence he dug Kidd's money is to be seen to this day; and the neighboring swamp and old Indian fort are often haunted on stormy nights by a figure on horseback, in morning gown and white cap, which is doubtless the troubled spirit of the usurer. In fact, the story has resolved itself into a proverb, and is the origin of that popular saying, so prevalent throughout New England, of "The Devil and Tom Walker."

CONCERNING WASHINGTON IRVING

1. Name some of the authors and books that were important in the English Romantic Movement. What were three important trends in the movement?

2. How did Irving become acquainted with the ideas of the Romantic Movement?

3. Name several examples of Irving's writing which show romantic influences.

CONCERNING "THE DEVIL AND TOM WALKER"

1. What is the significance of each of the following details?

(a) Captain Kidd's treasure

(b) a newly hewn tree with the name Crownin-shield upon it

(c) an indelible black mark on Tom's forehead

(d) a silver teapot

(e) a bundle tied up in a checked apron

(f) a Boston counting house

(g) a Bible

(h) an iron chest filled with chips and shavings

Using these details as a guide, give a brief synopsis of the story.

2. Give examples of Tom Walker's meanness and miserliness. What other qualities does he have? Why do you think Irving endowed him with this particular combination of qualities?

3. Whom do you find the more despicable character, Tom or his wife? Give reasons for your answer.

4. After his first meeting with the devil, what alternatives did Tom have to face? How did he happen to decide as he did?

5. This story ends with Tom's death. Is it, therefore, a tragic story? Account for your answer.

6. What touches of humor do you find in Irving's portrayal of the devil and of Tom and his wife?

7. One tendency of romantic writers was at times to show their own personalities and attitudes in the stories they wrote. How, specifically, does Irving here show this tendency? In what other ways does the story show the influence of romantic writers on Irving?

Know your words

Each adjective in the first column below has an antonym in the second column. Copy the first word in the first column on a sheet of paper; then choose its antonym from the second column and write it on the same line. Continue in the same way with the other words. You may use the Glossary if necessary.

parsimonious	simple
propitiatory	rare
ostentatious	squeamish
	begrimed
inflexible	pliant
superfluous	antagonistic
ill-gotten	false
	generous
melancholy	necessary
authentic	joyous
	patient
testy	honest
prevalent	expedient

🐦 VI HISTORIAN AND BIOGRAPHER

In 1826, Irving went to Spain, going there, as he had gone to England, because he was drawn by romantic associations. As he wrote, "From earliest boyhood, when, on the banks of the Hudson, I first poured over the pages of an old Spanish history about the wars of Granada,[1] that city has ever been a subject of my waking dreams." He now turned to the writing of history and biography, each tinged, naturally enough, with

---

[1] *wars of Granada* (grə näʹdə). Granada, in southern Spain, was ruled by the Moors throughout the Middle Ages. In 1492 the Christians under Ferdinand and Isabella conquered Granada and drove the Moors from Spain.

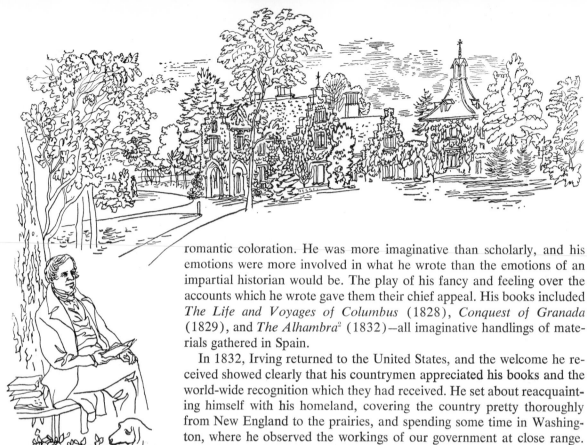

romantic coloration. He was more imaginative than scholarly, and his emotions were more involved in what he wrote than the emotions of an impartial historian would be. The play of his fancy and feeling over the accounts which he wrote gave them their chief appeal. His books included *The Life and Voyages of Columbus* (1828), *Conquest of Granada* (1829), and *The Alhambra*[2] (1832)—all imaginative handlings of materials gathered in Spain.

In 1832, Irving returned to the United States, and the welcome he received showed clearly that his countrymen appreciated his books and the world-wide recognition which they had received. He set about reacquainting himself with his homeland, covering the country pretty thoroughly from New England to the prairies, and spending some time in Washington, where he observed the workings of our government at close range. Then he bought an old stone cottage at Tarrytown on the Hudson,[3] and remodeled it into Sunnyside, the home where he remained the rest of his days, with the exception of the years 1842-1846, which he spent in Madrid as Minister to Spain.

His important books during this period fell into two classes. One group, based upon his own travels in the West and upon various documents, dealt with aspects of Western life and history. *A Tour on the Prairies* (1835) showed Irving as a visitor to a part of the country in which, even as he watched, a new phase of our history was developing. Historians are grateful for his detailed pictures of the frontier in that period. *Astoria* (1836) and *The Adventures of Captain Bonneville* (1837) recount the adventures of fur traders and explorers in the Far West. The second group includes two biographies, one—*Oliver Goldsmith* (1849)—of an eighteenth-century English writer who was one of Irving's literary idols, and the other—*Life of Washington* (1855-1859)—of the American patriot for whom Irving was named.

All these books showed that Irving, in his last years, was still a master stylist; but only the volume which sets forth the legends and the romance of the Alhambra and a few passages which give vivid pictures of life in the West compete in interest or importance with his writings before 1826.

---

[2]*The Alhambra* (al ham′brə), a book concerned with the history and legends of the Alhambra, the palace near Granada of the Moorish kings in Spain.

[3]*Tarrytown on the Hudson,* a small town a few miles up the Hudson River from New York City.

Yet the career which ended in mid-nineteenth century had been, as a whole, both admirable and important. During its course, Irving reëstablished links between the Old World and the new nation which had come into being about the time he was born; he proved that an American writer could be a fine artist; and he brought the spirit of romance to American letters.

The following passage shows Irving as a portrayer of life in the Far West of his day.

The Camp of the Wild Horse

Through a chance meeting in 1832 with Henry L. Ellsworth, a government commissioner of Indian affairs, Irving had an opportunity to explore the Indian country in what is now the state of Oklahoma. Escorted by a hundred Rangers from the army, Ellsworth, Irving, and their party went deep into the land of the Indians. The selection that follows describes a camp along the Arkansas River.

WE HAD ENCAMPED in a good neighborhood for game, as the reports of rifles in various directions speedily gave notice. One of our hunters soon returned with the meat of a doe, tied up in the skin, and slung across his shoulders. Another brought a fat buck across his horse. Two other deer were brought in, and a number of turkeys. All the game was thrown down in front of the Captain's fire, to be portioned out among the various messes. The spits and camp kettles were soon in full employ, and throughout the evening there was a scene of hunters' feasting and profusion.

We had been disappointed this day in our hopes of meeting with buffalo, but the sight of the wild horse had been a great novelty, and gave a turn to the conversation of the camp for the evening. There were several anecdotes told of a famous gray horse which has ranged the prairies of this neighborhood for six or seven years, setting at naught every attempt of the hunters to capture him. They say he can pace and rack (or amble) faster than the fleetest horses can run. Equally marvelous accounts

were given of a black horse on the Brassos,[1] who grazed the prairies on that river's banks in the Texas.[2] For years he outstripped all pursuit. His fame spread far and wide; offers were made for him to the amount of a thousand dollars; the boldest and most hard-riding hunters tried incessantly to make prize of him, but in vain. At length he fell a victim to his gallantry, being decoyed under a tree by a tame mare, and a noose dropped over his head by a boy perched among the branches.

The capture of the wild horse is one of the most favorite achievements of the prairie tribes; and, indeed, it is from this source that the Indian hunters chiefly supply themselves. The wild horses which range those vast grassy plains, extending from the Arkansas to the Spanish settlements,[3] are of various forms and colors, betraying their various descents. Some resemble the common English stock, and are probably descended from horses which have escaped from our border settlements. Others are of a low but strong make, and are supposed to be of the Andalusian[4] breed, brought out by the Spanish discoverers.

Some fanciful speculatists have seen in them descendants of the Arab stock, brought into Spain from Africa, and thence transferred to this country; and have pleased themselves with

---

[1] *Brassos,* the Brazos (brä′zōs) River, which runs through east-central Texas to the Gulf of Mexico.

[2] *the Texas,* the area, then a part of Mexico, which later became the state of Texas.

[3] *from the Arkansas...Spanish settlements,* from the territory which became the state of Arkansas to the towns founded by the Spanish among the Indians of New Mexico and southwestern Texas.

[4] *Andalusian* (an′də lü′zhən *or* an′də lü′shən), from Andalusia, a region in southern Spain.

the idea that their sires may have been of the pure coursers of the desert, that once bore Mahomet and his warlike disciples[5] across the sandy plains of Arabia.

The habits of the Arab seem to have come with the steed. The introduction of the horse on the boundless prairies of the Far West changed the whole mode of living of their inhabitants. It gave them that facility of rapid motion, and of sudden and distant change of place, so dear to the roving propensities of man. Instead of lurking in the depths of gloomy forests, and patiently threading the mazes of a tangled wilderness on foot, like his brethren of the North, the Indian of the West is a rover of the plain; he leads a brighter and more sunshiny life, almost always on horseback, on vast flowery prairies and under cloudless skies.

I was lying by the Captain's fire, late in the evening, listening to stories about those coursers of the prairies, and weaving speculations of my own, when there was a clamor of voices and a loud cheering at the other end of the camp; and word was passed that Beatte, the half-breed,[6] had brought in a wild horse.

In an instant every fire was deserted; the whole camp crowded to see the Indian and his prize. It was a colt about two years old, well-grown, finely limbed, with bright prominent eyes and a spirited yet gentle demeanor. He gazed about him with an air of mingled stupefaction and surprise at the men, the horses, and the campfires; while the Indian stood before him with folded arms, having hold of the other end of the cord which noosed his captive, and gazing on him with a most imperturbable aspect. If the horse, however, manifested the least restiveness, Beatte would immediately worry him with the lariat, jerking him first on one side, then on the other, so as almost to throw him on the ground; when he had thus rendered him passive, he would resume his statuelike attitude and gaze at him in silence.

The whole scene was singularly wild: the tall grove, partially illumined by the flashing fires of the camp, the horses tethered here and there among the trees, the carcasses of deer hanging around, and in the midst of all, the wild huntsman and his wild horse, with an admiring throng of rangers, almost as wild.

In the eagerness of their excitement, several of the young rangers sought to get the horse by purchase or barter, and even offered extravagant terms; but Beatte declined all their offers. "You give great price now," said he; "tomorrow you be sorry, and take back."

The young men importuned him with questions about the mode in which he took the horse, but his answers were dry and laconic; he evidently looked down upon them with contempt as greenhorns, little versed in the noble science of woodcraft.

Afterwards, however, when he was seated by our fire, I readily drew from him an account of his exploit; for, though taciturn among strangers and little prone to boast of his actions, yet his taciturnity, like that of all Indians, had its times of relaxation.

He informed me that on leaving the camp he had returned to the place where we had lost sight of the wild horse. Soon getting upon its track, he followed it to the banks of the river. Here, the prints being more distinct in the sand, he perceived that one of the hoofs was broken and defective, so he gave up the pursuit.

As he was returning to the camp, he came upon a gang of six horses, which immediately made for the river. He pursued them across the stream, left his rifle on the river bank, and, putting his horse to full speed, soon came up with the fugitives. He attempted to noose one of them, but the lariat hitched on one of his ears, and he shook it off. The horses dashed up a hill, he followed hard at their heels, when, of a sudden, he saw their tails whisking in the air, and they plunging down a precipice. It was too late to stop. He shut his eyes, held in his breath, and went over with them—neck or nothing. The descent was between twenty and thirty feet, but they all came down safe upon a sandy bottom.

---

[5]*Mahomet* (mə hom′it) *and his warlike disciples.* Mohammed (Mahomet) founded Islam (is′ləm), or the Mohammedan religion, in Arabia in the seventh century and encouraged his disciples to use force against those who would not accept its doctrines.

[6]*Beatte* (bā ät′), *the half-breed*, an interpreter hired by the party. Irving says Beatte was of French and Osage parentage, and often refers to him as "the Indian," but Beatte himself claimed to be all French.

He now succeeded in throwing his noose around a fine young horse. As he galloped alongside of him, the two horses passed each side of a sapling, and the end of the lariat was jerked out of his hand. He regained it, but an intervening tree obliged him again to let it go. Having once more caught it, and coming to a more open country, he was enabled to play the young horse with the line until he gradually checked and subdued him, so as to lead him to the place where he had left his rifle.

He had another formidable difficulty in getting him across the river, where both horses stuck for a time in the mire, and Beatte was nearly unseated from his saddle by the force of the current and the struggles of his captive. After much toil and trouble, however, he got across the stream, and brought his prize safe into camp.

For the remainder of the evening, the camp remained in a high state of excitment; nothing was talked of but the capture of wild horses. Every youngster of the troop was for this harum-scarum kind of chase; everyone promised himself to return from the campaign in triumph, bestriding one of these wild coursers of the prairies. Beatte had suddenly risen to great importance; he was the prime hunter, the hero of the day. Offers were made him by the best-mounted rangers to let him ride their horses in the chase provided he would give them a share of the spoil. Beatte bore his honors in silence, and closed with none of the offers. Our stammering, chattering, gasconading little Frenchman,[7] however, made up for his taciturnity, by vaunting as much upon the subject as if it were he that had caught the horse. Indeed he held forth so learnedly in the matter, and boasted so much of the many horses he had taken, that he began to be considered an oracle; and some of the youngsters were inclined to doubt whether he were not superior even to the taciturn Beatte.

The excitement kept the camp awake later than usual. The hum of voices, interrupted by occasional peals of laughter, was heard from the groups around the various fires, and the

---

[7]*Frenchman,* Antoine Deshetres (än twän′ dez etr′), called Tonish by Irving. He had been hired by the party in St. Louis to act as guide and interpreter.

night was considerably advanced before all had sunk to sleep.

With the morning dawn the excitement revived, and Beatte and his wild horse were again the gaze and talk of the camp. The captive had been tied all night to a tree among the other horses. He was again led forth by Beatte, by a long halter or lariat, and, on his manifesting the least restiveness, was, as before, jerked and worried into passive submission. He appeared to be gentle and docile by nature, and had a beautifully mild expression of the eye. In his strange and forlorn situation, the poor animal seemed to seek protection and companionship in the very horse which had aided to capture him.

Seeing him thus gentle and tractable, Beatte, just as we were about to march, strapped a light pack upon his back, by way of giving him the first lesson in servitude. The native pride and independence of the animal took fire at this indignity. He reared, and plunged, and kicked, and tried in every way to get rid of the degrading burden. The Indian was too potent for him. At every paroxysm he renewed the discipline of the halter, until the poor animal, driven to despair, threw himself prostrate on the ground, and lay motionless, as if acknowledging himself vanquished. A stage hero, representing the despair of a captive prince, could not have played his part more dramatically. There was absolutely a moral grandeur in it.

The imperturbable Beatte folded his arms, and stood for a time looking down in silence upon his captive; until seeing him perfectly subdued, he nodded his head slowly, screwed his mouth into a sardonic smile of triumph, and, with a jerk of the halter, ordered him to rise. He obeyed, and from that time forward offered no resistance. During that day he bore his pack patiently, and was led by the halter; but in two days he followed voluntarily at large among the supernumerary horses of the troop.

I could not but look with compassion upon this fine young animal, whose whole course of existence had been so suddenly reversed. From being a denizen of these vast pastures, ranging at will from plain to plain and mead to mead, cropping of every herb and flower, and drinking of every stream, he was suddenly reduced to perpetual and painful servitude, to pass his life under the harness and the curb, amid, perhaps, the din and dust and drudgery of cities. The transition in his lot was such as sometimes takes place in human affairs and in the fortunes of towering individuals—one day, a prince of the prairies—the next day, a pack horse!

CONCERNING WASHINGTON IRVING

1. What circumstances led Irving to go to Spain? What books resulted from his Spanish sojourn?

2. What were Irving's weaknesses as historian and biographer? What were his strong points? Why are the books of Irving's last years on the whole less important than his earlier writings?

CONCERNING "THE CAMP OF THE WILD HORSE"

1. Why were the stories of the famous gray horse told around the campfire particularly likely to appeal to Irving?

2. In what way do the three paragraphs beginning with "The capture of the wild horse..." (page 353, column 2, paragraph 1) prepare the reader to understand what follows?

3. Select the descriptions that give you the most vivid pictures of Beatte; of the captured horse.

4. How do Irving's personality and his feelings become evident in this selection? Would you say that here Irving is still the romantic writer? Explain your answer.

5. In what ways is this selection representative of Irving's last period?

The Larger View

I. Each of the following passages is by Franklin or Irving. Who wrote each passage? How is each passage characteristic of its author?

1. The fondness for rural life among the higher classes of the English has had a great and salutary effect upon the national character. I do not know a finer race of men than the English gentlemen. Instead of the softness and effeminacy which characterize the men of rank in most countries, they exhibit a union of elegance and strength, a robustness of frame and freshness of complexion, which I am inclined to attribute to their living so much in the open air, and pursuing so eagerly the invigorating recreations of the country. These hardy exercises produce also a healthful tone of mind and spirits, and a manliness and simplicity of manners, which even the follies and dissipations of the town cannot easily pervert, and can never entirely destroy. In the country, too, the different orders of society seem to approach more freely, to be more disposed to blend and operate favorably upon each other.

2. There was a salt marsh that bounded part of the millpond, on the edge of which, at high water, we used to stand to fish for minnows. By much trampling, we had made it a mere quagmire. My proposal was to build a wharf there fit for us to stand upon, and I showed my comrades a large heap of stones, which were intended for a new house near the marsh, and which would very well suit our purpose. Accordingly, in the evening, when the workmen were gone, I assembled a number of my playfellows, and working with them diligently like so many emmets, sometimes two or three to a stone, we brought them all away and built our little wharf. The next morning the workmen were surprised at missing the stones, which were found in our wharf. Inquiry was made after the removers; we were discovered and complained of; several of us were corrected by our fathers; and, though I pleaded the usefulness of the work, mine convinced me that nothing was useful which was not honest.

3. How full of interest everything is connected with the old times in Spain! I am more and more delighted with the old literature of the country, its chronicles, plays, and romances. It has the wild vigor and luxuriance of the forests of my native country, which, however savage and entangled, are more captivating to imagination than the finest parks and cultivated woodlands.

II. Talk over the following questions with your classmates. Use any ideas you have gained in outside reading to enrich the discussion.

1. Using the ideas of romanticism in literature you have gained in studying Irving, decide which of the following selections might be considered romantic: "A Test of Fortitude," by James Fenimore Cooper (page 62); "The Leader of the People," by John Steinbeck (page 82); "Four Generations," by Ruth Suckow (page 112); "The Gray Champion," by Nathaniel Hawthorne (page 182); and "A Tooth for Paul Revere," by Stephen Vincent Benét (page 206). Be ready to defend your answers.

2. How permanent is Irving's appeal? In other words, do you find his writings are still interesting and readable? In your opinion which of Irving's works will be read longest? Why do you think so?

3. What qualities do you find to be consistent in Irving's work?

MORE GOOD READING

BENÉT, LAURA, *Washington Irving, Explorer of American Legend.* (Dodd) This is an account of Irving's boyhood in old New York, his carefree youth, and his first trip to Europe. It presents an interesting picture of young Irving.

BROOKS, VAN WYCK, *The World of Washington Irving.* (Dutton) The America of Irving's time from New England to the South and the opening West are all brilliantly drawn. Here also are Irving's contemporary men of letters, Cooper and Poe. Read all of it or pick out a chapter.

COLVER, ANNE, *Theodosia, Daughter of Aaron Burr.* (Rinehart) Theodosia Burr was born in New York the same year as Irving. She was eleven when her mother died, and Theodosia assumed the position of lady of the manor. Girls will enjoy this sympathetic biography.

COOPER, JAMES FENIMORE, *The Deerslayer.* (Scribner) While Irving concerned himself with legends of Europe and Colonial America, Cooper was writing his novels about the Indians of New York State. *The Deerslayer* introduces Natty Bumppo, or Hawkeye, one of the most famous characters in American fiction. *The Last of the Mohicans* (Scribner), which continues the story, is even more exciting.

HELLMAN, GEORGE S., *Washington Irving, Esqr.* (Knopf) Mature readers will enjoy this biography, which presents Irving's full life in a readable, easy manner. The facsimiles of Irving's letters and manuscripts add an extra interest.

IRVING, WASHINGTON, *Alhambra; Palace of Mystery and Splendor;* Tales selected and arranged by Mabel Williams. (Macmillan) If you, like Irving, are charmed by old legends and exotic places, you will find pleasure in these beautifully written tales of an old Moorish palace.

IRVING, WASHINGTON, *The Bold Dragoon and Other Ghostly Tales;* selected and edited by A. C. Moore. (Knopf) The five short stories included are among the best stories of the supernatural ever written.

IRVING, WASHINGTON, *Knickerbocker's History of New York;* edited by A. C. Moore. (Doubleday) The editor has removed the passages which slow down the narrative; what remains is the best of Irving's sparkling account of old New York. For sheer fun study the Daugherty illustrations.

IRVING, WASHINGTON, *The Sketch Book of Geoffrey Crayon, Gent.* (Putnam) If by any chance you haven't read "Rip Van Winkle," "The Spectre Bridegroom," and "The Legend of Sleepy Hollow," read them now. Some of the world's most famous stories came from Irving's *Sketch Book.*

POE, EDGAR ALLAN, *Tales;* with an introduction by Hervey Allen. (Random) The best stories of Irving's contemporary from the South are collected here. You can choose mystery or horror—or both.

PROUDFIT, ISABEL, *James Fenimore Cooper.* (Messner) Cooper's life and interests differed greatly from Irving's. You'll enjoy this biography of an author who lived at the edge of the wilderness and immortalized men of action in his stories.

THE EARLY NATIONAL PERIOD

LITERATURE	HISTORICAL EVENTS	
	Washington reëlected President	1792
	Eli Whitney invented the cotton gin	1793
1796 George Washington, "Farewell Address"		
1800 Mason Weems, *Life of Washington*		
1801 *Evening Post* established by Alexander Hamilton	Jefferson inaugurated third President	1801
	Louisiana purchased from Napoleon for $15,000,000	1803
	Lewis and Clark Expedition set out for the Northwest	
1807 Washington Irving and others, *Salmagundi*	Robert Fulton demonstrated his steamboat on the Hudson River	1807
	Embargo Act prohibited all ships from leaving American ports	
1808 William Cullen Bryant, *The Embargo*		
1809 Washington Irving, *Knickerbocker's History of New York*		
	United States declared war on Great Britain	1812
	Washington captured by the British	1814
	Treaty of Ghent ended War of 1812	
1815 Philip Freneau, *Poems on American Affairs*		
1817 William Cullen Bryant, "Thanatopsis"	First steamship crossed the Atlantic Ocean in 26 days	1818
1819 Washington Irving, *The Sketch Book*	Florida acquired from Spain	1819
	Missouri Compromise adopted	1820
1821 William Cullen Bryant, *Poems*		
James Fenimore Cooper, *The Spy*		
1822 Washington Irving, *Bracebridge Hall*		
James Fenimore Cooper, *The Pilot*		
1824 Washington Irving, *Tales of a Traveller*		
	Erie Canal completed	1825
1826 James Fenimore Cooper, *Last of the Mohicans*	Thomas Jefferson and John Adams, last surviving signers of the Declaration of Independence, died	1826
1827 Edgar Allan Poe, *Tamerlane and Other Poems*		
1828 Noah Webster, *American Dictionary of the English Language*		
Washington Irving, *Life and Voyages of Columbus*		
1829 Edgar Allan Poe, *Al Aaraaf, Tamerlane, and Minor Poems*	Andrew Jackson inaugurated seventh President	1829
Washington Irving, *Conquest of Granada*		

Washington Irving   1783-1859

358

SOME PROMINENT WRITERS OF THE EARLY NATIONAL PERIOD

WILLIAM CULLEN BRYANT, 1794-1878

Bryant, the son of a country doctor, was born in a village in western Massachusetts. His first verses appeared in a newspaper when he was ten; "Thanatopsis" (see pages 551-552) was written at seventeen; and its publication in 1817 made its author famous. By this time young Bryant was already a successful lawyer who composed poetry in his spare time. In 1821 the publication of a small volume—*Poems*—formed a landmark in American literary history. Four years later Bryant deserted Massachusetts for New York and the certainties of law for the uncertainties of a literary life. He soon went to work for the *Evening Post,* a newspaper which had been founded by Alexander Hamilton. In 1829 he became its editor-in-chief, and from then until his death in 1878 he was first of all the editor of this newspaper—a great, liberal editor known for his fearless championship of what he believed right. Throughout his life he continued to write poetry, although not in great quantity, and he translated the *Iliad* and the *Odyssey.* Succeeding generations of Americans will remember him as both an influential newspaper editor and one of the first of our great poets.

JAMES FENIMORE COOPER, 1789-1851

James Fenimore Cooper, the son of a wealthy landowner, grew up in the frontier community of Cooperstown on Otsego Lake in central New York. He was sent away to school—first in Albany and then at Yale College. Expelled from Yale in 1806, he first shipped to England as a common seaman, then served as a midshipman in the United States Navy. He married, settled down, and, at thirty, was a gentleman farmer and a capitalist, but had shown no inclination toward authorship. According to tradition he turned to writing when, reading aloud to his wife a story of English country life, he remarked he could do as well himself. His first novel, based on English models, was not very good, but his second attempt, *The Spy* (1821), a Revolutionary War novel, was enormously successful. Like Irving, Cooper was influenced by Sir Walter Scott. His greatest novels, the Leatherstocking Tales, placed heroic characters against a wild and romantic background. In Natty Bumppo, frontiersman hero of *The Last of the Mohicans, The Deerslayer* (see "A Test of Fortitude" on pages 62-70), and other novels, he created one of the greatest characters in American fiction. His sea tales such as *The Red Rover* and *The Pilot* were almost equally successful. No one disputes his claim to fame as the first great American novelist.

PHILIP FRENEAU, 1752-1832

Freneau, who was born a quarter century before the Revolution and died during Jackson's term as President, bridges the gap between the Colonial and Early National Periods. A wealthy youth, Freneau was educated at Princeton. During the Revolutionary War he served both in the militia and as a blockade runner. His wartime experiences left him with a fierce hatred of the British which inspired him to write ballads and satirical pieces and won him the title "poet of the American Revolution." After the war Freneau went to sea again, but he continued to write, and in 1786 *The Poems of Philip Freneau* was published. In 1790 he married and turned to newspaper work. As founder and editor of the *National Gazette* he became a powerful spokesman for Jefferson's political ideas. During the rest of his long life he worked on other newspapers, returned to sea again, and continued to write poetry. He is remembered today as a ballad writer, a journalist, and, principally, as the first American poet to discover the beauties in the everyday world and the appeal of the Indian as a subject for verse.

EDGAR ALLAN POE, 1809-1849

Poe, the son of a wandering theatrical family, was orphaned at the age of two. Taken into the home of John Allan, a wealthy merchant of Richmond, Virginia, he was brought up as the pampered son of the family. After attending school in England and Richmond, he entered the University of Virginia. But friction which had begun earlier between the brilliant but moody boy and his foster father grew greater, and within a year he was withdrawn from the university. He served briefly in the army, entered West Point but was soon dismissed, and in 1832 broke finally with Mr. Allan. Poe had by this time published three volumes of poetry—none very successful financially. Now, driven to make a living by his pen, he turned to writing prose tales and later to editing magazines. His tales won him some measure of fame; he was acknowledged a brilliant editor; and by 1845 when *The Raven and Other Poems* (see "The Raven," pages 554-557) was published, even his poetry had won wide popularity. But Poe's pride, his fiery temper, and his emotional outbreaks kept him moving from one magazine to another, and in spite of critical acclaim he still lacked money. In 1835 he had married his cousin—fragile, thirteen-year-old Virginia Clemm. She was never well, and until her death in 1847 Poe's life was a constant battle against her illness, his own emotional troubles, and poverty. He himself died under mysterious circumstances two years later.

UNIT IX: HENRY DAVID THOREAU
(*representing* AMERICA'S "GOLDEN DAY")

THE DECADES just preceding the War Between the States were great ones in the history of American literature. Historians have called that period, when a number of our finest authors were in their prime, "America's Golden Day." A cantankerous and eccentric but very interesting writer, Henry David Thoreau,[1] who lived between 1817 and 1862, is a fine representative of that period.

One historian who wrote a book about our literature in those decades called his book *The Flowering of New England*. The title underlines the fact that New England, in those years, was clearly the literary and cultural capital of America. A surprisingly large number of our best authors were living and writing in New England—Henry Wadsworth Longfellow, James Russell Lowell, Oliver Wendell Holmes, Ralph Waldo Emerson, Richard Henry Dana, Francis Parkman, and Nathaniel Hawthorne, to name only a few. Thoreau was a New Englander, too; in fact, no man's roots dug deeper into Yankee earth, and no man was a more complete down-Easter than he.

The period was one during which two great interests were the world of nature and the world of human affairs. Throughout the world men were discovering new attractions and new meanings in the out-of-doors. And no one in those years or later enjoyed fields, forests, mountains, and streams more—or learned more from them—than Thoreau did. Also, the period was one during which men examined society and social institutions anew. And Thoreau had important things to say about what he considered the weaknesses of our social and political structure.

❧ I CRAFTSMAN AND WOODSMAN

Concord, Massachusetts, Thoreau's birthplace and his home through his whole lifetime, was a little country village. Thoreau was fond of it from the start. "I," he wrote at least half-seriously, "have never got over my surprise that I should have been born in the most estimable place in all the world, and in the very nick of time, too." Readers of Thoreau have noticed that he always was comparing other places, invariably to their disadvantage, with the wonderful town of Concord.

"I think," Thoreau said in 1841, when he was twenty-four, "I could write a poem to be called 'Concord.' For subject matter I should have

---

[1] *Thoreau* (thə rō′ *or* thō′rō).

the River, the Woods, the Ponds, the Hills, the Fields, the Swamps and Meadows, the Streets and Buildings, and the Villagers. Then Morning, Noon, and Evening, Spring, Summer, Autumn, and Winter, Night, Indian Summer, and the Mountains in the Horizon." As his outline shows, Thoreau was particularly fond of the world of nature that was an easy distance from any Concord doorway. In his boyhood, he enjoyed exploring the thick woods and the old orchards nearby. He enjoyed hunting hares, partridges, and wild pigeons in the forests, shore birds in the water meadows and swamps, muskrats and ducks along the river. Swimming and boating by day, spearing fish by torchlight at night, he appreciated the rivers which flowed through the town. In winter, he liked to skate on the ice-filled streams and ponds, and he enjoyed sledding so much that he once said he would miss it in heaven.

Four years of study at Harvard followed by graduation in 1837 did not lessen Thoreau's affection for the out-of-doors or for the home town to which he promptly returned. Now a somewhat more scientific interest in nature supplemented his instinctive enjoyment of it. His sister, Sophia, the family botanist, introduced him to the study of plants. His brother, John, who over the years had compiled a long list of Concord birds, passed along the list for Henry to study. Thus started the growth of a knowledge of the flowers, birds, and animals around Concord which in time was to surpass that of both Sophia and John.

This interest in the world of nature was important in the new school which John and Henry Thoreau founded in Concord in 1838. The school was a most unusual one for those strict times, because its two teachers did not think that children should be flogged. ("I," said Thoreau, "have always regarded cowhide as a nonconductor.") The hope was that students would like school so well that discipline would not be necessary—and the hope was realized. The brothers took part in the sports of the students, and led them on field trips during which they studied flowers, birds, and animals, and even at times did some surveying. The school closed in 1841 because of John's poor health (he died shortly after), but it was long remembered as a pioneering experiment pointing the way toward twentieth-century ideas about education.

Thoreau, looking for a new way to earn a livelihood, sought for one which would give him as much time out-of-doors as possible. College graduate though he was, he liked white-collar work less than open-air manual labor. Further, he had real talent for such work. A friend and neighbor, Ralph Waldo Emerson, himself awkward with any tools, never

could stop admiring Thoreau's amazing skills. "There was a wonderful fitness," he wrote, "of body and mind. He could pace sixteen rods more accurately than another man could measure them with rod and chain....He could estimate the measure of a tree very well by his eye; he could estimate the weight of a calf or a pig, like a dealer. From a box containing a bushel or more of loose pencils, he could take up with his hands fast enough just a dozen pencils at every grasp."

Such a gifted worker found that he could get all the work he wanted, but he did not work steadily at any one chore. Because he liked variety, he did jobs of many sorts. In answer to an inquiry from a classmate in 1847 about his occupation, he wrote airily: "I don't know whether mine is a profession, or a trade, or what not. I am a Schoolmaster, a private Tutor, a Surveyor, a Gardener, a Farmer, a Painter (I mean a House Painter), a Carpenter, a Mason, a Day Laborer, a Pencil Maker, a Glass-paper Maker, a Writer, and sometimes a Poetaster."

Actually, Thoreau did work, whenever he needed money for his simple wants, in many different capacities. To cite a few examples: Surveyor Thoreau marked off boundaries and drew several good maps of Concord which still survive. Mason Thoreau built walls, some of which stand today. Pencil-maker Thoreau manufactured a product which won prizes at an exposition. Carpenter and Gardener Thoreau was a handy man around the Emerson household.

But this versatile workman dropped his tools and became his own master whenever he could afford it, in order that he might have afternoons, nights, or whole days at a time to study and enjoy the world of nature. He was no longer a hunter in the usual sense as he walked about the neighboring countryside. Now he left his gun behind and studied animals as they lived rather than as they died. He carried a box in which to press and preserve plants; he had a field glass and a magnifying glass and a big knife. Sometimes he traveled by boat, on the Assabet River or the wider Concord River. More often he walked, moving along the edges of the marshes, slogging through the swamps, exploring the hill and lake regions—always on the alert to discover what went on in that wild world.

Those who saw Thoreau in the fields and forests felt that he was as much at home there as most people were in their parlors. He put on the proper dress for any kind of terrain or weather. His homespun coat and pants withstood the scratches of brambles and the tears of scrub oak. According to the weather, he wore heavy cowhide boots, light boots, or rubber boots. Although he was a thin little man, he was tough and muscular: his hands were strong and nimble, and his legs were sturdy. "When he walked to get over the ground," said a neighbor, "one thought of a tireless machine." There was an almost animal-like sharpness to his senses. His gray-blue eyes, peering out from under bushy brows, were unusually keen. They could distinguish the tiniest insects among the plants and dead leaves on the ground. He had a giant Roman nose which was as efficient as it was impressive. Whenever he picked a plant, he liked to sniff it long enough to make its scent a part of his acquaintance with it. His sense of hearing and his sense of touch were equally keen.

Emerson, impressed though he was by Thoreau's "most adapted and serviceable body," was equally impressed—as others were—by the wisdom he acquired on his wide-ranging explorations. "He knew the country like a fox or a bird," said Emerson, "and passed through it as freely by paths of his own." Emerson told how, in the spring, Thoreau could predict to the day when each wild flower would be in bloom. "Snakes coiled around his leg," Emerson testified; "the fishes swam into his hand, and he took them out of the water; he pulled the woodchuck out of his hole by the tail and took the foxes under his protection from the hunters."

In Thoreau's day, many authors were writing fine literature about nature—William Wordsworth, Samuel Taylor Coleridge, John Keats, and Alfred Lord Tennyson in England, William Cullen Bryant, Ralph Waldo Emerson, and James Russell Lowell in New England. Thoreau was outstanding as a writer on nature even in such a group. His writings are a good substitute for a trip into the fields, partly because they make nature very real to us, partly because they direct our attention to details in the scene which only such a keen explorer could discover, partly because they convey to us the joy which Thoreau himself experienced as he made his many field trips. "Henry," said one Concord housewife, "talks about Nature just as if she'd been born and brought up in Concord." The following passages are typical.

Chasing a Fox

THE FASHIONS of the wood are more fluctuating than those of Paris. Snow, rime, ice, green and dry leaves incessantly make new patterns. There are all the shapes and hues of the kaleidoscope, and the designs and ciphers of books of heraldry,[1] in the outline of the trees. Every time I see a nodding pine top, it seems as if a new fashion of wearing plumes had come into vogue.

You glance up these paths, closely embraced by bent trees, as through the side aisles of a cathedral, and expect to hear a choir chanting from their depths. You are never so far in them as they are far before you. Their secret is where you are not, and where your feet can never carry you.

Fair Haven pond is scored with the trails of foxes, and you may see where they have gam-

boled and gone through a hundred evolutions, which testify to a singular listlessness and leisure in nature....Suddenly looking down the river, I saw a fox some sixty rods off, making across the hills on my left. As the snow lay five inches deep, he made but slow progress, but it was no impediment to me. So, yielding to the instinct of the chase, I tossed my head aloft, and bounded away, snuffing the air like a foxhound, and spurning the world and human society at each bound. It seemed the woods rang with the hunter's horn, and Diana and all the satyrs[2] joined in the chase and cheered me on.

In the meanwhile I gained rapidly on the fox, but he showed a remarkable presence of mind, for instead of keeping up the face of the hill, which was steep and unwooded in that part, he kept along the slope in the direction of the forest, though he lost ground by it. Notwithstanding his fright, he took no step which was not beautiful. The course on his part was a series of most graceful curves. It was a sort of leopard canter, I should say, as if he were

[1]*designs...books of heraldry.* Books of heraldry are collections of the various designs and symbolic characters (ciphers) that in earlier ages were used as a mark of identification on shields, carriages, etc., by members of the nobility.

[2]*Diana and all the satyrs.* Diana was the Roman goddess of the hunt. The satyrs were Greek gods of the woods who were part man and part beast.

nowise impeded by the snow, but were husbanding his strength all the while. When he doubled, I wheeled and cut him off, bounding with fresh vigor, Antaeus-like,[3] recovering my strength each time I touched the snow. Having got near enough for a fair view, just as he was slipping into the wood, I gracefully yielded him the palm.[4] He ran as if there were not a bone in his back, occasionally dropping his muzzle to the snow for a rod or two, and then tossing his head aloft, when satisfied of his course. When he came to a declivity, he put his forefeet together and slid down it like a cat. He trod so softly that you could not have heard from any nearness, and yet with such expression that it would not have been quite inaudible at any distance. So hoping this experience would prove a useful lesson to him, I returned to the village by the highway of the river.

[3]*Antaeus-like*, like the giant Antaeus (an tē′əs), whose strength was renewed whenever he touched the earth. According to Greek legend, Hercules strangled him by lifting him high in the air.

[4]*yielded him the palm*, admitted defeat by him. The palm leaf is a symbol of victory.

~

The Battle of the Ants

O NE DAY when I went out to my woodpile, or rather my pile of stumps, I observed two large ants, the one red, the other much larger, nearly half an inch long, and black, fiercely contending with one another. Having once got hold, they never let go, but struggled and wrestled and rolled on the chips incessantly. Looking farther, I was surprised to find the chips were covered with such combatants—that it was not a *duellum,* but a *bellum,*[1] a war between two races of ants, the red always pitted against the black, and frequently two red ones to one black. The legions of these Myrmidons[2]

[1]*not a "duellum"* (dü el′əm) *but a "bellum"* (bel′əm), not merely a duel between two contestants but a war between many.

[2]*Myrmidons* (mèr′mi donz), warriors of ancient Thessaly, according to Greek legend. Thoreau compares the warring ants to these ancient fighters.

covered all the hills and vales in my woodyard, and the ground was already strewn with the dead and dying, both red and black.

It was the only battle which I have ever witnessed, the only battlefield I ever trod while the battle was raging; internecine war; the red republicans on the one hand, and the black imperialists[3] on the other. On every side they were engaged in deadly combat, yet without any noise that I could hear, and human soldiers never fought so resolutely.

I watched a couple that were fast locked in each other's embraces, in a little sunny valley amid the chips, now at noonday prepared to fight till the sun went down, or life went out. The smaller red champion had fastened himself like a vise to his adversary's front, and through all the tumblings on that field never for an instant ceased to gnaw at one of his feelers near the root, having already caused the other to go by the board; while the stronger black one dashed him from side to side, and, as I saw on looking nearer, had already divested him of several of his members. They fought with more pertinacity than bulldogs. Neither manifested the least disposition to retreat. It was evident that their battle cry was "Conquer or die."

In the meanwhile there came along a single red ant on the hillside of this valley, evidently full of excitement, who either had dispatched his foe or had not yet taken part in the battle (probably the latter, for he had lost none of his limbs); whose mother had charged him to return with his shield or upon it.[4] Or perchance he was some Achilles, who had nourished his wrath apart, and had now come to avenge or rescue his Patroclus.[5] He saw this unequal com-

[3]*red republicans…black imperialists.* At the time this selection was published in 1854, Europe had recently undergone several revolutions in which the people of a number of countries had rebelled against their kings and emperors.

[4]*whose mother…with his shield or upon it.* According to tales of ancient Greece, this was the command given by Spartan mothers to their sons when the sons went off to war. It means: Die rather than surrender.

[5]*Achilles* (ə kil′ēz) …*Patroclus* (pə trō′kləs). Because of a quarrel with Agamemnon (ag′ə mem′non), the Greek commander-in-chief in the Trojan War, Achilles, one of the greatest fighters, sulked in his tent. But when he heard that his friend Patroclus had been killed, he hurried into the battle to avenge him.

bat from afar. He drew near with rapid pace till he stood on his guard within half an inch of the combatants; then, watching his opportunity, he sprang upon the black warrior, and commenced his operations near the root of his right foreleg, leaving the foe to select among his own members.

And so there were three united for life, as if a new kind of attraction had been invented which put all other locks and cements to shame. I should not have wondered by this time to find that they had their respective musical bands stationed on some eminent chip, and playing their national airs the while, to excite the slow and cheer the dying combatants. I was myself excited somewhat even as if they had been men. The more you think of it, the less the difference. And certainly there is not the fight recorded in Concord history,[6] at least, if in the history of America, that will bear a moment's comparison with this, whether for the numbers engaged in it, or for the patriotism and heroism displayed. For numbers and for carnage it was an Austerlitz[7] or Dresden.[8] Concord Fight! Two killed on the patriots' side,[9] and Luther Blanchard wounded! Why, here every ant was a Buttrick[10]—"Fire! for God's sake fire!"—and thousands shared the fate of Davis and Hosmer. There was not one hireling there. I have no doubt that it was a principle they fought for, as much as our ancestors, and not to avoid a three-penny tax on their tea[11]; and the results of this battle will be as important and memorable to those whom it concerns as those of the battle of Bunker Hill, at least.

I took up the chip on which the three I have particularly described were struggling, carried it into my house, and placed it under a tumbler on my window sill, in order to see the issue. Holding a microscope to the first-mentioned red ant, I saw that, though he was assiduously gnawing at the near foreleg of his enemy, having severed his remaining feeler, his own breast was all torn away, exposing what vitals he had there to the jaws of the black warrior, whose breast-plate was apparently too thick for him to pierce; and the dark carbuncles of the sufferer's eyes shone with ferocity such as war only could excite. They struggled half an hour longer under the tumbler, and when I looked again the black soldier had severed the heads of his foes from their bodies, and the still living heads were hanging on either side of him like ghastly trophies at his saddlebow, still apparently as firmly fastened as ever, and he was endeavoring with feeble struggles, being without feelers and with only the remnant of a leg, and I know not how many other wounds, to divest himself of them; which after half an hour more he accomplished.

I raised the glass, and he went off over the window sill in that crippled state. Whether he finally survived that combat, and spent the remainder of his days in some Hôtel des Invalides,[12] I do not know; but I thought that his industry would not be worth much thereafter. I never learned which party was victorious, nor the cause of the war; but I felt for the rest of that day as if I had had my feelings excited and harrowed by witnessing the struggle, the ferocity and carnage, of a human battle before my door.

---

[6]*the fight recorded in Concord history,* the second battle of the Revolutionary War, on April 19, 1775.

[7]*Austerlitz* (ôs'tər lits), battle fought in old Austria (now Czechoslovakia) where in 1805 Napoleon defeated the Russians and Austrians. Many thousands were killed.

[8]*Dresden,* the last of Napoleon's great victories, in which he defeated the Russian, Austrian, and Prussian forces in 1813. Dresden is in Germany.

[9]*Two killed on the patriots' side.* Thoreau is writing of the mid-morning fight at the North Bridge when the militia advanced and attacked the British on guard there. Two Americans, Captain Isaac Davis and a man named Hosmer (both mentioned below), were killed.

[10]*Buttrick,* the major in command of the Concord militia in the fight at the North Bridge.

[11]*a three-penny tax on their tea,* a reference to the Boston Tea Party and the colonists' objections to taxation without representation.

[12]*Hôtel des Invalides* (ō tel' dä zäɴ vä lēd'), a hospital in Paris for old or sick soldiers.

CONCERNING HENRY DAVID THOREAU

1. How did the fact that Thoreau grew up in a small town rather than in a city affect his interests as a man? What advantage did he take of the opportunities Concord and the surrounding country offered?

2. What features of the school John and Henry Thoreau founded were most unusual for that day? Can you give any reasons why you would like to attend such a school?

3. What were Thoreau's ideas on earning a living?

CONCERNING "CHASING A FOX" AND "THE BATTLE OF THE ANTS"

1. In paragraph 2 on page 363 you read: "[Thoreau's] writings are a good substitute for a trip into the fields, partly because they make nature very real to us, partly because they direct our attention to details in the scene which only such a keen explorer could discover, partly because they convey to us the joy which Thoreau himself experienced." Select details from the selections you have read which illustrate each part of this statement.

2. What details in "Chasing a Fox" show that Thoreau was very aware of beauty in nature?

3. Point out passages in "The Battle of the Ants" in which ants are compared to men. What does the nature of the comparisons imply about men? How does Thoreau's comparison help him convey his message effectively?

4. Thoreau was a scholar as well as a woodsman. What evidence of this do you find in the selections you have read?

Know your words

Since Thoreau often uses a common word in an unusual sense, we are likely to miss his meaning. Examine the sentence on page 365 in which he tells us that the three battling ants were "united for life, as if a new kind of *attraction* had been invented which put all other locks and cements to shame." Obviously, Thoreau is not using *attraction* in its usual sense of "that which allures." Turn to the Glossary or a dictionary and select the definition that does fit the context. Then reword the sentence, without using the word *attraction,* in such a way as to make it clear. Explain, too, why the following words are particularly appropriate in the sentence: *united, locks,* and *cement.*

❧ II HUMOROUS PHILOSOPHER

Thoreau's study of nature did not end with his merely perceiving and recording details in the lives of plants and animals; he had other interests. "All science," he wrote, "is merely a makeshift, a means to an end. All nature is to be regarded as it concerns man."

This attitude was one which many poets and philosophers shared in Thoreau's day and which many share in our day. The men of that time had a renewed interest in nature because they felt that if they could truly understand the deeper meaning of it, they could learn great philosophical truths. They tried as William Blake (1757-1827), the English poet, had recently tried,

> To see a world in a grain of sand,
> And a heaven in a wild flower;

or they believed, as Alfred Tennyson (1809-1892), another English poet, did, that one who understood "a flower in a crannied wall" would "know what God and man is." God, they reasoned, is everywhere. Therefore if a small detail were really apprehended, great insights would result. "A drop is a small ocean," said Thoreau's friend and neighbor, Emerson, and "A man is related to all nature." So Thoreau was interested in deeper meanings. "It is the subject of the vision, the truth alone, that concerns me," he wrote. "The philosopher for whom rainbows can be explained away never saw them. With regard to such objects, I find that it is not they themselves (with which the men of science deal) that concern me; the point of interest is somewhere *between* me and the rainbows."

Thoreau, in other words, was rather more a philosopher than he was a scientist. Like most good philosophers, he had some ideas which were hard to communicate. Chiefly these ideas concern the relationship between nature and goodness and truth. These difficult ideas are not unusual ones: they are shared by many people who believe that God is everywhere—in the world of mountains, forests, rivers, and lakes as well as in men's hearts.

But though Philosopher Thoreau had as hard a time as anybody else explaining these mystical ideas, he managed to make many of his unusual ideas extraordinarily easy (for philosophical ideas) to understand. He made a special effort to write clearly: he hated big words and sloppy sentences. "It is on the whole better," he wrote, "as it is simpler, to use the common language." Furthermore, because this Yankee craftsman and woodsman was such a practical man, he hardly ever disappeared from the view of the ordinary reader in a cloud of generalities. Even his most profound writings were those of a man who planted his hobnail boots firmly on the Concord earth and refused to try to fly.

Thoreau was also helped as a writer by the fact that he was a humorist. His face was solemn, but his gray-blue eyes had a distinct twinkle in them. "There was a lurking humor in almost all that he said," a close associate testified. The elfish humor entered, too, into almost everything he wrote: it emphasized important points, added interest, and helped clarify Thoreau's ideas.

The humor ranged from the lowest levels to the highest. He loved puns and plays upon words. "Hard are the times," he wrote, "when the infant's shoes are *second-foot.*" Again, complaining about the discomforts of travel, "[Railway] *cars,*" he said, "sound like *cares* to me." He loved paradoxes, for instance: "The poor rich man! all he has is what he has bought. What I see is mine." Again: "When the farmer has got his house, he may not be the richer but the poorer for it, and it may be the house that has got him." He was good at using comic figures of speech, as in "His face expressed no more curiosity than a custard pudding," or "The chub is a soft fish, and tastes like boiled brown paper salted." He often used dry logic well, for instance: "Some circumstantial evidence is very strong, as when you find a trout in the milk," or "I went to the store the other day to buy a bolt for our front door, for, as I told the storekeeper, the Governor was coming here to Concord. 'Aye,' said he, 'and the Legislature too.' 'Then I will take two bolts,' said I."

But Thoreau's best humor pointed to his own foibles or to those of his neighbors, brute and human: it was the humor not of words or of logic but of character. Like a joking farmer, he often pretends to be simpleminded—to say sharp things entirely by accident. "I should not talk so much about myself," he wrote once, for instance, "if there were anybody else whom I know as well. Unfortunately, I am confined to this theme by the narrowness of my experience." Again he tells how once, when he was sitting by a pond, thinking deep philosophical thoughts, a friend came by and asked him to go fishing. Thoreau, so he says, told the friend, "I will go with you gladly soon, but I am just concluding a serious meditation. I think I am near the end of it. Leave me alone, then, for a while. But that we may not be delayed, you shall be digging the bait meanwhile." His sense of humor thus passes a hard test: he manages to laugh even at himself.

Like other Yankee humorists, Thoreau saw not only his own peculiar quirks but also those of his neighbors. Animals at times amused him because they had all-too-human traits, and he wrote of them in ways which communicated their laughable qualities. Constantly, too, he noticed and set down funny, unusual, or interesting details about people whom he met. The following passages from Thoreau's journals show him in his rôle of a philosopher with an eye for the humorous eccentricities of his fellow men.

Miss Mary Emerson

Nov. 13

JUST SPENT a couple of hours (eight to ten) with Miss Mary Emerson[1] at Holbrook's; the wittiest and most vivacious woman that I know, certainly that woman among my acquaintance whom it is most profitable to meet, the least frivolous, who will most surely provoke to good conversation. She is singular, among women at least, in being really and perseveringly interested to know what thoughtful people think. She relates herself surely to the intellectual wherever she goes.

It is perhaps her greatest praise and peculiarity that she, more surely than any other woman, gives her companion occasion to utter his best thought. In spite of her own biases, she can entertain a large thought with hospitality, and is not prevented by any intellectuality in it, as women commonly are.

In short, she is a genius, as woman seldom is, reminding you less often of her sex than any woman whom I know. Thus she is capable of a masculine appreciation of poetry and philosophy. I never talked with any other woman who I thought accompanied me so far in describing a poetic experience. Miss Fuller[2] is the only woman I think of in this connection, and of her[3]

rather from her fame than from my knowledge of her.

Miss Emerson expressed tonight a singular want of respect for her own sex, saying that they were frivolous, almost without exception, that woman was the weaker vessel, etc.; and that into whatever family she might go, she depended more upon the clown[4] for society than upon the lady of the house. Men are more likely to have opinions of their own.

Just in proportion to the outward poverty is the inward wealth. In cold weather fire burns with a clearer flame.

---

[4]*the clown,* the rude or uncultured member of the family.

⤜

I Attend a Party

Nov. 14

IN THE EVENING I went to a party. It is a bad place to go—thirty or forty persons, mostly young women, in a small room, warm and noisy. Was introduced to two young women. The first was as lively and loquacious as a chickadee, had been accustomed to the society of watering places, and therefore could get no refreshment out of such a dry fellow as I. The other was said to be pretty-looking, but I rarely look people in their faces, and, moreover, I could not hear what she said, there was such a clacking—could only see the motion of her lips when I looked that way. I could imagine better places for conversation, where there should be

---

[1]*Miss Mary Emerson,* an aunt of Ralph Waldo Emerson. She had a greater influence on Emerson's moral and intellectual development than any of his teachers. At the time Thoreau describes her she was seventy-six years old.

[2]*Miss Fuller,* Margaret Fuller (1810-1850), one of the most intellectual and scholarly of American women. Even more brilliant as a conversationalist than as a writer, she was an associate of Emerson and of the literary group in Concord and Boston.

[3]*and of her,* and I think of her.

a certain degree of silence surrounding you, and less than forty talking at once.

Why, this afternoon even I did better. Old Mr. Joseph Hosmer and I ate luncheon of cracker and cheese together in the woods. I heard all he said, though it was not much, to be sure, and he could hear me; and then he talked out of such a glorious repose, taking a leisurely bite at the cracker and cheese between his words, and so some of him was communicated to me, and some of me to him, I trust.

These parties, I think, are a part of the machinery of modern society, that young people may be brought together to form marriage connections.

What is the use in going to see people whom yet you never see, and who never see you?

I Chase a Pig

Aug. 8, 3:30 P.M.

WHEN I CAME FORTH, thinking to empty my boat and go a-meditating along the river—for the full ditches and drenched grass forbade other routes, except the highway—and this is one advantage of a boat—I learned to my chagrin that Father's pig was gone. He had leaped out of the pen some time since his breakfast, but his dinner was untouched. Here was an ugly duty not to be shirked—a wild shoat that weighed but ninety to be tracked, caught, and penned—an afternoon's work, at least (if I were lucky enough to accomplish it so soon), prepared for me, quite different from what I had anticipated. I felt chagrined, but I could not ignore the fact nor shirk the duty that lay so near to me. Do the duty that lies nearest to thee.

I proposed to Father to sell the pig as he was running (somewhere) to a neighbor who had talked of buying him, making a considerable reduction. But my suggestion was not acted on,

and the responsibilities of the case all devolved on me, for I could run faster than Father. Father looked to me, and I ceased to look to the river.

Well, let us see if we can track him. Yes, this is the corner where he got out, making a step of his trough. Thanks to the rain, his tracks are quite distinct. Here he went along the edge of the garden over the water- and muskmelons, then through the beans and potatoes, and even along the front-yard walk I detect the print of his divided hoof, his two sharp toes (*ungulæ*[1]). It's a wonder we did not see him. And here he passed out under the gate, across the road—how naked he must have felt!—into a grassy ditch, and whither next? Who knows how many miles off he is! Perhaps he has taken the back track and gone to Brighton,[2] or Ohio! At most, probably we shall only have the satisfaction of glimpsing the nimble beast at a distance, from time to time, as he trots swiftly through the green meadows and cornfields.

But, now I speak, what is that I see pacing deliberately up the middle of the street forty rods off? It is *he*. As if to tantalize, to tempt us to waste our afternoon without further hesitation, he thus offers himself. He roots a foot or two and then lies down on his belly in the middle of the street. But think not to catch him a-napping. He has his eyes about, and his ears too. He has already been chased. He gives that wagon a wide berth, and now, seeing me, he turns and trots back down the street. He turns into a front yard. Now if I can only close that gate upon him ninety-nine hundredths of the work is done; but ah! he hears me coming afar off, he foresees the danger, and, with swinish cunning, he scampers out. My neighbor in the street tries to head him; he jumps to this side the road, then to that, before him; but the third time the pig was there first and went by.

---

[1]*ungulæ* (ung′gū lē). This word for hoofed toes gives the name *ungulates* (ung′gū lātz) to the large group of mammals having hoofs.

[2]*Brighton*, in Thoreau's time a village near Boston, now part of the city.

"Whose is it?" he shouts.

"It's ours."

He bolts into that neighbor's yard and so across his premises. He has been twice there before, it seems; he knows the road; see what work he has made in his flower garden! He must be fond of bulbs. Our neighbor picks up one tall flower with its bulb attached, holds it out at arm's length. He is excited about the pig; it is a subject he is interested in. But where is he gone now? The last glimpse I had of him was as he went through the cow yard; here are his tracks again in this cornfield, but they are lost in the grass. We lose him; we beat the bushes in vain; he may be far away. But hark! I heard a grunt. Nevertheless for half an hour I do not see him that grunted. At last I find fresh tracks along the river, and again lose them.

Each neighbor whose garden I traverse tells me some anecdote of losing pigs, or the attempt to drive them, by which I am not encouraged. Once more he crosses our first neighbor's garden and is said to be in the road. But I am not there yet; it is a good way off. At length my eyes rest on him again, after three-quarters of an hour's separation. There he trots with the whole road to himself, and now again drops on his belly in a puddle. Now he starts again, seeing me twenty rods off, deliberates, considers which way I want him to go, and goes the other. There was some chance of driving him along the sidewalk, or letting him go rather, till he slipped under our gate again, but of what avail would that be? How corner and catch him who keeps twenty rods off? He never lets the open side of the triangle be less than a half a dozen rods wide. There was one place where a narrower street turned off at right angles with the main one, just this side our yard, but I could not drive him past that. Twice he ran up the narrow street, for he knew I did not wish it, but though the main street was broad and open and no traveler in sight, when I tried to drive him past this opening he invariably turned his piggish head toward me, dodged from side to side, and finally ran up the narrow street or down the main one, as if there were a high barrier erected before him.

But really he is no more obstinate than I. I cannot but respect his tactics and his independence. He will be he, and I may be I. He is not unreasonable because he thwarts me, but only the more reasonable. He has a strong will. He stands upon his idea. There is a wall across the path, not where a man bars the way, but where he is resolved not to travel. Is he not superior to man therein?

Once more he glides down the narrow street, deliberates at a corner, chooses wisely for him, and disappears through an openwork fence eastward.

At this stage an Irishman was engaged to assist. "I can catch him," says he, with Bonapartean confidence.[3] He thinks him a family Irish pig. His wife is with him, bareheaded, and his little flibbertigibbet of a boy, seven years old. "Here, Johnny, do you run right off there" (at the broadest possible angle with his own course).

"Oh, but he can't do anything."

"Oh, but I only want him to tell me where he is—to keep sight of him." Michael soon discovers that he is not an Irish pig, and his wife and Johnny's occupation are soon gone.

Ten minutes afterward I am patiently tracking him step by step through a cornfield, a nearsighted man helping me, and then into garden after garden far eastward, and finally into the highway, at the graveyard; but hear and see nothing. One suggests a dog to track him. Father is meanwhile selling him to the blacksmith, who also is trying to get sight of him.

After fifteen minutes since he disappeared eastward, I hear that he has been to the river twice far on the north, through the first neighbor's premises. I wend that way. He crosses the street far ahead, Michael behind; he dodges up an avenue. I stand in the gap there, Michael at the other end, and now he tries to corner him. But it is a vain hope to corner him in a yard. I see a carriage manufactory door open. "Let him go in there, Flannery." For once the pig and I are of one mind; he bolts in, and the door is closed. Now for a rope. It is a large barn, crowded with carriages. The rope is at length

---

[3]*Bonapartean* (bō′nə pär′ti ən) *confidence,* confidence like that of Napoleon Bonaparte, conqueror of most of Europe in the early nineteenth century.

obtained; the windows are barred with carriages lest he bolt through. He is resting quietly on his belly in the further corner, thinking unutterable things.

Now the course recommences within narrower limits. Bump, bump, bump he goes against wheels and shafts. We get no hold yet. He is all ear and eye. Small boys are sent under the carriages to drive him out. He froths at the mouth and deters them. At length he is stuck for an instant between the spokes of a wheel, and I am securely attached to his hind leg. He squeals deafeningly, and is silent. The rope is attached to a hind leg. The door is opened, and the *driving* commences. Roll an egg as well. You may drag him, but you cannot drive him. But he is in the road, and now a thundershower greets us. I leave Michael with the rope in one hand and a switch in the other and go home. He seems to be gaining a little westward. But, after long delay, I look out and find that he makes but doubtful progress. A boy is made to face him with a stick, and it is only when the pig springs at him savagely that progress is made homeward. He will be killed before he is driven home. I get a wheelbarrow and go to the rescue. Michael is alarmed. The pig is rabid, snaps at him. We drag him across the barrow, hold him down, and so, at last, get him home. I am wet through and supperless, covered with mud and wheel grease, without any rare flowers.

CONCERNING HENRY DAVID THOREAU

1. What did Thoreau mean by writing, "The philosopher for whom rainbows can be explained away never saw them"? How is this statement related to his general attitude toward nature?

2. How were Thoreau's ideas related to those of other writers of his period?

3. Why are Thoreau's ideas easier to grasp than those of many philosophers?

CONCERNING "MISS MARY EMERSON,"
"I ATTEND A PARTY," AND
"I CHASE A PIG"

1. Which of the elements of humor mentioned in the essay as typical of Thoreau's writing (pages 367-368) do you find in each of the selections? Cite specific examples. In your opinion is the humor effective? Why, or why not?

2. Judging from the selections you have read, what was Thoreau's opinion of women? Do you see a possible connection between this opinion and the fact that Thoreau never married?

3. Read again the last paragraph in "I Chase a Pig." Why are the short, abrupt sentences appropriate to the ideas and the tone of this paragraph? What does Thoreau gain by using many short, easily understood words?

Know your words

When Thoreau wrote of his young lady companion at an evening party that she was *"loquacious* as a chickadee" he meant that she talked a lot. *Loquacious* is derived from the Latin word *loqui,* meaning "to speak." Many other useful English words have been derived from this same word.

On a sheet of paper complete the statements below, making clear how the idea of "speak" appears in each italicized word. Use the dictionary if necessary.

1. The parents wished the child to take *elocution* lessons because....

2. *Ventriloquism* is a difficult art because....

3. *Colloquialisms* have a place in fiction because....

4. Thoreau avoided *circumlocutions* because....

5. On a crowded stage *soliloquies* often seem absurd because....

&* III THE WALDEN IDEA

Thoreau the Craftsman and Woodsman and Thoreau the Humorous Philosopher may be clearly seen in one of Thoreau's books which has become a classic in our country's literature—*Walden, or Life in the Woods,* published in 1854. This book is interesting also because it tells us Thoreau's solution for a problem which was beginning to become important in his day and which is even more important in ours.

The problem arose because of a development you have seen taking place in our country—the growth of science and industry (pages 139-177). In New England, even before the War Between the States, a man with such sharp eyes as Thoreau had could see early signs of the great change. Not far from Concord, two factory villages, Lowell and Lawrence, were growing like mushrooms. Nearer at hand railway tracks and telegraph wires were changing the look of the landscape; train whistles which Thoreau heard by day and by night screamed news of the growing importance of the machine. Newspapers told of factories springing up along the Eastern seacoast, of steamboats plying the rivers, the Great Lakes, and the oceans. Americans were beginning to struggle with the changes brought into their lives by the machine age.

Different groups offered varied solutions. One group urged American laborers to band together in a political party: in one election in New York City, such a party polled 30% of the vote. Another group favored trade unions: in 1837 delegates from such unions in a dozen different cities met and formed a National Trades Union. Several groups tried living in communities which embodied new social and economic organizations. One of the first of these was New Harmony, founded on a thirty-thousand-acre tract in Indiana by Robert Owen, an English reformer. Some thousand eager colonists made the long trek west to try life in a community where property was held jointly and labor shared, but after four years under seven different constitutions or plans of government the project failed in 1829. At Fruitlands in Harvard, Massachusetts, Amos Bronson Alcott[1] founded another community based on the sharing of labor, but this project lasted only a short time. The most famous of the experimental communities was Brook Farm, founded in 1841 at West Roxbury near Boston by George Ripley and a group of earnest social reformers. Authors and laborers, Harvard students and farmers, even men from foreign lands, came to try life in this coöperative community where everyone must work and where the pay was the same for all kinds of work. Men who worked in the dairy barn received about the same wages as the scholars who taught in the excellent school. The social life—picnics and dances, concerts and lectures—was open to all. But after six years this project, too, failed.

Thoreau also tried his experiment: he set up his model community. It was a one-man community located by Walden Pond, about a mile from Concord, out beyond the poorhouse. "Experiment" might seem to some to be too high-falutin a name to apply to Thoreau's unpretentious stay out in a hut by a pond, and it would have astonished Thoreau's fellow townsmen if they had heard that his report on that stay was to be an American literary masterpiece. Here are the simple facts:

Emerson, who had bought some ground alongside Walden Pond, gave Thoreau permission to go out there and live. In return, Thoreau was to clear the briar bushes from part of the property. In March, 1845, Thoreau went out to Emerson's lot, carrying a borrowed ax. He cut a good share of his own timber, and bought a laborer's shack for the boards and nails

---

[1] *Amos Bronson Alcott,* father of Louisa May Alcott, the author of *Little Women.*

in it. He built a hut so small that a friend called it a "sentry box." Beginning July 4, 1845, Thoreau lived in his pondside hut for two years and two months. Often he heard passers-by saying incredulously, "Does he *live* here?" He was not living in the wilds away from his fellowmen: he walked into town whenever he felt like it, and sometimes invited himself for dinner at friends' houses; and his friends frequently called on him. Thoreau found that by doing day labor now and then, and by selling farm produce, he could spend only a small part of his time working and get along easily. This left a large share of his time for studying nature, visiting friends, and writing a book. When he finished writing his book, Thoreau left his hut on Walden Pond forever.

That was all there was to the "experiment" which Thoreau told about in his most famous book, *Walden*. The chief reasons for the lasting importance of this book are these: (1) Since much of this book is written in Thoreau's typical humorous style, many have found it amusing. (2) The descriptions of plant and animal life as he observed them at Walden are as fascinating as any Thoreau ever wrote (for instance, "The Battle of the Ants," pages 364-365). (3) The account by Thoreau, the fine craftsman, of his way of building his hut and living in the woods has an interest not unlike that of such a book, say, as *Robinson Crusoe*. (4) The book set forth what might be called "the Walden Idea"—its author's suggestion about what a man might do to cope with the problems of the machine age.

Thoreau, like many others who have thought about the results of the machine in our lives, noticed that possible luxuries were multiplied. The bare necessities of life were four—food, shelter, clothing, and fuel. If these were reduced to a bare minimum, they were pretty easy to get. As for luxuries, such as great accumulations of property or money, or travel by train, one could easily get along without them. Everything beyond the bare necessities was a luxury for which you spent part of your precious lifetime. Thoreau, practical Yankee that he was, wanted to consider what kind of bargain he was getting. The question he asked was, "How much of your energy should you spend to buy unimportant luxuries?" His answer was, "None at all."

His idea was simple enough. It was that the less time you spend doing what is unimportant, the more time you can spend in doing what is important. For Thoreau, the important things of life were exploring nature, reading books, thinking, and writing. His simple way of living gave him plenty of time for all these activities. In his day and in ours, many people spend so much time acquiring luxuries that they never have time to live. Thoreau would claim that their luxuries cost too much. The following excerpts from *Walden* set forth the idea very well.

Why I Went to the Woods

I WENT TO THE WOODS because I wished to live deliberately, to front only the essential facts of life, and see if I could not learn what it had to teach, and not, when I came to die, discover that I had not lived. I did not wish to live what was not life, living is so dear; nor did I wish to practice resignation, unless it was quite necessary. I wanted to live deep and suck out all the marrow of life, to live so sturdily and Spartanlike[1] as to put to rout all that was not life, to cut a broad swath and shave close, to drive life into a corner, and reduce it to its lowest terms, and, if it proved to be mean, why then to get the whole and genuine meanness of it, and publish its meanness to the world; or if it were sublime, to know it by experience, and be able to give a true account of it in my next excursion.[2] For most men, it appears to me, are in a strange uncertainty about it, whether it is of the devil or of God, and have *somewhat hastily* concluded that it is the chief end of man here to "glorify God and enjoy Him forever."[3]

Still we live meanly, like ants, though the fable tells us that we were long ago changed into men[4]; like pygmies we fight with cranes[5]; it is error upon error, and clout upon clout, and our best virtue has for its occasion a superfluous and evitable wretchedness. Our life is frittered away by detail. An honest man has hardly need to count more than his ten fingers or in extreme cases he may add his ten toes, and lump the rest. Simplicity, simplicity, simplicity! I say, let your affairs be as two or three, and not a hundred or a thousand; instead of a million count half a dozen, and keep your accounts on your thumbnail. In the midst of this chopping sea of civilized life, such are the clouds and storms and quicksands and thousand-and-one items to be allowed for, that a man has to live, if he would not founder and go to the bottom and not make his port at all, by dead reckoning,[6] and he must be a great calculator indeed who succeeds. Simplify, simplify. Instead of three meals a day, if it be necessary eat but one; instead of a hundred dishes, five; and reduce other things in proportion. Our life is like a German Confederacy, made up of petty states,[7] with its boundary forever fluctuating, so that even a German cannot tell you how it is bounded at any moment. The nation itself, with all its so-called internal improvements, which, by the way, are all external and superficial, is just such an unwieldy and overgrown establishment, cluttered with furniture and tripped up by its own traps, ruined by luxury and heedless expense, by want of calculation and a worthy aim, as the million households in the land; and the only cure for it as for them is in a rigid economy, a stern and more than Spartan simplicity of life and elevation of purpose. It lives too fast. Men think that it is essential that the *Nation* have commerce, and export ice, and talk through a telegraph, and ride thirty miles an hour, without a doubt, whether *they* do or not; but whether we should live like baboons or like men is a little uncertain. If we do not get out sleepers, and forge rails, and devote days and nights to the work, but go to tinkering upon our *lives* to improve them, who will build railroads? And if railroads are not built, how shall we get to heaven in season? But if we stay at home and mind our business, who will want railroads? We do not ride on the railroad; it rides upon us.

[1]*Spartanlike,* like the Spartans, a people of ancient Greece who were noted for the value they placed on simplicity and severity in their daily living.

[2]*my next excursion,* my next or future life.

[3]*"glorify God and enjoy Him forever,"* the answer in the Westminster Catechism to the question, "What is the chief end of man?"

[4]*like ants...changed into men.* According to Hopi (hō′pē) Indian lore, the first people were ants.

[5]*like pygmies we fight with cranes.* Homer and other ancient writers believed that the pygmies, dwarf inhabitants of Africa, carried on warfare with the cranes.

[6]*dead reckoning,* calculation of a ship's position by using a compass and studying the record of the voyage, and without using observations of the sun and stars.

[7]*a German Confederacy, made up of petty states.* At the time Thoreau wrote *Walden,* Germany as a nation did not exist. Until the rise of Napoleon at the end of the eighteenth century, there had been a German emperor, but he was a mere figurehead; in each of the several hundred German states the real ruler was its prince or duke. At the Congress of Vienna (1814-1815), which met to reorganize Europe after Napoleon's defeat, the German states were reduced in number from several hundred to thirty-eight and a loose German Confederation was formed. However, the real power remained with the heads of the states. In 1871 Bismarck, a statesman from Prussia, the strongest of the German states, welded Germany into an empire.

My House by Walden Pond

THE EXACT COST of my house, paying the usual price for such materials as I used, but not counting the work, all of which was done by myself, was as follows; and I give the details because very few are able to tell exactly what their houses cost, and fewer still, if any, the separate cost of the various materials which compose them.

Boards	. . . . $8.03½, mostly shanty boards.	
Refuse shingles for roof and sides	. . . . . 4.00	
Laths	. . . . 1.25	
Two second-hand windows with glass.	2.43	
One thousand old brick	. . . . 4.00	
Two casks of lime	. . . . 2.40	That was high.
Hair	31	More than I needed.
Mantel-tree iron[1]	15	
Nails	. . . . 3.90	
Hinges and screws	14	
Latch	10	
Chalk	01	
Transportation	. . . . . . 1.40	I carried a good part
In all	. . . . $28.12½	on my back.

These are all the materials excepting the timber, stones, and sand, which I claimed by squatter's right. I have also a small woodshed adjoining, made chiefly of the stuff which was left after building the house. I intend to build me a house which will surpass any on the main street in Concord in grandeur and luxury, as soon as it pleases me as much and will cost me no more than my present one.

I thus found that the student who wishes for a shelter can obtain one for a lifetime at an expense not greater than the rent which he now pays annually. If I seem to boast more than is becoming, my excuse is that I brag for humanity rather than for myself; and my shortcomings and inconsistencies do not affect the truth of my statement. Notwithstanding much cant and hypocrisy—chaff which I find it difficult to separate from my wheat, but for which I am as sorry as

any man—I will breathe freely and stretch myself in this respect, it is such a relief to both the moral and physical system; and I am resolved that I will not through humility become the devil's attorney.[2] I will endeavor to speak a good word for the truth. At Cambridge College[3] the mere rent of a student's room, which is only a little larger than my own, is thirty dollars each year, though the corporation[4] had the advantage of building thirty-two side by side and under one roof, and the occupant suffers the inconvenience of many and noisy neighbors, and perhaps a residence in the fourth story....Of the present economical and social arrangements I was more independent than any farmer in Concord, for I was not anchored to a house or farm, but could follow the bent of my genius, which is a very crooked one, every moment....

By surveying, carpentry, and day labor of various other kinds in the village in the meanwhile, for I have as many trades as fingers, I had earned $13.34. The expense of food for eight months, namely, from July 4 to March 1, the time when these estimates were made, though I lived there more than two years—not counting potatoes, a little green corn, and some peas, which I had raised, nor considering the value of what was on hand at the last date, was:

Rice	. . . . $1.73½	
Molasses	. . . . . . 1.73	Cheapest form of the saccharine.
Rye meal	. . . . . . 1.04¾	
Indian meal[5]	. . . . .99¾	Cheaper than rye.
Pork	22	
Flour	88	Costs more than Indian meal, both money and trouble.
Sugar	80	
Lard	65	
Apples	25	
Dried apples	22	
Sweet potatoes	. . .10	
One pumpkin	06	
One watermelon	. .02	
Salt	03	

All experiments which failed

<hr>

[1]*mantel-tree iron,* a piece of iron across the top of a fireplace to support the masonry above.

[2]*the devil's attorney,* a liar.
[3]*Cambridge College,* Harvard University, which is located in Cambridge, Massachusetts.
[4]*the corporation,* the governing board of the college.
[5]*Indian meal,* meal made from corn, or corn meal.

Yes, I did eat $8.74, all told; but I should not thus unblushingly publish my guilt, if I did not know that most of my readers were equally guilty with myself, and their deeds would look no better in print. The next year I sometimes caught a mess of fish for my dinner, and once I went so far as to slaughter a woodchuck which ravaged my beanfield—effect his transmigration, as a Tartar would say[6]—and devour him, partly for experiment's sake; but though it afforded me a momentary enjoyment, notwithstanding a musky flavor, I saw that the longest use would not make that a good practice, however it might seem to have your woodchucks ready dressed by the village butcher.

Clothing and some incidental expenses within
   the same dates, though little can be inferred
   from this item, amounted to $8.40¾
Oil and some household utensils 2.00

So that all the pecuniary outgoes, excepting for washing and mending, which for the most part were done out of the house, and their bills have not yet been received—and these are all and more than all the ways by which money necessarily goes out in this part of the world—were:

House $28.12½
Farm, one year[7] 14.72½
Food eight months 8.74
Clothing, etc., eight months 8.40¾
Oil, etc., eight months 2.00
    In all $61.99¾

I address myself now to those of my readers who have a living to get. To meet this I have:

For farm produce sold $23.44
Earned by daylabor 13.34
    In all $36.78

which subtracted from the sum of the outgoes leaves a balance of $25.21¾ on the one side—this being very nearly the means with which I started, and the measure of expenses to be incurred—and on the other, besides the leisure and independence and health thus secured, a comfortable house for me as long as I choose to occupy it.

These statistics, however accidental and therefore uninstructive they may appear, as they have a certain completeness, have a certain value also. Nothing was given me of which I have not rendered some account. It appears from the above estimate that my food alone cost me in money about twenty-seven cents a week. It was, for nearly two years after this: rye and Indian meal without yeast, potatoes, rice, a very little salt pork, molasses, and salt and my drink —water. It was fit that I should live on rice, mainly, who loved so well the philosophy of India. To meet the objections of some inveterate cavilers, I may as well state that if I dined out occasionally, as I always had done, and I trust shall have opportunities to do again, it was frequently to the detriment of my domestic arrangements. But the dining out, being, as I have stated, a constant element, does not in the least affect a comparative statement like this.

I learned from my two years' experience that it would cost incredibly little trouble to obtain one's necessary food, even in this latitude; that a man may use as simple a diet as the animals, and yet retain health and strength. I have made a satisfactory dinner, satisfactory on several accounts, simply off a dish of purslane (*Portulaca oleracea*[8]) which I gathered in my cornfield, boiled, and salted. I give the Latin on account of the savoriness of the trivial name. And pray what more can a reasonable man desire, in peaceful times, in ordinary noons, than a sufficient number of ears of green sweet corn boiled, with the addition of salt? Even the little variety that I used was a yielding to the demands of appetite, and not of health. Yet men have come to such a pass that they frequently starve, not for want of necessaries, but for want of luxuries; and I know a good woman who thinks that her son lost his life because he took to drinking water only. . . .

---

[6]*effect his transmigration, as a Tartar would say*. The Tartars were a horde of Mongols and Turks who overran parts of Europe during the Middle Ages. Thoreau is saying that like many primitive people they believed that at death the soul passed into another body (transmigration).

[7]*Farm, one year*. This item covers the expenses incurred by Thoreau in his planting and cultivating of a 2½-acre farm.

---

[8]*Portulaca oleracea* (pōr′chü lā′kə ol′ėr ā′sē ə), the botanical name for purslane.

CONCERNING HENRY DAVID THOREAU

1. What social and economic problems disturbed thoughtful people in Thoreau's day? Describe some of the attempts to solve these problems. What was Thoreau's way of attacking the problem?

2. Why is *Walden* considered an important book?

CONCERNING THE SELECTIONS
FROM "WALDEN"

1. In the first paragraph of "Why I Went to the Woods" Thoreau explains exactly the reasons back of his experiment. Tell in your own words what he means by each of the following sentences, paying particular attention to the italicized words and expressions.

(*a*) I went to the woods because I wished *to live deliberately, to front* only the essential facts of life, and see if I could not learn what it had to teach, and not, when I came to die, *discover that I had not lived.*

(*b*) I did not wish *to live what was not life,* living is so *dear.*

(*c*) I wanted *to live deep and suck out all the marrow of life,* to live so sturdily and Spartanlike as to put to rout all that was not life, to cut a broad swath and shave close, to drive life into a corner, and reduce it to its lowest terms, and, if it proved to be mean, why then to get the whole and genuine meanness of it.

2. State Thoreau's idea of simplicity as it is developed in the third paragraph of this selection. Comment on the aptness of his comparison of modern life to a German Confederacy.

3. Is there a conflict between simplicity, as Thoreau understood it, and progress? Explain. What virtue, if any, do you find in Thoreau's viewpoint?

4. What did Thoreau mean by writing, "We do not ride on the railroad; it rides upon us" (page 374, column 2, last paragraph)? Relate this paradox to his ideas about simplicity.

5. Triumphantly Thoreau records the total cost of his house by Walden Pond as being only $28.12½. What, in your opinion, was his chief reason for wishing to keep down the cost?

6. What qualities and abilities did Thoreau possess that made it possible for him to make a success of the experiment he describes in "My House by Walden Pond"? Do you think his plan would prove successful for the average man today? Explain your answer.

IV REBEL

One evening in July, 1846, Thoreau walked from Walden to Concord to pick up a mended shoe at the cobbler's shop. In town, he was met by Sam Staples, the sheriff and tax collector. Sam arrested him.

The reason was that Thoreau had not paid his poll tax,[1] and the reason for his refusing to pay it was this: that he did not want to support certain activities of the government. Back in 1838, he had refused to pay taxes which had been levied to support a church which he did not attend. In 1846, he refused to pay his poll tax because, like many others, he was opposed to the Mexican War for which he could find no justification.

Sam felt awkward about arresting this man whom he had known for many years, this man with whom he'd had many pleasant conversations. He said, "I'll pay your tax, Henry, if you're hard up." Thoreau apparently said that he had the $1.50 needed to pay the tax, but he just refused to pay, anyhow. Why, he reasoned, should he support a government whose actions he believed immoral? So Sam regretfully locked Thoreau up in jail.

A story that is told in Concord to this day is that while Thoreau was in jail, his friend, Ralph Waldo Emerson, visited him. Emerson believed as Thoreau did, but he had paid the poll tax. The story has it that their talk went this way: Emerson said, "Henry, why are you here?" And the prisoner answered, "Waldo, why are you *not* here?"

---

[1]*poll* (pōl) *tax,* a tax that had to be paid by all individuals who were entitled to vote.

The next morning, much to Thoreau's disgust, someone in his family—his Aunt Maria, probably—sneaked over to the jail and paid the tax and the fees. But the visitor to Concord from Walden had made known his principles and had spent a night in jail to show that he believed in them.

Thoreau's experiences in jail as well as his beliefs concerning government are considered in an essay called "Civil Disobedience," published in 1849. In this essay Thoreau adopted an extreme attitude toward the long-admired American quality of self-reliance. That quality had been bred especially by life on the frontier, where the rugged individual chafed against controls of every sort. Relatively few Americans, however, had gone so far as Thoreau now did in believing that a man should refuse to let his rights as an individual be interfered with in any way by the government, and by the time Thoreau died, in 1862, the belief in such extreme individualism was even less general.

It is doubtful if Thoreau influenced very many Americans of his day—or later times—to adopt the ideas for which he willingly went to jail. But in the twentieth century in far-off India the great leader Mahatma Gandhi was to read Thoreau's essay and put his ideas into practice in what was an extraordinarily successful rebellion against the British Empire.

A summary of Thoreau's attitude toward the relations between the individual and the state is contained in the motto quoted by him in the opening sentence of the following selection.

FROM *Civil Disobedience*

I HEARTILY ACCEPT the motto, "That government is best which governs least"; and I should like to see it acted up to more rapidly and systematically. Carried out, it finally amounts to this, which also I believe—"That government is best which governs not at all"; and when men are prepared for it, that will be the kind of government which they will have. Government is at best but an expedient; but most governments are usually, and all governments are sometimes, inexpedient. The objections which have been brought against a standing army, and they are many and weighty, and deserve to prevail, may also at last be brought against a standing government. The standing army is only an arm of the standing government. The government itself, which is only the mode which the people have chosen to execute their will, is equally liable to be abused and perverted before the people can act through it. Witness the present Mexican War, the work of comparatively a few individuals using the standing government as their tool; for, in the outset, the people would not have consented to this measure.

This American government—what is it but a tradition, though a recent one, endeavoring to transmit itself unimpaired to posterity, but each instant losing some of its integrity? It has not the vitality and force of a single living man, for a single man can bend it to his will. It is a sort of wooden gun to the people themselves. But it is not the less necessary for this; for the people must have some complicated machinery or other, and hear its din, to satisfy that idea of government which they have. Governments show thus how successfully men can be imposed on, even impose on themselves, for their own advantage. It is excellent, we must all allow. Yet this government never of itself furthered any enterprise, but by the alacrity with which it got out of its way. *It* does not keep the country free. *It* does not settle the West. *It* does not educate. The character inherent in the American people has done all that has been accomplished; and it would have done somewhat more if the government had not sometimes got in its way. For government is an expedient by which men would fain succeed in letting one another alone; and, as has been said, when it is most expedient, the governed are most let alone by it. Trade and commerce, if they were not made of India rubber, would never manage to bounce over the obstacles which legislators are continually putting in their way; and, if one were to judge these men wholly by the effects of their actions and not partly by their intentions, they would deserve to be classed and punished with those mischievous persons who put obstructions on the railroads.

But, to speak practically and as a citizen, unlike those who call themselves no-government men, I ask for, not at once no government, but *at once* a better government. Let every man make known what kind of government would command his respect, and that will be one step toward obtaining it....

I have paid no poll tax for six years. I was put into jail once on this account, for one night; and, as I stood considering the walls of solid stone, two or three feet thick, and the iron grating which strained the light, I could not help being struck with the foolishness of that institution which treated me as if I were mere flesh and blood and bones, to be locked up. I wondered that it should have concluded at length that this was the best use it could put me to, and had never thought to avail itself of my services in some way. I saw that, if there was a wall of stone between me and my townsmen, there was a still more difficult one to climb or break through before they could get to be as free as I was. I did not for a moment feel confined, and the walls seemed a great waste of stone and mortar. I felt as if I alone of all my townsmen had paid my tax. They plainly did not know how to treat me, but behaved like persons who are underbred. In every threat and in every compliment there was a blunder; for they thought that my chief desire was to stand on the other side of that stone wall. I could not but smile to see how industriously they locked the door on my meditations, which followed them out again without let or hindrance, and *they* were really all that was dangerous. As they could not reach me, they had resolved to punish my body; just as boys, if they cannot come at some person against whom they have a spite, will abuse his dog. I saw that the State was half-witted, that it was timid as a lone woman with her silver spoons, and that it did not know its friends from its foes, and I lost all my remaining respect for it, and pitied it.

Thus the State never intentionally confronts a man's sense, intellectual or moral, but only his body, his senses. It is not armed with superior wit or honesty, but with superior physical force. I was not born to be forced. I will breathe after my own fashion. Let us see who is the strongest. What force has a multitude? They only can force me who obey a higher law than I. They force me to become like themselves. I do not hear of *men* being *forced* to live this way or that by masses of men. What sort of life were that to live? When I meet a government which says to me, "Your money or your life," why should I be in haste to give it my money? It may be in a great strait,[1] and not know what to do: I cannot help that. It must help itself; do as I do. It is not worth the while to snivel about it. I am not responsible for the successful working of the machinery of society. I am not the son of the engineer. I perceive that, when an acorn and a chestnut fall side by side, the one does not remain inert to make way for the other, but both obey their own laws, and spring and grow and flourish as best they can, till one, perchance, overshadows and destroys the other. If a plant cannot live according to its nature, it dies; and so a man.

The night in prison was novel and interesting enough. The prisoners in their shirt sleeves were enjoying a chat and the evening air in the doorway when I entered. But the jailer said, "Come, boys, it is time to lock up"; and so they dispersed, and I heard the sound of their steps returning into the hollow apartments. My roommate was introduced to me by the jailer as

---

[1] *in a great strait,* in great difficulty.

"a first-rate fellow and a clever[2] man." When the door was locked, he showed me where to hang my hat, and how he managed matters there. The rooms were whitewashed once a month; and this one, at least, was the whitest, most simply furnished, and probably the neatest apartment in the town. He naturally wanted to know where I came from, and what brought me there; and, when I had told him, I asked him in my turn how he came there, presuming him to be an honest man, of course; and, as the world goes, I believe he was. "Why," said he, "they accuse me of burning a barn; but I never did it." As near as I could discover, he had probably gone to bed in a barn when drunk, and smoked his pipe there; and so a barn was burnt. He had been there some three months waiting for his trial to come on, and would have to wait as much longer; but he was quite domesticated and contented, since he got his board for nothing, and thought that he was well treated.

He occupied one window, and I the other; and I saw that if one stayed there long, his principal business would be to look out the window. I had soon read all the tracts that were left there, and examined where former prisoners had broken out, and where a grate had been sawed off, and heard the history of the various occupants of that room; for I found that even here there was a history and a gossip which never circulated beyond the walls of the jail. Probably this is the only house in the town where verses are composed, which are afterward printed in a circular form, but not published. I was shown quite a long list of verses which were composed by some young men who had been detected in an attempt to escape, who avenged themselves by singing them.

I pumped my fellow-prisoner as dry as I could, for fear I should never see him again; but at length he showed me which was my bed, and left me to blow out the lamp.

It was like traveling into a far country, such as I had never expected to behold, to lie there for one night. It seemed to me that I never had heard the town clock strike before, nor the eve-

ning sounds of the village; for we slept with the windows open, which were inside the grating. It was to see my native village in the light of the Middle Ages, and our Concord was turned into a Rhine stream, and visions of knights and castles passed before me. They were the voices of old burghers[3] that I heard in the streets. I was an involuntary spectator and auditor of whatever was done and said in the kitchen of the adjacent village inn—a wholly new and rare experience to me. It was a closer view of my native town. I was fairly inside of it. I never had seen its institutions before. This is one of its peculiar institutions; for it is a shire town.[4] I began to comprehend what its inhabitants were about.

In the morning, our breakfasts were put through the hole in the door, in small oblong-square tin pans, made to fit, and holding a pint of chocolate, with brown bread, and an iron spoon. When they called for the vessels again, I was green enough to return what bread I had left; but my comrade seized it, and said that I should lay that up for lunch or dinner. Soon after he was let out to work at haying in a neighboring field, whither he went every day, and would not be back till noon; so he bade me good day, saying that he doubted if he should see me again.

When I came out of prison—for someone interfered, and paid that tax—I did not perceive that great changes had taken place on the common, such as he observed who went in a youth and emerged a tottering and gray-headed man[5]; and yet a change had to my eyes come over the scene—the town, and State, and country—greater than any that mere time could effect. I saw yet more distinctly the State in which I lived. I saw to what extent the people among whom I lived could be trusted as good neighbors and friends; that their friendship was for summer weather only; that they did not greatly propose to do right; that they were a distinct race from

---

[3]*old burghers,* citizens of a town in the Middle Ages.

[4]*a shire town,* a county seat. The jail in which Thoreau was confined in Concord was the county jail.

[5]*who went in a youth...gray-headed man.* This is a reference to Silvio Pellico (sēl′vē ō pel′lē kō), an Italian poet and dramatist, whose health had been broken by his sufferings in prison. The record of his experiences, entitled *My Prisons,* was translated into many languages.

---

[2]*clever,* honest, kind, obliging. The word *clever* was used colloquially in this sense in New England in Thoreau's time.

me by their prejudices and superstitions, as the Chinamen and Malays[6] are; that in their sacrifices to humanity they ran no risks, not even to their property; that after all they were not so noble but they treated the thief as he had treated them, and hoped, by a certain outward observance and a few prayers, and by walking in a particular straight though useless path from time to time, to save their souls. This may be to judge my neighbors harshly; for I believe that many of them are not aware that they have such an institution as the jail in their village.

It was formerly the custom in our village, when a poor debtor came out of jail, for his acquaintances to salute him, looking through their fingers, which were crossed to represent the grating of a jail window, "How do ye do?" My neighbors did not thus salute me, but first looked at me, and then at one another, as if I had returned from a long journey.

I was put in jail as I was going to the shoemaker's to get a shoe which was mended. When I was let out the next morning, I proceeded to finish my errand, and, having put on my mended shoe, joined a huckleberry party, who were impatient to put themselves under my conduct; and in half an hour—for the horse was soon tackled—was in the midst of a huckleberry field, on one of our highest hills, two miles off, and then the State was nowhere to be seen.

This is the whole history of "My Prisons."[7]...

The authority of government, even such as I am willing to submit to—for I will cheerfully obey those who know and can do better than I, and in many things even those who neither know nor can do so well—is still an impure one: to be strictly just, it must have the sanction and consent of the governed. It can have no pure right over my person and property but what I concede to it. The progress from an absolute to a limited monarchy,[8] from a limited monarchy to a democracy, is a progress toward a true respect for the individual. Even the Chinese philosopher[9] was wise enough to regard the individual as the basis of the empire. Is a democracy, such as we know it, the last improvement possible in government? Is it not possible to take a step further towards recognizing and organizing the rights of man? There will never be a really free and enlightened State until the State comes to recognize the individual as a higher and independent power, from which all its own power and authority are derived, and treats him accordingly. I please myself with imagining a State at last which can afford to be just to all men, and to treat the individual with respect as a neighbor; which even would not think it inconsistent with its own repose if a few were to live aloof from it, not meddling with it, nor embraced by it, who fulfilled all the duties of neighbors and fellowmen. A State which bore this kind of fruit, and suffered it to drop off as fast as it ripened, would prepare the way for a still more perfect and glorious State, which also I have imagined, but not yet anywhere seen.

---

[9]*the Chinese philosopher,* Confucius (kən fū′shəs), who lived about five hundred years before Christ.

CONCERNING HENRY DAVID THOREAU

1. Why may Thoreau be considered a rebel? What was the reaction of each of the following to his rebellion: the sheriff, Ralph Waldo Emerson, Thoreau's Aunt Maria? What is your reaction?

2. What circumstances in early nineteenth-century American life had fostered attitudes like Thoreau's?

3. What has been the importance of Thoreau's idea of civil disobedience in the twentieth century?

CONCERNING "CIVIL DISOBEDIENCE"

1. In the first paragraph of the selection Thoreau wrote: "Government is at best but an expedient; but most governments are usually, and all governments are sometimes, inexpedient." Explain this statement. Trace the arguments in the first two paragraphs by which Thoreau seeks to prove his point. What points can you advance to support or refute his argument?

2. On his being put in jail Thoreau commented: "I could not help being struck with the foolishness of that institution which treated me as if I were mere

---

[6]*Malays* (mā′lāz *or* mə lāz′), members of the brown race living on a peninsula of southeast Asia and on adjacent islands.

[7]*"My Prisons,"* the title of Pellico's book. (See footnote 5.)

[8]*an absolute...limited monarchy.* An absolute monarchy is one in which the ruler has unlimited power; a limited monarchy is one in which the ruler's powers are limited by the laws of the nation.

flesh and blood and bones, to be locked up" (page 379, column 1, paragraph 2). What did he mean? What did he consider the essential elements of a man's make-up? The unessential elements? Why did he consider himself to be more free inside the jail than his fellowmen who were outside?

3. What things about his night in prison did Thoreau find "novel and interesting"?

4. How did Thoreau's reactions to his night in prison differ from what the ordinary man would feel? What effect did his imprisonment have on the way he regarded his fellow townsmen?

5. Judging from the last paragraph of the selection, what was Thoreau's idea of the "free and enlightened State"? To what extent do your ideas on this subject agree or disagree with his?

The Larger View

I. One of the paragraphs below was written by Thoreau, the other by Irving. On a sheet of paper write the number indicating each paragraph and after the number write the name of the man who you believe wrote the paragraph; then list all the clues on which you base your decision.

1. Our first essay was along a mountain brook, among the highlands of the Hudson; a most unfortunate place for the execution of those piscatory tactics which had been invented along the velvet margins of quiet English rivulets. It was one of those wild streams that lavish, among our romantic solitudes, unheeded beauties, enough to fill the sketch book of a hunter of the picturesque. Sometimes it would leap down rocky shelves, making small cascades, over which the trees threw their broad balancing sprays, and long nameless weeds hung in fringes from the impending banks, dripping with diamond drops. Sometimes it would brawl and fret along a ravine in the matted shade of a forest, filling it with murmurs; and, after this termagant career, would steal forth into open day with the most placid, demure face imaginable; as I have seen some pestilent shrew of a housewife, after filling her home with uproar and ill-humor, come dimpling out of doors, swimming and curtsying, and smiling upon all the world.

2. I can easily walk ten, fifteen, twenty, any number of miles, commencing at my own door, without going by any house, without crossing a road except where the fox and the mink do: first along by the river, and then the brook, and then the meadow and the woodside. There are square miles in my vicinity which have no inhabitant.

From many a hill I can see civilization and the abodes of man afar. The farmers and their works are scarcely more obvious than woodchucks and their burrows. Man and his affairs, church and state and school, trade and commerce, and manufactures and agriculture, even politics, the most alarming of them all—I am pleased to see how little space they occupy in the landscape. Politics is but a narrow field, and that still narrower highway yonder leads to it....I pass from it as from a bean field into the forest, and it is forgotten. In one half-hour I can walk off to some portion of the earth's surface where a man does not stand from one year's end to another, and there, consequently, politics are not, for they are but as the cigar smoke of a man.

II. Discuss the following questions.

1. The chronological chart on pages 384-385 provides information about some of Thoreau's contemporaries. With which of these men are you familiar? What writings of theirs have you read in earlier sections of this book or elsewhere? Are there any authors who are completely unknown to you?

2. On page 360 you read that Thoreau was "a cantankerous and eccentric but very interesting writer." Using what you have read about Thoreau and his writings themselves as evidence, prove or disprove the truth of the statement.

3. Benjamin Franklin was a scientist, an inventor, a diplomat, and an author. Besides being an author, Washington Irving was Minister to Spain. Does Thoreau have any importance aside from literature itself? Explain your answer.

MORE GOOD READING

ALCOTT, LOUISA MAY, *Little Women*. (Little) One of the most popular girls' stories ever written, this novel pictures a family who lived in Concord in Thoreau's period. If through some quirk of circumstance you've missed the story of Meg, Jo, Beth, and Amy up to now, don't delay any longer to read it.

BROOKS, VAN WYCK, *The Flowering of New England*. (Dutton) There is no better way for the mature student to get the atmosphere of Thoreau's time and to learn about his contemporaries and their relations toward one another than by reading this always interesting literary history.

CANBY, HENRY SEIDEL, *Thoreau*. (Houghton) This is a fine biography of one of the most interesting personalities in American literature.

DANA, RICHARD HENRY, *Two Years Before the Mast*. (Houghton) In the 1830's Richard Dana, a Harvard student, left his studies because of failing eye-sight to sail on the brig *Pilgrim* to California. His story of the hard voyage is perhaps the best record ever made of life on a sailing ship.

HAWTHORNE, HILDEGARDE, *Romantic Rebel; the Story of Nathaniel Hawthorne*. (Appleton) Perhaps because she knew her material so well and had access to family records and letters, Hildegarde Hawthorne's biography of her grandfather is as interesting as a novel. This intimate knowledge of the New England group aided her also in writing the following biographies: *Youth's Captain; the Story of Ralph Waldo Emerson* (Longmans); *Poet of Craigie House; the Story of Henry Wadsworth Longfellow* (Appleton); *Happy Autocrat, a Life of Oliver Wendell Holmes* (Longmans); and *Concord's Happy Rebel; Henry David Thoreau* (Longmans).

HAWTHORNE, NATHANIEL, *The House of the Seven Gables*. (Houghton) This is the story of Hephzibah Pyncheon and the sinister happenings in an old Puritan family of Salem. Hawthorne's *The Blithedale Romance* (Dutton) pictures the Brook Farm Community of which Hawthorne was a member for a time.

HEWES, MRS. AGNES DANFORTH, *Glory of the Seas*. (Knopf) The scene of this story is Boston in the days of Donald McKay and clipper ships. The principal character is John Seagrave, a shipping clerk who dreamed of California.

HOLMES, OLIVER WENDELL, *Autocrat of the Breakfast Table*. (Macmillan) The wit of Oliver Wendell Holmes sparks these imaginary conversations around a boarding-house table.

LONGSTRETH, THOMAS M., *Two Rivers Meet in Concord*. (Westminster) Jim Minot, growing up in the Concord of Emerson and Thoreau, groped for a rich and satisfying way of life. How Thoreau's homespun philosophy affected him and how romance changed his life are parts of a vivid story.

MEIGS, CORNELIA, *Invincible Louisa*. (Little) Louisa May Alcott's father was an eccentric but brilliant man. To the Alcott home in Concord came Thoreau, Emerson, and others of the Concord group. You'll find this a very well-written, exceedingly interesting biography.

SCUDDER, TOWNSEND, *Concord: American Town*. (Little) The experiences of the citizens of Concord—from Thomas Wheeler, Indian fighter, to Joe Wheeler, veteran of World War II—make up this unique history of the events, movements, and ideas that have helped shape American life.

THARP, LOUISE HALL, *The Peabody Sisters of Salem*. (Little) There were three of them. Gentle Mary became the wife of the educator, Horace Mann. Beautiful Sophia married Nathaniel Hawthorne. Dynamic Elizabeth was an intellectual leader, a friend of Emerson's. Together their lives make a fascinating biography.

THOREAU, HENRY DAVID, *Heart of Thoreau's Journals*, edited by Odell Shepard. (Houghton) The most interesting passages from Thoreau's journals of twenty-four years have been collected here. This is a book to browse in, reading a little here, a little there.

THOREAU, HENRY DAVID, *Walden*. (Houghton) The mature reader will find delight in Thoreau's humor, his easily understood philosophy, his eccentricity, and his common sense.

LITERATURE	HISTORICAL EVENTS
	Andrew Jackson inaugurated seventh President 1829
	The first locomotive used in America
1830 Oliver Wendell Holmes, "Old Ironsides"	
	Oregon Trail came into general use 1832
	New York City established free public schools
	Cyrus H. McCormick invented the reaper 1833
1835 Washington Irving, *Tour on the Prairies*	Samuel Colt patented the revolver 1835
	The Alamo fell to the Mexicans 1836
1839 Henry Wadsworth Longfellow, *Voices of the Night*	
1840 Richard Henry Dana, *Two Years Before the Mast*	
Edgar Allan Poe, *Tales of the Grotesque and Arabesque*	
1841 James Fenimore Cooper, *The Deerslayer*	
Ralph Waldo Emerson, *Essays* (First Series)	
	Samuel Morse's telegraph used between Washington and Baltimore 1844
	Charles Goodyear vulcanized rubber
1845 Edgar Allan Poe, *The Raven and Other Poems*	
	War with Mexico 1846
	Ether first used successfully as an anesthetic
	Elias Howe patented the sewing machine
1847 Ralph Waldo Emerson, *Poems*	Lincoln elected to Congress from Illinois 1847
	The Mormons migrated to Great Salt Lake
1848 James Russell Lowell, *Fable for Critics; The Biglow Papers, First Series; The Vision of Sir Launfal*	Gold discovered in California, causing the famous "rush" 1848
	Mexico ceded what is now California, Nevada, Utah, and Arizona
1849 Henry David Thoreau, "Civil Disobedience"	
Francis Parkman, *The Oregon Trail*	
1850 Nathaniel Hawthorne, *The Scarlet Letter*	
1851 Nathaniel Hawthorne, *The House of the Seven Gables*	The clipper ship *Flying Cloud* made a record of 89 days from New York to San Francisco 1851
	Matthew C. Perry "opened" Japan to the Western World 1853
	Railroad extended west to Chicago
1854 Henry David Thoreau, *Walden*	
1855 Henry Wadsworth Longfellow, *Hiawatha*	
1858 Henry Wadsworth Longfellow, *The Courtship of Miles Standish*	
Oliver Wendell Holmes, *The Autocrat of the Breakfast-Table*	
	Washington Irving died 1859
	The first oil well drilled
1860 Ralph Waldo Emerson, *Conduct of Life*	Lincoln elected President 1860

Henry David Thoreau 1817-1862

SOME PROMINENT WRITERS OF AMERICA'S "GOLDEN DAY"

RALPH WALDO EMERSON, 1803-1882

Boston-born Ralph Waldo Emerson was a member of a minister's large family. Upon graduating from Harvard he taught school for a while. Then, following in his ancestors' footsteps, he became a minister. Three years later, when Emerson found himself out of sympathy with certain church rituals, he resigned and went abroad, where he visited some of Europe's best thinkers. After his return he saw his first book, *Nature*, published. This book met with a generally mild reception, but when Emerson delivered two ringing addresses, "The American Scholar" and "The Divinity School Address," he found his true power and became great. His diction, "like homespun cloth-of-gold," and his message of the individual worth of each man made him one of the most inspiring speakers of all times. Emerson's many published essays were often condensations of lectures, the best known and most frequently quoted essay in American literature being his "Self-Reliance" (see pages 283-285). He wrote some memorable poems, too, such as "Forbearance," "Each and All," and "Concord Hymn."

NATHANIEL HAWTHORNE, 1804-1864

Nathaniel Hawthorne was born in Salem, Massachusetts, the son of a sea captain who died four years later leaving a household in reduced circumstances and steeped in gloom, solitude, and stern family pride. In these surroundings Hawthorne's young imagination brooded upon his more sinister Puritan ancestors, a preoccupation which later contributed greatly to some of his best novels and stories. He left Salem to attend Bowdoin College, but returned to spend the next twelve years in almost complete seclusion from the world. Then, at the age of thirty-five, he went to work at the Boston Custom House. He later married Sophia Peabody, held a job at the Salem Custom House, and from 1853 to 1857 was consul at Liverpool, England. Meanwhile, two collections of short stories, *Twice-Told Tales* and *Mosses from an Old Manse*, had appeared, and fame, slow in starting, had caught up with him with *The Scarlet Letter*. His success was further established by *The House of the Seven Gables, The Blithedale Romance, The Marble Faun,* and several books of essays.

OLIVER WENDELL HOLMES, 1809-1894

"A man of family" is the term Holmes himself used in noting the fortunate background into which he was born at Cambridge. He was educated at private schools and at Harvard. Then, deciding on a career in medicine, he studied abroad, practiced in Boston, and finally became professor in the medical school at Harvard. Doctor Holmes' lectures were often scheduled for the end of the day when his wit and freshness were counted on to keep the students awake. And, by the same token, he kept his friends and followers amused with worldly, polished, and clever verses. One of the most popular poems of the period was his patriotic "Old Ironsides," but he himself claimed "The Chambered Nautilus" (see page 563) to be his most inspired and most truly poetic piece. However, it was in conversational prose, when *The Autocrat of the Breakfast-Table* began to appear in the then new *Atlantic Monthly* magazine, that Holmes' literary reputation became established—a reputation that has held up well.

HENRY WADSWORTH LONGFELLOW, 1807-1882

This best-loved American poet of his period was born in Portland, Maine, and carefully sheltered during childhood. Never troubled by poverty, he supplemented his education at Bowdoin with studies abroad, taught modern languages first at Bowdoin and then at Harvard, and lived out his years in a peaceful old house in Cambridge. He was characterized at the height of his fame as "the white Mr. Longfellow," but such suggested serenity was won only after a youth of inner storm and struggle. Longfellow's fame as an author began to flourish with a collection of verse, *Voices of the Night,* and steadily increased with such works as *Hiawatha, Evangeline, The Courtship of Miles Standish*, and *Tales of a Wayside Inn.*

JAMES RUSSELL LOWELL, 1819-1891

Like Holmes, this most versatile of the Cambridge group of authors could claim to be "a man of family." He was born in Cambridge and educated at private schools, at Harvard, and abroad. He studied and practiced law, held various positions on magazines and newspapers, became professor of modern languages at Harvard when Longfellow retired, was the first editor of the *Atlantic Monthly*, and served as American minister first to Spain and then to England. He had a passion for democracy which at times caused lifted eyebrows among staid Cambridge society, especially when he insisted that his servants eat their meals at his table. Along about 1848 it became common to hear quoted catchy bits from his Yankee dialect poem, *The Biglow Papers.* In the same year his sparklingly witty *Fable for Critics* and his metrical romance, *The Vision of Sir Launfal,* appeared. Lowell was perhaps at his richest in his nature lyrics and in his fine prose essays.

UNIT X: WALT WHITMAN
(representing THE PERIOD OF CONFLICT)

WALT WHITMAN was born only two years after Thoreau. However, he was slower in finding himself than Thoreau was; he was profoundly influenced by the war years of 1861-1865; and he lived thirty years beyond Thoreau's death. Therefore he is thought of as a writer of the period after Thoreau.

Extraordinary though he was as a personality, Whitman clearly was shaped by the times during which he lived. His living and his writing showed the growing importance of the city, of industry and science, in American life. He used new forms for his poetry. His ideas about democracy, nationalism, internationalism, and immortality were molded by the thinking of his times.

❧ I THE EARLY WHITMAN

Walter Whitman, born May 31, 1819, on a farm at West Hills, Long Island, moved to Brooklyn with his family when he was four, and lived there until he was well-grown. He was, nevertheless, a child of the country. Brooklyn itself in the poet's youth was really a quiet little village. While living there, he roamed the nearby countryside, and frequently he paid long visits to his grandparents on their Long Island farms.

Many of his memories of his boyhood were of woodlands, orchards, and grain fields, of the farmyard and farm animals—sheep, pigs, horses, noisy broods of chicks. His youth, too, was associated with the country. After learning the printer's trade, he not only set type but also reported for little local newspapers. He ranged through the farm districts to collect news from the farmers. Between 1836 and 1841, when the printing business was slack, he taught in a number of schools. He "boarded out" with the families of his students, and found his acquaintance with farm people (as he said later) "one of my best experiences and deepest lessons in human nature."

In an America still chiefly rural, Whitman in his early years was a rural American. But one of the great developments of Whitman's lifetime was to be the growth of the city and the movement of many Americans from the farm or the village to the metropolis. It is not surprising, therefore, that Whitman in time was drawn toward city life. Work of the sort he wanted and living of the sort he appreciated were to be found in nearby New York. So between 1839 and 1848 he worked on newspapers in New York as well as in Brooklyn, and he greatly enjoyed the big city.

He was fascinated by the crowds on the ferry boats. He went regularly to theaters, concert halls, and opera houses. He dined and chatted with

a Bohemian group of authors[1] in Pfaff's basement restaurant under the Broadway sidewalks. He found pleasure in the sight of the moving Broadway crowds. On that great street, as he said, there was "always something novel or inspiriting."

He was particularly fond of riding the Broadway omnibuses and talking with their colorful drivers. These men were, he felt, "a strange, natural, quick-eyed and wondrous race." "How many hours," he wrote, "forenoons and afternoons—how many exhilarating nighttimes I have had...riding the whole length of Broadway, listening to some yarn... or perhaps I declaiming some stormy passage from *Julius Caesar* or *Richard*[2] (you could roar as loudly as you chose in that heavy, dense, uninterrupted street bass[3]). Yes, I knew all the drivers then: Broadway Jack, Dressmaker, Balky Bill, George Storms, Old Elephant, his brother Young Elephant (who came afterward), Tippy, Pop Rice, Big Frank, Yellow Frank, Yellow Joe, Pete Callahan, Patsey Dee, and dozens more...."

Whitman, country-bred though he was, apparently tried to show that he was at home in the city by becoming a good deal of a dandy. Descriptions of him at the time picture him as a graceful six-footer with a neatly trimmed pointed beard and dressed in the height of fashion. He wore a stylish beaver hat at an angle; he had a boutonnière on the lapel of his frock coat[4]; he carried a cane. His trousers were immaculate and fashionable, and his boots were brightly polished. The only picture we have of him in this period reminds us of an old-time fashion plate.

And just as his clothes resembled those turned out by the most popular tailors, his writings at this time resembled those of the most popular authors. As yet, Whitman had not learned how to turn his own life and his own thoughts into literature. Practically none of his knowledge and feeling—about farms and farmers, about city streets and their teeming life—came into what he wrote. In a period during which sentimentalism and moralizing were the mode, Walter Whitman wrote and published pathetic stories, a hectic and preachy "temperance novel,"[5] and poems which were trite in their wording and sentimental in their feeling. Turn the page for one of his early poems.

[1] *a Bohemian group of authors,* a group of writers who were free and easy or unconventional in their ideas, dress, manners, etc.
[2] *"Julius Caesar" or "Richard,"* tragedies by Shakespeare.
[3] *heavy...street bass,* the low-toned but loud and constant noises of the street.
[4] *frock coat,* a fitted coat reaching about to the knees and equally long in front and back.
[5] *temperance novel,* a novel having as its theme the evils of drinking.

Young Grimes

WHEN OLD GRIMES died, he left a son—
  The graft of worthy stock;
In deed and word he shows himself
  A chip of the old block.

In youth, 'tis said, he liked not school—   5
  Of tasks he was no lover;
He wrote sums in a ciphering book,
  Which had a pasteboard cover.

Young Grimes ne'er went to see the girls
  Before he was fourteen;   10
Nor smoked, nor swore, for that he knew
  Gave Mrs. Grimes much pain.

He never was extravagant
  In pleasure, dress, or board;
His Sunday suit was of blue cloth,   15
  At six and eight a yard.[1]

But still there is, to tell the truth,
  No stinginess in him;
And in July he wears an old
  Straw hat with a broad brim.   20

No devotee in fashion's train
  Is good old Grimes's son;
He sports no cane—no whiskers wears,
  Nor lounges o'er the town.

He does not spend more than he earns   25
  In dissipation's round;
But shuns with care those dangerous rooms
  Where vice and sin abound.

It now is eight and twenty years
  Since young Grimes saw the light;   30
And no house in the land can show
  A fairer, prouder sight.

For there his wife, prudent and chaste,
  His mother's age made sweet,
His children trained in virtue's path,   35
  The gazer's eye will meet.

Upon a hill, just off the road
  That winds the village side,
His farmhouse stands, within whose door
  Ne'er entered Hate or Pride.   40

But Plenty and Benevolence
  And Happiness are there—
And underneath that lowly roof
  Content smiles calm and fair.

Reader, go view the cheerful scene—   45
  By it how poor must prove
The pomp, and tinsel, and parade,
  Which pleasure's followers love.

Leave the wide city's noisy din—
  The busy haunts of men—   50
And here enjoy a tranquil life,
  Unvexed by guilt or pain.

CONCERNING WALTER WHITMAN

1. How did Whitman earn a living before 1848?
2. List Whitman's interests and enthusiasms in (*a*) the country, (*b*) the city. How might these likings have been reflected in his writings?
3. What kinds of works did the early Whitman produce? How might these works be criticized?

CONCERNING "YOUNG GRIMES"

1. How does young Grimes, as Whitman pictures him, compare with Whitman at this period?
2. Most young poets show that they are beginners by using faulty rhymes, limping rhythms, and awkward phrasings. Point out examples of any or all of these.
3. Is this poem (*a*) "trite in its wording" and (*b*) "sentimental in its feeling"? In answering, prove your claims by pointing to definite passages.
4. "Practically none of his knowledge and feeling... came into what he wrote," says the biography. Illustrate the point from "Young Grimes."

[1]*At six and eight a yard,* at six shillings and eight pence, or about $1.60, a yard. At the time Whitman wrote the poem (1839), most woolens were imported from England and their prices were quoted in English money.

It is safe to say that if Whitman had continued to write the sort of verse he turned out in the first years of his career no one would be likely to remember him today. But in the late 1840's and the early 1850's, something changed the man, and the change showed in his work. Some revolution in his personality, in his way of thinking and feeling, in his way of writing, made him a different—and a great—poet.

The results of the change were shown in a book which Whitman published at his own expense in 1855. This was the first edition of *Leaves of Grass*. Even the portrait of Whitman on the title page provided a sharp contrast with the elegant dandy pictured earlier. Here was a man with a rough, untrimmed beard. His hat was battered. He was in shirtsleeves, and the open collar of his shirt revealed the top of flannel underwear. His trousers, far from being elegant, were the dungarees of a laboring man. This, the book revealed, was not *Walter* Whitman but *Walt* Whitman—a seemingly new personality.

The poems differed as much from the earlier poems as Walt differed from Walter. Here, for instance, was the opening of a new poem:

There was a child went forth every day,
And the first object he looked upon and received with wonder or pity or love or
    dread, that object he became,
And that object became part of him for the day or a certain part of the day...or
    for many years or stretching cycles of years.

The early lilacs became part of the child,
And grass, and white and red morning-glories, and white and red clover, and the
    song of the phoebe bird,
And the March-born lambs, and the sow's pink-faint litter, and the mare's foal, and
    the cow's calf, and the noisy brood of the barnside or by the mire of the pondside
    ...and the fish suspending themselves so curiously below there...and the beauti-
    ful curious liquid...and the water plants with their graceful flat heads...all
    became part of him.

Notice that rhyme has disappeared, and that the rhythm is quite different from that of the conventional poetry of the period. Notice too that instead of echoing the ideas and words of other poets—instead of writing what he now called "a poem distilled from poems"—Whitman is talking, in a new manner, of life as he himself has known it. He is giving a very personal interpretation of his Long Island boyhood. He expresses himself in language which is more like common talk, more simple and idiomatic, than most poets were using at that time. And this poem represents the whole book of poems which Printer Whitman set up in type and printed with his own hands.

What had brought about the change? Whitman himself thought that he wrote the new poems because he had grown up—that some thirty years of preparation merely came to fruition. "I found myself possessed," he wrote, "at the age of thirty-one to thirty-three, with a special desire and conviction...a desire that had been flitting through my previous life, or hovering on the flanks, most indefinitely hitherto, had steadily advanced to the front, defined itself, and finally dominated everything else."

The Period of Conflict   389

Students find that several other influences were at work. They notice, for instance, that Whitman was a great reader of the Bible, and that some of his rhythms are much like those of the poetic parts of that book. They point out that Whitman was, like many in his day, much interested in oratory. It was a time when many of the greatest leaders were great public speakers, too—Daniel Webster, Wendell Phillips, Henry Clay, Edward Everett, and others. In New York, Whitman had haunted the law courts and had heard great speakers in many meetings. He was to write enviously of the power of the public speaker:

O the orator's joys!
To inflate the chest—to roll the thunder of the voice from the ribs and throat,
To make the people rage, weep, desire, with yourself,
To lead America—to quell America with a great tongue.

The passages from Shakespeare which Whitman intoned on omnibuses were declamatory speeches. It was not strange, therefore, such critics claim, that the form—the organization and the rhythm—of Whitman's new poetry resembled that of oratory. Whitman always believed that his poems should be read pretty much as orations were, that they should be chanted and intoned.

Critics also point out that various earlier poets had prepared the way for the new verse form, which is of a type commonly called "free verse." During the first part of the nineteenth century, quite a few poets in England and the United States had experimented with verse forms which broke away from the regular rhythms of the older poetry. In England, there had been Coleridge and Blake; in America, Emerson, Thoreau, and Lowell—and in both countries there had been less famous experimenters than these. Whitman, therefore, in writing his free verse, merely pushed to an extreme what others had done on a smaller scale.

So much for the new form of Whitman's poetry. But what of the new substance, the new attitudes, the new feelings which it presented? Probably the substance was drawn in part from life itself, in part from the influence of certain books which the poet read.

Whitman's work, it happened, introduced him to some aspects of American living and thinking which were important in his new songs. As a newspaper reporter and as a schoolteacher, he had come to know how farmers lived, how they felt about many subjects. In 1848, having been employed by a New Orleans newspaper, he journeyed for the first time beyond Long Island and New York. By coach he followed the trail of the pioneers through Cumberland Gap[1] to Wheeling, then went by boat down the Ohio and the Mississippi. When his work in New Orleans was completed, he traveled home again by way of the pioneer highway first used by the early French explorers—the Mississippi River and the Great Lakes. During his journeys of five thousand miles, not only did he see life in parts of the country far beyond New York; in addition, he caught the frontier point of view. Then, when he returned to Brooklyn, Whit-

---

[1]*Cumberland Gap,* a mountain pass in the Cumberland Mountains where Virginia, Kentucky, and Tennessee meet.

man worked for a while as a carpenter, helping his father erect houses in the fast-growing city.

From the time that Andrew Jackson, the great champion of the rights of the common man, had been elected president in 1829, the United States had gradually been extending its concept of democracy. The great majority of farmers, frontiersmen, and workmen—followers of Jackson—were struggling to gain further social and economic rights. They wanted equality of opportunity, so that they might flourish in what they believed was a great land of opportunity. Whitman, as the costume he wore in his new picture showed, aligned himself with this group of toilers.

And it happened that Whitman's reading, in this period of his development, emphasized similar ideas. Very important to him were the writings of Ralph Waldo Emerson, who, in those days, was writing philosophical essays which stirred many readers. Emerson was urging his fellow countrymen to do their own thinking, to be independent and self-sufficient, to be democratic. "We will walk on our own feet; we will work with our own hands; we will speak our own minds," he had proclaimed in one of his most famous utterances. Professor Mark Van Doren says properly that Emerson's service to many Americans was "to fill them with a sense of their individual importance, and to convince them that as citizens of a New World they were under obligation to make a fresh start in the life of man." Whitman spoke of Emerson's importance to his own development: "I was simmering, simmering. Emerson brought me to a boil."

So the new Whitman, employing the new verse form which he had developed, preached the individualistic ideas about democracy prevalent in the swaggering new country. There was something of the workman's or the pioneer's self-confidence about him as he—to quote his own words—shouted his "barbaric yawp over the rooftops of the world." "I wear my hat as I please," he boasted, "indoors or out." He wrote, in his "Song of the Broad-Axe," of "the beauty of all adventurous and daring persons," "the beauty of independence, departure, actions that rely on themselves," and of the "boundless impatience of restraint" which he thought all Americans should have.

Whitman actually thought of himself as having a mission to voice America's concept of democracy for his countrymen. He regarded himself as a typical American, one whose life and thought qualified him for this august mission. He sang:

Fall behind me States!
A man before all—myself, typical, before all.
I have given alms to everyone that asked, stood up for the stupid and crazy, devoted
    my income and labor to others,
Hated tyrants, argued not concerning God, had patience and indulgence toward the
    people, taken off my hat to nothing known or unknown,
Gone freely with powerful uneducated persons, with the young and with the
    mothers of families...
I swear I will have each quality of my race in myself.

So he sang for America what its beliefs were to be. There follow extracts from two poems typical of this period in Whitman's development. In both you will observe his democratic faith in the individual.

FROM *To You*

1

WHOEVER YOU ARE, I fear you are walking
    the walks of dreams,
I fear these supposed realities are to melt from
    under your feet and hands,
Even now your features, joys, speech, house,
    trade, manners, troubles, follies, costume,
    crimes, dissipate away from you,
Your true soul and body appear before me,
They stand forth out of affairs, out of com-
    merce, shops, work, farms, clothes, the house,
    buying, selling, eating, drinking, suffering,
    dying.   5

2

Whoever you are, now I place my hand upon
    you, that you be my poem,
I whisper with my lips close to your ear,
I have loved many women and men, but I love
    none better than you.

3

O I have been dilatory and dumb,
I should have made my way straight to you long
    ago,   10
I should have blabbed nothing but you, I should
    have chanted nothing but you.

4

I will leave all and come and make the hymns
    of you,
None has understood you, but I understand you,
None has done justice to you, you have not
    done justice to yourself,
None but has found you imperfect, I only find
    no imperfection in you,   15
None but would subordinate you, I only am he
    who will never consent to subordinate you....

5

O I could sing such grandeurs and glories about
    you!
You have not known what you are, you have
    slumbered upon yourself all your life,
Your eyelids have been the same as closed most
    of the time,
What you have done returns already in mock-
    eries....   20

6

The mockeries are not you,
Underneath them and within them I see you
    lurk,
I pursue you where none else has pursued you,
Silence, the desk, the flippant expression, the
    night, the accustomed routine, if these con-
    ceal you from others or from yourself, they
    do not conceal you from me....

7

There is no endowment in man or woman that
    is not tallied in you,   25
There is no virtue, no beauty in man or woman,
    but as good is in you,
No pluck, no endurance in others, but as good
    is in you,
No pleasure waiting for others, but an equal
    pleasure waits for you....

8

Whoever you are! claim your own at any
    hazard!
These shows of the East and West[1] are tame
    compared to you,   30
These immense meadows, these interminable
    rivers, you are immense and interminable as
    they,
These furies, elements, storms, motions of
    nature, throes of apparent dissolution, you
    are he or she who is master or mistress over
    them,
Master or mistress in your own right over na-
    ture, elements, pain, passion, dissolution.

[1] *shows of the East and West,* wonders of nature in all
parts of the world.

〜

FROM *By Blue Ontario's Shore*

IT IS NOT the earth, it is not America who is
    so great,
It is I who am great or to be great, it is you up
    there, or any one,
It is to walk rapidly through civilizations, gov-
    ernments, theories,
Through poems, pageants, shows, to form in-
    dividuals.

Underneath all, individuals,   5
I swear nothing is good to me now that ignores
     individuals,
The American compact[1] is altogether with in-
     dividuals,
The only government is that which makes
     minute of[2] individuals,
The whole theory of the universe is directed
     unerringly to one single individual—namely
     to you....

O I see flashing that this America is only you
     and me,   10
Its power, weapons, testimony, are you and
     me,
Its crimes, lies, thefts, defections, are you and
     me,
Its Congress is you and me, the officers, capitols,
     armies, ships, are you and me,
Its endless gestations of new States are you and
     me,
Natural and artificial are you and me,   15
Freedom, language, poems, employments, are
     you and me,
Past, present, future, are you and me.

I dare not shirk any part of myself,
Not any part of America good or bad,
Not to build for that which builds for man-
     kind,   20
Not to balance ranks, complexions, creeds, and
     the sexes,
Not to justify science nor the march of equality,
Nor to feed the arrogant blood of the brawn
     beloved of time.

I am for those that have never been mastered,
For men and women whose tempers have never
     been mastered   25
For those whom laws, theories, conventions, can
     never master.

I am for those who walk abreast with the whole
     earth,
Who inaugurate one to inaugurate all.

---

[1]*The American compact,* the bond that ties together the
individuals of all the states in their common government.
[2]*makes minute of,* takes careful note of.

I will not be outfaced by irrational things,
I will penetrate what it is in them that is sar-
     castic upon me,   30
I will make cities and civilizations defer to me,
This is what I have learnt from America—it is
     the amount, and it I teach again.

CONCERNING WALT WHITMAN

1. The picture of Whitman in the first edition of
Leaves of Grass showed him dressed as a workman
rather than as the dandy he had earlier been. What
significance do you find in this fact? What experiences
had probably changed Whitman's outlook on life?

2. What was Emerson's influence on Whitman?

3. How were Whitman's new interests and philosophy reflected in the things he wrote about?

4. How did the form of Whitman's new poetry
differ from the form of his earlier poems? What influences had probably helped shape his new style?

CONCERNING THE POEMS

FROM *"To You"*

1. Who is the "you" of the poem? Is it any particular person? Cite lines which support your answer.

2. What is the theme of the poem?

3. In stanzas 1, 4, and 6, what kind of unusual
knowledge of "you" does Whitman claim he has?

4. Because of this special knowledge, what praises
of "you" is he able to sing?

5. What does stanza 3 mean? How does it show
that Whitman has turned his back on his past work?

6. How are Whitman's attitude and message related
to (a) the American thought of the time and (b) his
new philosophy?

7. Contrast this poem with "Young Grimes." How
is Whitman's manner of writing in "To You" (his
rhythms, his choice of words) typical of the new Whitman rather than the early Whitman?

FROM *"By Blue Ontario's Shore"*

1. What, according to Whitman, constitutes the
greatness of America? How is this idea related to that
developed in "To You"?

2. What are some of the things which Whitman
lists in lines 10-17 as being "you and me"? Can you
think of other similar features that are "you and me"?

3. In what way are the ideas expressed in lines 24-32
related to the American attitude concerning democracy
at the time the poem was written?

4. Why is Whitman's frequent use of "I" in the last
stanza less egotistical than it would be in the work of
another poet?

Free verse

Although the type of verse which Walt Whitman used in *Leaves of Grass* differed greatly from that which Longfellow, Holmes, and Whittier were writing at the same time, yet it was not something completely new. Free verse, as distinguished from conventional verse, had appeared in the Psalms of David and the Song of Solomon centuries before Christ; Frenchmen and Germans had experimented with the form. But it remained for Whitman to make the modern world aware that poetry need possess neither rhyme nor regular rhythm.

The term "free verse" explains itself—it is free: free of the demands of rhyme, free of the necessity for a certain number of accents in a line. Free verse must have rhythm, but it may be an irregular cadence which allows the poet to gain a variety of rhythmical effects. Because of this freedom of cadence, the rhythm of free verse is usually worked out not in a single line, as is true of conventional verse forms, but in a stanza.

Like all poetry, free verse is designed to be read aloud. (You won't really understand how skillfully verse form and substance are fused in Whitman's poetry until you hear it well read.) Choose a stanza that you like and understand from "To You" or from "By Blue Ontario's Shore." Practice reading it aloud until the rhythm and force of the verse roll out easily. (Remember that Whitman himself believed that poetry should be chanted; but take care not to make your reading "sing-songy.") Then read the stanza for your classmates.

III POET IN WARTIME

Readers of the present day see *Leaves of Grass* as the book in which Whitman's poetic powers became evident, but most readers of this unusual work at the time thought very little of it. The poet Whittier read a little in the copy which Walt sent him and then disgustedly flung the book into the blazing grate. Workers in a New York newspaper office listened to excerpts and roared with laughter. Reviewers either ignored the book or sternly criticized it. But Whitman, serenely sure that his poetry would in time be appreciated, prepared a second edition, with several new poems, in 1856, and a third in 1860. And as the years passed, Whitman enlarged and revised his collection of poems in editions which were published in 1867, 1871, 1876, 1881, 1888, 1889, and 1891. Most of these editions down to the last years of Whitman's life were not favorably received. Although he gained some enthusiastic admirers, and although their number grew as the years passed, the kind of poetry Whitman wrote made slow progress.

Whitman's career was a constant merging of observations and feelings into one great book—a single-minded concern with one great expression. Since Whitman kept weaving his new poems from new experiences, since these poems became parts of his growing book, and since the book represented growth and change in his thought, he came in time to think of *Leaves of Grass* as a kind of autobiography. Moreover it was valuable, he believed, because this depiction of the life of one man—"Walt Whitman, an American"—represented the lives of many others. To some extent at any rate, his belief was justified. When, for instance, he told of the profound impression which the War Between the States made upon him, he spoke for many millions upon whom the bitter war left lasting imprints. And for him, as for America, the war was a turning point.

Perhaps because of his Quaker background, Whitman did not enlist as a soldier when the war came. His first-hand experience of the war began in 1862, when he went to Virginia to care for his brother George, who had been wounded. His brother had almost recovered when the poet arrived, but Whitman found that he could be useful in the field hospital. He worked there, and in time he helped convoy some of the wounded to a Washington hospital. In Washington, he volunteered as a male nurse, and he served in the various hospitals and in nearby army camps until late in 1864.

His great rolling body and his bearded bronzed face became familiar in the hospitals. He visited the wards and tried to supply what the wounded and sick men needed—sweets, perhaps, or tobacco, or writing paper, or money. He read to some, wrote letters for others. His chief service, in his opinion, however, was simply indicating a personal interest in the men. "The American soldier," he wrote, "is full of affection and the yearning for affection. And it comes wonderfully grateful to him to have this yearning gratified when he is laid up with painful wounds or illness, far away from home, among strangers." Again, he wrote in a letter: "Mother, I have real pride in telling you that I have the consciousness of saving quite a number of lives by saving the soldiers from giving up—and being a good deal with them. The men say it is so, and the doctors say it is so—and I will candidly confess I can see it is true, though I say it of myself. I know you will like to hear it, so I tell you." Our knowledge of psychology helps us understand that Whitman probably was reporting accurately on his achievements. His friendliness was an antidote for shock and stimulated the will to live. The following poems are based upon Whitman's wartime experiences.

Beat! Beat! Drums!

Beat! beat! drums!—blow! bugles! blow!
   Through the windows—through doors—
   burst like a ruthless force,
Into the solemn church, and scatter the congregation,
Into the school where the scholar is studying;
Leave not the bridegroom quiet—no happiness
   must he have now with his bride,   5
Nor the peaceful farmer any peace, plowing his
   field or gathering his grain,
So fierce you whirr and pound you drums—so
   shrill you bugles blow.

Beat! beat! drums!—blow! bugles! blow!
Over the traffic of cities—over the rumble of
   wheels in the streets;
Are beds prepared for sleepers at night in the
   houses? no sleepers must sleep in those
   beds,   10

No bargainers' bargains by day—no brokers or
   speculators—would they continue?
Would the talkers be talking? would the singer
   attempt to sing?
Would the lawyer rise in the court to state his
   case before the judge?
Then rattle quicker, heavier drums—you bugles
   wilder blow.

Beat! beat! drums!—blow! bugles! blow!   15
Make no parley—stop for no expostulation,
Mind not the timid—mind not the weeper or
   prayer,
Mind not the old man beseeching the young
   man,
Let not the child's voice be heard, nor the
   mother's entreaties,
Make even the trestles to shake the dead where
   they lie awaiting the hearses,   20
So strong you thump O terrible drums—so loud
   you bugles blow.

When Lilacs Last in the Dooryard Bloomed

Walt Whitman first saw Lincoln in 1861, and was much impressed by his appearance. Later, in Washington, seeing the President almost daily, Whitman came to have great faith in him and love for him.

Lincoln was assassinated April 14, 1865, and Whitman heard the news the next day in Brooklyn. "There were many lilacs in full bloom," said Whitman later. "I find myself always reminded of the great tragedy of that day by the sight and odor of these blossoms. It never fails."

This memory went into the poem which Whitman wrote about Lincoln's death. In it, lilacs became the symbol of human love and memory; a fallen star symbolized the death of Lincoln; a bird's song symbolized the consolation of immortality. The poem pictures (in stanzas 5-7) the movement of Lincoln's funeral train from Washington to the burial place in Springfield, Illinois. Like most elegies, it begins with lamentation (stanzas 1-12), and after a transition (stanza 13) concludes with consolation (stanzas 14-16).

1

W HEN LILACS last in the dooryard bloomed,
  And the great star early drooped in the
western sky in the night,
I mourned, and yet shall mourn with ever-
  returning spring.

Ever-returning spring, trinity sure to me you
  bring,
Lilac blooming perennial and drooping star in
  the west,   5
And thought of him I love.

2

O powerful western fallen star!
O shades of night—O moody, tearful night!
O great star disappeared—O the black murk
  that hides the star!
O cruel hands that hold me powerless—O help-
  less soul of me!   10
O harsh surrounding cloud that will not free
  my soul.

3

In the dooryard fronting an old farmhouse near
  the whitewashed palings,
Stands the lilac bush tall-growing with heart-
  shaped leaves of rich green,
With many a pointed blossom rising delicate,
  with the perfume strong I love,
With every leaf a miracle—and from this bush
  in the dooryard,   15
With delicate-colored blossoms and heart-
  shaped leaves of rich green,
A sprig with its flower I break.

4

In the swamp in secluded recesses,
A shy and hidden bird is warbling a song.
Solitary the thrush,   20
The hermit withdrawn to himself, avoiding the
  settlements,
Sings by himself a song.

Song of the bleeding throat,
Death's outlet song of life (for well dear brother
  I know,
If thou wast not granted to sing thou would'st
  surely die).   25

5

Over the breast of the spring, the land, amid
  cities,
Amid lanes and through old woods, where lately
  the violets peeped from the ground, spotting
  the gray debris,
Amid the grass in the fields each side of the
  lanes, passing the endless grass,
Passing the yellow-speared wheat, every grain
  from its shroud in the dark brown fields
  uprisen,
Passing the apple-tree blows[1] of white and pink
  in the orchards,   30
Carrying a corpse to where it shall rest in the
  grave,
Night and day journeys a coffin.

---

[1] *blows*, blossoms.

6

Coffin that passes through lanes and streets,
Through day and night with the great cloud
  darkening the land,
With the pomp of the inlooped flags with the
  cities draped in black,   35
With the show of the States themselves as of
  crape-veiled women standing,
With processions long and winding and the
  flambeaus of the night,
With the countless torches lit, with the silent
  sea of faces and the unbared heads,
With the waiting depot, the arriving coffin, and
  the somber faces,
With dirges through the night, with the thousand
  voices rising strong and solemn,   40
With all the mournful voices of the dirges
  poured around the coffin,
The dim-lit churches and the shuddering organs
  —where amid these you journey,
With the tolling tolling bells' perpetual clang,
Here, coffin that slowly passes,
I give you my sprig of lilac.   45

7

(Nor for you, for one alone,
Blossoms and branches green to coffins all I
  bring,
For fresh as the morning, thus would I chant
  a song for you O sane and sacred death.

All over bouquets of roses,
O death, I cover you over with roses and early
  lilies,   50
But mostly and now the lilac that blooms the
  first,
Copious I break, I break the sprigs from the
  bushes,
With loaded arms I come, pouring for you,
For you and the coffins all of you O death.)

8

O western orb sailing the heaven,   55
Now I know what you must have meant as a
  month since I walked,
As I walked in silence the transparent shadowy
  night,
As I saw you had something to tell as you bent
  to me night after night,

As you drooped from the sky low down as if to
  my side (while the other stars all looked on),
As we wandered together the solemn night (for
  something I know not what kept me from
  sleep),   60
As the night advanced, and I saw on the rim of
  the west how full you were of woe,
As I stood on the rising ground in the breeze
  in the cool transparent night,
As I watched where you passed and was lost in
  the netherward black[2] of the night,
As my soul in its trouble dissatisfied sank, as
  where you sad orb,
Concluded, dropt in the night, and was gone. 65

9

Sing on there in the swamp,
O singer bashful and tender, I hear your notes,
  I hear your call,
I hear, I come presently, I understand you,
But a moment I linger, for the lustrous star has
  detained me,
The star my departing comrade holds and
  detains me.   70

10

O how shall I warble myself for the dead one
  there I loved?
And how shall I deck my song for the large
  sweet soul that has gone?
And what shall my perfume be for the grave
  of him I love?

Sea-winds blown from east and west,
Blown from the Eastern sea and blown from
  the Western sea, till there on the prairies
  meeting,   75
These and with these and the breath of my
  chant,
I'll perfume the grave of him I love.

11

O what shall I hang on the chamber walls?
And what shall the pictures be that I hang on
  the walls,
To adorn the burial-house of him I love?   80

---

[2]*netherward black,* the darkness that seems to hug the
region near the horizon.

Pictures of growing spring and farms and homes,

With the Fourth-month[3] eve at sundown, and the gray smoke lucid and bright,

With floods of the yellow gold of the gorgeous, indolent, sinking sun, burning, expanding the air,

With the fresh sweet herbage under foot, and the pale green leaves of the trees prolific,

In the distance the flowing glaze, the breast of the river, with a wind-dapple here and there, 85

With ranging hills on the banks, with many a line against the sky, and shadows,

And the city at hand with dwellings so dense, and stacks of chimneys,

And all the scenes of life and the workshops, and the workmen homeward returning.

12

Lo, body and soul—this land,

My own Manhattan with spires, and the sparkling and hurrying tides, and the ships, 90

The varied and ample land, the South and the North in the light, Ohio's shores and flashing Missouri,

And ever the far-spreading prairies covered with grass and corn.

Lo, the most excellent sun so calm and haughty,

The violet and purple morn with just-felt breezes,

The gentle soft-born measureless light, 95

The miracle spreading bathing all, the fulfilled noon,

The coming eve delicious, the welcome night and the stars,

Over my cities shining all, enveloping man and land.

13

Sing on, sing on you gray-brown bird,

Sing from the swamps, the recesses, pour your chant from the bushes, 100

Limitless out of the dusk, out of the cedars and pines.

Sing on dearest brother, warble your reedy song,

Loud human song, with voice of uttermost woe.

O liquid and free and tender!

O wild and loose to my soul—O wondrous singer! 105

You only I hear—yet the star holds me (but will soon depart),

Yet the lilac with mastering odor holds me.

14

Now while I sat in the day and looked forth,

In the close of the day with its light and the fields of spring, and the farmers preparing their crops,

In the large unconscious scenery of my land with its lakes and forests, 110

In the heavenly aerial beauty (after the perturbed winds and the storms),

Under the arching heavens of the afternoon swift passing, and the voices of children and women,

The many-moving sea tides, and I saw the ships how they sailed,

And the summer approaching with richness, and the fields all busy with labor,

And the infinite separate houses, how they all went on, each with its meals and minutia of daily usages, 115

And the streets how their throbbings throbbed, and the cities pent—lo, then and there,

Falling upon them all and among them all, enveloping me with the rest,

Appeared the cloud, appeared the long black trail,

And I knew death, its thought, and the sacred knowledge of death.

Then with the knowledge of death as walking one side of me, 120

And the thought of death close-walking the other side of me,

And I in the middle as with companions, and as holding the hands of companions,

---

[3]*Fourth-month,* April, the month in which Lincoln was assassinated.

I fled forth to the hiding receiving night that
talks not,
Down to the shores of the water, the path by
the swamp in the dimness,
To the solemn shadowy cedars and ghostly
pines so still.   125

And the singer so shy to the rest received me,
The gray-brown bird I know received us com-
rades three,
And he sang the carol of death, and a verse for
him I love.
From deep secluded recesses,
From the fragrant cedars and the ghostly pines
so still,   130
Came the carol of the bird.

And the charm of the carol rapt me,
As I held as if by their hands my comrades in
the night,
And the voice of my spirit tallied the song of
the bird.

Come lovely and soothing death,   135
Undulate round the world, serenely arriving,
arriving,
In the day, in the night, to all, to each,
Sooner or later delicate death.

Praised be the fathomless universe,
For life and joy, and for objects and knowledge
curious,   140
And for love, sweet love—but praise! praise!
praise!
For the sure-enwinding arms of cool-enfolding
death.

Dark mother always gliding near with soft feet,
Have none chanted for thee a chant of fullest
welcome?   144
Then I chant it for thee, I glorify thee above all,
I bring thee a song that when thou must indeed
come, come unfalteringly.

Approach strong deliveress,
When it is so, when thou hast taken them I
joyously sing the dead,
Lost in the loving floating ocean of thee,
Laved in the flood of thy bliss O death.   150

From me to thee glad serenades,
Dances for thee I propose saluting thee, adorn-
ments and feastings for thee,
And the sights of the open landscape and the
high-spread sky are fitting,
And life and the fields, and the huge and
thoughtful night.

The night in silence under many a star,   155
The ocean shore and the husky whispering wave
whose voice I know,
And the soul turning to thee O vast and well-
veiled death,
And the body gratefully nestling close to thee.

Over the treetops I float thee a song,
Over the rising and sinking waves, over the
myriad fields and the prairies wide,   160
Over the dense-packed cities all and the teem-
ing wharves and ways,
I float this carol with joy, with joy to thee
O death.

15

To the tally of my soul,
Loud and strong kept up the gray-brown bird,
With pure deliberate notes spreading, filling the
night.   165

Loud in the pines and cedars dim,
Clear in the freshness moist and the swamp
perfume,
And I with my comrades there in the night.

While my sight that was bound in my eyes
unclosed,
As to long panoramas of visions.   170

And I saw askant the armies,
I saw as in noiseless dreams hundreds of battle-
flags,
Borne through the smoke of the battles and
pierced with missiles I saw them,
And carried hither and yon through the smoke,
and torn and bloody,
And at last but a few shreds left on the staffs
(and all in silence),   175
And the staffs all splintered and broken.

I saw battle corpses, myriads of them,
And the white skeletons of young men, I saw
    them,
And I saw the debris and debris of all the slain
    soldiers of the war,
But I saw they were not as was thought,   180
They themselves were fully at rest, they suffered
    not,
The living remained and suffered, the mother
    suffered,
And the wife and the child and the musing com-
    rade suffered,
And the armies that remained suffered.

16

Passing the visions, passing the night,   185
Passing, unloosing the hold of my comrades'
    hands,
Passing the song of the hermit bird and the
    tallying song of my soul,
Victorious song, death's outlet song, yet varying
    ever-altering song,
As low and wailing, yet clear the notes, rising
    and falling, flooding the night,
Sadly sinking and fainting, as warning and warn-
    ing, and yet again bursting with joy,   190
Covering the earth and filling the spread of the
    heaven,
As that powerful psalm in the night I heard
    from recesses,
Passing, I leave thee lilac with heart-shaped
    leaves,
I leave thee there in the dooryard, blooming,
    returning with spring.

I cease from my song for thee,   195
From my gaze on thee in the west, fronting the
    west, communing with thee,
O comrade lustrous with silver face in the
    night.

Yet each to keep and all, retrievements out of
    the night,
The song, the wondrous chant of the gray-
    brown bird,
And the tallying chant, the echo aroused in my
    soul,   200
With the lustrous and drooping star with the
    countenance full of woe,

With the holders holding my hand nearing the
    call of the bird,
Comrades mine and I in the midst, and their
    memory ever to keep, for the dead I loved so
    well,
For the sweetest, wisest soul of all my days and
    lands—and this for his dear sake,
Lilac and star and bird twined with the chant
    of my soul,   205
There in the fragrant pines and the cedars dusk
    and dim.

CONCERNING WALT WHITMAN

1. How was *Leaves of Grass* received by most
people in Whitman's time? Can you account for this
feeling about the book? What do the numerous revised and enlarged editions show about Whitman's
confidence in the book?

2. In what way did Whitman consider his book important?

3. What do you believe was the greatest value of
Whitman's wartime experiences?

CONCERNING THE POEMS

"Beat! Beat! Drums!"

1. What do the drums of the poem symbolize?

2. Mention some of the kinds of people who hear
the beating drum. Why should the poet tell of the
sound reaching so many kinds of people?

3. The effects of the drums differ from stanza to
stanza. In stanza 1, for instance, the drums are merely
heard. What are their effects, by contrast, in stanzas 2
and 3? How does the poem mount to a climax in
stanza 3?

4. One critic says: "Under the strong emotional
stress of a country engaged in a deadly combat, Whitman's rhythms became more regular." Compare the
poem in this respect with those on pages 392 and 393.
Find lines which echo the rhythmic beat of the drums.

"When Lilacs Last in the Dooryard Bloomed"

1. What is the trinity that Whitman mentions in
the first stanza as returning with every spring?

2. In the early stanzas, the fallen star represents
Lincoln. Read the lines in stanzas 1 and 2 that indicate
this meaning, and show how these lines express Whitman's attitude toward Lincoln.

3. Stanza 3 identifies the lilac as a symbol of human
love and memory. How does the description of the
lilac show that it is well suited for this meaning?

4. What details are stressed in the description of the funeral procession (stanzas 5-6)? Why do you think these particular details are emphasized?

5. According to stanza 7, whom besides Lincoln is the nation mourning? Why is the entire stanza placed in parentheses?

6. Stanzas 10-12 are Whitman's lamentation for Lincoln. What is his particular concern in stanza 10? Are the first three lines of stanza 11 to be understood literally or figuratively? Explain them. How do the remainder of this stanza and stanza 12 elaborate the idea introduced in these lines? Why is Whitman's lament appropriate for Lincoln?

7. How do you interpret lines 120-125?

8. What is the feeling toward death in the lyric which begins "Come lovely and soothing death" (line 135)? How do this lyric and the succeeding stanzas vary in tone and mood from the earlier portions of the poem?

9. What does this poem show concerning Whitman's feeling about (*a*) the war, (*b*) Lincoln, (*c*) the nation after the war?

Know your words

Walt Whitman enjoyed using words of French origin in his poems. *Flambeau, debris,* and *bouquet,* all of which occur in "When Lilacs Last in the Dooryard Bloomed," are such words. The language of France has contributed many useful words to the English language, just as did the language of ancient Rome; but whereas most Latin words in time acquired English pronunciations, many French words have kept some of the characteristics of French pronunciation. For this reason it is necessary to check carefully the pronunciation of words derived from the French language. Give the correct pronunciation and meaning of *flambeau, debris,* and *bouquet.* (Consult the Glossary to make sure you are right.)

The italicized words in the sentences below are also of French origin. Determine the pronunciation of each by consulting the Glossary. Be prepared (1) to read the sentence aloud as it stands, and (2) to read the sentence, substituting another word or words for the italicized word.

1. Our host at the annual dinner was considered a real *gourmet.*

2. The trappers' usual *rendezvous* was a low bluff beside the river.

3. The *ingénue* wore clothes of a type well suited to a *petite* person.

4. His *ennui* disappeared as he learned that the task would require all his ingenuity.

5. People rushed out of the burning house in various kinds of *dishabille.*

6. In his hurry he left his *portmanteau* at the station.

7. A series of *tableaus* representing the growth of the United States concluded the program given by the students.

❧ IV POSTWAR THEMES

The experiences Whitman had as a nurse could not but influence him as a poet. His daily association with the wounded, the sick, and the dying gave him a broader knowledge of life. It taught him, too, the value of physical health, unimpaired strength. After his wartime experiences, however, he also saw more clearly the importance of suffering and the importance of good relationships between human beings. Shortly after the end of the conflict, he was singing not only of men as individuals but also of men suffering and striving together as a group:

> One's self I sing, a simple separate person,
> Yet utter the word Democratic, the word En Masse.

"Who except myself, America," he asked, "has conceived what your children en masse really are?" The war had made him more humane, more coöperative—had made him aware not only of freedom but also of responsibility.

Doubtless Whitman's own physical suffering also had its influence. An accidental wound in his hand in August, 1863, was followed by blood

poisoning. He suffered from malaria. And he worked harder than he should have in the hospitals. Eventually Whitman, who had never been sick, was forced to go to bed for several days at a time. He had "spells of deathly faintness." The doctors were saying, he wrote home, that he was "going too strong." Finally, he was forced to end his hospital work and return home to Brooklyn. After partial recovery, he returned to Washington in 1865, and worked in various government departments. But he was never to recover his health. In 1869, he was having his "spells" again, and the use of his limbs was impaired. In 1873, he suffered a paralytic stroke which left him partially crippled. He left Washington for Camden, New Jersey, where he lived during the final years of his life.

Whitman, between 1865 and his death, was no longer proclaiming himself "one of the roughs." He was called by his friends "the good gray poet." Admirers who traveled from many parts of the country or even across the ocean to visit him felt that this name was appropriate. He sat in an upper room of his house with books, newspapers, galley proofs, and manuscripts littering the floor about him. But visitors forgot their chaotic surroundings as they looked at the aged poet sitting motionless in his chair. His complexion was as pink as ever. But the face showed the effects of age and suffering; the heavy-lidded blue eyes, glazed and thoughtful, looked into the distance; and the magnificent white beard seemed to emphasize the poet's dignity. There was a spiritual quality in his appearance. Painters, sculptors, and photographers found him a wonderful subject. His songs lacked the vigor, the brutal force, of his earliest songs. They were more pensive and more serene. And his thoughts of men and of life led him to develop new themes.

One developing theme concerned mankind. In his first period, as we have seen, his emphasis was all upon the individual. But in Whitman's thinking there was a growing recognition of the dependence of man upon man—a theme which had been only briefly developed in his earlier poems. The war, naturally enough, emphasized Whitman's love for the United States as a nation. Now in the years after the War Between the States, as America became more and more of a force in world affairs, Whitman looked beyond the boundaries of his own country. He wrote a poem to France in 1871, to Brazil—newly made a republic—in the same year, to Spain in 1873. The poet who had believed that America must break away from the Old World ways now emphasized the fact that our country could learn much from the older nations. His "Passage to India" tells of the physical, intellectual, and spiritual unity of all the nations of the world.

Another developing theme concerned death. In the early years of his career, Whitman had thought little of this subject. In 1855, when he first published *Leaves of Grass,* death to him had simply meant that the physical body returned to nature:

> I bequeath myself to the dirt to grow from the grass I love,
> If you want me again look for me under your boot soles.

But Whitman's experiences in caring for the wounded during the War Between the States had caused him to see death as an important element in the whole career of man. The tragic death of Lincoln had strengthened this feeling. Whitman's own illness, too, had forced him to come face to face with the problems of man's mortality. Long before, like Emerson and Thoreau, Whitman had seen the significance and importance of all material things. Now he came to see that even death was a part of the total scheme. He became convinced that "the untold want by life and land ne'er granted" could be satisfied only when the voyager reached the land of death. The only true life, he said in his songs, must be that which followed death. And so Whitman became a great poet of immortality.

He faced death with serene confidence. His doctor, Richard Maurice Bucke, wrote: "I watched for years...in his sick-room, when from day to day and month to month his life was scarcely worth a week's purchase, and he knew it well; and I learned there for the first time in what spirit a truly heroic soul confronted death. Equally removed from fear and bravado; maintaining absolute equanimity; patient and forbearing; at times suffering but never complaining—so far from it, indeed, that he would rarely acknowledge he was in pain—for many weary, lingering months he awaited with calmness and resignation the inevitable end. He never for a moment lost the sweetness and charm of his habitual manner." The end came March 26, 1892.

During his last years, Whitman began to win solid recognition. A number of the leading literary men of England praised and published his work, and more and more Americans came to admire it. After his death, his reputation continued to grow, and today he is generally classed among the greatest American poets.

The following poems represent Whitman's final period.

FROM *Passage to India*

1

Singing my days,
Singing the great achievements of the present,
Singing the strong light works of engineers,
Our modern wonders (the antique ponderous
  Seven[1] outvied):

In the Old World the east, the Suez Canal,[2]   5
The New by its mighty railroad[3] spanned.

2

Passage to India!
Lo soul, seest thou not God's purpose from the
  first?
The earth to be spanned, connected by network,
The oceans to be crossed, the distant brought
  near,   10
The lands to be welded together.

---

[1]*Seven,* the seven wonders of the ancient world. These were the pyramids of Egypt, the great lighthouse at Alexandria in Egypt, the hanging gardens of Babylon, the temple of Diana at Ephesus (efʹi səs) in Asia Minor, the statue of Jupiter by Phidias (fidʹi əs), the Mausoleum (magnificent tomb) at Halicarnassus (halʹi kär nasʹəs) in Asia Minor, and the Colossus of Rhodes, a huge statue of the god Apollo.

[2]*Suez* (sü ezʹ *or* süʹez) *Canal,* completed in 1867 and formally opened two years later. It separated Asia and Africa by cutting through the Isthmus of Suez, and shortened the passage to India from Europe by thousands of miles.

[3]*mighty railroad,* the Union Pacific, the first railroad linking East and West. It was completed in 1869.

A worship new I sing,
You captains, voyagers, explorers, yours,
You engineers, you architects, machinists, yours,
You, not for trade or transportation only,   15
But in God's name, and for thy sake O soul.

3

Passage to India!
Lo soul for thee of tableaus twain.
I see in one the Suez Canal initiated, opened,
I see the procession of steamships, the Empress
    Eugenie's leading the van,[4]   20
I mark from on deck the strange landscape, the
    pure sky, the level sand in the distance,
I pass swiftly the picturesque groups, the work-
    men gathered,
The gigantic dredging machines.

In one again, different (yet thine, all thine, O
    soul, the same),
I see over my own continent the Pacific railroad
    surmounting every barrier,   25
I see continual trains of cars winding along the
    Platte[5] carrying freight and passengers,
I hear the locomotives rushing and roaring, and
    the shrill steam whistle,
I hear the echoes reverberate through the grand-
    est scenery in the world,
I cross the Laramie plains,[6] I note the rocks in
    grotesque shapes, the buttes,
I see the plentiful larkspur and wild onions, the
    barren, colorless, sage deserts,   30
I see in glimpses afar or towering immediately
    above me the great mountains, I see the Wind
    River and the Wasatch Mountains,[7]

I see the Monument Mountain[8] and the Eagle's
    Nest,[9] I pass the Promontory,[10] I ascend the
    Nevadas,[11]
I scan the noble Elk Mountain[12] and wind
    around its base,
I see the Humboldt Range,[13] I thread the valley
    and cross the river,
I see the clear waters of Lake Tahoe,[14] I see
    forests of majestic pines,   35
Or crossing the great desert, the alkaline plains,
    I behold enchanting mirages of waters and
    meadows,
Marking through these and after all, in duplicate
    slender lines,
Bridging the three or four thousand miles of
    land travel,
Tying the Eastern to the Western sea,
The road between Europe and Asia.   40
(Ah Genoese, thy dream![15] thy dream!
Centuries after thou art laid in thy grave,
The shore thou foundest verifies thy dream.)

4

Passage to India!
Struggles of many a captain, tales of many a
    sailor dead,   45
Over my mood stealing and spreading they
    come,
Like clouds and cloudlets in the unreached sky.

Along all history, down the slopes,
As a rivulet running, sinking now, and now
    again to the surface rising,
A ceaseless thought, a varied train—lo, soul, to
    thee, thy sight, they rise,   50

---

[4]*the Empress Eugenie's leading the van.* Since the Suez
Canal had been constructed by a French company, the
honor of leading the ships of various countries through it
at the formal opening fell to a French ship. Guest of honor
on this ship was Empress Eugenie (œ zhā nē´), wife of
Napoleon III, emperor of France.

[5]*Laramie plains,* level uplands in eastern Wyoming.

[6]*the Platte,* a river which rises in Colorado, crosses
Nebraska, and joins the Missouri fifteen miles south of
Omaha. The Union Pacific follows it across Nebraska.
Footnotes 5-14 identify places Whitman mentions as being
visible from the Union Pacific. However, since he had
never traveled west of the Mississippi, he was uncertain
of his geography, and several of the places are mentioned
in incorrect order.

[7]*the Wind River and the Wasatch* (wô´sach) *Mountains.*
The Wind River Mountains in western Wyoming form part
of the Continental Divide; the Wasatch Mountains rise
west of them in Utah.

[8]*Monument Mountain,* probably Monument Peak near
Elko in northeastern Nevada.

[9]*Eagle's Nest,* probably a reference to Eagle's Rest, a
peak in the Teton Mountains south of Yellowstone Park.

[10]*the Promontory,* the point near Salt Lake, Utah, at
which the railroad gangs laying the track west met those
coming east from California and a golden spike, symbolizing completion of the railroad, was driven.

[11]*the Nevadas,* the Sierra Nevadas, a mountain range
dividing Nevada from California.

[12]*Elk Mountain,* one of the highest peaks in the Medicine Bow Range in south central Wyoming.

[13]*Humboldt Range,* a mountain range in western Nevada.

[14]*Lake Tahoe* (tä´hō or tā´hō), a mountain lake in
California and Nevada.

[15]*Genoese* (jen´ō ēz´), *thy dream.* Columbus, who was
born in Genoa, Italy, was seeking a route to India when
he discovered America.

The plans, the voyages again, the expeditions;
Again Vasco da Gama[16] sails forth,
Again the knowledge gained, the mariner's
  compass,
Lands found and nations born, thou born
  America.
For purpose vast, man's long probation filled, 55
Thou rondure[17] of the world at last accom-
  plished.

5

O vast Rondure, swimming in space,
Covered all over with visible power and beauty,
Alternate light and day and the teeming spiritual
  darkness,
Unspeakable high processions of sun and moon
  and countless stars above,   60
Below, the manifold grass and waters, animals,
  mountains, trees,
With inscrutable purpose, some hidden pro-
  phetic intention,
Now first it seems my thought begins to span
  thee.

6

Year at whose wide-flung door I sing!
Year of the purpose accomplished!   65
Year of the marriage of continents, climates
  and oceans!
O sun and moon and all you stars! Sirius and
  Jupiter![18]
Passage to you!

Passage, immediate passage! the blood burns in
  my veins!
Away O soul! hoist instantly the anchor!   70
Cut the hawsers—haul out—shake out every sail!
Have we not stood here like trees in the ground
  long enough?
Have we not groveled here long enough, eating
  and drinking like mere brutes?
Have we not darkened and dazed ourselves
  with books long enough?

Sail forth—steer for the deep waters only,   75
Reckless O soul, exploring, I with thee, and
  thou with me,
For we are bound where mariner has not yet
  dared to go,
And we will risk the ship, ourselves and all.

O my brave soul!
O farther farther sail!   80
O daring joy, but safe! are they not all the seas
  of God?
O farther, farther, farther sail!

~

Joy, Shipmate, Joy!

JOY, shipmate, joy!
  (Pleased to my soul at death I cry);
Our life is closed, our life begins,
The long, long anchorage we leave,
The ship is clear at last, she leaps!   5
She swiftly courses from the shore,
Joy, shipmate, joy.

CONCERNING WALT WHITMAN

1. How do the lines

One's self I sing, a simple separate person,
Yet utter the word Democratic, the word En Masse,

indicate Whitman's viewpoint toward men in his later years? How does this viewpoint differ from his earlier viewpoint? What experiences brought about the change?

2. How did the emergence of the United States as a world power affect Whitman's thinking?

3. How did Whitman's view of death change as he became older?

4. What change took place in the way other people regarded Whitman in the last years of his life?

CONCERNING THE POEMS

FROM "*Passage to India*"

1. Why were the completion of the Suez Canal and of the Union Pacific Railroad important to Whitman? In what way does he see God's purpose (line 8) in these engineering feats?

---

[16]*Vasco da Gama* (väs'kŏ də gä'mə), Portuguese navigator who rounded the Cape of Good Hope and made the first journey by sea from Europe to India in 1497-1498.
[17]*rondure* (ron'jər), roundness. In the next line Whitman addresses the world as "the round earth" (Rondure).
[18]*Sirius* (sir'i əs) *and Jupiter,* the brightest fixed star and the largest planet.

2. Why do you think Whitman describes in detail the route of the Union Pacific (lines 25-40)? What is the effect of this passage upon you?

3. What do you think is Whitman's reason for mentioning Columbus and Vasco da Gama in the poem?

4. Read again lines 69-82. What is the voyage to which Whitman refers in these lines? What lines indicate that Whitman regards this voyage as more important and more hazardous than the usual voyage of discovery?

5. What new concept of mankind does Whitman reveal in this poem? How does he reveal it?

"Joy, Shipmate, Joy!"

1. Discover all the figures of speech which refer to a ship and a voyage.

2. What does each such figure stand for? How do you know?

3. What general attitude or idea is developed by the poem?

4. How are the thought and feeling of the poem related to Whitman's postwar development?

Extending interests

1. Many poets have written about death, and the ideas they have expressed and the ways in which they have expressed them have varied as greatly as the poets themselves. Pick out a poem on this subject and practice reading it aloud. Then present it orally before the class and compare its author's attitude toward death with Whitman's. Among poems you might read are: "The Reaper and the Flowers" or "Nature," by Henry Wadsworth Longfellow; "Up-Hill," by Christina Rossetti; "Prospice," by Robert Browning; "Requiem," by Robert Louis Stevenson; "Invictus," by William Ernest Henley; "Crossing the Bar," by Alfred Lord Tennyson; and "L'Envoi," by Rudyard Kipling. All these may be found in *The Home Book of Verse,* edited by Burton Stevenson.

2. "Passage to India" expresses Whitman's belief in the need for coöperation among men of all nations. If Whitman were alive today, what do you think would be his viewpoint toward the various agencies designed to promote union among nations and to secure a better living standard for all peoples? Be as specific as possible in your discussion.

The Larger View

I. During what part of Whitman's life was each of the following written? Justify your answers by discussing the ideas and the form of each passage.

1. O, many a panting, noble heart
　　Cherishes in its deep recess
　The hope to win renown o'er earth
　　From Glory's prized caress.

2. A child said *What is the grass?* fetching it to
　　me with full hands,
　How could I answer the child? I do not know
　　what it is any more than he.

　...I guess it is the handkerchief of the Lord,
　A scented gift and remembrancer designedly
　　dropt,
　Bearing the owner's name someway in the cor-
　　ners, that we may see and remark, and say
　　Whose?
　Or I guess it is a uniform hieroglyphic,

And it means, sprouting alike in broad zones
　　and narrow zones,
Growing among black folks as among white,
Kanuck, Tuckahoe, Congressman, Cuff, I give
　　them the same, I receive them the same.

3. My science-friend, my noblest woman-friend
　....
　Ended our talk—"The sum, concluding all we
　　know of old or modern learning, intuitions
　　deep,
　Of all Geologies—Histories—of all Astronomy—
　　of Evolution, Metaphysics all,
　Is, that we all are onward, onward, speeding
　　slowly, surely bettering,
　Life, life an endless march, an endless army
　　(no halt, but it is duly over),
　The world, the race, the soul—in space and time
　　the universes,
　All bound as is befitting each—all surely going
　　somewhere."

II. Talk over the following questions with your classmates. Be sure that you base your discussion not only on what you have learned in class but also on ideas gleaned from your outside reading.

1. Compare and contrast Thoreau's and Whitman's views of the individual. Which was more interested in his fellowmen? How do you know?

2. How did Thoreau's and Whitman's views of government differ? Would Thoreau, in your opinion, have been more sympathetic with Whitman's earlier, or his later, conception of democracy? Why?

3. Whitman is often called "the poet of American democracy." What recurring themes in his poems make this a fit title for him? In what sense is he more the spokesman of democracy than Thoreau or Irving?

4. Which poems of Whitman do you like best? Which least? Why?

MORE GOOD READING

ALDRICH, THOMAS BAILEY, *Story of a Bad Boy*. (Houghton) First published in 1860, this famous book of reminiscences of a New England boyhood presents a true-to-life picture of what it was like to grow up in America in the years before the War Between the States.

BROOKS, VAN WYCK, *The Times of Melville and Whitman*. (Dutton) The author gives a vivid picture of Whitman and his contemporaries, of literary happenings and historical events in the last half of the nineteenth century.

CANBY, HENRY SEIDEL, *Walt Whitman, an American*. (Houghton) The mature reader will find much of value in this sensitive study of Whitman by a prominent twentieth-century critic.

CHURCHILL, WINSTON, *The Crisis*. (Macmillan) War and romance are intermingled in this exciting novel of homes divided during the War Between the States. (The author was an American novelist of the nineteenth century, not the great British statesman.)

CORMACK, MARIBELLE, *Recruit for Abe Lincoln*. (Appleton) This is the story of Jeff, who wanted to join the army but couldn't because of a crippled arm. As a telegrapher at the War Department, he came to know Lincoln.

DEUTSCH, BABETTE, *Walt Whitman; Builder for America*. (Messner) In this biography especially written for high-school students, the author paints a sympathetic picture of Whitman against the background of his time. You'll know both Whitman and your country better after reading it.

FISH, CARL RUSSELL, *Rise of the Common Man (1830-1850)*. (Macmillan) The student interested in social and political history will find this account of the age which sought to make America a democratic society stimulating and worthwhile.

HUBBARD, FREEMAN H., *Vinnie Ream and Mr. Lincoln*. (McGraw) This charming fictionized biography is the story of the girl who modeled the realistic statue of Lincoln which stands in the Capitol. It presents a delightfully intimate picture of home and family life in the middle of the nineteenth century.

LONGSTRETH, THOMAS M., *Tad Lincoln; the President's Son*. (Westminster) Humor and suspense distinguish this picture of Washington in 1861-1865 seen through Tad Lincoln's eyes.

MEADER, STEPHEN W., *Whaler 'Round the Horn*. (Harcourt) This whaling story of Melville's time is crammed with the adventure of sailing ships, shipwreck, and a deserted island. You'll find Rodney Glenn's voyage around Cape Horn on the *Pelican* exciting all the way.

Walt Whitman; selected and with notes by Mark Van Doren. (Viking) Although the emphasis in this collection is on *Leaves of Grass,* the prose writings in which Whitman explained and justified his poetry as well as some of his other prose writings have been included.

WHITMAN, WALT, *Leaves of Grass*. (Doubleday) The real student will wish to read more of one of the most famous books in American literature than this textbook has provided.

LITERATURE	HISTORICAL EVENTS
1850 John Greenleaf Whittier, *Songs of Labor and Other Poems* Herman Melville, *White Jacket* Nathaniel Hawthorne, *The Scarlet Letter* John C. Calhoun, "Speech on the Slavery Question" Daniel Webster, "Seventh of March Speech" 1851 Herman Melville, *Moby Dick* 1852 Harriet Beecher Stowe, *Uncle Tom's Cabin*	Compromise of 1850 passed, admitting California as a free state 1850
1854 Henry David Thoreau, *Walden*	Kansas-Nebraska Act passed, establishing "squatter sovereignty" in those territories 1854 Republican Party organized as protest against Kansas-Nebraska Act
1855 Walt Whitman, *Leaves of Grass* Henry Wadsworth Longfellow, *Hiawatha* Paul Hamilton Hayne, *Poems*	
1857 *Atlantic Monthly* founded in Boston with James Russell Lowell as editor *Russell's Magazine* founded in Charleston, South Carolina, with Paul Hamilton Hayne as editor	Dred Scott Decision handed down by the Supreme Court 1857
1859 Washington Irving, *Life of Washington*	Lincoln-Douglas debates on the slavery question 1858 held in Illinois Silver discovered in the Comstock Lode at 1859 Virginia City, Nevada Oregon admitted as thirty-third state John Brown made his raid on Harper's Ferry Washington Irving died
1860 Henry Timrod, *Poems* Walt Whitman, *Leaves of Grass* (third edition) Ralph Waldo Emerson, *Conduct of Life* Nathaniel Hawthorne, *The Marble Faun*	Abraham Lincoln elected sixteenth President 1860 South Carolina seceded from the Union
	The War Between the States began 1861 Confederate States of America organized at Montgomery, Alabama, with Jefferson Davis as President Telegraphic communication established across the continent Henry David Thoreau died 1862
1863 John Greenleaf Whittier, "Barbara Frietchie" Abraham Lincoln, "Emancipation Proclamation" and "Gettysburg Address" Henry Wadsworth Longfellow, *Tales of a Wayside Inn*	The North won the battle of Gettysburg and 1863 forced the surrender of Vicksburg
1864 William Cullen Bryant, *Thirty Poems* 1865 Abraham Lincoln, "Second Inaugural Address" Walt Whitman, "When Lilacs Last in the Dooryard Bloomed" 1866 John Greenleaf Whittier, *Snow-Bound* 1867 Henry Timrod, "Ode"	Lincoln reëlected President 1864 Lee surrendered to Grant at Appomattox, Virginia 1865 Lincoln assassinated

Walt Whitman 1819-1892

408

SOME PROMINENT WRITERS OF THE PERIOD OF CONFLICT

PAUL HAMILTON HAYNE, 1830-1886

After the death of his father, Paul Hamilton Hayne was brought up in the Charleston home of his uncle, Robert Y. Hayne, a southern aristocrat who won fame as a statesman. Young Hayne grew up with every advantage that wealth and family could offer. After graduating from the College of Charleston, he studied law; but writing poetry interested him more than his law cases. His *Poems* (1855) won praise from Northern critics, as did two subsequent volumes. In 1857 he became editor of a new periodical launched by the Charleston literary group, *Russell's Magazine*, which flourished until the outbreak of war in 1861. Hayne served briefly in the Confederate army, but was invalided out because of ill health. After the war Hayne faced a different world. His home and library destroyed and his income gone, he went to live at "Copse Hill" in the pine woods near Augusta, Georgia. Here he supported his wife and child by his writing. It is the poems of this period that have won Hayne an enduring place among American lyric poets.

HERMAN MELVILLE, 1819-1891

Herman Melville was the son of a New York City merchant. When the boy was thirteen, his father died in debt; and for the next five years Herman, forced by poverty to leave school, clerked in a bank and in his brother's Albany store and worked on a farm. At eighteen, disappointed with life in general, he shipped for Liverpool as a common seaman. On his return he taught school and tried his hand at writing. At twenty-one he again went to sea, this time on a whaling ship bound for the South Seas. This voyage, which lasted almost four years, was the most decisive event in Melville's life. For out of his wanderings on the sea and his adventures on the islands of the South Pacific came ultimately his most important books—*Typee* (1846), *Omoo* (1846), and his masterpiece *Moby Dick* (1851). Melville lived for forty years after *Moby Dick* was written, but never again reached the heights he had achieved in his story of Captain Ahab and the great white whale. After about 1860 he was a forgotten author. It was not until the 1920's that his works were rediscovered and he was acclaimed as one of the strongest and most original of American writers.

ABRAM JOSEPH RYAN, 1838-1886

The son of Irish immigrants, Abram Joseph Ryan was born at Hagerstown, Maryland. With his parents he moved to St. Louis. He was educated there and at Niagara Falls, where he was ordained a Roman Catholic priest in 1856. Although he had spent most of his life in the North, his loyalties remained with the South, and in 1862 he joined the Confederate army as a chaplain. His kindliness, his great courage, and his humanitarianism made him a beloved figure in the army, yet his greatest service to the South was his poetry, which voiced the spirit of a people. After the war he served as pastor in various Southern cities and edited several Southern journals. *Father Ryan's Poems* (1879) went into several editions.

HENRY TIMROD, 1828-1867

Henry Timrod of Charleston, South Carolina, was ten years old when his father died of injuries received in the Seminole War in Florida. His widowed mother did her best to give Henry a good education. At Coates School he became a close friend of wealthy young Paul Hamilton Hayne. After a year and a half at the University of Georgia, he became successively a lawyer and a tutor to plantation families. Like Hayne, he turned to writing poetry and was a contributor to *Russell's Magazine*. He had published one book of lyrics—*Poems* (1860) —when the advent of war abruptly changed his life. Timrod enlisted in the Confederate army, but because of ill health was able to serve less than a year. The last years of his life were a struggle against poverty and disease. Yet through all these adversities Timrod continued to write poetry—the best poems of his career. He died poor but he left as a legacy a body of genuine poetry.

JOHN GREENLEAF WHITTIER, 1807-1892

John Greenleaf Whittier was born on a farm near Haverhill, Massachusetts, into a devout Quaker family. He attended country schools, worked on his father's farm and as a shoemaker. His simple and hard-working life made him see things through the eyes of the common man. As he grew older he became increasingly interested in the antislavery movement. He edited various periodicals devoted to the abolitionist cause and flooded the newspapers with poems attacking slavery. Occasionally he wrote poems and ballads based on local scenes and happenings. When the War Between the States ended, Whittier turned all his energies to the type of poetry on which his fame today rests—the portrayal of New England people and New England landscape in simple lyric poetry. In 1866 *Snow-Bound,* his greatest success, appeared. Other volumes including *Among the Hills and Other Poems* (1869) and *Ballads of New England* (1870) helped to establish Whittier's place in literature as one of the greatest of local-color poets.

UNIT XI: SAMUEL L. CLEMENS
(*representing* THE PERIOD OF NEW OUTLOOKS)

Trends which began in America in the days of Thoreau and Whitman were speeded up by the war of 1861-1865. For example, the industrial trend which Thoreau had noticed while living in his hut on Walden Pond became increasingly evident. Also the trend toward the cities, which had drawn Whitman to Manhattan, became more and more important. Natural results, of course, were changes in the way most Americans lived. When America changed from what was primarily a farming nation to a nation in which industry and urban life took the lead, practically everybody felt the transformation in one way or another.

It is understandable that the authors who arose in the new America of factory and city, of widespread transportation systems, differed from pre-war authors. Before the war, most of the important writers had been born and had lived on the Eastern seacoast, particularly in New England. After the war, fewer leading writers were natives of this section. Far more were from the sections now becoming increasingly important—the South, the Middle West, the Middle Eastern seaboard where cities flourished, and even the Far West. Before the war, most prominent authors had been aristocrats by birth; now most leading authors were from rising middle-class or even poor families. Before the war, most authors had been educated in some Eastern college—a large share of them in Harvard. Now leading authors such as Bret Harte, William Dean Howells, Joaquin Miller, Joel Chandler Harris, George W. Cable, and Sarah Orne Jewett were not college educated—were not even, in most instances, high-school educated.

It would have been strange if authors with such different backgrounds had not produced literature quite different from that of a younger America. The newer writings, in general, were much less scholarly, much less genteel, than the earlier ones had been. Some had less polish. But the newer writings were likely to be more robust, to have more of life in them. They were likely, finally, to be influenced less by Europe—to be influenced more by the great new American nation which was becoming an important force in the world.

Samuel L. Clemens—or, to use his pen name, Mark Twain—was typical of the new group of American authors. His parents were Western pioneers who, shortly before his birth, had moved westward from Tennessee to the Missouri frontier. He was born in Florida, Missouri, in

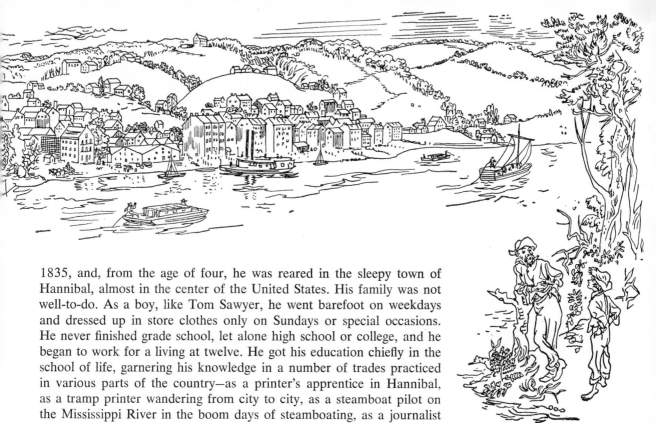

1835, and, from the age of four, he was reared in the sleepy town of
Hannibal, almost in the center of the United States. His family was not
well-to-do. As a boy, like Tom Sawyer, he went barefoot on weekdays
and dressed up in store clothes only on Sundays or special occasions.
He never finished grade school, let alone high school or college, and he
began to work for a living at twelve. He got his education chiefly in the
school of life, garnering his knowledge in a number of trades practiced
in various parts of the country—as a printer's apprentice in Hannibal,
as a tramp printer wandering from city to city, as a steamboat pilot on
the Mississippi River in the boom days of steamboating, as a journalist
and author in the Far West and in the cities of the East. What he wrote
had the gusto of the West; at its best it was full of the picturesque life
he had known intimately. In many ways, it was representative of the
new America.

❧ I JOURNALIST

Sam Clemens had about six years of formal schooling, first under an
old-fashioned schoolmarm and later under an old-fashioned schoolmaster. His informal schooling, gained from personal experience in a
riverside town with wild country on three sides of it, probably was more
valuable. Playing with other youngsters in the forests, visiting his uncle's
farm in the summertime, watching the Mississippi steamboats, and talking with grown-ups about life on the river, he acquired a great deal of
forest lore, farm lore, and river lore. He learned how to observe keenly
and minutely—a necessary skill on the frontier. A man who met him in
Europe years later wrote, "He has the peculiar Indianlike or American
faculty of observing innumerable little things which no European would
ever think of. There is, I think, a great deal of 'hard old Injun' in him."
He acquired a thirst for information—for facts and figures—which was
to prove to be fine equipment for a journalist.

In 1847, when Sam Clemens' father died, the family was left in
rather bad financial circumstances. The next year, therefore, Sam quit
school and was apprenticed as a printer to Joseph P. Ament, who was
the editor and printer of a Hannibal newspaper. After finishing his apprenticeship, Sam went to work as a printer for his brother Orion, who
had just started to publish his own home-town newspaper. The earliest

clear description of Clemens shows him as a skinny, sandy-haired youngster of twelve, standing at his printer's case, setting type, and singing a song with the refrain, "If I ever git up, I'll stay up—if I kin."

Orion's paper, *The Hannibal Journal,* was a small-town publication ("Terms: One Dollar a Year, if paid in Advance; if not paid within Six Months One Dollar and Fifty Cents; if not paid within Twelve Months, TWO DOLLARS"). Sam's work in the printshop was highly educational. He set up in type stories of all sorts, including, probably, humorous stories culled from Eastern newspapers. From such models, he doubtless learned a great deal about writing.

At about sixteen, Sam began to show what he had learned when he wrote and published in the *Journal* some pieces of his own. They included comic poems about the girls he had been courting, jesting comments on the news (some using outrageous puns), and jibes at fellow townsfolk. Once when the young journalist wrote humorously about the editor of another Hannibal newspaper, the offended gentleman called with a shotgun; but when he found how young the offender was, he merely tweaked Sam's ears. For an Eastern humorous magazine, he wrote a story about the way a Hannibal yokel got the best of a perfumed dandy from a steamboat, "The Dandy Frightening the Squatter."

Sam was seventeen when he left his brother's small-town newspaper and set out to see the world. For the next ten years he worked at various jobs, but on the side he constantly cultivated his skill as a writer. For the first four years Sam set type on newspapers in such cities as St. Louis, New York, and Philadelphia to pay his way. He sent back travel letters to Orion, who boastfully printed them as contributions from "Our Traveling Correspondent." For a time he returned West to work for Orion, now located in Iowa. Then the lure of the great river beside which he had grown up asserted itself, and in 1857 Sam realized an old ambition by becoming, first, a pilot's apprentice on the Mississippi River, and then, after eighteen months, a full-fledged pilot.

Sam loved and took pride in piloting a Mississippi River steamboat, but in 1861 the war closed river traffic and brought his career as pilot to an end. For a brief time he tried out soldiering with a group of Confederate volunteers. In the meantime, Orion had been appointed secretary of the newly organized Nevada Territory—an area rich in silver and gold. Sam determined to go West also and to earn his fortune as a miner. But he had no luck. The year 1862 found him living in a flimsy cabin in the Esmerelda mining settlement, suffering from the cold and harassed by the high price of mining-camp food. When he was asked to become a reporter for the *Territorial Enterprise,* published in Virginia City, a hundred and thirty miles away, he decided to accept and walked half the distance to the new job. While working in Virginia City, Clemens adopted his pen name, Mark Twain.

The job of reporting in a lively mine town was fascinating. "Our duty," he and a fellow reporter wrote, " is to keep the universe thoroughly posted concerning murders and street fights, and balls, and theaters, and pack trains, and churches, and lectures, and schoolhouses, and city hay wagons, and the thousand other things which it is in the province of local reporters to keep track of." After two years in Virginia City, he went to San Francisco to work for newspapers there, either as reporter or correspondent, from 1864 to 1867.

In 1867 the man from the Middle West went abroad for the first time—to France, Italy, Spain, and Palestine. Some of his newspaper stories about this trip were revised and published as *The Innocents Abroad,* his first important book, in 1869. With the proceeds of this highly successful book, Clemens bought a Buffalo newspaper which he published between 1870 and 1871. When he sold *The Buffalo Express,* his associations with newspapers ended, but he continued to write for magazines and, until the last years of his long life, to write such journalistic books as *Roughing It* (1871), *A Tramp Abroad* (1879), *Life on the Mississippi* (1883), and *Following the Equator* (1897). All these books are made up of the sorts of things he had been writing for years as a newspaper man, or journalist.

As a journalist, Mark had several valuable talents. For one thing, he had a knack for being on the spot when interesting events were transpiring. It was his good luck, for example, to be a pilot on the Mississippi River in the liveliest days of steamboating; and he therefore could set forth his colorful experiences in *Life on the Mississippi.* It was his good luck, again, to be in the Far West during a period when the West was particularly zestful and interesting; a result was his book, *Roughing It,* about his Western experiences.

For another thing, Mark Twain had an eye for details. He could observe, arrange, and set down exactly the concrete facts about a scene or a happening which created a vivid picture in the mind of the reader. Whether he was describing a miner's hut or a volcano, a jackass rabbit or the Egyptian Sphinx, he could notice and record precisely those elements which brought them plainly before the reader's eyes.

Finally, Mark Twain was effective as a journalist because he could consistently interest the reader by recording his own highly individual notions, reactions, and ideas. His friends found his crotchets, his prejudices, his foibles constantly fascinating. His lively personality and his unconventional attitudes colored his writings. Scores of Americans had gone to Europe before Twain did, and had written books about their trips. But most travel books lacked the appeals that made Twain's *The Innocents Abroad* immediately and lastingly popular: his scornful accounts of idiotic sightseers unable to form their own opinions of what they saw, his biting ridicule of foreign manners and customs, and his exaggerated claims for the superiority of American scenes over foreign scenes. From a sharp-tongued mother, he had inherited a keen sense of humor, and this gift was nurtured by his work as a printer, his work as a pilot, and his life among fun-loving miners. Hence he could see humorous elements in almost any situation, and he could write humor ranging from subtle satire to broad slapstick which delighted his readers. Like a good talker who has interesting things to say about practically any subject, Twain could treat a wide range of subjects and constantly interest the reader. Here are his reports on two of his varied experiences.

The Boys' Ambition

Like all the other boys in the river town of Hannibal, young Sam Clemens had one consuming ambition in life. The following selection from *Life on the Mississippi* tells about that ambition and, incidentally, gives a vivid picture of the part the river steamer played in American life for many years.

WHEN I was a boy, there was but one permanent ambition among my comrades in our village on the west bank of the Mississippi River. That was, to be a steamboatman. We had transient ambitions of other sorts, but they were only transient. When a circus came and went, it left us all burning to become clowns; the first Negro minstrel show that ever came to our section left us all suffering to try that kind of life; now and then we had a hope that if we lived and were good, God would permit us to be pirates. These ambitions faded out, each in its turn; but the ambition to be a steamboatman always remained.

Once a day a cheap, gaudy packet arrived upward from St. Louis, and another downward from Keokuk.[1] Before these events, the day was glorious with expectancy; after them, the day was a dead and empty thing. Not only the boys, but the whole village, felt this. After all these years I can picture that old time to myself now, just as it was then: the white town drowsing in the sunshine of a summer's morning; the streets empty, or pretty nearly so; one or two clerks sitting in front of the Water Street stores, with their splint-bottomed chairs[2] tilted back against the walls, chins on breasts, hats slouched over their faces, asleep—with shingle-shavings enough around to show what broke them down; a sow and a litter of pigs loafing along the sidewalk, doing a good business in watermelon rinds and seeds; two or three lonely little freight piles scattered about the levee; a pile of skids on the slope of the stone-paved wharf, and the fragrant town drunkard asleep in the shadow of them; two or three wood flats[3] at the head of the wharf, but nobody to listen to the peaceful lapping of the wavelets against them; the great Mississippi, the majestic, the magnificent Mississippi, rolling its mile-wide tide along, shining in the sun; the dense forest away on the other side; the point above the town, and the point below, bounding the river-glimpse and turning it into a sort of sea, and withal a very still and brilliant and lonely one. Presently a film of dark smoke appears above one of those remote points: instantly a Negro drayman, famous for his quick eye and prodigious voice, lifts up the cry, "S-t-e-a-m-boat a-comin'!" and the scene changes! The town drunkard stirs, the clerks wake up, a furious clatter of drays follows, every house and store pours out a human contribution, and all in a twinkling the dead town is alive and moving. Drays, carts, men, boys, all go hurrying from many quarters to a common center, the wharf. Assembled there, the people fasten their eyes upon the coming boat as upon a wonder they are seeing for the first time. And the boat *is* rather a handsome sight, too. She is long and sharp and trim and pretty; she has two tall, fancy-topped chimneys, with a gilded device of some kind swung between them; a fanciful pilot house, all glass and gingerbread, perched on top of the texas deck[4] behind them; the

---

[1]*Keokuk* (kē′ə kuk), a Mississippi River town in the southeastern corner of Iowa, about fifty miles above Hannibal.

[2]*splint-bottomed chairs,* chairs with seats woven of thin strips (splints) of wood. (Chairs of this sort are frequently called *split-bottomed* chairs.)

[3]*wood flats,* small flat-bottomed boats.

[4]*texas deck,* the deck adjacent to the pilot house and officers' quarters.

paddle boxes[5] are gorgeous with a picture or with gilded rays above the boat's name; the boiler deck, the hurricane deck,[6] and the texas deck are fenced and ornamented with clean white railings; there is a flag gallantly flying from the jack staff[7]; the furnace doors are open and the fires glaring bravely; the upper decks are black with passengers; the captain stands by the big bell, calm, imposing, the envy of all; great volumes of the blackest smoke are rolling and tumbling out of the chimneys—a husbanded grandeur created with a bit of pitch pine just before arriving at a town; the crew are grouped on the forecastle; the broad stage[8] is run far out over the port bow, and a deck hand stands picturesquely on the end of it with a coil of rope in his hand; the pent steam is screaming through the gauge cocks; the captain lifts his hand, a bell rings, the wheels stop; then they turn back, churning the water to foam, and the steamer is at rest. Then such a scramble as there is to get aboard, and to get ashore, and to take in freight and to discharge freight, all at one and the same time; and such a yelling and cursing as the mates facilitate it all with! Ten minutes later the steamer is under way again, with no flag on the jack staff and no black smoke issuing from the chimneys. After ten more minutes the town is dead again, and the town drunkard asleep by the skids once more.

My father was a justice of the peace, and I supposed he possessed the power of life and death over all men, and could hang anybody that offended him. This was distinction enough for me as a general thing; but the desire to be a steamboatman kept intruding, nevertheless. I first wanted to be a cabin boy, so that I could come out with a white apron on and shake a tablecloth over the side, where all my old comrades could see me; later I thought I would rather be the deck hand who stood on

the end of the stage-plank with the coil of rope in his hand, because he was particularly conspicuous. But these were only daydreams—they were too heavenly to be contemplated as real possibilities.

By and by one of our boys went away. He was not heard of for a long time. At last he turned up as apprentice engineer or "striker" on a steamboat. This thing shook the bottom out of all my Sunday-school teachings. That boy had been notoriously worldly, and I just the reverse; yet he was exalted to this eminence, and I left in obscurity and misery. There was nothing generous about this fellow in his greatness. He would always manage to have a rusty bolt to scrub while his boat tarried at our town, and he would sit on the inside guard[9] and scrub it, where we all could see him and envy him and loathe him. And whenever his boat was laid up he would come home and swell around the town in his blackest and greasiest clothes, so that nobody could help remembering that he was a steamboatman; and he used all sorts of steamboat technicalities in his talk, as if he were so used to them that he forgot common people could not understand them. He would speak of the "labboard"[10] side of a horse in an easy, natural way that would make one wish he was dead. And he was always talking about "St. Looy" like an old citizen; he would refer casually to occasions when he was "coming down Fourth Street," or when he was "passing by the Planter's House," or when there was a fire and he took a turn on the brakes of "the old Big Missouri"; and then he would go on and lie about how many towns the size of ours were burned down there that day. Two or three of the boys had long been persons of consideration among us because they had been to St. Louis once and had a vague general knowledge of its wonders, but the day of their glory was over now. They lapsed into a humble silence, and learned to disappear when the ruthless cub engineer approached. This fellow had money, too, and hair oil. Also an ignorant silver

---

[5]*paddle boxes,* the wooden coverings built over the upper part of the paddle wheels. These paddle wheels, which were located one at each side, propelled the ship.

[6]*the boiler deck, the hurricane deck.* The boiler deck is that part of the upper deck situated immediately over the boilers; the hurricane deck is the topmost deck.

[7]*jack staff,* a short pole erected at the front of the vessel.

[8]*stage,* stage-plank, or gangplank.

---

[9]*inside guard,* part of the steamboat's deck which curved out over the paddle wheel.

[10]*"labboard,"* larboard, the left or port side of a ship looking forward from the stern.

watch and a showy brass watch chain. He wore a leather belt and used no suspenders. If ever a youth was cordially admired and hated by his comrades, this one was. No girl could withstand his charms. He "cut out" every boy in the village. When his boat blew up at last, it diffused a tranquil contentment among us such as we had not known for months. But when he came home the next week, alive, renowned, and appeared in church all battered up and bandaged, a shining hero, stared at and wondered over by everybody, it seemed to us that the partiality of Providence for an undeserving reptile had reached a point where it was open to criticism.

This creature's career could produce but one result, and it speedily followed. Boy after boy managed to get on the river. The minister's son became an engineer. The doctor's and the postmaster's sons became mud clerks[11]; the wholesale liquor dealer's son became a barkeeper on a boat; four sons of the chief merchant, and two sons of the county judge, became pilots. Pilot was the grandest position of all. The pilot, even in those days of trivial wages, had a princely salary—from a hundred and fifty to two hundred and fifty dollars a month, and no board to pay. Two months of his wages would pay a preacher's salary for a year. Now some of us were left disconsolate. We could not get on the river—at least our parents would not let us.

So, by and by, I ran away. I said I would never come home again till I was a pilot and could come in glory. But somehow I could not manage it. I went meekly aboard a few of the boats that lay packed together like sardines at the long St. Louis wharf, and humbly inquired for the pilots, but got only a cold shoulder and short words from mates and clerks. I had to make the best of this sort of treatment for the time being, but I had comforting daydreams of a future when I should be a great and honored pilot, with plenty of money, and could kill some of these mates and clerks and pay for them.

---

[11]*mud clerks,* second clerks on river steamers. They were so called because it was their duty to go ashore at unimportant stops, often mere mud banks, to receive or check off freight.

Flush Times in Silverland

When Sam Clemens became a newspaper reporter in Virginia City, Nevada, in 1862, the raw little town was the center of one of the greatest mining booms in United States history. Three years earlier the Comstock Lode, a fabulously rich vein of silver and gold four miles long, had been discovered on the slope of Mount Davidson. Miners from all parts of the country had rushed to the new strike, and almost overnight a town had sprung up. This is the "Silverland" of which Clemens writes in the following selection from *Roughing It.*

SIX MONTHS after my entry into journalism the grand flush times of Silverland began, and they continued with unabated splendor for three years. All difficulty about filling up the local department[1] ceased, and the only trouble now was how to make the lengthened columns hold the world of incidents and happenings that came to our literary net every day.

Virginia City had grown to be the "livest" town for its age and population that America had ever produced. The sidewalks swarmed with people—to such an extent, indeed, that it was generally no easy matter to stem the human tide. The streets themselves were just as crowded with quartz wagons,[2] freight teams, and other vehicles. The procession was endless. So great was the pack that buggies frequently had to wait half an hour for an opportunity to cross the principal street.

Joy sat on every countenance, and there was a glad, almost fierce intensity in every eye, that told of the money-getting schemes that were seething in every brain and the high hope that held sway in every heart. Money was as plenty as dust; every individual considered himself wealthy, and a melancholy countenance was nowhere to be seen. There were military companies, fire companies, brass bands, banks, hotels, theaters, hurdy-gurdy houses,[3] wide-

---

[1]*local department,* a local-events section of a newspaper.
[2]*quartz wagons,* wagons carrying the quartz in which the silver was found.
[3]*hurdy-gurdy houses,* cheap dance halls where liquor was served.

open gambling palaces, political powwows, civic processions, street fights, murders, inquests, riots, a whisky mill[4] every fifteen steps, a board of aldermen, a mayor, a city surveyor, a city engineer, a chief of the fire department, with first, second, and third assistants, a chief of police, city marshal, and a large police force, two boards of mining brokers, a dozen breweries, and half a dozen jails and station houses[5] in full operation, and some talk of building a church. The flush times were in magnificent flower! Large fireproof brick buildings were going up in the principal streets, and the wooden suburbs were spreading out in all directions. Town lots soared up to prices that were amazing.

The great Comstock Lode stretched its opulent length straight through the town from north to south, and every mine on it was in diligent process of development. One of these mines alone employed 675 men, and in the matter of elections the adage was, "as the *Gould and Curry*[6] goes, so goes the city." Laboring men's wages were four and six dollars a day, and they worked in three shifts or gangs, and the blasting and picking and shoveling went on without ceasing, night and day.

The city of Virginia roosted royally midway up the steep side of Mount Davidson, 7200 feet above the level of the sea, and in the clear Nevada atmosphere was visible from a distance of fifty miles! It claimed a population of fifteen thousand to eighteen thousand, and all day long half of this little army swarmed the streets like bees and the other half swarmed among the drifts and tunnels of the Comstock hundreds of feet down in the earth directly under those same streets. Often we felt our chairs jar, and heard the faint boom of a blast down in the interior of the earth under the office.

The mountainside was so steep that the entire town had a slant to it like a roof. Each street was a terrace, and from each to the next street below the descent was forty or fifty feet. The fronts of the houses were level with the street they faced, but their rear first floors were propped on lofty stilts; a man could stand at a rear first-floor window of a C Street house and look down the chimneys of the row of houses below him facing D Street.

My salary was increased to forty dollars a week. But I seldom drew it. I had plenty of other resources, and what were two broad twenty-dollar gold pieces to a man who had his pockets full of such, and a cumbersome abundance of bright half dollars besides? (Paper money has never come into use on the Pacific coast.) Reporting was lucrative and every man in the town was lavish with his money and his feet.[7]

New claims were taken daily, and it was the friendly custom to run straight to the newspaper offices, give the reporter forty or fifty feet, and get him to go and examine the mine

[4]*whisky mill,* saloon.

[5]*station houses,* police stations.

[6]*Gould and Curry,* the richest of the mining companies. In 1862 stock in this company reached $6300 a share.

[7]*feet,* the local term for shares of stock in the mining companies.

and publish a notice of it. They did not care a fig what you said about the property so you said something.

There was *nothing* in the shape of a mining claim that was not salable. We received presents of feet every day. If we needed a hundred dollars or so, we sold some; if not, we hoarded it away, satisfied that it would ultimately be worth a thousand dollars a foot. I had a trunk about half full of stock. When a claim made a stir in the market and went up to a high figure, I searched through my pile to see if I had any of its stock—and generally found it.

The prices rose and fell constantly; but still a fall disturbed us little, because a thousand dollars a foot was our figure, and so we were content to let it fluctuate as much as it pleased till it reached it.

My pile of stock was not all given to me by people who wished their claims noticed. At least half of it was given me by persons who had no thought of such a thing, and looked for nothing more than a simple verbal "thank you"; and you were not even obliged by law to furnish that. If you are coming up the street with a couple of baskets of apples in your hands, and you meet a friend, you naturally invite him to take a few. That describes the condition of things in Virginia in the flush times. Every man had his pockets full of stock, and it was the actual *custom* of the country to part with small quantities of it to friends without the asking. Very often it was a good idea to close the transaction instantly when a man offered a stock present to a friend, for the offer was only good and binding at that moment. Mr. Stewart (senator, now, from Nevada) one day told me he would give me twenty feet of *Justis* stock if I would walk over to his office. It was worth five or ten dollars a foot. I asked him to make the offer good for next day, as I was just going to dinner. He said he would not be in town; so I risked it and took my dinner instead of the stock. Within the week the price went up to seventy dollars and afterward to a hundred and fifty, but nothing could make that man yield. I suppose he sold that stock of mine and placed the guilty proceeds in his own pocket.

CONCERNING SAMUEL CLEMENS

1. In what ways was Clemens, in background, rearing, and experience, typical of the American writers of his period?

2. Trace Clemens' various activities from his boyhood to the publication of *The Innocents Abroad* in 1869. How, in general, did his various experiences prove of value to him as a writer? Name specific books that grew out of his different activities.

3. Name three talents that were particularly valuable to Clemens as a journalist and explain the importance of each to his success.

CONCERNING CLEMENS'
JOURNALISTIC WRITINGS

"The Boys' Ambition"

1. In paragraph 1, the author mentions three transient, or passing, ambitions of the boys of Hannibal. What is Clemens' purpose in mentioning these passing ambitions?

2. Paragraph 2 is a very long one, but it is not difficult to follow if you notice Clemens' careful arrangement of his materials. In sentence 1 he states a simple fact. (What is it?) In sentence 2 he states the topic of the whole paragraph. (What contrast does he indicate that he is going to show?) Where does he start and end the "before" picture? Where does he start and end the "after" picture? What does he place between the "before" and "after" pictures? Point out some of the details that are most helpful to you in sensing the mood of each section of the paragraph.

3. Paragraph 2, column 1, page 416, begins with the word *So,* which indicates that it follows from something which has gone before. From what does it follow?

4. In what ways does Clemens introduce humor into the story of the local boy who became an apprentice engineer?

"Flush Times in Silverland"

1. What were the unique physical features of Virginia City as Clemens describes it?

2. Pick out the details that give you the most vivid picture of the "flush times" Clemens is writing about. What is Clemens' attitude to the period he is describing? How is that attitude indicated?

3. If you were preparing a humorous anthology, would you include "Flush Times in Silverland"? Why, or why not?

4. Why may this selection and the preceding one be considered journalistic writing? What qualities of good journalism do they possess?

Know your words

On a sheet of paper answer each of the following questions. Be ready to explain why you decided as you did. Use the Glossary if necessary.

1. If the drayman on the steamboat called out in a *prodigious* voice, did he speak clearly, call out loudly, or swear?

2. If the steamboat was *husbanding* its pitch pine, was it using it sparingly, wasting it, or using it to make a grand effect?

3. When the "striker" used steamboat *technicalities* in his talk, was he swearing in the fashion of river-men, using terms that applied especially to steamboats, or bragging about his adventures?

4. If life in Virginia City was *opulent,* was it marked by a display of wealth, an atmosphere of violence, or the presence of poverty?

5. When Twain speaks of silver half dollars as *cumbersome,* does he mean they are valuable, commonplace, or awkward to carry around?

6. If reporting in Virginia City was *lucrative,* was it exciting, profitable, or dangerous?

7. When the price of mining stock *fluctuated,* did it reach its highest value, hit its lowest value, or vary irregularly?

❧ II YARNSPINNER

During many periods of his life, Mark Twain found vast entertainment in listening to the oral stories of yarnspinners. Storytelling was a chief form of amusement on the frontier, and even as a boy Mark heard many fireside yarns. You will remember that in "Life on the Farm" (pages 229-233) he tells us that the best-loved evening occupation of the children was to gather around old Uncle Dan'l in the kitchen and listen in the firelight to his stories.

A few years later, as a printer's devil[1] and printer, Mark put into type many a story which its author had told in the fashion of an oral story-teller. Still later, on the Mississippi steamboats as they moved up and down the river, Twain listened with joy to the yarns spun by fellow pilots or passengers. "Above all," says Bernard De Voto, Twain's biographer, "there was the talk of men...heard in early evenings...tales of feuds and voyages, of mistaken identities, piracies, murders, hangings...revenge, ghosts—much that Mark's tropical imagination was to play with all his life...."

Later still, in the Far West, Twain loved to listen to stories and to tell them. His country-wide fame began when, after hearing one fine story which was going the rounds, he retold it for the delight of others. He and some companions were staying at Jim Gillis' cabin on Jackass Hill in the Tuolumne mining district[2] in the winter of 1864-65. When the weather was good, Mark and his friends engaged in pocket mining,[3] without much luck. When the weather was bad—and many days were rainy and muddy—they gathered around the fireplace in Gillis' cabin and swapped yarns, or they entered into yarnspinning sessions in the Angel's Camp Hotel over in Calaveras County. One story they heard was told by Ben Coon, a solemn, rather stupid fellow who apparently saw nothing

---

[1]*printer's devil,* young helper or errand boy in a printing shop.

[2]*Tuolumne* (twol'um nə) *mining district,* an area in central California adjoining Calaveras (kal'ə vā'rəs) County, where the mining town of Angel's Camp was located.

[3]*pocket mining,* searching for gold that occurs in pockets or small areas.

humorous about it. Twain and Gillis listened to it with great solemnity, but when they left the hotel, they repeated bits of the story to one another and howled with laughter. They thought it was one of the funniest stories they had ever heard, and soon they were both telling it to anyone who would listen. In a notebook which he was keeping at the time, Mark wrote down the main points in the story:

Coleman with his jumping frog—bet stranger $50.00—stranger had no frog, and C. got him one; in the meantime stranger filled C.'s frog full of shot and he couldn't jump. The stranger's frog won.

In due time, Mark told the story to Artemus Ward, a famous humorist of the day. Ward found it delightful, and he urged Twain to write it down so that it might be printed. When it appeared in an Eastern magazine in 1865, it was an overnight literary sensation. Soon newspapers all over the United States were publishing the story, and Americans everywhere were reading it with howls of laughter. Mark Twain had won his first nation-wide fame.

From that time on, Mark Twain frequently introduced the oral type of story into his accounts of personal experiences. As Bernard De Voto has said, "He took the humorous anecdote, combined it with auto-biographical reminiscence, and so achieved the narrative form best adapted to his mind." Many of his books thus became accounts of Twain's life or his travels interspersed with anecdotes. This is true of all the books mentioned in paragraph 1, page 413. In *The Innocents Abroad,* for example, the author used the story of his progress through Europe and Palestine as a framework for various anecdotes. Some of these anecdotes were brief; others were developed into little stories complete in themselves. The same pattern of autobiography combined with anecdotes was followed by Twain in *Roughing It, A Tramp Abroad, Life on the Mississippi,* and *Following the Equator.* Since these volumes were published over a long period of time—from 1869 to 1897—we can see that Mark Twain's skill as a yarnspinner was important to him throughout the major part of his career as an author.

"The humorous story," Mark Twain once said, "is strictly a work of art—high and delicate art—and only an artist can tell it." He might have added that *reading* the humorous story is also a high and delicate art. The following yarns offer proof of both points.

Bugs

This yarn is part of a letter that Mark Twain wrote to a girl friend in 1857. The girl, Annie Taylor, had gone to college and had written to ask her swain to write a theme for her. Mark said he couldn't—and then proceeded to write a most unusual one. The humor, like much humor produced by American yarnspinners, is based upon the resemblances—and differences—between human beings and other living creatures.

BUGS! Yes, B-U-G-S! What of Bugs? Why, perdition take the bugs! That is all. Night before last I stood at the little press until nearly two o'clock, and the flaring gaslight over my head attracted all the varieties of bugs which are to be found in natural history, and they all had the same praiseworthy recklessness about flying into the fire.

They at first came in little social crowds of a dozen or so, but soon increased in numbers, until a religious mass meeting of several millions was assembled on the board before me, presided over by a venerable beetle, who occupied the most prominent lock of my hair as his chair of state, while innumerable lesser dignitaries of the same tribe were clustered around him, keeping order, and at the same time endeavoring to attract the attention of the vast assemblage to their own importance by industriously grating their teeth.

It must have been an interesting occasion—perhaps a great bug jubilee commemorating the triumph of the locusts over Pharaoh's crops in Egypt many centuries ago.[1] At least, good seats, commanding an unobstructed view of the scene, were in great demand; and I have no doubt small fortunes were made by certain delegates from Yankeeland by disposing of comfortable places on my shoulders at round premiums. In fact, the advantages which my altitude afforded were so well appreciated that I soon began to look like one of those big cards in the museum covered with insects impaled on pins.

The big "president" beetle (who, when he frowned, closely resembled the music teacher when the pupils are out of time) rose and ducked his head, and, crossing his arms over his shoulders, stroked them down to the tip of his nose several times, and after thus disposing of the perspiration, stuck his hands under his wings, propped his back against a lock of hair, and then bobbing his head at the congregation, remarked, "B-u-z-z!" To which the congregation devoutly responded, "B-u-z-z!" Satisfied with this promptness on the part of his flock, he took a more imposing perpendicular against another lock of hair, and, lifting his hands to command silence, gave another melodious "b-u-z-z!" on a louder key (which I suppose to have been the keynote). After a moment's silence the whole congregation burst into a grand anthem, three dignified daddy-longlegs, perched near the gas burner, beating quadruple time during the performance. Soon a treble and alto duet, sung by forty-seven thousand mosquitoes and twenty-three thousand houseflies, came in, and then, after another chorus, a tenor and bass duet by thirty-two thousand locusts and ninety-seven thousand pinch bugs[2] was sung. Then another grand chorus, "Let Every Bug Rejoice and Sing" (we used to sing "heart" instead of "bug"), terminated the performance, during which eleven treble singers split their throats from head to heels, and the patriotic "daddies" who beat time hadn't a stump of a leg left.

It would take a ream of paper to give all the ceremonies of this great mass meeting. Suffice it to say that the little press "chawed up" half a bushel of the devotees, and I combed 976 beetles out of my hair the next morning, every one of whose throats stretched wide open, for their gentle spirits had passed away while they yet sung—and who shall say that they will not receive their reward? I buried their motionless forms with musical honors in John's hat.

---

[1] *the triumph of the locusts . . . many centuries ago.* The plague of locusts was one of the ten plagues sent by God upon the Egyptians when their ruler refused to let Moses lead the Israelites out of Egypt. (Exodus, Chapter 10.)

[2] *pinch bugs*, beetles.

"Bugs," from a letter written by Samuel Clemens in 1857, originally published in *The Kansas City Star Magazine.* Copyright, 1926, by *The Kansas City Star.*

The Celebrated Jumping
Frog of Calaveras County

IN COMPLIANCE with the request of a friend of mine, who wrote me from the East, I called on good-natured, garrulous old Simon Wheeler, and inquired after my friend's friend, *Leonidas W*. Smiley, as requested to do, and I hereunto append the result. I have a lurking suspicion that *Leonidas W*. Smiley is a myth; that my friend never knew such a personage; and that he only conjectured that if I asked old Wheeler about him, it would remind him of his infamous *Jim* Smiley, and he would go to work and bore me nearly to death with some exasperating reminiscence of him as long and as tedious as it should be useless to me. If that was the design, it succeeded.

I found Simon Wheeler dozing comfortably by the barroom stove of the dilapidated tavern in the decayed mining camp of Angel's, and I noticed that he was fat and baldheaded, and had an expression of winning gentleness and simplicity upon his tranquil countenance. He roused up, and gave me good day. I told him a friend of mine had commissioned me to make some inquiries about a cherished companion of his boyhood named *Leonidas W*. Smiley—*Rev. Leonidas W*. Smiley, a young minister of the Gospel, who he had heard was at one time a resident of Angel's Camp. I added that if Mr. Wheeler could tell me anything about this Rev. Leonidas W. Smiley, I would feel under many obligations to him.

Simon Wheeler backed me into a corner and blockaded me there with his chair, and then sat down and reeled off the monotonous narrative which follows this paragraph. He never smiled, he never frowned, he never changed his voice from the gentle-flowing key to which he tuned his initial sentence, he never betrayed the slightest suspicion of enthusiasm; but all through the interminable narrative there ran a vein of impressive earnestness and sincerity which showed me plainly that, so far from his imagining that there was anything ridiculous or funny about his story, he regarded it as a really important matter, and admired its two heroes as men of transcendent genius in *finesse*. I let him go on in his own way, and never interrupted him once.

"Rev. Leonidas W. H'm, Reverend Le— well, there was a feller here once by the name of *Jim* Smiley, in the winter of '49—or maybe it was the spring of '50—I don't recollect exactly, somehow, though what makes me think it was one or the other is because I remember the big flume wasn't finished when he first came to the camp. But anyway, he was the curiousest man about always betting on anything that turned up you ever see, if he could get anybody to bet on the other side; and if he couldn't, he'd change sides. Any way that suited the other man would suit *him*—any way just so's he got a bet, *he* was satisfied. But still he was lucky, uncommon lucky; he most always come out winner. He was always ready and laying for a chance; there couldn't be no solit'ry thing mentioned but that feller'd offer to bet on it, and take any side you please, as I was just telling you. If there was a horse race, you'd find him flush or you'd find him busted at the end of it; if there was a dog fight, he'd bet on it; if there was a cat fight, he'd bet on it; if there was a chicken fight, he'd bet on it. Why, if there was two birds setting on a fence, he would bet you which one would fly first; or if there was a camp meeting,[1] he would be there reg'lar to bet on Parson Walker, which he judged to be the best exhorter about there, and so he was too, and a good man. If he even see a straddlebug[2] start to go anywheres, he would bet you how long it would take him to get wherever he was going to, and if you took him up, he would foller that straddlebug to Mexico but what he would[3] find out where he was bound for and how long he was on the road.

"Lots of the boys here has seen Smiley, and can tell you about him. Why, it never made no difference to *him*—he'd bet on *any*thing—the dangdest feller. Parson Walker's wife laid very sick once, for a good while, and it seemed as

---

[1] *camp meeting*, religious meeting held outdoors or in a tent, usually lasting several days.

[2] *straddlebug*, any one of several species of long-legged beetles.

[3] *but what he would*, in order to.

if they warn't going to save her; but one morning he come in, and Smiley asked how she was, and he said she was considerable better—thank the Lord for His inf'nite mercy—and coming on so smart that with the blessing of Prov'dence she'd get well yet; and Smiley, before he thought, says, 'Well, I'll resk two-and-a-half that she don't anyway.'

"Thish-yer Smiley had a mare—the boys called her the fifteen-minute nag, but that was only in fun, you know, because of course she was faster than that—and he used to win money on that horse, for all she was so slow and always had the asthma, or the distemper, or the consumption, or something of that kind. They used to give her two or three hundred yards' start, and then pass her under way; but always at the fag end of the race she'd get excited and desperate-like, and come cavorting and straddling up, and scattering her legs around limber, sometimes in the air, and sometimes out to one side among the fences, and kicking up m-o-r-e dust and raising m-o-r-e racket with her coughing and sneezing and blowing her nose—and *always* fetch up at the stand just about a neck ahead, as near as you could cipher it down.

"And he had a little small bull pup, that to look at him you'd think he wan't worth a cent but to set around and look ornery and lay for a chance to steal something. But as soon as money was up on him he was a different dog; his under jaw'd begin to stick out like the fo'castle of a steamboat, and his teeth would uncover and shine like the furnaces.[4] And a dog might tackle him and bullyrag him, and bite him, and throw him over his shoulder two or three times, and Andrew Jackson—which was the name of the pup—Andrew Jackson would never let on but what *he* was satisfied, and hadn't expected nothing else—and the bets being doubled and doubled on the other side all the time, till the money was all up; and then all of a sudden he would grab that other dog jest by the j'int of his hind leg and freeze to it—not chaw, you understand, but only just grip and hang on till they throwed up the sponge, if it was a year.

"Smiley always come out winner on that pup, till he harnessed a dog once that didn't have no hind legs, because they'd been sawed off by a circular saw, and when the thing had gone along far enough, and the money was all up, and he come to make a snatch for his pet holt, he saw in a minute how he'd been imposed on, and how the other dog had him in the door,[5] so to speak, and he 'peared surprised, and then he looked sorter discouraged-like, and didn't try no more to win the fight, and so he got shucked out[6] bad. He give Smiley a look, as much as to say his heart was broke, and it was *his* fault, for putting up a dog that hadn't no hind legs for him to take holt of, which was his main dependence in a fight, and then he limped off a piece and laid down and died. It was a good pup, was that Andrew Jackson, and would have made a name for hisself if he'd lived, for the stuff was in him and he had genius—I know it, because he hadn't had no opportunities to speak of, and it don't stand to reason that a dog could make such a fight as he could under them circumstances if he hadn't no talent. It always makes me feel sorry when I think of that last fight of his'n, and the way it turned out.

"Well, thish-yer Smiley had rat terriers, and chicken cocks, and tomcats and all them kind of things, till you couldn't rest, and you couldn't fetch nothing for him to bet on but he'd match you. He ketched a frog one day, and took him home, and said he calk'lated to edercate him; and so he never done nothing for three months but set in his back yard and learn that frog to jump. And you bet he *did* learn him, too. He'd give him a little punch behind, and the next minute you'd see that frog whirling in the air like a doughnut—see him turn one summer-set, or maybe a couple, if he got a good start, and come down flat-footed and all right, like a cat. He got him up so in the matter of catching flies, and kep' him in practice so constant, that he'd nail a fly every time as far as he could see him.

---

[4]*the furnaces,* furnaces on a steamboat. Clemens is continuing the comparison of the bull pup to a steamboat.

[5]*had him in the door,* had him at a disadvantage.
[6]*shucked out,* beaten.

"Smiley said all a frog wanted was education, and he could do 'most anything—and I believe him. Why, I've seen him set Dan'l Webster down here on this floor—Dan'l Webster was the name of the frog—and sing out, 'Flies, Dan'l, flies!' and quicker'n you could wink he'd spring straight up and snake a fly off'n the counter there, and flop down on the floor ag'in as solid as a gob of mud, and fall to scratching the side of his head with his hind foot as indifferent as if he hadn't no idea he'd been doin' any more'n any frog might do. You never see a frog so modest and straightfor'ard as he was, for all he was so gifted. And when it come to fair and square jumping on a dead level, he could get over more ground at one straddle than any animal of his breed you ever see. Jumping on a dead level was his strong suit, you understand; and when it come to that, Smiley would ante up money on him as long as he had a red.[7] Smiley was monstrous proud of his frog, and well he might be, for fellers that had traveled and been everywheres all said he laid over any frog that ever *they* see.

"Well, Smiley kept the beast in a little lattice box, and he used to fetch him downtown sometimes and lay for a bet. One day a feller—a stranger in the camp, he was—come across him with his box, and says:

" 'What might it be that you've got in the box?'

"And Smiley says, sorter indifferent-like, 'It might be a parrot, or it might be a canary, maybe, but it ain't—it's only just a frog.'

"And the feller took it, and looked at it careful, and turned it round this way and that, and says, 'H'm—so 'tis. Well, what's *he* good for?'

" 'Well,' Smiley says, easy and careless, 'he's good enough for *one* thing, I should judge—he can outjump ary frog in Calaveras County.'

"The feller took the box again, and took another long, particular look, and give it back to Smiley, and says, very deliberate, 'Well, I don't see no p'ints about that frog that's any better'n any other frog.'

" 'Maybe you don't,' Smiley says. 'Maybe you understand frogs and maybe you don't understand 'em; maybe you've had experience, and maybe you ain't only a amature, as it were. Anyways, I've got *my* opinion, and I'll resk forty dollars that he can outjump any frog in Calaveras County.'

"And the feller studied a minute, and then says, kinder sad-like, 'Well, I'm only a stranger here, and I ain't got no frog; but if I had a frog, I'd bet you.'

"And then Smiley says, 'That's all right—that's all right—if you'll hold my box a minute, I'll go and get you a frog.' And so the feller took the box, and put up his forty dollars along with Smiley's, and set down to wait.

"So he set there a good while thinking and thinking to himself, and then he got the frog out and prized his mouth open and took a teaspoon and filled him full of quail shot—filled him pretty near up to his chin—and set him on the floor.

"Smiley he went to the swamp and slopped around in the mud for a long time, and finally he ketched a frog, and fetched him in, and give him to this feller, and says:

" 'Now, if you're ready, set him alongside of Dan'l, with his forepaws just even with Dan'l's, and I'll give the word.' Then he says, 'One—two—three—jump!' and him and the feller touched up the frogs from behind, and the new frog hopped off, but Dan'l give a heave and hysted up his shoulders—so—like a Frenchman, but it wan't no use—he couldn't budge; he was planted as solid as an anvil, and he couldn't no more stir than if he was anchored out. Smiley was a good deal surprised, and he

[7]*a red,* a red cent, or any money at all.

was disgusted too, but he didn't have no idea what the matter was, of course.

"The feller took the money and started away; and when he was going out at the door, he sorter jerked his thumb over his shoulder—this way—at Dan'l, and says again, very deliberate, 'Well, *I* don't see no p'ints about that frog that's any better'n any other frog.'

"Smiley he stood scratching his head and looking down at Dan'l a long time, and at last he says, 'I do wonder what in the nation that frog throw'd off for—I wonder if there ain't something the matter with him—he 'pears to look mighty baggy, somehow.' And he ketched Dan'l by the nap of the neck, and lifted him up, and says, 'Why blame my cats if he don't weigh five pound!' and turned him upside down, and he belched out a double handful of shot. And then Smiley see how it was, and he was the maddest man—he set the frog down and took out after that feller, but he never ketched him. And——"

Here Simon Wheeler heard his name called from the front yard, and got up to see what was wanted. And turning to me as he moved away, he said: "Just set where you are, stranger, and rest easy—I ain't going to be gone a second."

But, by your leave, I did not think that a continuation of the history of the enterprising vagabond *Jim* Smiley would be likely to afford me much information concerning the Rev. *Leonidas W.* Smiley, and so I started away.

At the door I met the sociable Wheeler returning, and he buttonholed me and recommenced:

"Well, thish-yer Smiley had a yaller one-eyed cow that didn't have no tail, only just a short stump like a bannanner, and——"

"Oh! hang Smiley and his afflicted cow!" I muttered, good-naturedly, and bidding the old gentleman good day, I departed.

CONCERNING MARK TWAIN

1. In what places did Mark Twain encounter oral storytelling?

2. How did his liking for yarnspinning influence his writing?

"Bugs"

1. A critic says: "The bugs in this story become increasingly 'human' as the narrative progresses." Trace the stages in this development, picking out details in the latter stages which do most to make the bugs seem like human beings.

2. Select and read aloud several sentences which help you see and hear the bugs quite clearly.

3. Compare the humor of "Bugs" with that of Franklin's "Ephemera" (pages 313-314).

"The Celebrated Jumping Frog"

1. How did Twain happen to write this story? What devices did he use to develop it from a brief entry in a notebook to a well-rounded yarn?

2. Which of Jim Smiley's animals did you find most amusing? Why was Jim willing to bet forty dollars on "Dan'l Webster"? Explain why you consider Jim's loss of the bet (*a*) sad or (*b*) amusing.

3. How does the narrator of the story imply that he is bored by his call on Wheeler? Cite evidence to support your opinion that he was, or was not, actually bored.

Helping the reader see and hear

Modern readers sometimes have trouble understanding exactly why the yarns in Mark Twain's books were considered very funny in his day. Probably the explanation lies in the fact that Twain's contemporaries, unlike us, were accustomed to being entertained by oral stories. Thus when they read a printed yarn like "The Celebrated Jumping Frog," they could easily do two things: (1) In their mind's eye, they could see Simon Wheeler distinctly. (2) In their mind's ear, they could hear the very sound of Wheeler's voice. And what they saw and heard amused them tremendously.

We moderns can increase our enjoyment of Twain's humor if we practice using *our* mental eyes and ears. If we try it, we will discover that Mark Twain has given us considerable aid. Test this out by rereading the first three paragraphs of the Jumping Frog story with your mental eyes wide open. How do you picture Simon Wheeler? What sort of person is he? What humor do you find in the *serious* attitude he takes toward the story he is about to tell? How has Mark Twain helped you form your impressions of Simon Wheeler?

Next read the first paragraph of Wheeler's story (page 422, column 2, paragraph 1), listening for the sound of Wheeler's voice. You will quickly note two ways in which Twain helps you hear that voice: by misspelling certain words and by italicizing others. (Give some examples, and explain how they aid your hearing.) If you listen sharply, you will notice also the skillful manner in which Twain has suggested the natural rhythm, the rise and fall, of Wheeler's speech. The best way for you to get the feel of this rhythm is to practice reading aloud sentences like the one beginning "If there was a horse race...." When you feel that you can reproduce the humorous, rhythmical quality of Wheeler's voice, perhaps you will want to read aloud at least a part of his yarn to the class.

➤ III FICTION WRITER

Mark Twain won his greatest fame and his high position among American men of letters, not for his journalistic reports or his imaginative yarns, but for his two best-known novels—*The Adventures of Tom Sawyer* (1876) and *The Adventures of Huckleberry Finn* (1884). Yet both these novels, in which Twain pictured life in his home section during the period of his boyhood, had much in common with his earlier writings.

Like Twain's journalistic reports, *Tom Sawyer* and *Huckleberry Finn* were crammed with concrete details which he had observed, remembered fully, and set down. Readers were able to get an experience almost like that of living in the times and places which he pictured. Sometimes historians quote passages from his books to show clearly what life of the sort he portrayed had been like. *The Adventures of Tom Sawyer,* for instance, offered a fine picture of the town of Hannibal (St. Petersburg in the book) in the day of Twain's boyhood—the houses, the church, the school—and the green countryside and the river which every boy who lived there came to know. It captured the qualities of the people of Hannibal, from the judge to the town drunkard, from the Sunday-school superintendent to the mischievous boys of the town. *The Adventures of Huckleberry Finn* pictured an even broader scene—the river and the towns alongside the river from Missouri to Arkansas, and the life of the river and the towns. Twain seems to have tried to get into this novel as many classes of people and as many customs and typical scenes as possible. The result was a great panorama of life in the Mississippi Valley in the middle of the nineteenth century.

Like Twain's yarns, his best fiction was full of the characteristic talk of Americans. A note which he placed in the opening pages of *Huckleberry Finn* shows how much care he took to render American speech accurately:

In this book a number of dialects are used, to wit: the Missouri Negro dialect; the extremest form of the backwoods Southwestern dialect; the ordinary 'Pike County' dialect; and four modified varieties of this last. The shadings have not been done in a haphazard fashion, or by guesswork; but painstakingly, and with the trustworthy guidance and support of personal familiarity with these several forms of speech.

It is remarkable how well Clemens was able to echo the rhythms, the turns of phrase, the idioms of ordinary talk. Like his yarns, his best fiction introduces us to fascinating characters and happenings which have been produced by Mark's lively imagination.

426   *Samuel L. Clemens*

Yet though his novels resemble his journalistic stories and his yarns, they differ greatly in some respects. For one thing, when Twain was writing a first-rate novel, he could give its episodes or even the whole book a well-rounded plot structure. In *Tom Sawyer,* for instance, he told by means of several threads of narrative the story of how Tom moved from childhood to the threshold of maturity. Again, one of the developments running throughout the whole of *Huckleberry Finn* is Huck's growing affection and respect for his Negro companion, Jim.

Also different from the journalistic reports and yarns is the tone of Mark's best fiction—one of longing for "the good old days." In the years between 1871 and 1891, when he wrote his two masterpieces, Twain's days as a Hannibal youngster, as a tramp printer, as a river pilot, and as a Western miner and newspaper man were far behind him. He was living in a big, elaborate mansion in Hartford, Connecticut, a great rambling house which he had built with the returns from his writings. He and his family had a coachman and several servants; they entertained lavishly; they frequently took trips to Europe. He was on friendly terms with the great financial and literary figures of the day. But it often seemed to him that the past had been the best time after all, and often he could not recall the old days without being homesick for them. When he heard from an old Hannibal schoolmate in 1870, he wrote: "The fountains of my great deep are broken up and I have rained reminiscences for four-and-twenty hours. The old life has swept before me like a panorama; the old days have trooped by in their old glory again; the old faces have looked out of the mists of the past; old footsteps have sounded in my listening ears; old hands have clasped mine; old voices have greeted me...." Again, years later, he wrote, "Those were pleasant days; none since have been so pleasant, none so well worth living over again. For the romance of life is the only part of it that is overwhelmingly valuable, and romance dies with youth."

It was in such a spirit of tenderness and longing that Twain wrote of the America of his boyhood. His feeling colored what he wrote, and the scenes he pictured often had more charm, more beauty, or more laughable comedy than the actual scenes upon which they were based ever had had. They were lifelike, to be sure, but they showed life in a rather more idyllic form than it ever had managed to achieve. Yet Twain, grown to manhood, knew about the tragedy of life, too, and he did not neglect the faults of the men and women and children whom he portrayed, nor did he neglect their troubles and sorrows. The result was a rich depiction of America during Twain's boyhood and youth.

Huck Visits the Grangerfords

The Adventures of Huckleberry Finn, as Twain has said, "is a story which details some passages in the life of an ignorant village boy, Huck Finn, son of the town drunkard.... He has run away from his persecuting father, and from a persecuting good widow who wishes to make a nice, truth-telling, respectable boy of him; and with him a slave of the widow's has also escaped. They have found a fragment of a lumber raft, and are floating down the river by night, and hiding in the willows by day." Twilight is falling as the following incident begins. Huck Finn is the narrator.

W E WENT ALONG during three hours and more. Well, the night got gray and ruther thick, which is the next meanest thing to fog. You can't tell the shape of the river, and you can't see no distance. It got to be very late and still, and then along comes a steamboat up the river. We lit the lantern, and judged she would see it. Upstream boats didn't generly come close to us; they go out and follow the bars and hunt for easy water under the reefs; but nights like this they bull right up the channel against the whole river.

We could hear her pounding along, but we didn't see her good till she was close. She aimed right for us. Often they do that and try to see how close they can come without touching; sometimes the wheel bites off a sweep, and then the pilot sticks his head out and laughs, and thinks he's mighty smart. Well, here she comes, and we said she was going to try and shave us; but she didn't seem to be sheering off a bit. She was a high one, and she was coming in a hurry, too, looking like a black cloud with rows of glowworms around it; but all of a sudden she bulged out, big and scary, with a long row of wide-open furnace doors shining like red-hot teeth, and her monstrous bows and guards[1] hanging right over us. There was a yell at us, and a jingling of bells to stop the engines, a powwow of cussing, and whis-

tling of steam—and as Jim went overboard on one side and I on the other, she came smashing straight through the raft.

I dived—and I aimed to find the bottom, too, for a thirty-foot wheel had got to go over me, and I wanted it to have plenty of room. I could always stay under water a minute; this time I reckon I stayed under a minute and a half. Then I bounced for the top in a hurry, for I was nearly busting. I popped out to my armpits and blowed the water out of my nose, and puffed a bit. Of course there was a booming current; and of course that boat started her engines again ten seconds after she stopped them, for they never cared much for raftsmen; so now she was churning along up the river, out of sight in the thick weather, though I could hear her.

I sung out for Jim about a dozen times, but I didn't get any answer; so I grabbed a plank that touched me while I was treading water, and struck out for shore, shoving it ahead of me. But I made out to see that the drift of the current was toward the left-hand shore, which meant that I was in a crossing[2]; so I changed off and went that way.

It was one of these long, slanting, two-mile crossings; so I was a good long time in getting over. I made a safe landing, and clumb up the bank. I couldn't see but a little ways, but I went poking along over rough ground for a quarter of a mile or more, and then I run across a big old-fashioned double log house before I noticed it. I was going to rush by and get away, but a lot of dogs jumped out and went to howling and barking at me, and I knowed better than to move another peg.

In about a minute somebody spoke out a window without putting his head out, and says: "Be done, boys![3] Who's there?"

I says: "It's me."

"Who's me?"

"George Jackson, sir."

---

[1]*guards,* the parts of the boat's deck which curved out over the paddle wheels.

[2]*a crossing,* a place in a river at which the channel, which follows the current, shifts from one side of the river to the other.

[3]*Be done, boys!* The voice is addressing the dogs, commanding them to stop their barking.

"What do you want?"

"I don't want nothing, sir. I only want to go along by, but the dogs won't let me."

"What are you prowling around here this time of night for—hey?"

"I warn't prowling around, sir: I fell overboard off of the steamboat."

"Oh, you did, did you? Strike a light there, somebody. What did you say your name was?"

"George Jackson, sir. I'm only a boy."

"Look here, if you're telling the truth you needn't be afraid—nobody'll hurt you. But don't try to budge; stand right where you are. Rouse out Bob and Tom, some of you, and fetch the guns. George Jackson, is anybody with you?"

"No, sir, nobody."

I heard the people stirring around the house now, and see a light. The man sung out:

"Snatch that light away, Betsy, you old fool—ain't you got any sense? Put it on the floor behind the front door. Bob, if you and Tom are ready, take your place."

"All ready."

"Now, George Jackson, do you know the Shepherdsons?"

"No, sir; I never heard of them."

"Well, that may be so, and it mayn't. Now, all ready. Step forward, George Jackson. And mind, don't you hurry—come mighty slow. If there's anybody with you, let him keep back—if he shows himself, he'll be shot. Come along now. Come slow; push the door open yourself—just enough to squeeze in, d'you hear?"

I didn't hurry; I couldn't if I'd wanted to. I took one slow step at a time and there warn't a sound, only I thought I could hear my heart. The dogs were as still as the humans, but they followed a little behind me. When I got to the three log doorsteps, I heard them unlocking and unbarring and unbolting. I put my hand on the door and pushed it a little and a little more till somebody said, "There, that's enough—put your head in." I done it, but I judged they would take it off.

The candle was on the floor, and there they all was, looking at me, and me at them, for about a quarter of a minute: Three big men with guns pointed at me, which made me wince, I tell you; the oldest, gray and about sixty, the other two thirty or more—all of them fine and handsome—and the sweetest old gray-headed lady, and back of her two young women which I couldn't see right well. The old gentleman says:

"There; I reckon it's all right. Come in."

As soon as I was in, the old gentleman he locked the door and barred it and bolted it, and told the young men to come in with their guns, and they all went in a big parlor that had a new rag carpet on the floor, and got together in a corner that was out of the range of the front windows—there warn't none on the side. They held the candle, and took a good look at me, and all said, "Why, *he* ain't a Shepherdson—no, there ain't any Shepherdson about him." Then the old man said he hoped I wouldn't mind being searched for arms, because he didn't mean no harm by it—it was only to make sure. So he didn't pry into my pockets, but only felt outside with his hands, and said it was all right. He told me to make myself easy and at home, and tell all about myself; but the old lady says:

"Why, bless you, Saul, the poor thing's as wet as he can be; and don't you reckon it may be he's hungry?"

"True for you, Rachel—I forgot."

So the old lady says: "Betsy, you fly around and get him something to eat as quick as you can, poor thing; and one of you girls go and wake up Buck and tell him—oh, here he is himself. Buck, take this little stranger and get the wet clothes off from him and dress him up in some of yours that's dry."

Buck looked about as old as me—thirteen or fourteen or along there, though he was a little bigger than me. He hadn't on anything but a shirt, and he was very frowzy-headed. He came in gaping and digging one fist into his eyes, and he was dragging a gun along with the other one. He says: "Ain't they no Shepherdsons around?"

They said, no, 'twas a false alarm.

"Well," he says, "if they'd 'a' ben some, I reckon I'd 'a' got one."

They all laughed, and Bob says: "Why, Buck, they might have scalped us all, you've been so slow in coming."

"Well, nobody came after me, and it ain't right. I'm always kept down; I don't get no show."

"Never mind, Buck, my boy," says the old man, "you'll have show enough, all in good time, don't you fret about that. Go 'long with you now, and do as your mother told you."

When we got upstairs to his room, he got me a coarse shirt and a roundabout and pants of his, and I put them on. While I was at it he asked me what my name was, but before I could tell him he started to tell me about a bluejay and a young rabbit he had catched in the woods day before yesterday, and he asked me where Moses was when the candle went out. I said I didn't know; I hadn't heard about it before, no way.

"Well, guess," he says.

"How'm I going to guess," says I, "when I never heard tell of it before?"

"But you can guess, can't you? It's just as easy."

"*Which* candle?" I says.

"Why, any candle," he says.

"I don't know where he was," says I; "where was he?"

"Why, he was in the *dark!* That's where he was!"

"Well, if you knowed where he was, what did you ask me for?"

"Why, blame it, it's a riddle, don't you see? Say, how long are you going to stay here? You got to stay always. We can just have booming times—they don't have no school now. Do you own a dog? I've got a dog—and he'll go in the river and bring out chips that you throw in. Do you like to comb up Sundays, and all that kind of foolishness? You bet I don't, but Ma she makes me. Confound these ole britches! I reckon I'd better put 'em on, but I'd ruther not, it's so warm. Are you all ready? All right. Come along, old hoss."

Cold corn pone, cold corn-beef, butter and buttermilk—that is what they had for me down there, and there ain't nothing better that ever I've come across yet. Buck and his ma and all of them smoked cob pipes, except Betsy, who was gone, and the two young women. They all smoked and talked, and I eat and talked. The young women had quilts around them, and their hair down their backs. They all asked me questions, and I told them how Pap and me and all the family was living on a little farm down at the bottom of Arkansaw, and my sister Mary Ann run off and got married and never was heard of no more, and Bill went to hunt them and he warn't heard of no more, and Tom and Mort died, and then there warn't nobody but just me and Pap left, and he was just trimmed down to nothing, on account of his troubles; so when he died I took what there was left, because the farm didn't belong to us, and started up the river, deck passage,[4] and fell overboard; and that was how I come to be here. So they said I could have a home there as long as I wanted it. Then it was most daylight and everybody went to bed.

I went to bed with Buck, and when I waked up in the morning, drat it all, I had forgot what my name was. So I laid there about an hour trying to think, and when Buck waked up I says: "Can you spell, Buck?"

[4]*deck passage,* traveling on the deck of a steamboat. This was the cheapest way to travel.

"Yes," he says.

"I bet you can't spell my name," says I.

"I bet you what you dare I can," says he.

"All right," says I, "go ahead."

"G-e-o-r-g-e- J-a-x-o-n—there now," he says.

"Well," says I, "you done it, but I didn't think you could. It ain't no slouch of a name to spell—right off without studying."

I set it down, private, because somebody might want *me* to spell it next, and so I wanted to be handy with it and rattle it off like I was used to it.

It was a mighty nice family, and a mighty nice house, too. I hadn't seen no house out in the country before that was so nice and had so much style. It didn't have an iron latch on the front door, nor a wooden one with a buckskin string, but a brass knob to turn, the same as houses in town. There warn't no bed in the parlor, nor a sign of a bed; but heaps of parlors in towns has beds in them. There was a big fireplace that was bricked on the bottom, and the bricks was kept clean and red by pouring water on them and scrubbing them with another brick; sometimes they wash them over with red water paint that they call Spanish brown, same as they do in town. They had big brass dog irons that could hold up a saw log. There was a clock on the middle of the mantelpiece, with a picture of a town painted on the bottom half of the glass front, and a round place in the middle of it for the sun, and you could see the pendulum swinging behind it. It was beautiful to hear that clock tick; and sometimes when one of these peddlers had been along and scoured her up and got her in good shape, she would start in and strike a hundred and fifty before she got tuckered out. They wouldn't took any money for her.

Well, there was a big outlandish parrot on each side of the clock, made out of something like chalk, and painted up gaudy. By one of the parrots was a cat made of crockery, and a crockery dog by the other; and when you pressed down on them they squeaked, but didn't open their mouth nor look different nor interested. They squeaked through underneath. There was a couple of big wild-turkey-wing fans spread out behind those things. On the table in the middle of the room was a kind of a lovely crockery basket that had apples and oranges and peaches and grapes piled up in it, which was much redder and yellower and prettier than real ones is, but they warn't real because you could see where pieces had got chipped off and showed the white chalk, or whatever it was, underneath.

This table had a cover made out of beautiful oilcloth, with a red and blue spread-eagle painted on it, and a painted border all around. It came all the way from Philadelphia, they said. There was some books, too, piled up perfectly exact, on each corner of the table. One was a big family Bible full of pictures. One was *Pilgrim's Progress,* about a man that left his family, it didn't say why. I read considerable in it now and then. The statements was interesting, but tough. Another was *Friendship's Offering,* full of beautiful stuff and poetry; but I didn't read the poetry. Another was Henry Clay's speeches, and another was Dr. Gunn's *Family Medicine,* which told you all about what to do if a body was sick or dead. There was a hymn book, and a lot of other books. And there was nice split-bottom chairs, and perfectly sound, too—not bagged down in the middle and busted, like an old basket.

They had pictures hung on the walls—mainly Washingtons and Lafayettes, and battles, and Highland Marys,[5] and one called "Signing the Declaration." There was some that they called crayons, which one of the daughters which was dead made her own self when she was only fifteen years old. They was different from any pictures I ever see before—blacker, mostly, than is common. One was a woman in a slim black dress, belted small under the armpits, with bulges like a cabbage in the middle of the sleeves, and a large black scoop-shovel bonnet[6] with a black veil, and white slim ankles crossed about with black tape, and very wee black slippers, like a chisel, and she was leaning pensive on a tombstone on her right elbow, under

---

[5]*Highland Marys,* pictures of beautiful girls. The name "Highland Mary" refers to Mary Campbell, to whom the Scotch poet Robert Burns wrote some of his finest poetry.

[6]*scoop-shovel bonnet,* a bonnet with a long, narrow front which shaded the face.

a weeping willow, and her other hand hanging down her side holding a white handkerchief and a reticule, and underneath the picture it said "Shall I Never See Thee More Alas." Another one was a young lady with her hair all combed up straight to the top of her head, and knotted there in front of a comb like a chair back, and she was crying into a handkerchief and had a dead bird laying on its back in her other hand with its heels up, and underneath the picture it said "I Shall Never Hear Thy Sweet Chirrup More Alas." There was one where a young lady was at a window looking up at the moon, and tears running down her cheeks; and she had an open letter in one hand with black sealing wax showing on one edge of it, and she was mashing a locket with a chain to it against her mouth, and underneath the picture it said "And Art Thou Gone Yes Thou Art Gone Alas."

These was all nice pictures, I reckon, but I didn't somehow seem to take to them, because if ever I was down a little they always give me the fantods.[7] Everybody was sorry the girl died, because she had laid out a lot more of these pictures to do, and a body could see by what she had done what they had lost. But I reckoned that with her disposition she was having a better time in the graveyard. She was at work on what they said was her greatest picture when she took sick, and every day and every night it was her prayer to be allowed to live till she got it done, but she never got the chance. It was a picture of a young woman in a long white gown, standing on the rail of a bridge all ready to jump off, with her hair all down her back, and looking up to the moon, with the tears running down her face, and she had two arms folded across her breast, and two arms stretched out in front, and two more reaching up toward the moon—and the idea was to see which pair would look best, and then scratch out all the other arms; but, as I was saying, she died before she got her mind made up and now they kept this picture over the head of the bed in her room, and every time her birthday come they hung flowers on it.

---

[7]*the fantods,* the fidgets. [*Slang*]

Other times it was hid with a little curtain. The young woman in the picture had a kind of a nice sweet face, but there was so many arms it made her look too spidery, seemed to me.

This young girl kept a scrapbook when she was alive, and used to paste obituaries and accidents and cases of patient suffering in it out of the *Presbyterian Observer,* and write poetry after them out of her own head. It was very good poetry. This is what she wrote about a boy by the name of Stephen Dowling Bots that fell down a well and was drownded:

ODE TO STEPHEN DOWLING BOTS, DEC'D.

> And did young Stephen sicken,
>   And did young Stephen die?
> And did the sad hearts thicken,
>   And did the mourners cry?
>
> No; such was not the fate of
>   Young Stephen Dowling Bots;
> Though sad hearts round him thickened,
>   'Twas not from sickness' shots.
>
> No whooping cough did rack his frame,
>   Nor measles drear with spots;
> Not these impaired the sacred name
>   Of Stephen Dowling Bots.
>
> Despised love struck not with woe
>   That head of curly knots,
> Nor stomach troubles laid him low,
>   Young Stephen Dowling Bots.
>
> O no. Then list with tearful eye,
>   Whilst I his fate do tell,
> His soul did from this cold world fly
>   By falling down a well.
>
> They got him out and emptied him;
>   Alas it was too late;
> His spirit was gone for to sport aloft
>   In the realms of the good and great.

If Emmeline Grangerford could make poetry like that before she was fourteen, there ain't no telling what she could 'a' done by and by. Buck said she could rattle off poetry like nothing. She didn't ever have to stop to think. He said she would slap down a line, and if she couldn't find anything to rhyme with it would just scratch it out and slap down another one, and go ahead. She warn't particular; she could write about anything you choose to give her to write about just so it was sadful. Every time a man died, or a woman died, or a child died, she would be on hand with her "tribute" before he was cold. She called them tributes. The neighbors said it was the doctor first, then Emmeline, then the undertaker—the undertaker never got in ahead of Emmeline but once, and then she hung fire on a rhyme for the dead person's name, which was Whistler. She warn't ever the same after that; she never complained, but she kinder pined away and did not live long.

Poor thing, many's the time I made myself go up to the little room that used to be hers and get out her poor old scrapbook and read in it when her pictures had been aggravating me and I had soured on her a little. I liked all that family, dead ones and all, and warn't going to let anything come between us. Poor Emmeline made poetry about all the dead people when she was alive, and it didn't seem right that there warn't nobody to make some about her now she was gone; so I tried to sweat out a verse or two myself, but I couldn't seem to make it go somehow.

It was a double house, and the big open place betwixt them was roofed and floored, and sometimes the table was set there in the middle of the day, and it was a cool, comfortable place. Nothing couldn't be better. And warn't the cooking good, and just bushels of it too!

Col. Grangerford was a gentleman, you see. He was a gentleman all over; and so was his family. He was wellborn, as the saying is, and that's worth as much in a man as it is in a horse, so the Widow Douglas[8] said.

Col. Grangerford was very tall and very slim, and had a darkish-paly complexion, not a sign of red in it anywheres; he was clean-shaved every morning all over his thin face, and he had the thinnest kind of lips, and the thinnest kind of nostrils, and a high nose, and heavy eyebrows, and the blackest kind of eyes, sunk so deep back that they seemed like they was looking out of caverns at you, as you may say.

His forehead was high, and his hair was gray and straight and hung to his shoulders. His hands was long and thin, and every day of his life he put on a clean shirt and a full suit from head to foot made out of linen so white it hurt your eyes to look at it; and on Sundays he wore a blue tail coat with brass buttons on it. He carried a mahogany cane with a silver head to it. There warn't no frivolishness about him, not a bit, and he warn't ever loud. He was as kind as he could be—you could feel that, you know, and so you had confidence. Sometimes he smiled and it was good to see; but when he straightened himself up like a liberty pole, and the lightning begun to flicker out from under his eyebrows, you wanted to climb a tree first, and find out what the matter was afterwards.

When him and the old lady come down in the morning, all the family got out of their chairs and give them good day, and didn't set down again till they had set down.

Bob was the oldest and Tom next—tall, beautiful men with very broad shoulders and brown faces, and long black hair and black eyes. They dressed in white linen from head to foot, like the old gentleman, and wore broad Panama hats.

---

[8] *the Widow Douglas,* the good widow from whose home Huck has run away.

Then there was Miss Charlotte; she was twenty-five, and tall and proud and grand, but as good as she could be when she warn't stirred up; but when she was, she had a look that would make you wilt in your tracks, like her father. She was beautiful.

So was her sister, Miss Sophia, but it was a different kind. She was gentle and sweet like a dove, and she was only twenty.

Each person had somebody to wait on them—Buck too. My boy had a monstrous easy time, because I warn't used to having anybody do anything for me, but Buck's was on the jump most of the time.

This was all there was of the family now, but there used to be more—three sons; they got killed; and Emmeline that died.

Sometimes a stack of people would come there, horseback, from ten or fifteen miles around, and stay five or six days, and have such junketings round about and on the river, and dances and picnics in the woods daytimes, and balls at the house nights. These people was mostly kinfolks of the family. The men brought their guns with them. It was a handsome lot of quality, I tell you.

There was another clan of aristocracy around there—five or six families—mostly of the name of Shepherdson. They was as high-toned and wellborn and rich and grand as the tribe of Grangerfords. The Shepherdsons and Grangerfords used the same steamboat landing, which was about two mile above the Grangerfords' house; so sometimes when I went up there with a lot of our folks, I used to see a lot of the Shepherdsons there on their fine horses.

One day Buck and me was away out in the woods hunting, and heard a horse coming. We was crossing the road. Buck says: "Quick! Jump for the woods!"

We done it, and then peeped down the woods through the leaves. Pretty soon a splendid young man came galloping down the road, setting his horse easy and looking like a soldier. He had his gun across his pommel. I had seen him before. It was young Harney Shepherdson. I heard Buck's gun go off at my ear, and Harney's hat tumbled off from his head. He grabbed his gun and rode straight to the place where we was hid. But we didn't wait. We started through the woods on a run. The woods warn't thick, so I looked over my shoulder to dodge the bullet, and twice I seen Harney cover Buck with his gun; and then he rode away the way he come—to get his hat, I reckon, but I couldn't see. We never stopped running till we got home. The old gentleman's eyes blazed a minute—'twas pleasure, mainly, I judged—then his face sort of smoothed down, and he says, kind of gentle: "I don't like that shooting from behind a bush. Why didn't you step into the road, my boy?"

"The Shepherdsons don't, Father. They always take advantage."

Miss Charlotte she held her head up like a queen while Buck was telling his tale, and her nostrils spread and her eyes snapped. The two young men looked dark, but never said nothing. Miss Sophia she turned pale, but the color come back when she found the man warn't hurt.

Soon as I could get Buck down by the corn cribs under the trees by ourselves, I says: "Did you want to kill him, Buck?"

"Well, I bet I did."

"What did he do to you?"

"Him? He never done nothing to me."

"Well, then, what did you want to kill him for?"

"Why, nothing—only it's on account of the feud."

"What's a feud?"

"Why, where was you raised? Don't you know what a feud is?"

"Never heard of it before—tell me about it."

"Well," says Buck, "a feud is this way: A man has a quarrel with another man, and kills him; then that other man's brother kills *him;* then the other brothers, on both sides, goes for one another; then the *cousins* chip in—and by and by everybody's killed off, and there ain't no more feud. But it's kind of slow, and takes a long time."

"Has this one been going on long, Buck?"

"Well, I should *reckon!* It started thirty years ago, or some'ers along there. There was trouble 'bout something, and then a lawsuit to settle it; and the suit went agin one of the men, and so he up and shot the man that won the suit—which he would naturally do, of course. Anybody would."

"What was the trouble about, Buck?"

"Laws, how do *I* know? It was all so long ago."

"Don't anybody know?"

"Oh, yes, Pa knows, I reckon, and some of the other old people; but they don't know now what the row was about in the first place."

"Has there been many killed, Buck?"

"Yes; right smart chance of funerals. But they don't always kill. Pa's got a few buckshot in him; but he don't mind it, 'cuz he don't weigh much anyway. Bob's been carved up some with a bowie, and Tom's been hurt once or twice."

"Has anybody been killed this year, Buck?"

"Yes; we got one, and they got one. 'Bout three months ago my cousin Bud, fourteen year old, was riding through the woods on t'other side of the river, and didn't have no weapon with him, which was blame' foolishness, and in a lonesome place he hears a horse a-coming behind him, and sees old Baldy Shepherdson a-linkin'[9] after him with his gun in his hand and his white hair a-flying in the wind; and 'stead of jumping off and taking to the brush, Bud 'lowed he could outrun him; so they had it, nip and tuck, for five mile or more, the old man a-gaining all the time. So at last Bud seen it warn't any use, so he stopped and faced around so as to have the bullet holes in front, you know, and the old man he rode up and shot him down. But he didn't git much chance to enjoy his luck, for inside of a week our folks laid *him* out."

"I reckon that old man was a coward, Buck."

"I reckon he *warn't* a coward. Not by a blame' sight. There ain't a coward amongst them Shepherdsons—not a one. And there ain't no cowards amongst the Grangerfords either. Why, that old man kep' up his end in a fight one day for half an hour against three Grangerfords, and come out winner. They was all a-horseback; he lit off of his horse and got behind a little woodpile, and kep' his horse

before him to stop the bullets; but the Grangerfords stayed on their horses and capered around the old man, and peppered away at him, and he peppered away at them. Him and his horse went home pretty leaky and crippled, but the Grangerfords had to be *fetched* home—and one of 'em was dead, and another died the next day. No, sir; if a body's out hunting for cowards, he don't want to fool anytime amongst them Shepherdsons, becuz they don't breed any of that *kind*."

Next Sunday we all went to church, about three mile, everybody a-horseback. The men took their guns along, so did Buck, and kept them between their knees or stood them handy against the wall. The Shepherdsons done the same. It was pretty ornery preaching—all about brotherly love, and suchlike tiresomeness; but everybody said it was a good sermon, and they all talked it over going home, and had such a powerful lot to say about faith and good works and free grace and preforeordestination,[10] and I don't know what all, that it did seem to me to be one of the roughest Sundays I had run across yet.

About an hour after dinner everybody was dozing around, some in their chairs and some in their rooms, and it got to be pretty dull. Buck and a dog was stretched out on the grass in the sun sound asleep. I went up to our room, and judged I would take a nap myself. I found that sweet Miss Sophia standing in her door, which was next to ours, and she took me in her room and shut the door very soft, and asked me if I liked her, and I said I did; and she asked me if I would do something for her and not tell anybody, and I said I would. Then she said she'd forgot her Testament, and left it in the seat at church between two other books, and would I slip out quiet and go there and fetch it to her, and not say nothing to nobody. I said I would. So I slid out and slipped off up the road, and there warn't anybody at the church, except maybe a hog or two, for there warn't any lock on the door, and hogs likes

[9]*a-linkin'*, hurrying.

[10]*preforeordestination.* Huck is combining *predestination* and *foreordination*, both of which mean "that which has been determined by God from all eternity."

a puncheon floor in summertime because it's cool. If you notice, most folks don't go to church only when they've got to; but a hog is different.

Says I to myself, something's up; it ain't natural for a girl to be in such a sweat about a Testament. So I give it a shake, and out drops a little piece of paper with *"Half past two"* wrote on it with a pencil. I ransacked it, but couldn't find anything else. I couldn't make anything out of that, so I put the paper in the book again, and when I got home and upstairs there was Miss Sophia in her door waiting for me.

She pulled me in and shut the door; then she looked in the Testament till she found the paper, and as soon as she read it, she looked glad; and before a body could think she grabbed me and give me a squeeze and said I was the best boy in the world, and not to tell anybody. She was mighty red in the face for a minute, and her eyes lighted up, and it made her powerful pretty. I was a good deal astonished, but when I got my breath, I asked her what the paper was about, and she asked me if I had read it, and I said no, and she asked me if I could read writing, and I told her no,

only coarse hand,[11] and then she said the paper warn't anything but a bookmark to keep her place, and I might go and play now.

I went off down to the river, studying over this thing, and pretty soon I noticed that my boy was following along behind. When we was out of sight of the house, he looked back and around a second, and then comes a-running, and says: "If you'll come down into de swamp, I'll show you a whole stack o' water moccasins."

So I says: "All right; trot ahead."

I followed a half a mile; then he struck out over the swamp and waded ankle-deep as much as another half mile. We come to a little flat piece of land which was dry and very thick with trees and bushes and vines, and he says: "You shove right in dah jist a few steps; dah's whah dey is. I's seed 'm befo'; I don't k'yer to see 'em no mo'."

Then he slopped right along and went away, and pretty soon the trees hid him. I poked into the place a ways and come to a little open patch as big as a bedroom all hung around with vines, and found a man laying there asleep—and, by jings, it was my old Jim!

I waked him up, and I reckoned it was going to be a grand surprise to him to see me again, but it warn't. He nearly cried he was so glad, but he warn't surprised. Said he swum along behind me that night, and heard me yell every time, but dasn't answer, because he didn't want nobody to pick *him* up and take him into slavery again. Says he: "I got hurt a little, en couldn't swim fas', so I wuz a considerable ways behine you towards de las'; when you landed, I reck'ned I could ketch up wid you on de lan' 'dout havin' to shout at you, but when I see dat house, I begin to go slow. I 'uz off too fur to hear what dey say to you—I wuz 'fraid o' de dogs; but when it 'uz all quiet ag'in, I knowed you's in de house, so I struck out for de woods to wait for day. Early in de mawnin' some er de hands come along, gwyne to de field, en dey tuk me en showed me dis place, whah de dogs can't track me on account o' de water, en dey brings me truck to eat every night, en tells me how you's a-gittin' along."

[11]*coarse hand*, a large, clumsy type of writing.

"Why didn't you tell my Jack to fetch me here sooner, Jim?"

"Well, 'twarn't no use to 'sturb you, Huck, tell we could do sumfn—but we's all right now. I ben a-buyin' pots en pans en vittles, as I got a chanst, en a-patchin' up de raf' nights when——"

"*What* raft, Jim?"

"Our ole raf'."

"You mean to say our old raft warn't smashed all to flinders?"

"No, she warn't. She was tore up a good deal —one en' of her was; but dey warn't no great harm done, only our traps[12] was mos' all los.' Ef we hadn' dive' so deep en swum so fur under water, en de night hadn't been so dark, en we warn't so sk'yered, en ben sich punkin-heads, as de sayin' is, we'd a seed de raf'. But it's jis' as well we didn't, 'kase now she's all fixed up ag'in mos' as good as new, en we's got a new lot o' stuff, in de place o' what us los'."

"Why, how did you get hold of the raft again, Jim—did you catch her?"

"How I gwyne to ketch her en I out in de woods? No; some er de hands foun' her ketched on a snag along heah in de ben', en dey hid her in a crick 'mongst de willows, en dey wuz so much jawin' 'bout which un 'um she b'longs to de mos' dat I come to heah 'bout it pretty soon, so I ups en settles de trouble by tellin' 'um she don' b'long to none uv 'um, but to you en me; en I ast 'm if dey gwyne to grab a young genlman's propaty, en git a hid'n[13] for it? Den I gin 'm ten cents apiece, en dey 'uz mighty well satisfied, en wisht some mo' raf's 'ud come along en make 'm rich ag'in. Dey's mighty good to me, dese folks is, en whatever I wants 'm to do fur me I doan' have to ast 'm twice, honey. Dat Jack's a good boy."

"Yes, he is. He ain't ever told me you was here; told me to come, and he'd show me a lot of water moccasins. If anything happens, *he* ain't mixed up in it. He can say he never seen us together, and it'll be the truth."

I don't want to talk much about the next day. I reckon I'll cut it pretty short. I waked up about dawn, and was a-going to turn over and go to sleep again when I noticed how still it was— didn't seem to be anybody stirring. That warn't usual. Next I noticed that Buck was up and gone. Well, I gets up, a-wondering, and goes downstairs—nobody around; everything as still as a mouse. Just the same outside. Thinks I, what does it mean?

Down by the woodpile I comes across my Jack, and says: "What's it all about?"

Says he: "Don't you know?"

"No," says I, "I don't."

"Well, den, Miss Sophia's run off! 'deed she has. She run off in de night some time—nobody don't know jis' when—run off to get married to dat young Harney Shepherdson, you know— leastways, so dey 'spec. De fambly foun' it out 'bout half an hour ago—maybe a little mo'—en I *tell* you, dey warn't no time los'. Sich another hurryin' up guns en hosses *you* never see! De women folks has gone for to stir up de relations, en ole Mars Saul en de boys tuck dey guns en rode up de river road for to try to ketch dat young man en kill him 'fo' he kin git acrost de river wid Miss Sophia. I reck'n dey's gwyne to be mighty rough times."

"Buck went off 'thout waking me up."

"Well, I reck'n he *did!* Dey warn't gwyne to mix you up in it. Mars Buck he loaded up his gun en 'lowed he's gwyne to fetch home a Shepherdson or bust. Well, dey'll be plenty un 'm dah, I reck'n, en you bet you he'll fetch one."

I took up the river road as hard as I could put. By and by I begin to hear guns a good ways off. When I come in sight of the log store and the woodpile where the steamboats land, I worked along under the trees and brush till I got to a good place, and then I clumb up into the forks of a cottonwood that was out of reach, and watched. There was a wood rank[14] four foot high a little ways in front of the tree, and first I was going to hide behind that; but maybe it was luckier I didn't.

There was four or five men cavorting around on their horses in the open place before the

---

[12]*traps*, equipment.
[13]*hid'n*, hiding, or whipping.

[14]*wood rank*, one length of corded wood, or a pile eight feet long.

log store, cussing and yelling, and trying to get at a couple of young chaps that was behind the wood rank alongside of the steamboat landing; but they couldn't come it. Every time one of them showed himself on the river side of the woodpile, he got shot at. The two boys was squatting back to back behind the pile, so they could watch both ways.

By and by the men stopped cavorting around and yelling. They started riding toward the store; then up gets one of the boys, draws a steady bead over the wood rank, and drops one of them out of his saddle. All the men jumped off of their horses and grabbed the hurt one and started to carry him to the store; and that minute the two boys started on the run. They got halfway to the tree I was in before the men noticed. Then the men see them, and jumped on their horses and took out after them. They gained on the boys, but it didn't do no good, the boys had too good a start; they got to the woodpile that was in front of my tree, and slipped in behind it, and so they had the bulge[15] on the men again. One of the boys was Buck, and the other was a slim young chap about nineteen years old.

The men ripped around awhile, and then rode away. As soon as they was out of sight, I sung out to Buck and told him. He didn't know what to make of my voice coming out of the tree at first. He was awful surprised. He told me to watch out sharp and let him know when the men come in sight again; said they was up to some devilment or other.

I wished I was out of that tree, but I dasn't come down. Buck begun to cry and rip, and 'lowed that him and his cousin Joe (that was the other young chap) would make up for this day yet. He said his father and his two brothers was killed and two or three of the enemy. Said the Shepherdsons laid for them in ambush. Buck said his father and brothers ought to waited for their relations—the Shepherdsons was too strong for them. I asked him what was become of young Harney and Miss Sophia. He said they'd got across the river and was safe. I was glad of that; but the way Buck did take

on because he didn't manage to kill Harney that day he shot at him—I hain't ever heard anything like it.

All of a sudden, bang! bang! bang! goes three or four guns—the men had slipped around through the woods and come in from behind without their horses! The boys jumped for the river—both of them hurt—and as they swum down the current the men run along the bank shooting at them and singing out, "Kill them, kill them!" It made me so sick I most fell out of the tree. I ain't a-going to tell *all* that happened—it would make me sick again. I wished I hadn't ever come ashore that night to see such things. I ain't ever going to get shut of them—lots of times I dream about them.

I stayed in the tree till it begun to get dark, afraid to come down. Sometimes I heard guns away off in the woods; and twice I seen little gangs of men gallop past the log store with guns; so I reckoned the trouble was still a-going on. I was mighty downhearted; so I made up my mind I wouldn't ever go anear the house again, because I reckoned I was to blame, some-how. I judged that that piece of paper meant that Miss Sophia was to meet Harney some-wheres at half past two and run off; and I judged I ought to told her father about that paper and the curious way she acted, and then maybe he would 'a' locked her up, and this awful mess wouldn't ever happened.

When I got down out of the tree I crept along down the river bank a piece, and found the two bodies laying in the edge of the water, and tugged at them till I got them ashore; then I covered up their faces, and got away as quick as I could. I cried a little when I was covering up Buck's face, for he was mighty good to me.

It was just dark now. I never went near the house, but struck through the woods and made for the swamp. Jim warn't on his island, so I tramped off in a hurry for the crick, and crowded through the willows, red-hot to jump aboard and get out of that awful country. The raft was gone! My souls, but I was scared! I couldn't get my breath for most a minute. Then I raise a yell. A voice not twenty-five foot from me says: "Good lan'! is dat you, honey? Doan' make a noise."

[15]*had the bulge,* had the advantage or upper hand.

It was Jim's voice—nothing ever sounded so good before. I run along the bank a piece and got aboard, and Jim he grabbed me and hugged me, he was so glad to see me. He says: "Laws bless you, chile, I 'uz right down sho' you's dead ag'in. Jack's been heah; he says he reck'n you's ben shot, kase you didn' come home no mo'; so I's jes' dis minute a'startin' de raf' down towards de mouf er de crick, so's to be all ready for to shove out en leave soon as Jack comes ag'in en tells me for certain you *is* dead. Lawsy, I's mighty glad to git you back ag'in, honey."

I says: "All right—that's mighty good; they won't find me, and they'll think I've been killed and floated down the river—there's something up there that'll help them think so—so don't you lose no time, Jim, but just shove off for the big water as fast as ever you can."

I never felt easy till the raft was two mile below there and out in the middle of the Mississippi. Then we hung up our signal lantern, and judged that we was free and safe once more. I hadn't had a bite to eat since yesterday, so Jim he got out some corn dodgers and buttermilk, and pork and cabbage and greens—there ain't nothing in the world so good when it's cooked right—and whilst I eat my supper we talked and had a good time. I was powerful glad to get away from the feuds, and so was Jim to get away from the swamp. We said there warn't no home like a raft, after all. Other places do seem so cramped up and smothery, but a raft don't. You feel mighty free and easy and comfortable on a raft.

Two or three days and nights went by; I reckon I might say they swum by, they slid along so quiet and smooth and lovely. Here is the way we put in the time. It was a monstrous big river down there—sometimes a mile and a half wide. We run nights, and laid up and hid daytimes; soon as night was most gone we stopped navigating and tied up—nearly always in the dead water under a towhead[16]; and then cut young cottonwoods and willows, and hid the raft with them. Then we set out the lines.[17]

Next we slid into the river and had a swim, so as to freshen up and cool off; then we set down on the sandy bottom where the water was about knee-deep, and watched the daylight come.

Not a sound anywhere—perfectly still—just like the whole world was asleep, only sometimes the bullfrogs a-cluttering, maybe. The first thing to see, looking away over the water, was a kind of dull line—that was the woods on t'other side; you couldn't make nothing else out; then a pale place in the sky; then more paleness spreading around; then the river softened up away off, and warn't black any more, but gray; you could see little dark spots drifting along ever so far away—trading scows, and such things; and long black streaks—rafts; sometimes you could hear a sweep screaking; or jumbled-up voices, it was so still, and sounds come so far; and by and by, you could see a streak on the water which you know by the look of the streak that there's a snag there in a swift current which breaks on it and makes that streak look that way; and you see the mist curl up off of the water, and the east reddens up, and the river, and you make out a log cabin in the edge of the woods, away on the bank on t'other side of the river, being a wood-yard, likely, and piled by them cheats so you can throw a dog through it anywheres[18]; then the nice breeze springs up, and comes fanning you from over there, so cool and fresh and sweet to smell on account of the woods and the flowers; but sometimes not that way, because they've left dead fish laying around, gars and such, and they do get pretty rank; and next you've got the full day, and everything smiling in the sun, and the songbirds just going it!

---

[18]*wood-yard . . . throw a dog through it anywheres.* Huck means that at the wood-yard, a place at which firewood for steamboats was sold, the wood was piled loosely so that the purchaser got less than he paid for.

CONCERNING MARK TWAIN

1. How did Twain's best novels resemble and differ from his other writings?

2. How do *Tom Sawyer* and *Huckleberry Finn* represent Twain's attitude toward his past life?

---

[16]*towhead,* a sandbar covered with cottonwoods.
[17]*set out the lines,* set out fishing lines.

1. How does Huck arrive at the Grangerfords?

2. What does the reception which he receives indicate about the attitude of the Grangerfords toward (*a*) the Shepherdsons, (*b*) other people?

3. What do you learn about Buck's characteristics both from his first appearance in the parlor (page 429) and from his first conversation with Huck (page 430)? Is his later behavior consistent with the traits he shows here? Explain your answer.

4. What episodes in the early portions of the selection show Huck's ingenuity and his ability to fend for himself?

5. What idea of the Grangerford family do you gain from Huck's description of the house (pages 431-432)? What do you learn about Huck himself and about his background from this description?

6. What kind of person was Emmeline Grangerford? Why is Huck's picture of her amusing?

7. Characterize Colonel Grangerford, Bob, Tom, Charlotte, and Sophia. How do their characteristics and past history set the stage for what happens later?

8. What part does Huck play in bringing on another outbreak of the feud?

9. How did the feud affect Huck and the various members of the Grangerford family?

10. Like other authors, Twain not only pictures life in his books, but he also comments upon life. What is his attitude toward feuding? How, exactly, is that attitude indicated by Huck's telling of the Grangerford episode?

11. What part does Jim play in this selection? Sum up your impressions of him.

12. Where in the selection do you find evidence of Mark Twain's attitude toward the days of his boyhood? What was that attitude? How is it conveyed?

Mark Twain's use of dialogue

No one knew better than Mark Twain the various uses of dialogue and the importance of dialogue to journalistic writing, yarns, and fiction. Good dialogue serves three purposes: (1) It can make a character real to the reader by reproducing the way he talks and by showing through what he says the kind of person he is. (2) It can provide background information that the reader needs to know in order to understand a particular episode. And (3) it can advance the action of the story.

In "Huck Visits the Grangerfords" Mark Twain uses dialogue skillfully for each of these purposes. Sometimes one purpose is dominant, but all are often combined. Locate each of the dialogues listed below and point out what purpose or purposes each dialogue serves.

1. Huck's initial dialogue with Colonel Grangerford (pages 428-429).

2. Huck's dialogue with Buck at the corn cribs (pages 434-435).

3. Huck's conversation with Jim (pages 436-437).

4. Huck's conversation with his boy Jack (page 437).

The Larger View

I. Talk over the following questions with your classmates, bringing to the discussion information you have gathered from previous study and from reading.

1. Is there any aspect of Mark Twain's writing that you would consider romantic? (See the discussion of romantic literature on page 343.) Explain your answer.

2. What examples can you offer to show that Mark Twain was a close observer of nature? What differences do you notice between the treatment of nature in his writings and in Thoreau's?

3. What evidence would you cite to show that Mark Twain was a thoroughgoing American?

4. Why do you think that Mark Twain will, or will not, continue to be widely read in America?

II. Prepare a report for the class on one of the following topics:

1. The Mississippi River in song and story

2. The river steamboat (Illustrations will make your talk more interesting and will make it easier for your hearers to understand the various features of a steamboat.)

3. Famous steamboats and steamboat races

4. Celebrated gold and silver strikes

5. Virginia City today

6. Ghost towns of the West

ANDREWS, KENNETH R., *Nook Farm, Mark Twain's Hartford Circle*. (Harvard) This interesting book will introduce the mature student to Mark Twain and his literary neighbors in Hartford during the author's best years as a writer.

CLEMENS, SAMUEL, *The Adventures of Tom Sawyer*. (Harper) This book and its sequel, *The Adventures of Huckleberry Finn* (Harper), are as American as the Mississippi River, and they are brimful of adventure and humor.

CLEMENS, SAMUEL, *A Connecticut Yankee in King Arthur's Court*. (Harper) This amusing tale is based on the adventures which befall a Yankee who finds himself an associate of Arthur and his Knights of the Round Table.

CLEMENS, SAMUEL, *Life on the Mississippi*. (Harper) Clemens' own experiences as a pilot are the heart of this famous account of life on a Mississippi River steamboat.

CLEMENS, SAMUEL, *The Prince and the Pauper*. (Harper) By a strange accident the boy-king Edward VI changes places with a street waif. The adventures which follow bring out the courage and humanity of both.

CLEMENS, SAMUEL, *Roughing It*. (Harper) Exaggeration and high spirits characterize Clemens' humorous account of his trip across the plains to California and then to Hawaii in the 1860's.

DE VOTO, BERNARD, *Mark Twain's America*. (Little) This is a fine presentation of Clemens and his times by an outstanding authority.

FERBER, EDNA, *Show Boat*. (Doubleday) *The Cotton Blossom Floating Palace Theatre* was towed up and down the Mississippi and its tributaries, giving shows at towns and hamlets. This fascinating novel of the Hawks-Ravenal family presents a unique aspect of life on the river.

GABRILOWITSCH, C. C., *My Father, Mark Twain*. (Harper) This intimate biography by Mark Twain's daughter is an interesting picture of an always interesting man.

HAVIGHURST, WALTER, *Upper Mississippi; a Wilderness Saga*. (Rinehart) This fine history chronicles the romance and terror of early life on and beside the Mississippi River.

HOWELLS, WILLIAM DEAN, *The Rise of Silas Lapham*. (Houghton) An outstanding novel of Mark Twain's period, this is a story for mature readers of a man who unexpectedly becomes rich and moves to Boston where his contacts with city people give rise to many humorous situations.

MEIGS, CORNELIA, *Vanished Island*. (Macmillan) Boys particularly will enjoy the adventures of Don Perry, who becomes a stoker on the *Mary Morton*, a Mississippi River steamboat.

MINER, LOUIS S., *Wild Waters*. (Messner) This is the story of river traffic on the upper Mississippi in the days before 1860 and of a seventeen-year-old boy who had his own way to make. You'll find it an exciting tale.

PAINE, ALBERT BIGELOW, *Boy's Life of Mark Twain*. (Harper) This condensation from a longer biography gives an intimate account of a life that in itself possessed many of the characteristics of a good story.

PATTEE, FRED LOUIS, *A History of American Literature Since 1870*. (Appleton) The mature student who would like to know more of Samuel Clemens and his contemporaries will find this book a source of valuable material.

PROUDFIT, ISABEL, *Riverboy; the Story of Mark Twain*. (Messner) This lively and entertaining biography, which was written especially for students, is particularly interesting for the glimpses it furnishes of the people and experiences behind Clemens' books.

PURDY, CLAIRE LEE, *He Heard America Sing; the Story of Stephen Foster*. (Messner) The days of river steamboats and the overland trails come to life again in this easily read biography of one of America's most beloved song writers.

QUICK, HERBERT and EDWARD, *Mississippi Steamboatin'*. (Holt) This readable history augments the picture given in Mark Twain's famous book on the Mississippi.

WESTCOTT, EDWARD NOYES, *David Harum*. (Appleton) Humor attaches to David Harum, who was a shrewd country banker, but romance follows John Lenox and Mary Blake. This is a fine novel of Mark Twain's period.

LITERATURE	HISTORICAL EVENTS

Samuel Clemens 1835-1910

1865 Samuel Clemens, "The Celebrated Jumping Frog of Calaveras County"

| | Alaska purchased from Russia | 1867 |
| 1868 Bret Harte, "The Luck of Roaring Camp" | Fourteenth Amendment ratified | 1868 |

Louisa May Alcott, *Little Women*

1869 Bret Harte, "Outcasts of Poker Flat"   Union Pacific Railroad completed line linking 1869
   Samuel Clemens, *Innocents Abroad*   East and West
   Thomas Bailey Aldrich, *Story of a Bad Boy*

   Rockefeller organized Standard Oil Company   1870

1871 James Russell Lowell, *My Study Window*

1875 Sidney Lanier, "Corn"
1876 Samuel Clemens, *Adventures of Tom Sawyer*   Bell telephone patented   1876

1878 Sidney Lanier, "The Marshes of Glynn"   William Cullen Bryant died   1878
1879 George W. Cable, *Old Creole Days*   Edison invented the incandescent lamp   1879
1880 Joel Chandler Harris, *Uncle Remus: His Songs and Sayings*
1881 Henry James, *Portrait of a Lady*   American Red Cross organized   1881
   Henry Wadsworth Longfellow and Ralph Waldo 1882
   Emerson died

1883 Samuel Clemens, *Life on the Mississippi*
   John Bannister Tabb, *Poems*
1884 Samuel Clemens, *Adventures of Huckleberry Finn*
   Mary Noailles Murfree, *In the Tennessee Mountains*
   Sidney Lanier, *Poems*
1885 William Dean Howells, *The Rise of Silas Lapham*

1887 Thomas Nelson Page, *In Ole Virginia*

1889 Samuel Clemens, *A Connecticut Yankee at King Arthur's Court*   Oklahoma opened for settlement   1889
1890 Emily Dickinson, *Poems*
1891 Hamlin Garland, *Main-Travelled Roads*
   Mary E. Wilkins Freeman, *A New England Nun and Other Stories*

   World's Columbian Exposition held in Chicago 1893

1895 Stephen Crane, *The Red Badge of Courage*
1896 Sarah Orne Jewett, *The Country of the Pointed Firs*
1897 John Bannister Tabb, *Lyrics*

   Spanish-American War began   1898

   Pacific cable laid   1903

1904 O. Henry, *Cabbages and Kings*

SOME PROMINENT WRITERS OF THE PERIOD OF NEW OUTLOOKS

STEPHEN CRANE, 1871-1900

Stephen Crane, a minister's son, was born in Newark, New Jersey. After two years of college, he turned to journalism. While working as a reporter in New York, he wrote his most famous book, *The Red Badge of Courage* (1895), a story of the war between North and South as seen through the eyes of a panic-stricken private. Crane's reporting carried him to Texas and Mexico, and, under war conditions, to Greece and Cuba. After his marriage in 1896 he lived in England. He died in 1900. Despite the brevity of his life, his poems, short stories, and novels have assured him a lasting place in American literature.

EMILY DICKINSON, 1830-1886

The known facts about Emily Dickinson's life are few. The daughter of a sternly religious lawyer in Amherst, Massachusetts, she nevertheless managed to be a happy, fun-loving girl. She was well educated in the Amherst Academy and at Mount Holyoke College. Then for some reason which remains a mystery, she went into seclusion in her Amherst home and remained a recluse for the rest of her life, writing poetry but refusing to publish it. The first collection of her poetry was issued in 1890, four years after her death. Today she is regarded as one of the greatest woman poets in all literature.

HAMLIN GARLAND, 1860-1940

Born on a Wisconsin farm, Hamlin Garland moved with his family first to Iowa, then to South Dakota. At twenty-four he went to Boston to study and write. A visit home suddenly opened his eyes to a life whose hardships he had heretofore taken for granted. When he returned East he wrote the realistic tales collected in *Main-Travelled Roads* (1891), his best work. During the next decades Garland wrote many novels on Western themes; these are notable chiefly for their fair treatment of the Indian. (See "Lone Wolf's Old Guard," pages 200-205.) After 1916 Garland attained new popularity for a series of biographies based on early remembrances. These included *A Son of the Middle Border* (1917) and *A Daughter of the Middle Border* (1922), for which he was awarded a Pulitzer Prize.

BRET HARTE, 1836-1902

Although Bret Harte is always thought of in connection with California gold-mining towns, he actually lived in the West only from 1854 to 1871. He was born in Albany, New York. After his widowed mother moved the family to San Francisco, he joined them there. He worked at various jobs until the publication of "The Luck of Roaring Camp" (see pages 522-528) shot him to immediate fame. Other stories of the same type increased his popularity, and in 1871 he started East to write for the *Atlantic Monthly*. He wrote a few more excellent stories, but for the most part his work was repetitious. From 1888 until his death he lived in England.

O. HENRY, 1862-1910

William Sydney Porter, who achieved world-wide fame under the pen name of "O. Henry," was born in Greensboro, North Carolina. After clerking in a drug store there, he went to Texas. While working as a bank teller in Austin, a charge of embezzlement led him to flee to Central America, only to return because of his wife's illness. He was convicted and in 1897 sent to the federal penitentiary at Columbus, Ohio, for three years. While there he began to write short stories under his pen name. His last ten years were spent in New York where he wrote his finest stories. Collections such as *Cabbages and Kings* and *The Four Million*, from which "The Gift of the Magi" (pages 530-533) is taken, have enjoyed a continuing popularity.

SIDNEY LANIER, 1842-1881

The son of a lawyer, Sidney Lanier grew up in Macon, Georgia. Shortly after his graduation from Oglethorpe College, war broke out between the North and the South. Lanier enlisted as a Confederate soldier and served throughout the war. During the 1870's he lived in Baltimore, where he pursued his ambition to be both musician and poet. In spite of his ill health he played flute with the Peabody Symphony Orchestra, lectured on literature at Johns Hopkins University, wrote several fine prose works on English literature, and produced his most outstanding lyrics.

JOHN BANNISTER TABB, 1845-1909

John Bannister Tabb was born into the old planter aristocracy of Virginia. Because of his poor eyesight he was tutored at home. When the War Between the States broke out, he tried to enlist in the Confederate army. Rejected because of his eyesight, he became a blockade runner. At the end of the war, his family fortune gone, Tabb turned to teaching to support himself, and began to write poetry. In 1872 he joined the Roman Catholic Church and in 1884 he was ordained a priest. Father Tabb gradually gained a reputation as a fine poet. Collections such as *Poems* (1883) and *Lyrics* (1897) show his genuine lyric gift.

UNIT XII: STEPHEN VINCENT BENET
(*representing* THE TWENTIETH CENTURY)

STEPHEN VINCENT BENÉT[1] was born in Bethlehem, Pennsylvania, in July, 1898, during the Spanish-American War. This war, won by the United States in four months, had one far-reaching effect: the United States emerged from it as a recognized world power. In the years that followed, America's destiny became more and more involved with that of other nations. Between 1917 and 1918 the United States joined with the allied nations in fighting World War I, which had started in 1914. Beginning in 1929 and on into the 1930's, our country suffered a terrible depression along with other countries of the world. Between 1941 and 1945, we found ourselves completely dedicated to winning World War II. After that war, our inevitable ties with Europe were clearer than ever. Meanwhile, our nation underwent tremendous changes. The rise of science and industry, of the machine and the city, gave men's lives different patterns from any that Americans had followed before.

These world-shaking events, of course, meant that any author who lived in our own century, as Benét did, had his life and work shaped by forces very different from those which had shaped the careers and writings of earlier authors whom we have studied—even of Mark Twain, who died in 1910. In his own way, Benét, like his contemporaries, was molded by the trying times during which he lived.

❧ I REBEL OF THE 1920's

It was apparently difficult if not impossible for a member of the Benét family to avoid becoming an author. Although the men of the Benét tribe for three generations had been professional soldiers, they had also been enthusiastic about books. Stephen's grandfather had been a translator of books into English and the author of books of his own. His father, a colonel and a vivid personality, constantly read aloud to his family and discussed poets and novelists with his friends and his children. Mrs. Benét, too, was passionately fond of reading. All three children of this couple —an older brother and sister as well as Stephen—in time became professional writers.

William Rose Benét recalled that his brother Steve began to show a literary bent at a comically early age: "He was discovered by my mother seated on the nursery floor with a book on his lap, reading aloud, although he had not yet learned to read. He was reading aloud to a mouse —or so he informed her. Unfortunately the mouse protruded from an ordinary mousetrap—and was quite dead."

As the years passed, Steve read so much, often in dim corners and

---

[1]*Benét* (bi nā′).

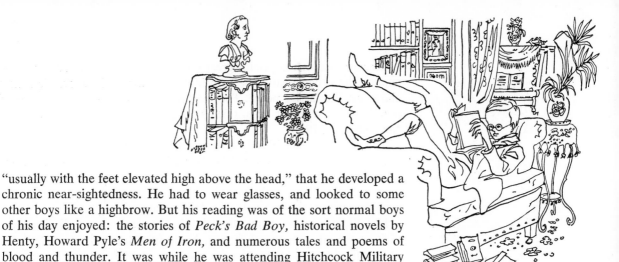

"usually with the feet elevated high above the head," that he developed a chronic near-sightedness. He had to wear glasses, and looked to some other boys like a highbrow. But his reading was of the sort normal boys of his day enjoyed: the stories of *Peck's Bad Boy*, historical novels by Henty, Howard Pyle's *Men of Iron*, and numerous tales and poems of blood and thunder. It was while he was attending Hitchcock Military Academy in California that Steve himself began to write some rather gory poems and stories. One stanza of a poem went like this:

> I have been on the old tramp steamer
> When heads were quickly bashed,
> When dead men rolled in the scuppers
> And revolvers spit and flashed.

Another poem won a three-dollar prize in a contest. Steve, aged thirteen, spent his prize money on various things to eat as he took the long train ride from California to the family's new home in Georgia. His first book of poetry, *Five Men and Pompey*, was published in 1915, the year he entered Yale at the age of seventeen.

Benét attended Yale during a period when several gifted young authors were studying there; three of them (Archibald MacLeish, Thornton Wilder, and Philip Barry) were, like Benét, destined to be Pulitzer Prize[2] winners. Stimulated by working with such a group, Benét cultivated his talents as a writer for student publications—*The Record* (a humorous monthly) and *The Yale Literary Magazine*.

During Benét's first college years, World War I was being fought abroad, but America had not yet entered the conflict. In 1917 the United States declared war. Benét, a junior, promptly tried to enlist, but was rejected by the army because of his near-sightedness. He spent the war years working for the State Department. At the end of the war in 1918 he returned to Yale and received both his B.A. and M.A. degrees[3] there.

In the postwar 1920's, many of the young men and women of America were embittered and disillusioned. If you read about America's wartime spirit, her part in the war, and then about the Peace of Versailles, you can understand why. The soldiers and many of the civilians who served

[2]*Pulitzer* (pū′lit sər *or* pùl′it sər) *Prize*, one of sixteen awards given yearly for outstanding work in some phase of journalism, literature, music, or art. The awards are named for a celebrated newspaperman.

[3]*B.A. and M.A. degrees*, a first degree, Bachelor of Arts (B.A.), and the more advanced degree, Master of Arts (M.A.).

The quatrain quoted on this page is from "My Brother Steve," by William Rose Benét in *The Saturday Review of Literature*, November 15, 1941. Used by permission of *The Saturday Review of Literature*.

in the war had high hopes for great results. They believed that the aftermath of the struggle would be a world-wide triumph of democratic beliefs and a just and lasting peace. They had faith that even the loss of lives of friends in battle might be justified by the aftermaths of Armistice Day, November 11, 1918.

The years of peace bitterly disappointed such idealists. Democracy did not triumph in Europe. Even in the United States, various politicians proved to be unworthy servants of a democracy, and some profiteers used their wealth to gain privileges. The Treaty of Versailles, instead of perpetuating peace, sowed seeds of a future war.

For these reasons many thoughtful Americans were disillusioned. Writers voiced widespread disgust. Some books bitterly recounted the futile sufferings of soldiers in the war, for example, John Dos Passos' *Three Soldiers* (1921). Other books, like Sinclair Lewis' *Babbitt* (1922), attacked the blind complacency of Americans. Still other works, such as Elmer Rice's play, *The Adding Machine* (1923), stressed the unfortunate effects of an ever-widening mechanical civilization. A large number of authors told of the effect of disillusionment upon American youth—their loss of faith, their tendency to become cynical, their feeling that the best thing to do was to forget the hopeless world and to enjoy themselves. A young man named F. Scott Fitzgerald, who had been a student at Princeton University, voiced this new viewpoint in *This Side of Paradise* (1920), a sensationally successful book. It was the first of many which showed the rebellion of what was called "flaming youth."

Benét was a contemporary of Fitzgerald, and his last years in college were those in which "flaming youth" was much in evidence. A few years later, many young Americans, seeking new slants on life, flocked to Europe. Great numbers of artists and writers like Fitzgerald and Ernest Hemingway went to Paris, to live and work there. Benét himself spent one year in Paris.

Benét's poems at this time take up the themes of the period. "Colloquy of the Statues" tells of his resentment of World War I and its aftermath, as do "Carol: New Style" and a poem, "The Walkers," about strike pickets on Fifth Avenue. He also wrote two novels, *The Beginning of Wisdom* (1921) and *Young People's Pride* (1922). These books did for the young men of Yale what *This Side of Paradise* had done for the Princetonians. The novels, as Horace Gregory and Marya Zaturenska have said, "represented a self-consciously restless generation whose stay at college was an introduction to the more exciting adventures of seeing New York, Chicago, Paris, and the Riviera soon after the First World War. The books were written with almost telegraphic speed, and they were models of what the 'younger generation' breathed, felt, and wore, and at last communicated their observations to readers of books...."

Benét, then, down to 1922, went through experiences in many ways like those of other authors in the period. He learned to write before the war. When he began to find a public in the postwar period, the feeling he had about the conflict and its aftermath colored his poems and his novels. These recorded and interpreted his experiences and those of his rebellious, "lost" generation.

Carol: New Style

IF JESUS CHRIST *should come again,*
On Christmas day, on Christmas day,
To bother the minds of gentlemen
On Christmas day in the morning?

The first one said as he passed by,   5
As he passed by, as he passed by,
"I see three thieves a-hanging high,
This Christmas day in the morning."

The second one said, "What sinful men!
What sinful men, what sinful men!   10
Hanging is too good for them,
On Christmas day in the morning."

The third one said, "Oh stay your word!
Stay your word, oh stay your word!
Do you not see that one's the Lord,   15
This Christmas day in the morning?

"I know him by his weary head,
His weary head, his weary head."
Whereat they all fell sore adread,
That Christmas day in the morning.   20

"How sad this is we all avow,
Yes indeed, we all avow!
But what shall we do about it now,
On Christmas day in the morning?"

PRIMUS[1]
"I'll run away as fast as I may,   25
As fast as I may, as fast as I may,
And pretend I haven't been out all day,
On Christmas day in the morning."

SECUNDUS
"I'll buy Him a shroud that's spick and span,
Spick and span, spick and span,   30
For I was always a generous man,
On Christmas day in the morning."

---

[1]*Primus* (prī′məs), the first speaker. The other men are also identified by Latin terms in the next stanzas as Secundus (se kun′dəs), the second speaker, and Tertius (tèr′shi əs), the third speaker.

TERTIUS
"But what if we should cut Him down,
Cut Him down, cut Him down?"

SECUNDUS ET PRIMUS
"You fool, do you want to arouse the town,   35
On Christmas day in the morning?"

"My speech was rash," the third one said,
The third one said, the third one said.
"We're surer of God when we know He's dead,
On any day in the morning."   40

They knelt in the snow and prayed and bowed,
Prayed and bowed, prayed and bowed,
And the two dead thieves laughed out aloud
On Christmas day in the morning.

As Jesus Christ was hanging high,   45
Hanging high, hanging high,
He saw three Christians, passing by,
On Christmas day in the morning.

CONCERNING STEPHEN VINCENT BENÉT

1. In what ways did Benét's environment make it natural for him to turn toward writing as a career?

2. How did the United States in which Benét grew up differ from that of earlier American authors?

3. What was the effect of the years following World War I on many American writers? In what ways does Benét's work at this period represent the writings of his contemporaries?

CONCERNING "CAROL: NEW STYLE"

1. The mood of the traditional carol is one of joy or reverence. How does Benét, in stanza 1, suggest the quite different mood of his "new style" carol?

2. What is the first reaction of each of the three gentlemen to the sight of three men hanging on crosses (lines 5-24)?

3. How does Primus react to the disclosure that the center man is Christ? What is Secundus' reaction? What does the reaction of each show about his character? Why is Tertius as blameworthy as the other two men?

4. What irony do you find in lines 41-44? In the word *Christians* in line 47?

5. What idea is Benét trying to develop in "Carol: New Style"? How is this poem typical of the mood of many Americans in the years following World War I?

The results of World War I were of many sorts; such a great contest naturally changed ways of thinking and feeling. In America, one effect resembled that which had followed other wars: there was a new turning to American history—a new interest in our past. People turned to American history for varied reasons. Some readers and writers found it pleasant to escape from immediate unpleasant realities by revisiting, in imaginative works, a more remote America. Some reëxamined the old America to see whether it, like the nation of the 1920's, had flaws. Some were interested in tracing current difficulties to their beginnings. And some hoped to find in the old America some codes of living—some values—which might help solve problems of the day. Whatever the cause, authors wrote and readers bought and read vast quantities of historical works. Among the best sellers popular in this period were such varied works as the following: *The Rise of American Civilization* (1927), a history by Charles and Mary Beard; *Anthony Adverse* (1933), a historical novel by Hervey Allen; *Gone With the Wind* (1936), a novel of the South in the 1860's by Margaret Mitchell; and *Abraham Lincoln: The Prairie Years* (1926), a long and detailed biography by Carl Sandburg.

Stephen Benét's upbringing and his interests caused him to welcome this trend and to follow it gladly. The grandfather for whom he was named had been enough of a historian to translate a history of the Battle of Waterloo[1] from French into English. When Steve was a boy, his father had argued for hours with him about the tactics used in the war between the North and the South and had introduced him to some good histories of that war. Stephen's early reading of historical novels for boys had been supplemented by later reading from novelists, biographers, and poets who had drawn upon history for subject matter.

In 1925 he wrote a historical novel, *Spanish Bayonet*, which did not sell very well. From this, he turned to short-story writing, and his short stories, by contrast, were highly remunerative. In 1926, however, he accepted a relatively small fellowship from a foundation and set out for Paris, where he planned to write a long poem dealing with the War Between the States.[2] His decision to give up the income which his stories had been bringing in—income he needed to support his wife and child—was a hard one for him to make. As his brother, William, commented:

> To a certain extent every writer has to be a gambler; but it takes entrails, with a family to support, to turn away from the lucrative field and embark upon a questionable project....[But] the book had to be written. It sprang from inner necessity. ...Steve dug in, toted masses of books home...,and went to work re-creating the American Civil War. Those long armchair discussions with his father...must have recurred to him vividly. His utter surprise when the finished book became a best seller is a story that has often been told. When asked by a ship-news reporter what it felt like, he characteristically remarked that to him it was as though he had given birth to a grand piano.

---

[1]*Battle of Waterloo,* the battle in which Napoleon was finally defeated in 1815 at Waterloo in Belgium.
[2]*fellowship...War Between the States.* The Guggenheim (gug′en hĭm) Foundation, an organization set up to finance creative work in the arts or in scientific research, granted Benét a sum of money (a fellowship) to support him while he was working on his poem.

John Brown's Body— so the long poem on which Benét had worked two years was named—was published in 1928. It was an attempt to re-create the impact of the war of 1861-1865 upon Americans who experienced it. It intertwined several stories—of Northern men and Southern men who went to war; of women who stayed at home; of political and military leaders who directed the war effort. In its unfolding of several plots, its characterization, its handling of backgrounds, it used some of the techniques of recent novelists. It also used the varied measures of modern poetry, ranging all the way from simple stanzas to free verse. But its fairly complex technique did not interfere with its clarity or its interest. Readers sensed the enthusiasm, the detailed historical knowledge, which lay behind the book, and followed the narrative with excitement. Perhaps an important fact was that other historical works had whetted their interest. Regardless of the reasons, the book was distributed to thousands of members of a book club, and it sold widely. It was awarded a Pulitzer Prize as an outstanding book of poetry and became a textbook in high schools and colleges.

Benét was enabled by this successful venture to write at a rather more leisurely pace and to create many poems and stories which utilized his deep interest in the American past. Some of his best writings developed a talent which had been first evidenced in some passages in *John Brown's Body*—a talent to mingle legend and humor with history.

Such a mingling was in tune with the taste of the times. One discovery made by many Americans after World War I was that the United States had delightful folklore of its own. For a long time (since the 1860's, as a matter of fact) scholars had been collecting American folk songs—ballads and Negro spirituals. Now not a few but many people began to appreciate such songs, as the success of various collections (for instance, Carl Sandburg's *American Songbag,* 1927) showed. (In this book you will find several such songs on pages 76-81, 274-275.) Furthermore, various authors retold, in widely read books, humorous legends of such comic American heroes as Paul Bunyan (pages 240-244), John Henry (pages 147-155), and Pecos Bill (pages 73-75). In Carl Sandburg's *Lincoln: The Prairie Years,* the author made use of ballad lore, folk tales, and folk humor to make vivid and understandable his subject's background.

Some years before, Benét had written a few poems in the spirit and form of the old ballads. Now he wrote many such poems, some of them published in the book *Ballads and Poems* (1931) and still others in *A Book of Americans* (1933), written in collaboration with his wife, Rosemary. In the latter volume, legendary and historical Americans, from colonial times on, were celebrated in balladlike little poems.

American folklore was echoed also in some of Benét's best stories, to which he gave a distinctive touch of humor. His father early had shown his son how to take things humorously, and through the years, Benét had cultivated his sense of the ridiculous. "In talk," wrote a friend, Basil Davenport, "he seems to 'make fun' of everything, not in the sense of ridicule, but with the humor that comes from looking at everything with a really original mind....That is the Benét who...can write a new legend so perfectly that it seems to have been always a part of our folklore." Benét wrote such short stories in the manner of a teller of the tall tale. His characters were figures who had actually lived or who had been invented by the folk in the past. These tales were inventive to the point of being fantastic, but they were told in the language of common speech and they were constantly flavored with salty humor. Examples are "The Devil and Daniel Webster" (pages 452-461), "Johnny Pye and the Fool-Killer," "The Angel Was a Yankee," "A Tooth for Paul Revere" (pages 206-215), and "Jacob and the Indians."

Americans have been particularly fond of those poems and stories by Benét which tell of their past in traditional forms. Here are some examples.

Stonewall Jackson's Last Charge

Ten miles west of Fredericksburg in Virginia lies a crossroads hamlet named Chancellorsville. Near here Colonel Alexander Spotswood had established the iron furnace about which he proudly told Colonel William Byrd. (See pages 52-54.) Years of cutting the trees to furnish charcoal for the furnaces had produced in time a tangled area of second-growth timber called the Wilderness. It was here that the Battle of Chancellorsville was fought in May, 1863. The Confederate Army, led by the gallant Thomas Jonathan ("Stonewall") Jackson, turned back the Union troops. In the following selection from *John Brown's Body* Stephen Vincent Benét records the price that Jackson paid for his victory.

I N THE DENSE HEART of the thicketed Wilderness,
Stonewall Jackson lies dying for four long days.
They have cut off his arm, they have tried such arts as they know,
But no arts can now save him.
When he was hit
By the blind chance bullet-spatter from his own lines,   5
In the night, in the darkness, they stole him off from the field
To keep the men from knowing, but the men knew.

The dogs in the house will know when there's something wrong,
You do not have to tell them.
He marched his men
That grim first day across the whole Union front   10
To strike a sleepy right wing with a sudden stone
And roll it up—it was his old trick of war
That Lee and he could play like finger and thumb!
It was the last time they played so.
When the blue-coated
Unprepared ranks of Howard[1] saw that storm, 15
Heralded by wild rabbits and frightened deer,
Burst on them yelling, out of the whispering woods,
They could not face it. Some men died where they stood,
The storm passed over the rest. It was Jackson's storm,
It was his old trick of war, for the last time played.   20
He must have known it. He loosed it and drove it on,
Hearing the long yell shake like an Indian cry
Through the dense black oaks, the clumps of second-growth pine,
And the red flags reel ahead through the underbrush.

---

[1]*Howard*, General O. O. Howard of the Union Army.

"Stonewall Jackson's Last Charge," from *John Brown's Body* in *Selected Works of Stephen Vincent Benét*, published by Rinehart & Co., Inc. Copyright, 1927, 1928 by Stephen Vincent Benét.

It was the hour he did not stop to taste,   25
Being himself. He saw it and found it good,
But night was falling, the Union center still held,
Another attack would end it. He pressed ahead
Through the dusk, pushing Little Sorrel, as if
the horse
Were iron, and he were iron, and all his men   30
Not men but iron, the stalks of an iron broom
Sweeping a dirt floor clean—and yet, as he rode,
A canny captain, planning a ruthless chess[2]
Skillfully as night fell. The night fell too soon.
It is hard to tell your friend from your enemy   35
In such a night. So he rode too far in advance
And, turning back toward his lines, unrecog-
nized,
Was fired upon in the night, in the stumbling
darkness,
By his own men. He had ridden such rides
before
Often enough and taken the chance of them,   40
But this chance was his bane.

            He lay on the bed
After the arm had been lopped from him, grim
and silent,
Refusing importunate Death with terrible eyes.
Death was a servant and Death was a sulky dog
And Death crouched down by the Lord in the
Lord's own time,   45
But he still had work to finish that Death would
spoil.
He would live in spite of that servant.

                     Now and then
He spoke, with the old curt justice that never
once
Denied himself or his foe or any other
The rigid due they deserved, as he saw that
due.   50
He spoke of himself and his storm. "A success-
ful movement.
I think the most successful I ever made."
—He had heard that long yell shake like an
Indian cry
Through the ragged woods and seen his flags
go ahead.
Later on, they brought him a stately letter from
Lee   55

[2]*planning a ruthless chess,* planning the movements of
army groups as chess players plan the movements of the
various pieces to win a game of chess.

That said in Lee's gracious way, "You have
only lost
Your left arm, I my right."

               The dour mouth opened.
"Better ten Jacksons should fall than one Lee,"
it said
And closed again, while the heart went on with
its task
Of beating off foolish, unnecessary Death.   60

The slow time wore. They had to tell him at last
That he must die. The doctors were brave
enough,
No doubt, but they looked awhile at the man on
the bed
And summoned his wife to do it. So she told
him.
He would not believe at first. Then he lay
awhile   65
Silent, while some slow, vast reversal of skies
Went on in the dying brain. At last he spoke.
"All right," he said.

             She opened the Bible and read.
It was Spring outside the window, the air was
warm,
The rough, plank house was full enough of the
Spring.   70
They had had a good life together, those two
middle-aged
Calm people, one reading aloud now, the other
silent.

They had passed hard schools. They were in
    love with each other
And had been for many years. Now that tale
    was told.
They had been poor and odd, found each other
    trusty,   75
Begotten children, prayed, disliked to be parted,
Had family jokes, known weather and other
    matters,
Planned for an age: they were famous now, he
    was dying.

The clock moved on, the delirium began.
The watchers listened, trying to catch the
    words;   80
Some awed, one broken-hearted, a few, no
    doubt,
Not glad to be there precisely, but in a way
Glad that, if it must happen, they could be
    there.
It is a human emotion.
                    The dying man
Went back at first to his battles, as soldiers
    do.   85
He was pushing a new advance
With the old impatience and skill, over tangled
    ground,
A cloudy drive that did not move as he willed
Though he had it clear in his mind. They were
    slow today.
"Tell A. P. Hill[3] to push them—push the at-
    tack—   90
Get up the guns!"
              The cloudy assault dispersed.
There was no more cannon. The ground was
    plain enough now.

He lay silent, seeing it so, while the watchers
    listened.
He had been dying once, but that was a dream.
The ground was plain enough now.   95
He roused himself and spoke in a different
    voice.
"Let us cross the river," he said, "and rest under
    the shade of the trees."

---

[3] *A. P. Hill*, a brilliant Confederate general whose division
formed part of Jackson's corps. Hill was severely wounded
at Chancellorsville.

452   STEPHEN VINCENT BENÉT

The Devil and Daniel Webster

IT'S A STORY they tell in the border country,
where Massachusetts joins Vermont and
New Hampshire.

Yes, Dan'l Webster's dead—or, at least, they
buried him. But every time there's a thunderstorm around Marshfield, they say you can hear
his rolling voice in the hollows of the sky. And
they say that if you go to his grave and speak
loud and clear, "Dan'l Webster—Dan'l Webster!" the ground'll begin to shiver and the trees
begin to shake. And after a while you'll hear a
deep voice saying, "Neighbor, how stands the
Union?" Then you better answer the Union
stands as she should, rock-bottomed and cop-
per-sheathed, one and indivisible, or he's liable
to rear right out of the ground. At least, that's
what I was told when I was a youngster.

You see, for a while, he was the biggest man
in the country. He never got to be President,
but he was the biggest man. There were thousands that trusted in him right next to God
Almighty, and they told stories about him that
were like the stories of patriarchs and such.
They said, when he stood up to speak, stars and
stripes came right out in the sky, and once he
spoke against a river and made it sink into the
ground. They said, when he walked the woods
with his fishing rod, Killall, the trout would
jump out of the streams right into his pockets,
for they knew it was no use putting up a fight
against him; and when he argued a case, he
could turn on the harps of the blessed and the
shaking of the earth underground. That was
the kind of man he was, and his big farm up at
Marshfield was suitable to him. The chickens
he raised were all white meat down through
the drumsticks, the cows were tended like children, and the big ram he called Goliath had
horns with a curl like a morning-glory vine and
could butt through an iron door. But Dan'l
wasn't one of your gentlemen farmers; he knew
all the ways of the land, and he'd be up by

"The Devil and Daniel Webster," from *Selected Works of
Stephen Vincent Benét,* published by Rinehart & Company,
Inc. Copyright, 1936, by Stephen Vincent Benét.

candlelight to see that the chores got done. A man with a mouth like a mastiff, a brow like a mountain and eyes like burning anthracite—that was Dan'l Webster in his prime. And the biggest case he argued never got written down in the books, for he argued it against the devil, nip and tuck and no holds barred. And this is the way I used to hear it told.

There was a man named Jabez Stone, lived at Cross Corners, New Hampshire. He wasn't a bad man to start with, but he was an unlucky man. If he planted corn, he got borers; if he planted potatoes, he got blight. He had good-enough land, but it didn't prosper him; he had a decent wife and children, but the more children he had, the less there was to feed them. If stones cropped up in his neighbor's field, boulders boiled up in his; if he had a horse with the spavins, he'd trade it for one with the staggers and give something extra. There's some folks bound to be like that, apparently. But one day Jabez Stone got sick of the whole business.

He'd been plowing that morning and he'd just broke the plowshare on a rock that he could have sworn hadn't been there yesterday. And, as he stood looking at the plowshare, the off horse[1] began to cough—that ropy[2] kind of cough that means sickness and horse doctors. There were two children down with measles, his wife was ailing, and he had a whitlow on his thumb. It was about the last straw for Jabez Stone. "I vow," he said, and he looked around him kind of desperate—"I vow it's enough to make a man want to sell his soul to the devil! And I would, too, for two cents!"

Then he felt a kind of queerness come over him at having said what he'd said; though, naturally, being a New Hampshireman, he wouldn't take it back. But, all the same, when it got to be evening and, as far as he could see, no notice had been taken, he felt relieved in his mind, for he was a religious man. But notice is always taken, sooner or later, just like the Good Book[3] says. And, sure enough, next day, about suppertime, a soft-spoken, dark-dressed stranger drove up in a handsome buggy and asked for Jabez Stone.

Well, Jabez told his family it was a lawyer, come to see him about a legacy. But he knew who it was. He didn't like the looks of the stranger, nor the way he smiled with his teeth. They were white teeth, and plentiful—some say they were filed to a point, but I wouldn't vouch for that. And he didn't like it when the dog took one look at the stranger and ran away howling, with his tail between his legs. But having passed his word, more or less, he stuck to it, and they went out behind the barn and made their bargain. Jabez Stone had to prick his finger to sign, and the stranger lent him a silver pin. The wound healed clean, but it left a little white scar.

After that, all of a sudden, things began to pick up and prosper for Jabez Stone. His cows got fat and his horses sleek, his crops were the envy of the neighborhood, and lightning might strike all over the valley, but it wouldn't strike his barn. Pretty soon, he was one of the prosperous people of the county; they asked him to stand for selectman,[4] and he stood for it; there began to be talk of running him for state senate. All in all, you might say the Stone family was as happy and contented as cats in a dairy. And so they were, except for Jabez Stone.

He'd been contented enough, the first few years. It's a great thing when bad luck turns; it drives most other things out of your head. True, every now and then, especially in rainy weather, the little white scar on his finger would give him a twinge. And once a year, punctual as clockwork, the stranger with the handsome buggy would come driving by. But the sixth year, the stranger lighted, and after that, his peace was over for Jabez Stone.

The stranger came up through the lower field, switching his boots with a cane—they were handsome black boots, but Jabez Stone never liked the look of them, particularly the toes. And, after he'd passed the time of day, he said, "Well, Mr. Stone, you're a hummer! It's a very pretty property you've got here, Mr. Stone."

---

[1] *off horse,* the horse on the right-hand side in a team.
[2] *ropy,* roupy, or hoarse.
[3] *the Good Book,* the Bible.

[4] *to stand for selectman,* to run for a position on the board of town officers.

"Well, some might favor it and others might not," said Jabez Stone, for he was a New Hampshireman.

"Oh, no need to decry your industry!" said the stranger, very easy, showing his teeth in a smile. "After all, we know what's been done, and it's been according to contract and specifications. So when—ahem—the mortgage falls due next year, you shouldn't have any regrets."

"Speaking of that mortgage, mister," said Jabez Stone, and he looked around for help to the earth and the sky, "I'm beginning to have one or two doubts about it."

"Doubts?" said the stranger, not quite so pleasantly.

"Why, yes," said Jabez Stone. "This being the U.S.A. and me always having been a religious man." He cleared his throat and got bolder. "Yes, sir," he said, "I'm beginning to have considerable doubts as to that mortgage holding in court."

"There's courts and courts," said the stranger, clicking his teeth. "Still, we might as well have a look at the original document." And he hauled out a big black pocketbook, full of papers. "Sherwin, Slater, Stevens, Stone," he muttered. "I, Jabez Stone, for a term of seven years—Oh, it's quite in order, I think."

But Jabez Stone wasn't listening, for he saw something else flutter out of the black pocketbook. It was something that looked like a moth, but it wasn't a moth. And as Jabez Stone stared at it, it seemed to speak to him in a small sort of piping voice, terrible small and thin, but terrible human. "Neighbor Stone!" it squeaked. "Neighbor Stone! Help me! For God's sake, help me!"

But before Jabez Stone could stir hand or foot, the stranger whipped out a big bandanna handkerchief, caught the creature in it, just like a butterfly, and started tying up the ends of the bandanna.

"Sorry for the interruption," he said. "As I was saying——"

But Jabez Stone was shaking all over like a scared horse.

"That's Miser Stevens' voice!" he said, in a croak. "And you've got him in your handkerchief!"

The stranger looked a little embarrassed.

"Yes, I really should have transferred him to the collecting box," he said with a simper, "but there were some rather unusual specimens there and I didn't want them crowded. Well, well, these little contretemps will occur."

"I don't know what you mean by contertan," said Jabez Stone, "but that was Miser Stevens' voice! And he ain't dead! You can't tell me he is! He was just as spry and mean as a woodchuck, Tuesday!"

" 'In the midst of life—' "[5] said the stranger, kind of pious. "Listen!" Then a bell began to toll in the valley and Jabez Stone listened, with the sweat running down his face. For he knew it was tolled for Miser Stevens and that he was dead.

"These long-standing accounts," said the stranger with a sigh; "one really hates to close them. But business is business."

He still had the bandanna in his hand, and Jabez Stone felt sick as he saw the cloth struggle and flutter.

"Are they all as small as that?" he asked hoarsely.

---

[5]"In the midst of life——," "In the midst of life we are in death," from "The Burial of the Dead," in *The Book of Common Prayer.*

"Small?" said the stranger. "Oh, I see what you mean. Why, they vary." He measured Jabez Stone with his eyes, and his teeth showed. "Don't worry, Mr. Stone," he said. "You'll go with a very good grade. I wouldn't trust you outside the collection box. Now, a man like Dan'l Webster, of course—well, we'd have to build a special box for him, and even at that, I imagine the wing spread would astonish you. But, in your case, as I was saying——"

"Put that handkerchief away!" said Jabez Stone, and he began to beg and pray. But the best he could get at the end was a three-years' extension, with conditions.

But till you make a bargain like that, you've got no idea of how fast four years can run. By the last months of those years, Jabez Stone's known all over the state and there's talk of running him for governor—and it's dust and ashes in his mouth. For every day, when he gets up, he thinks, "There's one more night gone," and every night when he lies down, he thinks of the black pocketbook and the soul of Miser Stevens, and it makes him sick at heart. Till, finally he can't bear it any longer, and, in the last days of the last year, he hitches up his horse and drives off to seek Dan'l Webster. For Dan'l was born in New Hampshire, only a few miles from Cross Corners, and it's well known that he has a particular soft spot for old neighbors.

It was early in the morning when he got to Marshfield, but Dan'l was up already, talking Latin to the farm hands and wrestling with the ram, Goliath, and trying out a new trotter and working up speeches to make against John C. Calhoun.[6] But when he heard a New Hampshireman had come to see him, he dropped everything else he was doing, for that was Dan'l's way. He gave Jabez Stone a breakfast that five men couldn't eat, went into the living history of every man and woman in Cross Corners, and finally asked him how he could serve him.

Jabez Stone allowed that it was a kind of mortgage case.

"Well, I haven't pleaded a mortgage case in a long time, and I don't generally plead now, except before the Supreme Court," said Dan'l, "but if I can, I'll help you."

"Then I've got hope for the first time in ten years," said Jabez Stone, and told him the details.

Dan'l walked up and down as he listened, his hands behind his back, now and then asking a question, now and then plunging his eyes at the floor, as if they'd bore through it like gimlets. When Jabez Stone had finished, Dan'l puffed out his cheeks and blew. Then he turned to Jabez Stone and a smile broke over his face like the sunrise over Monadnock.[7]

"You've certainly given yourself the devil's own row to hoe, Neighbor Stone," he said, "but I'll take your case."

"You'll take it?" said Jabez Stone, hardly daring to believe.

"Yes," said Dan'l Webster. "I've got about seventy-five other things to do and the Missouri Compromise[8] to straighten out, but I'll take your case. For if two New Hampshiremen aren't a match for the devil, we might as well give the country back to the Indians."

Then he shook Jabez Stone by the hand and said, "Did you come down here in a hurry?"

"Well, I admit I made time," said Jabez Stone.

"You'll go back faster," said Dan'l Webster, and he told 'em to hitch up Constitution and Constellation to the carriage. They were matched grays with one white forefoot, and they stepped like greased lightning.

Well, I won't describe how excited and pleased the whole Stone family was to have the great Dan'l Webster for a guest, when they finally got there. Jabez Stone had lost his hat on the way, blown off when they overtook a wind, but he didn't take much account of that.

---

[6]*John C. Calhoun,* a representative and later a senator from South Carolina; Webster's great antagonist.

[7]*Monadnock* (mə nad′nok), a mountain in southwestern New Hampshire.

[8]*Missouri Compromise,* an agreement in 1820 between proslavery and antislavery forces according to which Maine was admitted to the Union as a free state and Missouri as a slave state; the rest of the Louisiana Purchase north of 36° 30″ was to remain free.

But after supper he sent the family off to bed, for he had most particular business with Mr. Webster. Mrs. Stone wanted them to sit in the front parlor, but Dan'l Webster knew front parlors and said he preferred the kitchen. So it was there they sat, waiting for the stranger, with a jug on the table between them and a bright fire on the hearth—the stranger being scheduled to show up on the stroke of midnight, according to specifications.

Well, most men wouldn't have asked for better company than Dan'l Webster and a jug. But with every tick of the clock Jabez Stone got sadder and sadder. His eyes roved round, and though he sampled the jug you could see he couldn't taste it. Finally, on the stroke of 11:30 he reached over and grabbed Dan'l Webster by the arm.

"Mr. Webster, Mr. Webster!" he said, and his voice was shaking with fear and a desperate courage. "For God's sake, Mr. Webster, harness your horses and get away from this place while you can!"

"You've brought me a long way, neighbor, to tell me you don't like my company," said Dan'l Webster, quite peaceable, pulling at the jug.

"Miserable wretch that I am!" groaned Jabez Stone. "I've brought you a devilish way, and now I see my folly. Let him take me if he wills. I don't hanker after it, I must say, but I can stand it. But you're the Union's stay and New Hampshire's pride! He mustn't get you, Mr. Webster! He mustn't get you!"

Dan'l Webster looked at the distracted man, all gray and shaking in the firelight, and laid a hand on his shoulder.

"I'm obliged to you, Neighbor Stone," he said gently. "It's kindly thought of. But there's a jug on the table and a case in hand. And I never left a jug or a case half finished in my life."

And just at that moment there was a sharp rap on the door.

"Ah," said Dan'l Webster, very coolly, "I thought your clock was a trifle slow, Neighbor Stone." He stepped to the door and opened it. "Come in!" he said.

The stranger came in—very dark and tall he looked in the firelight. He was carrying a box under his arm—a black, japanned box with little air holes in the lid. At the sight of the box, Jabez Stone gave a low cry and shrank into a corner of the room.

"Mr. Webster, I presume," said the stranger, very polite, but with his eyes glowing like a fox's deep in the woods.

"Attorney of record for Jabez Stone," said Dan'l Webster, but his eyes were glowing too. "Might I ask your name?"

"I've gone by a good many," said the stranger carelessly. "Perhaps Scratch will do for the evening. I'm often called that in these regions."

Then he sat down at the table and poured himself a drink from the jug. The liquor was cold in the jug, but it came steaming into the glass.

"And now," said the stranger, smiling and showing his teeth, "I shall call upon you, as a law-abiding citizen, to assist me in taking possession of my property."

Well, with that the argument began—and it went hot and heavy. At first, Jabez Stone had a flicker of hope, but when he saw Dan'l Webster being forced back at point after point, he just scrunched in his corner, with his eyes on that japanned box. For there wasn't any doubt as to the deed or the signature—that was the worst of it. Dan'l Webster twisted and turned and thumped his fist on the table, but he couldn't get away from that. He offered to compromise the case; the stranger wouldn't hear of it. He pointed out the property had increased in value, and state senators ought to be worth more; the stranger stuck to the letter of the law. He was a great lawyer, Dan'l Webster, but we know who's the King of Lawyers,[9] as the Good Book tells us, and it seemed as if, for the first time, Dan'l Webster had met his match.

Finally, the stranger yawned a little. "Your spirited efforts on behalf of your client do you credit, Mr. Webster," he said, "but if you have no more arguments to adduce, I'm rather pressed for time——" and Jabez Stone shuddered.

_____
[9] *the King of Lawyers*, the devil.

Dan'l Webster's brow looked dark as a thundercloud.

"Pressed or not, you shall not have this man!" he thundered. "Mr. Stone is an American citizen, and no American citizen may be forced into the service of a foreign prince. We fought England for that in '12 and we'll fight all hell for it again!"

"Foreign?" said the stranger. "And who calls me a foreigner?"

"Well, I never yet heard of the dev—of your claiming American citizenship," said Dan'l Webster with surprise.

"And who with better right?" said the stranger, with one of his terrible smiles. "When the first wrong was done to the first Indian, I was there. When the first slaver put out for the Congo,[10] I stood on her deck. Am I not in your books and stories and beliefs, from the first settlements on? Am I not spoken of, still, in every church in New England? 'Tis true the North claims me for a Southerner and the South for a Northerner, but I am neither. I am merely an honest American like yourself—and of the best descent—for, to tell the truth, Mr. Webster, though I don't like to boast of it, my name is older in this country than yours."

"Aha!" said Dan'l Webster, with the veins standing out in his forehead, "then I stand on the Constitution! I demand a trial for my client!"

"The case is hardly one for an ordinary court," said the stranger, his eyes flickering. "And, indeed the lateness of the hour—"

"Let it be any court you choose, so it is an American judge and an American jury!" said Dan'l Webster in his pride. "Let it be the quick or the dead; I'll abide the issue!"[11]

"You have said it," said the stranger, and pointed his finger at the door. And with that, and all of a sudden, there was a rushing of wind outside and a noise of footsteps. They came, clear and distinct, through the night. And yet, they were not like the footsteps of living men.

"In God's name, who comes by so late?" cried Jabez Stone.

"The jury Mr. Webster demands," said the stranger, sipping at his boiling glass. "You must pardon the rough appearance of one or two; they will have come a long way."

And with that the fire burned blue and the door blew open and twelve men entered, one by one.

If Jabez Stone had been sick with terror before, he was blind with terror now. For there was Walter Butler, the Loyalist, who spread fire and horror through the Mohawk Valley[12] in the times of the Revolution; and there was Simon Girty, the renegade, who saw white men burned at the stake and whooped with the Indians to see them burn. His eyes were green, like a catamount's, and the stains on his hunting shirt did not come from the blood of the deer. King Philip[13] was there, wild and proud as he had been in life, with the great gash in his head that gave him his death wound, and cruel Governor Dale, who broke men on the wheel.[14] There was Morton of Merry Mount,[15] who so vexed the Plymouth Colony, with his flushed, loose, handsome face and his hate of the godly. There was Teach, the bloody pirate,[16] with his black beard curling on his breast. The Reverend John Smeet, with his strangler's hands and his Geneva gown,[17] walked as daintily as he had to the gallows. The red print of the rope was still around his neck, but he carried a perfumed handkerchief in one hand. One and all, they came into the room with the fires of hell still upon them, and the stranger named their names and their deeds as they came, till the tale of twelve was told. Yet the stranger had told the truth—they had all played a part in America.

---

[10]the Congo, a great river in central Africa flowing into the Atlantic Ocean.

[11]I'll abide the issue, I'll accept the verdict.

---

[12]the Mohawk Valley, a valley in New York State.

[13]King Philip, Indian chief of New England who led a war against the colonists from 1675 to 1676.

[14]Governor Dale, who broke men on the wheel. Thomas Dale, a governor of Virginia in the first years of the colony, was noted for his cruel laws and punishments. The wheel was a contrivance on which men were bound; their bones were broken by its action.

[15]Morton of Merry Mount, Thomas Morton, founder in 1625 of Merry Mount on the present site of Quincy, Massachusetts. His settlement was opposed by the Puritans because his settlers retained the customs of the Church of England and traded weapons with the Indians.

[16]Teach, the bloody pirate. Edward Teach, commonly called Blackbeard, operated along the coasts of Virginia and the Carolinas. He was notorious for his cruelty.

[17]Geneva gown, a minister's wide-sleeved black robe.

"Are you satisfied with the jury, Mr. Webster?" said the stranger mockingly, when they had taken their places.

The sweat stood upon Dan'l Webster's brow, but his voice was clear.

"Quite satisfied," he said. "Though I miss General Arnold[18] from the company."

"Benedict Arnold is engaged upon other business," said the stranger, with a glower. "Ah, you asked for a justice, I believe."

He pointed his finger once more, and a tall man, soberly clad in Puritan garb, with the burning gaze of the fanatic, stalked into the room and took his judge's place.

"Justice Hathorne[19] is a jurist of experience," said the stranger. "He presided at certain witch trials once held in Salem. There were others who repented of the business later, but not he."

"Repent of such notable wonders and undertakings?" said the stern old justice. "Nay, hang them—hang them all!" And he muttered to himself in a way that struck ice into the soul of Jabez Stone.

Then the trial began, and, as you might expect, it didn't look anyways good for the defense. And Jabez Stone didn't make much of a witness in his own behalf. He took one look at Simon Girty and screeched, and they had to put him back in his corner in a kind of swoon.

It didn't halt the trial, though; the trial went on, as trials do. Dan'l Webster had faced some hard juries and hanging judges in his time, but this was the hardest he'd ever faced, and he knew it. They sat there with a kind of glitter in their eyes, and the stranger's smooth voice went on and on. Every time he'd raise an objection, it'd be "Objection sustained," but whenever Dan'l objected, it'd be "Objection denied." Well, you couldn't expect fair play from a fellow like this Mr. Scratch.

It got to Dan'l in the end, and he began to heat, like iron in the forge. When he got up to speak he was going to flay that stranger with every trick known to the law, and the judge and jury too. He didn't care if it was contempt of court or what would happen to him for it. He didn't care any more what happened to Jabez Stone. He just got madder and madder, thinking of what he'd say. And yet, curiously enough, the more he thought about it, the less he was able to arrange his speech in his mind.

Till, finally, it was time for him to get up on his feet, and he did so, all ready to bust out with lightnings and denunciations. But before he started he looked over the judge and jury for a moment, such being his custom. And he noticed the glitter in their eyes was twice as strong as before, and they all leaned forward. Like hounds just before they get the fox, they looked, and the blue mist of evil in the room thickened as he watched them. Then he saw what he'd been about to do, and he wiped his forehead, as a man might who's just escaped falling into a pit in the dark.

For it was him they'd come for, not only Jabez Stone. He read it in the glitter of their eyes and in the way the stranger hid his mouth with one hand. And if he fought them with their own weapons, he'd fall into their power; he knew that, though he couldn't have told you how. It was his own anger and horror that burned in their eyes; and he'd have to wipe that out or the case was lost. He stood there for a moment, his black eyes burning like anthracite. And then he began to speak.

He started off in a low voice, though you could hear every word. They say he could call on the harps of the blessed when he chose. And this was just as simple and easy as a man could talk. But he didn't start out by condemning or reviling. He was talking about the things that make a country a country, and a man a man.

And he began with the simple things that everybody's known and felt—the freshness of a fine morning when you're young, and the taste of food when you're hungry, and the new day that's every day when you're a child. He took them up and he turned them in his hands. They were good things for any man. But without freedom, they sickened. And when he talked of those enslaved, and the sorrows of slavery, his voice got like a big bell. He talked of the early days of America and the men who had made those days. It wasn't a spread-eagle speech, but

---

[18]*General Arnold*, Benedict Arnold, an American general in the Revolutionary War, who turned traitor.

[19]*Justice Hathorne*, John Hathorne, an ancestor of the author Nathaniel Hawthorne.

he made you see it. He admitted all the wrong that had ever been done. But he showed how, out of the wrong and the right, the suffering and the starvations, something new had come. And everybody had played a part in it, even the traitors.

Then he turned to Jabez Stone and showed him as he was—an ordinary man who had had hard luck and wanted to change it. And, because he'd wanted to change it, now he was going to be punished for all eternity. And yet there was good in Jabez Stone, and he showed that good. He was hard and mean, in some ways, but he was a man. There was sadness in being a man, but it was a proud thing too. And he showed what the pride of it was till you couldn't help feeling it. Yes, even in hell, if a man was a man, you'd know it. And he wasn't pleading for any one person any more, though his voice rang like an organ. He was telling the story and the failures and the endless journey of mankind. They got tricked and trapped and bamboozled, but it was a great journey. And no demon that was ever foaled could know the inwardness of it —it took a man to do that.

The fire began to die on the hearth and the wind before morning to blow. The light was get-

ting gray in the room when Dan'l Webster finished. And his words came back at the end to New Hampshire ground, and the one spot of land that each man loves and clings to. He painted a picture of that, and to each one of that jury he spoke of things long forgotten. For his voice could search the heart, and that was his gift and his strength. And to one, his voice was like the forest and its secrecy, and to another like the sea and the storms of the sea; and one heard the cry of his lost nation in it, and another saw a little harmless scene he hadn't remembered for years. But each saw something. And when Dan'l Webster finished he didn't know whether or not he'd saved Jabez Stone. But he knew he'd done a miracle. For the glitter was gone from the eyes of judge and jury, and, for the moment, they were men again, and knew they were men.

"The defense rests," said Dan'l Webster, and stood there like a mountain. His ears were still ringing with his speech, and he didn't hear anything else till he heard Judge Hathorne say, "The jury will retire to consider its verdict."

Walter Butler rose in his place and his face had a dark, gay pride on it.

"The jury has considered its verdict," he said,

and looked the stranger full in the eye. "We find for the defendant, Jabez Stone."

With that the smile left the stranger's face, but Walter Butler did not flinch.

"Perhaps 'tis not strictly in accordance with the evidence," he said, "but even the damned may salute the eloquence of Mr. Webster."

With that, the long crow of a rooster split the gray morning sky, and judge and jury were gone from the room like a puff of smoke and as if they had never been there. The stranger turned to Dan'l Webster, smiling wryly.

"Major Butler was always a bold man," he said. "I had not thought him quite so bold. Nevertheless, my congratulations, as between two gentlemen."

"I'll have that paper first, if you please," said Dan'l Webster, and he took it and tore it into four pieces. It was queerly warm to the touch. "And now," he said, "I'll have you!" and his hand came down like a bear trap on the stranger's arm. For he knew that once you bested anybody like Mr. Scratch in fair fight, his power on you was gone. And he could see that Mr. Scratch knew it too.

The stranger twisted and wriggled, but he couldn't get out of that grip. "Come, come, Mr. Webster," he said, smiling palely. "This sort of thing is ridic—ouch!—is ridiculous. If you're worried about the costs of the case, naturally, I'd be glad to pay—"

"And so you shall!" said Dan'l Webster, shaking him till his teeth rattled. "For you'll sit right down at that table and draw up a document, promising never to bother Jabez Stone nor his heirs or assigns nor any other New Hampshire-man till doomsday! For any hades we want to raise in this state, we can raise ourselves, without assistance from strangers."

"Ouch!" said the stranger. "Ouch! Well, they never did run very big to the barrel, but—ouch!—I agree."

So he sat down and drew up the document. But Dan'l Webster kept his hand on his coat collar all the time.

"And now, may I go?" said the stranger, quite humble, when Dan'l'd seen the document was in proper and legal form.

"Go?" said Dan'l, giving him another shake. "I'm still trying to figure out what I'll do with you. For you've settled the costs of the case, but you haven't settled with me. I think I'll take you back to Marshfield," he said, kind of reflective. "I've got a ram there named Goliath that can butt through an iron door. I'd kind of like to turn you loose in his field and see what he'd do."

Well, with that the stranger began to beg and plead. And he begged and he pled so humble that finally Dan'l, who was naturally kind-hearted, agreed to let him go. The stranger seemed terrible grateful for that and said, just to show they were friends, he'd tell Dan'l's fortune before leaving. So Dan'l agreed to that, though he didn't take much stock in fortunetellers ordinarily. But naturally the stranger was a little different.

Well, he pried and he peered at the lines in Dan'l's hands. And he told him one thing and another that was quite remarkable. But they were all in the past.

"Yes, that's all true, and it happened," said Dan'l Webster. "But what's to come in the future?"

The stranger grinned, kind of happily, and shook his head.

"The future's not as you think it," he said. "It's dark. You have a great ambition, Mr. Webster."

"I have," said Dan'l firmly, for everybody knew he wanted to be President.

"It seems almost within your grasp," said the stranger, "but you will not attain it. Lesser men will be made President and you will be passed over."

"And, if I am, I'll still be Daniel Webster," said Dan'l. "Say on."

"You have two strong sons," said the stranger, shaking his head. "You look to found a line. But each will die in war and neither reach greatness."

"Live or die, they are still my sons," said Dan'l Webster. "Say on."

"You have made great speeches," said the stranger. "You will make more."

"Ah," said Dan'l Webster.

"But the last great speech you make will turn many of your own against you," said the stranger. "They will call you Ichabod[20]; they will call you by other names. Even in New England, some will say you have turned your coat[21] and sold your country, and their voices will be loud against you till you die."

"So it is an honest speech, it does not matter what men say," said Dan'l Webster. Then he looked at the stranger and their glances locked.

"One question," he said. "I have fought for the Union all my life. Will I see that fight won against those who would tear it apart?"

"Not while you live," said the stranger grimly, "but it will be won. And after you are dead, there are thousands who will fight for your cause, because of words that you spoke."

"Why, then, you long-barreled, slab-sided, lantern-jawed, fortune-telling note shaver!" said Dan'l Webster, with a great roar of laughter, "be off with you to your own place before I put my mark on you! For, by the thirteen original colonies, I'd go to the Pit itself to save the Union!"

And with that he drew back his foot for a kick that would have stunned a horse. It was only the tip of his shoe that caught the stranger, but he went flying out of the door with his collecting box under his arm.

"And now," said Dan'l Webster, seeing Jabez Stone beginning to rouse from his swoon, "let's see what's left in the jug, for it's dry work talking all night. I hope there's pie for breakfast, Neighbor Stone."

---

[20]*Ichabod*, a Hebrew word meaning "inglorious." John Greenleaf Whittier wrote a poem about Webster by this title to express the disappointment of the antislavery forces when Webster supported the Compromise of 1850.

[21]*have turned your coat*, have become a traitor.

But they say that whenever the devil comes near Marshfield, even now, he gives it a wide berth. And he hasn't been seen in the state of New Hampshire from that day to this. I'm not talking about Massachusetts or Vermont.

CONCERNING STEPHEN VINCENT BENÉT

1. What were some of the reasons that caused people to turn to studying and reading American history after World War I? How did this interest in history affect Benét's career?

2. Why was *John Brown's Body* a popular success? How did this influence Benét's subsequent writing?

CONCERNING BENÉT'S HISTORICAL
WRITINGS

"Stonewall Jackson's Last Charge"

1. What is Stonewall Jackson's situation as the selection opens? What device does the poet use to explain how this situation has come about? At what point does the action again move forward?

2. What idea of Jackson's character and personality do you gain from this selection? Read aloud the lines that you think show his dominant traits most clearly. Give your reasons for believing this is, or is not, a sympathetic portrait.

3. What did General Lee mean by writing to Jackson, "You have only lost your left arm, I my right"? How does the material about Jackson contained in the selection help you understand why Lee would feel this way? Can you cite any evidence from history to prove that Lee's idea was true?

4. Critics have said that Benét used some of the techniques of the modern novel in writing *John Brown's Body*. What evidence of this can you find in this selection?

"The Devil and Daniel Webster"

1. In what way does the first paragraph of the selection hint that what follows is probably a tall tale? How do the next two paragraphs develop this idea?

2. What were the terms of Jabez' contract with the devil? Why did he turn to Daniel Webster for help?

3. Outline the arguments that Lawyer Webster used in his attempt to persuade the devil that Jabez should be freed from the agreement. On what grounds did Webster demand a trial by jury?

4. What did the members of the jury and the judge all have in common? Into what fatal trap did Daniel Webster almost fall as he began to argue his case? On what line of argument did he finally win it?

5. In the history books Daniel Webster is recorded as a lawyer of great eloquence and a man who fought throughout his life to save the Union. Show how Benét works both these elements of Webster's career into this story.

6. In speaking of Benét's legends the biographical sketch says (page 450): "These tales were inventive to the point of being fantastic, but they were told in the language of common speech and they were constantly flavored with salty humor." Illustrate each of these points by citing examples from "The Devil and Daniel Webster."

7. Compare this selection with "The Devil and Tom Walker" (pages 344-351). What similarities in plot do you find? In what respects does one portrayal of the devil differ from the other? What differences in character do you find between Tom Walker and Jabez Stone? What characteristics of folklore are common to both stories? Which story do you like better, and why?

Know your words

When you read that Daniel Webster's ram was called Goliath, you probably inferred that he was named after the Biblical giant whom David killed with a pebble from his slingshot. You probably also decided that, like the first Goliath, this Goliath was large, fierce, and immensely strong.

Over the centuries the name *Goliath* has come to be used as a synonym for "giant." Other much-used proper names have also taken on a more general, often figurative, meaning. Look up the italicized words in the sentences below in an unabridged dictionary. Determine both the original meaning of the word and its meaning in the particular sentence. Then on a sheet of paper rewrite each sentence in such a way as to make its meaning clear without using the italicized word. Below each sentence briefly give the original meaning of the italicized word.

1. Mathematics has always been my *Waterloo*.
2. All compromise had failed and the nation waited *Armageddon*.
3. Looking back from maturity he saw his childhood as a remote *Arcadian* time.
4. The *Lilliputian* in blue jeans advanced slowly, gravely, and fearfully toward me.
5. All through high school she had been the class *Cinderella*.
6. I object to inviting that *Jonah* to our party.
7. Although he was a *Methuselah* according to the calendar, he was young in interest and enthusiasm.

➷ III REALIST

Benét's first book, *Five Men and Pompey*, published the year he entered Yale, was made up of dramatic sketches in poetic form. The sketches quite possibly were influenced by the young man's reading of Robert Browning, a nineteenth-century English poet who had written fine examples of the dramatic monologue—a poem in which an individual shows his true character by what he says. Like Browning, young Benét obviously was interested in understanding what "made people tick" and in showing their motives, both good and vicious, in his poems. This remained a lifelong interest.

Such curiosity about the causes for human actions is not, of course, peculiar to any period. Always the great writers have had such curiosity and have been skilled in showing character and the actions springing from character. But in Benét's day, the relating of men's deeds to men's natures took a particular form that was rather new. Like a few writers of the nineteenth century, a large majority of the great modern authors took pride in showing life, so they said, "realistically." On many occasions, Benét, like these others, was a "realist," a writer of realism.

What was meant by realism? You may remember that "Four Generations," by Ruth Suckow (pages 112-119), was described as a realistic short story because it pictured ordinary men and women caught in the disappointments usual in most lives. If you look further into the meaning of the term, you will find that writers and critics over the years have used the word *realism* in many senses—so many in fact that no one definition can be given of which all would approve. Yet, running through much of the talk about realism, you will find the following ideas:

1. Realism, instead of picturing life in far-off times and distant places, tends to show the life of the author's own day. For instance, in his novel *Main Street* (1920) Sinclair Lewis mirrored life in a Midwestern town during the very years in which the book was written. Quite possibly the great eagerness of moderns to cope with problems of life about them was responsible for such concentration upon present-day life.

2. Realism, instead of picturing characters as being better and more self-sufficing than they are in life, tries to show human beings with frailties and handicaps such as they have in the actual world. Thus Theodore Dreiser's *An American Tragedy* (1925) showed a weak youth driven to a tragic death by his inheritance and his upbringing. Quite possibly the emphasis in men's thinking upon heredity and environment as shapers of character led to this similar emphasis in fiction.

3. Realism, instead of showing men's thoughts and feelings in the old-fashioned way, often bases its depictions upon the new findings of the psychologists. Characters in stories and novels, in other words, are frequently shown suffering from phobias, complexes, peculiar quirks which Freud and other students of the human mind had discussed. Sherwood Anderson's collection of realistic short stories, *Winesburg, Ohio* (1919), was one of many books in which a large share of the men and women had psychopathic tendencies.

Benét, as a student and as a wide reader, enjoyed books about American life as it was being lived in his own day. Furthermore, as a commercial writer, he must have noted the liking of the public for books using realistic methods. For these reasons, among others, he often employed the methods of the realists in his poems and stories. As early as 1917, a lifelike poem, "Portrait of a Boy," told of a child's psychological reactions to a whipping. Reviewing Benét's poetry collection, *Young Adventure* (1918), critic Babette Deutsch spoke of the psychological insight of one poem and "the shocking realism" of another. Benét's novel, *The Beginning of Wisdom* (1921), in addition to portraying "flaming youth," traced the development of a sensitive boy whose life was shaped by the forces in the America of his day. Critic Henry Seidel Canby noted that *John Brown's Body* "owes much to the wave of realism in our literature," and cited as proof the use of many unheroic characters and the psychological detail.

In his short stories, as in his novels and poems, Benét often wrote about his own times, his own country; he showed the effects of time and place upon his characters; and he often probed for psychological motives. "The Story About the Anteater" (1928) dealt with the psychological adjustments of a modern married couple; "Too Early Spring" (1933) with the problems of present-day adolescence; "Everybody Was Very Nice" (1936) with some of the psychological reasons for widespread divorce in the present century. These are typical of Benét's realistic short stories—as is the story (published in 1942) which follows.

Famous

I T ISN'T that we aren't proud of him—anybody would be proud of their father's being Jordan Blake. Why, everybody at school knows the songs from *Random Rose* and *Hey Diddle Diddle,*[1] and the rest of them. And, whenever he has a new show, they talk about Victor Herbert[2] and Gilbert and Sullivan[3] and all the boys. And I've been offered as much as twenty dollars for the photograph of Carolina Clay with "To Jerry Blake, whose father wrote 'Random Rose,' from Carolina." But, naturally, when you're famous, it keeps you pretty busy being famous. It isn't like having the ordinary sort of father, if you know what I mean.

Not that I've got any complaints. I liked school and I liked camp. And if I wanted anything, all I had to do was write to Miss Hacker[4] and there'd be a check and a note. He'd always sign the note himself and sometimes he'd stick in a couple of the funny little drawings he makes on telephone pads. The fellows thought those were keen. And some awfully soupy fathers come up to visit the school.

I would like to have had him come up when I graduated. But it would have made an awful mess. Because I'd written most of the Sixth Form[5] show—words and music—and that was one thing Father was serious about. He'd leave you alone about most things, but he'd never even let me take piano. He said one song writer in the family was enough. And he said it with that cold little smile he uses on managers, sometimes. So I had to pick it up by myself—and get Nub Parsons to put his name on the show. But

even so, if Father had ever heard that score, he'd have recognized it. I'd swiped a couple of things from him, you see—little things of his that never quite jelled. Of course I couldn't develop them the way he would have—but they sounded fairly keen in the show. Anyway, he'd have spotted them, in a minute.

So I got Miss Hacker on the wire, and told her I knew he'd be awfully busy and not to bother. And a couple of days later, I got a funny little drawing from him showing me graduating with a sort of halo, and him looking at me from New York with a spyglass. So I knew it was all right, and it took a weight off my mind. Though, when the other fathers showed up, on Visitors' Day, I felt a little different. I guess you're bound to feel that way.

And now I was home, with school done and college ahead, and that was a funny feeling. Though things were always a little funny, that first day home. My school always seemed to get out ahead of Bibs' school; so she wouldn't be there, and it would be just the two of us. And each time, on the train, I'd think that things were going to be different this time. I don't mean anything sappy. And it's bound to be different, with a famous person. But I'd visited the Parsons' a lot—and Nub and his father got along pretty well. What I mean is, they could talk about things, in spite of Mr. Parsons being a Republican and a deacon, whereas Nub is going to write a big, vital book called *Proletarians, Unite!* as soon as he's through Harvard and has the real beans on the situation. He wanted to put a song about Proletarians Unite in the show, but I told him they were hard words to set.

But Father—well, he isn't exactly Mr. Parsons' type. You'd pick him out of any bunch of people, in the first place—and he'd be standing a little away from the rest of them, looking dark and keen and a little like a black-and-white sword. He isn't handsome, exactly, because you've seen the caricatures—but he looks as young as he does in the caricatures. I've seen him after he's been up all night at a rehearsal, and his tie was still tied in the neat, slim knot and there wasn't a speck of cigarette ash on his

---

[1] *"Random Rose"* and *"Hey Diddle Diddle."* These are the names of imaginary musical comedies by Jordan Blake, the father of the narrator, Jerry Blake.

[2] *Victor Herbert,* an American composer of operettas notable for their tuneful, catchy songs.

[3] *Gilbert and Sullivan,* Sir William Gilbert and Sir Arthur Sullivan, English collaborators on comic operas. Gilbert wrote the words and Sullivan composed the music.

[4] *Miss Hacker,* Jordan Blake's secretary.

[5] *Sixth Form.* Jerry attended a private school whose students were divided according to the English system into forms. The sixth form was the most advanced class and corresponded to the senior class in high school.

clothes. He gives you a very cool impression, and yet people like him a lot. Even managers like Jakie Rosebaum like him—and if you put Jakie in a tank with an alligator, you couldn't tell which eyes were which. In fact, all the people in the theater like him—though some of them say he's snooty, which nobody can help, and they wouldn't say it to me.

But I think he was different, before Mother died. Bibs can hardly remember that time, but I can. I guess Mother was the only person he ever loved, and children aren't the same thing, though he's pretty fond of Bibs. But he used to play with us a lot then and the house felt different. Mother was a swell person. They ran away when he was in Harvard and trouped in vaudeville for three years. It made a big scandal at the time—both their families came from Boston and were quite Back Bay.[6] Then Father wrote *Hey Diddle Diddle*—and they produced it right after the Armistice when he was still in France—and that made him Jordan Blake, and the families came around. So we've met our uncles and cousins socially, and most of them are pretty stuffy, if you ask us. Which is one thing Father isn't, even when he's being sarcastic.

But, to get back to coming home—he'd be waiting when the train pulled in, a little away from the crowd. And we'd shake hands and he'd say, "Hello, Jerry—how's the infant phenomenon?" and I'd say, "Fine." And then, of course, in the car, he'd ask questions and I'd try to tell him about things at school. But it's odd how little you can tell. It's awfully important at the time, but when you come to talk about it, it boils down to Bill Latimer being a good egg and the Latin master a slave-driver and the scores of games and things. I always thought it would last longer but it never did.

And all the time I'd be crazy to talk to him about people like Carolina and Noel Porter and the new show of his and the old ones. But he'd only talk about those when he forgot. I guess he felt we were too young, but we'd have understood. It used to get Bibs awfully mad when she

was younger and got sent to bed earlier, knowing people like Carolina and Noel were downstairs while she was having milk toast with the governess. I was luckier that way, because sometimes when he was sketching a song, he'd forget to send me out of the room. And I picked up quite a lot. But he always remembered, finally—and then, generally, I'd be sent to my cousins the week before camp.

But this summer, I was sure things were going to be different. I knew Jakie wanted him to do a show for that big barn of a 63rd Street Theater in the fall—and it would be the top, just to hear about that. I even had some ideas for a theater as big as that.

But when I got off the train, the old spell fell over me, as the books say, and pretty soon I found I was telling Father about Nub Parsons being a good egg and the science master being a twirp and the scores of the games. And finally, when Father said he'd taken a house at Blue Point for the summer, it was just like a blow with a dull instrument, it didn't hurt as much as it stunned.

"Well?" said Father, when he'd finished telling me. "Anything wrong? You don't seem to greet the idea with cheers, Jerry."

"Oh yes, I do," I said, prevaricating politely. Because Blue Point is all right, in its way, but it's where Uncle Lambert goes with his family. And not even the presence of the Parsons' could make up for Uncle Lambert—especially as Nub would be away, investigating the proletariat in a coal mine, which is what he was doing.

Then I thought a minute. "Will Bibs be there?" I said. "Or is she going to camp again?"

He looked at me a little queerly. "No, Bibs will not be going to camp," he said. "After all, she's fourteen. I'd like to see something of her."

"Well, that's an idea," I said. I didn't mean to be fresh or reproachful or anything—I thought we were just talking.

"As you so aptly remark," he said, with his cool little smile, "it might be an idea. In fact, we might be a reunited family for the summer. Learn to know each others' hearts and chat around the fireside. What would you say to that, Jerry?"

---

[6] *Back Bay*, aristocratic. Back Bay is a fashionable Boston residential section on the south bank of the Charles River.

Well, I could tell from the way he was trying to laugh it off that the very idea was an awful chore for him.

"Okey-doke," I said, because I was rattled, looking at him, and that's another expression he hates.

"How often have I told you, Jerry?" he said, and then he stopped. "Sorry," he said, quite nicely, "I forgot you were grown-up." He pulled on his cigarette and started to say something, but I was thinking.

"Look here," I said. "How are you going to work at Blue Point? The sea-damp's awfully bad for pianos. Or so they tell me."

The little frown came back on his forehead.

"I may not be working," he said. "I may take a vacation."

"But the *Times* said," I said, "that you were doing a show for Caro—for Miss Clay in the fall, with Jakie—and another one for——" I'd forgotten I wasn't supposed to know about his plans.

"Don't believe all you see in the papers, Jerry," he said quietly. "If I do do Carolina's show—and, by the way, I wouldn't call her Carolina, you're still a little young for that—I suppose I could commute from New York."

"Why, yes, you could do that," I said, and he said, "Why yes, I could. It might be better all around," in that queer way. "Jerry!" he said. And then he said, "Oh, well, what about those entrance exams, next fall? Do you need any tutoring? The system's changed since my time——"

So I told him, and it took quite a while and couldn't have been very interesting. At least, it wasn't for me—I wanted to ask him if he'd seen Jimmy Manistee, the new comedian, and what he thought of him. But it got us along to bedtime.

But when Bibs came home the next day and I broke the news to her, she said, "How perfectly foul! I was going to be a group-leader at camp, this summer. And now I'll have to tag around Blue Point with that slat-eyed Cousin Lucy of ours for company—and she's a human meat ball if I ever saw one."

"Is that the English they teach you at Miss Foster's?" I said.

"Oh, don't talk like Father," she said. "If

we've got to, we've got to. But I bet somebody eats snakes before the summer's over."

And I could not but feel that her prognostications were likely to be justified. It was all right the first week, while we were still getting settled. But after that, the grimness set in.

He didn't even bring down our regular servants or Miss Hacker. He got a special bunch straight from Boston that were about as cozy as iced codfish. We joined the Blue Point Club, which is highly select and quite as much fun any day as a first-class mortician's, and we swam at the right hours and played golf at the right hours and took the sand out of our toes at the right hours, the way you always do in a place like that. I didn't particularly mind—I'd been places like that before—and now and then, I'd sneak some fishing with Mr. Parsons. And Bibs, who's a devil, spent most of her time trying to break down our Cousin Lucy's morale, in a quiet way. But the whole thing simply seemed like an awful waste. And when I heard Father talking to Uncle Lambert about the gold standard and agreeing with every word he said, I knew something was terribly wrong. Uncle Lambert looks like a walrus and he thinks that civilization fell when women got the vote. I got up nerve enough to ask Father if nothing could be done about him, and he just remarked coldly that Uncle Lambert had put us up for the Club.[7]

And yet, I knew that he wasn't enjoying it. I was next to him once, when we entered the Blue Point Club at the proper bathing hour, and I heard him mutter, "Oh, God! Oh, Montreal!"

And once, when I was going out fishing with Mr. Parsons, I looked back, and he was standing on the porch with the funniest look on his face. Naturally, Bibs and I pretended we were having a good time, but it was hard work. There wasn't any life in the house, somehow, with Miss Hacker away and long-distance never ringing and Father never coming out of the study in his black-and-silver dressing gown and telling us, quietly but snootily, to go and drown ourselves in bathtubs if we had to but keep out of

_____
[7] *put us up for the Club.* As a member of the Blue Point Club, Uncle Lambert had the privilege of recommending the admission of others.

his way for the next eight hours because he was working on a song. Nowadays, he hardly touched the piano at all.

"In fact, if this is life with the famous," remarked Bibs, one day, when we were on the float alone, "give me old Camp Owatchee any time. At least there, you knew you could live through it because you always had. I'm writing a novel called *Rumble Seat Romance* and reading the snappy parts out loud to Cousin Lucy, in deadly secrecy. They make her say, 'Oh, Bibs!' But even that doesn't help much. Do you know that Father told me not to roll my stockings, this morning?"

"That's nothing," I said. "He asked me not to smoke in front of Aunt Susan. Said she didn't approve of the deadly weed for the young."

"As a glittering and sophisticated parent, Father is a flop," said Bibs. "Before, I thought we were going to have a nice time knowing him. Now, every time he looks at me, I wonder if he's going to send me to a nunnery. I don't think he approves of his daughter Barbara. Or maybe it's both of us. Though Uncle Lambert said you were a fine, clean, manly boy the other day. Jerry—ouch, leggo of my arm, you fool! And, if Uncle Lambert thinks that—all right, go ahead and drown!"

By that time we were both in the water and after we scrapped, we felt better. Only then we went back to the house and it was grim. Bibs went to bed early, as usual—I suspected her of writing *Rumble Seat Romance* when she was supposed to be asleep—and Father and I sat up. But you couldn't have called it conversation— we'd both start to talk at once and then we'd both say "Sorry" and then we'd neither of us say anything. Till, finally, I said I was going to the movies. They only change the bill twice a week at Blue Point and I'd already seen it. But anything was better than just sitting here, making him uncomfortable because I was around.

And driving over there, I thought of the times I'd brought people like Nub Parsons back to the apartment and how, maybe, they'd hardly see Father most of the time, but when they did see him, they'd be pretty impressed. Because they knew he was famous and yet he never treated them like kids and sometimes, if he wasn't busy, he'd do songs. And people like Carolina and Bill Fields[8] and George Kaufman[9] would be coming in and out. And the fellows used to kind of envy me and ask Father to come up to school.

And now, I just didn't get what he was about. Or why we were at Blue Point or anything. I didn't know if we were there because he wanted to build up some social stuff for Bibs—or because it was what he really wanted, instead of being friends with us—or what. And each time we sat down to talk, we got politer and farther apart. It had me jumping. And I couldn't help feeling that, whatever it was, was my fault.

Then, across the aisle, in the movie theater, I heard two old rock-ribbed dowagers talking. And one of them was saying, "Well, I did think the Jordan Blakes would bring something a little new to Blue Point. And the children are passable enough. But the man seems just as stodgy as his brother."

The second dowager made a reproving noise with her tongue, and the first one went on.

"Oh, don't click at me, Harriet!" she said.

---

[8]*Bill Fields,* W. C. Fields, famous comedian of stage, motion pictures, and radio.
[9]*George Kaufman,* a writer and director of plays and musical comedies.

"I've known Lambert Blake since he wore short coats and he's always been as dull as ditchwater. But I went to *Random Rose* four times—yes, Harriet, I did!—and I always wanted to ask the man who wrote it where he got the idea for that screamingly funny scene in the perambulator. But when I did, the other night, at the Hayes', he just muttered and looked shy. I hoped at least he'd have some of his interesting friends down—I'm dying to see Carolina Clay. But I suppose he thinks they're too good to waste on Blue Point."

"Oh no, it isn't that," said her companion, quickly. "Don't you know why he's here? He's trying to get over the drug habit—that's why he's so nervous and shy. I got it all from Maisie—and that's why he never touches the piano—it brings the craving on. That nice boy of his is dreadfully worried about it, everybody says——"

"Oh, is that it?" said the other old sea horse. "Tsh, tsh! Well, that explains the other night. I knew it must be something that——"

Then their voices dropped and I didn't hear any more. But I knew I had to do something. For it was all too plain. If people like that could notice that the Blake family wasn't itself, affairs were serious. And, somehow or other, I must be the false card in the deck.

It must be me, for there wasn't anything else to explain it—Bibs was too young. This was the first summer he hadn't done a lick of work—and it was the first summer I'd been home. So obviously, I hadn't turned out the way he expected or wanted—and it was getting him down. I even remembered a line I'd seen in one of the gossip columns, "Whispers say that the new Jordan Blake show is off for the fall, Jick Blake's having family trouble or something."

Well, it's pretty serious when you have to think a thing through like that. But I'm modern. I know there's no reason you should like anybody, just because he's your son. They prove that in books, these days. And if you're famous, why, naturally, grown-up children tie you down and get in your way. I didn't feel bitter about it—I tried not to. It was probably something pretty psychological that Father couldn't help. With one of those Greek names, maybe. But it all boiled down to the fact that things had been

all right for him when I was at school—and now they weren't all right. So what was I going to do?

Of course it would have been pleasant if we'd gotten along and could talk like Nub and Mr. Parsons. Because Bibs, after all, is a girl and you can't talk the same way to a girl. But Father was a famous person—and he'd supported me pretty darn well for seventeen years. St. Henry's isn't a cheap school. And all I was doing now was to get on his nerves so he couldn't work and make people think he was a dope fiend. I hadn't meant to do it, but it made me a good deal of a heel. Well, nobody likes to have a heel for a son.

It shook me up pretty badly—for you don't like to think of yourself as a heel, even when you have to. And I don't remember much of the road, coming back. But, when I drove up to the house, I noticed the piano was going—and a nice, tricky melody, too, a Jick Blake melody. But it stopped as soon as my headlights hit the window. And that made me surer than ever. He didn't even want to play when I was around.

I didn't sleep so well that night—I was too busy thinking whether I ought to pull out and join Nub in his coal mine or whether it wouldn't be better, on the whole, if I just made for the South Seas. You get crazy ideas sometimes. But we simply couldn't go on the way we were going. And the move was up to me. I had to get out somehow and I didn't quite know how. He'd be all right alone with Bibs—after all, she looked like Mother. Or maybe I wasn't even their son —maybe they'd adopted me and never told me and now he was scared to, because I hadn't turned out well. But if they had, I wished that he would tell me. It would be some sort of relief.

And then, darn it, when I did get to sleep, I overslept and came down to find that Father had been called to New York.

Well, in one way, of course that made things easier, because I could just hike out and leave a note on the telephone desk, the way they do in the movies, if I had to. But I didn't like to leave Bibs alone in the house with those frozen-faced servants. And yet I didn't want to hash the whole thing over with her—it felt too sore. She didn't think I was a heel, but probably she was wrong. And I was stewing the whole thing over in my mind—and jittering—when the telephone rang after lunch. And it was Carolina Clay, of all people.

"Oh, hello, Carolina—Dad's in New York," I said. I guess my voice sounded stiff.

"Are you telling me?" she said. "I've just seen your respectable father and he's breaking Jakie Rosebaum's heart because he hasn't got a score in his left-hand pocket. But I've invited myself down to your house for the weekend—so just run up the flag and be ready to pass me through Customs. I understand you need a certified blue-blood test to get into Blue Point."

"But, Carolina!" I said. "But Dad—is he coming down with you? But—"

She laughed her wonderful laugh over the phone.

"He thinks he's bringing me down tomorrow," she said, "but he's not. I'm starting now, with Mother. We're just in from the Coast and we're covered with dust and yes-men and I'm aching for fresh air. I'm bringing the monkey, by the way. Get some anchovies for him, will you, darling? He loves anchovies—the sinister little thing."

"But Caro—" I said, and she just said, "Kisses, darling," and rang off. And I went and held my head in my hands. Because it would be swell, of course, to see Carolina again, and she was more fun than anybody. But I didn't much want to see anybody. And what she'd do to Blue Point I couldn't think. And Father would hold me responsible, if she did. I thought of giving it all up and leaving for the South Seas right away. But that would have been cowardly.

She had the monkey on her shoulder when she got out of the car. And about 400-gauge stockings. And nineteen bags. And the kind of dress you don't see on anybody else. And she's older than Father and she can be as young as Bibs. And the servants nearly fell dead. And within five minutes we were all of us talking at the tops of our voices—Bibs and me and Carolina and her mother—and it seemed like old times.

Then we went for a swim at the Club and Uncle Lambert was there. And Carolina had her arm in mine when I introduced him to her

and I could see in one brief glance that my reputation was gone, and probably Father's too. And I didn't care—I felt swell. Because it was like old times. I even forgot about Father and what I meant to do. When she's gay, she can make you forget anything except being gay.

And then we were back at the house and her mother was upstairs showing Bibs six new ways to do her hair—her mother's a grand old sport and Bibs always has been crazy about her—and Carolina was asking me what I'd been doing. She knew about my writing songs—she always had. And I felt so good that I started playing some of the numbers from *Sixth Form Follies* and she picked up the hot number and started to go to town with it and it really sounded keen —as keen as I'd hoped it would.

"Gee, that's grand, Carolina!" I said. "I mean the way you sing it."

"I'd be a fool if I couldn't sing it," she said. "It's a real blues. Has Jicky heard it? He ought to."

"Oh, gee, Carolina!" I said, and before I knew what I was doing, I was crying on her shoulder. I hadn't cried since I was eight and I felt terribly ashamed.

She didn't try to be motherly or anything like that. She just said, "That's okay, sport," and let me use her handkerchief. And then we talked. We talked a lot. I suppose she meant her mother to keep Bibs upstairs. She may have. But I don't care. She's a pretty wise woman. If I'd talked like that to anybody else, I'd have felt like crawling into a hole in the ground.

About in the middle she said, "I always told Jicky he was a raging idiot, but the man wouldn't listen to reason." And then we talked some more. And when we'd finished, she said, "Blue Point is right. Nobody could have named it more fitly. Now do you know what we're going to do?"

"No, Carolina," I said.

"I am going to have a highball," she said. "I need it. And you are going to sleep for half an hour on that couch. Now don't argue with Carolina."

Well, I wouldn't have believed it, but as soon as I lay down, I was off, and I slept for an hour. When I woke, it was time to dress for dinner and I felt a lot better. I suppose it does happen to you, that way, when you're tired.

Then we all went to the Waldens' party—Mrs. Walden was the old sea horse I'd heard talking in the movies, and her Saturday night suppers for young and old are one of the more gruesome features of Blue Point. I won't describe what Carolina did to that. She didn't have to do anything, really—she was just Carolina Clay. She wasn't a bit vo-do-de-do—she can do that too, when she wants, but she didn't want. She was sweet and she wore a little cotton dress, with her hair done straight at the sides. But before she'd been there ten minutes, Uncle Lambert was telling her the story of his life, and male and female alike were fighting to bring her lobster salad.

I don't know how she got the whole party maneuvered over to our house, when they asked her to sing. It was just one of the things she does. She started off with some old things, "Roses of Picardy" and "Poor Butterfly" and even "Swing Low, Sweet Chariot" for the old folks. Then she went into *Random Rose*—I was playing her accompaniments, of course. And just as she was in the middle of "Love's a Dangerous Thing," I looked up and saw Father in the doorway.

His face was whiter than I'd ever seen it and his eyes were frowning and he looked like a black-and-silver sword. But I wasn't afraid of him a bit—I wasn't afraid of him. I went on with the accompaniment and even put in a couple of tricks with my left hand.

She didn't give him time to protest—she didn't give him time to do anything. As soon as she'd finished the song, she said, "And now, nice people, we're lucky. Because there's one song in *Random Rose* that needs a man's voice—'Silver Stars.' And we've got the composer himself to play it for us. All right, Jordan Blake."

Well, nobody could have helped himself when she spoke in that voice. Or almost nobody. But Father wasn't looking at her, queerly enough. He was looking at me—I'd swung round on my stool. And there was something funny in his face. It wasn't as if he were angry, even. It was almost as if he were frightened.

"Come on, Dad—please!" I said, and, for some reason, they all laughed and started to

clap. I saw Father stiffen a little at the laughter. And then he walked over to the piano, like a man in a dream, and sat down.

He went through the first verse and chorus. It's an old song, as songs go, but they still make records of it. And, on the second verse, I felt Carolina poke me, and I joined in. My voice isn't anything much but I know that song.

He looked up at me while they were clapping.

"You didn't look at the music," he said.

"I don't have to," I said. "Not with your songs."

And then they were clapping and clapping and, all of a sudden, his fingers were easy on the keys. We did "Nice Pair of Eyes" and "Roaming the World" and Carolina did "My House in Yonkers" and all three of us did the trio from *Harum-Scarum*. Then Carolina made me do "Sixth Form Blues." I felt scared, doing it, but they seemed to like it all right. I looked at Father, in the middle. He didn't say anything, but his left hand was picking out the tune.

We could have kept them there all night if we'd wanted. But Carolina knows how to break up a party, too. They didn't know they were being broken up—they thought it was their own idea. And when the last of them were gone, Carolina turned to Father.

"You'll excuse me for borrowing your house, Jick," she said. "And Jerry and Bibs. But, at any rate, we showed Blue Point a real Bohemian revel."[10] She glanced around at the room and the empty glasses. "And on nothing stronger than ginger ale and chicken sandwiches. It's a miracle."

"Blue Point flows with ginger ale," said Father. "It's about the only thing it does flow with. But I don't understand about the sandwiches. I didn't think it could be done."

"Oh, Mother went out and bullied those Mayflower descendants you have in the kitchen," said Carolina. "Mother can be a terrible bully when she likes."

"I've never dared," said Father. "They know I'm not a Cabot.[11] It's something in my left eye."

But I'm glad your Mother did. I hope it means they're leaving tomorrow," and he looked relieved.

"If they do," said Carolina, "Mother and I will cook up the famous *spaghetti à la Clay,* and we'll take the children on a beach picnic. We might do that anyway."

"We might," said Father. "Try and keep us from not."

"Shall we ask your brother Lambert?" said Carolina. "He's such a dear man. Such a sprite. He told me all about his liver and tried to hold my hand in the pantry."

"I guess there's no use trying to establish a good social position with you around," said Father, but he didn't seem to mind.

"The best authorities are agreed on that point," said Carolina. She turned to me. "Good night, Jerry," she said. "And thanks to you and Bibs for your charming hospitality. I've been trying to marry your father for eight or nine years now, but he doesn't seem to think I'd make a good stepmother. Maybe you could convince him. Or maybe I'll just turn around and marry Lambert. It must be wonderful to have a husband with a liver. So convenient when you run out of cornflakes."

Then she laughed her marvelous laugh and ran upstairs. "Good night, Toots, you maniac!" Father called after her, and his eyes were crinkly and amused. Then he turned and looked at me, and for a minute we didn't say anything.

"Carolina's kidding," he said finally. "You know that."

"I wouldn't mind if she wasn't," I said. "She's a grand girl."

"She is," he said. "We both knew your mother." He hesitated a second. "Let's go out in the garden," he said. "It's smoky in here."

We went out and walked up and down for a little while. It wasn't hard, not saying anything, it was easy. Like not saying anything with any of your friends.

I was thinking about the drawings Carolina had shown me—the funny little drawings he sends instead of letters. He'd sent her these and they were funny, and not so funny. They were funny enough. But he thought we wanted another kind of father—somebody like Uncle

---

[10] *a real Bohemian revel,* a free and easy, unconventional, but very gay party.

[11] *a Cabot,* a member of one of the oldest and most aristocratic Boston families.

Lambert or Mr. Parsons. And he thought we were right. And it was in the drawings. He'd wanted to see me graduate, but he'd thought he'd better stay away. Of course, that was cuckoo of him. But I could understand it, because I'd felt the same way about him. And then Carolina told me about the file in his office. That's a secret between us and I'll never tell him I know. But it's got everything in it from Bibs' first kindergarten work to that darn fool newspaper picture of me when I got the Raeburn Medal. I never thought he saved those things.

He gave me a cigarette and we both lit up.

"I've never told you much about your mother," he said. "You were young—and she wouldn't have wanted me to go in for the sob stuff. She had what she wanted, you see. She said she'd rather have children than live to be seventy—and she thought you and Bibs were swell. You can ask Carolina, if you like. But that was the last thing she said, 'Well, Jick, I've had what I wanted.' It makes it hard to talk about." He stopped a minute. "I won't want you to think she was an angel," he said. "She had a temper like the Irish Free State and she never was on time in her life except in the theater. And there wasn't anybody like her. It made it hard to talk about—even to Carolina, for a long time. You see, she wouldn't have wanted me to do the sob stuff."

"That's all right," I said. "I understand."

"Do you think Bibs does?" he said, and his voice wasn't like his ordinary one. "She was fond of Bibs."

"If she doesn't, I'll get it across to her," I said.

"I wish you would," he said. "Bibs is rather a problem to me."

"Oh, she's got her wheels in line," I said. "She has, honestly. She'll go a little haywire when she's eighteen and probably write a bum child-prodigy novel. And then she'll marry somebody who'll chase her around the house with a shotgun if she tries any tricks and have eight children and end up as a darn good Indian." And, funnily enough, I knew when I said it that that was going to be true.

"Well, that's some comfort for a worried parent," he said. "She used to scare me stiff when she was younger." I saw the end of his cigarette glow red. "In fact, you both did," he said. "I depended on your mother so much for all of that. You won't understand that till you're married. Well, I had to go on working, afterwards —it was the only thing I knew how to do."

"They were pretty expensive schools," I said.

"Why not?" he said. "Your mother and I used to say that the best was none too good for the Blakes. When we were heating bouillon cubes over a Sterno on the road,"[12] he made a little noise in his throat. "I got some things wrong," he said. "I ought to have known. But people keep telling you about the right environment for kids. Where did you pick up the piano?"

"I used to wake myself up at night after you'd gone out," I said. "And then there was a fellow at camp—you didn't say anything about camp."

I could feel him grin through the darkness though I couldn't see it.

"I learned from a cross-eyed German who played in a rathskeller," he said. "And Lambert told on me and I got the licking of my life. Your grandfather always liked Lambert. But *his* father lost a lot of honest Boston money, trying to manage an opera troupe in the Fifties. So that's three of us."

He chuckled and pulled on his cigarette again.

"Carolina said I was an idiot," he said. "And she was right. But I didn't want you to get into anything because of me. And when you're inside the game—well, it doesn't look the way it does from the outside. It's a tough game, you know. And sometimes you get thinking the other thing might be better. Till you try it. And then you know. It works both ways, of course. Do you really want to go to Harvard, by the way?"

"Uh-huh," I said. "I want harmony and counterpoint and all the theory I can get. And work on shows in the summer—the practical stuff. Lord, I haven't done anything yet!"

---

[12]*heating bouillon cubes over a Sterno on the road.* "Sterno" is the trade name of a kind of solid alcohol used for heating food. When the Blakes were starting out in theatrical business, they traveled from one small town to another, lived in cheap hotel rooms, and cooked over a Sterno can.

"We'll get Jakie down for a weekend," he said. "And you can listen in on the new one—you'll be a help. I want to do a real light opera and he tells me I can't, but we'll show him. I'm sick of just working for hit numbers and ringing the same old changes. And I want to have him hear your blues. There's one spot in it that's a little tricky—you've got to allow for the singer, now and then. But the rest goes right to town. I can show the spot, tomorrow, with Carolina. And we'll go through the whole score. Okey, son?"

"Okey-doke," I said.

CONCERNING STEPHEN VINCENT BENÉT

1. Explain briefly what is meant by realism in literature. How does it differ from romanticism?

2. What aspects of Stephen Vincent Benét's writing may be considered realistic? Do any of his writings show romantic tendencies? Explain your answer.

CONCERNING "FAMOUS"

1. What question does the first sentence of the story raise in your mind? What answer to your question do the first four paragraphs give you?

2. Jerry Blake compares his relations with his father to those of Nub with Mr. Parsons. What differences does he find in these two father-and-son relationships? What has led to these differences?

3. Which of these words might be used to describe Carolina Clay: high-spirited, vivacious, vain, wise, foolish, sympathetic, fickle? Give reasons for your choices.

4. What brings about the end of the misunderstanding between Jerry and his father? Who deserves the chief credit for ending the misunderstanding?

5. Give your reasons for liking or disliking each of these characters: Jordan Blake, Carolina Clay, Bibs, Uncle Lambert.

6. Explain why "Famous" is considered a realistic story.

Understanding the first-person story

Perhaps the most difficult problem facing the writer of a first-person story is to make clear to the reader the sort of person the narrator ("I") is. Obviously the author cannot have the narrator say of himself, "I am a very sensitive person," or "I am very intelligent." The author must find other and more subtle ways to make the narrator emerge as a distinct personality. He must build a character through the words the narrator uses in telling his story, the way he thinks, the things he says to others, and the things he does.

At this point you probably feel that you know Jerry Blake quite well. Make a list of his outstanding problems and of his qualities. Estimate his chances for future success. Then discuss with your classmates the way you got to know Jerry.

❧ IV PATRIOT

During the 1920's, many people had begun to examine America and her citizens with critical eyes; many authors had written realistically (and at times bitterly) about the lives of twentieth-century Americans. But as time went on both the American public and the writers who mirrored its attitudes began to see signs of hope. Strangely enough, this change from disillusionment to a more constructive attitude began during the hard times of the 1930's. The positive measures taken by Americans (both locally and nationally) to improve conditions for the underprivileged, caused our countrymen to think better of the United States. Furthermore, the dictatorships which arose in Europe during the 1930's made our government and our free people, by contrast, look very good indeed. Eventually, when we entered World War II, the people solidly backed the war effort. When it came to choosing between dictatorship and democracy, Americans did not hesitate.

Such attitudes found expression in the works of many writers. Poet Carl Sandburg, who in the 1920's had protested against the exploitation of some of the poor, in 1936 published a book-length poem voicing solid belief in Americans—*The People, Yes.* Sinclair Lewis, who in 1922 had attacked the businessman in his novel *Babbitt,* was, in 1935, warning Americans, in *It Can't Happen Here,* that dictatorship *could* come to the United States. Ernest Hemingway, prophet of cynicism in the 1920's, had the hero of *For Whom the Bell Tolls* (1940) conclude that the democratic way of life was worth fighting—even dying—for. These, and other works like them, betokened a widespread new faith, a newly awakened patriotism.

Benét, who had never been as dubious about America as some, became a leading spokesman for the belief that the United States was capable of high achievements. He was convinced, too, that America should join other free nations in overcoming the mortal enemies of democracy. He came of a family, it will be remembered, in which three generations had been army officers. Even in childhood he had steeped himself in native traditions. He never had felt that an author should remain aloof from the disputes of the day. At about thirteen, his brother William recalled, he wrote a poem which "stigmatized 'The Proud Man,' imagining himself sitting aloof from the world, till at last a glance from the window showed him how all mankind had passed him by and gone beyond him....My brother...never cared much about an ivory tower."

In sympathy with advocates of change in America, Benét wrote poems such as "Metropolitan Nightmare" (1933) and "Ode to Walt Whitman" (1935), which urged reforms. A large part of a book of poems, *Burning City* (1936), was eloquent in its advocacy of social and political change. He collaborated with another writer on a motion picture, *Power and the Land* (1940), issued by the Rural Electrification Administration.

Believing that America, in addition to improving its internal situation, should join in fighting totalitarianism, he used his pen to make known his convictions. In 1935, he warned his countrymen against the menace of the power state in "Litany for Dictatorships," and in 1936, in the story "Blood of the Martyrs," he denounced the suppression of freedom of speech by the Nazis. In *Zero Hour* (1940), a book to which five other authors contributed, in the poem "Nightmare at Noon" (1940), and in the radio play "Listen to the People" (1941), he urged as inevitable the defense of the American way of living against the forces which threatened it. "We made this thing, this dream," says the narrator of the radio play:

> We made it and we make it and it's ours.
> We shall maintain it. It shall be sustained.

The radio drama was broadcast on July 4, 1941, almost exactly five months before Pearl Harbor and our country's entrance into World War II. Once we had declared war, Benét used all his energy, all his skill as a writer, to aid the war effort. Particularly effective were several radio plays, notably "They Burned the Books," which helped clarify our aims and, in contrast, those of the enemy. He wrote whenever called upon, and on his script often penciled a note such as this one: "Perhaps this will help. Change it as you will—I have no pride in authorship in times like these. Just get it said."

Benét did not live to see the triumph for which he worked: he died March 13, 1943, two years before the surrender of Japan. His plays were published in 1945, after his death, in a volume called *We Stand United.* Of them, Norman Corwin, outstanding radio dramatist, wrote:

They are mostly tough and hard driving and sharp-edged. Though they are deadly serious there are more than occasional moments of the old Benét humor, and now and then a lyric passage of goose-pimpling beauty. There is anger and scorn in them, as one might expect from a poet and patriot who hated Fascism long before Munich and the shooting.[1] There is also in them the pride in America and her people, the stout affirmation of her democracy which inhabits so much of his work in other media.

"Listen to the People" summarizes much of the thought and feeling of Stephen Vincent Benét, patriot.

[1]*Munich* (mū′nik) *and the shooting.* Munich is the German city at which Neville Chamberlain, Prime Minister of England, signed an agreement with Adolf Hitler, dictator of Germany, in 1938, agreeing that certain parts of Czechoslovakia should be ceded to Germany. In spite of this appeasement, which Chamberlain believed would guarantee "peace in our time," World War II broke out a year later.

Listen to the People

[*Orchestra: Music up and out.*]

NARRATOR. This is Independence Day,
   Fourth of July, the day we mean to keep,
Whatever happens and whatever falls
Out of a sky grown strange;
This is firecracker day for sunburnt kids,   5
The day of the parade,
Slambanging down the street.
Listen to the parade!

There's J. K. Burney's float,
Red-white-and-blue crêpe paper on the wheels,
The Fire Department and the local Grange,[1] 11
There are the pretty girls with their hair curled
Who represent the Thirteen Colonies,
The Spirit of East Greenwich, Betsy Ross,
Democracy, or just some pretty girls.   15
There are veterans and the Legion Post[2]

[1]*local Grange,* the local branch of an organization founded by farmers in 1867 to advance their welfare.
[2]*Legion Post,* the local branch of the American Legion, an organization formed by servicemen of World War I.

From "Listen to the People," from *Selected Works of Stephen Vincent Benét,* published by Rinehart & Company, Inc. Copyright, 1941, by Stephen Vincent Benét.

(Their feet are going to hurt when they get
    home),
The band, the flag, the band, the usual crowd,
Good-humored, watching, hot,
Silent a second as the flag goes by,   20
Kidding the local cop and eating popsicles,
Jack Brown and Rosie Shapiro and Dan Shay,
Paul Bunchick and the Greek who runs the
    Greek's,
The black-eyed children out of Sicily,
The girls who giggle and the boys who push,   25
All of them there and all of them a nation.
And, afterwards,
There'll be ice cream and fireworks and a
    speech
By Somebody the Honorable Who,
The lovers will pair off in the kind dark   30
And Tessie Jones, our honor graduate,
Will read the Declaration.
That's how it is. It's always been that way.
That's our Fourth of July, through war and
    peace,
That's our Fourth of July.   35

And a lean farmer on a stony farm
Came home from mowing, buttoned up his
    shirt
And walked ten miles to town,
Musket in hand.
He didn't know the sky was falling down   40
And, it may be, he didn't know so much.
But people oughtn't to be pushed around
By kings or any such.
A workman in the city dropped his tools.
An ordinary, small-town kind of man   45
Found himself standing in the April sun,
One of a ragged line
Against the skilled professionals of war,
The matchless infantry who could not fail,
Not for the profit, not to conquer worlds,   50
Not for the pomp or the heroic tale
But first, and principally, since he was sore.
They could do things in quite a lot of places,
They shouldn't do them here, in Lexington.

He looked around and saw his neighbors'
    faces...   55
AN ANGRY VOICE. *Disperse, ye villains! Why
don't you disperse?*

A CALM VOICE. *Stand your ground, men. Don't
fire unless fired upon. But if they mean to
have a war, let it begin here!*

NARRATOR (resuming). Well, that was that. And
    later, when he died
Of fever or a bullet in the guts,
Bad generalship, starvation, dirty wounds   60
Or any one of all the thousand things
That kill a man in wars,
He didn't die handsome but he did die free
And maybe that meant something. It could be.
Oh, it's not pretty! Say it all you like!   65
It isn't a bit pretty. Not one bit.
But that is how the liberty was won.
That paid for the firecrackers and the band.

A YOUNG VOICE (radical). Well, what do you
    mean, you dope?
Don't you know this is an imperialist, capitalist
    country, don't you?   70
Suppose some old guy with chin whiskers did
    get his pants shot off at a place called Lex-
    ington?
What does it mean to me?

AN OLDER VOICE (conservative). My dear fel-
    low, I myself am a son of a son of a son of
    the American Revolution,
But I can only view the present situation with
    the gravest alarm.
The Constitution is dead and labor doesn't
    know its place.   75

A TOTALITARIAN VOICE (*persuasive*). My
worthy American listeners.
I am giving you one more chance.
Don't you know that we are completely invin-
cible, don't you?
Won't you just admit that we are the wave of
the future,[3] won't you?
You are a very nice, mongrel, disgusting peo-
ple—   80
But, naturally, you need new leadership.
We can supply it. We've sent the same brand to
fourteen nations.
It comes in the shape of a bomb and it beats as
it sweeps as it cleans.
For those of you who like order, we can supply
order.
We give the order. You take it.   85
Now be sensible—give up this corrupt and
stupid nonsense of democracy.

RADICAL VOICE. Forget everything but the class
struggle. Forget democracy.
CONSERVATIVE VOICE. Look back wistfully to
the good old, grand old days—the days when
the
Boys said "The public be damned!" and got
away with it.   89
TOTALITARIAN VOICE. Just a little collaboration
and you too can be part of the New Order.[4]
Democracy is finished. We are the future!
[*Music up and ominous.*]
NARRATOR (*resuming*). The sky is dark, now,
over the parade.
The sky's an altered sky, a sky that might be.
There's J. K. Burney's float

With funny-colored paper on the wheels   95
Or no—excuse me—used to be J. K.'s
But the store's under different management
Like quite a lot of stores.
You see, J. K. got up in church one day,
After it all had happened and walked out,   100
The day they instituted the new order.
They had a meeting. Held it in the church.
He just walked out. That's all.
That's all there is to say about J. K.
Though I remember just the way he looked,   105
White-faced and chin stuck out.
I think they could have let the church alone.
It's kind of dreary, shutting up the church.
But don't you say I said so. Don't you say!
Listen to the parade!   110
There are the pretty girls with their hair curled,
Back from the labor camp.[5]
They represent the League of Strength Through
Joy.[6]
At least, I guess it's that.
No, they don't go to high school any more.   115
They get told where they go. We all get told.
And, now and then, it happens like Jack Brown,
Nice fellow, Jack. Ran the gas station here.
But he was married to a You-Know-Who.
Fond of her, too.   120
I don't know why we never used to mind.
Why, she walked round like anybody else,
Kept her kids clean and joined the Ladies'
Social.
Just shows you, doesn't it? But that's all done.
And you won't see her in the crowd today,   125
Her or the kids or Jack,
Unless you look six feet under the ground,
The lime-washed ground, the bitter **prison**
ground
That hides the martyrs and the innocent,
And you won't see Dan Shay.   130
Dan was a union man
And now we don't have unions any more.

---

[3]*the wave of the future,* the way things are going to be
in coming years. The phrase implies that democracy is
based on a worn-out, impractical idea and must give way
to dictatorship.
[4]*the New Order,* a name applied to totalitarian governments by their supporters.

[5]*labor camp.* In Nazi Germany all boys and girls had
to put in a year working on farms or in other labor before
beginning college or going to work. For the boys this
labor-camp work was combined with military training.
[6]*League of Strength Through Joy,* a Nazi workers'
organization designed to provide workers with vacation
trips, sports events, and cultural progams. Since the words
"strength through joy" were also used as a slogan by the
Nazi youth organizations, Benét uses them here to suggest
an organization of Nazi girls.

They wouldn't even let him take his specs,
The day the troopers came around for him.
Listen to the parade!   135
The marching, marching, marching feet,
All with the same hard stamp!
The bands, the bands, the bands, the flags, the
    flags,
The sharp, mechanical, inhuman cheer
Dragged from the straining throats of the stiff
    crowd!   140
It's Independence—sorry, my mistake!—
It's National Day—the Day of the New Order!
We let it happen—we forgot the old
Bleak words of common sense, "Unite or Die,"
And the clock struck—and the bad dream was
    here.   145
A VOICE. You can't do this to me. We got laws.
    We got courts. We got unions.
A VOICE. You can't do this to me. The Consti-
    tution forbids it.
A VOICE. I was always glad to coöperate.
A VOICE. It looked to me like good business.
A VOICE. It looked to me like the class strug-
    gle.   150
A VOICE. It looked to me like peace in our time.
TOTALITARIAN VOICE. Thank you, ladies and
    gentlemen.
Democracy is finished. You are finished. We
    are the present!
                [Music up and down.]
NARRATOR. That is one voice. You've heard it.
    Don't forget it.
And don't forget it can be slick or harsh,   155
Violent or crooning, but it's still the same,
And it means death.

Are there no other voices? None at all?
No voice at all out of the long parade
That marched so many years,   160
Out of the passion of the Puritans,
The creaking of the wagons going west,
The guns of Sharpsburg,[7] the unnumbered dead,
Out of the baffled and bewildered hosts
Who came here for a freedom hardly known.   165

Out of the bowels of the immigrant ship,
The strange, sick voyage, the cheating and the
    scorn
And yet, at the end, Liberty.
Liberty with a torch in her right hand,
Slowly worked out, deceived a thousand
    times,   170
But never quite forgotten, always growing,
Growing like wheat and corn.
"I remember a man named Abe Lincoln.
I remember the words he used to say."
Oh, we can call on Lincoln and Tom Paine,[8]
Adams and Jefferson.   176
Call on the great words spoken that remain
Like the great stars of evening, the fixed stars,
But that is not enough.
The dead are mighty and are part of us   180
And yet the dead are dead.
                            This is our world,
Our time, our choice, our anguish, our decision.
This is our world. We have to make it now,
A hundred and thirty millions of us have to
And make it well, or suffer the bad dream.   185
What have we got to say?
A WOMAN'S VOICE. I don't know, I'm a woman
    with a house,
I do my work. I take care of my man.
I've got a right to say how things should be.
I've got a right to have my kids grow up   190
The way they ought to grow. Don't stop me
    there.
Don't tread on me, don't hinder me, don't
    cross me.
NARRATOR. What have we got to say,
People, you people?
MAN'S VOICE. I guess I haven't thought about
    it much.   195
I been too busy. Way I figure it
It's this way. We've got something. If it's
    crummy
The bunch of us can change what we don't like
In our own way and mean it.
I got a cousin back in the old country.   200
He says it's swell there but he couldn't change
A button on his pants without an order
From somebody's pet horse. Maybe he likes it.

---

[7]*Sharpsburg*, a town in Maryland. The Battle of Antie-
tam (an tēʹtəm), or Sharpsburg, was fought on its outskirts September 17, 1862. More men were killed or
wounded in this battle than on any other day of the
War Between the States.

---

[8]*Tom Paine*, an English-born American patriot who
wrote "Common Sense" and other pamphlets urging that
the colonies declare their independence of England.

I'm sticking here. That's all. Well, sign me off.
NARRATOR. People, you people, living every-
 where,   205
Sioux Falls and Saugatuck and Texarkana,
Memphis and Goshen, Harrodsburg and Troy,
People who live at postmarks with queer names,
Blue Eye and Rawhide, Santa Claus and
 Troublesome,
People by rivers, people of the plains, 210
People whose contour plows bring back the
 grass
To a dust-bitten and dishonored earth,
And those who farm the hillside acres still
And raise up fortitude between the stones,
Millions in cities, millions in the towns, 215
People who spit a mile from their front doors
And gangling kids, ballplaying in the street,
All races and all stocks, all creeds and cries,
And yet one people, one, and always striving....
A MAN. I'm on relief.[9]   220
I know what they say about us on relief,
Those who never were there.
All the same, we made the park.
We made the road and the check-dam[10] and the
 culvert.
Our names are not on the tablets. Forget our
 names.   225
But, when you drive on the road, remember us,
 also.
Remember Johnny Lombardo and his pick,
Remember us, when you build democracy,
For we, too, were part and are part.
NARRATOR. One nation, one. 230
And the voices of young and old, of all who
 have faith,
Jostling and mingling, speaking from the
 ground,
Speaking from the old houses and the pride,
Speaking from the deep hollows of the heart.
MAN'S VOICE. I was born in '63. 235
There were many then who despaired of the
 Republic,

Many fine and solid citizens.
They had good and plausible reasons and were
 eloquent.
I grew up in the Age of Brass, the Age of Steel.
I have known and heard of three wars. 240
All through my life, whenever the skies were
 dark,
There came to me many fine and solid citizens,
Wringing their hands, despairing of the Re-
 public,
Because we couldn't do this and shouldn't do
 that.
And yet, each time, I saw the Republic grow 245
Like a great elm tree, through each fault and
 failure,
And spread its branches over all the people.
Look at the morning sun. There is the Republic.
Not yesterday, but there, the breaking day.
TOTALITARIAN VOICE. But, my worthy Ameri-
 can listeners,   250
All this is degenerate talk.
The future rolls like a wave and you cannot
 fight it.
A VOICE. Who says we can't?
A VOICE. Who says so?
A VOICE. How does he get that way? 255
A VOICE. You mean to tell me
A little shrimp like that could run the world,
A guy with a trick mustache and a bum salute,
Run us, run you and me?
TOTALITARIAN VOICE. You mistake me. 260
Others have often made the same mistake
Often and often and in many countries.
I never play upon a people's strength.
I play upon their weaknesses and fears.
I make their doubts my allies and my spies. 265
My secret weapon is no secret weapon.
It is to turn all men against all men
For my own purposes. It is to use
Good men to do my work without their knowl-
 edge,
Not only the secret traitor and the spy. 270
It is to raise a question and a doubt
Where there was faith. It is to subjugate
Men's minds before their bodies feel the steel.
It is to use
All envy, all despair, all prejudice 275
For my own work.
If you've an envy or a prejudice

---

 [9]*on relief,* living on money supplied by national and state governments to provide the bare necessities of life for the unemployed. During the early 1930's, millions of Americans were kept alive by relief funds. Later such organizations as the Works Progress Administration (WPA) provided public projects to give work to the unemployed.
 [10]*check-dam,* a low levee designed to hold water in a certain area until it sinks into the ground.

I'll play on it and use it to your ruin.
My generals are General Distrust,
General Fear, General Half-A-Heart,   280
General It's-Too-Late,
General Greed and Major-General Hate,
And they go walking in civilian clothes
In your own streets and whisper in your ears.
For I'm not betting only on the tanks,   285
The guns, the planes, the bombers,
But on your own division and disunion,
On your own minds and hearts to let me in,
For, if that happens, all I wish for happens.
So what have you to say?   290
What have you got to bet against my bet?
Where's your one voice?
AMERICAN VOICE. Our voice is not one voice
    but many voices.
Not one man's, not the greatest, but the peo-
    ple's.
The blue sky and the forty-eight states of the
    people.   295
Many in easy times but one in the pinch
And that's what some folks forget.
Our voice is all the objectors and dissenters
And they sink and are lost in the ground swell
    of the people
Once the people rouse, once the people wake
    and listen.   300
People, you people, growing everywhere,
What have you got to say?
A VOICE. We are the people, listen to us now.
A VOICE. Says you we're puny? We built
    Boulder Dam,[11]
We built Grand Coulee[12] and the TVA.[13]   305
We built them out of freedom and our sweat.
VOICE. Says you we're faint of heart and little
    of mind?
We poured like wheat through the gaps of the
    Appalachians.
We made the seas of wheat, the seas of corn.
We made five states a sea of wheat and corn. 310
VOICE (laughing). We built the cities and the
    skyscrapers,

All the proud steel. We built them up so high
The eagles lost their way.
VOICE. That's us. When did you do a job like
    that?
VOICE. Wasn't enough.   315
VOICE. No, and you bet it wasn't.
Not with the apple-sellers in the streets,
Not with the empty shops, the hungry men.[14]
But we learned some things in that darkness and
    kept free.
We didn't fold up and yell for a dictator.   320
VOICE. We lost our way for a while, but we've
    found our way.
We know it and we'll hold it and we'll keep it.
We'll tell it to the world. We're saying it.
VOICE. Freedom to speak and pray.
VOICE. Freedom from want and fear.   325
VOICE. That's what we're building.
                        Now and here and now.
NARRATOR. People, you people, risen and
    awake....
VOICE. That's what we're building and we'll
    build it here.
That's what we're building and we'll build it
    now,
Build it and make it shine across the world, 330
A refuge and a fortress and a hope,
Breaking old chains and laughing in the sun.
This is the people's cause, the people's might.
We have set up a standard for the free
And it shall not go down.   335
That's why we drill the plate and turn the wheel,
Build the big planes.
That's why a million and a half of us
Learn here and now how free men stand in
    arms.
Don't tread on us, don't hinder us, don't cross
    us.   340
We won't have tyranny here.
VOICE. We don't give one long low hoot for
    your master race.
We think your slick new order's a bowl of
    raspberries.
We'll pick the small and the free and the en-
    during,

---

[11]*Boulder Dam*, now called Hoover Dam. The highest dam in the world, it is on the Colorado River in Nevada.

[12]*Grand Coulee* (grand′ kü′li), a dam on the Columbia River in Washington, the largest dam ever built.

[13]*TVA*, Tennessee Valley Authority, an organization set up in 1933 to build power dams, control floods, and enrich the land in the entire watershed of the Tennessee River.

---

[14]*apple-sellers...hungry men*, references to the depression years of the 1930's. Men selling apples on street corners to eke out a bare living were a familiar sight in cities.

Wherever we find them and wherever they are. 345

We won't have tyranny here.

VOICE. We'll stick by Rosie Shapiro and Dan Shay,

Paul Bunchick and the Greek who runs the Greek's,

And all of 'em like that, wherever they are.

We'll stick by the worn old stones in Salem churchyard, 350

The Jamestown church and the bones of the Alamo.[15]

We won't have tyranny here.

VOICE. It's a long way out of the past and a long way forward.

It's a tough way too, and there's plenty of trouble in it.

It's a black storm crowding the sky and a cold wind blowing, 355

Blowing upon us all.

See it and face it. That's the way it is.

That's the way it'll be for a time and a time.

Even the easy may have little ease.

Even the meek may suffer in their meekness. 360

But we've ridden out storms before and we'll ride out this one,

Ride it out and get through.

It won't be done by the greedy and the go-easies.

It'll be done by the river of the people,

The mountain of the people, the great plain 365

Grown to the wheat of the people,

It'll be done by the proud walker, Democracy,

The walker in proud shoes.

Get on your feet, Americans, and say it!

Forget your grievances, wherever you are, 370

The little yesterday's hates and the last year's discord,

This is your land, this is your independence,

This is the people's cause, the people's might.

Say it and speak it loud—united, free...

MANY VOICES. United, free. 375

VOICE. Whatever happens and whatever falls,

We pledge ourselves to liberty and faith.

MANY VOICES. To liberty and faith.

VOICE. We pledge ourselves to justice, law and hope

And a free government by our own men 380

For us, our children, and our children's children.

MANY VOICES. For us, our children, and our children's children.

VOICE. Not for an old dead world but a new world rising.

[Music up and down.]

NARRATOR. You've heard the long parade

And all the voices that cry out against it. 385

[Quietly.]

What do the people say?

Well, you've just heard some questions and some answers,

Not all, of course. No man can say that's all.

But look in your own minds and memories

And find out what you find and what you'd keep. 390

It's time we did that and it won't be earlier.

I don't know what each one of you will find,

It may be only half a dozen words

Carved on a stone, carved deeper in the heart,

It might be all a life, but look and find it— 395

Sun on Key West, snow on New Hampshire hills,

Warm rain on Georgia and the Texas wind

Blowing across an empire and all part,

All one, all indivisible and one—

Find it and keep it and hold on to it, 400

For there's a buried thing in all of us,

Deeper than all the noise of the parade,

The thing the haters never understand

And never will, the habit of the free.

Out of the flesh, out of the minds and hearts 405

Of thousand upon thousand common men,

Cranks, martyrs, starry-eyed enthusiasts,

Slow-spoken neighbors, hard to push around,

Women whose hands were gentle with their kids

And men with a cold passion for mere justice. 410

We made this thing, this dream,

We made it and we make it and it's ours.

We shall maintain it. It shall be sustained.

ALL VOICES (up). WE SHALL MAINTAIN IT. IT SHALL BE SUSTAINED.

[Music up to climax.]

(CURTAIN)

---

[15]*Alamo* (al′ə mō), a mission in San Antonio, Texas, captured by the Mexicans in 1836 during the war between Texas and Mexico after a siege of thirteen days. All its defenders, including Davy Crockett, died fighting.

CONCERNING STEPHEN VINCENT BENÉT

1. What was the mood of much American writing in the 1920's? How and why did this mood change in the following decade?

2. What did Stephen Vincent Benét's brother mean by saying that Stephen "never cared much about an ivory tower"? How did he show that his was not an "ivory-tower" attitude?

CONCERNING "LISTEN TO THE PEOPLE"

1. Contrast the two parades described in lines 1-35 and in lines 92-142. What change had taken place in the interval between the two parades? What had the men represented by Conservative Voice, Radical Voice, and Totalitarian Voice each done to bring about this change?

2. Why do you think Benét introduced the Lexington episode (lines 36-68) just after the description of the first parade and before the Radical, Conservative, and Totalitarian Voices?

3. When the Narrator in line 158 calls for other voices to answer the Totalitarian Voice, what voices answer him? Why do you think these particular types of people are chosen to speak for all Americans?

4. The Totalitarian Voice in lines 260-290 outlines the way in which dictatorships overcome democracies. What are the various points the voice makes? Explain why you do or do not believe these are the ways in which democracies have been actually overcome.

5. This radio drama was first broadcast five months before Pearl Harbor, December 7, 1941. By September, 1945, the Nazis had been totally crushed. Would you say, then, that this play is out-of-date today? Explain your answer.

Appreciating a play with a purpose

"Listen to the People" is a play with a purpose. In it Benét used every device he had learned through years of successful writing to arouse the American people, to show them the dangers of disunity, and to urge them to fight totalitarian promises. With these ideas of the purposes for which the play was written in mind, arrange with your teacher to have the entire radio drama read aloud, with various students reading the parts of the different voices. (Students selected to read parts should practice reading them aloud before the class performance.)

After the performance answer the following questions: Why do you think Benét wrote his play in verse rather than in prose? Why do you believe he varied the types of poetry he used in the play? What do you think his purpose was in including everyday slang expressions as well as lines of real poetry? What do you think was the mood of the radio audience as the play ended?

The Larger View

The unit you have just studied is the last of the six units tracing the growth of American literature from colonial times to the present day. Use the following statements as the basis of a discussion to check your knowledge of important men and great movements in literature in the United States.

1. The writings of Stephen Vincent Benét represent several different currents of twentieth-century ideas and beliefs.

2. As a realist Benét writes in the manner most typical of his age.

3. In some of his writings Benét shows a relationship to Washington Irving.

4. Benét's radio plays served somewhat the same purpose in the twentieth century that Franklin's political writings did in the eighteenth century.

5. In "Civil Disobedience" Thoreau speaks for the individual; in "Listen to the People" Benét speaks for the group.

6. Like Mark Twain, Benét shows the broad ideas of democracy that Whitman preached in *Leaves of Grass*.

7. Each generation of American authors has been somewhat influenced by the work of earlier writers, has discarded some of the characteristics of the past, and has added new themes, new tendencies, and new ways of thinking and writing.

MORE GOOD READING

In addition to the books listed below, you will find many fine novels and biographies by twentieth-century writers in the bibliographies in Part I of this book. For example, if you wish to read a historical novel, you might try Hervey Allen's "The Forest and the Fort" (page 95) or Kenneth Roberts' "Northwest Passage" (page 96). Among realistic novels you might choose Sinclair Lewis' "Arrowsmith" (page 177). Consult the bibliographies for other twentieth-century books you will enjoy.

BARNES, MARGARET AYER, *Within This Present.* (Houghton) This novel tells of the effect of World War I, the postwar boom, and the depression on a wealthy Chicago family. It is principally the story of a man and woman whose marriage is threatened by changing times.

BENÉT, ROSEMARY and STEPHEN VINCENT, *A Book of Americans.* (Rinehart) This clever light verse about American heroes masks its seriousness under a sparkling cover of humor.

BENÉT, STEPHEN VINCENT, *John Brown's Body.* (Farrar) Fact and fiction are skillfully interwoven in this fine narrative poem of brave men and steadfast women of both the North and the South during the War Between the States.

BENÉT, STEPHEN VINCENT, *Twenty-Five Short Stories.* (Sun Dial) This excellent collection contains historical tales, sketches of modern life, and stories warning against totalitarianism.

BENÉT, STEPHEN VINCENT, *Western Star.* (Rinehart) For this fine narrative poem of the Virginia and New England settlements in their perilous early days, Benét was posthumously awarded the Pulitzer Prize.

CHASE, MARY ELLEN, *Mary Peters.* (Macmillan) The strength and beauty of life in a Maine seacoast village underlie this slow-moving but rewarding novel of Mary and John Peters.

FERBER, EDNA, *Cimarron.* (Doubleday) From the famous run that opened up the Oklahoma country to settlers to the time oil was struck, this exciting novel follows the adventures of Yancey Cravat and his wife, Sabra.

GALE, ZONA, *Miss Lulu Bett.* (Appleton) Humor and pathos are mingled in this warmly human but realistic story of Lulu Bett's life as a drudge, and of her final release.

GEISMAR, MAXWELL, *The Last of the Provincials.* (Houghton) Serious students will enjoy the readable accounts of American novelists who were Benét's contemporaries found in this book and in the same author's *Writers in Crisis* (Houghton).

GLASGOW, ELLEN, *Battle-ground.* (Doubleday) The first half of this thoughtful novel pictures the life of wealthy Virginians in the days before 1860; the second half is a vivid portrayal of the changes wrought by war.

LEWIS, SINCLAIR, *Main Street.* (Harcourt) This is the satiric tale of Gopher Prairie, a smug little town, and of the young doctor's wife who tries futilely to uplift its complacent people. *Babbitt* (Harcourt) is also a satiric novel and so successful a one that the name of its principal character has become a synonym for all middle-class, overly enthusiastic town-boosters.

MITCHELL, MARGARET, *Gone With the Wind.* (Macmillan) Few books have achieved greater popularity in America than this story of Rhett Butler and Scarlett O'Hara in the years before, during, and after the War Between the States.

SAROYAN, WILLIAM, *The Human Comedy.* (Harcourt) This story of a family during World War II manages in a relatively small number of pages to give a meaningful account of the values Americans find in their way of life.

STEINBECK, JOHN, *The Moon Is Down.* (Viking) In this short, simply written novel of conquerors in an invaded country, the author affirms that free men and women can never be conquered.

TARKINGTON, BOOTH, *Alice Adams.* (Grosset) This is an honest picture of the struggles for social success of a girl in a Midwestern small town. Alice is sometimes amusing and sometimes pathetic, but she is always a real person.

WHARTON, EDITH, *Ethan Frome.* (Scribner) This is a grim story written with great artistry. It concerns a discouraged farmer, his complaining wife, and a girl who still finds joy in life. It has a climax that few other novels can equal.

THE TWENTIETH CENTURY

LITERATURE	HISTORICAL EVENTS	
	Wright brothers made first airplane flight	1903
1906 O. Henry, *The Four Million*	Radio tube invented	1906
	Model-T Ford put into mass production	1909
	Admiral Peary discovered the North Pole	
	The steamship *Titanic* sunk	1912
1913 Vachel Lindsay, *General William Booth Enters into Heaven and Other Poems*		
Robert Frost, *A Boy's Will*		
	Panama Canal opened	1914
	World War I started in Europe	
1915 Edgar Lee Masters, *Spoon River Anthology*		
1916 Carl Sandburg, *Chicago Poems*		
Edwin Arlington Robinson, *The Man Against the Sky*		
1917 Hamlin Garland, *A Son of the Middle Border*	United States declared war on Germany	1917
	Armistice with Germany signed	1918
	Treaty of Versailles ended World War I	1919
1920 Sinclair Lewis, *Main Street*	First meeting of the League of Nations held	1920
Eugene O'Neill, *The Emperor Jones* and *Beyond the Horizon*	Woman suffrage became effective through the Nineteenth Amendment	
1924 Samuel Clemens, *Autobiography*		
1925 Theodore Dreiser, *An American Tragedy*		
1926 Ruth Suckow, *Iowa Interiors*	First talking movie appeared	1926
1927 Thornton Wilder, *The Bridge of San Luis Rey*	Lindbergh made first solo flight across Atlantic	1927
Carl Sandburg, *The American Songbag*		
1928 Stephen Vincent Benét, *John Brown's Body*		
1929 Thomas Wolfe, *Look Homeward, Angel*		
Ernest Hemingway, *A Farewell to Arms*		
	Japanese occupied Manchuria	1931
	Franklin D. Roosevelt elected President	1932
	Hitler became Chancellor of Germany	1933
1934 Eugene O'Neill, *Ah, Wilderness!*	Congress granted Philippine independence, which became effective July 4, 1946	1934
	Drought and dust storms attacked Midwest	
1935 Douglas Southall Freeman, *R. E. Lee: A Biography*	United States government set up work relief program for the unemployed	1935
1937 John Dos Passos, *U. S. A.*		
1938 Thornton Wilder, *Our Town*		
1939 John Steinbeck, *The Grapes of Wrath*	Great Britain and France declared war on Germany	1939
Carl Sandburg, *Abraham Lincoln: The War Years*		
1940 Ernest Hemingway, *For Whom the Bell Tolls*		
	Pearl Harbor attacked by Japanese	1941
	United States declared war on Japan, Germany, and Italy	
1943 Thornton Wilder, *The Skin of Our Teeth*		
1944 Stephen Vincent Benét, *Western Star*		
	President Roosevelt died	1945
	World War II ended	
1949 Robert Frost, *Complete Poems, 1949*		
	United States sent troops to fight in Korea	1950
1952 James Thurber, *Thurber Album*		

Stephen Vincent Benét 1898-1943

SOME PROMINENT WRITERS OF THE TWENTIETH CENTURY

JOHN DOS PASSOS, 1896-

Chicago-born John Dos Passos was the son of a New York lawyer who traveled around quite a bit with his family while the boy was growing up. Shortly after graduating with honors from Harvard in 1916, Dos Passos went to Spain to study. However, World War I changed his plans and he served first with a French ambulance unit and later in the United States Medical Corps. After the war he traveled as a newspaper correspondent in Europe and America. His first book was published in 1919, but his literary reputation dates from *Three Soldiers,* which appeared two years later and is considered one of the best American novels dealing with the war. In 1925 Dos Passos really hit his stride with *Manhattan Transfer,* a portrait of New York City, and in 1937 three of his later works, *The 42nd Parallel, 1919,* and *The Big Money* (see "Tin Lizzie," pages 157-160), were combined to make *U. S. A.,* one of the most impressive social writings yet produced in America.

THEODORE DREISER, 1871-1945

Theodore Dreiser was the twelfth in a family of thirteen children. He was born in Terre Haute, Indiana, the son of a German immigrant who owned a woolen mill that burned down, bringing poverty to the family. After a year at Indiana University Dreiser went to Chicago where he held such odd jobs as washing dishes, shoveling coal, and collecting bills. Then until 1905 he was a newspaperman working on city papers from Chicago to New York, and after that he was connected with various magazines. Too advanced in realism for their times, Dreiser's early novels caused much discussion, not being generally accepted by the public. It was with the appearance of *An American Tragedy* in 1925 that the times caught up with Dreiser, and his importance has been increasingly recognized.

DOUGLAS SOUTHALL FREEMAN, 1886-1953

Douglas Southall Freeman was born in Lynchburg, Virginia, but his family moved to Richmond when he was six years old. Freeman graduated from Richmond College in 1904 and then won his doctor's degree from Johns Hopkins four years later. His first book, *Calendar of Confederate Papers,* was published in 1908. After writing editorials for Richmond newspapers for several years, Freeman was made editor of the *News-Leader* in which he later bought an interest. In 1914 he was asked to write a short biography of Robert E. Lee. However, in undertaking this, Freeman uncovered such a wealth of new material that the short biography grew into four volumes which were finally published in 1935 under the title *R. E. Lee: A Biography.* (See "Surrender at Appomattox," pages 623-628.) So excellent is this work that it won the Pulitzer Prize.

ROBERT FROST, 1875-

Ten years after Robert Frost was born in San Francisco his father died, and his mother moved her children back to New England where nine generations of forebears had lived. In Lawrence, Massachusetts, Frost was selected the valedictorian of his high-school class. He entered Dartmouth in 1892, but shortly withdrew. During the next few years he worked in a mill, took a tramping trip through the South, taught for a while, worked on a newspaper, and then studied for two years at Harvard. Living on a farm in New Hampshire, Frost found in the next eleven years that farming was not profitable enough, and he turned to teaching as well. Since his teens he had been writing poetry, but twenty years of effort in that direction had earned him only about two hundred dollars. In spite of this, Frost at thirty-six determined to concentrate on poetry. He moved his family to England where, during the next two years, a British firm published *A Boy's Will* and *North of Boston.* When Frost returned to America in 1915, he was a well-established poet. Nevertheless, he again took up farming and teaching, gaining distinction as a teacher at Amherst, the University of Michigan, and Middlebury. Frost has charmed his readers with many books of poems, receiving in 1924, 1931, 1937, and 1943 the Pulitzer Prize.

ERNEST HEMINGWAY, 1898-

This great novelist and master of the short story was born in Oak Park, Illinois. Following high school he got a job reporting on the *Kansas City Star,* but a few months later left for Italy to serve in World War I, in which he was severely wounded. While working in Paris as a newspaper correspondent he produced his first successful novel, *The Sun Also Rises,* in 1926, and three years later appeared *A Farewell to Arms,* which drew upon his war experiences. Through the years Hemingway worked as a correspondent and continued to write novels and short stories based on significant happenings in his own life. Out of impressions gained from reporting the Spanish Civil War came perhaps his most popular novel, *For Whom the Bell Tolls,* published in 1940. Because Hemingway's stories skillfully interpret the typical experiences and attitudes of his times, he is considered an outstanding spokesman for his own generation.

SINCLAIR LEWIS, 1885-1951

Sinclair Lewis, the son of a country doctor, was born and grew up in Sauk Center, Minnesota. His mother died when he was only five years old. Small-town life did not at all suit "Red" Lewis and he determined to get to the citified East. Earning most of his way by newspaper work, he attended Yale, from which he was graduated in 1908. By 1920 Lewis had held various literary jobs, devoted four years to free-lance writing, and seen a number of his things published. Then came *Main Street,* a novel that struck out at smug provincialism and won for Lewis great popularity and acclaim. From then on most of his writings, including *Babbitt, Arrowsmith,* and *Dodsworth,* were concerned with debunking whatever seemed false to him in American life. For *Arrowsmith* Lewis was offered the Pulitzer Prize, which he spectacularly refused on principle. However, in 1930 he traveled to Sweden to receive the Nobel Prize, thus becoming the first American writer to be so honored.

VACHEL LINDSAY, 1879-1931

Vachel Lindsay's parents had settled in Springfield, Illinois, by the time their son was born. He grew up as a member of an intensely evangelical religious sect. He was an idolizer of Andrew Jackson, Walt Whitman, and Lincoln, and an admirer of impassioned oratory. After attending Hiram College in Ohio, he studied art in Chicago and New York. Because he had tremendous faith in the importance of art and literature and hoped to convert his countrymen to his beliefs, he went on many tramping trips and lecture tours, later recounting some of his experiences in *Adventures While Preaching the Gospel of Beauty,* published in 1914. On one of these trips in 1912 he composed the poem "General William Booth Enters into Heaven" (see pages 584-585), which was to win him his first acclaim. Originally appearing in the magazine *Poetry,* it became the title selection in his first published collection of poems a year later. This book was followed by others, the last ones being *Every Soul Is a Circus* in 1929 and *Selected Poems* in 1931.

EDGAR LEE MASTERS, 1868-1950

Edgar Lee Masters was born in Garnett, Kansas, and reared in Petersburg and Lewiston, Illinois, the "Spoon River country" he was to make famous. He attended Knox College for a year, read law in his father's law office, and was admitted to the bar in 1891. The next year he went to Chicago where he established a flourishing law practice which he abandoned in 1920 in order to devote all his time to writing. Meanwhile Masters had acquired experience as a reporter, as a printer, and as a contributor to magazines and newspapers. And in 1915 he had published *Spoon River Anthology*, a collection of imaginary epitaphs from an Illinois graveyard. (For selections see pages 257 and 587.) This book is considered one of the most original pieces of writing in American literature. Besides other collections of verse, Masters wrote novels, stories for boys, and biographies.

EUGENE O'NEILL, 1888-1953

The greatest dramatist America has yet produced was born in New York City, the son of the famous actor James O'Neill. After a youth of varied experience including a year at Princeton, vaudeville, prospecting, shipping as a seaman, reporting, and venturing into business, O'Neill became ill at the age of twenty-three. During his recovery he decided on a career as a dramatist and seriously began writing one-act plays. Then he spent a year studying at Harvard. Between 1917 and 1920 ten of his short plays were produced in New York, the first one being *Bound East for Cardiff.* In 1920 O'Neill received the Pulitzer Prize for his first long play, *Beyond the Horizon,* and later the same prize was given him for *Anna Christie* in 1922 and *Strange Interlude* in 1928. These plays and many others of his such as *The Emperor Jones, Ah, Wilderness!* and *The Great God Brown* were performed—and are still being performed—both in this country and abroad. As his fame grew, honors were heaped upon him, the most notable being the Nobel Prize, which he received in 1936.

EDWIN ARLINGTON ROBINSON, 1869-1935

Edwin Arlington Robinson spent his youth in Gardiner, Maine, the "Tilbury Town" of his poems, near the village of Head Tide where he was born. At the age of seven he was reading Shakespeare, and at eleven he was writing verse. Financial difficulties subsequent to the death of his father brought an end to Robinson's schooling after two years at Harvard. In 1897, following his mother's death, he moved from Gardiner to New York City where he led a simple, hermitlike existence, working at whatever he could get whenever the pinch of poverty became too great, but always writing poetry. In 1916 *The Man Against the Sky* brought him his first real recognition. In his fifties Robinson's belated fame finally arrived. Ironically, however, it is for his early poems, the Tilbury Town portraits such as "Miniver Cheevy" (see pages 587-588), that he is most often acclaimed today. Robinson published over twenty volumes of poetry, and was three times awarded the Pulitzer Prize—for *Collected Poems* in 1922, for *The Man Who Died Twice* in 1925, and for *Tristram* in 1928.

CARL SANDBURG, 1878-

Carl Sandburg, the son of a blacksmith, was born in Galesburg, Illinois, and left school at thirteen to drive a milk wagon. After trying several jobs he took to traveling—hobo style—earning his way in such places as wheat fields and hotel kitchens. It was while he was serving in the Spanish-American War that he decided to get more education, and when his enlistment was up, he worked his way through Lombard College at Galesburg. After that Sandburg became a traveling salesman for stereopticon slides. A few years later he was a journalist, then secretary to Milwaukee's mayor, and in 1912 he drifted to Chicago where he worked on several publications and wrote poetry. In 1916 his first important book, *Chicago Poems*, appeared. This was followed by other collections including *Smoke and Steel* and *The People, Yes*. Sandburg also gained fame as a ballad singer. He appeared on many platforms with his guitar and sang songs collected on his travels. These were published in *The American Songbag* in 1927. But Sandburg's most spectacular task was his biography of Lincoln in two parts—*The Prairie Years* (see "Young Abe Lincoln," pages 617-622), published in 1926, and *The War Years*, published in 1939.

JOHN STEINBECK, 1902-

This foremost novelist of the Great Depression was born in Salinas, California, and grew up in a rich valley where deep impressions were made on him by the strike-tormented agricultural and factory workers. He attended Stanford University for four years as a special student, studying science mostly and developing a lasting interest in marine biology. However, he had already decided to become a writer and was contributing to the university magazines. He later reported on a New York City newspaper for a while. Because his first three books were financial failures, he fell back on such jobs as hod-carrying, surveying, and fruit-picking. In 1935 Steinbeck's popularity began with a book that is said to have been rejected by nine publishers. This was *Tortilla Flat*, a series of stories about Mexicans on the Monterey peninsula. His novelette *Of Mice and Men* became a best seller in 1937, and in 1939 *The Grapes of Wrath*, a novel which dealt with migratory workers, earned the Pulitzer Prize.

RUTH SUCKOW, 1892-

The daughter of a minister, Ruth Suckow was born at Hawarden and spent her childhood in various other towns and cities in Iowa. She went to college at Grinnell, Iowa, for three years, attended dramatic school in Boston, and obtained her master's degree from the University of Denver where she taught literature for a year. While there Miss Suckow developed an interest in beekeeping which later led to her operating her own beeyard in Iowa for six years. Meanwhile she was writing short stories and getting them published. In 1924 her first novel, *The Country People*, appeared. And that was followed by other novels and some fine collections of stories such as *Iowa Interiors*, in which "Four Generations" (pages 112-119) appeared. Miss Suckow is an outstanding regional writer, mostly setting her scenes in the Midwest and writing about German immigrants, like her grandparents, who settled there.

THORNTON WILDER, 1897-

Thornton Wilder was born in Madison, Wisconsin, and when he was nine years old was taken to China where his father held posts as Consul-General. He went to college in California, then at Oberlin, Ohio, and was graduated from Yale in 1920, after having served for a year in World War I. He next studied for a while in Rome, taught French, and obtained his master's degree from Princeton in 1925. That year his first novel, *The Cabala*, was published, and a year later his first play, *The Trumpet Shall Sound*, was produced. Neither of these works made much impression on the general public, but in 1927 *The Bridge of San Luis Rey*, a novel, won the Pulitzer Prize and became a best seller. Wilder continued to write and travel abroad. He went on lecture tours and spent some time as a University of Chicago lecturer before settling in New Haven, Connecticut. Since 1935 Wilder has pretty much devoted himself to writing plays and has won two Pulitzer Prizes in that field—for *Our Town* in 1938 and for *The Skin of Our Teeth* in 1943.

THOMAS WOLFE, 1900-1938

Thomas Wolfe's father was a stonecutter; his mother, a boarding-house keeper. He was born in Asheville, North Carolina, and grew up there until, at the age of fifteen, he entered the University of North Carolina, from which he was graduated in 1920. He then went to Harvard where, while obtaining his master's degree, he developed a longing to become a playwright. Soon discovering that his success did not rest in the field of writing plays, he turned to teaching at New York University, traveling abroad, and writing prose with such intensity that he often wrote most of the night after teaching all day, with brief time out for consuming canned beans and coffee. In 1929 his first book, *Look Homeward, Angel*, was published and met with a spectacular reception. On this book and on *Of Time and the River, The Web and the Rock*, and *You Can't Go Home Again* Wolfe's reputation as a great romantic genius rests securely.

Changing Literary Patterns

IN THE FIRST three divisions of this book, you have seen how literature has pictured the story of our nation's growth, voiced the hopes and ideals of the American people, and expressed the varied personalities of our great authors. Now in the last division of the book you are to see how certain types of our literature developed and how these types were influenced by the changing way of life of the American people.

More than three centuries have passed since little bands of colonists began to settle the eastern seaboard. During this period, the audiences for which literature was written have changed greatly. Great modifications have taken place in American tastes, ways of living, ways of enjoying leisure time. In early colonial days, only a small part of the population learned to read, but as educational opportunities increased, greater and greater proportions learned. A small, select audience therefore was gradually supplanted by a vast democratic one with widely varying backgrounds and interests. The pious colonists read the Bible, sermons, and instructive books; they shunned fiction and looked on the theater as wicked. But their descendants came in time to consider fiction, drama, movies, and radio and television shows worth while. A century ago the ordinary man worked from dawn to dusk; today his great-grandchildren have ample leisure time for reading of all forms of literature.

As the audience changed, new mediums of literary expression became popular and old mediums developed new tendencies. Newspapers and magazines, unknown in the wilderness colonies, were founded and published in ever-increasing numbers. The theater discarded candlelight for gaslight, gaslight for electric light; and with each change playwrights arose to produce entertainment for larger and larger audiences. The motion picture, the radio, and television encouraged writers to hit upon brand-new ways to tell stories through pictures and sounds. The field of literature was broadened by the lifting of puritanic restrictions, by the discoveries of scientists, and by the studies in human behavior made by psychologists and sociologists. Short stories, biographies, novels, essays, poetry, and scientific works all began to reflect the new knowledge and the new interests of the reading audience.

This section of *The United States in Literature* will show you some aspects of our literary history in the short story, lyric poetry, humor, biography, and drama.

UNIT XIII: THE AMERICAN SHORT STORY

SHORT STORIES are so commonplace in our magazines and books today that we have trouble conceiving of a time when readers did not find them everywhere. Yet the short story—in American literature and in world literature as well—did not become an outstanding type until about a century and a half ago. Up to the early years of the nineteenth century, longer works of fiction, essays, and poems were the types that literary people liked best.

The writers of our country in the early nineteenth century, interestingly enough, played an important part in giving the short story a high place in popularity all over the world. One reason was that several Americans with real talent for this form happened to be launching their careers in that period. Another reason was that the market for short stories, as a rule, was better than that for essays, poems, or novels. Periodicals of several kinds, particularly daily newspapers, monthly magazines, and annual "gift books," created a demand which authors were happy to supply.

You will remember that Washington Irving, whom you studied in Unit VIII (pages 322-359), was one of the earliest great American authors. When he began to write, the essay—the chief charm of which was the expression of the author's personality—was still very popular. Irving wrote many delightful essays, among them "Christmas" (pages 333-342), but he also modified the essay in the direction of the short story. "For my part," he wrote a friend, "I consider a story [i.e., the plot] merely as a frame on which to stretch the materials; it is the play of thought, and sentiment, and language, the weaving in of characters, lightly, yet expressively delineated; the familiar and faithful exhibition of scenes in common life, and the half-concealed vein of humor that is often playing through the whole—these are among what I aim at...." Irving's success in writing a story according to this definition is proved by such a tale as "The Devil and Tom Walker" (pages 344-351). Although in this story, as in "Rip Van Winkle," "The Legend of Sleepy Hollow," and others by Irving, the readers were interested in the events unfolded, they were even more interested in meeting the charming author who was telling the story.

After Irving, the short story had a gradual development during which a great variety of ways of telling stories was evolved. We shall look,

now, at a number of stories by outstanding authors—Edgar Allan Poe, Nathaniel Hawthorne, Bret Harte, O. Henry, Stephen Crane, and Ernest Hemingway. Each of these authors represents some particular phase in the growth of the short story. Through studying typical stories by these men, we will aim at gaining an understanding of the variety and the artistry of the short story as it has developed in the United States.

I EDGAR ALLAN POE (1809-1849)[1]

Edgar Allan Poe went about his story writing in a very different way from Irving. Poe had a wonderfully logical mind, and when he used it to decide how a tale could best be written, he hit upon a sure-fire formula. The chief aim of a writer of a tale, he reasoned, ought to be to create an effect upon the mind and feelings of a reader. The writer, therefore, should start by deciding what effect he wanted to create. Then, in writing, he should try to make everything that happened, and every word he wrote, help achieve that effect. Two kinds of stories which Poe wrote according to this formula were chiefly responsible for his fame—the detective story (discussed below) and the supernatural tale (discussed on page 502).

Inventor of the Detective Story

Poe really was the inventor of the detective story, which he called the "ratiocinative," or "reasoning," tale. In such a tale, Poe held, the effect intended was "to perplex the curiosity of the reader, and whet his desire for elucidation" (that is, explanation). He therefore invented two devices which helped him achieve this effect—devices which were to be widely used by later detective-story writers. Poe's first device was one that we might call "the device of the baffled friend." He gave his brilliant detective a friend, and had this friend narrate the story. The friend was not very good at solving mysteries. The reader, allowed to see the mysterious happenings through the baffled narrator's eyes, shared his increasing puzzlement. When the narrator had just about concluded that the problem could never be solved, Poe used his second device. This consisted in having the detective disclose his own solution of the mystery and then "elucidate" by unfolding, step by step, the chain of reasoning by which he had ferreted out the truth.

"The Purloined Letter" is a good example of Poe's detective stories.

---

[1]For a biographical sketch of Poe, see page 359. Poe as a poet is discussed on page 549.

The Purloined Letter

EDGAR ALLAN POE

Nil sapientiae odiosius acumine nimio.

—Seneca[1]

AT PARIS, just after dark one gusty evening in the autumn of 18–, I was enjoying the twofold luxury of meditation and a meerschaum, in company with my friend C. Auguste Dupin, in his little back library, or book closet, *au troisième,*[2] No. 33 Rue Dunôt,[3] Faubourg St. Germain.[4] For one hour at least we had maintained a profound silence; while each, to any casual observer, might have seemed intently and exclusively occupied with the curling eddies of smoke that oppressed the atmosphere of the chamber. For myself, however, I was mentally discussing certain topics which had formed matter for conversation between us at an earlier period of the evening; I mean the affair of the Rue Morgue and the mystery attending the murder of Marie Rogêt.[5] I looked upon it, therefore, as something of a coincidence, when the door of our apartment was thrown open and admitted our old acquaintance, Monsieur G—, the Prefect of the Parisian police.[6]

We gave him a hearty welcome; for there was nearly half as much of the entertaining as of the contemptible about the man, and we had not seen him for several years. We had been sitting in the dark, and Dupin now arose for the purpose of lighting a lamp. But he sat down again, without doing so, upon G—'s saying that he had called to ask the opinion of my friend about some official business which had occasioned a great deal of trouble.

"If it is any point requiring reflection," observed Dupin, as he forbore to enkindle the wick, "we shall examine it to better purpose in the dark."

"That is another of your odd notions," said the Prefect, who had a fashion of calling everything "odd" that was beyond his comprehension, and thus lived amid an absolute legion of "oddities."

"Very true," said Dupin, as he supplied his visitor with a pipe and rolled toward him a comfortable chair.

"And what is the difficulty now?" I asked. "Nothing more in the assassination way, I hope?"

"Oh, no; nothing of that nature. The fact is, the business is *very* simple indeed, and I make no doubt that we[7] can manage it sufficiently well ourselves; but then I thought Dupin would

---

[1] "*Nil sapientiae . . . nimio,*" nothing is so odious to wisdom as too great shrewdness. Seneca (sen′i kə), the author of this saying, was a Roman philosopher who lived at about the time of Christ.

[2] *au troisième* (ō trwä′zē yem), on the third floor. Actually this was the fourth floor, as the French begin their count above the ground floor.

[3] *No. 33 Rue Dunôt* (rü′ dʏ nō′). This is the street address. *Rue* is the French word for "street."

[4] *Faubourg St. Germain* (fō bür′ saɴ zhὲr′maɴ′), a section of Paris.

[5] *the affair of the Rue Morgue* (rü môrg′) . . . *Marie Rogêt* (rō zhä′). The reference is to two of Poe's own stories, "The Murders in the Rue Morgue" and "The Mystery of Marie Rogêt."

[6] *a coincidence . . . Monsieur G—, the Prefect of the Parisian police.* Monsieur G—, the head of the Parisian police force, had vainly attempted to solve both the murders in the Rue Morgue and the murder of Marie Rogêt. Both mysteries had been solved by Dupin.

[7] *we,* the Parisian police force.

BREININ

like to hear the details of it, because it is so excessively *odd*."

"Simple and odd," said Dupin.

"Why, yes; and not exactly that, either. The fact is, we have all been a good deal puzzled because the affair *is* so simple, and yet baffles us altogether."

"Perhaps it is the very simplicity of the thing which puts you at fault," said my friend.

"What nonsense you *do* talk!" replied the Prefect, laughing heartily.

"Perhaps the mystery is a little *too* plain," said Dupin.

"Oh, good heavens! who ever heard of such an idea?"

"A little *too* self-evident."

"Ha! ha! ha!—ha! ha! ha!—ho! ho! ho!" roared our visitor, profoundly amused. "Oh, Dupin, you will be the death of me yet!"

"And what, after all, *is* the matter on hand?" I asked.

"Why, I will tell you," replied the Prefect, as he gave a long, steady, and contemplative puff, and settled himself in his chair. "I will tell you in a few words; but, before I begin, let me caution you that this is an affair demanding the greatest secrecy, and that I should most probably lose the position I now hold were it known that I confided it to anyone."

"Proceed," said I.

"Or not," said Dupin.

"Well, then. I have received personal information from a very high quarter that a certain document of the last importance has been purloined from the royal apartments.[8] The individual who purloined it is known. This beyond a

8*the royal apartments.* At the time of the story France was ruled by a king.

doubt; he was seen to take it. It is known, also, that it still remains in his possession."

"How is this known?" asked Dupin.

"It is clearly inferred," replied the Prefect, "from the nature of the document, and from the non-appearance of certain results which would at once arise from its passing *out* of the robber's possession; that is to say, from his employing it as he must design in the end to employ it."

"Be a little more explicit," I said.

"Well, I may venture so far as to say that the paper gives its holder a certain power in a certain quarter where such power is immensely valuable."

"Still I do not quite understand," said Dupin.

"No? Well, the disclosure of the document to a third person, who shall be nameless, would bring in question the honor of a personage of most exalted station; and this fact gives the holder of the document an ascendancy over the illustrious personage whose honor and peace are so jeopardized."

"But this ascendancy," I interposed, "would depend upon the robber's knowledge of the loser's knowledge of the robber. Who would dare—"

"The thief," said G—, "is the Minister D—,[9] who dares all things, those unbecoming, as well as those becoming, a man. The method of the theft was not less ingenious than bold. The document in question—a letter,[10] to be frank—had been received by the personage robbed while alone in the royal boudoir. During its perusal she was suddenly interrupted by the entrance of the other exalted personage, from whom especially it was her wish to conceal it. After a hurried and vain endeavor to thrust it in a drawer, she was forced to place it, open as it was, upon a table. The address, however, was uppermost, and, the contents thus unexposed, the letter escaped notice. At this juncture enters the Minister D—. His lynx eye immediately perceives the paper, recognizes the handwriting

of the address, observes the confusion of the personage addressed, and fathoms her secret. After some business transactions, hurried through in his ordinary manner, he produces a letter somewhat similar to the one in question, opens it, pretends to read it, and then places it close to the other. Again he converses for some fifteen minutes upon the public affairs. At length in taking leave he takes also from the table the letter to which he had no claim. Its rightful owner saw, but of course dared not call attention to the act, in the presence of the third personage, who stood at her elbow. The Minister decamped, leaving his own letter—one of no importance—upon the table."

"Here, then," said Dupin to me, "you have precisely what you demand to make the ascendancy complete—the robber's knowledge of the loser's knowledge of the robber."

"Yes," replied the Prefect; "and the power thus attained has, for some months past, been wielded, for political purposes, to a very dangerous extent. The personage robbed is more thoroughly convinced every day of the necessity of reclaiming her letter. But this, of course, cannot be done openly. In fine, driven to despair, she has committed the matter to me."

"Than whom," said Dupin, amid a perfect whirlwind of smoke, "no more sagacious agent could, I suppose, be desired, or even imagined."

"You flatter me," replied the Prefect; "but it is possible that some such opinion may have been entertained."

"It is clear," said I, "as you observe, that the letter is still in possession of the Minister, since it is this possession—and not any employment of the letter—which bestows the power. With the employment the power departs."

"True," said G—; "and upon this conviction I proceeded. My first care was to make thorough search of the Minister's *hôtel*[11]; and here my chief embarrassment lay in the necessity of searching without his knowledge. Beyond all things, I have been warned of the danger which would result from giving him reason to suspect our design."

[9]*the Minister D—.* This man was the head (minister) of a department in the government.

[10]*a letter.* At the time of the story, letters were written on one side of a sheet of paper, which was then folded and sealed with wax. The address was written upon the outside, no envelope being used.

[11]*hôtel* (ō tel'), home. *Hôtel* is the French word for "private residence."

"But," said I, "you are quite *au fait*[12] in these investigations. The Parisian police have done this thing often before."

"Oh, yes; and for this reason I did not despair. The habits of the Minister gave me, too, a great advantage. He is frequently absent from home all night. His servants are by no means numerous. They sleep at a distance from their master's apartment, and, being chiefly Neapolitans,[13] are readily made drunk. I have keys, as you know, with which I can open any chamber or cabinet in Paris. For three months a night has not passed, during the greater part of which I have not been engaged, personally, in ransacking the D— *hôtel*. My honor is interested, and, to mention a great secret, the reward is enormous. So I did not abandon the search until I had become fully satisfied that the thief is a more astute man than myself. I fancy that I have investigated every nook and corner of the premises in which it is possible that the paper can be concealed."

"But is it not possible," I suggested, "that although the letter may be in possession of the Minister, as it unquestionably is, he may have concealed it elsewhere than upon his own premises?"

"This is barely possible," said Dupin. "The present peculiar condition of affairs at court, and especially of those intrigues in which D— is known to be involved, would render the instant availability of the document—its susceptibility of being produced at a moment's notice—a point of nearly equal importance with its possession."

"Its susceptibility of being produced?" said I.

"That is to say, of being *destroyed*," said Dupin.

"True," I observed; "the paper is clearly then upon the premises. As for its being upon the person of the Minister, we may consider that as out of the question."

"Entirely," said the Prefect. "He has been twice waylaid, as if by footpads, and his person rigorously searched under my own inspection."

"You might have spared yourself this trouble," said Dupin. "D—, I presume, is not altogether a fool, and, if not, must have anticipated these waylayings as a matter of course."

"Not *altogether* a fool," said G—, "but then he's a poet, which I take to be only one remove from a fool."

"True," said Dupin, after a long and thoughtful whiff from his meerschaum, "although I have been guilty of certain doggerel myself."

"Suppose you detail," said I to the Prefect, "the particulars of your search."

"Why, the fact is, we took our time, and we searched *everywhere*. I have had long experience in these affairs. I took the entire building, room by room, devoting the nights of a whole week to each. We examined, first, the furniture of each apartment. We opened every possible drawer; and I presume you know that, to a properly trained police agent, such a thing as a *secret* drawer is impossible. Any man is a dolt who permits a *secret* drawer to escape him in a search of this kind. The thing is *so* plain. There is a certain amount of bulk—of space— to be accounted for in every cabinet. Then we have accurate rules. The fiftieth part of a line could not escape us. After the cabinets we took the chairs. The cushions we probed with the fine, long needles you have seen me employ. From the tables we removed the tops."

"Why so?"

"Sometimes the top of a table, or other similarly arranged piece of furniture, is removed by the person wishing to conceal an article. Then the leg is excavated, the article deposited within the cavity, and the top replaced. The bottoms and tops of bedposts are employed in the same way."

"But could not the cavity be detected by sounding?" I asked.

"By no means, if, when the article is deposited, a sufficient wadding of cotton be placed around it. Besides, in our case we were obliged to proceed without noise."

"But you could not have removed—you could not have taken to pieces *all* articles of furniture in which it would have been possible to make a deposit in the manner you mention. A letter

---

[12]*au fait* (ō fe′), expert. [*French*]
[13]*Neapolitans* (nē′ə pol′ə tənz), natives of Naples in Italy.

may be compressed in a thin spiral roll, and in this form it might be inserted into the rung of a chair, for example. You did not take to pieces all the chairs?"

"Certainly not; but we did better. We examined the rungs of every chair in the *hôtel,* and indeed, the jointings of every description of furniture, by the aid of a most powerful microscope. Had there been any traces of recent disturbance, we should not have failed to detect it instantly. A single grain of gimlet dust, for example, would have been as obvious as an apple. Any disorder in the gluing—any unusual gaping in the joints—would have sufficed to insure detection."

"I presume you looked to the mirrors, between the boards and the plates, and you probed the beds and the bedclothes, as well as the curtains and carpets?"

"That, of course; and when we had absolutely completed every particle of furniture in this way, then we examined the house itself. We divided its entire surface into compartments, which we numbered, so that none might be missed; then we scrutinized each individual square inch throughout the premises, including the two houses immediately adjoining, with the microscope, as before."

"The two houses adjoining!" I exclaimed. "You must have had a great deal of trouble."

"We had; but the reward offered is prodigious."

"You include the *grounds* about the houses?"

"All the grounds are paved with brick. They gave us comparatively little trouble. We examined the moss between the bricks, and found it undisturbed."

"You looked among D——'s papers, of course, and into the books of the library?"

"Certainly; we opened every package and parcel. We not only opened every book, but we turned over every leaf in each volume, not contenting ourselves with a mere shake, according to the fashion of some of our police officers. We also measured the thickness of every book *cover,* with the most accurate admeasurement, and applied to each the most jealous scrutiny of the microscope. Had any of the bindings been recently meddled with, it would have been utterly impossible that the fact should have escaped observation. Some five or six volumes, just from the hands of the binder, we carefully probed, longitudinally, with the needles."

"You explored the floors beneath the carpets?"

"Beyond doubt. We removed every carpet, and examined the boards with the microscope."

"And the paper on the walls?"

"Yes."

"You looked into the cellars?"

"We did."

"Then," I said, "you have been making a miscalculation, and the letter is *not* upon the premises, as you suppose."

"I fear you are right there," said the Prefect. "And now, Dupin, what would you advise me to do?"

"To make a thorough re-search of the premises."

"That is absolutely needless," replied G——. "I am not more sure that I breathe than I am that the letter is not at the *hôtel.*"

"I have no better advice to give you," said Dupin. "You have, of course, an accurate description of the letter?"

"Oh, yes." And here the Prefect, producing a memorandum book, proceeded to read aloud a minute account of the internal, and especially of the external, appearance of the missing document. Soon after finishing the perusal of this description, he took his departure, more entirely depressed in spirits than I had ever known the good gentleman before.

In about a month afterwards he paid us another visit, and found us occupied very nearly as before. He took a pipe and a chair, and entered into some ordinary conversation. At length I said, "Well, but G——, what of the purloined letter? I presume you have at last made up your mind that there is no such thing as overreaching the Minister?"

"Confound him, say I—yes. I made the reexamination, however, as Dupin suggested—but it was all labor lost, as I knew it would be."

"How much was the reward offered, did you say?" asked Dupin.

"Why, a very great deal—a *very* liberal reward. I don't like to say how much precisely;

but one thing I *will* say, that I wouldn't mind giving my individual check for fifty thousand francs[14] to anyone who could obtain me that letter. The fact is, it is becoming of more and more importance every day; and the reward has been lately doubled. If it were trebled, however, I could do no more than I have done."

"Why, yes," said Dupin, drawlingly, between the whiffs of his meerschaum, "I really—think, G——, you have not exerted yourself—to the utmost in this matter. You might—do a little more, I think, eh?"

"How? In what way?"

"Why (puff, puff), you might (puff, puff) employ counsel in the matter, eh (puff, puff, puff)? Do you remember the story they tell of Abernethy[15]?"

"No; hang Abernethy!"

"To be sure! Hang him and welcome. But, once upon a time, a certain rich miser conceived the design of sponging upon this Abernethy for a medical opinion. Getting up, for this purpose, an ordinary conversation in a private company, he insinuated his case to the physician as that of an imaginary individual.

" 'We will suppose,' said the miser, 'that his symptoms are such and such; now, doctor, what would *you* have directed him to take?'

" 'Take!' said Abernethy, 'why, take *advice,* to be sure.' "

"But," said the Prefect, a little discomposed, "I am *perfectly* willing to take advice, and to pay for it. I would *really* give fifty thousand francs to anyone who would aid me in the matter."

"In that case," replied Dupin, opening a drawer and producing a checkbook, "you may as well fill me up a check for the amount mentioned. When you have signed it, I will hand you the letter."

I was astounded. The Prefect appeared absolutely thunderstricken. For some minutes he remained speechless and motionless, looking incredulously at my friend with open mouth and eyes that seemed starting from their sockets.

Then, apparently recovering himself in some measure, he seized a pen, and after several pauses and vacant stares, finally filled up and signed a check for fifty thousand francs, and handed it across the table to Dupin. The latter examined it carefully and deposited it in his pocketbook; then, unlocking an escritoire, took thence a letter and gave it to the Prefect. This functionary grasped it in a perfect agony of joy, opened it with a trembling hand, cast a rapid glance at its contents, and then, scrambling and struggling to the door, rushed at length unceremoniously from the room and from the house.

When he had gone, my friend entered into some explanations.

"The Parisian police," he said, "are exceedingly able in their way. They are persevering, ingenious, cunning, and thoroughly versed in the knowledge which their duties seem chiefly to demand. Thus, when G—— detailed to us his mode of searching the premises at the *Hôtel D——,* I felt entire confidence in his having made a satisfactory investigation—so far as his labors extended."

"So far as his labors extended?" said I.

"Yes," said Dupin. "The measures adopted were not only the best of their kind, but carried out to absolute perfection. Had the letter been deposited within the range of their search, these fellows would, beyond a question, have found it."

I merely laughed—but he seemed quite serious in all that he said.

"The measures, then," he continued, "were good in their kind, and well executed. Their defect lay in their being inapplicable to the case, and to the man. A certain set of highly ingenious resources are, with the Prefect, a sort of Procrustean bed to which he forcibly adapts his designs.[16] But he perpetually errs by being too deep or too shallow for the matter in hand; and many a schoolboy is a better reasoner than he. I knew one about eight years of age, whose success at guessing in the game of 'even and

---

[14]*fifty thousand francs,* almost $10,000 at the time Poe wrote his story.

[15]*Abernethy* (ab′ər nē′thi *or* ab′ər neth′i), a famous but eccentric English surgeon who lived from 1764 to 1831.

[16]*A certain set . . . his designs.* The Procrustean bed takes its name from Procrustes (prō krus′tēz), a robber in Greek mythology, who either stretched his victims or cut off their legs to make them fit the length of his bed. Just as Procrustes tried to make all men fit one bed, so the Prefect tried to use the same devices to solve all problems.

odd' attracted universal admiration. This game is simple, and is played with marbles. One player holds in his hand a number of these toys, and demands of another whether that number is even or odd. If the guess is right, the guesser wins one; if wrong, he loses one.

"The boy to whom I allude won all the marbles of the school. Of course he had some principle of guessing; and this lay in mere observation and admeasurement of the astuteness of his opponents. For example, an arrant simpleton is his opponent, and, holding up his closed hand, asks, 'Are they even or odd?' Our schoolboy replies, 'Odd,' and loses. But upon the second trial he wins, for he then says to himself, 'The simpleton had them even upon the first trial, and his amount of cunning is just sufficient to make him have them odd upon the second; I will therefore guess odd.' He guesses odd, and wins. Now, with a simpleton a degree above the first he would have reasoned thus: 'This fellow finds that in the first instance I guessed odd, and in the second he will propose to himself, upon the first impulse, a simple variation from even to odd, as did the first simpleton. But then a second thought will suggest that this is too simple a variation, and finally he will decide upon putting it even as before. I will therefore guess even.' He guesses even, and wins. Now, this mode of reasoning in the schoolboy, whom his fellows termed 'lucky'—what, in its last analysis, is it?"

"It is merely," I said, "an identification of the reasoner's intellect with that of his opponent."

"It is," said Dupin.

"And the identification," I said, "of the reasoner's intellect with that of his opponent's, depends, if I understand you right, upon the accuracy with which the opponent's intellect is admeasured."

"For its practical value it depends upon this," replied Dupin. "The Prefect and his cohort fail so frequently, first, by default of this identification, and secondly, by ill-admeasurement of the intellect with which they are engaged. They consider only their *own* ideas of ingenuity; and, in searching for anything hidden, they advert only to the modes in which *they* would have hidden it. They are right in this much—

that their own ingenuity is a faithful representative of that of *the mass;* but when the cunning of the individual is diverse in character from their own, the felon foils them, of course. This always happens when the felon's cunning is above their own, and very usually when it is below. They have no variation of principle in their investigations. What, for example, in this case of D——, has been done to vary the principle of action? What is all this boring, and probing, and sounding, and scrutinizing with the microscope, and dividing the surface of the building into registered square inches? What is it all but *the application* of the one principle or set of principles of search, principles which are based upon the one set of notions regarding human ingenuity, to which the Prefect has long been accustomed? Do you not see he has taken it for granted that *all* men proceed to conceal a letter—not exactly in a gimlet hole bored in a chair leg—but, at least in *some* out-of-the-way hole or corner? And do you not see, also, that such *recherché*[17] nooks for concealment are adapted only for ordinary occasions and would be adopted only by ordinary intellects? You will now understand why, had the purloined letter been hidden anywhere within the limits of the Prefect's examination, its discovery would have been a matter altogether beyond question. This functionary, however, has been thoroughly mystified; and the remote source of his defeat lies in the supposition that the Minister is a fool because he has acquired renown as a poet. All fools are poets; this the Prefect *feels,* and he is merely guilty of a *non distributio medii*[18] in thence inferring that all poets are fools."

"But is this really the poet?" I asked. "There are two brothers, I know; and both have attained reputation in letters. The Minister, I believe, has written learnedly on the Differential Calculus.[19] He is a mathematician and no poet."

"You are mistaken; I know him well; he is

---

[17]*recherché* (re shär shā′ or rə shär′shā), carefully thought up; hidden. [*French*]

[18]*non distributio medii* (nōn dis′tri bü′tē ō me′di ē), a Latin phrase meaning a mistake in reasoning known as the undistributed middle term. In this case it means that because the Prefect believes all fools are poets, in his mind it follows that all poets are fools.

[19]*Differential Calculus*, an advanced branch of mathematics.

both. As poet *and* mathematician he would reason well; as mere mathematician he could not have reasoned at all, and thus would have been at the mercy of the Prefect. I know him as courtier, too, and as a bold *intrigant*.[20] Such a man, I considered, could not fail to be aware of the ordinary policial modes of action.[21] He could not have failed to anticipate—and events have proved that he did not fail to anticipate—the waylayings to which he was subjected. He must have foreseen, I reflected, the secret investigations of his premises. His frequent absences from home at night, which were hailed by the Prefect as certain aids to his success, I regarded only as ruses, to afford opportunity for thorough search to the police, and thus the sooner to impress them with the conviction to which G——, in fact, did finally arrive—the conviction that the letter was not upon the premises. I felt, also, that G——'s whole train of thought would necessarily pass through the mind of the Minister. It would imperatively lead him to despise all the ordinary *nooks* of concealment. *He* could not, I reflected, be so weak as not to see that the most intricate and remote recess of his *hôtel* would be as open as his commonest closets to the eyes, to the probes, to the gimlets, and to the microscopes of the Prefect. I saw, in fine, that he would be driven, as a matter of course, to *simplicity*. You will remember, perhaps, how desperately the Prefect laughed when I suggested, upon our first interview, that it was just possible this mystery troubled him so much on account of its being so *very* self-evident."

"Yes," said I, "I remember his merriment well. I really thought he would have fallen into convulsions."

"There is a game of puzzles," continued Dupin, "which is played upon a map. One party playing requires another to find a given word—the name of town, river, state, or empire—any word, in short, upon the motley and perplexed surface of the chart. A novice in the game generally seeks to embarrass his opponents by giving them the most minutely lettered names; but

the adept selects such words as stretch in large characters, from one end of the chart to the other. These, like over-large street signs over shops, escape observation by dint of being excessively obvious. But this is a point, it appears, somewhat above or beneath the understanding of the Prefect. He never once thought it probable, or possible, that the Minister had deposited the letter immediately beneath the nose of the whole world by way of best preventing any portion of that world from perceiving it.

"But the more I reflected upon the daring, dashing, and discriminating ingenuity of the Minister—upon the fact that the document must always have been at *hand,* if he intended to use it to good purpose, and upon the decisive evidence, obtained by the Prefect, that it was not hidden within the limits of that dignitary's ordinary search—the more satisfied I became that, to conceal this letter, the Minister had resorted to the comprehensive and sagacious expedient of not attempting to conceal it at all.

"Full of these ideas, I prepared myself with a pair of green spectacles, and called one fine morning, quite by accident, at the Ministerial *hôtel.* I found D—— at home, yawning, lounging, and dawdling, as usual, and pretending to be in the last extremity of ennui. He is perhaps, the most really energetic human being now alive—but that is only when nobody sees him.

"To be even with him, I complained of my weak eyes and lamented the necessity of the spectacles, under cover of which I cautiously and thoroughly surveyed the whole apartment, while seemingly intent only upon the conversation of my host.

"I paid especial attention to a large writing table near which he sat, and upon which lay confusedly some miscellaneous letters and other papers, with one or two musical instruments and a few books. Here, however, after a long and very deliberate scrutiny, I saw nothing to excite particular suspicion.

"At length my eyes, in going the circuit of the room, fell upon a trumpery filigree card rack of pasteboard, that hung, dangling by a dirty blue ribbon, from a little brass knob just beneath the middle of the mantelpiece. In this rack, which had three or four compartments, were

---

[20]*intrigant* (in′tri gǝnt), intriguer or schemer. [*French*]
[21]*policial modes of action*, methods usually followed by the police.

five or six visiting cards and a solitary letter. This last was much soiled and crumpled. It was torn nearly in two, across the middle—as if a design, in the first instance, to tear it entirely up as worthless had been altered, or stayed, in the second. It had a large black seal, bearing the D— cipher[22] *very* conspicuously, and was addressed, in a diminutive female hand, to D—, the Minister himself. It was thrust carelessly, and even, as it seemed, contemptuously, into one of the upper divisions of the rack.

"No sooner had I glanced at this letter than I concluded it to be that of which I was in search. To be sure, it was, to all appearance, radically different from the one of which the Prefect had read us so minute a description. Here, the seal was large and black, with the D— cipher; there, it was small and red, with the ducal arms of the S— family. Here, the address, to the Minister, was diminutive and feminine; there, the superscription, to a certain royal personage, was markedly bold and decided. The size alone formed a point of correspondence. But, then, the *radicalness* of these differences, which was excessive—the dirt, the soiled and torn condition of the paper, so inconsistent with the *true*, methodical habits of D—, and so suggestive of a design to delude the beholder into an idea of the worthlessness of the document—these things, together with the hyperobtrusive situation of this document, full in the view of every visitor, were exactly in accordance with the conclusions to which I had previously arrived.

"I protracted my visit as long as possible, and while I maintained a most animated discussion with the Minister, upon a topic which I knew well had never failed to interest and excite him, I kept my attention really riveted upon the letter. In this examination, I committed to memory its external appearance and arrangement in the rack; and I also fell, at length, upon a discovery which set at rest whatever trivial doubt I might have entertained. In scrutinizing the edges of the paper, I observed them to be more *chafed* than seemed necessary.

They presented the *broken* appearance which is manifested when a stiff paper, having been once folded and pressed with a folder, is refolded in a reversed direction, in the same creases or edges which had formed the original fold. This discovery was sufficient. It was clear to me that the letter had been turned, as a glove, inside out, redirected, and resealed. I bade the Minister good morning, and took my departure at once, leaving a gold snuffbox upon the table.

"The next morning I called for the snuffbox, when we resumed, quite eagerly, the conversation of the preceding day. While thus engaged, however, a loud report, as if of a pistol, was heard immediately beneath the windows of the *hôtel,* and was succeeded by a series of fearful screams and the shoutings of a mob. D— rushed to a casement, threw it open, and looked out. In the meantime, I stepped to the card rack, took the letter, put it in my pocket, and replaced it by a facsimile, so far as regards externals— which I had carefully prepared at my lodgings —imitating the D— cipher very readily by means of a seal formed of bread.

"The disturbance in the street had been occasioned by the frantic behavior of a man with a musket. He had fired it among a crowd of women and children. It proved, however, to have been without ball, and the fellow was suffered to go his way as a lunatic or a drunkard. When he had gone, D— came from the window, whither I had followed him immediately upon securing the object in view. Soon afterwards I bade him farewell. The pretended lunatic was a man in my own pay."

"But what purpose had you," I asked, "in replacing the letter by a facsimile? Would it not have been better, at the very first, to have seized it openly and departed?"

"D—," replied Dupin, "is a desperate man, and a man of nerve. His *hôtel,* too, is not without attendants devoted to his interest. Had I made the wild attempt you suggest, I might never have left the Ministerial presence alive. The good people of Paris might have heard of me no more. But I had an object apart from these considerations. You know my political prepossessions. In this matter I act as a partisan

---

[22] *a large black seal...D— cipher.* The seal of black sealing wax, which had been used to fasten the letter, was imprinted with the monogram (cipher) of the D— family.

of the lady concerned. For eighteen months the Minister has had her in his power. She has now him in hers—since, being unaware that the letter is not in his possession, he will proceed with his exactions as if it was. Thus will he inevitably commit himself at once to his political destruction. His downfall, too, will not be more precipitate than awkward. It is all very well to talk about the *facilis descensus Averni*[23]; but in all kinds of climbing, as Catalani[24] said of singing, it is far more easy to get up than to come down. In the present instance I have no sympathy—at least no pity—for him who descends. He is that *monstrum horrendum,*[25] an unprincipled man of genius.

"I confess, however, that I should like very well to know the precise character of his thoughts, when, being defied by her whom the Prefect terms 'a certain personage,' he is reduced to opening the letter which I left for him in the card rack."

"How? Did you put anything particular in it?"

"Why—it did not seem altogether right to leave the interior blank—that would have been insulting. D——, at Vienna once, did me an evil turn, which I told him, quite good-humoredly, that I should remember. So, as I knew he would feel some curiosity in regard to the identity of the person who had outwitted him, I thought it a pity not to give him a clue. He is well acquainted with my manuscript,[26] and I copied into the middle of the blank sheet the words:
　　　　　　　—Un dessein si funeste,
　S'il n'est digne d'Atrée, est digne de Thyeste.[27]

They are to be found in Crébillon's *Atrée.*"[28]

---

[23]*facilis descensus Averni* (fä′ki lis dā skān′səs ə wėr′nē), easy is the descent to Avernus (the Lower World). This famous old saying is from Virgil's *Aeneid.*

[24]*Catalani* (kä′tä lä′nē), a famous Italian soprano, who lived from 1779 to 1849.

[25]*monstrum horrendum* (mōn′strum hôr ren′dum), dreadful monster. The Latin words are from Virgil's *Aeneid.*

[26]*my manuscript,* my handwriting.

[27]"*Un dessein...digne de Thyeste,*" so evil a plan, if not worthy of Atreus (ā′trüs *or* ā′tri əs), is worthy of Thyestes (thī es′tēz). In Greek mythology the brothers Atreus and Thyestes are symbols of savagery and treachery.

[28]*Crébillon's* (krā′bē yonz′) "*Atrée*" (ä trā′). *Atrée,* which tells the story of Atreus, was written by the French tragic poet, Prosper J. de Crébillon (1674–1762).

HOW GOOD IS YOUR "RATIOCINATION"?

1. What did Poe believe should be the effect of the ratiocinative, or reasoning, tale? In your opinion did he succeed in "The Purloined Letter" in achieving this effect?

2. In many stories the author sets down happenings according to their order in time. Poe once pointed out, however, that in a ratiocinative tale the author may deliberately perplex the reader by *not* presenting incidents in the order of their occurrence. Write on the blackboard the main events in the story in the order in which they actually occurred. Point out how Poe changed this order and the way the changes contributed to the effect he wished to create.

3. At what point in the story did you realize that neither Dupin nor the narrator thinks highly of the Prefect's ability? Why, according to Dupin, is the Prefect unable to find the missing letter?

4. Early in the story Dupin suggests to the Prefect that the mystery is "a little *too* self-evident." What clue does this statement provide to Dupin's reasoning in solving the mystery? Trace the steps in his reasoning process from the time he first hears of the missing letter until the time he recovers it.

5. There is at least one serious logical flaw in the story which you may discover from Dupin's statement: "It [the letter] had a large black seal, bearing the D—— cipher *very* conspicuously, and was addressed, in a diminutive feminine hand, to D——, the Minister himself" (page 500). What is the flaw here? Do you consider this flaw serious enough to spoil the story? Can you find any other flaws?

6. Of what value is the use of "the device of the baffled friend" in this story? In what ways does the baffled narrator help the reader? How would the tale differ if it were told by either Dupin or by an author who revealed the thoughts of the detective from the very beginning? Do you think you would like the story as well if it were told in either of these ways? Why, or why not?

Know your words

There's a certain amount of detective work involved in figuring out the meaning of a word by studying its context. Check your skill at this kind of problem solving by rewriting the following sentences, making the meaning clear without using the italicized words. You may use the Glossary as a check on the correctness of your work.

1. The *disclosure* of the document to a third person ...would bring in question the honor of a personage of most *exalted station;* and this fact gives the holder of the document an *ascendancy* over the *illustrious* personage whose honor and peace are so *jeopardized.*

2. The Parisian police...are *persevering, ingenious,* cunning, and thoroughly *versed* in the knowledge which their duties seem chiefly to demand.

3. Here, the address, to the Minister, was *diminutive* and feminine; there, the *superscription,* to a certain royal personage, was *markedly bold* and decided.

4. In the meantime, I stepped to the card rack, took the letter, put it in my pocket, and replaced it by a *facsimile,* so far as regards *externals*—which I had carefully prepared at my lodgings—imitating the D—— cipher very readily by means of a seal formed of bread.

Extending interests

One of Poe's most famous disciples in the field of the detective story was Sir Arthur Conan Doyle, whose sleuth, Sherlock Holmes, has become even more widely known than his creator. You will find it interesting to point out points of comparison between some Sherlock Holmes story known to the class and "The Purloined Letter." A comparison of the Holmes adventure "A Scandal in Bohemia" with "The Purloined Letter" would be particularly interesting, since some of the details in Doyle's story were suggested by Poe's tale.

Poe as a Writer of Supernatural Tales

Besides being supreme as a teller of detective stories, Poe excelled in another form of the short story—the tale of the supernatural. Among the best of his supernatural stories are "Berenice," "Shadow," "Ligeia," and the tale printed on pages 503-513, "The Fall of the House of Usher."

Poe's supernatural tales were not, as some believe, the products of a disordered mind, or of a mind stimulated by drink and drugs. Horror stories—"Gothic tales" as they were then called—were all the rage in Poe's day, and he wrote them to satisfy a definite demand. But Poe's supernatural stories have been remembered, while others of his day have been forgotten. The reason is simply that he had a well-worked-out formula for writing them, and he used it with great skill and imagination, while most other authors were satisfied with less effective methods.

As in writing his detective stories, Poe constructed each of his Gothic tales according to a pattern—a pattern which he explained in an article on the art of writing stories and poems. First of all, Poe said, the storyteller must decide upon the effect he wishes to achieve, such as terror or horror. Then everything in the tale—every incident, every combination of events, every word—must be chosen for its aid in establishing this chosen effect. If the author succeeds in this aim, the mood of his story will be successfully and powerfully transferred to the mind of the reader.

In "The Fall of the House of Usher" we can observe clearly Poe's methods of creating in the mind of the reader the mood chosen by the author. For one thing, Poe has one of the characters (comparable to the "I" in "The Purloined Letter") narrate the story. This narrator is an intelligent, normal, level-headed man. Yet as the story opens he experiences an unexplained feeling of oppression—a feeling that the reader finds himself sharing. And as the story continues, the reader comes more and more to feel the same spell of terror that haunts the narrator.

A second way in which Poe creates a particular mood in the mind of the reader is found in his choice of words. Poe knew, as few men do, the power of words to suggest emotion as well as meaning. As you read "The Fall of the House of Usher" you will observe again and again the power of Poe's words to suggest the things he wants you to see and hear, the emotions he wants you to feel.

The Fall of the House of Usher

EDGAR ALLAN POE

DURING THE WHOLE of a dull, dark, and soundless day in the autumn of the year, when the clouds hung oppressively low in the heavens, I had been passing alone, on horseback, through a singularly dreary tract of country. At length I found myself, as the shades of the evening drew on, within view of the melancholy House of Usher. I know not how it was —but, with the first glimpse of the building, a sense of insufferable gloom pervaded my spirit. I say insufferable, for the feeling was unrelieved by any of that half-pleasurable, because poetic, sentiment with which the mind usually receives even the sternest natural images of the desolate or terrible. I looked upon the scene before me —upon the mere house, and the simple landscape features of the domain, upon the bleak walls, upon the vacant eye-like windows, upon a few rank sedges, and upon a few white trunks of decayed trees—with an utter depression of soul which I can compare to no earthly sensation more properly than to the after-dream of the reveler upon opium: the bitter lapse into everyday life, the hideous dropping off of the veil. There was an iciness, a sinking, a sickening of the heart, an unredeemed dreariness of thought which no goading of the imagination could torture into aught of the sublime. What was it—I paused to think—what was it that so unnerved me in the contemplation of the House of Usher? It was a mystery all insoluble; nor could I grapple with the shadowy fancies that crowded upon me as I pondered. I was forced to fall back upon the unsatisfactory conclusion that while, beyond doubt, there *are* combinations of very simple natural objects which have the power of thus affecting us, still the analysis of this power lies among considerations beyond our depth. It was possible, I reflected, that a mere different arrangement of the details of the picture would be sufficient to modify, or perhaps to annihilate, its capacity for sorrowful impression. Acting upon this idea, I reined my horse to the precipitous brink of a black and lurid tarn that lay in unruffled luster by the dwelling, and gazed down—but with a shudder even more thrilling than before—upon the remodeled and inverted images of the gray sedge, and the ghastly tree stems, and the vacant and eye-like windows.

Nevertheless, in this mansion of gloom I now proposed to myself a sojourn of some weeks. Its proprietor, Roderick Usher, had been one of my boon companions in boyhood; but many years had elapsed since our last meeting. A letter, however, had lately reached me in a distant part of the country—a letter from him—which in its wildly importunate nature had admitted of no other than a personal reply. The MS.[1] gave evidence of nervous agitation. The writer spoke of acute bodily illness, of a mental disorder which oppressed him, and of an earnest desire to see me, as his best, and indeed his only, personal friend, with a view of attempting, by the cheerfulness of my society, some alleviation of his malady. It was the manner in which all this, and much more, was said—it was the apparent *heart* that went with his request—which allowed me no room for hesitation. I accordingly obeyed forthwith what I still considered a very singular summons.

Although as boys we had been even intimate associates, yet I really knew little of my friend. His reserve had been always excessive and habitual. I was aware, however, that his very ancient family had been noted, time out of mind, for a peculiar sensibility of temperament, displaying itself in many works of exalted art, and manifested of late in repeated deeds of unobtrusive charity, as well as in a passionate devotion to the intricacies of musical science. I had learned, too, the very remarkable fact that the stem of the Usher race, all time-honored as it was, had put forth at no period any enduring branch. In other words, the entire family lay in the direct line of descent, and had always, with very trifling and very temporary variation, so lain. It was this deficiency, perhaps, of collateral issue, and the consequent undeviating transmission from sire to son of the patrimony with the name, which had, at length, so identified the two as to merge the original title of the

[1] *MS.*, manuscript.

estate in the quaint and equivocal appellation of the "House of Usher"—an appellation which seemed to include, in the minds of the peasantry who used it, both the family and the family mansion.[2]

[2]*It was this deficiency . . . family mansion.* Since the Ushers' property had passed on directly from father to son for many generations (never to any collateral heir, such as a nephew or niece of another name), the term "House of Usher" had come to mean both the house and the family.

I have said that the sole effect of my somewhat childish experiment, that of looking down within the tarn, had been to deepen the first singular impression. When I again uplifted my eyes to the house itself from its image in the pool, there grew in my mind a strange fancy—a fancy so ridiculous, indeed, that I but mention it to show the vivid force of the sensations which oppressed me. I had so worked upon my imag-

ination as really to believe that about the whole
mansion and domain there hung an atmosphere
peculiar to themselves and their immediate vicinity. It was an atmosphere which had no
affinity with the air of heaven, but which had
reeked up from the decayed trees, and the gray
wall, and the silent tarn; a pestilent and mystic
vapor, dull, sluggish, faintly discernible, and
leaden-hued.

Shaking off from my spirit what *must* have been a dream, I scanned more narrowly the real aspect of the building. Its principal feature seemed to be that of an excessive antiquity. The discoloration of ages had been great. Minute fungi overspread the whole exterior, hanging in a fine tangled web-work from the eaves. Yet all this was apart from any extraordinary dilapidation. No portion of the masonry had fallen; and there appeared to be a wild inconsistency between its still perfect adaptation of parts and the crumbling condition of the individual stones. Beyond this indication of extensive decay, however, the fabric gave little token of instability. Perhaps the eye of a scrutinizing observer might have discovered a barely perceptible fissure, which, extending from the roof of the building in front, made its way down the wall in a zigzag direction, until it became lost in the sullen waters of the tarn.

Noticing these things, I rode over a short causeway to the house. A servant took my horse, and I entered the Gothic archway[3] of the hall. A valet, of stealthy step, thence conducted me, in silence, through many dark and intricate passages to the studio of his master. Much that I encountered on the way contributed, I know not how, to heighten the vague sentiments of which I have already spoken. While the objects around me—while the carvings of the ceilings, the somber tapestries of the walls, the ebon blackness of the floors, and the phantasmagoric armorial trophies which rattled as I strode, were but matters such as I had been accustomed to from my infancy, I still wondered to find how unfamiliar were the fancies which ordinary images were stirring up. On one of the staircases, I met the physician of the family. His countenance, I thought, wore a mingled expression of low cunning and perplexity. He accosted me with trepidation and passed on. The valet now threw open a door and ushered me into the presence of his master.

The room in which I found myself was very large and lofty. The windows were long, narrow, and pointed, and at a vast distance from the black oaken floor. Feeble gleams of en-crimsoned light made their way through the trellised panes, and served to render sufficiently distinct the more prominent objects around. The eye, however, struggled in vain to reach the remoter angles of the chamber, or the recesses of the vaulted and fretted ceiling. Dark draperies hung upon the walls. The general furniture was profuse, comfortless, antique, and tattered. Many books and musical instruments lay scattered about, but failed to give any vitality to the scene. I felt that I breathed an atmosphere of sorrow. An air of stern, deep, and irredeemable gloom hung over and pervaded all.

Upon my entrance, Usher arose from a sofa on which he had been lying at full length. He greeted me with a vivacious warmth which had much in it, I at first thought, of an overdone cordiality—of the constrained effort of the *ennuyé*[4] man of the world. A glance, however, at his countenance convinced me of his perfect sincerity. We sat down; and for some moments, while he spoke not, I gazed upon him with a feeling half of pity, half of awe. Surely man had never before so terribly altered, in so brief a period, as had Roderick Usher! It was with difficulty that I could bring myself to admit the identity of the wan being before me with the companion of my early boyhood. Yet the character of his face had been at all times remarkable: a cadaverousness of complexion; an eye, large, liquid, and luminous beyond comparison; lips somewhat thin and very pallid, but of a surpassingly beautiful curve; a nose of a delicate Hebrew model, but with a breadth of nostril unusual in similar formations; a finely molded chin, speaking, in its want of prominence, of a want of moral energy; hair of a more than web-like softness and tenuity. These features made up altogether a countenance not easily to be forgotten. And now in the mere exaggeration of the prevailing character of these features, and of the expression they were wont to convey, lay so much of change that I doubted to whom I spoke. The now ghastly pallor of the skin, and the now miraculous luster of the eye, above all things startled and even awed me. The silken

---

[3]*Gothic archway*, a pointed arch like those used by the cathedral builders of the later Middle Ages in Europe.

[4]*ennuyé* (än wē ā′), bored. [*French*]

hair, too, had been suffered to grow all un-heeded, and as, in its wild, gossamer texture, it floated rather than fell about the face, I could not, even with effort, connect its arabesque ex-pression with any idea of simple humanity.[5]

In the manner of my friend I was at once struck with an incoherence, an inconsistency. I soon found this to arise from a series of feeble and futile struggles to overcome an excessive nervous agitation. For something of this nature I had indeed been prepared, no less by his let-ter than by reminiscences of certain boyish traits. His action was alternately vivacious and sullen. His voice varied rapidly from a tremu-lous indecision, when the animal spirits seemed utterly in abeyance, to energetic concision, dur-ing the periods of his most intense excitement.

It was with the latter voice that he spoke of the object of my visit, of his earnest desire to see me, and of the solace he expected me to afford him. He entered, at some length, into what he conceived to be the nature of his malady. It was, he said, a constitutional and a family evil, and one for which he despaired to find a remedy—a mere nervous affection, he im-mediately added, which would undoubtedly soon pass off. It displayed itself in a host of unnat-ural sensations. He suffered much from a mor-bid acuteness of the senses: the most insipid food was alone endurable; he could wear only garments of certain texture; the odors of all flowers were oppressive; his eyes were tortured by even a faint light; and there were but pecul-iar sounds, and these from stringed instru-ments, which did not inspire him with horror.

To an anomalous species of terror I found him a bounden slave. "I shall perish," said he, "I *must* perish in this deplorable folly. Thus, thus, and not otherwise, shall I be lost. I dread the events of the future, not in themselves, but in their results. I shudder at the thought of any, even the most trivial, incident, which may oper-ate upon this intolerable agitation of soul. I have, indeed, no abhorrence of danger, except in its absolute effect—in terror. In this unnerved —in this pitiable condition, I feel that the period

will sooner or later arrive when I must abandon life and reason together, in some struggle with the grim phantasm, FEAR."

I learned, moreover, at intervals, and through broken hints, another singular feature of his mental condition. He was enchained by certain superstitious impressions in regard to the dwell-ing which he tenanted—and whence, for many years, he had never ventured forth—an influence which some peculiarities in the mere form and substance of his family mansion, had, he said, obtained over his spirit—an effect which the physique of the gray walls and turrets, and of the dim tarn into which they all looked down, had, at length, brought about upon the morale of his existence.

He admitted, however, although with hesita-tion, that much of the peculiar gloom which thus afflicted him could be traced to a more natural origin—to the severe and long-continued illness, indeed to the evidently approaching dis-solution, of a tenderly beloved sister—his sole companion for long years, his last and only rela-tive on earth. Her decease, he said, with a bit-terness which I can never forget, would leave him—him the hopeless and the frail—the last of the ancient race of the Ushers. While he spoke, the lady Madeline, for so was she called, passed slowly through a remote portion of the apart-ment, and, without having noticed my presence, disappeared. I regarded her with an utter aston-ishment not unmingled with dread, and yet I found it impossible to account for such feelings. A sensation of stupor oppressed me, as my eyes followed her retreating steps. When a door, at length, closed upon her, my glance sought in-stinctively and eagerly the countenance of the brother. But he had buried his face in his hands, and I could only perceive that a far more than ordinary wanness had overspread the emaciated fingers through which trickled many passionate tears.

The disease of the lady Madeline had long baffled the skill of her physicians. A settled apathy, a gradual wasting away of the person, and frequent, although transient, affections of a partially cataleptical character, were the un-usual diagnosis. Hitherto she had steadily borne up against the pressure of her malady, and had

---

[5] *I could not ... humanity,* I could see no resemblance between the fantastic (arabesque) expression of Usher's face and that of ordinary men.

not betaken herself finally to bed. But, on the closing in of the evening of my arrival at the house, she succumbed, as her brother told me at night with inexpressible agitation, to the prostrating power of the destroyer. I learned that the glimpse I had obtained of her person would thus probably be the last I should obtain.

For several days ensuing, her name was unmentioned by either Usher or myself; and during this period I was busied in earnest endeavors to alleviate the melancholy of my friend. We painted and read together; or I listened, as if in a dream, to the wild improvisations of his speaking guitar. And thus, as a closer and still closer intimacy admitted me more unreservedly into the recesses of his spirit, the more bitterly did I perceive the futility of all attempt at cheering a mind from which darkness poured forth upon all objects of the moral and physical universe, in one unceasing radiation of gloom.

I shall ever bear about me a memory of the many solemn hours I thus spent alone with the master of the House of Usher. Yet I should fail in any attempt to convey an idea of the exact character of the studies, or of the occupations, in which he involved me. His long, improvised dirges will ring forever in my ears. Among other things, I hold painfully in mind a certain singular perversion and amplification of the wild air of the last waltz of Von Weber.[6] From the paintings over which his elaborate fancy brooded, and which grew, touch by touch, into vaguenesses at which I shuddered, I would in vain endeavor to educe more than a small portion which should lie within the compass of merely written words.[7] By the utter simplicity, by the nakedness of his designs, he arrested and overawed attention. If ever mortal painted an idea, that mortal was Roderick Usher. For me at least, there arose, out of the pure abstractions which the hypochondriac contrived to throw upon his canvas, an intensity of intolerable awe.

One of the phantasmagoric conceptions of my friend may be shadowed forth, although feebly, in words. A small picture presented the interior of an immensely long and rectangular vault or tunnel, with low walls, smooth, white, and without interruption or device. Certain accessory points of the design served well to convey the idea that this excavation lay at an exceeding depth below the surface of the earth. No outlet was observed in any portion of its vast extent, and no torch or other artificial source of light was discernible; yet a flood of intense rays bathed the whole in a ghastly and inappropriate splendor.

I have just spoken of that morbid condition which rendered all music intolerable to the sufferer, with the exception of certain effects of stringed instruments. It was, perhaps, the narrow limits to which he thus confined himself upon the guitar, which gave birth, in great measure, to the fantastic character of his performances. But the fervid *facility* of his impromptus could not be so accounted for. They must have been, and were, in the notes, as well as in the words of his wild fantasias—for he not unfrequently accompanied himself with rhymed verbal improvisations. The words of one of these rhapsodies I have easily remembered. I was, perhaps, the more forcibly impressed with it, as he gave it, because, in the under or mystic current of its meaning, I fancied that I perceived, and for the first time, a full consciousness, on the part of Usher, of the tottering of his lofty reason upon her throne. The verses, which were entitled "The Haunted Palace," ran very nearly, if not accurately, thus:

> In the greenest of our valleys
>   By good angels tenanted,
> Once a fair and stately palace—
>   Radiant palace—reared its head.
> In the monarch Thought's dominion,
>   It stood there;
> Never seraph spread a pinion
>   Over fabric half so fair.
>
> Banners yellow, glorious, golden,
>   On its roof did float and flow—
> This—all this—was in the olden
>   Time long ago—
> And every gentle air that dallied,
>   In that sweet day,
> Along the ramparts plumed and pallid,
>   A wingèd odor went away.

---

[6]*Von Weber* (fon vā′bər), a German composer who lived from 1786 to 1826.

[7]*I would in vain . . . written words.* Words are inadequate to describe most of Usher's highly imaginative paintings.

Wanderers in that happy valley
Through two luminous windows saw
Spirits moving musically
To a lute's well-tunèd law,
Round about a throne where, sitting,
Porphyrogene,[8]
In state his glory well-befitting,
The ruler of the realm was seen.

And all with pearl and ruby glowing
Was the fair palace door,
Through which came flowing, flowing, flowing,
And sparkling evermore,
A troop of Echoes whose sweet duty
Was but to sing,
In voices of surpassing beauty,
The wit and wisdom of their king.

But evil things, in robes of sorrow,
Assailed the monarch's high estate;
(Ah, let us mourn, for never morrow
Shall dawn upon him, desolate!)
And round about his home the glory
That blushed and bloomed
Is but a dim-remembered story
Of the old time entombed.

And travelers now within that valley
Through the red-litten[9] windows see
Vast forms that move fantastically
To a discordant melody;
While, like a ghastly rapid river,
Through the pale door
A hideous throng rush out forever,
And laugh—but smile no more.

I well remember that suggestions arising from this ballad led us into a train of thought, wherein there became manifest an opinion of Usher's which he maintained with great pertinacity. This opinion, in its general form, was that of the sentience of all vegetable things.[10] But in his disordered fancy the idea had assumed a more daring character, and trespassed, under certain conditions, upon the kingdom of inorganization.[11] I lack words to express the full extent or the earnest *abandon* of his persuasion. The belief, however, was connected, as I have pre-viously hinted, with the gray stones of the home of his forefathers. The conditions of the sentience had been here, he imagined, fulfilled in the method of collocation of these stones—in the order of their arrangement, as well as in that of the many fungi which overspread them, and of the decayed trees which stood around—above all, in the long undisturbed endurance of this arrangement, and in its reduplication in the still waters of the tarn. Its evidence—the evidence of the sentience—was to be seen, he said (and I here started as he spoke), in the gradual, yet certain condensation of an atmosphere of their own about the waters and the walls. The result was discoverable, he added, in that silent yet terrible influence which for centuries had molded the destinies of his family, and which made *him* what I now saw him—what he was. Such opinions need no comment, and I will make none.

Our books—the books which, for years, had formed no small portion of the mental existence of the invalid—were, as might be supposed, in strict keeping with this character of phantasm. We pored together over such works as the *Ververt* and *Chartreuse* of Gresset[12]; the *Belphegor* of Machiavelli; the *Heaven and Hell* of Swedenborg; the *Subterranean Voyage of Nicholas Klimmer* by Holberg; the *Chiromancy* of Robert Flud, of Jean D'Indaginé, and of De La Chambre; the *Journey into the Blue Distance* of Tieck; and the *City of the Sun* of Campanella. One favorite volume was a small octavo edition of the *Directorium Inquisitorum* by the Dominican Eymeric de Gironne, and there were passages in Pomponius Mela, about the old African Satyrs and Ægipans,[13] over which Usher would sit dreaming for hours. His chief delight, however, was found in the perusal of an exceedingly rare and curious book in quarto Gothic[14]—the manual of a forgotten church.

---

[8]*Porphyrogene* (pôr′fi rō jēn′), of a royal house or "born to the purple." The word *porphyrogene* is derived from *porphyry*, the name for a sort of purple rock.
[9]*red-litten*, red-lighted.
[10]*the sentience* (sen′shəns) *of all vegetable things*, the ability of all plants to feel.
[11]*the kingdom of inorganization*, the mineral world.

[12]*the "Ververt"* (vär vär′) *and "Chartreuse"* (shär trœz′) *of Gresset* (gre′se′). Gresset was a French poet of the eighteenth century. The works of his mentioned here, as well as all the others listed in the paragraph, dealt with mystical or supernatural ideas.
[13]*Ægipans* (ē′gi panz′), creatures with horns, ears, and legs like goats.
[14]*in quarto Gothic*, with large pages printed in heavy black type.

I could not help thinking of the wild ritual of this manual, and of its probable influence upon the hypochondriac, when one evening, having informed me abruptly that the lady Madeline was no more, he stated his intention of preserving her corpse for a fortnight, previously to its final interment, in one of the numerous vaults within the main walls of the building. The worldly reason, however, assigned for this singular proceeding was one which I did not feel at liberty to dispute. The brother had been led to his resolution, so he told me, by consideration of the unusual character of the malady of the deceased, of certain obtrusive and eager inquiries on the part of her medical men, and of the remote and exposed situation of the burial ground of the family. I will not deny that when I called to mind the sinister countenance of the person whom I met upon the staircase, on the day of my arrival at the house, I had no desire to oppose what I regarded as at best but a harmless, and by no means an unnatural, precaution.

At the request of Usher, I personally aided him in the arrangements for the temporary entombment. The body having been encoffined, we two alone bore it to its rest. The vault in which we placed it had been so long unopened that our torches, half smothered in its oppressive atmosphere, gave us little opportunity for investigation. It was small, damp, and entirely without means of admission for light; lying, at great depth, immediately beneath that portion of the building in which was my own sleeping apartment. It had been used, apparently, in remote feudal times, for the worst purposes of a dungeon keep, and in later days as a place of deposit for powder, or some other highly combustible substance, as a portion of its floor, and the whole interior of a long archway through which we reached it, were carefully sheathed with copper. The door, of massive iron, had been, also, similarly protected. Its immense weight caused an unusually sharp, grating sound as it moved upon its hinges.

Having deposited our mournful burden upon trestles within this region of horror, we partially turned aside the yet unscrewed lid of the coffin,

and looked upon the face of the tenant. A striking similitude between the brother and sister now first arrested my attention. Usher, divining, perhaps, my thoughts, murmured out some few words from which I learned that the deceased and himself had been twins, and that sympathies of a scarcely intelligible nature had always existed between them. Our glances, however, rested not long upon the dead—for we could not regard her unawed. The disease had left, as usual in all maladies of a strictly cataleptical character, the mockery of a faint blush upon the face, and that suspiciously lingering smile upon the lip which is so terrible in death. We replaced and screwed down the lid, and, having secured the door of iron, made our way, with toil, into the scarcely less gloomy apartments of the upper portion of the house.

And now, some days of bitter grief having elapsed, an observable change came over the features of the mental disorder of my friend. His ordinary manner had vanished. His ordinary occupations were neglected or forgotten. He roamed from chamber to chamber with hurried, unequal, and objectless step. The pallor of his countenance had assumed, if possible, a more ghastly hue—but the luminousness of his eye had utterly gone out. The once occasional huskiness of his tone was heard no more; and a tremulous quaver, as if of extreme terror, habitually characterized his utterance. There were times, indeed, when I thought his unceasingly agitated mind was laboring with some oppressive secret, to divulge which he struggled for the necessary courage. At times, again, I was obliged to resolve all into the mere inexplicable vagaries of madness, for I beheld him gazing upon vacancy for long hours, in an attitude of the profoundest attention, as if listening to some imaginary sound. It was no wonder that his condition terrified—that it infected me. I felt creeping upon me, by slow yet certain degrees, the wild influences of his own fantastic yet impressive superstitions.

It was, especially, upon retiring to bed late in the night of the seventh or eighth day after the placing of the lady Madeline within the dungeon, that I experienced the full power of such feelings. Sleep came not near my couch, while the hours waned and waned away. I struggled to reason off the nervousness which had dominion over me. I endeavored to believe that much, if not all, of what I felt was due to the bewildering influence of the gloomy furniture of the room—of the dark and tattered draperies which, tortured into motion by the breath of a rising tempest, swayed fitfully to and fro. But my efforts were fruitless. An irrepressible tremor gradually pervaded my frame; and at length there sat upon my very heart an incubus of utterly causeless alarm. Shaking this off with a gasp and a struggle, I uplifted myself upon the pillows, and peering earnestly within the intense darkness of the chamber, hearkened to certain low and indefinite sounds which came, through the pauses of the storm, I knew not whence. Overpowered by an intense sentiment of horror, unaccountable yet unendurable, I threw on my clothes with haste—for I felt that I should sleep no more during the night. I endeavored to arouse myself from the pitiable condition into which I had fallen by pacing rapidly to and fro through the apartment.

I had taken but few turns in this manner, when a light step on an adjoining staircase arrested my attention. I presently recognized it as that of Usher. In an instant afterwards he rapped with a gentle touch at my door, and entered, bearing a lamp. There was a species of mad hilarity in his eyes—an evidently restrained hysteria in his whole demeanor. His air appalled me—but anything was preferable to the solitude which I had so long endured, and I even welcomed his presence as a relief.

"And you have not seen it?" he said abruptly, after having stared about him for some moments in silence—"you have not then seen it? But, stay! you shall." Thus speaking, and having carefully shaded his lamp, he hurried to one of the casements and threw it freely open to the storm.

The impetuous fury of the entering gust nearly lifted us from our feet. It was, indeed, a tempestuous yet sternly beautiful night, and one wildly singular in its terror and its beauty. A whirlwind had apparently collected its force in our vicinity, for there were frequent and violent alterations in the direction of the wind. The exceeding density of the clouds, which hung so low as to press upon the turrets of the house, did not prevent our perceiving the lifelike velocity with which they flew careering from all points against each other, without passing away into the distance. I say that even their exceeding density did not prevent our perceiving this; yet we had no glimpse of the moon or stars, nor was there any flashing forth of the lightning. But the under surfaces of the huge masses of agitated vapor, as well as all terrestrial objects immediately around us, were glowing in the unnatural light of a faintly luminous and distinctly visible gaseous exhalation which enshrouded the mansion.

"You must not—you shall not behold this!" said I, shudderingly, to Usher, as I led him with a gentle violence from the window to a seat. "These appearances, which bewilder you, are merely electrical phenomena not uncommon. Or it may be that they have their ghastly origin in the rank miasma of the tarn. Let us close this casement; the air is chilling and dangerous to your frame. Here is one of your favorite romances. I will read, and you shall listen—and so we will pass away this terrible night together."

The antique volume which I had taken up was the *Mad Trist* of Sir Launcelot Canning.[15] It was the only book immediately at hand; and I indulged a vague hope that the excitement which now agitated the hypochondriac might find relief—for the history of mental disorder is full of similar anomalies—even in the uncouth old tale. Could I have judged, indeed, by the wild, overstrained air of vivacity with which he hearkened, or apparently hearkened, to the words of the tale, I might well have congratulated myself upon the success of my design.

I had arrived at that well-known portion of the story where Ethelred, the hero of the *Trist,* having sought in vain for peaceable admission into the dwelling of the hermit, proceeds to make good an entrance by force. Here, it will be remembered, the words of the narrative run thus:

And Ethelred, who was by nature of a doughty heart, and who was now mighty withal, on account of the

---

[15] *"Mad Trist" of Sir Launcelot Canning.* Both book and author were invented by Poe.

powerfulness of the wine which he had drunken, waited no longer to hold parley with the hermit, who, in sooth, was of an obstinate and maliceful turn. Feeling the rain upon his shoulders, and fearing the rising of the tempest, Ethelred uplifted his mace outright, and with blows made quickly room in the plankings of the door for his gauntleted hand. And now pulling therewith sturdily, he so cracked, and ripped, and tore all asunder that the noise of the dry and hollow-sounding wood alarumed and reverberated throughout the forest.

At the termination of this last sentence I started, and for a moment paused; for it appeared to me—although I at once concluded that my excited fancy had deceived me—it appeared to me that from some very remote portion of the mansion there came, indistinctly, to my ears what might have been the echo, but a stifled and dull one certainly, of the very cracking and ripping sound which Sir Launcelot had so particularly described. It was, beyond doubt, the coincidence alone which had arrested my attention; for, amid the rattling of the sashes of the casements, and the ordinary commingled noises of the still increasing storm, the sound, in itself, had nothing, surely, which should have interested or disturbed me.

I continued the story:

But the good champion Ethelred, now entering within the door, was sore enraged and amazed to perceive no signal of the maliceful hermit; but, in the stead thereof, a dragon of a scaly and prodigious demeanor, and of a fiery tongue, which sate in guard before a palace of gold, with a floor of silver; and upon the wall there hung a shield of shining brass with this legend enwritten,

Who entereth herein, a conqueror hath bin[16];
Who slayeth the dragon, the shield he shall win.

And Ethelred uplifted his mace, and struck upon the head of the dragon, which fell before him, and gave up his pesty breath, with a shriek, so horrid and harsh, and withal so piercing, that Ethelred had fain to close his ears with his hands against the dreadful noise of it, the like whereof was never before heard.

Here again I paused abruptly, and now with a feeling of wild amazement; for there could be no doubt whatever that, in this instance, I did actually hear, although from what direction it proceeded I found it impossible to say, a low

—————
[16]bin, been.

and apparently distant, but harsh, protracted, and most unusual screaming or grating sound.

Oppressed, as I certainly was, by a thousand conflicting sensations, in which wonder and extreme terror were predominant, I still retained sufficient presence of mind to avoid exciting, by any observation, the sensitive nervousness of my companion. I was by no means certain that he had noticed the sounds in question; although, assuredly, a strange alteration had during the last few minutes taken place in his demeanor. From a position fronting my own, he had gradually brought round his chair so as to sit with his face to the door of the chamber. Thus I could but partially perceive his features, although I saw that his lips trembled as if he were murmuring inaudibly. His head had dropped upon his breast—yet I knew that he was not asleep, from the wide and rigid opening of the eye as I caught a glance of it in profile. The motion of his body, too, was at variance with this idea—for he rocked from side to side with a gentle yet constant and uniform sway. Having rapidly taken notice of all this, I resumed the narrative of Sir Launcelot, which thus proceeded:

And now the champion, having escaped from the terrible fury of the dragon, bethought himself of the brazen shield, and of the breaking up of the enchantment which was upon it. Removing the carcass from out of the way before him, he approached valorously over the silver pavement of the castle to where the shield was upon the wall; which in sooth tarried not for his full coming, but fell down at his feet upon the silver floor with a mighty great and terrible ringing sound.

No sooner had these syllables passed my lips than—as if a shield of brass had indeed, at the moment, fallen heavily upon a floor of silver—I became aware of a distinct, hollow, metallic, and clangorous, yet apparently muffled, reverberation. Completely unnerved, I leaped to my feet; but the measured rocking movement of Usher was undisturbed. I rushed to the chair in which he sat. His eyes were bent fixedly before him, and throughout his whole countenance there reigned a stony rigidity. But as I placed my hand upon his shoulder, there came a strong shudder over his whole person. A sickly smile quivered about his lips; and I saw that he spoke in a low, hurried, and gibbering murmur, as if unconscious of my presence. Bending closely over him, I at length drank in the hideous import of his words.

"Not hear it? Yes, I hear it, and *have* heard it. Long — long — long — many minutes, many hours, many days have I heard it. Yet I dared not—oh, pity me, miserable wretch that I am— I dared not—I *dared* not speak! *We have put her living in the tomb!* Said I not that my senses were acute? I *now* tell you that I heard her first feeble movements in the hollow coffin. I heard them—many, many days ago—yet I dared not— *I dared not speak!* And now—tonight—Ethelred —ha! ha!—the breaking of the hermit's door, and the death cry of the dragon, and the clangor of the shield!—say, rather, the rending of her coffin, and the grating of the iron hinges of her prison, and her struggles within the coppered archway of the vault! Oh, whither shall I fly? Will she not be here anon? Is she not hurrying to upbraid me for my haste? Have I not heard her footstep on the stair? Do I not distinguish that heavy and horrible beating of her heart? Madman!"—here he sprang furiously to his feet, and shrieked out his syllables, as if in the effort he were giving up his soul—*"Madman! I tell you that she now stands without the door!"*

As if in the superhuman energy of his utterance there had been found the potency of a spell, the huge, antique panels to which the speaker pointed threw slowly back, upon the instant, their ponderous and ebony jaws. It was the work of the rushing gust—but then without those doors there *did* stand the lofty and enshrouded figure of the lady Madeline of Usher! There was blood upon her white robes, and the evidence of some bitter struggle upon every portion of her emaciated frame. For a moment she remained trembling and reeling to and fro upon the threshold. Then, with a low, moaning cry, fell heavily inward upon the person of her brother, and, in her violent and now final death agonies, bore him to the floor a corpse, and a victim to the terrors he had anticipated.

From that chamber, and from that mansion, I fled aghast. The storm was still abroad in all its wrath as I found myself crossing the old causeway.

Suddenly there shot along the path a wild light, and I turned to see whence a gleam so unusual could have issued; for the vast house and its shadows were alone behind me. The radiance was that of the full, setting, and blood-red moon, which now shone vividly through that once barely discernible fissure, of which I have before spoken as extending from the roof of the building, in a zigzag direction, to the base. While I gazed, this fissure rapidly widened— there came a fierce breath of the whirlwind —the entire orb of the satellite burst at once upon my sight—my brain reeled as I saw the mighty walls rushing asunder—there was a long, tumultuous shouting sound like the voice of a thousand waters—and the deep and dank tarn at my feet closed sullenly and silently over the fragments of the "House of Usher."

HOW DOES POE CAST HIS SPELL?

1. How does the title, "The Fall of the House of Usher," describe in brief the theme of the entire story?

2. What are the most significant details of the house and its surroundings? What relationship does Roderick Usher find between himself and his house?

3. What details of Usher's appearance, ideas, and tastes suggest to the narrator that his host is on the verge of insanity?

4. What is the nature of the lady Madeline's illness? What is its importance to the plot?

5. Read again the description of the picture Usher has painted (the paragraph beginning at the bottom of column 1, page 508). In what way does this painting foreshadow Madeline's entombment?

6. How do you interpret Usher's poem, "The Haunted Palace" (pages 508-509)? What does this song foreshadow? What did this dirge tell the narrator about Usher's knowledge of himself and of his fears?

7. Trace the events of the last night of Usher's life. What peculiar happenings catch the narrator up in Usher's own terrors? Specifically, what event brings about Usher's death? Why should this event have a fatal effect upon him?

8. In what ways does the description of the house in the last paragraph echo the opening description?

9. Beginning with the narrator's approach to the House of Usher, point out passages which show the changes in his reactions up to the end of the story. If the sympathetic reader shares the emotions of the narrator, how will his emotions change while reading the story? Was the effect upon you what Poe evidently intended it to be?

Appreciating the tone of the story

Edgar Allan Poe was always a poet in his use of words. As pointed out on page 502, he regarded words not merely as symbols to convey meaning, but also as means of stirring the reader's emotions. Consider the opening paragraph of "The Fall of the House of Usher." Poe is beginning a tale whose effect is to be one of terror; it is important that the reader immediately sense the gloom and mystery that the narrator feels as he approaches the House of Usher. Read again, slowly, the first long paragraph, noting words and phrases that are particularly helpful in conveying to you the atmosphere of the scene. Select several of these words and phrases for analysis. Why, for example, are the adjectives *dull, dark,* and *soundless* good ones for describing the day on which the narrator set out alone on his journey? Why do you think Poe chooses an *autumn* day rather than a day in spring or summer or winter? How, and with what effect, does Poe describe the clouds? Perhaps you will want to select and talk over several additional words and phrases in the paragraph which are especially effective in establishing the tone of the opening scene of the story.

Prepare to read aloud to the class a passage of a dozen lines or so in which the words themselves made a deep impression on your mind and emotions. Practice delivering the passage in such a way as to make your classmates share your feelings.

II NATHANIEL HAWTHORNE (1804-1864)[1]

Back on pages 491 and 502 we glanced at some of Poe's ideas on how a short story should be written. These ideas are found in an essay which Poe wrote as a review of *Twice-Told Tales,* a collection of short stories by Nathaniel Hawthorne. In this review Poe said that Hawthorne wrote in the way that Poe admired, subordinating everything to effect. If Hawthorne did this, however, his understanding of "effect" was very different from that of Poe. Hawthorne, born and reared in pious New England, could not help believe that ideas or moral themes were very important elements in fiction. A typical story by Hawthorne, therefore, was held together by the idea which it served to express. "In all my stories, I think," he wrote, "there is one idea running through them like an iron rod, and to which all other ideas are referred or subordinate." You have seen an example of Hawthorne's theory of the short story in "The Gray Champion" (pages 182-188), which builds up throughout to the idea, or moral, expressed in the final paragraph.

"The Gray Champion," like many stories by Hawthorne, was based on colonial history. He liked to set his stories in the distant past or in far-off places, because tales removed from everyday life allowed an author to mingle a great deal of imaginative detail with the reality. He liked, he once said, to locate his stories "in a neutral territory, somewhere between the real world and the fairyland, where the Actual and the Imaginary meet, and each imbues itself with the other." Having set his story in such a realm, the author may so manage characters, happenings, and settings as to make all of them help him express an idea. Hawthorne does this by giving details allegorical or symbolic significance. As you read "Dr. Heidegger's Experiment," notice how the author handles various details in such a way as to emphasize the one dominant idea or moral of the whole story.

_____
[1] For a biographical sketch of Hawthorne see page 385.

Dr. Heidegger's Experiment

NATHANIEL HAWTHORNE

THAT VERY singular man, old Dr. Heidegger, once invited four venerable friends to meet him in his study. There were three white-bearded gentlemen, Mr. Medbourne, Colonel Killigrew, and Mr. Gascoigne, and a withered gentlewoman, whose name was the Widow Wycherly. They were all melancholy old creatures, who had been unfortunate in life, and whose greatest misfortune it was that they were not long ago in their graves. Mr. Medbourne, in the vigor of his age, had been a prosperous merchant, and had lost his all by a frantic speculation, and was now little better than a mendicant. Colonel Killigrew had wasted his best years, and his health and substance, in the pursuit of sinful pleasures, which had given birth to a brood of pains, such as the gout, and divers other torments of soul and body. Mr. Gascoigne was a ruined politician, a man of evil fame, or at least had been so, till time had buried him

from the knowledge of the present generation, and made him obscure instead of infamous. As for the Widow Wycherly, tradition tells us that she was a great beauty in her day; but, for a long while past, she had lived in deep seclusion, on account of certain scandalous stories, which had prejudiced the gentry of the town against her. It is a circumstance worth mentioning that each of these three old gentlemen, Mr. Medbourne, Colonel Killigrew, and Mr. Gascoigne, were early lovers of the Widow Wycherly, and had once been on the point of cutting each other's throats for her sake. And, before proceeding further, I will merely hint that Dr. Heidegger and all his four guests were sometimes thought to be a little beside themselves,[1] as is not unfrequently the case with old people, when worried either by present troubles or woeful recollections.

"My dear old friends," said Dr. Heidegger, motioning them to be seated, "I am desirous of your assistance in one of those little experiments with which I amuse myself here in my study."

If all stories were true, Dr. Heidegger's study must have been a very curious place. It was a dim, old-fashioned chamber, festooned with cobwebs and besprinkled with antique dust. Around the walls stood several oaken bookcases, the lower shelves of which were filled with rows of gigantic folios and black-letter quartos,

---

[1] *a little beside themselves*, a little out of their heads, or slightly insane.

and the upper with little parchment-covered duodecimos. Over the central bookcase was a bronze bust of Hippocrates,[2] with which, according to some authorities, Dr. Heidegger was accustomed to hold consultations in all difficult cases of his practice. In the obscurest corner of the room stood a tall and narrow oaken closet, with its door ajar, within which doubtfully appeared a skeleton. Between two of the bookcases hung a looking glass, presenting its high and dusty plate within a tarnished gilt frame. Among many wonderful stories related of this mirror, it was fabled that the spirits of all the doctor's deceased patients dwelt within its verge, and would stare him in the face whenever he looked thitherward. The opposite side of the chamber was ornamented with the full-length portrait of a young lady, arrayed in the faded magnificence of silk, satin, and brocade, and with a visage as faded as her dress. Above half a century ago, Dr. Heidegger had been on the point of marriage with this young lady; but, being affected with some slight disorder, she had swallowed one of her lover's prescriptions, and died on the bridal evening.

The greatest curiosity of the study remains to be mentioned; it was a ponderous folio volume, bound in black leather, with massive silver clasps. There were no letters on the back, and nobody could tell the title of the book. But it was well known to be a book of magic; and once when a chambermaid had lifted it, merely to brush away the dust, the skeleton had rattled in its closet, the picture of the young lady had stepped one foot upon the floor, and several ghastly faces had peeped forth from the mirror; while the brazen head of Hippocrates frowned, and said, "Forbear!"

Such was Dr. Heidegger's study. On the summer afternoon of our tale, a small round table, as black as ebony, stood in the center of the room, sustaining a cut-glass vase of beautiful form and elaborate workmanship. The sunshine came through the window, between the heavy festoons of two faded damask curtains,

and fell directly across this vase; so that a mild splendor was reflected from it on the ashen visages of the five old people who sat around. Four champagne glasses were also on the table.

"My dear old friends," repeated Dr. Heidegger, "may I reckon on your aid in performing an exceedingly curious experiment?"

Now Dr. Heidegger was a very strange old gentleman, whose eccentricity had become the nucleus for a thousand fantastic stories. Some of these fables, to my shame be it spoken, might possibly be traced back to mine own veracious self; and if any passages of the present tale should startle the reader's faith, I must be content to bear the stigma of a fictionmonger.

When the doctor's four guests heard him talk of his proposed experiment, they anticipated nothing more wonderful than the murder of a mouse in an air pump, or the examination of a cobweb by the microscope, or some similar nonsense, with which he was constantly in the habit of pestering his intimates. But without waiting for a reply, Dr. Heidegger hobbled across the chamber, and returned with the same ponderous folio, bound in black leather, which common report affirmed to be a book of magic. Undoing the silver clasps, he opened the volume and took from among its black-letter pages a rose, or what was once a rose, though now the green leaves and crimson petals had assumed one brownish hue, and the ancient flower seemed ready to crumble to dust in the doctor's hand.

"This rose," said Dr. Heidegger, with a sigh, "this same withered and crumbling flower, blossomed five-and-fifty years ago. It was given me by Sylvia Ward, whose portrait hangs yonder; and I meant to wear it in my bosom at our wedding. Five-and-fifty years it has been treasured between the leaves of this old volume. Now, would you deem it possible that this rose of half a century could ever bloom again?"

"Nonsense!" said the Widow Wycherly, with a peevish toss of her head. "You might as well ask whether an old woman's wrinkled face could ever bloom again."

"See!" answered Dr. Heidegger.

---

[2]*Hippocrate*s (hi pok′rə tēz), a Greek physician who lived several hundred years before Christ. He is called the father of medicine.

He uncovered the vase, and threw the faded rose into the water which it contained. At first it lay lightly on the surface of the fluid, appearing to imbibe none of its moisture. Soon, however, a singular change began to be visible. The crushed and dried petals stirred, and assumed a deepening tinge of crimson, as if the flower were reviving from a deathlike slumber; the slender stalk and twigs of foliage became green; and there was the rose of half a century, looking as fresh as when Sylvia Ward had first given it to her lover. It was scarcely full-blown; for some of its delicate red leaves curled modestly around its moist bosom, within which two or three dewdrops were sparkling.

"That is certainly a very pretty deception," said the doctor's friends; carelessly, however, for they had witnessed greater miracles at a conjurer's show; "pray, how was it effected?"

"Did you never hear of the Fountain of Youth," asked Dr. Heidegger, "which Ponce de León, the Spanish adventurer, went in search of, two or three centuries ago?"

"But did Ponce de León ever find it?" said the Widow Wycherly.

"No," answered Dr. Heidegger, "for he never sought it in the right place. The famous Fountain of Youth, if I am rightly informed, is situated in the southern part of the Floridian peninsula, not far from Lake Macaco. Its source is overshadowed by several gigantic magnolias, which, though numberless centuries old, have been kept as fresh as violets, by the virtues of this wonderful water. An acquaintance of mine, knowing my curiosity in such matters, has sent me what you see in the vase."

"Ahem!" said Colonel Killigrew, who believed not a word of the doctor's story; "and what may be the effect of this fluid on the human frame?"

"You shall judge for yourself, my dear Colonel," replied Dr. Heidegger; "and all of you, my respected friends, are welcome to so much of this admirable fluid as may restore to you the bloom of youth. For my own part, having had much trouble in growing old, I am in no hurry to grow young again. With your permission, therefore, I will merely watch the progress of the experiment."

While he spoke, Dr. Heidegger had been filling the four champagne glasses with the water of the Fountain of Youth. It was apparently impregnated with an effervescent gas, for little bubbles were continually ascending from the depths of the glasses, and bursting in silvery spray at the surface. As the liquor diffused a pleasant perfume, the old people doubted not that it possessed cordial and comfortable properties; and, though utter skeptics as to its rejuvenescent power, they were inclined to swallow it at once. But Dr. Heidegger besought them to stay a moment.

"Before you drink, my respectable old friends," said he, "it would be well that, with the experience of a lifetime to direct you, you should draw up a few general rules for your guidance, in passing a second time through the perils of youth. Think what a sin and shame it would be, if, with your peculiar advantages, you should not become patterns of virtue and wisdom to all the young people of the age."

The doctor's four venerable friends made him no answer except by a feeble and tremulous laugh, so very ridiculous was the idea that, knowing how closely repentance treads behind the steps of error, they should ever go astray again.

"Drink, then," said the doctor, bowing. "I rejoice that I have so well selected the subjects of my experiment."

With palsied hands they raised the glasses to their lips. The liquor, if it really possessed such virtues as Dr. Heidegger imputed to it, could not have been bestowed on four human beings who needed it more woefully. They looked as if they had never known what youth or pleasure was, but had been the offspring of Nature's dotage, and always the gray, decrepit, sapless, miserable creatures who now sat stooping round the doctor's table, without life enough in their souls or bodies to be animated even by the prospect of growing young again. They drank off the water, and replaced their glasses on the table.

Assuredly there was an almost immediate improvement in the aspect of the party, not unlike what might have been produced by a glass of generous wine, together with a sudden glow of cheerful sunshine, brightening over all their visages at once. There was a healthful suffusion on their cheeks, instead of the ashen hue that had made them look so corpselike. They gazed at one another, and fancied that some magic power had really begun to smooth away the deep and sad inscriptions which Father Time had been so long engraving on their brows. The Widow Wycherly adjusted her cap, for she felt almost like a woman again.

"Give us more of this wondrous water!" cried they, eagerly.

"We are younger—but we are still too old! Quick—give us more!"

"Patience, patience!" quoth Dr. Heidegger, who sat watching the experiment, with philosophic coolness. "You have been a long time growing old. Surely, you might be content to grow young in half an hour! But the water is at your service."

Again he filled their glasses with the liquor of youth, enough of which still remained in the vase to turn half the old people in the city to the age of their own grandchildren. While the bubbles were yet sparkling on the brim, the doctor's four guests snatched their glasses from the table, and swallowed the contents at a single gulp. Was it delusion? Even while the draft was passing down their throats, it seemed to have wrought a change on their whole systems. Their eyes grew clear and bright; a dark shade deepened among their silvery locks; they sat around the table, three gentlemen of middle age, and a woman hardly beyond her buxom prime.

"My dear widow, you are charming!" cried Colonel Killigrew, whose eyes had been fixed upon her face, while the shadows of age were flitting from it like darkness from the crimson daybreak.

The fair widow knew, of old, that Colonel Killigrew's compliments were not always measured by sober truth; so she started up and ran to the mirror, still dreading that the ugly visage of an old woman would meet her gaze. Meanwhile, the three gentlemen behaved in such a manner as proved that the water of the Fountain of Youth possessed some intoxicating qualities; unless, indeed, their exhilaration of spirits were merely a lightsome dizziness, caused by the sudden removal of the weight of years. Mr. Gascoigne's mind seemed to run on political topics, but whether relating to the past, present, or future, could not easily be determined, since the same ideas and phrases have been in vogue these fifty years. Now he rattled forth full-throated sentences about patriotism, national glory, and the people's right; now he muttered some perilous stuff or other, in a sly and doubtful whisper, so cautiously that even his own conscience could scarcely catch the secret; and now, again, he spoke in measured accents, and a deeply deferential tone, as if a royal ear were listening to his well-turned periods.[3] Colonel Killigrew all this time had been trolling forth a jolly bottle song, and ringing his glass in symphony with the chorus, while his eyes wandered toward the buxom figure of the Widow Wycherly. On the other side of the table, Mr. Medbourne was involved in a calculation of dollars and cents, with which was strangely intermingled a project for supplying the East Indies with ice, by harnessing a team of whales to the polar icebergs.

As for the Widow Wycherly, she stood before the mirror curtsying and simpering to her own image, and greeting it as the friend whom she loved better than all the world beside. She thrust her face close to the glass, to see whether some long-remembered wrinkle or crow's-foot had indeed vanished. She examined whether the snow had so entirely melted from her hair that the venerable cap could be safely thrown aside. At last, turning briskly away, she came with a sort of dancing step to the table.

"My dear old doctor," cried she, "pray favor me with another glass!"

"Certainly, my dear madam, certainly!" replied the complaisant doctor; "see! I have already filled the glasses."

---

[3] *well-turned periods*, neatly phrased sentences.

There, in fact, stood the four glasses, brimful of this wonderful water, the delicate spray of which, as it effervesced from the surface, resembled the tremulous glitter of diamonds. It was now so nearly sunset that the chamber had grown duskier than ever; but a mild and moon-like splendor gleamed from within the vase, and rested alike on the four guests and on the doctor's venerable figure. He sat in a high-backed, elaborately carved oaken armchair, with a gray dignity of aspect that might have well befitted that very Father Time whose power had never been disputed, save by this fortunate company. Even while quaffing the third draft of the Fountain of Youth, they were almost awed by the expression of his mysterious visage.

But, the next moment, the exhilarating gush of young life shot through their veins. They were now in the happy prime of youth. Age, with its miserable train of cares and sorrows and diseases, was remembered only as the trouble of a dream, from which they had joyously awoke. The fresh gloss of the soul, so early lost, and without which the world's successive scenes had been but a gallery of faded pictures, again threw its enchantment over all their prospects. They felt like new-created beings, in a new-created universe.

"We are young! We are young!" they cried exultingly.

Youth, like the extremity of age, had effaced the strongly marked characteristics of middle life, and mutually assimilated them all. They were a group of merry youngsters, almost maddened with the exuberant frolicsomeness of their years. The most singular effect of their gaiety was an impulse to mock the infirmity and decrepitude of which they had so lately been the victims. They laughed loudly at their old-fashioned attire, the wide-skirted coats and flapped waistcoats of the young men, and the ancient cap and gown of the blooming girl. One limped across the floor, like a gouty grandfather; one set a pair of spectacles astride of his nose, and pretended to pore over the black-letter pages of the book of magic; a third seated himself in an armchair and strove to imitate the venerable dignity of Dr. Heidegger. Then all shouted mirthfully, and leaped about the room. The Widow Wycherly—if so fresh a damsel could be called a widow—tripped up to the doctor's chair, with a mischievous merriment in her rosy face.

"Doctor, you dear old soul," cried she, "get up and dance with me!" And then the four young people laughed louder than ever, to think what a queer figure the poor old doctor would cut.

"Pray excuse me," answered the doctor, quietly. "I am old and rheumatic, and my dancing days were over long ago. But either of these gay young gentlemen will be glad of so pretty a partner."

"Dance with me, Clara!" cried Colonel Killigrew.

"No, no, I will be her partner!" shouted Mr. Gascoigne.

"She promised me her hand fifty years ago!" exclaimed Mr. Medbourne.

They all gathered round her. One caught both her hands in his passionate grasp—another threw his arm about her waist—the third buried his hand among the glossy curls that clustered beneath the widow's cap. Blushing, panting, struggling, chiding, laughing, her warm breath fanning each of their faces by turns, she strove to disengage herself, yet still remained in their triple embrace. Never was there a livelier picture of youthful rivalship, with bewitching beauty for the prize. Yet, by a strange deception, owing to the duskiness of the chamber, and the antique dresses which they still wore, the tall mirror is said to have reflected the figures of the three old, gray, withered grandsires, ridiculously contending for the skinny ugliness of a shriveled grandam.

But they were young; their burning passions proved them so. Inflamed to madness by the coquetry of the girl-widow, who neither granted nor quite withheld her favors, the three rivals began to interchange threatening glances. Still keeping hold of the fair prize, they grappled fiercely at one another's throats. As they struggled to and fro, the table was overturned, and the vase dashed into a thousand fragments. The precious Water of Youth flowed in a bright stream across the floor, moistening the wings of a butterfly, which, grown old in the decline of summer, had alighted there to die. The insect fluttered lightly through the chamber, and settled on the snowy head of Dr. Heidegger.

"Come, come, gentlemen! Come, Madam Wycherly," exclaimed the doctor, "I really must protest against this riot."

They stood still and shivered; for it seemed as if gray Time were calling them back from their sunny youth, far down into the chill and darksome vale of years. They looked at old Dr. Heidegger, who sat in his carved armchair, holding the rose of half a century, which he had rescued from among the fragments of the shattered vase. At the motion of his hand the four rioters resumed their seats; the more readily because their violent exertions had wearied them, youthful though they were.

"My poor Sylvia's rose!" ejaculated Dr. Heidegger, holding it in the light of the sunset clouds; "it appears to be fading again."

And so it was. Even while the party were looking at it, the flower continued to shrivel up till it became as dry and fragile as when the doctor had first thrown it into the vase. He shook off the few drops of moisture which clung to its petals.

"I love it as well thus as in its dewy freshness," observed he, pressing the withered rose to his withered lips. While he spoke, the butterfly fluttered down from the doctor's snowy head, and fell upon the floor.

His guests shivered again. A strange chillness, whether of the body or spirit they could not tell, was creeping gradually over them all. They gazed at one another and fancied that each fleeting moment snatched away a charm and left a deepening furrow where none had been before.

Was it an illusion? Had the changes of a lifetime been crowded into so brief a space, and were they now four aged people, sitting with their old friend, Dr. Heidegger?

"Are we grown old again, so soon!" cried they, dolefully.

In truth, they had. The Water of Youth possessed merely a virtue more transient than that of wine. The delirium which it created had effervesced away. Yes! they were old again. With a shuddering impulse, that showed her a woman still, the widow clasped her skinny hands before her face, and wished that the coffin lid were over it, since it could be no longer beautiful.

"Yes, friends, ye are old again," said Dr. Heidegger; "and lo! the Water of Youth is all lavished on the ground. Well—I bemoan it not; for if the fountain gushed at my very doorstep, I would not stoop to bathe my lips in it—no, though its delirium were for years instead of moments. Such is the lesson ye have taught me!"

But the doctor's four friends had taught no such lesson to themselves. They resolved forthwith to make a pilgrimage to Florida, and quaff at morning, noon, and night from the Fountain of Youth.

WHAT IS HAWTHORNE'S IDEA?

1. Hawthorne's desire to locate his stories in a half-*imaginary* world caused him to deal with (*a*) distant times, (*b*) distant places, or (*c*) people withdrawn from ordinary life. Which does he deal with here? Point out passages which justify your answer.

2. Hawthorne's eagerness to locate his stories in a half-*real* world caused him at times (*a*) to give his characters experiences and attitudes common in everyday life, and (*b*) to describe scenes in minute, concrete detail. Which of these things does he do here? Point out passages which support your answer.

3. Read again the description of Dr. Heidegger's study (pages 515-516). What details give an air of reality to the description? What details add an atmosphere of unreality or an imaginative quality? In what way does Dr. Heidegger's explanation of his elixir (page 517, column 1, paragraphs 3-5) combine these two qualities?

4. Describe briefly each of the four old people who take part in Dr. Heidegger's experiment. In what way is the behavior of each after drinking the liquid typical of such a character? Why do you think Hawthorne created such disreputable old people for this tale? How would the mood of the story have differed had he created good, likable characters?

5. What symbolism do you find in the spilling of the Water of Youth? Why is the butterfly such a wonderful detail?

6. Frequently Hawthorne uses mirrors in his stories to show truths not perceived by those reflected in them. Does he so use the mirror in this story? Explain your answer.

7. In many of his stories of the strange and mysterious, Hawthorne uses a clever device to make the events seem believable to the reader. Instead of insisting that his story is true, he slyly suggests that he himself has the same doubts that the reader must feel. Pleased that Hawthorne isn't trying to fool him, the reader soon finds himself sharing the author's feeling that, after all, these events *might* have happened. Does Hawthorne use this device in "Dr. Heidegger's Experiment"? If so, give illustrations.

8. How does Hawthorne's characterization of Dr. Heidegger prepare us for his statements in the next to the last paragraph? What were Dr. Heidegger's reasons for not drinking of the Water of Youth? Explain why you believe that Dr. Heidegger does or does not express the main idea that Hawthorne wished to express.

Contrasting Poe and Hawthorne

Edgar Allan Poe and Nathaniel Hawthorne were both masters of the short story, but they differed greatly in their ideas of what the short story should do. Poe believed the primary function of the short story was to play upon the emotions by establishing a certain mood; he cared not at all for ideas or for teaching a moral. Hawthorne, on the other hand, thought the short story should appeal to the mind through the presentation of one important idea. Poe appealed first to the reader's aesthetic sense, Hawthorne to his moral sense.

Imagine that Poe had written "Dr. Heidegger's Experiment." What mood do you think he would have tried to establish? How do you think the story itself would differ? Now suppose that Hawthorne had written "The Fall of the House of Usher." What moral idea do you think he might have developed through the tale? How might he have developed this idea?

III BRET HARTE (1836-1902)[1]

The short stories of Poe and Hawthorne, you will remember, depended not at all upon the exact location of their setting. Poe usually placed his stories in far-off lands. Hawthorne, as he once put it, preferred scenes made unreal by moonlight to scenes lighted by everyday sunlight. Indeed, vagueness of place was a great advantage to Poe and Hawthorne in impressing upon their readers the effects that they wished to achieve.

Quite different from Poe's and Hawthorne's settings were those of another group of short-story writers who won popularity in the last decades of the nineteenth century. These writers, seeking to satisfy the desire of readers to learn how people lived in every section of America, produced many realistic stories revealing the customs and peculiarities of specific localities. Such writers were called "local colorists." Their stories helped interpret every section of the country to all the other sections.

The new movement lasted from about 1868 to about 1900. Its first important leader was Bret Harte, who made good use of local color in his tales of the Far West. Harte lived in California at just the right time for direct observation of its fast-changing life. He watched a motley horde of people, lured by the news of gold, pouring into the state. He noted the lack of law and order, the primitive living conditions on the outskirts of civilization. And he wrote vivid, realistic stories of what he saw, setting each one in a typical locality, such as Roaring Camp or Poker Flat or Red Gulch. Readers in the staid old East were delighted with Harte's local-color narratives about this raw new frontier, with their mixture of rough life and tender feeling, of humor and pathos. "The Luck of Roaring Camp" is a fine example.

---

[1]For a biographical sketch of Bret Harte see page 443.

The Luck of Roaring Camp

BRET HARTE

THERE WAS COMMOTION in Roaring Camp. It could not have been a fight, for in 1850 that was not novel enough to have called together the entire settlement. The ditches and claims were not only deserted, but "Tuttle's grocery" had contributed its gamblers, who, it will be remembered, calmly continued their game the day that French Pete and Kanaka Joe shot each other to death over the bar in the front room. The whole camp was collected before a rude cabin on the outer edge of the clearing. Conversation was carried on in a low tone, but the name of a woman was frequently repeated. It was a name familiar enough in the camp—"Cherokee Sal."

Perhaps the less said of her the better. She was a coarse, and it is to be feared, a very sinful woman. But at that time she was the only woman in Roaring Camp, and was just then lying in sore extremity, when she most needed the ministration of her own sex. Dissolute, abandoned, and irreclaimable, she was yet suffering a martyrdom hard enough to bear even when veiled by sympathizing womanhood, but now terrible in her loneliness. The primal curse[1] had come to her in that original isolation which must have made the punishment of the first transgression so dreadful. It was, perhaps, part of the expiation of her sin, that, at a moment when she most lacked her sex's intuitive tenderness and care, she met only the half-contemptuous faces of her masculine associates. Yet a few of the spectators were, I think, touched by her sufferings. Sandy Tipton thought it was "rough on Sal," and, in the contemplation of her condition, for a moment rose superior to the fact that he had an ace and two bowers in his sleeve.[2]

It will be seen also, that the situation was novel. Deaths were by no means uncommon in Roaring Camp, but a birth was a new thing. People had been dismissed from the camp effectively, finally, and with no possibility of return; but this was the first time that anybody had been introduced *ab initio*.[3] Hence the excitement.

"You go in there, Stumpy," said a prominent citizen known as Kentuck, addressing one of the loungers. "Go in there, and see what you kin do. You've had experience in them things."

Perhaps there was a fitness in the selection. Stumpy, in other climes, had been the putative head of two families; in fact, it was owing to some legal informality in these proceedings that Roaring Camp—a city of refuge—was indebted to his company. The crowd approved the choice, and Stumpy was wise enough to bow to the majority. The door closed upon the extempore surgeon and midwife, and Roaring Camp sat down outside, smoked its pipe, and awaited the issue.

The assemblage numbered about a hundred men. One or two of these were actual fugitives from justice, some were criminal, and all were

---

[1]*The primal curse*. This is a reference to God's words to Eve after she and Adam had sinned: "In sorrow thou shalt bring forth children." (Genesis 3:16.)

[2]*an ace and two bowers in his sleeve*. In some card games the bowers, which are two of the jacks, are the two highest cards in the game. Cheating gamblers hid high extra cards in their sleeves to substitute for the poor cards in their hands.

[3]*ab initio* (äb in i′ti ō), from the very beginning. [*Latin*]

reckless. Physically, they exhibited no indication of their past lives and character. The greatest scamp had a Raphael face,[4] with a profusion of blond hair; Oakhurst, a gambler, had the melancholy air and intellectual abstraction of a Hamlet[5]; the coolest and most courageous man was scarcely over five feet in height, with a soft voice and an embarrassed timid manner. The term *roughs* applied to them was a distinction rather than a definition. Perhaps in the minor details of fingers, toes, ears, etc., the camp may have been deficient, but these slight omissions did not detract from their aggregate force. The strongest man had but three fingers on his right hand; the best shot had but one eye.

Such was the physical aspect of the men that were dispersed around the cabin. The camp lay in a triangular valley, between two hills and a river. The only outlet was a steep trail over the summit of a hill that faced the cabin, now illuminated by the rising moon. The suffering woman might have seen it from the rude bunk

[4]*a Raphael* (raf′i əl) *face*, a beautiful and sweet face such as those of the Biblical characters painted by Raphael, a great Italian artist who lived from 1483 to 1520.

[5]*Hamlet*, the principal character in the tragedy of the same name by William Shakespeare. Hamlet was a melancholy, intellectual man who pondered deeply on the tragic problem he faced.

whereon she lay—seen it winding like a silver thread until it was lost in the stars above.

A fire of withered pine boughs added sociability to the gathering. By degrees the natural levity of Roaring Camp returned. Bets were freely offered and taken regarding the result. Three to five that "Sal would get through with it"; even, that the child would survive; side bets as to the sex and complexion of the coming stranger. In the midst of an excited discussion an exclamation came from those nearest the door, and the camp stopped to listen. Above the swaying and moaning of the pines, the swift rush of the river, and the crackling of the fire rose a sharp, querulous cry—a cry unlike anything heard before in the camp. The pines stopped moaning, the river ceased to rush, and the fire to crackle. It seemed as if Nature had stopped to listen too.

The camp rose to its feet as one man! It was proposed to explode a barrel of gunpowder, but, in consideration of the situation of the mother, better counsels prevailed, and only a few revolvers were discharged; for, whether owing to the rude surgery of the camp, or some other reason, Cherokee Sal was sinking fast. Within an hour she had climbed, as it were, that rugged road that led to the stars, and so passed out of

Roaring Camp, its sin and shame forever. I do not think that the announcement disturbed them much, except in speculation as to the fate of the child. "Can he live now?" was asked of Stumpy. The answer was doubtful. The only other being of Cherokee Sal's sex and maternal condition in the settlement was a donkey. There was some conjecture as to fitness, but the experiment was tried. It was less problematical than the ancient treatment of Romulus and Remus,[6] and apparently as successful.

When these details were completed, which exhausted another hour, the door was opened, and the anxious crowd, who had already formed themselves into a queue, entered in single file. Beside the low bunk or shelf, on which the figure of the mother was starkly outlined below the blankets, stood a pine table. On this a candle box was placed, and within it, swathed in staring red flannel, lay the last arrival at Roaring Camp. Beside the candle box was placed a hat. Its use was soon indicated. "Gentlemen," said Stumpy, with a singular mixture of authority and *ex officio* complacency[7]— "Gentlemen will please pass in at the front door, round the table, and out at the back door. Them as wishes to contribute anything toward the orphan will find a hat handy." The first man entered with his hat on; he uncovered, however, as he looked about him, and so, unconsciously, set an example to the next.

In such communities good and bad actions are catching. As the procession filed in, comments were audible—criticisms addressed, perhaps, rather to Stumpy, in the character of showman—"Is that him?" "Mighty small specimen"; "Hasn't more'n got the color"; "Ain't bigger nor a derringer." The contributions were as characteristic: a silver tobacco box; a doubloon; a navy revolver, silver mounted; a gold specimen; a very beautifully embroidered lady's handkerchief (from Oakhurst the gambler); a diamond breastpin; a diamond ring (suggested by the pin, with the remark from the giver that he "saw that pin and went two diamonds better"); a slung shot[8]; a Bible (contributor not detected); a golden spur; a silver teaspoon (the initials, I regret to say, were not the giver's); a pair of surgeon's shears; a lancet; a Bank of England note for £5[9]; and about $200 in loose gold and silver coin. During these proceedings Stumpy maintained a silence as impassive as the dead on his left—a gravity as inscrutable as that of the newly born on his right.

Only one incident occurred to break the monotony of the curious procession. As Kentuck bent over the candle box half curiously, the child turned, and in a spasm of pain, caught at his groping finger, and held it fast for a moment. Kentuck looked foolish and embarrassed. Something like a blush tried to assert itself in his weather-beaten cheek. "The d—d little cuss!" he said, as he extricated his finger, with, perhaps, more tenderness and care than he might have been deemed capable of showing. He held that finger a little apart from its fellows as he went out, and examined it curiously. The examination provoked the same original remark in regard to the child. In fact, he seemed to enjoy repeating it. "He rastled with my finger," he remarked to Tipton, holding up the member, "the d—d little cuss!"

It was four o'clock before the camp sought repose. A light burnt in the cabin where the watchers sat, for Stumpy did not go to bed that night. Nor did Kentuck. He drank quite freely and related with great gusto his experience, invariably ending with his characteristic condemnation of the newcomer. It seemed to relieve him of any unjust implication of sentiment, and Kentuck had the weaknesses of the nobler sex. When everybody else had gone to bed, he walked down to the river, and whistled reflectingly. Then he walked up the gulch, past the cabin, still whistling with demonstrative unconcern. At a large redwood tree he paused and retraced his steps, and again passed the cabin. Halfway down to the river's bank he again

---

[6]*the ancient treatment of Romulus and Remus.* According to Roman myth, Romulus, the founder and first king of Rome, and his brother Remus were nourished by a wolf.

[7]*ex officio* (eks ə fish'i ō) *complacency*, self-satisfaction deriving from the office held.

[8]*a slung shot,* a weapon made of a piece of metal or stone fastened to a short strap or chain.

[9]*a Bank of England note for £5,* a piece of paper money worth five pounds drawn on the Bank of England. At the time of the story a five-pound note was worth about $25 in United States money.

paused, and then returned and knocked at the door. It was opened by Stumpy.

"How goes it?" said Kentuck, looking past Stumpy toward the candle box.

"All serene," replied Stumpy.

"Anything up?"

"Nothing."

There was a pause—an embarrassing one—Stumpy still holding the door. Then Kentuck had recourse to his finger, which he held up to Stumpy. "Rastled with it—the d——d little cuss," he said, and retired.

The next day Cherokee Sal had such rude sepulture as Roaring Camp afforded. After her body had been committed to the hillside, there was a formal meeting of the camp to discuss what should be done with her infant. A resolution to adopt it was unanimous and enthusiastic. But an animated discussion in regard to the manner and feasibility of providing for its wants at once sprung up. It was remarkable that the argument partook of none of those fierce personalities with which discussions were usually conducted at Roaring Camp. Tipton proposed that they should send the child to Red Dog—a distance of forty miles—where female attention could be procured. But the unlucky suggestion met with fierce and unanimous opposition. It was evident that no plan which entailed parting from their new acquisition would for a moment be entertained. "Besides," said Tom Ryder, "them fellows at Red Dog would swap it, and ring in somebody else on us." A disbelief in the honesty of other camps prevailed at Roaring Camp as in other places.

The introduction of a female nurse in the camp also met with objection. It was argued that no decent woman could be prevailed to accept Roaring Camp as her home, and the speaker urged that "they didn't want any more of the other kind." This unkind allusion to the defunct mother, harsh as it may seem, was the first spasm of propriety—the first symptom of the camp's regeneration. Stumpy advanced nothing. Perhaps he felt a certain delicacy in interfering with the selection of a possible successor in office. But when questioned, he averred stoutly that he and Jinny—the mammal before alluded to—could manage to rear the child. There was

something original, independent, and heroic about the plan that pleased the camp. Stumpy was retained. Certain articles were sent for to Sacramento. "Mind," said the treasurer, as he pressed a bag of gold dust into the expressman's hand, "the best that can be got—lace, you know, and filigree work and frills—d——n the cost!"

Strange to say, the child thrived. Perhaps the invigorating climate of the mountain camp was compensation for material deficiencies. Nature took the foundling to her broader breast. In that rare atmosphere of the Sierra foothills[10]—that air pungent with balsamic odor, that ethereal cordial, at once bracing and exhilarating, he may have found food and nourishment, or a subtle chemistry that transmuted donkey's milk to lime and phosphorus.[11] Stumpy inclined to the belief that it was the latter and good nursing. "Me and that donkey," he would say, "has been father and mother to him! Don't you," he would add, apostrophizing the helpless bundle before him, "never go back on us."

By the time he was a month old, the necessity of giving him a name became apparent. He had generally been known as "the Kid," "Stumpy's boy," "the Cayote" (an allusion to his vocal powers), and even by Kentuck's endearing diminutive of "the d——d little cuss." But these were felt to be vague and unsatisfactory, and were at last dismissed under another influence. Gamblers and adventurers are generally superstitious, and Oakhurst one day declared that the baby had brought "the luck" to Roaring Camp. It was certain that of late they had been successful. "Luck" was the name agreed upon, with the prefix of Tommy for greater convenience. No allusion was made to the mother, and the father was unknown. "It's better," said the philosophical Oakhurst, "to take a fresh deal all round. Call him Luck, and start him fair." A day was accordingly set apart for the christening. What was meant by this ceremony the reader may imagine, who has already gathered some idea of the reckless irreverence of Roaring Camp. The master of ceremonies was one "Boston," a noted wag, and the occasion seemed

10 *the Sierra* (si er'ə) *foothills*, the low hills at the base of the Sierra Nevada Mountains in eastern California.

11 *lime and phosphorus*, substances necessary for growth.

to promise the greatest facetiousness. This ingenious satirist had spent two days in preparing a burlesque of the church service, with pointed local allusions. The choir was properly trained and Sandy Tipton was to stand godfather. But after the procession had marched to the grove with music and banners, and the child had been deposited before a mock altar, Stumpy stepped before the expectant crowd.

"It ain't my style to spoil fun, boys," said the little man, stoutly, eyeing the faces around him, "but it strikes me that this thing ain't exactly on the squar. It's playing it pretty low down on this yer baby to ring in fun on him that he ain't goin' to understand. And ef there's going to be any godfathers round, I'd like to see who's got any better rights than me."

A silence followed Stumpy's speech. To the credit of all humorists be it said that the first man to acknowledge its justice was the satirist, thus stopped of his fun. "But," said Stumpy, quickly, following up his advantage, "we're here for a christening, and we'll have it. I proclaim you Thomas Luck, according to the laws of the United States and the State of California, so help me God." It was the first time that the name of the Deity had been uttered otherwise but profanely in the camp. The form of christening was perhaps even more ludicrous than the satirist had conceived; but strangely enough, nobody saw it and nobody laughed. Tommy was christened as seriously as he would have been under a Christian roof, and cried and was comforted in as orthodox fashion.

And so the work of regeneration began in Roaring Camp. Almost imperceptibly a change came over the settlement. The cabin assigned to Tommy Luck—or The Luck, as he was more frequently called—first showed signs of improvement. It was kept scrupulously clean and whitewashed. Then it was boarded, clothed and papered. The rosewood cradle—packed eighty miles by mule—had, in Stumpy's way of putting it, "sorter killed the rest of the furniture." So the rehabilitation of the cabin became a necessity. The men who were in the habit of lounging in at Stumpy's to see "how The Luck got on" seemed to appreciate the change, and, in self-defense, the rival establishment of "Tuttle's grocery" bestirred itself, and imported a carpet and mirrors. The reflections of the latter on the appearance of Roaring Camp tended to produce stricter habits of personal cleanliness. Again Stumpy imposed a kind of quarantine upon those who aspired to the honor and privilege of holding The Luck. It was a cruel mortification to Kentuck—who, in the carelessness of a large nature and the habits of frontier life, had begun to regard all garments as a second cuticle, which, like a snake's, only sloughed off through decay—to be debarred this privilege from certain prudential reasons. Yet such was the subtle influence of innovation that he thereafter appeared regularly every afternoon in a clean shirt, and face still shining from his ablutions. Nor were moral and social sanitary laws neglected. Tommy, who was supposed to spend his whole existence in a persistent attempt to repose, must not be disturbed by noise. The shouting and yelling which had gained the camp its infelicitous title were not permitted within hearing distance of Stumpy's. The men conversed in whispers, or smoked with Indian gravity. Profanity was tacitly given up in these sacred precincts, and throughout the camp a popular form of expletive, known as "D——n the luck!" and "Curse the luck!" was abandoned, as having a new personal bearing. Vocal music was not interdicted, being supposed to have a soothing, tranquilizing quality, and one song, sung by Man-o'-War Jack, an English sailor from Her Majesty's[12] Australian colonies, was quite popular as a lullaby. It was a lugubrious recital of the exploits of "the *Arethusa,* Seventy-four," in a muffled minor, ending with a prolonged dying fall at the burden of each verse, "On b-o-o-o-ard of the *Arethusa.*" It was a fine sight to see Jack holding The Luck, rocking from side to side as if with the motion of a ship, and crooning forth this naval ditty. Either through the peculiar rocking of Jack or the length of his song—it contained ninety stanzas, and was continued with conscientious deliberation to the bitter end—the lullaby generally had the desired effect. At such times the men would

---

[12]*Her Majesty,* Queen Victoria, ruler of England from 1837 to 1901.

lie at full length under the trees, in the soft summer twilight, smoking their pipes and drinking in the melodious utterances. An indistinct idea that this was pastoral happiness pervaded the camp. "This 'ere kind o' think," said the Cockney Simmons, meditatively reclining on his elbow, "is 'evingly." It reminded him of Greenwich.[13]

On the long summer days The Luck was usually carried to the gulch, from whence the golden store of Roaring Camp was taken. There, on a blanket spread over pine boughs, he would lie while the men were working in the ditches below. Latterly, there was a rude attempt to decorate this bower with flowers and sweet-smelling shrubs, and generally someone would bring him a cluster of wild honeysuckles, azaleas, or the painted blossoms of Las Mariposas.[14] The men had suddenly awakened to the fact that there were beauty and significance in these trifles, which they had so long trodden carelessly beneath their feet. A flake of glittering mica, a fragment of variegated quartz, a bright pebble from the bed of the creek, became beautiful to eyes thus cleared and strengthened, and were invariably put aside for The Luck. It was wonderful how many treasures the woods and hillsides yielded that "would do for Tommy." Surrounded by playthings such as never child out of fairyland had before, it is to be hoped that Tommy was content. He appeared to be serenely happy, albeit there was an infantine gravity about him, a contemplative light in his round gray eyes, that sometimes worried Stumpy. He was always tractable and quiet, and it is recorded that once, having crept beyond his "corral"—a hedge of tessellated pine boughs, which surrounded his bed—he dropped over the bank on his head in the soft earth, and remained with his mottled legs in the air in that position for at least five minutes with unflinching gravity. He was extricated without a murmur. I hesitate to record the many other instances of his sagac-

ity, which rest, unfortunately, upon the statements of prejudiced friends. Some of them were not without a tinge of superstition. "I crep' up the bank just now," said Kentuck one day, in a breathless state of excitement, "and dern my skin if he wasn't talking to a jaybird as was a-sittin' on his lap. There they was, just as free and sociable as anything you please, a-jawin' at each other just like two cherrybums."[15] Howbeit, whether creeping over the pine boughs or lying lazily on his back blinking at the leaves above him, to him the birds sang, the squirrels chattered, and the flowers bloomed. Nature was his nurse and playfellow. For him she would let slip between the leaves golden shafts of sunlight that fell just within his grasp; she would send wandering breezes to visit him with the balm of bay and resinous gums; to him the tall redwoods nodded familiarly and sleepily, the bumblebees buzzed, and the rooks cawed a slumberous accompaniment.

Such was the golden summer of Roaring Camp. They were flush times—and The Luck was with them. The claims had yielded enormously. The camp was jealous of its privileges and looked suspiciously on strangers. No encouragement was given to immigration, and, to make their seclusion more perfect, the land on either side of the mountain wall that surrounded the camp they duly preëmpted. This, and a reputation of singular proficiency with the revolver, kept the reserve of Roaring Camp inviolate. The expressman—their only connecting link with the surrounding world—sometimes told wonderful stories of the camp. He would say, "They've a street up there in Roaring, that would lay over any street up there in Red Dog. They've got vines and flowers round their houses, and they wash themselves twice a day. But they're mighty rough on strangers, and they worship an Injun baby."

With the prosperity of the camp came a desire for further improvement. It was proposed to build a hotel in the following spring, and to invite one or two decent families to reside there for the sake of The Luck, who might perhaps profit by female companionship. The sacrifice

[13]*Cockney Simmons . . . Greenwich* (grin′ij *or* gren′ich). To Simmons, who came from and spoke the dialect of a poor, crowded section of London, the atmosphere was like that of Greenwich, a much more green and open section of the city.

[14]*the painted blossoms of Las Mariposas* (läs mar′i pō′-səs), the tuliplike flowers of the Mariposa lily.

[15]*cherrybums,* cherubim, or angels.

that this concession to the sex cost these men, who were fiercely skeptical in regard to its general virtue and usefulness, can only be accounted for by their affection for Tommy. A few still held out. But the resolve could not be carried into effect for three months, and the minority meekly yielded in the hope that something might turn up to prevent it. And it did.

The winter of '51 will long be remembered in the foothills. The snow lay deep on the sierras, and every mountain creek became a river, and every river a lake. Each gorge and gulch was transformed into a tumultuous watercourse that descended the hillsides, tearing down giant trees and scattering its drift and debris along the plain. Red Dog had been twice under water, and Roaring Camp had been forewarned. "Water put the gold into them gulches," said Stumpy; "it's been here once and will be here again!" And that night the North Fork suddenly leaped over its banks, and swept up the triangular valley of Roaring Camp.

In the confusion of rushing water, crashing trees, and crackling timber, and the darkness which seemed to flow with the water and blot out the fair valley, but little could be done to collect the scattered camp. When the morning broke, the cabin of Stumpy nearest the riverbank was gone. Higher up the gulch they found the body of its unlucky owner; but the pride—the hope—the joy—The Luck—of Roaring Camp had disappeared. They were returning with sad hearts, when a shout from the bank recalled them.

It was a relief boat from down the river. They had picked up, they said, a man and an infant, nearly exhausted, about two miles below. Did anybody know them, and did they belong here?

It needed but a glance to show them Kentuck lying there, cruelly crushed and bruised, but still holding The Luck of Roaring Camp in his arms. As they bent over the strangely assorted pair, they saw that the child was cold and pulseless.

"He is dead," said one.

Kentuck opened his eyes.

"Dead?" he repeated feebly.

"Yes, my man, and you are dying, too."

A smile lit the eyes of the expiring Kentuck. "Dying!" he repeated, "he's a-taking me with him—tell the boys I've got The Luck with me now"; and the strong man, clinging to the frail babe as a drowning man is said to cling to a straw, drifted away into the shadowy river that flows forever to the unknown sea.

HOW DOES HARTE USE LOCAL COLOR?

1. Are happenings in this story the result of conditions in the mining camp, or might they have taken place almost anywhere? In other words, is the local color functional, or is it merely decorative?

2. The first two paragraphs set the scene, and are therefore very important in this local-color story. Describe in your own words the character of Roaring Camp and of its inhabitants. How has the author managed to tell you what the town is like?

3. Why does Roaring Camp reform? Trace the stages in its reformation. Explain why the reformation does or does not seem believable to you.

4. One device Harte was famous for (perhaps he'd learned it from the English novelist, Charles Dickens) was that of making characters memorable by giving them combinations of traits or a contrast between traits and appearance not usually found in the same person. For example, "The greatest scamp had a Raphael face with a profusion of blond hair" (page 523, column 1, lines 2-4). What incongruous traits do you find in Stumpy and in Kentuck? Cite any other examples of incongruous traits you can find.

5. Harte once wrote of Dickens: "I observe that whenever an accident, a murder, or death is about to happen, there is something in the furniture, in the locality, in the atmosphere, that foreshadows and suggests it...." Does this comment apply to any passages in this story? If so, which ones?

Bret Harte and the earlier humorists

In the days before the War Between the States, a group of storytellers far different from Hawthorne and Poe flourished in the United States. These men wrote stories of the type that Americans were telling around campfires and in country stores. The tales were about characters, customs, and happenings peculiar to a certain section of the country, and humor was one of their dominant characteristics.

Bret Harte gave much of the credit for his way of telling local-color stories to this group of earlier humorists. Their humor, he said, "was concise...yet suggestive...delightfully extravagant—or a miracle of understatement. It voiced not only the dialect, but the habits of thought of a people or locality....By degrees it developed character with its incident, often in a few lines, giving a striking photograph of a community or a section, but always reached its conclusion without an unnecessary word."

Illustrate from "The Luck of Roaring Camp" one or more of the points that Harte makes here about the humorists' (and his own) way of telling a story.

Extending interests

Many of Bret Harte's contemporaries of the local-color school wrote short stories that are just as entertaining to readers today as they were to their first audience. Among such authors are George Washington Cable, Edward Eggleston, Thomas Nelson Page, Mark Twain, Mary Noailles Murfree, Joel Chandler Harris, Sarah Orne Jewett, and Mary E. Wilkins Freeman.

Plan to read one or more stories by one of these authors, or by Bret Harte. Pay particular attention to the section of the country the writer represents and to the way in which he uses local color. If you can arrange with your teacher for a class period at which the stories may be discussed, you will find it interesting to exchange information about the various local-color stories members of the class have read. You will find collections of short stories by some of the individual writers listed in the bibliography on page 546. Others are represented in collections like the following: *Golden Tales of Our America, Golden Tales of the Far West, Golden Tales of the Old South,* and *Golden Tales of New England,* all edited by May Lamberton Becker; *Short Stories for English Courses,* edited by Rosa Mary Mikels; and *American Short Stories,* edited by Fred Lewis Pattee.

❧ IV O. HENRY (1862-1910)[1]

During the final years of the local-color movement, a new type of short story became popular with American readers. This kind of story, which reached the height of its development between 1873 and 1910, has been described by Professor Henry Seidel Canby as "the story of light and surprising situations whose point is revealed by a twist of the plot at the very end"—the story of "the surprise ending."

The surprise ending was not an entirely new thing. It had first come into popularity among the humorous yarnspinners who greatly influenced Bret Harte's work. (See "Bret Harte and the Earlier Humorists," above.) The new stories differed, however, from the old-fashioned yarns because of another influence, that of famous French short-story writers of the day. From them authors learned to write stories that were more sure-footed, more economical of words, and faster moving than the old yarns had been.

One of the best writers of stories with a surprise ending was William Sidney Porter, who wrote under the pen name O. Henry. Like the local colorists, he habitually set his stories in a particular area, and he wrote of a number of locales. However, he is chiefly famous for his pictures of the lives of the ordinary folk of New York City—"the four million," as he called them in the title of one of his books to distinguish them from "the four hundred," the very exclusive list of social leaders of New York.

O. Henry was a master of irony and humor—sometimes supplied by character portrayal, sometimes by the lifelike dialogue, sometimes by his style. Above all he was skilled in unfolding his stories in such a way as to keep the reader in suspense until the end, and then to deliver a "punch line" or "twist" at the conclusion.

[1]For a biographical sketch of O. Henry see page 443.

The Gift of the Magi

O. HENRY

ONE DOLLAR and eighty-seven cents. That was all. And sixty cents of it was in pennies. Pennies saved one and two at a time by bulldozing the grocer and the vegetable man and the butcher until one's cheeks burned with the silent imputation of parsimony that such close dealing implied. Three times Della counted it. One dollar and eighty-seven cents. And the next day would be Christmas.

There was clearly nothing to do but flop down on the shabby little couch and howl. So Della did it. Which instigates the moral reflec-tion that life is made up of sobs, sniffles, and smiles, with sniffles predominating.

While the mistress of the home is gradually subsiding from the first stage to the second, take a look at the home. A furnished flat at $8 per week. It did not exactly beggar description, but it certainly had that word on the lookout for the mendicancy squad.

In the vestibule below was a letter box into which no letter would go, and an electric button from which no mortal finger could coax a ring. Also appertaining thereunto was a card bearing the name Mr. James Dillingham Young.

The *Dillingham* had been flung to the breeze during a former period of prosperity when its possessor was being paid $30 per week. Now, when the income was shrunk to $20, the letters of *Dillingham* looked blurred, as though they were thinking seriously of contracting to a modest and unassuming *D*. But whenever Mr. James Dillingham Young came home and reached his flat above he was called Jim and greatly hugged by Mrs. James Dillingham Young, already introduced to you as Della. Which is all very good.

Della finished her cry and attended to her cheeks with the powder rag. She stood by the window and looked out dully at a gray cat walking a gray fence in a gray back yard. Tomorrow would be Christmas Day, and she had only $1.87 with which to buy Jim a present. She had been saving every penny she could for months, with this result. Twenty dollars a week doesn't go far. Expenses had been greater than she had calculated. They always are. Only $1.87 to buy a present for Jim. Her Jim. Many a happy hour she had spent planning for something nice for him. Something fine and rare and sterling—something just a little bit near to being worthy of the honor of being owned by Jim.

There was a pier glass between the windows of the room. Perhaps you have seen a pier glass in an $8 flat. A very thin and very agile person may, by observing his reflection in a rapid sequence of longitudinal strips, obtain a fairly accurate conception of his looks. Della, being slender, had mastered the art.

Suddenly she whirled from the window and stood before the glass. Her eyes were shining brilliantly, but her face had lost its color within twenty seconds. Rapidly she pulled down her hair and let it fall to its full length.

Now, there were two possessions of the James Dillingham Youngs in which they both took a mighty pride. One was Jim's gold watch that had been his father's and his grandfather's. The other was Della's hair. Had the Queen of Sheba[1] lived in the flat across the air shaft, Della would have let her hair hang out the window some day to dry just to depreciate Her Majesty's jewels and gifts. Had King Solomon been the janitor, with all his treasures piled up in the basement, Jim would have pulled out his watch every time he passed, just to see him pluck at his beard from envy.

So now Della's beautiful hair fell about her, rippling and shining like a cascade of brown waters. It reached below her knee and made itself almost a garment for her. And then she did it up again nervously and quickly. Once she faltered for a minute and stood still while a tear or two splashed on the worn red carpet.

On went her old brown jacket; on went her old brown hat. With a whirl of skirts and with the brilliant sparkle still in her eyes, she fluttered out of the door and down the stairs to the street.

Where she stopped, the sign read: "Mme. Sofronie. Hair Goods of All Kinds." One flight up Della ran, and collected herself, panting. Madame, large, too white, chilly, hardly looked the *Sofronie*.

"Will you buy my hair?" asked Della.

"I buy hair," said Madame. "Take yer hat off and let's have a sight at the looks of it."

Down rippled the brown cascade.

"Twenty dollars," said Madame, lifting the mass with a practiced hand.

"Give it to me quick," said Della.

Oh, and the next two hours tripped by on rosy wings. Forget the hashed metaphor.[2] She was ransacking the stores for Jim's present.

She found it at last. It surely had been made for Jim and no one else. There was no other like it in any of the stores, and she had turned all of them inside out. It was a platinum fob chain, simple and chaste in design, properly proclaiming its values by substance alone and not by meretricious ornamentation—as all good things

---

[1] *the Queen of Sheba*, a queen of ancient Abyssinia who visited King Solomon of Israel to learn of his great wisdom. She brought magnificent gifts. (I Kings 10:1-13.)

[2] *hashed metaphor*. The author is referring to his own mixed comparison in the preceding sentence. If hours *trip* by, it should be on *feet*, not *wings*.

should do. It was even worthy of The Watch. As soon as she saw it she knew that it must be Jim's. It was like him. Quietness and value—the description applied to both. Twenty-one dollars they took from her for it, and she hurried home with the 87 cents. With that chain on his watch Jim might be properly anxious about the time in any company. Grand as the watch was, he sometimes looked at it on the sly on account of the old leather strap that he used in place of a chain.

When Della reached home her intoxication gave way a little to prudence and reason. She got out her curling irons and lighted the gas and went to work repairing the ravages made by generosity added to love. Which is always a tremendous task, dear friends—a mammoth task.

Within forty minutes her head was covered with tiny, close-lying curls that made her look wonderfully like a truant schoolboy. She looked at her reflection in the mirror long, carefully, and critically.

"If Jim doesn't kill me," she said to herself, "before he takes a second look at me, he'll say I look like a Coney Island chorus girl.[3] But what could I do—oh! what could I do with a dollar and eighty-seven cents?"

At seven o'clock the coffee was made and the frying pan was on the back of the stove hot and ready to cook the chops.

Jim was never late. Della doubled the fob chain in her hand and sat on the corner of the table near the door that he always entered. Then she heard his step on the stair away down on the first flight, and she turned white for just a moment. She had a habit of saying little silent prayers about the simplest everyday things, and now she whispered: "Please, God, make him think I am still pretty."

The door opened and Jim stepped in and closed it. He looked thin and very serious. Poor fellow, he was only twenty-two—and to be burdened with a family! He needed a new overcoat and he was without gloves.

Jim stopped inside the door, as immovable as a setter at the scent of quail. His eyes were fixed upon Della, and there was an expression in them that she could not read, and it terrified her. It was not anger, nor surprise, nor disapproval, nor horror, nor any of the sentiments that she had been prepared for. He simply stared at her fixedly with that peculiar expression on his face.

Della wriggled off the table and went for him.

"Jim, darling," she cried, "don't look at me that way. I had my hair cut off and sold it because I couldn't live through Christmas without giving you a present. It'll grow out again—you won't mind, will you? I just had to do it. My hair grows awfully fast. Say 'Merry Christmas,' Jim, and let's be happy. You don't know what a nice—what a beautiful, nice gift I've got for you."

"You've cut off your hair?" asked Jim laboriously, as if he had not arrived at that patent fact yet, even after the hardest mental labor.

"Cut it off and sold it," said Della. "Don't you like me just as well, anyhow? I'm me without my hair, ain't I?"

Jim looked about the room curiously.

"You say your hair is gone?" he said, with an air almost of idiocy.

"You needn't look for it," said Della. "It's sold, I tell you—sold and gone, too. It's Christmas Eve, boy. Be good to me, for it went for you. Maybe the hairs of my head were numbered," she went on with a sudden serious sweetness, "but nobody could ever count my love for you. Shall I put the chops on, Jim?"

Out of his trance Jim seemed quickly to wake. He enfolded his Della. For ten seconds let us regard with discreet scrutiny some inconsequential object in the other direction. Eight dollars a week or a million a year—what is the difference? A mathematician or a wit would give you the wrong answer. The Magi[4] brought valuable gifts, but that was not among them. This dark assertion will be illuminated later on.

Jim drew a package from his overcoat pocket and threw it upon the table.

"Don't make any mistake, Dell," he said, "about me. I don't think there's anything in the

---

[3]*Coney Island chorus girl*, a girl who dances at Coney Island, a famous amusement park on Long Island in New York.

[4]*The Magi* (mā′jī *or* maj′ī), the three Wise Men from the East who brought gifts to the Infant Jesus. (Matthew 2:1-2, 7-13.)

way of a haircut or a shave or a shampoo that could make me like my girl any less. But if you'll unwrap that package you may see why you had me going awhile at first."

White fingers and nimble tore at the string and paper. And then an ecstatic scream of joy; and then, alas! a quick feminine change to hysterical tears and wails, necessitating the immediate employment of all the comforting powers of the lord of the flat.

For there lay The Combs—the set of combs, side and back, that Della had worshiped for long in a Broadway window. Beautiful combs, pure tortoise shell, with jeweled rims—just the shade to wear in the beautiful vanished hair. They were expensive combs, she knew, and her heart had simply craved and yearned over them without the least hope of possession. And now they were hers, but the tresses that should have adorned the coveted adornments were gone.

But she hugged them to her bosom, and at length she was able to look up with dim eyes and a smile and say: "My hair grows so fast, Jim!"

And then Della leaped up like a little singed cat and cried, "Oh, oh!"

Jim had not yet seen his beautiful present. She held it out to him eagerly upon her open palm. The dull precious metal seemed to flash with a reflection of her bright and ardent spirit.

"Isn't it a dandy, Jim? I hunted all over town to find it. You'll have to look at the time a hundred times a day now. Give me your watch. I want to see how it looks on it."

Instead of obeying, Jim tumbled down on the couch and put his hands under the back of his head and smiled.

"Dell," said he, "let's put our Christmas presents away and keep 'em a while. They're too nice to use just at present. I sold the watch to get the money to buy your combs. And now suppose you put the chops on."

The Magi, as you know, were wise men—wonderfully wise men—who brought gifts to the Babe in the manger. They invented the art of giving Christmas presents. Being wise, their gifts were no doubt wise ones, possibly bearing the privilege of exchange in case of duplication.

And here I have lamely related to you the uneventful chronicle of two foolish children in a flat who most unwisely sacrificed for each other the greatest treasures of their house. But in a last word to the wise of these days let it be said that of all who give gifts these two were the wisest. Of all who give and receive gifts, such as they are wisest. Everywhere they are wisest. They are the Magi.

WHAT IS THE ART OF THE SURPRISE-ENDING STORY?

1. What information does the author withhold until the very end in order to prepare for the surprise ending? What clue has the author given earlier in the story that might prepare the alert reader for this conclusion?

2. How does the last paragraph of the selection help explain the title? Would you like the story better if the last paragraph were removed? Why, or why not?

3. What means does the author use to assure the reader's sympathy for Jim and Della?

4. Cite details which show that this story is located in New York City. In your opinion is the local color here as functional as that in "The Luck of Roaring Camp"; that is, to what extent does the plot of each story depend on its particular locality? Explain your answer.

5. O. Henry has a way of speaking directly to the reader now and then, as when he writes, "Which instigates the moral reflection that life is made up of sobs, sniffles, and smiles, with sniffles predominating" (page 530, column 1, paragraph 2). Find other examples of such asides. What purposes do they serve?

6. Would you say that the humor in this story derives mainly from (a) the plot or (b) O. Henry's style? Read aloud passages that uphold your viewpoint.

Extending interests

Among the authors who with O. Henry brought the surprise-ending story to prominence were Henry Cuyler Bunner, Thomas Bailey Aldrich, and Frank Stockton. Plan to read several more stories by O. Henry or stories by one or more of these authors. Then arrange with your teacher for a class period at which the stories may be discussed. Pay particular attention to these points: Was the ending really a surprise? Did local color play any part in the story? Each of the following collections contains several good "twist" stories: *American Short Stories*, edited by Fred Lewis Pattee; *Representative Modern Short Stories* and *Best American Humorous Short Stories*, both edited by Alexander Jessup.

V STEPHEN CRANE (1871-1900)[1]

O. Henry and some of his contemporaries did much to perfect the art of unfolding stories. Another group of writers in their period believed that other matters were more important. They reasoned thus: (1) New ways of living were posing new questions to Americans. (2) These ways of living were stimulating new ideas and philosophies about life. (3) It was the task of the short-story writer—as well as the novelist—to represent these ideas in his work.

Different authors within this group went about their task in different ways. Some—for example, Hamlin Garland (1860-1940)—wrote fiction which embodied ideas about economics. Some, notably Henry James (1843-1916), dealt with the problems of the international scene. Quite a few presented new views of human nature, and were at the time called "naturalists." Prominent among this last group—which had adherents in France as well as in the United States—was Stephen Crane. Like his fellow naturalists, Crane believed that men's lives were often more sordid and terrible than they had been previously pictured. He also believed that the course of men's lives was more influenced by forces beyond their control than earlier authors had seen. These beliefs were reflected in Crane's writing. He included more distressing details than his predecessors had, and often he showed lowly characters suffering because they had a bad inheritance or because economic need or the harsh world of nature shaped their lives in undesirable patterns.

The rapidly developing science of psychology also had its influence upon Crane's works. Often his stories derived much of their power from the insights they gave into the minds of characters. A typical story showed a character gripped by a strong emotion. Crane conveyed that emotion by what critics have called "impressionism." This name means that as he described what the characters experienced, he selected details, and he described elements in the scene, in such a way as to convey the emotions of the characters. In "The Open Boat," for instance, he thus describes the sea as it is viewed from a tiny dinghy by the survivors of a wreck: "There was a terrible grace in the move of the waves, and they came in silence, save for the snarling of the crests." Or he describes a shark, hopefully following the little boat at night, as "a gleaming trail of phosphorescence" which "might have been made by a monstrous Knife." Thus, with deft, quick touches, Crane suggests the *menace* that the survivors feel in the snarling sea and its sharp-toothed monsters.

The following story of an incident in the War Between the States has been called by Carl Van Doren "pure, concentrated Crane."

---

[1]For a biographical sketch of Crane see page 443.

A Mystery of Heroism

STEPHEN CRANE

THE DARK UNIFORMS of the men were so coated with dust from the incessant wrestling of the two armies that the regiment almost seemed a part of the clay bank which shielded them from the shells. On the top of the hill a battery was arguing in tremendous roars with some other guns, and to the eye of the infantry the artillerymen, the guns, the caissons, the horses, were distinctly outlined upon the blue sky. When a piece was fired, a red streak as round as a log flashed low in the heavens, like a monstrous bolt of lightning. The men of the battery wore white duck trousers, which somehow emphasized their legs; and when they ran and crowded in little groups at the bidding of the shouting officers, it was more impressive than usual to the infantry.

Fred Collins, of A Company, was saying: "Thunder! I wisht I had a drink. Ain't there any water round here?"

Then somebody yelled: "There goes th' bugler!"

As the eyes of half the regiment swept in one machinelike movement, there was an instant's picture of a horse in a great convulsive leap of a death wound and a rider leaning back with a crooked arm and spread fingers before his face. On the ground was the crimson terror of an exploding shell, with fibers of flame that seemed like lances. A glittering bugle swung clear of the rider's back as fell headlong the horse and the man. In the air was an odor as from a conflagration.

Sometimes they of the infantry looked down at a fair little meadow which spread at their feet. Its long green grass was rippling gently in a breeze. Beyond it was the gray form of a house half torn to pieces by shells and by the busy axes of soldiers who had pursued firewood. The line of an old fence was now dimly marked by long weeds and by an occasional post. A shell had blown the wellhouse to fragments. Little lines of gray smoke ribboning upward from some embers indicated the place where had stood the barn.

From beyond a curtain of green woods there came the sound of some stupendous scuffle, as if two animals of the size of islands were fighting. At a distance there were occasional appearances of swift-moving men, horses, batteries, flags, and with the crashing of infantry volleys were heard, often, wild and frenzied cheers. In the midst of it all Smith and Ferguson, two privates of A Company, were engaged in a heated discussion which involved the greatest questions of the national existence.

The battery on the hill presently engaged in a frightful duel. The white legs of the gunners scampered this way and that way, and the officers redoubled their shouts. The guns, with their demeanors of stolidity and courage, were typical of something infinitely self-possessed in this clamor of death that swirled around the hill.

One of a "swing" team[1] was suddenly smitten quivering to the ground, and his maddened

brethren dragged his torn body in their struggle to escape from this turmoil and danger. A young soldier astride one of the leaders swore and fumed in his saddle and furiously jerked at the bridle. An officer screamed out an order so violently that his voice broke and ended the sentence in a falsetto shriek.

The leading company of infantry regiment was somewhat exposed, and the colonel ordered it moved more fully under the shelter of the hill. There was the clank of steel against steel.

A lieutenant of the battery rode down and passed them, holding his right arm carefully in his left hand. And it was as if this arm was not at all a part of him, but belonged to another man. His sober and reflective charger went slowly. The officer's face was grimy and perspiring, and his uniform was tousled as if he had been in direct grapple with an enemy. He smiled grimly when the men stared at him. He turned his horse toward the meadow.

Collins, of A Company, said: "I wisht I had a drink. I bet there's water in that there ol' well yonder!"

"Yes; but how you goin' to git it?"

For the little meadow which intervened was now suffering a terrible onslaught of shells. Its green and beautiful calm had vanished utterly. Brown earth was being flung in monstrous handfuls. And there was a massacre of the young blades of grass. They were being torn, burned, obliterated. Some curious fortune of the battle had made this gentle little meadow the object of the red hate of the shells, and each one as it exploded seemed like an imprecation in the face of a maiden.

The wounded officer who was riding across this expanse said to himself: "Why, they couldn't shoot any harder if the whole army was massed here!"

A shell struck the gray ruins of the house, and as, after the roar, the shattered wall fell in fragments, there was a noise which resembled the flapping of shutters during a wild gale of winter. Indeed, the infantry paused in the shelter of the bank appeared as men standing upon a shore contemplating a madness of the sea. The angel of calamity had under its glance the battery upon the hill. Fewer white-legged men

---

[1] a "swing" team, the middle pair of horses in a team of six.

labored about the guns. A shell had smitten one of the pieces, and after the flare, the smoke, the dust, the wrath of this blow were gone, it was possible to see white legs stretched horizontally upon the ground. And at that interval to the rear where it is the business of battery horses to stand with their noses to the fight, awaiting the command to drag their guns out of the destruction, or into it, or wheresoever these incomprehensible humans demanded with whip and spur—in this line of passive and dumb spectators, whose fluttering hearts yet would not let them forget the iron laws of man's control of them—in this rank of brute-soldiers there had been relentless and hideous carnage. From the ruck of bleeding and prostrate horses, the men of the infantry could see one animal raising its stricken body with its forelegs and turning its nose with mystic and profound eloquence toward the sky.

Some comrades joked Collins about his thirst.

"Well, if yeh want a drink so bad, why don't yeh go git it?"

"Well, I will in a minnet, if yeh don't shut up!"

A lieutenant of artillery floundered his horse straight down the hill with as little concern as if it were level ground. As he galloped past the colonel of the infantry, he threw up his hand in swift salute. "We've got to get out of that," he roared angrily. He was a black-bearded officer, and his eyes, which resembled beads, sparkled like those of an insane man. His jumping horse sped along the column of infantry.

The fat major, standing carelessly with his sword held horizontally behind him and with his legs far apart, looked after the receding horseman and laughed. "He wants to get back with orders pretty quick, or there'll be no batt'ry left," he observed.

The wise young captain of the second company hazarded to the lieutenant-colonel that the enemy's infantry would probably soon attack the hill, and the lieutenant-colonel snubbed him.

A private in one of the rear companies looked out over the meadow, and then turned to a companion and said, "Look there, Jim!" It was the wounded officer from the battery, who some time before had started to ride across the meadow, supporting his right arm carefully with his left hand. This man had encountered a shell, apparently, at a time when no one perceived him, and he could now be seen lying face downward with a stirruped foot stretched across the body of his dead horse. A leg of the charger extended slantingly upward, precisely as stiff as a stake. Around this motionless pair the shells still howled.

There was a quarrel in A Company. Collins was shaking his fist in the faces of some laughing comrades. "Dern yeh! I ain't afraid t' go. If yeh say much, I will go!"

"Of course, yeh will! You'll run through that there medder, won't yeh?"

Collins said, in a terrible voice: "You see now!"

At this ominous threat his comrades broke into renewed jeers.

Collins gave them a dark scowl, and went to find his captain. The latter was conversing with the colonel of the regiment.

"Captain," said Collins, saluting and standing at attention—in those days all trousers bagged at the knees—"Captain, I want t' get permission to go git some water from that there well over yonder!"

The colonel and the captain swung about simultaneously and stared across the meadow. The captain laughed. "You must be pretty thirsty, Collins?"

"Yes, sir, I am."

"Well—ah," said the captain. After a moment, he asked, "Can't you wait?"

"No, sir."

The colonel was watching Collins's face. "Look here, my lad," he said, in a pious sort of voice—"Look here, my lad"—Collins was not a lad—"don't you think that's taking pretty big risks for a little drink of water?"

"I dunno," said Collins uncomfortably. Some of the resentment toward his companions, which perhaps had forced him into this affair, was beginning to fade. "I dunno w'ether 'tis."

The colonel and the captain contemplated him for a time.

"Well," said the captain finally.

"Well," said the colonel, "if you want to go, why, go."

Collins saluted. "Much obliged t' yeh."

As he moved away the colonel called after him. "Take some of the other boys' canteens with you, an' hurry back, now."

"Yes, sir, I will."

The colonel and the captain looked at each other then, for it had suddenly occurred that they could not for the life of them tell whether Collins wanted to go or whether he did not.

They turned to regard Collins, and as they perceived him surrounded by gesticulating comrades, the colonel said: "Well, by thunder! I guess he's going."

Collins appeared as a man dreaming. In the midst of the questions, the advice, the warnings, all the excited talk of his company mates, he maintained a curious silence.

They were very busy in preparing him for his ordeal. When they inspected him carefully, it was somewhat like the examination that grooms give a horse before a race; and they were amazed, staggered, by the whole affair. Their astonishment found vent in strange repetitions.

"Are yeh sure a-goin'?" they demanded again and again.

"Certainly I am," cried Collins at last, furiously.

He strode sullenly away from them. He was swinging five or six canteens by their cords. It seemed that his cap would not remain firmly on his head, and often he reached and pulled it down over his brow.

There was a general movement in the compact column. The long animal-like thing moved slightly. Its four hundred eyes were turned upon the figure of Collins.

"Well, sir, if that ain't th' derndest thing! I never thought Fred Collins had the blood in him for that kind of business."

"What's he goin' to do, anyhow?"

"He's goin' to that well there after water."

"We ain't dyin' of thirst, are we? That's foolishness."

"Well, somebody put him up to it, an' he's doin' it."

"Say, he must be a desperate cuss."

When Collins faced the meadow and walked away from the regiment, he was vaguely conscious that a chasm, the deep valley of all prides, was suddenly between him and his comrades. It was provisional, but the provision was that he return as a victor. He had blindly been led by quaint emotions, and laid himself under an obligation to walk squarely up to the face of death.

But he was not sure that he wished to make a retraction, even if he could do so without shame. As a matter of truth, he was sure of very little. He was mainly surprised.

It seemed to him supernaturally strange that he had allowed his mind to maneuver his body into such a situation. He understood that it might be called dramatically great.

However, he had no full appreciation of anything, excepting that he was actually conscious of being dazed. He could feel his dulled mind groping after the form and color of this incident. He wondered why he did not feel some keen agony of fear cutting his sense like a knife. He wondered at this, because human expression had said loudly for centuries that men should feel afraid of certain things, and that all men who did not feel this fear were phenomena —heroes.

He was, then, a hero. He suffered that disappointment which we would all have if we discovered that we were ourselves capable of those deeds which we most admire in history and legend. This, then, was a hero. After all, heroes were not much.

No, it could not be true. He was not a hero. Heroes had no shames in their lives, and, as for him, he remembered borrowing fifteen dollars from a friend and promising to pay it back the next day, and then avoiding that friend for ten months. When, at home, his mother had aroused him for the early labor of his life on the farm, it had often been his fashion to be irritable, childish, diabolical; and his mother had died since he had come to the war.

He saw that, in this matter of the well, the canteens, the shells, he was an intruder in the land of fine deeds.

He was now about thirty paces from his comrades. The regiment had just turned its many faces toward him.

From the forest of terrific noises there suddenly emerged a little uneven line of men. They fired fiercely and rapidly at distant foliage on which appeared little puffs of white smoke. The spatter of skirmish firing was added to the thunder of guns on the hill. The little line of men ran forward. A color-sergeant fell flat with his flag as if he had slipped on ice. There was hoarse cheering from this distant field.

Collins suddenly felt that two demon fingers were pressed into his ears. He could see nothing but flying arrows, flaming red. He lurched from the shock of this explosion, but he made a mad rush for the house, which he viewed as a man submerged to the neck in a boiling surf might view the shore. In the air little pieces of shell howled, and the earthquake explosions drove him insane with the menace of their roar. As he ran, the canteens knocked together with a rhythmical tinkling.

As he neared the house, each detail of the scene became vivid to him. He was aware of some bricks of the vanished chimney lying on the sod. There was a door which hung by one hinge.

Rifle bullets called forth by the insistent skirmishers came from the far-off bank of foliage. They mingled with the shells and the pieces of shells until the air was torn in all directions by hootings, yells, howls. The sky was full of fiends who directed all their wild rage at his head.

When he came to the well, he flung himself face downward and peered into its darkness. There were furtive silver glintings some feet from the surface. He grabbed one of the canteens and, unfastening its cap, swung it down by the cord. The water flowed slowly in with an indolent gurgle.

And now, as he lay with his face turned away, he was suddenly smitten with the terror. It came upon his heart like the grasp of claws. All the power faded from his muscles. For an instant he was no more than a dead man.

The canteen filled with a maddening slowness, in the manner of all bottles. Presently he recovered his strength and addressed a screaming oath to it. He leaned over until it seemed as if he intended to try to push water into it with his hands. His eyes as he gazed down into the well shone like two pieces of metal, and in their expression was a great appeal and a great curse. The stupid water derided him.

There was the blaring thunder of a shell. Crimson light shone through the swift-boiling smoke and made a pink reflection on part of the wall of the well. Collins jerked out his arm and canteen with the same motion that a man would use in withdrawing his head from a furnace.

He scrambled erect and glared and hesitated. On the ground near him lay the old well bucket, with a length of rusty chain. He lowered it swiftly into the well. The bucket struck the water and then, turning lazily over, sank. When, with hand reaching tremblingly over hand, he hauled it out, it knocked often against the walls of the well and spilled some of its contents.

In running with a filled bucket, a man can adopt but one kind of gait. So, through this terrible field over which screamed practical angels of death, Collins ran in the manner of a farmer chased out of a dairy by a bull.

His face went staring white with anticipation —anticipation of a blow that would whirl him around and down. He would fall as he had seen other men fall, the life knocked out of them so suddenly that their knees were no more quick to touch the ground than their heads. He saw the long blue line of the regiment, but his comrades were standing looking at him from the edge of an impossible star. He was aware of some deep wheel ruts and hoofprints in the sod beneath his feet.

The artillery officer who had fallen in this meadow had been making groans in the teeth of the tempest of sound. These futile cries, wrenched from him by his agony, were heard only by shells, bullets. When wild-eyed Collins came running, this officer raised himself. His face contorted and blanched from pain, he was about to utter some great beseeching cry. But suddenly his face straightened, and he called: "Say, young man, give me a drink of water, will you?"

Collins had no room amid his emotions for surprise. He was mad from the threats of destruction.

"I can't!" he screamed, and in his reply was a full description of his quaking apprehension. His cap was gone and his hair was riotous. His clothes made it appear that he had been dragged over the ground by the heels. He ran on.

The officer's head sank down, and one elbow crooked. His foot in its brassbound stirrup still stretched over the body of his horse, and the other leg was under the steed.

But Collins turned. He came dashing back. His face had now turned gray, and in his eyes was all terror. "Here it is! here it is!"

The officer was as a man gone in drink. His arm bent like a twig. His head drooped as if his neck were of willow. He was sinking to the ground, to lie face downward.

Collins grabbed him by the shoulder. "Here it is. Here's your drink. Turn over. Turn over, man, for God's sake!"

With Collins hauling at his shoulder, the officer twisted his body and fell with his face turned toward that region where lived the unspeakable noises of the swirling missiles. There was the faintest shadow of a smile on his lips as he looked at Collins. He gave a sigh, a little primitive breath like that from a child.

Collins tried to hold the bucket steadily, but his shaking hands caused the water to splash all over the face of the dying man. Then he jerked it away and ran on.

The regiment gave him a welcoming roar. The grimed faces were wrinkled in laughter.

His captain waved the bucket away. "Give it to the men!"

The two genial, skylarking young lieutenants were the first to gain possession of it. They played over it in their fashion.

When one tried to drink, the other teasingly knocked his elbow. "Don't, Billie! You'll make me spill it," said the one. The other laughed.

Suddenly there was an oath, the thud of wood on the ground, and a swift murmur of astonishment among the ranks. The two lieutenants glared at each other. The bucket lay on the ground, empty.

HOW DOES CRANE TREAT THE SHORT STORY?

1. Why does Collins make his dangerous journey? Since Crane doesn't tell you explicitly, how does he make it possible for you to understand Collins' motives?

2. What sort of man is Collins? Do his particular characteristics account for his actions, or does Crane imply that forces beyond his control lead him on?

3. Read again the examples of Crane's use of "impressionism" on page 534. Then reread paragraph 2, column 1, page 536 and paragraph 5, column 2, page 536, selecting descriptive passages which are noteworthy in suggesting the emotions of the spectators.

4. Reread the part of the story which describes Collins' trip to the well and his return (page 538, column 2, paragraph 2, to page 540, column 1, paragraph 9). Select the details which show Collins' emotions during this hazardous journey.

5. What are the reactions of Collins' fellow soldiers to his dash for water? Why does Collins himself feel he must be a hero? Explain why you do or do not agree that he is a hero.

6. Crane is noted for his irony. Why is the spilling of the water at the end of the story ironic? What irony do you find in the title itself?

Know your words

The word *carnage,* which Stephen Crane uses to suggest the awful blood and slaughter of the battle-field, derives from the Latin word *caro,* meaning "flesh." Many other English words, some of them very different in their present meaning from the original Latin word, have been derived from some form of this word. For example, the word *carnival* was made by uniting a form of *caro,* "flesh," and *levare,* "to put away." Originally *carnival* meant the days of celebration before Lent, at which time the eating of meat was forbidden. The italicized words in the sentences below are all derived from the Latin word *caro.* Rewrite each sentence, substituting another word or group of words for the one italicized. You may use the Glossary if necessary. In a class discussion be ready to point out the connection between the original Latin word and the modern English meaning.

1. The lion is a *carnivorous* animal, but the elephant eats only plants.

2. As the man looked back on his childhood and remembered his mother's care and devotion, he thought of her as the *incarnation* of all virtues.

3. For generations the *carnelian* necklace had been the most prized family heirloom.

4. The rays of the setting sun *incarnadined* the sky.

5. The villain of the novel was a fiend *incarnate.*

From its first appearance in American literature up to the present day, the short story has been very popular, and in our own period the variety of short stories is greater than ever before. Modern counterparts of Poe's horror stories and of his detective stories may be found in magazines and collections of short stories. At rare intervals allegorical tales of the type written by Hawthorne appear. A group called "regionalists" carry on, in modified ways, the tradition of the local-color narrative.[2] O. Henry has his modern followers in the surprise-ending story. The interest in psychology shown by Stephen Crane and his group is one of the bases of the realism of many modern authors.[3] The historical tale has become an important type of twentieth-century short story.[4] In fact, so varied are the short stories of today that it is impossible to suggest any one trend which is followed generally. Yet certainly the kind of story written by Ernest Hemingway represents one of the dominant types.

Hemingway has created many fine short stories which people read both for their view of life and their interesting technique. Many of these short stories emphasize the reactions of characters to a world which is not too kind. Some deal with the discovery by young men of the cruelty, intentional or unintentional, of human beings. Some deal with the disillusionment brought by war or by the peace following war. For Hemingway served in World War I and had experiences which bred serious doubts about the values he had once taken for granted. He did, however, discover some values in which he believes. For one thing, he admires people who do not whine about their disillusionment, who find what joy they can in life—in physical well-being, in amusement, in companionship, in love. In time, too, he discovered a belief in the duty of the individual to defend the democratic way of life against the rising tide of dictatorship.

The stories Hemingway writes are well adapted to the expression of his views. They present a fragment of life, but often lack a "plot" in the sense of a completed action. They are as economical of words, as informal in their diction, as are his tight-lipped heroes. They communicate emotion by selecting vivid sensory details, and they show how characters feel chiefly by telling what these characters perceive and how these characters act. The author's problem, as Hemingway sees it, is "knowing what you truly felt, rather than what you were supposed to feel" and then writing down "the real thing, the sequence of motion and fact which made the emotion."

---

[1]For a biographical sketch of Hemingway see page 485.

[2]Refer to "The Leader of the People," by John Steinbeck (pages 82-92) and "Four Generations," by Ruth Suckow (pages 112-119) for examples of the way present-day regionalists handle local color.

[3]See pages 462-463 for a discussion of realism in modern American literature. "Famous," by Stephen Vincent Benét (pages 464-473), and "Four Generations," by Ruth Suckow (pages 112-119), are examples of modern stories influenced by realistic ideas.

[4]For a discussion of the short story based on history see pages 449-450. Refer also to the following short stories: "Lone Wolf's Old Guard," by Hamlin Garland (pages 200-205); "A Tooth for Paul Revere," by Stephen Vincent Benét (pages 206-216); "The Devil and Daniel Webster," by Stephen Vincent Benét (pages 452-461).

In Another Country

ERNEST HEMINGWAY

IN THE FALL the war[1] was always there, but we did not go to it any more. It was cold in the fall in Milan[2] and the dark came very early. Then the electric lights came on, and it was pleasant along the streets looking in the windows. There was much game hanging outside the shops, and the snow powdered in the fur of the foxes and the wind blew their tails. The deer hung stiff and heavy and empty, and small birds blew in the wind and the wind turned their feathers. It was a cold fall and the wind came down from the mountains.

We were all at the hospital every afternoon, and there were different ways of walking across the town through the dusk to the hospital. Two of the ways were alongside canals, but they were long. Always, though, you crossed a bridge across a canal to enter the hospital. There was a choice of three bridges. On one of them a woman sold roasted chestnuts. It was warm, standing in front of her charcoal fire, and the chestnuts were warm afterward in your pocket. The hospital was very old and very beautiful, and you entered through a gate and walked across a courtyard and out a gate on the other side. There were usually funerals starting from the courtyard. Beyond the old hospital were the new brick pavilions, and there we met every afternoon and were all very polite and interested in what was the matter, and sat in the machines that were to make so much difference.

The doctor came up to the machine where I was sitting and said: "What did you like best to do before the war? Did you practice a sport?"

I said: "Yes, football."

"Good," he said. "You will be able to play football again better than ever."

My knee did not bend and the leg dropped straight from the knee to the ankle without a calf, and the machine was to bend the knee and

make it move as in riding a tricycle. But it did not bend yet, and instead the machine lurched when it came to the bending part. The doctor said: "That will all pass. You are a fortunate young man. You will play football again like a champion."

In the next machine was a major who had a little hand like a baby's. He winked at me when the doctor examined his hand, which was between two leather straps that bounced up and down and flapped the stiff fingers, and said: "And will I too play football, captain-doctor?" He had been a very great fencer, and before the war the greatest fencer in Italy.

The doctor went to his office in the back room and brought a photograph which showed a hand that had been withered almost as small as the major's, before it had taken a machine course, and after was a little larger. The major held the photograph with his good hand and looked at it very carefully. "A wound?" he asked.

"An industrial accident," the doctor said.

---

[1] *the war*, World War I.

[2] *Milan* (mi lan′), a city in northern Italy.

"Very interesting, very interesting," the major said, and handed it back to the doctor.

"You have confidence?"

"No," said the major.

There were three boys who came each day who were about the same age I was. They were all three from Milan, and one of them was to be a lawyer, and one was to be a painter, and one had intended to be a soldier, and after we were finished with the machines, sometimes we walked back together to the Café Cova, which was next door to the Scala.[3] We walked the short way through the communist quarter because we were four together. The people hated us because we were officers, and from a wine shop some one called out, "A basso gli ufficiali!"[4] as we passed. Another boy who walked with us sometimes and made us five wore a black silk handkerchief across his face because he had no nose then and his face was to be rebuilt. He had gone out to the front from the military academy and been wounded within an hour after he had gone into the front line for the first time. They rebuilt his face, but he came from a very old family and they could never get the nose exactly right. He went to South America and worked in a bank. But this was a long time ago, and then we did not any of us know how it was going to be afterward. We only knew then that there was always the war, but that we were not going to it any more.

We all had the same medals, except the boy with the black silk bandage across his face, and he had not been at the front long enough to get any medals. The tall boy with a very pale face who was to be a lawyer had been a lieutenant of Arditi[5] and had three medals of the sort we each had only one of. He had lived a very long time with death and was a little detached. We were all a little detached, and there was nothing that held us together except that we met every afternoon at the hospital. Although, as we walked to the Cova through the tough part of town, walking in the dark, with light and

singing coming out of the wine shops, and sometimes having to walk into the street when the men and women would crowd together on the sidewalk so that we would have had to jostle them to get by, we felt held together by there being something that had happened that they, the people who disliked us, did not understand.

We ourselves all understood the Cova, where it was rich and warm and not too brightly lighted, and noisy and smoky at certain hours, and there were always girls at the tables and the illustrated papers on a rack on the wall....

The boys at first were very polite about my medals and asked me what I had done to get them. I showed them the papers, which were written in very beautiful language and full of *fratellanza* and *abnegazione*,[6] but which really said, with the adjectives removed, that I had been given the medals because I was an American. After that their manner changed a little toward me, although I was their friend against outsiders. I was a friend, but I was never really one of them after they had read the citations, because it had been different with them and they had done very different things to get their medals. I had been wounded, it was true; but we all knew that being wounded, after all, was really an accident. I was never ashamed of the ribbons, though, and sometimes, after the cocktail hour, I would imagine myself having done all the things they had done to get their medals; but walking home at night through the empty streets with the cold wind and all the shops closed, trying to keep near the street lights, I knew that I would never have done such things, and I was very much afraid to die, and often lay in bed at night by myself, afraid to die and wondering how I would be when I went back to the front again.

The three with the medals were like hunting hawks; and I was not a hawk, although I might seem a hawk to those who had never hunted; they, the three, knew better and so we drifted apart. But I stayed good friends with the boy who had been wounded his first day at the front, because he would never know now how he would have turned out; so he could never be

---

[3] *the Scala,* La Scala (lä skä′lä), Milan's world-famous opera house.

[4] *A basso gli ufficiali,* down with the officers. [*Italian*]

[5] *a lieutenant of Arditi* (är dē′tē), a lieutenant in a picked group of volunteers which served as storm troops of the Italian infantry.

[6] *"fratellanza"* (frä′tel län′zä) *and "abnegazione"* (äb′nē-gä tzyō′ne), brotherhood and self-denial. [*Italian*]

accepted either, and I liked him because I thought perhaps he would not have turned out to be a hawk either.

The major, who had been the great fencer, did not believe in bravery, and spent much time while we sat in the machines correcting my grammar. He had complimented me on how I spoke Italian, and we talked together very easily. One day I had said that Italian seemed such an easy language to me that I could not take a great interest in it; everything was so easy to say. "Ah, yes," the major said. "Why, then, do you not take up the use of grammar?" So we took up the use of grammar, and soon Italian was such a difficult language that I was afraid to talk to him until I had the grammar straight in my mind.

The major came very regularly to the hospital. I do not think he ever missed a day, although I am sure he did not believe in the machines. There was a time when none of us believed in the machines, and one day the major said it was all nonsense. The machines were new then and it was we who were to prove them. It was an idiotic idea, he said, "a theory, like another." I had not learned my grammar, and he said I was a stupid impossible disgrace, and he was a fool to have bothered with me. He was a small man and he sat straight up in his chair with his right hand thrust into the machine and looked straight ahead at the wall while the straps thumped up and down with his fingers in them.

"What will you do when the war is over if it is over?" he asked me. "Speak grammatically!"

"I will go to the States."

"Are you married?"

"No, but I hope to be."

"The more of a fool you are," he said. He seemed very angry. "A man must not marry."

"Why, Signor Maggiore[7]?"

"Don't call me 'Signor Maggiore.' "

"Why must not a man marry?"

"He cannot marry. He cannot marry," he said angrily. "If he is to lose everything, he should not place himself in a position to lose that. He should not place himself in a position to lose. He should find things he cannot lose."

He spoke very angrily and bitterly, and looked straight ahead while he talked.

"But why should he necessarily lose it?"

"He'll lose it," the major said. He was looking at the wall. Then he looked down at the machine and jerked his little hand out from between the straps and slapped it hard against his thigh. "He'll lose it," he almost shouted. "Don't argue with me!" Then he called to the attendant who ran the machines. "Come and turn this damned thing off."

He went back into the other room for the light treatment and the massage. Then I heard him ask the doctor if he might use his telephone and he shut the door. When he came back into the room, I was sitting in another machine. He was wearing his cape and had his cap on, and he came directly toward my machine and put his arm on my shoulder.

"I am so sorry," he said, and patted me on the shoulder with his good hand. "I would not be rude. My wife has just died. You must forgive me."

"Oh——" I said, feeling sick for him. "I am *so* sorry."

He stood there biting his lower lip. "It is very difficult," he said. "I cannot resign myself."

He looked straight past me and out through the window. Then he began to cry. "I am utterly unable to resign myself," he said, and choked. And then crying, his head up looking at nothing, carrying himself straight and soldierly, with tears on both his cheeks and biting his lips, he walked past the machines and out the door.

The doctor told me that the major's wife, who was very young and whom he had not married until he was definitely invalided out of the war, had died of pneumonia. She had been sick only a few days. No one expected her to die. The major did not come to the hospital for three days. Then he came at the usual hour, wearing a black band on the sleeve of his uniform. When he came back, there were large framed photographs around the wall, of all sorts of wounds before and after they had been cured by the machines. In front of the machine the

---

[7]*Signor Maggiore* (sē′nyōr mäj jô′re), Mr. Major. In Italy it is a sign of respect to prefix an officer's rank with *Signor.*

major used were three photographs of hands like his that were completely restored. I do not know where the doctor got them. I always understood we were the first to use the machines. The photographs did not make much difference to the major because he only looked out of the window.

WHAT IS HEMINGWAY'S POINT OF VIEW?

1. A critic has pointed out that the opening paragraph offers a number of symbolic details which stand for the " 'other countries' which the lonely characters portrayed in the story sense but do not enter." These countries are: "the country of battle from which [the characters'] wounds have removed them; that of peace which [the characters] glimpse through lighted windows from darkened streets; the country of nature symbolized by the game; and the country, finally, of death—connoted by the cold, the dark, and by the wind which blows from the mountains." How is the exclusion of the soldiers from these "countries" important in this story?

2. Not only are the soldiers, as a group, shut off from other groups; as individuals, they are separated from one another. How do they happen to be separated? Have their war experiences had anything to do with their loneliness? Explain.

3. Judging from what you have read on page 541 about the characters in Hemingway's stories, to what extent is the narrator typical of the characters Hemingway admires? Are the other characters typical?

4. How does the major differ from the other invalids? Why did his wife's illness cause him to quarrel as he did with the narrator? Why does the story of what happened to him offer a fitting climax for this story?

5. What is unusual about Hemingway's style? What contrasts do you find between his manner of writing and Poe's (pages 492-513), Hawthorne's (pages 515-520), Harte's (pages 522-528)? According to your experience, is his way of writing representative of present-day writers?

The Larger View

I. Plan a discussion of the American short story to summarize important things you have learned in studying this literary form. As examples to illustrate the various points you will wish to make, include not only authors and stories you have studied in class but also authors and stories you have become acquainted with through outside reading. You may wish to add other topics to those listed below as a guide to the discussion. Some classes will find it more interesting to divide into groups, each group presenting a discussion of one topic before the class.

1. An overview of the development of the short story from Irving to Hemingway.

2. Poe's contributions to the short-story form and his influence on subsequent writers.

3. The local-color group and their present-day successors.

4. The strengths and weaknesses of the surprise-ending story.

5. The influence of Crane on the modern short story.

6. The factors necessary to a good short story.

7. Reasons for the past and present popularity of the short story in the United States.

II. Most of the best modern short stories appear originally in magazines. With your teacher's help, draw up a list of current magazines which publish good stories. Read several stories, jotting down the name and issue of the magazine and the name and author of each story. In a class discussion try to arrive at answers to the following questions:

1. Do most of the stories satisfy the requirements for a good short story?

2. Do the stories fall into any of the categories (supernatural, surprise ending, regional, etc.) that you have studied in this unit? What kinds of story seem to be predominant today?

3. Are today's stories as interesting as those of yesterday? Why, or why not?

4. Have you come across an author whose stories you particularly like? If so, how can you best follow up your interest in that author?

MORE GOOD READING

CLARKE, FRANCES ELIZABETH (compiler), *Valiant Dogs; Great Dog Stories of Our Day*. (Macmillan) Since you are studying the growth of the short story in America, you will want to pick out only the American stories in this collection. Be sure to read "Hector," by Henry Cuyler Bunner, and "Dark-Brown Dog," by Stephen Crane.

CROSS, ETHAN ALLAN (editor), *Book of the Short Story*. (American Book) Ignore the foreign stories this time and select the American masterpieces. You will find they range all the way from Poe to Hemingway. The volume also contains fine material on the history and techniques of the short story.

FREEMAN, MARY E. WILKINS, *Best Stories of Mary E. Wilkins*, selected and with an introduction by H. W. Lanier. (Harper) These stories by the most realistic of the local colorists present vivid pictures of village life in Massachusetts.

GARLAND, HAMLIN, *Main-Travelled Roads*. (Harper) The drudgery and difficulty of farm life as well as its rewards are reflected in these tales of the Middle West.

HARTE, BRET, *Best of Bret Harte*, selected by Wilhelmina Harper and A. M. Peters. (Houghton) You'll find drama, humor, and pathos in these tales of mining camps in the Far West.

HAVIGHURST, WALTER (editor), *Masters of the Modern Short Story*. (Harcourt) Choose the American short stories assembled in this fine collection. You'll find plenty of variety in stories by such diversified writers as Edith Wharton, William Faulkner, Ernest Hemingway, John Steinbeck, William Saroyan, and Eudora Welty.

HAWTHORNE, NATHANIEL, *Hawthorne's Short Stories*, edited and with an introduction by Newton Arvin. (Knopf) You will find "The Maypole of Merry Mount," "Drowne's Wooden Image," and other stories that Americans have cherished for generations in this excellent collection.

HENRY, O., *The Four Million*. (Doubleday) If you enjoyed "The Gift of the Magi," you'll want to read more of O. Henry's sparkling, surprise-ending stories of the ordinary people of New York.

JEWETT, SARAH ORNE, *The Country of the Pointed Firs*. (Houghton) Life in a Maine village is the setting for these gentle, well-written tales by one of the best of the local colorists.

LONDON, JACK, *Best Short Stories*. (Sun Dial) If you haven't read "To Build a Fire," do it now. You'll find it and London's other tales gripping stories of the frozen Northern frontier.

PATTEE, FRED LEWIS, *Development of the American Short Story; an Historical Survey*. (Harper) The mature reader who is interested will find the section of this book dealing with the short story today particularly worth-while.

POE, EDGAR ALLAN, *Tales;* with an introduction by Hervey Allen. (Random House) The two stories Poe referred to in the first paragraph of "The Purloined Letter" are here as well as the best of Poe's other horror and detective stories.

RAWLINGS, MARJORIE KINNAN, *When the Whippoorwill——*. (Scribner) With humor and tenderness and a great insight into the lives of people, a modern regionalist writes of the folks who live along the back roads of Florida.

STEELE, WILBUR DANIEL, *Best Stories*. (Doubleday) Whether you're most interested in the mystery or in the atmosphere, you'll agree that "Footfalls" is a fascinating story. And you'll like many other tales by this fine Southern writer.

STOCKTON, FRANK RICHARD, *The Lady or the Tiger? and Other Stories*. (Scribner) Don't miss these stories by one of the best of O. Henry's colleagues in the surprise ending.

STUART, JESSE, *Clearing in the Sky and Other Stories*. (McGraw) Jesse Stuart was born in the Kentucky hills, and his knowledge of the country and of the people who live there adds to the charm and interest of these stories.

TAGGARD, ERNESTINE (editor), *Here We Are; Stories from Scholastic Magazine*. (McBride) Sinclair Lewis, Dorothy Canfield Fisher, and John Steinbeck are among the authors in this fine collection of stories.

WHITE, WILLIAM A. P. (editor), *Great American Detective Stories*. (World Publishing) The masters of the detective story from Edgar Allan Poe to Ellery Queen unravel their mysteries.

ALMOST FROM the very beginnings of literary history, men have felt the need of expressing their emotions in brief, songlike poems. Such poems are called lyrics, and although over the centuries the lyric has assumed various poetic forms—among them the sonnet, the ode, and the elegy—it has always remained a melodious expression of the poet's own feelings. In a good lyric the poet has recorded his thought and emotion in such a fresh and vivid manner that the reader feels his own imagination quickened and his memory awakened. Thus, after reading a lyric, we say, "I understand and share that experience, that feeling; the poet has said for me what I have experienced but could not express." Poetry viewed in this way is timeless, and a lyric written a thousand years ago may be more important to us at the moment than a poem written yesterday. Consider how many people of our troubled age have found comfort and reassurance in an ancient Hebrew poem beginning, "The Lord is my shepherd."

Viewed in another way, however, poetry is a reflection of the minds and hearts of men at the time when it was written. In this unit we shall glance at a few high points in the development of lyric poetry in America. From this survey we can learn who the great lyric poets of America are, what they have written about in the successive periods of our history, and how the art of lyric poetry has changed and flourished as a part of our literary heritage.

❧ I EARLY ROMANTIC POETS

Lyric poetry that was distinctively American in flavor did not develop until about the time of the Revolutionary War. During the colonial period few good lyrics were written. The American colonists, struggling against the hardships of their life in a new land, had little time for the cultivation of the arts, and what time they had was spent in keeping alive the culture of the lands from which they had come. Thus the early poetry of America tends to treat English subjects rather than American themes. Since religion was an important factor in colonial life, much of the poetry of this period dealt with religious ideas. For example, "Housewifery," by Edward Taylor (page 46), voiced the colonists' religious faith, while Michael Wigglesworth's long poem, "The Day of Doom," presented a gloomy picture of the terrors of the Last Judgment.

About the time of the American Revolution a new spirit in literature which expressed itself in what we now call the Romantic Movement (see pages 343-344) began to develop among the English poets and their American contemporaries. Over thirty years before Irving published

547

his *Sketch Book,* an American poet, Philip Freneau,[1] was writing lyrics that were genuinely romantic in mood. In time the Romantic Movement developed different aspects, but in lyric poetry its chief characteristics were: (1) A new interest in man as man, an interest shown by respect for the rights and liberties of each individual regardless of his birth or social rank; (2) a love of nature—the out-of-doors; (3) a love and respect for beauty in many newly discovered forms.

American poets found romanticism well suited to their needs. The theme of man's rights naturally appealed to the liberty-seeking colonists, and poets related it to their struggle for freedom. American poets found also that nature in their own land inspired them just as English nature inspired the English poets; that the honeysuckle is just as beautiful as the hawthorne or primrose; and that an Indian burying ground can arouse feelings of respect and wonder as much as an English churchyard. This discovery of the materials of poetry right at hand marks the beginnings of a genuine American lyric verse, although in poetic forms and in basic ideas it was for a long time imitative of English models. Three names stand out among those of early American romantic poets—Philip Freneau, William Cullen Bryant, and Edgar Allan Poe.

Philip Freneau (1752-1832)[2]

Born in New York in 1752, Freneau was a young man and an aspiring poet at the time of the Revolutionary War. The war changed the currents of his life. Fighting with the colonial militia, running the British blockade, and being confined on a British prison ship left him with a fierce hatred of the enemy which he expressed in vigorous prose and satirical verse. He is remembered today, however, less for his wartime verses than for the lovely lyrics of the years after the war. In these, for the first time, an American poet, moved by the spirit of the new Romantic Movement, used distinctively American scenes and American themes as subjects for poetry of a high order.

William Cullen Bryant (1794-1878)[3]

A few years after the colonies had won their independence, William Cullen Bryant was born in a small Massachusetts town. Although in his youth he was strongly influenced by the English poets of the eighteenth century, this influence faded as his own genius matured. When only seventeen years old he wrote the greater part of his famous poem, "Thanatopsis." Published six years later, it was considered by many critics superior to any poem previously written in America.

Bryant as a poet is thoughtful and gentle, powerfully influenced by nature. While many aspects of the out-of-doors inspired him to write first-rate poetry, he was particularly moved by the silence and solitude of nature. Reared in pious, moralizing New England and respected as a man of upright character, Bryant wrote poetry expressive of a strong sense of duty. He thus combines the moral force of the eighteenth-

---

[1]*Freneau* (fri nō′).
[2]For a biographical sketch of Freneau see page 359.
[3]For a short biography of Bryant see page 359.

century poets with the love of nature and lyric freedom of the romantics. This combination was of great importance to the development of American poetry.

Edgar Allan Poe (1809-1849)[4]

The forty years of Poe's life were brilliant, tragic, and intense. He began writing poetry as a very young man. He published two books of poetry by his twentieth year, and another two years later. Until the year of his death, he found time, between writing stories and critical articles, to compose poems. Although most of Poe's verse is highly original in subject and form, it reflects two common interests of Romantic poets: a feeling of wonder and awe inspired by mysterious and supernatural subjects, and a delight in melodious expression. In some poems Poe appeared to be more interested in producing a magic pattern of beautiful sounds than in expressing an idea.

In the making of verses Poe was a technical craftsman of the first rank. In addition, he was able to analyze and describe, in clear and forceful language, the way he went about creating his artistic effects in poetry. Hence his influence on the development of American poetry has been great both through his poems themselves and through his essays on the techniques of composing verse.

Poems by Freneau, Bryant, and Poe follow.

[4]For a biographical sketch of Poe see page 359; for material on Poe as a short-story writer see pages 491 and 502.

The Wild Honeysuckle

PHILIP FRENEAU

This poem and the one which follows it illustrate Freneau's discovery of materials for poetry in the everyday world about him.

FAIR FLOWER, that dost so comely grow,
  Hid in this silent, dull retreat,
Untouched thy honeyed blossoms blow,
  Unseen thy little branches greet;
    No roving foot shall crush thee here, 5
    No busy hand provoke a tear.

By Nature's self in white arrayed,
  She bade thee shun the vulgar eye,
And planted here the guardian shade,
  And sent soft waters murmuring by; 10
    Thus quietly thy summer goes,
    Thy days declining to repose.

Smit with those charms, that must decay,
  I grieve to see your future doom;
They died—nor were those flowers more gay, 15
  The flowers that did in Eden bloom;
    Unpitying frosts and autumn's power
    Shall leave no vestige of this flower.

From morning suns and evening dews
  At first thy little being came; 20
If nothing once, you nothing lose,
  For when you die you are the same;
    The space between is but an hour,
    The frail duration of a flower.

The Indian Burying Ground

PHILIP FRENEAU

The key to this poem is found in the first two stanzas,
in which the poet points out the contrast between the
way white men are buried (in prone position) and the
way Indians are buried (in upright position).

IN SPITE OF ALL the learned have said,
  I still my old opinion keep;
The posture that we[1] give the dead
  Points out the soul's eternal sleep.

Not so the ancients of these lands—   5
  The Indian, when from life released,
Again is seated with his friends,
  And shares again the joyous feast.

His imaged birds, and painted bowl,
  And venison, for a journey dressed,[2]   10
Bespeak the nature of the soul,
  Activity, that knows no rest.

His bow for action ready bent,
  And arrows with a head of stone,
Can only mean that life is spent,   15
  And not the old ideas gone.

---

[1] *we*, the white Americans.
[2] *venison, for a journey dressed*, deer meat, dried or
otherwise prepared to keep it from spoiling. Food was
placed in the grave to provide nourishment for the dead
man on his journey to a future life.

Thou, stranger, that shalt come this way,
  No fraud upon the dead commit—
Observe the swelling turf, and say
  "They do not lie, but here they sit."   20

Here still a lofty rock remains,
  On which the curious eye may trace
(Now wasted half of[3] wearing rains)
  The fancies of a ruder race.

Here still an aged elm aspires,   25
  Beneath whose far-projecting shade
(And which the shepherd still admires)
  The children of the forest played.

There oft a restless Indian queen
  (Pale Sheba with her braided hair[4])   30
And many a barbarous form is seen,
  To chide the man that lingers there.

By midnight moons, o'er moistening dews,
  In habit for the chase arrayed,
The hunter still the deer pursues,   35
  The hunter and the deer, a shade!

And long shall timorous fancy see
  The painted chief, and pointed spear,
And reason's self shall bow the knee
  To shadows and delusions here.   40

---

[3] *of*, by.
[4] *Pale Sheba with her braided hair*. The poet is comparing the pale ghost of an Indian queen, which he imagines
as haunting the spot, to Sheba, a queen of Biblical times.

Thanatopsis

WILLIAM CULLEN BRYANT

Since the word *thanatopsis* is a combination of Greek words meaning "a view of death," Bryant announces through his title that the poem discusses a way of considering death.

The following outline of the main divisions of "Thanatopsis" will help you grasp its ideas: (1) *Lines 1-8:* Nature speaks in various ways to those who love her. (2) *Lines 8-17:* Turn to Nature when thoughts of death bring sadness to you. (3) *Lines 17-30:* From Nature we learn that death comes to all. (4) *Lines 31-57:* Nature comforts us with a reminder that we do not go alone to our resting place but will lie down in the company of all who have lived before us, including all the great of the past. (5) *Lines 58-72:* Dying unmourned is not important, since all who live must die. (6) *Lines 73-81:* We must live in such a way that we shall not fear death but meet it with trust.

To HIM who in the love of Nature holds
Communion with her visible forms, she speaks
A various language; for his gayer hours
She has a voice of gladness, and a smile
And eloquence of beauty, and she glides   5
Into his darker musings with a mild
And healing sympathy that steals away
Their sharpness ere he is aware. When thoughts
Of the last bitter hour come like a blight
Over thy spirit, and sad images   10
Of the stern agony, and shroud, and pall,
And breathless darkness, and the narrow house[1]
Make thee to shudder and grow sick at heart—
Go forth, under the open sky, and list
To Nature's teachings, while from all around—
Earth and her waters, and the depths of air— 16
Comes a still voice—
          Yet a few days, and thee
The all-beholding sun shall see no more
In all his course; nor yet in the cold ground,
Where thy pale form was laid with many tears,
Nor in the embrace of ocean shall exist   21
Thy image. Earth, that nourished thee, shall claim

Thy growth, to be resolved to earth again,
And, lost each human trace, surrendering up
Thine individual being, shalt thou go   25
To mix forever with the elements,
To be a brother to the insensible rock
And to the sluggish clod which the rude swain
Turns with his share[2] and treads upon. The oak
Shall send his roots abroad and pierce thy mold.   30
Yet not to thine eternal resting place
Shalt thou retire alone; nor couldst thou wish
Couch more magnificent. Thou shalt lie down
With patriarchs of the infant world—with kings,
The powerful of the earth—the wise, the good,
Fair forms, and hoary seers of ages past,   36
All in one mighty sepulcher. The hills
Rock-ribbed and ancient as the sun; the vales
Stretching in pensive quietness between;
The venerable woods; rivers that move   40
In majesty; and the complaining brooks
That make the meadows green; and, poured round all
Old Ocean's gray and melancholy waste—
Are but the solemn decorations all
Of the great tomb of man. The golden sun,   45
The planets, all the infinite host of heaven,
Are shining on the sad abodes of death
Through the still lapse of ages. All that tread
The globe are but a handful to the tribes
That slumber in its bosom. Take the wings   50
Of morning, pierce the Barcan wilderness,[3]
Or lose thyself in the continuous woods
Where rolls the Oregon,[4] and hears no sound
Save his own dashings—yet the dead are there;
And millions in those solitudes, since first   55
The flight of years began, have laid them down
In their last sleep—the dead reign there alone.
So shalt thou rest, and what if thou withdraw
In silence from the living, and no friend
Take note of thy departure? All that breathe 60
Will share thy destiny. The gay will laugh
When thou art gone, the solemn brood of care
Plod on, and each one as before will chase
His favorite phantom; yet all these shall leave

---

[1] *the narrow house*, the grave.

[2] *share*, plow blade.
[3] *Barcan wilderness*, the desert land of Cyrenaica (sir'i nā'i kə), formerly the ancient kingdom of Barca, in northern Africa.
[4] *the Oregon*, the old name for the Columbia River, which flows between Oregon and Washington.

Their mirth and their employments, and shall
   come   65
And make their bed with thee. As the long train
Of ages glides away, the sons of men,
The youth in life's green spring, and he who
   goes
In the full strength of years, matron and maid,
The speechless babe, and the gray-headed
   man—   70
Shall one by one be gathered to thy side,
By those who in their turn shall follow them.

So live, that when thy summons comes to join
The innumerable caravan which moves
To that mysterious realm, where each shall
   take   75
His chamber in the silent halls of death,
Thou go not, like the quarry slave at night,
Scourged to his dungeon, but, sustained and
   soothed
By an unfaltering trust, approach thy grave
Like one who wraps the drapery of his couch 80
About him, and lies down to pleasant dreams.

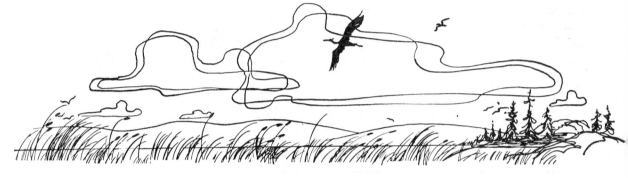

To a Waterfowl

WILLIAM CULLEN BRYANT

The sight of a lone bird flying across the evening sky
leads the poet to ask what force guides its purposeful
flight. Bryant wrote the poem when he was away from
home and anxiously seeking guidance in finding his
lifework.

WHITHER, midst falling dew
    While glow the heavens with the last
     steps of day,
Far, through their rosy depths, dost thou pursue
    Thy solitary way?

    Vainly the fowler's eye   5
Might mark thy distant flight to do thee wrong,
As, darkly seen against the crimson sky,
    Thy figure floats along.

    Seek'st thou the plashy brink
Of weedy lake, or marge of river wide,   10
Or where the rocking billows rise and sink
    On the chafed oceanside?

    There is a Power whose care
Teaches thy way along that pathless coast—
The desert and illimitable air—   15
    Lone wandering, but not lost.

    All day thy wings have fanned,
At that far height, the cold, thin atmosphere,
Yet stoop not, weary, to the welcome land,
    Though the dark night is near.   20

    And soon that toil shall end;
Soon shalt thou find a summer home, and rest,
And scream among thy fellows; reeds shall
   bend,
    Soon, o'er thy sheltered nest.

    Thou'rt gone, the abyss of heaven   25
Hath swallowed up thy form; yet, on my heart
Deeply hath sunk the lesson thou hast given,
    And shall not soon depart.

    He, who, from zone to zone,
Guides through the boundless sky thy certain
   flight,   30
In the long way that I must tread alone,
    Will lead my steps aright.

Israfel

EDGAR ALLAN POE

To the Mohammedans, Israfel (iz′ rə fel) is the angel of music, the one who will sound the trumpet at the resurrection of all men from their graves. In this poem, through speaking of the music of Israfel, Poe states the wish of all poets—to express the greatest thoughts in the world in the sweetest music possible. In fact, the poem stands so well for Poe's own beliefs about the function of poetry that biographers have often applied the name "Israfel" to him.

And the angel Israfel, whose heart strings are a lute, and who has the sweetest voice of all God's creatures.
— The Koran[1]

IN HEAVEN a spirit doth dwell
  Whose heartstrings are a lute;
None sing so wildly well
As the angel Israfel,
And the giddy stars (so legends tell),   5
Ceasing their hymns,[2] attend the spell
  Of his voice, all mute.

Tottering above
  In her highest noon,[3]
The enamored moon   10
Blushes with love,
  While, to listen, the red levin[4]
(With the rapid Pleiads, even,
Which were seven[5])
  Pauses in Heaven.   15

And they say (the starry choir
  And the other listening things)
That Israfeli's fire
Is owing to that lyre
By which he sits and sings,   20
The trembling living wire
  Of those unusual strings.

But the skies that angel trod,
  Where deep thoughts are a duty,
Where Love's a grown-up god,   25
  Where the Houri[6] glances are
Imbued with all the beauty
  Which we worship in a star.

Therefore thou art not wrong,
  Israfeli, who despisest   30
An unimpassioned song;
To thee the laurels belong,
  Best bard, because the wisest!
Merrily live, and long!

The ecstasies above   35
  With thy burning measures suit;
Thy grief, thy joy, thy hate, thy love,
  With the fervor of thy lute—
Well may the stars be mute!

Yes, Heaven is thine; but this   40
  Is a world of sweets and sours;
  Our flowers are merely—flowers,
And the shadow of thy perfect bliss
  Is the sunshine of ours.

If I could dwell   45
Where Israfel
  Hath dwelt, and he where I,
He might not sing so wildly well
  A mortal melody,
While a bolder note than this might swell   50
  From my lyre within the sky.

[1]*The Koran* (kô rän′ *or* kō′ran), the sacred book of the Mohammedans.

[2]*And the giddy stars...ceasing their hymns.* It was an ancient belief that the stars gave forth heavenly music as they moved in their courses.

[3]*her highest noon,* the position at which the moon is highest in the sky.

[4]*levin* (lev′in), lightning.

[5]*Pleiads* (plē′adz *or* plī′adz) ... *seven,* a group of seven stars usually called the Pleiades (plē′ə dēz *or* plī′ə dēz). According to Greek mythology these stars were once the seven daughters of Atlas, the giant who supported the world on his shoulders.

[6]*Houri* (hŭ′ri *or* hou′ri), a beautiful spirit of the Mohammedan paradise.

The Raven

EDGAR ALLAN POE

"The Raven" is one of the best known and most often quoted of American poems. As you read it, note the devices and details Poe uses to create melody and to create a mood of mystery and melancholy.

ONCE UPON a midnight dreary, while I pon-
    dered, weak and weary,
Over many a quaint and curious volume of for-
    gotten lore—
While I nodded, nearly napping, suddenly there
    came a tapping,
As of someone gently rapping, rapping at my
    chamber door.
" 'Tis some visitor," I muttered, "tapping at
    my chamber door—   5
    Only this and nothing more."

Ah, distinctly I remember it was in the bleak
    December,
And each separate dying ember wrought its
    ghost upon the floor.
Eagerly I wished the morrow; vainly I had
    sought to borrow
From my books surcease of sorrow—sorrow for
    the lost Lenore—   10
For the rare and radiant maiden whom the
    angels named Lenore—
    Nameless here for evermore.

And the silken, sad, uncertain rustling of each
    purple curtain
Thrilled me—filled me with fantastic terrors
    never felt before;
So that now, to still the beating of my heart,
    I stood repeating,   15
" 'Tis some visitor entreating entrance at my
    chamber door;
Some late visitor entreating entrance at my
    chamber door,
    This it is and nothing more."

Presently my soul grew stronger; hesitating then
    no longer,
"Sir," said I, "or Madam, truly your forgiveness
    I implore;   20

But the fact is I was napping, and so gently
    you came rapping,
And so faintly you came tapping, tapping at my
    chamber door,
That I scarce was sure I heard you"—here I
    opened wide the door—
    Darkness there and nothing more.

Deep into that darkness peering, long I stood
    there wondering, fearing,   25
Doubting, dreaming dreams no mortal ever
    dared to dream before;
But the silence was unbroken, and the stillness
    gave no token,
And the only word there spoken was the whis-
    pered word "Lenore?"
This I whispered, and an echo murmured back
    the word "Lenore!"
    Merely this and nothing more.   30

Back into the chamber turning, all my soul
    within me burning,
Soon again I heard a tapping somewhat louder
    than before.
"Surely," said I, "surely that is something at my
    window lattice;
Let me see, then, what thereat is, and this mys-
    tery explore;
Let my heart be still a moment and this mystery
    explore;   35
    'Tis the wind and nothing more!"

Tell me what thy lordly name is on the Night's
    Plutonian[2] shore!"
    Quoth the Raven, "Nevermore."

Open here I flung the shutter, when, with many
    a flirt and flutter,
In there stepped a stately Raven of the saintly
    days of yore.
Not the least obeisance made he; not a minute
    stopped or stayed he;
But, with mien of lord or lady, perched above
    my chamber door,   40
Perched upon a bust of Pallas[1] just above my
    chamber door—
    Perched, and sat, and nothing more.

Then this ebon bird beguiling all my fancy into
    smiling
By the grave and stern decorum of the counte-
    nance it wore,
"Though thy crest be shorn and shaven, thou,"
    I said, "art sure no craven,   45
Ghastly grim and ancient Raven wandering
    from the Nightly shore—

Much I marveled this ungainly fowl to hear
    discourse so plainly,
Though its answer little meaning—little rele-
    vancy bore;   50
For we cannot help agreeing that no living
    human being
Ever yet was blessed with seeing bird above his
    chamber door,
Bird or beast upon the sculptured bust above
    his chamber door,
    With such name as "Nevermore."

But the Raven, sitting lonely on the placid bust,
    spoke only   55
That one word, as if his soul in that one word
    he did outpour.
Nothing further then he uttered, not a feather
    then he fluttered,
Till I scarcely more than muttered—"Other
    friends have flown before;

[1]*Pallas* (pal′əs), one of the names of Athena, who, in
Greek mythology, was the goddess of wisdom.

[2]*Plutonian* (plü tō′ni ən), of the spirit world ruled over
by Pluto, Greek and Roman god of the lower world.

On the morrow *he* will leave me, as my hopes
  have flown before."
Then the bird said, "Nevermore."   60

Startled at the stillness broken by reply so
  aptly spoken,
"Doubtless," said I, "what it utters is its only
  stock and store,
Caught from some unhappy master whom un-
  merciful disaster
Followed fast and followed faster till his songs
  one burden bore—
Till the dirges of his hope that melancholy
  burden bore   65
  Of 'Never—nevermore.' "

But the Raven still beguiling all my fancy into
  smiling,
Straight I wheeled a cushioned seat in front of
  bird and bust and door;
Then, upon the velvet sinking, I betook myself
  to linking
Fancy unto fancy, thinking what this ominous
  bird of yore,   70
What this grim, ungainly, ghastly, gaunt, and
  ominous bird of yore
  Meant in croaking "Nevermore."

This I sat engaged in guessing, but no syllable
  expressing
To the fowl whose fiery eyes now burned into
  my bosom's core;
This and more I sat divining, with my head at
  ease reclining   75
On the cushion's velvet lining that the lamplight
  gloated o'er,[3]
But whose velvet violet lining with the lamplight gloating o'er
  She shall press, ah, nevermore!

Then, methought, the air grew denser, perfumed from an unseen censer
Swung by seraphim[4] whose footfalls tinkled on
  the tufted floor.   80

"Wretch,"[5] I cried, "thy God hath lent thee—
  by these angels he hath sent thee
Respite—respite and nepenthe, from thy memories of Lenore,
Quaff, oh quaff this kind nepenthe and forget
  this lost Lenore!"
  Quoth the Raven, "Nevermore."

"Prophet!" said I, "thing of evil! prophet still,
  if bird or devil!   85
Whether Tempter sent, or whether tempest
  tossed thee here ashore,
Desolate yet all undaunted, on this desert land
  enchanted—
On this home by Horror haunted—tell me truly,
  I implore:
Is there—*is* there balm in Gilead?[6]—tell me—tell
  me, I implore!"
  Quoth the Raven, "Nevermore."   90

"Prophet!" said I, "thing of evil—prophet still,
  if bird or devil!
By that Heaven that bends above us, by that
  God we both adore,
Tell this soul with sorrow laden if, within the
  distant Aidenn,[7]
It shall clasp a sainted maiden whom the angels
  name Lenore—
Clasp a rare and radiant maiden whom the
  angels name Lenore!"   95
  Quoth the Raven, "Nevermore."

"Be that word our sign of parting, bird or
  fiend!" I shrieked, upstarting.
"Get thee back into the tempest and the Night's
  Plutonian shore!
Leave no black plume as a token of that lie thy
  soul hath spoken!
Leave my loneliness unbroken! quit the bust
  above my door!   100
Take thy beak from out my heart, and take thy
  form from off my door!"
  Quoth the Raven, "Nevermore."

[5]*Wretch.* The narrator is here addressing himself.
[6]*is there balm in Gilead* (gilʹi əd)? Is there no comfort
for my sorrow? In Jeremiah 8:22 the prophet asks whether
no healing ointment (balm) can be found in Gilead, a
region in ancient Palestine east of the Jordan River.
Gradually the words came to have the figurative meaning
which Poe uses.
[7]*Aidenn* (āʹden), the Moslem paradise.

[3]*the lamplight gloated o'er.* The rays of the light were
refracted or turned aside by the velvet material with which
the seat was covered.
[4]*seraphim* (serʹə fim), angels of one of the highest
orders.

And the Raven, never flitting, still is sitting,
    still is sitting
On the pallid bust of Pallas just above my
    chamber door;
And his eyes have all the seeming of a demon's
    that is dreaming,   105
And the lamplight o'er him streaming throws
    his shadow on the floor;
And my soul from out that shadow that lies
    floating on the floor
  Shall be lifted—nevermore!

CONCERNING THE POETS AND THE POEMS

Philip Freneau

1. Why are "The Wild Honeysuckle" and "The Indian Burying Ground" considered romantic poems? Why are they classified as lyrics?

2. In the first stanza of "The Indian Burying Ground" Freneau says that the method of burial used by the white man indicates "the soul's eternal sleep." What does he say the Indian mode of burial indicates? How does he develop this idea in the last three stanzas?

3. What is Freneau's attitude toward the Indian? Is this attitude normal for the time when he wrote, or is it unusual?

William Cullen Bryant

1. What attitude toward death does Bryant express in "Thanatopsis"? In what way does his love of nature influence his feeling about death? What lines best express his strong moral sense?

2. Do you find the ideas expressed in "Thanatopsis" consoling or disturbing? Explain your answer.

3. Compare "Thanatopsis" with the lyric beginning "Come lovely and soothing death" from Whitman's "When Lilacs Last in the Dooryard Bloomed" (pages 396-400). Are any of Bryant's ideas similar to those expressed by Whitman? Which poem do you like better?

4. In what way does "To a Waterfowl" indicate Bryant's pious New England heritage? Interpret in your own words the message which Bryant says the waterfowl has given.

5. Prepare to read aloud to the class lines in "To a Waterfowl" which show Bryant's accurate observation of nature.

Edgar Allan Poe

1. From Poe's description of Israfel's song, what characteristics of poetry do you think that Poe himself most admires? Can you find any of these characteristics in this poem?

2. What is the meaning of the last stanza of "Israfel"?

3. What is the setting of "The Raven"? What details make it a peculiarly appropriate setting for the entrance of the mysterious bird?

4. How does the lonely student first greet the raven? Trace the changes in the student's attitude from the bird's entrance to the end of the poem. What is the student's final mood?

5. What characteristics of romantic poetry do you find in "Israfel" and "The Raven"? What romantic elements can you point out in "Annabel Lee" (pages 270-271)?

Poe as a maker of music

The magic which "The Raven" has exerted over several generations of readers lies less in its idea or its slight story than in its matchless melody. Glancing at some of the devices which Poe has used to haunt the ear and to create a mood of mystery and melancholy will add to your appreciation of the poem.

(*a*) *Rhyme.* The end rhyme, or rhyme at the end of a line, is only one of the rhyming devices Poe has used. Far more unusual and elaborate is his use of *internal rhyme* within the lines. Read the first stanza slowly. Notice that *dreary* in the first line rhymes with *weary* at its end, that the word *napping* in line 3 rhymes both with *tapping* at the end of the line and with *rapping* in line 4.

(*b*) *Alliteration*, the repetition of the initial sound of two or more closely related words or accented syllables, is richly used throughout the poem. Again referring to the first stanza, notice the alliterative effect of "*weak* and *weary*" in the first line, of "*quaint* and *curious*" in line 2, and of "*I nodded, nearly napping*" in line 3.

(*c*) *Assonance*, the resemblance in the sound of the vowel in two or more accented syllables, adds greatly to the musical effect of the poem. In the first stanza note that the sound of the *o* in *pondered* (line 1) is repeated in *volume* (line 2) and *nodded* (line 3), and that this sound in turn is closely related to the *o* sounds in *forgotten lore* (line 2).

(*d*) *Repetition*, the deliberate repeating of a word or phrase, is particularly striking throughout the poem. Notice, for example, how Poe has repeated in the last line of stanzas 1, 3, 4, 5, and 6 the phrase *and nothing more*.

Choose a stanza of "The Raven" that you find exceptionally musical and prepare to read it aloud to the class. Be ready also to point out examples of rhyme, alliteration, assonance, or repetition which Poe used to make this particular music.

By 1829 New England led the still young United States in commerce and industry. Such leadership brought wealth and leisure to the established families and a culture which favored the development of the creative arts. Hence, as a result of her advantages in material progress, the New England poets dominated the literary scene until the outbreak of war in 1861. The poets of this period are distinguished by the blending of two powerful influences: (1) the English tradition in poetry, which united the polish and elegance of eighteenth-century verse with the emotional force of the romantic poets, and (2) a new spirit of American independence and self-reliance. The leading New England poets—Longfellow, Whittier, Holmes, Lowell, and Emerson—show in varying degrees the effect of these influences.

Henry Wadsworth Longfellow (1807-1882)[1]

Among the major New England poets, the one most influenced by European verse patterns was Henry Wadsworth Longfellow. Affected, perhaps, by his years of study abroad and his research as professor of modern languages at Harvard, he wrote a number of translations from European poets, or composed poems on American themes in forms suggested by European poems. For example, in style and meter his *Hiawatha* reflects the Finnish national epic, the *Kalevala*.

However, there was also a strong native strain in Longfellow's poems. By his use of simple, everyday words and of sentences which followed the pattern of common speech, he made poetry the property of the ordinary man. Because of his New England consciousness of moral problems, he was enabled to write poems which embodied the feelings of the great body of the people. Thus, because of the skill in versifying which he had acquired from foreign models, because of his simplicity, and because of his sound and conventional morality, he was able to reach the hearts of common people. During his life and for many years after his death, he enjoyed a popularity exceeding that of any other American poet.

John Greenleaf Whittier (1807-1892)[2]

Like Longfellow, Whittier was affected both by foreign influences and by the place of his birth. He was born on a farm near Haverhill, Massachusetts, in 1807—the same year in which Longfellow was born. The Whittiers were Quakers, and John Greenleaf often showed in his poems the moral fervor of his religious sect. He was a great admirer of another farm-bred poet, the Scotchman Robert Burns, and his best songs often resembled Burns' poetry in various ways. Like Burns he wrote of the world of nature about him and of common experiences; he used simple, everyday language; and he believed strongly in the equality of all men.[3] Whittier came to rank high among the poets whose works communicated the flavor and the atmosphere of a particular region.

---

[1]For a biographical sketch of Longfellow see page 385.
[2]For a short biography of Whittier see page 409.
[3]See "The Poor Voter on Election Day" (page 200) for an illustration of Whittier's democratic spirit.

Oliver Wendell Holmes (1809-1894)[4]

In wit, polish, and cleverness Oliver Wendell Holmes stood foremost among the writers of his times. His style in verse reflects the elegance and attention to perfection of phrase of the eighteenth-century English poets; but his subject matter comes from the circumstances of his life. A physician and teacher of anatomy at Harvard by profession, he turned to poetry as an avocation and a means of delighting his friends. Because of his skill in writing witty and polished poems for particular occasions, he was in great demand as a local poet laureate, no important occasion being complete without a poem read by Dr. Holmes. Much of his verse is of this character, pleasant to read but failing to appeal to any deep emotions. Only once, in "The Chambered Nautilus," did Holmes himself feel that he had written genuine poetry. This poem showed the skill typical of much he wrote, and also moralized in a way New Englanders liked.

James Russell Lowell (1819-1891)[5]

Like Dr. Holmes, James Russell Lowell was a professor at Harvard, succeeding in 1856 to the chair in modern languages formerly occupied by Longfellow. Also like Dr. Holmes, Lowell utilized the wit and patterns of eighteenth-century English verse for his models. But here the similarity ends, for Lowell had an understanding of America and of her future not to be found in the polished Dr. Holmes. Although like Holmes and Longfellow he used older verse patterns and foreign models when he wished to, he also freely developed his own patterns and styles when he felt the need for them. The *Biglow Papers,* which gained real popularity for Lowell, were completely original and thoroughly American. Mr. Ezekiel Biglow is a horse-sense philosopher. His native New England dialect is accurately portrayed and provides a vehicle for Lowell's wit and humor as well as for common-sense ideas, and, if need be, for pathos.

Ralph Waldo Emerson (1803-1882)[6]

Of all the New England group of this rich, literary period, Emerson was most independent of European influence. He was supremely an individualist; his continuous plea is for man to be himself, to be independent and self-reliant, to cast off convention and conformity. (See the selection from "Self-Reliance" on pages 283-285.) Yet he shared with the English romanticists and his neighbor and friend Thoreau (see pages 360-385) two important attitudes: a love of nature and a profound belief in truth which strikes into man's heart and mind by intuition. This belief is called *transcendentalism;* it means that man is able to receive ultimate truth from a source above and beyond (transcending) what can be experienced by the senses. This belief, in addition to Emerson's strong moral sense, makes his poetry in general more the quiet counsel of a teacher than the impassioned outburst of a lyric poet.[7]

---

[4]For a biographical sketch of Holmes see page 385.
[5]See the short biography of Lowell on page 385.
[6]For a biographical sketch of Emerson see page 385.
[7]For a poem which differs from Emerson's usual "quiet counsel" see "Give All to Love" (pages 271-272).

My Lost Youth

HENRY WADSWORTH LONGFELLOW

Longfellow makes use of a verse from a Lapland poem to form the refrain of this poem about his memories of childhood. This verse sets the mood of the poem, and by its repetition, gives a haunting quality to the poet's thoughts. The "beautiful town" is his boyhood home, Portland, Maine.

OFTEN I THINK of the beautiful town
    That is seated by the sea;
Often in thought go up and down
The pleasant streets of that dear old town,
    And my youth comes back to me.   5
      And a verse of a Lapland song
      Is haunting my memory still:
      "A boy's will is the wind's will,
And the thoughts of youth are long, long
    thoughts."

I can see the shadowy lines of its trees,   10
    And catch, in sudden gleams,
The sheen of the far-surrounding seas,
And islands that were the Hesperides[1]
    Of all my boyish dreams.
      And the burden of that old song,   15
      It murmurs and whispers still:
      "A boy's will is the wind's will,
And the thoughts of youth are long, long
    thoughts."

I remember the black wharves and the slips,
    And the sea tides tossing free;   20
And Spanish sailors with bearded lips,
And the beauty and mystery of the ships,
    And the magic of the sea.
      And the voice of that wayward song
      Is singing and saying still: 25
      "A boy's will is the wind's will,
And the thoughts of youth are long, long
    thoughts."

I remember the bulwarks by the shore,
    And the fort upon the hill;
The sunrise gun, with its hollow roar,   30
The drumbeat repeated o'er and o'er,
    And the bugle wild and shrill.
      And the music of that old song
      Throbs in my memory still:
      "A boy's will is the wind's will,   35
And the thoughts of youth are long, long
    thoughts."

I remember the sea fight[2] far away,
    How it thundered o'er the tide!
And the dead captains, as they lay
In their graves, o'erlooking the tranquil bay   40
    Where they in battle died.
      And the sound of that mournful song
      Goes through me with a thrill:
      "A boy's will is the wind's will,
And the thoughts of youth are long, long
    thoughts."   45

I can see the breezy dome of groves,
    The shadows of Deering's Woods;
And the friendships old and the early loves
Come back with a Sabbath sound, as of doves
    In quiet neighborhoods.   50
      And the verse of that sweet old song,
      It flutters and murmurs still:

---

[1]*Hesperides* (hes per′ə dēz), the Fortunate Isles of Greek mythology where the garden which produced the magic golden apples was located.

[2]*the sea fight,* a naval battle between the American brig *Enterprise* and the English brig *Boxer,* which occurred off Portland in 1813. The *Enterprise* won the engagement, but the captains of both ships were killed and were buried side by side on the shore.

"A boy's will is the wind's will,
And the thoughts of youth are long, long
thoughts."

I remember the gleams and glooms that dart   55
    Across the schoolboy's brain;
The song and the silence in the heart,
That in part are prophecies, and in part
    Are longings wild and vain.
        And the voice of that fitful song   60
        Sings on, and is never still:
        "A boy's will is the wind's will,
And the thoughts of youth are long, long
thoughts."

There are things of which I may not speak;
    There are dreams that cannot die;   65
There are thoughts that make the strong heart
    weak,
And bring a pallor into the cheek,
    And a mist before the eye.
        And the words of that fatal song
        Come over me like a chill: 70
        "A boy's will is the wind's will,
And the thoughts of youth are long, long
thoughts."

Strange to me now are the forms I meet
    When I visit the dear old town;
But the native air is pure and sweet,   75
And the trees that o'ershadow each well-known
    street,
    As they balance up and down,
        Are singing the beautiful song,
        Are sighing and whispering still:
        "A boy's will is the wind's will,   80
And the thoughts of youth are long, long
thoughts."

And Deering's Woods are fresh and fair,
    And with joy that is almost pain
My heart goes back to wander there,
And among the dreams of the days that were,   85
    I find my lost youth again.
        And the strange and beautiful song,
        The groves are repeating it still:
        "A boy's will is the wind's will,
And the thoughts of youth are long, long
thoughts."   90

The Arsenal at Springfield

HENRY WADSWORTH LONGFELLOW

The arsenal at Springfield, Massachusetts, which was established by the Continental Congress in Revolutionary War days, is one of the oldest in the United States. Longfellow's visit to this arsenal brought forth the question—still unanswered today—"Why must there be war?"

THIS IS the Arsenal. From floor to ceiling,
    Like a huge organ, rise the burnished arms;
But from their silent pipes no anthem pealing
    Startles the villages with strange alarms.

Ah! what a sound will rise, how wild and
    dreary,   5
    When the death-angel touches those swift
    keys!
What loud lament and dismal Miserere[1]
    Will mingle with their awful symphonies!

I hear even now the infinite fierce chorus,
    The cries of agony, the endless groan,   10
Which, through the ages that have gone before
    us,
    In long reverberations reach our own.

On helm and harness rings the Saxon hammer,[2]
    Through Cimbric forest roars the Norse-
    man's song,[3]
And loud, amid the universal clamor,   15
    O'er distant deserts sounds the Tartar[4] gong.

---

[1]*Miserere* (miz′ə rā′rā), a prayer of petition in time of trouble. *Miserere* is the first word of the Latin version of the Psalm which begins "Have mercy upon me, O Lord."

[2]*On helm and harness...Saxon hammer.* This is a reference to the forging of helmets (helms) and other armor (harness) by the ancient inhabitants of Germany. In this and the following stanza Longfellow suggests the sounds made as various nations of the past prepared for warfare.

[3]*Cimbric* (sim′brik) *forests...Norseman's song.* The reference is probably to Jutland, a peninsula of Denmark. Jutland is believed to have been the original home of the Cimbri, a warlike northern tribe who invaded Roman territory and were destroyed in northern Italy in 101 B. C.

[4]*Tartar.* The Tartars were a mixed horde of Mongols and Turks who overran Asia and eastern Europe during the Middle Ages.

I hear the Florentine, who from his palace
  Wheels out his battle bell[5] with dreadful din,
And Aztec priests upon their teocallis[6]
  Beat the wild war drum made of serpent's
    skin;   20

The tumult of each sacked and burning village:
  The shout that every prayer for mercy
    drowns;
The soldiers' revels in the midst of pillage;
  The wail of famine in beleaguered towns;

The bursting shell, the gateway wrenched
    asunder,   25
  The rattling musketry, the clashing blade;
And ever and anon, in tones of thunder,
  The diapason of the cannonade.

Is it, O man, with such discordant noises,
  With such accursed instruments as these, 30
Thou drownest Nature's sweet and kindly
    voices,
  And jarrest the celestial harmonies?

Were half the power, that fills the world with
    terror,
  Were half the wealth, bestowed on camps
    and courts,
Given to redeem the human mind from error, 35
  There were no need of arsenals nor forts—

The warrior's name would be a name abhorrèd!
  And every nation, that should lift again
Its hand against a brother, on its forehead
  Would wear forevermore the curse of Cain![7]

Down the dark future, through long genera-
    tions,   41
  The echoing sounds grow fainter and then
    cease;

And like a bell, with solemn, sweet vibrations,
  I hear once more the voice of Christ say,
    "Peace!"

Peace! and no longer from its brazen portals 45
  The blast of War's great organ shakes the
    skies!
But beautiful as songs of the immortals,
  The holy melodies of love arise.

The Trailing Arbutus

JOHN GREENLEAF WHITTIER

In this and the following poem two leading characteristics of Whittier are disclosed: his response to
nature in its simple forms, and his deeply religious
attitude toward life.

I WANDERED lonely where the pine trees
    made
Against the bitter East their barricade,
  And, guided by its sweet
Perfume, I found, within a narrow dell,
The trailing spring flower tinted like a shell   5
  Amid dry leaves and mosses at my feet.

From under dead boughs, for whose loss the
    pines
Moaned ceaseless overhead, the blossoming
    vines
  Lifted their glad surprise,
While yet the bluebird smoothed in leafless
    trees   10
His feathers ruffled by the chill sea breeze,
  And snowdrifts lingered under April skies.

As, pausing o'er the lonely flower I bent,
I thought of lives thus lowly, clogged and pent,
  Which yet find room,   15
Through care and cumber, coldness and decay,
To lend a sweetness to the ungenial day,
  And make the sad earth happier for their
    bloom.

Dear Lord and Father of Mankind

JOHN GREENLEAF WHITTIER

DEAR LORD and Father of Mankind,
  Forgive our foolish ways!
Reclothe us in our rightful mind,
In purer lives Thy service find,
  In deeper reverence, praise.   5

In simple trust like theirs who heard
  Beside the Syrian sea
The gracious calling of the Lord,[1]
Let us, like them, without a word,
  Rise up and follow Thee.   10

O Sabbath rest by Galilee!
  O calm of hills above,
Where Jesus knelt to share with Thee
The silence of eternity
  Interpreted by love!   15

With that deep hush subduing all
  Our words and works that drown
The tender whisper of Thy call,
As noiseless let Thy blessing fall
  As fell Thy manna down.[2]   20

Drop Thy still dews of quietness,
  Till all our strivings cease;
Take from our souls the strain and stress,
And let our ordered lives confess
  The beauty of Thy peace.   25

Breathe through the heats of our desire
  Thy coolness and Thy balm;
Let sense be dumb, let flesh retire;
Speak through the earthquake, wind, and fire,
  O still, small voice[3] of calm!   30

---

[1] *like theirs who heard...the Lord.* This is a reference to Christ's calling Peter and the others who were fishermen on the Sea of Galilee to follow Him and become His apostles. (Matthew 4:18-22.) During Christ's lifetime Galilee was part of the Roman province of Syria.

[2] *as fell Thy manna down.* After the Israelites had been led out of Egypt by Moses, they spent forty years wandering in the wilderness before finding the Promised Land. During those years of wandering, food from heaven (manna) was miraculously supplied. (Exodus 16:14-36.)

[3] *still, small voice,* a reference to the voice of the Lord as He spoke to Elijah. (I Kings 19:12-13.)

The Chambered Nautilus

OLIVER WENDELL HOLMES

"The Chambered Nautilus" was first published in *The Autocrat of the Breakfast Table,* a collection of leisurely imaginary conversations. In introducing the poem, Holmes wrote: "I will read you a few lines... suggested by looking at a section of one of those chambered shells to which is given the name of pearly nautilus...The name [*nautilus* from the Greek *naus,* "ship"] shows that it has long been compared to a ship." In describing the shell itself Holmes wrote of "the series of enlarging compartments successively dwelt in by the animal that inhabits the shell, which is built in a widening spiral." It is from this "widening spiral" that the poet draws his lesson.

THIS IS the ship of pearl, which, poets feign,
  Sails the unshadowed main—
    The venturous bark that flings
On the sweet summer wind its purpled wings
In gulfs enchanted,[1] where the Siren sings,[2]   5
  And coral reefs lie bare,
Where the cold sea-maids[3] rise to sun their
    streaming hair.

Its webs of living gauze[4] no more unfurl;
  Wrecked is the ship of pearl!
Where its dim dreaming life was wont to dwell,
As the frail tenant shaped his growing shell,   11
    And ever-chambered cell,
      Before thee lies revealed—
Its irised[5] ceiling rent, its sunless crypt un-
    sealed!

Year after year beheld the silent toil   15
    That spread his lustrous coil;
      Still, as the spiral grew,
He left the past year's dwelling for the new,

---

[1] *gulfs enchanted.* The chambered nautilus lives in the South Pacific and Indian Oceans, distant and enchanted places to Holmes, who had spent most of his life in New England.

[2] *the Siren sings.* According to Greek mythology the sirens were nymphs who by their sweet singing lured sailors to destruction.

[3] *sea-maids,* mermaids.

[4] *webs of living gauze,* tentacles, or feelers.

[5] *irised,* containing the colors of the rainbow as pearl does.

Stole with soft step its shining archway through,
    Built up its idle door,   20
Stretched in his last-found home, and knew the
    old no more.

Thanks for the heavenly message brought by
    thee,
    Child of the wandering sea,
    Cast from her lap, forlorn!
From thy dead lips a clearer note is born   25
Than ever Triton blew from wreathèd horn![6]
    While on mine ear it rings,
Through the deep caves of thought I hear a
    voice that sings:

Build thee more stately mansions, O my soul,
    As the swift seasons roll!   30
    Leave thy low-vaulted past!
Let each new temple, nobler than the last,
Shut thee from heaven with a dome more vast,
    Till thou at length art free,
Leaving thine outgrown shell by life's unresting
    sea!   35

---

[6]*Triton* (trī′tən) *blew from wreathèd horn.* According to Greek mythology Triton was the god of the sea. His horn makes the roaring of the ocean.

My Aunt

OLIVER WENDELL HOLMES

In an age when practically no career was open to a gentlewoman other than marriage, the position of an elderly spinster was half pathetic, half humorous. The unmarried aunt who resided in the homes of her relatives was a common figure of society in Holmes' time. Holmes here explains how his own aunt came to be what she was.

MY AUNT! my dear unmarried aunt!
    Long years have o'er her flown;
Yet still she strains the aching clasp
    That binds her virgin zone[1];
I know it hurts her—though she looks   5
    As cheerful as she can;

---

[1]*virgin zone*, maiden's waist.

Her waist is ampler than her life,
    For life is but a span.

My aunt! my poor deluded aunt!
    Her hair is almost gray;   10
Why will she train that winter curl
    In such a springlike way?
How can she lay her glasses down,
    And say she reads as well,
When, through a double convex lens,   15
    She just makes out to spell?

Her father—grandpapa! forgive
    This erring lip its smiles—
Vowed she should make the finest girl
    Within a hundred miles;   20
He sent her to a stylish school;
    'Twas in her thirteenth June;
And with her, as the rules required,
    "Two towels and a spoon."

They braced my aunt against a board,   25
    To make her straight and tall;
They laced her up, they starved her down,
    To make her light and small;
They pinched her feet, they singed her hair,
    They screwed it up with pins—   30
Oh, never mortal suffered more
    In penance for her sins.

So, when my precious aunt was done,
    My grandsire brought her back
(By daylight, lest some rabid youth   35
    Might follow on the track);
"Ah!" said my grandsire, as he shook
    Some powder in his pan,[2]
"What could this lovely creature do
    Against a desperate man!"   40

Alas! nor chariot, nor barouche,
    Nor bandit cavalcade,
Tore from the trembling father's arms
    His all-accomplished maid.
For her how happy had it been!   45
    And Heaven had spared to me
To see one sad, ungathered rose
    On my ancestral tree.

---

[2]*pan*, the firing pan of an old musket.

To the Dandelion

JAMES RUSSELL LOWELL

Of all our wild flowers the dandelion is perhaps commonest and least desired, yet Lowell makes it the subject not only of his sensitive response to nature, but also of his convictions concerning the true democracy of mankind.

D EAR COMMON FLOWER, that grow'st beside the way,
Fringing the dusty road with harmless gold,
   First pledge of blithesome May,
Which children pluck, and, full of pride, uphold,
   High-hearted buccaneers, o'erjoyed that they
An El Dorado[1] in the grass have found,   6
   Which not the rich earth's ample round
May match in wealth—thou art more dear to me
Than all the prouder summer blooms may be.

Gold such as thine ne'er drew the Spanish prow[2]   10
Through the primeval hush of Indian seas,
   Nor wrinkled the lean brow
Of age, to rob the lover's heart of ease;
   'Tis the spring's largess, which she scatters now
To rich and poor alike, with lavish hand,   15
   Though most hearts never understand
To take it at God's value, but pass by
The offered wealth with unrewarded eye.

Thou art my tropics and mine Italy;
To look at thee unlocks a warmer clime;   20
   The eyes thou givest me
Are in the heart, and heed not space or time.
   Not in mid June the golden-cuirassed bee[3]

Feels a more summerlike warm ravishment
   In the white lily's breezy tent,   25
His fragrant Sybaris,[4] than I, when first
From the dark green thy yellow circles burst.

Then think I of deep shadows on the grass,
Of meadows where in sun the cattle graze,
   Where, as the breezes pass,   30
The gleaming rushes lean a thousand ways,
   Of leaves that slumber in a cloudy mass,
Or whiten in the wind, of waters blue
   That from the distance sparkle through
Some woodland gap, and of a sky above,   35
Where one white cloud like a stray lamb doth move.

My childhood's earliest thoughts are linked with thee;
The sight of thee calls back the robin's song,
   Who, from the dark old tree
Beside the door, sang clearly all day long,   40
   And I, secure in childish piety,
Listened as if I heard an angel sing
   With news from heaven, which he could bring
Fresh every day to my untainted ears,
   When birds and flowers and I were happy peers.   45

How like a prodigal doth nature seem,
When thou, for all thy gold, so common art!
   Thou teachest me to deem
More sacredly of every human heart,
   Since each reflects in joy its scanty gleam   50
Of heaven, and could some wondrous secret show
   Did we but pay the love we owe,
And with a child's undoubting wisdom look
On all these living pages of God's book.

---

[1]*El Dorado* (el′də rä′dō), a legendary city of gold.
[2]*the Spanish prow,* the ships of the Spanish explorers of the sixteenth century who came to the New World in search of gold.
[3]*golden-cuirassed* (-kwi rasd′) *bee,* bee encased in golden armor. This is a figurative way of saying that the bee's body looked as if it were sheathed in body armor (cuirass).

---

[4]*the white lily's breezy tent, his fragrant Sybaris* (sib′ə ris). To the bee the lily was as rich a place as Sybaris, an ancient Grecian city in southern Italy once noted for its luxury.

The Courtin'

JAMES RUSSELL LOWELL

It is interesting to contrast the humor of Lowell with
that of Holmes. In "My Aunt" we find an aristocratic
subject and a treatment which would appeal particularly to upper classes of society. In "The Courtin',"
which first appeared in the *Biglow Papers*, we find a
very humble subject, a theme of universal appeal, and
the use of dialect for realism and for humor.

GOD MAKES sech nights, all white an' still
    Fur 'z you can look or listen,
Moonshine an' snow on field an' hill,
    All silence an' all glisten.

Zekle crep' up quite unbeknown   5
    An' peeked in thru' the winder,
An' there sot Huldy all alone,
    'ith no one nigh to hender.

A fireplace filled the room's one side
    With half a cord o' wood in—   10
There warn't no stoves (tell[1] comfort died)
    To bake ye to a puddin'.

The wa'nut logs shot sparkles out
    Towards the pootiest,[2] bless her,
An' leetle flames danced all about   15
    The chiny on the dresser.

Agin the chimbley crook-necks[3] hung,
    An' in amongst 'em rusted
The ole queen's-arm[4] thet Gran'ther Young
    Fetched back from Concord busted.   20

The very room, coz she was in,
    Seemed warm from floor to ceilin',
An' she looked full ez rosy agin
    Ez the apples she was peelin'.

'Twas kin' o' kingdom-come[5] to look   25
    On sech a blessed cretur,
A dog rose[6] blushin' to a brook
    Ain't modester nor sweeter.

He was six foot o' man, A-1,
    Clear grit an' human natur';   30
None couldn't quicker pitch a ton[7]
    Nor dror a furrer[8] straighter.

He'd sparked it with full twenty gals,
    Had squired 'em, danced 'em, druv 'em,
Fust this one, an' then thet, by spells—   35
    All is, he couldn't love 'em.

But long o' her his veins 'ould run
    All crinkly like curled maple,
The side she breshed felt full o' sun
    Ez a south slope in Ap'il.   40

She thought no v'ice had sech a swing
    Ez hisn in the choir;
My! when he made Ole Hunderd[9] ring,
    She *knowed* the Lord was nigher.

An' she'd blush scarlit, right in prayer,   45
    When her new meetin'-bunnet
Felt somehow thru' its crown a pair
    O' blue eyes sot upun it.

Thet night, I tell ye, she looked *some!*
    She seemed to've gut a new soul,   50
For she felt sartin-sure he'd come,
    Down to her very shoe sole.

She heered a foot, an' knowed it tu,
    A-raspin' on the scraper—
All ways to once her feelin's flew   55
    Like sparks in burnt-up paper.

He kin' o' l'itered[10] on the mat
    Some doubtfle o' the sekle,[11]
His heart kep' goin' pity-pat
    But hern went pity Zekle.   60

---

[1] *tell*, until.
[2] *pootiest*, prettiest.
[3] *crook-necks*, squashes with crooked necks.
[4] *queen's-arm*, a musket which takes its name from Queen
Anne who ruled England from 1702 to 1714.
[5] *kingdom-come*, as if one had already arrived in heaven.

[6] *dog rose*, the common wild rose.
[7] *pitch a ton*, pitch a ton of hay.
[8] *dror a furrer*, draw (plow) a furrow.
[9] *Ole Hunderd*, the hymn, "Praise God from Whom
All Blessings Flow," which is regularly sung as a part of
many Protestant church services.
[10] *l'itered*, loitered.
[11] *sekle*, sequel, or outcome.

An' yet she gin her cheer a jerk
  Ez though she wished him furder,
An' on her apples kep' to work,
  Parin' away like murder.

"You want to see my Pa, I s'pose?"   65
  "Wal...no....I come dasignin'—"
"To see my Ma? She's sprinklin' clo'es
  Agin tomorrer's i'nin'."

To say why gals acts so or so,
  Or don't, 'ould be presumin';   70
Mebby to mean *yes* an' say *no*
  Comes nateral to women.

He stood a spell on one foot fust,
  Then stood a spell on t'other,
An' on which one he felt the wust   75
  He couldn't ha' told ye nuther.

Says he, "I'd better call agin";
  Says she, "Think likely, Mister";
Thet last word pricked him like a pin,
  An'....Wal, he up an' kist her.   80

When Ma bimeby upon 'em slips,
  Huldy sot pale ez ashes,
All kin' o' smily roun' the lips
  An' teary roun' the lashes.

For she was jes' the quiet kind   85
  Whose naturs never vary,
Like streams that keep a summer mind
  Snowhid in Jenooary.

The blood clost roun' her heart felt glued
  Too tight for all expressin',   90
Tell mother see how metters stood,
  An' gin 'em both her blessin'.

Then her red come back like the tide
  Down to the Bay o' Fundy,[12]
An' all I know is they was cried   95
  In meetin'[13] come nex' Sunday.

---

[12]*Bay o' Fundy*, an inlet of the Atlantic Ocean, separating New Brunswick from Nova Scotia. It is remarkable for the great rise and fall of its tides.

[13]*cried in meetin'*. The marriage bans, signifying their intention to wed, were announced by the minister at church service.

The Snowstorm

RALPH WALDO EMERSON

Alive to the wonder and beauty of common events
around him, Emerson speaks in this poem of the
savage beauty of a New England snowstorm. To him
the north wind is a "fierce artificer," or craftsman,
building magnificent structures of driven snow. From
this idea of the wind as a builder, Emerson evolves the
contrast which ends the poem.

Announced by all the trumpets of the sky,
    Arrives the snow, and, driving o'er the
    fields,
Seems nowhere to alight. The whited air
Hides hills and woods, the river, and the
    heaven,
And veils the farmhouse at the garden's end. 5
The sled and traveler stopped, the courier's feet
Delayed, all friends shut out, the housemates
    sit
Around the radiant fireplace, enclosed
In a tumultuous privacy of storm.

    Come see the north wind's masonry.   10
Out of an unseen quarry evermore
Furnished with tile, the fierce artificer
Curves his white bastions with projected roof
Round every windward stake, or tree, or door.
Speeding, the myriad-handed, his wild work 15
So fanciful, so savage, nought cares he
For number or proportion. Mockingly,
On coop or kennel he hangs Parian wreaths[1];
A swanlike form invests the hidden thorn,
Fills up the farmer's lane from wall to wall, 20
Maugre the farmer's sighs; and at the gate
A tapering turret overtops the work.

---

[1]*Parian* (păr′i ən) *wreaths,* snowy wreaths seemingly
carved of fine white marble like that from the Greek
island of Paros.

And when his hours are numbered,[2] and the
    world
Is all his own, retiring, as he were not,[3]
Leaves, when the sun appears, astonished Art 25
To mimic in slow structures, stone by stone,
Built in an age, the mad wind's night work,
The frolic architecture of the snow.

---

[2]*when his hours are numbered,* when the storm is almost
over.
[3]*the world...retiring, as he were not,* during the night
while people are at rest the storm retires, dying away as
if it had never been.

The Rhodora

On Being Asked, Whence Is the Flower?[1]

RALPH WALDO EMERSON

The rhodora—a low shrub with delicate purplish-pink
flowers which appear before the leaves do—grows
wild throughout New England. Yet just as Lowell
considered the dandelion a worthy subject for poetry,
so Emerson chose this common flower to illuminate a
profound idea.

In May, when sea winds pierced our solitudes,
    I found the fresh rhodora in the woods,
Spreading its leafless blooms in a damp nook,
To please the desert and the sluggish brook.
The purple petals, fallen in the pool,   5
Made the black water with their beauty gay;
Here might the redbird come his plumes to
    cool,
And court the flower that cheapens his array.
Rhodora! if the sages ask thee why
This charm is wasted on the earth and sky, 10
Tell them, dear, that if eyes were made for
    seeing,
Then Beauty is its own excuse for being:
Why thou wert there, O rival of the rose!
I never thought to ask, I never knew;
But, in my simple ignorance, suppose 15
The selfsame Power that brought me there
    brought you.

---

[1]*Whence Is the Flower,* what is the reason for the
existence of the flower.

CONCERNING THE POETS AND THE POEMS

Henry Wadsworth Longfellow

1. Name some of the memories of boyhood that Longfellow speaks of in "My Lost Youth." What relationship do you find between these memories and the refrain that Longfellow uses?

2. What is the mood of the poem? How do both the title and the refrain help emphasize this mood?

3. What detail of the arsenal at Springfield makes Longfellow think of an organ? Trace his use of this figure of speech throughout the poem.

4. Read aloud the lines from "The Arsenal at Springfield" that offer Longfellow's solution to the threat of war. Can you mention any instances of progress in attempting to follow this idea?

5. Through his years of study and travel abroad, Longfellow became well acquainted with European literature and history. Cite lines from the poems which show the influence of this background.

John Greenleaf Whittier

1. What lesson does Whittier learn from the trailing arbutus? Read aloud lines from the poem which show Whittier's close observation of nature.

2. How does "Dear Lord and Father of Mankind" reflect the poet's Quaker background?

Oliver Wendell Holmes

1. Why does Holmes compare the chambered nautilus to a ship? Where does this figure of speech end?

2. Compare stanzas 3 and 5. What information does the poet give you in stanza 3? What use does he make of this factual material in stanza 5?

3. In what ways does Holmes create humor in his description of his aunt? What does the poem satirize? Prepare to read aloud lines which you particularly enjoy.

4. Is "The Chambered Nautilus" or "My Aunt" more typical of Holmes as a poet? Explain your answer.

James Russell Lowell

1. In what respects is "To the Dandelion" a nature poem? In what ways does it differ from "The Trailing Arbutus"? In what way does each of the poets end his poem? What attitude toward mankind does each poet hold?

2. In "The Courtin'" what other means in addition to dialect does Lowell use to create humor?

3. Does Lowell make Zekle and Huldy seem ridiculous? What do you feel is his attitude toward them? Contrast this attitude with that of Holmes toward his aunt.

Ralph Waldo Emerson

1. Compare "The Snowstorm" as a nature poem with "The Trailing Arbutus" and with "To the Dandelion." Which poem do you think reveals the most feeling? Which one is most descriptive? How does the ending of "The Snowstorm" differ from that of the other two poems?

2. How, according to Emerson, does the north wind's masonry differ from that of man? Which is superior? Why?

3. What is the question that Emerson raises in "The Rhodora"? Read the question aloud and explain Emerson's answers.

4. Emerson and Whittier each wrote a poem about a humble flower hidden away in an obscure place. Contrast the ideas that the poets evolved from a very similar situation.

Understanding meter

We read a poem primarily for pleasure. It may be the pleasure of a comforting or inspiring thought, or the pleasure of rhythmic and beautiful language. We take it for granted that all poems have rhythm, regular or irregular, and that many poems use rhyme. However, some knowledge of the regular rhythms, called *meters*, that are used in all but free verse, will add to our enjoyment of poetry.

The basis of meter is the *foot*. Each foot contains one accented syllable and one or more unaccented syllables. The arrangement of accented and unaccented syllables in a foot gives us four basic meters:

(a) *The iamb*. This metrical foot, which consists of an unaccented syllable followed by an accented syllable ($\smile$ /), as in the word *delight*, is the measure most commonly used in verse written in the English language. Notice how the accents fall in the lines from Freneau's poem "The Wild Honeysuckle":

No rov | ing foot | shall crush | thee here, |

No bus | y hand | pro voke | a tear |

(b) *The trochee*. This two-syllabled metrical foot is the opposite of the iamb. Here the accented syllable precedes the unaccented syllable (/ $\smile$), as in the word *golden*. Longfellow used this meter in *Hiawatha*:

Out of | child hood | in to | man hood |

Now had | grown my | Hi a | wath a. |

(c) *The anapest*. This three-syllabled measure consists of two short or unaccented syllables followed by one long or accented syllable ($\smile\smile$ /), as in the word *introduce*. It is seldom sustained throughout an entire poem, but many poets gain variety and a swift-moving effect by combining anapestic with iambic feet. The following lines from "Sandolphon," by Longfellow, illustrate this meter:

From the spir | its on earth | that a dore |

From the souls | that en treat | and im plore. |

(*d*) *The dactyl.* Like the anapest, the dactyl is a three-syllabled foot, but in the dactyl the long or accented syllable precedes the two unaccented syllables (∕◡◡), as in the word *happiness*. Few poems are written entirely in dactylic feet, but Longfellow used this meter frequently in "The Courtship of Miles Standish":

Noth ing was | heard in the | room but the | hur ry ing |

pen of the | strip ling. |

Few poems are written in metrical feet of a single kind. Poets worth their salt tend to avoid the monotony of a completely regular beat by using *substitute feet*. For example, *strip′ling* is a trochee at the end of a dactylic line by Longfellow quoted above. Such departures from regular rhythm may not only destroy monotony; they also may emphasize important words.

Poetry varies not only in meter but also in the number of feet in a line. A line of poetry containing only one foot is said to be written in *monometer;* a line of two feet is called *dimeter;* a line of three feet gives us *trimeter.* Thus, the lines from "Sandolphon" scanned above are said to be written in *anapestic trimeter.*

Tetrameter, a line of four metrical feet, is frequently used by poets. "The Wild Honeysuckle" is written in *iambic tetrameter* and the meter of *Hiawatha* is *trochaic tetrameter.*

Pentameter is a line of five metrical feet. *Iambic pentameter* is used in sonnets (see "Understanding a Sonnet," page 286) and in the dignified unrhymed lines which we call *blank verse.* Bryant's "Thanatopsis" (pages 551-552) and Emerson's "The Snowstorm" (page 568) are written in blank verse.

Compare the verse structure of "The Snowstorm" with that of "The Trailing Arbutus" and "To the Dandelion." What effect does the verse pattern of each have on the mood and feeling of the poem?

Examine the meters of some of the other poems you have studied in this unit. Indicate on the blackboard the scansion of several lines from various poems. Can you find substitute feet used for emphasis? Can you find examples of more than one meter in a single poem? Which meter predominates?

Extending interests

Taken as a group, no American poets have been more popular or better loved than those who flourished in New England during its "Golden Age." Your parents and your grandparents learned poems by Longfellow, Whittier, and their contemporaries in school. Ask some member of your family for his favorite poem by one of these writers. Find the poem and practice reading it aloud. Then arrange with your teacher for a poetry-reading hour at which these favorite poems of the past may be read and the reasons for their popularity discussed.

❧ III FOUR SOUTHERN POETS

Just as the New England poets celebrated the landscape and life of their section in their lyrics, the poets of the South wrote songs that expressed the beauties of nature and the way of life in their part of the United States. Four names—Henry Timrod, Paul Hamilton Hayne, Abram Joseph Ryan, and Sidney Lanier—stand out among those of Southern poets.

The emergence of a group of first-rate poets came later in the South than it had in New England. Longfellow had finished college and was studying abroad when Timrod, the oldest of the Southern quartet, was born; and all of the New England group we have studied had achieved fame before the first of the Southerners had reached his full powers. In fact, it was the War Between the States and the years of strain and conflict which accompanied it which brought the creative powers of these Southern artists to maturity.

Henry Timrod (1828-1867)[1]

Southern-born and Southern-educated, Henry Timrod of Charleston, South Carolina, is often called "the Laureate of the Confederacy." Before the outbreak of the war in 1861 he had published one volume of poetry, but it was the war itself and his service in the Confederate army which brought forth his full powers as a poet.

Timrod was influenced by the English romantic poets. To romantic ardor he added a precision in his use of words and a restraint in his expression of emotion. Because he was able to avoid the fiery anger which mars much war verse, he produced some genuine poetry.

Paul Hamilton Hayne (1830-1886)[2]

Like his lifelong friend Timrod, Paul Hamilton Hayne was born and educated in Charleston, South Carolina. Before the outbreak of the war he had published three volumes of poetry and had won generous praise from the New England group. The war changed the course of his life. His Charleston home was burned, his library destroyed, his income ended. He retired to Augusta, Georgia, built himself a simple cottage in a pine grove, and began to write his best poetry. He lacked Timrod's strength and control. Too often his work was imitative of the English singers. But he had a feeling for nature which was sincere and often moving, and at his best he wrote poetry which successfully evoked the romantic mood of the Old South.

Abram Joseph Ryan (1838-1886)[3]

A Roman Catholic priest, Abram Joseph Ryan served as chaplain with a Southern regiment from 1862 until the end of the war. His grief at the death of a younger brother in battle and the defeat of the cause in which he so strongly believed inspired his best poetry. Poems like "The Conquered Banner" (page 573) are notable for dignity as well as pathos and restrained but deep emotion. Because he expressed so well the spirit of the South in defeat, Ryan is called "the poet of the Lost Cause."

Sidney Lanier (1842-1881)[4]

Of the four Southern poets, Sidney Lanier was least influenced by the war. Although he fought loyally and long in the Confederate army and spent five months as a prisoner of war, his poetry was formed less by his wartime experiences than by his subsequent training in music. In his poems Lanier constantly experimented with musical effects and with melodies; he also attempted at times to reproduce the structure of symphonies. His poetry is full of the emotional richness of an artist's imagination. This richness led him at times to write too emotionally or to use figures of speech which were confused and overelaborate. Nevertheless, he is a poet to be respected and remembered for the grace and clearness with which he pictured the Southern landscape.

---

[1] For a brief biography of Timrod see page 409.
[2] For a biographical sketch of Hayne see page 409.
[3] For a brief biography of Ryan see page 409.
[4] For a biographical sketch of Lanier see page 443.

Ode

HENRY TIMROD

This poem was first published in the Charleston *Courier* under the title "Ode Sung on the Occasion of Decorating the Graves of the Confederate Dead, at Magnolia Cemetery, Charleston, S. C." It is probably the most famous of all Timrod's poems.

SLEEP SWEETLY in your humble graves,
  Sleep, martyrs of a fallen cause;
Though yet no marble column[1] craves
  The pilgrim here to pause.

In seeds of laurel in the earth,   5
  The blossom of your fame is blown,
And somewhere, waiting for its birth,
  The shaft is in the stone!

Meanwhile, behalf[2] the tardy years
  Which keep in trust your storied tombs,   10
Behold! your sisters bring their tears,
  And these memorial blooms.

Small tributes! but your shades will smile
  More proudly on these wreaths today,
Than when some cannon-molded pile   15
  Shall overlook this bay.

Stoop, angels, hither from the skies!
  There is no holier spot of ground
Than where defeated valor lies,
  By mourning beauty crowned!   20

---

[1] *no marble column.* At the time Timrod wrote his "Ode," no monument had been erected in Charleston to the soldiers of the Confederacy. Later, as Timrod prophesies in stanzas 2 and 4, a fine monument was erected.
[2] *behalf,* in behalf of.

Aspects of the Pines

PAUL HAMILTON HAYNE

Living in a cottage in a pine grove, Hayne came to know and love the great surrounding trees. This poem, which describes the pines in various aspects from dawn to darkness, shows Hayne's careful observation of nature and explains why he is often called "the poet of the pines."

TALL, SOMBER, GRIM, against the morning sky
  They rise, scarce touched by melancholy airs,
Which stir the fadeless foliage dreamfully,
  As if from realms of mystical despairs.

Tall, somber, grim, they stand with dusky gleams   5
  Brightening to gold within the woodland's core,
Beneath the gracious noontide's tranquil beams—
  But the weird winds of morning sigh no more.

A stillness, strange, divine, ineffable,
  Broods round and o'er them in the wind's surcease,   10
And on each tinted copse and shimmering dell
  Rests the mute rapture of deep-hearted peace.

Last, sunset comes—the solemn joy and might
  Borne from the west when cloudless day declines—
Low, flutelike breezes sweep the waves of light,   15
  And, lifting dark green tresses of the pines,

Till every lock is luminous—gently float,
  Fraught with hale odors up the heavens afar,
To faint when twilight on her virginal throat
  Wears for a gem the tremulous vesper star. 20

The Conquered Banner

ABRAM J. RYAN

FURL THAT BANNER, for 'tis weary;
� Round its staff 'tis drooping dreary;
  Furl it, fold it—it is best;
For there's not a man to wave it,
And there's not a sword to save it,   5
And there's not one left to lave it
In the blood which heroes gave it;
And its foes now scorn and brave it;
  Furl it, hide it—let it rest!

Take that Banner down! 'tis tattered;   10
Broken is its staff and shattered;
And the valiant hosts are scattered,
  Over whom it floated high.
Oh, 'tis hard for us to fold it,
Hard to think there's none to hold it,   15
Hard that those who once unrolled it
  Now must furl it with a sigh!

Furl that Banner—furl it sadly!
Once ten thousand hailed it gladly,
And ten thousands wildly, madly,   20
  Swore it should forever wave—
Swore that foeman's sword should never
Hearts like theirs entwined dissever,
Till that flag should float forever
  O'er their freedom or their grave!   25

Furl it! for the hands that grasped it,
And the hearts that fondly clasped it,
  Cold and dead are lying low;
And that Banner—it is trailing,
While around it sounds the wailing   30
  Of its people in their woe.

For, though conquered, they adore it—
Love the cold, dead hands that bore it,
Weep for those who fell before it,
Pardon those who trailed and tore it—   35
But, oh, wildly they deplore it,
  Now who furl and fold it so!

Furl that Banner! True, 'tis gory,
Yet 'tis wreathèd round with glory,
And 'twill live in song and story   40

Though its folds are in the dust!
For its fame on brightest pages,
Penned by poets and by sages,
Shall go sounding down the ages—
  Furl its folds though now we must.   45

Furl that Banner, softly, slowly,
Treat it gently—it is holy,
  For it droops above the dead.
Touch it not—unfold it never;
Let it droop there, furled forever—   50
  For its people's hopes are fled!

The Marshes of Glynn

SIDNEY LANIER

This best known of Lanier's poems was inspired by the wide marshes which border the ocean near Brunswick, Georgia. Lanier begins his poem by describing the live-oak forest that runs down to the marshes (lines 1-20). As sunset approaches he discovers that he has escaped from the problems of men and that the vastness of forest and marsh no longer fills him with fear (lines 21-34). Unafraid, he steps to the edge of the forest and looks out over marsh and sea (lines 35-48). He describes the marsh curving beside the sea (lines 49-60). The sight of the marsh stretching wide and the confidence of the marsh hen who builds her nest on the watery shore revive his confidence in the goodness of God (lines 61-78). This confidence becomes triumphant as he watches the order and beauty of the flood tide coming in (lines 79-105).

Lanier's musical background shows itself in the rhythms and the patterns of sound which distinguish this poem.

GLOOMS of the live oaks, beautiful-braided
  and woven
With intricate shades of the vines that myriad-
  cloven
  Clamber the forks of the multiform boughs—
    Emerald twilights—
    Virginal shy lights,   5
Wrought of the leaves to allure to the whisper
  of vows,

When lovers pace timidly down through the
    green colonnades
Of the dim sweet woods, of the dear dark
    woods,
    Of the heavenly woods and glades,
That run to the radiant marginal sand beach
    within   10
        The wide sea-marshes of Glynn—

Beautiful glooms, soft dusks in the noonday
    fire—
Wildwood privacies, closets of lone desire,
Chamber from chamber parted with wavering
    arras of leaves—
Cells for the passionate pleasure of prayer to
    the soul that grieves,   15
Pure with a sense of the passing of saints
    through the wood,
Cool for the dutiful weighing of ill with good—

O braided dusks of the oak and woven shades
    of the vine,
While the riotous noonday sun of the June day
    long did shine
Ye held me fast in your heart and I held you
    fast in mine;   20
But now when the noon is no more, and riot is
    rest,
And the sun is a-wait at the ponderous gate of
    the West,
And the slant yellow beam down the wood aisle
    doth seem
Like a lane into heaven that leads from a
    dream—
Ay, now, when my soul all day hath drunken
    the soul of the oak,   25

And my heart is at ease from men, and the
    wearisome sound of the stroke
    Of the scythe of time and the trowel of trade
    is low,
    And belief overmasters doubt, and I know
    that I know,
    And my spirit is grown to a lordly great
    compass within,
That the length and the breadth and the sweep
    of the marshes of Glynn   30
Will work me no fear like the fear they have
    wrought me of yore

When length was fatigue, and when breadth was
    but bitterness sore,
And when terror and shrinking and dreary un-
    nameable pain
Drew over me out of the merciless miles of the
    plain—

Oh, now, unafraid, I am fain to face   35
    The vast sweet visage of space.
To the edge of the wood I am drawn, I am
    drawn,
Where the gray beach glimmering runs, as a
    belt of the dawn,
    For a mete and a mark
        To the forest dark—   40
            So:
Affable live oak, leaning low—
Thus—with your favor—soft, with a reverent
    hand
(Not lightly touching your person, Lord of the
    land!)
Bending your beauty aside, with a step I stand
On the firm-packed sand,   46
            Free
By a world of marsh that borders a world of
    sea.
    Sinuous southward and sinuous northward
    the shimmering band
    Of the sand beach fastens the fringe of the
    marsh to the folds of the land.   50
Inward and outward to northward and south-
    ward the beach lines linger and curl
As a silver-wrought garment that clings to and
    follows the firm sweet limbs of a girl.
Vanishing, swerving, evermore curving again
    into sight,
Softly the sand beach wavers away to a dim
    gray looping of light.
And what if behind me to westward the wall of
    the woods stands high?   55
The world lies east: how ample, the marsh and
    the sea and the sky!

A league and a league of marsh grass, waist-
high, broad in the blade,
Green, and all of a height, and unflecked with
a light or a shade,
Stretch leisurely off, in a pleasant plain,
To the terminal blue of the main.   60

Oh, what is abroad in the marsh and the terminal sea?
   Somehow my soul seems suddenly free
From the weighing of fate and the sad discussion of sin,
By the length and the breadth and the sweep of
the marshes of Glynn.

Ye marshes, how candid and simple and noth-
ing-withholding and free   65
Ye publish yourselves to the sky and offer yourselves to the sea!
Tolerant plains, that suffer the sea and the rains
and the sun,
Ye spread and span like the catholic man who
hath mightily won
God out of knowledge and good out of infinite
pain
And sight out of blindness and purity out of a
stain.   70

As the marsh hen secretly builds on the watery
sod,
Behold I will build me a nest on the greatness
of God;
I will fly in the greatness of God as the marsh
hen flies
In the freedom that fills all the space 'twixt the
marsh and the skies;
By so many roots as the marsh grass sends in
the sod   75
I will heartily lay me a-hold on the greatness of
God;
Oh, like to the greatness of God is the greatness
within

The range of the marshes, the liberal marshes
of Glynn.

And the sea lends large, as the marsh; lo, out of
his plenty the sea
Pours fast; full soon the time of the flood tide
must be: 80
Look how the grace of the sea doth go
About and about through the intricate channels
that flow
         Here and there,
              Everywhere,
Till his waters have flooded the uttermost creeks
and the low-lying lanes,   85
And the marsh is meshed with a million veins,
That like as with rosy and silvery essences flow
   In the rose-and-silver evening glow.
              Farewell, my lord Sun!
The creeks overflow; a thousand rivulets run 90
'Twixt the roots of the sod; the blades of the
marsh grass stir;
Passeth a hurrying sound of wings that west-
ward whirr;
Passeth, and all is still; and the currents cease
to run;
And the sea and the marsh are one.

How still the plains of the waters be!   95
The tide is in his ecstasy.
The tide is at his highest height—
         And it is night.

And now from the Vast of the Lord will the
waters of sleep
Roll in on the souls of men,   100
But who will reveal to our waking ken
The forms that swim and the shapes that creep
              Under the waters of sleep?
And I would I could know what swimmeth
below when the tide comes in
On the length and the breadth of the marvelous
marshes of Glynn.   105

CONCERNING THE POETS AND THE POEMS

Henry Timrod and Abram Ryan

1. Compare Timrod's "Ode" with "The Conquered Banner" by Ryan. How are these poems related in circumstance? How would you describe the mood of each of these poems?

2. Why do you think these poems have remained popular when so much verse on similar themes is quickly forgotten?

Paul Hamilton Hayne

1. In "Aspects of the Pines" at what times of day does Hayne describe the trees? What effect does the mention of the wind in each stanza have on the poem as a whole?

2. What words or phrases picture the pines most vividly for you? What words or phrases express the feelings which the pines arouse in the poet?

3. When Hayne writes, "But the weird winds of morning *sigh* no more," he is using figurative language. Why is this a particularly suitable figure of speech? Point out other examples of effective figurative language in the poem.

Sidney Lanier

1. Which of the following words might be used to describe the spirit of various parts of "The Marshes of Glynn": (*a*) hope, (*b*) confidence, (*c*) doubt, (*d*) affirmation, (*e*) weariness, (*f*) despair? Explain the reasons for your choices, quoting lines from the poem to uphold your viewpoint.

2. Read aloud the first two stanzas of the poem. What is the rhyme scheme? What meter predominates? Pick out good examples of repetition, alliteration, and assonance.

3. Prepare to read aloud to the class several lines of "The Marshes of Glynn" that you feel are notable for their musical features. Explain why you consider these lines musical. (Considering the points noted in question 2 should help your analysis.)

Know your words

Most of the words poets use are no different from those used in prose writings or in conversation. But occasionally poets find it desirable to make use of words that the dictionary classifies as *poetic* or *archaic*. These are half-remembered words of former generations whose use is now mainly literary. The italicized words in the lines of poetry below are all such words. Determine the meaning of each italicized word. Then tell why you think the poet used it rather than a word in common use today.

> ...vainly I had sought to borrow
> From my books *surcease* of sorrow...
> > —*The Raven*

> Go forth, under the open sky, and *list*
> To Nature's teachings...
> > —*Thanatopsis*

> Seek'st thou the plashy brink
> Of weedy lake, or *marge* of river wide...
> > —*To a Waterfowl*

> Then this *ebon* bird beguiling all my fancy into smiling...
> > —*The Raven*

> This is the ship of pearl, which, poets feign,
> Sails the unshadowed *main*—
> The venturous *bark* that flings
> On the sweet summer wind its purpled wings...
> > —*The Chambered Nautilus*

> A swanlike form invests the hidden thorn,
> Fills up the farmer's lane from wall to wall,
> *Maugre* the farmer's sighs...
> > —*The Snowstorm*

> And there's not one left to *lave* it
> In the blood which heroes gave it...
> > —*The Conquered Banner*

> Oh, now, unafraid, I am *fain* to face
> The vast sweet visage of space.
> > —*The Marshes of Glynn*

❧ IV VOICES SPEAKING AMERICAN

In 1855 Henry Wadsworth Longfellow's *Hiawatha* appeared and was acclaimed throughout the United States. In the same year a man in Brooklyn set in type and published at his own expense a book of poems. The man was Walt Whitman and the book was *Leaves of Grass*—the most important book in the history of American poetry.

As you learned in studying the unit on Walt Whitman (pages 386-409), *Leaves of Grass* at first was little noticed, and what notice it had was generally scornful. Whitman's poetry differed too radically from that to which people were accustomed to gain an audience. Yet Whitman spoke with an authentic American voice and the passage of years has convinced the world of the greatness of his poetry. Two other poets who belonged to no particular group and who were strong and original singers should be considered with Whitman. These are Emily Dickinson and John Bannister Tabb.

Walt Whitman (1819-1892)

The 1855 edition of *Leaves of Grass* spoke of common subjects in common language. The poems undoubtedly used the language of Americans, but they were more notable for strength than for lyric passages, for originality than for beautiful imagery. In subsequent editions of *Leaves of Grass* Whitman matured into a style less formless and more melodious than that of his earlier poems. He began to produce beautiful lyrics like the one from "When Lilacs Last in the Dooryard Bloomed" which begins "Come lovely and soothing death" (page 399). Critics today view Whitman not only as a great original poet but also as the author of excellent lyrics.

Emily Dickinson (1830-1886)[1]

Although she lived through approximately the same span of time as Walt Whitman, Emily Dickinson differed from him in every way except in the freshness and vigor of her verse. Born in Amherst, Massachusetts, as a young woman she became a recluse in her own home and remained so for the rest of her life. Only two of her poems were published in her lifetime, one of them without her consent. Since the first volume of her poems appeared in 1890 and the most recent in 1945, in influence she is a poet of our own times rather than of the period in which she lived.

Emily Dickinson is admired and loved for the simplicity and directness of her language, the freshness of her images, and the freedom with which she used verse forms, rhyme, language, and even grammar to produce her effects. Very original, almost entirely uninfluenced by other poets, she is a late and delicate voice in the New England chorus of singers. Her delicate sense of humor and her use of fresh, unexpected images give her poetry truly unique qualities.

John Bannister Tabb (1845-1909)[2]

It was Sidney Lanier who first directed John Bannister Tabb to the writing of poetry. Tabb had been a blockade runner for the Confederacy during the War Between the States. When he was captured and imprisoned, he found that one of his fellow prisoners was Lanier. Some years after the war Tabb entered the priesthood of the Roman Catholic Church and spent many quiet years teaching literature. The poetry which he wrote did not resemble Lanier's rolling rhythms. In Tabb's response to nature, in the simplicity of his language, and in his verse forms he resembles Emily Dickinson more than any other poet.

[1]For a brief biography of Emily Dickinson see page 443.
[2]For a short biographical sketch of John Bannister Tabb see page 443.

For You O Democracy

WALT WHITMAN

Whitman's love for America and his faith in her greatness as a democracy are exuberantly expressed in this short lyric.

COME, I will make the continent indis-
    soluble,
I will make the most splendid race the sun ever
    shone upon,
I will make divine magnetic lands,
        With the love of comrades,
            With the lifelong love of comrades. 5

I will plant companionship thick as trees along
    all the rivers of America, and along the
    shores of the great lakes, and all over the
    prairies,
I will make inseparable cities with their arms
    about each other's necks,
        By the love of comrades,
            By the manly love of comrades,

For you these from me, O Democracy, to serve
    you ma femme[1]!   10
For you, for you I am trilling these songs.

———
[1]ma femme (mä fäm′), my loved one.

When I Heard the Learn'd Astronomer

WALT WHITMAN

As a poet Whitman expresses his preference for the stars as objects of beauty, bringing comfort to his spirit, rather than as subject matter for a coldly scientific lecture.

WHEN I HEARD the learn'd astronomer,
    When the proofs, the figures, were
    ranged in columns before me,
When I was shown the charts and diagrams, to
    add, divide, and measure them,
When I sitting heard the astronomer where he
    lectured with much applause in the lecture
    room,
How soon unaccountable I became tired and
    sick,   5
Till rising and gliding out I wandered off by
    myself,
In the mystical moist night air, and from time
    to time,
Looked up in perfect silence at the stars.

I'll Tell You How the Sun Rose

EMILY DICKINSON

The delight that readers find in Emily Dickinson's poems comes partly from the simplicity of her subjects and language, and partly from the vivid and unexpected way in which she says things. If you read her poems with an alert imagination, you will find that you are seeing ordinary things in a new and different way.

I'LL TELL YOU how the sun rose—
    A ribbon at a time.
The steeples swam in amethyst,
The news like squirrels ran.

The hills untied their bonnets,   5
The bobolinks begun.
Then I said softly to myself,
"That must have been the sun!"

*   *   *   *

But how he set, I know not.
There seemed a purple stile   10
Which little yellow boys and girls
Were climbing all the while

Till when they reached the other side,
A dominie in gray
Put gently up the evening bars,   15
And led the flock away.

———
"I'll Tell You How the Sun Rose," from *Poems of Emily
Dickinson,* edited by Martha Dickinson Bianchi,
by permission of Little, Brown & Co.

The Snake

EMILY DICKINSON

A NARROW fellow in the grass
   Occasionally rides;
You may have met him—did you not?
His notice instant is.

The grass divides as with a comb,   5
A spotted shaft is seen;
And then it closes at your feet
And opens further on.

He likes a boggy acre,
A floor too cool for corn,   10
Yet when a boy, and barefoot,
I more than once, at noon,

Have passed, I thought, a whiplash
Unbraiding in the sun—
When, stooping to secure it,   15
It wrinkled, and was gone.

Several of nature's people
I know, and they know me;
I feel for them a transport
Of cordiality;   20

But never met this fellow,
Attended or alone,
Without a tighter breathing,
And zero at the bone.

"The Snake" from *Poems of Emily Dickinson*, edited by Martha Dickinson
Bianchi, by permission of Little, Brown & Co.

To a Wood Violet

JOHN BANNISTER TABB

Father Tabb responds to nature with simplicity and
wonder. The finding of a flower and the haunting song
of a bird awaken responses in him which anyone can
share.

IN THIS secluded shrine,
   O miracle of grace,
No mortal eye but mine
   Hath looked upon thy face.

No shadow but mine own   5
   Hath screened thee from the sight
Of heaven, whose love alone
   Hath led me to thy light.

Whereof—as shade to shade
   Is wedded in the sun—   10
A moment's glance hath made
   Our souls forever one.

The Whippoorwill

JOHN BANNISTER TABB

FROM YONDER wooded hill
  I hear the whippoorwill,
Whose mate or wandering echo answers him
  Athwart the lowlands dim.

He calls not through the day;   5
But when the shadows gray
  Across the sunset draw their lengthening veil,
  He tells his twilight tale.

What unforgotten wrong
Haunts the ill-omened song?   10
  What scourge of fate has left its loathèd mark
  Upon the cringing dark?

"Whip! Whippoorwill!"
O sobbing voice, be still!
  Tell not again, O melancholy bird,   15
  The legend thou hast heard!

CONCERNING THE POETS AND THE POEMS

Walt Whitman

1. What attitude toward America do you find in "For You O Democracy"? What is Whitman's attitude toward the people of America? Compare these attitudes with those expressed by Whitman in the selections from "To You" and "By Blue Ontario's Shore" (pages 392-393).

2. In "When I Heard the Learn'd Astronomer" what is Whitman's feeling about the lecture? Why does he prefer to wander off by himself? Would you say that this poem shows that Whitman had no interest in science? Explain your answer.

Emily Dickinson

1. What is the relationship between the first two stanzas of "I'll Tell You How the Sun Rose" and the last two?

2. What lines in "The Snake" present the speaker's reaction toward this creature? What is his feeling toward most of "nature's people"?

3. Both "I'll Tell You How the Sun Rose" and "The Snake" are written in quatrains with the second and fourth lines rhyming. What is peculiar about some of the stanzas? Why do you believe the poet let them remain this way? Do these peculiarities increase or decrease your pleasure in the poems?

John Bannister Tabb

1. What similarities do you find in the ideas expressed in "To a Wood Violet" and "The Rhodora" (page 568)?

2. What ideas float through Father Tabb's imagination as he listens to the song of the whippoorwill at twilight? What would you say is the mood of the lyric?

3. In what ways are the poems of John Bannister Tabb like those of Emily Dickinson? In what ways do they differ? If you like the lyrics of one of these two poets better than those of the other, explain your preference.

Understanding imagery

In the discussion of Emily Dickinson's poetry on page 577 you read that one of the notable things about it is "the freshness of the images." Just what are *images*? C. Day Lewis in *Poetry for You* describes them as "word pictures painted by the poet in such a way as to appeal to the reader's imagination." They may make an appeal to any one of the senses, or to more than one. Often they occur in figures of speech. Images are "fresh" when they say things in a new and unexpected way.

In "I'll Tell You How the Sun Rose" Emily Dickinson describes sunrise and sunset almost entirely by the use of images. For example, she says, "the sun rose a ribbon at a time." What picture does this image give you? Select other images in this poem and explain them. What images in "The Snake" appealed most to your imagination?

John Bannister Tabb also was a master of imagery. In "The Whippoorwill" he uses several images which make a particular appeal to the sense of hearing. Locate these images as you read this poem through again and then explain how they intensify the mood of the poem.

The lyric voice of America lifted in songs of new sorts in the twentieth century. Some of these many singers have produced large numbers of outstanding lyrics; others are known chiefly for a particular poem or even for a few lines. Twentieth-century poets have varied greatly in the techniques of their verses. Some have been strongly influenced by the free-verse forms that Whitman had used so powerfully; others have followed the more conventional forms of Longfellow and Whittier. But all have found subjects in almost every aspect of American life and thought, from religion and philosophy to jazz.

The year 1913 marks a milestone in American verse. In this year two important new poets gained recognition: Vachel Lindsay, through *General William Booth Enters into Heaven and Other Poems,* and Robert Frost, through *A Boy's Will.*

Vachel Lindsay (1879-1931)[1]

The agricultural Middle West, with its strong belief in democracy and its equally strong religious beliefs, profoundly influenced the poetry of Vachel Lindsay. Born in Springfield, Illinois, as a young man he studied art in Chicago and New York. Firmly convinced of the importance of art and literature in the lives of all people, he went on tramping trips across the United States. He was a preacher in a hobo costume. He had a message, the Gospel of Beauty, which he preached to all who would listen. Using the rhythms of ragtime and jazz, he brought poetry to people who would not listen to conventional voices. On occasion he would recite his poems while his audience stamped their feet or clapped their hands in tempo with the rhythm of his verse. Lindsay's rhythmic lyrics had a great effect on the development of twentieth-century poetry.

Robert Frost (1875-   )[2]

Although Robert Frost is utterly unlike Vachel Lindsay in most respects, he, like Lindsay, writes modern poems which vividly portray an agricultural section of America. Frost has lived most of his life in New England, where nine generations of ancestors lived before him, and his work is in the tradition of New England writers like Emerson and Emily Dickinson. The subject matter, the expressions, and the intonations of his poems are pure "north of Boston." He speaks quietly and shyly, as a rule very simply. Yet those who first heard him recognized a new and authentic voice of poetry; they listened and brought others to listen. Thus over the years from 1913 to the present, Robert Frost has spoken confidentially to Americans, who have opened their ears and hearts to him.

[1]For a biographical sketch of Vachel Lindsay see page 486.
[2]For additional material on Robert Frost see page 485.

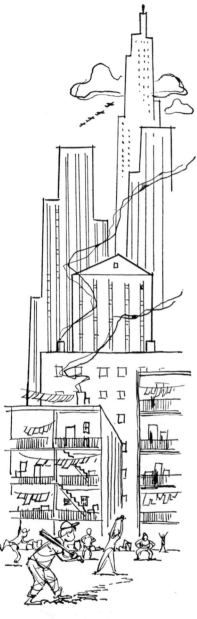

Edgar Lee Masters (1869-1950)[3]

The voice in which Edgar Lee Masters addressed America was totally different from the restrained New England accents of Robert Frost. Like Vachel Lindsay, Illinois-born Masters was a Midwestern experimentalist. He was a flourishing Chicago lawyer in 1915 when his *Spoon River Anthology*[4] appeared, striking a new note in American poetry—a note of critical self-appraisal and of disillusionment with life. *Spoon River Anthology* was immediately popular and has continued to attract new readers. It has also influenced a school of followers—both poets and writers of prose—who, like Masters, have held America up for critical and often cynical analysis.

Edwin Arlington Robinson (1869-1935)[5]

It was in 1916, with the publication of *The Man Against the Sky,* that Edwin Arlington Robinson first became widely known. For almost twenty years he had been living quietly in New York and writing poetry, but he had remained obscure. The success of *The Man Against the Sky* did not mean that in it Robinson had presented better verse than he had formerly written, but rather that the American people had grown ready for poetry that was often difficult to understand and somber in mood. In the years from 1916 until his death Robinson was acknowledged by critics as an outstanding poet; three times he was awarded the Pulitzer Prize. However, because the beauty of his poetry is not always evident on first reading and because the poems are concerned with the analysis of individual characters, he is less known to the general reader than are Robert Frost and Carl Sandburg.

Carl Sandburg (1878-   )[6]

Like Edwin Arlington Robinson, Carl Sandburg first rose to fame in 1916. The book that gained him recognition as a new and striking American voice was *Chicago Poems*. Sandburg, like Vachel Lindsay and Edgar Lee Masters, was born in Illinois. Like Lindsay, he had traveled over America as a hobo, he had a message, and he used the accompaniments of rhythm and music to reach his audiences. Today he still strums his guitar and sings his rhythms as he did over half a century ago. His message is social—it is people who count, not material things. The heart of his message lies in *The People, Yes,* which was published in 1937 and has been widely quoted. In the vigorous and often rough rhythms of his poetry as well as in his democratic ideas, Sandburg follows the tradition of Whitman and Lindsay.

---

[3]For a short biography of Edgar Lee Masters see page 486.
[4]See the headnote to "Henry Cogdal" (page 191) for an explanation of the scheme of *Spoon River Anthology*.
[5]For a biographical sketch of Edwin Arlington Robinson see page 486.
[6]For a short biography of Carl Sandburg see page 487.

Counteé Cullen (1903-1946)

The influence of the English romantic poets of the nineteenth century and of Edwin Arlington Robinson may be found in the melodious lyrics of Counteé Cullen. He himself wrote of his poetry, "Most things I write I do for the sheer love of the music in them." His lyrics of the thoughts and feelings, the joys and sorrows of the poetic Negro race have added a rich strain to American poetry.

Archibald MacLeish (1892-   )

The twofold career of Archibald MacLeish as poet and public official makes him a rather unique figure among today's literary men. In his youth, like others of the so-called "lost generation," he passed through a period of disillusionment. This period of depression gave way in time to a strong faith in America and her future. It was this appreciation of life in freedom which motivated his fine radio plays; he showed his patriotism also by serving as director of the Office of Facts and Figures during World War II and as a delegate to the San Francisco session to draw up a charter for the United Nations.

MacLeish's love of America shines out through his lyrics. His poems are notable also for his command of cadence and rhythm.

Karl Shapiro (1913-   )

One of America's leading critics wrote, *"Person, Place and Thing* seems to me to be the most impressive first volume of verse to be published in the 1940's." This book marked Karl Shapiro's appearance as a poet. Baltimore-born Karl Shapiro has lived the quiet life of a student and teacher, serving as poetry consultant to the Library of Congress, as Professor of English at Johns Hopkins University, and as editor of *Poetry: a Magazine of Verse.* Among the features that make his poetry outstanding are the variety of his subjects and the clarity of his visual images.

* * *

A fine modern poet whom you have previously studied is Stephen Vincent Benét (pages 444-487). Other modern American poets ranging from William Vaughn Moody (pages 155-157) to Sara Teasdale (page 272) were briefly introduced in earlier units. But in addition to these, there are dozens of important names in American poetry which it has been impossible to include in this brief survey. The best way to get acquainted with them is to dip into such anthologies of poetry as those listed on page 594.

In spite of the criticism that Americans are concerned only with material things, the history of our poetry shows that a spirit of love of beauty and of faith in humanity pervades our culture. And this spirit is just as vigorous today as it has been at any period of our history.

General William Booth Enters into Heaven

VACHEL LINDSAY

William Booth, who was born in England in 1829, was the founder of the Salvation Army. A great-hearted man with an enormous sympathy for the poor and degraded, he set up his organization with the hope of bringing the comforts of religion to these unfortunates. As the leader of the "army," he became "General" Booth.

Shortly after Booth's death in 1912, Vachel Lindsay composed this poem. In it he visualizes the scene as General Booth, followed by all the unfortunates he had led to religion, entered into the presence of God.

To be sung to the tune of THE BLOOD OF THE LAMB[1] *with indicated instruments.*

I

[Bass drum beaten loudly.]

Booth led boldly with his big bass drum—
    (Are you washed in the blood of the Lamb?)
The saints smiled gravely, and they said: "He's come."
(Are you washed in the blood of the Lamb?)
Walking lepers followed, rank on rank,   5
Lurching bravos from the ditches dank,
Drabs from the alleyways and drug fiends pale—
Minds still passion-ridden, soul-powers frail—
Vermin-eaten saints with moldy breath,
Unwashed legions with the ways of death— 10
(Are you washed in the blood of the Lamb?)

[Banjos.]

Every slum had sent its half-a-score
The round world over. (Booth had groaned for more.)
Every banner that the wide world flies
Bloomed with glory and transcendent dyes. 15
Big-voiced lasses made their banjos bang!

Tranced, fanatical, they shrieked and sang—
"Are you washed in the blood of the Lamb?"
Hallelujah! It was queer to see
Bull-necked convicts with that land make free!   20
Loons with bazoos[2] blowed a blare, blare, blare
On, on, upward through the golden air.
(Are you washed in the blood of the Lamb?)

II

[Bass drum slower and softer.]
Booth died blind, and still by faith he trod,
Eyes still dazzled by the ways of God.   25
Booth led boldly and he looked the chief—
Eagle countenance in sharp relief,
Beard a-flying, air of high command
Unabated in that holy land.

[Sweet flute music.]
Jesus came from out the courthouse door,   30
Stretched His hands above the passing poor.
Booth saw not, but led his queer ones there
Round and round the mighty courthouse square.
Yet in an instant all that blear review
Marched on spotless, clad in raiment new.   35
The lame were straightened, withered limbs uncurled,
And blind eyes opened on a new, sweet world.

[Bass drum louder.]
Drabs and vixens in a flash made whole!
Gone was the weasel-head, the snout, the jowl!
Sages and sibyls now, and athletes clean,   40
Rulers of empires, and of forests green!

[Grand chorus of all instruments. Tambourines to the foreground.]
The hosts were sandaled and their wings were fire!
(Are you washed in the blood of the Lamb?)
But their noise played havoc with the angel choir.
(Are you washed in the blood of the Lamb?) 45
Oh, shout Salvation! it was good to see

----

[1]"*The Blood of the Lamb,*" a hymn much used in the Salvation Army. "The Lamb" is Christ, and the refrain line, "Are you washed in the blood of the Lamb?" calls on the sinner to repent and receive Christ's forgiveness.

[2]*bazoos,* simple musical instruments played by singing or humming into them.

Kings and princes by the Lamb set free.
The banjos rattled and the tambourines
Jing-jing-jingled in the hands of queens!

[*Reverently sung, no instruments.*]
And when Booth halted by the curb for
  prayer   50

He saw his Master through the flag-filled air.
Christ came gently with a robe and crown
For Booth the soldier, while the throng knelt
  down.
He saw King Jesus. They were face to face,
And he knelt a-weeping in that holy place. 55
(Are you washed in the blood of the Lamb?)

Stopping by Woods on a Snowy Evening

ROBERT FROST

In this and the following poem, Robert Frost speaks
so simply that at first you may think he says very
little. But underneath the simple words you will find
expressed very important attitudes toward life, and
convictions formed from experience. The homely facts
of New England farm life provide symbols by which
Frost expresses his philosophy.

WHOSE WOODS these are I think I know.
    His house is in the village though;
He will not see me stopping here
To watch his woods fill up with snow.

My little horse must think it queer   5
To stop without a farmhouse near
Between the woods and frozen lake
The darkest evening of the year.

He gives his harness bells a shake
To ask if there is some mistake.   10
The only other sound's the sweep
Of easy wind and downy flake.

The woods are lovely, dark, and deep,
But I have promises to keep,
And miles to go before I sleep,   15
And miles to go before I sleep.

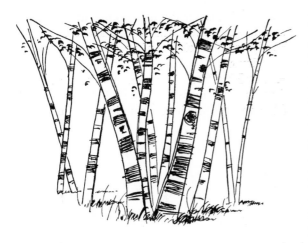

Birches

ROBERT FROST

WHEN I SEE birches bend to left and right
    Across the line of straighter, darker trees,
I like to think some boy's been swinging them.
But swinging doesn't bend them down to stay.
Ice storms do that. Often you must have seen them   5
Loaded with ice a sunny winter morning
After a rain. They click upon themselves
As the breeze rises, and turn many-colored
As the stir cracks and crazes their enamel.
Soon the sun's warmth makes them shed crystal shells   10
Shattering and avalanching on the snow crust—
Such heaps of broken glass to sweep away
You'd think the inner dome of heaven had fallen.
They are dragged to the withered bracken by the load,
And they seem not to break; though once they are bowed   15
So low for long, they never right themselves;
You may see their trunks arching in the woods
Years afterwards, trailing their leaves on the ground
Like girls on hands and knees that throw their hair
Before them over their heads to dry in the sun.   20
But I was going to say when Truth broke in
With all her matter-of-fact about the ice storm
I should prefer to have some boy bend them
As he went out and in to fetch the cows—
Some boy too far from town to learn baseball,   25
Whose only play was what he found himself,
Summer or winter, and could play alone.
One by one he subdued his father's trees
By riding them down over and over again
Until he took the stiffness out of them,   30
And not one but hung limp, not one was left
For him to conquer. He learned all there was
To learn about not launching out too soon
And so not carrying the tree away
Clear to the ground. He always kept his poise   35
To the top branches, climbing carefully
With the same pains you use to fill a cup
Up to the brim, and even above the brim.
Then he flung outward, feet first, with a swish,
Kicking his way down through the air to the ground.   40
So was I once myself a swinger of birches
And so I dream of going back to be.
It's when I'm weary of considerations,
And life is too much like a pathless wood
Where your face burns and tickles with the cobwebs   45
Broken across it, and one eye is weeping
From a twig's having lashed across it open.
I'd like to get away from earth awhile
And then come back to it and begin over.
May no fate willfully misunderstand me   50
And half grant what I wish and snatch me away
Not to return. Earth's the right place for love:
I don't know where it's likely to go better.
I'd like to go by climbing a birch tree,
And climb black branches up a snow-white trunk   55
Toward heaven, till the tree could bear no more,
But dipped its top and set me down again.
That would be good both going and coming back.
One could do worse than be a swinger of birches.

Lucinda Matlock

EDGAR LEE MASTERS

In the short poems from *Spoon River Anthology* which follow, two women speak from their graves. One was a vigorous woman of the poet's own imagining; the other was the sweetheart of Abraham Lincoln. What they say reveals their lives to us, and if we are alert, will cause us to reconsider critically our own lives.

I WENT to dances at Chandlerville,
　　And played snap-out at Winchester.
One time we changed partners,
Driving home in the moonlight of middle June,
And then I found Davis.　　　　　　　　　5
We were married and lived together for seventy
　　years,
Enjoying, working, raising the twelve children,
Eight of whom we lost
Ere I had reached the age of sixty.
I spun, I wove, I kept the house, I nursed the
　　sick,　　　　　　　　　　　　　　10
I made the garden, and for holiday
Rambled over the fields where sang the larks,
And by Spoon River gathering many a shell,
And many a flower and medicinal weed—
Shouting to the wooded hills, singing to the
　　green valleys.　　　　　　　　　　15
At ninety-six I had lived enough, that is all,
And passed to a sweet repose.
What is this I hear of sorrow and weariness,
Anger, discontent, and drooping hopes?
Degenerate sons and daughters,　　　　20
Life is too strong for you—
It takes life to love Life.

"Lucinda Matlock," from *Spoon River Anthology*, copyright, 1915, by Edgar Lee Masters. Reprinted by permission of Ellen C. Masters.

Anne Rutledge

EDGAR LEE MASTERS

O UT OF ME, unworthy and unknown,
　　The vibrations of deathless music;
"With malice toward none, with charity for all."[1]
Out of me the forgiveness of millions toward
　　millions,
And the beneficent face of a nation　　　5
Shining with justice and truth.
I am Anne Rutledge who sleep beneath these
　　weeds,
Beloved in life of Abraham Lincoln,
Wedded to him, not through union,
But through separation.　　　　　　　　10
Bloom forever, O Republic,
From the dust of my bosom!

[1]*"With malice toward none, with charity for all,"* from Lincoln's Second Inaugural Address. See pages 219-221.

"Anne Rutledge," from *Spoon River Anthology*, copyright, 1915, by Edgar Lee Masters. Reprinted by permission of Ellen C. Masters.

Miniver Cheevy

EDWIN ARLINGTON ROBINSON

Those who cannot face the realities of life sometimes take refuge by imagining the pleasures of living in the romantic past. Miniver Cheevy was such a person.

M INIVER CHEEVY, child of scorn,
　　Grew lean while he assailed the sea-
　　sons;
He wept that he was ever born,
　　And he had reasons.

Miniver loved the days of old　　　　　5
　　When swords were bright and steeds were
　　prancing;

"Miniver Cheevy" reprinted from *The Town down the River* by Edwin Arlington Robinson; copyright 1910 by Charles Scribner's Sons, 1938 by Ruth Nivison; used by permission of the publishers.

The vision of a warrior bold
   Would set him dancing.

Miniver sighed for what was not,
   And dreamed, and rested from his labors; 10
He dreamed of Thebes[1] and Camelot,[2]
   And Priam's neighbors.[3]

Miniver mourned the ripe renown
   That made so many a name so fragrant;
He mourned Romance, now on the town,[4]   15
   And Art, a vagrant.

Miniver loved the Medici,[5]
   Albeit he had never seen one;
He would have sinned incessantly
   Could he have been one.   20

Miniver cursed the commonplace
   And eyed a khaki suit with loathing;
He missed the medieval grace
   Of iron clothing.

Miniver scorned the gold he sought,   25
   But sore annoyed was he without it;
Miniver thought, and thought, and thought,
   And thought about it.

Miniver Cheevy, born too late,
   Scratched his head and kept on thinking;   30
Miniver coughed, and called it fate,
   And kept on drinking.

----

[1]*Thebes* (thēbz), an ancient city of Greece.

[2]*Camelot* (kam′ə lot), a legendary British city, famous as the place from which King Arthur ruled over his Knights of the Round Table.

[3]*Priam's neighbors.* Priam (prī′əm), the last king of Troy, an ancient city in Asia Minor, was killed in the Trojan War. His neighbors were the Greeks, who, under Agamemnon, conquered Troy.

[4]*on the town,* living on charity, a pauper.

[5]*the Medici* (med′ə chē), the ruling family of Florence, Italy, during the fifteenth and sixteenth centuries. They were notable both for their generous patronage of art and for their lavish living and wicked lives.

The Dark Hills

EDWIN ARLINGTON ROBINSON

The sight of dark hills against the sunset sky fills the poet with a feeling of peace and confidence.

Dark hills at evening in the west,
   Where sunset hovers like a sound
Of golden horns that sang to rest
Old bones of warriors under ground,
Far now from all the bannered ways   5
Where flash the legions of the sun,
You fade—as if the last of days
Were fading, and all wars were done.

The Harbor

CARL SANDBURG

Like "Chicago" (page 252), "The Harbor" presents a glimpse of the city in which Sandburg has spent much of his life. It is notable for a theme which recurs in many of his poems—the sudden glimpses of beauty which may be found in even the most commonplace or sordid surroundings.

Passing through huddled and ugly walls
   By doorways where women
Looked from their hunger-deep eyes,
Haunted with shadows of hunger-hands,
Out from the huddled and ugly walls   5
I came sudden, at the city's edge,
On a blue burst of lake,
Long lake waves breaking under the sun
On a spray-flung curve of shore;
And a fluttering storm of gulls,   10
Masses of great gray wings
And flying white bellies
Veering and wheeling free in the open.

Jazz Fantasia

CARL SANDBURG

Many of the qualities which made Sandburg famous are to be found in "Jazz Fantasia." It combines a typically modern and American theme, strong rhythms, and harsh, unpoetic language.

DRUM on your drums, batter on your banjos, sob on the long cool winding saxophones. Go to it, O jazzmen.

Sling your knuckles on the bottoms of the happy tin pans, let your trombones ooze, and go husha-husha-hush with the slippery sandpaper.

Moan like an autumn wind high in the lonesome treetops, moan soft like you wanted somebody terrible, cry like a racing car slipping away from a motorcycle-cop, bang-bang! you jazzmen, bang altogether drums, traps, banjos, horns, tin cans—make two people fight on the top of a stairway and scratch each other's eyes in a clinch tumbling down the stairs.

Can the rough stuff...Now a Mississippi steamboat pushes up the night river with a hoo-hoo-hoo-oo...and the green lanterns calling to the high soft stars...a red moon rides on the humps of the low river hills ...Go to it, O jazzmen.

Any Human to Another

COUNTEÉ CULLEN

Counteé Cullen speaks a truth here that all Americans must heed. No grief, sorrow, or wrong can strike at one group of Americans without affecting us all. No man can reach full happiness so long as others about him are denied the path to happiness.

THE ILLS I sorrow at
Not me alone
Like an arrow,
Pierce to the marrow,
Through the fat   5
And past the bone.

Your grief and mine
Must intertwine
Like sea and river,
Be fused and mingle,   10
Diverse yet single,
Forever and forever.

Let no man be so proud
And confident,
To think he is allowed   15
A little tent
Pitched in a meadow
Of sun and shadow
All his little own.

Joy may be shy, unique,   20
Friendly to a few,
Sorrow never scorned to speak
To any who
Were false or true.

Your every grief   25
Like a blade
Shining and unsheathed
Must strike me down.
Of bitter aloes wreathed,
My sorrow must be laid   30
On your head like a crown.

Brave New World

ARCHIBALD MACLEISH

This poem is a question addressed to all of us, today,
in a world made tense by anxiety and mistrust.
Where is the freedom our American ancestors fought
for? asks MacLeish. Are we hiding the tiny flame of
liberty which should now be blazing to all the world?
Why are we frightened when freedom was won to
release us from fear?

BUT YOU, Thomas Jefferson,
   You could not lie so still,
You could not bear the weight of stone
On the quiet hill,

You could not keep your green-grown peace   5
Nor hold your folded hand
If you could see your new world now,
Your new sweet land.

There was a time, Tom Jefferson,
When freedom made free men.   10
The new-found earth and the new-freed mind
Were brothers then.

There was a time when tyrants feared
The new world of the free.
Now freedom is afraid and shrieks   15
At tyranny.

Words have not changed their sense so soon
Nor tyranny grown new.
The truths you held, Tom Jefferson,
Will still hold true.   20

What's changed is freedom in this age.
What great men dared to choose
Small men now dare neither win
Nor lose.

Freedom, when men fear freedom's use   25
But love its useful name,
Has cause and cause enough for fear
And cause for shame.

We fought a war for freedom's name
And won it on our own.   30
We fought to free a world and raised
A wall of stone.

Your countrymen who could have built
The hill fires of the free
To set the dry world all ablaze   35
With liberty—

To burn the brutal thorn in Spain
Of bigotry and hate[1]
And the dead lie and the brittle weed
Beyond the Plate:[2]   40

Who could have heaped the bloody straw,
The dung of time, to light
The Danube[3] in a sudden flame
Of hope by night—

Your countrymen who could have hurled   45
Their freedom like a brand
Have cupped it to a candle spark
In a frightened hand.

Freedom that was a thing to use
They've made a thing to save   50
And staked it in and fenced it round
Like a dead man's grave.

You, Thomas Jefferson,
You could not lie so still,
You could not bear the weight of stone   55
On your green hill,

You could not hold your angry tongue
If you could see how bold
The old stale bitter world plays new—
And the new world old.   60

---

[1] *the brutal thorn...bigotry and hate*, a reference to the
dictatorship of Francisco Franco in Spain.
[2] *the dead lie...beyond the Plate*. These lines refer to the
dictatorship of Juan Perón (pə rōn′) in Argentina. The
Plata (plä′tä), to which the poet gives an English pronunciation, is Argentina's principal waterway.
[3] *to light the Danube*, to bring the hope of freedom to
the eastern European countries along the Danube River.
These countries are now under Russian Communist rule.

A Cut Flower

KARL SHAPIRO

Like Robert Frost, Karl Shapiro finds symbols for interpreting life in the common things about him. You will be interested in deciphering his use of the cut flower in this poem and the attitude toward life he expresses through it.

I STAND on slenderness all fresh and fair
  I feel root firmness in the earth far down
I catch in the wind and loose my scent for bees
That sack my throat for kisses and suck love.
What is the wind that brings thy body over? 5
Wind, I am beautiful and sick. I long
For rain that strikes and bites like cold and
  hurts.
Be angry, rain, for dew is kind to men
When I am cool from sleep and take my bath.

Who softens the sweet earth about my feet? 10
Touches my face so often and brings water?
Where does she go, taller than any sunflower
Over the grass like birds? Has she a root?
These are great animals that kneel to us,
Sent by the sun perhaps to help us grow. 15
I have seen death. The colors went away,
The petals gasped at nothing and curled tight.
Then the whole head fell off and left the sky.

She tended me and held me by my stalk.
Yesterday I was well, and then the gleam, 20
The thing sharper than frost cut me in half.
I fainted and was lifted high. I feel
Waist-deep in rain. My face is dry and drawn.
My beauty leaks into the glass like rain.
When first I opened to the sun I thought 25
My colors would be parched. Where are my
  bees?
Must I die now? Is this a part of life?

October 1

KARL SHAPIRO

Most people have at some time passed with little interest the clutter of furniture on the sidewalk which signalizes moving day. But to the poet this ordinary sight is sufficient to suggest the stories hidden in the life of every individual.

THAT SEASON when the leaf deserts the
  bole
And half-dead seesaws through the Octo-
  ber air
Falling face-downward on the walks to
  print
The decalcomania of its little soul—
Hardly has the milkman's sleepy horse 5
On wooden shoes echoed across the blocks,
When with its back jaws open like a dredge
The van comes lumbering up the curb to some-
  one's door and knocks.

And four black genii muscular and shy
Holding their shy caps enter the first
  room 10
Where someone hurriedly surrenders up
The thick-set chair, the mirror half awry,
Then to their burdens stoop without a
  sound.
One with his bare hands rends apart the
  bed,
One stuffs the china barrel with stale
  print,[1] 15
To bear the sofa toward the door with dark
  funereal tread.

The corner lamp,[2] the safety eye of night,
Enveloped in the sun blinks and goes
  blind
And soon the early risers pick their way
Through kitchenware and pillows bolt up-
  right. 20
The bureau on the sidewalk with bare back

---

[1] *stale print*, old newspapers.
[2] *The corner lamp*, the street light.

And wrinkling veneer is most disgraced,
The sketch of Paris suffers in the wind,
Only the bike, its nose against the wall, does
    not show haste.

Two hours—the movers mop their necks
    and look   25
Filing through dust and echoes back and
    forth.
The halls are hollow and all the floors are
    cleared
Bare to the last board, to the most secret
    nook;
But on the street a small chaos survives
That slowly now the leviathan ingests,[3] 30
And schoolboys and stenographers stare at
The truck, the house, the husband in his hat
    who stands and rests.

He turns with miserable expectant face
And for the last time enters. On the wall
A picture stain spreads from the nail hole
    down.   35
Each object live and dead has left its trace.
He leaves his key; but as he quickly goes
This question comes behind: Did someone
    die?
Is someone rich or poor, better or worse?
What shall uproot a house and bring this care
    into his eye?   40

---

[3] *the leviathan ingests,* the moving van takes in the load.
The poet is comparing the van as it is loaded to a huge
animal (leviathan) taking food into its body (ingesting).

CONCERNING THE POETS
AND THE POEMS

Vachel Lindsay

1. What earthly scene does the heavenly scene
described in "General William Booth Enters into
Heaven" resemble? Explain why you believe this
resemblance adds to or detracts from the effectiveness
of the poem.

2. Notice that the poem is written in a marching
rhythm. What devices does Lindsay use to emphasize
the idea of a march?

3. *Onomatopoeia* is the use of words whose sound
suggests their meaning. What onomatopoeic words
do you find in this poem? What is their effect?

4. Read aloud the descriptive details that you find
most vivid and explain what you think this imagery
adds to the effectiveness of the poem.

Robert Frost

1. What do "Stopping by Woods on a Snowy Evening" and "Birches" tell you about Frost's background
and his interests? What additional information does
"Mowing" (page 239) give you?

2. How do birches ordinarily become bent? How
does the poet like to believe this happens? What does
this fancy tell you about the poet?

3. What larger idea does Frost draw from his
remembrance of being "a swinger of birches"? Can
you find any meaning beyond the actual description
in "Stopping by Woods on a Snowy Evening"?

4. What verse form does Frost use in "Birches"?
Why do you think he chose this form?

Edgar Lee Masters

1. What kind of woman do you find Lucinda Matlock to be from her own story? What qualities did she
have in common with Fiddler Jones? (See page 257.)
With the printer in "Henry Cogdal" (page 191)?

2. What claim does Anne Rutledge make in her
epitaph? From what you know of her story, do you
feel that this claim is justified?

3. In your opinion, what accounts for the popularity
of these "Spoon River" poems?

Edwin Arlington Robinson

1. Do you think Miniver Cheevy would have been
contented in Camelot? Would he have enjoyed "the
medieval grace of iron clothing"? Explain.

2. Do you believe with Miniver Cheevy that romance and adventure are to be found only in the past?
Why, or why not?

3. What similarity of mood and idea do you find in
"The Dark Hills" and "Credo" (page 286)?

Carl Sandburg

1. What idea did you gain from "The Harbor"?
What is the theme of "Jazz Fantasia"? Contrast the
mood of these poems. Which resembles "Chicago"
(page 252) more? Select the poem of Sandburg's you
liked best and give the reasons for your preference.

2. Compare "Jazz Fantasia" with Lindsay's "General William Booth Enters into Heaven." What characteristics are common to both poems? How do they
differ in purpose?

Counteé Cullen

1. Restate in your own words the idea Counteé
Cullen outlines in the first stanza of "Any Human to

Another." What does the second stanza add to the idea of the first?

2. What does the "little tent" (line 16) stand for? What other images does the poet use to make his idea vivid?

3. Explain the relationship between the first and last stanzas.

4. Do you agree with the idea developed in this poem? Why, or why not?

Archibald MacLeish

1. An *apostrophe* is a figure of speech in which an abstract quality, an absent person, or an imaginary person is addressed as though present. Point out MacLeish's use of an apostrophe in this poem. Why do you think he chose this particular person to apostrophize?

2. In describing freedom what metaphor does the poet use? Read aloud and explain the stanzas through which this figure runs.

3. What does the poet say is happening to freedom today? Explain what is meant by lines 49-52 and 59-60. Give your reasons for accepting or rejecting as true the idea these lines express.

Karl Shapiro

1. In "A Cut Flower" what question does the flower ask in the first stanza? What aspects of the flower's life does this question suggest? How are the questions asked in the second stanza related to the flower's life?

2. What is the mood of the questions in the third stanza? Where earlier in the poem has the reader been prepared for the idea of death?

3. In a symbolic sense, what is the meaning of the poem? What attitude toward life does Shapiro express?

4. In "October 1" Shapiro again uses questions to bring out the idea of the poem. What is the idea?

5. Why may "October 1" be considered a lyric poem?

The Larger View

I. Talking over the following questions with your classmates will help you see the relationship of American poetry to American living, distinguish between the various schools of poetry, and put your ideas about lyric poetry in order.

1. What is a lyric? Why are the lyrics of a particular period a good indication of the prevailing mood and disposition of that generation?

2. What is meant by romanticism in poetry? Name some American poets of the past whom you consider romantics. What poets of the present show romantic tendencies?

3. Would you consider any of the poets whom you have studied realists? Explain your answer.

4. Which of the poems you have studied are linked by their subject matter to a particular period in history or to a certain event?

5. Poetry may give an indication of the poet's background in various ways. Among these are (a) the subject matter itself, (b) the descriptive details, (c) the point of view. From among the poems you have studied choose those which best give this kind of information and explain the reasons for your selections.

6. In which poets of the twentieth century is Whitman's influence most apparent? Which poets of this century more nearly follow the conventional patterns of earlier poets?

7. Do you find any significant differences between most twentieth-century poetry and that of earlier times? If you do, explain what they are.

8. Of all the poems you have studied, which do you like best? Explain as clearly as you can why this is your favorite poem.

II. Arrange with your teacher for a bulletin-board display of lyric poetry clipped from (or copied out of) current magazines. In order to be sure that all the poems in the collection are liked and understood by the class, as each poem is brought in it might be read aloud by the one finding it or by the teacher. A brief discussion would allow fellow students to express their ideas as to the advisability of using the poem. Nature poems, lyrics of childhood, and others that suggest strong visual images might be illustrated by class members who enjoy drawing. When the collection is complete, the class might vote to ascertain which poem is most popular with the group.

MORE GOOD READING

If you are interested in knowing more about the lives and works of some of the older poets you have studied in this unit, you may wish to refer to various books that are listed in the bibliographies of the "Men and Books" units. For example, on page 383 you will find mention of Hildegarde Hawthorne's biographies of Emerson, Longfellow, and Holmes. Van Wyck Brooks' "The Flowering of New England," also annotated on page 383, contains fine critical and biographical accounts of the major New England poets. The always-interesting Edgar Allan Poe is treated in Brooks' "The World of Washington Irving," which is described on page 357. The same critic's "The Times of Melville and Whitman," which is listed on page 407, has good critical accounts of Sidney Lanier and the other Southern writers of his period.

BENÉT, WILLIAM ROSE (editor), *Fifty Poets; an American Anthology*. (Dodd) This very interesting collection contains one poem by each of fifty contemporary American poets. In most cases the poets themselves chose the poem to be included. Each poem is preceded by the poet's statement of the mood or circumstance which led to the creation of the poem. Another good Benét collection is *Poems for Youth; an American Anthology* (Dutton). These poems, which are arranged chronologically, were selected for their simplicity and directness.

BONTEMPS, ARNA WENDELL (compiler), *Golden Slippers; an Anthology of Negro Poetry for Young Readers*. (Harper) While your chief interest in this appealing selection will be the lyrics, you probably won't be able to resist entirely the narrative and humorous poetry also included. The brief biographies will add to your understanding of the poets and the poems.

CLARK, HARRY HAYDEN (editor), *Major American Poets*. (American Book) Some of the greatest figures in American poetry—Freneau, Poe, Bryant, Longfellow, Lowell, Whittier, Holmes, Emerson, Lanier, Whitman, Dickinson, Lindsay, and Robinson—are included here. The notes in the appendix trace the main outline of each poet's art and illuminate individual poems.

Oxford Book of American Verse; chosen and with an introduction by F. O. Matthiessen. (Oxford) The entire range of American poetry from colonial times to the present is covered.

STEDMAN, EDMUND C. (editor), *American Anthology, 1787-1900*. (Houghton) The poems and the poets of our first hundred years of existence as a nation are represented in this excellent collection. The poems are well chosen, and the chronological arrangement and brief biographical dictionary add to the usefulness of the anthology.

UNTERMEYER, LOUIS (editor), *American Poetry from the Beginning to Whitman*. (Harcourt) No one has compiled better anthologies of poetry than Untermeyer, who is himself a poet. In this chronologically arranged volume, the selections from each poet are accompanied by a biographical sketch. The companion volume, *Modern American Poetry; a Critical Anthology* (Harcourt), treats poetry from Whitman to the present. Lengthy biographical and critical sketches precede the poems of each of the ninety-three writers represented. An excellent preface discusses various tendencies and schools of poetry of the period. A supplementary volume, *Anthology of the New England Poets* (Random House), treats over thirty distinguished poets of this section from the seventeenth century to the present day.

WILLIAMS, OSCAR (editor), *Little Treasury of American Poetry*. (Scribner) Over four hundred poems chronologically arranged provide an outline of American poetry from early times to the younger poets of the present day. You may be especially interested in the appendix, which gives portraits of sixty-seven poets.

UNIT XV: AMERICAN HUMOR

THE PEOPLE of other countries for a long time have been much amused by our humor. There is widespread agreement that regardless of our lack of success in creating some forms of literature (the epic, for instance) our funny writings have consistently been of a pretty high order. "It has long been the English habit," wrote British critic Andrew Lang in 1892, "to look for most of our broad fun across the Atlantic. If you see the tears running down from the eyes of a fellow countryman riding in a railway carriage, if he be writhing with mirth too powerful for expression, the odds are that he has got hold of a Yankee book." Not only the British but also people of other countries think our humor "peculiarly American." For these reasons (and also because our humor makes wonderful reading) it is worth while for the student to know something of its development.

❧ I THE DEVELOPMENT OF AMERICAN HUMOR

Humor which had a great appeal and was, moreover, clearly American was slow in developing. Colonial humor was, naturally enough, quite hard to tell from British humor. The thread of well-mannered humor that runs through William Byrd's "Neighbors in Virginia" (pages 52-54) and even the satiric humor of Franklin's "The Ephemera" (pages 313-314) and "Dialogue Between Franklin and the Gout" (pages 314-317) greatly resembled that of eighteenth-century English humorists. Even after the Revolutionary War, much humor produced in America was quite like that of Great Britain. For instance, Washington Irving's amusing writings about old New Amsterdam (pages 47-51 and 326-328) were very much in the vein of such idols of his as Jonathan Swift and Oliver Goldsmith.

Huldy and Zekle from "The Courtin'"
Illustrated by Augustus Hoppin in 1858

The election of Andrew Jackson in 1828 marked the triumph of the common man—the frontiersman, the laborer—in politics and signalized the development of a new type of distinctly American humor. The common man was its dominant character, and since the common man might be a Western frontiersman, a down-East peddler, or a Missouri farmer, this new humor often took off the qualities of natives of various sections of the country.[1] "Crockett's Morning Hunt" (page 72), for example, is typical of the picture the humorous yarnspinners usually drew of a frontiersman—a man characterized by exuberance, rough activity, and courage to surmount any hardship. James Russell Lowell's "The Courtin'" (pages 566-567), which appeared in the *Biglow Papers* in mid-nineteenth century, is an amusing picture of a rural New Englander and his girl.

In the years after the War Between the States, this tendency of the yarnspinner to picture characters of a particular section of the country influenced the growth of the local-color movement.[2] Some of the best local colorists, like Bret Harte and Mark Twain, were also humorists. They differed from the prewar yarnspinners in writing well-plotted short stories instead of rambling yarns, in being more sympathetic toward the comic figures they pictured, and in creating complex human characters rather than mere cartoonlike figures.

During this same postwar period, another group of humorists was evolving far less complex comic figures. These characters might live anywhere in the country, and their homes, speech, ways of thinking and acting belonged to no particular section. Often these relatively simple characters were what Mark Twain once called "genial idiots"—well-intentioned but muddle-headed blunderers in thoughts and actions. The humorists who created these characters frequently made people laugh more at the humor of words than at the humor of character. They played with words in all sorts of ways. Perhaps they spelled them badly, or misused them, or turned them into puns. Or perhaps they fashioned sentences which behaved surprisingly. Artemus Ward, for instance, wrote, "If I was in the politics business, I should git carriages to take the cripples, the infirm, and the indignant to the Poles." Again, of "a bright-eyed little girl of about twelve summers," he wrote, "I was so pleased with the little girl's brightness that I could have kissed the dear child, and I would if she'd been six years older." Humorists of this group were called "funny men" or "literary comedians."

---

[1] See "Bret Harte and the Earlier Humorists" (pages 528-529).
[2] See the discussion of local-color writers under the heading "Bret Harte" (page 521).

Mark Twain, the greatest of all our humorists,[3] operated both as a "funny man" and as a local colorist. He was a "funny man" when he wrote about "The calm confidence of a Christian with four aces." He was a local colorist when he pictured life on the Mississippi during his youth[4] or described the silver-mining towns of the West.[5] Sometimes, as in his great novel *The Adventures of Huckleberry Finn,* he mingled the two kinds of humor. Most of the humor in "Huck Visits the Grangerfords" (pages 428-439) is that of the local colorist, but the poem about Stephen Dowling Bots attributed to Emmeline Grangerford (page 432) is typical of the literary comedian.

❧ II CONTEMPORARY AMERICAN HUMOR

America today consists of many kinds of people with varying tastes. It therefore contains not one audience for humor, but many. To appeal to these varied audiences, many kinds of humor including comic strips, radio shows, cartoons, magazine articles of many sorts, and books ranging all the way from slapstick to subtle humor have come into being. Among these varied works, one may recognize not only the older types of humor but also some types which are rather new.

Huck Finn from The Adventures of Huckleberry Finn
Illustrated by Edward Windsor Kemble in 1884

One old-time trend which still flourishes is that of writing tall tales in the way the yarnspinners of long ago might have told them. "The Saga of Pecos Bill," by Edward O'Reilly (pages 73-75) and "John Henry and the Machine in West Virginia," by Walter Blair (pages 147-155) are written in this manner. Again, we find in modern fiction the humorous story reminiscent of the local colorists. "O'Meara, the *Mayflower,* and Mrs. MacLirr," by Don Marquis (pages 103-111) and "Mr. K*a*p*l*a*n Cuts a Gordian Knot," by Leonard Q. Ross (pages 120-124) are such stories.

Although contemporary humorists are thus continuing the forms of earlier native humor, there is a striking difference in the point of view of these modern writers. The cocksure characters who were the heroes in older American humor are now pictured as admirable but quaint—laughably behind the times. And the unsure or maladjusted characters who were the butts of earlier humor are now sympathetically portrayed. In other words, in a world wherein problems seem all but unsolvable, the humorist and the readers laugh together at modern man and his bewilderment. Varied examples of current humorous writing follow.

[3]For a discussion of Mark Twain see Unit XI (pages 410-443).
[4]See "The Boys' Ambition" (pages 414-416).
[5]See "Flush Times in Silverland" (pages 416-418).

Father Opens My Mail

CLARENCE DAY

One of the traditions of American humor is that of amusingly portraying lifelike characters against vivid local backgrounds. Clarence Day found in his own father a matchless subject, and New York City of the 1880's and 1890's provided an always picturesque and interesting background. He blended these elements to produce *Life with Father,* from which this selection and "A Holiday with Father" (pages 234-238) are taken.

In "Father Opens My Mail," as in other stories of the series, Father Day has as a foil a member of his family, here his son. Young Day is exactly the sort of person bound to baffle his perfectly systematic and (by his own lights) completely logical parent, and the elder Day is equally sure to harass his son. The clash of these differing temperaments makes good comedy.

Clarence Day writes in the easy colloquial style characteristic of most modern humorists. His viewpoint, too, is the viewpoint of modern comedy. Today's reader, looking out on a world in which nothing seems secure, sees Father, so sure of himself and his standards, as "quaint." And the reader's sympathy and understanding are more with the son, who, in his unsureness of himself, echoes the temper of the present.

THERE WAS A TIME in my boyhood when I felt that Father had handicapped me severely in life by naming me after him, "Clarence." All literature, so far as I could see, was thronged with objectionable persons named Clarence. Percy was bad enough, but there had been some good fighters named Percy.[1] The only Clarence in history was a duke who did something dirty at Tewkesbury, and who died a ridiculous death afterwards in a barrel of malmsey.[2]

As for the Clarences in the fiction I read, they were horrible. In one story, for instance, there were two brothers, Clarence and Frank. Clarence was a "vain, disagreeable little fellow," who was proud of his curly hair and fine clothes, while Frank was a "rollicking boy who was ready to play games with anybody." Clarence didn't like to play games, of course. He just minced around looking on.

One day when the mother of these boys had gone out, this story went on, Clarence "tempted" Frank to disobey her and fly their kite on the roof. Frank didn't want to, but Clarence kept taunting him and daring him until Frank was stung into doing it. After the two boys went up to the roof, Frank got good and dirty, running up and down and stumbling over scuttles, while Clarence sat there, giving him orders, and kept his natty clothes tidy. To my horror, he even spread out his handkerchief on the trap door to sit on. And to crown all, this sneak told on Frank as soon as their mother came in.

This wasn't an exceptionally mean Clarence, either. He was just run-of-the-mill.[3] Some were worse.

So far as I could ever learn, however, Father had never heard of these stories, and had never dreamed of there being anything objectionable in his name. Quite the contrary. And yet as a boy he had lived a good rough-and-tumble boy's life. He had played and fought on the city streets, and kept a dog in Grandpa's stable, and stolen rides to Greenpoint Ferry on the high, lurching bus. In the summer he had gone to West Springfield and had run down Shad Lane through the trees to the house where Grandpa was born, and had gone barefoot and

---

[1] *some good fighters named Percy.* A noble English family of this name was noted for great warriors. Most famous member of the family was Sir Henry Percy, called Hotspur, who was killed while battling the forces of Henry IV in 1403.

[2] *a duke...malmsey* (mäm'zi). George, Duke of Clarence, was a younger brother of Edward IV of England. He lived during the fifteenth century at a time when rival families were claiming the throne, and he sided first with one and then the other. Thus, at Tewkesbury (tūks'bĕr i) he supported his brother, whom he had previously opposed. In 1478 he was accused of treason by his brother the king and condemned to death. According to rumor he died by being drowned in a large cask of malmsey wine.

[3] *run-of-the-mill,* ordinary, neither very good nor very bad.

driven the cows home just as though he had been named Tom or Bill.

He had the same character as a boy, I suppose, that he had as a man, and he was too independent to care if people thought his name fancy. He paid no attention to the prejudices of others, except to disapprove of them. He had plenty of prejudices himself, of course, but they were his own. He was humorous and confident and level-headed, and I imagine that if any boy had tried to make fun of him for being named Clarence, Father would simply have laughed and told him he didn't know what he was talking about.

I asked Mother how this name had ever happened to spring up in our family. She explained that my great-great-grandfather was Benjamin Day, and my great-grandfather was Henry, and consequently my grandfather had been named Benjamin Henry. He in turn had named his eldest son Henry and his second son Benjamin. The result was that when Father was born there was no family name left. The privilege of choosing a name for Father had thereupon been given to Grandma, and unluckily for the Day family she had been reading a novel, the hero of which was named Clarence.

I knew that Grandma, though very like Grandpa in some respects, had a dreamy side which he hadn't, a side that she usually kept to herself in her serene quiet way. Her romantic choice of this name probably made Grandpa smile, but he was a detached sort of man who didn't take small matters seriously, and who drew a good deal of private amusement from the happenings of everyday life. Besides, he was partly to blame in this case, because that novel was one he had published himself in his magazine.

I asked Mother, when she had finished, why I had been named Clarence too.

It hadn't been her choice, Mother said. She had suggested all sorts of names to Father, but there seemed to be something wrong with each one. When she had at last spoken of naming me after him, however, he had said at once that that was the best suggestion yet—he said it sounded just right.

Father and I would have had plenty of fric-

tion in any case. This identity of names made things worse. Every time that I had been more of a fool than he liked, Father would try to impress on me my responsibilities as his eldest son, and above all as the son to whom he had given his name, as he put it. A great deal was expected, it seemed to me, of a boy who was named after his father. I used to envy my brothers, who didn't have anything expected of them on this score at all.

I envied them still more after I was old enough to begin getting letters. I then discovered that when Father "gave" me his name he had also, not unnaturally, I had to admit, retained it himself, and when anything came for Clarence S. Day he opened it, though it was sometimes for me.

He also opened everything that came addressed to Clarence S. Day, Jr. He didn't do this intentionally, but unless the "Jr." was clearly written, it looked like "Esq.,"[4] and anyhow Father was too accustomed to open all Clarence Day letters to remember about looking carefully every time for a "Jr." So far as mail and express went, I had no name at all of my own.

For the most part nobody wrote to me when I was a small boy except firms whose advertisements I had read in the *Youth's Companion*[5] and to whom I had written requesting them to send me their circulars. These circulars described remarkable bargains in magicians' card outfits, stamps and coins, pocket knives, trick spiders, and imitation fried eggs, and they seemed interesting and valuable to me when I got them. The trouble was that Father usually got them and at once tore them up. I then had to write for such circulars again, and if Father got the second one too, he would sometimes explode with annoyance. He became particularly indignant one year, I remember, when he was repeatedly urged to take advantage of a special bargain sale of false whiskers. He said that he couldn't understand why these offerings kept pouring in. I knew why, in this case, but at other times I was often surprised myself at

---

[4]*"Esq.,"* Esquire, a title of respect.
[5]*"Youth's Companion,"* a magazine for young people. Beginning in 1827 it was published for over a century.

the number he got, not realizing that as a result of my postcard request my or our name had been automatically put on several large general mailing lists.

During this period I got more of my mail out of Father's wastebasket than I did from the postman.

At the age of twelve or thirteen I stopped writing for these childish things and turned to a new field. Father and I, whichever of us got at the mail first, then began to receive not merely circulars but personal letters beginning:

Dear Friend Day:

In reply to your valued request for one of our Mammoth Agents' Outfits, kindly forward post-office order for $1.49 to cover cost of postage and packing, and we will put you in a position to earn a large income in your spare time with absolutely no labor on your part, by taking subscriptions for *The Secret Handbook of Mesmerism,* and our *Tales of Blood* series.

And one spring, I remember, as the result of what I had intended to be a secret application on my part, Father was assigned "the exclusive rights for Staten Island[6] and Hoboken[7] of selling the Gem Home Popper for Pop Corn. Housewives buy it at sight."

After Father had stormily endured these afflictions for a while, he and I began to get letters from girls. Fortunately for our feelings, these were rare, but they were ordeals for both of us. Father had forgotten, if he ever knew, how silly young girls can sound, and I got my first lesson in how unsystematic they were. No matter how private and playful they meant their letters to be, they forgot to put "Jr." on the envelope every once in so often. When Father opened these letters, he read them all the way through, sometimes twice, muttering to himself over and over: "This is very peculiar. I don't understand this at all. Here's a letter to me from some person I never heard of. I can't see what it's about." By the time it had occurred to him that possibly the letter might be for me, I was red and embarrassed and even

angrier at the girl than at Father. And on days when he had read some of the phrases aloud to the family, it nearly killed me to claim it.

Lots of fellows whom I knew had been named after their fathers without having such troubles. But although Father couldn't have been kinder-hearted or had any better intentions, when he saw his name on a package or envelope it never dawned on him that it might not be for him. He was too active in his habits to wait until I had a chance to get at it. And as he was also single-minded and prompt to attend to unfinished business, he opened everything automatically and then did his best to dispose of it.

This went on even after I grew up, until I had a home of my own. Father was always perfectly decent about it, but he never changed. When he saw I felt sulky, he was genuinely sorry and said so, but he couldn't see why all this should annoy me, and he was surprised and amused that it did. I used to get angry once in a while when something came for me which I particularly hadn't wished him to see and which I would find lying opened, on the hall table, marked "For Jr.?" when I came in; but nobody could stay angry with Father—he was too utterly guiltless of having meant to offend.

He often got angry himself, but it was mostly at things, not at persons, and he didn't mind a bit (as a rule) when persons got angry at him. He even declared, when I got back from college, feeling dignified, and told him that I wished he'd be more careful, that he suffered from these mistakes more than I did. It wasn't *his* fault, he pointed out, if my stupid correspondents couldn't remember my name, and it wasn't any pleasure to him to be upset at his breakfast by finding that a damned lunatic company in Battle Creek[8] had sent him a box of dry bread crumbs, with a letter asserting that this rubbish would be good for his stomach. "I admit I threw it into the fireplace, Clarence, but what else could I do? If you valued this preposterous concoction, my dear boy, I'm sorry. I'll buy another box for you today, if you'll tell me where I can get it. Don't feel

---

[6]*Staten Island,* an island south of Manhattan in New York Bay.

[7]*Hoboken,* a city in New Jersey across the Hudson River from New York City.

[8]*Battle Creek,* a city in southern Michigan. One of its principal industries is the manufacture of breakfast foods.

badly! I'll buy you a barrel. Only I hope you won't eat it."

In the days when Mrs. Pankhurst and her friends were chaining themselves to lampposts in London in their campaign for the vote,[9] a letter came from Frances Hand[10] trustfully asking "Dear Clarence" to do something to help woman suffrage—speak at a meeting, I think. Father got red in the face. "Speak at one of their meetings!" he roared at Mother. "I'd like nothing better! You can tell Mrs. Hand that it would give me great pleasure to inform all those crackpots in petticoats exactly what I think of their antics."

"Now, Clare," Mother said, "you mustn't talk that way. I like that nice Mrs. Hand, and anyhow this letter must be for Clarence."

One time I asked Father for his opinion of a low-priced stock I'd been watching. His opinion was that it was not worth a damn. I thought this over, but I still wished to buy it, so I placed a scale order with another firm instead of with Father's office,[11] and said nothing about it. At the end of the month this other firm sent me a statement, setting forth each of my little transactions in full, and of course they forgot to put the "Jr." at the end of my name. When Father opened the envelope, he thought at first in his excitement that this firm had actually opened an account for him without being asked. I found him telling Mother that he'd like to wring their damned necks.

"That must be for me, Father," I said, when I took in what had happened.

We looked at each other.

"You bought this stuff?" he said incredulously. "After all I said about it?"

"Yes, Father."

He handed over the statement and walked out of the room.

Both he and I felt offended and angry. We

stayed so for several days, too, but we then made it up.

Once in a while when I got a letter that I had no time to answer I used to address an envelope to the sender and then put anything in it that happened to be lying around on my desk—a circular about books, a piece of newspaper, an old laundry bill—anything at all, just to be amiable, and yet at the same time to save myself the trouble of writing. I happened to tell several people about this private habit of mine at a dinner one night—a dinner at which Alice Duer Miller[12] and one or two other writers were present. A little later she wrote me a criticism of Henry James[13] and ended by saying that I needn't send her any of my old laundry bills because she wouldn't stand it. And she forgot to put on the "Jr."

"In the name of God," Father said bleakly, "this is the worst yet. Here's a woman who says I'd better not read the *Golden Bowl*,[14] which I have no intention whatever of doing, and she also warns me for some unknown reason not to send her my laundry bills."

The good part of all these experiences, as I realize now, was that in the end they drew Father and me closer together. My brothers had only chance battles with him. I had a war. Neither he nor I relished its clashes, but they made us surprisingly intimate.

---

[12]*Alice Duer Miller*, an American novelist and poet. She was born in 1874—the same year as Clarence Day—and died in 1942.

[13]*Henry James*, a great American novelist who lived from 1843 to 1916.

[14]*"Golden Bowl,"* a novel by Henry James published in 1904.

UNDERSTANDING CLARENCE
—ESQ. AND JR.

1. Contrast the attitudes of the older and the younger Day toward the name *Clarence*. What do you learn about each character from his feeling about his name? How is Father's attitude toward his name related to his treatment of his son's mail?

2. Trace the changes in the nature of the author's mail. About how old was he at the time of the "laundry bill" episode? How do the changes mentioned (*a*) show his development and (*b*) emphasize the difficulty of dealing with Father?

---

[9]*Mrs. Pankhurst...campaign for the vote.* Mrs. Emmeline Pankhurst was a leader in the struggle of English women to receive the vote. She and her followers resorted to violent means to gain recognition.

[10]*Frances Hand*, a friend of Clarence Day Jr.'s who was active in the struggle for woman suffrage.

[11]*I placed a scale order...Father's office.* Clarence Day sent an order to a stockbroker directing him to buy stock at intervals instead of all at once. Mr. Day was also a stockbroker.

3. Does the sketch prepare you for the last paragraph? Explain your answer.

4. Do you agree that Father is pictured as quaint and the author as sympathetic? Justify your answer.

5. Compare this selection with "A Holiday with Father" (pages 234-238). In what ways is the relationship between father and son similar in the two sketches? What elements make these selections humorous? Which do you find more amusing?

6. Prepare to read to the class examples from "Father Opens My Mail" of what you consider an "easy colloquial style." How does this style add to the humor of the selection?

Every Day Is Monday

OGDEN NASH

It is an old tradition in American humor for poets to create illiterate characters who write bad poetry. This poetry often was laughable because both its meter and its rhyming got out of control. The farmer poets that James Russell Lowell used in his *Biglow Papers* at times put too many words into a line and rhymed *woman* with *inhuman, feeble* with *people,* and *presume we* with *Montezumy.* After the War Between the States, humorists and their readers continued to laugh at bad poets; witness Mark Twain's success with Emmeline Grangerford (page 432).

In modern times, Ogden Nash has made good use of the comic style of a hard-working but ineffective songster. He pretends to be mastered by rhymes instead of being their master. Often, he stretches his lines far beyond their metrical limits before he can end them with a rhyme; again and again, he has to misspell and mispronounce words in order to make them chime with others. In these ways, he follows the path of the naive poets of the nineteenth century.

Though Nash's verse is deliberately childlike, the ideas which it expresses are often those of a harassed and discontented twentieth-century man. He writes of the unhappiness and discomfort he suffers whether the sun shines or not, of his annoyance with people of many sorts, of his dislike not only for sickness but also for convalescence, of a world which in general pushes him around. Thus he uses the awkward verse of an untrained singer to tell about the woes of a world-weary sophisticate—and the contrast between form and content helps make his verse amusing.

Monday is the day that everything starts all over again,
Monday is the day when just as you are beginning to feel peaceful you have to get up and get dressed and put on your old gray bonnet and drive down to Dover again,[1]
It is the day when life becomes grotesque again,
Because it is the day when you have to face your desk again;
It is a day with no fun about it,   5
Because it is the first of a series of days filled with one task or another that something has to be done about it.
When the telephone rings on Saturday or Sunday you are pleased because it probably means something pleasing and you take the call with agility,
But when it rings on any other day it just usually means some additional responsibility,
And if in doubt,
Why the best thing to do is to answer it in a foreign accent or if you are a foreigner answer it in a native accent and say you are out.   10
Oh, there is not a weekday moment that can't wring a sigh from you,
Because you are always being confronted with people who want to sell you something, or if they don't want to sell you something, there is something they want to buy from you,
And every shining hour swaggers arrogantly up to you demanding to be improved,[2]
And apparently not only to improve it, but also to shine it, is what you are behooved.
Oh for a remedy, oh for a panacea, oh for a something, oh yes, oh for a coma or swoon,
Yes indeed, oh for a coma that would last from nine A.M. on Monday until Saturday noon.

---

[1] *put on your old gray bonnet...Dover again.* These words were suggested by "Put on Your Old Gray Bonnet," a song published in 1909. It concerns two people who celebrate their golden-wedding anniversary by riding down to Dover.

[2] *And every shining hour...improved.* This line and the following one are funnier if you realize that Nash is making fun of a serious poem by Isaac Watts (1674-1748):
How doth the little busy bee
Improve each shining hour...

"Every Day Is Monday." Copyright, 1938, by Ogden Nash. From *I'm a Stranger Here Myself* by Ogden Nash, by permission of Little, Brown & Co.

This Is Going to Hurt Just a Little Bit

OGDEN NASH

ONE THING I like less than most things is
    sitting in a dentist chair with my mouth
    wide open,
And that I will never have to do it again is a
    hope that I am against hope hopen.
Because some tortures are physical and some
    are mental,
But the one that is both is dental.
It is hard to be self-possessed   5
With your jaw digging into your chest,
So hard to retain your calm
When your fingernails are making serious
    alterations in your life line or love line
    or some other important line in your
    palm;
So hard to give your usual effect of cheery
    benignity
When you know your position is one of the two
    or three in life most lacking in dignity   10
And your mouth is like a section of road that
    is being worked on,
And it is all cluttered up with stone crushers
    and concrete mixers and drills and steam
    rollers and there isn't a nerve in your head
    that you aren't being irked on.
Oh, some people are unfortunate enough to be
    strung up by thumbs,
And others have things done to their gums,
And your teeth are supposed to be being pol-
    ished,   15
But you have reason to believe they are being
    demolished,
And the circumstance that adds most to your
    terror
Is that it's all done with a mirror,
Because the dentist may be a bear, or as the
    Romans used to say, only they were referring
    to a feminine bear when they said it, an
    ursa,[1]

---

[1]*they were referring...an "ursa"* (ĕr′sə). In Latin the
word *ursa* is used for the feminine of *bear* and *ursus* for
the masculine.

But all the same how can you be sure when he
    takes his crowbar in one hand and mirror
    in the other he won't get mixed up, the way
    you do when you try to tie a bow tie with
    the aid of a mirror, and forget that left is
    right and *vice versa?*   20
And then at last he says That will be all; but
    it isn't because he then coats your mouth
    from cellar to roof
With something that I suspect is generally used
    to put a shine on a horse's hoof,
And you totter to your feet and think, Well it's
    all over now and after all it was only this
    once,
And he says come back in three monce.
And this, O Fate, is I think the most vicious
    circle that thou ever sentest,   25
That Man has to go continually to the dentist
    to keep his teeth in good condition when the
    chief reason he wants his teeth in good con-
    dition is so that he won't have to go to the
    dentist.

WHAT'S WRONG WITH OGDEN NASH'S WORLD?

1. What plaint does Ogden Nash make in "Every Day Is Monday"? Point out examples in which he exaggerates to make his case amusing.

2. Why is the last statement of "This Is Going to Hurt Just a Little Bit" a proper climax to this woeful song?

3. Select from the poems examples of (a) lines which run longer than they should before the author finds a chance to end them with a rhyme, (b) words which have to be misspelled and mispronounced in order to rhyme.

4. Read aloud to the class the lines from each poem which you think are funniest. Are they humorous because of (a) what Nash says, (b) the meter and rhyme he uses, or (c) both?

5. Why is the verse Nash writes like the world in which he lives?

6. Read and laugh with Robert Benchley as he describes "The Tooth, the Whole Tooth, and Nothing But the Tooth," in *Love Conquers All*. Which visit to the dentist is funnier–Robert Benchley's or Ogden Nash's?

Love Song

DOROTHY PARKER

"Love Song" is not what it seems. Far from taking the usual starry-eyed and romantic attitude toward love, in this and other lyrics Dorothy Parker often assumes the rôle of a disillusioned woman. Her poems are deflations: they start with airy flights into romantic dreamlands and end with swoops into rude awakenings. At times they deflate the glamorous male, at other times the wistful female who expects love to be an everlasting bed of roses without thorns. You may not agree with Dorothy Parker's attitude, but you will recognize it as typical of twentieth-century humor.

My OWN DEAR LOVE he is strong and bold
    And he cares not what comes after.
His words ring sweet as a chime of gold,
    And his eyes are lit with laughter.
He is jubilant as a flag unfurled— 5
    Oh, a girl, she'd not forget him.
My own dear love, he is all my world—
    And I wish I'd never met him.

My love, he's mad, and my love, he's fleet,
    And a wild young wood-thing bore him! 10
The ways are fair to his roaming feet,
    And the skies are sunlit for him.
As sharply sweet to my heart he seems
    As the fragrance of acacia.
My own dear love, he is all my dreams— 15
    And I wish he were in Asia.

My love runs by like a day in June,
    And he makes no friends of sorrows.
He'll tread his galloping rigadoon[1]
    In the pathway of the morrows. 20
He'll live his days where the sunbeams start,
    Nor could storm or wind uproot him.
My own dear love, he is all my heart—
    And I wish somebody'd shoot him.

---

[1]*rigadoon* (rĭg′ə dün′), a lively, old-fashioned dance.

IS THIS A LOVE SONG?

1. What changes would you have to make to turn "Love Song" into an old-fashioned, romantic song?

2. "I Shall Not Care," by Sara Teasdale (page 272) is also a twentieth-century lyric on love. What similarities do you find in the situation in this poem and "Love Song"? What differences do you find in the viewpoint?

3. Considered as poetry, how does "Love Song" differ from Ogden Nash's verse?

The Waltz

DOROTHY PARKER

In her prose sketches as in her poems, Dorothy Parker's subject matter typically is the comedy of relationships between the sexes. Her subject, of course, does not belong to any particular period, but her treatment of it is modern. Writing in a period when even courtship and love have had some of their romantic glow rubbed away, Miss Parker makes fun of the suffering any woman or girl undergoes who is so unfortunate as to have anything to do with men.

WHY, *thank you so much. I'd adore to.* I don't want to dance with him. I don't want to dance with anybody. And even if I did, it wouldn't be him. He'd be well down among the last ten. I've seen the way he dances; it looks like something you do on Saint Walpurgis Night.[1] Just think, not a quarter of an hour ago, here I was sitting, feeling so sorry for the poor girl he was dancing with. And now *I'm* going to be the poor girl. Well, well. Isn't it a small world?

And a peach of a world, too. A true little corker. Its events are so fascinatingly unpredictable, are not they? Here I was, minding my own business, not doing a stitch of harm to any living soul. And then he comes into my life,

---

[1]*Saint Walpurgis* (väl pûr′gĭs) *Night,* the night of April 30, when witches were supposed to revel with the devil.

all smiles and city manners, to sue me for the favor of one memorable mazurka. Why, he scarcely knows my name, let alone what it stands for. It stands for Despair, Bewilderment, Futility, Degradation, and Premeditated Murder, but little does he wot. I don't wot his name, either; I haven't any idea what it is. Jukes[2] would be my guess from the look in his eyes. How do you do, Mr. Jukes? And how is that dear little brother of yours, with the two heads?

Ah, now why did he have to come around me, with his low requests? Why can't he let me lead my own life? I ask so little—just to be left alone in my quiet corner of the table, to do my brooding over all my sorrows. And he must come, with his bows and his scrapes and his may-I-have-this-ones. And I had to go and tell him that I'd adore to dance with him. I cannot understand why I wasn't struck right down dead. Yes, and being struck dead would look like a day in the country, compared to struggling out a dance with this boy. But what could I do? Everyone else at the table had got up to dance, except him and me. There was I, trapped. Trapped like a trap in a trap.

What can you say, when a man asks you to dance with him? I most certainly will *not* dance with you. Why, thank you, I'd like to awfully, but I'm having pains. Oh, yes, *do* let's dance together—it's so nice to meet a man who isn't a scaredy-cat about catching my beriberi. No. There was nothing for me to do, but say I'd adore to. Well, we might as well get it over with. All right, Cannonball, let's run out on the field. You won the toss; you can lead.

Why, I think it's more of a waltz, really. Isn't it? We might just listen to the music a second. Shall we? Oh, yes, it's a waltz. Mind? Why, I'm simply thrilled. I'd love to waltz with you.

I'd love to waltz with you. I'd love to waltz with you. I'd love to have my tonsils out, I'd love to be in a midnight fire at sea. Well, it's too late now. We're getting under way. *Oh.*

Oh, dear. Oh, dear, dear, dear. Oh, this is even worse than I thought it would be. I suppose that's the one dependable law of life—everything is always worse than you thought it was going to be. Oh, if I had any real grasp of what this dance would be like, I'd have held out for sitting it out. Well, it will probably amount to the same thing in the end. We'll be sitting it out on the floor in a minute, if he keeps this up.

I'm so glad I brought it to his attention that this is a waltz they're playing. Heaven knows what might have happened, if he had thought it was something fast; we'd have blown the sides right out of the building. Why does he always want to be somewhere that he isn't? Why can't we stay in one place just long enough to get acclimated? It's this constant rush, rush, rush, that's the curse of American life. That's the reason that we're all of us so—*Ow!* For heaven's sake, don't *kick,* you idiot; this is only second down. Oh, my shin. My poor, poor shin, that I've had ever since I was a little girl!

Oh, no, no, no. Goodness, no. It didn't hurt the least little bit. And anyway it was my fault. Really it was. Truly. Well, you're just being sweet, to say that. It really was all my fault.

I wonder what I'd better do—kill him this instant, with my naked hands, or wait and let him drop in his traces. Maybe it's best not to make a scene. I guess I'll just lie low, and watch the pace get him. He can't keep this up indefinitely—he's only flesh and blood. Die he must, and die he shall, for what he did to me. I don't want to be of the oversensitive type, but you can't tell me that kick was unpremeditated. Freud[3] says that there are no accidents. I've led no cloistered life, I've known dancing partners who have spoiled my slippers and torn my dress; but when it comes to kicking, I am Outraged Womanhood. When you kick me in the shin, *smile.*

Maybe he didn't do it maliciously. Maybe it's just his way of showing his high spirits. I suppose I ought to be glad that one of us is having such a good time. I suppose I ought to think

---

[2]*Jukes,* a name given by sociologists to designate a New York State family which had an unusual record over several generations of crime, pauperism, and low moral standards.

[3]*Freud* (froid), an Austrian physician who developed a theory and technique of psychoanalysis. He lived from 1856 to 1939.

myself lucky if he brings me back alive. Maybe it's captious to demand of a practically strange man that he leave your shins as he found them. After all, the poor boy's doing the best he can. Probably he grew up in the hill country, and never had no larnin'. I bet they had to throw him on his back to get shoes on him.

Yes, it's lovely, isn't it? It's simply lovely. It's the loveliest waltz. Isn't it? Oh, I think it's lovely, too.

Why, I'm getting positively drawn to the Triple Threat here. He's my hero. He has the heart of a lion, and the sinews of a buffalo. Look at him—never a thought of the consequences, never afraid of his face, hurling himself into every scrimmage, eyes shining, cheeks ablaze. And shall it be said that I hung back? No, a thousand times no. What's it to me if I have to spend the next couple of years in a plaster cast? Come on, Butch, right through them! Who wants to live forever?

Oh. Oh, dear. Oh, he's all right, thank goodness. For a while I thought they'd have to carry him off the field. Ah, I couldn't bear to have anything happen to him. I love him. I love him better than anybody in the world. Look at the spirit he gets into a dreary, commonplace waltz; how effete the other dancers seem, beside him. He is youth and vigor and courage, he is strength and gaiety and—*Ow!* Get off my instep, you hulking peasant! What do you think I am, anyway—a gangplank? *Ow!*

No, of course it didn't hurt. Why, it didn't a bit. Honestly. And it was all my fault. You see, that little step of yours—well, it's perfectly lovely, but it's just a tiny bit tricky to follow at first. Oh, did you work it up yourself? You really did? Well, aren't you amazing! Oh, now I think I've got it. Oh, I think it's lovely. I was watching you do it when you were dancing before. It's awfully effective when you look at it.

It's awfully effective when you look at it. I bet I'm awfully effective when you look at me. My hair is hanging along my cheeks, my skirt is swaddling about me, I can feel the cold damp of my brow. I must look like something out of "The Fall of the House of Usher." This sort of thing takes a fearful toll of a woman my age. And he worked up his little step himself,

he with his degenerate cunning. And it was just a tiny bit tricky at first, but now I think I've got it. Two stumbles, slip, and a twenty-yard dash; yes. I've got it. I've got several other things, too, including a split shin and a bitter heart. I hate this creature I'm chained to. I hated him the moment I saw his leering, bestial face. And here I've been locked in his noxious embrace for the thirty-five years this waltz has lasted. Is that orchestra never going to stop playing?

Oh, they're going to play another encore. Oh, goody. Oh, that's lovely. Tired? I should say I'm not tired. I'd like to go on like this forever.

I should say I'm not tired. I'm dead, that's all I am. Dead, and in what a cause! And the music is never going to stop playing, and we're going on like this, Double-Time Charlie and I, throughout eternity. I suppose I won't care any more, after the first hundred thousand years. I suppose nothing will matter then, not heat nor pain nor broken heart nor cruel, aching weariness. Well. It can't come too soon for me.

I wonder why I didn't tell him I was tired. I wonder why I didn't suggest going back to the table. I could have said let's just listen to the music. Yes, and if he would, that would be the first bit of attention he has given it all evening. George Jean Nathan[4] said that the lovely rhythms of the waltz should be listened to in stillness and not be accompanied by strange gyrations of the human body. I think that's what he said. I think it was George Jean Nathan. Anyhow, whatever he said and whoever he was and whatever he's doing now, he's better off than I am. That's safe. Anybody who isn't waltzing with this Mrs. O'Leary's cow[5] I've got here is having a good time.

Still if we were back at the table, I'd probably have to talk to him. Look at him—what could you say to a thing like that! Did you go to the circus this year, what's your favorite kind of ice cream, how do you spell *cat?* I guess I'm as well off here. As well off as if I were in a cement mixer in full action.

---

[4]*George Jean Nathan,* a noted American drama critic.

[5]*Mrs. O'Leary's cow.* According to popular belief, the great Chicago fire of 1871 was started when Mrs. O'Leary's cow kicked over a lantern in the cow barn.

I'm past all feeling now. The only way I can tell when he steps on me is that I can hear the splintering of bones. And all the events of my life are passing before my eyes. There was the time I was in a hurricane in the West Indies, there was the day I got my head cut open in the taxi smash, there was the night the drunken lady threw a bronze ash tray at her own true love and got me instead, there was that summer that the sailboat kept capsizing. Ah, what an easy, peaceful time was mine, until I fell in with Swifty, here. I didn't know what trouble was, before I got drawn into this *danse macabre.*[6] I think my mind is beginning to wander. It almost seems to me as if the orchestra were stopping. It couldn't be, of course; it could never, never be. And yet in my ears there is a silence like the sound of angel voices....

Oh, they've stopped, the mean things. They're not going to play any more. Oh, darn. Oh, do you think they would? Do you really think so, if you gave them twenty dollars? Oh, that would be lovely. And look, do tell them to play this same thing. I'd simply adore to go on waltzing.

------

[6]*danse macabre* (däNs′ mə′kä′brə), dance of death. In this dance a figure of death, usually a skeleton, leads the living to the grave. [*French*]

WHAT IS THE MOOD OF "THE WALTZ"?

1. How does "The Waltz" differ from a typical piece which might have been written under the same title a hundred years ago? What words would you probably use to describe it? What words would you use to describe Dorothy Parker's piece?

2. What contrast do you find between what the girl says and what she thinks? How does this pattern of alternate speaking and thinking add to the humor of the selection? What is the effect of the last paragraph?

3. Compare "Love Song" and "The Waltz."

Extending interests

A man's idea of the comedy between the sexes may vary from a woman's. Boys may enjoy writing a male version of "The Waltz," using Dorothy Parker's technique of alternating what is said and thought by the character. Both boys and girls will find it fun to attempt a humorous verse in which, like Ogden Nash, they hold forth on something that annoys them.

University Days

JAMES THURBER

One of the types of American humor most popular today results in part from the development of modern psychology. Just as the "funny men" of the late nineteenth century often pretended to be genial idiots, many humorists of today make the reader laugh by pretending to be neurotics—people nervously unable to adjust to life. As Bernard De Voto says, "The literary comedians after the Civil War presented themselves as Perfect Fools, whereas our modern comedians present themselves as Perfect Neurotics."

James Thurber is an outstanding humorist of this school. He himself says of "the Perfect Neurotics": "They lead an existence of jumpiness and apprehension. In the house of Life they have the feeling that they have never taken off their overcoats. They have a genius for getting into minor difficulties: they walk into the wrong apartments, they drink furniture polish for stomach bitters, they drive their cars into the prize tulip beds of haughty neighbors." Of course, such descriptions don't necessarily apply to the authors themselves. But they do apply to the comic characters they portray or humorously pretend to be.

I PASSED all the other courses that I took at my university, but I could never pass botany. This was because all botany students had to spend several hours a week in a laboratory looking through a microscope at plant cells, and I could never see through a microscope. I never once saw a cell through a microscope. This used to enrage my instructor. He would wander around the laboratory pleased with the progress all the students were making in drawing the involved and, so I am told, interesting structure of flower cells, until he came to me. I would just be standing there. "I can't see anything," I would say. He would begin patiently enough, explaining how anybody can see through a microscope, but he would always end up in a fury, claiming that I could *too* see through a microscope but just pretended that I couldn't. "It takes away from the beauty of

------

"He Was Beginning to Quiver All Over Like Lionel Barrymore."

flowers anyway," I used to tell him. "We are not concerned with beauty in this course," he would say. "We are concerned solely with what I may call the *mechanics* of flars." "Well," I'd say, "I can't see anything." "Try it just once again," he'd say, and I would put my eye to the microscope and see nothing at all, except now and again a nebulous milky substance—a phenomenon of maladjustment. You were supposed to see a vivid, restless clockwork of sharply defined plant cells. "I see what looks like a lot of milk," I would tell him. This, he claimed, was the result of my not having adjusted the microscope properly, so he would readjust it for me, or rather, for himself. And I would look again and see milk.

I finally took a deferred pass, as they called it, and waited a year and tried again. (You had to pass one of the biological sciences or you couldn't graduate.) The professor had come back from vacation brown as a berry, bright-eyed, and eager to explain cell structure again to his classes. "Well," he said to me, cheerily, when we met in the first laboratory hour of the semester, "we're going to see cells this time, aren't we?" "Yes, sir," I said. Students to right of me and to left of me and in front of me were seeing cells; what's more, they were quietly drawing pictures of them in their notebooks. Of course, I didn't see anything.

"We'll try it," the professor said to me, grimly, "with every adjustment of the microscope known to man. As God is my witness, I'll arrange this glass so that you see cells through it or I'll give up teaching. In twenty-two years of botany, I—" He cut off abruptly for he was beginning to quiver all over, like Lionel Barrymore,[1] and he genuinely wished to hold onto his temper; his scenes with me had taken a great deal out of him.

So we tried it with every adjustment of the microscope known to man. With only one of them did I see anything but blackness or the familiar lacteal opacity, and that time I saw, to my pleasure and amazement, a variegated constellation of flecks, specks, and dots. These I hastily drew. The instructor, noting my activity, came back from an adjoining desk, a smile on his lips and his eyebrows high in hope. He looked at my cell drawing. "What's that?" he demanded, with a hint of a squeal in his voice. "That's what I saw," I said. "You didn't, you didn't, you *did*n't!" he screamed, losing control of his temper instantly, and he bent over and squinted into the microscope. His head snapped up. "That's your eye!" he shouted. "You've fixed the lens so that it reflects! You've drawn your eye!"

Another course that I didn't like, but somehow managed to pass, was economics. I went to that class straight from the botany class, which didn't help me any in understanding either subject. I used to get them mixed up. But not as mixed up as another student in my economics class who came there direct from a physics laboratory. He was a tackle on the football team, named Bolenciecwcz. At that time Ohio State University had one of the best football teams in the country, and Bolenciecwcz was one of its outstanding stars. In order to be eligible to play it was necessary for him to

keep up in his studies, a very difficult matter, for while he was not dumber than an ox he was not any smarter. Most of his professors were lenient and helped him along. None gave him more hints, in answering questions, or asked him simpler ones than the economics professor, a thin, timid man named Bassum. One day when we were on the subject of transportation and distribution, it came Bolenciecwcz's turn to answer a question. "Name one means of transportation," the professor said to him. No light came into the big tackle's eyes. "Just any means of transportation," said the professor. Bolenciecwcz sat staring at him. "That is," pursued the professor, "any medium, agency, or method of going from one place to another." Bolenciecwcz had the look of a man who is being led into a trap. "You may choose among steam, horse-drawn, or electrically propelled vehicles," said the instructor. "I might suggest the one which we commonly take in making long journeys across land." There was a profound silence in which everybody stirred uneasily, including Bolenciecwcz and Mr. Bassum. Mr. Bassum abruptly broke this silence in an amazing manner. "Choo-choo-choo," he said, in a low voice, and turned instantly scarlet. He glanced appealingly around the room. All of us, of course, shared Mr. Bassum's desire that Bolenciecwcz should stay abreast of the class in economics, for the Illinois game, one of the hardest and most important of the season, was only a week off. "Toot, toot, too-tooooooot!" some student with a deep voice moaned, and we all looked encouragingly at Bolenciecwcz. Somebody else gave a fine imitation of a locomotive letting off steam. Mr. Bassum himself rounded off the little show. "Ding, dong, ding, dong," he said hopefully. Bolenciecwcz was staring at the floor now, trying to think, his great brow furrowed, his huge hands rubbing together, his face red.

"How did you come to college this year, Mr. Bolenciecwcz?" asked the professor. "*Chuffa*, chuffa, *chuffa*, chuffa."

"M'father sent me," said the football player.

"What on?" asked Bassum.

"I git an 'lowance," said the tackle, in a low, husky voice, obviously embarrassed.

[1]*Lionel Barrymore*, a famous actor, one of the celebrated Barrymore family. He was born in 1878.

"No, no," said Bassum. "Name a means of transportation. What did you *ride* here on?"

"Train," said Bolenciecwcz.

"Quite right," said the professor. "Now, Mr. Nugent, will you tell us——"

If I went through anguish in botany and economics—for different reasons—gymnasium work was even worse. I don't even like to think about it. They wouldn't let you play games or join in the exercises with your glasses on and I couldn't see with mine off. I bumped into professors, horizontal bars, agricultural students, and swinging iron rings. Not being able to see, I could take it but I couldn't dish it out. Also, in order to pass gymnasium (and you had to pass it to graduate) you had to learn to swim if you didn't know how. I didn't like the swimming pool, I didn't like the swimming, and I didn't like the swimming instructor, and after all these years I still don't. I never swam but I passed my gym work anyway, by having another student give my gymnasium number (978) and swim across the pool in my place. He was a quiet, amiable blonde youth, number 473, and he would have seen through a microscope for me if we could have got away with it, but we couldn't get away with it. Another thing I didn't like about gymnasium work was that they made you strip the day you registered. It is impossible for me to be happy when I am stripped and being asked a lot of questions. Still, I did better than a lanky agricultural student who was cross-examined just before I was. They asked each student what college he was in—that is, whether Arts, Engineering, Commerce, or Agriculture. "What college are you in?" the instructor snapped at the youth in front of me. "Ohio State University," he said promptly.

It wasn't that agricultural student but it was another a whole lot like him who decided to take up journalism, possibly on the ground that when farming went to hell he could fall back on newspaper work. He didn't realize, of course, that that would be very much like falling back full-length on a kit of carpenter's tools. Haskins didn't seem cut out for journalism, being too embarrassed to talk to anybody and unable to use a typewriter, but the editor of the college paper assigned him to the cow barns, the sheep house, the horse pavilion, and the animal husbandry department generally. This was a genuinely big "beat,"[2] for it took up five times as much ground and got ten times as great a legislative appropriation as the College of Liberal Arts.[3] The agricultural student knew animals, but nevertheless his stories were dull and colorlessly written. He took all afternoon on each of them, on account of having to hunt for each letter on the typewriter. Once in a while he had to ask somebody to help him hunt. *C* and *L*, in particular, were hard letters for him to find. His editor finally got pretty much annoyed at the farmer-journalist because his pieces were so uninteresting. "See here, Haskins," he snapped at him one day. "Why is it we never have anything hot from you on the horse pavilion? Here we have two hundred head of horses on this campus—more than any other university in the Western Conference[4] except Purdue[5]—and yet you never get any real low-down on them. Now shoot over to the horse barns and dig up something lively." Haskins shambled out and came back in about an hour; he said he had something. "Well, start it off snappily," said the editor. "Something people will read." Haskins set to work and in a couple of hours brought a sheet of typewritten paper to the desk; it was a two-hundred word story about some disease that had broken out among the horses. Its opening sentence was simple but arresting. It read: "Who has noticed the sores on the tops of the horses in the animal husbandry building?"

Ohio State was a land grant university[6] and therefore two years of military drill was compulsory. We drilled with old Springfield rifles and studied the tactics of the Civil War even

---

[2]"*beat*," the area in which a newspaperman is responsible for reporting all happenings of interest.

[3]*the College of Liberal Arts*, the division of the university which included literature, languages, history, philosophy, and other subjects studied for culture rather than for immediate practical use.

[4]*Western Conference*, a group of Midwestern universities organized into a league in athletics.

[5]*Purdue*, a university at Lafayette, Indiana, noted particularly for its schools of agriculture and engineering.

[6]*a land grant university*, a university which received its land as a gift from the government. Such a gift was made to aid public education.

though the World War[7] was going on at the time. At eleven o'clock each morning thousands of freshmen and sophomores used to deploy over the campus, moodily creeping up on the old chemistry building. It was good training for the kind of warfare that was waged at Shiloh[8] but it had no connection with what was going on in Europe. Some people used to think there was German money behind it, but they didn't dare say so or they would have been thrown in jail as German spies. It was a period of muddy thought and marked, I believe, the decline of higher education in the Middle West.

As a soldier I was never any good at all. Most of the cadets were glumly indifferent soldiers, but I was no good at all. Once General Littlefield, who was commandant of the cadet corps, popped up in front of me during regimental drill and snapped, "You are the main trouble with this university!" I think he meant that my type was the main trouble with the university but he may have meant me individually. I was mediocre at drill, certainly—that is, until my senior year. By that time I had drilled longer than anybody else in the Western Conference, having failed at military at the end of each preceding year so that I had to do it all over again. I was the only senior still in uniform. The uniform which, when new, had made me look like an interurban railway conductor, now that it had become faded and too tight made me look like Bert Williams in his bellboy act.[9] This had a definitely bad effect on my morale. Even so, I had become by sheer practise little short of wonderful at squad maneuvers.

One day General Littlefield picked our company out of the whole regiment and tried to get it mixed up by putting it through one movement after another as fast as we could execute them: squads right, squads left, squads on right into line, squads right about, squads left front into line, etc. In about three minutes one hundred and nine men were marching in one direction and I was marching away from them at an angle of forty degrees, all alone. "Company, halt!" shouted General Littlefield, "That man is the only man who has it right!" I was made a corporal for my achievement.

The next day General Littlefield summoned me to his office. He was swatting flies when I went in. I was silent and he was silent too, for a long time. I don't think he remembered me or why he had sent for me, but he didn't want to admit it. He swatted some more flies, keeping his eyes on them narrowly before he let go with the swatter. "Button up your coat!" he snapped. Looking back on it now I can see that he meant me although he was looking at a fly, but I just stood there. Another fly came to rest on a paper in front of the general and began rubbing its hind legs together. The general lifted the swatter cautiously. I moved restlessly and the fly flew away. "You startled him!" barked General Littlefield, looking at me severely. I said I was sorry. "That won't help the situation!" snapped the General, with cold military logic. I didn't see what I could do except offer to chase some more flies toward his desk, but I didn't say anything. He stared out the window at the faraway figures of coeds crossing the campus toward the library. Finally, he told me I could go. So I went. He either didn't know which cadet I was or else he forgot what he wanted to see me about. It may have been that he wished to apologize for having called me the main trouble with the university; or maybe he had decided to compliment me on my brilliant drilling of the day before and then at the last minute decided not to. I don't know. I don't think about it much any more.

COLLEGE LIFE AND HARD TIMES

1. Which of James Thurber's college experiences seemed most frustrating to you? What made this experience humorous?

2. Why do you think Thurber included the story of the football player who couldn't learn economics and the journalism student who couldn't write a story?

3. In your opinion does the character pictured here fit Thurber's description of "the Perfect Neurotic"? Explain your answer, giving illustrations from the selection to prove your point.

---

[7]*the World War,* the First World War, 1914-1918.

[8]*Shiloh* (shī′lō), a place in southwestern Tennessee at which one of the important battles of the War Between the States was fought in 1862.

[9]*Bert Williams in his bellboy act.* Bert Williams (1876?-1922) was a star of vaudeville and musical comedy.

CARTOON HUMOR

"Is this seat taken?"

Burr Shafer in *The Saturday Review of Literature.*
Copyright 1951 by Saturday Review Association, In

"Do you spell 'hunt' with one dog or two?"

Charles D. Pearson in *The Saturday Review of Literatur*
Copyright 1951 by Saturday Review Association, Inc.

*"Sometimes I wish I were a boy so I wouldn't
have to wear blue jeans."*

*"Well, if I Called the Wrong Number, Why
Did You Answer the Phone?"*

The Larger View

I. An informal discussion of humorous selections that you and your classmates have read and of programs you have seen or listened to should give you a good time and help you gain even more pleasure from various types of humor in the future. The following questions may serve as a basis for such a class discussion.

1. What humorous writings have you read that belong to the same general class as Clarence Day's "Father Opens My Mail"? What similarities did you find between these selections and Clarence Day's sketch? Did you think any of these selections funnier than "Father Opens My Mail"? Which ones? Why?

2. Name some humorous verse you have read recently. Was it regularly constructed verse like Dorothy Parker's or did it have queer rhymes and overlong lines like Ogden Nash's? What made it funny?

3. Of all the humorous selections—verse or prose—you have read, which did you like best? Try to describe it briefly in such a way that your classmates will be eager to read it.

4. Who is your favorite radio or television comedian? Why do you think he is amusing?

II. Arrange with your teacher for a bulletin-board display of cartoons. All members of the class might coöperate in bringing cartoons they particularly like to class; a committee might then work with the teacher to select and arrange the cartoons to be exhibited. When all students have had an opportunity to look at the completed exhibit, talk over the following points:

1. What is the purpose of the caption? Is it necessary that every cartoon have a caption?

2. What makes a cartoon good?

3. In your opinion which is the best cartoon in the collection? Why do you think so?

4. Explain why you would, or would not, include in your collection any of the cartoons on this page and the facing page.

BECKER, MAY LAMBERTON (editor), *Home Book of Laughter*. (Dodd) American humorists from Mark Twain and O. Henry to Clarence Day and James Thurber are represented in this fine collection of sketches and stories.

BENCHLEY, ROBERT, *Inside Benchley*. (Harper) This collection and another omnibus volume, *Benchley Beside Himself* (Harper), contain most of the funniest pieces ever written by one of America's favorite "funny men."

DALY, THOMAS AUGUSTINE (compiler), *Little Book of American Humorous Verse*. (McKay) Verse that Americans have laughed at from "Yankee Doodle" to the present day is included in this amusing collection.

DAY, CLARENCE, *Life with Father*. (Knopf) You've had a taste of the sympathetic humor that has made this book one of the most popular of our times. You'll want to read more of it and to become acquainted also with *Life with Mother* (Knopf), more sketches of life in the amazing Day household.

GILBRETH, FRANK, and CAREY, ERNESTINE, *Cheaper by the Dozen*. (Crowell) A brother and sister write a hilarious account of growing up in a family in which the efficiency-engineer father tries to apply business methods to raising a family of twelve.

GUITERMAN, ARTHUR, *Brave Laughter*. (Dutton) Guiterman's skill in versifying, plus his sense of the ridiculous and his bent for satire, makes these verses very entertaining reading.

HERZBERG, MAX, and MONES, LEON (editors), *Humor of America*. (Appleton) In addition to a fine collection of prose, verse, and cartoons, this book contains an introductory section with much interesting information on the various types of humor.

KIMBROUGH, EMILY, *It Gives Me Great Pleasure*. (Dodd) Girls particularly will enjoy the experiences of this lady lecturer as she travels from place to place finding humor in every situation.

MARQUIS, DON, *lives and times of archy and mehitabel*. (Doubleday) Few funnier books have ever been written than this, supposedly pecked out on the typewriter by archy, the educated cockroach, who cannot manage the shift key to form capital letters. His friend, mehitabel the cat, figures in many of his adventures.

NASH, OGDEN, *The Face Is Familiar*. (Little) With Ogden Nash one verse invariably leads to another, and soon you'll find yourself quoting favorite lines to your friends. *Family Reunion* (Little), another collection with emphasis on parents, children, husbands, and wives, is also worth investigating.

PAPASHVILY, GEORGE and HELEN, *Anything Can Happen*. (Harper) The queer English, the strange adventures, and the unfailing good humor of this immigrant from Russia combine to make his story, written with his American wife, one of the most amusing and most likable books of recent years.

SCOGGIN, MARGARET (editor), *Chucklebait; Funny Stories for Everyone*. (Knopf) Save the examples of English humor included here for another time and concentrate on the American writers. There's enough variety to provide something for every taste. *More Chucklebait* (Knopf) is an equally good collection.

SKINNER, CORNELIA OTIS, *That's Me All Over*. (Dodd) The zest that has made life an exciting adventure sparks these witty sketches by a writer who is also a fine actress.

THURBER, JAMES, *The Thurber Carnival*. (Grosset) Many of the famous Thurber cartoons are here, as well as sketches like "University Days" and some of the best of Thurber's short stories. This is a real feast for the Thurber fan.

UNTERMEYER, LOUIS (editor), *A Treasury of Laughter*. (Simon) It's almost impossible to name a type of humor that isn't included in this generous collection. From limericks to tall tales and from jokes to boners, they're all here.

WHITE, ELWYN and KATHERINE (editors), *A Subtreasury of American Humor*. (Coward) This is a good book for browsing. Just sample a little verse here and a little prose there and you'll find yourself having a very amusing time.

UNIT XVI: AMERICAN BIOGRAPHY

E VERY LIST of "best seller" books in recent years has included one or
more distinguished biographies, and on several occasions a particular biography has stood for a time at the head of the list of
nonfictional works. This evidence of the popularity of biography among
present-day readers marks the victory of a form of writing which has had
a long history in America.

In colonial America there were no biographies of the kind being produced so abundantly today. Nevertheless, some interesting bits of biography appeared among the writings of the colonists. For example, in the
chronicles written to record public and church events, a writer sometimes
produced a readable sketch of a preacher or a government official. Again,
writers of diaries and travel accounts often drew miniature portraits
of their friends or relatives or new acquaintances—or themselves. Examples of such biographical items have already been examined in
"Captain Smith Among the Indians" (pages 25-27) and "Neighbors in
Virginia" (pages 52-54). A larger and more enduring colonial biography
was that of Benjamin Franklin, written by himself and hence called his
autobiography. An extract from Franklin's lively account of his busy
life and active mind appears on pages 296-301.

❧ I POST-REVOLUTIONARY BIOGRAPHY

It was not until after the Revolutionary War that biography as such
appeared in any quantity, and even then it was of dubious literary value.
Most popular of early post-Revolution biographies was *The Life and
Memorable Actions of George Washington,* written by Mason Weems
and published about 1800. The author, a clergyman popularly called
Parson Weems, fed the public demand for a superhuman hero by creating events that never occurred in Washington's life, such as the famous
"cherry tree" episode.

Fifty-nine years after the publication of Parson Weems' volume, there
appeared a quite different life of George Washington, written by Washington Irving. While it does not appeal widely to modern tastes, it represents an important advance on Weems' work: (1) Although Irving presented George Washington with sympathetic admiration, he avoided
making him, as Weems had done, a stuffed shirt of incredible virtue.
(2) Irving's *Life of Washington* filled five large volumes, against the one
thin volume by Weems. Unlike Weems, who had been satisfied to write
mere sketches of the "memorable actions" of his hero, Irving supplied a
detailed account of Washington's life in relation to his time in order to
show his growth as the leader best fitted to guide the colonies through
revolution to independence. (3) Unlike Weems, who had little narrative

skill, Irving knew how to tell a story entertainingly, whether that story concerned the imaginary Rip Van Winkle or the flesh-and-blood George Washington.

Throughout the nineteenth century and on into the early twentieth century, authors continued to write biography pretty much in the pattern set by Washington Irving. Like him, they chose subjects they admired greatly; and if they did not deliberately suppress or falsify facts unfavorable to their heroes, neither did they stress such facts. By and large, biographers wrote eulogies; they seemed to be saying to their readers, "Here is a man or a woman on whom you might well pattern your own life."

II CONTEMPORARY BIOGRAPHY

In the 1920's a revolution broke out against the practice of eulogizing the subjects of biographies. Biographers must no longer ignore or gloss over their characters' faults. In fact, many writers now took just the opposite tack and showed Washington or Lincoln or Longfellow as knaves or fools, or both. Some authors used "psychological" analysis to prove that men or women formerly admired had been anything but virtuous and praiseworthy. The works of these "debunkers" were read with avid curiosity for a while. But the public soon discovered that a totally black portrait of a person can be as dull and false as an all-white one. Readers turned to a still newer type of biography, and found it admirable and satisfying.

The popularity of the new biography can be accounted for, at least in part, by certain things that writers of this form of literature have discovered: (1) They have learned, like Irving, to tell a compelling story, one that holds constant narrative interest and moves steadily forward to a climax. (2) They have learned to avoid tediously long passages of description or character analysis. Instead they have liberally sprinkled their pages with such attention-holders as bits of lively conversation, amusing anecdotes, and revealing letters. (3) They have found out that readers want to know a man and the background against which he moved as they really were, not idealized and prettified beyond belief. Mark Twain once remarked that there is nothing harder to endure than a good example; and this expresses the attitude of readers today toward the subject of a biography. More inspiring to us than any plaster saint is the man or woman who had human faults like our own but who nevertheless struggled on to reach a particular goal.

The appeals of fine biography can be fully appreciated only through reading complete such biographies as those listed on pages 639-640. But these appeals can at least be savored in the brief modern biographical selections you have already read in this book[1] and those that follow.

---

[1]See "America's First Great Lady," by Donald Culross Peattie (pages 28-31); "The First Day," by George and Helen Papashvily (pages 98-102); "Tin Lizzie," by John Dos Passos (pages 157-160); "Reed of Virginia," by Charles Morrow Wilson (pages 160-166); "Wheels in His Head," by M. M. Musselman (pages 166-171); "Practical Politics," by Fiorello La Guardia (pages 194-199); "Life on the Farm," by Samuel Clemens (pages 229-233); "A Holiday with Father" and "Father Opens My Mail," by Clarence Day (pages 234-238 and 598-602); and "Circus at Dawn," by Thomas Wolfe (pages 253-256).

Young Abe Lincoln

CARL SANDBURG

Many biographies of Abraham Lincoln have been written, but none presents a more detailed and sympathetic picture of the man and his times than the monumental, six-volume life by Carl Sandburg. Sandburg had already won fame as a poet and as a collector of American ballads and songs when he began the biography he was so well fitted to write. Like Lincoln, he grew up in the Middle West; his boyhood was hard, with little schooling; he found satisfaction in dealing with people of all kinds; and he has the kind of honest mind that sees things as they are and can still make the best of them.

The two volumes of *Abraham Lincoln: The Prairie Years* (1926) and the four volumes of *Abraham Lincoln: The War Years* (1939) are more than just another life of Lincoln. They are the biography of the places where Lincoln lived and the story of the times in which he lived. Like a painter with a huge canvas and a comprehensive vision, Sandburg gives us the whole picture of the man, the place, and the time. Thus in these volumes the great figure of Lincoln moves against a real and alive background, and we see him as both product and creator of the events of his life span.

The following selection, which is taken from *Abraham Lincoln: The Prairie Years*, pictures Lincoln as a sturdy youth in a frontier settlement of southern Indiana.

SIXTEEN-YEAR-OLD ABE had worked on the farm of James Taylor, at the mouth of Anderson Creek, on that great highway of traffic, the Ohio River. Besides plowing and doing barn and field work, he ran the ferryboat across the Ohio. Two travelers wanted to get on a steamboat one day, and after Abe sculled them to it and lifted their trunks on board they threw him a half dollar apiece; it gave him a new feeling; the most he had ever earned before that was at butchering for thirty-one cents a day. And when one of the half dollars slipped from him and sank in the river, that too gave him a new feeling.

At Anderson Creek ferry, he saw and talked with settlers, land buyers and sellers, traders, hunters, peddlers, preachers, gamblers, politicians, teachers, and men shut-mouthed about their business. Occasionally came a customer who looked as if he might be one of the "half-horse, half-alligator men" haunting the Ohio watercourse those years. There was river talk about Mike Fink,[1] known on the Ohio as the "Snapping Turtle" and on the Mississippi as "The Snag," the toughest of the half-horse, half-alligator crowd; he was a famous marksman, and aiming his rifle from his keelboat floating the Ohio had shot off the tails of pigs running loose in the bottom lands[2]; once Mike ordered his wife off his barge, covered her with autumn leaves while he threatened to shoot her, set fire to the leaves, so that Mrs. Fink ran with clothes and hair on fire and jumped into the river, to hear her husband saying, "Ye will make eyes at the men on other boats, will ye?"

Along the water front of Louisville, Mike Fink had backed up his claim, "I can outrun, outhop, outjump, throw down, drag out, and lick any man in the country; I'm a Salt River roarer; I love the wimming and I'm chock-full of fight." They tried him for crimes in Louisville and acquitted him for lack of sufficient evidence; he waved a red bandanna for a good-by and told them he would come back to face their other indictments.

Among the bad men of the river, rough-and-tumble fighting included gouging of eyes, thumb-chewing, knee-lifting, head-butting, the biting off of noses and ears, and the tearing loose of underlips with the teeth. "Fights was fights in them days."

Travelers had a proverb that a tavern was hardly safe if the proprietor had a nose or an ear off. It was a sign the landlord couldn't take care of himself.

Lawyers with books in their saddlebags took the ferryboat across the Ohio; law and order was coming to that wild young country, they

---

[1] *Mike Fink,* a half-legendary boatman on the Ohio and Mississippi rivers.

[2] *bottom lands,* low lands along a river.

believed; they could remember only ten years back how the law of the Territory of Indiana[3] provided that a horse thief should have two hundred lashes with a whip on his bare back and stay in jail till the horse was paid for, and the second time he was caught horse-stealing he was shot or hanged; for stealing cattle or hogs the thief had his shirt taken off and was given thirty-nine lashes.

Old-timers came along who could tell how the Indians in 1809 were stealing horses, burning barns and fences, killing settlers, running off with cattle and chickens, and how General Hopkins with 1200 soldiers burned the Indian villages along the Wabash, their log cabins, gardens, orchards, stationed rangers to hunt down every Indian they found, till the time came when there was not a red man on the Wabash or south of that river in the state of Indiana.

The ferry boy at Anderson Creek watched and listened to this human drift across the Ohio River—the bushwhackers[4] and bad men who called themselves bad, and the others who called themselves good. Civilization went by, boats and tools breaking ways. Steamboats came past in a slow and proud pageantry making their fourteen- to twenty-day passage from New Orleans to Pittsburgh; geography became fact to the boy looking on; flags on the steamboats were a sign of that long stretch of country the steamboats were crossing. Strings of flatboats passed, loaded with produce—pork, turkeys, chicken, corn meal, flour, whiskey, venison hams, hazelnuts, skins, furs, ginseng; this was farm produce for trading at river ports to merchants or to plantation owners for feeding slaves. Other trading boats carried furniture, groceries, clothes, kitchenware, plows, wagons, harness; this was from manufacturing centers, consignments to storekeepers and traders. Houseboats, arks, sleds,[5] flatboats with small cabins in which families lived and kept house, floated toward their new homesteads; on these

the women were washing, the children playing. The life flow of a main artery of American civilization, at a vivid line of growth, was a piece of pageantry there at Anderson Creek.

Young Abe was out with ax, saw, and drawknife building himself a light flatboat at Bates' Landing, a mile and a half down the river from Anderson Creek. He was eighteen years old, a designer, builder, navigator; he cut down trees, hewed out planks, pegged and cleated together the bottoms and sides of his own boat, wood from end to end.

Pieces of money jingled in his pockets. Passengers paid him for sculling them from Bates' Landing out to steamboats in the middle of the Ohio River.

He studied words and figurations on pieces of money. Thirteen stars stood for the first Thirteen States of the Union. The silver print of an eagle spreading its wings and lifting a fighting head was on the half dollar. As though the eagle were crying high, important words,

<hr />

[3] *the Territory of Indiana.* Indiana was still a territory at the time Sandburg is describing. It was admitted to the Union as a state in 1816.

[4] *bushwhackers,* people who live in the wilderness.

[5] *arks, sleds,* types of clumsy, roughly made river boats.

above its beak was inscribed *E Pluribus Unum*[6]; this meant the many states should be One, young Abe learned.

Circled with the thirteen stars were the head and bust of a motherly looking woman. On her forehead was the word *Liberty*. Just what did *She* mean?

Waiting for passengers and looking out on the wide Ohio to the drooping trees that dipped their leaves in the water on the farther shore, he could think about money and women and eagles.

A signal came from the opposite shore one day and Lincoln rowed across the river. As he stepped out of his boat two men jumped out of the brush. They took hold of him and said they were going to "duck" him in the river. They were John and Lin Dill, brothers who operated a ferry and claimed Abe had been transporting passengers contrary to the law of Kentucky.

As they sized up Abe's lean husky arms they decided not to throw him in the river. He might be too tough a customer. Then all three went to Squire Samuel Pate, justice of the peace, near Lewisport.[7]

A warrant for the arrest of Abraham Lincoln was sworn out by John T. Dill. And the trial began of the case of "The Commonwealth of Kentucky versus Abraham Lincoln," charged with violation of "An Act Respecting the Establishment of Ferries."

Lincoln testified he had carried passengers from the Indiana shore out to the middle of the river, never taking them to the Kentucky shore. And the Dill brothers, though sore and claiming the defendant Lincoln had wronged them, did not go so far as to testify he had "for reward set any person over a river," in the words of the Kentucky statute.

Squire Pate dismissed the warrant against Lincoln. The disappointed Dills put on their hats and left. Lincoln sat with Squire Pate for a long talk. If a man knows the law about a business he is in, it is a help to him, the Squire told young Abe.

They shook hands and parted friends. Afterwards on days when no passengers were in sight and it was "law day" at Squire Pate's down the river, Abe would scull over and watch the witnesses, the constables, the Squire, the machinery of law, government, justice.

The State of Indiana, he learned, was one thing, and the State of Kentucky, something else. A water line in the middle of a big river ran between them. He could ask: "Who makes state lines? What *are* state lines?"

In the year 1825, ox teams and pack horses came through Gentryville[8] carrying people on their way to a place on the Wabash River they called New Harmony.[9] A rich English businessman named Robert Owen had paid $132,-000 for land and $50,000 for live stock, tools, and merchandise, and had made a speech before the Congress at Washington telling how he and his companions were going to try to find a new way for people to live their lives together, without fighting, cheating, or exploiting each other, where work would be honorable yet there would be time for play and learning; they would share and share alike, each for all and all for each. In January, 1826, Owen himself, with a party of thirty people, came down the Ohio River in what was called the "boatload of knowledge."

More ox wagons and pack horses kept coming past the Gentryville crossroads; about a thousand people were joined in Owen's scheme at New Harmony on the Wabash. The scheme lighted up Abe Lincoln's heart. His eyes were big and hungry as a hoot owl's as he told Dennis Hanks,[10] "There's a school and thousands of books there and fellers that know everything in creation." The schooling would have cost him about $100 a year and he could have worked for his board. But Tom Lincoln had other plans for his son Abe.

Across the next three years the boy grew longer of leg and arm, tougher of bone and

[6]"*E Pluribus Unum*" (ē plūr'ə bəs ū'nəm), a Latin phrase meaning "out of many, one." It is the motto of the United States.

[7]*Lewisport*, a Kentucky town on the Ohio River.

[8]*Gentryville*, a crossroads hamlet in southern Indiana near the Pigeon Creek clearings where Lincoln lived.

[9]*New Harmony*. For another mention of this town see the discussion of experimental communities in Thoreau's time on page 372.

[10]*Dennis Hanks*, a cousin of Lincoln.

sinew, with harder knuckles and joints. James Gentry, with the largest farms in the Pigeon Creek clearings, and a landing on the Ohio River, was looking the big boy over. He believed Abe could take his pork, flour, meal, bacon, potatoes, and produce to trade down the Mississippi River for cotton, tobacco, and sugar. Young Abe was set to work on a flatboat; he cut the oaks for a double bottom of stout planks, and a deck shelter, two pairs of long oars at bow and stern, a check-post,[11] and a setting pole for steering.

As the snow began to melt, a little before the first frogs started shrilling, in that year of 1828, they loaded the boat and pushed off.

In charge of the boat Mr. Gentry had placed his son Allen, and in charge of Allen he had placed Abe Lincoln, to hold his own against any half-horse, half-alligator bushwhackers who might try to take the boat or loot it, and leave the bones of those they took from, at Cave-in-Rock on the Illinois shore, or other spots

---

[11]*check-post,* a post used to secure the boat.

---

where the skeletons of flatboatmen had been found years after the looters sold the cargo down the river. The honesty of Abe, of course, had been the first point Mr. Gentry considered; and the next point had been whether he could handle the boat in the snags and sand bars. The two young men pushed off on their trip of a thousand miles to New Orleans, on a wide, winding waterway, where the flatboats were tied up at night to the river bank, and floated and poled by day amid changing currents, strings of other flatboats, and in the paths of the proud white steamboats.

Whitecaps rose and broke with their foam feathers, a mile, two miles, beyond the limit of eyesight, as fresh winds blew along the Ohio River. Cave-in-Rock was passed on the Illinois shore, with its sign, "Wilson's Liquor Vault and House of Entertainment," with a doorway 25 feet high, 80 feet wide, and back of that entrance a cavern 200 feet deep, a 14-foot chimney leading to an upper room, where one time later were found 60 human skeletons, most of them rivermen lured and trapped by

the Wilson gang that camped at Hurricane Island near by.

Timber-covered river bluffs stood up overlooking the river like plowmen resting big shoulders between the plow handles; twisted dumps and runs of clay banks were like squatters who had lost hope and found rheumatism and malaria; lone pine trees had silhouetted their dry arms of branches on reefs where they dissolved and reappeared in river-mist lights as if they struggled to tell some secret of water and sky before going under.

The nineteen-year-old husky from Indiana found the Mississippi River as tricky with comic twists as Aesop's fables,[12] as mystical, boding, and promising as the family Bible. Sand bars, shoals, and islands were scattered along with the look of arithmetic numbers. Sudden rains, shifting winds, meant new handling of oars. A rising roar and rumble of noise might be rough water ahead or some whimsical current tearing through fallen tree branches at the riverside. A black form seems to be floating up-river through a gray drizzle; the coming out of the sun shows it is an island point, standing still; the light and air play tricks with it.

The bends of the river ahead must be watched with ready oars and sweeps or the flatboat naturally heads in to shore. Strong winds crook the course of the boat, sometimes blowing it ashore; one of the crew must hustle off in a rowboat, tie a hawser to a tree or stump, while another man on the big boat has a rope at the check-post; and they slow her down. Warning signals must be given at night, by waving a lantern or firewood, to other craft.

So the flatboat, "the broadhorn," went down the Father of Waters, four to six miles an hour, the crew frying their own pork and corn-meal cakes, washing their own shirts, sewing on their own buttons.

Below Baton Rouge,[13] among the sugar plantations known as the "Sugar Coast," they tied up at the plantation of Madame Duquesne one evening, put their boat in order, spoke their good nights to any sweet stars in the sky, and dropped off to sleep. They woke to find seven rowdies on board trying to steal the cargo and kill the crew; the long-armed Indiana husky swung a crab-tree club, knocked them galley-west, chased them into the woods, and laid a bandanna on a gash over the right eye that left a scar for life as it healed. Then they cut loose the boat and moved down the river.

At New Orleans they traded, sold the rest of their cargo of potatoes, bacon, hams, flour, apples, jeans, in exchange for cotton, tobacco, and sugar, and sold the flatboat for what it would bring as lumber. And they lingered and loitered a few days, seeing New Orleans, before taking steamer north.

On the streets and by-streets of that town, which had floated the flags of French, British, and American dominion, young Abraham Lincoln felt the pulses of a living humanity with far heartbeats in wide, alien circles over the earth: English sailors who sang "Ranzo" and "Boney," "Hangin' Johnny," and "O Fare-you-well, My Bonny Young Girls"; Dutchmen and French in jabber and exclamative; Swedes, Norwegians, and Russians with blond and reddish mustaches and whiskers; Spaniards and Italians with knives and red silk handkerchiefs; New York, Philadelphia, Boston, Rome, Amsterdam became human facts; it was London those men came from ejaculating, "Ow can ye blime me?"

Women in summer weather wearing slippers and boots; creoles with dusks of eyes; quadroons and octoroons with elusive soft voices; streets lined with saloons where bets were laid on steamboat races; talk ran fast about the construction, then going on, of the New Orleans & Pontchartrain Railroad, to be one of the first steam railroads in America and the world; slaves passed handcuffed into gangs headed for cotton fields of one, two, six thousand acres in size; and everywhere was talk about slaves.

As young Abe Lincoln and Allen Gentry made their way back home to the clearings of Pigeon Creek, Indiana, the tall boy had his thoughts. He had crossed half the United States,

---

[12]*Aesop's* (ē′səpz) *fables,* stories about animals written by a Greek slave over five hundred years before the birth of Christ. Although all the fables point a moral, many do it in a humorous way.

[13]*Baton Rouge* (bat′ən rüzh′), a town on the Mississippi River in southeastern Louisiana, the capital of the state.

it seemed, and was back home after three-months' vacation with eight-dollars-a-month pay in his pocket and a scar over the right eye.

That year Indiana University was to print its first catalogue, but Abe Lincoln didn't show up among the students who registered. He was between the plow handles or pulling fodder or sinking the ax in trees and brush, and reading between times *Pilgrim's Progress*,[14] a history of the United States, the life of Francis Marion,[15] the life of Ben Franklin, and the book he borrowed from Dave Turnham, the constable. The title page of the book said it contained "The Revised Laws of Indiana, adopted and enacted by the general assembly at their eighth session. To which are prefixed the Declaration of Independence, the Constitution of the United States, the Constitution of the State of Indiana, and sundry other documents connected with the Political History of the Territory and State of Indiana. Arranged and published by the authority of the General Assembly."

The science of government, theories of law, and schemes of administration spread themselves before the young man's mind as he crept along from page to page, wrestling with those statutes of Indiana and other documents. Crimes and punishments were listed there, in black and white, fine distinctions between murder and manslaughter, between burglary, robbery, larceny, forgery, trespass, nuisance, fraud; varied circumstances of assault and battery, affray, unlawful assembly, rout and riot.

Lives of masses of people spread out before him in a panorama as he read the statutes. He read that there are crimes which shall be deemed "infamous," and any man found guilty of an infamous crime "shall thereafter be rendered incapable of holding any office of honor, trust, or profit, of voting at any election, of serving as a juror, of giving testimony within this state." He read in Section 60 on page 48, "Every person of the age of fourteen years or upwards, who shall profanely curse or damn, or shall

profanely swear by the name of God, Jesus Christ, or the Holy Ghost, shall be fined not less than one, nor more than three dollars, for each offence." Sharp lines were drawn between murder and manslaughter; a murderer shall be a person "of sound memory and discretion, who shall unlawfully kill any reasonable creature in being and under the peace of this state, with malice aforethought"; a manslaughterer shall be a person "who without malice, either express or implied, shall unlawfully kill another person, either voluntarily upon a sudden heat, or involuntarily, but in the commission of some unlawful act." It seemed, too, there was a stream of people born or gone wrong, for the state to take care of, the criminals in jails and prisons, the paupers in poorhouses, the insane and feeble-minded in asylums, wives with runaway husbands, and children born out of wedlock.

It was tough plowing through that book, with the satisfaction, however, that he could keep what he earned.

ABE LINCOLN AND THE FRONTIER

1. What impression of a frontier society do you get from Carl Sandburg's account? Name some of the details that helped you build up this idea.

2. In this account Sandburg seldom describes Lincoln directly; rather he pictures him in action against his frontier background, and lets the reader infer what sort of youth Lincoln was. Point out passages in the biography which show that Lincoln possessed the following qualities: (a) intelligence, (b) ambition, (c) eagerness to learn, (d) honesty, (e) courage, and (f) imagination.

3. In two paragraphs near the end of the selection Sandburg explains in some detail the contents of *The Revised Laws of Indiana*. What was the value to Lincoln of this particular book? How do you think his study of it helped him toward maturity?

4. It is generally agreed that the events and circumstances of a person's childhood and youth set the pattern for his achievement in later life. In what ways might the experiences of the frontier have fitted Lincoln for the difficult tasks he later assumed? What were the foundations for the trust he inspired in people?

5. In telling the story of Lincoln as a young man, what seems to be the author's purpose? In what ways does he try to accomplish his purpose? Explain why you think he has, or has not, succeeded in his attempt.

---

[14]"*Pilgrim's Progress*," an allegory of the Christian life by John Bunyan published in 1678.

[15]*Francis Marion*, a Revolutionary War general who, because he operated in the lowlands of the South, was called "the Swamp Fox."

The Surrender at Appomattox

DOUGLAS SOUTHALL FREEMAN

The great Southern leader, Robert E. Lee, has been the subject of many biographies, but in attention to detail, in accuracy, and in character portrayal none has equaled Douglas Southall Freeman's *R. E. Lee*. Freeman, like Lee, was a Virginian. For almost twenty years prior to the publication of his four-volume biography in 1934-35, he steeped himself in his subject. No detail of Lee's life was too trivial to investigate; no campaign or battle was too intricate to be mastered. The resulting biography, which won the Pulitzer Prize in 1935, gives us a portrait of Lee not only as a great general but also as a fine gentleman and a lovable human being.

The following selection, which is taken from the fourth volume of *R. E. Lee*, presents General Lee in the last days of the bloody conflict between the North and the South. It is April, 1865, as Lee moves toward the tiny village of Appomattox (ap′ə mat′əks) Court House near Lynchburg, Virginia. There he is to discuss terms for the surrender of his army with General Grant, commander of the armies of the United States.

GRANT already had offered...to have the surrender arranged through officers designated for that purpose, in order that the Confederate leader might be spared humiliation, but Lee probably never thought of passing on to others this unpleasant task....

In the company of Marshall,[1] Babcock,[2] and Tucker, the daring orderly, Lee started up the road, and beyond the thin and silent line of battle on the hillside. At the stream, Traveler[3] wanted to drink. Lee waited until his faithful mount had his fill. Then he went on.

How often he had ridden that strong steed and in scenes how various!...Jackson[4] had ridden with him, the battle light in his eyes, the laughing Stuart, the nervous Hill, the diligent Pender, the gallant Rodes—all of them dead now, and he alone, save for those silent companions, was on his last ride as commander of the Army of Northern Virginia. Thirty-nine years of devotion to military duty had come to this...and this, too, was duty.

As the little cavalcade passed toward the village of Appomattox, Lee had to arouse himself and arrange the details: Grant had left it to him to select the place of meeting. Would Marshall go ahead and find a suitable house? Obediently, the colonel trotted off. Lee remained with Babcock. They did not talk—how could they?

After a while the orderly returned to say that Colonel Marshall had found a room for the conference. Lee went on and, under the soldier's guidance, drew rein beyond the courthouse in the yard of a house on the left-hand side of the road to Lynchburg. The residence belonged to Major Wilmer McLean....

Lee dismounted in the yard and after the orderly took Traveler, he walked toward the wide steps that led to the covered porch which ran the whole width of the house. Entering the central hall, at the top of the steps, he turned into the front room on his left, a typical parlor of a middle-class Virginia home. Colonel Marshall went with him. Colonel Babcock accompanied Lee, also, with the explanation that as General Grant would soon arrive, the orderly could easily direct him to the place....

Half an hour passed, perhaps the longest half hour in Lee's whole life. If there was any conversation, it was in snatches and was slow, labored, and vague. About 1:30 o'clock there was a clatter in the road, the sound of approach of a large body of mounted men.

They drew nearer, they halted, they dis-

[1] *Marshall*, Colonel Charles Marshall, General Lee's military secretary.

[2] *Babcock*, Lieutenant-Colonel Orville E. Babcock, a Union officer. He served as aide-de-camp, or assistant, to General Grant.

[3] *Traveler*, Lee's famous iron-gray horse, which served as his mount during the war.

[4] *Jackson*, Stonewall Jackson, one of the most brilliant of the Southern generals. He and the other men named in the paragraph were all officers who had served with Lee.

mounted. Some of them climbed the steps. Babcock went to the door and opened it. A man of middle height, slightly stooped and heavily bearded, came in alone. He was dressed for the field, with boots and breeches mud-bespattered. He took off his yellow thread gloves as he stepped forward. Lee had never seen him to remember him, but he knew who he was and, rising with Marshall, he started across the room to meet General Grant. They shook hands quietly with brief greetings. Then Grant sat down at the table in the middle of the room, and Lee returned to his place. Marshall stood to the left and somewhat behind him. Babcock had a few whispered words with Grant, then went from the room and out on the porch. He soon was back, followed by a full dozen Federal officers, Sheridan and Ord among them....

The conversation began: "I met you once before, General Lee," Grant said in his normal tones, "while we were serving in Mexico,[5] when you came over from General Scott's headquarters to visit Garland's brigade, to which I then belonged. I have always remembered your appearance, and I think I should have recognized you anywhere."

"Yes," answered Lee quietly, "I know I met you on that occasion, and I have often thought of it and tried to recollect how you looked, but I have never been able to recall a single feature."

Mention of Mexico aroused many memories. Grant pursued them with so much interest and talked of them so readily that the conversation went easily on until the Federal[6] was almost forgetting what he was about. Lee felt the weight of every moment and brought Grant back with words that seemed to come naturally, yet must have cost him anguish that cannot be measured.

"I suppose, General Grant," he said, "that the object of our present meeting is fully understood. I asked to see you to ascertain upon what terms you would receive the surrender of my army."

Grant did not change countenance or exhibit the slightest note of exultation in his reply. "The terms I propose are those stated substantially in my letter of yesterday—that is, the officers and men surrendered to be paroled and disqualified from taking up arms again until properly exchanged, and all arms, ammunition and supplies to be delivered up as captured property."

Lee nodded an assent that meant more than his adversary realized. The phantom of a proud army being marched away to prison disappeared as Grant spoke, and the hope Lee had first expressed to Taylor that morning[7] was confirmed. "Those," said he, "are about the conditions I expected would be proposed."

"Yes," Grant answered, "I think our correspondence indicated pretty clearly the action that would be taken at our meeting; and I hope it may lead to a general suspension of hostilities and be the means of preventing any further loss of life."

That, of course, was a theme that Lee's conception of his duty as a soldier would not permit him to discuss. It was his to obey orders and to direct the forces in the field. The civil authorities had the sole power, he held, to make peace of the sort General Grant had in mind. So he merely inclined his head again.

Grant talked on of peace and its prospects. Lee waited and then, courteously, but in a manifest desire to finish the business in hand, he said: "I presume, General Grant, we have both carefully considered the proper steps to be taken, and I would suggest that you commit to writing the terms you have proposed, so that they may be formally acted upon."

"Very well, I will write them out."

Lee sat in silence and looked straight ahead as Grant called for his manifold order book, opened it, lit his pipe, puffed furiously, wrote steadily for a while with his pencil, paused, reflected, wrote two sentences and then quickly completed the text. Grant went over it in an

---

[5]*while we were serving in Mexico.* Grant and Lee, both West Point graduates, had received their first battle experience during the Mexican War.

[6]*the Federal,* Grant.

[7]*the hope...that morning.* In a conversation with Colonel Walter H. Taylor that morning, Lee had told Taylor that he had hopes the terms of surrender would be generous.

undertone with one of his military secretaries, who interlined a few words. Lee did not follow any of this. He sat as he was until Grant rose, crossed to him, and put the manifold book in his hands, with the request that he read over the letter.

Lee probably was at his tensest then, for he busied himself with little mechanical acts as though to master his nerves. He placed the book on the table. He took his spectacles from his pocket. He pulled out his handkerchief. He wiped off the glasses, he crossed his legs, he set his glasses very carefully on his nose, and then he took up the order book for a slow, careful reading:

Appomattox C. H.,[8] Va.
Apr. 9th, 1865.

Gen. R. E. Lee,
Comd. C. S. A.[9]
Gen.

In accordance with the substance of my letter to you of the 8th instant[10] I propose to receive the surrender of the Army of N. Va. on the following terms, to wit:

[8]*C. H.,* Court House.
[9]*C. S. A.,* Confederate States of America.
[10]*the substance of...the 8th instant.* Grant is referring to the letter mentioned earlier which he had written the previous day. In it he had outlined the terms on which a surrender might be carried out.

Rolls of all the officers and men to be made in duplicate, one copy to be given to an officer designated by me, the other to be retained by such officer or officers as you may designate. The officers to give their individual paroles not to take up arms against the

—At this point, Lee turned the page and read on—

Government of the United States until properly and each company or regimental commander sign a like parole for the men of their command.

Lee stopped in his reading, looked up, and said to Grant: "After the words *until properly,* the word *exchanged* seems to be omitted. You doubtless intended to use that word."

"Why, yes," answered Grant, "I thought I had put in the word *exchanged.*"

"I presumed it had been omitted inadvertently, and with your permission I will mark where it should be inserted."

"Certainly."

Lee felt for a pencil, but could not find one. Colonel Horace Porter[11] stepped forward and offered his. Lee took it, thanked him, placed the book on the table, inserted the caret, and resumed his reading:

[11]*Colonel Horace Porter,* a Union officer and an American Indian.

The arms, artillery and public property to be parked and stacked and turned over to the officer appointed by me to receive them.

This will not embrace the side arms of the officers, nor their private horses or baggage. This done, each officer and man will be allowed to return to their homes not to be disturbed by United States authority so long as they observe their paroles and the laws in force where they may reside.

Very respectfully,

U. S. Grant, Lt. Gl.

There was a slight change in Lee's expression as he read the closing sentences, and his tone was not without warmth as now he looked up at Grant and said: "This will have a very happy effect on my army."

"Unless you have some suggestions to make in regard to the form in which I have stated the terms," Grant resumed, "I will have a copy of the letter made in ink and sign it."

Lee hesitated: "There is one thing I would like to mention. The cavalrymen and artillerists own their own horses in our army. Its organization in this respect differs from that of the United States. I would like to understand whether these men will be permitted to retain their horses."

"You will find," answered Grant, "that the terms as written do not allow this. Only the officers are allowed to take their private property."

Lee read over the second page of the letter again. For months he had agonized over his field transportation and cavalry mounts. He knew what the army's horses would mean to the South, stripped as it had been of all draft animals, and he wanted those of his men who owned mounts to have them for the spring plowing. His face showed his wish. His tongue would not go beyond a regretful "No, I see the terms do not allow it; that is clear."

Grant read his opponent's wish, and, with the fine consideration that prevailed throughout the conversation—one of the noblest of his qualities, and one of the surest evidences of his greatness—he did not humiliate Lee by forcing him to make a direct plea for a modification of terms that were generous. "Well, the subject is quite new to me. Of course, I did not know that any private soldiers owned their animals, but I think this will be the last battle of the war—I sincerely hope so—and that the surrender of this army will be followed soon by that of all the others, and I take it that most of the men in the ranks are small farmers, and as the country has been so raided by the two armies, it is doubtful whether they will be able to put in a crop to carry themselves and their families through the next winter without the aid of the horses they are now riding, and I will arrange it this way: I will not change the terms as now written, but I will instruct the officers I shall appoint to receive the paroles to let all the men who claim to own a horse or mule take the animals home with them to work their little farms."

It could not have been put more understandingly or more generously. Lee showed manifest relief and appreciation. "This will have the best possible effect upon the men," he said; "it will be very gratifying and will do much toward conciliating our people."

While Grant set about having his letter copied, Lee directed Marshall to draft a reply. In the wait that followed, Grant brought up and introduced the officers who had remained silent in the background. Lee shook hands with those who extended theirs and bowed to the others, but he spoke only to General Seth Williams, a warm friend during his superintendency at West Point[12]....

When the introductions were over, Lee turned again to General Grant. "I have a thousand or more of your men as prisoners, General Grant, a number of them officers whom we have required to march along with us for several days. I shall be glad to send them into your lines as soon as it can be arranged, for I have no provisions for them. I have, indeed, nothing for my own men. They have been living for the last few days principally upon parched corn, and are badly in need of both rations and forage. I telegraphed to Lynchburg, directing several trainloads of rations to be sent on by rail from there, and when they arrive I should be glad to have the present wants of my men supplied from them."

---

[12]*during his superintendency at West Point.* From 1852 to 1855 Lee served as head of the military academy.

There was a stir among the listeners at this remark, and they looked at Sheridan, for, unknown to Lee, he had the previous night captured at Appomattox Station the rations that had come down from Lynchburg. Those that had been sent up from Farmville had been found by the Federals farther down the road. Grant did not add to Lee's distress by a recountal of these seizures. He merely said, "I should like to have our men within our lines as soon as possible. I will take steps at once to have your army supplied with rations, but I am sorry we have no forage for the animals. We have had to depend upon the country for our supply of forage. Of about how many men does your present force consist?"

Lee reflected for a moment: "Indeed, I am not able to say. My losses in killed and wounded have been exceedingly heavy, and besides, there have been many stragglers and some deserters. All my reports and public papers, and, indeed, my own private letters, had to be destroyed on the march to prevent them from falling into the hands of your people. Many companies are entirely without officers, and I have not seen any returns for several days; so that I have no means of ascertaining our present strength."

Grant had estimated Lee's numbers at 25,000 and he asked, "Suppose I send over 25,000 rations, do you think that will be a sufficient supply?"

"I think it will be ample," Lee is said by Horace Porter to have replied. "And it will be a great relief, I assure you," he added instantly. Colonel Marshall's memory of Lee's answer was that he said 25,000 rations would be "more than enough."

General Sheridan then came forward and requested that he might copy two dispatches he had sent Lee that day, in such a hurry that he had not written them out for his records. These dispatches were protests against alleged violations of the truce. Lee took out the dispatches from his pocket and said he was sure that if the truce had been violated it was through a misunderstanding.

By this time, Marshall had finished his draft of Lee's acceptance of Grant's terms of surrender. It began with a sentence which would indicate that the agreement had been reached by correspondence. Lee modified this because he thought it would create a false impression. He made, perhaps, a few other changes, and then he had Marshall copy the document. The Federals had borrowed Marshall's ink in order to write their answer, and now, Marshall, having no paper with him, had to procure some from their stock.

The finished letter was now brought Lee and was read over by him:

Lieut-Gen. U. S. Grant,
    Commanding Armies of the United States.

    General: I have received your letter of this date containing the terms of surrender of the Army of Northern Virginia as proposed by you. As they are substantially the same as those expressed in your letter of the 8th instant, they are accepted. I will proceed to designate the proper officers to carry the stipulations into effect.

    Very respectfully, your obedient servant,

Lee put his signature to this without a quiver. Marshall sealed it and went over to Parker, who already had Grant's letter waiting for him, duly signed and in an addressed envelope. They made the exchange and the surrender was complete. It was then about 3:45 P.M.

The rest was casual and brief. Grant explained why he was without his sword. Lee is said to have remarked that he usually wore his when with the army in the field. Then Lee requested that Grant notify Meade[13] of the surrender, so that firing might not break out and men be slain to no purpose. He requested also, that pending the actual surrender, the two armies be kept separate, so that personal encounters would be avoided. Grant acquiesced immediately and suggested that time might be saved if two of his officers rode to Meade through the Confederate lines.

Lee thereupon rose, shook hands with General Grant, bowed to the spectators, and passed from the room. He went through the hall to the porch, where several Federal officers at once sprang to their feet and saluted. Putting on his

---

[13]*Meade*, General George Meade, a Union officer, best known for the victory of his armies at Gettysburg. At this time he commanded the Army of the Potomac.

hat, Lee mechanically but with manifest courtesy returned their salute and with measured tread crossed the porch. At the head of the steps, he drew on his gauntlets, and absently smote his hands together several times as he looked into space—across the valley to the hillside where his faithful little army lay. In a moment he aroused himself and, not seeing his mount, called in a voice that was hoarse and half-choked, "Orderly! Orderly!" Quickly Tucker answered from the corner of the house, where he was holding Traveler's rein as the steed grazed.

Lee walked down the steps and stood in front of the animal while the man replaced the bridle. Lee himself drew the forelock from under the brow band and parted and smoothed it. Then, as Tucker stepped aside, Lee mounted slowly and with an audible sigh. At that moment General Grant stepped down from the porch on his way to the gate, where his horse was waiting. Stopping suddenly, Grant took off his hat, but did not speak. The other Federals followed the courteous example of their chief. Lee raised his hat, without a word, turned his horse and rode away to an ordeal worse than a meeting with Grant—the ordeal of breaking the news to his soldiers and of telling them farewell.

THE MEETING AT APPOMATTOX

1. This selection presents General Lee during only a few hours of one afternoon; yet from it a very clear picture of the man emerges. What qualities of Lee are made apparent to you through reading the selection? How do you learn of these qualities?

2. What idea of General Grant do you gain?

3. In making a movie short on the surrender at Appomattox, a director would probably find Freeman's account one of his best sources of information. What details might he gain from this source on (a) setting, (b) individuals present, (c) description of characters, (d) action? Why do you think Freeman included details of this sort in a biography?

Contrasting two biographies

In "The Surrender at Appomattox" Lee's name appears in the first sentence, and from here on throughout the entire selection the reader never loses sight of the defeated leader. We ride with him to Appomattox; we suffer with him as he awaits Grant; we share with him his concern lest his men lose their horses; and we feel his anguish as he departs to break the news of surrender to his men.

In "Young Abe Lincoln" the first sentence also introduces the biographer's subject, but throughout the remainder of the selection Sandburg's method is very different from Freeman's. Approximately what proportion of the selection focuses directly upon Lincoln and what proportion might be considered background? What device has the biographer used to relate the background to the subject? About how many episodes in Lincoln's life does the selection treat of? Could a method such as Sandburg uses here be used as successfully with "The Surrender at Appomattox," which covers only one episode? In general, to what extent do you believe the character of the subject matter determines the method of the biographer?

Country Schoolteacher

JESSE STUART

The selection which follows is quite different from the two preceding ones. Those were biographical, small excerpts from detailed lives of great men whose every act is now a part of history. This is autobiographical, a portion of Jesse Stuart's warm-hearted and enthusiastic account of his years as a teacher entitled *The Thread That Runs So True.*

Jesse Stuart, whom the world knows today as poet and novelist, was born and raised in W-Hollow in the Kentucky mountains. He was not yet eighteen when he began his teaching career at Lonesome Valley rural school, thirty miles from his home. Five years later, having in the intervening years worked in a steel mill and made his way through college, he was engaged as the only teacher in the new rural high school of Winston, Kentucky. The school was a crumbling old building which had once been used as a lodge hall, but here for the first time the boys and girls of Winston, cut off from the outside world by high mountain walls and the lack of hard roads, had a chance for a high-school education.

WHEN I had first come to Winston, I wondered what my pupils did for recreation. I wondered what I would do for recreation. I had thought reading was about the only kind of recreation. It didn't take me long to learn differently. One evening in September I was invited to Bill Madden's home. He was one of my pupils. His father had invited six or seven of the local musicians in to play for us. We sat in the yard where the grass was dying and the peach-tree leaves had turned golden and the moon was high in the sky above us. We listened to this local band play with their banjos, fiddles, guitar, mandolin, and accordion from seven until eleven. They never played the same tune twice, and often when they played a fast breakdown, one of the listeners would dance. I had never heard old-time music sound as beautiful as this, in the moonlight of the mild September evening.

There was hardly a family in this big vicinity who didn't have a musician. This was part of their recreation. People had learned to play musical instruments to furnish their own music just as they had learned to plant, cultivate, and harvest crops for their food supply. They depended upon themselves for practically everything.

I went with my pupils, their parents, and neighbors to cornhuskings, apple-peelings, bean-stringings,[1] square dances, and to the belling of the bride[2] when there was a wedding. Often we rode mules many miles through darkness or moonlight to these community events....This was the most democratic recreation I had ever seen.

Not one of my pupils had ever seen a stage play. If one had ever seen a movie, I'd never heard of it. They didn't have to leave land-locked Winston to find recreation. They had it at home. They created it just as they created most of their necessities of life. As the autumn days wore on they popped corn over the blazing wood fires and made molasses-and-popcorn balls. There was somewhere to go every night. I couldn't accept all the invitations. Each pupil invited me to his home to spend the night. This was an old custom, for in the past years the teacher had boarded with his pupils, since his salary wasn't enough to enable him to pay his board and have anything left.

When the hunting season came, I hunted quail with my pupils. I hunted rabbits with them in the Tiber[3] weed fields. My pupils were good marksmen. But I gave them a few surprises at some of the shots I made. I had never told them about my years of hunting experience. I went to the autumn-coloring hills to hunt possums. And I taught them—as I had tried to teach them high-school subjects—a little about possum hunting: that on the still and misty,

---

[1]*cornhuskings, apple-peelings, bean-stringings,* social gatherings at which the neighbors came together to help one another get their crops ready for winter use.
[2]*the belling of the bride,* a shivaree (shiv ə rē′), or noisy serenade for a newly married couple.
[3]*the Tiber,* the river that flows through the valley.

warm nights when not a leaf stirred was the time to catch possums and coons. When I learned more about the terrain of the east and west walls,[4] where the persimmons and papaws grew, I showed them where to find the possums. They—as I had once done—hunted for animal pelts, shipped them, and bought books and clothes with the money. I showed them how to take better care of their pelts....

When the leaves changed color in the valley and the sun was bright as a brush-pile flame, I went on long hikes with my pupils. We'd take a hike to the autumn-colored hills soon as the school day was over. We'd take food to cook over an open fire on the summit of one of the walls that enclosed the valley. Sometimes the girls would go with us. The hike to the highest summits was often a strenuous climb....

Down in the valley we could see every splash of color. Green leaves were there still, for the Tiber mists had protected them against the biting frost. There were blood-red shoe-make[5] leaves, golden sycamore and poplar leaves, slate-colored water-birch leaves, and the dull- and bright-gold willow leaves. And down in the valley the corn shocks stood like wigwams in an Indian village. We could see the bright knee-high corn stubble glittering in the autumn sun. We could see the brown meadow stubble, too, where the hay had been mown and piled in high mounds with poles through the center.

Often I walked alone beside the Tiber in autumn. For there was a somberness that put me in a mood that was akin to poetry. I'd

watch the big sycamore leaves zigzag from the interlocking branches above to the clear blue Tiber water and drift away like tiny golden ships. I'd find the farewell-to-summer[6] in bloom along this river. Then a great idea occurred to me. It wasn't about poetry. It was about schools.

I thought if every teacher in every school in America—rural, village, city, township, church, public, or private—could inspire his pupils with all the power he had, if he could teach them as they had never been taught before to live, to work, to play, and to share, if he could put ambition into their brains and hearts, that would be a great way to make a generation of the greatest citizenry America had ever had. All of this had to begin with the little unit. Each teacher had to do his share. Each teacher was responsible for the destiny of America, because the pupils came under his influence. The teacher held the destiny of a great country in his hand as no member of any other profession could hold it. All other professions stemmed from the products of his profession....

When I told my pupils about a scholastic contest with Landsburgh High School, I watched their expressions. They were willing and ready for the challenge. The competitive spirit was in them.

"We must review everything we have covered in our textbooks," I told them. "We must cover more territory in our textbooks too. Hold up your right hands if you are willing!"

Every pupil raised his hand.

Right then we started to work. In addition to regular assignments, my pupils began reviewing all of the old assignments we had covered.

Despite the challenge ahead and all the reviewing and study we planned to do, we never stopped play. The Tiber River was frozen over. The ring of skates and merry laughter broke the stillness of the winter nights. We skated on the white winding ribbon of ice beneath the high, cold winter moon....

Over the weekends we'd go to Tiber, where we'd cut holes in the ice and gig fish. The boys

[4]*walls,* the hills that enclosed the valley in which Winston was situated.

[5]*shoe-make,* sumac.

[6]*farewell-to-summer,* a late-blooming aster.

and I would rabbit-hunt up and down the Tiber Valley in the old stubble fields now covered with snow and swept by wind....When we hunted, the girls didn't go with us, but when we skated, fished, and rode sleighs, they went along. There was a long gentle slope not far from the schoolhouse, we found ideal for our sleighs. It was almost a mile to the end of our sleigh run. We went over the river bank and downstream for many yards on the Tiber ice. We rode sleighs during the noon hour, before and after school.

On winter days when the snow had melted, leaving the dark earth a sea of sloppy mud, we designed floor games for our little one-room school. They were simple games such as throwing bolts in small boxes. And we played darts. We also played a game called "fox and goose." We made our fox-and-goose boards and we played with white, yellow, and red grains of corn. We had to make our own recreation. I never saw a distracted look on a pupil's face. I never heard one complain that the short, dark winter days were boresome because there wasn't anything to do. I think each pupil silently prayed for the days to be longer. We were a united little group. We were small, but we were powerful. We played hard, and we studied hard. We studied and played while the December days passed.

That day in early January, we dismissed school....This was the big day for us. It was too bad that another blizzard had swept our rugged land and that a stinging wind was smiting the valleys and the hills. But this didn't stop the boys and me from going. Leona Maddox, my best Latin pupil, couldn't go along. Her father, Alex Maddox, wouldn't let her ride a mule seventeen miles to Landsburgh to compete in a contest on a day like this. I couldn't persuade him to let her go.

On that cold blizzardy morning, Budge Waters[7] rode his mule to school very early and built a fire in the potbellied stove. When the rest of us arrived on our mules at approximately seven o'clock, Budge had the schoolroom warm. We tied our mules to the fence, stood before the fire, and warmed ourselves before we started on our journey. Then we unhitched our mules from the fence and climbed into the saddles. Little clouds of frozen snow in powdery puffs arose from the mules' hoofs as six pupils and their teacher rode down the road.

Though the force of wind in the Tiber Valley was powerful, it was at our backs. The wind was strong enough to give our mules more momentum. We made good time until we left the valley and climbed the big hill. Here, we faced the wind. It was a whipping wind—stinging, biting wind on this mountain—that made the water run from our eyes and our mules' eyes, but for us there was no turning back. We were going to Landsburgh High School. That was that. We were determined to meet this big school—big to us, for they outnumbered us twenty-six to one. Soon we were down in Hinton Valley. Then we rode to the top of the Raccoon Hill, where we faced the stinging wind again.

"Mr. Stuart, I have been thinking," Budge Waters said, as we rode along together, "if you can sleep in a fodder shock when it's twelve degrees below zero, we can take this contest from Landsburgh High School! I've not forgotten how you walked seventeen miles to carry us books.[8] All of your pupils remember. We'll never let you down!"

Budge Waters thought of this because we were riding down the mountain where I had slept that night. Then we rode down into the Raccoon Valley, and Billie Leonard, only thir-

---

[7]*Budge Waters,* a remarkably brilliant boy, the best student in the school.

[8]*I've not forgotten...carry us books.* Mr. Stuart had set out on foot to walk the seventeen miles to Landsburgh and bring back some books for his pupils. Lost in a blinding snowstorm, he had suffered great hardships. But he brought the books back.

teen years old, complained of numbness in his hands, feet, and lips. He said he felt as if he was going to sleep....We stopped at a home, tied our mules to the fence, and went in and asked to warm. Bert Patton, a stranger to us, piled more wood on the open fire until we were as warm as when we had left the schoolhouse. We told him who we were and where we were going.

"On a day like this!" he said, shaking his head sadly.

We climbed into the saddles again. We were over halfway now. The second hitch would put us at Landsburgh High School. We had valley all the way to Landsburgh, with walls of rugged hills on each side for windbreaks.

At eleven o'clock we rode across the Landsburgh High School yard, and hitched our mules to the fence around the athletic field. There were faces against the windowpanes watching us. Then we walked inside the high school, where Principal Ernest Charters met and welcomed us. He told us that he was surprised we had come on a day like this and that we had been able to arrive so soon.

In the principal's office my pupils and I huddled around the gas stove while we heard much laughter in the high-school corridors. The Landsburgh High School pupils thought we were a strange-looking lot. Many came inside their principal's office to take a look at us. We were regarded with curiosity, strangeness, and wonder. Never before had these pupils seen seven mules hitched to their schoolyard fence. Never before had they competed scholastically with so few in number—competitors who had reached them by muleback. The Landsburgh High School principal didn't feel about the contest the way we felt. To him, this was just a "setup" to test his pupils for the district contest which would soon be held. He told me this when he went after the sealed envelopes that held the questions. We warmed before the gas stove while he made arrangements for the contest.

"These questions were made out by the state department of education," he said when he returned. "I don't know how hard they are."

My pupils stood silently by the stove and looked at each other. We were asked to go to one of the largest classrooms. A Landsburgh High School teacher had charge of giving the tests. When the Landsburgh High School pupils came through the door to compete against my pupils, we knew why Principal Charters had selected this large classroom. My pupils looked at each other, then at their competitors.

I entered redheaded Jesse Jarvis to compete with ten of their plane-geometry pupils. I entered Billie Leonard against twenty-one of their selected algebra pupils.

"Budge, you'll have to represent us in grammar, English literature, and history," I said. "And I believe I'll put you in civil government. Is that all right?"

"Yes," he agreed. Budge had never had a course in civil government. All he knew about it was what he had read in connection with history.

"Robert Batson, you enter in history and grammar.

"Robin Baylor, you enter in algebra.

"Snookie Baylor, you enter in algebra and plane geometry.

"Sorry, Mr. Charters," I said, "we don't have anyone to enter in Latin. My best Latin pupil, Leona Maddox, couldn't make this trip."

After the contest had begun, I left the room. Miss Bertha Madden was in charge. I took our mules to Walter Scott's barn on the east end of Landsburgh, where I fed and watered them.

With the exception of an interval when the contestants ate a quick lunch, the contest lasted until 2:30 P.M. I had one pupil, Budge Waters, in four contests. I had planned to enter him in two. Just as soon as Budge had finished with civil government, we started grading the papers. All the pupils were requested to leave the room.

We graded the papers with keys. Mr. Charters, Miss Madden, and two other teachers, and I did the grading. Mr. Charters read the answers on the keys, and we checked the answers. Once or twice we stopped long enough to discuss what stiff questions these were. We wondered how far we would have gotten if we—all of us, college graduates—had taken the same test. One of the teachers asked me, while we graded these papers, if Budge Waters had ever seen these questions before.

When we were through grading the papers, Mr. Charters called the contestants into the classroom.

"I want to read you the scores of this contest," he said. His voice was nervous.

"Budge Waters, winner in English literature.

"Budge Waters, winner in grammar.

"Budge Waters, winner in history with almost a perfect score.

"Budge Waters, winner in civil government.

"Why didn't you bring just this one boy?" Principal Charters asked me.

"Because I've got other good pupils," I quickly retorted.

"Billie Leonard, winner in algebra, with plenty of points to spare.

"Jesse Jarvis, second in plane geometry.

"Snookie Baylor and Robin Baylor tied for second place in algebra.

"Congratulations," said Principal Charters, "to your pupils and to you, on your success. It looks as though Winston High will represent this county in the district scholastic contest. I've never heard of such a remarkable thing."

When we left the Landsburgh High School we heard defeated pupils crying because "a little mudhole in the road like Winston beat us."

In a few minutes our mule cavalcade passed the Landsburgh High School. Faces were against the windowpanes and many pupils waved jubilantly to us as we rode by, our coattails riding the wind behind our saddles, and the ends of our scarfs bright banners on the wind. We rode victoriously down the main street of Landsburgh on our way home.

MAN AND TEACHER

1. Jesse Stuart saw the teacher's duty as helping pupils "to live, to work, to play, and to share." Judging from this selection, would you say he was successful in carrying out this idea? Cite examples from the text to support your answer.

2. To what causes do you attribute the unusual success of the Winston pupils in the contest?

3. Although in this autobiographical selection the author constantly directs the reader's attention to his pupils, we gain a clear idea of the author himself. What qualities would you say Jesse Stuart possessed? How did you learn he had these qualities?

4. Contrast this selection with Mark Twain's account of his own experiences in "Life on the Farm" (pages 229-233) and "The Boys' Ambition" (pages 414-416). Point out the ways in which each author makes use of sensory imagery to give a vivid background to his story. In which of these selections do you get the clearest picture of the man who is telling the story?

Know your words

The English language is the richest, most flexible in the world. One reason is the fact that practically every nation has contributed words to it. You have learned that many commonly used English words are of Latin origin and that French words also have become an important part of the language. But many of the simple words Jesse Stuart uses in "Country Schoolteacher" are neither Latin nor French in derivation. Tracing the origin of some of them will give you a better idea of how the English language came to be the rich instrument that it is.

Look up, in an unabridged dictionary, the italicized words in the sentences below. On a sheet of paper write the word, and after the word note the language or languages from which it was derived.

1. Recreation in Winston was very *democratic*.
2. Groups of people got together to play *banjos, guitars,* and *mandolins*.
3. In autumn the boys hunted *raccoons* and *opossums* on the mountainsides where *papaws* and *persimmons* grew.
4. Scarlet *sumac* glowed in the valley, and the yellow corn *shocks* stood like *wigwams*.
5. In winter *skating* and *sleighing* were popular.

The Priceless Gift of Laughter

All biographies are not book-length. There have always been shorter biographies, usually recountings of a great man's life written for children. But of recent years short biographies for adults have become increasingly popular. Often called *profiles,* these vivid and readable accounts usually treat of contemporary figures. In easily read, often colloquial language, they touch the highlights in the careers of military men and artists, manufacturers and explorers. Occasionally, as in the news magazines, these profiles are unsigned by the author. The sketch of James Thurber, which is printed below, typifies this type of biography.

JAMES GROVER THURBER was born in Columbus in 1894, second of the three children of Charles Leander and Mary Agnes Fisher Thurber. Their other sons were William, a year older than Jim, and Robert, two years younger.

Charley Thurber, the boys' father, was tall, thin, an inveterate wearer of derby hats and by profession an unsuccessful politician. Although he kept running for various offices until he was nearly sixty-five, he never got elected to any. When there were six leading candidates for five offices, Charley Thurber would invariably finish sixth. Too honest to play ball with a political machine,[1] and too amiable and gentle to be a winning maverick,[2] he was a chronic also-ran.

In return for his unflagging idealism and perseverance, he received appointments that were largely drudgery: secretary to two governors of Ohio (Asa Bushnell and William McKinley[3]), to a mayor of Columbus; member of a committee to investigate hazing at West Point; state organizer for Teddy Roosevelt's unsuccessful Bull Moose campaign for the presidency in 1912,[4] etc. In a piece called "Gentleman from Indiana,"[5] Jim has written lovingly and beautifully of his father.

In contrast to her mild, quiet husband, who never scolded the boys, Mamie Thurber was a hurled hand grenade. The class comic in school, a star at amateur theatricals, for a while she considered running away from home and going on the professional stage. Her stern Methodist father scotched that, clamping down on even the amateur theatricals, but it made no difference. Mamie kept right on performing.

---

[1] *to play ball with a political machine,* to engage in dishonest dealings in order to gain votes as the political organization demanded.

[2] *maverick* (mav′ər ik), a man who runs independently of a regular political party.

[3] *William McKinley,* later president of the United States. He served from 1897 until he was assassinated in 1901.

[4] *Teddy Roosevelt's unsuccessful Bull Moose campaign...in 1912.* In 1909, having filled out McKinley's term and served a term of his own, Roosevelt retired from the Presidency. But in 1912 he decided 'o run again for president as a Progressive. He lost. Hi party was nicknamed the "Bull Moose" party.

[5] *"Gentleman from Indiana."* Thurber calls his father by this name because the older Thurber was born and raised in Indiana.

"The Priceless Gift of Laughter." Courtesy of *Time.* Copyright Time Inc., 1951.

Once at a buffet luncheon she found a bowl of uncooked eggs waiting to be used for eggnogs. "You know, I've always wanted to throw a dozen eggs," she said to nobody in particular. Whereupon she selected a dozen and threw them at the nearest wall, not missing it once.

Another time, she attended an overflow meeting conducted by a faith healer, who with his exhortations and layings-on-of-hands had set Columbus afire. Somehow she got hold of a stretcher, lay down on it, and had a couple of friends carry her toward the platform. Half way down the aisle, Mamie flipped to her feet, yelling, "I can walk! I can walk! It's the first time I've walked in forty years!" Hundreds wept or screamed at the miracle.

Mamie Thurber has gone on performing. Her husband died in 1939 at the age of seventy-two, but she is still at it, an amazing old lady of eighty-five, with piercing grey eyes under black brows, and none of her staggering faculties impaired. Wolcott Gibbs, of *The New Yorker*, has written of Thurber's "sure grasp of confusion." Nobody who ever heard Jim's mother tell a long, detailed, uproarious misadventure story would wonder where his sureness of grasp came from. There are old-timers in Columbus who insist that Jim is but his mother's pale copy.

The five Thurbers constituted a family unit, but they were also a kind of club. Things were apt to be quite electric around the house; just how electric Jim has described in *My Life and Hard Times*, a book which many Thurberites consider his most durable masterpiece.[6] Sometimes it got a little overwhelming for Charley Thurber. In Jim's story, "The Night the Bed Fell," occurs the sentence, "It happened, then, that my father had decided to sleep in the attic...to be away where he could think."

Thurber family sessions were marked by plenty of mimicry. William and Robert were good mimics (and still are), but Jim was even better. One day, during their young manhood, he phoned William and pretended to be a tailor, claiming in dialect to have made a suit for him

which had not been called for, and demanding to be paid. Flabbergasted, William swore he had never ordered the suit and finally put his mother on the phone. After some angry argument, she challenged the tailor to describe William. "Ha!" said Jim. "It's a fine mudder dat don't even know her own son."

Outside the family, Jim was shy through grammar and high school and his first two years at Ohio State University, where he did little else than sit reading in the library with his hair in his eyes, looking like an emaciated sheep dog. After testing him, the psychology department reported that he had a remarkable memory. Unkempt, unloved, and unknown, he was on his way to a Phi Beta Kappa key,[7] perhaps to a life of scholarship.

But one fateful day in a junior-year English class, the professor, William Lucius Graves, read aloud a student theme entitled, "My Literary Enthusiasms," in which the dime novels of the day were wittily treated. Before he had a chance to announce the writer's name, the bell rang, and the students streamed out. Thurber found himself walking alongside Elliott Nugent, who was everything on the campus that Thurber was not—athlete, social success, best actor in the dramatic club, class president, idol of the coeds.[8]

"Gee, that was a swell piece, wasn't it?" Nugent remarked to the weedy stranger beside him. "I wonder who wrote it." Thurber swallowed, "I did," he said in a dim voice. Nugent stared at Thurber, then introduced himself. The two became best and lifelong friends.

Nugent made Thurber get his hair cut and buy a new blue suit, then got him into his own fraternity, Phi Kappa Psi. Thurber blossomed and expanded. He became an editor of the college daily and editor-in-chief of the humorous monthly, acted for the dramatic club, was elected to the senior honor society.

---

[6]*"My Life and Hard Times"...masterpiece.* "University Days" (pages 607-611) is taken from this book.

[7]*a Phi Beta Kappa* (fī' bā'tə kap'ə) *key,* a small gold key which signifies membership in a national society of college students who have ranked high in scholarship.

[8]*Elliott Nugent...idol of the coeds.* Nugent's campus success endured into his later life. He won fame as actor, director, and playwright. He and Thurber wrote one play, *The Male Animal,* together, and Nugent was the star of the production.

He did not wait to graduate, for by then the U.S. was at war with Germany and he wanted to do something about it. Unable to enlist in the armed forces because of his eye,[9] he entered the State Department and served a year and a half as code clerk at the American embassy in Paris. With that memory of his, Jim was an outstanding code clerk. One of his colleagues in the code room was a young Yale poet named Stephen Vincent Benét.

After returning from Paris in 1920, Thurber went to work as a reporter on the Columbus *Dispatch*, where he stayed three years, mostly covering the City Hall beat.[10] To Thurber's city editor, the pattern of a perfect lead for all stories whatsoever was: "John Holtsapple, 63, prominent Columbus galosh manufacturer, died of complications last night, at his home, 396 N. Persimmon Blvd." Any attempts by the staff to get wit or originality into the paper usually landed on the spike.[11] The city editor who began by addressing Thurber as "Author" and "Phi Beta Kappa," came to respect him, but Thurber still sees this Legree[12] in a recurring anxiety dream: "He runs up to my desk with a shoe in his hand and says, 'We've got just ten minutes to get this shoe in the paper.' Boy, do I move!"

In 1922, Thurber married Althea Adams, then a sophomore at Ohio State and one of the prettiest girls on the campus. He was chafing to write something better than city-council doings, but had little confidence in his ability to make good outside Columbus. Urged on by Althea, he finally decided to assault New York by way of France, which he had loved in his code-clerk days. When they had saved up $125, they took off.

After the novel Jim started in a Normandy[13] farmhouse had petered out, the Thurbers went to Paris. He got a job on the Paris edition of the Chicago *Tribune* at $12 a week. The Paris *Trib*'s cable tolls were in keeping with the princely salaries it paid its staff: a fat fifty words of variegated news arrived from America each night. Once Jim was handed a flimsy containing the line, "Christy Mathewson died Saranac,"[14] and from memory and by Ouija board[15] wrote a column obituary on the great New York Giants pitcher.

The summer of 1951 marks the twenty-fifth anniversary of Jim Thurber's arrival in New York City. Knowing only Columbus and Paris, he loathed New York at first, with its roar, its dirt, its jostle, and the brash ways of its citizenry. But he got a job as reporter on the *Evening Post,* which reduced its price from 5¢ to 3¢ the day he went to work.

That fall and winter, he bombarded *The New Yorker*, a struggling humorous weekly little more than a year old, with twenty pieces, all of which were rejected. Althea argued that he was sweating too much over them and suggested that he bat one out in forty-five minutes. On his next Sunday off, he did. It was about a man who got caught in a revolving door. *The New Yorker* bought it.

During the four years he was a reporter, Thurber registered countless impressions that he could not have gotten into any newspaper. These were filed away in his memory, and he began working them into enchanting monologues for the amusement of his friends. In the '20s and '30s, to sit with drink in hand and listen to Jim Thurber off on a free-association talking marathon[16] was an indescribable pleasure. When he used to mimic Harold Ross,[17] he even looked like Ross, an incredible accomplishment.

---

[9]*Unable to enlist...because of his eye.* At the age of six Thurber lost his left eye when one of his brothers accidentally shot him with an arrow. The other eye began to fail after about forty years and Thurber became almost blind.

[10]*the City Hall beat.* Reporters got leads for news stories at the City Hall.

[11]*landed on the spike,* were rejected by the editor.

[12]*Legree* (lə grē′). Simon Legree is a character in *Uncle Tom's Cabin,* by Harriet Beecher Stowe. A brutal and hard-driving planter, his name has come to symbolize any cruel boss.

[13]*Normandy,* a district in northwestern France.

[14]*Saranac,* a health resort situated on Saranac Lake in the Adirondack Mountains of northern New York.

[15]*by Ouija* (wē′jə) *board,* by guesswork. The Ouija board is a fortunetelling device that is supposed to answer questions.

[16]*a free-association talking marathon,* a long monologue in which one subject led freely and without interruption to another.

[17]*Harold Ross,* editor of *The New Yorker.* He died in 1951.

One night in 1927 at a small party in Greenwich Village,[18] Thurber met E. B. White, who was already doing "Notes and Comments" on the front page of *The New Yorker's* "Talk of the Town" section.[19] White was immediately taken with him; a little later, he recommended him to Ross as a "Talk" reporter and writer.

Not long after Ross hired him, Thurber was puzzled to find that he had a secretary, which he had never heard of a reporter having; he supposed that things were different on magazines. He was amazed when she handed him the office weekly payroll to sign, and the fine print of the "Goings On" department[20] to check and O.K. He asked her why, and her answer left him thunderstruck. "Because you're the managing editor," she said.

In that era, *New Yorker* managing editors had a life expectancy hardly greater than that of May flies.[21] In addition to hiring and firing managing editors, Ross was combating his restlessness by having the office walls torn down. The editorial floor was cluttered with scaffolding; workmen bashed out plaster and lath with sledge hammers and crowbars; a chalky haze permeated the halls, assailing the lungs of staff and visiting contributors.

Thurber wanted to write. He hated being managing editor, but Ross kept encouraging him. Once in an editorial conference, Ross snarled, "This week's issue has more mistakes in it than any we ever published. Who's responsible?" Hope rising in his breast, Thurber shot up his hand. "Good," Ross said. "Only honest managing editor I ever had."

Thurber stood it for six months and, in spite of his misery as an executive, managed to write seven pieces that were accepted, but for which he did not get paid. At last Ross said, "I guess you're a writer. All right then, write." So Thurber continued to write pieces and, in addition,

he and White and one legman[22] for seven and one-half straight years got out "The Talk of the Town," which, nowadays, requires virtually a platoon. Between them, White and Thurber pretty much set the tone of the magazine.

Thurber learned a great deal from White, and he is the first to acknowledge the debt. "I learned more about writing from White than from anybody," he has said. "He taught me to write a simple declarative sentence. I still send my things to him to read."

Of his old colleague, White has written: "Most writers would be glad to settle for any one of ten of Thurber's accomplishments. He has written the funniest memoirs, fables, reports, satires, fantasies, complaints, fairy tales, and sketches of the past twenty years, has gone into the drama and the cinema, and on top of that has littered the world with thousands of drawings. Most writers and artists can be compared fairly easily with contemporaries. Thurber inhabits a world of his own.

"When I first knew him, his mind was unbelievably restless and made him uncomfortable at all hours. Now, almost twenty-five years later, I can't see that it has relaxed. He still pulls at his hair and trembles all over, as though he were about to sell his first piece. His thoughts have always been a tangle of baseball scores, Civil War tactical problems, Henry James,[23] personal maladjustments, terrier puppies, literary tide rips,[24] ancient myths and modern apprehensions. Through this jungle stalk the unpredictable ghosts of his relatives in Columbus, Ohio."

In 1935, Jim and Althea were divorced. Their daughter, Rosemary, has just finished her sophomore year at the University of Pennsylvania. She has shown marked acting talent, perhaps inherited from her paternal grandmother. Thurber is an affectionate father; he and his daughter get along splendidly.

Jim always had a taste for handsome women, and the year of his divorce he married Helen

---

[18]*Greenwich* (gren'ich) *Village,* a section of New York City famous as a district in which artists and writers live.
[19]*"Talk of the Town" section,* several pages of brief articles or comments on all kinds of topics, some humorous, some serious.
[20]*the "Goings On" department,* a section in *The New Yorker* which gives information about current theater productions, movies, sports events, musical affairs, etc.
[21]*May flies,* insects which mature rapidly and then quickly die.

---

[22]*legman,* reporter, or man who goes out on foot to get the news.
[23]*Henry James,* a famous American novelist who lived from 1843 to 1916.
[24]*literary tide rips,* matters of current interest or note in the literary world.

Wismer, a clergyman's daughter, Mount Holyoke[25] graduate and the former editor of a string of pulp magazines.[26] She expertly manages his business and his home, and has helped him enormously in conquering his blindness. The Thurbers spend part of every winter and spring in Hot Springs, Virginia, and Bermuda.[27] Summer and fall they live in their beautiful twelve-room, ninety-year-old house on sixty-five acres of land in West Cornwall, Connecticut.

Ambivalent is probably the word for Thurber. Although he believes he is essentially optimistic about the human species, he tends to nurse doubt when he rolls the subject around in his mind: "The human species is both horrible and wonderful. Occasionally, I get very mad at human beings, but there's nothing you can do about it. I like people and hate them at the same time. I wouldn't draw them in cartoons, if I didn't think they were horrible; and I wouldn't write about them, if I didn't think they were wonderful."

That, however, might be what his wife calls Jim's Friday Opinion. By the following Monday he may have reversed himself, or be fretting over something different. For humorists, there are not many fixed rules; about the only thing they are consistently against is pomposity.

During wassail, Thurber's ambivalence can snap loose and he may be given to bursts of hooting and hollering. A *New Yorker* editor once returned to the office after a stormy evening at the Algonquin Hotel[28] and thoughtfully announced, "Thurber is the greatest guy in the world up to 5 P.M." Those who love Thurber ascribe such outbursts to old-fashioned artistic temperament and simply shrug them off. They know that when real troubles arise, there is nobody more steadfast and generous. The jams he has helped and comforted friends through are without number.

[25]*Mount Holyoke,* a college for women situated at South Hadley, Massachusetts.
[26]*pulp magazines,* magazines printed on cheap paper made of wood pulp and usually containing cheap or sensational material.
[27]*Bermuda,* a group of British islands lying in the Atlantic almost six hundred miles off the coast of North Carolina.
[28]*the Algonquin Hotel,* a favorite meeting place of literary men.

1. This biography first appeared as an unsigned article in a news magazine. With what groups of readers do you believe it was most popular? What did you like best about it?

2. What idea of James Thurber do you get from reading this article? Do you see any resemblances between Thurber, as he is presented here, and the writer as he pictures himself in "University Days" (pages 607-611)? Explain. What light does your comparison throw upon Thurber's way of writing?

3. What picture of James Thurber's father and mother does the article give you? Why do you think material on them was included in the profile?

4. Contrast the style of this article with that of the other selections you have read in this unit. Which selection is most colloquial in the form of its sentences and in its use of words? Which is most poetical? Which moves forward most rapidly?

Know your words

Explain why each of these statements is true or false:

1. All her life Mrs. Thurber has been an *inveterate* performer.
2. James Thurber's *ambivalence* gradually prevented him from seeing very well.
3. He always hated *pomposity* because he himself was a man of few words.
4. E. B. White and Harold Ross were *contemporaries* of James Thurber.
5. Thurber's skill in *mimicry* was apparent in his imitations of Harold Ross.

Extending interests

If you've enjoyed this profile of Thurber, you'll be interested in reading more of these brief modern biographies. Among magazines you might consult for articles of this type are *The New Yorker, Time, Life, The Saturday Evening Post, Coronet, Colliers,* and *The Reader's Digest.* Arrange with your teacher for a class period at which you and your classmates may exchange information about the profiles you have read. Questions like the following may serve as a guide to the discussion:

1. What class of men—military leaders, business men, authors, etc.—are most frequently written about?
2. How would you describe the style of most of these profiles?
3. Why do you think these brief biographies are extremely popular today?

The Larger View

I. Talk over the following questions. The reading you have done will help you make a valuable contribution to the group discussion, but an alert, thoughtful mind will help even more.

1. Biography has been a popular literary form since the days of the ancient Greeks and Romans. How do you account for its long-continued popularity? What do you believe is the chief reason for its great popularity today?

2. It is said that more biographies of Lincoln have been written than of any other American. What aspects of Lincoln's life and character do you think have led to his popularity as a subject for biography?

3. You have read that Franklin wrote his *Autobiography* as a guide to conduct for his son. Why do you believe Jesse Stuart wrote *The Thread That Runs So True*, from which "Country School-teacher" is taken? What reasons do you believe impelled other authors whose autobiographies you have read to write their life stories?

4. Which of the selections you have studied in this unit did you like best? Give reasons for your choice. Did you enjoy any biography you read independently more than the selections? If you did, give its name and author and tell why you preferred it.

5. What, in general, are the qualities that you think any good biography must have?

II. Write a brief biographical sketch of some member of your family or of a friend. If you keep in mind the things you have learned about what constitutes a good biography, you can probably turn out a very interesting sketch. Perhaps you can arrange with your teacher to have the best of these short profiles read aloud in class.

MORE GOOD READING

Many of the finest American biographies and autobiographies have been listed in previous bibliographies in this text. For example, on page 95 you will find mention of John Bakeless' life of Daniel Boone, and on page 96 Constance Rourke's account of Davy Crockett is annotated. The autobiographies of three famous foreign-born Americans—Louis Adamic, Mary Antin, and Edward Bok—are listed on page 137. If you're interested in the biography of a scientist, consult page 177. "The Story of Television: the Life of Philo T. Farnsworth," by George Everson, "George Washington Carver," by Rackham Holt, and "Albert Einstein," by Alma Levinger are all listed here. "Yankee from Olympus; Justice Holmes and His Family," by Catherine Drinker Bowen, annotated on page 225, is a fine biography, as is "Paul Revere and the World He Lived In," by Esther Forbes, noted on page 226. The "Men and Books" unit bibliographies are rich in the stories of literary men, for example, Franklin's famous "Autobiography," on page 319, and Paine's life of Mark Twain, on page 441.

ANTHONY, KATHERINE, *Dolly Madison; Her Life and Times.* (Doubleday) The wife of the fourth President of the United States, a lady whose charm, gaiety, and love of pretty clothes have become legendary, is the subject of this excellent biography. The great figures of Madison, Jefferson, and others move through its pages.

AVERILL, ESTHER, *King Philip, the Indian Chief.* (Harper) As chief of the Wampanoag Indians, King Philip led his people in a war against the New England colonists in the seventeenth century. From this skillful biography the misunderstood Indian chief emerges as a noble figure.

BAKER, RACHEL, *First Woman Doctor; the Story of Elizabeth Blackwell, M.D.* (Messner) Ambitious girls will find courage and inspiration in the story of this woman who fought the prejudices of the 1840's in her struggle to become a doctor.

BOWEN, CATHERINE DRINKER, *John Adams and the American Revolution*. (Little) If you're looking for a first-rate biography, don't miss this splendid account of John Adams' first forty years. Through watching one man as he moves from childhood to maturity, you'll gain a far better understanding of the events which were climaxed by the signing of the Declaration of Independence.

CUNNINGHAM, VIRGINIA, *Paul Laurence Dunbar and His Song*. (Dodd) The life of this talented Negro poet, its successes and its failures, provides unusual and absorbing reading.

EPSTEIN, BERYL and SAMUEL, *Great Houdini; Magician Extraordinary*. (Messner) If you've ever stared wide-eyed at a magician's tricks, you won't be able to resist this entertaining biography of the man who could walk through brick walls and make an elephant disappear from the stage of a theater.

EWEN, DAVID, *Story of George Gershwin*. (Holt) This account of a brilliant musician was written from Ewen's memories of him. You will find the same author's *Story of Irving Berlin* (Holt) an equally fascinating book.

GUNTHER, JOHN, *Roosevelt in Retrospect; a Profile in History*. (Harper) An ace reporter turns his hand to biography and writes an honest study of a great and interesting man. You'll find that reading this biography will help you understand the present-day world.

HEISER, VICTOR GEORGE, *An American Doctor's Odyssey*. (Norton) In forty-five countries scattered around the world Dr. Heiser studied disease, fought epidemics, and worked for public health. But this is not only an inspiring account of a doctor's work—it's also a fascinating adventure story.

JOHNSON, OSA, *I Married Adventure*. (Lippincott) For twenty years the author and her husband, the moving-picture explorer Martin Johnson, adventured in the jungles. This is the exciting story of those years.

KIMBROUGH, EMILY, *Innocents from Indiana*. (Harper) When Emily was eleven and her brother was four, the family moved from Muncie, Indiana, to Chicago. This is the warmly human account of a small-town family's laughs and heartaches in adjusting to life in a city.

ROURKE, CONSTANCE, *Audubon*. (Harcourt) Audubon ventured into Kentucky in the time of Daniel Boone. This is as much a story of adventure in new lands as it is the biography of an artist and naturalist.

SANDBURG, CARL, *Abe Lincoln Grows Up*. (Harcourt) This adaptation from *Abraham Lincoln: The Prairie Years* tells the story of Lincoln's life until he left home at nineteen. It is especially designed for adolescent readers.

STEFFENS, LINCOLN, *Autobiography*. (Harcourt) Steffens was a reporter who devoted his energy to fighting corruption in government. His autobiography is a stirring account of a vital and interesting career.

STUART, JESSE, *The Thread That Runs So True*. (Scribner) Since you've already had a taste of Stuart's delightful record of his teaching days in "Country Schoolteacher," you'll need no further inducement to read the rest of this engrossing autobiography.

TAVES, ISABELLA (editor), *There Were Giants in the Land*. (Rinehart) The authors of these fifty-six biographical sketches of great Americans from Nathan Hale to Woodrow Wilson are all noted writers. These are excellent short biographies.

WARFIELD, FRANCES, *Cotton in My Ears*. (Viking) If you'd like a humorous but courageous account of a young woman's struggle with deafness, read this inspiring autobiography.

UNIT XVII: DRAMA IN AMERICA

DRAMA was a long time developing in America. Colonial America lacked the large centers of population necessary for the support of the theater, and the Puritans were hostile to plays. In New England they were completely outlawed. The cavalier spirit of the South, however, was more hospitable to the drama. A theater was built in Williamsburg, Virginia, as early as 1716, and in Charleston, South Carolina, in 1735. To these theaters, Lewis Hallam brought his "American Company" in 1752, and, except for occasional seasons in New York and Philadelphia, found his main support in Southern towns.

But even though theatrical history began in America with the coming of the American Company, native drama was a long way off. The repertoire of this company consisted of some twenty plays, all by British authors. Americans saw few non-British plays.

❧ I THE DEVELOPMENT OF AMERICAN DRAMA

After the Revolutionary War there was a noticeable lessening of prejudice against the drama. In 1789 Philadelphia repealed its old law against stage plays, and in 1794 Boston had its first theater. The effect of this change in attitude was almost immediate. Native-born Americans began to take over the show business and to use the drama as a means of expressing American character. The most famous as well as the best constructed of the early American plays is *The Contrast,* by Royall Tyler (1757-1826). Throughout this play native American qualities were contrasted with foreign. The stage "Yankee" was introduced, a character who for the next hundred years was to make his regular appearance in American plays to outwit the foreign and the sophisticated with his shrewd horse sense.

Tyler was followed by two professional dramatists, William Dunlap (1766-1839) and John Howard Payne (1791-1852). Each was a prolific writer, but each relied heavily upon foreign themes and models.

As the years passed, drama moved westward with the frontier. By 1830 the American theater extended to the river towns along the Ohio and the Mississippi. New Orleans, St. Louis, and Chicago provided theatrical centers and a frontier audience whose influence upon American drama was felt until the end of the century. Authors as well as managers became very conscious of the box office. The "star" system, familiar in moving pictures today, began to replace the repertory company. Managers began to bid for the most sensational devices of the drama. Actors ranted and swaggered and outdid even the thunderous and impassioned oratory of the day. The successful author had to use all the devices of

melodrama that he could command and to write for the star, whose sole test of a play was the opportunity it provided for him to shine.

Uncle Tom's Cabin, a dramatization of Harriet Beecher Stowe's attack upon slavery, was typical of the plays of this era. It was filled with scenes that kept the audience alternating between laughter and tears, and it presented an array of typed characters, from the saintly Little Eva to the mustached villain, Simon Legree. The wide popularity of this melodrama was a clear indication of the public taste.

II CHANGING TRENDS

Although the theater flourished during the second half of the nine-teenth century, the dramas written by Americans were not particularly good. Melodramas continued to be the principal fare for theatergoers. Toward the close of the century, however, three significant trends gave promise of a new era: (1) Authors began to develop realism in setting, character, and action. (2) They began to discover the drama in real-life problems and to deal with it in their plays. (3) They began to use char-acter and setting as symbols of ideas and to interpret life by this means. Two skilled authors of the period were Clyde Fitch (1865-1909) and William Vaughn Moody (1869-1910).

Fitch proved his skill at historical drama in *Nathan Hale* (1898) and *Barbara Frietchie* (1899). In *The Truth* (1906) he wrote a psycholog-ical study that foreshadowed the mastery that was soon to be revealed by Eugene O'Neill. The most significant play before 1910, however, was by William Vaughn Moody, a man who gained fame as both poet[1] and play-wright. His best play was *The Great Divide,* a study of American char-acter which shows how love refines and ennobles the hero, a crude Westerner, and finally breaks down the Puritan reserve of his wife.

III DRAMA TODAY

The drama of our time offers great opportunities to dramatists, pro-ducers, and audiences. No longer limited to the stage and the printed page, plays are given daily at the neighborhood movie theater and through the magic of radio and television in our very homes. We have become a drama-consuming people. And as never before we are ap-proaching the balance between the interests of author, actor, producer, and the public that is essential for the production of great drama.

Let us look at the circumstances that have brought about this happy situation. Europe played a part in making it possible. Toward the close of the nineteenth century, a Norwegian playwright, Henrik Ibsen, devel-oped a new concept concerning drama. He believed that drama should mirror life and comment upon the evils of society. Ibsen's plays were so powerful that he brought about a renaissance in European drama.

Ibsen's influence was particularly felt in France, Ireland, Russia, and Germany. In each of these countries, groups experimented with the drama. Americans traveling in Europe were so impressed with the force and originality of the new drama that, when they returned to the United

---

[1]For an example of Moody's work as a poet see "The Brute" (pages 155-157).

States, they won others with their enthusiasm. Small groups here and there began writing and producing plays for the sake of artistic expression rather than for commercial gain. Thus the little-theater movement began and spread to almost every sizable community in the nation.

At the same time several colleges began to offer work in writing and producing plays. Under competent instructors at such universities as Harvard, Yale, Stanford, North Carolina, and the Catholic University of America, bands of students worked together in laboratory theaters and frequently produced authors, actors, and directors of a very high order.

It was not long before the little theaters and the drama workshops in colleges and universities began to influence the commercial theater. The American audience which saw their plays soon became more critical and demanded greater artistry and originality from the theater. Three of the little-theater groups became very successful commercial producers and shaped the course of American drama. They are the Theater Guild, formerly the Washington Square Players, organized in 1915; the Provincetown Players, also founded in 1915; and the Group Theater, organized in 1931 by some insurgent members of the Theater Guild. During the last thirty years, many leading figures in the American theater have been associated with one or more of these groups.

Eugene O'Neill (1888-1953)[2]

Heading the list of American writers of the new drama is Eugene O'Neill. The son of an actor, he became familiar with the stage early in life. As a youth he wandered about the world, prospecting for gold in Honduras, shipping to foreign parts as an able seaman. His observations of people and places during these years furnished the inspiration for his first dramas—three one-act plays produced by the Provincetown Players in 1916. Critics have called this performance "the most important event in the recent history of our theater."

O'Neill applied his powers to long plays with even greater success. He experimented constantly, time and again proving that the theater could be utilized in various ways. For example, he wrote *The Emperor Jones* (1921) in eight scenes instead of the usual three acts, and he used flashbacks, which appeared before the eyes of the tortured hero, to show the effect of fear upon human life. In *The Hairy Ape* (1922) he used masked figures to dramatize the struggle of man seeking his rightful place in the mechanized industrial world. In the spectacular *Strange Interlude* (1928) he used soliloquies to unfold in nine acts (really three plays in one) an intense psychological study of a very selfish woman.

O'Neill was a serious writer who devoted himself to the task of interpreting some of the more complex problems of living. He had faults: his characters were rarely normal flesh-and-blood men and women, and he lacked the humor that often tempers the work of supremely great dramatists. In spite of these limitations, he has probed life more thoroughly than any other dramatist of our time and has interpreted some of its tragic aspects in plays that are of a high order.

[2]For a brief biography of Eugene O'Neill see page 486.

Ile

EUGENE O'NEILL

"Ile" is typical of the one-act plays which won the earliest recognition of Eugene O'Neill's ability as a dramatist. Its setting is an ice-bound whaling ship; most of the characters are men. The main character is a monomaniac; that is, he is mentally unbalanced because of an abnormal concentration upon a single idea or object. Here it is whale oil ("ile"). As you read the play, observe the author's treatment of a psychological situation. Watch for evidence of his skill in portraying character, creating atmosphere, and developing a tragic situation to a powerful climax.

CHARACTERS

BEN, *the cabin boy*
THE STEWARD
CAPTAIN KEENEY
SLOCUM, *second mate*[1]
MRS. KEENEY
JOE, *a harpooner*
   Members of the crew of the steam whaler,
        Atlantic Queen

Scene: CAPTAIN KEENEY'S *cabin on board the steam whaling ship* Atlantic Queen—*a small, square compartment about eight feet high with a skylight in the center looking out on the poop deck. On the left (the stern of the ship) a long bench with rough cushions is built in against the wall. In front of the bench, a table. Over the bench, several curtained portholes.*

In the rear, left, a door leading to the CAPTAIN'S *sleeping quarters. To the right of the door a small organ, looking as if it were brand-new, is placed against the wall.*

On the right, to the rear, a marble-topped sideboard. On the sideboard, a woman's sewing basket. Farther forward, a doorway leading

---

[1]*second mate*, the man third in command on the ship. (The captain of the ship and the first mate are his superiors.)

to the companionway, and past the officers' quarters to the main deck.

In the center of the room, a stove. From the middle of the ceiling a hanging lamp is suspended. The walls of the cabin are painted white.

There is no rolling of the ship, and the light which comes through the skylight is sickly and faint, indicating one of those gray days of calm when ocean and sky are alike dead. The silence is unbroken except for the measured tread of someone walking up and down on the poop deck overhead.

It is nearing two bells—one o'clock—in the afternoon of a day in the year 1895.

At the rise of the curtain there is a moment of intense silence. Then the STEWARD *enters and commences to clear the table of the few dishes which still remain on it after the* CAPTAIN'S *dinner. He is an old, grizzled man dressed in dungaree pants, a sweater, and a woolen cap with ear-flaps. His manner is sullen and angry. He stops stacking up the plates and casts a quick glance upward at the skylight; then tiptoes over to the closed door in rear and listens with his ear pressed to the crack. What he hears makes his face darken and he mutters a furious curse. There is a noise from the doorway on the right and he darts back to the table.*

BEN *enters. He is an overgrown, gawky boy with a long, pinched face. He is dressed in sweater, fur cap, etc. His teeth are chattering with the cold and he hurries to the stove, where he stands for a moment shivering, blowing on his hands, slapping them against his sides, on the verge of crying.*

THE STEWARD *(in relieved tones—seeing who it is).* Oh, 'tis you, is it? What're ye shiverin' 'bout? Stay by the stove where ye belong and ye'll find no need of chatterin'.

BEN. It's c-c-cold. *(Trying to control his chattering teeth—derisively.)* Who d'ye think it were—the Old Man?

THE STEWARD *(makes a threatening move—* BEN *shrinks away).* None o' your lip, young un, or I'll learn ye. (More kindly.) Where was it ye've been all o' the time—the fo'c's'tle²?

BEN. Yes.

THE STEWARD. Let the Old Man see ye up for'ard monkeyshinin' with the hands and ye'll get a hidin' ye'll not forget in a hurry.

BEN. Aw, he don't see nothin'. (A trace of awe in his tones—he glances upward.) He jest walks up and down like he didn't notice nobody —and stares at the ice to the no'th'ard.

THE STEWARD (the same tone of awe creeping into his voice). He's always starin' at the ice. (In a sudden rage, shaking his fist at the skylight.) Ice, ice, ice! Damn the ice! Holdin' us in for nigh on a year—nothin' to see but ice— stuck in it like a fly in molasses!

BEN (apprehensively). Ssshh! He'll hear ye.

THE STEWARD (raging). Aye, damn him, and damn the Arctic seas, and damn this stinkin' whalin' ship of his, and damn me for a fool to ever ship on it! (Subsiding as if realizing the uselessness of this outburst—shaking his head— slowly, with deep conviction.) He's a hard man—as hard a man as ever sailed the seas.

BEN (solemnly). Aye.

THE STEWARD. The two years we all signed up for are done this day. Two years o' this dog's life, and no luck in the fishin', and the hands half starved with the food runnin' low, rotten as it is; and not a sign of him turnin' back for home! (Bitterly.) Home! I begin to doubt if ever I'll set foot on land again. (Excitedly.) What is it he thinks he's goin' to do? Keep us all up here after our time is worked out till the last man of us is starved to death or frozen? We've grub enough hardly to last out the voyage back if we started now. What are the men goin' to do 'bout it? Did ye hear any talk in the fo'c's'tle?

BEN (going over to him—in a half whisper). They said if he don't put back south for home today they're goin' to mutiny.

THE STEWARD (with grim satisfaction). Mutiny? Aye, 'tis the only thing they can do; and serve him right after the manner he's treated them— 's if they weren't no better nor dogs.

BEN. The ice is all broke up to s'uth'ard.

They's clear water s'far 's you can see. He ain't got no excuse for not turnin' back for home, the men says.

THE STEWARD (bitterly). He won't look nowheres but no'th'ard where they's only the ice to see. He don't want to see no clear water. All he thinks on is gettin' the ile— 's if it was our fault he ain't had good luck with the whales. (Shaking his head.) I think the man's mighty nigh losin' his senses.

BEN (awed). D'you really think he's crazy?

THE STEWARD. Aye, it's the punishment o' God on him. Did ye ever hear of a man who wasn't crazy do the things he does? (Pointing to the door in rear.) Who but a man that's mad would take his woman—and as sweet a woman as ever was—on a stinkin' whalin' ship to the Arctic seas to be locked in by the rotten ice for nigh on a year, and maybe lose her senses forever—for it's sure she'll never be the same again.

BEN (sadly). She useter be awful nice to me before—(his eyes grow wide and frightened)— she got—like she is.

THE STEWARD. Aye, she was good to all of us. 'Twould have been hell on board without her; for he's a hard man—a hard, hard man— a driver if there ever was one. (With a grim laugh.) I hope he's satisfied now—drivin' her on till she's near lost her mind. And who could blame her? 'Tis a God's wonder we're not a ship full of crazed people—with the ice all the time, and the quiet so thick you're afraid to hear your own voice.

BEN (with a frightened glance toward the door on right). She don't never speak to me no more—jest looks at me 's if she didn't know me.

THE STEWARD. She don't know no one—but him. She talks to him—when she does talk— right enough.

BEN. She does nothin' all day long now but sit and sew—and then she cries to herself without makin' no noise. I've seen her.

THE STEWARD. Aye, I could hear her through the door awhile back.

BEN (tiptoes over to the door and listens). She's cryin' now.

THE STEWARD (furiously—shaking his fist). Blast him for the devil he is!

---

²the fo'c's'tle, the forecastle (fōk′səl or fōr′kas′əl), the sailors' quarters in the forward part of the ship.

[*There is the noise of someone coming slowly down the companionway stairs. The* STEWARD *hurries to his stacked-up dishes. He is so nervous from fright that he knocks off the top one, which falls and breaks on the floor. He stands aghast, trembling with dread.* BEN *is violently rubbing off the organ with a piece of cloth which he has snatched from his pocket.* CAPTAIN KEENEY *appears in the doorway on right and comes into the cabin, removing his fur cap as he does so. He is a man of about forty, around five-ten in height but looking much shorter on account of the enormous proportions of his shoulders and chest. His face is massive and deeply lined, with gray-blue eyes of a bleak hardness, and a tightly clenched, thin-lipped mouth. His thick hair is long and gray. He is dressed in a heavy blue jacket and blue pants stuffed into his sea-boots.*

He is followed into the cabin by the SECOND MATE, *a rangy six-footer with a lean weather-beaten face. The* MATE *is dressed about the same as the* CAPTAIN. *He is a man of thirty or so.*]

KEENEY (*comes toward the* STEWARD *with a stern look on his face. The* STEWARD *is visibly frightened and the stack of dishes rattles in his trembling hands.* KEENEY *draws back his fist and the* STEWARD *shrinks away. The fist is gradually lowered and* KEENEY *speaks slowly*). 'Twould be like hittin' a worm. It is nigh on two bells, Mr. Steward, and this truck not cleared yet.

THE STEWARD (*stammering*). Y-y-yes, sir.

KEENEY. Instead of doin' your rightful work ye've been below here gossipin' old woman's talk with that boy. (*To* BEN, *fiercely.*) Get out o' this, you! Clean up the chart room.[3] (BEN *darts past the* MATE *to the open doorway.*) Pick up that dish, Mr. Steward!

THE STEWARD (*doing so with difficulty*). Yes, sir.

KEENEY. The next dish you break, Mr. Steward, you take a bath in the Bering Sea[4] at the end of a rope.

THE STEWARD (*tremblingly*). Yes, sir.

----

[3]*chart room*, place where compass, maps, etc. are kept.
[4]*Bering* (bēr′ing *or* bãr′ing) *Sea*, a sea between Alaska and Siberia.

[*He hurries out. The* SECOND MATE *walks slowly over to the* CAPTAIN.]

MATE. I warn't 'specially anxious the man at the wheel should catch what I wanted to say to you, sir. That's why I asked you to come below.

KEENEY (*impatiently*). Speak your say, Mr. Slocum.

MATE (*unconsciously lowering his voice*). I'm afeared there'll be trouble with the hands by the look o' things. They'll likely turn ugly, every blessed one o' them, if you don't put back. The two years they signed up for is up today.

KEENEY. And d' you think you're tellin' me somethin' new, Mr. Slocum? I've felt it in the air this long time past. D'you think I've not seen their ugly looks and the grudgin' way they worked?

[*The door in rear is opened and* MRS. KEENEY *stands in the doorway. She is a slight, sweet-faced little woman, primly dressed in black. Her eyes are red from weeping and her face drawn and pale. She takes in the cabin with a frightened glance and stands as if fixed to the spot by some nameless dread, clasping and unclasping her hands nervously. The two men turn and look at her.*]

KEENEY (*with rough tenderness*). Well, Annie?

MRS. KEENEY (*as if awakening from a dream*). David, I— (*She is silent. The* MATE *starts for the doorway.*)

KEENEY (*turning to him—sharply*). Wait!

MATE. Yes, sir.

KEENEY. D'you want anything, Annie?

MRS. KEENEY (*after a pause, during which she seems to be endeavoring to collect her thoughts*). I thought maybe—I'd go up on deck, David, to get a breath of fresh air. (*She stands humbly awaiting his permission. He and the* MATE *exchange a significant glance.*)

KEENEY. It's too cold, Annie. You'd best stay below today. There's nothin' to look at on deck—but ice.

MRS. KEENEY (*monotonously*). I know—ice, ice, ice! But there's nothing to see down here but these walls. (*She makes a gesture of loathing.*)

KEENEY. You can play the organ, Annie.

MRS. KEENEY (dully). I hate the organ. It puts me in mind of home.

KEENEY (a touch of resentment in his voice). I got it jest for you.

MRS. KEENEY (dully). I know. (She turns away from them and walks slowly to the bench on left. She lifts up one of the curtains and looks through a porthole; then utters an exclamation of joy.) Ah, water! Clear water! As far as I can see! How good it looks after all these months of ice! (She turns round to them, her face transfigured with joy.) Ah, now I must go up on deck and look at it, David!

KEENEY (frowning). Best not today, Annie. Best wait for a day when the sun shines.

MRS. KEENEY (desperately). But the sun never shines in this terrible place.

KEENEY (a tone of command in his voice). Best not today, Annie.

MRS. KEENEY (crumbling before this command—abjectly). Very well, David. (She stands there staring straight before her as if in a daze. The two men look at her uneasily.)

KEENEY (sharply). Annie!

MRS. KEENEY (dully). Yes, David.

KEENEY. Me and Mr. Slocum has business to talk about—ship's business.

MRS. KEENEY. Very well, David. (She goes slowly out, rear, and leaves the door three-quarters shut behind her.)

KEENEY. Best not have her on deck if they's goin' to be any trouble.

MATE. Yes, sir.

KEENEY. And trouble they's goin' to be. I feel it in my bones. (Takes a revolver from his coat pocket and examines it.) Got your'n?

MATE. Yes, sir.

KEENEY. Not that we'll have to use 'em—not if I know their breed of dog—jest to frighten 'em up a bit. (Grimly.) I ain't never been forced to use one yit; and trouble I've had by land and by sea s'long as I kin remember, and will have till my dyin' day, I reckon.

MATE (hesitatingly). Then you ain't goin'—to turn back?

KEENEY. Turn back? Mr. Slocum, did you ever hear o' me pointin' s'uth for home with only a measly four hundred barrel of ile in the hold?

MATE (hastily). No, sir—but the grub's gittin' low.

KEENEY. They's enough to last a long time yit, if they're careful with it; and they's plenty o' water.

MATE. They say it's not fit to eat—what's left; and the two years they signed on fur is up today. They might make trouble for you in the courts when we git home.

KEENEY. Let them make what law trouble they kin! I've got to git the ile! (Glancing sharply at the MATE.) You ain't turnin' no sea-lawyer, be you, Mr. Slocum?

MATE (flushing). Not by a sight, sir.

KEENEY. What do the fools want to go home fur now? Their share o' the four hundred barrel wouldn't keep 'em in chewin' terbacco.

MATE (slowly). They wants to git back to their folks an' things, I s'pose.

KEENEY (looking at him searchingly). 'N you want to turn back, too. (The MATE looks down confusedly before his sharp gaze.) Don't lie, Mr. Slocum. It's writ down plain in your eyes. (With grim sarcasm.) I hope, Mr. Slocum, you ain't agoin' to jine the men agin me.

MATE (indignantly). That ain't fair, sir, to say sich things.

KEENEY (with satisfaction). I warn't much afeard o' that, Tom. You been with me nigh on ten year and I've learned ye whalin'. No man kin say I ain't a good master, if I be a hard one.

MATE. I warn't thinkin' of myself, sir— 'bout turnin' home, I mean. (Desperately.) But Mrs. Keeney, sir—seems like she ain't jest satisfied up here, ailin' like—what with the cold an' bad luck an' the ice an' all.

KEENEY (his face clouding—rebukingly but not severely). That's my business, Mr. Slocum. I'll thank you to steer a clear course o' that. (A pause.) The ice'll break up soon to no'th'ard. I could see it startin' today. And when it goes and we git some sun Annie'll perk up. (Another pause—then he bursts forth.) It ain't the money what's keepin' me up in the northern seas, Tom. But I can't go back to Homeport with a measly four hundred barrel of ile. I'd die fust. I ain't never come back home in all my days without a full ship. Ain't that truth?

MATE. Yes, sir; but this voyage you been icebound, an'—

KEENEY (scornfully). And d'you s'pose any of 'em would believe that—any o' them skippers I've beaten voyage after voyage? Can't you hear 'em laughin' and sneerin'—Tibbots 'n' Harris 'n' Simms and the rest—and all o' Homeport makin' fun o' me? "Dave Keeney what boasts he's the best whalin' skipper out o' Homeport comin' back with a measly four hundred barrel of ile?" (The thought of this drives him into a frenzy, and he smashes his fist down on the marble top of the sideboard.) I got to git the ile, I tell you. How could I figger on this ice? It's never been so bad before in the thirty year I been acomin' here. And now it's breakin' up. In a couple o' days it'll be all gone. And they's whale here, plenty of 'em. I know they is and I ain't never gone wrong yit. I got to git the ile! I got to git it, and I ain't agoin' home till I do git it!

[There is the sound of subdued sobbing from the door in rear. The two men stand silent for a moment, listening. Then KEENEY goes over to the door and looks in. He hesitates for a moment as if he were going to enter—then closes the door softly. JOE, the harpooner, an enormous six-footer with a battered, ugly face, enters from right and stands waiting for the CAPTAIN to notice him.]

KEENEY (turning and seeing him). Don't stand there like a gawk, Harpooner. Speak up!

JOE (confusedly). We want—the men, sir— they wants to send a depitation[5] aft to have a word with you.

KEENEY (furiously). Tell 'em to go to— (Checks himself and continues grimly.) Tell 'em to come. I'll see 'em.

JOE. Aye, aye, sir. (He goes out.)

KEENEY (with a grim smile). Here it comes, the trouble you spoke of, Mr. Slocum, and we'll make short shift of it. It's better to crush such things at the start than let them make headway.

MATE (worriedly). Shall I wake up the First and Fourth,[6] sir? We might need their help.

KEENEY. No, let them sleep. I'm well able to handle this alone, Mr. Slocum.

[There is the shuffling of footsteps from outside and five of the crew crowd into the cabin, led by JOE. All are dressed alike—sweaters, sea-boots, etc. They glance uneasily at the CAPTAIN, twirling their fur caps in their hands.]

KEENEY (after a pause). Well? Who's to speak fur ye?

JOE (stepping forward with an air of bravado). I be.

KEENEY (eying him up and down coldly). So you be. Then speak your say and be quick about it.

JOE (trying not to wilt before the CAPTAIN's glance and avoiding his eyes). The time we signed up for is done today.

KEENEY (icily). You're tellin' me nothin' I don't know.

JOE. You ain't p'intin' fur home yit, far 's we kin see.

KEENEY. No, and I ain't agoin' to till this ship is full of ile.

JOE. You can't go no further no'th with the ice afore ye.

KEENEY. The ice is breaking up.

JOE (after a slight pause during which the others mumble angrily to one another). The grub we're gittin' now is rotten.

KEENEY. It's good enough fur ye. Better men than ye are have eaten worse.

[There is a chorus of angry exclamations.]

JOE (encouraged by this support). We ain't agoin' to work no more 'less you puts back for home.

KEENEY (fiercely). You ain't, ain't you?

JOE. No; and the law courts'll say we was right.

KEENEY. We're at sea now and I'm the law on this ship! (Edging up toward the harpooner.) And every mother's son of you what don't obey orders goes in irons.

[There are more angry exclamations from the crew. MRS. KEENEY appears in the doorway in rear and looks on with startled eyes. None of the men notice her.]

JOE (with bravado). Then we're agoin' to mutiny and take the old hooker home ourselves. Ain't we, boys?

---

[5]depitation, deputation, or group of men to speak for the crew.
[6]the First and Fourth, men who, along with the second and third mates, were directly responsible to Captain Keeney for the operation of the ship.

[*As he turns his head to look at the others,* KEENEY'S *fist shoots out to the side of his jaw.* JOE *goes down in a heap and lies there.* MRS. KEENEY *gives a shriek and hides her face in her hands. The men pull out their sheath-knives and start a rush, but stop when they find themselves confronted by the revolvers of* KEENEY *and the* MATE.]

KEENEY (*his eyes and voice snapping*). Hold still! (*The men stand huddled together in a sullen silence.* KEENEY'S *voice is full of mockery.*) You've found out it ain't safe to mutiny on this ship, ain't you? And now git for'ard where ye belong, and— (*He gives* JOE'S *body a contemptuous kick.*) Drag him with you. And remember, the first man of ye I see shirkin' I'll shoot dead as sure as there's a sea under us, and you can tell the rest the same. Git for'ard now! Quick! (*The men leave in cowed silence, carrying* JOE *with them.* KEENEY *turns to the* MATE *with a short laugh and puts his revolver back in his pocket.*) Best get up on deck, Mr. Slocum,

and see to it they don't try none of their skulkin' tricks. We'll have to keep an eye peeled from now on. I know 'em.

MATE. Yes, sir.

[*He goes out, right.* KEENEY *hears his wife's hysterical weeping and turns around in surprise —then walks slowly to her side.*]

KEENEY (*putting an arm around her shoulder—with gruff tenderness*). There, there, Annie. Don't be afeard. It's all past and gone.

MRS. KEENEY (*shrinking away from him*). Oh, I can't bear it— Oh, I can't bear it any longer!

KEENEY (*gently*). Can't bear what, Annie?

MRS. KEENEY (*hysterically*). All this horrible brutality, and these brutes of men, and this terrible ship, and this prison cell of a room, and the ice all around, and the silence. (*After this outburst she calms down and wipes her eyes with her handkerchief.*)

KEENEY (*after a pause during which he looks down at her with a puzzled frown*). Remember,

I warn't hankerin' to have you come on this voyage, Annie.

MRS. KEENEY. I wanted to be with you, David, don't you see? I didn't want to wait back there in the house all alone as I've been doing these last six years since we were married—waiting, and watching, and fearing—with nothing to keep my mind occupied—not able to go back teaching school on account of being Dave Keeney's wife. I used to dream of sailing on the great, wide, glorious ocean. I wanted to be by your side in the danger and vigorous life of it all. I wanted to see you the hero they make you out to be in Homeport. And instead—(her voice grows tremulous)—all I find is ice and cold—and brutality! (Her voice breaks.)

KEENEY. I warned you what it'd be, Annie. "Whalin' ain't no ladies' tea party," I says to you, and "You better stay to home where you've got all your woman's comforts." (Shaking his head.) But you was so set on it.

MRS. KEENEY (wearily). Oh, I know it isn't your fault, David. You see, I didn't believe you. I guess I was dreaming about the old Vikings in the story books[7] and I thought you were one of them.

KEENEY (protestingly). I done my best to make it as cozy and comfortable as could be. (MRS. KEENEY looks around her in wild scorn.) I even sent to the city for that organ for ye, thinkin' it might be soothin' to ye to be playin' it times when they was calms and things was dull-like.

MRS. KEENEY (wearily). Yes, you were very kind, David. I know that. (She goes to left and lifts the curtains from the porthole and looks out—then suddenly bursts forth:) I won't stand it—I can't stand it—pent up by these walls like a prisoner. (She runs over to him and throws her arms around him, weeping. He puts his arm protectingly over her shoulders.) Take me away from here, David! If I don't get away from here, out of this terrible ship, I'll go mad! Take me home, David! I can't think any more. I feel as if the cold and the silence were crushing down on my brain. I'm afraid. Take me home!

—————
[7] the old Vikings in the story books, the Scandinavians who sailed the oceans in the early Middle Ages as they appeared in romantic tales.

KEENEY (holds her at arm's length and looks at her face anxiously). Best go to bed, Annie. You ain't yourself. You got fever. Your eyes look so strange-like. I ain't never seen you look this way before.

MRS. KEENEY (laughing hysterically). It's the ice and the cold and the silence—they'd make anyone look strange.

KEENEY (soothingly). In a month or two, with good luck, three at the most, I'll have her filled with ile and then we'll give her everything she'll stand and p'int for home.

MRS. KEENEY. But we can't wait for that—I can't wait. I want to get home. And the men won't wait. They want to get home. It's cruel, it's brutal for you to keep them. You must sail back. You've got no excuse. There's clear water to the south now. If you've a heart at all, you've got to turn back.

KEENEY (harshly). I can't, Annie.

MRS. KEENEY. Why can't you?

KEENEY. A woman couldn't rightly understand my reason.

MRS. KEENEY (wildly). Because it's a stupid, stubborn reason. Oh, I heard you talking with the second mate. You're afraid the other captains will sneer at you because you didn't come back with a full ship. You want to live up to your silly reputation even if you do have to beat and starve men and drive me mad to do it.

KEENEY (his jaw set stubbornly). It ain't that, Annie. Them skippers would never dare sneer to my face. It ain't so much what anyone'd say —but—(he hesitates, struggling to express his meaning)—you see—I've always done it—since my first voyage as skipper. I always come back —with a full ship—and—it don't seem right not to—somehow. I been always first whalin' skipper out o' Homeport, and—don't you see my meanin', Annie? (He glances at her. She is not looking at him, but staring dully in front of her, not hearing a word he is saying.) Annie! (She comes to herself with a start.) Best turn in, Annie, there's a good woman. You ain't well.

MRS. KEENEY (resisting his attempts to guide her to the door in rear). David! Won't you please turn back?

KEENEY (gently). I can't, Annie—not yet

awhile. You don't see my meanin'. I got to git the ile.

MRS. KEENEY. It'd be different if you needed the money, but you don't. You've got more than plenty.

KEENEY (impatiently). It ain't the money I'm thinkin' of. D'you think I'm mean as that?

MRS. KEENEY (dully). No—I don't know—I can't understand—(Intensely.) Oh, I want to be home in the old house once more and see my own kitchen again, and hear a woman's voice talking to me and be able to talk to her. Two years! It seems so long ago—as if I'd been dead and could never go back.

KEENEY (worried by her strange tone and the faraway look in her eyes). Best go to bed, Annie. You ain't well.

MRS. KEENEY (not appearing to hear him). I used to be lonely when you were away. I used to think Homeport was a stupid, monotonous place. Then I used to go down on the beach, especially when it was windy and the breakers were rolling in, and I'd dream of the fine, free life you must be leading. (She gives a laugh which is half a sob.) I used to love the sea then. (She pauses; then continues with slow intensity.) But now—I don't ever want to see the sea again.

KEENEY (thinking to humor her). 'Tis no fit place for a woman, that's sure. I was a fool to bring ye.

MRS. KEENEY (after a pause—passing her hand over her eyes with a gesture of pathetic weariness). How long would it take us to reach home—if we started now?

KEENEY (frowning). 'Bout two months, I reckon, Annie, with fair luck.

MRS. KEENEY (counts on her fingers—then murmurs with a rapt smile). That would be August, the latter part of August, wouldn't it? It was on the twenty-fifth of August we were married, David, wasn't it?

KEENEY (trying to conceal the fact that her memories have moved him—gruffly). Don't you remember?

MRS. KEENEY (vaguely—again passes her hand over her eyes). My memory is leaving me —up here in the ice. It was so long ago. (A pause—then she smiles dreamily.) It's June now. The lilacs will be all in bloom in the front yard —and the climbing roses on the trellis to the side of the house—they're budding. (She suddenly covers her face with her hands and commences to sob.)

KEENEY (disturbed). Go in and rest, Annie. You're all worn out cryin' over what can't be helped.

MRS. KEENEY (suddenly throwing her arms around his neck and clinging to him). You love me, don't you, David?

KEENEY (in amazed embarrassment at this outburst). Love you? Why d'you ask me such a question, Annie?

MRS. KEENEY (shaking him fiercely). But you do, don't you, David? Tell me!

KEENEY. I'm your husband, Annie, and you're my wife. Could there be aught but love between us after all these years?

MRS. KEENEY (shaking him again—still more fiercely). Then you do love me. Say it!

KEENEY (simply). I do, Annie.

MRS. KEENEY (gives a sigh of relief—her hands drop to her sides. KEENEY regards her anxiously. She passes her hand across her eyes and murmurs half to herself). I sometimes think if we could only have had a child—(KEENEY turns away from her, deeply moved. She grabs his arm and turns him around to face her— intensely.) And I've always been a good wife to you, haven't I, David?

KEENEY (his voice betraying his emotion). No man has ever had a better, Annie.

MRS. KEENEY. And I've never asked for much from you, have I, David? Have I?

KEENEY. You know you could have all I got the power to give ye, Annie.

MRS. KEENEY (wildly). Then do this, this once, for my sake, for God's sake—take me home! It's killing me, this life—the brutality and cold and horror of it. I'm going mad. I can feel the threat in the air. I can hear the silence threatening me—day after gray day and every day the same. I can't bear it. (Sobbing.) I'll go mad, I know I will. Take me home, David, if you love me as you say. I'm afraid. For the love of God, take me home!

[She throws her arms around him, weeping against his shoulder. His face betrays the tremendous struggle going on within him. He

holds her out at arm's length, his expression softening. For a moment his shoulders sag, he becomes old, his iron spirit weakens as he looks at her tear-stained face.]

KEENEY (*dragging out the words with an effort*). I'll do it, Annie—for your sake—if you say it's needful for ye.

MRS. KEENEY (*with wild joy—kissing him*). God bless you for that, David!

[*He turns away from her silently and walks toward the companionway. Just at that moment there is a clatter of footsteps on the stairs and the* SECOND MATE *enters the cabin.*]

MATE (*excitedly*). The ice is breakin' up to no'th'ard, sir. There's a clear passage through the floe, and clear water beyond, the lookout says.

[KEENEY *straightens himself like a man coming out of a trance.* MRS. KEENEY *looks at the* MATE *with terrified eyes.*]

KEENEY (*dazedly—trying to collect his thoughts*). A clear passage? To no'th'ard?

MATE. Yes, sir.

KEENEY (*his voice suddenly grim with deter-* mination). Then get her ready and we'll drive her through.

MATE. Aye, aye, sir.

MRS. KEENEY (*appealingly*). David!

KEENEY (*not heeding her*). Will the men turn to willin' or must we drag 'em out?

MATE. They'll turn to willin' enough. You put the fear o' God into 'em, sir. They're meek as lambs.

KEENEY. Then drive 'em—both watches. (*With grim determination.*) They's whale t'other side o' this floe and we're agoin' to git 'em.

MATE. Aye, aye, sir.

[*He goes out hurriedly. A moment later there is the sound of scuffling feet from the deck outside and the* MATE'S *voice shouting orders.*]

KEENEY (*speaking aloud to himself—derisively*). And I was agoin' home like a yaller dog!

MRS. KEENEY (*imploringly*). David!

KEENEY (*sternly*). Woman, you ain't adoin' right when you meddle in men's business and weaken 'em. You can't know my feelin's. I got to prove a man to be a good husband for ye to take pride in. I got to git the ile, I tell ye.

MRS. KEENEY (supplicatingly). David. Aren't you going home?

KEENEY (ignoring this question—commandingly). You ain't well. Go and lay down a mite. (He starts for the door.) I got to git on deck.

[He goes out. She cries after him in anguish, "David!" A pause. She passes her hand across her eyes—then commences to laugh hysterically and goes to the organ. She sits down and starts to play wildly an old hymn. KEENEY reënters from the doorway to the deck and stands looking at her angrily. He comes over and grabs her roughly by the shoulder.]

KEENEY. Woman, what foolish mockin' is this? (She laughs wildly and he starts back from her in alarm.) Annie! What is it? (She doesn't answer him. KEENEY's voice trembles.) Don't you know me, Annie?

[He puts both hands on her shoulders and turns her around so that he can look into her eyes. She stares up at him with a stupid expression, a vague smile on her lips. He stumbles away from her, and she commences softly to play the organ again.]

KEENEY (swallowing hard—in a hoarse whisper, as if he had difficulty in speaking). You said—you was agoin' n ad—God!

[A long wail is heard from the deck above, "Ah, bl-o-o-o-ow!" A moment later the MATE's face appears through the skylight. He cannot see MRS. KEENEY.]

MATE (in great excitement). Whales, sir—a whole school of 'em—off the starb'd[8] quarter 'bout five miles away—big ones!

KEENEY (galvanized into action). Are you lowerin' the boats?

MATE. Yes, sir.

KEENEY (with grim decision). I'm acomin' with ye.

MATE. Aye, aye, sir. (Jubilantly.) You'll git the ile now right enough, sir.

[His head is withdrawn and he can be heard shouting orders.]

KEENEY (turning to his wife). Annie! Did you hear him? I'll git the ile. (She doesn't an-

swer or seem to know he is there. He gives a hard laugh, which is almost a groan.) I know you're foolin' me, Annie. You ain't out of your mind—(anxiously)—be you? I'll git the ile now right enough—jest a little while longer, Annie—then we'll turn home'ard. I can't turn back now, you see that, don't you? I've got to git the ile. (In sudden terror.) Answer me! You ain't mad, be you?

[She keeps on playing the organ, but makes no reply. The MATE's face appears again through the skylight.]

MATE. All ready, sir.

[KEENEY turns his back on his wife and strides to the doorway, where he stands for a moment and looks back at her in anguish, fighting to control his feelings.]

MATE. Comin', sir?

KEENEY (his face suddenly grown hard with determination). Aye.

[He turns abruptly and goes out. MRS. KEENEY does not appear to notice his departure. Her whole attention seems centered in the organ. She sits with half-closed eyes, her body swaying a little from side to side to the rhythm of the hymn. Her fingers move faster and faster and she is playing wildly and discordantly as the curtain falls.]

INTERPRETING A PSYCHOLOGICAL DRAMA

1. Drama thrives upon conflict. What are the conflicts in this play? Which is the greatest? At what point do you first discover the existence of this conflict? At what point does its outcome seem to be determined? At what point is it actually determined?

2. What coincidence brought about Captain Keeney's final decision? Did this decision surprise you? Give reasons for your answer.

3. What sort of person is Mrs. Keeney when you first meet her? According to the conversation of others, what kind of woman had she been earlier? What is her situation as the play ends?

4. What does the presence of an organ on a whaling ship tell you about (a) Captain Keeney, (b) Mrs. Keeney? How is it symbolic of the relationship between them?

5. In your opinion may this play be considered a tragedy? Explain your answer.

6. Why is "Ile" classified as a psychological drama?

---

[8]starb'd, starboard (stär'bərd or stär'bōrd), on the right of the ship when facing forward.

Understanding Captain Keeney

When a play is to be read, it is possible to give the reader clues as to what kind of characters he is to meet. Thus, the headnote to "Ile" tells you that Captain Keeney is a monomaniac. But when a play is to be acted, it is up to the playwright to make the personalities he has created understandable through the way they act and the things they say, and through the way other characters react to them and speak about them.

Imagine yourself at a performance of "Ile." The first person to come on stage is the Steward. Before he says a word, what mood have his actions conveyed to you? Ben enters, and he and the Steward talk. What do you learn from their conversation about Captain Keeney? Then the Captain himself appears. How does he treat Ben and the Steward? Is he the sort of man the previous talk has led you to expect? What do you learn about him through his conversation with his wife? How does Captain Keeney's talk with Slocum, the second mate, add to your knowledge of him?

Trace the actions and words of Captain Keeney from the entrance of Joe, the harpooner, to the end of the play, reading aloud lines that you feel are particularly significant in showing the Captain's character. Do you agree that he is a monomaniac? How has the playwright guided you in making this conclusion?

Know your words

In reading "Ile" you doubtless noticed quite a few words, such as *chart room* and *starboard,* which the seamen used in referring to the ship. A specialized vocabulary of this type is often developed in connection with a particular trade or profession and is called the *vernacular* of that occupation. Some of the italicized words in the sentences below belong to the vernacular of seamen; others are words which belong to the common body of English. On a sheet of paper, after the number 1, write the italicized words from the first sentence, labeling them *V* (vernacular) or *C* (common). Then rewrite the sentence, substituting another word or group of words for each word in italics. Continue in the same manner with each sentence. You may use the headnote, the footnotes, and the Glossary for help.

1. The *monomaniac* entered the *cabin* at the *stern* of the vessel.
2. Standing at the doorway leading to the *companionway* was a veteran of the sea dressed in *dungarees*.
3. The *novice* looked through the *porthole*.
4. The *skipper* smashed his fist down on the top of the *sideboard*.
5. The *monotony* seemed unendurable to the men in the *forecastle*.
6. Keeney's desire to fill the *hold* with oil led to his brutal treatment of the *deputation*.

Thornton Wilder (1897-   )[1]

Eugene O'Neill was not alone in searching for more effective ways of writing plays. Another American dramatist, Thornton Wilder, was already known as a fine novelist when his play *Our Town* won a Pulitzer Prize in 1938. This play, which gained immediate recognition for its author as a leading American playwright, was an experimental drama produced with no scenery and few stage properties; much of its action was carried forward by monologues. In *The Skin of Our Teeth* (1942) Wilder again experimented by having the actors step out of character in order to comment upon the play and by having the play itself rehearsed before the audience. Wilder's experimentations are also evident in his one-act plays. "The Happy Journey to Trenton and Camden," which begins on the next page, requires no scenery and few stage properties. Interest centers in a few likable, everyday people rather than in an involved plot. Like Wilder's longer plays, it demonstrates what a gifted playwright can do to free the stage from outworn conventions and to promote alive and popular drama.

---

[1]For a brief biography of Thornton Wilder see page 487.

The Happy Journey to Trenton and Camden

THORNTON WILDER

No scenery is required for this play. Perhaps a few dusty flats may be seen leaning against the brick wall at the back of the stage.

The five members of the Kirby family and the STAGE MANAGER *compose the cast.*

The STAGE MANAGER *not only moves forward and withdraws the few properties that are required, but he reads from a typescript the lines of all the minor characters. He reads them clearly, but with little attempt at characterization, scarcely troubling himself to alter his voice, even when he responds in the person of a child or a woman.*

As the curtain rises the STAGE MANAGER *is leaning lazily against the proscenium pillar at the audience's left. He is smoking.*

ARTHUR *is playing marbles in the center of the stage.*

CAROLINE *is at the remote back right talking to some girls who are invisible to us.*

MA KIRBY *is anxiously putting on her hat before an imaginary mirror.*

MA. Where's your pa? Why isn't he here? I declare, we'll never get started.

ARTHUR. Ma, where's my hat? I guess I don't go if I can't find my hat.

MA. Go out into the hall and see if it isn't there. Where's Caroline gone to now, the plagued child?

ARTHUR. She's out waitin' in the street talkin' to the Jones girls.—I just looked in the hall a thousand times, Ma, and it isn't there. *(He spits for good luck before a difficult shot and mutters:)* Come on, baby.

MA. Go and look again, I say. Look carefully.

[ARTHUR *rises, runs to the right, turns around swiftly, returns to his game, flinging himself on the floor with a terrible impact and starts shooting an aggie.*]

ARTHUR. No, Ma, it's not there.

MA *(serenely).* Well, you don't leave Newark without that hat, make up your mind to that. I don't go no journeys with a hoodlum.

ARTHUR. Aw, Ma!

[MA *comes down to the footlights and talks toward the audience as through a window.*]

MA. Oh, Mrs. Schwartz!

THE STAGE MANAGER *(consulting his script).* Here I am, Mrs. Kirby. Are you going yet?

MA. I guess we're going in just a minute. How's the baby?

THE STAGE MANAGER. She's all right now. We slapped her on the back and she spat it up.

MA. Isn't that fine!—Well now, if you'll be good enough to give the cat a saucer of milk in the morning and the evening, Mrs. Schwartz, I'll be ever so grateful to you—Oh, good afternoon, Mrs. Hobmeyer!

THE STAGE MANAGER. Good afternoon, Mrs. Kirby, I hear you're going away.

MA *(modest).* Oh, just for three days, Mrs. Hobmeyer, to see my married daughter, Beulah, in Camden.[1] Elmer's got his vacation week from the laundry early this year, and he's just the best driver in the world.

[CAROLINE *comes "into the house" and stands by her mother.*]

THE STAGE MANAGER. Is the whole family going?

MA. Yes, all four of us that's here. The change ought to be good for the children. My married daughter was downright sick a while ago—

THE STAGE MANAGER. Tchk—tchk—tchk! Yes. I remember you tellin' us.

MA. And I just want to go down and see the child. I ain't seen her since then. I just won't rest easy in my mind without I see her. *(To* CAROLINE.*)* Can't you say good afternoon to Mrs. Hobmeyer?

CAROLINE *(blushes and lowers her eyes and*

---

[1] *Camden* (kam′dən), a city in southwestern New Jersey across the Delaware River from Philadelphia. It is about seventy miles from Newark, where the Kirbys live.

says woodenly). Good afternoon, Mrs. Hobmeyer.

THE STAGE MANAGER. Good afternoon, dear. Well, I'll wait and beat these rugs until after you're gone, because I don't want to choke you. I hope you have a good time and find everything all right.

MA. Thank you, Mrs. Hobmeyer, I hope I will. Well, I guess that milk for the cat is all, Mrs. Schwartz, if you're sure you don't mind. If anything should come up, the key to the back door is hanging by the icebox.

ARTHUR and CAROLINE. Ma! Not so loud. Everybody can hear yuh.

MA. Stop pullin' my dress, children. *(In a loud whisper.)* The key to the back door I'll leave hangin' by the icebox and I'll leave the screen door unhooked.

THE STAGE MANAGER. Now have a good trip, dear, and give my love to Loolie.

MA. I will, and thank you a thousand times. *(She returns "into the room.")* What can be keeping your pa?

ARTHUR. I can't find my hat, Ma.

[*Enter* ELMER *holding a hat.*]

ELMER. Here's Arthur's hat. He musta left it in the car Sunday.

MA. That's a mercy. Now we can start.—Caroline Kirby, what've you done to your cheeks?

CAROLINE *(defiant-abashed).* Nothin'.

MA. If you've put anything on 'em, I'll slap you.

CAROLINE. No, Ma, of course I haven't—*(hanging her head)*—I just rubbed'm to make'm red. All the girls do that at high school when they're goin' places.

MA. Such silliness I never saw. Elmer, what kep' you?

ELMER *(always even-voiced and always looking out a little anxiously through his spectacles).* I just went to the garage and had Charlie give a last look at it, Kate.

MA. I'm glad you did. I wouldn't like to have no breakdown miles from anywhere. Now we can start. Arthur, put those marbles away. Anybody'd think you didn't want to go on a journey to look at yuh.

[*They go out through the "hall," take the short steps that denote going downstairs, and find themselves in the street.*]

ELMER. Here, you boys, you keep away from that car.

MA. Those Sullivan boys put their heads into everything.

[*The* STAGE MANAGER *has moved forward four chairs and a low platform. This is the automobile. It is in the center of the stage and faces the audience. The platform slightly raises the two chairs in the rear.* PA'S *hands hold an imaginary steering wheel and continually shift gears.* CAROLINE *sits beside him.* ARTHUR *is behind him and* MA *behind* CAROLINE.*]

CAROLINE *(self-consciously).* Good-by, Mildred. Good-by, Helen.

THE STAGE MANAGER. Good-by, Caroline. Good-by, Mrs. Kirby. I hope y'have a good time.

MA. Good-by, girls.

THE STAGE MANAGER. Good-by, Kate. The car looks fine.

MA *(looking upward toward a window).* Oh, good-by, Emma! *(Modestly.)* We think it's the best little Chevrolet in the world—Oh, good-by, Mrs. Adler!

THE STAGE MANAGER. What, are you going away, Mrs. Kirby?

MA. Just for three days, Mrs. Adler, to see my married daughter in Camden.

THE STAGE MANAGER. Have a good time.

[*Now* MA, CAROLINE, *and the* STAGE MANAGER *break out into a tremendous chorus of good-bys. The whole street is saying good-by.* ARTHUR *takes out his pea shooter and lets fly happily into the air. There is a lurch or two and they are off.*]

ARTHUR *(in sudden fright).* Pa! Pa! Don't go by the school. Mr. Biedenbach might see us!

MA. I don't care if he does see us. I guess I can take my children out of school for one day without having to hide down back streets about it.

[ELMER *nods to a passerby.*]

MA *(asks without sharpness).* Who was that you spoke to, Elmer?

ELMER. That was the fellow who arranges our banquets down to the Lodge, Kate.

MA. Is he the one who had to buy four hun-

dred steaks? *(Pa nods.)* I declare, I'm glad I'm not him.

ELMER. The air's getting better already. Take deep breaths, children.

[*They inhale noisily.*]

ARTHUR. Gee, it's almost open fields already. "Weber and Heilbronner Suits for Well-dressed Men." Ma, can I have one of them some day?

MA. If you graduate with good marks, perhaps your father'll let you have one for graduation.

CAROLINE *(whining).* Oh, Pa! do we have to wait while that whole funeral goes by?

[*Pa takes off his hat. Ma cranes forward with absorbed curiosity.*]

MA. Take off your hat, Arthur. Look at your father. Why, Elmer, I do believe that's a lodge-brother of yours. See the banner? I suppose this is the Elizabeth[2] branch.

––––––––
[2]*Elizabeth,* a city in New Jersey adjoining Newark.

[ELMER *nods.* MA *sighs: Tchk–tchk–tchk. They all lean forward and watch the funeral in silence, growing momentarily more solemnized. After a pause,* MA *continues almost dreamily:*]

MA. Well, we haven't forgotten the one that we went on, have we? We haven't forgotten our good Harold. He gave his life for his country, we mustn't forget that. *(She passes her finger from the corner of her eye across her cheek. There is another pause.)* Well, we'll all hold up the traffic for a few minutes some day.

THE CHILDREN *(very uncomfortable).* Ma!

MA *(without self-pity).* Well I'm ready, children. I hope everybody in this car is ready. *(She puts her hand on* PA's *shoulder.)* And I pray to go first, Elmer. Yes. (PA *touches her hand.)*

THE CHILDREN. Ma, everybody's looking at you. Everybody's laughing at you.

MA. Oh, hold your tongues! I don't care

what a lot of silly people in Elizabeth, New Jersey, think of me.—Now we can go on. That's the last.

[*There is another lurch and the car goes on.*]

CAROLINE. "Fit-Rite Suspenders. The Working Man's Choice." Pa, why do they spell *Rite* that way?

ELMER. So that it'll make you stop and ask about it, Missy.

CAROLINE. Papa, you're teasing me.—Ma, why do they say "Three Hundred Rooms Three Hundred Baths"?

ARTHUR. "Miller's Spaghetti: The Family's Favorite Dish." Ma, why don't you ever have spaghetti?

MA. Go along, you'd never eat it.

ARTHUR. Ma, I like it now.

CAROLINE (*with gesture*). Yum-yum. It looks wonderful up there. Ma, make some when we get home?

MA (*dryly*). "The management is always happy to receive suggestions. We aim to please."

[*The whole family finds this exquisitely funny. The children scream with laughter. Even* ELMER *smiles.* MA *remains modest.*]

ELMER. Well, I guess no one's complaining, Kate. Everybody knows you're a good cook.

MA. I don't know whether I'm a good cook or not, but I know I've had practice. At least I've cooked three meals a day for twenty-five years.

ARTHUR. Aw, Ma, you went out to eat once in a while.

MA. Yes. That made it a leap year.

[*This joke is no less successful than its predecessor. When the laughter dies down,* CAROLINE *turns around in an ecstasy of well-being and kneeling on the cushions says:*]

CAROLINE. Ma, I love going out in the country like this. Let's do it often, Ma.

MA. Goodness, smell that air, will you! It's got the whole ocean in it.—Elmer, drive careful over that bridge. This must be New Brunswick we're coming to.—Elmer, don't run over that collie dog. (*She follows the dog with her eyes.*) Looked kinda peaked to me. Needs a good honest bowl of leavings. Pretty dog, too. (*Her eyes fall on a billboard.*) That's a pretty advertisement for Chesterfield cigarettes, isn't it? Looks like Beulah, a little.

ARTHUR. Ma?

MA. Yes.

ARTHUR ("*route*" *rhymes with* "*out*"). Can't I take a paper route with the Newark *Daily Post*?

MA. No, you cannot. No, sir. I hear they make the paper boys get up at four-thirty in the morning. No son of mine is going to get up at four-thirty every morning, not if it's to make a million dollars. Your *Saturday Evening Post* route on Thursday mornings is enough.

ARTHUR. Aw, Ma.

MA. No, sir. No son of mine is going to get up at four-thirty and miss the sleep God meant him to have.

ARTHUR (*sullenly*). Hmm! Ma's always talking about God. I guess she got a letter from Him this morning.

[MA *rises, outraged.*]

MA. Elmer, stop that automobile this minute. I don't go another step with anybody that says things like that. Arthur, you get out of this car. Elmer, you give him another dollar bill. He can go back to Newark, by himself. I don't want him.

ARTHUR. What did I say? There wasn't anything terrible about that.

ELMER. I didn't hear what he said, Kate.

MA. God has done a lot of things for me and I won't have Him made fun of by anybody. Go away. Go away from me.

CAROLINE. Aw, Ma—don't spoil the ride.

MA. No.

ELMER. We might as well go on, Kate, since we've got started. I'll talk to the boy tonight.

MA (*slowly conceding*). All right, if you say so, Elmer. But I won't sit beside him. Caroline, you come, and sit by me.

ARTHUR (*frightened*). Aw, Ma, that wasn't so terrible.

MA. I don't want to talk about it. I hope your father washes your mouth out with soap and water. Where'd we all be if I started talking about God like that, I'd like to know! We'd be in the speakeasies and night clubs and places like that, that's where we'd be.—All right, Elmer, you can go on now.

CAROLINE. What did he say, Ma? I didn't hear what he said.

MA. I don't want to talk about it.

[*They drive on in silence for a moment, the shocked silence after a scandal.*]

ELMER. I'm going to stop and give the car a little water, I guess.

MA. All right, Elmer. You know best.

ELMER *(to a garage hand)*. Could I have a little water in the radiator—to make sure?

THE STAGE MANAGER *(in this scene alone he lays aside his script and enters into a rôle seriously)*. You sure can. *(He punches the tires.)* Air, all right? Do you need any oil or gas?

ELMER. No, I think not. I just got fixed up in Newark.

MA. We're on the right road for Camden, are we?

THE STAGE MANAGER. Yes, keep straight ahead. You can't miss it. You'll be in Trenton in a few minutes. *(He carefully pours some water into the hood.)* Camden's a great town, lady, believe me.

MA. My daughter likes it fine—my married daughter.

THE STAGE MANAGER. Ye'? It's a great burg all right. I guess I think so because I was born near there.

MA. Well, well. Your folks still live there?

THE STAGE MANAGER. No, my old man sold the farm and they built a factory on it. So the folks moved to Philadelphia.

MA. My married daughter Beulah lives there because her husband works in the telephone company.—Stop pokin' me, Caroline!—We're all going down to see her for a few days.

THE STAGE MANAGER. Ye'?

MA. She's been sick, you see, and I just felt I had to go and see her. My husband and my boy are going to stay at the Y.M.C.A. I hear they've got a dormitory on the top floor that's real clean and comfortable. Have you ever been there?

THE STAGE MANAGER. No. I'm Knights of Columbus[3] myself.

MA. Oh.

THE STAGE MANAGER. I used to play basket-

ball at the Y though. It looked all right to me. *(He has been standing with one foot on the rung of* MA'S *chair. They have taken a great fancy to one another. He reluctantly shakes himself out of it and pretends to examine the car again, whistling.)* Well, I guess you're all set now, lady. I hope you have a good trip; you can't miss it.

EVERYBODY. Thanks. Thanks a lot. Good luck to you.

[*Jolts and lurches.*]

MA *(with a sigh)*. The world's full of nice people. That's what I call a nice young man.

CAROLINE *(earnestly)*. Ma, you oughtn't to tell'm all everything about yourself.

MA. Well, Caroline, you do your way and I'll do mine. He looked kinda thin to me. I'd like to feed him up for a few days. His mother lives in Philadelphia and I expect he eats at those dreadful Greek places.

CAROLINE. I'm hungry. Pa, there's a hot dog stand. K'n I have one?

ELMER. We'll all have one, eh, Kate? We had such an early lunch.

MA. Just as you think best, Elmer.

ELMER. Arthur, here's half a dollar. Run over and see what they have. Not too much mustard either.

[ARTHUR *descends from the car and goes off-stage right.* MA *and* CAROLINE *get out and walk a bit.*]

MA. What's that flower over there? I'll take some of those to Beulah.

CAROLINE. It's just a weed, Ma.

MA. I like it.—My, look at the sky, wouldya! I'm glad I was born in New Jersey. I've always said it was the best state in the Union. Every state has something no other state has got.

[*They stroll about humming. Presently* AR-THUR *returns with his hands full of imaginary hot dogs which he distributes. He is still very much cast down by the recent scandal. He finally approaches his mother and says falteringly:*]

ARTHUR. Ma, I'm sorry. I'm sorry for what I said. *(He bursts into tears and puts his forehead against her elbow.)*

MA. There. There. We all say wicked things at times. I know you didn't mean it like it

---

[3] *Knights of Columbus*, society of Roman Catholic men.

sounded. *(He weeps still more violently than before.)* Why, now, now! I forgive you, Arthur, and tonight before you go to bed you ... *(She whispers.)* You're a good boy at heart, Arthur, and we all know it.

[CAROLINE *starts to cry too.*]

MA *(suddenly joyously alive and happy).* Sakes alive, it's too nice a day for us all to be cryin'. Come now, get in. You go up in front with your father, Caroline. Ma wants to sit with her beau. I never saw such children. Your hot dogs are all getting wet. Now chew them fine, everybody.—All right, Elmer, forward march. Caroline, whatever are you doing?

CAROLINE. I'm spitting out the leather, Ma.

MA. Then say: Excuse me.

CAROLINE. Excuse me, please.

MA. What's this place? Arthur, did you see the post office?

ARTHUR. It said Laurenceville.

MA. Hmm. School kinda. Nice. I wonder what that big yellow house set back was.—Now it's beginning to be Trenton.

CAROLINE. Papa, it was near here that George Washington crossed the Delaware. It was near Trenton, Mama. He was first in war and first in peace, and first in the hearts of his countrymen.

MA *(surveying the passing world, serene and didactic).* Well, the thing I like about him best was that he never told a lie. *(The children are duly cast down. There is a pause.)* There's a sunset for you. There's nothing like a good sunset.

ARTHUR. There's an Ohio license in front of us. Ma, have you ever been to Ohio?

MA. No.

[*A dreamy silence descends upon them.* CAROLINE *sits closer to her father.* MA *puts her arm around* ARTHUR.]

ARTHUR. Ma, what a lotta people there are in the world, Ma. There must be thousands and thousands in the United States. Ma, how many are there?

MA. I don't know. Ask your father.

ARTHUR. Pa, how many are there?

ELMER. There are a hundred and twenty-six million, Kate.

MA *(giving a pressure about* ARTHUR's *shoulder).* And they all like to drive out in the evening with their children beside'm. *(Another pause.)* Why doesn't somebody sing something? Arthur, you're always singing something; what's the matter with you?

ARTHUR. All right. What'll we sing? *(He sketches:)*

> In the Blue Ridge mountains of Virginia,
> On the trail of the lonesome pine...

No, I don't like that any more. Let's do:

> I been workin' on de railroad
> All de liblong day.
> I been workin' on de railroad
> Just to pass de time away.

[CAROLINE *joins in at once. Finally even* MA *is singing. Even* PA *is singing.* MA *suddenly jumps up with a wild cry:*]

MA. Elmer, that signpost said Camden, I saw it.

ELMER. All right, Kate, if you're sure.

[*Much shifting of gears, backing, and jolting.*]

MA. Yes, there it is. "Camden—five miles." Dear old Beulah. Now, children, you be good and quiet during dinner. She's just got out of bed after a big sorta operation, and we must all move around kinda quiet. First you drop me and Caroline at the door and just say hello, and then you men-folk go over to the Y.M.C.A. and come back for dinner in about an hour.

CAROLINE *(shutting her eyes and pressing her fists passionately against her nose).* I see the first star. Everybody make a wish.

> Star light, star bright,
> First star I seen tonight.
> I wish I may, I wish I might
> Have the wish I wish tonight.

(Then solemnly.) Pins. Mama, you say "needles." *(She interlocks little fingers with her mother.)*

MA. Needles.

CAROLINE. Shakespeare. Ma, you say "Longfellow."

MA. Longfellow.

CAROLINE. Now it's a secret and I can't tell it to anybody. Ma, you make a wish.

MA *(with almost grim humor).* No, I can make wishes without waiting for no star. And

I can tell my wishes right out loud too. Do you want to hear them?

CAROLINE (resignedly). No, Ma, we know'm already. We've heard'm. (She hangs her head affectedly on her left shoulder and says with unmalicious mimicry:) You want me to be a good girl and you want Arthur to be honest-in-word-and-deed.

MA (majestically). Yes. So mind yourself.

ELMER. Caroline, take out that letter from Beulah in my coat pocket by you and read aloud the places I marked with red pencil.

CAROLINE (working). "A few blocks after you pass the two big oil tanks on your left..."

EVERYBODY (pointing backward). There they are!

CAROLINE. "...you come to a corner where there's an A and P store on the left and a firehouse kitty-corner to it..." (They all jubilantly identify these landmarks.) "...turn right, go two blocks, and our house is Weyerhauser St. Number 471."

MA. It's an even nicer street than they used to live in. And right handy to an A and P.

CAROLINE (whispering). Ma, it's better than our street. It's richer than our street. Ma, isn't Beulah richer than we are?

MA (looking at her with a firm and glassy eye). Mind yourself, missy. I don't want to hear anybody talking about rich or not rich when I'm around. If people aren't nice I don't care how rich they are. I live in the best street in the world because my husband and children live there. (She glares impressively at CAROLINE a moment to let this lesson sink in, then looks up, sees BEULAH, and waves.) There's Beulah standing on the steps lookin' for us.

[BEULAH has appeared and is waving. They all call out: Hello, Beulah—Hello. Presently they are all getting out of the car. BEULAH kisses her father long and affectionately.]

BEULAH. Hello, Papa. Good old Papa. You look tired, Pa. Hello, Mama. Lookit how Arthur and Caroline are growing!

MA. They're bursting all their clothes.—Yes, your pa needs a rest. Thank Heaven, his vacation has come just now. We'll feed him up and let him sleep late. Pa has a present for you, Loolie. He would go and buy it.

BEULAH. Why, Pa, you're terrible to go and buy anything for me. Isn't he terrible?

MA. Well, it's a secret. You can open it at dinner.

ELMER. Where's Horace, Loolie?

BEULAH. He was kep' over a little at the office. He'll be here any minute. He's crazy to see you all.

MA. All right. You men go over to the Y and come back in about an hour.

BEULAH (as her father returns to the wheel, stands out in the street beside him). Go straight along, Pa, you can't miss it. It just stares at yuh. (She puts her arm around his neck and rubs her nose against his temple.) Crazy old Pa, goin' buyin' things! It's me that ought to be buyin' things for you, Pa.

ELMER. Oh, no! There's only one Loolie in the world.

BEULAH (whispering, as her eyes fill with tears). Are you glad I'm still alive, Pa?

[She kisses him abruptly and goes back to the house steps. THE STAGE MANAGER removes the automobile with the help of ELMER and ARTHUR who go off waving their good-bys.]

BEULAH. Well, come on upstairs, Ma, and take off your things. Caroline, there's a surprise for you in the back yard.

CAROLINE. Rabbits?

BEULAH. No.

CAROLINE. Chickens?

BEULAH. No. Go and see. (CAROLINE runs off-stage. BEULAH and MA gradually go upstairs.) There are two new puppies. You be thinking over whether you can keep one in Newark.

MA. I guess we can. It's a nice house, Beulah. You just got a lovely home.

BEULAH. When I got back from the hospital, Horace had moved everything into it, and there wasn't anything for me to do.

MA. It's lovely.

[The STAGE MANAGER pushes out a bed from the left. Its foot is toward the right. BEULAH sits on it, testing the springs.]

BEULAH. I think you'll find the bed comfortable, Ma.

MA (taking off her hat). Oh, I could sleep on a heapa shoes, Loolie! I don't have no trouble sleepin'. *(She sits down beside her.)* Now let me look at my girl. Well, well, when I last saw you, you didn't know me. You kep' saying: "When's Mama comin'? When's Mama comin'?" But the doctor sent me away.

BEULAH *(puts her head on her mother's shoulder and weeps).* It was awful, Mama. It was awful. She didn't even live a few minutes, Mama. It was awful.

MA *(looking far away).* God thought best, dear. God thought best. We don't understand why. We just go on, honey, doin' our business. *(Then almost abruptly—passing the back of her hand across her cheek.)* Well, now, what are we giving the men to eat tonight?

BEULAH. There's a chicken in the oven.

MA. What time didya put it in?

BEULAH *(restraining her).* Aw, Ma, don't go yet. I like to sit here with you this way. You always get the fidgets when we try and pet yuh, Mama.

MA *(ruefully, laughing).* Yes, it's kinda foolish. I'm just an old Newark bag-a-bones. *(She glances at the backs of her hands.)*

BEULAH *(indignantly).* Why, Ma, you're good-lookin'! We always said you were good-lookin'. And besides, you're the best ma we could ever have.

MA *(uncomfortable).* Well, I hope you like me. There's nothin' like being liked by your family. Now I'm going downstairs to look at the chicken. You stretch out here for a minute and shut your eyes. Have you got everything laid in for breakfast before the shops close?

BEULAH. Oh, you know! Ham and eggs.

[They both laugh.]

MA. I declare I never could understand what men see in ham and eggs. I think they're horrible.—What time did you put the chicken in?

BEULAH. Five o'clock.

MA. Well, now, you shut your eyes for ten minutes. (BEULAH *stretches out and shuts her eyes.* MA *descends the stairs absent-mindedly singing:)*

> There were ninety and nine that safely lay
> In the shelter of the fold,
> But one was out on the hills away,
> Far off from the gates of gold....

[And the curtain falls.]

1. In "Ile" you learned about the characters partially through the way they reacted to various conflicts. How do you learn to know the characters in "The Happy Journey"? Characterize Ma, Pa, Caroline, Arthur, and Beulah. Would you call them normal, flesh-and-blood human beings? Why, or why not?

2. What is the force of the word *journey* in the title of the play? What does the use of this word tell you about the characters in the play?

3. What is the central idea of this play?

4. Would you say that there is a conflict in "The Happy Journey"? If not, what makes it a play?

5. Why do you think Thornton Wilder designed "The Happy Journey" to be staged without scenery? What, in general, are the advantages of this type of staging? The disadvantages?

Four chairs and imagination

Perhaps you have become accustomed to thinking of scenery and stage properties as essential to producing a play. Yet elaborate settings are a comparatively recent development in the centuries-old history of drama. In Shakespeare's day a sign hanging on a pillar at the side of the stage announced the setting—"A Forest" or "A Street in Verona." Since there was no curtain to separate actors from audience, the playgoers watched while a chair was dragged on stage to represent a king's throne. All the details of the setting were filled in by the spectators' imagination, which could transform a bare stage into a leafy forest and an old chair to a throne hung with crimson and gold.

In modern plays such as "The Happy Journey to Trenton and Camden," the audience is once again called upon to take an active part in the play—to furnish the imagination which sets the stage. Try acting out "The Happy Journey" with this in mind. Those chosen for the various rôles should read their parts over several times to be sure of vivid and correct interpretation; memorizing is not necessary. If the spectators are in the correct frame of mind as they settle back to enjoy the play, four chairs will become an automobile, the actors will become the Kirby family, and the classroom walls will give way to billboards and hot-dog stands flashing by as the Kirbys roll along on their journey.

Other Prominent Dramatists

Among dramatists who have achieved recognition because of their versatility as well as their mastery of dramatic technique, two names stand out—Maxwell Anderson and Robert Sherwood. Although Anderson has been successful with realistic plays, prose satire, musical-comedy satire, and fantasy, his chief claim to distinction lies in his verse plays. In dramas such as *Elizabeth the Queen* (1930), *Mary of Scotland* (1933), *Valley Forge* (1934), and *Winterset* (1935), he proved that poetry could be used successfully to set the mood and carry forward the action on the modern stage. Robert Sherwood's versatility is evident when one considers that he has written historical plays, social comedy, and lyrics for musical comedy. However, his greatest achievement has been giving expression to fundamental American ideals in such plays as *Abe Lincoln in Illinois* (1938) and *There Shall Be No Night* (1940).

Many other dramatists today are well known for their fine plays. Among these plays are the delightful satirical comedies of George Kaufman, the sympathetic folk plays of Marc Connelly and Paul Green, and the intensely dramatic social-problem plays of Elmer Rice, Clifford Odets, and Arthur Miller.

Theresa Helburn, whose one-act play "Enter the Hero" is printed below, is best known as a director of the Theater Guild. Through her efforts and those of others who have worked actively for the various theater organizations, the American theater has gradually become a rich and satisfying part of our literary heritage.

Enter the Hero

THERESA HELBURN

CHARACTERS

RUTH CAREY	HAROLD LAWSON
ANNE CAREY	MRS. CAREY

The scene presents an upstairs sitting room in a comfortable house in a small city. The wall on the spectator's left is broken by a fireplace, and beyond that a door leading into the hall. At the back of the stage is a deep bay window from which one may have a view up and down the street. A door in the right wall leads to ANNE CAREY'S *bedroom. The sitting room, being* ANNE'S *particular property, is femininely furnished in chintz. A table desk with several drawers occupies an important place in the room, which is conspicuously rich in flowers.*

The curtain rises on an empty stage. RUTH CAREY, ANNE'S *pretty younger sister, enters hurriedly, carrying a large box; she wears a hat and coat.*

RUTH. Oh, Anne, here's *another* box of flowers! Anne, where are you?

VOICE FROM ANNE'S BEDROOM. In here. I thought you had gone out.

RUTH *(opening door left)*. I was just going when the expressman left these—and I wanted to see them. *(Looking into the bedroom.)* Oh, how pretty your dress is. Turn around. Just adorable! May I open these?

THE VOICE FROM THE BEDROOM. Yes, but hurry. It's late.

RUTH *(throwing her sister a kiss)*. You dear! It's almost like having a fiancé of my own. Three boxes in two days! He's adorably extravagant. Oh, Anne, exquisite white roses! Come, look!

[ANNE CAREY *appears in the bedroom door. Her manner in this scene shows nervousness and suppressed excitement.*]

ANNE. Yes, lovely. Get a bowl, Ruth. Quickly.

RUTH. I will. Here's a card. *(She hands* ANNE *an envelope, goes to the door, then stops.)* What does he say, Anne? May I see?

[ANNE, *who has read the card quickly with a curious little smile, hands it back to her without turning.*]

RUTH *(reading)*.

The red rose whispers of passion,
And the white rose breathes of love;
Oh, the red rose is a falcon,
And the white rose is a dove.

But I send you a cream-white rosebud
With a flush on its petals' tips
For the love that is purest and sweetest
Has a kiss of desire on the lips.

Oh, how beautiful! Did he make that up, do you suppose? I didn't know he was a real poet.

ANNE *(who has been pinning some of the roses on her dress)*. Anyone in love is a poet.

RUTH. It's perfectly beautiful! *(She takes a pencil and little notebook out of her pocket.)* May I copy it in my "Harold Notebook"?

ANNE. Your *what*?

RUTH. I call it my "Harold Notebook." I've put down bits of his letters that you read to me, the lovery bits that are too beautiful to forget. Do you mind?

ANNE. You silly child!

RUTH. Here, you may see it....That's from the second letter he wrote you from Rio de Janeiro. I just couldn't get over that letter. You know I made you read it to me three times. It was so—so delicate. I remembered this passage—see. "A young girl seems to me as exquisite and frail as a flower. Anne, your face is always before me, and I know now what I was too stupid to realize before, that it was you and you only who made life bearable for me last winter when I was a stranger and alone." Oh, Anne—*(sighing rapturously)*—that's the sort of love letters I've dreamed of getting. I don't suppose I ever shall.

ANNE *(still looking over the notebook with her odd smile)*. Have you shown this to anyone?

RUTH. Only to Caroline—in confidence. *(Pauses to see how* ANNE *will take it.)* But really, Anne, everyone knows about Harold. You've told Madge and Eleanor, and I'm sure they've told the others. They don't say anything to us, but they do to Caroline, and she tells me. *(Watching* ANNE's *face.)* You're not angry, are you, Anne?

ANNE. Yes, rather. *(Then eagerly.)* What do they say?

RUTH. Oh, all sorts of things. Some of them horrid, of course! You can't blame them for being jealous. Here you are having just the sort of experience that any one of them would give their eyeteeth to have. *I'd* be jealous if you weren't my sister. As it is, I seem to get some of the glory myself.

ANNE (*pleased, but disparaging*). But every girl has this experience sooner or later.

RUTH. Oh, not in this way. Everything that Harold does is beautiful, ideal. Jane Fenwick showed me some of Bob's letters. They were so dull, so prosaic! All about his salary and the corn crop. I was disgusted with them. So was she, I think, when she saw Harold's letters.

ANNE. Oh, you showed them to Jane, too?

RUTH (*a bit frightened*). No, really I didn't. Caroline did. I lent her my notebook once overnight, and she gave Jane a peek—in the *strictest* confidence. Jane really needed it. She was getting so cocky about Bob. Girls are funny things, aren't they?

ANNE (*who has been keenly interested in all of* RUTH's *gossip*). What do you mean?

RUTH. It isn't so much the man, as the idea of a man—someone to dream about, and to talk about. When I think of getting engaged—I suppose I shall get engaged some day—I never think of being really, really kissed by a man—

ANNE. What do you think of?

RUTH. I always think of telling Caroline about it, showing my ring to her and to Madge. Oh, Madge is green with envy. I believe she thought Harold sort of liked her. (ANNE *turns away.*) She was so excited when she saw him in New York. She said she would have got off the bus and chased him, but he went into a house. ...Anne, why didn't you tell us—me, at least—that Harold was back from South America, before we heard it from Madge?

ANNE. Just because...I wanted to avoid all this...It was hard enough to have him within a few hours' distance and know he could not get to me. But it was easier when no one else knew. Don't you understand?

RUTH. Yes, dear, of course I do—but still—

ANNE (*impatiently*). Now Ruth, it's quarter past four. You promised—

RUTH. I'm going...right straight off...unless —Oh, Anne, mayn't I stay and have just one peek? I won't let him see me, and then I'll run straight away.

ANNE. Oh, for heaven's sake, don't be naughty and silly! Clear out now, quickly, or— (*Changing her tone suddenly.*) Ruth, dear, put yourself in my place. Think how you would feel if you were going to see the man you loved for the first time. That's what it really is. Think of it! Two years ago when he went away we were just the merest friends—and now—

RUTH. And now you're engaged to be married! Oh, isn't it the most romantic thing! Of course you want to be alone. Forgive me. Oh, Anne, how excited you must be!

ANNE (*with rather histrionic intensity*). No, I'm strangely calm. And yet, Ruth, I'm afraid, terribly afraid.

RUTH. Why, what of?

ANNE (*acting*). I don't know...of everything ...of the unknown. All this has been so wonderful, if anything should happen, I don't think I could bear it. I think I should die.

RUTH. Nonsense, dear, what can happen? You're just on edge. Well, I'll be off. I'll join Mother at Aunt Nellie's. Give my love to Harold. You know I've never called him anything but Mr. Lawson to his face. Isn't that funny? Good-by, dear. (*Throwing* ANNE *a kiss.*) You look so sweet.

ANNE (*her hands on* RUTH's *shoulders for an impressive moment*). Good-by, Ruth. Good-by. (*They kiss.*)

[RUTH *goes. Left alone, a complete change comes over* ANNE. *She drops the romantic attitude. She is nervously determined. She quickly arranges the flowers, takes out the box, etc., straightens the room, and surveys herself rapidly in the mirror. There is a sound of wheels outside.* ANNE *goes to the bay window and looks out. Then she stands erect in the grip of an emotion that is more like terror than anticipation. Hearing the sound of footsteps on the stair she is panic-stricken and about to bolt, but at the sound of voices she pulls herself together and stands motionless.*]

MAN'S VOICE (*outside*). In here? All right!

[HAROLD LAWSON *enters, a well set-up bronzed, rather commonplace young man of about twenty-eight. He sees no one on his entry, but as he advances into the room,* ANNE *comes down from the bay window.*]

HAROLD. Hello, Miss Carey, how are you? Splendid to see you again, after all this time. (ANNE *looks at him without speaking, which slightly embarrasses him.*) You're looking fine. How's your mother—and little Ruth?

ANNE (*slowly*). Welcome home.

HAROLD. Oh, thanks. It's rather nice to be back in God's country. But it's not for long this time.

ANNE. Are you going away again?

HAROLD. Yes, I've another appointment. This one in India, some big salt mines. Not bad, eh? I made pretty good in Brazil, they tell me.

ANNE (*nervously*). Sit down.

HAROLD. Thanks. Hot for September, isn't it? Though I ought to be used to heat by this time. Sometimes the thermometer would run a hundred and eight for a week on end. Not much fun, that.

ANNE. No, indeed.

HAROLD (*settling back comfortably to talk about himself*). You know I loathed it down there at first. What with all the foreigners and the rotten weather and the bugs—thought I'd never get into the swing. Wanted to chuck engineering for any old job that was cool, but after a while—

ANNE. How long have you been home?

HAROLD. About three weeks. I'd really been meaning to come out here and have a look round my old haunts, but there was business in New York, and I had to go South and see my family—you know how time flies. Then your note came. It was mighty jolly of you to ask me out here. By the way, how did you know I was back?

ANNE (*after a pause*). Madge Kennedy caught sight of you in New York.

HAROLD. Did she really? How is little Madge? And that odd brother of hers. Is he just as much of a fool as ever? I remember once he said to me—

ANNE. Oh, I didn't ask you here to talk about Madge Kennedy's family.

HAROLD (*taken aback*). No...no, of course not. I—er—I've been wondering just why you did ask me. You said you wanted to talk to me about something.

ANNE (*gently*). Weren't you glad to come?

HAROLD. Why, of course I was. Of course. And then your note fired my curiosity—your asking me to come straight to you before seeing anyone else.

ANNE. Aren't you glad to be here with me?

HAROLD. Why, surely, of course, but— (*Pause.*)

ANNE. You see, people seemed to expect you would come to see me first of all. I rather expected it myself. Don't you understand?

HAROLD (*very uncomfortable*). No...I'm afraid I don't....

ANNE. From the way you acted before you went away I thought you, yourself, would want to see me first of all.

HAROLD. Before I went away? What do you mean?

ANNE. You know well enough what I mean. The parties those last weeks—the theater we went to—the beautiful flowers you sent Mother —the letter—

HAROLD. But—but—why, I was going away. You and your people had been awfully nice to me, a perfect stranger in town. I was simply trying to do the decent thing. Good Lord! You don't mean to say you thought—

ANNE (*watching him very closely*). Yes, it's true, I thought—and everyone else thought—I've been waiting these two years for you to come back.

[*She drops her face into her hands. Her shoulders shake.*]

HAROLD (*jumping up*). Great Heavens! I never imagined—Why, Miss Carey, I—oh, I'm terribly sorry! (*She continues to sob.*) Please don't do that—please! I'd better go away—I'll clear out—I'll go straight off to India—I'll never bother you again.

[*He has seized his hat, and is making, in a bewildered way, for the door, when she intercepts him.*]

ANNE. No. You mustn't go away!

HAROLD. But what can I do?

ANNE (*striking a tragic attitude*). You mean to say you don't care at all—that you have never cared?

HAROLD. Really, Miss Carey, I—

ANNE. For heaven's sake, don't call me Miss Carey. Call me Anne.

HAROLD. Miss Carey...Anne...I...Oh, you'd better let me go—let me get away before anyone knows I'm here—before they think—

ANNE. It's too late. They think already.

HAROLD. Think what? What do you mean?

ANNE. Oh, this is terrible! Sit down, Harold, and listen to me. *(She pushes him into a chair and begins to talk very rapidly, watching intently the effect of her words upon him.)* You see, when you went away, people began to say things about us—you and me—about your caring. I let them go on. In fact I believed them. I suppose it was because I wanted so much to believe them. Oh, what a fool I've been! What a fool! *(She covers her face with her hands. He gets up intending vaguely to comfort her, but she thinks he is making another move to go, and jumps to her feet.)* And now you want to clear out like a thief in the night, and leave me to be laughed at! No, no, you can't do that! You must help me. You've hurt me to the very soul. You mustn't humiliate me before the world.

HAROLD. I'll do anything I can, Miss Carey.

ANNE. Anne!

HAROLD. Anne, I mean. But how?

ANNE *(after a moment's thought, as if the idea had just come to her)*. You must stay here. You must pretend for a few days—for a week at most, that we're engaged.

HAROLD. I can't do that, you know. Really, I can't.

ANNE *(going to him)*. Why not? Only a little while. Then you'll go away to India. We'll find it's been a mistake. I'll break it off—it will only be a pretense, of course, but at least no one will know what a fool I've been.

HAROLD *(after a moment's hesitation)*. Miss Carey—Anne, I mean—I'll do anything I can, but not that. A man can't do that. You see, there's a girl, an English girl, down in Brazil, I—

ANNE. Oh, a girl! Another! Well, after all, what does that matter? Brazil is a long way off. She need never know.

HAROLD. She might hear. You can't keep things like this hid. I wouldn't risk that. You'd better let me clear out before your family gets home. No one need ever know I've been here.

[*Again he makes a move toward the door.* ANNE *stands motionless.*]

ANNE. You can't go. You can't. It's more serious than you imagine.

HAROLD. Serious? What do you mean?

ANNE. Come here. *(He obeys. She sits in a big chair, but avoids looking at him. There is a delicate imitation of a tragic actress in the way she tells her story.)* I wonder if I can make you understand? It means so much to me that you should—so much! Harold, you know how dull life is here in this little town. You were glad enough to get away after a year of it, weren't you? Well, it's worse for a girl, with nothing to do but sit at home—and dream—of you. Yes, that's what I did, until, at last, when I couldn't stand it any longer, I wrote you.

HAROLD *(quickly)*. I never got the letter, Miss Carey. Honor bright, I didn't.

ANNE. Perhaps not, but nevertheless you answered it.

HAROLD. Answered it? What are you talking about?

ANNE. Would you like to see your answer? *(She goes to the desk, takes a packet of letters out of a drawer, selects one, and hands it to him.)* Here it is—your answer. You see it's postmarked Rio de Janeiro.

HAROLD *(taking it wonderingly)*. This does look like my writing. *(Reads.)* "Anne, my darling—" I say, what does this mean?

ANNE. Go on.

HAROLD *(reading)*. "I have your wonderful letter. It came to me like rain in the desert. Can it be true, Anne, that you do care? I ask myself a hundred times what I have done to deserve this. A young girl seems to me as exquisite and frail as a flower——" Great Scott! You don't think *I* could have written such stuff! What in the world!

ANNE *(handing over another letter)*. Here's the next letter you wrote me, from the mine. It's a beautiful one. Read it.

HAROLD *(tears it open angrily, and reads)*. "I have been out in the night under the stars. Oh, that you were here, my beloved! It is easy to stand the dust and the turmoil of the mine without you, but beauty that I cannot share with you hurts me like a pain——"

[*He throws the letter on the table and turns toward her, speechless.*]

ANNE (*inexorably*). Yes, that's an exceptionally beautiful one. But there are more—lots more. Would you like to see them?

HAROLD. But I tell you, I never wrote them. These aren't my letters.

ANNE. Whose are they, then?

HAROLD (*walking up and down furiously*). God knows! This is some outrageous trick. You've been duped, you poor child. But we'll get to the bottom of this. Just leave it to me. I'll get detectives. I'll find out who's back of it! I'll—

[*He comes face to face with her and finds her looking quietly at him with something akin to critical interest.*]

HAROLD. Good Lord. What's the matter with me! You don't believe those letters. You couldn't think I wrote them, or you wouldn't have met me as you did, quite naturally, as an old friend. *You understand!* For heaven's sake, make it clear to me!

ANNE. I am trying to...I told you there had to be...answers...I was afraid to send my letters to you, but there had to be answers. (HAROLD *stares at her.*) So I wrote them myself.

HAROLD. You wrote them yourself!

ANNE. Yes.

HAROLD. These? These very letters?

ANNE. Yes. I had to.

HAROLD. Good God! (*He gazes at the litter of letters on the desk in stupefied silence.*) But the handwriting.

ANNE. Oh, that was easy. I had the letter you wrote to Mother.

HAROLD. And you learned to imitate my handwriting?

ANNE (*politely*). It was very good writing.

HAROLD (*in sudden apprehension*). No one has seen these things—have they?

ANNE. They arrived by mail.

HAROLD. You mean people saw the envelopes. Yes, that's bad enough...But you haven't shown them to anyone? (*At her silence he turns furiously upon her.*) Have you?...Have you?

ANNE (*who enjoys her answer and its effect upon him*). Only parts—never a whole letter.

But it was such a pleasure to be able to talk about you to someone. My only pleasure.

HAROLD. Good heavens! You told people I wrote these letters? That we were engaged?

ANNE. I didn't mean to, Harold. Really, I didn't. But I couldn't keep it dark. There were your telegrams.

HAROLD. My telegrams?

[*She goes to desk and produces a bundle of dispatches.*]

ANNE (*brazen in her sincerity*). You used to write me every time you changed your address. You were very thoughtful, Harold. But, of course, I couldn't keep those secret like your letters.

HAROLD (*standing helplessly, with the telegrams loose in his fingers*). My telegrams! Good Lord! (*He opens one and reads.*) "Leaving Rio for fortnight of inspection in interior. Address care Señor Miguel—" *My* telegrams!

[*He flings the packet violently on the table thereby almost upsetting a bowl of roses which he hastens to preserve.*]

ANNE. And then there were your flowers. I see you are admiring them.

[HAROLD *withdraws as if the flowers were charged with electricity.*]

HAROLD. What flowers?

ANNE. These—these—all of them. You sent me flowers every week while you were gone.

HAROLD (*overcome*). Good God!

[*He has now reached the apex of his amazement and becomes sardonic.*]

ANNE. Yes. You were extravagant with flowers, Harold. Of course I love them, but I had to scold you about spending so much money.

HAROLD. Spending so much money? And what did I say when you scolded me?

ANNE (*taken aback only for a moment by his changed attitude*). You sent me a bigger bunch than ever before—and—wait a minute—here's the card you put in it.

[*She goes to the same fatal desk and produces a package of florist's cards.*]

HAROLD. Are all those my cards too?

ANNE. Yes.

HAROLD (*laughing a bit wildly*). I'm afraid I *was* a bit extravagant!

ANNE. Here's the one! You wrote: "If all

that I have, and all that I am, is too little to lay before you, how can these poor flowers be much?"

HAROLD. I wrote that? Very pretty—very. I'd forgotten I had any such knack at sentiments.

ANNE. And then, right away, you sent me the ring.

HAROLD *(jumps, startled out of his sardonic pose)*. Ring! What ring?

ANNE. My engagement ring. You were very extravagant that time.

HAROLD *(looking fearfully at her hands)*. But I don't see...You're not wearing...?

ANNE. Not there—here, next to my heart. *(She takes out a ring which hangs on a chain inside her frock, and presses it to her lips, looking at him deeply.)* I adore sapphires, Harold.

[*A new fear comes into* HAROLD's *eyes. He begins to humor her.*]

HAROLD. Yes. Yes. Of course. Everyone likes sapphires, Anne. It is a beauty. Yes. *(He comes very close to her, and speaks very gently, as if to a child.)* You haven't shown your ring to anyone, have you, Anne?

ANNE. Only to a few people—one or two.

HAROLD. A few people! Good heavens! *(Then he controls himself, takes her hands gently in his, and continues speaking, as if to a child.)* Sit down, Anne; we must talk this over a little—very quietly, you understand, very quietly. Now to begin with, when did you first—

ANNE *(breaks away from him with a little laugh)*. No, I'm not crazy. Don't be worried. I'm perfectly sane. I had to tell you all this to show how serious it was. Now you know. What are you going to do?

HAROLD. Do? *(He slowly straightens up as if the knowledge of her sanity had relieved him of a heavy load.)* I'm going to take the next train back to New York.

ANNE. And leave me to get out of this before people all alone?

HAROLD. You got into it without my assistance, didn't you? Great Scott, you forged those letters in cold blood—

ANNE. Not in cold blood, Harold. Remember, I cared.

HAROLD. I don't believe it. *(Accusingly.)* You enjoyed writing those letters!

ANNE. Of course I enjoyed it. It meant thinking of you, talking of—

HAROLD. Rot! Not of me, really. You don't think I am really the sort of person who could write that—that drivel!

ANNE *(hurt)*. Oh, I don't know. After a while I suppose you and my dream got confused.

HAROLD. But it was the rankest—

ANNE. Oh, I'm not so different from other girls. We're all like that. *(Repeating* RUTH's *phrase reminiscently.)* We must have someone to dream about—to talk about. I suppose it's because we haven't enough to do. And then we girls that stay at home don't have any—any real adventures like working girls.

HAROLD *(surprised at this bit of reasoning)*. That's a funny excuse to give!

ANNE. Well, it's true. I know I went rather far. After I got started I couldn't stop. I didn't want to, either. It took hold of me. So I went on and on and let people think whatever they wanted. But if you go now and people find out what I've done, they'll think I'm really mad—or something worse. Life will be impossible for me here, don't you see—impossible. (HAROLD *is silent.*) But if you stay, it will be so easy. Just a day or two. Then you will have to go to India. Is that much to ask? *(Acting.)* And you save me from disgrace, from ruin!

[HAROLD *remains silent, troubled.*]

ANNE *(becoming excited).* You must help me. You *must.* After I've been so frank with you, you can't go back on me now. I've never in my life talked to anyone like this—so openly. You *can't* go back on me! If you leave me here to be laughed at, mocked at by everyone, I don't know what I shall do. I shan't be responsible. If you have any kindness, any chivalry...Oh, for God's sake, Harold, help me, help me! *(Kneels at his feet.)*

HAROLD. I don't know...I'm horribly muddled...All right, I'll stay!

ANNE. Good! Good! Oh, you are fine! I knew you would be. Now everything will be so simple. *(The vista opens before her.)* We will be very quiet here for a couple of days. We won't see many people, for of course it isn't announced. And then you will go...and I will write you a letter....

HAROLD *(disagreeably struck by the phrase).* Write me a letter? What for?

ANNE *(ingenuously).* Telling you that I have been mistaken. Releasing you from the engagement...and you will write me an answer... sad but manly...reluctantly accepting my decision....

HAROLD. Oh, I am to write an answer, sad but manly— Good God! Suppose you don't release me after all!

ANNE. Don't be silly, Harold. I promise. Can't you trust me?

HAROLD. Trust you? *(His eyes travel quickly from the table littered with letters and dispatches to the flowers that ornament the room, back to the table, and finally to the ring that now hangs conspicuously on her breast. She follows the look and instinctively puts her hand to the ring.)* Trust you? By Jove, no, I don't trust you! This is absurd. I don't stay another moment. Say what you will to people. I'm off. This is final.

ANNE *(who has stepped to the window).* You can't go now. I hear Mother and Ruth coming.

HAROLD. All the more reason. *(He finds his hat.)* I bolt.

ANNE *(blocking the door).* You can't go, Harold! Don't corner me. I'll fight like a wildcat if you do.

HAROLD. Fight?

ANNE. Yes. A pretty figure you'll cut if you bolt now. They'll think you a cad—an out-and-out cad! Haven't they seen your letters come week by week, and your presents? And you have written to Mother, too—I have your letter. There won't be anything bad enough to say about you. They'll say you jilted me for that English girl in Brazil. It will be true, too. And it will get about. She'll hear of it, I'll see to that—and then——

HAROLD. But it's a complete lie! I can explain——

ANNE. You'll have a hard time explaining your letters and your presents—and your ring. There's a deal of evidence against you——

HAROLD. See here, are you trying to blackmail me? Oh, this is too ridiculous!

ANNE. They're coming! I hear them on the stairs! What are you going to tell them?

HAROLD. The truth. I must get clear of all this. I tell you——

ANNE *(suddenly clinging to him).* No, no, Harold! Forgive me; I was just testing you. I will get you out of this. Leave it to me.

HAROLD *(struggling with her).* No, I won't leave anything to you, *ever.*

ANNE *(still clinging tightly).* Harold, remember I am a woman—and I love you.

[*This brings him up short a moment to wonder, and in this moment there is a knock at the door.*]

ANNE *(abandoning HAROLD).* Come in.

[*There is a discreet pause.*]

MRS. CAREY'S VOICE *(off-stage).* May we come in?

ANNE *(angrily).* Yes!

[HAROLD, *who has moved toward the door, meets* MRS. CAREY *as she enters. She throws her arms about his neck and kisses him warmly. She is followed by* RUTH.]

MRS. CAREY. Harold! My dear boy!

RUTH *(clutching his arm).* Hello, Harold. I am so glad.

[HAROLD, *temporarily overwhelmed by the onslaught of the two women, is about to speak.* ANNE *interrupts dramatically.*]

ANNE. Wait a moment, Mother. Before you say anything more I must tell you that Harold and I are no longer engaged!

[MRS. CAREY *and* RUTH *draw away from* HAROLD *in horror-struck surprise.*]

MRS. CAREY. No longer engaged? Why... What...?

HAROLD. Really, Mrs. Carey, I—

ANNE *(interrupts, going to her mother).* Mother, dear, be patient with me, trust me, I beg of you—and please, please don't ask me any questions. Harold and I have had a very hard—a very painful hour together. I don't think I can stand any more.

[*She is visibly very much exhausted, gasping for breath.*]

MRS. CAREY. Oh, my poor child, what is it? What has he done?

[*She supports* ANNE *on one side while* RUTH *hurries to the other.*]

HAROLD. Really, Mrs. Carey, I think I can explain.

ANNE. No, Harold, there's no use trying to explain. There are some things a woman feels, about which she cannot reason. I know I am doing right.

HAROLD *(desperately).* Mrs. Carey, I assure you—

ANNE *(as if on the verge of a nervous crisis).* Oh, please, *please,* Harold, don't protest any more. I am not blaming you. Understand, Mother, I am not blaming him. But my decision is irrevocable. I thought you understood. I beg you to go away. You have just time to catch the afternoon express.

HAROLD. Nonsense, Anne, you must let me—

ANNE *(wildly).* No, no, Harold, it is finished! Don't you understand? Finished! *(She abandons the support of her mother and* RUTH *and goes to the table.)* See, here are your letters—*(She throws the packet into the fire.)* All your letters—*(She throws the dispatches into the fire.)* Don't, please, continue this unendurable situation any longer. Go, I beg of you, go! *(She is almost hysterical.)*

HAROLD. But I tell you I must—

ANNE *(falling back in her mother's arms).* Make him go, Mother! Make him go!

MRS. CAREY. Yes, go! Go, sir! Don't you see you are torturing the child? I insist you go.

RUTH. Yes, she is in a dreadful state.

[*Here* MRS. CAREY *and* RUTH *fall into simultaneous urgings.*]

HAROLD *(who has tried in vain to make himself heard).* All right, I'm going; I give up!

[*He seizes his hat and rushes out, banging the door behind him.* ANNE *breaks away from her mother and sister, totters rapidly to the door, and calls gently down the stairs.*]

ANNE. Not in anger, I beg of you, Harold! I am not blaming you. Good-by.

[*The street door is heard to bang.* ANNE *collapses in approved tragedy style.*]

ANNE *(gasping).* Get some water, Ruth. I shall be all right in a moment.

[RUTH *rushes into the bedroom.*]

MRS. CAREY. Oh, my dear child, calm yourself. Mother is here, dear. She will take care of you. Tell me, dear, tell me.

[RUTH *returns with the water.* ANNE *sips a little.*]

ANNE. I will, Mother—I will...everything... later. *(She drinks.)* But now I must be alone. Please, dear, go away...for a little while. I must be alone—*(rising and moving to the fire)*—with the ruin of my dreams.

[*She puts her arms on the chimney shelf and drops her head on them.*]

RUTH. Come, Mother! Come away!

MRS. CAREY. Yes, I am coming. We shall be in the next room Anne, when you want us. Right here.

ANNE *(as they go out, raises her head and murmurs).* Dust and ashes! Dust and ashes!

[*As soon as they have gone,* ANNE *straightens up slowly. She pulls herself together after the physical strain of her acting. Then she looks at the watch on her wrist and sighs a long triumphant sigh. Her eye falls on the desk and she sees the package of florist's cards still there. She picks them up, returns with them to the fire and is about to throw them in, when her eye is caught by the writing on one. She takes it out and reads it. Then she takes another—and another. She stops and looks away dreamily. Then slowly, she moves back to the desk, drops the cards into a drawer, and locks it. She sits brooding at the desk and the open paper before her seems to fascinate her. As if in a dream she picks up a pencil. A creative look comes into her eyes. Resting her chin on her left hand, she begins slowly to write, murmuring to herself.*]

ANNE *(reading as she writes).* "Anne, my dearest...I am on the train...broken, shattered ...Why have you done this to me...why have you darkened the sun...and put out the stars... put out the stars...Give me another chance, Anne; don't shut me out of your life utterly... I cannot bear it...I..."
[*The curtain has fallen slowly as she writes.*]

GETTING TO KNOW ANNE

1. What is the situation when the curtain rises? At what point did you receive the first hint that Anne's romance was not all that she pictured it? Name in order the things that confirmed your suspicions.

2. What sort of young man is Harold? What contrast do you find between his conversation and the letters he is supposed to have written? Do you agree with him that the letters are "drivel" or do you admire them as Ruth did?

3. Harold asks Anne if she is trying to blackmail him. What is your answer to this question? What reasons did Anne offer as excuse for her actions? In your opinion do they excuse her? Why, or why not?

4. Is Anne a different person at the end of the play from what she is at the beginning? Explain.

5. What makes "Enter the Hero" a good play?

Know your words

In order to help actors dramatize a play, the author supplies stage directions which indicate how each character is to react to various situations. If you plan to act out "Enter the Hero" successfully, it will be necessary to interpret these stage directions accurately. Several of them, with accompanying dialogue, are listed below. In deciding how the dialogue is to be spoken, pay particular attention to the italicized words in the stage directions. You may use the Glossary for help.

1. ANNE (pleased, but *disparaging*). But every girl has this experience sooner or later.

2. ANNE (with rather *histrionic* intensity). No, I'm strangely calm. And yet, Ruth, I'm afraid, terribly afraid.

3. ANNE (*inexorably*). Yes, that's an exceptionally beautiful one. But there are more—lots more. Would you like to see them?

4. HAROLD (He has now reached the *apex* of his amazement and becomes *sardonic*.)...Spending so much money? And what did I say when you scolded me?

5. ANNE (repeating RUTH's phrase *reminiscently*). We must have someone to dream about....

6. HAROLD. Write me a letter? What for?
ANNE (*ingenuously*). Telling you that I have been mistaken. Releasing you from the engagement...

❧ IV RADIO AND TELEVISION DRAMA

By means of radio and television more people enjoy dramas today than ever before. Some of these are the greatest dramas of the past and present, condensed and adapted for new mediums. Other plays are adaptations of stories, as is the radio play "Sixteen" (pages 258-263). Still others are written to dramatize the life of a great person, to commemorate some historical event, to make vivid some story or set of conditions in the world today, or to arouse respect for and loyalty to American ideals. Stephen Vincent Benét's "Listen to the People" (pages 475-482) is a fine example of this last type of drama.

Compared to stage plays, which have a history centuries old, radio and television dramas are in their infancy. Many of the plays presented are commonplace; much remains to be learned. But at their best both radio and television dramas indicate what may yet be achieved in the creation of character and in the interpretation of great human problems.

The Pharmacist's Mate

BUDD SCHULBERG
(based on the newspaper story by
GEORGE WELLER)

Few television plays have had more to offer or have been more enthusiastically received than "The Pharmacist's Mate." Some members of the audience were particularly interested in it because George Weller had won a Pulitzer Prize for the newspaper story on which the play was based. Others liked especially the fact that the play was a *documentary*, or a presentation in dramatic form of something that had really happened. But the great bulk of the television audience were carried along simply by the excitement of watching an action-filled drama that was well written and well staged.

If you are to get the same thrill from this play that the television audience received, you must open your imaginative eyes and ears wide. You must be ready to "follow the camera," picking up the various characters, visualizing their facial expressions, and, from what you see and hear, interpreting the emotions of men at a tense moment on a submarine.

CHARACTERS

JIMMY BRUCE, *Pharmacist's Mate*[1]
LT. COMMANDER MILLER, *Skipper*
FLOYD HUDSON, *Executive Officer*[2]
APPRENTICE SEAMAN TOMMY FORD, *Patient*
ENSIGN RIGGS, *Diving Officer*[3]

---

[1]*Pharmacist's Mate,* the seaman in complete charge of the sick bay, or the place on the ship used as a hospital.
[2]*Executive Officer,* the officer who ranks next to the commanding officer and is his representative at all times.
[3]*Diving Officer,* the officer in charge of controlling the depth of the submarine.

Other Members of the Crew

FANELLI	HELMSMAN
GOODMAN	MESSENGER
O'BRIEN	SONARMAN[4]
RADIOMAN	YOUNG PETTY OFFICER
SWEDE	LEROY JOHNSON
LT. DAVISON	QUARTERMASTER WILLIAMS

FIRST ACEY-DEUCY[5] PLAYER
SECOND ACEY-DEUCY PLAYER

Fade in[6] *on view of the sea as seen in an enlarged circle through a submarine periscope. The sea is disturbed, boiling up. Dissolve to*[7] *interior view of conning tower. Present are the* EXECUTIVE OFFICER *at the periscope, the* QUARTERMASTER, *working the periscope for him, the* HELMSMAN *and, off to the starboard side, the* SONARMAN. *The* EXECUTIVE OFFICER, LT. FLOYD HUDSON, *is in his late twenties, good-looking, tight-lipped, serious to the point of being disagreeable. He is walking the periscope around.*[8]

HUDSON (*turning from the periscope and addressing the* QUARTERMASTER). Down periscope, Williams.

WILLIAMS. Aye, aye, sir.

[HUDSON *goes to the squawk box*[9] *near the wheel. Close shot of* HUDSON.]

---

[4]*Sonarman* (sō'när man'), the sound operator. He is in charge of using the apparatus for detecting enemy ships when the submarine is submerged.
[5]*Acey-Deucy,* a gambling game in which both cards and dice are used.
[6]*Fade in,* bring slowly into sight.
[7]*Dissolve to,* change picture gradually to.
[8]*walking the periscope around,* making a complete turn of the periscope to search for enemy ships or airplanes.
[9]*squawk box,* intercommunication system of ship.

HUDSON (into the squawk box). Lt. Hudson in the conning tower. Lt. Hudson in the conning tower. Are you listening, Skipper?

VOICE OF SKIPPER (on squawk box). Go ahead, Hudson.

HUDSON. Still all clear. Nothing in sight. And it's all clear from the sonarman, too.

VOICE OF SKIPPER. Very well. Come up for a look every twenty minutes. And don't bother reporting again until you sight something.

HUDSON. Aye, aye, sir. (Pause.) Ensign Riggs. Ensign Riggs, run at 90 feet until 1350 and then come back to periscope depth.[10]

[Cut to[11] control room, below the conning tower. Present are the diving officer, young, sandy-haired ENSIGN RIGGS; the two planesmen, who operate the imposing wheels that affect the angle and depth and control of the boat; men on the trim and air manifolds[12]; a chief of the watch[13]; and stand-by men and messengers.]

RIGGS (getting his order from the squawk box). Aye, aye, Hudson.

[He turns to check the enormous depth-control gauge and addresses the planesmen.]

RIGGS. Five-degree down angle. Level off at 90.

[One planesman nods and the giant wheel begins to turn. The depth-gauge needle drops. Cut back to conning tower.]

WILLIAMS (standing near and addressing the youthful HELMSMAN). Man, this is one night I wouldn't mind a little shore duty. Christmas Eve in Pearl.[14] (Sighs.) Oughta be quite a brawl.

[LT. HUDSON, behind him, overhears.]

HUDSON. They didn't send us out here to go to Christmas parties, Williams; they sent us to——

WILLIAMS (rather tolerantly, with an old, wrinkled smile). I know, I know, Lieutenant.

If we can spot the enemy troopships and get a report back on their course, the islands fall into our hands like ripe apples. But Christmas Eve —a guy can dream, can't he?

HUDSON (sharply, humorlessly). Not when he's on watch. We can't slack off up here. We're out here to find them. They must be somewhere.

WILLIAMS (dead-pan). I'm sure they are, sir.

[New camera angle: HUDSON turns to consult with SONARMAN in the background. In the foreground are WILLIAMS and the HELMSMAN.]

HELMSMAN (in a mumble). Pretty serious fella—that new Exec.

WILLIAMS. Aw, he's just a little Academy-happy.[15] The Old Man[16] will straighten him out.

[Fade to corridor leading to galley, etc. The "Old Man" appears. He is in his early thirties, not as good-looking in a conventional way as the EXECUTIVE OFFICER. Also in contrast to LT. HUDSON, he is relaxed, and underlying his control of every situation there is a current of good humor. He looks into the galley. SWEDE, the cook, big and easygoing, turns around with a wide grin. He looks much too rough to be an expert on fancy pastry; but just the same, he is. He works in shorts and he is bare to the waist, exhibiting some fancy tattooing.]

SWEDE (respectfully, but familiarly). Cap'n.

MILLER. What've you got for us tonight, Swede?

SWEDE. Well, seein' it's Christmas, I thought I'd break out some steaks.

MILLER. And a cake?

SWEDE. Wait'll you see it. It's gonna have red and green lights that pop up and spell Merry Christmas.

MILLER (grinning). Good boy. You know what they say on a sub, Swede. Good chow is the skipper's secret weapon. What else is there to do on a pigboat but hunt and hide—and sleep and eat?

SWEDE. You can say that again, Cap'n. This is gonna be a rum cake that'll make 'em forget all about home cooking.

---

[10]run at 90 feet...periscope depth, keep the submarine 90 feet below the surface until 1:50 P.M. and then come up to the depth at which the periscope can be used for observation. Naval time is reckoned from midnight counting continuously for twenty-four hours; thus 1350 would be 1:50 P.M.

[11]Cut to, change picture to view of.

[12]the trim and air manifolds. The trim manifold shifts water from some tanks to others to keep the boat level; the air manifold blows water from tanks into the sea to level the boat when surfacing.

[13]chief of the watch, man responsible for the men on duty during a four-hour period.

[14]Pearl, Pearl Harbor, the great United States naval base in the Hawaiian Islands.

---

[15]Academy-happy. Williams means that Hudson, a recent graduate of the Naval Academy at Annapolis, is overproud of his training and commission as an officer in the regular Navy.

[16]The Old Man, the commander of the ship.

MILLER (*suddenly more serious*). I doubt that, Swede—even though you are the best cook I ever had aboard. (*Picking up something to munch on.*) You know, when you get to be as old as I am, you learn something—to pick your cooks even more carefully than your gunnery officers.

[*During the above conversation* SWEDE *is not idle. He is kneading dough, checking his oven, etc. Now he takes some fried potatoes off the griddle.*]

SWEDE. Thanks, Cap'n. But if I had a little more room, I could really show you something.

MILLER (*picking up a potato slice*). That's how we all feel. But on a pigboat, you make do. Good luck with the cake, Swede. You better plan to serve it pretty early. I doubt if we'll have much time for celebration after sundown.

SWEDE. Aye, aye, sir.

[COM. MILLER *goes on down the corridor toward the bow.* SWEDE *grins, picks up a plate of French fries, and turns toward the dinette next door. Cut to dinette.* SWEDE *enters, sets the plate down.*]

SWEDE. Free sample, fellers. Wrap your molars around these.

[*He exits. Half a dozen men are crowded into this dinette. A couple of petty officers are playing acey-deucy; another, a first-class gunner's mate*[17]—*squat, husky, tough-looking veteran-submariner* O'BRIEN—*is kibitzing.* FANELLI, *a dark-haired young seaman, is trying to read a pocketbook while an apprentice seaman,* TOMMY FORD, *who hardly looks old enough to be away from home, is trying, in the midst of all this relaxed confusion, to write a letter.*]

FIRST ACEY-DEUCY PLAYER. Boy, I'll bet that girl of yours will be pining for you to-night—

SECOND ACEY-DEUCY PLAYER. Come on, play your cards. You haven't even got a girl.

FIRST PLAYER (*winking to the others*). Why should I? I c'n always take yours.

FANELLI. All right, knock it off, you guys. I'm trying to read.

O'BRIEN (*in a false soprano*). I'm trying to read.

---

[17]*first-class gunner's mate*, a seaman having charge of munitions.

[*Everyone except the letter writer laughs.*]

FANELLI (*putting the book down*). Christmas. At least on a CV[18] they'd have a tree…maybe a regular party with a band…and look at us …the only way we know it's Christmas is by short wave.

[*Camera centers on* TOMMY FORD *trying to write his letter. As he writes, he looks off meditatively, not hearing the adlib cracks, his mind thousands of miles away. While he goes on writing, we peek at his letter in an insert.*]

Dear Mom and Pop. Sure seems funny to be away from you for the first time on Christmas Eve….

[*The pen pauses. Wider camera angle of dinette while* TOMMY *goes on writing.*]

SECOND ACEY-DEUCY PLAYER. A year ago I was home-sweet-home, eating hot mince pie and then my girl came in and gave me this watch and when I turned it over it said—

EVERYONE (*except* TOMMY *who continues to write*). To my dearest from his Bibsey.

SECOND ACEY-DEUCY PLAYER (*disgusted*). Aw, nothing's sacred around you guys.

O'BRIEN. That home-baked hot mince pie and a good ten-cent cigar after the turkey and your arm around the old lady's waist. (*Sighs.*) Last Christmas I got so bloomin' sentimental about it I went down and got this little art job.

[*He rolls up his sleeves to show his powerful forearm. Close-up of tattoo on forearm showing* "Mike" *and* "Kate" *in a Christmas wreath. As he flexes his muscle, their heads go back and forth as in a kiss. Camera cuts back to group laughing.*]

ADLIB. What a man! (*Etc.*)

[*Close-up of* TOMMY *ignoring the banter. Insert of letter.*]

Tonight I can just see the tree by the fireplace, and the kids and Mary Lou….

O'BRIEN (*out of camera range*). You had him, if you'da rolled a six.

SECOND ACEY-DEUCY PLAYER (*out of camera range*). I know what they keep you around for, Obie—in case they run out of high-pressure air they've always got you.

---

[18]*CV*, aircraft carrier.

O'BRIEN (out of camera range, flaring up). Listen, Jackson, I was wearin' Dolphins[19] when you—

[In a wider camera angle TOMMY FORD looks up, still oblivious of the group around him. The memory his words evoke makes it difficult for him to go on.]

FANELLI (looking up from his book again). Slow it down to two knots, you guys. You're racing your motors.

[TOMMY tries to go on writing, then stops as his hand goes to his right side; a small sound of pain escapes him. The others look up.]

O'BRIEN (sympathetically). Whatsa matter, Tommy?

TOMMY. I dunno. I had a gut ache all night. Feels like a knife in there.

FIRST ACEY-DEUCY PLAYER. It's those biscuits we had last night. I tell ya that Swede is trying to poison us. It's sabotage, that's what it is.

O'BRIEN. Why don't you see the quack[20]; let him put you on the binnacle list.[21]

TOMMY (talking with effort but trying to minimize the pain). Aw, I guess I'll be all right. Maybe I did wolf too many of those biscuits down last night.

SECOND ACEY-DEUCY PLAYER. Whatta ya wanna bet the Swede worked in a cement factory before he got this job?

[TOMMY rubs his right side, obviously in distress, yet trying not to make too much of it.]

O'BRIEN. No kidding, boy, I'd do something about that.

TOMMY. I did. I took some tablets the Chief[22] gave me this morning.

FIRST ACEY-DEUCY PLAYER. Oh, great. Just because the Chief knows how to doctor a Diesel,[23] he thinks he's a great medical man.

[20]the quack, a joking reference to the pharmacist's mate.

[21]binnacle list, sick list, so called because it is posted near the binnacle, a case containing a ship's compass and a lamp for night use.

[22]the Chief, the chief petty officer, the highest rating among enlisted men.

[23]Diesel (dē'zəl or dē'səl), the oil-burning engine used to run the submarine.

[19]Dolphins, insignia worn by officers and enlisted men on a submarine. A man wins his Dolphin only after finishing school and qualifying—or demonstrating that he knows the complete operation of the boat—on his first submarine.

SECOND ACEY-DEUCY PLAYER. Well, he can't kill you any quicker than the quack—that's for sure.

[A MESSENGER enters.]

MESSENGER. Fanelli, Ford, O'Brien—five minutes and you're on watch, fellows.

[The MESSENGER exits. The three he alerted rise and start toward the door.]

FANELLI. Back to the salt mines, Tommy.

TOMMY (trying to grin). Right, Joe.

[O'BRIEN, the veteran submariner, gunner's mate first-class, older than the others, puts his hand on TOMMY's shoulder.]

O'BRIEN. That's a tough job on the planes,[24] kid. I wouldn't stand watch if I looked the way you do.

TOMMY. Aw, if I was back at the base I guess I'd see the doc. But out here, with something liable to happen any second—well, I c'n take it for four hours, and then I'll hit the sack.

O'BRIEN (easily). Know what I always say, lad? "Do what you're man enough to do."

[Cut to control room. In the background we can see TOMMY and FANELLI relieving the planesmen. In the foreground are COM. MILLER, ENSIGN RIGGS, and LT. DAVISON, a hulking, affable young Southerner.]

MILLER. I'll be in the wardroom if you need me for anything, Riggs.

RIGGS. Yes, sir.

MILLER (to DAVISON). Come on, Jeff. I'll give you another chess lesson.

DAVISON. Chess? When we're practically up on the enemy beach?

MILLER (smiling). That's the time for chess.

[They start off toward the forward compartments. As they do so, they pass PHARMACIST'S MATE JIMMY BRUCE, on his way aft. MILLER says, "Jimmy," and gives him an offhand salute, a habitual gesture. JIMMY grins, mumbles a respectful "Cap'n," and we follow him as he continues on toward the rear compartments. Cut back to dinette as JIMMY BRUCE enters. He is a blond, wiry kid from Arkansas, about twenty-two years old. He has unruly hair and is cocky in an unobjectionable way, quick to grin. As soon as they see him, the ACEY-DEUCY PLAYERS set up a cross fire of banter that is apparently a stylized bit of by-play on the sub.]

FIRST ACEY-DEUCY PLAYER. Hi ya, ducky?

BRUCE. Waddya mean, ducky?

FIRST ACEY-DEUCY PLAYER. The quack, quack, quack. (They laugh.)

SECOND ACEY-DEUCY PLAYER. How's everything back in Ar-kansas?

BRUCE. It's not Ar-kansas, it's—(then realizing it is a rib)—aw, why don't you guys get a new joke?

[He sits down and pulls out a comic book.]

FIRST ACEY-DEUCY PLAYER. Hey, quack, I got a hangnail that's painin' me somethin' awful.

SECOND ACEY-DEUCY PLAYER. Put 'im on the binnacle list so you c'n goldbrick[25] together.

BRUCE (jovially). Keep on callin' me quack and I'll cut that hangnail off—right up to here. (He indicates the player's neck.)

SECOND ACEY-DEUCY PLAYER. No kiddin', Brucie, how come you rate this soft job? The only noncombatant on the whole darn boat. Nothin' to do but sit around readin' comics.

BRUCE. Oh, sure. All I've got to do is stand regular watches like the rest of you, and doctor up you goof-offs on the side.

FIRST ACEY-DEUCY PLAYER. Listen to the boy. He never had it so good.

BRUCE (grinning). Sure, it's a breeze—as long as everyone stays in one piece around here.

[He settles down comfortably with his comic book; the ACEY-DEUCY PLAYERS chatter up a little adlib on their game. Dissolve to periscope cutting through the rough sea. Then dissolve to conning tower. EXECUTIVE OFFICER HUDSON appears up the ladder from the control room, takes over the periscope lookout from the Chief, and peers intently at the sea and the sky. Cut to interior of control room. TOMMY on the bow plane is perspiring from the effort to overcome his pain.]

RIGGS. Mind your bubble,[26] Ford. Hold her to a half-degree down angle.

---

[24]the planes, the wheels that affect the angle, depth, and control of the submarine. Tommy is to serve as planesman for this watch.

[25]goldbrick, get out of work.

[26]bubble. Above each plane is an instrument called a level filled with a fluid in which a bubble rides. When the submarine is level, the bubble is at dead center. It moves to indicate whether the boat is pointing up or down.

TOMMY (through his teeth). Aye, aye, sir.

[Shot of depth indicator. It is fluctuating, showing that the boat is in danger of broaching.[27] Close shot of RIGGS.]

RIGGS (observing the indicator). Flood auxiliary from sea—one thousand pounds.

[Close shot of O'BRIEN at trim manifold. He is opening the valve, and watching the gauge.]

YOUNG PETTY OFFICER. Auxiliaries are flooding, sir.

[Close shot of air manifold.]

O'BRIEN. One thousand pounds flooded in auxiliary. Trim manifold secure.

[Wider angle shot of control room angled toward planes. ENSIGN RIGGS comes up and looks over TOMMY'S shoulder critically.]

RIGGS. You've got a two-degree down angle. Come on, Ford, stay awake.

[TOMMY wipes the sweat from his forehead and, operating the plane automatically, adjusts the angle of the boat. Cut to wardroom. COM. MILLER has sat down to his game of chess with LT. DAVISON. To one side are charts which MILLER has been working on.]

DAVISON (in his slow drawl). Chess. Sure never thought I'd learn to play a brainy game like chess.

MILLER (with a slight smile, as he takes two of DAVISON'S pawns with his knight). What makes you think you've learned, Jeff?

DAVISON. Sure beats me how you figured that out, Skipper. I thought I had you trapped.

MILLER (studying the board). If you hope to skipper one of these boats some day, Jeff, this game can give you some pointers. A sub is like this king. Everything on the board is hunting you. And you can't use it to strike without fatally exposing yourself. (He makes another move on the board and DAVISON winces.) To stay alive, you always have to be at least two or three jumps ahead.

[Over the squawk box in the corner we hear:]

SQUAWK BOX. Wardroom, this is the conning tower, Lt. Hudson. Is the Captain there?

MILLER (operating the squawk box). What's the story, Floyd?

SQUAWK BOX. We've sighted smoke, sir. Maybe fifteen miles. Bearing 0-2-7.[28]

MILLER. Very well.

[He rises and pushes the chessboard back, moving as quickly as possible in the cramped quarters.]

DAVISON (over the squawk box). Okay, Hudson. The Skipper's on his way up.

[Cut to conning tower. HUDSON is peering through the periscope again. The rough sea makes it difficult to maintain depth control.]

WILLIAMS (over the squawk box). Mr. Hudson wants you to run at 55 feet.

SQUAWK BOX (Riggs' voice). I need more speed.

[HUDSON goes to the squawk box.]

HUDSON. All right. But slow her down as soon as you can maintain trim at one-third speed.

SQUAWK BOX. Aye, aye, sir.

HUDSON. Down periscope.

[QUARTERMASTER WILLIAMS begins to comply. Cut to control room, ENSIGN RIGGS at the squawk box.]

RIGGS. All ahead two-thirds.

[Cut to engine room: the engineman responds. Dissolve to exterior of submarine moving through water. Cut to conning tower as COM. MILLER appears up the ladder from the control room.]

HUDSON. I think I have a destroyer bearing 0-3-5. And it looks like another one off our port bow. Hull down.[29]

MILLER. Very well. Let me have a look as soon as we get back to one-third.

[After a pause, we hear over the squawk box:]

RIGGS' VOICE. I can hold her at 55.

MILLER. Very well. Up periscope.

[WILLIAMS raises the periscope. Meanwhile MILLER turns to the SONARMAN.]

MILLER. Do you have the target bearing 0-3-5?

SONARMAN. Still all clear for me, sir.

MILLER. Keep searching in that quadrant. Let me know as soon as you pick them up. (He turns

---

[27]broaching, coming to the surface.

[28]Bearing 0-2-7. Numbers are used to indicate the angle from which a ship is approaching.

[29]Hull down, a submariner's expression meaning "Only the mast and stacks are visible; the hull is invisible."

and peers intently into the periscope. *After a moment's study he speaks with quiet satisfaction.*) That looks like our little friends, all right. (*Studies them further.*) We'll continue to close and track them at periscope depth until sundown. (*To* QUARTERMASTER WILLIAMS.) What time is it, Williams?

WILLIAMS. 1517 hours, sir.

MILLER. Very well. Keep tracking their course and speed and at 1530 we'll surface to get off our report.

HUDSON. Aye, aye, sir. (*After a pause.*) Sure wish we could take a crack at them now, Captain.

MILLER. So do I. But if our report brings our striking force[30] over in time to intercept them, that will more than make up for having to wait. (MILLER *returns to the periscope.*) Let's be very careful on these observations. We don't want some zoomy[31] to pick us up before we can accomplish this mission.

[*The boat pitches upward, almost throwing them off balance.*]

HUDSON (*on squawk box*). What's the matter down there? Can't you hold her at 55?

[*Cut to control room.* ENSIGN RIGGS *checks the depth gauge, which records 48, and then turns on* TOMMY FORD *who has been fighting collapse.*]

RIGGS (*angrily*). Come on, Ford. Watch that bubble.

FORD (*weakly*). Aye...aye, sir.

RIGGS. What's the matter with you today?

FORD. Sir, I'm not feeling well...there's something wrong. I...

RIGGS. Why didn't you say something right away so I could get you relieved?

FORD. Well, I—I thought I'd be all right, and ...(*He clutches his side.*)

RIGGS (*turning to a stand-by planesman*). Goodman, relieve the stern planes. Depth 55. One-degree down angle. And don't let the waves suck you up.

[SEAMAN GOODMAN *moves in to take* FORD's *place. As* FORD *rises he is suddenly seized with excruciating pain and slumps to the deck.* EN-

---

SIGN RIGGS *and a stand-by messenger kneel beside him.* ENSIGN RIGGS *looks up at the chief of the watch.*]

RIGGS. Get Bruce. Have him report here right away.

[TOMMY, *unconscious, writhes and groans.* RIGGS *rises and addresses the messenger and another stand-by.*]

RIGGS. Carry him in to my bunk.

[RIGGS *turns back to check the depth gauge. Cut to dinette.* JIMMY BRUCE *is reading his comic book. The acey-deucy game goes on.*]

SQUAWK BOX. Pharmacist's Mate Bruce. Pharmacist's Mate Bruce. Report to control room at once.

BRUCE (*pushing his comic book away reluctantly and rising*). Yeah, I got a cinch. All I have to do is sit down and one of you clumsy jokers is sure to bump his head on a hatchway. (*He folds his comic book into his pocket.*) I've been trying to finish "Lil Abner" for three days!

FIRST ACEY-DEUCY PLAYER (*as* BRUCE *exits*). Don't worry, boy, you got lots of time. At the rate we're going, we'll still be out here next Christmas.

SECOND ACEY-DEUCY PLAYER (*calling after* BRUCE *in a mimicking voice*). Calling Dr. Kildare.[32] Calling Dr. Kildare. Emergency case of hiccoughs in the control room.

[*The two men are laughing together at their wit as* JIMMY BRUCE *hurries out. Cut to Chief's room.* JIMMY BRUCE *enters.* TOMMY *is lying on the bunk, conscious now but in terrible pain.*]

BRUCE. Hello, Tommy. Let's have a look at you. (*He kneels at the bunk, feels* TOMMY's *head and sticks a thermometer in his mouth.* TOMMY *screws his face up against the pain.* BRUCE *takes a hypodermic needle from his kit.*) This'll make you ride a little more comfortable. (*He shoots the morphine. Then he sits on the edge of the bunk and feels* TOMMY's *pulse. There is a tense silence. The water can be heard sloshing against the boat's sides.* TOMMY *rolls his head as another spasm of pain seizes him.* JIMMY *seems worried by the pulsebeat.*)

BRUCE. How long has this been going on? (TOMMY *tries to answer with the thermometer*

---

[30]*our striking force,* nearby surface vessels to attack the enemy destroyers.
[31]*zoomy,* enemy aircraft.

[32]*Dr. Kildare,* a famous doctor in fiction and the movies.

in his mouth.) Hold it a second. I c'n never remember not to ask questions when I got that thing in their mouths. *(He removes the thermometer.)*

TOMMY *(speaking with great effort).* Since... yesterday.

[JIMMY *rises to study the thermometer in the light.*]

BRUCE. Why didn't you tell me right away?

TOMMY. I...I thought...

BRUCE. I'm the closest thing to a doctor they got on board, chum. Sometimes you fellas seem to forget that. *(He has been studying the thermometer.)* A hundred an'——*(He shakes his head.)*

[JIMMY *returns to the bunk and presses his hand on* TOMMY'S *abdomen.*]

BRUCE. Hurt there?

[TOMMY *shakes his head.* JIMMY *moves his hand and presses again.*]

BRUCE. There?

[TOMMY *shakes his head.* JIMMY *now presses the right lower abdomen.* TOMMY *gives a tense cry of pain.* JIMMY *maintains the pressure... and then suddenly releases it. The reaction on* TOMMY *is even greater than it was before.*]

BRUCE. Mmmmmm-hmmmm. Mmmmmm-hmmmm. *(Then suddenly.)* Take it easy a minute, kid. I better see the Skipper. *(He exits quickly.)*

[*Cut to control room.* COM. MILLER *is just coming down the ladder from the conning tower when* JIMMY BRUCE *appears.*]

BRUCE. Captain, c'n I talk to you a minute?

MILLER. Sure thing, son.

BRUCE. I just examined Tommy—Seaman Apprentice Ford. Looks to me like appendicitis—maybe acute.

MILLER. Any chance of holding out until we get back to port?

BRUCE. I don't see how, sir.

MILLER. Then what do you suggest, Jimmy?

BRUCE. Well, everything points to an immediate operation——if we had a surgeon on board.

MILLER. We never carry any *ifs* aboard these boats. *(Suddenly.)* Don't suppose you were ever called upon to perform an appendectomy?

BRUCE *(taken aback).* Are you kidding? *(Catching himself.)* I mean...no, sir. At Pearl,

before I won my Dolphins, all the training I had was as a cardiographer.[33]

MILLER. Ever seen this operation performed?

BRUCE. Well, I...I wheeled a fellow in for one once. That's about as close as I ever came.

MILLER. Think you can do it?

BRUCE. I...I...well, I'd hate to say "yes" for sure and then foul it up.

MILLER. Jimmy, there's nothing in the book says a pharmacist's mate has to perform any duty for which he hasn't been specifically trained. So I'm not going to order you to do this. I'm going to ask you to think it over for five minutes. *(Close on* BRUCE, *listening, as* MILLER *continues.)* If you say "yes" we'll give you all the coöperation possible. If you say "no," we'll give up our mission and see if we can't make it back to the tender[34] before——

BRUCE. Yes, sir, I understand.

[*Medium shot, holding the two.* JIMMY *starts to turn away, obviously troubled.*]

MILLER. And Jimmy...

[JIMMY BRUCE *turns around.*]

BRUCE. Yes, sir.

MILLER. Before we left the States, I had the opportunity of picking out every one of you men individually. For every one of you aboard there are at least ten others—almost as good. I didn't pick you for my pharmacist's mate because you happened to have a high rating as a technician—but because you impressed me as the kind of a man who could come through in emergencies.

[COM. MILLER'S *words seem to increase* JIMMY'S *confidence.*]

BRUCE. Yes, sir.

[COM. MILLER *turns and starts toward the ladder, passing* ENSIGN RIGGS.]

MILLER. How's she behaving, Bill?

RIGGS. This dirty weather's making her tough to handle. We nearly broached there a minute ago. *(He keeps his eye on the depth gauge while he is talking. Now, noticing that it is pointing a little too high, he acts promptly.)* Plane her down another five feet....

---

[33]*cardiographer* (kär′di og′rə fər), a technician who operates a machine which registers the movements of the heart and interprets the results.

[34]*tender*, submarine tender, a boat having aboard all supplies to replenish fuel, food, etc.

[COM. MILLER *has started up to the conning tower. Cut to conning tower. As* MILLER *appears,* LT. HUDSON *is studying the chart.*]

HUDSON. Two more destroyers approximately twelve miles off the bow. Looks like the screen for the main force all right!

MILLER. That's fine. I—hope we don't have to lose 'em.

HUDSON. Lose 'em? Why should we if we keep closing in?

MILLER. That's the hitch. One of our seamen —young Ford—has appendicitis. Needs an operation pronto, according to Bruce. If he thinks he can do it, and I agree to let him go ahead, we'd have to get down for at least an hour.

HUDSON. An hour! They'll be out of sight in an hour. We may never pick up their trail again.

MILLER. I know. I know, Floyd. I suppose you're right...from a military standpoint. *(Close shot of the two men, favoring* MILLER.*)* But, Floyd, one of these days you'll have your own command. Then you'll know a little more than you do now about the human side of this job. What makes these boats run? It's not the Diesels—they can always be replaced. It's the men —they aren't interchangeable. Not even young apprentice seamen like Tommy Ford.

[*Close-up* MILLER.]

MILLER. It didn't take just months and months to train them and work them in as a team. It took years—all their lives—to develop into the kind of men who can stand the gaff of living on top of each other for fifty days at a time under constant danger without getting on each other's nerves.

[*Medium shot favoring* MILLER.]

MILLER. No, Floyd, the life—even an outside chance to save the life—of one of my men still means more to me than the course and disposition of the whole enemy fleet.

HUDSON. In another hour or two we could crack the secret of a major enemy movement—

MILLER. In another hour or two a nice kid from Chautauqua, Kansas, may be dead because his Skipper was afraid to take a chance.

HUDSON. But this kid, Bruce, if you don't mind my saying so, still seems pretty wet behind the ears. I can't see him performing any miracles.

MILLER. Floyd, I've seen my share of miracles aboard these boats. I've seen the big brave fellows cave in and I've seen panicky, half-grown kids suddenly find out they're men. Keep tracking 'em to the last possible moment. I'll send word up as soon as I decide.

[*He starts down the ladder. Quick dissolve to corridor outside the Chief's room. As* COM. MILLER *appears, coming forward from the control room,* JIMMY BRUCE *enters the corridor from the Chief's room, where the body of* TOMMY FORD *can be seen in the background.*]

MILLER. What's the story, Jimmy?

BRUCE. I'll take a crack at it.

MILLER. Good boy. Only now, for the record, I'm ordering you to do it. So, just in case we're unlucky and a bunch of second-guessing, top-brass medics[35] decide we could've waited, at a court martial three stripes on your arm look better than the crow.[36] *(*MILLER *forces a grin.)* Only I wouldn't have put this up to you if I wasn't dead sure you had it in you.

BRUCE *(a little shaky).* Thanks, Skipper. I just wish I was as sure as you are.

MILLER *(placing his hand on* JIMMY'S *shoulder).* Better go in and see your patient. Put it up to him the same way I did you. This is a volunteer service. I want everybody to go in with his eyes open.

BRUCE *(his respect for the Skipper is obvious despite his conventional response).* Aye, aye, sir.

[*He turns toward the Chief's room. Cut to Chief's room. As* BRUCE *enters,* TOMMY *looks up and forces a weak grin.*]

BRUCE. Tommy, there's no sense giving you a snow job.[37] I'm gonna be level with you.

TOMMY. Okay, Jim.

BRUCE. If I just sit here picking my teeth and feeding you pills, I think you've had it.[38]

TOMMY *(in a whisper).* Yeah, I know.

BRUCE. So the Skipper's giving me the green light to operate. It's a heck of a thing to tell

---

[35]*top-brass medics,* doctors who hold high officer rank.

[36]*at a court-martial...the crow,* if the matter comes before a Navy court, my three stripes as a lieutenant commander will carry more weight than your insignia as an enlisted man (the crow).

[37]*giving you a snow job,* not telling you the truth.

[38]*you've had it,* it's the end for you.

you, but somehow I feel I've gotta say it—I'm not sure I know how. There's a chance that— *(He looks at* TOMMY, *almost begging.)* Well, it's plenty rugged either way. But I've gotta know if you think I should.

TOMMY. Whatever you say, Doc.

[JIMMY *straightens up.*]

BRUCE. That's the first time anybody on this boat ever called me anything but *quack. (He rises.)* Rest easy, kid. It's a tough point but we're gonna get lucky and make it.

[TOMMY, *wincing, but forcing back any sound, makes a feeble but definite circle of approval with his thumb and forefinger. Dissolve to control room.* COM. MILLER *talking into the general address system:*]

MILLER. Attention, all hands. We've got an emergency on our hands that calls for teamwork, and I want you all to know exactly what we're up against. We're going deeper so that Pharmacist's Mate Bruce can perform an appendectomy on Apprentice Seaman Ford.

[*Wider angle of room as all listen intently.*]

MILLER. I don't have to tell you what a ticklish job this is going to be. We'll have to keep her awful steady down there. Just a little better trim than we ever had before.

[*Quick flashes of men in torpedo room, engine room, pump room, etc., listening.*]

MILLER. Every one of you, wherever you're standing watch—the planesmen, you on the manifolds, you back there in the engine rooms —is going to be part of this thing. We've been in tough spots before and we've come through because each one of you knew that. So I've got a hunch you're all going to deliver this Christmas Eve for Tommy Ford and Jimmy Bruce. That is all. (MILLER *turns to* ENSIGN RIGGS.) Better check the pressure we've got in the boat. We'll need all the good air we can get because that ether's going to smell things up. Take her to a hundred feet. *(He turns away as* RIGGS *gives him an "Aye, aye, sir.")*

[*Exterior of submarine as it noses down into the sea. Dissolve to the control room, discovering* JIMMY BRUCE, *nervous but controlled;* COM. MILLER; LT. HUDSON; LT. DAVISON. *At the planes are* FANELLI *and* GOODMAN. *Keeping an eye on the bubble, the depth gauge, the*

Christmas tree,[39] *etc., is the diving officer,* ENSIGN RIGGS. *At one of the manifolds is the chunky, tattooed veteran* O'BRIEN.]

MILLER. Now, Jimmy, there's nothing in the book to cover this kind of deal. So we're going to stow rank and Navy regs.[40] From this point until the end of the operation, you're the boss. You pick your staff from any level you want—you tell us where you want us and what you want us to do.

[JIMMY BRUCE *still seems uncertain about his authority. During this period he should seem to be groping his way toward the confidence and strength he will eventually assert.*]

BRUCE. Aye, aye, sir. Can we have Tommy moved to the wardroom? See that he's made as comfortable as possible. And tell him I'll be with him as soon as I get everything squared away.

MILLER *(to* DAVISON*)*. Get a detail and take care of that, Jeff.

BRUCE. Now for my chief assistant...*(He looks around.)* I don't want you to think I'm giving you the business, Skipper, but I think I'd pick you even if you were an apprentice striker.[41]

MILLER. Thanks, Jimmy. I wanted to be in on every step of this thing. His life's in your hands, but I want there to be no doubt about the responsibility's being mine.

BRUCE. Now, I'm not sure exactly where to use him yet, but I'd like to have the Swede. He's one of those fellows who c'n do a little bit of everything, and also he's the luckiest gambler on the boat.

HUDSON. Sir, if I can butt in, don't you think it's a little more proper if all those in attendance were officers? After all—

MILLER *(rather sharply)*. Hudson, a good officer knows when to pull rank, and when to stow it. And, I don't want to disillusion you, but the best men in the Navy aren't always

---

[39]*the* Christmas tree, the board with red and green lights that controls the hydraulic system for the hull openings.

[40]*we're going to stow rank and Navy regs,* we're going to disregard a man's rank and Navy regulations governing relationships between ranks.

[41]*an apprentice striker,* a sailor learning new and specific duties to get a petty-officer's rating.

the ones with the gold on their sleeves. Now send a messenger for Swede Engstrum.

HUDSON *(silenced but obviously not convinced)*. Yes, sir.

BRUCE. Now for my nurse. *(Looks around again.)* Lemme see, I'd like to have O'Brien.

[COM. MILLER *crosses to* RIGGS.]

MILLER. Have a stand-by take over the trim manifold. We want to use O'Brien.

RIGGS. Aye, aye, sir.

[*He goes to* O'BRIEN, *taps him on the shoulder and points to the group around* BRUCE. O'BRIEN—*balding, bare-chested, and perspiring—joins the group.*]

BRUCE. Obie, you're going to be a nurse.

O'BRIEN. A nurse!

BRUCE. Yeah. I won't say you're the prettiest nurse I ever saw—(O'BRIEN'S *face wrinkles into a hard, likable grin)*—but you're another guy I'd like to have around if things really get tough.

O'BRIEN *(not at all maliciously)*. Okay, kid. If you c'n be a surgeon, I guess I c'n be a nurse.

BRUCE. Good deal, Pop. Now, let's see—an anesthetist. I want someone who's a real cool customer, and won't lose his head. *(He nods to* LT. HUDSON.) Lt. Hudson, I guess you'll fill the bill. I'll show you what I want when we get in there. Meanwhile, go check on the ether supply.

[LT. HUDSON *hesitates, resenting being ordered around by a mere pharmacist's mate.*]

BRUCE. Then I'd like Leroy Johnson—

HUDSON *(stopping just as he's turning away)*. Johnson—the mess boy?

BRUCE. I know, Lieutenant, but his old man happens to be a doctor, and I figure...

MILLER *(severely)*. That's all right, Jimmy. A surgeon doesn't need to know the rank or pedigree of his assistants. You're not handing out invitations to the Officers' Ball. You're picking *men.*

HUDSON *(rebuked again, leaving)*. I'll check on that ether, Skipper.

BRUCE. Now lessee—we'll need a recorder—someone to make sure that everything that goes in, comes out.

[*At this point* LT. DAVISON *has returned.* SWEDE *enters from left.*]

BRUCE. I guess that'll be your job, Mr. Davison.

DAVISON. Aye, aye, Doc.

BRUCE. I've got a list of all the stuff we're going to need and, brother, it's rough. No ether cone, no antiseptic powder, no scalpel—in fact, no surgical instruments of any kind. *(Shakes his head.)* They say one way to tell a submariner is the way he c'n open a bottle of beer with a fifty-cent piece. That's what we all gotta do now—get our noggins workin' on how t' make do.

SWEDE. I got some fine tea strainers in the galley. How about tryin' one of them for an ether cone?

BRUCE. I think ya got something there, Swede. Get on it. *(As* SWEDE *starts off.)* Oh, and while you're there, we're gonna need something for muscular retractors—that's to hold the wound open after I make the incision. I think maybe we c'n use some of your tablespoons, if we double 'em all the way back.

SWEDE *(heading back toward the control room)*. Back in a flash, Doc.

BRUCE. Antiseptic powder. Well, why don't we just grind up some sulfanilimide tablets? Leroy, find as many as you can in the medicine chest and powderize 'em for me.

LEROY. Right, Jimmy. *(He starts off.)*

BRUCE. Then we'll need something to sterilize the instruments.

O'BRIEN. We could use the alcohol in the torpedoes.

BRUCE. Good deal.

[O'BRIEN *hurries off.*]

BRUCE. Then there's lights. We'll need a lot more'n we got in there. Maybe we can string some floods from the overhead.[42]

DAVISON. I'll get Chief Childs to put a couple of his electricians on that.

BRUCE. Check. Let's see, that takes care of just about everything except—except the scalpel. All I could find was an old scalpel blade without a handle.

MILLER. Could you hold it with a pair of pliers?

BRUCE. Kinda clumsy, Skipper. Wait a min-

---

[42]*the overhead,* the ceiling.

ute; I think I've got it—those hemostats we use for pinching blood vessels. Maybe one of the machinists could rig that up for me.

MILLER. Okay, I'll get somebody on it. You better go in and have a look at your patient.

BRUCE. Yes, Commander.

[COM. MILLER *puts his hand on* JIMMY'S *shoulder.*]

MILLER. And remember what I told you, Jimmy. This deal is going to depend on you giving the orders. Until you get it all battened down, you're in command.

BRUCE (*suddenly*). Do you believe in God, sir?

MILLER (*seriously*). I certainly do, Jimmy. And I still believe He watches over all of us on earth.

BRUCE (*literally, with a deep sigh as he turns to enter the wardroom*). Boy, I just hope He doesn't have any trouble getting down here twenty fathoms below the surface.

[*Close shot of* LEROY JOHNSON *pounding tablets to powder. Close shot of* SWEDE *stretching gauze over a strainer to form a homemade ether cone. Close shot of* O'BRIEN *draining alcohol from a torpedo. Close shot of machinist rigging the scalpel with a hemostat. Close shot of electricians in wardroom rigging overhead lights. Close shot of* COM. MILLER *bending the Monel-metal spoons into retractors. Close shot of* JIMMY *in a corner of the wardroom, studying his handbook with a pencil in his hand. Cut to control room. Angle toward* FANELLI *and depth gauge, which is fluctuating.* RIGGS *enters to* FANELLI.]

RIGGS. Watch that bubble, Fanelli. Hold her to one-half degree.

FANELLI. It's rough holding her against the swells, sir.

RIGGS. I know it. Do the best you can.

[*Cut to conning tower. Close on* SONARMAN, *listening intently with earphones on. He turns to* QUARTERMASTER WILLIAMS.]

SONARMAN. All clear on sound.

[*Interior of wardroom. Close on clock showing time to be five minutes after two. Camera pans down*[43] *to full shot around table. Ready*

---

[43]*pans down,* gradually moves downward to cover a large area.

with the ether cans, behind* TOMMY'S *head, is* LT. HUDSON. *Near him is* SWEDE, *who holds the improvised ether cone. At the side of the table facing the camera are* JIMMY BRUCE *and* COM. MILLER. *At the foot of the table is* O'BRIEN, *and sitting near him,* LT. DAVISON, *with medical books open and paper and pencil to record the movements of the operation. All these men wear white reversed pajama coats and their faces are covered by gauze masks, all except their eyes, which express tenseness and anxiety. In the taut silence we can hear, over the sound of the water washing the hull, the ticking of the clock.*

Cut to the pantry. Here LEROY JOHNSON *is stationed. He is placing the bent-double spoons into a pot of boiling water and is ready to pass them through the small sliding panel that leads directly into the wardroom. Cut to wardroom.*]

BRUCE (*his voice tight in his throat, the tone belying his attempts at confident words and manners*). Well, Tommy, I guess we're all set. In a minute or two we're gonna start feeding you the ether. You're not gonna feel a thing.

TOMMY (*in a hoarse whisper*). Listen, Jimmy, I don't wantcha to think I'm chicken or anything, but just in case, you know, if something goes wrong, I wantcha to go see my folks. Tell 'em...Tell 'em...

BRUCE (*embarrassed*). Aw, knock it off. You're gonna see your own folks. Pretty lucky guy, prob'ly get a fat sixty-day leave outa this deal.

TOMMY. Okay, Doc. But, just in case...

BRUCE. Sure...sure...Now quit gabbin'. Think about something cheerful.

TOMMY (*to himself in a whisper*). I'll think about bein' home...Christmas Eve...Mary Lou...

[NOTE: *Through the above the trim of the submarine has been far from perfect. The boat has been pitching, not violently, but enough to be disturbing.* SWEDE, *at* TOMMY'S *head,* O'BRIEN, *at his feet, have been holding the patient in place on the table. Suddenly the submarine lurches upward.* TOMMY *groans.*]

BRUCE (*on edge*). Whatsa matter with those guys? Don't they know what they're doin'?

[COM. MILLER'S *manner, in contrast to* JIM-MY'S, *is controlled and quieting.*]

MILLER. Easy, Jimmy. Let me see if I can straighten them out.

[*He exits quickly. Cut to control room. The depth-gauge needle swings between 100 and 95. The planesmen are working the electrical.* ENSIGN RIGGS *hovers over them. After a pause* COM. MILLER *enters.*]

MILLER. What's the trouble, Bill?

RIGGS. It's so rough down here that it's hard to maintain depth control. The two best men I've got are having trouble.

MILLER. Okay. Let's ease her down another fifty feet and see if it's any better. We'll never get this job done without perfect depth control.

RIGGS. Aye, aye, sir. We'll do the best we can. (*Slight smile.*) And then we'll try to do even a little better than that.

[COM. MILLER *slaps* RIGGS *on the shoulder and turns back toward the wardroom.* RIGGS *turns to his men to give an order. Exterior of submarine as the boat noses down into a quieter layer. Interior of wardroom as the table becomes level at last. Everyone leaning in slightly toward* TOMMY, *all faces washed out in the glare of the overhanging flood lights.*]

JIMMY BRUCE (*in a strange, quiet voice*). That's better. Now if they can just hold like that. (*Pause.*) Gloves.

[O'BRIEN *comes forward and holds them for* JIMMY *while he sterilizes his hands in a ready bowl of alcohol. The fingers of the gloves are too long for* JIMMY'S *small hands and the rubber ends are ludicrously limp.*]

O'BRIEN. You look like Mickey Mouse, Doc.

[JIMMY *grins a little through his gauze, then turns back to the table and addresses* SWEDE.]

BRUCE. Okay, Swede. I guess we're ready for your strainer. (SWEDE *starts to lower it over* TOMMY'S *mouth.* JIMMY *turns to* HUDSON.) Now, just like I told you, drop a little...easy... onto the strainer. (HUDSON *appears to pour the ether too freely.*) I said *easy*. We've only got five pounds. And when you figure all this pressure—

[COM. MILLER *turns to the squawk box.*]

MILLER. See if the pressure's built up again. If so, pump it back to one-tenth.

[*Almost simultaneously,* HUDSON *has turned on* BRUCE.]

HUDSON. Look, Bruce, I'm doing what I—

BRUCE (*with a curt gesture*). Pipe down. Watch him close. And remember—another drop—another—until the eyes begin to dilate. (*To* TOMMY *softly.*) Now relax, Tommy—like you're sacking in[44] after a tough watch. Breathe deep. (*Takes a deep breath with him.*) Attaboy.

[*Close on* TOMMY *breathing deeply, his eyes going vague. Angle on faces peering down at him slowly going out of focus. The ticking of the clock can be heard. Dissolve to control room. The gauge now shows nearly 150 feet.* FANELLI *and* GOODMAN, *the two planesmen, are obviously on edge to keep the boat steady.*]

RIGGS. That's it, fellows. Now, try to hold to a maximum of a half-degree down angle.

[*Dissolve to wardroom.* TOMMY *is now unconscious. The clock on the wall shows twelve minutes after two.* JIMMY *bends over his patient and studies his face. The silence is oppressive.* JIMMY'S *face has begun to shine with perspiration under the lights.*]

BRUCE (*sounding jittery*). Well, I guess it's my move. (*He reaches out his hand.*) Scalpel.

[JOHNSON *removes scalpel from the improvised sterilizer and passes it through the panel to* O'BRIEN; O'BRIEN *takes scalpel from* JOHNSON *and hands it across to* JIMMY. JIMMY *stares at it almost as if afraid of it. His hesitation is noticeable. He nods at* LT. DAVISON.]

BRUCE. Davison, before I make the incision, maybe you better check me out again to make sure. Read that page I got turned down.

DAVISON (*opening the handbook*). "When a hospital corpsman on duty on a ship that has no medical officer is confronted with a case of acute appendicitis, his judgment is put perhaps to its supreme test...."

BRUCE (*impatiently*). Brother, you c'n say that again! But I mean further down where it's marked.

DAVISON. "In the case of appendectomies, it is the rare pharmacist's mate whose chances of proper diagnosis and successful operation are at all good...."

---

[44]*sacking in,* going to bed.

BRUCE (*reacting angrily*). Hey, you pinhead, you're in the wrong book—the other big red one —*General Surgery.*

[DAVISON *picks up the other volume, already opened to the right page.*]

DAVISON. "The incision begins above a line between the anterior superior iliac spine and the umbilicus, about four centimeters medial to the anterior spine."

[*Close on* JIMMY BRUCE *straining to understand.*]

DAVISON (*out of camera range*). "It extends downward and inward parallel to the fibers of the external oblique muscle and fascia...."

[*Now the sweat is really standing out on* JIMMY'S *face. He places his little finger on* TOMMY'S *hip, the thumb on his umbilicus.*]

BRUCE (*muttering to himself in intense concentration*). Downward and inward...between the anterior superior iliac....

[*Camera pans up and holds on clock ticking industriously. The minute hand moving slowly but at abnormal speed. We hear only* JIMMY'S *staccato demands:*]

BRUCE. A spoon....

DAVISON'S VOICE. One spoon.

BRUCE. Little more ether....

[*Camera shoots through panel as* JOHNSON'S *hand, encased in white glove, passes instruments through to wardroom.*]

BRUCE. Those tweezers...sponge...scalpel ...all right, quick—another spoon....

[*Close on* DAVISON *recording insertion.*]

DAVISON. Spoon two.

BRUCE'S VOICE. Hemostat....

[*Cut to control room medium close on* FANELLI *and* GOODMAN.]

FANELLI. Wonder how it's going?

[GOODMAN *turns to* ENSIGN RIGGS.]

GOODMAN. Any news yet, sir?

RIGGS (*shaking his head*). He's still hunting around. (*Checks gauge and bubble.*) Nice work, boys. Hold her right there.

[*Back to wardroom.* JIMMY'S *strained face reflects frustration and the dreadful possibility of failure.*]

BRUCE. Gee...this...oughta be the right place...but I...can't seem to find it.

[*Close on* HUDSON.]

HUDSON (*to* MILLER *in undertone*). What did I tell you? (*His eyes betray his lack of confidence in* BRUCE. *He looks at the clock.*)

MILLER (*with a firm warning gesture*). Shhh....

[*Close on clock showing that twenty minutes have passed. Back to full shot wardroom.*]

BRUCE. Sometimes these things aren't where they oughta be. Guess I'll hafta try the other side of the caecum. (*Pause.*) Better widen the incision. (*He reaches his hand out.*) Scalpel.

[COM. MILLER *doesn't pass it quite quickly enough for* JIMMY. *He snaps his fingers impatiently, his nerves in danger of cracking.*]

BRUCE. Come on, snap it up. I said the scalpel.

MILLER (*very quietly as he passes the scalpel to* BRUCE). Take it easy, son. You'll get there.

[COM. MILLER'S *manner seems to quiet* JIMMY. *When he addresses* DAVISON *now, he sounds more pulled together.*]

BRUCE. Hey, Davison, hold that picture up for me again.

[DAVISON *holds the open book up, right over* TOMMY'S *prostrate figure.* JIMMY *reads from it while he holds the scalpel poised over* TOMMY'S *body, which is hidden from us by the sheet.*]

BRUCE (*reading slowly*). "To retract the muscle medially, the anterior and posterior sheaths are—" (TOMMY *groans feebly.* JIMMY *looks up at* LT. HUDSON. *Curtly.*) Come on—more ether.

HUDSON (*hesitating*). How long do you think this will take?

BRUCE (*flaring up*). How should I know? Y'think I do 'em every day?

HUDSON. But we have only four pounds left. If it takes you—

BRUCE. I don't want back talk. I want ether.

HUDSON. Back talk? What do you think you're—

MILLER (*breaking in*). Come on, Floyd, leave it up to the doc. Follow instructions.

HUDSON (*sullenly*). Yes, sir. (*He pours more ether onto the strainer* SWEDE *is holding.*)

BRUCE (*to* MILLER). Now, have a spoon ready, and I mean *ready.*

MILLER (*soothingly*). Okay, Doc. Okay.

[*Cut to control room. The men are silently, tensely doing their jobs.* RIGGS *glances at the clock. It shows half an hour has passed. Cut to conning tower. The* HELMSMAN *is sweating it out, too. He turns to check the time. Cut to dinette. The two* ACEY-DEUCY PLAYERS *are also involved, though the game still goes on.*]

FIRST PLAYER. It's taking a long time.

SECOND PLAYER. Come on, roll those bones.

FIRST PLAYER (*taking a deep breath*). Get a load of that ether. What they tryin' t' do—asphyxiate all of us?

[*Back to wardroom. Somewhat drugged by the ether,* JIMMY *runs his hand over his face.* COM. MILLER *watches him solicitously.*]

MILLER. Is the ether getting you, Doc?

BRUCE (*impatiently*). Nah, come on, let's get on with it. What's the next line, Davison?

DAVISON (*reading from the surgery book*). "Injury to the ilio...ilio...."

BRUCE (*brusquely*). Ilioinguinal nerve.

DAVISON (*continuing*). "May result in paralysis...."

[*Close on* DAVISON *reacting. Close on* BRUCE.]

BRUCE (*cutting him off abruptly*). Okay, okay, I remember that. On your toes everybody. Another spoon ready.

[*We feel from his eyes and the strain of his face the fearful pressure of this critical moment. Close shot of* SWEDE. *Close shot of* O'BRIEN. *Close shot of* JOHNSON. *All are watching tensely. Close on* BRUCE *sweating profusely, straining, then suddenly relieved.*]

BRUCE. Got around the nerve okay. (*He probes further. We can hear the ticking of the clock. Suddenly he looks up in triumph.*) I see it! No wonder I couldn't find it. All covered with adhesions and the tip is gangrenous.

[*Group shot showing the response—relief—a momentary breather. Close on* BRUCE.]

BRUCE (*all business now, and with more confidence*). All right...now, fast...catgut...hemostat...another retractor....

DAVISON. Catgut for first suture.

[DAVISON *looks up at clock. Close on clock showing two minutes before half past two. Dissolve. Close on clock, now showing nearly five past three. Camera pans down to full show of wardroom. The room is full of foul ether vapors and* JIMMY *shows signs of nervous exhaustion.*]

BRUCE *(to* MILLER*).* Come on...clamps... hold it open so I c'n....

    [TOMMY *groans. Close on* TOMMY.]

TOMMY *(stirring and groping up toward the surface of consciousness, hardly audible).* Oh...

    [*Close group shot at table.*]

BRUCE *(anxiously).* More ether. He's coming out!

HUDSON. How much more do you think it's going to take?

BRUCE *(flaring up).* How many times must you ask me that? I'm trying my best. I—

HUDSON *(glancing at clock).* It's over an hour already. I just want to be sure we don't run out of ether before—

BRUCE *(facing him angrily).* If we do, Hudson, it'll be your fault and I'll—*(He seems almost ready to strike* HUDSON *who cuts in sharply.)*

HUDSON. Listen, Bruce, I don't care what you're doing. You're still an enlisted man and—

[COM. MILLER *takes control at this point in his authoritative, but very quiet, way.*]

MILLER. I think it's time to clear the air a little bit, fellows. Getting pretty foul in here. *(Looks across at* SWEDE.*)* Better get the blowers working, Swede.

[HUDSON *and* BRUCE *relax.* JIMMY *goes back to work.*]

BRUCE *(snapping his fingers).* More catgut ...hemostat...alcohol....

[*Cut to dinette. The* MESSENGER *who was seen previously kneeling over the fallen body of* TOMMY *appears in the entrance way.*]

FIRST ACEY-DEUCY PLAYER. How's it going?

MESSENGER *(looking up).* They say he's got hold of a whole mess of appendix.

SECOND PLAYER. That's the *mesoappendix* —the little knob near the base.

FIRST PLAYER. Listen to the man—another quack!

[*Cut to conning tower, angling toward* HELMSMAN *and* WILLIAMS.]

HELMSMAN *(glancing up at clock).* What's taking so long?

WILLIAMS. What's the diff, long as he makes it?

[*Medium close of* SONARMAN, *listening intently as he moves his dial.*]

HELMSMAN. That stinkin' ether'll put us all under before he's through.

[*Suddenly the* SONARMAN *cocks his head, moves his dial slowly back and holds it. He hears something. He listens more eagerly and signals* WILLIAMS.]

SONARMAN. Tell the Skipper I think I hear screws[45] bearing 0-3-9.

[*Dissolve to wardroom. Close of* BRUCE. *We cannot see his hands, of course, but he has reached a delicate phase of the operation—the purse-string suture.*]

BRUCE *(hoarsely).* Okay. Now, what's the next step?

DAVISON *(reading).* "The ends of the tied purse-string suture are again tied over the stump of the mesoappendix...."

BRUCE *(gritting his teeth).* The ends of the—

[*Suddenly they are interrupted by the squawk box.*]

SQUAWK BOX *(voice of* QUARTERMASTER WILLIAMS*).* Sound reports screws bearing 0-3-9, Skipper.

[*Close on* COM. MILLER, *reacting to this report of the presence of an enemy vessel. Wider angle of wardroom. The others also react to this new danger. They seem to hesitate for a moment.*]

BRUCE *(to* O'BRIEN*).* All right...more alcohol....Let the Skipper worry about that.

[COM. MILLER *goes to the squawk box.*]

MILLER *(to squawk box).* Let me know if they're closing. And get a turn count.[46]

[*He turns back to the table and looks at* BRUCE *questioningly.*]

BRUCE *(to himself).* Oh, brother! If I make a mistake now.

---

[45]*screws,* the propellers of a subchaser.
[46]*a turn count,* a count of the rate of speed at which the propellers of the approaching ship are turning, to determine the speed of the vessel.

SQUAWK BOX (voice of QUARTERMASTER WILLIAMS). The screws are highspeed, Skipper. Still closing. Bearing 0-3-6.

[MILLER looks at JIMMY.]

BRUCE. Go ahead, Skipper. I'll get Swede to relieve you. Better go fight your ship.

MILLER (turns back to the squawk box). I'm on my way up to take charge of evasive action. Rig for silent running. Change course—right fifteen degrees rudder. (He turns back to JIMMY, puts his hand on his shoulder a moment.) Back as soon as I can shake this baby, Jimmy.

BRUCE (so intent on what he is doing that he merely nods and goes on with his labors). Vaseline gauze. More catgut....

[COM. MILLER exits. Cut to control room angled toward plane wheels. ENSIGN RIGGS comes over to the planesmen.]

RIGGS. Shift the bow and stern planes to hand power.

FANELLI and GOODMAN. Aye, aye, sir.

[While they attend to this, RIGGS crosses back and gets on the squawk box.]

RIGGS. Secure the I.C. motor generators.[47] Secure the blower and air conditioning.

[As COM. MILLER appears on his way to the conning tower, the motors go off and the sudden quiet permits us to hear the water sloshing against the hull. Close on FANELLI and GOODMAN. Having to hold the planes with their own muscle power is a tremendous strain. Their arms tremble with the effort.]

RIGGS. Hold her with everything you've got, boys.

[FANELLI and GOODMAN can only nod as they put their strength against the wheels. Cut to interior of wardroom. The lights go out because of the cutting off of the generators.]

BRUCE. Now what's the matter?

HUDSON. They've cut off the generators.

BRUCE (cracking for a moment). Oh, brother, what a SNAFU![48] (Then he takes hold again.)

[There is a quick look between HUDSON and BRUCE, nothing more.]

_____

[47]Secure the I.C. motor generators, shut off the intercommunication motor generators.

[48]SNAFU, snarled up situation. The word snafu is derived from the initial letters of "situation normal—all fouled up." It is Army and Navy slang.

HUDSON. We can finish up with the emergency lanterns.

BRUCE. Right. Break 'em out. No stinkin' subchaser's gonna foul up this operation.

[HUDSON stares at him a moment, impressed, then sets to work with the others. And DAVISON, SWEDE, O'BRIEN, and HUDSON grab the lanterns and rapidly set them up so that they throw a strange but adequate light on the operating table.]

BRUCE (going back to his work). Okay. We've almost got it now.

[Cut to conning tower. COM. MILLER approaches the SONARMAN. The latter switches on the loud-speaker so MILLER and the audience can hear the sound of the approaching screws.]

SONARMAN. Closing fast. Bearing 0-2-3.

MILLER (to WILLIAMS). We'll keep turning away from them—left rudder another ten degrees.

WILLIAMS. Aye, aye, sir.

SONARMAN (calling out over the sound of the sonar). Still closing, sir. Bearing 0-2-1.

MILLER. Very well.

[Cut to control room. FANELLI and GOODMAN show perspiration on their faces as they strain to hold the boat steady. Cut to interior of dinette. The two ACEY-DEUCY PLAYERS are now silently sweating it out. One of them rattles the dice listlessly over and over. Cut to wardroom. With the ventilation system off, the effect of the ether fumes is overpowering. JIMMY pauses and holds his head, seemingly overcome for a moment.]

JIMMY. Oh, this ether.

[HUDSON'S reaction is surprisingly sympathetic.]

HUDSON. With those ventilators off, it's rough, kid. But at least it solves one thing for us—(indicates the unconscious form of TOMMY FORD)—it keeps him under. (To O'BRIEN.) Try holding a little alcohol under his nose. That'll pep him up.

BRUCE (looking at HUDSON warmly for the first time). Thanks. (Goes on with his work.)

[Cut to conning tower. Medium close at sonar table. The sound of the oncoming screws is considerably louder.]

SONARMAN. Seem to be coming right for us, Skipper. Bearing 1-8-8.

MILLER (to WILLIAMS, wearing earphones for silent running). Right fifteen degrees rudder. We'll try to get on their course in the opposite direction.

[Close on sonar apparatus as the sound of the screws grows louder. Cut to control room. FANELLI and GOODMAN, who can hear the approaching subchaser now, exchange a look of apprehension. Cut to dinette. The ACEY-DEUCY PLAYERS can hear it. They look at each other meaningfully. Back to wardroom.]

BRUCE (in a hoarse whisper). Another drain...alcohol...have the needle ready....

[The men in the wardroom too can hear the sound of the approaching enemy screws, but—except for a quick glance in the direction of the sound—all keep at their jobs. Cut to conning tower, close at sonar system. The sound of the enemy vessel is exceedingly loud now.]

SONARMAN. Closing, closing. Gonna pass right over us.

MILLER (in whisper to QUARTERMASTER WILLIAMS). All stop.

[Cut to control room. Now with all motors off, FANELLI and GOODMAN must strain harder than ever to hold the boat level. Their muscles stand out against the pressure of it.]

RIGGS (quietly). Hang on! Hang on!

[Cut to conning tower. The rumbling grows louder as the subchaser begins to pass over them. It sounds like an elevated railway. They all look up instinctively. Cut back to wardroom. The subchaser is passing over with a subway roar. Even JIMMY is interrupted by the terrible proximity of the enemy. He looks up with anxious eyes like the others. Then he takes hold again.]

BRUCE. Okay, let's keep going. Every second counts now.

[Reaction from HUDSON—increasingly impressed. Dissolve to interior of conning tower, close at sonar system. The sound indicates that the subchaser is now going away.]

SONARMAN (suppressing a tendency to smile). Screws now opening on one-eighty.[49]

MILLER (relieved, turning to WILLIAMS). All right. Make 50 R.P.M.'S[50] again. At 1540, if screws continue to open, return to normal running.

WILLIAMS (also showing his relief). Aye, aye, sir.

MILLER (to SONARMAN). Report to me when it's all clear. (He starts down the hatchway.)

[Exterior of submarine underway, submerged. Dissolve to wardroom. Close on clock showing the time as 3:40.]

BRUCE'S VOICE. Ready...scalpel.

[Camera pulls back to full shot of everyone including COM. MILLER, waiting tensely while JIMMY goes in with scalpel off scene. He bends down over the body and probes with his other gloved hand. Close on BRUCE so that you cannot see what he is holding.]

BRUCE (triumphantly). Well, there it is. Funny that a little thing like that c'n cause all this fuss. (He snaps back into his job, clicking with efficiency and confidence now.) All right now, let's get this thing battened down—sew Tommy back in one piece.

[Close shot favoring HUDSON. He looks at MILLER.]

HUDSON (recalling MILLER'S words at the beginning; muttering them to himself). "Panicky, half-grown kids suddenly find out they're men."

[MILLER just manages to overhear him and smiles.]

BRUCE (to HUDSON). What was that?

HUDSON. Nothing, Doc. Just talking to myself. Anything else you want me to do?

BRUCE. Just keep watching his eyes. We don't want him to come out of this too soon.

HUDSON (under his breath). Aye, aye.

SQUAWK BOX. Conning tower reporting on sound. All clear. All clear.

[MILLER grins. Goes to squawk box.]

MILLER. Return to normal running. Get the ventilators going. And bleed oxygen into the boat[51] so we can purify the air.

[49]*Screws now opening on one-eighty*, the propellers of the subchaser are now going away from the stern.

[50]*50 R.P.M.'S*, fifty revolutions per minute. The R.P.M.'s determine the speed of the motors.

[51]*bleed oxygen into the boat*, open the compressed-oxygen flasks in each compartment to get fresh oxygen into the boat.

SQUAWK BOX. Aye, aye, sir. Oh, and Skipper, how's it going down there?

MILLER (cheerfully). Operation appendix is just about secured.

[He returns to the table. In a moment the lights come on. The ventilator starts. The men breathe in with relief. Cut to control room.]

RIGGS. Return bow and stern planes to normal power.

[SEAMEN FANELLI and GOODMAN grin and heave deep sighs of relief. Cut to interior of conning tower. Close on HELMSMAN, grinning. Cut to dinette. Close on ACEY-DEUCY PLAYERS, also grinning. Wardroom again.]

BRUCE (briskly). Okay, before this final suture—one last check to make sure we haven't left anything inside of Tommy.

DAVISON (checking his list). Hemostats—eight.

MILLER (counting the ones removed). Er... eight...check.

DAVISON. Gauze drains—five.

MILLER. Check.

DAVISON. Retractors, that is, spoons—three.

MILLER (counting them). Three here... check.

VOICE OF LEROY JOHNSON. Wait a minute! (They turn toward his voice in the pantry. Cut to pantry. JOHNSON bends down to talk through sliding door.) I handed out four spoons, and I want every one of my spoons back!

[Cut to wardroom. BRUCE reaches in out of the scene.]

BRUCE. Leroy, you're really on the ball. Here's your spoon!

[Everyone laughs and the tension is released.]

MILLER. Okay, Doc, soon as you give us the all clear, we'll surface and air out the boat, and see if we can't reëstablish contact with our little friends.

[They turn back to finish the job. Dissolve to exterior of submarine surfacing. Then to interior of conning tower. Present, waiting with bursting lungs for the hatch to open, are all the principals at the operation. WILLIAMS throws open the hatch to the bridge. COM. MILLER, JIMMY BRUCE, SWEDE, O'BRIEN, LTS. HUDSON and DAVISON, and LEROY JOHNSON raise their faces to the open air, breathing luxuriously.

HUDSON turns around and smiles at JIMMY. We should have a feeling, without hitting it too hard, that this experience has mellowed him and brought him closer to the men.]

HUDSON (quietly). Nice work, Jimmy. I'm sorry I blew.

BRUCE. Aw, forget it, Mr. Hudson. You're a good man to have around.

HUDSON. Thanks, Jimmy. I feel the same way about you. (HUDSON relaxes slightly.)

SWEDE (suddenly lets out a wail of dismay). Oh, what I forgot!

O'BRIEN. Not another spoon?

SWEDE. My cake! My Christmas cake! It's been in the oven all this time! (He shoots down through the hatchway to the control room. Dissolve to galley.)

SWEDE (runs in, throws the oven door open and draws out his cake. It is burnt to ash. Half bitterly, half with humor). Serves me right for trying to get fancy on a pigboat. It happens every time.

[Back to conning tower with hatch to bridge open.]

MILLER. Well, Jimmy, I think you've got a Christmas present coming. I could have orders cut to send you home to college—pre-med. If ever I saw a great natural surgeon—

BRUCE. Me a surgeon? Are you kidding? I never want to go through anything like that again as long as I live. (MILLER, HUDSON, O'BRIEN, and the others grin.)

[The RADIOMAN enters.]

RADIOMAN. I got the report off, sir. Oh, and everybody back at the base is wishing us a Merry Christmas.

MILLER. That reminds me, men—we've been a little busy around here today or I would have said it sooner: Merry Christmas to all of you.

ADLIBS. Thanks, Skipper. Merry Christmas, sir.

[There is a general exchange of handshakes. BRUCE and HUDSON shake, too, but casually, like the others.]

MILLER (all business again). All right, men. Let's pull the plug[52] and get on with the job.

[Fade out.]

---

[52]pull the plug, dive.

UNDERSTANDING A TELEVISION PLAY

1. Which is the most important conflict in the play? What other conflicts can you name? How is each of the other conflicts related to the main conflict?

2. Trace Jimmy Bruce's development from the time he settles down with a comic book to his successful completion of the operation. In what ways does he bear out the Skipper's statement, "I've seen panicky, half-grown kids suddenly find out they're men"?

3. What are Commander Miller's outstanding qualities? Which of these qualities do you think are most important to a man in a position of authority?

4. What evidences of humor do you find in "The Pharmacist's Mate"? Why are these humorous touches included in an essentially serious drama?

5. The vernacular of submariners and the vernacular of doctors both are used in this television play. Which of these must you understand if you are to follow the play intelligently? Why is it unnecessary to understand the other?

6. How does a television play differ from (a) a stage play, (b) a radio play? What are the advantages of this form? Can you name any disadvantages?

Extending interests

While some excellent documentary moving pictures have been filmed, radio and television seem to be particularly well adapted to this form: (1) They can use a documentary at a time when it has news value. (2) They can reach a nation-wide audience simultaneously. (3) Their programs are of a length well suited to this type of drama.

Arrange with your teacher for a discussion of documentaries. What films of this type have you seen? What outstanding radio programs of this kind have you listened to? What television programs would you class as documentaries? What qualifications must a film, radio, or television drama possess to be rated a good documentary?

The Larger View

I. A series of round-table discussions would provide an interesting way to sum up your study of drama in America. A group of students wishing to work together might select one of their number as chairman to present the subject and to guide its development. In addition to the following items, you may suggest other topics for discussion:

1. The appeal of live staged plays will never be equaled by movies, radio plays, or TV plays.

2. The development of new types of drama on radio and television programs has strengthened the position of drama in America.

3. Conflict is less important in a stage play than in a movie, or a radio or television drama.

4. A poor play can present an interesting conflict; only a good play can present believable and living characters.

5. Twentieth-century playwrights have added variety, depth, and appeal to drama in America.

6. An alert and critical audience might greatly increase the quality of movies and radio and television dramas.

II. A committee of students might make a survey of the radio dramas listened to by members of the class, polling students on the following:

1. How many radio dramas do you listen to in an average week?

2. How do you make your selections; that is, do you listen to the same programs each week or do you consult a radio directory to discover new programs?

3. Do you read reviews of radio programs and tune in on those recommended?

4. What do you consider your favorite dramatic program?

5. Do you tune in on a documentary if you know one is to be broadcast?

6. How would you rate radio plays in general: poor, average, good?

After the survey has been completed, the committee might make a report of its findings for presentation to the class. A similar poll might be made on television plays.

MORE GOOD READING

ANDERSON, MAXWELL, *Eleven Verse Plays, 1929-1939.* (Harcourt) The fine poetry combined with the dramatic action of these plays will provide rewarding reading for the discriminating student.

CERF, BENNETT, and CARTMELL, VAN H. (editors), *Sixteen Famous American Plays.* (Garden City) The names of the authors of these plays—Sidney Howard, Marc Connelly, Eugene O'Neill, Robert Sherwood, Thornton Wilder, and others—read like a roll call of the most prominent modern American dramatists. The plays are worthy of the playwrights.

CORDELL, KATHRYN and WILLIAM (editors), *New Edition of the Pulitzer Prize Plays.* (Random House) Twenty plays, each one a winner of the valued Pulitzer award in the year of its presentation on the stage, are included in this fine collection.

CORNELL, KATHARINE, *I Wanted to Be an Actress.* (Random House) One of America's finest actresses traces her career from her start in stock companies to her present-day position as actress-manager. .

CORWIN, NORMAN, *Thirteen by Corwin.* (Holt) This collection of radio plays by a man outstanding in his field is notable for variety and readability.

FLEXNER, ELEANOR, *American Playwrights, 1918-1938.* (Simon) The student really interested in modern drama will find these critical studies of Eugene O'Neill, Robert Sherwood, Maxwell Anderson, and others valuable reading.

FULLER, EDMUND, *Pageant of the Theater.* (Crowell) This is a fine account of the history of drama from its earliest days to modern times. You will want to concentrate your attention on the last two chapters, "Our American Theater" and "From the Civil War to Today."

HART, MOSS, and KAUFMAN, GEORGE S., *You Can't Take It with You.* (Rinehart) The dignified parents of Alice's fiancé come to dinner on the wrong night and find Alice's family engaged in their usual peculiar occupations, which include raising snakes and testing fireworks. This is one of the best of comedies.

JACKSON, PHYLLIS WYNN, *Golden Footlights; the Merrymaking Career of Lotta Crabtree.* (Holiday) The make-up of this book evokes the period it treats of—California in gold-rush days. You will find that this account of the child star of the mining camps who became a success on Broadway is fascinating reading.

KAUFMAN, WILLIAM I. (editor), *Best TV Plays of the Year 1950-1951.* (Merlin Press) Whether or not you are a TV fan these outstanding television plays offer a wealth of entertainment.

LE GALLIENNE, EVA, *At 33.* (Longmans) This is the modest, honest, and humorous autobiography of a great American actress.

LINDSAY, HOWARD, and CROUSE, RUSSELL, *Clarence Day's Life with Father.* (Knopf) This is a perfect comedy built on Clarence Day's memories of life in an unusual family.

MALVERN, GLADYS, *Good Troupers All; the Story of Joseph Jefferson.* (Macrea) Joseph Jefferson, who was born in Philadelphia in 1829, spent seventy-one years of his full and successful life on the stage. Reading this interesting account of his life will give you a fine idea of drama in nineteenth-century America.

O'NEILL, EUGENE, *Nine Plays.* (Modern Library) O'Neill himself chose these plays as representative of his best work. The mature student will find them excellent reading.

QUINN, ARTHUR (editor), *Representative American Plays, from 1767 to the Present Day.* (Appleton) Glance through this collection, read the introduction to each play and perhaps a play or two, and you will have a much better understanding of the growth of American drama.

SHERWOOD, ROBERT, *Abe Lincoln in Illinois.* (Scribner) This play covers Lincoln's life from his first meeting with Anne Rutledge until he leaves Springfield for his inauguration as President. It's a fine, moving, American drama.

WILDER, THORNTON, *Our Town.* (Coward) Here is a thoroughly American play simply and beautifully written. You'll find that this story of life in Grovers Corners, New Hampshire, will make you see your own corner of America with new eyes.

GLOSSARY

The pronunciation of each word is shown just after the word, in this way: **ab bre vi ate** (ə brē′vi āt). The letters and signs used are pronounced as in the words below. The mark ′ is placed after a syllable with primary or strong accent, as in the example above. The mark ′ after a syllable shows a secondary or lighter accent, as in **ab bre vi a tion** (ə brē′vi ā′shən).

Some words, taken from foreign languages, are spoken with sounds that otherwise do not occur in English. Symbols for these sounds are given at the end of the table as "Foreign Sounds."

a	hat, cap	o	hot, rock	ə represents:	
ā	age, face	ō	open, go	a in about	
ã	care, air	ô	order, all	e in taken	
ä	father, far	oi	oil, voice	i in pencil	
		ou	house, out	o in lemon	
b	bad, rob			u in circus	
ch	child, much				
d	did, red	p	paper, cup		
		r	run, try	FOREIGN SOUNDS	
e	let, best	s	say, yes		
ē	equal, see	sh	she, rush	Y	as in French **du** (dY). Pronounce Y like ē with the lips rounded as for English ü in **rule.**
èr	term, learn	t	tell, it		
		th	thin, both		
f	fat, if	ŦH	then, smooth		
g	go, bag			œ	as in French **peu** (pœ). Pronounce œ like ā with the lips rounded as for ō.
h	he, how				
		u	cup, butter		
i	it, pin	u̇	full, put		
ī	ice, five	ü	rule, move	N	as in French **bon** (boN). The N is not pronounced, but shows that the vowel before it is nasal.
		ū	use, music		
j	jam, enjoy				
k	kind, seek	v	very, save		
l	land, coal	w	will, woman		
m	me, am	y	young, yet	H	as in German **ach** (aH). Pronounce H like k without closing the breath passage.
n	no, in	z	zero, breeze		
ng	long, bring	zh	measure, seizure		

<	from, derived from, taken from	*def.*	definition	*masc.*	masculine
?	possibly	*dial.*	dialect	*neut.*	neuter
abl.	ablative	*dim.*	diminutive	*pp.*	past participle
accus.	accusative	*fem.*	feminine	*ppr.*	present participle
cf.	compare	*gen.*	genitive	*ult.*	ultimately
		lang.	language	*var.*	variant

AF Anglo-French (= Anglo-Norman, the dialect of French spoken by the Normans in England, esp. 1066-c.1164)

Am.E American English (word originating in the United States)

Am.Ind. American Indian

E English

F French

G German

Gk. Greek

Gmc. Germanic (parent language of Gothic, Scandinavian, English, Dutch, German)

HG High German (speech of Central and Southern Germany)

Hindu. Hindustani (the commonest language of India)

Ital. Italian

L Latin (Classical Latin 200 B.C.-300 A.D.)

LG Low German (speech of Northern Germany)

LGk. Late Greek (300-700)

LL Late Latin (300-700)

M Middle

ME Middle English (1100-1500)

Med. Medieval

Med.Gk. Medieval Greek (700-1500)

Med.L Medieval Latin (700-1500)

MF Middle French (1400-1600)

MHG Middle High German (1100-1450)

MLG Middle Low German (1100-1450)

NL New Latin (after 1500)

O Old

OE Old English (before 1100)

OF Old French (before 1400)

OHG Old High German (before 1100)

Pg. Portuguese

Scand. Scandinavian (one of the languages of Northern Europe before Middle English times; Old Norse unless otherwise specified)

Skt. Sanskrit (the ancient literary language of India, from the same parent language as Persian, Greek, Latin, Germanic, Slavonic, and Celtic)

Sp. Spanish

VL Vulgar Latin (a popular form of Latin, the main source of French, Spanish, Italian, Portuguese, and Rumanian)

OTHER ABBREVIATIONS

adj.	adjective	*E*	Eastern	*pron.*	pronoun
adv.	adverb	*esp.*	especially	*sing.*	singular
Anat.	anatomy	*interj.*	interjection	*SW*	Southwestern
Ant.	antonym	*n.*	noun	*Syn.*	synonym
Brit.	British	*pl.*	plural	*U.S.*	United States
conj.	conjunction	*prep.*	preposition	*v.*	verb

The keys on pages 694 and 695 are from the *Thorndike-Barnhart High School Dictionary*, copyright, 1952, by Scott, Foresman and Company.

a ban don (ə ban′dən), *n.* freedom from restraint; lack of self-control: *The students cheered with abandon, waving their arms and shouting.* [< F]

a ban doned (ə ban′dənd), *adj.* wicked; immoral.

a bate ment (ə bāt′mənt), *n.* **1.** decrease; lessening. **2.** putting an end to. **3.** reduction.

ab di cate (ab′də kāt), *v.* **1.** give up or renounce formally; resign: *The king abdicated his throne, and his brother became king.* **2.** renounce office or power. [< L *abdicare* < *ab-* away + *dicare* proclaim]

a bey ance (ə bā′əns), *n.* temporary inactivity; state of suspended action: *The judge held the question in abeyance until he had the information necessary to make a decision.* [< AF *abeiance* expectation < L *ad-* at + VL *batare* gape]

ab hor rence (ab hôr′əns *or* ab hor′əns), *n.* a feeling of very great hatred; horror; disgust.

ab lu tion (ab lü′shən), *n.* **1.** a washing of one's person. **2.** cleansing as a religious ceremony of purification. [< L *ablutio, -onis* < *abluere* < *ab-* away + *luere* wash]

ab nor mal (ab nôr′məl), *adj.* deviating from the normal, the standard, or a type; markedly irregular; unusual: *It is abnormal for a man to be seven feet tall.* [< *ab-* from + *normal*] —**ab nor′mal ly,** *adv.* —**ab nor′mal ness,** *n.*

ab o rig i nal (ab′ə rij′ə nəl), *adj.* **1.** existing from the beginning; first; original; native: *aboriginal inhabitants.* **2.** of the earliest known inhabitants.

a bor tive (ə bôr′tiv), *adj.* **1.** coming to nothing; unsuccessful; fruitless: *The early attempts to make airplanes were abortive.* **2.** born before the right time.

ab sent ly (ab′sənt li), *adv.* inattentively.

ab strac tion (ab strak′shən), *n.* **1.** idea of a quality thought of apart from any particular object or real thing having that quality; idea that is not concrete. Whiteness and goodness are abstractions. **2.** formation of such an idea. **3.** being lost in thought.

a ca cia (ə kā′shə), *n.* a thorny North American tree with white flowers; the locust tree.

ac cede (ak sēd′), *v.* **1.** give in; agree (to). **2.** come (to); attain (to an office or dignity): *When the king died, his oldest son acceded to the throne.*

ac cel er ate (ak sel′ər āt), *v.* **1.** go or cause to go faster. **2.** hasten. **3.** change the speed of (a moving object). [< L *accelerare* < *ad-* to + *celer* swift]

ac ces so ry (ak ses′ə ri), *n.* **1.** an extra thing added to help something of more importance. **2.** person who helps an offender against the law. —*adj.* added; additional; extra.

ac cli mate (ə klī′mit *or* ak′lə māt), *v. Esp. U.S.* accustom or become accustomed to a new climate, surroundings, or conditions. [< F *acclimater* < *à* to (< L *ad-*) + *climat* climate (< L *clima*)]

ac cord (ə kôrd′), *v.* **1.** be in harmony; agree (with): *His account of the accident accords with yours.* **2.** grant. **3.** make agree; harmonize; reconcile. [< OF *acorder* < VL *acchordare* bring into harmony < L *ad-* to + *chorda* string]

ac cost (ə kôst′ *or* ə kost′), *v.* speak to first.

ac count a bil i ty (ə koun′tə bil′ə ti), *n.* responsibility.

ac qui esce (ak′wi es′), *v.* give consent by keeping silent. —**ac′qui es′cence,** *n.* —**Syn.** accede, assent.

ac quit (ə kwit′), *v.* **1.** declare (a person) not guilty (of an offense): *The jury acquitted the innocent man of the crime.* **2.** set free or release (from a duty, an obligation, etc.).

ac rid (ak′rid), *adj.* **1.** bitter or stinging. **2.** sharp or irritating in manner or temper. [< L *acer, acris* sharp]

ad duce (ə düs′ *or* ə dūs′), *v.* offer as a reason.

ad ept (*n.* ad′ept *or* ə dept′; *adj.* ə dept′), *n.* a thoroughly skilled or expert person. —*adj.* expert.

ad he sion (ad hē′zhən), *n.* **1.** a sticking fast. **2.** agreement. **3.** the growing together of tissues that should be separate.

ad lib (ad lib′), *v. Informal.* make up as one goes along. [shortened form of *ad libitum*]

a droit (ə droit′), *adj.* skillful: *A good teacher is adroit in asking questions.* [< F *adroit* < *à droit* rightly < L *ad-* to + *directus* straight] —**a droit′ly,** *adv.* —**a droit′ness,** *n.*

ad vert (ad vėrt′), *v.* direct attention; refer (to).

aer o stat (ār′ə stat), *n.* any lighter-than-air aircraft, such as a balloon or dirigible. —**aer′o stat′ic,** *adj.*

af fa ble (af′ə bəl), *adj.* easy to talk to; courteous and pleasant.

af fin i ty (ə fin′ə ti), *n.* **1.** natural attraction to a person or liking for a thing. **2.** resemblance; likeness.

af flu ence (af′lü əns), *n.* **1.** wealth. **2.** abundant supply.

aft (aft *or* äft), *adv.* at, near, or toward the stern.

ag glu ti nate (*v.* ə glü′tə nāt; *adj.* ə glü′tə nit *or* ə glü′tə nāt), *v.* stick together. —*adj.* stuck or joined together.

ag gre gate (*v.* ag′rə gāt; *n., adj.* ag′rə git *or* ag′rə gāt), *v.* collect; unite. —*n.* total: *The aggregate of all the gifts was $100.* —*adj.* total. [< L *aggregare* < *ad-* to + *grex* flock] —**ag′gre gate ly,** *adv.*

ag gres sion (ə gresh′ən), *n.* **1.** first step in an attack or quarrel; an unprovoked attack. **2.** practice of making assaults or attacks. [< L *aggressio, -onis* < *aggredi* < *ad-* to + *gradi* to step]

a ghast (ə gast′ *or* ə gäst′), *adj.* filled with horror; frightened; terrified. [pp. of obsolete *agast* terrify < OE *on-* on + *gæstan* frighten. Related to *ghost.*]

a gil i ty (ə jil′ə ti), *n.* ability to move quickly; liveliness.

a lac ri ty (ə lak′rə ti), *n.* **1.** brisk and eager action. **2.** cheerful willingness.

al be it (ôl bē′it), *conj.* although; even though.

al bu min (al bū′mən), *n.* in chemistry, any of a class of proteins soluble in water and found in the white of egg and in many other animal and plant tissues and juices.

al bu mi nous (al bū′mə nəs), *adj.* resembling albumin.

al ien ate (āl′yən āt *or* ā′li ən āt), *v.* turn away in feeling or affection; make unfriendly.

al le vi ate (ə lē′vi āt), *v.* make easier to endure (suffering of the body or mind); lessen: *Heat often alleviates pain.*

al lot (ə lot′), *v.* **1.** divide and distribute in parts or shares. **2.** give as a share; assign.

alms house (ämz′hous′ *or* älmz′hous′), *n.* home for persons who do not have enough money to live on.

al oe (al′ō), *n.* **1.** plant having a long spike of flowers and thick, narrow leaves. **2. aloes,** *pl.* a bitter drug made from the dried juice of the leaves of certain aloes. **3.** a symbol of bitterness or sorrow.

al pac a (al pak′ə), *n.* **1.** a South American animal with long, soft, silky hair or wool. It is a kind of llama. **2.** cloth made from its wool. **3.** glossy, wiry cloth made of wool and cotton, usually black.

am a zon (am′ə zon *or* am′ə zən), *n.* **1.** a tall, strong, masculine woman. **2.** Also, **Amazon.** in Greek legend, one of a legendary race of women warriors supposed to live near the Black Sea.

am big u ous (am big′ū əs), *adj.* **1.** having more than one possible meaning. **2.** doubtful; not clear: *He was left in an ambiguous position by his friend's failure to appear and help him.* —**Syn. 1.** equivocal. See **obscure.**

am biv a lence (am biv′ə ləns), *n.* state of having exactly opposite feelings toward the same person, thing, or action at the same time. —**am biv′a lent,** *adj.*

am ble (am′bəl), *n.* **1.** gait of a horse when it lifts first the two legs on one side and then the two on the other.

< = from, derived from, taken from; cf., compare; dial., dialect; dim., diminutive; lang., language; pp., past participle; ppr., present participle; pt., past tense; ult., ultimately; var., variant; ? = possibly.

2. easy, slow pace in walking. —*v.* **1.** walk at an easy, slow pace. **2.** (of a horse) move at an amble. [< OF *ambler* < L *ambulare* walk]

am e thyst (am′ə thist), *n.* a purple or violet variety of quartz, used for jewelry. —*adj.* purple; violet.

am i ca ble (am′ə kə bəl), *adj.* peaceable; friendly.

am i ty (am′ə ti), *n.* peace and friendship.

am phib i ous (am fib′i əs), *adj.* **1.** able to live both on land and in water. **2.** having two natures, or parts. [< Gk. *amphibios* living a double life < *amphi-* both + *bios* life]

am pli fi ca tion (am′plə fə kā′shən), *n.* expansion; an increase in power, sound, etc.

am pli tude (am′plə tüd *or* am′plə tūd), *n.* **1.** width; breadth; size. **2.** abundance; fullness.

an cho vy (an′chō vi, an′chə vi, *or* an chō′vi), *n.* a very small fish that looks somewhat like a herring. Anchovies are pickled or made into a paste which is used as an appetizer.

an es the tist (ən es′thə tist), *n.* person who supplies ether or other substances that cause the loss of sensation in a patient during an operation.

an i ma tion (an′ə mā′shən), *n.* liveliness; spirit.

an i mos i ty (an′ə mos′ə ti), *n.* violent hatred.

an ni hi late (ə nī′hi lāt), *v.* **1.** destroy completely. **2.** bring to ruin or confusion. —**an ni′hi la′tion,** *n.*

an nul (ə nul′), *v.* do away with; destroy the force of; make void. —*Syn.* abolish, cancel.

a nom a lous (ə nom′ə ləs), *adj.* irregular; abnormal.

a nom a ly (ə nom′ə li), *n.* **1.** irregularity. **2.** something abnormal: *A dog with six legs is an anomaly.*

an te (an′ti), *n.* stake in the game of poker that every player must put up before receiving a hand or drawing new cards. —*v. Informal.* **1.** put (one's stake) into the pool. **2.** pay (one's share).

an te ri or (an tēr′i ər), *adj.* toward the front; fore.

an thrax (an′thraks), *n.* an infectious, often fatal, disease of cattle, sheep, etc., that may be transmitted to human beings. [< LL < Gk. *anthrax* carbuncle, live coal]

an tic (an′tik), *adj.* grotesque; odd; fantastic. —*n.* **antics,** *pl.* a grotesque gesture or action; a silly trick.

an ti dote (an′ti dōt), *n.* **1.** medicine or remedy that counteracts a poison. **2.** remedy for any evil.

an tip o des (an tip′ə dēz), *n.pl.* **1.** two places on directly opposite sides of the earth: *The North Pole and the South Pole are antipodes.* **2.** place on the opposite side of the earth. **3.** two opposites or contraries: *Forgiveness and revenge are antipodes.* **4.** the direct opposite.

➔ **Antipodes** is plural in form and plural or singular in use for defs. 2 and 4.

an ti quar i an (an′ti kwär′i ən), *adj.* having to do with antiques. —*n.* **1.** student or collector of antiques. **2.** person who studies former times.

an ti quat ed (an′tə kwāt′id), *adj.* old-fashioned.

a pace (ə pās′), *adv.* swiftly; quickly; fast.

ap a thy (ap′ə thi), *n.* lack of interest or desire for activity; indifference.

ap er ture (ap′ər chúr *or* ap′ər chər), *n.* an opening; gap; hole. [< L *apertura* < *aperire* open]

a pex (ā′peks), *n.* **1.** the highest point; tip: *the apex of a triangle.* **2.** climax. [< L]

ap os tol ic (ap′əs tol′ik), *adj.* **1.** having to do with Christ's twelve disciples, the Apostles. **2.** like a religious leader.

a pos tro phize (ə pos′trə fīz), *v.* address some thing or absent person, usually with emotion.

ap pall ing (ə pôl′ing), *adj.* dismaying; terrifying.

ap pa ri tion (ap′ə rish′ən), *n.* **1.** ghost; phantom. **2.** something strange, remarkable, or unexpected which comes into view. **3.** act of appearing; appearance. [< LL *apparitio, -onis* < L *apparere*]

ap pel la tion (ap′ə lā′shən), *n.* name; title.

ap pend (ə pend′), *v.* add to a larger thing; attach.

ap per tain (ap′ər tān′), *v.* belong as a part; relate.

ap prais er (ə prāz′ər), *n.* **1.** person authorized to fix the value of property, imported goods, etc. **2.** person who estimates the value, amount, quality of (a thing or person).

ap pre hen sive (ap′ri hen′siv), *adj.* **1.** afraid; anxious. **2.** quick to understand. —**ap′pre hen′sive ly,** *adv.*

ap prise (ə prīz′), *v.* inform; notify; advise.

a quat ic (ə kwat′ik *or* ə kwot′ik), *adj.* **1.** growing or living in water: *Water lilies are aquatic plants.* **2.** taking place in or on water: *Swimming and sailing are aquatic sports.*

aq ua vi tae (ak′wə vī′tē), *n.* **1.** alcohol. **2.** brandy; whiskey, etc. [< NL *aqua vitae* water of life]

ar bi trar y (är′bə trer′i), *adj.* **1.** based on one's own wishes, notions, or will; not going by rule or law: *A good judge does not make arbitrary decisions.* **2.** tyrannical: *an arbitrary king.* —**ar′bi trar′i ly,** *adv.* —**ar′bi trar′i ness,** *n.* —*Syn.* **2.** despotic.

ar bu tus (är bū′təs), *n.* **1.** a trailing plant growing in E North America, that has clusters of fragrant, pink or white flowers very early in the spring. It is also called the Mayflower or trailing arbutus. **2.** shrub or tree of the same family as the heath, that has clusters of large white flowers and scarlet berries. [< L]

arch (ärch), *adj.* **1.** chief: *The arch rebel of all was Patrick Henry.* **2.** playfully mischievous.

ar du ous (är′jü əs), *adj.* **1.** hard to do; requiring much effort; difficult. **2.** using up much energy; strenuous. **3.** hard to climb; steep. [< L *arduus* steep] —**ar′du ous ly,** *adv.* —**ar′du ous ness,** *n.*

ar ma da (är mä′də *or* är mā′də), *n.* **1.** fleet of warships. **2.** fleet of airplanes. **3. the Armada,** the Spanish fleet that was sent to attack England in 1588. [< Sp. < L *armata* armed force, originally pp. neut. pl. of *armare* to arm]

ar mo ri al (är mô′ri əl *or* är mō′ri əl), *adj.* having to do with coats of arms or heraldry.

ar raign ment (ə rān′mənt), *n.* **1.** act of bringing before a court to answer a charge. **2.** unfavorable criticism.

ar rant (ar′ənt), *adj.* thoroughgoing; downright.

ar ras (ar′əs), *n.* **1.** kind of tapestry. **2.** curtain or hangings of tapestry. [from *Arras,* a city in France]

ar rest (ə rest′), *v.* **1.** seize by legal authority; take to jail or court. **2.** stop; check: *Filling a tooth arrests decay.* **3.** catch and hold. —*n.* **1.** a seizing by legal authority; a taking to jail or court. **2.** a stopping; checking.

ar ro gant (ar′ə gənt), *adj.* too proud; haughty. [< L *arrogans, -antis,* ppr. of *arrogare* < ad- to + *rogare* ask] —*Syn.* overbearing. —*Ant.* humble, meek.

ar tic u late (*adj.* är tik′ū lit; *v.* är tik′ū lāt), *adj.* **1.** uttered in distinct syllables or words. **2.** able to put one's thoughts into words. **3.** jointed. —*v.* **1.** speak distinctly: *Be careful to articulate your words so that everyone in the room can understand you.* **2.** fit together in a joint. [< L *articulatus,* pp. of *articulare* divide into single joints < *articulus*] —**ar tic′u late ly,** *adv.* —**ar tic′u la′tion,** *n.*

ar ti fice (är′tə fis), *n.* a clever device; trick.

ar tif i cer (är tif′ə sər), *n.* **1.** skilled workman; craftsman. **2.** maker; inventor.

ar ti san (är′tə zən), *n.* skilled workman; craftsman. [< F < Ital. *artigiano* < L *ars, artis* art]

as cend an cy (ə sen′dən si), *n.* controlling influence; domination; rule.

ash en (ash′ən), *adj.* like ashes; pale as ashes.

a skance (ə skans′), *adv.* **1.** with suspicion or disapproval: *The students looked askance at the suggestion for having classes on Saturday.* **2.** sideways; to one side.

a skant (ə skant′), *adv.* askance.

a skew (ə skū′), *adv., adj.* to one side; turned or twisted the wrong way: *Her hat is on askew.*

---

hat, āge, cãre, fär; let, ēqual, tėrm; it, īce; hot, ōpen, ôrder; oil, out; cup, pút, rüle, ūse; ch, child; ng, long; th, thin; ₮H, then; zh, measure; ə represents *a* in about, *e* in taken, *i* in pencil, *o* in lemon, *u* in circus.

as pen (as′pən), *n.* a poplar tree whose leaves tremble in the slightest breeze. —*adj.* quivering; trembling.

as phyx i ate (as fik′si āt), *v.* suffocate because of lack of oxygen and excess of carbon dioxide in the blood.

as pi ra tion (as′pə rā′shən), *n.* **1.** earnest desire; longing. **2.** act of drawing air into the lungs; breathing.

as sail ant (ə sāl′ənt), *n.* person who attacks: *The injured man did not know his assailant.*

as sem blage (ə sem′blij), *n.* **1.** group of persons gathered together. **2.** collection; group. **3.** meeting.

as sent (ə sent′), *v.* express agreement. —*n.* acceptance of a proposal, statement, etc.; agreement.

as sid u ous (ə sij′ü əs), *adj.* careful and attentive; diligent. —**as sid′u ous ly,** *adv.*

as sign (ə sīn′), *v.* **1.** give as a task, lesson. **2.** name definitely. **3.** transfer or hand over (property, a right, etc.) legally: *Mr. Jones assigned his home and farm to his creditors.* —*n.* person to whom property, a right, etc., is legally transferred.

as sim i late (ə sim′ə lāt), *v.* **1.** absorb; digest: *The girl reads so fast that she does not assimilate it all.* **2.** make or become like (people of a nation, etc.) in customs and viewpoint. [< L *assimilare* < *ad-* to + *similis* like]

as sist (ə sist′), *v.* **1.** help; aid. **2.** take part. [< F < L *assistere* < *ad-* by + *sistere* take a stand]

as tute (əs tüt′ *or* əs tūt′), *adj.* shrewd; crafty; sagacious. [< L *astutus* < *astus* sagacity] —**as tute′ness,** *n.*

a the ism (ā′thi iz əm), *n.* belief that there is no God.

a thwart (ə thwôrt′), *prep.* across.

a tro cious (ə trō′shəs), *adj.* **1.** wicked; brutal. **2.** *Informal.* very bad; abominable.

at ten u ate (ə ten′ü āt), *v.* **1.** weaken; reduce. **2.** make less dense; dilute. [< L *attenuare* < *ad-* + *tenuis* thin]

at trac tion (ə trak′shən), *n.* **1.** thing that delights or attracts people. **2.** force which tends to bring together, to unite closely, or to hold fast.

au di ble (ô′də bəl), *adj.* capable of being heard; loud enough to be heard. [< LL *audibilis* < L *audire* hear] —**au′di bly,** *adv.*

au di tor (ô′də tər), *n.* hearer; listener.

au gust (ô gust′), *adj.* inspiring admiration; majestic.

au ro ra bo re al is (ô rô′rə bô′ri al′is, ô rô′rə bō′ri al′is, ô rô′rə bô′ri ā′lis, *or* ô rô′rə bō′ri ā′lis), *n.* streamers or bands of light appearing in the northern sky at night; northern lights. [< NL]

au then tic (ô then′tik), *adj.* **1.** reliable. **2.** genuine. [< L *authenticus* < Gk. *authentikos* < *auto-* by oneself + *hentes* one who acts]

au to crat ic (ô′tə krat′ik), *adj.* absolute in authority; ruling without checks or limitations.

au to mo tive (ô′tə mō′tiv), *adj.* **1.** of automobiles. Automotive engineering deals with the design and construction of automobiles. **2.** self-moving; furnishing its own power.

au top sy (ô′top si *or* ô′təp si), *n.* medical examination of a dead body to find the cause of death. [< NL < Gk. *autopsia* < *auto-* for oneself + *opsis* a seeing]

av a lanche (av′ə lanch *or* av′ə länch), *n.* **1.** a large mass of snow and ice, or of dirt and rocks, sliding or falling down a mountainside. **2.** anything like an avalanche: *an avalanche of questions.* —*v.* move like an avalanche. [< F < Swiss F *lavenche* (< a pre-Latin Alpine language), influenced by F *avaler* go down < *à val* < L *ad vallem* to the valley]

a ver (ə vėr′), *v.* state to be true; assert.

av id (av′id), *adj.* eager; greedy: *The miser was avid for gold.* [< L *avidus* < *avere* desire eagerly] —**av′id ly,** *adv.* —**a vid′i ty,** *n.*

a vow (ə vou′), *v.* admit; acknowledge.

a ware (ə wãr′), *adj.* knowing; realizing; conscious: *I was too sleepy to be aware how cold it was.* [OE *gewær*]

a wry (ə rī′), *adv., adj.* **1.** with a twist or turn to one side: *Her hat was blown awry by the wind.* **2.** wrong.

ba cil lus (bə sil′əs), *n.* **1.** any of the rod-shaped bacteria. **2.** any of the bacteria.

bac te ri a (bak tēr′i ə), *n. pl. of* **bacterium.** very tiny and simple plants, so small that they can usually be seen only through a microscope. Certain bacteria cause diseases such as pneumonia, typhoid fever, etc.

bac te ri o log i cal (bak tēr′i ə loj′ə kəl), *adj.* having to do with bacteriology.

bac te ri ol o gist (bak tēr′i ol′ə jist), *n.* expert in bacteriology.

bac te ri ol o gy (bak tēr′i ol′ə ji), *n.* science that deals with bacteria.

bag a telle (bag′ə tel′), *n.* **1.** a mere trifle; thing of no importance. **2.** game somewhat like billiards. [< F < Ital. *bagatella*, dim. of *baga* berry]

ban dy (ban′di), *v.* **1.** throw back and forth; toss about. **2.** give and take; exchange: *To bandy words with a foolish person is a waste of time.*

bane (bān), *n.* **1.** cause of death, ruin, or harm. **2.** ruin.

ban shee (ban′shē), *n. Irish and Scottish.* spirit whose wails mean that there will soon be a death in the family.

ban ter (ban′tər), *n.* playful teasing; joking.

bark (bärk), *n.* **1.** ship with three masts, square-rigged on the first two masts and fore-and-aft-rigged on the other. **2.** *Poetic.* boat; ship. [< F *barque* < Ital. *barca* < LL]

Bark

ba rouche (bə rüsh′), *n.* a four-wheeled carriage with two seats facing each other and a folding top. [< dialectal G *barutsche* < Ital. < L *birotus* two-wheeled < *bi-* two + *rota* wheel]

bar ri cade (bar′ə kād′ *or* bar′ə kād), *n.* **1.** a rough, hastily made barrier for defense. **2.** any barrier or obstruction. —*v.* block or obstruct with a barricade: *The road was barricaded with fallen trees.* [< F *barricade*, apparently < Provençal *barricada* < *barrica* cask; originally, made of casks]

bar ter (bär′tər), *v.* **1.** trade by exchanging one kind of goods for other goods without using money. **2.** exchange. **3.** give (away) without an equal return. —*n.* **1.** act of bartering. **2.** exchange. **3.** something bartered. [< OF *barater* exchange]

➔ When **barter** means exchange, it is followed by *for*: *The colonists bartered calico for Indian land.* When it means give away without an equal return, it is followed by *away*: *He pretended to be happy about his new contract although he realized that he had bartered away his chance for fame.*

bas tion (bas′chən *or* bas′ti ən), *n.* **1.** a projecting part of a fortification. **2.** defense; fortification.

bay[1] (bā), *n.* **1.** the long, deep bark of a dog: *The hunters heard the distant bay of the hounds.* **2.** stand made by a hunted animal to face pursuers when escape is impossible. [ME *bay, abay* < OF *abai* a barking]

bay[2] (bā), *n.* a small evergreen tree with smooth, shiny leaves; laurel tree. [< OF *baie* < L *baca* berry]

bay[3] (bā), *adj.* reddish-brown. [< OF *bai* < L *badius*]

bay ou (bī′ü), *n. U.S.* a marshy inlet or outlet of a lake, river, or gulf in the southern United States. [Am.E; < Louisiana F < Choctaw *bayuk* small stream]

be di zen (bi dī′zən *or* bi diz′ən), *v.* dress in gaudy clothes; ornament with showy finery.

beg gar (beg′ər), *n.* person who lives by begging. —*v.* **1.** bring to poverty. **2.** make seem poor: *The grandeur of Niagara Falls beggars description.*

be grimed (bi grīmd′), *v.* made grimy; soiled and dirty.

< = from, derived from, taken from;　cf., compare;　dial., dialect;　dim., diminutive;　lang., language; pp., past participle;　ppr., present participle;　pt., past tense;　ult., ultimately;　var., variant;　? = possibly.

be grudge (bi gruj′), *v.* envy (somebody) the possession of; be reluctant to give (something); grudge.

be guile (bi gīl′), *v.* **1.** deceive; cheat: *His pleasant ways beguiled me into thinking that he was my friend.* **2.** take away from deceitfully or cunningly. **3.** entertain; amuse. **4.** while away (time) pleasantly.

be he moth (bi hē′məth *or* bē′ə məth), *n.* a huge animal mentioned in the Bible, possibly the hippopotamus.

be hoove (bi hüv′), *v.* **1.** be necessary for: *It behooves you to work hard if you want to keep this job.* **2.** be proper for. [OE *behōfian* to need]

be lea guer (bi lē′gər), *v.* **1.** besiege. **2.** surround.

be lie (bi lī′), *v.* **1.** give a false idea of; misrepresent. **2.** prove to be mistaken.

bel lig er ent (bə lij′ər ənt), *adj.* fond of fighting; warlike. —*n.* nation or person at war. [< L *belligerans, -antis,* ppr. of *belligerare* < *bellum* war + *gerere* wage] —**bel lig′er ent ly,** *adv.*

ben e dic tion (ben′ə dik′shən), *n.* **1.** the asking of God's blessings at the end of a church service. **2.** blessing.

be nef i cence (bə nef′ə səns), *n.* kindness.

be nef i cent (bə nef′ə sənt), *adj.* kind; doing good.

be nev o lent (bə nev′ə lənt), *adj.* kindly; charitable. —**Syn.** philanthropic. —**Ant.** malevolent.

be nign (bi nīn′), *adj.* **1.** gentle; kindly. **2.** favorable; mild: *a benign climate.*

be nig ni ty (bi nig′nə ti), *n.* kindliness; graciousness.

be numb (bi num′), *v.* **1.** make numb. **2.** make stupid, dull, or senseless.

ber i ber i (ber′i ber′i), *n.* disease affecting the nerves, accompanied by weakness, loss of weight, etc.

berth (bėrth), *n.* **1.** place to sleep on a ship, train, or airplane. **2.** a ship's place at a wharf. **3. give a wide berth to,** keep well away from.

be times (bi tīmz′), *adv.* **1.** early: *He rose betimes in the morning.* **2.** soon; before it is too late. [ME *bitime* by time]

be to ken (bi tō′kən), *v.* be a sign of; indicate; show.

bev y (bev′i), *n.* a small group: *a bevy of girls.*

bi as (bī′əs), *n.* **1.** a slanting or oblique line. **2.** opinion before there is reason for it; a leaning of the mind; prejudice. —*adj.* oblique; diagonal. —*v.* influence, usually unfairly.

big ot (big′ət), *n.* an intolerant, prejudiced person.

big ot ed (big′ət id), *adj.* sticking to an opinion, belief, party, etc., without reason and not tolerating other views.

big ot ry (big′ət ri), *n.* intolerance. —**Syn.** prejudice.

birch (bėrch), *n.* **1.** a slender tree whose smooth bark peels off in thin layers. **2.** bundle of birch twigs or a birch stick, used for whipping. —*v.* whip with a birch.

bit tern (bit′ərn), *n.* a small kind of heron that lives in marshes and has a peculiar booming cry. [< OF *butor*]

bi zarre (bə zär′), *adj.* odd; queer; fantastic; grotesque.

black mail (blak′māl′), *n.* **1.** money obtained from a person by threatening to tell something bad about him. **2.** act of blackmailing. —*v.* get or try to get blackmail from. [< *black* + *mail* rent, tribute, coin < OF *maille* < *medaille* coin, medal] —**black′mail′er,** *n.*

blanch (blanch *or* blänch), *v.* turn white or pale.

blas pheme (blas fēm′), *v.* speak about (God or sacred things) with abuse or contempt. —**blas′phe my,** *n.* —**blas′phe mous,** *adj.*

blear (blēr), *adj.* dim, blurred.

blench (blench), *v.* draw back; shrink away.

blithe some (blīᴛʜ′səm *or* blīth′səm), *adj.* gay; cheerful; happy. —**blithe′some ly,** *adv.* —**blithe′some ness,** *n.*

blowzed (blouzd), *adj.* high-colored, red-faced; fat and ruddy; untidy.

bode (bōd), *v.* be a sign of; indicate beforehand: *Dark clouds boded rain.*

bog gy (bog′i *or* bôg′i), *adj.* marshy; swampy.

bold (bōld), *adj.* **1.** without fear; daring. **2.** too free in manner; impudent: *The bold little boy made faces at us as we passed.* **3.** striking; vigorous; free; clear: *The mountains stood in bold outline against the sky.* **4.** steep; abrupt. [OE *bald*] **Syn. 1.** fearless, courageous, brave. **2. Bold, brazen, forward** mean too free in manner. **Bold** suggests lacking proper shame and modesty and pushing oneself forward too rudely: *He swaggered into school late with a bold look on his face.* **Brazen** means defiantly and insolently shameless: *He is brazen about being expelled.* **Forward** suggests being too sure of oneself, too disrespectful of others, too pert in pushing oneself forward: *With her forward ways, that girl will make no friends.* —**Ant. 1.** timid.

bole (bōl), *n.* trunk of a tree. [< Scand. *bolr*]

boll (bōl), *n.* a rounded seed pod or capsule of cotton or flax. [var. of *bowl*]

bonds man (bondz′mən), *n.* **1.** slave. **2.** serf in the Middle Ages.

bore (bôr *or* bōr), *n.* **1.** hole made by a revolving tool. **2.** a hollow space inside a pipe, tube, or gun barrel.

bor er (bôr′ər *or* bōr′ər), *n.* **1.** tool for boring holes. **2.** insect or worm that bores into wood, fruit, etc.

bou doir (bü′dwär *or* bü′dwôr), *n.* a lady's private sitting room or dressing room. [< F *boudoir* < *bouder* sulk]

bou quet (bō kā′ *or* bü kā′ *for* 1; bü kā′ *for* 2), *n.* **1.** bunch of flowers. **2.** fragrance; aroma. [< F *bouquet* little wood, dim. of OF *bosc* wood]

brace (brās), *n.* **1.** thing that holds parts together or in place. **2.** pair; couple: *a brace of ducks.*

brac ing (brās′ing), *adj.* giving strength; refreshing.

brack en (brak′ən), *n.* growth of ferns.

brae (brā), *n. Scottish.* slope; hillside.

brash (brash), *adj.* **1.** hasty; rash. **2.** impudent.

bra va do (brə vä′dō), *n.* a great show of boldness without much real courage; boastful defiance without much real desire to fight. [< Sp. *bravada* < *bravo*]

brave (brāv), *adj.* **1.** without fear. **2.** making a fine appearance; showy. **3.** *Archaic.* fine; excellent. —*v.* meet without fear. [< F < Ital. *bravo* brave, bold < Sp. *bravo* vicious (as applied to bulls), ? < L *pravus*] **Syn.** *adj.* **1. Brave, courageous** mean showing no fear. **Brave** suggests being able to face danger or trouble boldly and with determination, without giving in to fear: *The brave girl went into the burning house to save a baby.* **Courageous** suggests being fearless in the face of danger, having a strength and firmness of character that makes one able to make any trial or even to welcome it: *The courageous pioneers were not stopped by the dangers of the journey westward.* —**Ant.** **1.** cowardly, fearful.

brav er y (brāv′ər i *or* brāv′ri), *n.* showy dress; finery.

bra vo (brä′vō *or* brä′vō), *interj.* well done! fine! *n.* hired fighter or murderer.

brawn (brôn), *n.* **1.** muscle. **2.** muscular strength. **3.** boiled and pickled meat from a boar or hog.

bra zen (brā′zən), *adj.* **1.** like brass in color and strength. **2.** loud and harsh. **3.** shameless; impudent. —*v.* **1.** make shameless or impudent. **2. brazen a thing out or through,** act as if unashamed of it. —**bra′zen ly,** *adv.* —**Syn.** *adj.* **3.** See **bold.**

breast work (brest′wėrk′), *n.* a low, hastily built wall for defense.

bride well (brīd′wel), *n.* house of correction for vagrants and disorderly persons; jail. [from a former prison at St. Bride's well in London]

bridge (brij), *n.* **1.** structure built over a river, road, etc., so that people, trains, etc., can get across. **2.** platform above the deck of a ship for the officer in command. **3.** the upper part of the nose.

bri dle (brī′dəl), *n.* **1.** the head part of a horse's harness, used to hold back or control a horse. **2.** anything that holds back or controls. —*v.* **1.** put a bridle on. **2.** hold back; check; control.

bro ker (brō′kər), *n.* person who buys and sells stocks, bonds, grain, cotton, etc., for other people; agent.

hat, āge, cãre, fär; let, ēqual, tėrm; it, īce; hot, ōpen, ôrder; oil, out; cup, pùt, rüle, ūse; ch, child; ng, long; th, thin; ᴛʜ, then; zh, measure; ə represents *a* in about, *e* in taken, *i* in pencil, *o* in lemon, *u* in circus.

brusque (brusk), *adj.* abrupt in manner or speech; blunt. —**brusque′ly**, *adv.* —**brusque′ness**, *n.*

buc ca neer (buk′ə nēr′), *n.* pirate; sea robber.

buck ler (buk′lər), *n.* **1.** a small, round shield. **2.** protection; defense.

buf fet (bú fā′), *n.* piece of dining-room furniture for holding dishes, silver, and table linen; sideboard.

buf fet lunch eon (bú fā′ lun′chən), *n.* meal where the food is arranged on tables and buffet, and the guests serve themselves.

bull doze (búl′dōz), *v. U.S. Informal.* frighten by violence or threats; bully. [Am.E]

bul ly rag (búl′i rag′), *v. Informal.* bully; tease; abuse.

buoy an cy (boi′ən si *or* bü′yən si), *n.* **1.** power to float. **2.** tendency to rise. **3.** light-heartedness; cheerfulness.

bur den (bėr′dən), *n.* **1.** the main idea. **2.** chorus; refrain. [< OF *bourdon* humming, drone of bagpipe < LL *burda* pipe]

burgh er (bėr′gər), *n.* citizen of a burgh or town; citizen.

bur go mas ter (bėr′gə mas′tər *or* bėr′gə mäs′tər), *n.* mayor of a town in the Netherlands, Flanders, or Germany. [< Dutch *burgemeester* < *burg* borough + *meester* master]

bur lesque (bėr lesk′), *n.* a literary or dramatic composition in which a serious subject is treated ridiculously, or with mock seriousness. —*adj.* comical; making people laugh.

bur ly (bėr′li), *adj.* **1.** strong; sturdy; big. **2.** bluff; rough.

bus tle (bus′əl), *n.* pad used to puff out the upper back part of a woman's skirts.

butte (būt), *n.* in western United States, a steep hill standing alone. [Am.E < F]

bux om (buk′səm), *adj.* plump and good to look at; healthy and cheerful. [ME *buhsum* < OE *būgan* bend] —**bux′om ness**, *n.*

by-play (bī′plā′), *n.* action that is not part of the main action, especially on the stage.

by word (bī′wėrd′), *n.* **1.** a common saying; proverb. **2.** object of contempt; thing scorned.

cab in (kab′ən), *n.* **1.** a small, roughly built house; hut. **2.** room in a ship. **3.** place for passengers in an airplane or airship. [< F *cabane* < LL *capanna*]

ca dav er ous (kə dav′ər əs), *adj.* **1.** pale and ghastly. **2.** thin and worn.

ca dence (kā′dəns), *n.* **1.** rhythm. **2.** measure or beat of any rhythmical movement. **3.** fall of the voice.

cae cum (sē′kəm), *n.* first part of the large intestine.

cais son (kā′sən *or* kā′son), *n.* **1.** box for ammunition. **2.** wagon to carry ammunition. [< F *caisson* < *caisse* chest < L *capsa* box]

ca jole (kə jōl′), *v.* persuade by pleasant words; coax.

calk (kôk), *n.* **1.** a projecting piece on a horseshoe. **2.** *U.S.* a sharp, projecting piece of metal on the bottom of a shoe to prevent slipping. —*v.* put calks on. [< L *calx* heel *or* *calcar* spur]

cal low (kal′ō), *adj.* **1.** young and inexperienced. **2.** not fully developed.

ca nar y (kə nãr′i), *n.* **1.** a small, yellow songbird. **2.** wine from the Canary Islands.

can did (kan′did), *adj.* **1.** frank; sincere. **2.** fair; impartial. —**can′did ly**, *adv.* —**Syn.** **1.** truthful, ingenuous.

can ny (kan′i), *adj. Scottish.* **1.** shrewd. **2.** thrifty.

cant (kant), *n.* insincere talk. —*v.* use cant; talk in cant. [< L *cantus* song]

can tan ker ous (kan tang′kər əs), *adj.* hard to get along with because ready to make trouble and oppose anything suggested; ill-natured.

ca pon (kā′pon *or* kā′pən), *n.* a fattened rooster.

cap tious (kap′shəs), *adj.* hard to please; faultfinding.

car bun cle (kär′bung kəl), *n.* **1.** a very painful, inflamed swelling under the skin. **2.** a smooth, round garnet or other deep-red jewel.

ca reen (kə rēn′), *v.* lean to one side; tilt; tip.

ca reer (kə rēr′), *v.* rush along wildly; dash.

car et (kar′ət), *n.* mark (∧) to show where something should be put in, used in writing and in correcting proof.

car i ca ture (kar′ə kə chùr *or* kar′ə kə chər), *n.* **1.** picture, cartoon, description, etc., that ridiculously exaggerates the peculiarities or defects of a person or thing. **2.** a very poor imitation. —*v.* make a caricature of. [< F < Ital. *caricatura* < *caricare* overload, exaggerate] —**Syn.** *n.* **1.** burlesque.

cark ing (kär′king), *adj.* troublesome; worrying.

car nage (kär′nij), *n.* slaughter of a great number of people. [< F < Ital. *carnaggio* < L *caro* flesh]

car nel ian (kär nēl′yən), *n.* a red stone used in jewelry. It is a kind of quartz. [influenced by L *caro* flesh]

car niv o rous (kär niv′ə rəs), *adj.* flesh-eating. [< L *carnivorus* < *caro* flesh + *vorare* devour]

car ri on (kar′i ən), *adj.* feeding on dead flesh.

cat a lep sy (kat′ə lep′si), *n.* kind of fit during which a person loses consciousness and the power to feel, and his muscles become rigid. [< LL *catalepsis* < Gk. *katalepsis* seizure < *kata-* down + *lambanein* seize]

cat a lep ti cal (kat′ə lep′ti kəl), *adj.* **1.** of catalepsy. **2.** having catalepsy.

cat a mount (kat′ə mount), *n.* wildcat, such as a puma or lynx.

catch pole (kach′pōl′), *n.* a deputy sheriff or bailiff whose duties include arresting debtors.

cath o lic (kath′ə lik *or* kath′lik), *adj.* having sympathies with all; universal; broad-minded; liberal.

cause way (kôz′wā′), *n.* a raised road or path, usually built across wet ground, shallow water, etc.

cav al cade (kav′əl kād′ *or* kav′əl kād), *n.* procession of persons riding on horses or in carriages.

cav a lier (kav′ə lēr′), *n.* **1.** horseman; mounted soldier; knight. **2.** a courteous gentleman. **3.** a courteous escort for a lady. **4.** Cavalier, person who supported Charles I of England in his struggle with Parliament from 1641 to 1649. —*adj.* **1.** free and easy; offhand. **2.** proud and scornful; haughty; arrogant. [< F < Ital. *cavalliere* < *cavallo* horse < L *caballus*] —**cav′a lier′ly**, *adv.*

cav ern ous (kav′ər nəs), *adj.* large and hollow.

cav i ar (kav′i är′), *n.* a salty relish made from the eggs of sturgeon or other large fish.

cav il (kav′əl), *v.* find fault unnecessarily. —*n.* a petty objection; trivial criticism. [< F < L *cavillari* jeer] —**cav′-il er**, *n.*

ca vort (kə vôrt′), *v. U.S. Informal.* prance about.

ce ler i ty (sə ler′ə ti), *n.* swiftness; speed.

cel i ba cy (sel′ə bə si), *n.* unmarried state; single life.

cen ser (sen′sər), *n.* container in which incense is burned to produce a sweet, perfumed odor.

cen ti pede (sen′tə pēd′), *n.* a small wormlike animal with many pairs of legs. [< L *centipeda* < *centum* hundred + *pes* foot]

cer e bra tion (ser′ə brā′shən), *n.* thinking.

chafe (chāf), *v.* **1.** rub to make warm: *She chafed her cold hands.* **2.** wear or be worn away by rubbing. **3.** make or become sore by rubbing: *The stiff collar chafed the man's neck.* **4.** make angry: *His big brother's teasing chafed him.* **5.** become angry: *He chafed under his big brother's teasing.* —*n.* a chafing; irritation. [< OF *chaufer* < L *calefacere* < *calere* be warm + *facere* make]

cha grin (shə grin′), *n.* a feeling of disappointment or failure; humiliation.

cha ot ic (kā ot′ik), *adj.* confused; completely disordered.

char (chär), *v.* **1.** burn to charcoal. **2.** burn slightly; scorch.

< = from, derived from, taken from; cf., compare; dial., dialect; dim., diminutive; lang., language; pp., past participle; ppr., present participle; pt., past tense; ult., ultimately; var., variant; ? = possibly.

chase (chās), *v.* engrave.

chasm (kaz′əm), *n.* **1.** a deep opening or crack in the earth; gap. **2.** a wide difference of feelings or interests between people or groups: *The chasm between England and the American colonies grew wider and wider until it finally resulted in the American Revolution.* [< L *chasma* < Gk.] —Syn. **1.** fissure.

chas sis (shas′i *or* chas′i), *n.* frame, wheels, and machinery of a motor vehicle that support the body. [< F < VL *capsiceum* < L *capsa* box]

che ru bic (chə rü′bik), *adj.* **1.** of or like an angel; angelic. **2.** innocent; good. **3.** chubby.

cher u bim (cher′ə bim *or* cher′ū bim), *n. pl. of* **cherub.** cherubs; angels.

chick a dee (chik′ə dē), *n.* a small bird. Its cry sounds somewhat like its name. [Am.E; imitative]

chide (chīd), *v.* reproach; blame; scold: *She chided the little girl for soiling her dress.* [OE *cīdan*]

chol er a (kol′ər ə), *n.* an acute disease of the stomach and intestines, characterized by vomiting, cramps, and diarrhea.

chron ic (kron′ik), *adj.* **1.** of a disease, lasting a long time: *The doctor told him rheumatism was a chronic disease.* **2.** habitual. [< L *chronicus* < Gk. *chronikos* < *chronos* time]

chron o log i cal (kron′ə loj′ə kəl), *adj.* arranged in the order in which the events happened.

cir cum lo cu tion (sėr′kəm lō kū′shən), *n.* a roundabout way of speaking. "The wife of your father's brother" is a circumlocution for "Your aunt." [< L *circumlocutio, -onis* < *circum* around + *loqui* speak]

cir cum scribe (sėr′kəm skrīb′ *or* sėr′kəm skrīb′), *v.* **1.** draw a line around; mark the boundaries of. **2.** surround. **3.** limit; restrict. [< L *circumscribere* < *circum* around + *scribere* write]

ci ta tion (sī tā′shən), *n.* **1.** specific mention in an official dispatch. **2.** honorable mention for bravery in war.

clab ber (klab′ər), *n.* thick, sour milk. —*v.* become thick in souring; curdle. [< Irish *clabar* curds, short for *bainne clabair* bonnyclabber (curdled milk)]

clan gor (klang′gər *or* klang′ər), *n.* continued loud, harsh, ringing sound. —**clan′gor ous,** *adj.*

cleat (klēt), *n.* strip of wood or iron fastened across anything for support. —*v.* fasten to or with a cleat.

cler i cal (kler′ə kəl), *adj.* **1.** of a clerk or clerks. **2.** of a clergyman or the clergy.

clerk (klerk), *n.* **1.** salesman or saleswoman. **2.** person whose work is keeping records or accounts, etc., in an office. **3.** layman who has minor church duties. **4.** *Archaic.* clergyman.

clock (klok), *n.* an ornamental pattern sewn or woven on the side of a stocking, extending up from the ankle.

clock work (klok′werk′), *n.* **1.** machinery used to run a clock, consisting of gears, wheels, and springs. **2.** machinery like this. **3.** like clockwork, with great regularity and smoothness.

clog (klog), *v.* **1.** fill up; choke up: *Greasy water clogged the drain.* **2.** become filled or choked up. **3.** hinder; interfere with; hold back: *Heavy clothes clogged the swimmer.* —*n.* **1.** thing that hinders or interferes. **2.** any weight, such as a block of wood, fastened to the leg of an animal to hinder motion. **3.** a heavy shoe with a wooden sole. **4.** a lighter shoe with a wooden sole, used in dancing. **5.** dance in which wooden-soled shoes are worn. [ME *clogge* block]

clois tered (klois′tərd), *adj.* shut away in a quiet place.

clos et (kloz′it), *n.* **1.** a small room used for storing clothes, etc. **2.** a private room for prayer, study, etc.

clout (klout), *n. Informal.* a hit with the hand; rap; knock.

clo ven (klō′vən), *adj.* split; divided.

co ad ju tor (kō aj′ü tər *or* kō′ə jü′tər), *n.* assistant; helper.

co er cion (kō ėr′shən), *n.* use of force; act of compelling.

co e val (kō ē′vəl), *adj.* of the same age, date, or duration.

cof fer (kôf′ər *or* kof′ər), *n.* **1.** box, chest, or trunk, especially one used to hold money or other valuable things. **2.** coffers, *pl.* treasury; funds. [< OF *cofre* < L *cophinus* basket]

co gent (kō′jənt), *adj.* forcible; convincing: *cogent arguments.*

cog wheel (kog′hwēl′), *n.* wheel with teeth projecting from the rim for transmitting or receiving motion.

co hort (kō′hôrt), *n.* group; band; company.

coif (koif), *n.* cap or hood that fits closely around the head.

co in ci dent (kō in′sə dənt), *adj.* **1.** coinciding; happening at the same time. **2.** in agreement.

col lab o ra tion (kə lab′ə rā′shən), *n.* **1.** act of working together. **2.** act of aiding or coöperating traitorously.

col leen (kol′ēn *or* kə lēn′), *n. Irish.* girl.

col lo ca tion (kol′ō kā′shən), *n.* arrangement.

col lo qui al (kə lō′kwi əl), *adj.* used in everyday, informal talk, but not in formal speech or writing. *Beat (someone) all hollow* and *It's a cinch* are colloquial expressions. → **Colloquial** means conversational, used in speaking. Since the speech of people varies with their education, work, and social status, there are obviously many different types of colloquial English. Since the bulk of conversation is informal, *colloquial* suggests informal rather than formal English. It need not, however, mean the speech of uneducated people. As used in many dictionaries, *colloquial* refers to informal cultivated English.

col lo qui al ism (kə lō′kwi əl iz′əm), *n.* **1.** a colloquial word or phrase. **2.** a colloquial style or usage.

col lo quy (kol′ə kwi), *n.* conversation. [< L *colloquium* < *colloqui* < *com-* with + *loqui* speak]

col on nade (kol′ə nād′), *n.* series of columns set the same distance apart.

co ma (kō′mə), *n.* a prolonged unconsciousness caused by disease, injury, or poison; stupor. [< Gk. *koma*]

com bus ti ble (kəm bus′tə bəl), *adj.* capable of taking fire and burning; easily burned.

come ly (kum′li), *adj.* **1.** having a pleasant appearance; attractive. **2.** fitting; suitable; proper. —**come′li ness,** *n.* —Ant. **1.** ugly, homely, plain.

com min gle (kə ming′gəl), *v.* mingle together.

com mo di ous (kə mō′di əs), *adj.* **1.** roomy. **2.** convenient.

com mon wealth (kom′ən welth′), *n.* **1.** group of people who make up a nation; citizens of a state. **2.** a democratic state; republic. **3.** any one of the States of the United States. **4.** group of persons, nations, etc., united by some common interest.

com mune (*v.* kə mūn′; *n.* kom′ūn), *v.* talk intimately. —*n.* intimate talk; communion. [< OF *communer* < *comun*]

com mun ion (kə mūn′yən), *n.* **1.** act of sharing; a having in common. **2.** exchange of thoughts and feelings; intimate talk; fellowship. **3.** a close spiritual relationship. **4.** groups of people having the same religious beliefs. [< L *communio, -onis* < *communis*]

com mute (kə mūt′), *v. U.S.* travel regularly back and forth to work by train, bus, automobile, etc.

com pan ion way (kəm pan′yən wā′), *n.* **1.** stairway from the deck of a ship down to the rooms below. **2.** space where such a stairway is.

com pass (kum′pəs), *n.* **1.** instrument for showing directions, consisting of a needle that points to the magnetic north. **2.** space within limits; extent; range: *The old sailor had many adventures within the compass of his lifetime.*

com pa tri ot (kəm pā′tri ət), *n.* a fellow countryman.

com peer (kəm pēr′ *or* kom′pēr), *n.* **1.** equal. **2.** comrade. [< OF *comper* < L *compar* < *com-* with + *par* equal]

---

hat, āge, cāre, fär; let, ēqual, tėrm; it, īce; hot, ōpen, ôrder; oil, out; cup, pùt, rüle, ūse; ch, child; ng, long; th, thin; ₮H, then; zh, measure; ə represents *a* in about, *e* in taken, *i* in pencil, *o* in lemon, *u* in circus.

com pile (kəm pĭl′), *v.* **1.** collect and bring together in one list or account. **2.** make (a book, report, etc.) out of various materials. [< F < L *compilare* steal, originally, pile up < *com-* together + *pilare* press] —**com pil′er,** *n.*

com pla cen cy (kəm plā′sən si), *n.* self-satisfaction.

com plai sant (kəm plā′zənt *or* kom′plə zant), *adj.* **1.** obliging; gracious; courteous. **2.** yielding.

com pli ance (kəm plī′əns), *n.* **1.** act of doing as another wishes; act of yielding to a request or command. **2.** tendency to yield to others. **3. in compliance with,** according to.

com port ment (kəm pôrt′mənt *or* kəm pōrt′mənt), *n.* behavior.

com press (*v.* kəm pres′; *n.* kom′pres), *v.* squeeze together; make smaller by pressure. —*n.* **1.** pad of wet cloth applied to some part of the body to create pressure or to reduce inflammation. **2.** machine for compressing cotton into bales.

con ceit (kən sēt′), *n.* **1.** too high an opinion of oneself. **2.** a fanciful notion.

con cept (kon′sept), *n.* general notion; idea.

con cil i ate (kən sil′i āt), *v.* **1.** win over. **2.** reconcile; bring into harmony.

con ci sion (kən sizh′ən), *n.* expressing much in few words.

con coc tion (kon kok′shən *or* kən kok′shən), *n.* thing made up or prepared.

con com i tant (kon kom′ə tənt *or* kən kom′ə tənt), *adj.* accompanying; attending: *a concomitant result.*

con course (kon′kôrs, kong′kôrs, kon′kōrs, *or* kong′-kōrs), *n.* **1.** a running, flowing, or coming together. **2.** crowd. **3.** driveway; boulevard.

con cur rence (kən kėr′əns), *n.* **1.** having the same opinion; agreement. **2.** a working together.

con de scend ing (kon′di sen′ding), *adj.* **1.** stooping to the level of one's inferiors. **2.** patronizing. —**con′de-scend′ing ly,** *adv.*

con fla gra tion (kon′flə grā′shən), *n.* a big fire.

con form a ble (kən fôr′mə bəl), *adj.* **1.** similar. **2.** adapted; suited. **3.** in agreement; harmonious. **4.** obedient: *The boy was conformable to his father's wishes.* —**con form′a bly,** *adv.*

con form i ty (kən fôr′mə ti), *n.* **1.** similarity; correspondence; agreement. **2.** action in agreement with generally accepted standards of business, law, conduct, or worship; fitting oneself and one's actions to the ideas of others; compliance. **3.** obedience; submission.

con front (kən frunt′), *v.* **1.** meet face to face; stand facing. **2.** face boldly; oppose. **3.** bring face to face.

con ges tion (kən jes′chən), *n.* **1.** overcrowded or congested condition: *congestion of traffic.* **2.** too much blood in one part of the body: *An ice bag will relieve congestion.*

con ju ra tion (kon′jū rā′shən), *n.* **1.** act of invoking by a sacred name. **2.** a magic form of words used in conjuring; magic spell.

con jure (kun′jər *or* kon′jər *for 1;* kən jür′ *for 2*), *v.* **1.** summon a devil, spirit, etc. **2.** request earnestly; entreat: *I conjure you not to betray your country.*

con ning tow er (kon′ing tou′ər), *n.* a small tower on the deck of a submarine, used as an entrance and as a place for observation.

con san guin i ty (kon′sang gwin′ə ti), *n.* relationship by descent from the same parent or ancestor.

con ser va tor (kon′sər vā′tər *or* kən sėr′və tər), *n.* preserver; guardian.

con sign ment (kən sīn′mənt), *n.* shipment sent to a person or company for safekeeping or sale.

con sist ence (kən sis′təns), *n.* consistency.

con sist en cy (kən sis′tən si), *n.* **1.** degree of firmness or stiffness. **2.** a keeping to the same principles, course of action, etc.

con stel la tion (kon′stə lā′shən), *n.* **1.** a group of stars: *The Big Dipper is the easiest constellation to locate.* **2.** a brilliant gathering. [< LL *constellatio, -onis* < L *com-* together + *stella* star]

con ster na tion (kon′stər nā′shən), *n.* great dismay; paralyzing terror.

con stit u ent (kən stich′ü ənt), *n.* **1.** a necessary part of a whole. **2.** person who votes or appoints; voter.

con sti tu tion al (kon′stə tü′shən əl, kon′stə tū′shən-əl, kon′stə tüsh′nəl *or* kon′stə tūsh′nəl), *adj.* **1.** of or in the make-up of a person or thing: *A constitutional weakness makes him subject to colds.* **2.** of, in, or according to the basic laws of a nation, state, or group: *The Supreme Court must decide whether this law is constitutional.*

con strain (kən strān′), *v.* **1.** force; compel. **2.** confine; imprison. **3.** repress; restrain. [< OF *constreindre* < L *constringere* < *com-* together + *stringere* pull tightly]

con strained (kən strānd′), *adj.* **1.** forced. **2.** restrained; stiff; unnatural: *a constrained smile.*

con straint (kən strānt′), *n.* **1.** confinement. **2.** restraint. **3.** a holding back of natural feelings; forced or unnatural manner; embarrassment. **4.** force; compulsion. [< OF *constreinte* < *constreindre.* See CONSTRAIN.]

con sum mate (*v.* kon′sə māt; *adj.* kən sum′it), *v.* complete; fulfill. —*adj.* complete; perfect; in the highest degree: *The paintings of great artists show consummate skill.* —**con′sum ma′tion,** *n.*

con sump tive (kən sump′tiv), *adj.* **1.** having or likely to have tuberculosis of the lungs. **2.** destructive; wasteful.

con tem pla tive (kon′təm plā′tiv *or* kən tem′plə tiv), *adj.* thoughtful; meditative.

con tem po rar y (kən tem′pə rer′i), *n.* **1.** person who belongs to the same period of time as another or others: *Lincoln and Lee were contemporaries.* **2.** person, magazine, etc., of the same age or date. [< *con-* together + L *temporarius* belonging to time < *tempus* time]

con tempt i ble (kən temp′tə bəl), *adj.* deserving contempt or scorn; held in contempt; mean; low; worthless: *Cowards and cheats are contemptible.* —**con tempt′i ble ness,** *n.* —**con tempt′i bly,** *adv.*

con temp tu ous (kən temp′chü əs), *adj.* showing contempt; scornful: *a contemptuous look.* —**con temp′tu ous ly,** *adv.* —**con temp′tu ous ness,** *n.*

➤ Contemptuous and contemptible are sometimes confused. The distinction will be clear if one observes that in *contemptible* the suffix *-ible,* often, means deserving.

con tort (kən tôrt′), *v.* twist or bend out of shape: *The clown contorted his face.* [L *contortus,* pp. of *contorquere* < *com-* + *torquere* twist]

con tre temps (kôN′trə täN′), *n.* an unlucky accident; embarrassing or awkward happening.

con viv i al i ty (kən viv′i al′ə ti), *n.* fondness for eating and drinking with friends; good-fellowship.

con vo lu tion (kon′və lü′shən), *n.* coil; winding; twist.

con vul sion (kən vul′shən), *n.* **1.** involuntary contracting and relaxing of the muscles. **2.** violent disturbance. —**con vul′sive,** *adj.*

coon (kün), *n. Informal.* raccoon.

coot (küt), *n.* a wading and swimming bird with short wings and toes broadened by lobes of skin.

copse (kops), *n.* a thicket of small trees, bushes, shrubs.

co quet ry (kō′kə tri *or* kō ket′ri), *n.* **1.** flirting. **2.** trifling.

co quette (ko ket′), *n.* woman who tries to attract men merely to please her vanity; flirt. —**co quet′tish,** *adj.*

cor mo rant (kôr′mə rənt), *n.* **1.** a very large, greedy sea bird that has a pouch under the beak for holding captured fish. **2.** a greedy person.

cor re la tion (kôr′ə lā′shən *or* kor′ə lā′shən), *n.* the mutual relation of two or more things: *There is a close correlation between climate and crops.*

< = from, derived from, taken from; cf., compare; dial., dialect; dim., diminutive; lang., language; pp., past participle; ppr., present participle; pt., past tense; ult., ultimately; var., variant; ? = possibly.

cou gar (kü′gər), *n.* a large, tawny American wildcat; mountain lion.

coun te nance (koun′tə nəns), *n.* **1.** face; features. **2. keep one's countenance,** be calm. **3. keep (others) in countenance,** make easy and relaxed; keep from being ashamed.

coun ter bal ance (koun′tər bal′əns), *v.* set off or balance one influence, power, etc., with another; as, to counterbalance skill with strength.

coun ter part (koun′tər pärt′), *n.* **1.** copy; duplicate. **2.** person or thing closely resembling another: *This twin is her sister's counterpart.*

coun ter point (koun′tər point′), *n.* art of adding melodies to a given melody according to fixed rules. [< F *contrepoint*]

cour i er (kėr′i ər *or* kür′i ər), *n.* messenger sent in haste. [< F *courrier* < Ital. < L *currere* run]

cours er (kôr′sər *or* kōr′sər), *n. Poetic.* a swift horse.

court-mar tial (kôrt′mär′shəl *or* kōrt′mär′shəl), *n.* **1.** court of army or navy officers for trying offenders against military or naval laws. **2.** trial by such a court.

cov ert (kuv′ərt), *n.* **1.** shelter; hiding place. **2.** thicket in which animals hide.

cow (kou), *v.* make afraid; frighten. [< Scand. *kūga*] —**Syn.** scare, bully.

coy (koi), *adj.* **1.** shy; modest; bashful. **2.** pretending to be shy. [< F *coi* < L *quietus* at rest] —**coy′ly,** *adv.* —**coy′ness,** *n.*

crave (krāv), *v.* **1.** long for; yearn for; desire strongly: *The thirsty man craved water.* **2.** ask earnestly; beg: *crave a favor.* [OE *crafian* demand]

cra ven (krā′vən), *n.* coward.

Cre ole *or* **cre ole** (krē′ōl), *n.* **1.** a white person who is a descendant of the French who settled in Louisiana. **2.** the French language as spoken in Louisiana. **3.** a French or Spanish person born in Spanish America or the West Indies. **4. creole,** person who is part Negro and part Creole. —*adj.* of or having to do with the Creoles. [< F *créole* < Sp. < Pg. *crioulo* < *criar* bring up < L *creare* create]

cringe (krinj), *v.* **1.** shrink from danger or pain. **2.** bow down timidly.

crone (krōn), *n.* a withered old woman. [< MDutch *croonje* < OF *carogne* carcass, hag]

crotch et (kroch′it), *n.* odd notion; unreasonable whim.

crow's-foot (krōz′fút′), *n.* wrinkle at the outer corner of the eye.

cru cial (krü′shəl), *adj.* **1.** very important; critical; decisive. **2.** very trying.

crypt (kript), *n.* an underground room or vault.

cue ball (kū′ bôl′), *n.* the ball which a player strikes with his cue, the long tapering stick used in playing billiards.

cul prit (kul′prit), *n.* **1.** person guilty of a fault or crime; offender. **2.** prisoner in court accused of a crime.

cul tur al (kul′chər əl), *adj.* of or having to do with the civilization of a given race or a nation at a given time; that is, its customs, its arts, its conveniences, etc.

cul vert (kul′vərt), *n.* a small channel for water crossing under a road, railroad, canal, etc.

cum ber (kum′bər), *v.* burden; trouble: *Household cares cumber a busy mother.* —*n.* hindrance.

cum ber some (kum′bər səm), *adj.* clumsy; unwieldy: *The armor worn by knights seems cumbersome to us today.*

cum brous (kum′brəs), *adj.* cumbersome.

curt (kėrt), *adj.* short; rudely brief. [< L *curtus* cut short]

cur va ture (kėr′və chūr *or* kėr′və chər), *n.* **1.** a curving; abnormal curving: *curvature of the spine.* **2.** a curved piece or part; curve.

cus tom (kus′təm), *n.* **1.** a usual action; habit. **2. customs,** *pl.* **a.** taxes paid to the government on things

brought in from a foreign country. **b.** department of the government that collects these taxes.

cu ti cle (kū′tə kəl), *n.* the outer skin of vertebrates. [< L *cuticula,* dim. of *cutis* skin]

cyn ic (sin′ik), *n.* **1.** person inclined to believe that the motives for people's actions are insincere and selfish. **2.** a sneering, sarcastic person. —*adj.* cynical. —**cyn′i cism,** *n.*

cyn i cal (sin′ə kəl), *adj.* **1.** doubting the sincerity and goodness of others. **2.** sneering; sarcastic.
Syn. 1. Cynical, pessimistic mean doubting and mistrustful. **Cynical** emphasizes the idea of doubting the honesty and sincerity of people and their motives for doing things: *People cannot make friends with a person who is cynical about friendship.* **Pessimistic** emphasizes the idea of always looking on the dark side of things and expecting the unpleasant or worst to happen: *He has a very pessimistic attitude toward the value of this work.*

dal ly (dal′i), *v.* **1.** act in a playful manner: *The spring breeze dallies with the flowers.* **2.** flirt (with danger, temptation, a person, etc.); trifle: *He dallied with the offer for days, but finally refused it.* **3.** be idle; loiter. **4.** waste (time).

dam (dam), *n.* **1.** the female parent of four-footed animals. **2.** mother.

dan der (dan′dər), *n. Informal.* **1.** temper; anger. **2. get one's dander up,** get angry; lose one's temper.

dank (dangk), *adj.* unpleasantly damp; moist; wet.

das tard (das′tərd), *n.* a mean coward; sneak. —*adj.* mean and cowardly; sneaking. —**das′tard ly,** *adj.*

da ta (dā′tə, dat′ə, *or* dä′tə), *n. pl.* of **datum.** things known or granted; information from which conclusions can be drawn; facts.
→ **Data** is the plural of the seldom used singular *datum.* Since its meaning is often collective, referring to a group of facts as a unit, *data* is often used with a singular verb in informal English: *The data we have collected is not enough to be convincing.* Formal English continues to regard *data* as a plural rather than as a collective noun: *Our task is to analyze the data that have been secured.*

de bris (də brē′ *or* dā′brē), *n.* **1.** scattered fragments; ruins; rubbish: *The street was covered with debris from the explosion.* **2.** in geology, a mass of fragments of rock, etc.: *the debris left by a glacier.* [< F *débris* < OF *debrisier* < *de-* + *brisier* break]

de cal co ma ni a (di kal′kə mā′ni ə), *n.* design or picture treated so that it will stick fast to glass, wood, etc.

de camp (di kamp′), *v.* depart quickly or secretly.

de cant er (di kan′tər), *n.* a glass bottle with a stopper, used for serving wine or liquor.

de claim (di klām′), *v.* **1.** recite in public. **2.** speak in a loud and emotional manner. [< L *declamare* < *de-* + *clamare* cry]

dec la ma tion (dek′lə mā′shən), *n.* **1.** act or art of reciting in public; making a formal speech or speeches. **2.** selection of poetry, prose, etc., for reciting; formal speech. **3.** act of talking loudly and emotionally. **4.** loud and emotional talk.

de clam a to ry (di klam′ə tô′ri *or* di klam′ə tō′ri), *adj.* **1.** having to do with declamation. **2.** loud and emotional.

de cliv i ty (di kliv′ə ti), *n.* a downward slope.

de co rum (di kô′rəm *or* di kō′rəm), *n.* a being proper in action, speech, dress, etc.

de coy (di koi′), *v.* **1.** lure (wild birds, animals, etc.) into a trap or within gunshot. **2.** lead or tempt into danger.

de crep it (di krep′it), *adj.* broken down or weakened by old age; old and feeble. [< L *decrepitus* broken down < *de-* + *crepare* creak] —**de crep′i tude,** *n.*

de cry (di krī′), *v.* **1.** condemn. **2.** try to lower the value of; make little of.

de fec tion (di fek′shən), *n.* **1.** a falling away from loyalty, duty, religion, etc.; desertion. **2.** failure.

def er ence (def′ər əns), *n.* **1.** a yielding to the judgment or opinion of another. **2.** great respect.

def er en tial (def′ər en′shəl), *adj.* respectful.

---

hat, āge, cãre, fär; let, ēqual, tėrm; it, īce; hot, ōpen, ôrder; oil, out; cup, pùt, rüle, ūse; ch, child; ng, long; th, thin; ʈH, then; zh, measure; ə represents *a* in about, *e* in taken, *i* in pencil, *o* in lemon, *u* in circus.

de funct (di fungkt′), *adj.* dead; no longer existing.

de gen er a cy (di jen′ər ə si), *n.* degenerate condition.

de gen er ate (*v.* di jen′ər āt; *adj.* di jen′ər it), *v.* decline in physical, mental, or moral qualities; grow worse. —*adj.* showing a decline in physical, mental, or moral qualities: *The thief was a degenerate member of a fine family.*

deg ra da tion (deg′rə dā′shən), *n.* **1.** a degrading. **2.** being degraded: *Failure to obey orders caused the captain's degradation to the rank of a private.* **3.** degraded condition: *The drunkard, filthy and half-starved, lived in degradation.*

de grade (di grād′), *v.* make worse; lower: *You degrade yourself when you tell a lie.*

delft (delft), *n.* kind of glazed earthenware made in Holland, usually decorated in blue.

de lude (di lüd′), *v.* mislead; deceive. [< L *deludere* < *de-* to the detriment of + *ludere* play]

del uge (del′ūj), *n.* **1.** a great flood. **2.** a heavy fall of rain. **3.** any overwhelming rush: *Most stores have a deluge of orders just before Christmas.* **4. the Deluge,** in the Bible, the great flood in the days of Noah. Gen. 7. —*v.* **1.** flood. **2.** overwhelm: *The movie star was deluged with requests for his autograph.* [< OF < L *diluvium* < *diluere* < *dis-* away + *luere* wash]

de lu sion (di lü′zhən), *n.* **1.** act of deluding. **2.** state of being deluded. **3.** a false notion or belief: *The insane man had a delusion that he was the king.* **4.** a fixed belief maintained in spite of unquestionable evidence to the contrary. —**Syn. 1.** deception. [< L *delusio, -onis* < *deludere*. See DELUDE.]

delve (delv), *v.* search carefully for information.

de mean¹ (di mēn′), *v.* lower in dignity or standing; humble. [< *de-* down + *mean* low in quality]

de mean² (di mēn′), *v.* behave or conduct (oneself). [< OF *demener* < *de-* (< L) + *mener* lead < L *minare* drive]

de mean or (di mēn′ər), *n.* way a person looks and acts; behavior; conduct; manner. [ME *demenure* < *demenen* behave < OF *demener*. See DEMEAN².]

dem i tasse (dem′i tas′ *or* dem′i täs′), *n.* a very small cup of black coffee. [< F *demitasse* half-cup]

de moc ra cy (di mok′rə si), *n.* **1.** government that is run by the people who live under it. **2.** country, state, or community having such a government. The United States is a democracy. **3.** treatment of others as one's equals. [< F *démocratie* < Gk. *demokratia* < *demos* people + *kratos* rule]

dem o crat ic (dem′ə krat′ik), *adj.* **1.** of or like a democracy. **2.** treating all classes of people as one's equals.

de mo ni a cal (dē′mə nī′ə kəl), *adj.* **1.** devilish. **2.** frantic.

den i zen (den′ə zən), *n.* inhabitant; occupant.

de nom i nate (*v.* di nom′ə nāt; *adj.* di nom′ə nit *or* di nom′ə nāt), *v.* give a name to; name. —*adj.* called by a specific name. [< L *denominare* < *de-* + *nomen* name]

de nun ci a tion (di nun′si ā′shən *or* di nun′shi ā′shən), *n.* **1.** expression of strong disapproval. **2.** accusation. **3.** declaration of a curse, revenge, etc.; warning; threat.

de pic tion (di pik′shən), *n.* act of picturing; description.

de plor a ble (di plôr′ə bəl *or* di plōr′ə bəl), *adj.* **1.** regrettable: *a deplorable accident.* **2.** miserable.

de ploy (di ploi′), *v.* of troops, military units, etc., spread out from a column into a long battle line.

de pos i to ry (di poz′ə tô′ri *or* di poz′ə tō′ri), *n.* place where a thing is put for safekeeping; storehouse.

dep re cate (dep′rə kāt), *v.* express strong disapproval of: *Lovers of peace deprecate war.* [< L *deprecari* plead in excuse, avert by prayer < *de-* + *precari* pray] —**dep′re cat′ing ly,** *adv.* —**dep′re ca′tor,** *n.*

➔ **deprecate, depreciate.** Do not confuse *deprecate,* meaning to express strong disapproval of, with *depreciate,* meaning to lessen in value or price. Contrast these sentences: *I feel I must deprecate the*

course the club is following. Naturally the car depreciates after a number of years of service.

de pre ci ate (di prē′shi āt), *v.* lessen the value or price of. [< L *depretiare* < *de-* + *pretium* prize] ➔ See **depreciate** for usage note.

de ride (di rīd′), *v.* make fun of; laugh at in scorn; ridicule with contempt. [< L *deridere* < *de-* at + *ridere* laugh] —**de rid′er,** *n.* —**de rid′ing ly,** *adv.* —**Syn.** jeer, mock.

de ri sive (di rī′siv), *adj.* mocking. —**de ri′sive ly,** *adv.*

der rin ger (der′ən jər), *n. U.S.* a short pistol that has a large caliber. [Am.E; named after H. *Derringer,* Am. inventor]

des ert (dez′ərt), *n.* **1.** a dry, barren region. **2.** region that is not inhabited or cultivated; wilderness.

de spond en cy (di spon′dən si), *n.* loss of hope.

des pot ic (des pot′ik), *adj.* tyrannical; having unlimited power.

des pot ism (des′pət iz əm), *n.* tyranny; oppression.

de tached (di tacht′), *adj.* not influenced by others or by one's own interests and prejudices; impartial.

de tail (di tāl′ *or* dē′tāl), *n.* **1.** a small or unimportant part. **2.** a small group selected for or sent on some special duty: *The captain sent a detail of six soldiers to guard the road.*

de ter (di tèr′), *v.* discourage; keep back; hinder: *The extreme heat deterred us from going downtown.* [< L *deterrere* < *de-* from + *terrere* frighten]

de ter rent (di tèr′ənt *or* di ter′ənt), *adj.* holding back; hindering.

det ri ment (det′rə mənt), *n.* damage; injury; harm.

dev as tate (dev′əs tāt), *v.* make desolate; destroy; ravage: *A long war devastated the border towns.* [< L *devastare* < *de-* + *vastus* waste]

de void (di void′), *adj.* lacking (of): *devoid of sense.*

de volve (di volv′), *v.* **1.** transfer (duty, work, etc.) to someone else. **2.** be handed down to someone else; be transferred: *If the president is unable to handle his duties, they devolve upon the vice-president.*

dev o tee (dev′ə tē′), *n.* person deeply devoted to something.

di a bol i cal (dī′ə bol′e kəl), *adj.* devilish.

di ag no sis (dī′əg nō′sis), *n.* **1.** act or process of finding out what disease a person or animal has by examination and careful study of the symptoms: *The doctor used X rays and blood tests in his diagnosis.* **2.** decision reached after a careful study of symptoms or facts.

di a pa son (dī′ə pā′zən *or* dī′ə pā′sən), *n.* **1.** harmony. **2.** melody. **3.** a swelling musical sound. **4.** the whole range of a voice or instrument.

di dac tic (dī dak′tik *or* di dak′tik), *adj.* **1.** intended to instruct: *Aesop's "Fables" are didactic stories; each one has an instructive moral.* **2.** inclined to instruct others; teacherlike. [< Gk. *didaktikos* < *didaskein* teach]

dig ni tar y (dig′nə ter′i), *n.* person who has a position of honor. A bishop is a dignitary of the church.

di lap i dat ed (də lap′ə dāt′id), *adj.* falling to pieces; partly ruined through neglect. —**di lap′i da′tion,** *n.*

di la to ry (dil′ə tô′ri *or* dil′ə tō′ri), *adj.* tending to delay; not prompt.

di lem ma (də lem′ə), *n.* **1.** situation requiring a choice between two evils; any embarrassing or perplexing situation; a difficult choice. **2.** argument forcing an opponent to choose one of two alternatives equally unfavorable to him. [< LL < Gk. *dilemma* < *di-* two + *lemma* premise]

di min u tive (də min′ū tiv), *adj.* **1.** small; little; tiny. **2.** expressing smallness. [< Med.L *diminutivus* < L *diminutus, deminutus,* pp. of *diminuere, deminuere* lessen]

dint (dint), *n.* force: *By dint of hard work he succeeded.*

dirge (dèrj), *n.* a funeral song or tune. [contraction of L *dirige* direct (imperative of *dirigere*), first word in office for the dead]

< = from, derived from, taken from; cf., compare; dial., dialect; dim., diminutive; lang., language; pp., past participle; ppr., present participle; pt., past tense; ult., ultimately; var., variant; ? = possibly.

dis af fec tion (dis′ə fek′shən), *n.* discontent; state of being unfriendly, disloyal, or discontented.

dis ap pro ba tion (dis′ap rə bā′shən), *n.* disapproval.

dis a vow (dis′ə vou′), *v.* deny that one knows about, approves of, or is responsible for; disclaim.

dis bur den (dis bėr′dən), *v.* relieve of a burden: *The boy disburdened his mind to his brother by confessing what he had done.*

dis clo sure (dis klō′zhər), *n.* 1. act of making known. 2. thing disclosed.

dis com pose (dis′kəm pōz′), *v.* make uneasy.

dis con so late (dis kon′sə lit), *adj.* without hope; forlorn; unhappy; cheerless. —**dis con′so late ly,** *adv.*

dis cord ant (dis kôr′dənt), *adj.* 1. not in harmony. 2. not in agreement; not fitting together: *Many discordant views were expressed.*

dis crep an cy (dis krep′ən si), *n.* lack of harmony or agreement.

dis crim i nat ing (dis krim′ə nāt′ing), *adj.* able to distinguish or see differences in: *She was discriminating in her choice of friends.*

dis em bod y (dis′em bod′i), *v.* separate (a soul, spirit, etc.) from the body.

dis en gage (dis′en gāj′), *v.* 1. free from a pledge, obligation, etc. 2. detach; loosen.

dis ha bille (dis′ə bēl′), *n.* 1. informal dress. 2. garment worn in dishabille. 3. condition of being only partly dressed. [< F *déshabillé,* pp. of *déshabiller* < *dés-* (< L *dis-*) + *habiller* dress]

dis il lu sion (dis′i lü′zhən), *v.* free from false beliefs or optimistic ideas: *People are apt to become disillusioned as they grow old.*

dis mem ber (dis mem′bər), *v.* cut to pieces.

dis par age (dis par′ij), *v.* 1. try to lessen the importance or value of; belittle: *The coward disparaged the hero's brave rescue.* 2. lower the reputation of; discredit. [< OF *desparagier* match unequally < *des-* (< L *dis-*) + *parage* rank, lineage < L *par* equal] —**dis par′ag ing,** *adj.* —**dis par′ag ing ly,** *adv.* —**dis par′age ment,** *n.* —Syn. 1. depreciate.

dis pen sa tion (dis′pən sā′shən), *n.* 1. act of giving out: *the dispensation of charity to the poor.* 2. thing given out or distributed: *They gave thanks for the dispensations of Providence.* 3. official permission to disregard a rule.

dis port (dis pôrt′ *or* dis pōrt′), *v.* amuse (oneself); sport; play. —*n. Archaic.* pastime; amusement.

dis po si tion (dis′pə zish′ən), *n.* 1. habitual ways of acting toward others or of thinking about things; nature. 2. tendency; inclination. 3. act of putting in order or position; arrangement: *the disposition of soldiers in battle.* 4. management. 5. disposal.

dis qui si tion (dis′kwə zish′ən), *n.* a long or formal speech or writing about a subject.

dis sem i nate (di sem′ə nāt), *v.* scatter widely; spread abroad: *Missionaries disseminate Christian beliefs all over the world.* [< L *disseminare* < *dis-* in every direction + *semen* seed]

dis sev er (di sev′ər), *v.* separate; divide.

dis si pate (dis′ə pāt), *v.* 1. spread in different directions. 2. spend foolishly. 3. indulge too much in evil or foolish pleasures. [< L *dissipare* < *dis-* in different directions + *sipare* throw]

dis so lute (dis′ə lüt), *adj.* living an evil life.

dis so lu tion (dis′ə lü′shən), *n.* 1. a breaking up. 2. ruin; destruction. 3. death.

dis tem per (dis tem′pər), *n.* an infectious disease of animals, accompanied by a loss of strength.

di ver gent (di vėr′jənt *or* dī vėr′jənt), *adj.* varying; different.

di vers (dī′vərz), *adj.* several different; various.

di ver tisse ment (dē ver tēs mäɴ′), *n.* amusement.

di vest (də vest′ *or* dī vest′), *v.* 1. strip; rid. 2. force to give up; deprive: *Citizens were divested of their right to vote.*

di vine (də vīn′), *adj.* 1. like God or a god; heavenly. 2. very excellent; unusually good or great. —*n.* clergyman who knows much about theology. —*v.* find out or foretell by inspiration, by magic, or by guessing; predict. [< OF < L *divinus* of a diety < *divus* deity]

di vulge (də vulj′), *v.* make known; tell; reveal.

doc ile (dos′əl), *adj.* easily managed; obedient. —**do-cil′i ty,** *n.*

dod der (dod′ər), *v.* shake; tremble; totter.

doff (dof *or* dôf), *v.* 1. take off; remove: *He doffed his hat as the flag passed by.* 2. get rid of; throw aside. [contraction of *do off*]

dog ger el (dôg′ər əl *or* dog′ər əl), *n.* very poor poetry.

dog mat ic (dôg mat′ik *or* dog mat′ik), *adj.* 1. asserting opinions as if one were the highest authority. 2. asserted without proof. —**dog mat′i cal ly,** *adv.*

dog mat i cal (dôg mat′ə kəl *or* dog mat′ə kəl), *adj.* dogmatic.

dolt (dōlt), *n.* a dull, stupid person.

do mes ti cate (də mes′tə kāt), *v.* 1. tame. 2. make fond of home and family life. 3. cause to be or feel at home.

dom i nie (dom′ə ni *for 1;* dom′ə ni *or* dō′mə ni *for 2*), *n.* 1. *Esp. Scottish.* schoolmaster. 2. *Informal.* clergyman.

dot age (dōt′ij), *n.* weak-minded and childish condition caused by old age.

do tard (dō′tərd), *n.* person who is weak-minded and childish because of old age.

dou bloon (dub lün′), *n.* a former Spanish gold coin.

dough ty (dou′ti), *adj. Archaic or Humorous.* brave; valiant; strong: *doughty knights.*

dour (dür *or* dour), *adj.* 1. gloomy. 2. *Scottish.* stern; severe. [< L *durus* hard, stern]

dow a ger (dou′ə jər), *n.* 1. woman who holds some title or property from her dead husband. 2. *Informal.* a dignified, elderly lady.

dow er (dou′ər), *n.* 1. money, property, etc., that a woman brings to her husband when she marries him. 2. a natural gift, talent, or quality; endowment.

drab (drab), *n.* a dirty, untidy woman. —*adj.* 1. dull, unattractive. 2. dull brownish-gray.

draw (drô), *n.* land basin into or through which water drains; valley.

draw ing room (drô′ing rüm′ *or* rum′), *n.* room for receiving or entertaining guests; parlor.

draw knife (drô′nīf′), *n.* blade with a handle at each end, used to shave off surfaces.

dray (drā), *n.* a low, strong cart for hauling heavy loads.

driv el (driv′əl), *n.* stupid, foolish talk; silly nonsense.

droll er y (drōl′ər i *or* drōl′ri), *n.* 1. something odd and amusing; laughable trick. 2. quaint humor. 3. jesting.

drop sy (drop′si), *n.* an abnormal accumulation of watery fluid in certain tissues or cavities of the body.

du cal (dü′kəl *or* dū′kəl), *adj.* of a duke or dukedom.

dul cet (dul′sit), *adj.* soothing; sweet; pleasing.

dun ga ree (dung′gə rē′ *or* dung′gə rē), *n.* 1. a coarse cotton cloth, used for work clothes. 2. **dungarees,** *pl.* trousers or clothing made of this cloth. [< Hindu. *dungrī*]

du o dec i mo (dü′ō des′ə mō *or* dū′ō des′ə mō), *n.* 1. the page size of a book in which each leaf is one twelfth of a whole sheet of paper, or about 5 by 7½ inches. 2. book having pages of this size. [< L *in duodecimo* in a twelfth]

dy nam ic (dī nam′ik), *adj.* active; energetic; forceful.

eb on (eb′ən), *n.* ebony. —*adj. Poetic.* 1. made of ebony. 2. dark; black.

e bul lient (i bul′yənt), *adj.* 1. overflowing with excitement, liveliness, etc. 2. very enthusiastic.

ec cen tric i ty (ek′sen tris′ə ti), *n.* oddity; peculiarity.

---

hat, āge, cāre, fär; let, ēqual, tėrm; it, īce; hot, ōpen, ôrder; oil, out; cup, pūt, rüle, ūse; ch, child; ng, long; th, thin; ŦH, then; zh, measure; ə represents *a* in about, *e* in taken, *i* in pencil, *o* in lemon, *u* in circus.

e clipse (i klips′), *n.* **1.** a darkening of the sun, moon, etc., when some other heavenly body is in a position that partly or completely cuts off its light. **2.** loss of importance or reputation; failure for a time. —*v.* **1.** cut off or obscure the light from; darken. **2.** obscure the importance or reputation of; make less outstanding by comparison; surpass: *Napoleon eclipsed other generals of his time.* [< OF < L < Gk. *ekleipsis* < *ex-* out + *leipein* leave] —**Syn.** *v.* **2.** outshine, excel.

ec stat ic (ek stat′ik), *adj.* full of overwhelming joy.

e dict (ē′dikt), *n.* a public order by some authority; decree. [< L *edictum* < *edicere* < *ex-* out + *dicere* say]

e duce (i düs′ *or* i dūs′), *v.* bring out; draw forth; elicit.

ee rie (ēr′i), *adj.* causing fear; strange; weird.

ef fem i na cy (ə fem′ə nə si), *n.* unmanly weakness.

ef fer vesce (ef′ər ves′), *v.* **1.** give off bubbles of gas. **2.** be lively and gay. —**ef fer ves′cent,** *adj.*

ef fete (i fēt′), *adj.* worn out; exhausted.

ef fi gy (ef′ə ji), *n.* **1.** statue, etc., of a person; image: *The dead man's monument bore his effigy.* **2. burn** or **hang in effigy,** burn or hang a stuffed image of a person to show hatred or contempt. [< F *effigie* < L *effigies* < *effingere* < *ex-* out + *fingere* form]

e go ism (ē′gō iz əm *or* eg′ō iz əm), *n.* **1.** seeking the welfare of oneself only; selfishness. **2.** talking too much about oneself; conceit. ➤ See **egotism** for usage note.

e go tism (ē′gə tiz əm *or* eg′ə tiz əm), *n.* **1.** excessive use of *I, my,* and *me;* habit of thinking, talking, or writing too much of oneself. **2.** self-conceit. **3.** selfishness. [< *ego* + *-t-* + *ism*]

➤ **Egotism, egoism** mean a habit of thinking too much about self, but should not be confused. **Egotism** emphasizes conceit, boasting, and selfishness, and means always talking about oneself and one's own affairs and trying to get attention: *Henry's egotism keeps him from having friends.* **Egoism** emphasizes being self-centered and looking at everyone and everything only as it affects oneself and one's own welfare, but does not suggest boasting or annoying conceit, nor always selfishness: *We forget the natural egoism of a genius when he is charming.*

el bow-chair (el′bō chãr′), *n.* a chair with padded arms.

el o cu tion (el′ə kū′shən), *n.* **1.** art of public speaking, including the correct use of the voice, gestures, etc. **2.** manner of speaking or reading in public. [< L *elocutio, -onis* < *eloqui* < *ex-* out + *loqui* speak]

e lon gate (i lông′gāt *or* i long′gāt), *v.* lengthen; stretch. —*adj.* **1.** lengthened. **2.** long and thin: *the elongate leaf of a willow.* [< L *elongare* < *ex-* out + *longus* long] —**e lon ga′tion,** *n.*

e lu ci da tion (i lü′sə dā′shən), *n.* explanation; a making clear.

e ma ci ate (i mā′shi āt), *v.* make unnaturally thin; cause to lose flesh or waste away. [< L *emaciare* < *ex-* + *macies* leanness]

e man ci pa tion (i man′sə pā′shən), *n.* release from slavery or restraint; a setting free.

em bel lish (em bel′ish), *v.* **1.** decorate; adorn; ornament. **2.** make more interesting by adding real or imaginary details; elaborate: *He embellished the old stories, so that they sounded new.* [< OF *embelliss-,* stem of *embellir* < *en-* in (< L *in-*) + *bel* handsome < L *bellus*]

em bel lish ment (em bel′ish mənt), *n.* **1.** decoration; adornment; ornament. **2.** detail, often imaginary, added to a story, account, etc., more interesting.

em bod i ment (em bod′i mənt), *n.* person or thing symbolizing, or standing for, some idea, quality, etc.

em i nence (em′ə nəns), *n.* **1.** rank or position above all or most others; high standing; greatness; fame. **2.** a high place; lofty hill. —**Syn.** **1.** distinction, prominence, renown.

em met (em′it), *n. Archaic.* ant. [OE *æmete*]

e mol u ment (i mol′ū mənt), *n.* profit from a job; fee.

em prise (em prīz′), *n. Archaic.* **1.** adventure; daring undertaking. **2.** knightly daring.

en am ored (en am′ərd), *adj.* **1.** very much in love; very fond; charmed: *The enamored prince gave up his throne to marry the beautiful peasant girl.* **2. enamored of,** in love with; very fond of; charmed by.

en dow ment (en dou′mənt), *n.* **1.** money or property given to provide an income. **2.** ability; talent.

en gross (en grōs′), *v.* **1.** occupy wholly; take up all the attention of: *She was engrossed in a story.* **2.** copy or write in large letters; write a beautiful copy of. **3.** write out in formal style; express in legal form. [(def. 1) < *in gross* < *en gros* in a lump; (defs. 2, 3) < AF *engrosser* < *en-* in + *grosse* large writing, document] —**en gross′ing,** *adj.*

en join (en join′), *v.* **1.** order; direct; urge: *Parents enjoin good behavior on their children.* **2.** in law, issue an authoritative command. Through an injunction a judge may enjoin a person to do (or not do) some act. [< OF *enjoindre* < L *injungere* attack, charge < *in-* on + *jungere* join] —**Syn.** **1.** command, bid.

en masse (en mas′ *or* än mäs′), in a group. [< F]

en nui (än′wē), *n.* boredom. [< F]

en sconce (en skons′), *v.* **1.** shelter safely; hide. **2.** settle comfortably and firmly: *The cat ensconced itself in the armchair.* [< *en-* + *sconce* fortification, probably < Dutch *schans*]

en trée (än′trā), *n.* **1.** freedom or right to enter; access. **2.** *U.S.* the main dish of food at dinner or lunch. [< F *entrée,* fem. pp. of *entrer* enter]

en vi rons (en vī′rənz), *n.pl.* surrounding districts.

en vis age (en viz′ij), *v.* form a mental picture of: *The architect looked at the plans and envisaged the finished house.* [< F *envisager*]

ep i thet (ep′ə thet), *n.* a descriptive expression: *In "Richard the Lion-Hearted" the epithet is "the Lion-Hearted."*

e pit o me (i pit′ə mi), *n.* **1.** a condensed account. **2.** some thing or part that is typical or representative of the whole: *Solomon is often spoken of as the epitome of wisdom.*

e qua nim i ty (ē′kwə nim′ə ti *or* ek′wə nim′ə ti), *n.* calmness: *A wise man bears misfortune with equanimity.*

e qui lib ri um (ē′kwə lib′ri əm), *n.* **1.** state of balance. **2.** mental poise.

eq ui page (ek′wə pij), *n.* **1.** carriage with its horses, driver, and servants. **2.** equipment.

e quiv o cal (i kwiv′ə kəl), *adj.* **1.** having two or more meanings; intentionally vague. **2.** undecided. **3.** rousing suspicion. —**Syn.** **1.** doubtful. —**Ant.** **1.** clear, evident, definite.

e rad i cate (i rad′ə kāt), *v.* **1.** get entirely rid of; destroy completely: *Yellow fever has been eradicated in the United States.* **2.** pull out by the roots: *eradicate weeds from a garden.* [< L *eradicare* < *ex-* out + *radix* root] —**e rad′i ca′tor,** *n.*

ere long (ãr′lông′ *or* ãr′long′), *adv.* before long; soon.

er rant (er′ənt), *adj.* **1.** traveling in search of adventure; wandering; roving. **2.** wrong; mistaken; incorrect.

er rat ic (ə rat′ik), *adj.* **1.** uncertain; irregular. **2.** queer; odd: *erratic behavior.* [< L *erraticus* < *errare* err]

er u dite (er′ü dīt *or* er′ü dīt), *adj.* scholarly; learned.

es cri toire (es′krə twär′), *n.* a writing desk.

es ti ma ble (es′tə mə bəl), *adj.* deserving high regard.

eth i cal (eth′ə kəl), *adj.* having to do with standards of right and wrong; of ethics or morality.

e va sive (i vā′siv *or* i vā′ziv), *adj.* trying to avoid the truth by indefinite or misleading statements: *"Perhaps" is an evasive answer.*

e vince (i vins′), *v.* show clearly.

ev i ta ble (ev′ə tə bəl), *adj.* avoidable.

e voke (i vōk′), *v.* call forth; bring out.

< = from, derived from, taken from;   cf., compare;   dial., dialect;   dim., diminutive;   lang., language; pp., past participle;   ppr., present participle;   pt., past tense;   ult., ultimately;   var., variant;   ? = possibly.

ev o lu tion (ev'ə lü'shən), *n.* **1.** any process of formation or growth; gradual development. **2.** a motion that combines with similar motions to form a pattern: *the graceful evolutions of the ballet dancer.* **3.** a releasing; giving off; setting free: *the evolution of heat from burning coal.*

ex alt (eg zôlt'), *v.* **1.** raise in rank, honor, power, character, quality, etc. **2.** fill with pride, joy, or noble feeling. **3.** praise; honor; glorify. [< *exaltare* < *ex-* out, up + *altus* high] —**ex alt'ed,** *adj.*

ex cep tion (ek sep'shən), *n.* **1.** a leaving out. **2.** an unusual instance. **3.** objection.

ex cheq uer (eks chek'ər *or* eks'chek ər), *n.* treasury.

ex cru ci at ing (eks krü'shi āt'ing), *adj.* torturing: *excruciating pain.*

ex ha la tion (eks'hə lā'shən), *n.* something breathed out; air, vapor, smoke, odor, etc.

ex hil a rate (eg zil'ə rāt), *v.* put into high spirits; stimulate. [< L *exhilarare* < *ex-* thoroughly + *hilaris* merry] —**ex hil'a rat'ing,** *adj.* —**ex hil'a ra'tion,** *n.*

ex hor ta tion (eg'zôr tā'shən *or* ek'sôr tā'shən), *n.* strong urging; earnest advice or warning.

ex hort (eg zôrt'), *v.* advise or warn earnestly. [< L *exhortari* < *ex-* + *hortari* urge strongly] —**ex-hort'er,** *n.*

ex i gen cy (ek'sə jən si), *n.* **1.** usually, **exigencies,** *pl.* an urgent need: *The exigencies of business kept him from leaving town.* **2.** situation demanding immediate action or attention.

ex ot ic (eg zot'ik), *adj.* foreign; strange; not native; rare.

ex pe di en cy (eks pē'di ən si), *n.* **1.** usefulness; suitability for bringing about a desired result; desirability or fitness under the circumstances. **2.** personal advantage; self-interest.

ex pe di ent (eks pē'di ənt), *adj.* **1.** fit for bringing about a desired result. **2.** giving or seeking personal advantage. —*n.* means of bringing about a desired result. [< L *expediens, -entis,* ppr. of *expedire* to free from a net, set right < *ex-* out + *pes* foot]

ex pe di tious (eks'pə dish'əs), *adj.* quick; speedy; efficient and prompt. —**ex'pe di'tious ly,** *adv.*

ex pi a tion (eks'pi ā'shən), *n.* a giving of something to make up for a wrong, sin, etc.

ex ple tive (eks'plə tiv), *adj.* oath or meaningless exclamation.

ex plic it (eks plis'it), *adj.* definite; exact. —**Ant.** vague, indefinite, ambiguous.

ex ploi ta tion (eks'ploi tā'shən), *n.* selfish or unfair use.

ex pos tu la tion (eks pos'chú lā'shən), *n.* earnest reasoning with a person to protest against something he means to do or has done. —**Syn.** remonstrance.

ex tem po re (eks tem'pə ri), *adv.* offhand. —*adj.* made, done, or said on the spur of the moment.

ex ten u a tion (eks ten'ū ā'shən), *n.* something that lessens the seriousness of guilt; partial excuse.

ex ter mi nate (eks tėr'mə nāt), *v.* destroy completely: *This poison will exterminate rats.* [< LL *exterminare* destroy < L *exterminare* drive out < *ex-* out of + *terminus* boundary]

ex ter nal (eks tėr'nəl), *adj.* on the outside; outer. —*n.* **1.** an outer surface or part; outside. **2.** **externals,** *pl.* clothing, manners, outward acts, or appearances: *He judges people by mere externals.* [< L *externus* outside < *exterus* outside < *ex* out of]

ex tort (eks tôrt'), *v.* obtain (money, a promise, etc.) by threats, force, fraud, or illegal use of authority.

ex tri cate (eks'trə kāt), *v.* set free (from entanglements, difficulties, etc.); release.

ex u ber ant (eg zü'bər ənt), *adj.* **1.** very abundant; lavish: *exuberant health; an exuberant welcome.* **2.** profuse in growth.

ex ult ant (eg zul'tənt), *adj.* rejoicing greatly.

ex ul ta tion (eg'zul tā'shən *or* ek'sul tā'shən), *n.* act of exulting; great rejoicing; triumph: *There was exultation over the army's victory.*

fab ric (fab'rik), *n.* **1.** cloth. **2.** structure; framework: *the whole fabric of society.*

fa ce tious (fə sē'shəs), *adj.* said in fun; not to be taken seriously. —**fa ce'tious ly,** *adv.* —**fa ce'tious ness,** *n.*

fa cil i tate (fə sil'ə tāt), *v.* make easy; lessen the labor of; help forward: *A vacuum cleaner facilitates my housework.*

fac sim i le (fak sim'ə li), *n.* an exact copy or likeness; perfect reproduction. [< L *fac* make! + *simile,* neut., like]

fag ot (fag'ət), *n.* bundle of sticks tied together.

fain (fān), *Archaic* and *Poetic.* —*adv.* by choice; willingly. —*adj.* **1.** willing, but not eager. **2.** glad; willing. **3.** eager; desirous. [OE *fægen*]

fal set to (fôl set'ō), *n.* **1.** an unnaturally high-pitched voice, especially in a man. **2.** person who sings with a falsetto. —*adj.* of or for a falsetto; that sings in a falsetto. —*adv.* in a falsetto. [< Ital. *falsetto,* dim. of *falso* false < L *falsus*]

fa nat ic (fə nat'ik), *n.* person who is carried away beyond reason by his feelings or beliefs. —*adj.* enthusiastic or zealous beyond reason. [< L *fanaticus* inspired by divinity < *fanum* temple]

fa nat i cal (fə nat'ə kəl), *adj.* unreasonably enthusiastic; extremely eager or earnest. —**fa nat'i cal ly,** *adv.*

fan cy-free (fan'si frē'), *adj.* **1.** not in love. **2.** free to follow one's inclinations.

fan ta si a (fan tā'zhi ə, fan tā'zhə, *or* fan tā'zi ə), *n.* a musical composition following no fixed form or style. [< Ital. *fantasia* < L < Gk. *phantasia*]

fan ta sy (fan'tə si *or* fan'tə zi), *n.* **1.** play of the mind; imagination; fancy. **2.** a wild, strange fancy. **3.** picture existing only in the mind; queer illusion. Fantasies seem real to a delirious person. **4.** caprice; whim. **5.** in music, a fantasia. [< OF *fantasie* < L < Gk. *phattasia* appearance, image, ult. < *phainein* show.]

fas ci a (fash'i ə), *n.* band; long flat strip. [< L]

fas tid i ous (fas tid'i əs), *adj.* extremely refined or critical.

fa tal i ty (fā tal'ə ti *or* fə tal'ə ti), *n.* **1.** a fatal accident or happening; death. **2.** condition of being controlled by fate; inevitable necessity.

fath om (faṯH'əm), *n., pl.* **fath oms** or (*esp. collectively*) **fath om,** a unit of measure equal to 6 feet, used mostly in measuring the depth of water and the length of ships' ropes, cables, etc. —*v.* **1.** measure the depth of. **2.** get to the bottom of; understand fully. [OE *fæthm* width of the outstretched arms]

fath om less (faṯH'əm lis), *adj.* **1.** too deep to be measured. **2.** impossible to be fully understood: *the fathomless riddle of the universe.*

fawn (fôn), *v.* **1.** cringe and bow; act slavishly: *Many flattering relatives fawned on the rich old man.* **2.** of dogs, etc., show fondness by crouching, wagging the tail, licking the hand, etc. [OE *fagnian* < *fægen* fain]

fay (fā), *n.* fairy.

fea si ble (fē'zə bəl), *adj.* **1.** capable of being done or carried out easily. **2.** probable. **3.** suitable. —**fea'si bil'i-ty,** *n.*

fe lic i ty (fə lis'ə ti), *n.* **1.** happiness. **2.** good fortune. [< L *felicitas* < *felix* happy]

fel on (fel'ən), *n.* person who has committed a serious crime; criminal: *Murderers and thieves are felons.*

fer ret (fer'it), *n.* a white or yellowish-white weasel used for killing rats, hunting rabbits, etc. —*v.* **1.** hunt with ferrets. **2.** hunt; search: *The detectives ferreted out the criminal.* [< OF *fuiret,* ult. < L *fur* thief]

fer vid (fėr'vid), *adj.* showing great warmth of feeling; intensely emotional.

---

hat, āge, cāre, fär; let, ēqual, tėrm; it, īce; hot, ōpen, ôrder; oil, out; cup, pút, rüle, ūse; ch, child; ng, long; th, thin; ṮH, then; zh, measure; ə represents *a* in about, *e* in taken, *i* in pencil, *o* in lemon, *u* in circus.

fer vor (fèr′vər), *n.* **1.** great warmth of feeling; intense emotion: *The patriot's voice trembled as he spoke of his country with fervor.* **2.** intense heat. [< OF < L *fervor* < *fervere* boil]

fic tion mon ger (fik′shən mung′gèr), *n.* one who invents or spreads fictions or stories; a gossip.

fig ur a tion (fig′yər ā′shən), *n.* **1.** form; shape. **2.** a forming; shaping. **3.** representation by a likeness or symbol.

fil i al (fil′i əl), *adj.* of a son or daughter; due from a son or daughter: *The children treated their parents with filial respect.* [< LL *filialis* < L *filius* son, *filia* daughter]

fil i gree (fil′ə grē), *n.* lacy, delicate, or fanciful patterns in any material. —*adj.* ornamented with filigree.

fine (fīn), *n.* sum of money paid as a punishment. —*adv.* **in fine, a.** finally. **b.** in a few words.

fi nesse (fə nes′), *n.* delicacy of execution; skill. **2.** the skillful handling of a delicate situation to one's advantage: *A shrewd diplomat must be a master of finesse.*

fin ick y (fin′ə ki), *adj.* too dainty; too precise.

fis sure (fish′ər), *n.* split or crack.

flail (flāl), *n.* **1.** instrument for threshing grain by hand. **2.** weapon. —*v.* beat; thrash.

flam beau (flam′bō), *n.* **1.** a flaming torch. **2.** a large, decorated candlestick. [< F < OF *flambe* flame, ult. < L *flamma*]

flay (flā), *v.* **1.** strip off the skin. **2.** scold severely. **3.** rob; cheat. [OE *flēan*]

flib ber ti gib bet (flib′ər ti jib′it), *n.* **1.** a frivolous, flighty person. **2.** a chatterbox.

flim sy (flim′zi), *adj.* light and thin. —*n.* **1.** a thin paper used by reporters. **2.** a newspaper report on this paper.

flip pant (flip′ənt), *adj.* not respectful.

flirt (flèrt), *v.* **1.** make love without meaning it. **2.** trifle; toy: *He flirted with the idea of going to Europe, though he couldn't afford it.* **3.** move quickly; flutter: *She flirted her fan impatiently.* **4.** toss; jerk. —*n.* **1.** person who makes love without meaning it. **2.** a quick movement or flutter: *With a flirt of its tail, the bird flew away.* **3.** toss; jerk.

floe (flō), *n.* **1.** field of floating ice. **2.** a floating piece broken off from such a field.

flor id (flôr′id *or* flor′id), *adj.* **1.** highly colored; ruddy. **2.** flowery; ornate. [< L *floridus* < *flos* flower]

fluc tu ate (fluk′chü āt), *v.* **1.** rise and fall; change continually; vary irregularly. **2.** move in waves. [< L *fluctuare* < *fluctus* wave] —**fluc′tu a′tion,** *n.*

flume (flüm), *n.* large, inclined trough or chute for carrying water.

foal (fōl), *n.* a young horse, donkey, etc.; colt or filly. —*v.* give birth to (a foal). [OE *fola*]

fob (fob), *n.* a short watch chain, ribbon, etc., that hangs out of a watch pocket.

foi ble (foi′bəl), *n.* a weak point; weakness.

fo li o (fō′li ō), *n.* book of the largest size. A folio is usually any book more than 11 inches in height. —*adj.* of the largest size (of books).

fools cap (fülz′kap′), *n.* writing paper in sheets from 12 to 13½ inches wide and 15 to 17 inches long.

foot pad (fút′pad′), *n.* a highway robber who goes on foot only.

fop per y (fop′ər i), *n.* vain, empty-headed behavior.

fore cas tle (fōk′səl, fôr′kas′əl, fôr′käs′əl, fōr′kas′əl, *or* fōr′käs′əl), *n.* **1.** the upper deck in front of the foremast. **2.** the sailors' quarters in a merchant ship.

fore close (fôr klōz′ *or* fōr klōz′), *v.* **1.** prevent; exclude. **2.** take away the right to redeem (a mortgage). When the conditions of a mortgage are not met, the holder can foreclose and have the property sold to satisfy his claim.

for go (fôr gō′), *v.* do without; give up.

for mi da ble (fôr′mə də bəl), *adj.* hard to overcome; hard to deal with; to be dreaded. [< L *formidabilis* < *formidare* dread] —**for′mi da bly,** *adv.* —**Syn.** appalling, fearful.

for te (fôr′tā), *adj., adv.* in music, loud. [< Ital. *forte* strong < L *fortis*]

for ti fi ca tion (fôr′tə fə kā′shən), *n.* **1.** thing used in fortifying; fort, wall, ditch, etc. **2.** a fortified place.

for ti fy (fôr′tə fī), *v.* **1.** build forts, walls, etc.; strengthen against attack. **2.** strengthen. [< F *fortifier* < LL *fortificare*, ult. < L *fortis* strong + *facere* make]

for tis si mo (fôr tis′ə mō), *adj., adv.* in music, very loud. [< Ital. *fortissimo*, superlative of *forte* strong]

for tress (fôr′tris), *n.* a fortified place; fort. [< OF *forteresse* < *fort* strong < L *fortis*] —**Syn.** stronghold.

fowl (foul), *n.* **1.** hunt wild fowl.

fowl ing piece (foul′ing pēs′), *n.* a light gun for shooting wild birds.

fra cas (frā′kəs), *n.* disturbance; uproar; brawl.

fra ter ni ty (frə tèr′nə ti), *n.* **1.** *U.S.* group of men or boys joined together for fellowship or for some other purpose; society. **2.** group having the same interests, kind of work, etc. **3.** fraternal feeling; brotherhood. [< L *fraternitas* brotherhood]

fraught (frôt), *adj.* loaded; filled: *A battlefield is fraught with horror.*

free boot er (frē′büt′ər), *n.* pirate; buccaneer.

free ma son ry (frē′mā′sən ri), *n.* natural fellowship; common understanding based on similar experiences.

fresh et (fresh′it), *n.* **1.** flood caused by heavy rains or melted snow. **2.** rush of fresh water flowing into the sea.

fret (fret), *n.* an ornamental pattern made of straight lines combined at angles. —*v.* decorate with fretwork.

frond (frond), *n.* **1.** a divided leaf of a fern, palm, etc. **2.** anything resembling such a leaf.

fru gal (frü′gəl), *adj.* **1.** avoiding waste; saving; tending to avoid unnecessary spending: *A frugal housekeeper buys and uses food carefully.* **2.** costing little; barely sufficient: *He ate a frugal supper of bread and milk.* [< L *frugalis* < *frugi* economical] —**fru′gal ly,** *adv.*

fru gal i ty (frü gal′ə ti), *n.* thrift; avoidance of waste.

fru i tion (frü ish′ən), *n.* fulfillment: *After years of hard work his plans came to fruition.* [< LL *fruitio, -onis* < *frui* enjoy]

frus tra tion (frus trā′shən), *n.* **1.** a bringing to nothing; defeat. **2.** opposition.

func tion ar y (fungk′shən er′i), *n.* official.

fu ne re al (fū nēr′i əl), *adj.* **1.** of or suitable for a funeral. **2.** sad; gloomy; dismal.

furl (fèrl), *v.* roll up; fold up: *furl a sail, furl a flag.* —*n.* act of furling.

fur tive (fèr′tiv), *adj.* **1.** secret: *a furtive glance into the forbidden room.* **2.** sly; stealthy. [< L *furtivus* < *fur* thief]

fu tile (fū′təl), *adj.* **1.** not successful; useless. **2.** not important; trifling. [< L *futilis* pouring easily, worthless < *fundere* pour] —**fu′tile ly,** *adv.*

fu til i ty (fū til′ə ti), *n.* **1.** uselessness. **2.** unimportance.

gal ax y (gal′ək si), *n.* a brilliant or splendid group.

gall (gôl), *v.* **1.** make or become sore by rubbing: *The rough strap galled the horse's skin.* **2.** annoy; irritate.

gal ley (gal′i), *n.* **1.** a long, narrow ship of former times having oars and sails. **2.** kitchen of a ship.

gal li gas kins (gal′ə gas′kinz), *n.pl.* loose breeches.

gal va nize (gal′və nīz), *v.* **1.** apply an electric current to. **2.** arouse suddenly; startle. **3.** cover (iron or steel) with a thin coating of zinc to prevent rust.

gam bol (gam′bəl), *n.* a running and jumping about in play; caper; frolic. —*v.* frisk about; run and jump about in play: *Lambs gamboled in the meadow.* [< F *gambade* < Ital. *gambata* < *gamba* leg]

gam y (gām′i), *adj.* having a strong taste or smell like the flesh of wild animals or birds.

< = from, derived from, taken from; cf., compare; dial., dialect; dim., diminutive; lang., language; pp., past participle; ppr., present participle; pt., past tense; ult., ultimately; var., variant; ? = possibly.

gan gling (gang′gling), *adj.* awkwardly tall and slender; lank and loosely built.

gan grene (gang′grēn *or* gang grēn′), *n.* decay of a part of a living person or animal when the blood supply is interfered with by injury, infection, freezing, etc. —**gan′gre nous,** *adj.*

gar ru lous (gar′ə ləs *or* gar′ū ləs), *adj.* **1.** talking too much about trifles. **2.** using too many words. [< L *garrulus* < *garrire* chatter] **Syn.** **Garrulous, loquacious** mean talking much. **Garrulous** implies rambling talk about insignificant matters. **Loquacious** adds the idea of talking smoothly and easily and suggests a steady stream of words.

gas con ade (gas′kən ād′), *n.* extravagant boasting. —*v.* boast extravagantly.

gaunt let (gônt′lit *or* gänt′lit), *n.* **1.** a stout, heavy glove, usually of leather covered with plates of iron or steel, that was part of a knight's armor. **2.** a stout, heavy glove with a wide, flaring cuff.

gen er al i ty (jen′ər al′ə ti), *n.* **1.** a general statement; word or phrase not definite enough to have much meaning or value. **2.** general quality or condition.

ge ni i (jē′ni ī), *n. pl. of* **genius.** **1.** guardian spirits of a person, institution, etc. **2.** spirits.

gen til i ty (jen til′ə ti), *n.* **1.** membership in the aristocracy or upper class. **2.** refinement.

ge nus (jē′nəs), *n.* **1.** kind; sort; class. **2.** group of related animals or plants ranking below a family and above a species.

ges ta tion (jes tā′shən), *n.* formation and development of a new life, a new idea, etc.

ges tic u late (jes tik′ū lāt), *v.* make or use gestures.

ges tic u la tion (jes tik′ū lā′shən), *n.* **1.** act of gesticulating. **2.** gesture.

ghet to (get′ō), *n.* **1.** part of a city where Jews are required to live. **2.** part of a city where many Jews live. [< Ital.]

gib ber (jib′ər *or* gib′ər), *v.* chatter senselessly.

Gi la monster (hē′lə mon′stər), *n.* a large poisonous lizard of Arizona and New Mexico. [Am.E; named after *Gila* River, Arizona]

Gila monster
(1½ ft. long)

gim let (gim′lit), *n.* a small tool with a screw point, for boring holes.

gin seng (jin′seng), *n.* **1.** a low plant with a thick, branched root. **2.** this root, much used in medicine by the Chinese. [< Chinese *jên shên; jên* = man]

glass-pa per (glas′pā′pər), *n.* a paper with a layer of finely ground glass, used for smoothing and polishing.

gloam ing (glōm′ing), *n.* evening twilight; dusk. [OE *glōmung* < *glōm* twilight; influenced by *glow*]

glow er (glou′ər), *v.* an angry or sullen look.

glut (glut), *v.* fill full.

gnarled (närld), *adj.* knotted; twisted; rugged.

gon do la (gon′də lə), *n.* **1.** *U.S.* a large flat-bottomed river boat with pointed ends. **2.** a freight car that has low sides and no top.

good ly (gụd′li), *adj.* **1.** pleasant; excellent; fine: *a goodly land.* **2.** good-looking: *a goodly youth.* **3.** considerable: *a goodly quantity.* —**good′li ness,** *n.*

gor mand ize (gôr′mən dīz), *v.* stuff oneself with food; eat very greedily.

gos sa mer (gos′ə mər), *n.* film or thread of cobweb. —*adj.* like gossamer; very light and thin; filmy.

gouge (gouj), *n.* chisel with a curved blade. —*v.* **1.** cut with a gouge. **2.** dig out; tear out; force out.

gour met (gụr′mā′), *n.* person who is expert in judging and choosing fine foods, wines, etc. [< F < OF *groumet* wine tester]

gov ern ment (guv′ərn mənt *or* guv′ər mənt), *n.* **1.** rule or authority over a country, state, district, etc. **2.** rule; control.

gran dam (gran′dam), *n.* an old woman.

graph ic (graf′ik), *adj.* lifelike; vivid: *a graphic account of a battle.* —**graph′i cal ly,** *adv.*

grat is (grat′is *or* grā′tis), *adv., adj.* for nothing; free of charge. [< L *gratis,* ult. < *gratia* favor]

grat u la tion (grach′ụ lā′shən), *n.* rejoicing; joy.

gre gar i ous (grə gãr′i əs), *adj.* **1.** living in groups. **2.** fond of being with others. **3.** of or having to do with a flock or crowd. [< L *gregarius* < *grex* flock]

grid i ron (grid′ī′ərn), *n.* **1.** a cooking utensil consisting of a framework of parallel iron bars. **2.** a football field.

gri mace (grə mās′ *or* grim′is), *n.* a twisting of the face. —*v.* make grimaces. [< F < Sp. *grimazo* panic]

groin (groin), *n.* the hollow on either side of the body where the thigh joins the abdomen.

gross (grōs), *adj.* **1.** whole; entire. **2.** very bad. **3.** coarse; vulgar: *Her manners are too gross for a lady.* **4.** thick; heavy; dense: *the gross growth of a jungle.*

ground swell (ground′ swel′), *n.* **1.** broad, deep waves caused by a distant storm, earthquake, etc. **2.** a strong wave of feeling among a group of people.

grov el (gruv′əl *or* grov′əl), *v.* lie face downward; crawl at someone's feet; humble oneself.

gru el ing (grü′əl ing), *adj. Informal.* exhausting.

gull (gul), *v.* deceive; cheat. —*n.* person who is easily deceived or cheated.

gun wale (gun′əl), *n.* the upper edge of a ship's or boat's side.

gus to (gus′tō), *n.* **1.** hearty enjoyment. **2.** liking or taste.

gy ra tion (jī rā′shən), *n.* circular or spiral motion.

ha be as cor pus (hā′bi əs kôr′pəs), *n.* writ or order requiring that a prisoner be brought before a judge or into court to decide whether he is being held lawfully.

ha bit u al (hə bich′ü əl), *adj.* **1.** done by habit: *habitual courtesy.* **2.** being or doing something by habit. **3.** usual; customary. —**Syn.** **2.** chronic. **3.** accustomed.

hale¹ (hāl), *adj.* strong and well; healthy. [OE *hāl*] —**Syn.** sound, robust. —**Ant.** sickly.

hale² (hāl), *v.* **1.** drag by force. **2.** compel to go. [< OF *haler* < Gmc.]

hang (hang), *v.* **1.** fasten or be fastened to something above. **2.** **hang fire,** hesitate; delay.

har ass (har′əs *or* hə ras′), *v.* **1.** trouble by repeated attacks. **2.** disturb; worry; torment.

hard-fa vored (härd′fā′vərd), *adj.* having harsh or coarse features; ugly.

har di hood (här′di hụd), *n.* boldness; daring.

har row (har′ō), *v.* **1.** hurt; wound. **2.** arouse uncomfortable feelings in; distress; torment.

has sock (has′ək), *n.* a thick cushion to rest the feet on, sit on, or kneel on.

hatch way (hach′wā′), *n.* an opening in the deck of a ship to the lower part.

haunch (hônch *or* hänch), *n.* part of the body around the hip; the hip.

hav oc (hav′ək), *n.* **1.** very great destruction or injury. Tornadoes, severe earthquakes, and plagues create widespread havoc. **2.** **play havoc with,** injure severely; ruin; destroy. [< AF var. of OF *havot* plundering, devastation, especially in phrase *crier havot* cry havoc < Gmc.] —**Syn.** **1.** wreck, ruin.

haw ser (hô′zər *or* hô′sər), *n.* a large rope or small cable. Hawsers are used for mooring or towing ships.

haz ard ous (haz′ər dəs), *adj.* dangerous; risky; perilous.

hear say (hēr′sā′), *n.* common talk; gossip.

heart strings (härt′stringz′), *n.pl.* deepest feelings.

---

hat, āge, cãre, fär; let, ēqual, tėrm; it, īce; hot, ōpen, ôrder; oil, out; cup, pụt, rüle, ūse; ch, child; ng, long; th, thin; ᵺ, then; zh, measure; ə represents *a* in about, *e* in taken, *i* in pencil, *o* in lemon, *u* in circus.

hec tic (hek′tik), *adj.* **1.** flushed. **2.** feverish. **3.** *Informal.* much excited. **4.** *Informal.* very exciting.

helms man (helmz′mən), *n.* man who steers a ship.

he mo stat (hē′mō stat), *n.* device for stopping bleeding by compressing a blood vessel.

hench man (hench′mən), *n.* **1.** a trusted attendant or follower. **2.** an obedient, unscrupulous follower. [ME *henxstman* < OE *hengest* horse + *man;* originally, a groom]

her ald ry (her′əld ri), *n.* science or art dealing with coats of arms. Heraldry deals with a person's right to use a coat of arms, traces family descent, etc.

het er o ge ne ous (het′ər ə jē′ni əs *or* het′ər ə jēn′yəs), *adj.* **1.** different in kind; unlike; not at all similar; varied. **2.** made up of unlike elements or parts. [< Med.L *heterogeneus,* ult. < Gk. *heteros* other + *genos* kind]

hey day (hā′dā′), *n.* period of greatest strength, vigor, spirits, prosperity, etc.

hi lar i ty (hə lar′ə ti *or* hī lar′ə ti), *n.* noisy mirth.

hire ling (hīr′ling), *n.* person who works only for money, without interest or pride in the task.

his tri on ic (his′tri on′ik), *adj.* **1.** having to do with actors or acting. **2.** theatrical; insincere. [< L *histrionicus* < *histrio* actor]

hob gob lin (hob′gob′lən), *n.* **1.** elf. **2.** evil spirit.

hold (hōld), *n.* interior of a ship below the deck. A ship's cargo is carried in its hold. [var. of *hole*]

hol o caust (hol′ə kôst), *n.* **1.** an offering all of which is burned. **2.** complete destruction by fire, especially of animals or human beings. **3.** great or wholesale destruction. [< L *holocaustum* < Gk. *holokauston,* neut. of *holokaustos* < *holos* whole + *kaustos* burned]

hon ey dew (hun′i dü *or* hun′i dū′), *n.* a sweet substance on leaves and stems, secreted by tiny insects called aphids.

host (hōst), *n.* **1.** a large number; multitude. **2.** army.

how be it (hou bē′it), *adv.* nevertheless.

hoy den (hoi′dən), *n.* a boisterous, romping girl.

hulk ing (hul′king), *adj.* big and clumsy.

hu mil i a tion (hū mil′i ā′shən), *n.* a lowering of pride, dignity, or self-respect.

hus band (huz′bənd), *n.* **1.** man who has a wife. **2.** *Archaic.* manager. —*v.* **1.** manage carefully: *husband one's resources.* **2.** marry. **3.** *Archaic.* till (soil); cultivate (plants). [OE *hūsbōnda* < *hūs* house + *bōnda* head of family (< Scand. *bōndi*)]

hus band ry (huz′bənd ri), *n.* **1.** farming. **2.** management of one's affairs or resources. **3.** careful management; thrift.

hy per ob tru sive (hī′pər əb trü′siv), *adj.* exceedingly obtrusive.

hy po chon dri ac (hī′pə kon′dri ak), *n.* person suffering from unnatural anxiety about his health.

hy po der mic (hī′pə dèr′mik), *adj.* **1.** under the skin. **2.** injected under the skin: *The doctor used a hypodermic needle.*

hys te ri a (his tēr′i ə *or* his ter′i ə), *n.* **1.** general lack of self-control. **2.** senseless excitement.

id i om (id′i əm), *n.* **1.** phrase or expression whose meaning cannot be understood from the ordinary meanings of the words in it: *"How do you do?"* and *"I have caught cold" are English idioms.* **2.** a people's way of expressing themselves. **3.** dialect. **4.** individual manner of expression in music, art, etc.

id i o mat ic (id′i ə mat′ik), *adj.* **1.** using an idiom or idioms. **2.** of idioms; concerning idioms.

i dle (ī′dəl), *adj.* **1.** doing nothing. **2.** lazy. **3.** useless; worthless. **4.** without any good reason, cause, or foundation: *idle rumors.*

il i ac (il′i ak), *adj. Anat.* of or having to do with the broad upper portion of the hipbone.

il i o in gui nal nerve (il′i ō in′gwə nəl nèrv′), *n.* a nerve located between the ribs and the hipbones.

ill-got ten (il′got′ən), *adj.* dishonestly obtained.

il lim it a ble (i lim′ə tə bəl), *adj.* limitless; boundless; infinite.

il lit er ate (i lit′ər it), *adj.* **1.** unable to read or write. **2.** not cultured: *He writes in a very illiterate way.*

il lus tri ous (i lus′tri əs), *adj.* very famous; great; outstanding. [< L *illustris* lighted up, bright]

im bibe (im bīb′), *v.* **1.** drink; drink in. **2.** absorb. [< L *imbibere* < *in-* in + *bibere* drink]

im bue (im bū′), *v.* fill; inspire.

im me mo ri al (im′ə mô′ri əl *or* im′ə mō′ri əl), *adj.* extending back beyond the bounds of memory.

im mi nent (im′ə nənt), *adj.* likely to happen soon; about to occur: *The black clouds, thunder, and lightning show that a storm is imminent.* [< L *imminens, -entis,* ppr. of *imminere* overhang] —**im′mi nent ly,** *adv.*

Syn. Imminent, impending mean likely to happen soon. **Imminent** chiefly describes danger, death, etc., that seems to hang threateningly over a person and is likely to happen any minute without further warning: *Swept along by the swift current, he was in imminent danger of going over the falls.* **Impending** suggests hanging over one, often indefinitely, and keeping him in suspense, and means near and likely to happen at any time: *For weeks I have had a feeling of impending disaster.*

im mo bil i ty (im′ō bil′ə ti), *n.* **1.** a condition of complete lack of movement. **2.** a being firmly fixed or unable to be moved.

im mov a ble (i müv′ə bəl), *adj.* **1.** that cannot be moved; firmly fixed. **2.** not changing position. **3.** firm; steadfast. **4.** unfeeling. —**im mov′a bly,** *adv.*

im mune (i mūn′), *adj.* **1.** protected from disease. **2.** exempt: *immune from taxes.*

im mu ta ble (i mū′tə bəl), *adj.* never changing; unchangeable. —**Syn.** permanent.

im pair (im pãr′), *v.* make worse; damage; weaken: *Poor food impaired his health.* [< OF *empeirer,* ult. < L *in-* + *pejor* worse] —**Syn.** harm, hurt.

im pale (im pāl′), *v.* pierce through with anything pointed; fasten upon anything pointed.

im pas sive (im pas′iv), *adj.* **1.** without feeling or emotion. **2.** not feeling pain or injury; insensible.

im pend ing (im pen′ding), *adj.* **1.** likely to happen soon; threatening; about to occur. **2.** overhanging: *Above him were impending cliffs.* —**Syn.** **1.** See **imminent.**

im per cep ti ble (im′pər sep′tə bəl), *adj.* very slight; gradual. —**im′per cep′ti bly,** *adv.*

im pe ri al ist (im pēr′i əl ist), *n.* person who favors the policy of extending the rule or authority of one country over other countries and colonies.

im pe ri ous (im pēr′i əs), *adj.* **1.** haughty; arrogant; overbearing. **2.** necessary; urgent. [< L *imperiosus* commanding] —**im pe′ri ous ly,** *adv.* —**im pe′ri ous ness,** *n.*

im per turb a ble (im′pər tèr′bə bəl), *adj.* **1.** not capable of being excited or disturbed. **2.** calm.

im pla ca ble (im plā′kə bəl *or* im plak′ə bəl), *adj.* that cannot be appeased; relentless. —**Syn.** unforgiving, inexorable.

im port (*v.* im pôrt′, im pōrt′, im′pôrt *or* im′pōrt; *n.* im′pôrt *or* im′pōrt), *v.* **1.** bring in from a foreign country for sale or use. **2.** mean; signify: *What do these facts import?* **3.** be of importance. —*n.* **1.** thing imported. **2.** meaning. **3.** importance. [< L *importare* < *in-* in + *portare* carry]

im por tu nate (im pôr′chə nit), *adj.* asking repeatedly; annoyingly persistent; urgent. —**im por′tu nate ly,** *adv.*

im por tune (im′pôr tün′, im′pôr tūn′, *or* im pôr′chən), *v.* ask urgently or repeatedly; trouble with demands.

im pre ca tion (im′prə kā′shən), *n.* a curse.

im preg na ble (im preg′nə bəl), *adj.* that cannot be overthrown by force: *an impregnable fortress.*

< = from, derived from, taken from; cf., compare; dial., dialect; dim., diminutive; lang., language; pp., past participle; ppr., present participle; pt., past tense; ult., ultimately; var., variant; ? = possibly.

impregnate

im preg nate (im preg′nāt), *v.* **1.** fill (with); saturate. **2.** instill into (the mind); inspire.

im promp tu (im promp′tü *or* im promp′tū), *adv., adj.* without previous preparation: *a speech made impromptu.* —*n.* something impromptu. [< L *in promptu* in readiness]

im pro vi sa tion (im′prə vī zā′shən *or* im′prov ə zā′-shən), *n.* **1.** an improvising. **2.** something improvised.

im pro vise (im′prə vīz), *v.* **1.** compose or utter without preparation. **2.** prepare or provide offhand: *The boys improvised a tent out of two blankets and some long poles.*

im pu ta tion (im′pū tā′shən), *n.* **1.** a charging of a fault, etc., to a person; a blaming. **2.** hint of wrongdoing.

in ad vert ent (in′ad ver′tənt), *adj.* **1.** not attentive. **2.** not done on purpose. —**in′ad vert′ent ly,** *adv.*

in al ien a ble (in āl′yən ə bəl *or* in ā′li ən ə bəl), *adj.* that cannot be given away or taken away.

in can ta tion (in′kan tā′shən), *n.* **1.** set of words spoken to cast a magic spell. **2.** use of such words.

in car na dine (in kär′nə din, in kär′nə dīn, *or* in kär′-nə dēn), *v.* make blood-red or flesh-colored. [< F < Ital. *incarnadino,* ult. < L *in-* + *caro* flesh]

in car nate (*adj.* in kär′nit *or* in kär′nāt; *v.* in kär′-nāt), *adj.* embodied in flesh, especially in human form: *The villian was a fiend incarnate.* —*v.* **1.** make incarnate; embody. **2.** put into an actual form; realize: *The sculptor incarnated his vision in a beautiful statue.* [< L *incarnatus,* pp. of *incarnare* < *in-* + *caro* flesh]

in car na tion (in′kär nā′shən), *n.* **1.** embodiment. **2.** person or thing that represents some quality or idea: *A miser is an incarnation of greed.*

in ci dent (in′sə dənt), *n.* **1.** a happening; event. **2.** position at which one thing strikes upon another. —*adj.* falling or striking (upon): *rays of light incident upon a mirror.*

in cip i ent (in sip′i ənt), *adj.* just beginning; in an early stage. —**in cip′i ence,** *n.* —**in cip′i ent ly,** *adv.*

in co her ence (in′kō hēr′əns), *n.* failure to stick together; looseness. **2.** lack of logical connection. **3.** disconnected thought or speech: *the incoherence of a madman.*

in com pre hen si ble (in′kom pri hen′sə bəl), *adj.* impossible to understand. —**in′com pre hen′si bly,** *adv.*

in con se quen tial (in′kon sə kwen′shəl), *adj.* unimportant; trifling.

in con sist ent (in′kən sis′tənt), *adj.* **1.** lacking in agreement or harmony. **2.** lacking harmony between its different parts; not uniform. **3.** failing to keep to the same principles, course of action, etc.; changeable. —**in′con sist′en cy,** *n.*

in con test a ble (in′kən tes′tə bəl), *adj.* not to be disputed; unquestionable.

in cor ri gi ble (in kôr′ə jə bəl *or* in kor′ə jə bəl), *adj.* **1.** so firmly fixed (in bad ways, a bad habit, etc.) that nothing else can be expected: *an incorrigible liar.* **2.** so fixed that it cannot be changed or cured.

in cred i ble (in kred′ə bəl), *adj.* seeming too extraordinary to be possible; unbelievable: *The hero fought with incredible bravery.* —**in cred′i bly,** *adv.*

➜ **incredible, incredulous.** *Incredible* means unbelievable; *incredulous* means not ready to believe or showing a lack of belief: *His story of having seen a ghost seemed incredible to his family. If they look incredulous, show them the evidence.*

in cre du li ty (in′krə dü′lə ti *or* in′krə dū′lə ti), *n.* lack of belief; doubt. —**Syn.** unbelief, distrust.

in cred u lous (in krej′ú ləs), *adj.* **1.** not ready to believe; doubting. **2.** showing a lack of belief. —**in cred′u lous ly,** *adv.* ➜ See **incredible** for usage note.

in cu bus (in′kū bəs *or* ing′kū bəs), *n.* **1.** nightmare. **2.** an oppressive or burdensome thing.

in cul cate (in kul′kāt *or* in′kul kāt), *v.* impress by repetition; teach persistently.

in cum bent (in kum′bənt), *n.* person holding an office, position, church living, etc. —*adj.* resting (on a person) as a duty: *It is incumbent on the judge to be just.*

infringement

in de fat i ga ble (in′di fat′ə gə bəl), *adj.* tireless.

in dict ment (in dīt′mənt), *n.* **1.** a formal accusation; especially, the legal accusation presented by a grand jury. **2.** accusation.

in dif fer ent ly (in dif′ər ənt li *or* in dif′rənt li), *adv.* **1.** with lack of interest. **2.** moderately. **3.** poorly.

in di gent (in′də jənt), *adj.* poor; needy. [< L *indigens, -entis,* ppr. of *indigere* need]

in dis crim i nate (in′dis krim′ə nit), *adj.* **1.** confused. **2.** with no feeling for differences. —**in′dis crim′i nate ly,** *adv.*

in dis sol u ble (in′di sol′ū bəl), *adj.* not capable of being destroyed; lasting; firm.

in do lent (in′də lənt), *adj.* lazy; disliking work. —**in′-do lence,** *n.* —**in′do lent ly,** *adv.*

in dom i ta ble (in dom′ə tə bəl), *adj.* unconquerable; unyielding. —**in dom′i ta bly,** *adv.*

in du bi ta ble (in dü′bə tə bəl *or* in dū′bə tə bəl), *adj.* not to be doubted; certain. —**in du′bi ta bly,** *adv.*

in e bri ate (in ē′bri it), *adj.* intoxicated; drunk.

in ef fa ble (in ef′ə bəl), *adj.* **1.** too great to be described in words. **2.** that must not be spoken.

in es ti ma ble (in es′tə mə bəl), *adj.* **1.** too good, great, valuable, etc., to be measured or estimated.

in ex o ra ble (in ek′sə rə bəl), *adj.* relentless; unyielding. [< L *inexorabilis* < *in-* not + *ex-* successfully + *orare* entreat] —**in ex′o ra bly,** *adv.* —**Syn.** unrelenting, implacable. See **inflexible.**

in ex pe di ent (in′eks pē′di ənt), *adj.* not practicable, suitable, or wise. —**Syn.** inadvisable, unprofitable.

in ex pli ca ble (in eks′plə kə bəl *or* in′eks plik′ə bəl), *adj.* impossible to explain or understand; mysterious. [< L *inexplicabilis*] —**in ex′pli ca bly,** *adv.*

in ex tri ca ble (in eks′trə kə bəl), *adj.* **1.** that one cannot get out of. **2.** that cannot be disentangled or solved.

in fa mous (in′fə məs), *adj.* **1.** deserving or causing a very bad reputation; shamefully bad; extremely wicked. **2.** having a very bad reputation; in public disgrace: *A traitor's name is infamous.* —**in′fa mous ly,** *adv.*

in fa my (in′fə mi), *n.* **1.** very bad reputation; public disgrace: *Traitors are held in infamy.* **2.** shameful badness; extreme wickedness. [< L *infamia* < *in-* without + *fama* (good) reputation]

in fan tile (in′fən tīl *or* in′fən til), *adj.* **1.** like an infant; babyish; childish. **2.** in an early stage; just beginning to develop.

in fan tine (in′fən tin *or* in′fən tīn), *adj.* infantile; babyish; childish.

in fe lic i tous (in′fə lis′ə təs), *adj.* **1.** unsuitable. **2.** unfortunate.

in flex i ble (in flek′sə bəl), *adj.* **1.** firm; unyielding; steadfast. **2.** that cannot be changed; unalterable. **3.** not easily bent; stiff; rigid. —**in flex′i bly,** *adv.* —**in flex′i bil′i ty,** *n.*

Syn. 1. Inflexible, inexorable, unrelenting mean unyielding in character or purpose. **Inflexible** means unbending, holding fast or doggedly to what one has made up his mind to do, think, or believe: *You waste time when you argue with someone whose attitude is inflexible.* **Inexorable,** formal, means not to be influenced or affected by begging or pleading, but firm and pitiless: *The principal was inexorable in his decision.* **Unrelenting** means not softening and showing pity or lessening in force, harshness, or cruelty: *He was unrelenting in his hatred.* **3.** unbending, firm.

in form ant (in fôr′mənt), *n.* person who gives information to another: *My informant saw it happen.*

in frac tion (in frak′shən), *n.* **1.** a breaking of a law or obligation. **2.** a partial fracture.

in fringe ment (in frinj′mənt), *n.* **1.** a breaking (of a law): *infringement of the food and drug law.* **2.** the doing of an unlawful act against the person, property, or rights of another.

---

hat, āge, cãre, fär; let, ēqual, tèrm; it, īce; hot, ōpen, ôrder; oil, out; cup, pút, rüle, ūse; ch, child; ng, long; th, thin; ℋ, then; zh, measure; ə represents *a* in about, *e* in taken, *i* in pencil, *o* in lemon, *u* in circus.

in gen ious (in jēn′yəs), *adj.* **1.** clever; good at inventing. **2.** cleverly planned and made. [< L *ingeniosus* < *ingenium* natural talent]
➔ **Ingenious, ingenuous.** *Ingenious* means clever; skillful; *ingenuous* means frank; sincere; simple: *Fay is so ingenious that she will think of a way to do this work more easily. The ingenuous child had never thought of being suspicious of what others told her.*

in gé nue (aN′zhə nü; *French* aN zhā nY′), *n.* simple, innocent girl or young woman, especially as represented on the stage. [< F *ingénue*, originally fem. adj., ingenuous]

in gen u ous (in jen′ū əs), *adj.* **1.** frank; open; sincere. **2.** simple; natural; innocent. [< L *ingenuus*, originally, native, free born] —**Syn. 1.** candid. **2.** naive. ➔ See ingenious for usage note.

in her ent (in hēr′ənt *or* in her′ənt), *adj.* existing; abiding; belong to (a person or thing) as a quality or attribute: *In spite of flattery, she kept her inherent modesty.*

in no vate (in′ə vāt), *v.* make changes; bring in something new or new ways of doing things. [< L *innovare* < *in- + novus* new]

in no va tion (in′ə vā′shən), *n.* **1.** change made in the established way of doing things. **2.** making changes; bringing in new things or new ways of doing things.

in nu en do (in′ū en′dō), *n.* **1.** an indirect reference. **2.** an indirect suggestion against somebody.

in or di nate (in ôr′də nit), *adj.* excessive; unrestrained. [< L *inordinatus* < *in-* not + *ordo* order]

in quest (in′kwest), *n.* a legal inquiry, especially before a jury. An inquest is held to determine the cause of a death that may possibly have been the result of a crime.

in scru ta ble (in skrü′tə bəl), *adj.* that cannot be understood; so mysterious or obscure that one cannot make out its meaning. [< LL *inscrutabilis* < L *in-* not + *scrutari* examine, ransack < *scruta* trash] —**in scru′ta bly,** *adv.*

in sen si bly (in sen′sə bli), *adv.* by hardly noticeable degrees; little by little.

in sin u ate (in sin′ū āt), *v.* **1.** suggest indirectly; hint. **2.** push in or get in by an indirect, twisting way.

in sip id (in sip′id), *adj.* **1.** without much taste. **2.** dull; uninteresting. [< LL *insipidus* < L *in-* not + *sapidus* tasty]

in sist ence (in sis′təns), *n.* **1.** act of insisting. **2.** quality of being firm in a demand.

in spir it (in spir′it), *v.* put spirit into; encourage. —**in spir′it ing,** *adj.*

in sta bil i ty (in′stə bil′ə ti), *n.* lack of firmness.

in stan ta ne ous (in′stən tā′ni əs), *adj.* occurring, done, or made in an instant. —**in′stan ta′ne ous ly,** *adv.*

in sti gate (in′stə gāt), *v.* urge on; stir up: *Foreign agents instigated a rebellion.*

in still (in stil′), *v.* impart gradually: *Reading good books instills a love for really fine literature.*

in suf fer a ble (in suf′ər ə bəl *or* in suf′rə bəl), *adj.* intolerable; unbearable: *insufferable impudence.*

in su per a ble (in sü′pər ə bəl), *adj.* that cannot be passed over or overcome: *an insuperable barrier.*

in sur gent (in sėr′jənt), *n.* **1.** person who rises in revolt; rebel. **2.** *U.S.* rebel within a political party. —*adj.* rising in revolt; rebellious. [< L *insurgens, -entis,* ppr. of *insurgere* < *in-* against + *surgere* rise]

in te gral (in′tə grəl), *adj.* **1.** necessary to the completeness of the whole; essential. **2.** entire; complete. **3.** not fractional. [< LL *integralis* < L *integer* whole]

in teg ri ty (in teg′rə ti), *n.* **1.** honesty; sincerity; uprightness: *A man of integrity is respected.* **2.** wholeness; completeness: *Soldiers defend the integrity of their country against those who want part of it.* **3.** perfect condition; soundness. [< L *integritas* < *integer* whole]

in tel li gi ble (in tel′ə jə bəl), *adj.* capable of being understood; comprehensible. [< L *intelligibilis* < *intelligere*] —**in tel′li gi bly,** *adv.* —**Syn.** understandable, plain, clear.

in tem per ate (in tem′pər it *or* in tem′prit), *adj.* **1.** lacking in self-control; excessive. **2.** severe: *an intemperate winter.*

in ter dict (in′tər dikt′), *v.* prohibit.

in ter line (in′tər lin′), *v.* insert between the lines of.

in ter me di ar y (in′tər mē′di er′i), *n.* person who acts for one person with another; go-between. —*adj.* acting between.

in ter ment (in tėr′mənt), *n.* burial.

in ter mi na ble (in tėr′mə nə bəl), *adj.* endless; so long as to seem endless. [< LL *interminabilis,* ult. < L *in-* not + *terminare* to end]

in ter mit tent (in′tər mit′ənt), *adj.* stopping and beginning again; pausing at intervals.

in ter ne cine (in′tər nē′sin *or* in′tər nē′sīn), *adj.* **1.** destructive to both sides. **2.** deadly; destructive.

in ter po si tion (in′tər pə zish′ən), *n.* an interference in order to help.

in ter ur ban (in′tər ėr′bən), *adj.* between cities or towns. [Am.E]

in ti ma tion (in′tə mā′shən), *n.* indirect suggestion.

in tol er a ble (in tol′ər ə bəl), *adj.* unbearable; too much, too painful, etc., to be endured. [< L *intolerabilis*] —**in tol′er a bly,** *adv.* —**Syn.** unendurable, insufferable.

in tone (in tōn′), *v.* **1.** read or recite in a singing voice; chant. **2.** utter with a particular tone.

in tox i ca tion (in tok′sə kā′shən), *n.* **1.** drunkenness. **2.** great excitement. **3.** in medicine, poisoning.

in tri ca cy (in′trə kə si), *n.* **1.** complexity: *The intricacy of the plan made it hard to understand.* **2.** complication; something involved: *The plan was full of intricacies.*

in tu i tion (in′tü ish′ən *or* in′tū ish′ən), *n.* **1.** perception of truths, facts, etc., without reasoning: *By experience with all kinds of people Mr. Jones had developed great powers of intuition.* **2.** something so perceived. [< LL *intuitio, -onis* a gazing at < L *intueri* < *in-* at + *tueri* look] —**in tu′i tive,** *adj.*

in un da tion (in′un dā′shən), *n.* an overflowing; flood.

in val u a ble (in val′ū ə bəl *or* in val′ū bəl), *adj.* priceless; very precious; valuable beyond measure.

in vest (in vest′), *v.* **1.** use (money) to buy something that is expected to produce a profit, or income, or both. **2.** clothe; cover; surround: *Darkness invests the earth at night.* **3.** give power to.

in vet er ate (in vet′ər it), *adj.* habitual: *an inveterate smoker.* —**Syn.** chronic.

in vig or ate (in vig′ər āt), *v.* fill with life and energy.

in vin ci ble (in vin′sə bəl), *adj.* not to be overcome; unconquerable. [< L *invincibilis* < *in-* not + *vincere* conquer] —**in vin′ci bly,** *adv.* —**Syn.** indomitable.

in vi o late (in vī′ə lit *or* in vī′ə lāt), *adj.* uninjured; unbroken.

in ward ness (in′wərd nis), *n.* inner nature.

irk (ėrk), *v.* weary; disgust; annoy; trouble; bore.

i ron (ī′ərn), *n.* **1.** the commonest and most useful metal, from which tools, etc., are made. **2. irons,** *pl.* chains or bands of iron; handcuffs; shackles.

i ron i cal (ī ron′ə kəl), *adj.* **1.** expressing one thing and meaning the opposite: *"Speedy" would be an ironical name for a snail.* **2.** contrary to what would naturally be expected.

ir re claim a ble (ir′i klām′ə bəl), *adj.* that cannot be reclaimed. —**ir′re claim′a bly,** *adv.*

ir re deem a ble (ir′i dēm′ə bəl), *adj.* **1.** that cannot be bought back. **2.** beyond remedy; hopeless.

ir re press i ble (ir′i pres′ə bəl), *adj.* that cannot be held back, kept down, or kept in check. —**ir′re press′i bly,** *adv.*

ir rev o ca ble (i rev′ə kə bəl), *adj.* not to be recalled, withdrawn, or abolished: *an irrevocable decision.*

ir rup tion (i rup′shən), *n.* a breaking or bursting in.

< = from, derived from, taken from;   cf., compare;   dial., dialect;   dim., diminutive;   lang., language; pp., past participle;   ppr., present participle;   pt., past tense;   ult., ultimately;   var., variant;   ? = possibly.

ja pan (jə pan′), *n.* a hard, glossy varnish. —*v.* put japan on. [from *Japan*]

jape (jāp), *n.* 1. joke; jest. 2. trick.

jeal ous (jel′əs), *adj.* 1. full of envy; envious. 2. watchful in keeping or guarding something. 3. close; watchful; suspicious.

jeop ard ize (jep′ər dīz), *v.* risk; endanger; imperil: *Soldiers jeopardize their lives in war.*

jibe (jīb), *n.* jeer; scoff; sneer.

jo cose (jō kōs′), *adj.* jesting; humorous.

ju bi lant (jü′bə lənt), *adj.* 1. rejoicing. 2. expressing or showing joy. —**ju′bi lant ly**, *adv.* —**Syn.** 1. joyful, exultant.

ju di ci ar y (jü dish′i er′i), *n.* branch of government that administers justice. —*adj.* of or having to do with courts, judges, or the administration of justice.

junc ture (jungk′chər), *n.* 1. point of time. 2. state of affairs. 3. crisis. 4. joint. 5. a joining. 6. being joined.

jun ket ing (jung′kit ing), *n.* feasting; going on a pleasure trip.

ju ris dic tion (jür′is dik′shən), *n.* 1. right or power of administering law or justice. 2. authority; power; control. [< L *jurisdictio, -onis*, ult. < *jus* law + *dicere* say]

ka lei do scope (kə lī′də skōp), *n.* tube containing bits of colored glass and two mirrors. As it is turned, it reflects continually changing patterns.

keep (kēp), *v.* have; hold. —*n.* the strongest part of a castle.

ken (ken), *n.* 1. range of sight. 2. range of knowledge.

ker sey (kér′zi), *v.* a coarse, ribbed, woolen cloth with a cotton warp.

kib itz (kib′its), *v.* *Slang.* look on as an outsider and offer unwanted advice. [Am.E]

knav er y (nāv′ər i or nāv′ri), *n.* tricky, dishonest act.

knot (not), *n.* unit of speed used on ships; one nautical mile per hour: *The ship averaged 12 knots.*

KEEP

la bored (lā′bərd), *adj.* done with effort; forced; not easy or natural.

la con ic (lə kon′ik), *adj.* using few words; brief in speech or expression; concise. [< L < Gk. *lakonikos* Spartan; Spartans were noted for pithy speech]

lac te al (lak′ti əl), *adj.* milky. [< L *lacteus* < *lac* milk]

la goon (lə gün′), *n.* 1. pond or small lake connected with a larger body of water. 2. shallow water separated from the sea by low sandbanks. 3. water within a ring-shaped coral island. [< Ital. *laguna* < L *lacuna* pond]

lair (lār), *v.* make a lair; use as a home or resting place.

lan cet (lan′sit or län′sit), *n.* a small, sharp-pointed surgical knife, usually having two sharp edges.

lan guor ous (lang′gər əs), *adj.* 1. weak. 2. slow-moving; sluggish. —**lan′guor ous ly**, *adv.*

lar der (lär′dər), *n.* 1. pantry; place where food is kept. 2. stock of food. [< OF *lardier* < *lard* lard < L *lardum*]

lar gess (lär′jis), *n.* 1. generous giving. 2. a generous gift or gifts. [< OF *largesse* < *large* < L *largus* copious]

la tent (lā′tənt), *adj.* present but not active; hidden; concealed: *latent talents.* [< L *latens, -entis*, ppr. of *latere* lie hidden]

lat i tude (lat′ə tüd or lat′ə tūd), *n.* 1. distance north or south of the equator, measured in degrees. 2. room to act; scope; freedom from narrow rules. [< L *latitudo* < *latus* wide]

laud a ble (lôd′ə bəl), *adj.* worthy of praise.

lave (lāv), *v.* *Poetic.* 1. wash; bathe. 2. wash or flow against: *The stream laves its banks.* [OE *lafian* < L *lavare*]

league (lēg), *n.* measure of distance, usually about 3 miles.

leg a cy (leg′ə si), *n.* 1. money or other property left to a person by a will. 2. something that has been handed down from an ancestor or predecessor.

le git i mate (lə jit′ə mit), *adj.* 1. rightful; lawful; allowed. 2. conforming to accepted standards. [< Med.L *legitimatus* < L *legitimus* lawful < *lex* law]

len ient (lēn′yənt or lē′ni ənt), *adj.* mild; gentle; merciful. [< L *leniens, -entis*, ppr. of *lenire* soften < *lenis* mild] —**len′ient ly**, *adv.*

le thal (lē′thəl), *adj.* causing death; deadly: *lethal weapons, a lethal dose.* [< L *let(h)alis* < *letum* death]

lev ee (lev′i), *n.* 1. *U.S.* bank built to keep a river from overflowing. 2. a landing place for boats.

lev i ty (lev′ə ti), *n.* lack of proper seriousness.

lib er al (lib′ər əl or lib′rəl), *adj.* 1. generous: *a liberal donation.* 2. plentiful; abundant: *He put in a liberal supply of coal for the winter.* 3. broad-minded; not narrow in one's ideas: *a liberal thinker.* 4. favoring progress and reforms. —*n.* person favorable to progress and reforms.

lib er ty pole (lib′ər ti pōl′), *n.* a high flag pole with a flag or some other symbol of liberty mounted at the top.

lig a ture (lig′ə chür or lig′ə chər), *n.* 1. anything used to bind or tie up; bandage, cord, etc. 2. thread, string, etc., used to tie up a bleeding artery or vein. [< LL *ligatura* < L *ligare* bind]

light some (līt′səm), *adj.* 1. nimble; lively. 2. happy; gay; cheerful. 3. frivolous.

lim pid (lim′pid), *adj.* clear; transparent: *limpid water.*

lin e al (lin′i əl), *adj.* in the direct line of descent: *A grandson is a lineal descendant of his grandfather.*

lin e a ment (lin′i ə mənt), *n.* part or feature; part or feature of a face with attention to its outline.

lin sey-wool sey (lin′zi wůl′zi), *n.* a strong coarse fabric made of linen and wool or of cotton and wool.

lis some (lis′əm), *adj.* 1. lithe; limber. 2. nimble; active.

list (list), *v.* *Archaic* and *Poetic.* 1. listen. 2. listen to. [OE *hlystan* < *hlyst* hearing]

list less (list′lis), *adj.* seeming too tired to care about anything; not interested in things; not caring to be active. —**list′less ly**, *adv.* —**list′less ness**, *n.*

lists (lists), *n.pl.* 1. place where knights fought in tournaments. 2. any place or scene of combat. 3. **enter the lists**, join in a contest.

lith o graph (lith′ə graf or lith′ə gräf), *n.* picture made from a specially prepared stone or a metal plate.

liv ing (liv′ing), *n.* 1. act or condition of one that lives. 2. a means of obtaining what is needed to support life. 3. position in the church with the income attached.

loll (lol), *v.* 1. recline or lean in a lazy manner. 2. hang loosely or droop: *A dog's tongue lolls out in hot weather.*

lon gi tu di nal (lon′jə tü′də nəl or lon′jə tū′də nəl), *adj.* 1. of length; in length. 2. running lengthwise.

loon (lün), *n.* a worthless or stupid person.

loot (lüt), *n.* spoils; booty. —*v.* plunder; rob.

lop (lop), *v.* 1. cut; cut off. 2. cut branches, twigs, etc., from.

lo qua cious (lō kwā′shəs), *adj.* talking much; fond of talking. —**Syn.** See **garrulous**.

lu cid (lü′sid), *adj.* 1. easy to understand. 2. shining; bright. 3. sane. 4. clear; transparent.

lu cra tive (lü′krə tiv), *adj.* bringing in money; profitable. [< L *lucrativus* < *lucrari* to gain < *lucrum* gain]

lu cu bra tion (lü′kū brā′shən), *n.* a learned or carefully written production, especially one that is labored and dull.

hat, āge, cãre, fär; let, ēqual, tėrm; it, ĭce; hot, ōpen, ôrder; oil, out; cup, půt, rüle, ūse; ch, child; ng, long; th, thin; ŦH, then; zh, measure; ə represents *a* in about, *e* in taken, *i* in pencil, *o* in lemon, *u* in circus.

lu di crous (lü′də krəs), *adj.* amusingly absurd; ridiculous. [< L *ludicrus* < *ludus* sport] —**Syn.** laughable.
lu gu bri ous (lü gü′bri əs *or* lü gū′bri əs), *adj.* sad; mournful. —**Syn.** dismal, melancholy.
lu mi nous (lü′mə nəs), *adj.* **1.** shining by its own light. **2.** full of light; bright. **3.** easily understood; clear; enlightening. —**lu′mi nous ly,** *adv.* —**lu′mi nous ness,** *n.*
lu pine (lü′pən), *n.* any of several plants of the same family as peas and beans, that have long spikes of flowers, radiating clusters of grayish, hairy leaflets, and flat pods with bean-shaped seeds. [< L *lupinus, lupinum*]
lu rid (lür′id), *adj.* **1.** lighted up with a red or fiery glare. **2.** terrible; sensational; startling: *lurid crimes.*
lynx (lingks), *n.* sharp-sighted wildcat that has a short tail and rather long legs.

mac a ro ni (mak′ə rō′ni), *n.* a fashionable English dandy of the 18th century.
mack in tosh (mak′ən tosh), *n.* a waterproof coat. [named after the inventor, Charles *Macintosh*]
mag na nim i ty (mag′nə nim′ə ti), *n.* nobility of soul or mind; generosity in forgiving.
mag net ic (mag net′ik), *adj.* having the power to attract or charm; attractive.
mag net ism (mag′nə tiz əm), *n.* power to attract or charm: *A person with magnetism has many friends and admirers.*
main (mān), *adj.* most important; largest. —*n.* **1.** a large pipe for water, gas, etc. **2.** *Poetic.* the open sea; ocean. **3.** *Archaic.* mainland. [OE *mægen* power]
mal ad just ment (mal′ə just′mənt), *n.* bad fitting or adaptation (of one thing to another): *The new pupil's unhappiness was due to her maladjustment to strange surroundings.*
ma lev o lent (mə lev′ə lənt), *adj.* wishing evil to happen to others; showing ill will; spiteful. —**Syn.** malicious, resentful. —**Ant.** benevolent.
ma li cious (mə lish′əs), *adj.* showing active ill will; wishing to hurt others; spiteful. —**ma li′cious ly,** *adv.* —**ma li′cious ness,** *n.*
mam mal (mam′əl), *n.* an animal that has a backbone and that gives milk to its young.
man i fest (man′ə fest), *adj.* apparent to the eye or to the mind; plain; clear.
ma no ri al (mə nô′ri əl *or* mə nō′ri əl), *adj.* of a large estate with a fine mansion and much land.
man u fac to ry (man′ū fak′tə ri), *n.* factory.
marge (märj), *n. Poetic.* edge; border: *the marge of a stream.* [< F]
mark ed ly (mär′kid li), *adv.* in a marked manner or degree; conspicuously; noticeably; plainly.
ma son ry (mā′sən ri), *n.* work built by a mason; stonework; brickwork.
masque (mask *or* mäsk), *n.* **1.** amateur dramatic entertainment in which fine costumes, scenery, music, and dancing are more important than the story. **2.** masked ball.
mas tiff (mas′tif *or* mäs′tif), *n.* a large, strong dog with drooping ears and hanging lips.
ma te ri al ism (mə tēr′i əl iz′əm), *n.* tendency to care too much for the things of this world and neglect spiritual needs.
ma te ri al is tic (mə tēr′i əl is′tik), *adj.* of materialism.
mau gre (mô′gər), *prep. Archaic.* in spite of; notwithstanding. [< OF *maugre*, originally n., ill will, spite]
maw (mô), *n.* **1.** mouth. **2.** throat. **3.** stomach.
ma zur ka (mə zėr′kə), *n.* **1.** a lively Polish dance. **2.** music for it. [< Polish, woman of *Mazovia* in Poland]
mead (mēd), *n. Poetic.* meadow. [OE *mæd*]
meas ured (mezh′ərd *or* māzh′ərd), *adj.* **1.** regular. **2.** rhythmical. **3.** deliberate, not hasty or careless.

me di a (mē′di ə), *n. pl.* of **medium:** *Newspapers, magazines, billboards, and radio are important media for advertising.*
me di al (mē′di əl), *adj.* in the middle. —**me′di al ly,** *adv.*
me di o cre (mē′di ō′kər *or* mē′di ō′kər), *adj.* neither good nor bad; average; ordinary.
me di oc ri ty (mē′di ok′rə ti), *n.* mediocre quality.
me di um (mē′di əm), *n.* a means through which something is accomplished: *The author used the short story as a medium for expressing his hatred of tyranny.*
med ley (med′li), *n.* **1.** mixture of things that ordinarily do not belong together. **2.** piece of music made up of parts from other pieces.
meer schaum (mēr′shəm *or* mēr′shôm), *n.* a tobacco pipe made of a very soft, light stone.
mel an chol y (mel′ən kol′i), *n.* **1.** sadness. **2.** sober thoughtfulness. —*adj.* **1.** sad; gloomy. **2.** depressing. **3.** soberly thoughtful; pensive.
mel o dra ma (mel′ə drä′mə *or* mel′ə dram′ə), *n.* **1.** a sensational drama with exaggerated appeal to the emotions. **2.** any sensational writing, speech, or action.
me men to (mə men′tō), *n.* thing serving as a reminder: *The postcards are mementos of our trip abroad.*
mem oir (mem′wär), *n.* **1.** biography. **2. memoirs,** *pl.* record of facts and events written from personal knowledge or special information.
mem o ran dum (mem′ə ran′dəm), *n.* **1.** note to aid one's memory. **2.** an informal letter, note, or report.
men di can cy (men′də kən si), *n.* act of begging.
men di cant (men′də kənt), *n.* beggar.
me ni al (mē′ni əl *or* mēn′yəl), *adj.* belonging to or suited to a servant; low; mean. —*n.* servant who does the most unpleasant tasks. —**me′ni al ly,** *adv.*
mer ce nar y (mėr′sə ner′i), *adj.* working for money only. —*n.* soldier serving for pay in a foreign army. [< L *mercenarius* < *merces* wages]
mer e tri cious (mer′ə trish′əs), *adj.* attractive in a showy way; alluring by false charms: *A wooden building painted to look like marble is meretricious.*
mes mer ism (mes′mər iz əm *or* mez′mər iz əm), *n.* hypnotism. [named after F. A. *Mesmer* (1734-1815), who popularized the doctrine] —**mes′mer ize,** *v.*
met al line (met′əl in *or* met′əl īn), *adj.* of metal.
met a mor phose (met′ə môr′fōz *or* met′ə môr′fōs), *v.* change in form; transform: *The witch metamorphosed people into animals.*
mete (mēt), *n.* **1.** boundary. **2.** a boundary stone.
mi as ma (mī az′mə *or* mi az′mə), *n.* poisonous vapor rising from the earth and infecting the air.
mien (mēn), *n.* manner of holding the head and body; way of acting and looking: *George Washington had the mien of a soldier.* [probably < *demean;* influenced by F *mine* expression < Celtic] —**Syn.** bearing, demeanor, appearance.
mim ic ry (mim′ik ri), *n.* **1.** a making fun of by imitating. **2.** a close copy; imitation.
mince (mins), *v.* **1.** chop up into very small pieces. **2.** speak or do in an affectedly polite or elegant manner. **3. not to mince matters,** to speak plainly and frankly. **4.** walk with little short steps. [< OF *mincier*, ult. < L *minutus* small]
min i mize (min′ə mīz), *v.* reduce to the least possible amount or degree.
min is tra tion (min′is trā′shən), *n.* help; aid.
min strel sy (min′strəl si), *n.* **1.** art or practice of a minstrel. **2.** collection of songs and ballads. **3.** company of minstrels.
mi nu ti a (mi nü′shi ə *or* mi nū′shi ə), *n. pl.* **-ae** (ē). very small matter; trifling detail.
mi rage (mə razh′), *n.* **1.** a misleading appearance, usually in the desert or at sea, resulting from a reflection

---

< = from, derived from, taken from; cf., compare; dial., dialect; dim., diminutive; lang., language; pp., past participle; ppr., present participle; pt., past tense; ult., ultimately; var., variant; ? = possibly.

misadventure

of some distant scene in such a way as to give the impression that it is near. **2.** illusion; thing that does not exist. [< F *mirage* < *mirer* look at, ult. < L *mirare*]

mis ad ven ture (mis′əd ven′chər), *n.* an unfortunate accident; bad luck; mishap.

mis cal cu late (mis kal′kū lāt), *v.* make a mistake in figuring or reasoning.

mis rep re sen ta tion (mis′rep ri zen tā′shən), *n.* incorrect story or explanation.

mis shape (mis shāp′), *v.* shape badly; deform. —**mis shap′en,** *adj.*

mis sile (mis′əl), *n.* object that is thrown, hurled, or shot, such as a stone, a bullet, an arrow, or a lance.

mit i gate (mit′ə gāt), *v.* make or become mild; made or become milder; soften: *mitigate the punishment.*

mol li fy (mol′ə fī), *v.* soften; appease; mitigate: *mollify his wrath.* [< F < LL *mollificare* < *mollis* soft + *facere* make]

mo men tum (mō men′təm), *n.* force and speed with which a body moves.

Mo nel met al (mō nel′ met′əl), *n.* Trademark. a silver-colored metal made from copper and nickel.

mon o logue (mon′ə lôg *or* mon′ə log), *n.* **1.** a long speech by one person. **2.** entertainment by a single speaker. [< F < LGk. *monologos* < *monos* single + *logos* speech, discourse]

mo not o ny (mə not′ə ni), *n.* **1.** sameness of tone or pitch. **2.** lack of variety. **3.** wearisome sameness. [< Gk. *monotonia,* ult. < Gk. *monos* single + *tonos* tone]

mon stros i ty (mon stros′ə ti), *n.* animal, person, or thing that is so huge or otherwise unusual as to appear horrible or dreadful.

mo rale (mə ral′ *or* mə räl′), *n.* moral or mental condition as regards courage, confidence, enthusiasm: *The morale of the troops was high.*

mo rass (mə ras′), *n.* piece of low, soft, wet ground; swamp.

mor a to ri um (môr′ə tô′ri əm, môr′ə tō′ri əm, mor′ə tô′ri əm, *or* mor′ə tō′ri əm), *n.* **1.** a legal authorization to delay payments of money due. **2.** period during which such authorization is in effect. [< NL < L *morari* delay < *mora* a delay]

mor bid (môr′bid), *adj.* **1.** unhealthy; not wholesome: *a morbid liking for horror.* **2.** caused by disease; diseased: *Cancer is a morbid growth.*

mor ti cian (môr tish′ən), *n.* undertaker.

mote (mōt), *n.* speck of dust.

mot ley (mot′li), *adj.* **1.** of different colors like a clown's suit. **2.** made up of units not alike: *a motley collection.*

mud cat (mud′kat′), *n.* a catfish, which is not highly valued as food.

mul ti form (mul′tə fôrm), *adj.* having many different shapes, forms, or kinds.

mul ti plic i ty (mul′tə plis′ə ti), *n.* great many.

mul ti tu di nous (mul′tə tü′də nəs *or* mul′tə tū′də-nəs), *adj.* very numerous. —**mul′ti tu′di nous ly,** *adv.*

mum mer y (mum′ər i), *n.* **1.** performance of persons wearing masks, fancy costumes, etc. **2.** any useless or silly ceremony.

murk (mėrk), *n.* darkness; gloom.

muse (mūz), *n.* spirit that inspires a poet or composer.

mus ing (mūz′ing), *adj.* dreamy; meditative.

mus ket ry (mus′kit ri), *n.* shooting with muskets or rifles.

musk y (mus′ki), *adj.* having a strong and lasting odor.

mus ty (mus′ti), *adj.* **1.** having a smell or taste suggesting mold or damp. **2.** stale.

mu tu al (mū′chü əl), *adj.* **1.** done, said, felt, etc., by each toward the other; given and received: *mutual promises, mutual dislike.* **2.** each to the other: *mutual enemies.* —**mu′tu al ly,** *adv.*

oblivion

mys ti cal (mis′tə kəl), *adj.* **1.** having some secret meaning; beyond human understanding; mysterious. **2.** spiritually symbolic. The lamb and the dove are mystical symbols of the Christian religion.

mys ti fy (mis′tə fī), *v.* bewilder purposely; puzzle.

myth (mith), *n.* **1.** legend, usually attempting to account for something in nature. **2.** any invented story. **3.** an imaginary person or thing. [< NL < LL < Gk. *mythos* word, story]

na ive (nä ēv′), *adj.* simple in nature; like a child; artless.

nat ty (nat′i), *adj.* neatly smart in dress or appearance; trim and tidy.

nat u ral ize (nach′ə rəl īz *or* nach′rəl īz), *v.* **1.** admit (a foreigner) to citizenship. **2.** introduce and make at home in another country: *The English oak has become naturalized in parts of Massachusetts.* —**nat′u ral i za′tion,** *n.*

neb u lous (neb′ū ləs), *adj.* **1.** hazy; vague; confused. **2.** cloudlike. [< L *nebulosus* < *nebula* mist]

ne pen the (ni pen′thi), *n.* **1.** drug supposed to bring forgetfulness of sorrow. **2.** anything that does this.

nice (nīs), *adj.* **1.** pleasing; agreeable. **2.** exact; precise: *a nice ear for music.* **3.** minute; fine: *a nice distinction.* **4.** requiring care, skill, or tact: *a nice problem.* **5.** fastidious; dainty: *nice in his eating.* **6.** proper; suitable.

ni ce ty (nī′sə ti), *n.* **1.** exactness; delicacy. **2.** a fine point; detail. **3.** daintiness, refinement.

non com bat ant (non′kəm bat′ənt *or* non kom′bə-tənt), *n.* person who is not a fighter in the army or navy in time of war; civilian. Surgeons, nurses, chaplains, etc., are noncombatants even though with the army.

non com mit tal (non′kə mit′əl), *adj.* not committing oneself; not saying yes or no. [Am.E]

non con duc tor (non′kən duk′tər), *n.* substance that does not readily conduct heat, electricity, etc.

non con form ist (non′kən fôr′mist), *n.* person who refuses to conform to an established church or commonly accepted beliefs.

nos tal gic (nos tal′jik), *adj.* homesick. —**nos tal′-gia,** *n.*

no to ri e ty (nō′tə rī′ə ti), *n.* **1.** ill fame. **2.** being widely known. **3.** a well-known person.

no to ri ous (nō tô′ri əs *or* no tō′ri əs), *adj.* **1.** having a bad reputation. **2.** well-known. [< Med.L *notorius* < L *notus* known]

➔ **Notorious** means well-known for offensive reasons: *a notorious cheat;* **famous** means well-known for accomplishment or excellence: *a famous writer or aviator.*

nov ice (nov′is), *n.* beginner.

nox ious (nok′shəs), *adj.* very harmful; poisonous.

nub bin (nub′ən), *n.* **1.** a small lump or piece. **2.** U.S. a small or imperfect ear of corn.

nu cle us (nü′kli əs *or* nū′kli əs), *n.* **1.** a beginning to which additions are to be made. **2.** a central part or thing around which other parts or things are collected.

ob du rate (ob′dü rit *or* ob′dū rit), *adj.* **1.** stubborn. **2.** hardened in feelings or heart: *an obdurate criminal.* —**Syn.** **1.** obstinate.

o bei sance (ō bā′səns *or* ō bē′səns), *n.* deep bow expressing respect.

ob e lisk (ob′ə lisk), *n.* a tapering, four-sided shaft of stone with a top shaped like a pyramid.

o bit u ar y (ō bich′ü er′i), *n.* a notice of death, often with a brief account of the person's life.

ob lit er ate (ə blit′ər āt), *v.* blot out; destroy.

ob liv i on (ə bliv′i ən), *n.* **1.** condition of being entirely forgotten. **2.** forgetfulness. [< L *oblivio, -onis* < *oblivisci* forget, originally, even off, smooth out < *ob-* + *levis* smooth]

---

hat, āge, cāre, fär; let, ēqual, tėrm; it, īce; hot, ōpen, ôrder; oil, out; cup, put, rüle, ūse; ch, child; ng, long; th, thin; ᴛʜ, then; zh, measure; ə represents *a* in about, *e* in taken, *i* in pencil, *o* in lemon, *u* in circus.

ob scure (əb skūr′), *adj.* **1.** not clearly expressed: *an obscure passage in a book.* **2.** not expressing meaning clearly: *an obscure style of writing.* **3.** not well known: *an obscure little village.* **4.** not easily discovered; hidden: *an obscure meaning.* **5.** not distinct; not clear: *an obscure form.* **6.** dark; dim: *an obscure corner.* **7.** indefinite: *an obscure vowel.* —*v.* hide from view; make obscure; dim; darken: *Clouds obscure the sun.* [< OF < L *obscurus* < *ob-* up + *scur-* cover] —**ob scure′ly,** *adv.* —**ob scure′ness,** *n.*
Syn. *adj.* **1. Obscure, vague, ambiguous** mean not clearly expressed or understood. **Obscure** suggests that the meaning of something is hidden from the understanding, because it is not clearly or plainly expressed or the reader lacks the knowledge necessary for understanding: *Much legal language is obscure.* **Vague** means not definite, too general in meaning or statement or not clearly and completely thought out: *No one can be sure what a vague statement means.* **Ambiguous** means so expressed that either of two meanings is possible: *"She kissed her when she left" is an ambiguous statement.* **3.** unknown, undistinguished, humble. **4.** secluded. **6.** dusky.
ob se qui ous (əb sē′kwi əs), *adj.* polite or obedient from hope of gain or from fear; slavish.
ob tru sive (əb trü′siv), *adj.* inclined to put forward (ideas, opinions, etc.) unasked and unwanted.
oc ta vo (ok tā′vō *or* ok tä′vō), *n.* the page size of some books, usually about 6 by 9 inches. —*adj.* having this size. [< Med.L *in octavo* in an eighth]
oc to roon (ok′tə rün′), *n.* person having one eighth Negro blood or ancestry.
of fi ci ate (ə fish′i āt), *v.* perform the duties of any office.
o gle (ō′gəl), *v.* look at with desire; make eyes at. —*n.* an ogling look.
om niv o rous (om niv′ə rəs), *adj.* **1.** eating both animal and vegetable food: *Man is an omnivorous animal.* **2.** taking in everything; all-devouring: *An omnivorous reader reads all kinds of books.* [< L *omnivorus* < *omnis* all + *vorare* eat greedily]
on slaught (on′slôt′ *or* ôn′slôt′), *n.* a vigorous attack.
o pac i ty (ō pas′ə ti), *n.* **1.** quality or condition that does not permit light to show through. **2.** quality of being obscure or unclear in meaning. [< L *opacitas* < *opacus* dark]
op pres sive (ə pres′iv), *adj.* **1.** harsh; severe; unjust. **2.** hard to bear; burdensome. —**op pres′sive ly,** *adv.*
op u lent (op′ū lənt), *adj.* **1.** wealthy; rich. **2.** abundant. [< L *opulens, -entis* < *ops* power, resources]
or bit (ôr′bit), *n.* **1.** path of any heavenly body about another heavenly body. **2.** regular course of life or experience.
or chis (ôr′kis), *n.* orchid.
or deal (ôr dēl′ *or* ôr′dēl), *n.* a severe test or experience. [OE *ordæl* judgment] —**Syn.** trial.
ord nance (ôrd′nəns), *n.* **1.** cannon; artillery. **2.** military weapons of all kinds.
or ner y (ôr′nər i), *adj. Chiefly U.S. Informal or Dialect.* **1.** inferior. **2.** mean in disposition. [contraction of *ordinary*]
or tho dox (ôr′thə doks), *adj.* **1.** generally accepted, especially in religion. **2.** approved by custom; usual.
os ten si ble (os ten′sə bəl), *adj.* apparent; pretended; professed: *Her ostensible purpose was borrowing sugar, but she really wanted to see the new furniture.* [< F < L *ostendere* show < *ob-* toward + *tendere* stretch] —**os ten′si bly,** *adv.*
os ten ta tious (os′ten tā′shəs), *adj.* **1.** done for display; intended to attract notice. **2.** showing off. —**os ten-ta′tion,** *n.* —**Syn.** **1.** showy, gaudy.
o ver bear ing (ō′vər bãr′ing), *adj.* inclined to dictate; forcing others to one's own will.
o ver plus (ō′vər plus), *n.* surplus; too great an amount.
o ver reach (ō′vər rēch′), *v.* **1.** reach over. **2.** reach too far. **3.** get the better of by cunning. **4.** cheat.
o ver step (ō′vər step′), *v.* go beyond; exceed.

pa cif ic (pə sif′ik), *adj.* **1.** loving peace; not warlike. **2.** calm; quiet.
pack et (pak′it), *n.* a boat that carries mail, passengers, and goods.
pa dro ne (pä drō′nā *for 1;* pə drō′ni *for 2*), *n.* **1.** *Italian.* master; boss. **2.** man who controls and supplies Italian laborers.
pag eant ry (paj′ənt ri), *n.* **1.** a splendid show; gorgeous display; pomp. **2.** mere show; empty display.
pall (pôl), *n.* **1.** a heavy cloth of black, purple, or white velvet spread over a coffin, a hearse, or a tomb. **2.** a dark, gloomy covering: *A thick pall of smoke shut out the sun from the city.* [OE *pæll* < L *pallium* cloak]
pal lid (pal′id), *adj.* lacking color; pale: *a pallid complexion.* [< L *pallidus*]
pal lor (pal′ər), *n.* paleness. [< L]
pal met to (pal met′ō), *n.* any of several kinds of palm trees with fan-shaped leaves.
pal sied (pôl′zid), *adj.* **1.** paralyzed. **2.** shaking.
pal sy (pôl′zi), *n.* paralysis.
pan a ce a (pan′ə sē′ə), *n.* cure-all.
pan o ply (pan′ə pli), *n.* **1.** a complete suit of armor. **2.** complete equipment or covering: *an Indian in panoply of paint and feathers.*
pan o ram a (pan′ə ram′ə *or* pan′ə rä′mə), *n.* **1.** a wide, unbroken view of a surrounding region. **2.** a complete survey of some subject. **3.** picture unrolled a part at a time and made to pass continuously before the spectators.
pa paw (pô′pô), *n.* **1.** a small North American tree bearing oblong, yellowish, edible fruit with many beanlike seeds. **2.** this fruit. [Am.E; < Sp. *papaya*]
pa rade (pə rād′), *n.* **1.** procession. **2.** a great show or display. **3.** a military display or review of troops.
par a dox (par′ə doks), *n.* statement that may be true but seems to say two opposite things: *"More haste, less speed" is a paradox.*
par a gon (par′ə gon), *n.* model of perfection.
par ley (pär′li), *n.* **1.** conference. **2.** an informal discussion with an enemy about terms of surrender, etc.
par o dy (par′ə di), *n.* **1.** a humorous imitation of a serious writing. **2.** a poor imitation.
pa role (pə rōl′), *n.* **1.** conditional release from prison or jail before the full term is served. **2.** conditional release of soldiers from service while peace terms are being arranged. —*v.* put on parole; release on parole.
par ox ysm (par′ək siz əm), *n.* **1.** a severe, sudden attack. **2.** fit; convulsion: *a paroxysm of rage.*
par ry (par′i), *v.* ward off; turn aside; evade (a thrust, weapon, question, etc.). —*n.* act of parrying; avoiding.
par si mo ni ous (pär′sə mō′ni əs), *adj.* too economical; stingy. —**Ant.** generous, liberal, lavish.
par si mo ny (pär′sə mō′ni), *n.* stinginess.
par son age (pär′sən ij), *n.* house provided for a minister by a church.
par ti al i ty (pär′shi al′ə ti *or* pär shal′ə ti), *n.* **1.** a favoring of one more than another or others. **2.** fondness: *Children often have a partiality for candy.*
par ti san (pär′tə zən), *n.* a strong supporter of a person, party, or cause; one whose support is based on feeling rather than on reasoning. —*adj.* of a partisan.
pas ty (pas′ti), *n. Esp. Brit.* pie filled with game, fish.
pat ent (pā′tənt *or* pat′ənt), *adj.* **1.** evident; plain: *It is patent that cats dislike dogs.* **2.** open.
path o log i cal (path′ə loj′ə kəl), *adj.* dealing with diseases or concerned with diseases.
pa thos (pā′thos), *n.* quality in speech, writing, music, events, or a scene that arouses a feeling of pity or sadness.
pa tri arch (pā′tri ärk), *n.* **1.** father and ruler of a family or tribe. **2.** an old man deserving respect. [< L < Gk. *patriarches* < *patria* family + *archos* leader] —**pa tri-ar′chal,** *adj.*

< = from, derived from, taken from; cf., compare; dial., dialect; dim., diminutive; lang., language; pp., past participle; ppr., present participle; pt., past tense; ult., ultimately; var., variant; ? = possibly.

pat ri mo ny (pat′rə mō′ni), *n.* **1.** property inherited from one's father or ancestors. **2.** anything handed on to a person from his ancestors.

pa tron age (pā′trən ij *or* pat′rə nij), *n.* **1.** regular business given by customers. **2.** favor, encouragement, or support given by a patron. **3.** condescending favor: *an air of patronage.* **4.** power to give jobs or favors: *the patronage of a Congressman.* **5.** political jobs or favors.

pa tron ize (pā′trən īz *or* pat′rən īz), *v.* **1.** be a regular customer of. **2.** act as a patron toward; support or protect. **3.** treat in a condescending way.

peak ed (pēk′id), *adj.* sickly in appearance; faint or weak; thin.

pea vey (pē′vi), *n.* a strong stick that is tipped with an iron or steel point and has a hinged hook near the end. Lumbermen use peaveys in managing logs. [named after J. *Peavey*, the inventor]

pe cu ni ar y (pi kū′ni er′i), *adj.* of or having to do with money; in the form of money.

ped a gogue (ped′ə gog *or* ped′ə gôg), *n.* **1.** teacher. **2.** a narrow-minded teacher. [< OF < L < Gk. *paidagogos* < *pais* boy + *agogos* leader] —**ped′a gog′i cal**, *adj.*

ped ant (ped′ənt), *n.* person who displays his knowledge in an unnecessary or tiresome way.

peer (pēr), *n.* **1.** person of the same rank, ability, etc., as another; equal. **2.** man who has a title; man who is high and great by birth or rank. [< OF *per* < L *par* equal]

pelf (pelf), *n.* money or riches, thought of as bad or degrading. [< OF *pelfre* spoils]

pend ing (pen′ding), *prep.* **1.** while waiting for; until: *Pending his return, let us get everything ready.* **2.** during.

per am bu la tor (pər am′bū lā′tər), *n.* a small carriage in which a baby is pushed about.

per di tion (pər dish′ən), *n.* **1.** loss of one's soul and the joys of heaven. **2.** hell. **3.** utter loss.

per en ni al (pər en′i əl), *adj.* **1.** lasting through the whole year: *a perennial stream.* **2.** lasting for a very long time; enduring: *the perennial beauty of the hills.* **3.** having underground parts that live more than two years: *perennial garden plants.* —*n.* a perennial plant. Roses are perennials. [< L *perennis* lasting < *per-* through + *annus* year] —**per en′ni al ly**, *adv.*

per fi dy (pėr′fə di), *n.* a breaking faith; base treachery. [< L *perfidia*, ult. < *per-* + *fides* faith] —**per fid′i ous**, *adj.*

per force (pər fôrs′ *or* pər fōrs′), *adv.* by necessity.

pe riph er y (pə rif′ər i), *n.* an outside boundary.

per me ate (pėr′mi āt), *v.* **1.** spread through the whole of; pass through; soak through. **2.** penetrate. [< L *permeare* < *per* through + *meare* to pass]

per se vere (pėr′sə vēr′), *v.* continue steadily in doing something hard; persist. [< F < L *perseverare* < *per-* very + *severus* strict]

per sim mon (pər sim′ən), *n.* **1.** a North American tree with a plumlike fruit. **2.** fruit of this tree.

per son al i ty (pėr′sə nal′ə ti), *n.* **1.** qualities of a person. **2.** remark made about or against some person: *Personalities are not in good taste in general conversation.*

per son nel (pėr′sə nel′), *n.* persons employed in any work, business, or service.

per sua sion (pər swā′zhən), *n.* **1.** a persuading: *All our persuasion was of no use; she would not come.* **2.** firm belief. **3.** religious belief; creed.

per ti nac i ty (pėr′tə nas′ə ti), *n.* great persistence; holding firmly to a purpose, action, or opinion.

per turb (pər tėrb′), *v.* disturb greatly; make uneasy or troubled: *Mother was much perturbed by my illness.* [< L *perturbare* < *per-* thoroughly + *turbare* confuse] —**Syn.** excite, trouble, distress.

pe rus al (pə rüz′əl), *n.* a reading.

pes ti lent (pes′tə lənt), *adj.* **1.** often causing death. **2.** harmful to morals; destroying peace. **3.** troublesome.

pe ter (pē′tər), *v.* *U.S. Informal.* **peter out**, gradually come to an end; fail; give out.

pe tite (pə tēt′), *adj.* of small size; tiny, especially with reference to a woman or girl. [< F *petite*, fem. of *petit* little]

pet ty of fi cer (pet′i of′ə sər), *n.* a noncommissioned officer in the navy.

pet u lant (pech′ù lənt), *adj.* subject to little fits of bad temper; irritable over trifles.

phan tasm (fan′taz əm), *n.* thing seen only in one's imagination; unreal fancy: *the phantasms of a dream or fever.*

phan tas ma go ric (fan taz′mə gôr′ik), *adj.* of or pertaining to a shifting scene of real things, illusions, imaginary fancies, deceptions, and the like.

phe nom e non (fə nom′ə non), *n.*, *pl.* **-na** *or* (*esp. for def. 2*) **-nons.** **1.** fact, event, or circumstance that can be observed. **2.** something or someone extraordinary or remarkable.

phil an throp ic (fil′ən throp′ik), *adj.* charitable; benevolent.

phil o soph ic (fil′ə sof′ik), *adj.* wise; calm; reasonable. —**phil′o soph′i cal ly**, *adv.*

pho bi a (fō′bi ə), *n.* an insane fear arising from an unhealthy or gloomy state of mind.

phos pho res cent (fos′fə res′ənt), *adj.* showing light without burning or by very slow burning that seems not to give out heat.

phys i og no my (fiz′i og′nə mi *or* fiz′i on′ə mi), *n.* **1.** kind of features or type of face one has; one's face. **2.** the general aspect or looks of a countryside, a situation, etc.

phys i ol o gist (fiz′i ol′ə jist), *n.* expert in the science dealing with the normal functions of living things or their organs.

phy sique (fə zēk′), *n.* bodily structure.

pier glass (pēr′ glas′), *n.* a tall mirror.

pil lion (pil′yən), *n.* pad attached behind a saddle for a person to sit on.

pi lot house (pī′lət hous′), *n.* an enclosed place on the deck of a ship, sheltering the steering wheel and helmsman.

pique (pēk), *n.* wounded pride. —*v.* **1.** wound the pride of. **2.** arouse; stir up. **3.** **pique oneself on** *or* **upon**, feel proud about. [< F *piquer* prick, sting < *pic* a pick (< Gmc.)]

plash y (plash′i), *adj* marshy; wet.

pla toon (plə tün′), *n.* **1.** group of soldiers acting as a unit. **2.** a group.

plau si ble (plô′zə bəl), *adj.* **1.** appearing true, reasonable, or fair. **2.** apparently worthy of confidence but often not really so: *a plausible liar.*

pneu mat ic (nü mat′ik *or* nū mat′ik), *adj.* **1.** filled with air. **2.** worked by air.

po et as ter (pō′it as′tər), *n.* writer of rather bad poetry.

pol i tic (pol′ə tik), *adj.* **1.** wise in looking out for one's own interests. **2.** scheming; crafty. **3.** political.

pom mel (pum′əl *or* pom′əl), *n.* **1.** part of a saddle that sticks up at the front. **2.** a rounded knob on the hilt of a sword, dagger, etc.

pom pos i ty (pom pos′ə ti), *n.* **1.** pompous quality. **2.** pompous show of self-importance.

pom pous (pom′pəs), *adj.* **1.** trying to seem magnificent; fond of display; acting proudly; self-important. **2.** (of language, style, etc.) too lofty; not simple.

poop (püp), *n.* deck at the stern above the ordinary deck.

poor (pür), *adj.* **1.** having few things or nothing; needy. **2.** not good in quality; lacking something needed: *poor soil, poor health.* **3.** scanty. **4.** needing pity; unfortunate. **5.** not favorable: *a poor chance for recovery.* [< OF *povre* < L *pauper*]

port (pôrt *or* pōrt), *n.* the left side of a ship, when facing the bow. —*adj.* on the left side of a ship. See **aft** for diagram.

---

hat, āge, cāre, fär; let, ēqual, tėrm; it, ĭce; hot, ōpen, ôrder; oil, out; cup, pùt, rüle, ūse; ch, child; ng, long; th, thin; ŦH, then; zh, measure; ə represents *a* in about, *e* in taken, *i* in pencil, *o* in lemon, *u* in circus.

por tent (pôr′tent *or* pōr′tent), *n.* sign; omen.

port hole (pôrt′hōl′ *or* pōrt′hōl′), *n.* **1.** an opening in a ship's side to let in light and air. **2.** opening in a ship, wall, etc., through which to shoot.

port man teau (pôrt man′tō *or* pōrt man′tō), *n. Esp. Brit.* a stiff, oblong traveling bag with two compartments opening like a book. [< F *portmanteau* < *porter* carry + *manteau* mantle]

post (pōst), *n.* an established system for carrying letters, papers, packages, etc.; the mail. —*v.* **1.** send by post; mail. **2.** travel with post horses or by post chaise. **3.** travel with speed; hasten. —*adv.* by post; speedily. [< F < Ital. < L *posita*, fem. pp. of *ponere* place]

post boy (pōst′boi′), *n.* **1.** boy or man who carries mail. **2.** man who rides one of the horses drawing a carriage.

post chaise (pōst′ shāz′), a hired carriage formerly used for traveling.

po ta tion (pō tā′shən), *n.* **1.** act of drinking. **2.** a drink, especially of alcoholic liquor.

po ten cy (pō′tən si), *n.* **1.** power; strength: *the potency of an argument, the potency of a drug.* **2.** power to develop. [< L *potentia* < *potens*. See POTENT.]

po tent (pō′tənt), *adj.* **1.** powerful; having great power: *a potent remedy for a disease.* **2.** exercising great moral influence: *His good deeds had a potent effect on his comrades.* [< L *potens, -entis,* ppr. of unrecorded OL *potere* be powerful] —**po′tent ly,** *adv.* —**Syn. 1.** mighty, strong.

po ten ti al i ty (pə ten′shi al′ə ti), *n.* **1.** possibility as opposed to actuality; hidden power or capacity not yet developed. **2.** a possibility.

pow wow (pou′wou′), *n.* **1.** council of or with American Indians. **2.** *U.S. Informal.* any conference or meeting. [Am.E; < Algonquian]

pre car i ous (pri kãr′i əs), *adj.* **1.** dependent on the will or pleasure of another. **2.** dangerous; risky: *A soldier leads a precarious life.* [< L *precarius,* originally, obtainable by entreaty, ult. < *prex* prayer] —**Ant. 2.** certain, secure, safe, sure.

prec e dent (pres′ə dənt), *n.* case that may serve as an example or reason for a later case.

pre cip i tate (pri sip′ə tāt *or* pri sip′ə tit), *adj.* **1.** very hurried; sudden. **2.** with great haste and force; plunging or rushing; rash. [< L *praecipitare* < *praeceps* headlong] —**pre cip′i tate ly,** *adv.*

pre co cious (pri kō′shəs), *adj.* **1.** developed earlier than usual: *This very precocious child could read well at the age of four.* **2.** developed too early. [< L *praecox, -ocis,* ult. < *prae-* before (its time) + *coquere* ripen] —**pre co′cious ly,** *adv.* —**pre co′cious ness,** *n.*

pre ëmpt (pri empt′), *v.* **1.** secure before someone else can: *The cat had preëmpted the comfortable chair.* **2.** settle on (land) with the right to buy it before others.

pre fect (prē′fekt), *n.* the chief administrative official of a government district of France.

prel a cy (prel′ə si), *n.* **1.** position of clergymen of high rank. **2.** church government by these clergymen.

pre med i tate (prē med′ə tāt), *v.* consider; plan beforehand.

prem ise (prem′is), *n.* **1.** in logic, a statement assumed to be true and used to draw a conclusion. **2. premises,** *pl.* house or building with its grounds.

pre mo ni tion (prē′mə nish′ən *or* prem′ə nish′ən), *n.* a forewarning. [< earlier F < L *praemonitio, -onis,* ult. < *prae-* before + *monere* warn]

pre mon i to ry (pri mon′ə tô′ri *or* pri mon′ə tō′ri), *adj.* giving warning beforehand.

pre pos ses sion (prē′pə zesh′ən), *n.* favorable feeling or opinion formed beforehand; bias.

pre pos ter ous (pri pos′tər əs *or* pri pos′trəs), *adj.* contrary to nature, reason, or common sense; absurd; senseless: *It would be preposterous to shovel coal with a teaspoon.*

[< L *praeposterus* in reverse order, ult. < *prae-* before + *post* after] —**pre pos′ter ous ly,** *adv.* —**pre pos′ter ous ness,** *n.* —**Syn.** foolish, silly.

pre rog a tive (pri rog′ə tiv), *n.* right or privilege that nobody else has.

pres tige (pres tēzh′ *or* pres′tij), *n.* reputation, influence, or distinction based on what is known of one's abilities, achievements, opportunities, associations, etc.

pre ten sion (pri ten′shən), *n.* **1.** claim: *The young prince has pretensions to the throne.* **2.** a putting forward of a claim.

prev a lent (prev′ə lənt), *adj.* widespread; in general use; common: *Colds are prevalent in the winter.* [< L *praevalens, -entis,* ppr. of *praevalere* prevail]

pre var i cate (pri var′ə kāt), *v.* turn aside from the truth in speech or act; lie.

pri mal (prī′məl), *adj.* **1.** of early times; first. **2.** chief; fundamental. [< Med.L *primalis* < L *primus* first]

pri ma ry (prī′mer′i *or* prī′mə ri), *n.* a meeting or gathering of the voters of a political party in an election district to choose candidates for office.

prime (prīm), *v.* supply (a gun) with powder.

pri me val (prī mē′vəl), *adj.* **1.** of or having to do with the first age or ages, especially of the world. **2.** ancient. [< L *primaevus* early in life < *primus* first + *aevum* age]

pro ba tion (prō bā′shən), *n.* trial or testing of conduct, character, qualifications, etc.

prob lem at i cal (prob′ləm at′ə kəl), *adj.* having the nature of a problem; doubtful; uncertain; questionable.

pro cras ti nate (prō kras′tə nāt), *v.* put things off until later; delay; delay repeatedly. [< L *procrastinare,* ult. < *pro-* forward + *cras* tomorrow] —**Syn.** defer, postpone.

prod i gal (prod′ə gəl), *adj.* **1.** wasteful. **2.** abundant. —*n.* person who is wasteful or extravagant; spendthrift.

pro di gious (prə dij′əs), *adj.* **1.** very great; huge; vast: *The ocean contains a prodigious amount of water.* **2.** wonderful. [< L *prodigiosus* < *prodigium* prodigy, omen]

pro fan i ty (prə fan′ə ti), *n.* use of profane language; swearing.

pro fi cien cy (prə fish′ən si), *n.* knowledge; expert skill.

prof it eer (prof′ə tēr′), *n.* person who makes an unfair profit by taking advantage of public necessity.

pro fu sion (prə fū′zhən), *n.* great abundance.

prog nos ti cate (prog nos′tə kāt), *v.* predict from facts; forecast. —**prog nos′ti ca′tion,** *n.*

pro jec tile (prə jek′təl), *n.* object that can be thrown, hurled, or shot, such as a stone or a bullet.

pro jec tion (prə jek′shən), *n.* **1.** part that sticks out. **2.** a throwing or casting forward. **3.** a forming of projects or plans.

pro le tar i an (prō′lə tãr′i ən), *n.* person belonging to the lowest class in economic and social rank.

pro lif ic (prə lif′ik), *adj.* **1.** producing offspring abundantly: *prolific animals.* **2.** producing much: *a prolific tree, garden, imagination, or writer.*

pro lix i ty (prō lik′sə ti), *n.* too great length; tedious length of speech or writing.

prom on to ry (prom′ən tô′ri *or* prom′ən tō′ri), *n.* a high point of land extending from the coast into the water.

pron to (pron′tō), *adv. U.S. Informal.* promptly; right away. [Am.E; < Sp. *pronto* < L *promptus* prompt]

pro pen si ty (prə pen′sə ti), *n.* inclination.

prop er (prop′ər), *adj.* **1.** correct; fitting. **2.** respectable. **3.** *Archaic.* good-looking; handsome. [< OF < L *proprius*]

pro pi ti ate (prə pish′i āt), *v.* prevent or reduce the anger of; win the favor of; appease. —**pro pi′ti a′tion,** *n.*

pro pi ti a to ry (prə pish′i ə tô ri *or* prə pish′i ə tō′ri), *adj.* intended to propitiate; making propitiation: *a propitiatory offering.*

pro pi tious (prə pish′əs), *adj.* favorable: *propitious weather for a picnic.*

< = from, derived from, taken from; cf., compare; dial., dialect; dim., diminutive; lang., language; pp., past participle; ppr., present participle; pt., past tense; ult., ultimately; var., variant; ?=possibly.

pro pri e ty (prə prī′ə ti), *n.* **1.** quality of being proper; fitness. **2.** proper behavior: *Propriety demands that a boy tip his hat to a lady whom he knows.* **3. proprieties,** *pl.*, conventional standards or requirements of proper behavior. [< L *proprietas* < *proprius* proper] —**Syn. 1.** suitability. **2.** decorum, decency.

pro pul sion (prə pul′shən), *n.* **1.** a driving forward or onward. **2.** a forward-driving force or impulse. [< F]

pro sa ic (prō zā′ik), *adj.* like prose; matter-of-fact; ordinary; not exciting.

pro sce ni um (prō sē′ni əm), *n.* **1.** part of the stage in front of the curtain. **2.** curtain and the framework that holds it.

pros e cute (pros′ə kūt), *v.* **1.** bring before a court of law. **2.** carry out; follow up: *prosecute an inquiry into the reasons for the company's failure.*

pro spec tus (prə spek′təs), *n.* a printed statement describing and advertising something.

pro tract (prō trakt′), *v.* **1.** draw out; lengthen in time: *protract a visit.* **2.** slide out; thrust out; extend. [< L *protractus,* pp. of *protrahere* < *pro-* forward + *trahere* drag] —**pro tract′ed,** *adj.*

pro ver bi al (prə vėr′bi əl), *adj.* well-known: *the proverbial loyalty of dogs.*

prov i dence (prov′ə dəns), *n.* **1.** God's care and help. **2.** care for the future. **3. Providence,** God.

prov i den tial (prov′ə den′shəl), *adj.* fortunate.

pro vi sion al (prə vizh′ən əl), *adj.* for the time being; temporary: *a provisional agreement, a provisional governor.*

pro voc a tive (prə vok′ə tiv), *adj.* **1.** irritating; vexing. **2.** tending to call forth action, thought, etc.

pru dence (prü′dəns), *n.* **1.** wise thought before acting; good judgment. **2.** good management; economy.

pru den tial (prü den′shəl), *adj.* of, marked by, or showing prudence.

pseu do nym (sü′də nim), *n.* name used by an author instead of his real name.

psy cho log i cal (sī′kə loj′ə kəl), *adj.* **1.** of the mind. Memories and dreams are psychological facts. **2.** of psychology.

psy chol o gist (sī kol′ə jist), *n.* person skilled or trained in psychology.

psy chol o gy (sī kol′ə ji), *n.* the science of mind. Psychology tries to explain why people act, think, and feel as they do. [< NL *psychologia* < Gk. *psyche* soul, mind + *-logos* treating of]

psy cho path ic (sī′kə path′ik), *adj.* **1.** of or having to do with mental diseases. **2.** likely to become insane.

pud ding stone (pud′ing stōn′), *n.* rock composed of pebbles held together by cementlike stone.

pu er ile (pū′ər əl), *adj.* childish.

pum mel (pum′əl), *v.* beat; beat with the fists.

pun cheon (pun′chən), *n.* **1.** a large cask for liquor. **2.** slab of timber with the face roughly smoothed.

punc til i ous (pungk til′i əs), *adj.* **1.** very careful and exact: *A nurse should be punctilious in obeying the doctor's orders.* **2.** paying strict attention to details of conduct and ceremony. —**punc til′i ous ly,** *adv.*

pun gent (pun′jənt), *adj.* **1.** sharply affecting the organs of taste and smell. **2.** sharp; biting.

pur ga to ry (pėr′gə tô′ri *or* pėr′gə tō′ri), *n.* any condition or place of temporary suffering or punishment.

pur loin (pėr loin′), *v.* steal.

purse (pėrs), *v.* draw together; press into folds.

purs lane (pėrs′lān *or* pėrs′lən), *n.* a common plant that has small, yellow flowers and small, thick leaves.

pur sy (pėr′si), *adj.* **1.** shortwinded or puffy. **2.** fat.

pu ta tive (pū′tə tiv), *adj.* supposed; reputed.

pu trid (pū′trid), *adj.* **1.** rotten. **2.** thoroughly corrupt.

pyg my (pig′mi), *n.* a very small person; dwarf. —*adj.* very small.

quad rant (kwod′rənt), *n.* one of four equal segments of a circle used to locate objects on a navigation chart.

quad ri lat er al (kwod′rə lat′ər al), *n.* a plane figure having four sides and four angles.

qua drille (kwə dril′), *n.* **1.** a square dance for four couples that has five parts or movements. **2.** music for it.

quad roon (kwod rün′), *n.* person having one fourth Negro blood.

quaff (kwäf, kwaf, *or* kwôf), *v.* drink in large draughts; drink freely.

quag mire (kwag′mīr′ *or* kwog′mīr′), *n.* soft, muddy ground; boggy or miry place.

quail (kwāl), *v.* be afraid; shrink back in fear.

quar ry (kwôr′i *or* kwor′i), *n.* **1.** animal or person chased in a hunt; game. **2.** anything hunted or eagerly pursued.

quar ter mas ter (kwôr′tər mas′tər *or* kwôr′tər mäs′tər), *n.* in the navy, an officer on a ship who has charge of the steering, the compasses, signals, etc.

quar to (kwôr′tō), *n.* **1.** the page size (usually about 9 by 12 inches) of some books. **2.** book having this size.

quer u lous (kwer′ú ləs *or* kwer′ū ləs), *adj.* **1.** complaining; faultfinding. **2.** fretful. —**Syn. 2.** petulant.

queue (kū), *n.* **1.** braid of hair hanging down from the back of the head. **2.** a long line of people, automobiles, etc.

quire (kwīr), *n.* 24 or 25 sheets of paper of the same size and quality.

quirk (kwėrk), *n.* a peculiar way of acting.

quirt (kwėrt), *n.* a riding whip with a short, stout handle and a lash of braided leather. [Am.E; < Am.Sp. *cuarta,* originally, a long whip]

quiz zi cal (kwiz′ə kəl), *adj.* **1.** odd; queer; comical. **2.** that suggests making fun of others; teasing.

rab id (rab′id), *adj.* **1.** fanatical; violent. **2.** furious; raging. **3.** having rabies; mad: *a rabid dog.*

rac ism (rās′iz əm), *n.* prejudice in favor of certain races.

rac y (rās′i), *adj.* **1.** vigorous; lively. **2.** having an agreeably peculiar taste or flavor.

ra di a tion (rā′di ā′shən), *n.* **1.** act or process of giving out light, heat, etc. **2.** process of spreading like rays from a center.

rad i cal (rad′ə kəl), *adj.* **1.** going to the root; fundamental. **2.** favoring extreme changes or reforms; extreme. —*n.* **1.** person who favors extreme changes or reforms. **2.** anything fundamental or basic. [< LL *radicalis* < L *radix* root] —**rad′i cal ly,** *adv.* —**rad′i cal ness,** *n.*

rail (rāl), *v.* complain bitterly.

ram bunc tious (ram bungk′shəs), *adj.* *U.S. Slang.* **1.** wild and uncontrollable; unruly. **2.** noisy and violent.

ran cor (rang′kər), *n.* bitter resentment or ill will. —**Syn.** animosity.

rang y (rān′ji), *adj.* slender and long-limbed.

rank (rangk), *adj.* **1.** large and coarse. **2.** growing richly. **3.** having a strong, bad smell or taste. **4.** strongly marked; extreme: *rank ingratitude.*

ran sack (ran′sak), *v.* **1.** search thoroughly through. **2.** rob; plunder.

ra pi er (rā′pi ər), *n.* a light sword used for thrusting.

rare (rār), *adj.* **1.** seldom seen or found. **2.** not happening often: *a rare event.* **3.** unusually good or great: *Edison had rare powers as an inventor.* **4.** thin; not dense: *rare gases.* [< L *rarus*]
Syn. 1. Rare, scarce mean not often or easily found. **Rare** describes something uncommon or unusual at any time because it seldom occurs or only a few specimens exist, and often suggests excellence or value above the ordinary: *The Gutenberg Bible is a rare book.* **Scarce** describes something usually or formerly common or plentiful, but not existing or produced in large enough numbers or quantities at the present time: *Water is becoming scarce in some parts of the country.* **2.** infrequent, uncommon.

---

hat, āge, cãre, fär; let, ēqual, tèrm; it, īce; hot, ōpen, ôrder; oil, out; cup, put, rüle, ūse; ch, child; ng, long; th, thin; ŦH, then; zh, measure; ə represents *a* in about, *e* in taken, *i* in pencil, *o* in lemon, *u* in circus.

rar e fy (râr′ə fī), *v.* **1.** make less dense. **2.** become less dense. **3.** purify. [< L *rarefacere* < *rarus* rare + *facere* make]

rate (rāt), *v.* scold.

raths kel ler (räts′kel′ər), *n.* restaurant selling alcoholic drinks.

rau cous (rô′kəs), *adj.* hoarse; harsh-sounding.

rav ish ment (rav′ish mənt), *n.* rapture; ecstasy.

re cede (ri sēd′), *v.* **1.** go backward. **2.** withdraw: *He receded from the agreement.*

re cess (*n.* rē′ses for 1, ri ses′ or rē′ses for 2 and 3; *v.* ri ses′), *n.* **1.** time during which work stops: *There will be a short recess before the next meeting.* **2.** part in a wall set back from the rest; alcove; niche. **3.** an inner place or part; quiet, secluded place: *the recesses of a cave, the recesses of one's secret thoughts.* —*v.* **1.** take a recess. **2.** put in a recess; set back. **3.** make a recess in. [< L *recessus* a retreat < *recedere* recede] —**Syn.** *n.* **1.** respite.

re cip ro cal (ri sip′rə kəl), *adj.* **1.** in return: *Although I gave him many presents, I had no reciprocal gifts from him.* **2.** mutual: *reciprocal liking, reciprocal distrust.*

rec i proc i ty (res′ə pros′ə ti), *n.* **1.** mutual action. **2.** a mutual exchange, especially, an exchange of special privileges in regard to trade between two countries.

rec on noi ter (rek′ə noi′tər or rē′kə noi′tər), *v.* approach and examine in order to learn something; survey (the enemy, the enemy's strength or position, a region, etc.) in order to gain information for military purposes.

rec re ant (rek′ri ənt), *n.* **1.** coward. **2.** traitor.

rec ti tude (rek′tə tüd or rek′tə tūd), *n.* upright conduct or character; honesty; righteousness.

re cur rent (ri kėr′ənt), *adj.* occurring again; repeated.

re dress (*v.* ri dres′; *n.* rē′dres or ri dres′), *v.* set right; remedy. —*n.* a setting right; relief: *Any man deserves redress if he has been injured unfairly.*

re flec tive (ri flek′tiv), *adj.* thoughtful.

ref use (ref′ūs), *n.* useless stuff; waste; rubbish. —*adj.* rejected as worthless or of little value; discarded.

re gen er ate (ri jen′ər āt), *v.* **1.** give a new and better spiritual life to. **2.** improve the moral condition of; put new life and spirit into. **3.** reform. —**re gen′er a′tion,** *n.*

reg i men ta tion (rej′ə men tā′shən), *n.* **1.** formation into organized or uniform groups. **2.** a making uniform. **3.** subjection to control. In time of war there may be regimentation of our work, play, food, and clothing.

reg u lar (reg′ū lər), *adj.* **1.** fixed by custom or rule; usual; normal: *Six o'clock was his regular hour of rising.* **2.** coming, acting, or done again and again at the same time: *Saturday is a regular holiday.* **3.** steady; habitual. **4.** even in size, spacing, or speed; well-balanced: *regular features, regular teeth.* [< L *regularis* < *regula*]

re im burse (rē′im bėrs′), *v.* pay back. You reimburse a person for expenses made for you.

re ju ve nes cent (ri jü′və nes′ənt), *adj.* making young again.

rel a tive (rel′ə tiv), *adj.* **1.** related or compared to each other. **2.** relative to, **a.** about; concerning. **b.** in proportion to. **3.** depending for meaning on a relation to something else. *East* is a relative term.

re lent less (ri lent′lis), *adj.* without pity; unyielding; harsh: *The storm raged with relentless fury.*

rel e van cy (rel′ə vən si), *n.* being relevant.

rel e vant (rel′ə vənt), *adj.* bearing upon or connected with the matter in hand; to the point: *Be sure your questions are relevant to the subject being discussed.*

rem i nis cent (rem′ə nis′ənt), *adj.* **1.** recalling past events, etc.: *reminiscent talk.* **2.** awakening memories of something else; suggestive. —**rem′i nis′cent ly,** *adv.*

re mon strance (ri mon′strəns), *n.* protest; complaint.

re morse less (ri môrs′lis), *adj.* pitiless; cruel.

re mu ner a tive (ri mū′nər ā′tiv), *adj.* paying; profitable.

ren ais sance (ren′ə säns′, ren′ə säns, or ri nā′səns), *n.* **1.** revival; new birth. **2. the Renaissance, a.** the great revival of art and learning in Europe during the 14th, 15th, and 16th centuries. **b.** period of time when this revival occurred. **c.** style of art, architecture, etc., of this period. [< F *renaissance* < *renaître* be born again, ult. < L *renasci* → **renaissance.** The word is capitalized when it refers to the period of history: *art of the Renaissance.* It is not capitalized when it refers to a revival: *a renaissance of interest in old-time melodramas.*

ren coun ter (ren koun′tər), *n.* **1.** a hostile meeting; conflict; battle; duel. **2.** a chance meeting.

ren dez vous (rän′də vü), *n.* **1.** an appointment to meet at a fixed place or time. **2.** a meeting place; gathering place. —*v.* meet at a rendezvous. [< F *rendezvous* < *rendez vous* betake yourself!]

ren e gade (ren′ə gād), *n.* traitor.

re pair (ri pâr′), *v.* go (to a place).

rep a ra tion (rep′ə rā′shən), *n.* a giving of satisfaction or compensation for wrong or injury done.

rep er toire (rep′ər twär or rep′ər twôr), *n.* the list of plays, operas, parts, pieces, etc., that a company, an actor, a musician, or a singer is prepared to perform.

rep er to ry (rep′ər tô′ri or rep′ər tō′ri), *n.* **1.** repertoire. **2. repertory company,** a theatrical organization which prepares a number of plays and produces them in rotation.

re plete (ri plēt′), *adj.* abundantly supplied; filled. [< L *repletus,* pp. of *replere* < *re-* again + *plere* fill]

re pub li can ism (ri pub′lə kən iz′əm), *n.* form of government managed by representatives elected by the citizens.

res in ous (rez′ə nəs), *adj.* containing resin, a sticky substance that flows from certain plants and trees.

re solved (ri zolvd′), *adj.* **1.** firm in purpose. **2.** broken up into its original parts.

res o nance (rez′ə nəns), *n.* **1.** resounding quality. **2.** a reinforcing and prolonging of sound by reflection or by vibration of other objects.

res pite (res′pit), *n.* **1.** time of relief and rest; lull: *A thick cloud brought a respite from the glare of the sun.* **2.** a putting off; delay, especially, in carrying out a sentence of death; reprieve. [< OF < VL *respectus* delay < LL *respectus* expectation < L *respectare* wait for]

res tive (res′tiv), *adj.* **1.** restless; uneasy. **2.** hard to manage. **3.** refusing to go ahead. —**res′tive ness,** *n.*

ret i cent (ret′ə sənt), *adj.* disposed to keep silent or say little; not speaking freely; reserved in speech. [< L *reticens, -entis,* ppr. of *reticere* keep silent < *re-* back + *tacere* be silent] —**ret′i cent ly,** *adv.* —**Syn.** reserved, taciturn.

ret i cule (ret′ə kūl), *n.* a woman's small handbag.

ret i nue (ret′ə nü or ret′ə nū), *n.* a group of attendants or followers.

re trac tion (rē′trak′shən), *n.* a withdrawing of a promise, statement, etc.

re trac tor (ri trak′tər), *n.* a surgical instrument or appliance for drawing back an organ or part.

re ver ber ate (ri vėr′bər āt), *v.* echo back: *His voice reverberates from the high ceiling.*

re ver ber a tion (ri vėr′bėr ā′shən), *n.* **1.** echoing back of sound; echo. **2.** reflection of light or heat.

rev er ie (rev′ər i), *n.* dreamy thoughts.

re vert (ri vėrt′), *v.* turn back to former beliefs, outlooks, conditions, etc.

re vile (ri vīl′), *v.* call bad names; abuse with words. —**re vil′ing,** *adj.*

rhap so dy (rap′sə di), *n.* utterance or writing marked by extravagant enthusiasm.

rhet o ric (ret′ə rik), *n.* **1.** art of using words in speaking or writing. **2.** mere display in language.

rhe tor i cal (ri tôr′ə kəl or ri tōr′ə kəl), *adj.* **1.** of or having to do with rhetoric. **2.** pertaining to a question

---

< = from, derived from, taken from; cf., compare; dial., dialect; dim., diminutive; lang., language; pp., past participle; ppr., present participle; pt., past tense; ult., ultimately; var., variant; ? = possibly.

spo rad ic (spə rad′ik), *adj.* appearing or happening at intervals in time: *sporadic outbreaks.*

spread-ea gle (spred′ē′gəl), *adj.* **1.** having the form of an eagle with wings spread out. **2.** *U.S.* boastful.

springe (sprinj), *n.* snare for catching small game.

sprock et (sprok′it), *n.* **1.** one of a set of projections on the rim of a wheel, arranged so as to fit into the links of a chain. **2.** wheel made with sprockets.

spy glass (spī′glas′ or spī′gläs′), *n.* a small telescope.

squal id (skwol′id), *adj.* filthy; degraded; wretched.

squat ter (skwot′ər), *n.* **1.** person who settles on another's land without right. **2.** person who settles on public land to acquire ownership of it. **3.** person, animal, etc., that crouches or squats.

squeam ish (skwēm′ish), *adj.* **1.** easily shocked. **2.** too particular. **3.** easily turned sick.

squire (skwīr), *v.* escort (a lady).

stac ca to (stə kä′tō), in music: —*adj.* with breaks between the successive tones; disconnected; abrupt.

stag ger (stag′ər), *v.* **1.** sway or reel (from weakness, a heavy load, or drunkenness). **2.** become unsteady. —*n.* **1.** a swaying; reeling. **2. staggers,** a nervous disease of horses, cattle, etc., that makes them stagger or fall suddenly.

stag hound (stag′hound′), *n.* one of a breed of hounds resembling the foxhound but larger, used for hunting deer.

stance (stans), *n.* position of the feet of a player when making a stroke in golf or other games.

stanch (stänch or stanch), *adj.* **1.** firm; strong: *stanch walls.* **2.** loyal; steadfast: *a stanch friend.*

stand-by (stand′bī′), *n.* person or thing that can be relied upon; chief support; ready resource.

star board (stär′bərd, stär′bôrd, or stär′bōrd), *adj.* on the right side of a ship when facing forward. See *aft* for diagram.

stark (stärk), *adj.* **1.** downright; complete: *That fool is talking stark nonsense.* **2.** stiff: *The dog lay stark in death.* **3.** harsh; stern; **4.** *Archaic.* strong; sturdy. —*adv.* **1.** entirely; completely; **2.** in a stark manner. [OE *stearc* stiff, strong] —**stark′ly,** *adv.*

stat ics (stat′iks), *n.* **1.** branch of mechanics that deals with objects as held in balance by the forces acting on them. **2.** forces that hold objects together in resistance to forces that tend to separate them.

sta tion (stā′shən), *n.* **1.** place to stand in; place which a person is appointed to occupy in the performance of some duty. **2.** a regular stopping place: *a railroad station.* **3.** social position; rank. [< L *statio, -onis* < *stare* stand]

sta tion ar y en gine (stā′shən ãr i en′jən), *n.* a steam engine that is used in a permanent position.

stat u esque (stach′ü esk′), *adj.* like a statue in dignity, formal grace, or classic beauty. —**stat′u esque′ly,** *adv.*

stay (stā), *n.* **1.** a support; prop; brace. **2. stays,** *pl.* corset.

stealth y (stel′thi), *adj.* secret; sly. —**Syn.** furtive, sneaking.

steer age (stēr′ij), *n.* part of a passenger ship occupied by passengers traveling at the cheapest rate.

ster e o scope (ster′i ə skōp′ or stēr′i ə skōp′), *n.* instrument through which two pictures of the same object or scene are viewed, one by each eye. The object or scene thus viewed appears to have three dimensions, as it would if really seen.

ste ril i ty (stə ril′ə ti), *n.* **1.** inability to produce offspring. **2.** inability to produce results.

ster ling (ster′ling), *n.* sterling silver or things made of it. —*adj.* **1.** of standard quality; containing 92.5 per cent pure silver. **2.** genuine; excellent.

stern (stern), *n.* the hind part of a ship or boat. See *aft* for diagram.

stig ma (stig′mə), *n., pl.* **stig mas** or **stig ma ta.** **1.** mark of disgrace; stain or reproach on one's reputation.

2. a distinguishing mark or sign. **3.** the part of the pistil of a plant that receives the pollen.

stile (stīl), *n.* step or steps for getting over a fence.

stip u la tion (stip′ū lā′shən), *n.* **1.** agreement. **2.** condition in an agreement or bargain.

stodg y (stoj′i), *adj.* **1.** dull or uninteresting. **2.** heavy: *stodgy food.* **3.** heavily built: *a stodgy person.*

stol id (stol′id), *adj.* hard to arouse; not easily excited; showing no emotion. —**Syn.** stodgy.

stom ach er (stum′ək ər), *n.* a part of a woman's dress covering the stomach and chest.

stout (stout), *adj.* **1.** fat and large. **2.** firm; strong. **3.** brave; bold. —*n.* a strong, dark-brown beer.

strait (strāt), *n.* **1.** a narrow channel connecting two larger bodies of water. **2. straits,** *pl.* difficulty; distress.

strap ping (strap′ing), *adj. Informal.* tall, strong, and healthy: *a fine strapping girl.*

strat e gist (strat′ə jist), *n.* person trained or skilled in planning and management.

strip ling (strip′ling), *n.* youth; lad.

stump speak er (stump′ spēk′ər), *n.* person who makes speeches in various places during a political campaign.

stu pe fac tion (stü′pə fak′shən or stū′pə fak′shən), *n.* **1.** dazed or senseless condition. **2.** overwhelming amazement.

stu por (stü′pər or stū′pər), *n.* **1.** loss or lessening of the power to feel. **2.** intellectual or moral numbness. [< L *stupor* < *stupere* be dazed]

styl ize (stīl′īz), *v.* conform to a particular style.

sua vi ty (swä′və ti or swav′ə ti), *n.* smoothly agreeable quality of behavior; smooth politeness.

sub ac id (sub as′id), *adj.* slightly acid.

sub ju gate (sub′jü gāt), *v.* subdue; conquer. [< L *subjugare* < *sub-* under + *jugum* yoke]

sub stan tial ly (səb stan′shəl i), *adv.* as to the main or essential points.

suc co tash (suk′ə tash), *n.* corn and beans cooked together. [Am.E; < Algonquian]

suc cu lence (suk′ū ləns), *n.* juiciness.

suc cu lent (suk′ū lənt), *adj.* **1.** juicy: *a succulent fruit.* **2.** interesting; not dull. [< L *succulentus* < *succus* juice]

suc cumb (sə kum′), *v.* **1.** give way; yield: *He succumbed to temptation and stole the money.* **2.** die. **3. succumb to,** die of. [< L *succumbere* < *sub-* down + *cumbere* lie]

suf fer ance (suf′ər əns or suf′rəns), *n.* **1.** permission given only by a failure to object. **2.** patient endurance.

suf frage (suf′rij), *n.* **1.** a vote. **2.** the right to vote.

suf fu sion (sə fū′zhən), *n.* flush of color.

sul fa nil a mide (sul′fə nil′ə mīd or sul′fə nil′ə mid), *n.* a white, crystalline substance, derived from coal tar and used in treating various infections.

sul tri ness (sul′tri nes), *n.* quality of being hot, close, and moist.

sun dry (sun′dri), *adj.* several; various.

su per an nu at ed (sü′pər an′ū āt′id), *adj.* **1.** too old for work, service, etc. **2.** old-fashioned; out-of-date.

su per flu ous (sù pėr′flü əs), *adj.* **1.** more than is needed: *In writing telegrams omit superfluous words.* **2.** needless. [< L *superfluus,* ult. < *super-* over + *fluere* flow]

su per nu mer ar y (sü′pər nü′mər er′i or sü′pər nü′mər er′i), *adj.* more than the usual or necessary number.

su per scrip tion (sü′pər skrip′shən), *n.* **1.** a writing above, on, or outside of something. **2.** something written above or on the outside. **3.** address on a letter or parcel.

sup pos i ti tious (sə poz′ə tish′əs), *adj.* **1.** pretended; false; not genuine. **2.** assumed; supposed.

sur cease (sèr sēs′), *n. Archaic.* end; ceasing. [< OF *sursis,* pp. of *surseoir* refrain < L *supersedere*]

sur cin gle (sèr′sing gəl), *n.* strap around a horse's body to keep a saddle, blanket, or pack in place.

---

hat, āge, cãre, fär;   let, ēqual, tèrm;   it, īce;   hot, ōpen, ôrder;   oil, out;   cup, pút, rüle, ūse;   ch, child;
ng, long;   th, thin;   ŦH, then;   zh, measure;   ə represents *a* in about, *e* in taken, *i* in pencil, *o* in lemon, *u* in circus.

sur feit (sèr′fit), *n.* too much; excess. —*v.* overfeed.

sur mise (sər mīz′ *or* sèr′mīz), *n.* formation of an idea with little or no evidence; a guessing.

sus cep ti bil i ty (sə sep′tə bil′ə ti), *n.* **1.** quality or state of being easily influenced by feelings or emotions. **2.** quality of being open to certain treatment.

su ture (sü′chər), *n.* seam formed in sewing up a wound.

swale (swāl), *n.* a low, wet piece of land; low place.

swathe (swāᵮH), *v.* wrap up closely or fully.

sweep (swēp), *n.* **1.** dignified motion: *the sweep of verse* **2.** a curve, bend. **3.** a long oar.

sym bol ic (sim bol′ik), *adj.* **1.** used as a symbol: *A lily is symbolic of purity.* **2.** of a symbol; expressed by a symbol; using symbols. —**sym bol′i cal ly,** *adv.*

sym pho ny (sim′fə ni), *n.* **1.** an elaborate musical composition for an orchestra. **2.** harmony of sounds **3.** harmony of colors.

syn tax (sin′taks), *n.* study of sentence structure.

tab leau (tab′lō), *n., pl.* **-leaux** or **-leaus. 1.** a striking scene; picture. **2.** representation of a picture, statue, scene, etc., by a person or group posing in appropriate costume. [< F *tableau,* dim. of *table* table]

tac it (tas′it) *adj.* **1.** unspoken; silent. **2.** implied or understood without being openly expressed. [< L *tacitus,* pp. of *tacere* to be silent] —**tac′it ly,** *adv.*

tac i turn (tas′ə tèrn), *adj.* speaking very little. [< L *taciturnus* < *tacitus* tacit. See TACIT.] —**Syn.** reserved, reticent. —**Ant.** talkative, garrulous.

tac i tur ni ty (tas′ə tèr′nə ti), *n.* habit of keeping silent; disinclination to talk much.

tac ti cal (tak′tə kəl), *adj.* **1.** of tactics; concerning tactics. **2.** having to do with the disposal of military or naval forces in action against an enemy.

tac tics (tak′tiks), *n.* **1.** art or science of disposing military or naval forces in action. **2.** procedures to gain advantage or success; methods.

tal ly (tal′i), *n.* anything on which a score or account is kept. —*v.* **1.** mark on a tally; count up. **2.** label; tag. **3.** agree; correspond: *My count of votes tallies with yours.*

tan gent (tan′jənt), *n.* a sudden change from one course of action or thought to another.

tan ta lize (tan′tə līz), *v.* torment or tease by keeping something desired in sight but out of each, or by holding out hopes that are repeatedly disappointed. [< *Tantalus,* a legendary Greek king who was punished in Hades by having to stand in high water, over which were fruit-laden branches. Whenever he tried to drink or eat, the water or fruit withdrew from his reach]

tan ta mount (tan′tə mount), *adj.* equal in value, force, significance, etc.

tarn (tärn), *n.* a small lake or pool.

tar sal (tär′səl), *adj.* of or having to do with the tarsus, a bone or cartilage in the ankle.

taut (tôt), *adj.* **1.** tightly drawn; tense. **2.** tidy.

tav ern (tav′ərn), *n.* **1.** saloon. **2.** inn.

tax (taks), *v.* **1.** put a tax on. **2.** lay a heavy burden on; be hard for. **3.** reprove; accuse: *The teacher taxed Tom with having neglected his work.* [< L *taxare* estimate, compute, originally, censure]

tech ni cal (tek′nə kəl), *adj.* **1.** of or having to do with a mechanical or industrial art or applied science. **2.** of or having to do with the special facts of a science or art. **3.** treating a subject technically; using technical terms: *a technical lecture.*

tech ni cal i ty (tek′nə kal′ə ti), *n.* a technical matter, point, detail, term, expression, etc.

tech ni cian (tek nish′ən), *n.* person experienced in the technicalities of a subject.

tech nol o gy (tek nol′ə ji), *n.* the science of the industrial arts: *He studied engineering at a school of technology.*

teem (tēm), *v.* be full (of); abound; swarm: *The swamp teemed with mosquitoes.* [OE *tēman* < *tēam* progeny]

te mer i ty (tə mer′ə ti), *n.* reckless boldness; rashness.

tem po rize (tem′pə rīz), *v.* **1.** evade immediate action or decision in order to gain time, avoid trouble, etc. **2.** fit one's acts to the time or occasion.

te na cious (ti nā′shəs), *adj.* **1.** holding fast: *a person tenacious of his rights.* **2.** stubborn. **3.** able to remember.

ten u i ty (ten ū′ə ti *or* ti nü′ə ti), *n.* thinness; slightness.

ten ure (ten′yər), *n.* **1.** a holding; possessing. **2.** length of time of holding or possessing. **3.** conditions, terms, etc., on which anything is held or occupied.

ter ma gant (tèr′mə gənt), *n.* a violent, quarreling, scolding woman.

ter rain (te rān′ *or* ter′ān), *n.* land; tract of land, especially considered as to its natural features. [< F *terrain,* ult. < L *terra* earth]

ter res tri al (tə res′tri əl), *adj.* **1.** of the earth. **2.** living on the ground; not in the air or water or in trees. **3.** worldly; earthly. [< L *terrestris* < *terra* earth]

ter ror ism (ter′ər iz əm), *n.* condition of fear and submission produced by frightening people.

tes sel late (*v.* tes′ə lāt; *adj.* tes′ə lit *or* tes′ə lāt), *v.* make of small squares or blocks, or in a checkered pattern. —*adj.* made in small squares or blocks or in a checkered pattern.

tes ty (tes′ti), *adj.* easily irritated; impatient. [< AF *testif* headstrong < *teste* head < L *testa* pot] —**Syn.** petulant, cross.

the o ret ic (thē′ə ret′ik), *adj.* planned or worked out in the mind, not from experience.

there at (ᵮHãr at′), *adv.* **1.** when that happened; at that time. **2.** because of that. **3.** at that place; there.

tho rax (thô′raks *or* thō′raks), *n.* **1.** part of the body between the neck and the abdomen. **2.** the second division of an insect's body, between the head and the abdomen.

thorn (thôrn), *n.* **1.** a sharp-pointed growth on a stem or branch of a tree or plant. **2.** tree that has thorns on it.

thrall dom (thrôl′dəm), *n.* bondage; slavery.

throe (thrō), *n.* **1.** a violent pang; great pain. **2.** throes, *pl.* **a.** anguish; agony. **b.** a desperate struggle.

thun der strick en (thun′dər strik′ən), *adj.* astonished; amazed.

thwart (thwôrt), *v.* oppose and defeat. —*n.* seat across a boat, on which a rower sits.

till er (til′ər), *n.* bar or handle used to turn the rudder in steering a boat.

Canoe with thwarts

tim ber (tim′bər), *n.* **1.** wood for building and making things. **2.** essential quality or essence of a person: *Men of heroic timber built this country.*

tin der box (tin′dər boks′), *n.* box for holding tinder, flint, and steel for making a fire.

tine (tīn), *n.* a sharp projecting point or prong: *the tines of a fork.*

tip pler (tip′lər), *n.* a habitual drinker of alcoholic liquor.

ti tan ic (tī tan′ik), *adj.* having great size, strength, or power: *a titanic mountain, titanic energy.*

toil (toil), *n.* Often, **toils,** *pl.* net; snare.

tol er ant (tol′ər ənt), *adj.* **1.** willing to let other people do as they think best; willing to endure beliefs and actions of which one does not approve: *The United States government is tolerant toward all religious beliefs.* **2.** able to endure or resist the action of a drug, poison, etc. —**tol′er ant ly,** *adv.*

tome (tōm), *n.* book, especially a large, heavy book.

ton al (tōn′əl), *adj.* of or having to do with tones or tone.

< = from, derived from, taken from; cf., compare; dial., dialect; dim., diminutive; lang., language; pp., past participle; ppr., present participle; pt., past tense; ult., ultimately; var., variant; ? = possibly.

top er (tōp′ər), *n.* person who drinks a great deal of alcoholic liquor.

tor pid (tôr′pid), *adj.* **1.** dull; inactive; sluggish. **2.** not moving or feeling. **3.** numb. [< L *torpidus* < *torpere* be numb] —**tor′pid ly,** *adv.*

tor toise shell (tôr′təs shel′), *n.* the mottled yellow-and-brown shell of a turtle or tortoise. Tortoise shell is much used for combs and ornaments.

tor toise-shell (tôr′təs shel′), *adj.* **1.** made of tortoise shell. **2.** having the colors of a tortoise shell.

to tal i tar i an ism (tō′tal ə tãr′i ən iz′əm), *n.* system under which a government is controlled by one political party exclusively and no other political groups are permitted to exist.

tote (tōt), *v. U.S. Informal.* carry; haul.

touch stone (tuch′stōn′), *n.* **1.** a black stone used to test the purity of gold or silver by the color of the streak made on the stone by rubbing it with the metal. **2.** any means of testing; a test.

tract (trakt), *n.* **1.** a little book or pamphlet on a religious subject. **2.** any little book or pamphlet.

trac ta ble (trak′tə bəl), *adj.* easily managed or controlled; easy to deal with. —**Syn.** docile.

tran scend ent (tran sen′dənt), *adj.* surpassing ordinary limits; excelling; superior; extraordinary.

tran sient (tran′shənt), *adj.* **1.** passing soon; fleeting; not lasting. **2.** passing through and not staying long: *a transient guest.*

trans mute (trans mūt′ *or* tranz mūt′), *v.* change from one nature, substance, or form into another: *to transmute water power into electric power.* [< L *transmutare* < *trans-* thoroughly + *mutare* change]

tran spire (tran spīr′), *v.* **1.** take place; happen. **2.** leak out; become known.

→ **transpire.** The meaning happen, take place, was once regarded as not being in good use, but *transpire* is fairly common in cultivated English in this sense today.

trans port (*v.* trans pôrt′ *or* trans pōrt′; *n.* trans′pôrt *or* trans′pōrt), *v.* **1.** carry from one place to another. **2.** carry away by strong feeling: *She was transported with joy by the good news.* —*n.* **1.** a carrying from one place to another. **2.** a strong feeling.

trea dle (tred′əl), *n.* lever worked by the foot to operate a machine.

tread mill (tred′mil′), *n.* **1.** apparatus to turn something by having a person or animal walk on the moving steps of a wheel or of a sloping, endless belt. **2.** any wearisome or monotonous round of work or life.

trem or (trem′ər), *n.* **1.** an involuntary shaking or trembling. **2.** thrill of emotion or excitement.

trem u lous (trem′ū ləs), *adj.* **1.** trembling; quivering. **2.** timid; fearful. [< L *tremulus* < *tremere* tremble] —**trem′u lous ly,** *adv.* —**trem′u lous ness,** *n.* —**Syn.** **1.** shaking, vibrating.

trench er (tren′chər), *n.* a wooden platter on which meat was formerly served and carved.

trep i da tion (trep′ə dā′shən), *n.* fear; fright.

tres tle (tres′əl), *n.* **1.** frame used as a support. **2.** a supporting framework for carrying railroad tracks across a gap.

trite (trīt), *adj.* worn out by use; commonplace: *a trite phrase or saying.*

troll (trōl), *n.* in Scandinavian folklore, an ugly dwarf or giant living underground in caves, etc.

truck ing (truk′ing), *n.* exchange; barter.

trump er y (trump′ər i *or* trump′ri), *n.* something showy but without value; rubbish. —*adj.* showy but without value; trifling; worthless. [< F *tromperie* < *tromper* deceive]

trun cheon (trun′chən), *n.* **1.** stick; club. **2.** staff of office or authority.

trun dle bed (trun′dəl bed′), *n.* a low bed moving on small wheels or casters. It can be pushed under a regular bed when not in use.

truss (trus), *v.* **1.** tie; fasten. **2.** support (a roof, bridge, etc.) with trusses. **3.** *Archaic.* fasten or tighten (a garment). —*n.* beams or other supports connected to support a roof, bridge, etc.

tuf taf fe ta (tuf taf′ə tə), *n.* a silk fabric with a raised pattern.

tur bid (tėr′bid), *adj.* **1.** muddy; thick; not clear: *a turbid river.* **2.** confused; disordered: *a turbid imagination.*

tur moil (tėr′moil), *n.* commotion; disturbance: *Six robberies in one night put the village in a turmoil.*

tweak (twēk), *v.* seize and pull with a jerk and twist.

type script (tīp′skript′), *n.* typewritten manuscript.

ul tra con serv a tive (ul′trə kən sėr′və tiv), *n.* member of a political group which opposes any changes in national institutions. —*adj.* extremely opposed to change.

ul tra re fine ment (ul′trə ri fīn′mənt), *n.* an unusual or excessive fineness of taste, manners, or language.

um ber-brown (um′bər broun′), *adj.* reddish-brown.

um bil i cus (um bil′ə kəs *or* um′bə lī′kəs), *n.* the navel.

un a bashed (un′ə basht′), *adj.* not embarrassed, ashamed, or awed.

un ac count a ble (un′ə koun′tə bəl), *adj.* **1.** that cannot be accounted for or explained. **2.** not responsible. —**Syn.** **1.** inexplicable.

un as sum ing (un′ə süm′ing), *adj.* modest; not putting on airs.

un budg ing (un budg′ing), *adj.* not moving in the least; firmly fixed.

un der bred (un′dər bred′), *adj.* of inferior breeding or manners; vulgar.

un de vi at ing (un dē′vi āt′ing), *adj.* not turning aside (from a way, course, rule, truth, etc.).

un du late (*v.* un′jù lāt *or* un′dū lāt; *adj.* un′jù lit, un′jù lāt, un′dū lit, *or* un′dū lāt), *v.* **1.** move in waves. **2.** have a wavy form or surface. —*adj.* wavy.

un err ing (un ėr′ing *or* un er′ing), *adj.* making no mistakes; exactly right. —**un err′ing ly,** *adv.*

un fet ter (un fet′ər), *v.* remove fetters from; unchain.

un flag ging (un flag′ing), *adj.* not drooping or failing.

un flecked (un flekt′), *adj.* not sprinkled with spots or patches of color, light, etc.

un flinch ing (un flin′ching), *adj.* not drawing back from difficulty, danger, or pain; firm; resolute.

un gain ly (un gān′li), *adj.* awkward; clumsy.

u ni corn (ū′nə kôrn), *n.* an imaginary animal like a horse, but having a single long horn in the middle of its forehead. [< L *unicornis* < *unus* one + *cornu* horn]

u nique (ū nēk′), *adj.* **1.** having no like or equal; being the only one of its kind. **2.** *Informal.* rare; unusual. [< F < L *unicus*] —**u nique′ly,** *adv.* —**u nique′ness,** *n.*

→ **unique.** In formal usage *unique* means having no like or equal and therefore cannot be compared. In informal usage it has become generalized to mean rare or unusual, and is often compared with *more* or *most* or modified by *very* or *rather: Her clothes are rather unique.*

un kempt (un kempt′), *adj.* **1.** not combed. **2.** neglected; untidy.

un mit i gat ed (un mit′ə gāt′id), *adj.* **1.** not softened or lessened: *unmitigated harshness.* **2.** absolute.

un nerve (un nėrv′), *v.* deprive of nerve or self-control.

un pal at a ble (un pal′it ə bəl), *adj.* distasteful; unpleasant. —**Syn.** unappetizing, unsavory.

un pre ten tious (un′pri ten′shəs), *adj.* modest.

un prin ci pled (un prin′sə pəld), *adj.* lacking good moral principles; bad.

un re lent ing (un′ri len′ting), *adj.* **1.** not yielding to feelings of kindness or compassion; merciless. **2.** not

---

hat, āge, cãre, fär; let, ēqual, tėrm; it, īce; hot, ōpen, ôrder; oil, out; cup, pût, rüle, ūse; ch, child; ng, long; th, thin; ŦH, then; zh, measure; ə represents *a* in about, *e* in taken, *i* in pencil, *o* in lemon, *u* in circus.

slackening or relaxing in severity or determination. —Syn.
1. obdurate, relentless. See **inflexible.**

un re mit ting (un'ri mit'ing), *adj.* never ceasing.

un re quit ed (un'ri kwit'əd), *adj.* not paid for; for which no return has been made.

un ruf fled (un ruf'əld), *adj.* **1.** smooth. **2.** calm.

un sa vor y (un sā'vər i *or* un sāv'ri), *adj.* **1.** tasteless. **2.** morally unpleasant; offensive.

un seem ly (un sēm'li), *adj.* not suitable; improper.

un sheathe (un shēth'), *v.* draw (a sword, knife, or the like) from its case.

un spent (un spent'), *adj.* not tired or worn out; vigorous.

un war rant a ble (un wôr'ən tə bəl *or* un wor'ən tə-bəl), *adj.* not justifiable; illegal; improper.

un wield y (un wēl'di), *adj.* not easily handled or managed, because of size, shape, or weight; bulky and clumsy: *the unwieldly armor of knights, a fat unwieldly man.* —Syn. cumbersome.

un winc ing (un win'sing), *adj.* not drawing back or shrinking.

up braid (up brād'), *v.* find fault with; blame; reprove: *The captain upbraided his men for falling asleep.* —Syn. reproach.

ur gen cy (ėr'jən si), *n.* **1.** urgent character; need for immediate action or attention. **2.** insistence.

u su rer (ū'zhə rər), *n.* person who lends money at an extremely high or unlawful rate of interest.

u su ri ous (ū zhür'i əs), *adj.* taking extremely high or unlawful interest for the use of money.

u sur pa tion (ū'zər pā'shən *or* ū'sər pā'shən), *n.* the seizing and holding of the place or power of another by force or without right.

u til i tar i an (ū til'ə tār'i ən), *adj.* aiming at usefulness rather than beauty, style, etc.

ux o ri ous (uks ô'ri əs *or* uks ō'ri əs), *adj.* excessively or foolishly fond of one's wife. [< L *uxorius* < *uxor* wife]

va gar y (və gār'i *or* vā'gə ri), *n.* **1.** an odd fancy: *the vagaries of a dream.* **2.** odd action; freak.

vain glo ry (vān'glô'ri *or* vān'glō'ri), *n.* **1.** an extreme pride in oneself. **2.** worthless pomp or show.

val et (val'it *or* val'ā), *n.* **1.** servant who takes care of a man's clothes, helps him dress, etc. **2.** a similar servant in a hotel who cleans or presses clothes. —*v.* serve as a valet. [< F *valet,* var. of OF *vaslet*]

va lid i ty (və lid'ə ti), *n.* **1.** truth; soundness: *the validity of an argument.* **2.** legal soundness or force; being legally binding. **3.** effectiveness.

val or ous (val'ər əs), *adj.* valiant; brave; courageous. —**val'or ous ly,** *adv.* —**val'or ous ness,** *n.*

van[1] (van), *n.* the leading position in any procession or movement. [< *vanguard*]

van[2] (van), *n.* a covered truck or wagon. [< *caravan*]

var i e gat ed (vār'i ə gāt'id *or* vār'i gāt'id), *adj.* **1.** varied in appearance; marked with different colors: *variegated pansies.* **2.** having variety.

var mint (vär'mənt), *n.* *Informal* or *Dialect.* **1.** vermin. **2.** an objectionable animal or person.

vault ed (vôl'tid), *adj.* arched.

vaunt (vônt *or* vänt), *v., n.* boast. [< F < LL *vanitare* < *vanus* vain] —**vaunt'ing ly,** *adv.*

ve nal (vē'nəl), *adj.* **1.** willing to sell one's services or influence basely; open to bribes; corrupt: *Venal judges are a disgrace to a country.* **2.** influenced or obtained by bribery: *venal conduct.* [< L *venalis* < *venum* sale]

ven tril o quism (ven tril'ə kwiz əm), *n.* art or practice of speaking or uttering sounds with the lips nearly shut so that the voice may seem to come from some other source than the speaker. [< L *ventriloquus* ventriloquist < *venter* belly + *loqui* speak]

ve ra cious (və rā'shəs), *adj.* **1.** truthful. **2.** true. [< L *verax, -acis* < *verus* true]

ve rac i ty (və ras'ə ti), *n.* **1.** truthfulness. **2.** correctness. [< Med.L *veracitas* < L *verax.* See VERACIOUS.]

ver bal (vėr'bəl), *adj.* **1.** in words; of words: *A description is a verbal picture.* **2.** expressed in spoken words; oral: *a verbal promise.* [< L *verbalis* < *verbum* word, verb]

ver dant (vėr'dənt), *adj.* **1.** green: *a verdant valley.* **2.** inexperienced.

ver i est (ver'i ist), *adj.* utmost: *the veriest nonsense.*

ver min (vėr'mən), *n.* **1.** small animals that are troublesome or destructive. **2.** a vile, worthless person.

versed (vėrst), *adj.* experienced; practiced; skilled: *A doctor should be well versed in medical theory.*

ves per (ves'pər), *adj.* of evening.

vest ment (vest'mənt), *n.* **1.** garment. **2.** garment worn by a clergyman in performing sacred duties.

ves ture (ves'chər), *n.* clothing; garments.

vet er an (vet'ər ən *or* vet'rən), *n.* **1.** person who has served in the armed forces. **2.** person who has had much experience in some position, occupation, etc. [< L *veteranus* < *vetus* old]

vi and (vī'ənd), *n.* **1.** article of food. **2.** viands, *pl.* articles of choice food. [< OF *viande* < LL *vivenda* things for living < L *vivenda,* pl., to be lived]

vi brance (vī'brəns), *n.* state of being vibrant.

vi brant (vī'brənt), *adj.* **1.** vibrating. **2.** resounding.

vi ce ver sa (vī'sə vėr'sə *or* vīs vėr'sə), the other way round; conversely: *John blamed Harry, and vice versa (Harry blamed John).* [< L]

vict ual (vit'əl), *n.* Usually, **victuals,** *pl. Informal* or *Dialect.* food.

vin di cate (vin'də kāt), *v.* **1.** clear from suspicion, dishonor, hint, or charge of wrongdoing, etc. **2.** defend successfully against opposition.

vin di ca tion (vin'də kā'shən), *n.* a being vindicated.

vir tu al ly (vėr'chü əl i), *adv.* in effect, though not in name; actually; really.

vi sa (vē'zə), *n.* an official signature upon a passport or document, showing that it has been examined and approved. [< F *visa,* ult. < L *videre* see]

vis age (viz'ij), *n.* **1.** face. **2.** appearance. [< OF *visage* < *vis* face < L *visus* a look < *videre* see]

vis i bly (viz'ə bli), *adv.* so as to be visible; evidently.

vi sion (vizh'ən), *n.* **1.** power of seeing; sense of sight. **2.** power of perceiving by the imagination or by clear thinking. **3.** something seen in the imagination, in a dream, in one's thoughts, etc.: *The beggar had visions of great wealth.* [< L *visio, -onis* < *videre* see]

vi sion ar y (vizh'ən er'i), *adj.* **1.** not practical; dreamy. **2.** imaginary: *The visionary scene faded and John awoke.* —*n.* **1.** person who is not practical; dreamer. **2.** person who sees visions. —**vi'sion ar i ness,** *n.* —Syn. *adj.* **1.** fanciful. —Ant. *adj.* **1.** practical.

vis ta (vis'tə), *n.* **1.** view seen through a narrow opening or passage. **2.** such an opening or passage itself. **3.** a mental view: *Education should open up new vistas.* [< Ital. *vista,* ult. < L *videre* see]

vi va cious (vi vā'shəs *or* vī vā'shəs), *adj.* lively; sprightly; animated; gay.

vi vac i ty (vi vas'ə ti *or* vī vas'ə ti), *n.* liveliness.

vix en (vik'sən), *n.* **1.** a female fox. **2.** a bad-tempered or quarrelsome woman. [OE *fyxen* < *fox* fox]

vo cif er ate (vō sif'ər āt), *v.* cry out loudly or noisily.

vo cif er ous (vō sif'ər əs *or* vō sif'rəs), *adj.* loud and noisy; shouting; clamoring: *a vociferous person.*

vo lu mi nous (və lü'mə nəs), *adj.* **1.** forming, filling, or writing a large book or many books: *a voluminous report, a voluminous author.* **2.** of great size; very bulky.

vol un tar y (vol'ən ter'i *or* vol'ən tār'i), *adj.* of one's own free will; not forced. —**vol'un tar'i ly,** *adv.*

< = from, derived from, taken from;   cf., compare;   dial., dialect;   dim., diminutive;   lang., language;   pp., past participle;   ppr., present participle;   pt., past tense;   ult., ultimately;   var., variant;   ? = possibly.

vo lup tu ous (və lup′chü əs), *adj.* **1.** caring much for the pleasures of the senses. **2.** giving pleasure to the senses.

vo ra cious (və rā′shəs), *adj.* greedy in eating. —**vo rac′i ty,** *n.*

vul gar i ty (vul gar′ə ti), *n.* **1.** lack of refinement; lack of good breeding, manners, taste, etc.; coarseness. **2.** action, habit, speech, etc., showing vulgarity.

wag ger y (wag′ər i), *n.* **1.** a joking. **2.** joke.

wam pum (wom′pəm *or* wôm′pəm), *n.* beads made from shells, formerly used by American Indians as money and ornaments.

ward room (wôrd′rüm′ *or* wôrd′rum′), *n.* the living and eating quarters for all the commissioned officers on a warship except the commanding officer.

war i ly (wâr′ə li), *adv.* cautiously; carefully.

war ren (wôr′ən *or* wor′ən), *n.* **1.** piece of ground filled with burrows, where rabbits live or are raised. **2.** a crowded district or building.

was sail (wos′əl *or* was′əl), *n.* **1.** a drinking party; revel with drinking of healths. **2.** spiced ale or other liquor drunk at a wassail. **3.** a salutation meaning "Your health!"

wa ter ing place (wô′tər ing *or* wot′ər ing plās′), *n.* *Esp. Brit.* resort with springs containing mineral water.

wax (waks), *v.* **1.** grow bigger or greater. **2.** become.

whelp (hwelp), *n.* puppy or cub.

whim si cal (hwim′zə kəl), *adj.* having many odd notions or fancies; fanciful; odd. **whim′si cal ly,** *adv.*

whit low (hwit′lō), *n.* abscess on a finger or toe.

wil y (wīl′i), *adj.* crafty; cunning; sly.

wind jam mer (wind′jam′ər), *n.* *Informal.* **1.** a sailing ship. **2.** member of its crew. [Am.E]

wind ward (wind′wərd; *Nautical* win′dərd), *adj.* on the side toward the wind.

win some (win′səm), *adj.* charming; attractive.

wise (wīz), *n.* way; manner: *John is in no wise a student; he prefers sports and machinery.*

wit (wit), *v.* **1.** *Archaic.* know. **2.** **to wit,** that is to say; namely.

wot (wot), *v.* *Archaic.* know. "He wot" means "He knows."

wroth (rôth *or* roth), *adj.* angry. [OE *wrāth*]

wry (rī), *adj.* turned to one side; twisted: *She made a wry face to show her disgust.* —**wry′ly,** *adv.*

yard arm (yärd′ärm′), *n.* either end of a long, slender beam or pole used to support a square sail.

yawp (yôp *or* yäp), *Dialect or Informal.* —*v.* utter a loud, harsh cry. —*n.* a loud, harsh cry. [imitative]

yes man (yes′ man′), *n.* *Slang.* person who habitually agrees with his employer, superior officer, party, etc., without criticism.

yore (yôr *or* yōr), *adv.* **1.** **of yore,** of long ago; formerly; in the past. **2.** *Obsolete.* long ago; years ago.

zest (zest), *n.* **1.** keen enjoyment; relish: *The hungry man ate with zest.* **2.** a pleasant or exciting quality, flavor, etc.

zest ful (zest′fəl), *adj.* characterized by zest.

---

hat, āge, cãre, fär; let, ēqual, tėrm; it, īce; hot, ōpen, ôrder; oil, out; cup, pùt, rüle, ūse; ch, child; ng, long; th, thin; ᴛʜ, then; zh, measure; ə represents *a* in about, *e* in taken, *i* in pencil, *o* in lemon, *u* in circus.

For the pronunciation of certain foreign proper names the following symbols are used:

ʏ as in French **du** (dʏ).   Pronounce ʏ like ē with the lips rounded as for English ü in **rule.**
œ as in French **peu** (pœ).   Pronounce œ like ā with the lips rounded as for ō.
N as in French **bon** (bõN).   The N is not pronounced, but shows that the vowel before it is nasal.
 H as in German **ach** (aH).   Pronounce H like k without closing the breath passage.

A chil les (ə kil′ēz)
Ad a mic, Lou is (lü′is ad′ə mik)
Ad ams, Al the a (al thē′ə ad′əmz)
Ae ne id (ē nē′id)
Ae sop (ē′səp *or* ē′sop)
Ag a mem non (ag′ə mem′non)
A gra mon te, Ar is ti des (ar′is tī′dēz ä′grä môn′tā)
Al ham bra (al ham′brə)
Al len, Giles (jīlz′ al′ən)
Am a zon (am′ə zon *or* am′ə zən)
An dros, Sir Ed mund (sėr ed′mənd an′drōs)
An tae us (an tē′əs)
Ap pa ma tuck (ap′ə mat′ək; *Indian,* äp′pä mä′tuk)
Ap po mat tox (ap′ə mat′əks)
A ra pou la o po lus (ä′rä pü′lä ō pō′lús)
Ar ca di a (är kā′di ə)
Ar e thu sa (ar′i thü′zə *or* ar′i thü′sə)
Ar i el (är′i əl)
Assabet (as′ə bet)
A the na (ə thē′nə)
Aus ter litz (ôs′tər lits)
Az tec (az′tek)

Be atte (bā ät′)
Bel phe gor (bel′fē gôr)
Be nét, Ste phen Vin cent (stē′ven vin′sənt bi nā′)
Beu lah (bū′lə)
Bie den bach (bē′dən bäH)
Bo len cie cwcz (bō len′si wits)
Bonne ville (bon′vil)
Bril lon (brē yoN′)
Bul li vant (búl′i vənt)
Bun chick, Paul (pôl′ bun′chik)
Bush nell, Asa (ā′sə búsh′nəl)
But ter wick, Lige (līj′ but′ər wik)

Cab ot (kab′ət)
Ca fé No va (ka fā′ nō′və)
Cal a ve ras (kal′ə vä′rəs)
Cam pa nel la (käm′pä nel′lä)
Ca pa ho wo sick (kä′pä hō wō′sik)
Ca ra vel lo (kär ä vel′lō)
Char le magne (shär′lə mān)
Chau tau qua (shə tô′kwə)
Chee vy, Min i ver (min′ə vər chē′vi)
Chey enne (shī en′ *or* shī an′)
Chick a ha ma ni a (chik′ä hä mä′ni ä)
Chin gach gook (chin gäch′gúk)
Chi ro man cy (kī′rō man′si)
Chis holm (chiz′əm)
Cic e ro (sis′ə rō)
Cir ce (sėr′sē)
Clem ens, O ri on (ô rī′ən klem′ənz)
Com mu ni paw (kə mū′ni pô)
Con fu cius (kən fū′shəs)
Co per ni cus (kə pėr′nə kəs)
Cov e nant er (kuv′ə nən tər *or* kuv′ə nan′tər)
Crum paugh (krum′pô)
Cul len, Coun teé (koun′tē kul′ən)

D'Ar landes, Mar quis (mär kē′ där länd′)
De Gi ronne, Ey me ric (ā mə rēk′ də zhi ron′)
De La Cham bre (də lä shäN′brə)

Del mon i co, Lo ren zo Crist (lō ren′zō krist del-mon′i kō)
Des hetres, An toine (än twän′ dez etr′)
Deutsch, Ba bette (ba bet′ doitsch′)
Dic con (dik′ən)
D'In da gi né, Jean (zhän′ daN dä jē nā′)
Di rec to ri um In qui si to ri um (dē rek tō′ri əm in kwi zi tō′ri əm)
Drei ser, The o dore (thē′ə dōr drī′sər *or* drī′zər)
Dres den (drez′dən)
Du pin, C. Au guste (sā ō gʏst′ dʏ paN′)
Du quesne (dū kān′ *or* dü kān′)

El e a zar (el′i ā′zər)
E li (ē′lī)
E li jah (i lī′jə)
E piph a ny (i pif′ə ni)
Es me ral da (ez′mə ral′də)
Es pres so, Lou is (lü′is es pres′sō)
Eth el red (eth′əl red)
E ton (ē′tən)
Eu gé nie (œ zhā nē′)

Fa nel li (fä nel′li)
Fé ne lon (fān lôN′)
Fie gen baum (fē′gən boum′)
Flud, Rob ert (rob′ėrt flud′)
Franck, Cé sar (sā′zär′ frängk′)
Fran co, Fran cis co (fran sis′kō frang′kō)
Fran çois (fräN′ swä′)
Fre neau (fri nō′)
Freud (froid)
Fried man (frēd′mən)
Fuchs (fúHs)
Fun dy (fun′di)

Gael ic (gāl′ik)
Gal a te a (gal′ə tē′ə)
Gal i le o (gal′ə lē′ō *or* gal ə lā′ō)
Gan dhi, Ma hat ma (mə hät′mə *or* mə hat′mə gän′-di *or* gan′di)
Gas coigne (gəs koin′)
Ger man na (jėr man′ə)
Gi bral tar (jə brôl′tər)
Gid e on (gid′i ən)
Glynn (glin)
Goffe, Wil liam (wil′yəm gof′)
Gold berg, Ro chelle (rō shel′ gōld′bèrg)
Gor di an (gôr′di ən)
Gor di us (gôr′di us)
Gos nold (goz′nōld)
Gould and Cur ry (güld′ ənd kėr′i)
Gra na da (grə nä′də)
Graves end (grāvz′end′)
Green wich (grin′ij *or* gren′ich)
Guam (gwäm)

Ham or (ham′ər)
Has san (häs sän′)
Hei deg ger (hī′deg′ər)
He rod o tus (hə rod′ə təs)
Hes per i des (hes per′ə dēz)
Hi a wath a (hī′ə woth′ə *or* hē′ə woth′ə)
Hip poc ra tes (hi pok′rə tēz)

Ho bo ken (hō′bō kən)
Hol berg (hōl′berH)
Ho mer (hō′mər)
Hong Kong (hong′kong′ or hông′kông′)
Hor ace (hôr′is or hor′is)
Hume (hūm)

Ib sen, Hen rik (hen′rik ib′sən)
Ich a bod (ik′ə bod)
Ir o quois (ir′ə kwoi or ir′ə kwoiz)
Is ra fel (iz′rə fel)

Ja son (jā′sən)
Jer e mi ah (jer′ə mī′ə)
Jer i cho (jer′i kō)
Jo dy (jō′di)
Josh u a (josh′ü ə)
Jun to (jun′tō)

Ka le va la (kä′lā vä′lä)
Ka na ka Joe (kə nak′ə or kan′ə kə jō′)
Kant, Im man u el (i man′yů əl kant′; German känt′)
Kap lan, Hy man (hī′mən kap′lən)
Kee ney (kē′ni)
Ke hoe, Mike (mĭk′ kē′hō′)
Kil ken ny (kil ken′i)
Ki o was (kī′ō wāz or kī′ō wəz)
Klein (klīn)
Knowles (nōlz)
Koe nig, Sam (sam′ kā′nig)

La Guar di a, Fi o rel lo (fē′ō rel′ō lə gwär′di ə or lə gär′di ə)
La nier, Sid ney (sid′ni lə nir′ or lə nēr′)
La place, Pierre Si mon (pyer′ sē′môN′ lä pläs′)
Lar a mie (lar′ə mi)
Las A ni mas (läs ä′nē məs)
La zear, Jes se (jes′i lə zēr′)
Le Daim-Mose (lə daN′ mōz′)
Le Gar çon qui Bon di (lə gär sōN′ kē bôN di′)
Leigh, Joce lyn (jos′lin or jos′ə lin lē′)
Lil ien thal, Da vid (dā′vid lil′yen thäl)
Lind say, Va chel (vä′chəl lind′zi)
Lith u a ni an (lith′ü ā′ni ən)
Los Que ma dos (lōs kā mä′ᵮHōs)

Ma ca co (mə kä′kō)
Mach i a vel li (mak′i ə vel′i)
Mac Leish, Ar chi bald (ärch′ə bôld mək lēsh′)
Mac Lirr, Man a nan (man′ə nan mak lēr′)
Ma drid (mə drid′)
Ma gi (mä′jī or maj′ī)
Mag na li a Chris ti A mer i ca na (mag nā′li ə kris′ti ə mer′i kā′nə or ə mer′i ka′nə)
Ma lay a (mə lā′ə)
Mar quis, Don (don′ mär′kwis)
Mas sa po nax (mäs′sä pō′näks)
Mas sas soit (mas′ə soit′)
Math er, Cot ton (kot′ən maᵮH′ər)
Ma to a ka (mä′tō ä′kə)
Mau rice (mô′ris or mor′is)
Me de a (mi dē′ə)
Me la, Pom po ni us (pom pō′ni əs mā′lə)
Mer o no co mo co (mer′ō nō kō mō′kō)
Mi lan (mi lan′)
Mil ler, Joa quin (wä kēn′ mil′ər)
Mit nick (mit′nik)
Moi ra (moi′rə)
Mont gol fier (mōN gôl fyā′)
Mos ko witz (mos′kō wits)

Mou lin Jo ly (mü laN′ zhō lē′)
Mount Hol yoke (mount hōl′yōk)
Mus sel man (mus′əl mən)
Myr mi dons (mėr′mə donz)

Nan ta quoud (nän′tä kwoud)
Natch ez (nach′iz)
Nau si tes (nou sē′tās)
Na zi (nä′tsi or nat′si)
Nu gent, El li ott (el′i ət nü′gənt)

O a hu (ō ä′hü)
O' Mea ra (ō mä′rə)
On der donks (on′dėr donkz′)
O pe chan ka nough (ō′pə chän kä′nôH)
O ra paks (ō rä′päks)
O wat chee (ō wät′chē)

Pa ga no (pä gä′nō)
Pal las (pal′əs)
Pa maun kee (pə môn′kē; Indian pä moun′kā)
Pa pash vi ly, George (jôrj′ pä päsh′vi lē)
Pas pa heghs (päs pä′heHs)
Pas sy (pä sē′)
Pa tro clus (pə trō′kləs)
Pa tux et (pô tuk′sit; Indian pä túk′set)
Peat tie, Don ald Cul ross (don′əld kul′ros pēt′i)
Pe cos (pā′kōs)
Per di ta (pėr′di tə)
Pe rón, Juan (hwän′ pə rōn′)
Pfaff (pfäf)
Phi Kap pa Psi (fī′ kap′ə sī′)
Phryg i a (frij′i ə)
Pier sey (pir′si)
Pi nar del Ri o (pē när′ del rē′ō)
Pla to (plā′tō)
Platte (plat)
Plu to (plü′tō)
Po ca hon tas (pō′kə hon′təs)
Ponce de Le ón (pons′ də lē′ən; Spanish pôn′thā ᵮHā lā ôn′)
Pont char train (pon′chər trän)
Pow ha tan (pou′hə tan′)
Pro crus te an (prō krus′ti ən)
Pro me the us (prə mē′thi əs or prə mē′thüs)
Pu litz er (pů′lit sər or půl′it sər)
Py thag o ras (pi thag′ə rəs)

Rab e lais (rab′ə lā)
Raph a el (raf′i əl)
Rap i dan (rap′i dan′)
Rap pa han nock (rap′ə han′ək)
Re mus (rē′mus)
Reyn old (ren′əld)
Riv en oak (riv′ən ōk′)
Riv i er a (riv′i är′ə)
Ri voire, Ap po los (ä pō lō′ rē vwär′)
Ro dri guez (rô ᵮHrē′gäs)
Ro gêt, Ma rie (ma rē′ rō zhe′)
Rom u lus (rom′yə ləs)
Ro sen baum, Ja kie (jā′ki rō′zen boum)
Rue Morgue (rü môrg′)

Sac (sak)
Sal ma gun di (sal′mə gun′di)
Sam o set (sam′ō set)
Sa nar el li, Gui sep pe (jü zep′pā sä nä rel′lē)
Sar a nac (sar′ə nak)
Sat urn (sat′ərn)
Schauff ler, Rob ert Ha ven (ro′bərt hä′vən shôf′lər)

---

hat, āge, cãre, fär; let, ēqual, tėrm; it, īce; hot, ōpen, ôrder; oil, out; cup, pút, rüle, ūse; ch, child; ng, long; th, thin; ᵮH, then; zh, measure; ə represents *a* in about, *e* in taken, *i* in pencil, *o* in lemon, *u* in circus.

Schuldt, Ber nie (bėr′ni shúlt′)	**Tho reau, Hen ry Da vid** (hen′ri dā′vid thə rō′
Se ger, John (jon′ sē′gər)	or thō′rō)
Sha pi ro Karl (kärl′ shə pir′ō)	**Tieck** (tēk)
She ba (shē′bə)	**Tuol um ne** (twol′um nə)
Shi lo (shĭ′lō)	
Si er ra Ne vad a (si er′ə nə vad′ə or nə vä′də)	**Un cas** (ung′kəs)
Slav ic (släv′ik or slav′ik)	
Smi ley, Le on i das W. (lē on′ə dəs dub′əl yü	**Van Twil ler, Wou ter** (wou′tər van twil′ər;
smĭ′li)	*Dutch* vou′tər vän tvil′ər)
Soc ra tes (sok′rə tēz)	**Van Zandt** (van zant′)
So fro nie (sō frô nē′)	**Ver sailles** (vär sī′)
So lon (sō′lən or sō′lon)	**Vir gil** (vėr′jəl)
Som er set (sum′ər set)	**Vol taire** (vol tãr′)
Soph o cles (sof′ə klēz)	
Spfier schla ge, So phie (sō′fi shpfēr′shlä′gə)	**Ward, Ar te mus** (är tē′məs wôrd)
Stat en Is land (stat′ən ĭ′lənd)	**Wein stein** (wīn′stīn)
Stein beck, John (jon′ stĭn′bek)	**Wey a noke** (wā′ə nōk)
Stone, Ja bez (jā′bez stōn′)	**Wey er hau ser** (wĭ′ər hou′zər)
Stuy ve sant (stĭ′və sənt)	**Wich i ta** (wich′i tô)
Suck ow, Ruth (rüth′ sü′kō)	**Wis mer, Hel en** (hel′ən wiz′mər)
Su ez (sü ez′ or sü′ez)	**Wych er ley** (wich′ər li)
Su mach (sü′mak)	**Wynne** (win)
Swe den borg (swē′dən bôrg)	**Wythe, George** (jôrj′ with′)
Ta me nund (tä′mā núnd)	**Y saacs** (ē′säks)
Tants Wey a noke (tants′ wā′ə nok)	
Than a top sis (than′ə top′sis)	**Ze kle** (zē′kəl)
Thek y (thek′i)	**Zu ra beg** (zü′rä beg)

hat, āge, cãre, fär; let, ēqual, tėrm; it, ĭce; hot, ōpen, ôrder; oil, out; cup, pût, rüle, ūse; ch, child; ng, long; th, thin; ᴛʜ, then; zh, measure; ə represents *a* in about, *e* in taken, *i* in pencil, *o* in lemon, *u* in circus.

INDEX OF LITERARY TERMS

Definitions are given only of terms not defined or explained in the text. The numbers refer to pages on which the term is explained or an understanding of it developed.

731

INDEX OF TYPES OF LITERATURE

The references indicate the pages on which the selections illustrating the various types represented in THE UNITED STATES IN LITERATURE begin. Titles of selections are given only when the page references alone do not make clear what selections are referred to.

GENERAL INDEX

Titles of selections printed in the text and names of authors represented appear in capitals. General topics, including names of authors discussed but not represented by a selection, are printed in capitals and small letters. Selections discussed but not included in the text are printed in italics.

6 7 8 9 10 11 12 13 14 15 16 17 18 19 20 21 22 23 24 25   61 60 59 58 57